HOCKEY REGISTER

1988-89 EDITION

Editor/Hockey Register
LARRY WIGGE

Compiled by
FRANK POLNASZEK

Contributing Editor/Hockey Register
BARRY SIEGEL

President-Chief Executive Officer
RICHARD WATERS

Editor
TOM BARNIDGE

Director of Books and Periodicals
RON SMITH

Published by

The Sporting News

1212 North Lindbergh Boulevard
P.O. Box 56 — St. Louis, MO 63166

Copyright © 1988
The Sporting News Publishing Company

WITHDRAWN

A Times Mirror
Company

ISBN 0-89204-291-5   ISSN 0090-2292

Table of Contents

Players included are those who played in at least one National Hockey League game in 1987-88 and selected invitees to training camps.

Explanation of Abbreviations 3
Forwards and Defensemen 4
Goaltenders 362

ON THE COVER: Edmonton goalie Grant Fuhr led the NHL with 40 victories last season and captured the Vezina Trophy, awarded annually to the league's top goaltender.
                                                    —Photo by Paul Bereswill

EXPLANATION OF ABBREVIATIONS

A—Assists.
AHL—American Hockey League.
AJHL—Alberta Junior Hockey League.
ASHL—Alberta Senior Hockey League.
Avg.—Goals against per game average.
BCHL—British Columbia Hockey League.
CAHL—Central Alberta Hockey League.
CCHA—Central Collegiate Hockey Association.
Cent. OHA—Central Ontario Hockey Association.
CHL—California Hockey League or Central Hockey League.
CMJHL—Canadian Major Junior Hockey League.
CPHL—Central Pro Hockey League.
EHL—Eastern Hockey League.
EPHL—Eastern Pro Hockey League.
G—Goals scored.
Games—Games played.
Goals—Goals against.
IHL—International Hockey League.
MJHL—Manitoba Junior Hockey League or Midwest Junior Hockey League.
NAHL—North American Hockey League.
NEHL—Northeastern Hockey League.
NHL—National Hockey League.
NOHA—Northern Ontario Hockey Association.
NSHL—North Shore (New Brunswick) Hockey League.
NYMJHA—New York Metropolitan Junior Hockey Association.
OHA—Ontario Hockey Association.
OMJHL—Ontario Major Junior Hockey League.
OPHL—Ontario Provincial Hockey League.
Pen.—Minutes in penalties.
PHL—Prairie Hockey League.
Pts.—Points.
QHL—Quebec Hockey League.
QJHL—Quebec Junior Hockey League.
SHL—Southern Hockey League.
SJHL—Saskatchewan Junior Hockey League.
SOJHL—Southern Ontario Junior Hockey League.
TBJHL—Thunder Bay Junior Hockey League.
USHL—United States Hockey League.
WCHA—Western Collegiate Hockey Association.
WCHL—Western Canada Hockey League (Juniors).
WCJHL—Western Canada Junior League.
WHA—World Hockey Association.
WHL—Western Hockey League.
WHL—Western Hockey League (Junior "A" League since 1978-79).
WIHL—Western International Hockey League.
WOJHL—Western Ontario Junior Hockey League.
*—Indicates either led or was tied for league lead.
    Footnotes (a) indicates player was member of first all-star team.
    Footnotes (b) indicates player was member of second all-star team.
Scoring totals (goals plus assists) do not always balance in certain leagues due to un-balanced schedules and scoring system.
Junior "A" Ontario Hockey Association also includes Metro League and OHA Major Junior.
Quebec Junior Hockey League also includes Montreal Metro League and OJHL Major.

FORWARDS AND DEFENSEMEN

(a)—First team all-star selection. (b)—Second team.
*Indicates led league or tied for leadership.

CLIFF ABRECHT

Defense . . . 6' . . . 185 lbs. . . . Born, Toronto, Ont., May 24, 1963 . . . Shoots right.

Year	Team	League	Games	G.	A.	Pts.	Pen.
1982-83—Princeton Univ. (c)		ECAC	24	4	10	14	52
1983-84—Princeton Univ.		ECAC	23	9	9	18	62
1984-85—Princeton Univ.		ECAC	26	6	22	28	31
1985-86—Princeton Univ.		ECAC	30	15	26	41	42
1985-86—St. Catharines Saints		AHL	1	0	1	1	0
1986-87—Newmarket Saints		AHL	63	2	5	7	20
1987-88—Milwaukee Admirals		IHL	36	12	10	22	22
1987-88—Baltimore Skipjacks		AHL	33	2	9	11	18

(c)—June, 1983—Drafted by Toronto Maple Leafs as an underage junior in 1983 NHL entry draft. Seventh Maple Leafs pick, 168th overall, eighth round.

KEITH EDWARD ACTON

Center . . . 5'10" . . . 167 lbs. . . . Born, Newmarket, Ont., April 15, 1958 . . . Shoots left . . . (April 20, 1984)—Injured left wrist in playoff game at St. Louis.

Year	Team	League	Games	G.	A.	Pts.	Pen.
1974-75—Wexford Raiders		OPJHL	43	23	29	52	46
1975-76—Peterborough Petes		Jr."A"OHA	35	9	17	26	30
1976-77—Peterborough Petes		Jr."A"OHA	65	52	69	121	93
1977-78—Peterborough Petes (c)		Jr."A"OHA	68	42	86	128	52
1978-79—Nova Scotia Voyageurs		AHL	79	15	26	41	22
1979-80—Nova Scotia Voyageurs (b)		AHL	75	45	53	98	38
1979-80—Montreal Canadiens		NHL	2	0	1	1	0
1980-81—Montreal Canadiens		NHL	61	15	24	39	74
1981-82—Montreal Canadiens		NHL	78	36	52	88	88
1982-83—Montreal Canadiens		NHL	78	24	26	50	63
1983-84—Montreal Canadiens (d)		NHL	9	3	7	10	4
1983-84—Minnesota North Stars		NHL	62	17	38	55	60
1984-85—Minnesota North Stars		NHL	78	20	38	58	90
1985-86—Minnesota North Stars		NHL	79	26	32	58	100
1986-87—Minnesota North Stars		NHL	78	16	29	45	56
1987-88—Minnesota North Stars (e)		NHL	46	8	11	19	74
1987-88—Edmonton Oilers		NHL	26	3	6	9	21
NHL TOTALS			607	168	264	432	630

(c)—Drafted from Peterborough Petes by Montreal Canadiens in sixth round of 1978 amateur draft.
(d)—October, 1983—Traded with Mark Napier and third round 1984 draft pick (Kenneth Hodge) by Montreal Canadiens to Minnesota North Stars for Bobby Smith.
(e)—January, 1988—Traded by Minnesota North Stars to Edmonton Oilers for Moe Mantha.

GREG ADAMS

Center . . . 6'2" . . . 185 lbs. . . . Born, Nelson, B.C., August 1, 1963 . . . Shoots left . . . (April, 1986)—Tore tendon in right wrist during World Championship game at Moscow while playing for Team Canada.

Year	Team	League	Games	G.	A.	Pts.	Pen.
1980-81—Kelowna Wings		BCJHL	47	40	50	90	16
1981-82—Kelowna Wings		BCJHL	45	31	42	73	24
1982-83—Northern Arizona Univ.		NCAA	29	14	21	35	46
1983-84—Northern Arizona Univ. (c)		NCAA	47	40	50	90	16
1984-85—Maine Mariners		AHL	41	15	20	35	12
1984-85—New Jersey Devils		NHL	36	12	9	21	14
1985-86—New Jersey Devils		NHL	78	35	43	78	30
1986-87—New Jersey Devils (d)		NHL	72	20	27	47	19
1987-88—Vancouver Canucks		NHL	80	36	40	76	30
NHL TOTALS			266	103	119	222	93

(c)—June, 1984—Signed by New Jersey Devils as a free agent.
(d)—September, 1987—Traded with Kirk McLean by New Jersey Devils to Vancouver Canucks for Patrik Sundstrom, fourth-round 1988 draft pick (Matt Ruchty) and the option to flip second-round picks in 1988 entry draft (Jeff Christian).

GREGORY CHARLES ADAMS

Left Wing . . . 6'1" . . . 190 lbs. . . . Born, Duncan, B. C., May 31, 1960 . . . Shoots left . . . (September 26, 1986)—Suspended by NHL for first three games of season for an altercation in a pre-season game with Hartford . . . (February, 1987)—Hospitalized with a collapsed lung.

Year	Team	League	Games	G.	A.	Pts.	Pen.
1977-78—Nanaimo	BCJHL	62	53	60	113	150
1978-79—Victoria Cougars	WHL	71	23	31	54	151
1979-80—Victoria Cougars (c)	WHL	71	62	48	110	212
1980-81—Philadelphia Flyers	NHL	6	3	0	3	8
1980-81—Maine Mariners	AHL	71	19	20	39	158
1981-82—Maine Mariners	AHL	45	16	21	37	241
1981-82—Philadelphia Flyers (d)	NHL	33	4	15	19	105
1982-83—Hartford Whalers	NHL	79	10	13	23	216
1983-84—Washington Capitals (e)	NHL	57	2	6	8	133
1984-85—Binghamton Whalers	AHL	28	9	16	25	58
1984-85—Washington Capitals	NHL	51	6	12	18	72
1985-86—Washington Capitals	NHL	78	18	38	56	152
1986-87—Washington Capitals	NHL	67	14	30	44	184
1987-88—Washington Capitals (f)	NHL	78	15	12	27	153
NHL TOTALS		449	72	126	198	1023

(c)—August, 1980—Signed by Philadelphia Flyers as a free agent.
(d)—August, 1982—Traded by Philadelphia Flyers with Ken Linseman and Flyers' No. 1 draft choice (David A. Jensen) in 1983 to Hartford Whalers for Mark Howe. Hartford and Philadelphia also swapped third-round choices in 1983 draft.
(e)—October, 1983—Traded by Hartford Whalers to Washington Capitals for Torrie Robertson.
(f)—July, 1988—Traded by Washington Capitals to Edmonton Oilers for Geoff Courtnall.

JIM AGNEW

Defense . . . 6'1" . . . 179 lbs. . . . Born, Deloraine, Man., March 21, 1966 . . . Shoots left.

Year	Team	League	Games	G.	A.	Pts.	Pen.
1982-83—Brandon Wheat Kings	WHL	14	1	1	2	9
1983-84—Brandon Wheat Kings (c)	WHL	71	6	17	23	107
1984-85—Brandon Wheat Kings	WHL	19	3	15	18	82
1984-85—Portland Winter Hawks	WHL	44	5	24	29	223
1985-86—Portland Winter Hawks (a)	WHL	70	6	30	36	386
1986-87—Vancouver Canucks	NHL	4	0	0	0	0
1986-87—Fredericton Express	AHL	67	0	5	5	261
1987-88—Vancouver Canucks	NHL	10	0	1	1	16
1987-88—Fredericton Express	AHL	63	2	8	10	188
NHL TOTALS		14	0	1	1	16

(c)—June, 1984—Drafted as underage junior by Vancouver Canucks in NHL entry draft. Tenth Canucks pick, 157th overall, eighth round.

BRADLEY AITKEN

Left Wing and Center . . . 6'3" . . . 200 lbs. . . . Born, Scarborough, Ont., October 30, 1967 . . . Shoots left . . . (October, 1986)—Missed three weeks with a separated shoulder.

Year	Team	League	Games	G.	A.	Pts.	Pen.
1984-85—Peterborough Petes	OHL	63	18	26	44	36
1985-86—Peterborough Petes (c)	OHL	48	9	28	37	77
1985-86—Sault Ste. Marie Greyhounds (d)	OHL	20	8	19	27	11
1986-87—Sault Ste. Marie Greyhounds	OHL	52	27	38	65	86
1987-88—Pittsburgh Penguins	NHL	5	1	1	2	0
1987-88—Muskegon Lumberjacks	IHL	74	32	31	63	128
NHL TOTALS		5	1	1	2	0

(c)—February, 1986—Traded with future considerations by Peterborough Petes to Sault Ste. Marie Greyhounds for Graeme Bonar.
(d)—June, 1986—Drafted as underage junior by Pittsburgh Penguins in 1986 NHL entry draft. Third Penguins pick, 46th overall, third round.

MICAH AIVAZOFF

Center . . . 6' . . . 185 lbs. . . . Born, Powell River, B.C., May 4, 1969 . . . Shoots left.

Year	Team	League	Games	G.	A.	Pts.	Pen.
1985-86—Victoria Cougars	WHL	27	3	4	7	25
1986-87—Victoria Cougars	WHL	72	18	39	57	112
1987-88—Victoria Cougars (c)	WHL	69	26	57	83	79

(c)—June, 1988—Drafted by Los Angeles Kings in 1988 NHL entry draft. Sixth Kings pick, 109th overall, sixth round.

TOMMY ALBELIN

Defense . . . 6'1" . . . 185 lbs. . . . Born, Stockholm, Sweden, May 21, 1964 . . . Shoots left.

Year	Team	League	Games	G.	A.	Pts.	Pen.
1982-83	Djurgardens (c)	Sweden	17	2	5	7	4
1983-84	Djurgardens	Sweden	37	9	8	17	36
1984-85	Djurgardens	Sweden	....	...	....	....	....
1985-86	Djurgardens	Sweden	....	...	....	....	....
1986-87	Djurgardens	Sweden	33	7	5	12	49
1987-88	Quebec Nordiques	NHL	60	3	23	26	47
	NHL TOTALS		60	3	23	26	47

(c)—June, 1983—Drafted by Quebec Nordiques in NHL entry draft. Seventh Nordiques pick, 152nd overall, eighth round.

DAVE BRYAN ALLISON

Defense and Right Wing . . . 6'1" . . . 198 lbs. . . . Born, Ft. Francis, Ontario, April 14, 1959 . . . Shoots right . . . Injured right shoulder in 1976-77 . . . Slipped vertabra in back in 1977-78 . . . Brother of Mike Allison.

Year	Team	League	Games	G.	A.	Pts.	Pen.
1976-77	Cornwall Royals	QMJHL	63	2	11	13	180
1977-78	Cornwall Royals	QMJHL	60	9	29	38	302
1978-79	Cornwall Royals	QMJHL	66	7	31	38	*407
1979-80	Nova Scotia Voyageurs	AHL	49	1	12	13	119
1980-81	Nova Scotia Voyageurs	AHL	70	5	12	17	298
1981-82	Nova Scotia Voyageurs (c)	AHL	78	8	25	33	332
1982-83	Nova Scotia Voyageurs	AHL	70	3	22	25	180
1983-84	Montreal Canadiens	NHL	3	0	0	0	12
1983-84	Nova Scotia Voyageurs	AHL	53	2	18	20	155
1984-85	Sherbrooke Canadiens	AHL	4	0	1	1	19
1984-85	Nova Scotia Voyageurs	AHL	68	4	18	22	175
1985-86	Muskegon Lumberjacks	IHL	66	7	30	37	247
1986-87	Muskegon Lumberjacks	IHL	67	11	35	46	337
1987-88	Newmarket Saints	AHL	48	1	9	10	166
	NHL TOTALS		3	0	0	0	12

(c)—Led AHL Playoffs with 84 penalty minutes.

MICHAEL EARNEST ALLISON

Center . . . 6' . . . 202 lbs. . . . Born, Ft. Francis, Ont., March 28, 1961 . . . Shoots right . . . Brother of Dave Allison . . . (January 13, 1981)—Strained ligaments in right knee . . . (October 25, 1981)—Bruised kneecap . . . (January 20, 1982)—Sprained medial collateral ligament in right knee vs. N.Y. Islanders requiring surgery . . . (November 20, 1982) Strained ligaments in right knee at Toronto . . . (October, 1983)—Sprained left knee . . . (October, 1984)—Missed games with knee injury . . . (January, 1985)—Arthroscopic surgery to knee . . . (October, 1987)—Back injury . . . (January, 1988)—Groin injury.

Year	Team	League	Games	G.	A.	Pts.	Pen.
1977-78	New Westminster Bruins	WCHL	5	0	1	1	2
1977-78	Kenora Thistles	MJHL	47	30	36	66	70
1978-79	Sudbury Wolves	OMJHL	59	24	32	56	41
1979-80	Sudbury Wolves (c)	OMJHL	67	24	71	95	74
1980-81	New York Rangers	NHL	75	26	38	64	83
1981-82	Springfield Indians	AHL	2	0	0	0	0
1981-82	New York Rangers	NHL	48	7	15	22	74
1982-83	Tulsa Oilers	CHL	6	2	2	4	2
1982-83	New York Rangers	NHL	39	11	9	20	37
1983-84	New York Rangers	NHL	45	8	12	20	64
1984-85	New York Rangers	NHL	31	9	15	24	17
1985-86	New Haven Nighthawks	AHL	9	6	6	12	4
1985-86	New Qork Rangers (d)	NHL	28	2	13	15	22
1986-87	Toronto Maple Leafs	NHL	71	7	16	23	66
1987-88	Toronto Maple Leafs (e)	NHL	15	0	3	3	10
1987-88	Los Angeles Kings	NHL	37	16	12	28	57
	NHL TOTALS		389	86	133	219	430

(c)—June, 1980—Drafted as underage junior by New York Rangers in NHL entry draft. Second Rangers pick, 35th overall, second round.

(d)—August, 1986—Traded by New York Rangers to Toronto Maple Leafs for Walt Poddubny.

(e)—December, 1987—Traded by Toronto Maple Leafs to Los Angeles Kings for Sean McKenna.

JOSEPH ALOI

Defense . . . 6'3" . . . 195 lbs. . . . Born, New Haven, Conn., October 10, 1968 . . . Shoots right.

Year	Team	League	Games	G.	A.	Pts.	Pen.
1985-86—Hamden H.S.	Conn. H.S.	....	...	....	....	....	
1986-87—Hull Olympiques (c)	QHL	58	2	5	7	166	
1987-88—Hull Olympiques	QHL	66	0	18	18	171	

(c)—June, 1987—Drafted by Calgary Flames in 1987 NHL entry draft. Seventh Flames pick, 124th overall, sixth round.

ANTHONY AMONTE

Right Wing . . . 6' . . . 165 lbs. . . . Born, Weymouth, Mass., August 2, 1970 . . . Shoots left.

Year	Team	League	Games	G.	A.	Pts.	Pen.
1986-87—Thayer Academy	Mass. H.S.	....	25	32	57	....	
1987-88—Thayer Academy (c)	Mass. H.S.	....	30	38	68	....	

(c)—June, 1988—Drafted by New York Rangers in 1988 NHL entry draft. Third Rangers pick, 68th overall, fourth round.

DARRIN AMUNDSON

Center . . . 6'2" . . . 180 lbs. . . . Born, Duluth, Minn., November 13, 1968 . . . Shoots left . . . Son of Art Amundson, coach at Duluth East High School in 1986-87.

Year	Team	League	Games	G.	A.	Pts.	Pen.
1985-86—Duluth East High School	Minn. H.S.	22	10	26	36	....	
1986-87—Duluth East High School (c)	Minn. H.S.	24	20	37	57	....	
1987-88—Univ. of Minnesota/Duluth	WCHA	16	0	6	6	4	

(c)—June, 1987—Drafted by Winnipeg Jets in 1987 NHL entry draft. Fifth Jets pick, 100th overall, fifth round.

JOHN ANDERSEN

Left Wing . . . 6' . . . 175 lbs. . . . Born, Toronto, Ont., January 18, 1968 . . . Shoots left . . . Also plays Center.

Year	Team	League	Games	G.	A.	Pts.	Pen.
1984-85—Toronto Marlboros	OHL	54	1	9	10	4
1985-86—Oshawa Generals (c)	OHL	60	13	11	24	15
1986-87—Oshawa Generals	OHL	45	11	13	24	24
1987-88—Oshawa Generals (d)	OHL	28	13	13	26	30
1987-88—Hamilton Steelhawks	OHL	22	6	6	12	17

(c)—June, 1986—Drafted as underage junior by New Jersey Devils in 1986 NHL entry draft. Eleventh Devils pick, 213th overall, 11th round.

(d)—January, 1988—Traded by Oshawa Generals to Hamilton Steelhawks for Kirk Tomlinson.

DAVID ANDERSON

Right Wing . . . 6' . . . 190 lbs. . . . Born, Vancouver, B.C., July 30, 1962 . . . Shoots right.

Year	Team	League	Games	G.	A.	Pts.	Pen.
1981-82—Denver University	WCHA	43	10	10	20	42
1982-83—Denver University	WCHA	30	5	10	15	27
1983-84—Denver University	WCHA	38	23	27	50	75
1984-85—Denver University	WCHA	34	16	23	39	48
1985-86—Fort Wayne Komets (c)	IHL	79	33	41	74	156
1986-87—Maine Mariners	AHL	59	9	9	18	80
1987-88—Utica Devils	AHL	74	23	12	35	191

(c)—August, 1986—Signed by New Jersey Devils as a free agent.

GLENN CHRIS ANDERSON

Right Wing . . . 5'11" . . . 175 lbs. . . . Born, Vancouver, B.C., October 2, 1960 . . . Shoots left . . . Played on Canadian Olympic Team in 1980 . . . (November, 1980)—Knee surgery to remove bone chips . . . (Spring, 1982)—Nose surgery to correct breathing problem caused during a December 1, 1981 altercation with Mark Hunter of Montreal . . . (December 13, 1985)—Given eight-game suspension by NHL for stick-swinging incident at Winnipeg . . . Also plays Left Wing.

Year	Team	League	Games	G.	A.	Pts.	Pen.
1977-78—New Westminster Bruins	WHL	1	0	1	1	2
1978-79—Seattle Breakers	WHL	2	0	1	1	0
1978-79—Denver University (c)	WCHA	40	26	29	55	58
1979-80—Canadian Olympic Team	Int'l	49	21	21	42	46
1979-80—Seattle Breakers	WHL	7	5	5	10	4
1980-81—Edmonton Oilers	NHL	58	30	23	53	24
1981-82—Edmonton Oilers	NHL	80	38	67	105	71
1982-83—Edmonton Oilers	NHL	72	48	56	104	70
1983-84—Edmonton Oilers	NHL	80	54	45	99	65

Year	Team	League	Games	G.	A.	Pts.	Pen.
1984-85—Edmonton Oilers		NHL	80	42	39	81	69
1985-86—Edmonton Oilers		NHL	72	54	48	102	90
1986-87—Edmonton Oilers		NHL	80	35	38	73	65
1987-88—Edmonton Oilers		NHL	80	38	50	88	58
NHL TOTALS			602	339	366	705	512

(c)—August, 1979—Drafted by Edmonton Oilers in NHL entry draft. Third Oilers pick, 69th overall, fourth round.

JOHN MURRAY ANDERSON

Left Wing . . . 5'11" . . . 180 lbs. . . . Born, Toronto, Ont., March 28, 1957 . . . Shoots left . . . Missed part of 1975-76 season with shoulder separation . . . (December, 1981)—Elbow injury . . . (November, 1984)—Injured collarbone . . . (December 18, 1985)—Sprained back at Montreal . . . (January 20, 1986)—Injured shoulder vs. Montreal and missed one game . . . (March 1, 1988)—Missed final five weeks of season with injured rotator cuff suffered in a team practice.

Year	Team	League	Games	G.	A.	Pts.	Pen.
1973-74—Toronto Marlboros		Jr. "A" OHA	38	22	22	44	6
1974-75—Toronto Marlboros		Jr. "A" OHA	70	49	64	113	31
1975-76—Toronto Marlboros		Jr. "A" OHA	39	26	25	51	19
1976-77—Toronto Marlboros (a-c)		Jr. "A" OHA	64	57	62	119	42
1977-78—Dallas Black Hawks (b-d)		CHL	52	22	23	45	6
1977-78—Toronto Maple Leafs		NHL	17	1	2	3	2
1978-79—Toronto Maple Leafs		NHL	71	15	11	26	10
1979-80—Toronto Maple Leafs		NHL	74	25	28	53	22
1980-81—Toronto Maple Leafs		NHL	75	17	26	43	31
1981-82—Toronto Maple Leafs		NHL	69	31	26	57	306
1982-83—Toronto Maple Leafs		NHL	80	31	49	80	24
1983-84—Toronto Maple Leafs		NHL	73	37	31	68	22
1984-85—Toronto Maple Leafs (e)		NHL	75	32	31	63	27
1985-86—Quebec Nordiques (f)		NHL	65	21	28	49	26
1985-86—Hartford Whalers		NHL	14	8	17	25	2
1986-87—Hartford Whalers		NHL	76	31	44	75	19
1987-88—Hartford Whalers		NHL	63	17	32	49	20
NHL TOTALS			752	266	325	591	235

(c)—Drafted from Toronto Marlboros by Toronto Maple Leafs in first round of 1977 amateur draft.
(d)—Led in goals (11) and points (19) during playoffs.
(e)—August, 1985—Traded by Toronto Maple Leafs to Quebec Nordiques for Brad Maxwell.
(f)—March, 1986—Traded by Quebec Nordiques to Hartford Whalers for Risto Siltanen.

PERRY LYNN ANDERSON

Left Wing . . . 6' . . . 210 lbs. . . . Born, Barrie, Ont., October 14, 1961 . . . Shoots left . . . (March, 1984)—Broke bone in foot . . . (October 23, 1985)—Bruised right shoulder at N.Y. Rangers and missed five games . . . (December 17, 1985)—Bruised left knee vs. Philadelphia and missed five games . . . (January 13, 1986)—Strained abdominal muscle at Chicago and missed eight games . . . (January, 1988)—Concussion.

Year	Team	League	Games	G.	A.	Pts.	Pen.
1978-79—Kingston Canadians		OMJHL	60	6	13	19	85
1979-80—Kingston Canadians (c)		OMJHL	63	17	16	33	52
1980-81—Kingston Canadians		OHL	38	9	13	22	118
1980-81—Brantford Alexanders		OHL	31	8	27	35	43
1981-82—Salt Lake Golden Eagles (b)		CHL	71	32	32	64	117
1981-82—St. Louis Blues		NHL	5	1	2	3	0
1982-83—Salt Lake Golden Eagles		CHL	57	23	19	42	140
1982-83—St. Louis Blues		NHL	18	5	2	7	14
1983-84—Montana Magic		CHL	8	7	3	10	34
1983-84—St. Louis Blues		NHL	50	7	5	12	195
1984-85—St. Louis Blues (d)		NHL	71	9	9	18	146
1985-86—New Jersey Devils		NHL	51	7	12	19	91
1986-87—New Jersey Devils		NHL	57	10	9	19	105
1987-88—New Jersey Devils		NHL	60	4	6	10	222
NHL TOTALS			312	43	45	88	773

(c)—June, 1980—Drafted by St. Louis Blues as an underage junior in NHL entry draft. Fifth Blues pick, 117th overall, sixth round.
(d)—August, 1985—Traded by St. Louis Blues to New Jersey Devils for Rick Meagher and 1986 12th round draft choice (Bill Butler).

SHAWN ANDERSON

Defense . . . 6'1" . . . 190 lbs. . . . Born, Montreal, Que., February 7, 1968 . . . Shoots left . . .

Also plays Left Wing . . . (October, 1986)—Sprained knee . . . (January 20, 1987)—Missed four games with injured back at Minnesota . . . (March 3, 1987)—Separated shoulder at Philadelphia . . . (March 28, 1987)—Reseparated shoulder vs. Montreal . . . (December, 1987)—Injured ankle.

Year	Team	League	Games	G.	A.	Pts.	Pen.
1984-85—Lac St. Louis Midget		Que.AAA Mid.	42	23	42	65	100
1985-86—University of Maine		H. East	16	5	8	13	22
1985-86—Team Canada (c)		Int'l	33	2	6	8	16
1986-87—Rochester Americans		AHL	15	2	5	7	11
1986-87—Buffalo Sabres		NHL	41	2	11	13	23
1987-88—Buffalo Sabres		NHL	23	1	2	3	17
1987-88—Rochester Americans		AHL	22	5	16	21	19
NHL TOTALS			64	3	13	16	40

(c)—June, 1986—Drafted as underage player by Buffalo Sabres in 1986 NHL entry draft. First Sabres pick, fifth overall, first round.

BO MIKAEL ANDERSSON
(Known by middle name)

Center . . . 5'9" . . . 183 lbs. . . . Born, Malmo, Sweden, May 10, 1966 . . . Shoots left . . . (March 3, 1987)—Missed three weeks with sprained ankle at Philadelphia . . . (March, 1988)—Twisted ankle.

Year	Team	League	Games	G.	A.	Pts.	Pen.
1983-84—Vastra Frolunda (c)		Sweden	12	0	2	2	6
1984-85—Vastra Frolunda		Sweden	32	16	11	27	....
1985-86—Rochester Americans		AHL	20	10	4	14	6
1985-86—Buffalo Sabres		NHL	33	1	9	10	4
1986-87—Rochester Americans		AHL	42	6	20	26	14
1986-87—Buffalo Sabres		NHL	16	0	3	3	0
1987-88—Rochester Americans		AHL	35	12	24	36	16
1987-88—Buffalo Sabres		NHL	37	3	20	23	10
NHL TOTALS			86	4	32	36	14

(c)—June, 1984—Drafted by Buffalo Sabres in NHL entry draft. First Sabres pick, 18th overall, first round.

TRENT ANDISON

Left Wing . . . 5'10" . . . 190 lbs. . . . Born, Bracebridge, Ont., May 30, 1969 . . . Shoots left.

Year	Team	League	Games	G.	A.	Pts.	Pen.
1986-87—St. Mary's Jr. B		OHA	42	53	38	91	101
1987-88—Cornell University (c)		ECAC	27	21	17	38	22

(c)—June, 1988—Drafted by Minnesota North Stars in 1988 NHL entry draft. Eighth North Stars pick, 232nd overall, 12th round.

DAVID ANDREYCHUK

Center . . . 6'4" . . . 198 lbs. . . . Born, Hamilton, Ont., September 29, 1963 . . . Shoots right . . . (March, 1983)—Sprained knee . . . Played with Team Canada in 1982-83 World Junior Championship . . . (March, 1985)—Fractured collarbone . . . (September, 1985)—Twisted knee in first day of Buffalo training camp . . . (September, 1986)—Injured right knee during training camp when he collided with Phil Housley during a team scrimmage.

Year	Team	League	Games	G.	A.	Pts.	Pen.
1980-81—Oshawa Generals		OHL	67	22	22	44	80
1981-82—Oshawa Generals (c)		OHL	67	58	43	101	71
1982-83—Oshawa Generals		OHL	14	8	24	32	6
1982-83—Buffalo Sabres		NHL	43	14	23	37	16
1983-84—Buffalo Sabres		NHL	78	38	42	80	42
1984-85—Buffalo Sabres		NHL	64	31	30	61	54
1985-86—Buffalo Sabres		NHL	80	36	51	87	61
1986-87—Buffalo Sabres		NHL	77	25	48	73	46
1987-88—Buffalo Sabres		NHL	80	30	48	78	112
NHL TOTALS			422	174	242	416	331

(c)—June, 1982—Drafted as underage junior by Buffalo Sabres in NHL entry draft. Third Sabres pick, 16th overall, first round.

GREG ANDRUSAK

Defense . . . 6'1" . . . 180 lbs. . . . Born, Cranbrook, B.C., November 14, 1969 . . . Shoots right.

Year	Team	League	Games	G.	A.	Pts.	Pen.
1986-87—Kelowna Jr. A		BCJHL	45	10	24	34	95
1987-88—Univ. of Minnesota/Duluth (c)		WCHA	37	4	5	9	42

(c)—June, 1988—Drafted by Pittsburgh Penguins in 1988 NHL entry draft. Fifth Penguins pick, 88th overall, fifth round.

SERGE ANGLEHART

Defense . . . 6'2" . . . 190 lbs. . . . Born, Hull, Que., April 18, 1970 . . . Shoots right.

Year	Team	League	Games	G.	A.	Pts.	Pen.
1986-87	Outaouais Midget	Que. AAA	41	4	27	31	102
1987-88	Drummondville Voltigeurs (c)	QHL	44	1	8	9	122

(c)—June, 1988—Drafted as underage junior by Detroit Red Wings in 1988 NHL entry draft. Second Red Wings pick, 38th overall, second overall.

DAVID ARCHIBALD

Center . . . 6'1" . . . 195 lbs. . . . Born, Chillawack, B.C., April 14, 1969 . . . Shoots left . . . (January, 1984)—Shoulder surgery . . . (October, 1986)—Lacerated hand . . . (September, 1987)—Injured shoulder.

Year	Team	League	Games	G.	A.	Pts.	Pen.
1984-85	Portland Winter Hawks	WHL	47	7	11	18	10
1985-86	Portland Winter Hawks	WHL	70	29	35	64	56
1986-87	Portland Winter Hawks (c)	WHL	65	50	57	107	40
1987-88	Minnesota North Stars	NHL	78	13	20	33	26
	NHL TOTALS		78	13	20	33	26

(c)—June, 1987—Drafted as underage junior by Minnesota North Stars in 1987 NHL entry draft. First North Stars pick, sixth overall, first round.

JIM ARCHIBALD

Right Wing . . . 5'11" . . . 180 lbs. . . . Born, Craik, Sask., June 6, 1961 . . . Shoots right.

Year	Team	League	Games	G.	A.	Pts.	Pen.
1980-81	Moose Jaw Canucks (c)	SJHL	52	46	42	88	308
1981-82	Univ. of North Dakota	WCHA	41	10	16	26	96
1982-83	Univ. of North Dakota	WCHA	33	7	14	21	91
1983-84	Univ. of North Dakota	WCHA	44	21	15	36	156
1984-85	Univ. of North Dakota (a)	WCHA	41	37	24	61	197
1984-85	Springfield Indians	AHL	8	1	0	1	5
1984-85	Minnesota North Stars	NHL	4	1	2	3	11
1985-86	Springfield Indians	AHL	12	1	7	8	34
1985-86	Minnesota North Stars	NHL	11	0	0	0	32
1986-87	Springfield Indians	AHL	66	10	17	27	303
1986-87	Minnesota North Stars	NHL	1	0	0	0	2
1987-88	Kalamazoo Wings	IHL	12	0	1	1	73
	NHL TOTALS		16	1	2	3	45

(c)—June, 1981—Drafted by Minnesota North Stars in 1981 NHL entry draft. Eleventh North Stars pick, 139th overall, seventh round.

IAN ARMSTRONG

Defense . . . 6'4" . . . 200 lbs. . . . Born, Peterborough, Ont., January 25, 1965 . . . Shoots right.

Year	Team	League	Games	G.	A.	Pts.	Pen.
1981-82	Lakefield Jr. C	OHA	35	8	25	33	46
1985-83	Peterborough Petes	OHL	63	1	6	7	29
1983-84	Peterborough Petes (c)	OHL	67	1	23	24	66
1984-85	Peterborough Petes (d)	OHL	66	13	21	34	63
1985-86	Hershey Bears	AHL	66	0	8	8	42
1986-87	Hershey Bears	AHL	68	0	7	7	148
1987-88	Hershey Bears (e)	AHL	6	0	0	0	14
1987-88	Baltimore Skipjacks	AHL	75	7	8	15	200

(c)—June, 1983—Drafted as underage junior by Boston Bruins in 1983 NHL entry draft. Seventh Bruins pick, 142nd overall, seventh round.
(d)—June, 1985—Released by Boston Bruins and signed by Philadelphia Flyers as a free agent.
(e)—October, 1987—Loaned to Baltimore Skipjacks by Philadelphia Flyers.

TIM ARMSTRONG

Center . . . 5'11" . . . 170 lbs. . . . Born, Toronto, Ont., May 12, 1967 . . . Shoots right.

Year	Team	League	Games	G.	A.	Pts.	Pen.
1983-84	Markham Tier II Jr. A	OHA	42	24	41	65	41
1984-85	Toronto Marlboros (c)	OHL	63	17	45	62	28
1985-86	Toronto Marlboros	OHL	64	35	69	104	36
1986-87	Toronto Marlboros	OHL	66	29	55	84	61
1986-87	Newmarket Saints	AHL	5	3	0	3	2
1987-88	Newmarket Saints	AHL	78	19	40	59	26

(c)—June, 1985—Drafted as underage junior by Toronto Maple Leafs in 1985 NHL entry draft. Eleventh Maple Leafs pick, 211th overall, 11th round.

TROY ARNDT

Defense . . . 6' . . . 195 lbs. . . . Born, Regina, Sask., April 30, 1968 . . . Shoots left.

Year	Team	League	Games	G.	A.	Pts.	Pen.
1983-84—Weyburn Red Wings		WHL	56	3	8	11	63
1984-85—Portland Winter Hawks		WHL	65	5	14	19	172
1985-86—Portland Winter Hawks (c)		WHL	63	3	20	23	288
1986-87—Brandon Wheat Kings (d)		WHL	38	1	8	9	154
1987-88—New Westminster Bruins		WHL	36	4	6	10	82

(c)—June, 1986—Drafted as underage junior by Buffalo Sabres in 1986 NHL entry draft. Twelfth Sabres pick, 215th overall, 11th round.

(d)—October, 1986—Traded by Portland Winter Hawks to Brandon Wheat Kings for WHL rights to Roydon Gunn.

SCOTT ARNIEL

Left Wing . . . 6'1" . . . 170 lbs. . . . Born, Kingston, Ont., September 17, 1962 . . . Shoots left . . . Also plays Center . . . (February 26, 1987)—Missed three games due to a charley horse . . . (March, 1988)—Bruised abdominal muscle.

Year	Team	League	Games	G.	A.	Pts.	Pen.
1979-80—Cornwall Royals		QMJHL	61	22	28	50	51
1980-81—Cornwall Royals (c)		QMJHL	68	52	71	123	102
1981-82—Cornwall Royals		OHL	24	18	26	44	43
1981-82—Winnipeg Jets		NHL	17	1	8	9	14
1982-83—Winnipeg Jets		NHL	75	13	5	18	46
1983-84—Winnipeg Jets		NHL	80	21	35	56	68
1984-85—Winnipeg Jets		NHL	79	22	22	44	81
1985-86—Winnipeg Jets (d)		NHL	80	18	25	43	40
1986-87—Buffalo Sabres		NHL	63	11	14	25	59
1987-88—Buffalo Sabres		NHL	73	17	23	40	61
NHL TOTALS			467	103	132	235	369

(c)—June, 1981—Drafted as underage junior by Winnipeg Jets in NHL entry draft. Second Jets pick, 22nd overall, second round.

(d)—June, 1986—Traded by Winnipeg Jets to Buffalo Sabres for Gilles Hamel.

CHAD ARTHUR

Left Wing . . . 5'11" . . . 195 lbs. . . . Born, Dekalb, Ill., February 18, 1967 . . . Shoots left . . . Also plays Defense.

Year	Team	League	Games	G.	A.	Pts.	Pen.
1984-85—Stratford Jr. B (c)		OHA	40	22	21	43	159
1985-86—Bowling Green University		CCHA	35	3	4	7	50
1986-87—Bowling Green University		CCHA	20	6	4	10	41
1987-88—Bowling Green University		CCHA	40	8	8	16	58

(c)—June, 1985—Drafted as underage junior by Montreal Canadiens in NHL entry draft. Thirteenth Canadiens pick, 205th overall, 10th round.

BRENT KENNETH ASHTON

Left Wing . . . 6'1" . . . 200 lbs. . . . Born, Saskatoon, Sask., May 18, 1960 . . . Shoots left . . . Missed part of 1979-80 season with knee ligament injury . . . (October, 1985)—Missed two weeks with injured hip in training camp . . . Also plays Center . . . (September, 1986)—Tore left knee ligaments in pre-season altercation with Dave Semenko vs. Edmonton . . . (December 12, 1987)—Missed four games with eye injury at Montreal.

Year	Team	League	Games	G.	A.	Pts.	Pen.
1975-76—Saskatoon Blades		WCHL	11	3	4	7	11
1976-77—Saskatoon Blades		WCHL	54	26	25	51	84
1977-78—Saskatoon Blades		WCHL	46	38	28	66	47
1978-79—Saskatoon Blades (c)		WHL	62	64	55	119	80
1979-80—Vancouver Canucks		NHL	47	5	14	19	11
1980-81—Vancouver Canucks (d-e)		NHL	77	18	11	29	57
1981-82—Colorado Rockies		NHL	80	24	36	60	26
1982-83—New Jersey Devils		NHL	76	14	19	33	47
1983-84—Minnesota North Stars (f)		NHL	68	7	10	17	54
1984-85—Minnesota North Stars (g)		NHL	29	4	7	11	15
1984-85—Quebec Nordiques		NHL	49	27	24	51	38
1985-86—Quebec Nordiques		NHL	77	26	32	58	64
1986-87—Quebec Nordiques (h)		NHL	46	25	19	44	17
1986-87—Detroit Red Wings		NHL	35	15	16	31	22
1987-88—Detroit Red Wings (i)		NHL	73	26	27	53	50
NHL TOTALS			657	191	215	406	401

(c)—August, 1979—Drafted by Vancouver Canucks as underage junior in NHL entry draft. Second Canucks pick, 26th overall, second round.

(d)—July, 1981—Traded with a fourth-round draft pick in 1982 by Vancouver to Winnipeg Jets as compensation for Canucks signing of Ivan Hlinka, a Czechoslovakian player drafted by Winnipeg in a special draft on May 28, 1981.

(e)—July, 1981—Traded with a third-round 1982 draft pick (Dave Kasper) by Winnipeg Jets to Colorado Rockies for Lucien DeBlois

(f)—October, 1983—Traded by New Jersey Devils to Minnesota North Stars for Dave Lewis.

(g)—December, 1984—Traded with Brad Maxwell by Minnesota North Stars to Quebec Nordiques for Tony McKegney and Bo Berglund.

(h)—January, 1987—Traded with Gilbert Delorme and Mark Kumpel by Quebec Nordiques to Detroit Red Wings for John Ogrodnick, Doug Shedden and Basil McRae.

(i)—June, 1988—Traded by Detroit Red Wings to Winnipeg Jets for Paul MacLean.

BOB BABCOCK

Defense . . . 6'1" . . . 190 lbs. . . . Born, Agincourt, Ont., August 3, 1968 . . . Shoots left.

Year	Team	League	Games	G.	A.	Pts.	Pen.
1984-85	St. Michaels Midgets	OHA	40	8	30	38	140
1985-86	Sault Ste. Marie Greyhounds (c)	OHL	50	1	7	8	185
1986-87	Sault Ste. Marie Greyhounds	OHL	62	7	8	15	243
1987-88	Sault Ste. Marie Greyhounds	OHL	8	0	2	2	30
1987-88	Cornwall Royals	OHL	42	0	16	16	120

(c)—June, 1986—Drafted as underage junior by Washington Capitals in 1986 NHL entry draft. Eleventh Capitals pick, 208th overall, 10th round.

WARREN BABE

Left Wing . . . 6'2" . . . 190 lbs. . . . Born, Medicine Hat, Alta., September 7, 1968 . . . Shoots left . . . (October 19, 1987)—Nerve damage in leg after being slashed by Patrick Roy in game vs. Montreal.

Year	Team	League	Games	G.	A.	Pts.	Pen.
1984-85	Lethbridge Broncos	WHL	70	7	14	21	117
1985-86	Lethbridge Broncos (c)	WHL	63	33	24	57	125
1986-87	Kamloops Blazers	WHL	68	36	57	93	129
1987-88	Minnesota North Stars	NHL	6	0	1	1	4
1987-88	Kalamazoo Wings	IHL	6	0	0	0	7
1987-88	Kamloops Blazers	WHL	32	17	19	36	73
NHL TOTALS			6	0	1	1	4

(c)—June, 1986—Drafted as underage junior by Minnesota North Stars in 1986 NHL entry draft. First North Stars pick, 12th overall, first round.

DAVID MICHAEL BABYCH

Defense . . . 6'2" . . . 215 lbs. . . . Born, Edmonton, Alta., May 23, 1961 . . . Shoots left . . . Brother of Wayne Babych . . . First member of Winnipeg Jets to be voted to mid-season All-Star game (1983) starting team . . . (March, 1984)—Separated shoulder . . . (December, 1984)—Back spasms . . . (January, 1987)—Missed 12 games with a hip injury . . . (February, 1988)—Missed five games with a bruised knee.

Year	Team	League	Games	G.	A.	Pts.	Pen.
1977-78	Portland Winter Hawks	WCHL	6	1	3	4	4
1977-78	Ft. Sask. Traders (a-c-d)	AJHL	56	31	69	100	37
1978-79	Portland Winter Hawks	WHL	67	20	59	79	63
1979-80	Portland Winter Hawks (a-e-f)	WHL	50	22	60	82	71
1980-81	Winnipeg Jets	NHL	69	6	38	44	90
1981-82	Winnipeg Jets	NHL	79	19	49	68	92
1982-83	Winnipeg Jets	NHL	79	13	61	74	56
1983-84	Winnipeg Jets	NHL	66	18	39	57	62
1984-85	Winnipeg Jets	NHL	78	13	49	62	78
1985-86	Winnipeg Jets (g)	NHL	19	4	12	16	14
1985-86	Hartford Whalers	NHL	62	10	43	53	36
1986-87	Hartford Whalers	NHL	66	8	33	41	44
1987-88	Hartford Whalers	NHL	71	14	36	50	54
NHL TOTALS			589	105	360	465	526

(c)—Named winner of AJHL Rookie of the Year Trophy.

(d)—Named winner of AJHL Top Defenseman Trophy.

(e)—Named winner of WHL Top Defenseman Trophy.

(f)—June, 1980—Drafted as underage junior by Winnipeg Jets in NHL entry draft. First Jets pick, second overall, first round.

(g)—November, 1985—Traded by Winnipeg Jets to Hartford Whalers for Ray Neufeld.

JOEL BAILLARGEON

Left Wing . . . 6'1" . . . 205 lbs. . . . Born, Charlesbourg, Que., October 6, 1964 . . . Shoots left . . . (November, 1986)—Suspended three games by IHL for fighting . . . (November 27, 1987)—Lacerated Achilles tendon in AHL game vs. Newmarket.

Year	Team	League	Games	G.	A.	Pts.	Pen.
1981-82—Trois-Rivieres Draveurs		QMJHL	26	1	3	4	47
1982-83—Trois-Rivieres		QHL	29	4	5	9	197
1982-83—Hull Olympics (c)		QHL	25	15	7	22	76
1983-84—Chicoutimi Sagueneens		QHL	60	48	35	83	184
1983-84—Sherbrooke Jets		AHL	8	0	0	0	26
1984-85—Granby Bisons		QHL	32	25	24	49	160
1985-86—Sherbrooke Canadiens		AHL	56	6	12	18	115
1986-87—Fort Wayne Komets		IHL	4	1	1	2	37
1986-87—Sherbrooke Canadiens		AHL	44	9	18	27	137
1986-87—Winnipeg Jets		NHL	11	0	1	1	15
1987-88—Winnipeg Jets		NHL	4	0	1	1	12
1987-88—Moncton Golden Flames		AHL	48	8	14	22	133
NHL TOTALS			15	0	2	2	27

(c)—June, 1983—Drafted as underage junior by Winnipeg Jets in NHL entry draft. Seventh Jets pick, 109th overall, sixth round.

PETER GEORGE BAKOVIC

Right Wing . . . 6'1" . . . 190 lbs. . . . Born, Thunder Bay, Ont., January 31, 1965 . . . Shoots right.

Year	Team	League	Games	G.	A.	Pts.	Pen.
1982-83—Thunder Bay Jr. B		OHA	40	30	29	59	159
1983-84—Kitchener Rangers		OHL	28	2	6	8	87
1983-84—Windsor Spitfires		OHL	35	10	25	35	74
1984-85—Windsor Spitfires		OHL	58	26	48	74	*259
1985-86—Moncton Golden Flames (c)		AHL	80	18	36	54	349
1986-87—Moncton Golden Flames		AHL	77	17	34	51	280
1987-88—Vancouver Canucks (d)		NHL	10	2	0	2	48
1987-88—Salt Lake Golden Eagles		IHL	39	16	27	43	221
NHL TOTALS			10	2	0	2	48

(c)—October, 1985—Signed by Moncton Golden Flames as a free agent.

(d)—March, 1988—Traded with Brian Bradley and future considerations (Kevan Guy) by Calgary Flames to Vancouver Canucks for Craig Coxe.

MIGUEL BALDRIS

Defense . . . 6' . . . 195 lbs. . . . Born, Montreal, Que., January 30, 1968 . . . Shoots left.

Year	Team	League	Games	G.	A.	Pts.	Pen.
1984-85—Richelieu Rivermen		Que. Midget	37	12	28	40	42
1985-86—Shawinigan Cataracts (c)		QHL	67	2	30	32	101
1986-87—St. Jean Castors (d)		QHL	67	7	34	41	72
1987-88—St. Jean Castors		QHL	69	5	34	39	136

(c)—June, 1986—Drafted as underage junior by Buffalo Sabres in 1986 NHL entry draft. Seventh Sabres pick, 110th overall, sixth round.

(d)—October, 1986—Traded by Shawinigan Cataracts to St. Jean Castors for Francois Gravel.

JEFF BALLANTYNE

Defense . . . 6'1" . . . 195 lbs. . . . Born, Brampton, Ont., January 7, 1969 . . . Shoots left.

Year	Team	League	Games	G.	A.	Pts.	Pen.
1985-86—Owen Sound Jr. A		OHA	44	2	18	20	128
1986-87—Ottawa 67's (c)		OHL	65	2	13	15	75
1987-88—Ottawa 67's		OHL	16	1	4	5	21

(c)—June, 1987—Drafted as underage junior by Washington Capitals in 1987 NHL entry draft. First Capitals pick, 36th overall, second round.

DARIN BANISTER

Defense . . . 6' . . . 185 lbs. . . . Born, Calgary, Alta., January 16, 1967 . . . Shoots right.

Year	Team	League	Games	G.	A.	Pts.	Pen.
1985-86—Calgary Spurs		AJHL	51	16	42	58	127
1986-87—Univ. of Illinois/Chicago (c)		CCHA	38	4	16	20	38
1987-88—Univ. of Illinois/Chicago		CCHA	39	2	26	28	48

(c)—June, 1987—Drafted by Detroit Red Wings in 1987 NHL entry draft. Eleventh Red Wings pick, 200th overall, 10th round.

MARK BAR

Defense ... 6'3" ... 197 lbs. ... Born, Toronto, Ont., February 15, 1968 ... Shoots left.

Year	Team	League	Games	G.	A.	Pts.	Pen.
1984-85	Toronto Nationals	OHA	42	10	23	33	78
1985-86	Peterborough Petes (c)	OHL	56	2	24	26	98
1986-87	Peterborough Petes	OHL	36	2	12	14	38
1987-88	Peterborough Petes	OHL	64	4	9	13	93

(c)—June, 1986—Drafted as underage junior by Philadelphia Flyers in 1986 NHL entry draft. Fourth Flyers pick, 83rd overall, fourth round.

MARIO BARBE

Defense ... 6'1" ... 195 lbs. ... Born, Abitibi, Que., March 17, 1967 ... Shoots left.

Year	Team	League	Games	G.	A.	Pts.	Pen.
1983-84	Bourassa AAA	Que.Midget	42	7	13	20	63
1984-85	Chicoutimi Sagueneens (c)	QHL	64	2	13	15	211
1985-86	Granby Bisons	QHL	70	5	25	30	261
1986-87	Granby Bisons	QHL	65	7	25	32	356
1987-88	Granby Bisons	QHL	45	8	10	18	294

(c)—June, 1985—Drafted as underage junior by Edmonton Oilers in NHL entry draft. Ninth Oilers pick, 209th overall, 10th round.

DON BARBER

Left Wing ... 6'1" ... 205 lbs. ... Born, Victoria, B.C., December 2, 1964 ... Shoots left ... (October, 1987)—Injured knee.

Year	Team	League	Games	G.	A.	Pts.	Pen.
1982-83	Kelowna Buckaroos (c)	BCJHL	35	26	31	57	54
1983-84	St. Albert Saints	AJHL	53	42	38	80	74
1984-85	Bowling Green Univ.	CCHA	39	15	12	27	44
1985-86	Bowling Green Univ. (d)	CCHA	35	21	22	43	64
1986-87	Bowling Green Univ.	CCHA	43	29	34	63	109
1987-88	Bowling Green Univ.	CCHA	38	18	47	65	60

(c)—June, 1983—Drafted as underage junior by Edmonton Oilers in NHL entry draft. Fifth Oilers pick, 120th overall, sixth round.

(d)—December, 1985—Traded with Marc Habscheid and Emanuel Viveiros by Edmonton Oilers to Minnesota North Stars for Gord Sherven and Don Biggs.

MURRAY BARON

Defense ... 6'3" ... 210 lbs. ... Born, Prince George, B.C., June 1, 1967 ... Shoots left.

Year	Team	League	Games	G.	A.	Pts.	Pen.
1984-85	Vernon Lakers	BCJHL	50	10	15	25	200
1985-86	Vernon Lakers (c)	BCJHL	46	12	32	44	....
1986-87	Univ. of North Dakota	WCHA	41	4	10	14	62
1987-88	Univ. of North Dakota	WCHA	41	1	10	11	95

(c)—June, 1986—Drafted as underage player by Philadelphia Flyers in 1986 NHL entry draft. Seventh Flyers pick, 167th overall, eighth round.

DAVID BARR

Center ... 6'1" ... 185 lbs. ... Born, Edmonton, Alta., November 30, 1960 ... Shoots right ... Also plays Right Wing ... (March 19, 1986)—Sprained knee vs. Hartford ... (November, 1987)—Separated right shoulder ... (December, 1987)—Broken right foot.

Year	Team	League	Games	G.	A.	Pts.	Pen.
1977-78	Pincher Creek	AJHL	60	16	32	48	53
1978-79	Edmonton Oil Kings	WHL	72	16	19	35	61
1979-80	Lethbridge Broncos	WHL	60	16	38	54	47
1980-81	Lethbridge Broncos	WHL	72	26	62	88	106
1981-82	Erie Blades	AHL	76	18	48	66	29
1981-82	Boston Bruins (c)	NHL	2	0	0	0	0
1982-83	Baltimore Skipjacks	AHL	72	27	51	78	67
1982-83	Boston Bruins	NHL	10	1	1	2	7
1983-84	New York Rangers (d)	NHL	6	0	0	0	2
1983-84	Tulsa Oilers	CHL	50	28	37	65	24
1983-84	St. Louis Blues (e)	NHL	1	0	0	0	0
1984-85	St. Louis Blues	NHL	75	16	18	34	32
1985-86	St. Louis Blues	NHL	75	13	38	51	70
1986-87	St. Louis Blues (f)	NHL	2	0	0	0	0
1986-87	Hartford Whalers (g)	NHL	30	2	4	6	19
1986-87	Detroit Red Wings	NHL	37	13	13	26	49
1987-88	Detroit Red Wings	NHL	51	14	26	40	58
	NHL TOTALS		289	59	100	159	237

(c)—September, 1981—Signed by Boston Bruins as a free agent.
(d)—October, 1983—Traded by Boston Bruins to New York Rangers for Dave Silk.
(e)—March, 1984—Traded with third-round 1984 draft pick (Alan Perry) and cash by New York Rangers to St. Louis Blues for Larry Patey and NHL rights to Bob Brooke.
(f)—October, 1986—Traded by St. Louis Blues to Hartford Whalers for Tim Bothwell.
(g)—January, 1987—Traded by Hartford Whalers to Detroit Red Wings for Randy Ladouceur.

JOHN DAVID BARRETT

Defense . . . 6'1" . . . 210 lbs. . . . Born, Ottawa, Ont., July 1, 1958 . . . Shoots left . . . (December 16, 1980)—Separated left shoulder vs. Edmonton . . . Brother of former NHLer Fred Barrett . . . (October 17, 1984)—Broke right hand vs. N.Y. Islanders . . . (January 13, 1986)—Injured groin at Toronto . . . (January 20, 1987)—Broke left kneecap when struck by a shot at Vancouver . . . (1987-88)—Underwent extensive therapy on his kneecap.

Year	Team	League	Games	G.	A.	Pts.	Pen.
1976-77	Windsor Spitfires	OMJHL	63	7	17	24	168
1977-78	Windsor Spitfires (c)	OMJHL	67	8	18	26	133
1978-79	Milwaukee Admirals	IHL	42	8	13	21	117
1978-79	Kalamazoo Wings	IHL	31	1	12	13	54
1979-80	Kalamazoo Wings	IHL	52	8	33	41	63
1979-80	Adirondack Red Wings	AHL	28	0	4	4	59
1980-81	Adirondack Red Wings	AHL	21	4	11	15	63
1980-81	Detroit Red Wings	NHL	56	3	10	13	60
1981-82	Detroit Red Wings	NHL	69	1	12	13	93
1982-83	Detroit Red Wings	NHL	79	4	10	14	74
1983-84	Detroit Red Wings	NHL	78	2	8	10	78
1984-85	Detroit Red Wings	NHL	71	6	19	25	117
1985-86	Detroit Red Wings (d)	NHL	65	2	12	14	125
1985-86	Washington Capitals	NHL	14	0	3	3	12
1986-87	Washington Capitals	NHL	55	2	2	4	43
1987-88	Binghamton Whalers	AHL	5	0	2	2	6
1987-88	Minnesota North Stars (e)	NHL	1	0	1	1	2
1987-88	Kalamazoo Wings	IHL	2	0	1	1	2
	NHL TOTALS		488	20	77	97	604

(c)—June, 1978—Drafted by Detroit Red Wings in NHL amateur draft. Tenth Red Wings pick, 129th overall, eighth round.
(d)—March, 1986—Traded with Greg Smith by Detroit Red Wings to Washington Capitals for Darren Veitch.
(e)—February 29, 1988—Traded by Washington Capitals to Minnesota North Stars for a conditional seventh-round draft pick.

LEN BARRIE

Right Wing . . . 6' . . . 195 lbs. . . . Born, Kimberly, B.C., June 4, 1969 . . . Shoots right.

Year	Team	League	Games	G.	A.	Pts.	Pen.
1984-85	Kelowna	B.C. Mdgt.	20	51	55	106	24
1985-86	Calgary Spurs	AJHL	23	7	14	21	86
1985-86	Calgary Wranglers	WHL	32	3	0	3	18
1986-87	Victoria Cougars	WHL	68	20	19	39	173
1987-88	Victoria Cougars (c)	WHL	70	37	49	86	192

(c)—June, 1988—Drafted by Edmonton Oilers in 1988 NHL entry draft. Seventh Oilers pick, 124th overall, sixth round.

ROBIN BARTELL

Defense . . . 6' . . . 195 lbs. . . . Born, Drake, Sask., May 16, 1961 . . . Shoots left.

Year	Team	League	Games	G.	A.	Pts.	Pen.
1980-81	Prince Albert Raiders	SAJHL	86	22	63	85	....
1981-82	Prince Albert Raiders	SAJHL	83	17	73	90	....
1982-83	Univ. of Saskatchewan	CAHA	24	4	14	18	....
1983-84	Canadian Olympic Team	Oly.	....	...	....	....	....
1984-85	Switzerland	Switz.	....	...	....	....	....
1984-85	Moncton Golden Flames (c)	AHL	41	4	11	15	66
1985-86	Moncton Golden Flames	AHL	74	4	21	25	100
1985-86	Calgary Flames (d)	NHL	1	0	0	0	0
1986-87	Fredericton Express	AHL	10	0	2	2	15
1986-87	Vancouver Canucks	NHL	40	0	1	1	14
1987-88	Fredericton Express	AHL	37	1	10	11	54
	NHL TOTALS		41	0	1	1	14

(c)—December, 1984—Signed by Moncton Golden Flames as a free agent.
(d)—July, 1986—Signed by Vancouver Canucks as a free agent.

WADE BARTLEY

Defense . . . 6'1" . . . 190 lbs. . . . Born, Killarney, Manitoba, May 16, 1970 . . . Shoots right . . . (November, 1986)—Torn knee cartilage.

Year	Team	League	Games	G.	A.	Pts.	Pen.
1986-87—Dauphin Kings		MJHL	36	4	24	28	55
1987-88—Dauphin Kings (c)		MJHL	....	...	...	....	....

(c)—June, 1988—Drafted by Washington Capitals in 1988 NHL entry draft. Third Capitals pick, 41st overall, second round.

DAVID BASEGGIO

Defense . . . 6'1" . . . 185 lbs. . . . Born, Niagara Falls, Ont., October 28, 1967 . . . Shoots left . . . Brother of Rob Basaggio (teammate at Yale Univ.).

Year	Team	League	Games	G.	A.	Pts.	Pen.
1984-85—Niagara Falls Jr. B		OHA	39	16	45	61	88
1985-86—Yale University (c)		ECAC	30	7	17	24	54
1986-87—Yale University (b)		ECAC	29	8	17	25	52
1987-88—Yale University		ECAC	24	4	22	26	67

(c)—June, 1986—Drafted by Buffalo Sabres in 1986 NHL entry draft. Fifth Sabres pick, 68th overall, fourth round.

BOB BASSEN

Center . . . 5'10" . . . 180 lbs. . . . Born, Calgary, Alta., May 6, 1965 . . . Shoots left . . . Son of Hank Bassen (Goalie with Chicago, Detroit and Pittsburgh in NHL in mid '60s) . . . (October 12, 1985)—Injured knee at Los Angeles.

Year	Team	League	Games	G.	A.	Pts.	Pen.
1982-83—Medicine Hat Tigers		WHL	4	3	2	5	0
1983-84—Medicine Hat Tigers		WHL	72	29	29	58	93
1984-85—Medicine Hat Tigers (a-c)		WHL	65	32	50	82	143
1985-86—New York Islanders		NHL	11	2	1	3	6
1985-86—Springfield Indians		AHL	54	13	21	34	111
1986-87—New York Islanders		NHL	77	7	10	17	89
1987-88—New York Islanders		NHL	77	6	16	22	99
NHL TOTALS			165	15	27	42	194

(c)—June, 1985—Signed by New York Islanders as a free agent.

JOHN ROBERTSON (ROBBY) BATEMAN

Defense . . . 6'2" . . . 190 lbs. . . . Born, LaSalle, Que., February 24, 1968 . . . Shoots left.

Year	Team	League	Games	G.	A.	Pts.	Pen.
1984-85—Laurentide Pionniers		Que.AAA Mid.	39	5	12	17	56
1985-86—St. Lawrence College H.S. (c)		Que. H.S.	41	2	13	15	73
1986-87—University of Vermont		ECAC	32	2	3	5	78
1987-88—University of Vermont		ECAC	34	1	3	4	64

(c)—June, 1986—Drafted as underage player by Winnipeg Jets in 1986 NHL entry draft. Sixth Jets pick, 113th overall, sixth round.

GREG BATTERS

Right Wing . . . 6'1" . . . 196 lbs. . . . Born, Victoria, B.C., January 10, 1967 . . . Shoots right.

Year	Team	League	Games	G.	A.	Pts.	Pen.
1984-85—Victoria Cougars		WHL	54	16	17	33	87
1985-86—Victoria Cougars		WHL	71	27	26	53	164
1986-87—Victoria Cougars (c)		WHL	64	21	40	61	157
1987-88—Victoria Cougars		WHL	18	3	4	7	65
1987-88—Moose Jaw Warriors		WHL	32	7	12	19	99

(c)—June, 1987—Drafted by Los Angeles Kings in 1987 NHL entry draft. Fifth Kings pick, 111th overall, sixth round.

COLLIN BAUER

Defense . . . 6'1" . . . 175 lbs. . . . Born, Edmonton, Alta., September 6, 1970 . . . Shoots left.

Year	Team	League	Games	G.	A.	Pts.	Pen.
1986-87—Saskatoon Blades		WHL	61	1	25	26	37
1987-88—Saskatoon Blades (c)		WHL	70	9	53	62	66

(c)—June, 1988—Drafted by Edmonton Oilers in 1988 NHL entry draft. Fourth Oilers pick, 61st overall, third round.

KEN JAMES BAUMGARTNER

Defense . . . 6' . . . 200 lbs. . . . Born, Flin Flon, Manitoba, March 11, 1966 . . . Shoots left.

Year	Team	League	Games	G.	A.	Pts.	Pen.
1983-84—Prince Albert Raiders		WHL	57	1	6	7	203
1984-85—Prince Albert Raiders (c)		WHL	60	3	9	12	252
1985-86—Prince Albert Raiders (d)		WHL	70	4	23	27	277
1986-87—Chur		Switz.	....	...	....	....	....
1986-87—New Haven Nighthawks		AHL	13	0	3	3	99
1987-88—Los Angeles Kings		NHL	30	2	3	5	189
1987-88—New Haven Nighthawks		AHL	48	1	5	6	181
NHL TOTALS			30	2	3	5	189

(c)—June, 1985—Drafted as underage junior by Buffalo Sabres in 1985 NHL entry draft. Twelfth Sabres pick, 245th overall, 12th round.

(d)—January, 1986—Traded with Larry Playfair and Sean McKenna by Buffalo Sabres to Los Angeles Kings for Brian Engblom and Doug Smith.

TIM BEAN

Left Wing . . . 6'1" . . . 190 lbs. . . . Born, Sault Ste. Marie, Ont., March 9, 1967 . . . Shoots left.

Year	Team	League	Games	G.	A.	Pts.	Pen.
1982-83—North York Tier II		MTHL	45	9	11	20	57
1983-84—Belleville Bulls		OHL	63	12	13	25	131
1984-85—Belleville Bulls		OHL	31	10	11	21	60
1984-85—North Bay Centennials (c)		OHL	28	11	13	24	61
1985-86—North Bay Centennials		OHL	66	32	34	66	129
1986-87—North Bay Centennials		OHL	65	24	39	63	134
1987-88—Newmarket Saints		AHL	76	12	16	28	118

(c)—June, 1985—Drafted by Toronto Maple Leafs in 1985 NHL entry draft as an underage junior. Seventh Maple Leafs pick, 127th overall, seventh round.

PATRICK BEAUCHESNE

Defense . . . 6'2" . . . 205 lbs. . . . Born, Prince Albert, Sask., February 12, 1967 . . . Shoots left.

Year	Team	League	Games	G.	A.	Pts.	Pen.
1984-85—Medicine Hat Tigers		WHL	53	1	9	10	85
1985-86—Medicine Hat Tigers		WHL	4	0	0	0	10
1985-86—Moose Jaw Warriors		WHL	64	3	13	16	116
1986-87—Moose Jaw Warriors (c)		WHL	69	11	33	44	151
1987-88—Binghamton Whalers		AHL	2	0	0	0	14
1987-88—Moose Jaw Warriors		WHL	54	1	19	20	190

(c)—June 1987—Drafted by Washington Capitals in 1987 NHL entry draft. Fourth Capitals pick, 99th overall, fifth round.

YVES BEAUDOIN

Defense . . . 5'11" . . . 180 lbs. . . . Born, Pointe Aux Trembles, Que., January 7, 1965 . . . Shoots right.

Year	Team	League	Games	G.	A.	Pts.	Pen.
1981-82—Hull Olympics		QMJHL	50	2	18	20	39
1982-83—Hull Olympics		QHL	6	1	2	3	9
1982-83—Shawinigan Cataracts (c)		QHL	56	11	23	34	51
1983-84—Shawinigan Cataracts		QHL	68	14	43	57	93
1984-85—Shawinigan Cataracts (a)		QHL	58	20	38	58	78
1985-86—Binghamton Whalers		AHL	48	5	12	17	36
1985-86—Washington Capitals		NHL	4	0	0	0	0
1986-87—Binghamton Whalers		AHL	63	11	25	36	35
1986-87—Washington Capitals		NHL	6	0	0	0	5
1987-88—Binghamton Whalers		AHL	64	11	39	50	56
1987-88—Washington Capitals		NHL	1	0	0	0	0
NHL TOTALS			11	0	0	0	5

(c)—June, 1983—Drafted as underage junior by Washington Capitals in NHL entry draft. Sixth Capitals pick, 195th overall, tenth round.

COREY BEAULIEU

Defense . . . 6'1" . . . 210 lbs. . . . Born, Winnipeg, Manitoba, September 9, 1969 . . . Shoots left.

Year	Team	League	Games	G.	A.	Pts.	Pen.
1984-85—Winnipeg Stars		Man. Mdgt.	48	2	19	21	168
1985-86—Moose Jaw Warriors		WHL	68	3	1	4	111
1986-87—Moose Jaw Warriors		WHL	63	2	7	9	188
1987-88—Seattle Thunderbirds (c)		WHL	67	2	9	11	225

(c)—June, 1988—Drafted by Hartford Whalers in 1988 NHL entry draft. Fifth Whalers pick, 116th overall, sixth round.

NICHOLAS BEAULIEU

Left Wing . . . 6'1" . . . 200 lbs. . . . Born, Rimouski, Que., August 19, 1968 . . . Shoots left.

Year	Team	League	Games	G.	A.	Pts.	Pen.
1984-85—Richelieu Rivermen		Que. Midget	42	4	18	22	68
1985-86—Drummondville Voltigeurs (c)		QHL	70	11	20	21	93
1986-87—Drummondville Voltigeurs		QHL	69	19	34	53	198
1987-88—Laval Titans		QHL	64	39	56	95	240

(c)—June, 1986—Drafted as underage junior by Edmonton Oilers in 1986 NHL entry draft. Eighth Oilers pick, 168th overall, eighth round.

BRAD BECK

Defense . . . 5'11" . . . 185 lbs. . . . Born, Vancouver, B.C., February 10, 1964 . . . Shoots right.

Year	Team	League	Games	G.	A.	Pts.	Pen.
1980-81—Penticton Knights		BCJHL	....	10	24	34	....
1981-82—Penticton Knights (c)		BCJHL	52	13	32	45	116
1982-83—Michigan State Univ.		CCHA	42	5	15	20	40
1983-84—Michigan State Univ.		CCHA	42	2	7	9	67
1984-85—Michigan State Univ.		CCHA	42	5	18	23	60
1985-86—Michigan State Univ.		CCHA	41	3	15	18	40
1986-87—Saginaw Generals		IHL	82	10	24	34	114
1987-88—Saginaw Generals		IHL	80	8	22	30	159

(c)—June, 1982—Drafted as underage player by Chicago Black Hawks in NHL entry draft. Fifth Black Hawks pick, 91st overall, fifth round.

ROGER BELANGER

Right Wing and Center . . . 6' . . . 192 lbs. . . . Born, St. Catharines, Ont., December 1, 1965 . . . Shoots right . . . (October 31, 1984)—Sprained knee at New Jersey and missed 11 games . . . (January, 1985)—Sprained knee.

Year	Team	League	Games	G.	A.	Pts.	Pen.
1981-82—London Midgets		Ont. Midget	25	20	21	41	..
1982-83—London Knights		OHL	68	17	14	31	53
1983-84—Kingston Canadians (c)		OHL	67	44	46	90	66
1984-85—Hamilton Steelhawks		OHL	3	3	3	6	0
1984-85—Pittsburgh Penguins		NHL	44	3	5	8	32
1985-86—Baltimore Skipjacks		AHL	69	17	21	38	61
1986-87—Muskegon Lumberjacks		IHL	5	1	2	3	4
1986-87—Baltimore Skipjacks		AHL	32	9	11	20	14
1987-88—Muskegon Lumberjacks		IHL	5	1	3	4	6
1987-88—New Haven Nighthawks		AHL	2	0	0	0	0
NHL TOTALS			44	3	5	8	32

(c)—June, 1984—Drafted by Pittsburgh Penguins in NHL entry draft. Third Penguins pick, 16th overall, first round.

BRUCE BELL

Defense . . . 5'11" . . . 195 lbs. . . . Born, Toronto, Ont., February 15, 1965 . . . Shoots left.

Year	Team	League	Games	G.	A.	Pts.	Pen.
1981-82—Sault Ste. Marie Greyhounds		OHL	67	11	18	29	63
1982-83—Sault Ste. Marie Greyhounds		OHL	5	0	2	2	2
1982-83—Windsor Spitfires (c)		OHL	61	10	35	45	39
1983-84—Brantford Alexanders		OHL	63	7	41	48	55
1984-85—Quebec Nordiques		NHL	75	6	31	37	44
1985-86—St. Louis Blues (d)		NHL	75	2	18	20	43
1986-87—St. Louis Blues (e)		NHL	45	3	13	16	18
1987-88—Colorado Rangers		IHL	65	11	34	45	107
1987-88—New York Rangers (f)		NHL	13	1	2	3	8
NHL TOTALS			208	12	64	76	113

(c)—June, 1983—Drafted by Quebec Nordiques in NHL entry draft. Second Nordiques pick, 52nd overall, third round.

(d)—October, 1985—Traded by Quebec Nordiques to St. Louis Blues for Gilbert Delorme.

(e)—June, 1987—Traded with fourth-round 1988 draft pick and future considerations by St. Louis Blues to New York Rangers for Tony McKegney and Rob Whistle.

(f)—August, 1988—Traded with Walt Poddubny, Jari Gronstrand and fourth-round draft choice in 1989 by New York Rangers to Quebec Nordiques for Normand Rochefort and Jason Lafreniere.

BRAD BELLAND

Center . . . 6'1" . . . 185 lbs. . . . Born, Windsor, Ont., January 4, 1967 . . . Shoots right.

Year	Team	League	Games	G.	A.	Pts.	Pen.
1983-84—Windsor Jr. B		OHA	43	26	25	51	63
1984-85—Sudbury Wolves (c)		OHL	64	17	27	44	48
1985-86—Sudbury Wolves (d)		OHL	7	0	6	6	0
1985-86—Hamilton Steelhawks		OHL	52	20	20	40	40
1986-87—Cornwall Royals		OHL	50	28	25	53	31
1987-88—Cornwall Royals		OHL	61	22	46	68	71

(c)—June, 1985—Drafted by Chicago Black Hawks in NHL entry draft. Fifth Black Hawks pick, 95th overall, fifth round.

(d)—October, 1985—Traded by Sudbury Wolves to Hamilton Steelhawks for Mike Hudson and Keith Van Rooyen.

BRIAN BELLEFEUILLE

Left Wing . . . 6'2" . . . 185 lbs. . . . Born, Natick, Mass., March 21, 1967 . . . Shoots left.

Year	Team	League	Games	G.	A.	Pts.	Pen.
1984-85—Framingham North H.S.		Mass.	20	35	26	61	..
1985-86—Canterbury H.S. (c)		Mass.	31	57	58	115	..
1986-87—Univ. of Ill./Chicago		CCHA	2	0	0	0	2
1987-88—University of Maine		H. East	15	2	2	4	30

(c)—June, 1986—Drafted by Toronto Maple Leafs in 1986 NHL entry draft. Ninth Maple Leafs pick, 174th overall, ninth round.

BRIAN BELLOWS

Right Wing . . . 6' . . . 196 lbs. . . . Born, St. Catharines, Ont., September 1, 1964 . . . Shoots right . . . Also plays Center . . . (November, 1981)—Separated shoulder at Niagara Falls. Coached two games while recovering to become the youngest coach in OHL history (17) . . . (January, 1984)—Became youngest team captain in Minnesota North Stars history . . . (October, 1984)—Tendinitis in elbow . . . (October, 1986)—Missed 13 games with an injured wrist.

Year	Team	League	Games	G.	A.	Pts.	Pen.
1980-81—Kitchener Rangers		OHL	66	49	67	116	23
1981-82—Kitchener Rangers (a-c)		OHL	47	45	52	97	23
1982-83—Minnesota North Stars		NHL	78	35	30	65	27
1983-84—Minnesota North Stars		NHL	78	41	42	83	66
1984-85—Minnesota North Stars		NHL	78	26	36	62	72
1985-86—Minnesota North Stars		NHL	77	31	48	79	46
1986-87—Minnesota North Stars		NHL	65	26	27	53	54
1987-88—Minnesota North Stars		NHL	77	40	41	81	81
NHL TOTALS			453	199	224	423	346

(c)—June, 1982—Drafted as underage junior by Minnesota North Stars in NHL entry draft. First North Stars pick, second overall, first round.

ERIC (RICK) BENNETT

Left Wing . . . 6'3" . . . 200 lbs. . . . Born, Springfield, Mass., July 24, 1967 . . . Shoots left.

Year	Team	League	Games	G.	A.	Pts.	Pen.
1985-86—Wilbraham Monson Acad. (c)		Mass. H.S.	20	30	39	69	25
1986-87—Providence College		H. East	32	15	12	27	34
1987-88—Providence College		H. East	33	9	16	25	70

(c)—June, 1986—Drafted by Minnesota North Stars in 1986 NHL entry draft. Fourth North Stars pick, 54th overall, third round.

BRIAN BENNING

Defense . . . 6' . . . 175 lbs. . . . Born, Edmonton, Alta., June 10, 1966 . . . Shoots left . . . Brother of Jim Benning . . . (December, 1983)—Cracked bone in his right wrist and missed 38 games . . . (December 28, 1984)—Broke right leg vs. Victoria.

Year	Team	League	Games	G.	A.	Pts.	Pen.
1983-84—Portland Winter Hawks (c)		WHL	38	6	41	47	108
1984-85—Kamloops Blazers		WHL	17	3	18	21	26
1984-85—St. Louis Blues		NHL	4	0	2	2	0
1985-86—Team Canada		Int'l	60	6	13	19	43
1985-86—St. Louis Blues (d)		NHL	..	..	..	..	..
1986-87—St. Louis Blues		NHL	78	13	36	49	110
1987-88—St. Louis Blues		NHL	77	8	29	37	107
NHL TOTALS			159	21	67	88	217

(c)—June, 1984—Drafted as underage junior by St. Louis Blues in NHL entry draft. First Blues pick, 26th overall, second round.

(d)—No regular season record. Played six playoff games.

JAMES BENNING

Defense . . . 6' . . . 183 lbs. . . . Born, Edmonton, Alta., April 29, 1963 . . . Shoots left . . . Brother of Brian Benning . . . (February 8, 1986)—Injured ligaments in right knee vs. St. Louis.

Year	Team	League	Games	G.	A.	Pts.	Pen.
1978-79—Ft. Saskatchewan Traders		AJHL	45	14	57	71	10
1979-80—Portland Winter Hawks		WHL	71	11	60	71	42
1980-81—Portland Winter Hawks (a-c-d)		WHL	72	28	*111	139	61
1981-82—Toronto Maple Leafs		NHL	74	7	24	31	46
1982-83—Toronto Maple Leafs		NHL	74	5	17	22	47
1983-84—Toronto Maple Leafs		NHL	79	12	39	51	66
1984-85—Toronto Maple Leafs		NHL	80	9	35	44	55
1985-86—Toronto Maple Leafs		NHL	52	4	21	25	71
1986-87—Newmarket Saints		AHL	10	1	5	6	0
1986-87—Toronto Maple Leafs (e)		NHL	5	0	0	0	4
1986-87—Vancouver Canucks		NHL	54	2	11	13	40
1987-88—Vancouver Canucks		NHL	77	7	26	33	58
NHL TOTALS			495	46	173	219	387

(c)—Winner of WHL Top Defenseman Trophy.
(d)—June, 1981—Drafted as underage junior by Toronto Maple Leafs in NHL entry draft. First Toronto pick, sixth overall, first round.
(e)—December, 1986—Traded with Dan Hodgson by Toronto Maple Leafs to Vancouver Canucks for Rick Lanz.

PAUL BERALDO

Right Wing . . . 6' . . . 180 lbs. . . . Born, Stoney Creek, Ont., October 5, 1967 . . . Shoots right.

Year	Team	League	Games	G.	A.	Pts.	Pen.
1984-85—Grimsby Jr.B.		OHA	25	9	4	13	24
1985-86—Sault Ste. Marie Greyhounds (c)		OHL	61	15	13	28	48
1986-87—Sault Ste. Marie Greyhounds		OHL	63	39	51	90	117
1987-88—Maine Mariners		AHL	62	22	15	37	112
1987-88—Boston Bruins		NHL	3	0	0	0	0
NHL TOTALS			3	0	0	0	0

(c)—June, 1986—Drafted as underage junior by Boston Bruins in 1986 NHL entry draft. Sixth Bruins pick, 139th overall, seventh round.

PERRY BEREZAN

Center . . . 6'2" . . . 190 lbs. . . . Born, Edmonton, Alta., December 5, 1964 . . . Shoots right . . . (February, 1986)—Missed eight games with sinus problems . . . (March 19, 1986)—Broke ankle vs. Minnesota . . . (November, 1986)—Injured groin . . . (March, 1987)—Surgery for groin injury . . . (November, 1987)—Injured groin . . . (February, 1988)—Hand laceration.

Year	Team	League	Games	G.	A.	Pts.	Pen.
1981-82—St. Albert Saints		AJHL	47	16	36	52	47
1982-83—St. Albert Saints (c)		AJHL	57	37	40	77	110
1983-84—Univ. of North Dakota		WCHA	44	28	24	52	29
1984-85—Univ. of North Dakota		WCHA	42	23	35	58	32
1984-85—Calgary Flames		NHL	9	3	2	5	4
1985-86—Calgary Flames		NHL	55	12	21	33	39
1986-87—Calgary Flames		NHL	24	5	3	8	24
1987-88—Calgary Flames		NHL	29	7	12	19	66
NHL TOTALS			117	27	38	65	133

(c)—June, 1983—Drafted as underage junior by Calgary Flames in NHL entry draft. Third Flames pick, 55th overall, third round.

WILLIAM (BILL) BERG

Defense . . . 6' . . . 190 lbs. . . . Born, St. Catharines, Ont., October 21, 1967 . . . Shoots left . . . (March, 1985)—Broken ankle . . . (October, 1986)—Injured knee.

Year	Team	League	Games	G.	A.	Pts.	Pen.
1984-85—Grimsby Jr. B		OHA	42	10	22	32	153
1985-86—Toronto Marlboros (c)		OHL	64	3	35	38	143
1986-87—Toronto Marlboros		OHL	57	3	15	18	138
1986-87—Springfield Indians		AHL	4	1	1	2	4
1987-88—Springfield Indians		AHL	76	6	26	32	148

(c)—June, 1986—Drafted as underage junior by New York Islanders in 1986 NHL entry draft. Third Islanders pick, 59th overall, third round.

MIKE BERGER

Defense . . . 6'1" . . . 197 lbs. . . . Born, Edmonton, Alta., June 2, 1967 . . . Shoots right . . . (November, 1983)—Separated shoulder . . . (January, 1985)—Hyperextended left knee . . . (October, 1985)—Shoulder injury . . . (September, 1987)—Injured knee in Minnesota training camp . . . (October 27, 1988)—Bruised foot.

Year	Team	League	Games	G.	A.	Pts.	Pen.
1983-84	Lethbridge Broncos	WHL	41	2	9	11	60
1984-85	Lethbridge Broncos (c)	WHL	58	9	31	40	85
1985-86	Lethbridge Broncos	WHL	21	2	9	11	39
1985-86	Spokane Chiefs (b)	WHL	36	7	31	38	56
1986-87	Spokane Chiefs (b)	WHL	65	26	49	75	80
1986-87	Indianapolis Checkers	IHL	4	0	3	3	4
1987-88	Kalamazoo Wings	IHL	36	5	10	15	94
1987-88	Minnesota North Stars	NHL	29	3	1	4	65
	NHL TOTALS		29	3	1	4	65

(c)—June, 1985—Drafted as underage junior by Minnesota North Stars in NHL entry draft. Second North Stars pick, 69th overall, fourth round.

MARTIN BERGERON

Center . . . 6' . . . 185 lbs. . . . Born, Verdun, Que., January 20, 1968 . . . Shoots left.

Year	Team	League	Games	G.	A.	Pts.	Pen.
1985-86	Drummondville Voltigeurs	QHL	74	14	34	48	65
1986-87	Drummondville Voltigeurs	QHL	66	36	58	94	83
1987-88	Drummondville Voltigeurs (c)	QHL	69	45	64	109	99

(c)—June, 1988—Drafted by New York Rangers in 1988 NHL entry draft. Fourth Rangers pick, 99th overall, fifth round.

MARC BERGEVIN

Defense . . . 6' . . . 185 lbs. . . . Born, Montreal, Que., August 11, 1965 . . . Shoots left. . . (March 18, 1987)—Sprained neck at Toronto.

Year	Team	League	Games	G.	A.	Pts.	Pen.
1982-83	Chicoutimi Sagueneens (c)	QHL	64	3	27	30	113
1983-84	Chicoutimi Sagueneens	QHL	70	10	35	45	125
1983-84	Springfield Indians	AHL	7	0	1	1	2
1984-85	Chicago Black Hawks	NHL	60	0	6	6	54
1985-86	Chicago Black Hawks	NHL	71	7	7	14	60
1986-87	Chicago Black Hawks	NHL	66	4	10	14	66
1987-88	Chicago Black Hawks	NHL	58	1	6	7	85
1987-88	Saginaw Hawks	IHL	10	2	7	9	20
	NHL TOTALS		255	12	29	41	265

(c)—June, 1983—Drafted as underage junior by Chicago Black Hawks in NHL entry draft. Third Black Hawks pick, 59th overall, third round.

TIMOTHY BERGLUND

Center . . . 6'3" . . . 180 lbs. . . . Born, Crookston, Minn., January 11, 1965 . . . Shoots right.

Year	Team	League	Games	G.	A.	Pts.	Pen.
1982-83	Lincoln High School (c)	Minn. H.S.	20	26	22	48	....
1983-84	Univ. of Minnesota	WCHA	24	4	11	15	4
1984-85	Univ. of Minnesota	WCHA	46	7	12	19	16
1985-86	Univ. of Minnesota	WCHA	48	11	16	27	26
1986-87	Univ. of Minnesota	WCHA	49	18	17	35	48
1987-88	Fort Wayne Komets	IHL	13	2	1	3	9
1987-88	Binghamton Whalers	AHL	63	21	26	47	31

(c)—June, 1983—Drafted by Washington Capitals as underage junior in NHL entry draft. First Capitals pick, 75th overall, fourth round.

RON BERNACCI

Center . . . 5'10" . . . 175 lbs. . . . Born, Hamilton, Ont., February 21, 1967 . . . Shoots left.

Year	Team	League	Games	G.	A.	Pts.	Pen.
1983-84	Hamilton Jr. B	OHA	42	26	31	57	83
1984-85	Hamilton Steelhawks	OHL	57	20	19	39	65
1985-86	Hamilton Steelhawks	OHL	66	21	26	47	155
1986-87	Hamilton Steelhawks (c)	OHL	66	43	47	90	79
1987-88	Hamilton Steelhawks	OHL	60	31	53	84	124

(c)—June, 1987—Drafted by Toronto Maple Leafs in 1987 NHL entry draft. Tenth Maple Leafs pick, 196th overall, 10th round.

BRAD BERRY

Defense . . . 6'2" . . . 190 lbs. . . . Born, Barshaw, Alta., April 1, 1965 . . . Shoots left . . . (November 9, 1987)—Broken nose.

Year	Team	League	Games	G.	A.	Pts.	Pen.
1982-83—St. Albert Junior Saints (c)	AJHL	55	9	33	42	97
1983-84—Univ. of North Dakota	WCHA	32	2	7	9	8
1984-85—Univ. of North Dakota	WCHA	40	4	26	30	26
1985-86—Univ. of North Dakota	WCHA	40	6	29	35	26
1985-86—Winnipeg Jets	NHL	13	1	0	1	10
1986-87—Winnipeg Jets	NHL	52	2	8	10	60
1987-88—Winnipeg Jets	NHL	48	0	6	6	75
1987-88—Moncton Golden Flames	AHL	10	1	3	4	14
NHL TOTALS		113	3	14	17	145

(c)—June, 1983—Drafted as underage junior by Winnipeg Jets in NHL entry draft. Third Jets pick, 29th overall, second round.

KEN E. BERRY

Left Wing . . . 5'9" . . . 165 lbs. . . . Born, Barnaby, B.C., June 21, 1960 . . . Shoots left.

Year	Team	League	Games	G.	A.	Pts.	Pen.
1977-78—New Westminister Bruins	WCHL	5	0	0	0	0
1978-79—Denver University	WCHA	39	17	20	37	52
1979-80—Canadian Olympic Team (c)	Int'l	46	19	19	38	38
1979-80—Olympics	....	6	4	1	5	8
1980-81—Denver University (a-d)	WCHA	40	22	34	56	84
1980-81—Wichita Wind (e)	CHL	9	7	6	13	13
1981-82—Edmonton Oilers	NHL	15	2	3	5	9
1981-82—Wichita Wind	CHL	58	28	29	57	70
1982-83—Moncton Alpines	AHL	76	24	26	50	80
1983-84—Moncton Alpines	AHL	53	18	20	38	75
1983-84—Edmonton Oilers	NHL	13	2	3	5	10
1984-85—Nova Scotia Voyageurs (f)	AHL	71	30	27	57	40
1985-86—Bayreuth	W. Germ.	33	27	25	52	88
1985-86—Canadian Nat. Team	Int'l	8	1	2	3	20
1986-87—Canadian Nat. Team	Int'l	52	17	27	44	60
1987-88—Canadian Nat. Team	Int'l	67	22	23	45	55
1987-88—Vancouver Canucks (g)	NHL	14	2	3	5	6
NHL TOTALS		42	6	9	15	25

(c)—June, 1980—Drafted by Vancouver Canucks in NHL entry draft. Fifth Canucks pick, 112th overall, sixth round.

(d)—March, 1981—NHL rights traded with Garry Lariviere by Vancouver Canucks to Edmonton Oilers for Blair MacDonald.

(e)—March, 1981—Signed by Edmonton Oilers.

(f)—August, 1984—Traded with Gary Lariviere by Edmonton Oilers to New Jersey Devils for future considerations.

(g)—March, 1988—Signed by Vancouver Canucks as a free agent.

CRAIG BERUBE

Left Wing . . . 6'2" . . . 195 lbs. . . . Born, Calihoo, Alta., December 17, 1965 . . . Shoots left . . . (March, 1988)—Sprained left knee.

Year	Team	League	Games	G.	A.	Pts.	Pen.
1982-83—Kamloops Junior Oilers	WHL	4	0	0	0	0
1983-84—New Westminster Bruins	WHL	70	11	20	31	104
1984-85—New Westminster Bruins	WHL	70	25	44	69	191
1985-86—Kamloops Blazers	WHL	32	17	14	31	119
1985-86—Medicine Hat Tigers (c)	WHL	34	14	16	30	95
1986-87—Hershey Bears	AHL	63	7	17	24	325
1986-87—Philadelphia Flyers	NHL	7	0	0	0	57
1987-88—Hershey Bears	AHL	31	5	9	14	119
1987-88—Philadelphia Flyers	NHL	27	3	2	5	108
NHL TOTALS		34	3	2	5	165

(c)—March, 1986—Signed as free agent by Philadelphia Flyers.

JEFF BEUKEBOOM

Defense . . . 6'4" . . . 210 lbs. . . . Born, Ajax, Ont., March 28, 1965 . . . Shoots right . . . Brother of John Beukeboom and Brian Beukeboom. Nephew of Ed Kea (Atlanta/St. Louis, '73-'83) . . . First non-goalie to be drafted in first round not to have scored a goal in season prior to being drafted . . . (December, 1984)—Injured knee in World Junior Tournament in game vs. United States . . . (October 24, 1987)—Lacerated knuckle vs. Vancouver.

Year	Team	League	Games	G.	A.	Pts.	Pen.
1981-82—Newmarket		OPJHL	49	5	30	35	218
1982-83—Sault Ste. Marie Greyhounds (c)		OHL	70	0	25	25	143
1983-84—Sault Ste. Marie Greyhounds		OHL	61	6	30	36	178
1984-85—Sault Ste. Marie Greyhounds (a)		OHL	37	4	20	24	85
1985-86—Nova Scotia Oilers		AHL	77	9	20	29	175
1985-86—Edmonton Oilers (d)		NHL	....	...	....	....	....
1986-87—Nova Scotia Voyageurs		AHL	14	1	7	8	35
1986-87—Edmonton Oilers		NHL	44	3	8	11	124
1987-88—Edmonton Oilers		NHL	73	5	20	25	201
NHL TOTALS			117	8	28	36	325

(c)—June, 1983—Drafted as underage junior by Edmonton Oilers in NHL entry draft. First Oilers pick, 19th overall, first round.

(d)—No regular season record. Played one playoff game.

DON BIGGS

Center . . . 5'8" . . . 180 lbs. . . . Born, Mississauga, Ont., April 7, 1965 . . . Shoots right . . . (April, 1982)—Injured knee ligaments.

Year	Team	League	Games	G.	A.	Pts.	Pen.
1981-82—Mississauga Reds		MTHL	54	49	67	116	125
1982-83—Oshawa Generals (c)		OHL	70	22	53	75	145
1983-84—Oshawa Generals		OHL	58	31	60	91	149
1984-85—Oshawa Generals		OHL	60	48	69	117	105
1984-85—Springfield Indians		AHL	6	0	3	3	0
1984-85—Minnesota North Stars		NHL	1	0	0	0	0
1985-86—Springfield Indians (d)		AHL	28	15	16	31	46
1985-86—Nova Scotia Oilers		AHL	47	6	23	29	36
1986-87—Nova Scotia Oilers (e)		AHL	80	22	25	47	165
1987-88—Hershey Bears		AHL	77	38	41	79	151
NHL TOTALS			1	0	0	0	0

(c)—June, 1983—Drafted as underage junior by Minnesota North Stars in NHL entry draft. Ninth North Stars pick, 156th overall, eighth round.

(d)—December, 1985—Traded with Gord Sherven by Minnesota North Stars to Edmonton Oilers for Marc Habscheid, Emanuel Viveiros and Don Barber.

(e)—July, 1987—Signed as free agent by Philadelphia Flyers.

CHRIS BIOTTI

Defense . . . 6'3" . . . 198 lbs. . . . Born, Waltham, Mass., April 22, 1967 . . . Shoots left . . . (August, 1985)—Injured shoulder during U.S. Sports festival.

Year	Team	League	Games	G.	A.	Pts.	Pen.
1983-84—Belmont Hill H.S.		Mass. H.S.	23	10	20	30	....
1984-85—Belmont Hill H.S. (c)		Mass. H.S.	23	13	24	37	....
1985-86—Harvard University		ECAC	15	3	5	8	53
1986-87—Harvard University		ECAC	30	1	6	7	23
1987-88—Salt Lake Golden Eagles		IHL	72	5	19	24	73

(c)—June, 1985—Drafted by Calgary Flames in 1985 NHL entry draft. First Flames pick, 17th overall, first round.

GRANT BISCHOFF

Left Wing . . . 5'10" . . . 165 lbs. . . . Born, Anoka, Minn., October 26, 1968 . . . Shoots left . . . (March, 1986)—Broken thumb.

Year	Team	League	Games	G.	A.	Pts.	Pen.
1986-87—Grand Rapids H.S.		Minn. H.S.	23	26	31	57	....
1987-88—Univ. of Minnesota (c)		WCHA	40	14	22	36	14

(c)—June, 1988—Drafted by Minnesota North Stars in 1988 entry draft. Eighth North Stars pick, 211th overall, 11th round.

MICHAEL BISHOP

Defense . . . 6'2" . . . 187 lbs. . . . Born, Sarnia, Ont., June 15, 1966 . . . Shoots left. . . . (December, 1986)—Knee surgery . . . (October, 1987)—Fractured wrist in ECAC pre-season game.

Year	Team	League	Games	G.	A.	Pts.	Pen.
1983-84—Mooretown Flags Jr.C		OHA	40	24	24	48	91
1984-85—Sarnia Bees Jr.B (c)		OHA	43	9	32	41	104
1985-86—Colgate University		ECAC	25	9	8	17	63
1986-87—Colgate University		ECAC	30	7	17	24	68
1987-88—Colgate University		ECAC	31	8	24	32	49

(c)—June, 1985—Drafted as underage junior by Montreal Canadiens in 1985 NHL entry draft. Fourteenth Canadiens pick, 226th overall, 11th round.

STEVEN GUY BISSON

Defense . . . 6'1" . . . 175 lbs. . . . Born, Ottawa, Ont., May 24, 1968 . . . Shoots left . . . (September, 1985)—Broken thumb.

Year	Team	League	Games	G.	A.	Pts.	Pen.
1984-85—Ottawa Senators		OHA	49	1	15	16	96
1985-86—Sault Ste. Marie Greyhounds (c)		OHL	66	3	23	26	44
1986-87—Sault Ste. Marie Greyhounds		OHL	52	5	15	20	38
1987-88—Sault Ste. Marie Greyhounds		OHL	3	0	2	2	0
1987-88—Cornwall Royals		OHL	61	10	57	67	89

(c)—June, 1986—Drafted as an underage junior by Montreal Canadiens in 1986 NHL entry draft. Seventh Canadiens pick, 120th overall, sixth round.

SCOTT BJUGSTAD

Left Wing . . . 6'1" . . . 185 lbs. . . . Born St. Paul, Minn., June 2, 1981 . . . Shoots left . . . 1979 graduate of Minnesota Irondale High School where he was All-Conference for three years and All-State as a senior . . . Named prep All-America in Soccer . . . Member of 1984 U.S. Olympic Team . . . Also plays Center. . . . (March 15, 1987)—Pulled abdominal muscle at Chicago . . . (October 31, 1987)—Separated shoulder in game vs. Washington . . . (December, 1987)—Strained knee ligaments . . . (February, 1988)—Knee surgery.

Year	Team	League	Games	G.	A.	Pts.	Pen.
1979-80—University of Minnesota		WCHA	18	2	2	4	2
1980-81—University of Minnesota (c)		WCHA	35	12	13	25	34
1981-82—University of Minnesota		WCHA	36	29	14	43	24
1982-83—University of Minnesota		WCHA	44	43	48	91	30
1983-84—U.S. National Team		Int'l	54	31	20	51	28
1983-84—U.S. Olympic Team		Int'l	6	3	2	5	6
1983-84—Minnesota North Stars		NHL	5	0	0	0	2
1983-84—Salt Lake Golden Eagles		CHL	15	10	8	18	6
1984-85—Minnesota North Stars		NL	72	11	4	15	32
1984-85—Springfield Indians		AHL	5	2	3	5	2
1985-86—Minnesota North Stars		NHL	80	43	33	76	24
1986-87—Minnesota North Stars		NHL	39	4	9	13	43
1986-87—Springfield Indians		AHL	11	6	4	10	7
1987-88—Minnesota North Stars		NHL	33	10	12	22	15
NHL TOTALS			229	68	58	126	116

(c)—June, 1981—Drafted by Minnesota North Stars in NHL entry draft. Thirteenth North Stars pick, 181st overall, ninth round.

THOMAS BJUHR

Right Wing . . . 6'1" . . . 207 lbs. . . . Born, Stockholm, Sweden, August 28, 1966 . . . Shoots left.

Year	Team	League	Games	G.	A.	Pts.	Pen.
1984-85—AIK Jr. (c)		Sweden	33	38	18	56	28
1985-86—AIK		Sweden	14	0	1	1	8
1986-87—Portland Winter Hawks		WHL	39	28	26	54	23
1987-88—Adirondack Red Wings		AHL	58	4	2	6	21

(c)—June, 1985—Drafted by Detroit Red Wings in 1985 NHL entry draft. Seventh Red Wings pick, 134th overall, seventh round.

BRIAN BLAD

Defense . . . 6'2" . . . 195 lbs. . . . Born, Brockville, Ont., July 22, 1967 . . . Shoots left.

Year	Team	League	Games	G.	A.	Pts.	Pen.
1983-84—Windsor Spitfires		OHL	78	8	21	29	123
1984-85—Windsor Spitfires		OHL	56	1	7	8	126
1985-86—Windsor Spitfires		OHL	56	2	9	11	195
1986-87—Windsor Spitfires		OHL	15	1	1	2	30
1986-87—Belleville Bulls (c)		OHL	20	1	5	6	43
1987-88—Newmarket Saints		AHL	39	0	4	4	74
1987-88—Milwaukee Admirals		IHL	28	1	6	7	45

(c)—June, 1987—Drafted by Toronto Maple Leafs in 1987 NHL entry draft. Ninth Maple Leafs pick, 175th overall, ninth round.

JEFF BLAESER

Left Wing . . . 6'3" . . . 195 lbs. . . . Born, Parma, Ohio, November 5, 1970 . . . Shoots left.

Year	Team	League	Games	G.	A.	Pts.	Pen.
1986-87—St. John's Prep.		Mass. H.S.	..	15	22	37	..
1987-88—St. John's Prep. (c)		Mass. H.S.	..	14	20	34	..

(c)—June, 1988—Drafted by Pittsburgh Penguins in 1988 NHL entry draft. Seventh Penguins pick, 130th overall, seventh round.

MICHAEL WALTER BLAISDELL

Right Wing ... 6'1" ... 196 lbs. ... Born, Moose Jaw, Sask., January 18, 1960 ... Shoots right ... (November 6, 1985)—Pulled groin vs. Washington and missed two games ... (October 28, 1986)—Separated left shoulder at Hartford.

Year	Team	League	Games	G.	A.	Pts.	Pen.
1977-78—Regina Pats	WCHL	6	5	5	10	2
1977-78—Regina Blues	SJHL	60	70	46	116	43
1978-79—University of Wisconsin	WCHA	20	7	1	8	15
1979-80—Regina Pats (b-c)	WHL	63	71	38	109	62
1980-81—Adirondack Red Wings	AHL	41	10	4	14	8
1980-81—Detroit Red Wings	NHL	32	3	6	9	10
1981-82—Detroit Red Wings	NHL	80	23	32	55	48
1982-83—Detroit Red Wings (d)	NHL	80	18	23	41	22
1983-84—Tulsa Oilers	CHL	32	10	8	18	23
1983-84—New York Rangers	NHL	36	5	6	11	31
1984-85—New Haven Nighthawks	AHL	64	21	23	44	41
1984-85—New York Rangers	NHL	12	1	0	1	11
1985-86—Pittsburgh Penguins (e)	NHL	66	15	14	29	36
1986-87—Baltimore Skipjacks	AHL	43	12	12	24	47
1986-87—Pittsburgh Penguins	AHL	10	1	1	2	2
1987-88—Newmarket Saints	AHL	57	28	28	56	30
1987-88—Toronto Maple Leafs	NHL	18	3	2	5	2
NHL TOTALS		334	69	84	153	162

(c)—June, 1980—Drafted by Detroit Red Wings in NHL entry draft. First Red Wings pick, 11th overall, first round.

(d)—June, 1983—Traded with Mark Osborne and Willie Huber by Detroit Red Wings to New York Rangers for Ron Duguay, Eddie Johnstone and Eddie Mio.

(e)—October, 1985—Acquired by Pittsburgh Penguins in 1985 NHL waiver draft.

ROB BLAKE

Defense ... 6'3" ... 205 lbs. ... Born, Simcoe, Ont., December 10, 1969 ... Shoots right ... (April, 1987)—Dislocated shoulder.

Year	Team	League	Games	G.	A.	Pts.	Pen.
1986-87—Stratford Junior B	OHA	31	11	20	31	115
1987-88—Bowling Green Univ. (c)	CCHA	36	5	8	13	72

(c)—June, 1988—Drafted by Los Angeles Kings in 1988 NHL entry draft. Fourth Kings pick, 70th overall, fourth round.

JOHN BLESSMAN

Defense ... 6'3" ... 211 lbs. ... Born, Toronto, Ont., April 27, 1967 ... Shoots left.

Year	Team	League	Games	G.	A.	Pts.	Pen.
1983-84—Wexford Midgets	OHA	40	8	12	20	60
1984-85—Toronto Marlboros	OHL	25	1	3	4	42
1985-86—Toronto Marlboros	OHL	64	2	13	15	116
1986-87—Toronto Marlboros (c)	OHL	61	6	24	30	130
1987-88—Toronto Marlboros	OHL	23	8	11	19	64
1987-88—Utica Devils	AHL	24	0	2	2	50

(c)—June, 1987—Drafted by New Jersey Devils in 1987 NHL entry draft. Eighth Devils pick, 170th overall, ninth round.

JEFF BLOEMBERG

Defense ... 6'1" ... 200 lbs. ... Born, Listowel, Ont., January 31, 1968 ... Shoots right.

Year	Team	League	Games	G.	A.	Pts.	Pen.
1984-85—Listowell Jr. B	OHA	31	7	14	21	73
1985-86—North Bay Centennials (c)	OHL	60	2	11	13	76
1986-87—North Bay Centennials	OHL	60	5	13	18	91
1987-88—North Bay Centennials	OHL	46	9	26	35	60
1987-88—Colorado Rangers	IHL	5	0	0	0	0

(c)—June, 1986—Drafted as underage junior by New York Rangers in 1986 NHL entry draft. Fifth Rangers pick, 93rd overall, fifth round.

JOHN BLUM

Defense ... 6'3" ... 205 lbs. ... Born, Detroit, Mich., October 8, 1959 ... Shoots right.

Year	Team	League	Games	G.	A.	Pts.	Pen.
1980-81—University of Michigan		WCHA	....	8	32	40	....
1981-82—Wichita Wind (c)		CHL	79	8	33	41	247
1982-83—Moncton Alpines		AHL	76	10	30	40	219
1982-83—Edmonton Oilers		NHL	5	0	3	3	24
1983-84—Moncton Alpines		AHL	57	3	22	25	202
1983-84—Edmonton Oilers (d)		NHL	4	0	1	1	2
1983-84—Boston Bruins		NHL	12	1	1	2	30
1984-85—Boston Bruins		NHL	75	3	13	16	263
1985-86—Boston Bruins		NHL	61	1	7	8	80
1985-86—Moncton Golden Flames		AHL	12	1	5	6	37
1986-87—Washington Capitals (e-f)		NHL	66	2	8	10	133
1987-88—Boston Bruins		NHL	19	0	1	1	70
1987-88—Maine Mariners (g)		AHL	43	5	18	23	136
NHL TOTALS			242	7	34	41	602

(c)—May, 1981—Signed by Edmonton Oilers as a free agent.
(d)—March, 1983—Traded by Edmonton Oilers to Boston Bruins for Larry Melnyk.
(e)—October, 1986—Selected by Washington Capitals in 1987 NHL waiver draft.
(f)—June, 1987—Traded by Washington Capitals to Boston Bruins for future considerations.
(g)—August, 1988—Signed by Detroit Red Wings as a free agent.

JEFFREY BLUMER

Right Wing . . . 6'1" . . . 190 lbs. . . . Born, St. Paul, Minn., September 25, 1969.

Year	Team	League	Games	G.	A.	Pts.	Pen.
1986-87—Hill Murray H.S.		Minn. H.S.	27	22	37	59	..
1987-88—St. Thomas College (c)		MIAC	28	11	30	41	12

(c)—June, 1988—Drafted by New York Islanders in 1988 NHL entry draft. Twelfth Islanders' pick, 184th overall, ninth round.

BRENT BOBYCK

Left Wing . . . 5'11" . . . 180 lbs. . . . Born, Regina, Sask., April 26, 1968 . . . Shoots left.

Year	Team	League	Games	G.	A.	Pts.	Pen.
1985-86—Notre Dame Hounds (c)		Sask.	25	13	27	40	12
1986-87—Univ. of North Dakota		WCHA	46	8	11	19	16
1987-88—Univ. of North Dakota		WCHA	41	10	20	30	43

(c)—June, 1986—Drafted by Montreal Canadiens in 1986 NHL entry draft. Fourth Canadiens pick, 78th overall, fourth round.

BOB BODAK

Left Wing . . . 6'2" . . . 190 lbs. . . . Born, Thunder Bay, Ont., May 28, 1961 . . . Shoots left . . . (November, 1987)—Punctured sinus cavity.

Year	Team	League	Games	G.	A.	Pts.	Pen.
1983-84—Lakehead University		....	....	...	....	....	....
1984-85—Springfield Indians (c)		AHL	79	21	24	45	52
1985-86—Springfield Indians		AHL	4	0	0	0	4
1985-86—Moncton Golden Flames		AHL	58	27	15	42	114
1986-87—Moncton Golden Flames (d)		AHL	48	11	20	31	75
1987-88—Salt Lake Golden Eagles		IHL	44	12	10	22	117
1987-88—Calgary Flames		NHL	3	0	0	0	22
NHL TOTALS			3	0	0	0	22

(c)—September, 1984—Signed by Springfield Indians as a free agent.
(d)—January, 1986—Signed by Calgary Flames as a free agent.

DOUG BODGER

Defense . . . 6'2" . . . 200 lbs. . . . Born, Chemainus, B.C., June 18, 1966 . . . Shoots left . . . (February, 1985)—Missed four games with slight shoulder separation . . . (April, 1985)—Surgery to remove bone chip near big toe of left foot . . . (December, 1987)—Sprained knee.

Year	Team	League	Games	G.	A.	Pts.	Pen.
1982-83—Kamloops Junior Oilers (b)		WHL	72	26	66	92	98
1983-84—Kamloops Junior Oilers (a-c)		WHL	70	21	77	98	90
1984-85—Pittsburgh Penguins		NHL	65	5	26	31	67
1985-86—Pittsburgh Penguins		NHL	79	4	33	37	63
1986-87—Pittsburgh Penguins		NHL	76	11	38	49	52
1987-88—Pittsburgh Penguins		NHL	69	14	31	45	103
NHL TOTALS			289	34	128	162	285

(c)—June, 1984—Drafted as underage junior by Pittsburgh Penguins in NHL entry draft. Second Penguins pick, ninth overall, first round.

RICK BOH

Center . . . 5'10" . . . 180 lbs. . . . Born, Kamloops, B.C., May 18, 1964 . . . Shoots right.

Year	Team	League	Games	G.	A.	Pts.	Pen.
1983-84	Colorado College	WCHA	27	1	5	6	12
1984-85	Colorado College	WCHA	38	10	18	28	24
1985-86	Colorado College	WCHA	40	30	29	59	14
1986-87	Colorado College (b-c)	WCHA	38	22	42	64	37
1987-88	Minnesota North Stars	NHL	8	2	1	3	4
1987-88	Kalamazoo Wings	IHL	75	26	41	67	45
	NHL TOTALS		8	2	1	3	4

(c)—June, 1987—Selected by Minnesota North Stars in 1987 NHL supplemental draft.

SERGE BOISVERT

Right Wing . . . 5'9" . . . 175 lbs. . . . Born, Drummondville, Que., June 1, 1959 . . . Shoots right . . . Also plays Center.

Year	Team	League	Games	G.	A.	Pts.	Pen.
1977-78	Sherbrooke Beavers	QMJHL	55	17	33	50	19
1978-79	Sherbrooke Beavers	QMJHL	72	50	72	122	45
1979-80	Sherbrooke Beavers	QMJHL	69	52	72	124	47
1979-80	New Brunswick Hawks (c)	AHL	..	..	..	..	..
1980-81	New Brunswick Hawks	AHL	60	19	27	46	31
1981-82			...	..	..	..	..
1982-83	Toronto Maple Leafs (d)	NHL	17	0	2	2	4
1982-83	St. Catharines Saints	AHL	19	10	9	19	2
1982-83	Moncton Alpines	AHL	29	6	12	18	7
1983-84	Moncton Alpines	AHL	66	15	13	28	34
1984-85	Sherbrooke Canadiens (e)	AHL	63	38	41	79	8
1984-85	Montreal Canadiens	NHL	14	2	2	4	0
1985-86	Sherbrooke Canadiens (b)	AHL	69	40	48	88	18
1985-86	Montreal Canadiens	NHL	9	2	2	4	2
1986-87	Montreal Canadiens	NHL	1	0	0	0	0
1986-87	Sherbrooke Canadiens (b)	AHL	78	27	54	81	29
1987-88	Canadian Olympic Team	Int'l	71	29	28	57	36
1987-88	Montreal Canadiens	NHL	5	1	1	2	2
	NHL TOTALS		46	5	7	12	8

(c)—No regular season record. Scored four goals in seven playoff games.
(d)—January, 1983—Traded by Toronto Maple Leafs to Edmonton Oilers for Reid Bailey.
(e)—September, 1984—Signed by Montreal Canadiens as a free agent.

CLAUDE BOIVIN

Left Wing . . . 6'2" . . . 190 lbs. . . . Born, St. Foy, Que., March 1, 1970 . . . Shoots left.

Year	Team	League	Games	G.	A.	Pts.	Pen.
1986-87	Ste. Foy AAA	Que. Mdgt.	39	12	27	39	90
1987-88	Drummondville Voltigeurs (c)	QHL	63	23	26	49	233

(c)—June, 1988—Drafted by Philadelphia Flyers in 1988 NHL entry draft. First Flyers pick, 14th overall, first round.

SEAN BOLAND

Defense . . . 6'3" . . . 185 lbs. . . . Born, Toronto, Ont., February 18, 1968 . . . Shoots right.

Year	Team	League	Games	G.	A.	Pts.	Pen.
1984-85	Toronto Nationals	MTHL	60	17	24	41	90
1985-86	Toronto Marlboros (c)	OHL	52	2	10	12	85
1986-87	Toronto Marlboros	OHL	17	0	4	4	23
1987-88	Toronto Marlboros	OHL	52	3	21	24	143

(c)—June, 1986—Drafted as underage junior by Toronto Maple Leafs in 1986 NHL entry draft. Third Maple Leafs pick, 48th overall, third round.

GRAEME BONAR

Right Wing . . . 6'3" . . . 205 lbs. . . . Born, Toronto, Ont., January 21, 1966 . . . Shoots right . . . (September, 1986)—Broken wrist.

Year	Team	League	Games	G.	A.	Pts.	Pen.
1981-82	Henry Carr H.S.	MTJHL	35	27	24	51	32
1982-83	Windsor Spitfires	OHL	70	14	26	40	78
1983-84	Windsor Spitfires	OHL	21	5	9	14	37
1983-84	Sault Ste. Marie Greyhounds (c)	OHL	44	10	30	40	43
1984-85	Sault Ste. Marie Greyhounds (a)	OHL	66	*66	71	137	93

Year	Team	League	Games	G.	A.	Pts.	Pen.
1985-86—Sault Ste. Marie Greyhounds (d)	OHL	38	33	25	58	21
1985-86—Peterborough Petes (b)	OHL	18	20	15	35	20
1986-87—Sherbrooke Canadiens	AHL	21	6	6	12	7
1987-88—Sherbrooke Canadiens	AHL	8	1	1	2	2
1987-88—Saginaw Hawks	IHL	11	6	4	10	2
1987-88—Baltimore Skipjacks	AHL	6	2	1	3	0

(c)—June, 1984—Drafted as underage junior by Montreal Canadiens in NHL entry draft. Fifth Canadiens pick, 54th overall, third round.

(d)—February, 1986—Traded by Sault Ste. Marie Greyhounds to Peterborough Petes for Brad Aitken and future considerations.

JOHN BORRELL

Right Wing . . . 6'2" . . . 190 lbs. . . . Born, Shakopee, Minn., March 23, 1967 . . . Shoots right.

Year	Team	League	Games	G.	A.	Pts.	Pen.
1984-85—Burnsville H.S. (c)	Minn.H.S.	27	20	16	36	16
1985-86—University of Lowell	H. East	41	3	15	18	12
1986-87—University of Lowell	H. East	34	5	10	15	43
1987-88—University of Lowell	H. East	29	2	8	10	34

(c)—June, 1985—Drafted by Winnipeg Jets in 1985 NHL entry draft. Fifth Jets pick, 102nd overall, fifth round.

LUCIANO BORSATO

Center . . . 5'10" . . . 165 lbs. . . . Born, Richmond Hill, Ont., January 7, 1966 . . . Shoots right.

Year	Team	League	Games	G.	A.	Pts.	Pen.
1983-84—Bramalea Blues (c)	MTJHL	37	20	36	56	59
1984-85—Clarkson University	ECAC	33	15	17	32	37
1985-86—Clarkson University	ECAC	32	17	20	37	50
1986-87—Clarkson University	ECAC	31	16	*41	57	55
1987-88—Clarkson University (d)	ECAC	33	15	29	44	38
1987-88—Moncton Golden Flames	AHL	3	1	1	2	0

(c)—June, 1984—Drafted as underage junior by Winnipeg Jets in NHL entry draft. Seventh Jets pick, 135th overall, seventh round.

(d)—Named second-team All-America (East).

LAURIE JOSEPH BOSCHMAN

Center . . . 6' . . . 185 lbs. . . . Born, Major, Sask., June 4, 1960 . . . Shoots left . . . (December 7, 1980)—Finger tendon injury . . . (January, 1981)—Mononucleous . . . (December 7, 1983)—Dislocated shoulder at New Jersey . . . (April, 1988)—Surgery to reconstruct right shoulder.

Year	Team	League	Games	G.	A.	Pts.	Pen.
1976-77—Brandon	MJHL	47	17	40	57	139
1976-77—Brandon Wheat Kings	WCHL	3	0	1	1	0
1977-78—Brandon Wheat Kings	WCHL	72	42	57	99	227
1978-79—Brandon Wheat Kings (a-c)	WCHL	65	66	83	149	215
1979-80—Toronto Maple Leafs	NHL	80	16	32	48	78
1980-81—New Brunswick Hawks	AHL	4	4	1	5	47
1980-81—Toronto Maple Leafs	NHL	53	14	19	33	178
1981-82—Toronto Maple Leafs (d)	NHL	54	9	19	28	150
1981-82—Edmonton Oilers	NHL	11	2	3	5	37
1982-83—Edmonton Oilers (e)	NHL	62	8	12	20	183
1982-83—Winnipeg Jets	NHL	12	3	5	8	33
1983-84—Winnipeg Jets	NHL	61	28	46	74	234
1984-85—Winnipeg Jets	NHL	80	32	44	76	180
1985-86—Winnipeg Jets	NHL	77	27	42	69	241
1986-87—Winnipeg Jets	NHL	80	17	24	41	152
1987-88—Winnipeg Jets	NHL	80	25	23	48	227
NHL TOTALS		650	181	269	450	1693

(c)—August, 1979—Drafted by Toronto Maple Leafs in NHL entry draft. First Toronto pick, ninth overall, first round.

(d)—March, 1982—Traded by Toronto Maple Leafs to Edmonton Oilers for Walt Poddubny and Phil Drouillard.

(e)—March, 1983—Traded by Edmonton Oilers to Winnipeg Jets for Willy Lindstrom.

MICHEL (MIKE) BOSSY

Right Wing . . . 6' . . . 186 lbs. . . . Born, Montreal, Que., January 22, 1957 . . . Shoots right . . . Set NHL record for goals in season by a rookie (53 in 1977-78) . . . Set NHL record for

fastest 100 goals (129 games) . . . Tied NHL record with goals in 10 straight games 1977-78 (Since broken by Charlie Simmer). . . Tied NHL record of Rocket Richard for fastest 50 goals (in 50 games) 1980-81 (Since broken by Wayne Gretzky) . . . Set record for most goals in regular season plus playoffs (85) 1980-81 (Since broken by Wayne Gretzky) . . . Set record for most points in a playoff year (35) 1981 (Since broken by Wayne Gretzky) . . . Set record for most hat tricks in one season (9) 1980-81 (Since broken by Wayne Gretzky) . . . Set NHL record for fastest 250 goals (315 games) (Since broken by Wayne Gretzky) . . . Set record for most goals (69) by a right wing 1978-79 (Since broken by Jari Kurri) . . . Set record for most assists by a right wing (83) 1981-82 . . . Set record for most points by a right wing (147) 1981-82 . . . Injured left knee during 1983 playoffs . . . (October, 1983)—Pulled hip muscle . . . (January 28, 1984)—Sprained right knee in collision with Dwight Foster vs. Detroit . . . (September, 1984)—Injured right knee during training camp . . . (January 16, 1985)—Pulled muscle on left side at Edmonton . . . First NHL player to have eight consecutive 50-goal seasons (Since equalled by Wayne Gretzky) . . . Holds NHL record for career playoff goals with 85 (Broke Maurice Richard's record of 82) . . . (October, 1986)—Strained lower back. He had recurring muscle spasms throughout the season and missed several games . . . Brother-in-law of Pierre Creamer (Former coach of Pittsburgh Penguins) . . . Missed the 1987-88 season while he underwent therapy for abnormalities in the disks in his lower back.

Year	Team	League	Games	G.	A.	Pts.	Pen.
1972-73	Laval National	QJHL	4	1	2	3	0
1973-74	Laval National	QJHL	68	70	48	118	45
1974-75	Laval National (a)	QJHL	67	*84	65	149	42
1975-76	Laval National (b)	QJHL	64	79	57	136	25
1976-77	Laval National (b-c-d)	QJHL	61	75	51	126	12
1977-78	New York Islanders (b-e)	NHL	73	53	38	91	6
1978-79	New York Islanders (b)	NHL	80	*69	57	126	25
1979-80	New York Islanders	NHL	75	51	41	92	12
1980-81	New York Islanders (a-f)	NHL	79	*68	51	119	32
1981-82	New York Islanders (a-g-h)	NHL	80	64	83	147	22
1982-83	New York Islanders (a-h-i)	NHL	79	60	58	118	20
1983-84	New York Islanders (a-i)	NHL	67	51	67	118	8
1984-85	New York Islanders (b)	NHL	76	58	59	117	38
1985-86	New York Islanders (a-i)	NHL	80	61	62	123	14
1986-87	New York Islanders	NHL	63	38	37	75	33
1987-88	Did not play		....	...	....	....	....
	NHL TOTALS		752	573	553	1126	210

(c)—Most Gentlemanly Player Award winner.
(d)—Drafted from Laval National by New York Islanders in first round of 1977 amateur draft.
(e)—Won Calder Memorial Trophy and named THE SPORTING NEWS NHL Rookie of the Year.
(f)—Tied with Steve Payne (Minn.) for playoff lead in goals (17), tied Bryan Trottier (NYI) for playoff lead in assists (18) and led 1981 playoffs with 35 points.
(g)—Won Conn Smythe Trophy (Most Valuable Player in Stanley Cup Playoffs).
(h)—Led Stanley Cup Playoffs with 17 goals.
(i)—Won Lady Byng Trophy (Combination of Sportsmanship and Quality play).

TIM BOTHWELL

Defense . . . 6'3" . . . 195 lbs. . . . Born, Vancouver, B.C., May 6, 1955 . . . Shoots left . . . Missed part of 1974-75 season with broken ankle . . . Missed part of 1978-79 season with fractured cheekbone that required surgery . . . (October, 1981)—Badly strained stomach muscles . . . (March 1, 1983)—Cut tendons in left hand vs. Los Angeles . . . (January, 1984)—Injured ligament in right knee during CHL game . . . (October, 1985)—Missed seven games due to a parasitic infection caused by drinking tainted water . . . (March 17, 1986)—Missed four games with sprained right shoulder when checked in a team practice.

Year	Team	League	Games	G.	A.	Pts.	Pen.
1973-74	Burlington Mohawks	....	..	..	..	..	..
1974-75	Brown University JV	ECAC	9	6	9	15	14
1975-76	Brown University	ECAC	29	12	22	34	30
1976-77	Brown University (a)	ECAC	27	7	27	34	40
1977-78	Brown University (a-c)	ECAC	29	9	26	35	48
1978-79	New York Rangers	NHL	1	0	0	0	2
1978-79	New Haven Nighthawks	AHL	66	15	33	48	44
1979-80	New Haven Nighthawks	AHL	22	6	7	13	25
1979-80	New York Rangers	NHL	45	4	6	10	20
1980-81	New Haven Nighthawks	AHL	73	10	53	63	98
1980-81	New York Rangers	NHL	3	0	1	1	0
1981-82	Springfield Indians	AHL	10	0	4	4	7
1981-82	New York Rangers (d)	NHL	13	0	3	3	10
1982-83	St. Louis Blues	NHL	61	4	11	15	34
1983-84	Montana Magic	CHL	4	0	3	3	0
1983-84	St. Louis Blues	NHL	62	2	13	15	65

Year	Team	League	Games	G.	A.	Pts.	Pen.
1984-85—St. Louis Blues		NHL	79	4	22	26	62
1985-86—Hartford Whalers (e)		NHL	62	2	8	10	53
1986-87—Hartford Whalers (f)		NHL	4	1	0	1	0
1986-87—St. Louis Blues		NHL	72	5	16	21	46
1987-88—St. Louis Blues		NHL	78	6	13	19	76
NHL TOTALS			480	28	93	121	368

(c)—Signed by New York Rangers, May, 1978.
(d)—October, 1982—Claimed by St. Louis Blues in NHL waiver draft.
(e)—October, 1985—Sold by St. Louis Blues to Hartford Whalers.
(f)—October, 1986—Traded by Hartford Whalers to St. Louis Blues for Dave Barr.

BRUCE ALLAN BOUDREAU

Center ... 5'10" ... 170 lbs. ... Born, Toronto, Ont., January 9, 1955 ... Shoots left ... Set OMJHL record with 165 pts. in '74-75 (Broken in '75-76 by Mike Kaszycki's 170 pts.) ... Set OMJHL record with 68 goals in '74-75 (Broken in '77-78 by Bobby Smith's 69) ... (1983-84)—Assistant coach at St. Catharines ... (February, 1986)—Broke hand in AHL game.

Year	Team	League	Games	G.	A.	Pts.	Pen.
1972-73—Toronto Marlboros		Jr."A"OHA	61	38	49	87	22
1973-74—Toronto Marlboros (b-c)		Jr."A"OHA	53	46	67	113	51
1974-75—Toronto Marlboros (d-e)		Jr."A"OHA	69	*68	97	*165	52
1975-76—Johnstown Jets		NAHL	34	25	35	60	14
1975-76—Minnesota Fighting Saints (f)		WHA	30	3	6	9	4
1976-77—Dallas Black Hawks		CHL	58	*37	34	71	40
1976-77—Toronto Maple Leafs		NHL	15	2	5	7	4
1977-78—Dallas Black Hawks		CHL	22	13	9	22	11
1977-78—Toronto Maple Leafs		NHL	40	11	18	29	12
1978-79—Toronto Maple Leafs		NHL	26	4	3	7	2
1978-79—New Brunswick Hawks		AHL	49	20	38	58	22
1979-80—Toronto Maple Leafs		NHL	2	0	0	0	2
1979-80—New Brunswick Hawks		AHL	75	36	54	90	47
1980-81—New Brunswick Hawks		AHL	40	17	41	58	22
1980-81—Toronto Maple Leafs		NHL	39	10	14	24	18
1981-82—Cincinnati Tigers (b)		AHL	65	42	61	103	42
1981-82—Toronto Maple Leafs		NHL	12	0	2	2	6
1982-83—St. Catharines Saints		AHL	80	50	72	122	65
1982-83—Toronto Maple Leafs (g)		NHL	..	..	..	..	..
1983-84—St. Catharines Saints		AHL	80	47	62	109	44
1984-85—Baltimore Skipjacks (h)		AHL	17	4	7	11	4
1985-86—Chicago Black Hawks (i)		NHL	7	1	0	1	2
1985-86—Nova Scotia Oilers		AHL	65	30	36	66	36
1986-87—Nova Scotia Oilers		AHL	78	35	47	82	40
1987-88—Springfield Indians		AHL	80	42	*74	*116	84
NHL TOTALS			141	28	42	70	46
WHA TOTALS			30	3	6	9	4

(c)—May, 1974—Selected by Minnesota Fighting Saints in World Hockey Association amateur player draft.
(d)—Won Eddie Powers Memorial Trophy (leading scorer).
(e)—Drafted from Toronto Marlboros by Toronto Maple Leafs in third round of 1975 amateur draft.
(f)—August, 1976—Signed by Toronto Maple Leafs.
(g)—Played four playoff games (1 goal), none in regular season.
(h)—March, 1985—Signed by Baltimore Skipjacks as a free agent after completing season in West Germany.
(i)—August, 1985—Released by Detroit Red Wings and signed by Chicago Black Hawks as a free agent.

CHARLES BOURGEOIS

Defense ... 6'4" ... 205 lbs. ... Born, Moncton, N.B., November 11, 1959 ... Shoots right ... (January, 1987)—Missed 11 games with a virus and lost 10 pounds ... (November, 1987)—Broken jaw when struck by a puck vs. Detroit ... (December, 1987)—Shoulder separation ... (February, 1988)—Strained left ankle in game vs. Pittsburgh.

Year	Team	League	Games	G.	A.	Pts.	Pen.
1980-81—University of Moncton (a-c-d)		AUAA	24	8	23	31	..
1981-82—Oklahoma City Stars		CHL	13	2	2	4	17
1981-82—Calgary Flames		NHL	54	2	13	15	112
1982-83—Calgary Flames		NHL	15	2	3	5	21
1982-83—Colorado Flames		CHL	51	10	18	28	128
1983-84—Colorado Flames (a)		CHL	54	12	32	44	133
1983-84—Calgary Flames		NHL	17	1	3	4	35
1984-85—Calgary Flames		NHL	47	2	10	12	134

Year	Team	League	Games	G.	A.	Pts.	Pen.
1985-86—Calgary Flames (e)		NHL	29	5	5	10	128
1985-86—St. Louis Blues		NHL	31	2	7	9	116
1986-87—St. Louis Blues		NHL	66	2	12	14	164
1987-88—St. Louis Blues (f)		NHL	30	0	1	1	78
1987-88—Hartford Whalers		NHL	1	0	0	0	0
NHL TOTALS			290	16	54	70	788

(c)—Named to All Canada Team (East).
(d)—April, 1981—Signed by Calgary Flames as free agent.
(e)—February, 1986—Traded with Gino Cavallini and Eddy Beers by Calgary Flames to St. Louis Blues for Joe Mullen, Terry Johnson and Rik Wilson.
(f)—March, 1988—Traded with a third-round 1988 draft pick by St. Louis Blues to Hartford Whalers for a second-round 1989 draft pick.

GLEN ROBERT (BOB) BOURNE

Center and Left Wing . . . 6'3" . . . 195 lbs. . . . Born, Kindersley, Sask., June 21, 1954 . . . Shoots left . . . Signed a contract with Houston Astros at Covington, Va. and batted .257 . . . (October 17, 1981)—Pulled muscles in upper thigh . . . (October 8, 1983)—Scored first overtime goal in NHL since November 10, 1942 when Lynn Patrick scored in a N.Y. Rangers' 5-3 OT win vs. Chicago. Bourne's goal beat Washington Capitals, 7-6, at the Capital Centre at 2:01 of overtime . . . (November, 1984)—Took 21 stitches in head when hit by a shot during a team practice . . . (January 19, 1985)—Cut tendons in right hand at Los Angeles and required surgery . . . (September, 1985)—Injured ribs in training camp and missed first eight games . . . (November 30, 1985)—Injured mouth at Calgary and missed two games . . . (December, 1987)—Sprained knee.

Year	Team	League	Games	G.	A.	Pts.	Pen.
1971-72—Saskatoon Blades		WCHL	63	28	32	60	36
1972-73—Saskatoon Blades		WCHL	66	40	53	93	74
1973-74—Saskatoon Blades (c-d)		WCHL	63	29	42	71	41
1974-75—New York Islanders		NHL	77	16	23	39	12
1975-76—Fort Worth Texans (b)		CHL	62	29	44	73	80
1975-76—New York Islanders		NHL	14	2	3	5	13
1976-77—New York Islanders		NHL	75	16	19	35	30
1977-78—New York Islanders		NHL	80	30	33	63	31
1978-79—New York Islanders		NHL	80	30	31	61	48
1979-80—New York Islanders		NHL	73	15	25	40	52
1980-81—New York Islanders		NHL	78	35	41	76	62
1981-82—New York Islanders		NHL	76	27	26	53	77
1982-83—New York Islanders		NHL	77	20	42	62	55
1983-84—New York Islanders		NHL	78	22	34	56	75
1984-85—New York Islanders		NHL	44	8	12	20	51
1985-86—New York Islanders		NHL	62	17	15	32	36
1986-87—Los Angeles Kings (e)		NHL	78	13	9	22	35
1987-88—Los Angeles Kings (f)		NHL	72	7	11	18	28
NHL TOTALS			964	258	324	582	605

(c)—Drafted from Saskatoon Blades by Kansas City Scouts in third round of 1974 amateur draft.
(d)—September, 1974—NHL rights traded to New York Islanders by Kansas City Scouts for NHL rights to Larry Hornung and a player to be named later. (New York sent Bart Crashley to Kansas City to complete deal, September, 1974).
(e)—October, 1986—Selected by Los Angeles Kings in 1987 NHL waiver draft.
(f)—Won Bill Masterton Memorial Trophy (Perseverance, sportsmanship and dedication).

PHILLIPPE RICHARD BOURQUE

Defense . . . 6' . . . 180 lbs. . . . Born, Chelmsford, Mass., June 8, 1962 . . . Shoots left.

Year	Team	League	Games	G.	A.	Pts.	Pen.
1980-81—Kingston Canadians		OHL	47	4	4	8	46
1981-82—Kingston Canadians (c)		OHL	67	11	40	51	111
1982-83—Baltimore Skipjacks		AHL	65	1	15	16	93
1983-84—Baltimore Skipjacks		AHL	58	5	17	22	96
1983-84—Pittsburgh Penguins		NHL	5	0	1	1	12
1984-85—Baltimore Skipjacks		AHL	79	6	15	21	164
1985-86—Pittsburgh Penguins		NHL	4	0	0	0	2
1985-86—Baltimore Skipjacks		AHL	74	8	18	26	226
1986-87—Pittsburgh Penguins		NHL	22	2	3	5	32
1986-87—Baltimore Skipjacks		AHL	49	15	16	31	183
1987-88—Muskegon Lumberjacks (a-d)		IHL	52	16	36	52	66
1987-88—Pittsburgh Penguins		NHL	21	4	12	16	20
NHL TOTALS			52	6	16	22	66

(c)—July, 1982—Signed by Pittsburgh Penguins as a free agent.
(d)—Winner of Governors' Trophy (Top IHL defenseman).

RAYMOND JEAN BOURQUE

Defense . . . 5'11" . . . 197 lbs. . . . Born, Montreal, Que., December 28, 1960 . . . Shoots left . . . Set record for most points by a rookie defenseman 1979-80 (65 pts) (Broken by Larry Murphy of L.A. Kings in '80-81 with 76 pts.) . . . (November 11, 1980)—Broken jaw . . . Brother of Richard Bourque (203rd NHL '81 draft pick) . . . (October, 1981)—Injured left shoulder . . . (April 21, 1982)—Broke left wrist vs. Quebec in playoffs. During the summer he refractured the wrist and his left forearm . . . (October, 1982)—Broken bone over left eye when hit by puck during preseason game vs. Montreal.

Year	Team	League	Games	G.	A.	Pts.	Pen.
1976-77—Sorel Black Hawks		QMJHL	69	12	36	48	61
1977-78—Verdun Black Hawks (a)		QMJHL	72	22	57	79	90
1978-79—Verdun Black Hawks (a-c)		QMJHL	63	22	71	93	44
1979-80—Boston Bruins (a-d-e)		NHL	80	17	48	65	73
1980-81—Boston Bruins (b)		NHL	67	27	29	56	96
1981-82—Boston Bruins (a)		NHL	65	17	49	66	51
1982-83—Boston Bruins (b)		NHL	65	22	51	73	20
1983-84—Boston Bruins (a)		NHL	78	31	65	96	57
1984-85—Boston Bruins (a)		NHL	73	20	66	86	53
1985-86—Boston Bruins (b)		NHL	74	19	57	76	68
1986-87—Boston Bruins (a-f)		NHL	78	23	72	95	36
1987-88—Boston Bruins (a-f)		NHL	78	17	64	81	72
NHL TOTALS			658	193	501	694	526

(c)—August, 1979—Drafted by Boston Bruins in 1979 entry draft. First Bruins pick, eighth overall, first round.

(d)—Selected NHL Rookie of the Year in poll of players by THE SPORTING NEWS.

(e)—Won Calder Memorial Trophy (Top NHL Rookie).

(f)—Won James Norris Memorial Trophy (Top NHL Defenseman).

PAUL ANDRE BOUTILIER

Defense . . . 5'11" . . . 188 lbs. . . . Born, Sydney, N.S., May 3, 1963 . . . Shoots left . . . (November, 1984)—Required 66 stitches to close cut when struck by a shot during a team practice.

Year	Team	League	Games	G.	A.	Pts.	Pen.
1980-81—Sherbrooke Beavers (c)		QMJHL	72	10	29	39	95
1981-82—Sherbrooke Beavers		QMJHL	57	20	60	80	62
1981-82—New York Islanders		NHL	1	0	0	0	0
1982-83—St. Jean Beavers (d)		QHL	22	5	14	19	30
1982-83—New York Islanders		NHL	29	4	5	9	24
1983-84—Indianapolis Checkers		CHL	50	6	17	23	56
1983-84—New York Islanders		NHL	28	0	11	11	36
1984-85—New York Islanders		NHL	78	12	23	35	90
1985-86—New York Islanders		NHL	77	4	30	34	100
1986-87—Boston Bruins (e)		NHL	52	5	9	14	84
1986-87—Minnesota North Stars (f)		NHL	10	2	4	6	8
1987-88—Moncton Golden Flames		AHL	41	9	29	38	40
1987-88—New Haven Nighthawks		AHL	9	0	3	3	10
1987-88—Colorado Rangers		IHL	9	2	6	8	4
1987-88—New York Rangers (g)		NHL	4	0	1	1	6
1987-88—Winnipeg Jets (h)		NHL	6	0	0	0	6
NHL TOTALS			285	27	83	110	354

(c)—June, 1981—Drafted as underage junior by New York Islanders in 1981 NHL entry draft. First Islanders pick, 21st overall, first round.

(d)—January, 1983—QHL rights traded by St. Jean Beavers to Shawinigan Cataracts for Yves Lapointe.

(e)—September, 1986—Sent to Boston Bruins by arbitration judge as compensation for New York Islanders signing of free agent Brian Curran.

(f)—March, 1987—Traded by Boston Bruins to Minnesota North Stars for a fourth-round 1987 draft pick (Darwin McPherson).

(g)—October, 1987—Traded with Jari Gronstrand by Minnesota North Stars to New York Rangers for Dave Gagner and Jay Caufield.

(h)—December, 1987—Traded by New York Rangers to Winnipeg Jets for a fifth-round 1989 draft pick and future considerations.

RANDY KEITH JOSEPH BOYD

Defense . . . 5'11" . . . 192 lbs. . . . Born, Coniston, Ont., January 23, 1962 . . . Shoots left . . . (November 2, 1985)—Missed 14 games with injured ankle following collision with Alan Haworth vs. Washington.

Year	Team	League	Games	G.	A.	Pts.	Pen.
1979-80—Ottawa 67's (c)		OMJHL	65	3	21	24	148
1980-81—Ottawa 67's (a-d)		OHL	64	11	43	54	225

Year	Team	League	Games	G.	A.	Pts.	Pen.
1981-82—Ottawa 67's		OHL	26	9	29	38	51
1981-82—Pittsburgh Penguins		NHL	23	0	2	2	49
1982-83—Baltimore Skipjacks		AHL	21	5	10	15	43
1982-83—Pittsburgh Penguins		NHL	56	4	14	18	71
1983-84—Pittsburgh Penguins		NHL	5	0	1	1	6
1983-84—Baltimore Skipjacks		AHL	20	6	13	19	69
1983-84—Chicago Black Hawks (e)		NHL	23	0	4	4	16
1983-84—Springfield Indians		AHL	27	2	11	13	48
1984-85—Milwaukee Admirals (a)		IHL	68	18	55	73	162
1984-85—Chicago Black Hawks		NHL	3	0	0	0	6
1985-86—New York Islanders (f)		NHL	55	2	12	14	79
1986-87—New York Islanders		NHL	30	7	17	24	37
1986-87—Springfield Indians		AHL	48	9	30	39	96
1987-88—Vancouver Canucks (g)		NHL	60	7	16	23	64
NHL TOTALS			255	20	66	86	328

(c)—June, 1980—Drafted by Pittsburgh Penguins as underage junior in 1980 NHL entry draft. Second Penguins pick, 51st overall, third round.

(d)—Won Max Kaminsky Trophy (Top OHL Defenseman).

(e)—December, 1983—Traded by Pittsburgh Penguins to Chicago Black Hawks for Greg Fox.

(f)—October, 1985—Acquired by New York Islanders in 1985 NHL waiver draft.

(g)—October, 1987—Selected by Vancouver Canucks in 1987 NHL waiver draft.

STEVEN MICHAEL BOZEK

Left Wing . . . 5'11" . . . 170 lbs. . . . Born, Kelowna, B. C., November 26, 1960 . . . Shoots left . . . Set Los Angeles club record for most goals by a rookie in 1981-82 (since broken by Luc Robitaille) . . . (January 20, 1983)—Sprained left knee in game vs. Hartford . . . (October, 1984)—Torn ligament in baby finger of left hand in pre-season game . . . (January 19, 1986)—Strained both knees vs. New Jersey and missed two games . . . (March 12, 1986)—Injured knee vs. N.Y. Rangers . . . (October, 1987)—Strained knee ligaments . . . (March, 1988)—Hyperextended knee and strained back.

Year	Team	League	Games	G.	A.	Pts.	Pen.
1978-79—Northern Michigan Univ.		CCHA	33	12	12	24	21
1979-80—Northern Michigan Univ. (a-c)		CCHA	41	42	47	89	32
1980-81—Northern Michigan Univ. (a-d)		CCHA	44	*35	*55	*90	46
1981-82—Los Angeles Kings		NHL	71	33	23	56	68
1982-83—Los Angeles Kings (e)		NHL	53	13	13	26	14
1983-84—Calgary Flames		NHL	46	10	10	20	16
1984-85—Calgary Flames		NHL	54	13	22	35	6
1985-86—Calgary Flames		NHL	64	21	22	43	24
1986-87—Calgary Flames		NHL	71	17	18	35	22
1987-88—Calgary Flames		NHL	26	3	7	10	12
1987-88—St. Louis Blues (f)		NHL	7	0	0	0	2
NHL TOTALS			392	110	115	225	164

(c)—June, 1980—Drafted by Los Angeles Kings in 1980 NHL entry draft. Fifth Kings pick, 52nd overall, third round.

(d)—Selected to All-America (West) team.

(e)—June, 1983—Traded by Los Angeles Kings to Calgary Flames for Kevin LaVallee and Carl Mokosak.

(f)—March, 1988—Traded with Brett Hull by Calgary Flames to St. Louis Blues for Rob Ramage and Rick Wamsley.

RICHARD BRACCIA

Left Wing . . . 6' . . . 195 lbs. . . . Born, Revere, Mass., September 5, 1967 . . . Shoots left.

Year	Team	League	Games	G.	A.	Pts.	Pen.
1984-85—Avon Old Farms (c)		Conn. H.S.	....	26	32	58	....
1985-86—Boston College		H. East	9	0	3	3	20
1986-87—Boston College		H. East	39	4	5	9	52
1987-88—Boston College		H. East	11	2	2	4	10

(c)—June, 1985—Drafted by Chicago Black Hawks in 1985 NHL entry draft. Twelfth Black Hawks pick, 242nd overall, 12th round.

BRIAN BRADLEY

Center . . . 5'9" . . . 165 lbs. . . . Born, Kitchener, Ont., January 21, 1965 . . . Shoots right.

Year	Team	League	Games	G.	A.	Pts.	Pen.
1981-82—London Knights		OHL	62	34	44	78	34
1982-83—London Knights (c)		OHL	67	37	82	119	37
1983-84—London Knights		OHL	49	40	60	100	24
1984-85—London Knights		OHL	32	27	49	76	22

Year	Team	League	Games	G.	A.	Pts.	Pen.
1985-86—Calgary Flames		NHL	5	0	1	1	0
1985-86—Moncton Golden Flames		AHL	59	23	42	65	40
1986-87—Moncton Golden Flames		AHL	20	12	16	28	8
1986-87—Calgary Flames		NHL	40	10	18	28	16
1987-88—Canadian Olympic Team		Int'l	51	18	23	41	42
1987-88—Vancouver Canucks (d)		NHL	11	3	5	8	6
NHL TOTALS			56	13	24	37	22

(c)—June, 1983—Drafted by Calgary Flames as underage junior in 1983 NHL entry draft. Second Flames pick, 51st overall, third round.

(d)—March, 1988—Traded with Peter Bakovic and future considerations (Kevin Guy) by Calgary Flames to Vancouver Canucks for Craig Coxe.

NEIL BRADY

Center . . . 6'2" . . . 180 lbs. . . . Born, Montreal, Que., April 12, 1968 . . . Shoots left.

Year	Team	League	Games	G.	A.	Pts.	Pen.
1984-85—Calgary Northstars (b)		Alta. Midget	37	25	50	75	75
1985-86—Medicine Hat Tigers (c-d)		WHL	72	21	60	81	104
1986-87—Medicine Hat Tigers		WHL	57	19	64	83	126
1987-88—Medicine Hat Tigers		WHL	61	16	35	51	110

(c)—WHL Rookie of the Year (East).

(d)—June, 1986—Drafted as underage junior by New Jersey Devils in 1986 NHL entry draft. First Devils pick, third overall, first round.

CHRIS BRANT

Left Wing . . . 6'1" . . . 190 lbs. . . . Born, Belleville, Ont., August 26, 1965 . . . Shoots left.

Year	Team	League	Games	G.	A.	Pts.	Pen.
1981-82—Belleville Jr. B		OHA	36	10	32	42	13
1982-83—Kingston Canadians		OHL	67	1	17	18	53
1983-84—Kingston Canadians		OHL	7	4	4	8	14
1983-84—Sault Ste. Marie Greyhounds		OHL	60	9	12	21	50
1984-85—Sault Ste. Marie Greyhounds (c)		OHL	52	16	33	49	110
1985-86—Binghamton Whalers		AHL	73	7	6	13	45
1985-86—Salt Lake Golden Eagles		IHL	5	2	1	3	4
1986-87—Salt Lake Golden Eagles		IHL	67	27	38	65	107
1987-88—Binghamton Whalers		AHL	66	18	29	47	74

(c)—June, 1985—Drafted by Hartford Whalers in 1985 NHL entry draft. Fifth Whalers pick, 131st overall, seventh round.

ANDRE BRASSARD

Defense . . . 6' . . . 190 lbs. . . . Born, Arvida, Que., April 18, 1968 . . . Shoots left.

Year	Team	League	Games	G.	A.	Pts.	Pen.
1985-86—Longueuil Chevaliers		QHL	61	3	15	18	70
1986-87—Longueuil Chevaliers		QHL	66	3	26	29	164
1987-88—Trois-Rivieres Draveurs (c)		QHL	56	5	31	36	141

(c)—June, 1988—Drafted by New York Islanders in 1988 NHL entry draft. Fifth Islanders pick, 79th overall, fourth round.

CAM BRAUER

Defense . . . 6'3" . . . 200 lbs. . . . Born, Calgary, Alta., January 4, 1970 . . . Shoots left.

Year	Team	League	Games	G.	A.	Pts.	Pen.
1986-87—Calgary Midget		Alta. Mgt.	34	4	7	11	112
1987-88—R.P.I. (c)		ECAC	18	0	1	1	4

(c)—June, 1988—Drafted by Edmonton Oilers in 1988 NHL entry draft. Fifth Oilers pick, 82nd overall, fourth round.

ANDY BRICKLEY

Left Wing . . . 5'11" . . . 185 lbs. . . . Born, Melrose, Mass., August 9, 1961 . . . Shoots left . . . (December, 1983)—Strained ankle . . . (December, 1985)—Tendinitis in shoulder . . . (September, 1987)—Injured foot.

Year	Team	League	Games	G.	A.	Pts.	Pen.
1979-80—University of New Hampshire (c)		ECAC	27	15	17	32	8
1980-81—University of New Hampshire		ECAC	31	27	25	52	16
1981-82—University of New Hampshire (d)		ECAC	35	26	27	53	6
1982-83—Philadelphia Flyers		NHL	3	1	1	2	0
1982-83—Maine Mariners (b)		AHL	76	29	54	83	10

Year	Team	League	Games	G.	A.	Pts.	Pen.
1983-84—Springfield Indians	AHL	7	1	5	6	2
1983-84—Pittsburgh Penguins (e)	NHL	50	18	20	38	9
1983-84—Baltimore Skipjacks	AHL	4	0	5	5	2
1984-85—Baltimore Skipjacks	AHL	31	13	14	27	8
1984-85—Pittsburgh Penguins	NHL	45	7	15	22	10
1985-86—Maine Mariners (f-g-h)	AHL	60	26	34	60	20
1986-87—New Jersey Devils	NHL	51	11	12	23	8
1987-88—Utica Devils	AHL	9	5	8	13	4
1987-88—New Jersey Devils	NHL	45	8	14	22	14
NHL TOTALS		194	45	62	107	41

(c)—June, 1980—Drafted by Philadelphia Flyers in 1980 NHL entry draft. Tenth Flyers pick, 210th overall, tenth round.

(d)—Named to All-American Team (East).

(e)—October, 1983—Traded with Ron Flockhart, Mark Taylor and first-round 1984 draft pick (Roger Belanger) by Philadelphia Flyers to Pittsburgh Penguins for Rich Sutter and second (Greg Smyth) and third round (David McLay) 1984 draft picks.

(f)—August, 1985—Released by Pittsburgh Penguins.

(g)—September, 1985—Attended Hartford Whalers training camp as an unsigned free agent. Released at the conclusion of camp and signed with Maine Mariners as a free agent.

(h)—June, 1986—Signed by New Jersey Devils as a free agent.

MELVIN JOHN BRIDGMAN

Center . . . 6' . . . 185 lbs. . . . Born, Trenton, Ont., April 28, 1955 . . . Shoots left . . . Also plays Left Wing . . . (January 12, 1987)—Non-displaced fracture of left foot vs. Hartford.

Year	Team	League	Games	G.	A.	Pts.	Pen.
1971-72—Nanaimo Clippers	Jr."A" BCHL	....	...	....	....	....
1971-72—Victoria Cougars	WCHL	4	0	0	0	0
1972-73—Nanaimo Clippers	Jr."A" BCHL	49	37	50	87	13
1972-73—Victoria Cougars	WCHL	4	1	1	2	0
1973-74—Victoria Cougars	WCHL	62	26	39	65	149
1974-75—Victoria Cougars (a-c)	WCHL	66	66	91	*157	175
1975-76—Philadelphia Flyers	NHL	80	23	27	50	86
1976-77—Philadelphia Flyers	NHL	70	19	38	57	120
1977-78—Philadelphia Flyers	NHL	76	16	32	48	203
1978-79—Philadelphia Flyers	NHL	76	24	35	59	184
1979-80—Philadelphia Flyers	NHL	74	16	31	47	136
1980-81—Philadelphia Flyers	NHL	77	14	37	51	195
1981-82—Philadelphia Flyers (d)	NHL	9	7	5	12	47
1981-82—Calgary Flames	NHL	63	26	49	75	94
1982-83—Calgary Flames (e)	NHL	79	19	31	50	103
1983-84—New Jersey Devils	NHL	79	23	38	61	121
1984-85—New Jersey Devils	NHL	80	22	39	61	105
1985-86—New Jersey Devils	NHL	78	23	39	62	80
1986-87—New Jersey Devils (f)	NHL	51	8	31	39	80
1986-87—Detroit Red Wings	NHL	13	2	2	4	19
1987-88—Detroit Red Wings	NHL	57	6	11	17	42
1987-88—Adirondack Red Wings	AHL	2	1	2	3	0
NHL TOTALS		962	248	445	693	1615

(c)—Drafted from Victoria Cougars by Philadelphia Flyers in first round of 1975 amateur draft (Flyers obtained draft choice from Washington Capitals for Bill Clement and Don McLean, June, 1975).

(d)—November, 1981—Traded by Philadelphia Flyers to Calgary Flames for Brad Marsh.

(e)—July, 1983—Traded by Calgary Flames with Phil Russell to New Jersey Devils for Steve Tambellini and Joel Quenneville.

(f)—March, 1987—Traded by New Jersey Devils to Detroit Red Wings for Chris Cichocki and a third round 1987 draft pick. (New Jersey later traded that pick to Buffalo who then drafted Andrew MacIver).

ROD BRIND'AMOUR

Center . . . 6' . . . 185 lbs. . . . Born, Ottawa, Ont., August 9, 1970 . . . Shoots left . . . (November, 1985)—Broken wrist.

Year	Team	League	Games	G.	A.	Pts.	Pen.
1986-87—Notre Dame Midget	Sask. Mdgt.	33	38	50	88	66
1987-88—Notre Dame Jr. A (c)	SJHL	56	46	61	107	136

(c)—June, 1988—Drafted by St. Louis Blues in 1988 NHL entry draft. First Blues pick, ninth overall, first round.

LEE BRODEUR

Right Wing . . . 6'1" . . . 180 lbs. . . . Born, Grafton, N. Dak., February 14, 1966 . . . Shoots right

... (December, 1985)—Left University of North Dakota and transferred to Western Michigan University.

Year	Team	League	Games	G.	A.	Pts.	Pen.
1983-84—Grafton H.S. (c)	No.Dak.H.S.	23	40	36	76	42
1984-85—Univ. North Dakota	WCHA	13	0	2	2	6
1985-86—Western Michigan Univ.	CCHA	20	1	4	5	22
1986-87—Western Michigan Univ.	CCHA	26	3	4	7	8
1987-88—Western Michigan Univ.	CCHA	14	1	1	2	8

(c)—June, 1984—Drafted by Montreal Canadiens in 1984 NHL entry draft. Sixth Canadiens pick, 65th overall, fourth round.

ROBERT W. BROOKE

Right Wing ... 6'2" ... 185 lbs. ... Born, Melrose, Mass., December 18, 1960 ... Shoots right ... Holds Yale career records for goals (42), assists (113) and points (155) ... Also plays Center and Defense ... Played shortstop on Yale baseball team ... Member of 1984 U.S. Olympic Team ... (October 11, 1984)—Separated shoulder in opening game of season vs. Hartford ... (January, 1988)—Stiff neck.

Year	Team	League	Games	G.	A.	Pts.	Pen.
1979-80—Yale University (c)	ECAC	24	7	22	29	38
1980-81—Yale University	ECAC	27	12	30	42	59
1981-82—Yale University	ECAC	25	12	30	42	60
1982-83—Yale University (a-d)	ECAC	27	11	31	42	50
1983-84—U.S. National Team	Int'l	54	7	18	25	75
1983-84—U.S. Olympic Team	Int'l	6	1	2	3	10
1983-84—New York Rangers (e)	NHL	9	1	2	3	4
1984-85—New York Rangers	NHL	72	7	9	16	79
1985-86—New York Rangers	NHL	79	24	20	44	111
1986-87—New York Rangers (f)	NHL	15	3	5	8	20
1986-87—Minnesota North Stars	NHL	65	10	18	28	78
1987-88—Minnesota North Stars	NHL	77	5	20	25	108
NHL TOTALS		317	50	74	124	400

(c)—June, 1980—Drafted by St. Louis Blues in 1980 NHL entry draft. Third Blues pick, 75th overall, fourth round.

(d)—Named to All-America Team (East).

(e)—March, 1984—Traded with Larry Patey by St. Louis Blues to New York Rangers for Dave Barr, a third round (Alan Perry) 1984 draft pick and cash.

(f)—November, 1986—Traded with a fourth-round 1988 draft pick by New York Rangers to Minnesota North Stars for Tony McKegney, Curt Giles and a second-round (Troy Mallette) 1988 draft pick.

AARON BROTEN

Center ... 5'10" ... 168 lbs. ... Born, Roseau, Minn., November 14, 1960 ... Shoots left ... Brother of Neal Broten and Paul Broten ... Also plays Left Wing ... (February 15, 1986)—Sprained ankle vs. N.Y. Islanders ... (March 6, 1986)—Reinjured ankle vs. Detroit ... (March 19, 1986)—Reinjured ankle vs. Pittsburgh ... Holds New Jersey record for career assists.

Year	Team	League	Games	G.	A.	Pts.	Pen.
1979-80—University of Minnesota (c-d)	WCHA	41	25	47	72	8
1980-81—University of Minnesota (b-e)	WCHA	45	*47	*59	*106	24
1980-81—Colorado Rockies	NHL	2	0	0	0	0
1981-82—Ft. Worth Texans	CHL	19	15	21	36	11
1981-82—Colorado Rockies	NHL	58	15	24	39	6
1982-83—Wichita Wind	CHL	4	0	4	4	0
1982-83—New Jersey Devils	NHL	73	16	39	55	28
1983-84—New Jersey Devils	NHL	80	13	23	36	36
1984-85—New Jersey Devils	NHL	80	22	35	57	38
1985-86—New Jersey Devils	NHL	66	19	25	44	26
1986-87—New Jersey Devils	NHL	80	26	53	79	36
1987-88—New Jersey Devils	NHL	80	26	57	83	80
NHL TOTALS		519	137	256	393	250

(c)—Named top WCHA Rookie.

(d)—June, 1980—Drafted by Colorado Rockies in 1980 NHL entry draft. Fifth Rockies pick, 106th overall, sixth round.

(e)—WCHA Scoring Leader.

NEAL LaMOY BROTEN

Center ... 5'9" ... 160 lbs. ... Born, Roseau, Minn., November 29, 1959 ... Shoots left ... Brother of Aaron Broten and Paul Broten ... Scored game winning goal to give University of Minnesota 1979 NCAA Championship over North Dakota ... Member of 1980 U.S.

Olympic Gold Medal Team . . . (December 26, 1981)—Ankle fracture . . . Set NHL record for most points by American-born player (97), 1981-82 . . . Set NHL record for most goals by an American-born player (38), 1981-82 (broken by Joe Mullen in 1983-84) . . . Set NHL record for most assists by American-born player (60), 1981-82 . . . (1985-86)—Became first American-born player to score 100 points in one season in NHL . . . (October 30, 1986)—Dislocated shoulder . . . (March, 1987)—Torn shoulder ligaments . . . (November, 1987)—Separated shoulder . . . (February, 1988)—Reconstructive shoulder surgery.

Year	Team	League	Games	G.	A.	Pts.	Pen.
1978-79—University of Minnesota (c-d)		WCHA	40	21	50	71	18
1979-80—U. S. Olympic Team		Int'l	62	27	31	58	22
1980-81—University of Minnesota (a-e-f-g)		WCHA	36	17	54	71	56
1980-81—Minnesota North Stars		NHL	3	2	0	2	12
1981-82—Minnesota North Stars		NHL	73	38	60	98	42
1982-83—Minnesota North Stars		NHL	79	32	45	77	43
1983-84—Minnesota North Stars		NHL	76	28	61	89	43
1984-85—Minnesota North Stars		NHL	80	19	37	56	39
1985-86—Minnesota North Stars		NHL	80	29	76	105	47
1986-87—Minnesota North Stars		NHL	46	18	35	53	35
1987-88—Minnesota North Stars		NHL	54	9	30	39	32
NHL TOTALS			491	175	344	519	293

(c)—Named top WCHA Rookie player.
(d)—August, 1979—Drafted by Minnesota North Stars in 1979 NHL entry draft. Third North Stars pick, 42nd overall, second round.
(e)—Named to All-America Team (West).
(f)—Named to All-NCAA Tournament team.
(g)—First winner of Hobey Baker Memorial Trophy (Top U. S. College Hockey Player).

PAUL BROTEN

Center . . . 5'11" . . . 155 lbs. . . . Born, Roseau, Minn., October 27, 1965 . . . Shoots right . . . Brother of Aaron and Neal Broten . . . Also plays Right Wing.

Year	Team	League	Games	G.	A.	Pts.	Pen.
1983-84—Roseau H.S. (c)		Minn. H.S.	26	26	29	55	4
1984-85—Univ. of Minnesota		WCHA	44	8	8	16	26
1985-86—Univ. of Minnesota		WCHA	38	6	16	22	24
1986-87—Univ. of Minnesota		WCHA	48	17	22	39	52
1987-88—Univ. of Minnesota		WCHA	62	19	26	45	54

(c)—June, 1984—Drafted by New York Rangers in 1984 NHL entry draft. Third Rangers pick, 77th overall, fourth round.

ALLISTER BROWN

Defense . . . 6' . . . 185 lbs. . . . Born, Cornwall, Ont., November 12, 1965 . . . Shoots right . . . Brother of Phil and Newell Brown.

Year	Team	League	Games	G.	A.	Pts.	Pen.
1983-84—Univ. of New Hampshire (c)		ECAC	36	1	7	8	12
1984-85—Univ. of New Hampshire		H. East	42	4	7	11	18
1985-86—Univ. of New Hampshire		H. East	36	2	5	7	28
1986-87—Univ. of New Hampshire		H. East	33	0	10	10	38
1987-88—Univ. of New Hampshire		H. East	13	2	1	3	12
1987-88—Flint Spirits		IHL	2	0	1	1	0

(c)—June, 1984—Drafted by New York Islanders in 1984 NHL entry draft. Thirteenth Islanders pick, 249th overall, 12th round.

DAVID BROWN

Right Wing . . . 6'5" . . . 205 lbs. . . . Born, Saskatoon, Sask., October 12, 1962 . . . Shoots right . . . (March, 1985)—Bruised shoulder . . . (March, 1987)—Suspended five games for stick swinging incident . . . (October 16, 1987)—Suspended 15 games by NHL for crosschecking Tomas Sandstrom in game vs. N.Y. Rangers . . . (January, 1988)—Bruised left hand and wrist in game vs. Pittsburgh.

Year	Team	League	Games	G.	A.	Pts.	Pen.
1980-81—Spokane Flyers		WHL	9	2	2	4	21
1981-82—Saskatoon Blades (c)		WHL	62	11	33	44	344
1982-83—Maine Mariners (d)		AHL	71	8	6	14	*418
1982-83—Philadelphia Flyers		NHL	2	0	0	0	5
1983-84—Philadelphia Flyers		NHL	19	1	5	6	98
1983-84—Springfield Indians		AHL	59	17	14	31	150
1984-85—Philadelphia Flyers		NHL	57	3	6	9	165
1985-86—Philadelphia Flyers		NHL	76	10	7	17	277
1986-87—Philadelphia Flyers		NHL	62	7	3	10	274
1987-88—Philadelphia Flyers		NHL	47	12	5	17	114
NHL TOTALS			263	33	26	59	933

(c)—June, 1982—Drafted by Philadelphia Flyers in 1982 NHL entry draft. Seventh Flyers pick, 140th overall, seventh round.
(d)—Led AHL Playoffs with 107 penalty minutes.

DOUG BROWN

Right Wing . . . 5'11" . . . 190 lbs. . . . Born, Southborough, Mass., June 12, 1964 . . . Shoots right . . . Brother of Greg Brown.

Year	Team	League	Games	G.	A.	Pts.	Pen.
1982-83—Boston College		ECAC	22	9	8	17	0
1983-84—Boston College		ECAC	38	11	10	21	6
1984-85—Boston College		H. East	45	37	31	68	10
1985-86—Boston College (c)		H. East	38	16	40	56	16
1986-87—Maine Mariners		AHL	73	24	34	58	15
1986-87—New Jersey Devils		NHL	4	0	1	1	0
1987-88—New Jersey Devils		NHL	70	14	11	25	20
1987-88—Utica Devils		AHL	2	0	2	2	2
NHL TOTALS			70	14	11	25	20

(c)—August, 1986—Signed by New Jersey Devils as a free agent.

GREGORY BROWN

Defense . . . 6' . . . 185 lbs. . . . Born, Hartford, Conn., March 7, 1963 . . . Shoots right . . . Brother of Doug Brown.

Year	Team	League	Games	G.	A.	Pts.	Pen.
1984-85—St. Marks H.S.		Mass.	24	16	24	40	12
1985-86—St. Marks H.S. (c)		Mass.	19	22	28	50	30
1986-87—Boston College		H. East	37	10	27	37	22
1987-88—U.S. Olympic Team		Int'l	6	0	4	4	2

(c)—June, 1986—Drafted by Buffalo Sabres in 1986 NHL entry draft. Second Sabres pick, 26th overall, second round.

JEFF BROWN

Defense . . . 6'1" . . . 185 lbs. . . . Born, Ottawa, Ont., April 30, 1966 . . . Shoots right.

Year	Team	League	Games	G.	A.	Pts.	Pen.
1981-82—Hawkesbury Tier II		Ont. Jr.	49	12	47	59	72
1982-83—Sudbury Wolves		OHL	65	9	37	46	39
1983-84—Sudbury Wolves (c)		OHL	68	17	60	77	39
1984-85—Sudbury Wolves		OHL	56	16	48	64	26
1985-86—Sudbury Wolves (a-d)		OHL	45	22	28	50	24
1985-86—Quebec Nordiques		NHL	8	3	2	5	6
1985-86—Fredericton Express (e)		AHL	....	...	....	....	....
1986-87—Fredericton Express		AHL	26	2	14	16	16
1986-87—Quebec Nordiques		NHL	44	7	22	29	16
1987-88—Quebec Nordiques		NHL	78	16	37	53	64
NHL TOTALS			130	26	61	87	86

(c)—June, 1984—Drafted as underage junior by Quebec Nordiques in 1984 NHL entry draft. Second Nordiques pick, 36th overall, second round.
(d)—Shared Max Kaminsky Trophy (Top OHL Trophy) with Terry Carkner.
(e)—No regular season record. Played one playoff game.

KEITH JEFFREY BROWN

Defense . . . 6'1" . . . 192 lbs. . . . Born, Corner Brook, Nfld., May 6, 1960 . . . Shoots right . . . (December 23, 1981)—Torn ligaments in right knee . . . (January 26, 1983)—Separated right shoulder vs. Vancouver . . . (January, 1985)—Strained leg . . . (October, 1985)—Broken finger in three places in weight training accident and missed 10 games . . . (October, 1987)—Torn ligaments and damaged cartilage in left knee.

Year	Team	League	Games	G.	A.	Pts.	Pen.
1976-77—Ft. Saskatchewan Traders		AJHL	59	14	61	75	14
1976-77—Portland Winter Hawks		WCHL	2	0	0	0	0
1977-78—Portland Winter Hawks (b-c)		WCHL	72	11	53	64	51
1978-79—Portland Winter Hawks (a-d-e)		WHL	70	11	85	96	75
1979-80—Chicago Black Hawks		NHL	76	2	18	20	27
1980-81—Chicago Black Hawks		NHL	80	9	34	43	80
1981-82—Chicago Black Hawks		NHL	33	4	20	24	26
1982-83—Chicago Black Hawks		NHL	50	4	27	31	20
1983-84—Chicago Black Hawks		NHL	74	10	25	35	94
1984-85—Chicago Black Hawks		NHL	56	1	22	23	55

Year	Team	League	Games	G.	A.	Pts.	Pen.
1985-86—Chicago Black Hawks		NHL	70	11	29	40	87
1986-87—Chicago Black Hawks		NHL	73	4	23	27	86
1987-88—Chicago Black Hawks		NHL	24	3	6	9	45
NHL TOTALS			536	48	204	252	520

(c)—Shared WCHL Top Rookie with John Ogrodnick.

(d)—Named outstanding WHL defenseman.

(e)—August, 1979—Drafted as underage junior by Chicago Black Hawks in 1979 NHL entry draft. First Black Hawks pick, seventh overall, first round.

ROBERT BROWN

Center . . . 6' . . . 180 lbs. . . . Born, Kingston, Ont., October 4, 1968 . . . Shoots left . . . Holds WHL records for career assists (343) and points (522) . . . Set single season WHL record with 212 points in 1986-87 . . . (October, 1987)—Scored goals on his first three NHL shots.

Year	Team	League	Games	G.	A.	Pts.	Pen.
1983-84—Kamloops Jr. Oilers		WHL	50	16	42	58	80
1984-85—Kamloops Blazers		WHL	60	29	50	79	95
1985-86—Kamloops Blazers (a-c-d)		WHL	69	58	*115	*173	171
1986-87—Kamloops Blazers (a-c-e)		WHL	63	*76	*136	*212	101
1987-88—Pittsburgh Penguins		NHL	51	24	20	44	56
NHL TOTALS			51	24	20	44	56

(c)—Named WHL Most Valuable Player (West).

(d)—June, 1986—Drafted by Pittsburgh Penguins as underage junior in 1986 NHL entry draft. Fourth Penguins pick, 67th overall, fourth round.

(e)—Named WHL Player-of-the-Year.

JEFFREY BRUBAKER

Left Wing . . . 6'2" . . . 205 lbs. . . . Born, Hagerstown, Md., February 24, 1958 . . . Shoots left . . . Missed parts of 1979-80 season with dislocated shoulder and a sprained knee . . . (October, 1980)—Shoulder injury . . . (January, 1985)—Given three-game suspension for stick-swinging incident . . . (December 29, 1985)—Sprained left ankle at Vancouver.

Year	Team	League	Games	G.	A.	Pts.	Pen.
1974-75—St. Paul Vulcans		MWJHL	57	13	14	27	130
1975-76—St. Paul Vulcans		MWJHL	47	6	34	40	152
1976-77—Michigan State University		WCHA	18	0	3	3	30
1976-77—Peterborough Petes		Jr."A" OHA	26	0	5	5	143
1977-78—Peterborough Petes (c-d)		Jr."A" OHA	68	20	24	44	307
1978-79—New England Whalers		WHA	12	0	0	0	19
1978-79—Rochester Americans		AHL	57	4	10	14	253
1979-80—Hartford Whalers		NHL	3	0	1	1	2
1979-80—Springfield Indians		AHL	50	12	13	25	165
1980-81—Binghamton Whalers		AHL	38	18	11	29	138
1980-81—Hartford Whalers		NHL	43	5	3	8	93
1981-82—Montreal Canadiens (e)		NHL	3	0	1	1	32
1981-82—Nova Scotia Voyageurs		AHL	60	28	12	40	256
1982-83—Nova Scotia Voyageurs		AHL	78	31	27	58	183
1983-84—Calgary Flames (f)		NHL	4	0	0	0	19
1983-84—Colorado Flames		CHL	57	16	19	35	218
1984-85—Toronto Maple Leafs (g)		NHL	68	8	4	12	209
1985-86—Nova Scotia Oilers		AHL	19	4	3	7	41
1985-86—Toronto Maple Leafs (h)		NHL	21	0	0	0	67
1985-86—Edmonton Oilers		NHL	4	1	0	1	12
1986-87—Nova Scotia Oilers (i)		AHL	47	10	16	26	80
1986-87—Hershey Bears (j)		AHL	12	1	2	3	30
1987-88—New York Rangers		NHL	31	2	0	2	78
1987-88—Colorado Rangers		IHL	30	12	10	22	53
WHA TOTALS			12	0	0	0	19
NHL TOTALS			177	16	9	25	512

(c)—June, 1978—Selected by New England Whalers in World Hockey Association amateur players' draft and signed by Whalers.

(d)—Drafted from Peterborough Petes by Boston Bruins in sixth round of 1978 amateur draft.

(e)—October, 1981—Selected by Montreal Canadiens in 1981 NHL waiver draft.

(f)—October, 1983—Selected by Calgary Flames in 1983 NHL waiver draft.

(g)—October, 1984—Selected by Toronto Maple Leafs in 1984 NHL waiver draft.

(h)—December, 1985—Acquired by Edmonton Oilers on waivers from Toronto Maple Leafs.

(i)—March, 1987—Traded by Edmonton Oilers to Philadelphia Flyers for Dominic Campedelli.

(j)—July, 1987—Traded by Philadelphia Flyers to New York Rangers for future considerations.

DAVID BRUCE

Right Wing ... 5'11" ... 170 lbs. ... Born, Thunder Bay, Ont., October 7, 1964 ... Shoots right ... Also plays Center ... (November, 1987)—Mononucleosis ... (March, 1988)—Bruised foot.

Year	Team	League	Games	G.	A.	Pts.	Pen.
1981-82—Thunder Bay Kings		Tier II	35	27	31	58	74
1982-83—Kitchener Rangers (c)		OHL	67	36	35	71	199
1983-84—Kitchener Rangers		OHL	62	52	40	92	203
1984-85—Fredericton Express		AHL	56	14	11	25	104
1985-86—Fredericton Express		AHL	66	25	16	41	151
1985-86—Vancouver Canucks		NHL	12	0	1	1	14
1986-87—Fredericton Express		AHL	17	7	6	13	73
1986-87—Vancouver Canucks		NHL	50	9	7	16	109
1987-88—Fredericton Express		AHL	30	27	18	45	115
1987-88—Vancouver Canucks		NHL	28	7	3	10	57
NHL TOTALS			90	16	11	27	180

(c)—June, 1983—Drafted as underage junior by Vancouver Canucks in 1983 NHL entry draft. Second Canucks pick, 30th overall, second round.

JAMES MURRAY BRUMWELL
(Known by middle name)

Defense ... 6'1" ... 190 lbs. ... Born, Calgary, Alta., March 31, 1960 ... Shoots left ... (February, 1979)—Mononucleosis ... (January, 1982)—Back injury.

Year	Team	League	Games	G.	A.	Pts.	Pen.
1977-78—Calgary Canucks		AJHL	59	4	40	44	79
1977-78—Calgary Wranglers		WCHL	1	0	0	0	2
1977-78—Saskatoon Blades		WCHL	1	0	2	2	0
1978-79—Billings Bighorns		WHL	61	11	32	43	62
1979-80—Billings Bighorns		WHL	67	18	54	72	50
1980-81—Minnesota North Stars (c)		NHL	1	0	0	0	0
1980-81—Oklahoma City Stars		CHL	79	12	43	55	79
1981-82—Nashville South Stars		CHL	55	4	21	25	66
1981-82—Minnesota North Stars (d)		NHL	21	0	3	3	18
1982-83—Wichita Wind		CHL	11	4	1	5	4
1982-83—New Jersey Devils		NHL	59	5	14	19	34
1983-84—Maine Mariners		AHL	34	4	25	29	16
1983-84—New Jersey Devils		NHL	42	7	13	20	14
1984-85—Maine Mariners		AHL	64	8	31	39	52
1985-86—New Jersey Devils		NHL	1	0	0	0	0
1985-86—Maine Mariners		AHL	66	9	28	37	35
1986-87—Maine Mariners		AHL	69	10	38	48	30
1986-87—New Jersey Devils		NHL	1	0	0	0	2
1987-88—Utica Devils		AHL	77	13	53	66	44
1987-88—New Jersey Devils		NHL	3	0	1	1	2
NHL TOTALS			128	12	31	43	70

(c)—September, 1980—Signed by Minnesota North Stars as a free agent.
(d)—Claimed by New Jersey Devils in 1982 NHL waiver draft.

BENOIT BRUNET

Left Wing ... 5'11" ... 180 lbs. ... Born, Montreal, Que., August 24, 1968 ... Shoots left ... (September, 1987)—Injured ankle.

Year	Team	League	Games	G.	A.	Pts.	Pen.
1985-86—Hull Olympiques (c)		QHL	71	33	37	70	81
1986-87—Hull Olympiques (b)		QHL	60	43	67	110	105
1987-88—Hull Olympiques		QHL	62	54	89	143	131

(c)—June, 1986—Drafted as underage junior by Montreal Canadiens in 1986 NHL entry draft. Second Canadiens pick, 27th overall, second round.

BOB BRYDEN

Left Wing ... 6'3" ... 205 lbs. ... Born, Toronto, Ont., April 5, 1963 ... Shoots left.

Year	Team	League	Games	G.	A.	Pts.	Pen.
1982-83—Henry Carr H.S. (c)		Toronto H.S.	32	28	39	67	65
1983-84—Western Michigan Univ.		CCHA	36	17	12	29	60
1984-85—Western Michigan Univ.		CCHA	39	18	19	37	59
1985-86—Western Michigan Univ.		CCHA	44	23	28	51	85
1985-86—Team Canada		Int'l	3	0	1	1	2
1986-87—Western Michigan Univ. (b)		CCHA	43	*46	48	*94	84
1987-88—Sherbrooke Canadiens		AHL	66	21	16	37	75

(c)—June, 1983—Drafted by Montreal Canadiens in 1983 NHL entry draft. Tenth Canadiens pick, 158th overall, eighth round.

PAUL BRYDGES

Center . . . 5'11" . . . 177 lbs. . . . Born, Guelph, Ont., June 21, 1965 . . . Shoots right . . . (February 22, 1987)—Bruised his shoulder at Hartford and missed five games.

Year	Team	League	Games	G.	A.	Pts.	Pen.
1983-84	Guelph Platers	OHL	68	27	23	50	37
1984-85	Guelph Platers	OHL	57	22	24	46	39
1985-86	Guelph Platers (c)	OHL	62	17	40	57	88
1986-87	Rochester Americans	AHL	54	13	17	30	54
1986-87	Buffalo Sabres	NHL	15	2	2	4	6
1987-88	Rochester Americans	AHL	69	15	16	31	86
	NHL TOTALS		15	2	2	4	6

(c)—July, 1986—Signed by Buffalo Sabres as a free agent.

KELLY BUCHBERGER

Left Wing . . . 6'2" . . . 190 lbs. . . . Born, Langenburg, Sask., December 12, 1966 . . . Shoots left . . . (March 30, 1988)—Suspended six games by AHL for leaving the bench in a fight.

Year	Team	League	Games	G.	A.	Pts.	Pen.
1983-84	Melville Millionaires	SAJHL	60	14	11	25	139
1984-85	Moose Jaw Warriors (c)	WHL	51	12	17	29	114
1985-86	Moose Jaw Warriors	WHL	72	14	22	36	206
1986-87	Nova Scotia Oilers	AHL	70	12	20	32	257
1986-87	Edmonton Oilers (d)	NHL	....	...	....	....	....
1987-88	Edmonton Oilers	NHL	19	1	0	1	81
1987-88	Nova Scotia Oilers	AHL	49	21	23	44	206
	NHL TOTALS		19	1	0	1	81

(c)—June, 1985—Drafted as underage junior by Edmonton Oilers in 1985 NHL entry draft. Eighth Oilers pick, 188th overall, ninth round.
(d)—No regular season record. Played three playoff games.

WAYDE BUCSIS

Right Wing . . . 6'1" . . . 180 lbs. . . . Born, Prince Albert, Sask., January 18, 1968 . . . Shoots left.

Year	Team	League	Games	G.	A.	Pts.	Pen.
1985-86	Prince Albert Raiders	WHL	7	1	1	2	0
1986-87	Prince Albert Raiders	WHL	64	18	28	46	21
1987-88	Prince Albert Raiders (c)	WHL	70	37	54	91	27

(c)—June, 1988—Drafted by Hartford Whalers in 1988 NHL entry draft. Ninth Whalers pick, 200th overall, 10th round.

RANDY BUCYK

Center . . . 6' . . . 190 lbs. . . . Born, Edmonton, Alta., November 9, 1962 . . . Shoots left . . . Nephew of Johnny Bucyk (Hall of Famer and former Boston Bruin).

Year	Team	League	Games	G.	A.	Pts.	Pen.
1980-81	Northeastern Univ.	ECAC	26	9	7	16	18
1981-82	Northeastern Univ.	ECAC	33	19	17	36	10
1982-83	Northeastern Univ.	ECAC	28	16	20	36	16
1983-84	Northeastern Univ.	ECAC	29	16	13	29	11
1984-85	Sherbrooke Canadiens (c)	AHL	62	21	26	47	20
1985-86	Sherbrooke Canadiens	AHL	43	18	33	51	22
1985-86	Montreal Canadiens	NHL	17	4	2	6	8
1986-87	Sherbrooke Canadiens (d)	AHL	70	24	39	63	28
1987-88	Salt Lake Golden Eagles	IHL	75	37	45	82	68
1987-88	Calgary Flames	NHL	2	0	0	0	0
	NHL TOTALS		19	4	2	6	8

(c)—September, 1984—Signed by Montreal Canadiens as a free agent.
(d)—August, 1987—Signed by Calgary Flames as a free agent.

MICHAEL BRIAN BULLARD

Center . . . 5'10" . . . 183 lbs. . . . Born, Ottawa, Ont., March 10, 1961 . . . Shoots left . . . (February 21, 1982)—Scored winning goal with 4:29 to play to stop N.Y. Islanders 15-game win streak in 4-3 win at Pittsburgh . . . (October, 1982)—Missed first 20 games of the season with mononucleosis . . . (1981-82)—Set Pittsburgh club record for goals in a rookie season (36) . . . (December, 1984)—Chip fracture of left shoulder and missed 11

games . . . (January 31, 1985)—Arrested in Mount Lebanon, Pennsylvania when his car struck two people . . . (December 2, 1985)—Suffered cracked ribs vs. N.Y. Rangers and missed three games.

Year	Team	League	Games	G.	A.	Pts.	Pen.
1978-79—Brantford Alexanders		OMJHL	66	43	56	99	66
1979-80—Brantford Alexanders (b-c)		OMJHL	66	66	84	150	86
1980-81—Brantford Alexanders		OHL	42	47	60	107	55
1980-81—Pittsburgh Penguins		NHL	15	1	2	3	19
1981-82—Pittsburgh Penguins		NHL	75	36	27	63	91
1982-83—Pittsburgh Penguins		NHL	57	22	22	44	60
1983-84—Pittsburgh Penguins		NHL	76	51	41	92	57
1984-85—Pittsburgh Penguins		NHL	57	9	11	20	125
1985-86—Pittsburgh Penguins		NHL	77	41	42	83	69
1986-87—Pittsburgh Penguins		NHL	14	2	10	12	17
1986-87—Calgary Flames (d)		NHL	57	28	26	54	34
1987-88—Calgary Flames		NHL	79	48	55	103	68
NHL TOTALS			507	238	236	474	540

(c)—June, 1980—Drafted as underage junior by Pittsburgh Penguins in 1980 NHL entry draft. First Penguins pick, ninth overall, first round.

(d)—November, 1986—Traded by Pittsburgh Penguins to Calgary Flames for Dan Quinn.

STU BURNIE

Right Wing . . . 5'11" . . . 185 lbs. . . . Born, Orilla, Ont., May 7, 1962 . . . Shoots right.

Year	Team	League	Games	G.	A.	Pts.	Pen.
1982-83—Western Michigan Univ.		CCHA	36	12	7	19	50
1983-84—Western Michigan Univ.		CCHA	42	26	13	39	73
1984-85—Western Michigan Univ.		CCHA	39	21	16	37	49
1985-86—Western Michigan Univ. (b)		CCHA	42	43	36	79	78
1986-87—Springfield Indians (c)		AHL	76	21	30	51	62
1987-88—Springfield Indians		AHL	78	33	22	55	98

(c)—September, 1986—Signed by New York Islanders as a free agent.

SHAWN BURR

Center . . . 6'1" . . . 180 lbs. . . . Born, Sarnia, Ont., July 1, 1966 . . . Shoots left . . . (May, 1988)—Separated left shoulder in playoff game at Edmonton.

Year	Team	League	Games	G.	A.	Pts.	Pen.
1982-83—Sarnia Midgets		OPHL	52	50	85	135	125
1983-84—Kitchener Rangers (c-d)		OHL	68	41	44	85	50
1984-85—Kitchener Rangers		OHL	48	24	42	66	50
1984-85—Detroit Red Wings		NHL	9	0	0	0	2
1984-85—Adirondack Red Wings		AHL	4	0	0	0	2
1985-86—Kitchener Rangers (b)		OHL	59	60	67	127	83
1985-86—Adirondack Red Wings		AHL	3	2	2	4	2
1985-86—Detroit Red Wings		NHL	5	1	0	1	4
1986-87—Detroit Red Wings		NHL	80	22	25	47	107
1987-88—Detroit Red Wings		NHL	78	17	23	40	97
NHL TOTALS			172	40	48	88	210

(c)—June, 1984—Drafted as underage junior by Detroit Red Wings in 1984 NHL entry draft. First Red Wings pick, seventh overall, first round.

(d)—Won Emms Family Award (Top OHL Rookie).

RANDY BURRIDGE

Center . . . 5'9" . . . 170 lbs. . . . Born, Fort Erie, Ont., January 7, 1966 . . . Shoots left . . . (March 1, 1986)—Strained groin vs. New Jersey . . . (April, 1987)—Suspended during AHL playoffs.

Year	Team	League	Games	G.	A.	Pts.	Pen.
1982-83—Fort Erie Jr.B		OHA	42	32	56	88	32
1983-84—Peterborough Petes		OHL	55	6	7	13	44
1984-85—Peterborough Petes (c)		OHL	66	49	57	106	88
1985-86—Peterborough Petes		OHL	17	15	11	26	23
1985-86—Boston Bruins		NHL	52	17	25	42	28
1985-86—Moncton Golden Flames (d)		AHL	..	..	..	..	..
1986-87—Moncton Golden Flames		AHL	47	26	41	67	139
1986-87—Boston Bruins		NHL	23	1	4	5	16
1987-88—Boston Bruins		NHL	79	27	28	55	105
NHL TOTALS			154	45	57	102	149

(c)—June, 1985—Drafted by Boston Bruins in 1985 NHL entry draft. Seventh Bruins pick, 157th overall, eighth round.
(d)—No regular season record. Played three playoff games.

ADAM BURT

Defense . . . 6'2" . . . 195 lbs. . . . Born, Detroit, Mich., January 15, 1969 . . . Shoots left . . . (December, 1985)—Broken jaw.

Year	Team	League	Games	G.	A.	Pts.	Pen.
1985-86—North Bay Centennials		OHL	49	0	11	11	81
1986-87—North Bay Centennials (c)		OHL	57	4	27	31	138
1987-88—North Bay Centennials (b)		OHL	66	17	54	71	176

(c)—June, 1987—Drafted as underage junior by Hartford Whalers in 1987 NHL entry draft. Second Whalers pick, 39th overall, second round.

ROD DALE BUSKAS

Defense . . . 6'2" . . . 195 lbs. . . . Born, Wetaskiwin, Alta., January 7, 1961 . . . Shoots right . . . (February, 1985)—Shoulder injury . . . (December 26, 1985)—Bruised ribs vs. Boston and missed five games . . . (November, 1986)—Injured shoulder.

Year	Team	League	Games	G.	A.	Pts.	Pen.
1978-79—Red Deer Rustlers		AJHL	37	13	22	35	63
1978-79—Billings Bighorns		WHL	1	0	0	0	0
1978-79—Medicine Hat Tigers		WHL	35	1	12	13	60
1979-80—Medicine Hat Tigers		WHL	72	7	40	47	284
1980-81—Medicine Hat Tigers (c)		WHL	72	14	46	60	164
1981-82—Erie Blades		AHL	69	1	18	19	78
1982-83—Muskegon Mohawks		IHL	1	0	0	0	9
1982-83—Baltimore Skipjacks		AHL	31	2	8	10	45
1982-83—Pittsburgh Penguins		NHL	41	2	2	4	102
1983-84—Baltimore Skipjacks		AHL	33	2	12	14	100
1983-84—Pittsburgh Penguins		NHL	47	2	4	6	60
1984-85—Pittsburgh Penguins		NHL	69	2	7	9	191
1985-86—Pittsburgh Penguins		NHL	72	2	7	9	159
1986-87—Pittsburgh Penguins		NHL	68	3	15	18	123
1987-88—Pittsburgh Penguins		NHL	76	4	8	12	206
NHL TOTALS			373	15	43	58	841

(c)—June, 1981—Drafted by Pittsburgh Penguins in 1981 NHL entry draft. Fifth Penguins pick, 112th overall, sixth round.

GARTH BUTCHER

Defense . . . 6' . . . 194 lbs. . . . Born, Regina, Sask., January 8, 1963 . . . Shoots right . . . (October, 1984)—Shoulder separation.

Year	Team	League	Games	G.	A.	Pts.	Pen.
1978-79—Regina Canadians		AMHL	22	4	22	26	72
1979-80—Regina Tier II		SJHL	51	15	31	46	236
1979-80—Regina Pats		WHL	13	0	4	4	20
1980-81—Regina Pats (a-c)		WHL	69	9	77	86	230
1981-82—Regina Pats (a)		WHL	65	24	68	92	318
1981-82—Vancouver Canucks		NHL	5	0	0	0	9
1982-83—Kamloops Junior Oilers		WHL	5	4	2	6	4
1982-83—Vancouver Canucks		NHL	55	1	13	14	104
1983-84—Fredericton Express		AHL	25	4	13	17	43
1983-84—Vancouver Canucks		NHL	28	2	0	2	34
1984-85—Vancouver Canucks		NHL	75	3	9	12	152
1985-86—Vancouver Canucks		NHL	70	4	7	11	188
1986-87—Vancouver Canucks		NHL	70	5	15	20	207
1987-88—Vancouver Canucks		NHL	80	6	17	23	285
NHL TOTALS			383	21	61	82	979

(c)—June, 1981—Drafted as underage junior by Vancouver Canucks in 1981 NHL entry draft. First Canucks pick, 10th overall, first round.

LYNDON BYERS

Right Wing . . . 6'2" . . . 195 lbs. . . . Born, Nipawin, Sask., February 29, 1964 . . . Shoots right . . . (April, 1981)—Broken right wrist . . . (September, 1987)—Torn ligaments in right knee in collision in Boston training camp . . . (November, 1987)—Separated left shoulder . . . (March, 1988)—Bruised right hand . . . (April, 1988)—Bruised left thigh.

Year	Team	League	Games	G.	A.	Pts.	Pen.
1980-81—Notre Dame Hounds (b)		SCMHL	37	35	42	77	106
1981-82—Regina Pats (c-d)		WHL	57	18	25	43	169
1982-83—Regina Pats		WHL	70	32	38	70	153
1983-84—Regina Pats		WHL	58	32	57	89	154
1983-84—Boston Bruins		NHL	10	2	4	6	32
1984-85—Hershey Bears		AHL	27	4	6	10	55
1984-85—Boston Bruins		NHL	33	3	8	11	41
1985-86—Boston Bruins		NHL	5	0	2	2	9
1985-86—Moncton Golden Flames		AHL	14	2	4	6	26
1985-86—Milwaukee Admirals		IHL	8	0	2	2	22
1986-87—Moncton Golden Flames		AHL	27	5	5	10	63
1986-87—Boston Bruins		NHL	18	2	3	5	53
1987-88—Maine Mariners		AHL	2	0	1	1	18
1987-88—Boston Bruins		NHL	53	10	14	24	236
NHL TOTALS			119	17	31	48	371

(c)—September, 1981—Traded by Saskatoon Blades to Regina Pats for Todd Strueby.

(d)—June, 1982—Drafted as underage junior by Boston Bruins in NHL entry draft. Third Bruins pick, 39th overall, second round.

SHAWN BYRAM

Left Wing . . . 6'2" . . . 190 lbs. . . . Born, Neepawa, Manitoba, September 12, 1968 . . . Shoots left . . . Also plays Center.

Year	Team	League	Games	G.	A.	Pts.	Pen.
1984-85—Regina Canadians		Sask. Midget	25	12	21	33	38
1985-86—Regina Pats (c)		WHL	46	7	6	13	45
1986-87—Prince Albert Raiders		WHL	67	19	21	40	147
1987-88—Prince Albert Raiders		WHL	61	23	28	51	178

(c)—June, 1986—Drafted as underage junior by New York Islanders in 1986 NHL entry draft. Fourth Islanders pick, 80th overall, fourth round.

GERALD BZDEL

Defense . . . 6' . . . 190 lbs. . . . Born, Wyryard, Sask., March 13, 1968 . . . Shoots right . . . (March, 1985)—Torn ligaments in left knee.

Year	Team	League	Games	G.	A.	Pts.	Pen.
1984-85—Regina Pats		WHL	20	0	4	4	6
1985-86—Regina Pats (c)		WHL	72	2	15	17	107
1986-87—Seattle Thunderbirds		WHL	48	4	12	16	137
1987-88—Moose Jaw Warriors		WHL	72	4	17	21	217

(c)—June, 1986—Drafted as underage junior by Quebec Nordiques in 1986 NHL entry draft. Fifth Nordiques pick, 102nd overall, fifth round.

KELLY CAIN

Center . . . 5'6" . . . 180 lbs. . . . Born, Toronto, Ont., April 19, 1968 . . . Shoots left.

Year	Team	League	Games	G.	A.	Pts.	Pen.
1984-85—London Knights		OHL	59	8	17	25	74
1985-86—London Knights (c)		OHL	62	46	51	97	87
1986-87—London Knights (d)		OHL	5	4	3	7	18
1986-87—Kingston Canadians		OHL	52	7	19	26	7
1986-87—Kitchener Rangers		OHL	28	18	19	37	48
1987-88—Windsor Spitfires		OHL	66	57	76	133	66

(c)—June, 1986—Drafted as underage junior by Pittsburgh Penguins in 1986 NHL entry draft. Tenth Penguins pick, 193rd overall, 10th round.

(d)—October, 1986—Traded with Ed Kister and David Haas by London Knights to Kitchener Rangers for Peter Lisy, Ian Pound, Steve Marcolini and Greg Hankkio.

PAUL CAIN

Center . . . 5'10" . . . 180 lbs. . . . Born, Toronto, Ont., April 6, 1969 . . . Shoots right.

Year	Team	League	Games	G.	A.	Pts.	Pen.
1984-85—Toronto Red Wings		Ont. Mdgt.	40	36	38	74	26
1985-86—Cornwall Royals		OHL	62	11	12	23	21
1986-87—Cornwall Royals		OHL	60	13	27	40	8
1987-88—Cornwall Royals (c)		OHL	21	14	9	23	6

(c)—June, 1988—Drafted by New York Rangers in 1988 NHL entry draft. Ninth Rangers pick, 194th overall, 10th round.

GARY CALLAGHAN

Center . . . 5'11" . . . 176 lbs. . . . Born, Oshawa, Ont., August 12, 1967 . . . Shoots left . . . Also

plays Left Wing . . . (January, 1985)—Strained medial collateral ligament in left knee . . . (October 5, 1986)—Suspended for eight games by OHL for stick-swinging incident with Denis Larocque of Guelph.

Year	Team	League	Games	G.	A.	Pts.	Pen.
1983-84—Oshawa Parkway TV		OHA	57	76	56	132	54
1984-85—Belleville Bulls (c)		OHL	57	24	25	49	42
1985-86—Belleville Bulls		OHL	53	29	16	45	42
1986-87—Belleville Bulls		OHL	4	1	2	3	5
1986-87—Kitchener Rangers		OHL	52	29	28	57	18
1987-88—Binghamton Whalers		AHL	4	2	2	4	0
1987-88—Milwaukee Admirals		IHL	71	14	20	34	38

(c)—June, 1985—Drafted as underage junior by Hartford Whalers in NHL entry draft. Third Whalers pick, 68th overall, fourth round.

JOHN (JOCK) CALLANDER

Center . . . 6'1" . . . 170 lbs. . . . Born, Regina, Sask., April 23, 1961 . . . Shoots right . . . Brother of Drew Callander.

Year	Team	League	Games	G.	A.	Pts.	Pen.
1978-79—Regina Pats		WHL	19	3	2	5	0
1978-79—Regina Blues		SJHL	42	44	42	86	24
1979-80—Regina Pats		WHL	39	9	11	20	25
1980-81—Regina Pats		WHL	72	67	86	153	37
1981-82—Regina Pats (c-d)		WHL	71	79	111	*190	59
1982-83—Salt Lake Golden Eagles		CHL	68	20	27	47	26
1983-84—Montana Magic		CHL	72	27	32	59	69
1983-84—Toledo Goaldiggers		IHL	2	0	0	0	0
1984-85—Muskegon Lumberjacks		IHL	82	39	68	107	86
1985-86—Muskegon Lumberjacks (e)		IHL	82	39	72	111	121
1986-87—Muskegon Lumberjacks (a-f-g)		IHL	82	54	82	*136	110
1987-88—Muskegon Lumberjacks		IHL	31	20	36	56	49
1987-88—Pittsburgh Penguins		NHL	41	11	16	27	45
NHL TOTALS			41	11	16	27	45

(c)—Won Bob Brownridge Memorial Trophy (WHL scoring leader).
(d)—Led WHL playoffs with 26 assists.
(e)—Won Turner Cup Playoff MVP.
(f)—Co-winner of Leo P. Lamoureaux Memorial Trophy (IHL leading scorer) with Jeff Pyle.
(g)—Co-winner of James Gatschene Memorial Trophy (IHL MVP) with Jeff Pyle.

JIM CAMAZZOLA

Left Wing . . . 5'11" . . . 190 lbs. . . . Born, Burnaby, B.C., January 5, 1964 . . . Shoots left . . . Brother of Tony Camazzola.

Year	Team	League	Games	G.	A.	Pts.	Pen.
1982-83—Kamloops Junior Oilers (c)		WHL	66	57	58	115	54
1983-84—Seattle Breakers		WHL	3	1	1	2	0
1983-84—Kamloops Junior Oilers		WHL	29	26	24	50	25
1983-84—Chicago Black Hawks		NHL	1	0	0	0	0
1984-85—New Westminster Bruins		WHL	25	19	29	48	25
1985-86—Saginaw Generals		IHL	42	16	22	38	10
1985-86—Nova Scotia Oilers		AHL	3	0	0	0	0
1986-87—Nova Scotia Oilers		AHL	48	13	18	31	31
1986-87—Chicago Black Hawks (d)		NHL	2	0	0	0	0
1987-88—Maine Mariners		AHL	62	13	23	36	80
NHL TOTALS			3	0	0	0	0

(c)—June, 1982—Drafted as underage junior by Chicago Black Hawks in 1982 NHL entry draft. Tenth Black Hawks pick, 196th overall, 10th round.
(d)—July, 1987—Signed by Boston Bruins as a free agent.

WADE CAMPBELL

Defense . . . 6'4" . . . 220 lbs. . . . Born, Peace River, Alta., February 1, 1961 . . . Shoots right.

Year	Team	League	Games	G.	A.	Pts.	Pen.
1980-81—University of Alberta		CWJAA	24	3	15	18	46
1981-82—University of Alberta (c)		CWJAA	24	6	12	18	....
1982-83—Sherbrooke Jets		AHL	18	4	2	6	23
1982-83—Winnipeg Jets		NHL	42	1	2	3	50
1983-84—Winnipeg Jets		NHL	79	7	14	21	147
1984-85—Winnipeg Jets		NHL	40	1	6	7	21
1984-85—Sherbrooke Canadiens		AHL	28	2	6	8	70

Year	Team	League	Games	G.	A.	Pts.	Pen.
1985-86—Sherbrooke Canadiens		AHL	9	0	2	2	26
1985-86—Winnipeg Jets (d)		NHL	24	0	1	1	27
1985-86—Moncton Golden Flames		AHL	17	2	2	4	21
1985-86—Boston Bruins		NHL	8	0	0	0	15
1986-87—Moncton Golden Flames		AHL	64	12	23	35	34
1986-87—Boston Bruins		NHL	14	0	3	3	24
1987-88—Maine Mariners		AHL	69	11	29	40	118
1987-88—Boston Bruins		NHL	6	0	1	1	21
NHL TOTALS			213	9	27	36	305

(c)—September, 1982—Signed by Winnipeg Jets as a free agent.

(d)—January, 1986—Traded by Winnipeg Jets to Boston Bruins for Bill Derlago.

DOMINIC CAMPEDELLI

Defense . . . 6'1" . . . 185 lbs. . . . Born, Cohasset, Me., April 3, 1964 . . . Shoots left.

Year	Team	League	Games	G.	A.	Pts.	Pen.
1982-83—Boston College (c)		ECAC	26	1	10	11	26
1983-84—Boston College		ECAC	37	10	19	29	24
1984-85—Boston College (d)		H. East	44	5	44	49	74
1985-86—Sherbrooke Canadiens		AHL	38	4	10	14	27
1985-86—Montreal Canadiens		NHL	2	0	0	0	0
1986-87—Sherbrooke Canadiens (e)		AHL	7	3	2	5	2
1986-87—Hershey Bears (f)		AHL	45	7	15	22	70
1986-87—Nova Scotia Oilers		AHL	12	0	4	4	7
1987-88—Nova Scotia Oilers		AHL	70	3	17	20	117
NHL TOTALS			2	0	0	0	0

(c)—June, 1982—Drafted by Toronto Maple Leafs in 1982 NHL entry draft. Tenth Maple Leafs pick, 129th overall, seventh round.

(d)—September, 1985—Traded by Toronto Maple Leafs to Montreal Canadiens for third-round draft choice (Darryl Shannon) in 1986.

(e)—November, 1986—Traded by Montreal Canadiens to Philadelphia Flyers for Andre Villeneuve.

(f)—March, 1987—Traded by Philadelphia Flyers to Edmonton Oilers for Jeff Brubaker.

JEFF CAPELLO

Left Wing . . . 6'1" . . . 195 lbs. . . . Born, Ottawa, Ont., September 25, 1964 . . . Shoots left.

Year	Team	League	Games	G.	A.	Pts.	Pen.
1983-84—Univ. of Vermont		ECAC	26	9	11	20	8
1984-85—Univ. of Vermont		ECAC	29	8	10	18	16
1985-86—Univ. of Vermont (c)		ECAC	31	9	17	26	36
1986-87—Univ. of Vermont		ECAC	32	17	26	43	56
1987-88—Rochester Americans		AHL	69	15	23	38	53

(c)—June, 1986—Selected by Buffalo Sabres in 1986 NHL supplementary draft.

DAVID CAPUANO

Center . . . 6'2" . . . 190 lbs. . . . Born, Warwick, R.I., July 27, 1968 . . . Shoots left . . . Brother of Jack Capuano. . . . (August, 1986)—Broke hand at U.S. National Junior Team tryout camp at Lake Placid, N.Y.

Year	Team	League	Games	G.	A.	Pts.	Pen.
1984-85—Mt. St. Charles H.S.		R.I.	....	41	38	79	....
1985-86—Mt. St. Charles H.S. (c)		R.I.	22	39	48	87	20
1986-87—University of Maine		H. East	38	18	41	59	14
1987-88—University of Maine		H. East	42	34	51	85	51

(c)—June, 1986—Drafted by Pittsburgh Penguins in 1986 NHL entry draft. Second Penguins pick, 25th overall, second round.

JACK CAPUANO

Defense . . . 6'2" . . . 210 lbs. . . . Born, Cranston, R.I., July 7, 1966 . . . Shoots left . . . Brother of Dave Capuano.

Year	Team	League	Games	G.	A.	Pts.	Pen.
1983-84—Kent Prep. (c)		Conn.	....	10	8	18	....
1984-85—University of Maine		H. East	....	...	....	....	....
1985-86—University of Maine		H. East	39	9	13	22	59
1986-87—University of Maine (b)		H. East	42	10	34	44	20
1987-88—University of Maine (d)		H. East	43	13	37	50	87

(c)—June, 1984—Drafted by Toronto Maple Leafs in 1984 NHL entry draft. Fourth Maple Leafs pick, 88th overall, fifth round.

(d)—Named to first All-America team (East).

GUY CARBONNEAU

Center . . . 5'10" . . . 165 lbs. . . . Born, Sept Iles, Que., March 18, 1960 . . . Shoots right.

Year	Team	League	Games	G.	A.	Pts.	Pen.
1976-77	Chicoutimi Sagueneens	QMJHL	59	9	20	29	8
1977-78	Chicoutimi Sagueneens	QMJHL	70	28	55	83	60
1978-79	Chicoutimi Sagueneens (c)	QMJHL	72	62	79	141	47
1979-80	Chicoutimi Saguennens (b)	QMJHL	72	72	110	182	66
1979-80	Nova Scotia Voyageurs (d)	AHL	....	...	....	....	....
1980-81	Montreal Canadiens	NHL	2	0	1	1	0
1980-81	Nova Scotia Voyageurs	AHL	78	35	53	88	87
1981-82	Nova Scotia Voyageurs	AHL	77	27	67	94	124
1982-83	Montreal Canadiens	NHL	77	18	29	47	68
1983-84	Montreal Canadiens	NHL	78	24	30	54	75
1984-85	Montreal Canadiens	NHL	79	23	34	57	43
1985-86	Montreal Canadiens	NHL	80	20	36	56	57
1986-87	Montreal Canadiens	NHL	79	18	27	45	68
1987-88	Montreal Canadiens (e)	NHL	80	17	21	38	61
	NHL TOTALS		475	120	178	298	372

    (c)—August, 1979—Drafted by Montreal Canadiens as underage junior in NHL entry draft. Fourth Canadiens pick, 44th overall, third round.

    (d)—No regular season record. Played one playoff game.

    (e)—Won Frank Selke Trophy (Top NHL defensive forward).

TERRY CARKNER

Defense . . . 6'3" . . . 200 lbs. . . . Born, Smith Falls, Ont., March 7, 1966 . . . Shoots left . . . (January 24, 1988)—Suspended 10 games by NHL for leaving the bench during an altercation in game vs. Montreal.

Year	Team	League	Games	G.	A.	Pts.	Pen.
1982-83	Brockville Braves	COJHL	47	8	32	40	94
1983-84	Peterborough Petes (c)	OHL	66	4	21	25	91
1984-85	Peterborough Petes (b)	OHL	64	14	47	61	125
1985-86	Peterborough Petes (a-d)	OHL	54	12	32	44	106
1986-87	New Haven Nighthawks	AHL	12	2	6	8	56
1986-87	New York Rangers (e)	NH	52	2	13	15	120
1987-88	Quebec Nordiques (f)	NHL	63	3	24	27	159
	NHL TOTALS		115	5	37	42	279

    (c)—June, 1984—Drafted as underage junior by New York Rangers in NHL entry draft. First Rangers pick, 14th overall, first round.

    (d)—Shared Max Kaminsky Trophy (Top OHL Defenseman) with Jeff Brown.

    (e)—September, 1987—Traded with Jeff Jackson by New York Rangers to Quebec Nordiques for John Ogrodnick and David Shaw.

    (f)—July, 1988—Traded by Quebec Nordiques to Philadelphia Flyers for Greg Smyth and third-round draft choice in 1989.

KENT CARLSON

Left Wing and Defense . . . 6'3" . . . 200 lbs. . . . Born, Concord, N.H., January 11, 1962 . . . Shoots left . . . (January 8, 1985)—Broke right hand at N.Y. Islanders . . . (February, 1985)—Sprained shoulder during team practice . . . (February 18, 1986)—Missed eight games with back spasms . . . (September, 1986)—Missed the 1986-87 season following back fusion surgery . . . (April, 1987)—Surgery related nerve damage to right bicep.

Year	Team	League	Games	G.	A.	Pts.	Pen.
1981-82	St. Lawrence University (c)	ECAC	28	8	14	22	24
1982-83	St. Lawrence University	ECAC	36	10	23	33	56
1983-84	Montreal Canadiens	NHL	65	3	7	10	73
1984-85	Sherbrooke Canadiens	AHL	13	1	4	5	7
1984-85	Montreal Canadiens	NHL	18	1	1	2	33
1985-86	Sherbrooke Canadiens	AHL	35	11	15	26	79
1985-86	Montreal Canadiens (d)	NHL	2	0	0	0	0
1985-86	St. Louis Blues	NHL	26	2	3	5	42
1986-87	Did not play		....	...	....	....	....
1987-88	Peoria Rivermen	IHL	52	5	16	21	88
	NHL TOTALS		111	6	11	17	148

    (c)—June, 1982—Drafted by Montreal Canadiens in NHL entry draft. Third Canadiens pick, 32nd overall, second round.

    (d)—January, 1986—Traded by Montreal Canadiens to St. Louis Blues for Graham Herring and a fifth round 1986 draft pick (Eric Aubertin).

ANDERS CARLSSON

Center . . . 5'11" . . . 185 lbs. . . . Born, Gavle, Sweden, November 25, 1960 . . . Shoots left . . . (January, 1988)—Strained ligaments in right knee.

Year	Team	League	Games	G.	A.	Pts.	Pen.
1985-86—Sodertalje (c)		Sweden	36	12	26	38	20
1986-87—Maine Mariners		AHL	6	0	6	6	2
1986-87—New Jersey Devils		NHL	48	2	18	20	16
1987-88—Utica Devils		AHL	33	12	22	34	16
1987-88—New Jersey Devils		NHL	9	1	0	1	0
NHL TOTALS			57	3	18	21	16

(c)—June, 1986—Drafted by New Jersey Devils in NHL entry draft. Fifth Devils pick, 66th overall, fourth round.

RANDY ROBERT CARLYLE

Defense . . . 5'10" . . . 198 lbs. . . . Born, Sudbury, Ont., April 19, 1956 . . . Shoots left . . . Missed part of 1978-79 season with broken ankle . . . (October, 1982)—Injured back . . . (January, 1983)—Injured knee . . . (March, 1984)—Knee injury . . . (November 12, 1985)— Missed eight games with thigh injury . . . (December 7, 1985)—Missed four games after a calf contusion suffered vs. Los Angeles . . . (November, 1986)—Missed nine games with whiplash injury after being checked by Tiger Williams vs. Los Angeles.

Year	Team	League	Games	G.	A.	Pts.	Pen.
1973-74—Sudbury Wolves		Jr."A" OHA	12	0	8	8	21
1974-75—Sudbury Wolves		Jr."A" OHA	67	17	47	64	118
1975-76—Sudbury Wolves (b-c)		Jr."A" OHA	60	15	64	79	126
1976-77—Dallas Black Hawks		CHL	26	2	7	9	63
1976-77—Toronto Maple Leafs		NHL	45	0	5	5	51
1977-78—Dallas Black Hawks		CHL	21	3	14	17	31
1977-78—Toronto Maple Leafs (d)		NHL	49	2	11	13	31
1978-79—Pittsburgh Penguins		NHL	70	13	34	47	78
1979-80—Pittsburgh Penguins		NHL	67	8	28	36	45
1980-81—Pittsburgh Penguins (a-e)		NHL	76	16	67	83	136
1981-82—Pittsburgh Penguins		NHL	73	11	64	75	131
1982-83—Pittsburgh Penguins		NHL	61	15	41	56	110
1983-84—Pittsburgh Penguins (f)		NHL	50	3	23	26	82
1983-84—Winnipeg Jets		NHL	5	0	3	3	2
1984-85—Winnipeg Jets		NHL	71	13	38	51	98
1985-86—Winnipeg Jets		NHL	68	16	33	49	93
1986-87—Winnipeg Jets		NHL	71	16	26	42	93
1987-88—Winnipeg Jets		NHL	78	15	44	59	210
NHL TOTALS			784	128	417	545	1160

(c)—Drafted from Sudbury Wolves by Toronto Maple Leafs in second round of 1976 amateur draft.

(d)—Traded to Pittsburgh Penguins by Toronto Maple Leafs with George Ferguson for Dave Burrows, June, 1978.

(e)—Won James Norris Memorial Trophy (Top NHL Defenseman).

(f)—March, 1984—Traded by Pittsburgh Penguins to Winnipeg Jets for first round 1984 draft pick (Doug Bodger) and player to be named after the 1983-84 season (Moe Mantha).

TODD CARNELLEY

Defense . . . 5'11" . . . 190 lbs. . . . Born, Edmonton, Alta., September 18, 1966 . . . Shoots right . . . (December, 1984)—Tendinitis.

Year	Team	League	Games	G.	A.	Pts.	Pen.
1983-84—Kamloops Junior Oilers		WHL	70	7	23	30	66
1984-85—Kamloops Blazers (b-c)		WHL	56	18	29	47	69
1985-86—Kamloops Blazers		WHL	44	3	23	26	63
1986-87—Muskegon Lumberjacks		IHL	71	4	29	33	75
1987-88—Milwaukee Admirals		IHL	46	5	10	15	43

(c)—June, 1985—Drafted as underage junior by Edmonton Oilers in 1985 NHL entry draft. Second Oilers pick, 41st overall, second round.

NEIL CARNES

Center . . . 5'11" . . . 180 lbs. . . . Born, Farmington, Mich., August 19, 1970 . . . Shoots left.

Year	Team	League	Games	G.	A.	Pts.	Pen.
1986-87—Verdun Junior Canadiens		QHL	62	30	55	85	83
1987-88—Verdun Junior Canadiens (c)		QHL	61	31	57	88	117

(c)—June, 1988—Drafted by Montreal Canadiens in 1988 NHL entry draft. Third Canadiens pick, 46th overall, third round.

ROBERT CARPENTER

Center . . . 6' . . . 190 lbs. . . . Born, Beverly, Mass., July 13, 1963 . . . Shoots left . . . First to play in NHL directly from U.S. high school hockey . . . (1984-85)—Set NHL record for goals in a season by an American-born player . . . (January, 1988)—Torn rotator cuff.

Year	Team	League	Games	G.	A.	Pts.	Pen.
1979-80—St. Johns Prep. H.S. (a)		Mass. H.S.	....	28	37	65	....
1980-81—St. Johns Prep. H.S. (a-c)		Mass. H.S.	....	14	24	38	....
1981-82—Washington Capitals		NHL	80	32	35	67	69
1982-83—Washington Capitals		NHL	80	32	37	69	64
1983-84—Washington Capitals		NHL	80	28	40	68	51
1984-85—Washington Capitals		NHL	80	53	42	95	87
1985-86—Washington Capitals		NHL	80	27	29	56	105
1986-87—Washington Capitals (d)		NHL	22	5	7	12	21
1986-87—New York Rangers (e)		NHL	28	2	8	10	20
1986-87—Los Angeles Kings		NHL	10	2	3	5	6
1987-88—Los Angeles Kings		NHL	71	19	33	52	84
NHL TOTALS			531	200	234	434	507

(c)—June, 1981—Drafted as underage junior by Washington Capitals in 1981 NHL entry draft. First Capitals pick, third overall, first round.

(d)—January, 1987—Traded with second-round 1989 draft pick by Washington Capitals to New York Rangers for Mike Ridley, Kelly Miller and Bobby Crawford.

(e)—March, 1987—Traded with Tom Laidlaw by New York Rangers to Los Angeles Kings for Marcel Dionne, Jeff Crossman and a third-round 1989 draft pick.

JAMES CARSON

Center . . . 6' . . . 185 lbs. . . . Born, Southfield, Mich., July 20, 1968 . . . Shoots right . . . (October, 1986)—Youngest Los Angeles King in club history.

Year	Team	League	Games	G.	A.	Pts.	Pen.
1984-85—Verdun Buniors		QHL	68	44	72	116	16
1985-86—Verdun Juniors (b-c-d-e)		QHL	69	70	83	153	46
1986-87—Los Angeles Kings		NHL	80	37	42	79	22
1987-88—Los Angeles Kings (f)		NHL	80	55	52	107	45
NHL TOTALS			160	92	94	186	67

(c)—Won Frank Selke Trophy (Most Gentlemanly player).

(d)—Won Mike Bossy Trophy (Top Pro Prospect).

(e)—June, 1986—Drafted as underage junior by Los Angeles Kings in 1986 NHL entry draft. First Kings pick, second overall, first round.

(f)—August, 1988—Traded with Martin Gelinas and first-round draft choices in 1989, '91 and '93, plus cash in excess of $10 million by Los Angeles Kings to Edmonton Oilers for Wayne Gretzky, Marty McSorley and Mike Krushelnyski.

LINDSAY WARREN CARSON

Center . . . 6'2" . . . 190 lbs. . . . Born, Oxbow, Sask., November 21, 1960 . . . Shoots left . . . Also plays Left Wing . . . (October 15, 1983)—Broke left arm when checked vs. N.Y. Islanders . . . (November 24, 1985)—Broke knuckle on left hand vs. Pittsburgh and missed 17 games . . . (March, 1988)—Back spasms.

Year	Team	League	Games	G.	A.	Pts.	Pen.
1977-78—Saskatoon Blades		WCHL	62	23	55	78	124
1978-79—Saskatoon Blades		WHL	37	21	29	50	55
1978-79—Billings Bighorns (c)		WHL	40	13	22	35	50
1979-80—Billings Bighorns		WHL	70	42	66	108	101
1980-81—Maine Mariners		AHL	79	11	25	36	84
1981-82—Maine Mariners		AHL	54	20	31	51	92
1981-82—Philadelphia Flyers		NHL	18	0	1	1	32
1982-83—Philadelphia Flyers		NHL	78	18	19	37	68
1983-84—Springfield Indians		AHL	5	2	4	6	5
1983-84—Philadelphia Flyers		NHL	16	1	3	4	10
1984-85—Philadelphia Flyers		NHL	77	20	19	39	123
1985-86—Philadelphia Flyers		NHL	50	9	12	21	84
1986-87—Philadelphia Flyers		NHL	71	11	15	26	141
1987-88—Philadelphia Flyers (d)		NHL	36	2	7	9	37
1987-88—Hartford Whalers		NHL	27	5	4	9	30
NHL TOTALS			373	66	80	146	525

(c)—August, 1979—Drafted as underage junior by Philadelphia Flyers in 1979 NHL entry draft. Fourth Flyers pick, 56th overall, third round.

(d)—January, 1988—Traded by Philadelphia Flyers to Hartford Whalers for Paul Lawless.

JOHN CARTER

Left Wing . . . 5'10" . . . 175 lbs. . . . Born, Winchester, Mass., May 3, 1963 . . . Shoots left . . . (February, 1986)—Sprained knee in ECAC game . . . (March, 1987)—Bruised knee . . . (February, 1988)—Bruised knee.

Year	Team	League	Games	G.	A.	Pts.	Pen.
1982-83—R.P.I.		ECAC	29	16	22	38	33
1983-84—R.P.I. (b)		ECAC	38	35	39	74	52
1984-85—R.P.I. (a-c)		ECAC	37	43	29	72	52
1985-86—R.P.I. (d)		ECAC	27	23	18	41	68
1985-86—Boston Bruins		NHL	3	0	0	0	0
1986-87—Moncton Golden Flames		AHL	58	25	30	55	60
1986-87—Boston Bruins		NHL	8	0	1	1	0
1987-88—Boston Bruins		NHL	4	0	1	1	2
1987-88—Maine Mariners		AHL	76	38	38	76	145
NHL TOTALS			15	0	2	2	2

(c)—Named second-team All-American (East).
(d)—March, 1986—Signed by Boston Bruins as a free agent.

ANDREW CASSELS

Center . . . 6' . . . 167 lbs. . . . Born, Mississauga, Ont., July 23, 1969 . . . Shoots left . . . (January, 1986)—Broken wrist.

Year	Team	League	Games	G.	A.	Pts.	Pen.
1985-86—Bramalea Jr. B		OHA	33	18	25	43	26
1986-87—Ottawa 67's (c-d)		OHL	66	26	66	92	28
1987-88—Ottawa 67's (a-e-f)		OHL	61	48	*103	*151	39

(c)—Won Emms Family Award (OHL Rookie of the Year).
(d)—June, 1987—Drafted as underage junior by Montreal Canadiens in 1987 NHL entry draft. First Canadiens pick, 17th overall, first round.
(e)—Won Eddie Powers Memorial Trophy (Top OHL scorer).
(f)—Won Red Tilson Trophy (Outstanding Player).

BRUCE CASSIDY

Defense . . . 5'11" . . . 175 lbs. . . . Born, Ottawa, Ont., May 20, 1965 . . . Shoots left . . . (Summer, 1984)—Injured knee and missed training camp.

Year	Team	League	Games	G.	A.	Pts.	Pen.
1981-82—Hawkesbury Hawks		COJHL	37	13	30	43	32
1982-83—Ottawa 67's (c-d)		OHL	70	25	86	111	33
1983-84—Ottawa 67's (b)		OHL	67	27	68	95	58
1983-84—Chicago Black Hawks		NHL	1	0	0	0	0
1984-85—Ottawa 67's		OHL	28	13	27	40	15
1985-86—Chicago Black Hawks		NHL	1	0	0	0	0
1985-86—Nova Scotia Oilers		AHL	4	0	0	0	0
1986-87—Saginaw Generals		IHL	10	2	13	15	6
1986-87—Nova Scotia Oilers		IHL	19	2	8	10	4
1986-87—Chicago Black Hawks		NHL	2	0	0	0	0
1987-88—Chicago Black Hawks		NHL	21	3	10	13	6
1987-88—Saginaw Hawks		IHL	60	9	37	46	59
NHL TOTALS			25	3	10	13	6

(c)—Won Emms Family Award (OHL Rookie-of-the-Year).
(d)—June, 1983—Drafted as underage junior by Chicago Black Hawks in NHL entry draft. First Black Hawks pick, 18th overall, first round.

JAY CAUFIELD

Right Wing . . . 6'4" . . . 220 lbs. . . . Born, Lansdale, Penn., July 17, 1965 . . . Shoots right . . . Linebacker at University of North Dakota. He gave up his football career following a neck injury. . . . (October, 1986)—Injured knee.

Year	Team	League	Games	G.	A.	Pts.	Pen.
1984-85—University of North Dakota		WCHA	1	0	0	0	0
1985-86—New Haven Nighthawks (c)		AHL	42	2	3	5	40
1985-86—Toledo Goaldiggers		IHL	30	5	3	8	54
1986-87—New Haven Nighthawks		AHL	13	0	0	0	43
1986-87—Flint Spirit		IHL	14	4	3	7	59
1986-87—New York Rangers		NHL	13	2	1	3	45
1987-88—Kalamazoo Wings		IHL	65	5	10	15	273
1987-88—Minnesota North Stars (d)		NHL	1	0	0	0	0
NHL TOTALS			14	2	1	3	45

(c)—October, 1985—Signed by New York Rangers as a free agent.

(d)—October, 1987—Traded with Dave Gagner by New York Rangers to Minnesota North Stars for Jari Gronstrand and Paul Boutilier.

GINO CAVALLINI

Left Wing . . . 6'2" . . . 215 lbs. . . . Born, Toronto, Ont., November 24, 1962 . . . Shoots left . . . (January, 1988)—Missed 16 games with broken right hand.

Year	Team	League	Games	G.	A.	Pts.	Pen.
1981-82—Toronto St. Mikes		OJHL	37	27	56	83	..
1982-83—Bowling Green Univ.		CCHA	40	8	16	24	52
1983-84—Bowling Green Univ. (c)		CCHA	43	25	23	48	16
1984-85—Moncton Golden Flames		AHL	51	29	19	48	28
1984-85—Calgary Flames		NHL	27	6	10	16	14
1985-86—Moncton Golden Flames		AHL	4	3	2	5	7
1985-86—Calgary Flames (d)		NHL	27	7	7	14	26
1985-86—St. Louis Blues		NHL	30	6	5	11	36
1986-87—St. Louis Blues		NHL	80	18	26	44	54
1987-88—St. Louis Blues		NHL	64	15	17	32	62
NHL TOTALS			228	52	65	117	192

(c)—July, 1984—Signed by Calgary Flames as a free agent.
(d)—February, 1986—Traded with Eddy Beers and Charles Bourgeois by Calgary Flames to St. Louis Blues for Terry Johnson, Joe Mullen and Rik Wilson.

PAUL CAVALLINI

Defense . . . 6'2" . . . 202 lbs. . . . Born, Toronto, Ont., October 13, 1965 . . . Shoots left . . . (December 11, 1987)—Broke hand when slashed by Darren Veitch at Detroit.

Year	Team	League	Games	G.	A.	Pts.	Pen.
1983-84—Henry Carr H.S. (c)		MTHL	54	20	41	61	190
1984-85—Providence College		H. East	45	5	14	19	64
1985-86—Team Canada		Int'l.	52	1	11	12	95
1985-86—Binghamton Whalers		AHL	15	3	4	7	20
1986-87—Binghamton Whalers		AHL	66	12	24	36	188
1986-87—Washington Capitals		NHL	6	0	2	2	8
1987-88—Washington Capitals (d)		NHL	24	2	3	5	66
1987-88—St. Louis Blues		NHL	48	4	7	11	86
NHL TOTALS			78	6	12	18	160

(c)—June, 1984—Drafted as underage junior by Washington Capitals in NHL entry draft. Ninth Capitals pick, 205th overall, 10th round.
(d)—December, 1987—Traded by Washington Capitals to St. Louis Blues for a second-round 1988 draft pick (Wade Bartley).

JOHN DAVID CHABOT

(Given Name: John Kahibaitche)

Center . . . 6'1" . . . 185 lbs. . . . Born Summerside, P.E.I., May 18, 1962 . . . Shoots left . . . (February, 1988)—Fractured mastoin in ear.

Year	Team	League	Games	G.	A.	Pts.	Pen.
1979-80—Hull Olympics (c)		QMJHL	68	26	57	83	28
1980-81—Hull Olympics		QMJHL	70	27	62	89	24
1980-81—Nova Scotia Voyageurs		AHL	1	0	0	0	0
1981-82—Sherbrooke Beavers (a-d-e)		QMJHL	62	34	*109	143	40
1982-83—Nova Scotia Voyageurs		AHL	76	16	73	89	19
1983-84—Montreal Canadiens		NHL	56	18	25	43	13
1984-85—Montreal Canadiens (f)		NHL	10	1	6	7	2
1984-85—Pittsburgh Penguins		NHL	67	8	45	53	12
1985-86—Pittsburgh Penguins		NHL	77	14	31	45	6
1986-87—Pittsburgh Penguins (g)		NHL	72	14	22	36	8
1987-88—Detroit Red Wings		NHL	78	13	44	57	10
NHL TOTALS			360	68	173	241	51

(c)—June, 1980—Drafted as underage junior by Montreal Canadiens in 1980 NHL entry draft. Third Canadiens pick, 40th overall, second round.
(d)—September 1981—Traded by Hull Olympics to Sherbrooke Beavers for Tim Cranston and Rousell MacKenzie.
(e)—Won Michel Briere Trophy (Regular Season QMJHL MVP).
(f)—November, 1984—Traded by Montreal Canadiens to Pittsburgh Penguins for Ron Flockhart.
(g)—July, 1987—Signed by Detroit Red Wings as a free agent.

SEAN CHAMBERS

Defense . . . 6'2" . . . 215 lbs. . . . Born, Royal Oaks, Mich., October 11, 1966 . . . Shoots left . . . (February, 1988)—Dislocated shoulder in game at Toronto.

Year	Team	League	Games	G.	A.	Pts.	Pen.
1985-86—Univ. Alaska/Fairbanks		GWHC	25	15	21	36	34
1986-87—Univ. Alaska/Fairbanks (c)		GWHC	17	11	19	30	....
1986-87—Seattle Thunderbirds		WHL	28	8	25	33	58
1986-87—Fort Wayne Komets		IHL	12	2	6	8	0
1987-88—Minnesota North Stars		NHL	19	1	7	8	21
1987-88—Kalamazoo Wings		IHL	19	1	6	7	22
NHL TOTALS			19	1	7	8	21

(c)—June, 1987—Selected by Minnesota North Stars in 1987 NHL supplemental draft.

TODD CHANNEL

Right Wing . . . 5'10" . . . 185 lbs. . . . Born, Naperville, Ill., October 8, 1963 . . . Shoots right.

Year	Team	League	Games	G.	A.	Pts.	Pen.
1982-83—Miami of Ohio Univ.		CCHA	34	8	18	26	6
1983-84—Miami of Ohio Univ.		CCHA	34	14	14	28	4
1984-85—Miami of Ohio Univ.		CCHA	40	15	32	47	22
1985-86—Miami of Ohio Univ.		CCHA	38	27	27	54	18
1986-87—Binghamton Whalers (c)		AHL	12	1	4	5	4
1986-87—Salt Lake Golden Eagles		IHL	59	22	19	41	28
1987-88—Milwaukee Admirals		IHL	49	14	16	30	16

(c)—August, 1986—Signed by Hartford Whalers as a free agent.

CRAIG CHANNELL

Defense . . . 5'11" . . . 195 lbs. . . . Born, Moncton, N.B., April 24, 1962 . . . Shoots left.

Year	Team	League	Games	G.	A.	Pts.	Pen.
1979-80—Seattle Breakers		WHL	70	3	21	24	191
1980-81—Seattle Breakers		WHL	71	9	66	75	181
1981-82—Seattle Breakers (c)		WHL	71	9	79	88	244
1982-83—Sherbrooke Jets		AHL	65	0	15	15	109
1983-84—Sherbrooke Jets		AHL	80	5	18	23	112
1984-85—Sherbrooke Canadiens		AHL	1	0	0	0	0
1984-85—Fort Wayne Komets		IHL	78	10	35	45	110
1985-86—Fort Wayne Komets		IHL	69	7	28	35	116
1986-87—Fort Wayne Komets		IHL	81	12	42	54	90
1987-88—Fort Wayne Komets		IHL	81	11	29	40	108

(c)—September, 1982—Signed by Winnipeg Jets as a free agent.

RENE CHAPDELAINE

Defense . . . 6'1" . . . 195 lbs. . . . Born, Weyburn, Sask., September 27, 1966 . . . Shoots right.

Year	Team	League	Games	G.	A.	Pts.	Pen.
1984-85—Weyburn		SJHL	61	3	17	20	..
1985-86—Lake Superior State (c)		CCHA	40	2	7	9	24
1986-87—Lake Superior State		CCHA	28	1	5	6	51
1987-88—Lake Superior State		CCHA	35	1	9	10	44

(c)—June, 1986—Drafted by Los Angeles Kings in 1986 NHL entry draft. Seventh Kings pick, 149th overall, eighth round.

BRIAN CHAPMAN

Defense . . . 6' . . . 185 lbs. . . . Born, Brockville, Ont., February 10, 1968 . . . Shoots left. . . . (October 5, 1986)—Suspended 10 games by OHL.

Year	Team	League	Games	G.	A.	Pts.	Pen.
1984-85—Brockville Braves		Jr.A. OPHL	50	11	32	43	145
1985-86—Belleville Bulls (c)		OHL	66	6	31	37	168
1986-87—Belleville Bulls		OHL	54	4	32	36	142
1986-87—Binghamton Whalers (d)		AHL	....	...	....	....	....
1987-88—Belleville Bulls		OHL	63	11	57	68	180

(c)—June, 1986—Drafted as underage junior by Hartford Whalers in 1986 NHL entry draft. Third Whalers pick, 74th overall, fourth round.

(d)—No regular season record. Played one playoff game.

JOSE CHARBONNEAU

Right Wing . . . 6' . . . 195 lbs. . . . Born, Ferme-Neuve, Que., November 2, 1966 . . . Shoots right . . . (November, 1984)—Separated right shoulder . . . (December, 1984)—Reinjured shoulder . . . (January, 1985)—Aggravated shoulder.

Year	Team	League	Games	G.	A.	Pts.	Pen.
1983-84—Drummondville Voltigeurs		QHL	65	31	59	90	110
1984-85—Drummondville Voltigeurs (c)		QHL	46	34	40	74	91

Year	Team	League	Games	G.	A.	Pts.	Pen.
1985-86—Drummondville Voltigeurs		QHL	57	44	45	89	158
1986-87—Sherbrooke Canadiens		AHL	72	14	27	41	94
1987-88—Sherbrooke Canadiens		AHL	55	30	35	65	108
1987-88—Montreal Canadiens		NHL	16	0	2	2	6
NHL TOTALS			16	0	2	2	6

(c)—June, 1985—Drafted as underage junior by Montreal Canadiens in NHL entry draft. First Canadiens pick, 12th overall, first round.

TODD CHARLESWORTH

Defense . . . 6'1" . . . 185 lbs. . . . Born, Calgary, Alta., March 22, 1965 . . . Shoots left.

Year	Team	League	Games	G.	A.	Pts.	Pen.
1981-82—Gloucester Rangers		COJHL	50	13	24	37	67
1982-83—Oshawa Generals (c)		OHL	70	6	23	29	55
1983-84—Oshawa Generals		OHL	57	11	35	46	54
1983-84—Pittsburgh Penguins		NHL	10	0	0	0	8
1984-85—Pittsburgh Penguins		NHL	67	1	8	9	31
1985-86—Baltimore Skipjacks		AHL	19	1	3	4	10
1985-86—Muskegon Lumberjacks		IHL	51	9	27	36	78
1985-86—Pittsburgh Penguins		NHL	2	0	1	1	0
1986-87—Baltimore Skipjacks		AHL	75	5	21	26	64
1986-87—Pittsburgh Penguins		NHL	1	0	0	0	0
1987-88—Pittsburgh Penguins		NHL	6	2	0	2	2
1987-88—Muskegon Lumberjacks		IHL	64	9	31	40	49
NHL TOTALS			86	3	9	12	41

(c)—June, 1983—Drafted as underage junior by Pittsburgh Penguins in NHL entry draft. Second Penguins pick, 22nd overall, second round.

ERIC CHARRON

Defense . . . 6'3" . . . 190 lbs. . . . Born, Verdun, Que., January 14, 1970 . . . Shoots left.

Year	Team	League	Games	G.	A.	Pts.	Pen.
1986-87—Lac St. Louis AAA		Que. Mdgt.	41	1	8	9	92
1987-88—Trois-Rivieres Draveurs (c)		QHL	67	3	13	16	135

(c)—June, 1988—Drafted by Montreal Canadiens in 1988 NHL entry draft. First Canadiens pick, 20th overall, first round.

TIMOTHY CHASE

Center . . . 6'1" . . . 175 lbs. . . . Born, Midland, Mich., March 23, 1970 . . . Shoots left.

Year	Team	League	Games	G.	A.	Pts.	Pen.
1987-88—Tabor Academy (c)		Mass. H.S.	....	20	20	40	....

(c)—June, 1988—Drafted by Montreal Canadiens in 1988 NHL entry draft. Eighth Canadiens pick, 146th overall, seventh round.

ROBERT CHEEVERS

Center . . . 6'2" . . . 195 lbs. . . . Born, North Andover, Mass., October 29, 1968 . . . Shoots right . . . Son of Gerry Cheevers, former goaltender with Boston (NHL) and Cleveland (WHA).

Year	Team	League	Games	G.	A.	Pts.	Pen.
1985-86—North Andover H.S.		Mass. H.S.	....	20	35	55	....
1986-87—Boston College (c)		H. East	10	1	2	3	6
1987-88—Boston College		H. East	29	3	3	6	6

(c)—June, 1987—Drafted by Boston Bruins in 1987 NHL entry draft. Eighth Bruins pick, 140th overall, seventh round.

CHRIS CHELIOS

Defense . . . 6'1" . . . 187 lbs. . . . Born, Chicago, Ill., January 25, 1962 . . . Shoots right. . . . Member of 1984 U.S. Olympic Team . . . (January, 1985)—Sprained right ankle . . . (April, 1985)—Injured left knee . . . Older brother of Steve Chelios (QHL player) . . . (December 19, 1985)—Sprained knee at Quebec . . . (January 20, 1986)—Reinjured knee at Quebec . . . (October, 1986)—Back spasms . . . (February, 1987)—Missed four games with shoulder injury . . . (December, 1987)—Broke little finger of left hand vs. N.Y. Rangers . . . (February 7, 1988)—Bruised tailbone.

Year	Team	League	Games	G.	A.	Pts.	Pen.
1979-80—Moose Jaw Canucks		SJHL	53	12	31	43	118
1980-81—Moose Jaw Canucks (c)		SJHL	54	23	64	87	175
1981-82—University of Wisconsin		WCHA	43	6	43	49	50
1982-83—University of Wisconsin (b)		WCHA	45	16	32	48	62
1983-84—U.S. National Team		Int'l.	60	14	35	49	58

Year	Team	League	Games	G.	A.	Pts.	Pen.
1983-84—U.S. Olympic Team		Int'l.	6	0	4	4	8
1983-84—Montreal Canadiens		NHL	12	0	2	2	12
1984-85—Montreal Canadiens		NHL	74	9	55	64	87
1985-86—Montreal Canadiens		NHL	41	8	26	34	67
1986-87—Montreal Canadiens		NHL	71	11	33	44	124
1987-88—Montreal Canadiens		NHL	71	20	41	61	172
NHL TOTALS			269	48	157	205	462

(c)—June, 1981—Drafted as underage junior by Montreal Canadiens in 1981 NHL entry draft. Fifth Canadiens pick, 40th overall, second round.

RICHARD CHERNOMAZ

Right Wing . . . 5'10" . . . 175 lbs. . . . Born, Selkirk, Man., September 1, 1963 . . . Shoots right . . . Missed parts of 1981-82 season with recurring pain caused by separated shoulder . . . (January, 1983)—Injured knee ligaments . . . (November 27, 1984)—Sprained left knee in game vs. Minnesota and needed arthroscopic surgery.

Year	Team	League	Games	G.	A.	Pts.	Pen.
1979-80—Saskatoon		SJHL	51	33	37	70	75
1979-80—Saskatoon Blades		WHL	25	9	10	19	33
1980-81—Victoria Cougars (c)		WHL	72	49	64	113	92
1981-82—Victoria Cougars		WHL	49	36	62	98	69
1981-82—Colorado Rockies		NHL	2	0	0	0	0
1982-83—Victoria Cougars (a)		WHL	64	71	53	124	113
1983-84—Maine Mariners		AHL	69	17	29	46	39
1983-84—New Jersey Devils		NHL	7	2	1	3	2
1984-85—Maine Mariners		AHL	64	17	34	51	64
1984-85—New Jersey Devils		NHL	3	0	2	2	2
1985-86—Maine Mariners		AHL	78	21	28	49	82
1986-87—Maine Mariners		AHL	58	35	27	62	65
1986-87—New Jersey Devils (d)		NHL	25	6	4	10	8
1987-88—Calgary Flames		NHL	2	1	0	1	0
1987-88—Salt Lake Golden Eagles		IHL	73	48	47	95	122
NHL TOTALS			39	9	7	16	12

(c)—June, 1981—Drafted as underage junior by Colorado Rockies in 1981 NHL entry draft. Third Rockies pick, 26th overall, second round.

(d)—August, 1987—Signed as free agent by Calgary Flames.

KEVIN CHEVELDAYOFF

Defense . . . 6'1" . . . 200 lbs. . . . Born, Saskatoon, Sask., February 4, 1970 . . . Shoots right.

Year	Team	League	Games	G.	A.	Pts.	Pen.
1986-87—Brandon Wheat Kings		WHL	70	0	16	16	259
1987-88—Brandon Wheat Kings (c)		WHL	71	3	29	32	265

(c)—June, 1988—Drafted by New York Islanders in 1988 NHL entry draft. First Islanders pick, 16th overall, first round.

STEVE CHIASSON

Defense . . . 6'1" . . . 200 lbs. . . . Born, Barrie, Ont., April 14, 1967 . . . Shoots left . . . (October, 1985)—Hand injury . . . (February, 1988)—Separated right shoulder . . . (May, 1988)—Injured foot.

Year	Team	League	Games	G.	A.	Pts.	Pen.
1982-83—Peterborough Midgets		OHA	40	25	35	60	120
1983-84—Guelph Platers		OHL	55	1	9	10	112
1984-85—Guelph Platers (c)		OHL	61	8	22	30	139
1985-86—Guelph Platers		OHL	54	12	29	41	126
1986-87—Detroit Red Wings		NHL	45	1	4	5	73
1987-88—Adirondack Red Wings		AHL	23	6	11	17	58
1987-88—Detroit Red Wings		NHL	29	2	9	11	57
NHL TOTALS			74	3	13	16	130

(c)—June, 1985—Drafted as underage junior by Detroit Red Wings in 1985 NHL entry draft. Third Red Wings pick, 50th overall, third round.

COLIN CHIN

Center . . . 5'8" . . . 165 lbs. . . . Born, Fort Wayne, Ind., August 28, 1961 . . . Shoots left.

Year	Team	League	Games	G.	A.	Pts.	Pen.
1983-84—Univ. Illinois-Chicago		CCHA	35	11	25	36	14
1984-85—Univ. Illinois-Chicago (c)		CCHA	38	23	42	65	22
1985-86—Baltimore Skipjacks		AHL	78	17	28	45	38

Year	Team	League	Games	G.	A.	Pts.	Pen.
1986-87—Fort Wayne Komets		IHL	75	33	42	75	35
1987-88—Fort Wayne Komets		IHL	75	31	35	66	60

(c)—October, 1985—Signed by Pittsburgh Penguins as a free agent.

COLIN CHISHOLM

Defense . . . 6'3" . . . 210 lbs. . . . Born, Edmonton, Alta., February 25, 1963 . . . Shoots right.

Year	Team	League	Games	G.	A.	Pts.	Pen.
1980-81—Calgary Midget Wranglers		Midget	..	2	21	23	..
1981-82—Calgary Midget Wranglers		Midget	..	1	21	22	..
1982-83—University of Alberta		CWUAA	..	1	7	8	..
1983-84—University of Alberta		CWUAA	..	2	17	19	..
1984-85—University of Alberta		CWUAA	..	3	31	34	..
1985-86—University of Alberta		CWUAA	..	6	23	29	..
1986-87—Springfield Indians (c)		AHL	75	1	11	12	141
1986-87—Minnesota North Stars		NHL	1	0	0	0	0
1987-88—Kalamazoo Wings		IHL	44	1	3	4	59
NHL TOTALS			1	0	0	0	0

(c)—September, 1986—Signed by Minnesota North Stars as a free agent.

PETER CHOMA

Right Wing . . . 6'1" . . . 215 lbs. . . . Born, St. Catharines, Ont., September 10, 1968 . . . Shoots right.

Year	Team	League	Games	G.	A.	Pts.	Pen.
1984-85—St. Catharines Midget		OHA	43	38	32	70	87
1985-86—Hamilton Steelhawks (c)		OHL	18	2	3	5	13
1985-86—Belleville Bulls (d)		OHL	46	9	11	20	25
1986-87—Belleville Bulls		OHL	64	18	17	35	34
1987-88—Belleville Bulls		OHL	14	2	4	6	18
1987-88—Ottawa 67's		OHL	50	7	27	34	46

(c)—November, 1985—Traded with Jason Lafreniere and Lawrence Hinch by Hamilton Steelhawks to Belleville Bulls for Sean Doyl, John Purves and Brian Hoard.

(d)—June, 1986—Drafted as underage junior by Washington Capitals in 1986 NHL entry draft. Eighth Capitals pick, 145th overall, seventh round.

THOMAS CHORSKE

Right Wing . . . 6'1" . . . 185 lbs. . . . Born, Minneapolis, Minn., September 18, 1966 . . . Shoots right.

Year	Team	League	Games	G.	A.	Pts.	Pen.
1984-85—Minn. Southwest H.S. (c)		Minn. H.S.	23	44	26	70	..
1985-86—University of Minnesota		WCHA	39	6	4	10	6
1986-87—University of Minnesota		WCHA	47	20	22	42	20
1987-80—U.S. Olympic Team		Int'l	..	9	16	25	..

(c)—June, 1985—Drafted by Montreal Canadiens in 1985 NHL entry draft. Second Canadiens pick, 16th overall, first round.

DAVE CHRISTIAN

Center . . . 5'11" . . . 170 lbs. . . . Born, Warroad, Minn., May 12, 1959 . . . Shoots right . . . Member of 1978 U.S. National Junior Team and 1980 U.S. Olympic Gold Medal Team . . . Son of Bill Christian ('60 & '64 Olympic Teams), Nephew of Roger Christian ('60 & '64 Olympic Teams) and nephew of Gordon Christian ('56 Olympic Team) . . . His Father (Bill) and Uncle (Roger) own the Christian Brothers Hockey Stick Company . . . Also plays Right Wing . . . Brother of Edward Christian (Winnipeg '80 draft pick) . . . (December, 1982)— Torn shoulder muscles and missed 25 games . . . (November, 1986)—Missed four games with pulled muscle in right side.

Year	Team	League	Games	G.	A.	Pts.	Pen.
1977-78—University of North Dakota		WCHA	38	8	16	24	14
1978-79—University of North Dakota (c)		WCHA	40	22	24	46	22
1979-80—U.S. Olympic Team		Int'l	*66	10	28	38	32
1979-80—Winnipeg Jets		NHL	15	8	10	18	2
1980-81—Winnipeg Jets		NHL	80	28	43	71	22
1981-82—Winnipeg Jets		NHL	80	25	51	76	28
1982-83—Winnipeg Jets (d)		NHL	55	18	26	44	23
1983-84—Washington Capitals		NHL	80	29	52	81	28
1984-85—Washington Capitals		NHL	80	26	43	69	14
1985-86—Washington Capitals		NHL	80	41	42	83	15
1986-87—Washington Capitals		NHL	76	23	27	50	8
1987-88—Washington Capitals		NHL	80	37	21	58	26
NHL TOTALS			626	235	315	550	166

(c)—August, 1979—Drafted by Winnipeg Jets in 1979 NHL entry draft. Second Jets pick, 40th overall, second round.

(d)—June, 1983—Traded by Winnipeg Jets to Washington Capitals for first round draft pick in 1983 (Jets drafted Bobby Dollas).

JEFF CHRISTIAN

Left Wing . . . 6'1" . . . 185 lbs. . . . Born, Burlington, Ont., July 30, 1970 . . . Shoots left . . . Son of Gord Christian (Member of Hamilton Tiger Cats-CFL, 1967-72).

Year	Team	League	Games	G.	A.	Pts.	Pen.
1986-87	Dundas Blues	OHA Jr. 'C'	29	20	34	54	42
1987-88	London Knights (c)	OHL	64	15	29	44	154

(c)—June, 1988—Drafted by New Jersey Devils in 1988 NHL entry draft. Second Devils pick, 23rd overall, second round.

SHANE CHURLA

Right Wing . . . 6'1" . . . 200 lbs. . . . Born, Fernie, B.C., June 24, 1965 . . . Shoots right . . . (October, 1985)—Pulled stomach muscles . . . (October 5, 1986)—Suspended three games by AHL.

Year	Team	League	Games	G.	A.	Pts.	Pen.
1983-84	Medicine Hat Tigers	WHL	48	3	7	10	115
1984-85	Medicine Hat Tigers (c)	WHL	70	14	20	34	*370
1985-86	Binghamton Whalers	AHL	52	4	10	14	306
1986-87	Binghamton Whalers	AHL	24	1	5	6	249
1986-87	Hartford Whalers	NHL	20	0	1	1	789
1987-88	Binghamton Whalers	AHL	25	5	8	13	168
1987-88	Hartford Whalers (d)	NHL	2	0	0	0	14
1987-88	Calgary Flames	NHL	29	1	5	6	132
	NHL TOTALS		51	1	6	7	224

(c)—June, 1985—Drafted by Hartford Whalers in 1985 NHL entry draft. Fourth Whalers pick, 110th overall, sixth round.

(d)—January, 1988—Traded with Dana Murzyn by Hartford Whalers to Calgary Flames for Neil Sheehy, Carey Wilson and Lane McDonald.

JEFF CHYCHRUN

Defense . . . 6'4" . . . 190 lbs. . . . Born, Lasalle, Que., May 3, 1966 . . . Shoots right.

Year	Team	League	Games	G.	A.	Pts.	Pen.
1983-84	Kingston Canadians (c)	OHL	83	1	13	14	137
1984-85	Kingston Canadians	OHL	58	4	10	14	206
1985-86	Kingston Canadians	OHL	61	4	21	25	127
1985-86	Kalamazoo Wings (d)	IHL	....	...	....	....	....
1985-86	Hershey Bears (e)	AHL	....	...	....	....	....
1986-87	Hershey Bears	AHL	74	1	17	18	239
1986-87	Philadelphia Flyers	NHL	1	0	0	0	4
1987-88	Philadelphia Flyers	NHL	3	0	0	0	4
1987-88	Hershey Bears	AHL	55	0	5	5	210
	NHL TOTALS		4	0	0	0	8

(c)—June, 1984—Drafted as underage junior by Philadelphia Flyers in 1984 NHL entry draft. Second Flyers pick, 37th overall, second round.

(d)—No regular season record. Played three playoff games.

(e)—No regular season record. Played four playoff games.

DEAN CHYNOWETH

Defense . . . 6'1" . . . 185 lbs. . . . Born, Saskatoon, Sask., October 30, 1968 . . . Shoots right . . . Son of Ed Chynoweth, President of the Western Hockey League . . . (April, 1987)—Fractured rib and punctured lung during WHL playoff game . . . (September, 1985 April, 1986 and October, 1986)—Broken hand.

Year	Team	League	Games	G.	A.	Pts.	Pen.
1984-85	Calgary Buffaloes	Atla. Midget	26	5	13	18	104
1985-86	Medicine Hat Tigers	WHL	69	3	12	15	208
1986-87	Medicine Hat Tigers (c)	WHL	67	3	18	21	285
1987-88	Medicine Hat Tigers	WHL	64	1	21	22	274

(c)—June, 1987—Drafted as underage junior by New York Islanders in 1987 NHL entry draft. First Islanders pick, 13th overall, first round.

BARRY CHYZOWSKI

Center . . . 6' . . . 170 lbs. . . . Born, Edmonton, Alta., May 25, 1968 . . . Shoots right . . . Brother of Ron Chyzowski . . . (January 1986)—Separated shoulder.

Year	Team	League	Games	G.	A.	Pts.	Pen.
1984-85—Carnwood SSAC	Alta. Midget	36	32	39	71	10
1985-86—St. Albert Saints (a-c)	AJHL	45	34	34	68	33
1986-87—University of Minn./Duluth	WCHA	39	5	11	16	16
1987-88—University of Minn./Duluth	WCHA	41	22	34	56	14

(c)—June, 1986—Drafted by New York Rangers in 1986 NHL entry draft. Eighth Rangers pick, 156th overall, eighth round.

PETER CIAVAGLIA

Center . . . 5'10" . . . 160 lbs. . . . Born, Albany, N.Y., July 15, 1969 . . . Shoots left.

Year	Team	League	Games	G.	A.	Pts.	Pen.
1985-86—Nichols/Wheatfield Mid.	NY Midget	60	84	113	197	..
1986-87—Nichols/Wheatfield Jr. B (c)	NY Jr. B	..	53	84	137	...
1987-88—Harvard University	ECAC	30	10	23	33	16

(c)—June, 1987—Drafted by Calgary Flames in 1987 NHL entry draft. Eighth Flames pick, 145th overall, seventh round.

DINO CICCARELLI

Right Wing . . . 5'11" . . . 185 lbs. . . . Born, Sarnia, Ont., February 8, 1960 . . . Shoots right . . . (Spring, 1978)—Fractured midshaft of right femur that required the insertion of 16 inch metal rod in leg . . . Set NHL Playoff record for most goals as a rookie (14) in 1981 . . . First Minnesota player to score 50 goals in a season . . . (November, 1984)—Shoulder injury . . . (December, 1984)—Broken right wrist . . . (October 5, 1987)—Suspended three games by NHL for making contact with linesman Mark Pare during pre-season game vs. Chicago . . . (January 6, 1988)—Given 10-game suspension by NHL for stick swinging incident involving Luke Richardson at Toronto.

Year	Team	League	Games	G.	A.	Pts.	Pen.
1976-77—London Knights	OMJHL	66	39	43	82	45
1977-78—London Knights (b)	OMJHL	68	72	70	142	49
1978-79—London Knights (c)	OMJHL	30	8	11	19	25
1979-80—London Knights	OMJHL	62	50	53	103	72
1979-80—Oklahoma City Stars	CHL	6	3	2	5	0
1980-81—Oklahoma City Stars	CHL	48	32	25	57	45
1980-81—Minnesota North Stars	NHL	32	18	12	30	29
1981-82—Minnesota North Stars	NHL	76	55	51	106	138
1982-83—Minnesota North Stars	NHL	77	37	38	75	94
1983-84—Minnesota North Stars	NHL	79	38	33	71	58
1984-85—Minnesota North Stars	NHL	51	15	17	32	41
1985-86—Minnesota North Stars	NHL	75	44	45	89	53
1986-87—Minnesota North Stars	NHL	80	52	51	103	92
1987-88—Minnesota North Stars	NHL	67	41	45	86	79
NHL TOTALS			537	300	292	592	584

(c)—September, 1979—Signed by Minnesota North Stars as free agent.

CHRIS CICHOCKI

Right Wing . . . 5'10" . . . 185 lbs. . . . Born, Detroit, Mich., September 17, 1963 . . . Shoots right . . . Member of 1983 U.S. Junior National Team . . . (January 7, 1986)—Injured mouth at Washington and missed three games.

Year	Team	League	Games	G.	A.	Pts.	Pen.
1982-83—Michigan Tech.	CCHA	36	12	10	22	10
1983-84—Michigan Tech.	CCHA	40	25	20	45	36
1984-85—Michigan Tech. (c)	WCHA	40	30	24	54	14
1985-86—Adirondack Red Wings	AHL	9	4	4	8	6
1985-86—Detroit Red Wings	NHL	59	10	11	21	21
1986-87—Adirondack Red Wings	AHL	55	31	34	65	27
1986-87—Detroit Red Wings (d)	NHL	2	0	0	0	2
1986-87—Maine Mariners	AHL	7	2	2	4	0
1987-88—New Jersey Devils	NHL	5	1	0	1	2
1987-88—Utica Devils	AHL	69	36	30	66	66
NHL TOTALS			66	11	11	22	25

(c)—June, 1985—Signed by Detroit Red Wings as a free agent.

(d)—March, 1987—Traded with third-round 1987 draft pick by Detroit Red Wings to New Jersey Devils for Mel Bridgman. (The Devils later traded the pick to Buffalo who drafted Andrew MacIver).

ROBERT CIMETTA

Left Wing . . . 6' . . . 190 lbs. . . . Born, Toronto, Ont., February 15, 1970 . . . Shoots left . . . (October, 1986)—Fractured wrist.

Year	Team	League	Games	G.	A.	Pts.	Pen.
1986-87—Toronto Marlboros		OHL	66	21	35	56	65
1987-88—Toronto Marlboros (c)		OHL	64	34	42	76	90

(c)—June, 1988—Drafted by Boston Bruins in 1988 NHL entry draft. First Bruins pick, 18th overall, first round.

JOE CIRELLA

Defense . . . 6'2" . . . 205 lbs. . . . Born, Hamilton, Ont., May 9, 1963 . . . Shoots right . . . Brother of Carmine Cirella . . . (December 17, 1984)—Hit by stick vs. Edmonton and needed 12 stitches . . . (November 26, 1985)—Injured left knee vs. Winnipeg.

Year	Team	League	Games	G.	A.	Pts.	Pen.
1979-80—Hamilton Major Midgets		....	21	5	26	31	....
1980-81—Oshawa Generals (c)		OHL	56	5	31	36	220
1981-82—Oshawa Generals		OHL	3	0	1	1	10
1981-82—Colorado Rockies		NHL	65	7	12	19	52
1982-83—Oshawa Generals (a)		OHL	56	13	55	68	110
1982-83—New Jersey Devils		NL	2	0	1	1	4
1983-84—New Jersey Devils		NHL	79	11	33	44	137
1984-85—New Jersey Devils		NHL	66	6	18	24	143
1985-86—New Jersey Devils		NHL	66	6	23	29	147
1986-87—New Jersey Devils		NHL	65	9	22	31	111
1987-88—New Jersey Devils		NHL	80	8	31	39	191
NHL TOTALS			423	47	140	187	785

(c)—June, 1981—Drafted as underage junior by Colorado Rockies in 1981 NHL entry draft. First Rockies pick, fifth overall, first round.

KERRY CLARK

Right Wing . . . 6'1" . . . 195 lbs. . . . Born, Kelvington, Sask., August 21, 1968 . . . Shoots right.

Year	Team	League	Games	G.	A.	Pts.	Pen.
1984-85—Regina Pats		WHL	36	1	1	2	66
1985-86—Regina Pats		WHL	23	4	4	8	58
1985-86—Saskatoon Blades (c)		WHL	39	5	8	13	104
1986-87—Saskatoon Blades		WHL	54	12	10	22	229
1987-88—Saskatoon Blades		WHL	67	15	11	26	241

(c)—June, 1986—Drafted as underage junior by New York Islanders in 1986 NHL entry draft. Twelfth Islanders pick, 206th overall, 10th round.

WENDEL CLARK

Left Wing . . . 5'11" . . . 190 lbs. . . . Born, Kelvington, Sask., October 25, 1966 . . . Shoots left . . . (November, 1985)—Virus . . . (November 26, 1985)—Missed 14 games with broken right foot at St. Louis . . . Also plays Defense . . . (November, 1987)—Missed 23 games with back spasms . . . (October, 1987)—Tendinitis in right shoulder . . . (February, 1988)—Reinjured back.

Year	Team	League	Games	G.	A.	Pts.	Pen.
1983-84—Saskatoon Blades		WHL	72	23	45	68	225
1984-85—Saskatoon Blades (a-c-d)		WHL	64	32	55	87	253
1985-86—Toronto Maple Leafs (e)		NHL	66	34	11	45	227
1986-87—Toronto Maple Leafs		NHL	80	37	23	60	271
1987-88—Toronto Maple Leafs		NHL	28	12	11	23	80
NHL TOTALS			174	83	45	128	578

(c)—Won WHL Top Defenseman Trophy.

(d)—June, 1985—Drafted as underage junior by Toronto Maple Leafs in 1985 NHL entry draft. First Maple Leafs pick, first overall, first round.

(e)—Named NHL Rookie of the Year in poll of players by THE SPORTING NEWS.

DOUG CLARKE

Defense . . . 6' . . . 190 lbs. . . . Born, Toronto, Ont., February 29, 1964 . . . Shoots left.

Year	Team	League	Games	G.	A.	Pts.	Pen.
1983-84—Colorado College (c)		WCHA	35	6	26	32	70
1984-85—Colorado College (b)		WCHA	37	12	36	48	77
1985-86—Team Canada		Int'l	72	7	7	14	38
1986-87—Colorado College		WCHA	37	11	37	48	73
1987-88—Salt Lake Golden Eagles		IHL	71	11	26	37	14

(c)—June, 1984—Drafted by Vancouver Canucks in 1984 NHL entry draft. Twelfth Canucks pick, 219th overall, 11th round.

JOSEPH CLEARY

Defense ... 6' ... 190 lbs. ... Born, Buffalo, N.Y., January 17, 1970 ... Shoots right.

Year	Team	League	Games	G.	A.	Pts.	Pen.
1986-87—Cushing Academy		Mass. H.S.	..	15	30	45	..
1987-88—Stratford Cullitons (c)		OHA	41	20	37	57	160

(c)—June, 1988—Drafted by Chicago Black Hawks in 1988 NHL entry draft. Fourth Black Hawks pick, 92nd overall, fifth round.

SEAN CLEMENT

Defense ... 6'2" ... 185 lbs. ... Born, Winnipeg, Man., February 26, 1966 ... Shoots left ... (December, 1987)—Injured knee.

Year	Team	League	Games	G.	A.	Pts.	Pen.
1983-84—Brockville Braves (c)		COJHL	52	13	41	54	135
1984-85—Michigan State Univ.		CCHA	44	5	13	18	24
1985-86—Michigan State Univ.		CCHA	40	4	7	11	40
1986-87—Michigan State Univ.		CCHA	41	3	11	14	70
1987-88—Michigan State Univ.		CCHA	42	3	12	15	92

(c)—June, 1984—Drafted as underage junior by Winnipeg Jets in 1984 NHL entry draft. Third Jets pick, 72nd overall, fourth round.

KEVIN (CHET) CLEMENTS

Left Wing ... 5'11" ... 185 lbs. ... Born, McLennan, Alta., February 2, 1967 ... Shoots left.

Year	Team	League	Games	G.	A.	Pts.	Pen.
1983-84—Regina Pats		WHL	47	5	8	13	14
1984-85—Regina Pats (c)		WHL	70	31	16	47	40
1985-86—Regina Pats		WHL	71	26	32	58	70
1986-87—Brandon Wheat Kings		WHL	69	16	20	36	50
1987-88—Brandon Wheat Kings		WHL	11	7	6	13	12
1987-88—Regina Pats (d)		WHL	62	24	25	49	103

(c)—June, 1985—Drafted as underage junior by Pittsburgh Penguins in 1985 NHL entry draft. Fifth Penguins pick, 107th overall, sixth round.

(d)—November, 1987—Traded by Brandon Wheat Kings to Regina Pats for future considerations.

SCOTT CLEMENTS

Defense ... 6'1" ... 205 lbs. ... Born, Sudbury, Ont., May 1, 1962 ... Shoots left.

Year	Team	League	Games	G.	A.	Pts.	Pen.
1984-85—St. Catharines Saints (c)		AHL	13	1	8	9	19
1985-86—St. Catharines Saints		AHL	53	1	10	11	43
1985-86—Fredericton Express		AHL	20	0	2	2	4
1986-87—Newmarket Saints		AHL	70	1	15	16	77
1987-88—Newmarket Saints		AHL	76	3	11	14	53

(c)—May, 1985—Signed by Toronto Maple Leafs as a free agent.

SEAN CLIFFORD

Defense ... 6'1" ... 200 lbs. ... Born, North Bay, Ont., May 11, 1967 ... Shoots left.

Year	Team	League	Games	G.	A.	Pts.	Pen.
1985-86—Ohio State University		CCHA	12	0	2	2	18
1986-87—Ohio State University (c)		CCHA	42	3	8	11	107
1987-88—Ohio State University		CCHA	40	1	6	7	121

(c)—June, 1987—Drafted by Detroit Red Wings in 1987 NHL entry draft. Seventh Red Wings pick, 116th overall, sixth round.

SHAUN CLOUSTON

Right Wing ... 6' ... 205 lbs. ... Born, Viking, Alta., February 21, 1968 ... Shoots left.

Year	Team	League	Games	G.	A.	Pts.	Pen.
1985-86—Univ. of Alberta (c)		CWUAA	25	10	9	19	59
1986-87—Portland Winter Hawks		WHL	70	6	25	31	93
1987-88—Portland Winter Hawks		WHL	68	29	50	79	144

(c)—June, 1986—Drafted by New York Rangers in 1986 NHL entry draft. Third Rangers pick, 53rd overall, third round.

GLEN MACLEOD COCHRANE

Defense ... 6'3" ... 205 lbs. ... Born, Cranbrook, B. C., January 29, 1958 ... Shoots left ... (March, 1984)—Knee surgery ... (October, 1984)—Missed first 42 games of season following surgery to repair kneecap ... (September-October, 1985)—Missed first five games

of season due to pain in knee . . . (January 10, 1986)—Missed four games due to back spasms . . . (December, 1986)—Disc surgery.

Year	Team	League	Games	G.	A.	Pts.	Pen.
1974-75—The Pass Red Devils		AJHL	16	1	4	5	61
1975-76—The Pass Red Devils		AJHL	60	17	42	59	210
1975-76—Calgary Centennials		WCHL	3	0	0	0	0
1976-77—Calgary Centennials		WCHL	35	1	5	6	105
1976-77—Victoria Cougars		WCHL	36	1	7	8	60
1977-78—Victoria Cougars (c)		WCHL	72	7	40	47	311
1978-79—Philadelphia Flyers		NHL	1	0	0	0	0
1978-79—Maine Mariners		AHL	76	1	22	23	320
1979-80—Maine Mariners		AHL	77	1	11	12	269
1980-81—Maine Mariners		AHL	38	4	13	17	201
1980-81—Philadelphia Flyers		NHL	31	1	8	9	219
1981-82—Philadelphia Flyers		NHL	63	6	12	18	329
1982-83—Philadelphia Flyers		NHL	77	2	22	24	237
1983-84—Philadelphia Flyers		NHL	67	7	16	23	225
1984-85—Philadelphia Flyers (d)		NHL	18	0	3	3	100
1984-85—Hershey Bears		AHL	9	0	8	8	35
1985-86—Vancouver Canucks		NHL	49	0	3	3	125
1986-87—Vancouver Canucks (e)		NHL	14	0	0	0	52
1987-88—Chicago Black Hawks		NHL	73	1	8	9	204
NHL TOTALS			393	17	72	89	1491

(c)—Drafted from Victoria Cougars by Philadelphia Flyers in third round of 1978 amateur draft.
(d)—March, 1985—Traded by Philadelphia Flyers to Vancouver Canucks for future third round draft pick.
(e)—October, 1987—Selection by Chicago Black Hawks in NHL waiver draft.

PAUL DOUGLAS COFFEY

Defense . . . 6'1" . . . 185 lbs. . . . Born, Weston, Ont., June 1, 1961 . . . Shoots left . . . Became only third defenseman in NHL history to have a 100-point season (Potvin & Orr) with 126 points in 1983-84 . . . (May, 1985)—Set NHL record for most goals (12) assists (25) and points (37) in playoffs by a defenseman . . . (1985-86)—Set NHL record for most goals in one season by a defenseman, breaking Bobby Orr's mark of 46 goals in 1974-75 . . . (December, 1986)—Missed 10 games with recurring back spasms . . . (April 9, 1987)—Missed four playoff games when he sprained right shoulder vs. Los Angeles. . . . (December, 1987)—Slightly torn knee cartilage in a collision with referee Don Koharski.

Year	Team	League	Games	G.	A.	Pts.	Pen.
1977-78—Kingston Canadians		OHL	8	2	2	4	11
1977-78—North York Rangers		MTHL	50	14	33	47	64
1978-79—Sault Ste. Marie Greyhounds		OPJHL	68	17	72	89	99
1979-80—Sault Ste. Marie Grehhounds		OPJHL	23	10	21	31	63
1979-80—Kitchener Rangers (b-c)		OPJHL	52	19	52	71	130
1980-81—Edmonton Oilers		NHL	74	9	23	32	130
1981-82—Edmonton Oilers (b)		NHL	80	29	60	89	106
1982-83—Edmonton Oilers (b)		NHL	80	29	67	96	87
1983-84—Edmonton Oilers (b)		NHL	80	40	86	126	104
1984-85—Edmonton Oilers (a-d)		NHL	80	37	84	121	97
1985-86—Edmonton Oilers (a-d)		NHL	79	48	90	138	120
1986-87—Edmonton Oilers		NHL	59	17	50	67	49
1987-88—Pittsburgh Penguins (e)		NHL	46	15	52	67	93
NHL TOTALS			578	224	512	736	786

(c)—June, 1980—Drafted by Edmonton Oilers in NHL entry draft. First Oilers pick, sixth overall, first round.
(d)—Won James Norris Memorial Trophy (Top NHL Defenseman).
(e)—November, 1987—Traded with Dave Hunter and Wayne Van Dorp by Edmonton Oilers to Pittsburgh Penguins for Craig Simpson, Dave Hannan, Moe Mantha and Chris Joseph.

DARREN COLBOURNE

Right Wing . . . 6' . . . 190 lbs. . . . Born, Corner Brook, N.F., January 5, 1968 . . . Shoots left . . . (October, 1987)—Mononcleosis.

Year	Team	League	Games	G.	A.	Pts.	Pen.
1985-86—Oshawa Generals		OHL	46	4	3	7	16
1986-87—Oshawa Generals (c)		OHL	17	3	2	5	18
1986-87—Cornwall Royals		OHL	41	17	25	42	33
1987-88—Cornwall Royals (d)		OHL	61	47	51	98	66

(c)—December, 1986—Traded with Scott MacDonald by Oshawa Generals to Cornwall Royals for future considerations.
(d)—June, 1988—Drafted by Detroit Red Wings in 1988 NHL entry draft. Tenth Red Wings pick, 227th overall, 11th round.

DANTON COLE

Center . . . 5'10" . . . 180 lbs. . . . Born, Pontiac, Mich., January 10, 1967 . . . Shoots right . . . Also plays Right Wing.

Year	Team	League	Games	G.	A.	Pts.	Pen.
1984-85—Aurora Tigers (c)		OHA	41	51	44	95	91
1985-86—Michigan State Univ.		CCHA	43	11	10	21	22
1986-87—Michigan State Univ.		CCHA	44	9	15	24	16
1987-88—Michigan State Univ.		CCHA	46	20	36	56	38

(c)—June, 1985—Drafted by Winnipeg Jets in 1985 NHL entry draft. Sixth Jets pick, 123rd overall, sixth round.

PATRICK JOHN CONACHER

Center . . . 5'8" . . . 188 lbs. . . . Born, Edmonton, Alta., May 1, 1959 . . . Shoots left . . . (September 21, 1980)—Fractured left ankle in rookie scrimmage vs. Washington that required surgery . . . (November, 1982)—Injured shoulder . . . (December, 1984)—Severe groin injury . . . (February, 1988)—Sprained back.

Year	Team	League	Games	G.	A.	Pts.	Pen.
1977-78—Billings Bighorns		WCHL	72	31	44	75	105
1978-79—Billings Bighorns		WHL	39	25	37	62	50
1978-79—Saskatoon Blades (c)		WHL	33	15	32	47	37
1979-80—New York Rangers		NHL	17	0	5	5	4
1979-80—New Haven Nighthawks		AHL	53	11	14	25	43
1980-81—Did not play			..	..	..	..	..
1981-82—Springfield Indians		AHL	77	23	22	45	38
1981-82—Springfield Indians		AHL	77	23	22	45	38
1982-83—Tulsa Oilers		CHL	63	29	28	57	44
1982-83—New York Rangers		NHL	5	0	1	1	4
1983-84—Moncton Alpines		AHL	28	7	16	23	30
1983-84—Edmonton Oilers		NHL	45	2	8	10	31
1984-85—Nova Scotia Oilers (d)		AHL	68	20	45	65	44
1985-86—New Jersey Devils		NHL	2	0	2	2	2
1985-86—Maine Mariners		AHL	69	15	30	45	83
1986-87—Maine Mariners		AHL	56	12	14	26	47
1987-88—Utica Devils		AHL	47	14	33	47	32
1987-88—New Jersey Devils		NHL	24	2	5	7	12
NHL TOTALS			93	4	21	25	53

(c)—August, 1979—Drafted by New York Rangers in 1979 NHL entry draft. Third Rangers pick, 76th overall, fourth round.

(d)—August, 1985—Signed by New Jersey Devils as a free agent.

JAMIE COOK

Right Wing . . . 6'1" . . . 195 lbs. . . . Born, Bramalea, Ont., November 5, 1968 . . . Shoots right.

Year	Team	League	Games	G.	A.	Pts.	Pen.
1986-87—Bramalea Jr. B		OHL	37	21	28	49	46
1987-88—Bramalea Jr. B (c)		OHL	37	26	44	70	56

(c)—June, 1988—Drafted by Philadelphia Flyers in 1988 NHL entry draft. Eighth Flyers pick, 140th overall, seventh round.

TODD COPELAND

Defense . . . 6'2" . . . 200 lbs. . . . Born, Ridgewood, N.J., May 18, 1968 . . . Shoots left . . . (February, 1986)—Knee injury.

Year	Team	League	Games	G.	A.	Pts.	Pen.
1984-85—Belmont Hill H.S.		Mass.	23	8	25	33	18
1985-86—Belmont Hill H.S. (c)		Mass.	19	4	19	23	19
1986-87—University of Michigan		CCHA	34	2	10	12	57
1987-88—University of Michigan		CCHA	41	3	10	13	58

(c)—June, 1986—Drafted by New Jersey Devils in 1986 NHL entry draft. Second Devils pick, 24th overall, second round.

BOB CORKUM

Right Wing . . . 6'2" . . . 200 lbs. . . . Born, Salisbury, Mass., December 18, 1967 . . . Shoots right.

Year	Team	League	Games	G.	A.	Pts.	Pen.
1984-85—Triton Regional H.S.		Mass.	18	35	36	71	....
1985-86—University of Maine (c)		H. East	39	7	16	23	53
1986-87—University of Maine		H. East	35	18	11	29	24
1987-88—University of Maine		H. East	40	14	18	32	64

YVON CORRIVEAU

Left Wing . . . 6'1" . . . 195 lbs. . . . Born, Welland, Ont., February 8, 1967 . . . Shoots left . . . (March, 1985)—Shoulder injury.

Year	Team	League	Games	G.	A.	Pts.	Pen.
1983-84—Welland Cougars Jr.B		OHA	36	16	21	37	51
1984-85—Toronto Marlboros (c)		OHL	59	23	28	51	65
1985-86—Toronto Marlboros		OHL	59	54	36	90	75
1985-86—Washington Capitals		NHL	2	0	0	0	0
1986-87—Toronto Marlboros		OHL	23	14	19	33	23
1986-87—Binghamton Whalers		AHL	7	0	0	0	2
1986-87—Washington Capitals		NHL	17	1	1	2	24
1987-88—Binghamton Whalers		AHL	35	15	14	29	64
1987-88—Washington Capitals		NHL	44	10	9	19	84
NHL TOTALS			63	11	10	21	108

SHAYNE CORSON

Center and Left Wing . . . 6' . . . 175 lbs. . . . Born, Barrie, Ont., August 13, 1966 . . . Shoots left . . . (1986)—Named to World Junior Hockey Championship All-Star team . . . (January 24, 1987)—Broke jaw at St. Louis . . . (September, 1987)—Strained ligament in right knee during Montreal training camp . . . (March, 1988)—Injured groin . . . (April, 1988)—Knee injury.

Year	Team	League	Games	G.	A.	Pts.	Pen.
1982-83—Barrie Flyers		COJHL	23	13	29	42	87
1983-84—Brantford Alexanders (c)		OHL	66	25	46	71	165
1984-85—Hamilton Steelhawks		OHL	54	27	63	90	154
1985-86—Hamilton Steelhawks		OHL	47	41	57	98	153
1985-86—Montreal Canadiens		NHL	3	0	0	0	2
1986-87—Montreal Canadiens		NHL	55	12	11	23	144
1987-88—Montreal Canadiens		NHL	71	12	27	39	152
NHL TOTALS			129	24	38	62	298

ALAIN COTE

Left Wing . . . 5'10" . . . 203 lbs. . . . Born, Matane, Que., May 3, 1957 . . . Shoots left . . . Brother-in-law of Luc Dufour.

Year	Team	League	Games	G.	A.	Pts.	Pen.
1974-75—Chicoutimi Sagueneens		QJHL	57	15	29	44	43
1975-76—Chicoutimi Sagueneens		QJHL	72	35	49	84	93
1976-77—Chicoutimi Sagueneens (c-d)		QJHL	56	42	45	87	86
1977-78—Hampton Gulls		AHL	36	15	17	32	38
1977-78—Quebec Nordiques		WHA	27	3	5	8	8
1978-79—Quebec Nordiques (e)		WHA	79	14	13	27	23
1979-80—Quebec Nordiques		NHL	41	5	11	16	13
1979-80—Syracuse Firebirds		AHL	6	0	5	5	9
1980-81—Rochester Americans		AHL	23	1	6	7	14
1980-81—Quebec Nordiques		NHL	51	8	18	26	64
1981-82—Quebec Nordiques		NHL	79	15	16	31	82
1982-83—Quebec Nordiques		NHL	79	12	28	40	45
1983-84—Quebec Nordiques		NHL	77	19	24	43	41
1984-85—Quebec Nordiques		NHL	80	13	22	35	31
1985-86—Quebec Nordiques		NHL	78	13	21	34	29
1986-87—Quebec Nordiques		NHL	80	12	24	36	38
1987-88—Quebec Nordiques		NHL	76	4	18	22	26
WHA TOTALS			106	17	18	35	31
NHL TOTALS			641	101	182	283	369

ALAIN GABRIEL COTE

Defense . . . 6' . . . 200 lbs. . . . Born, Montmagny, Que., April 14, 1967 . . . Shoots right.

Year	Team	League	Games	G.	A.	Pts.	Pen.
1983-84—Quebec Remparts		QHL	60	3	17	20	40
1984-85—Quebec Remparts (c)		QHL	68	9	25	34	173
1985-86—Granby Bisons		QHL	22	4	12	16	48
1985-86—Moncton Golden Flames		AHL	3	0	0	0	0
1985-86—Boston Bruins		NHL	32	0	6	6	14
1986-87—Granby Bisons		QHL	43	7	24	31	185
1986-87—Boston Bruins		NHL	3	0	0	0	0
1987-88—Boston Bruins		NHL	2	0	0	0	0
1987-88—Maine Mariners		AHL	69	9	34	43	108
NHL TOTALS			37	0	6	6	14

(c)—June, 1985—Drafted as underage junior by Boston Bruins in NHL entry draft. First Bruins pick, 31st overall, second round.

SYLVAIN COTE

Defense ... 6' ... 170 lbs. ... Born, Quebec City, Que., January 19, 1966 ... Shoots right ... (1986)—Named to World Junior Championship All-Star Team.

Year	Team	League	Games	G.	A.	Pts.	Pen.
1982-83—Quebec Remparts		QHL	66	10	24	34	50
1983-84—Quebec Remparts (c)		QHL	66	15	50	65	89
1984-85—Hartford Whalers		NHL	67	3	9	12	17
1985-86—Hartford Whalers		NHL	2	0	0	0	0
1985-86—Hull Olympiques (a-d-e)		QHL	26	10	33	43	14
1986-87—Binghamton Whalers		AHL	12	2	4	6	0
1986-87—Hartford Whalers		NHL	67	2	8	10	20
1987-88—Hartford Whalers		NHL	67	7	21	28	30
NHL TOTALS			136	9	29	38	50

(c)—June, 1984—Drafted as underage junior by Hartford Whalers in 1984 NHL entry draft. First Whalers pick, 11th overall, first round.
(d)—Won Emile "Butch" Bouchard Trophy (Top Defenseman).
(e)—Shared Guy Lafleur Trophy (Playoff MVP) with Luc Robitaille.

NEAL COULTER

Right Wing ... 6'2" ... 110 lbs. ... Born, Toronto, Ont., January 2, 1963 ... Shoots right ... (December 6, 1985)—Sprained knee at Quebec ... (January, 1988)—Fractured left thumb.

Year	Team	League	Games	G.	A.	Pts.	Pen.
1979-80—Oakridge Midgets		...	60	35	30	65	150
1980-81—Toronto Marlboros (c)		OHL	18	4	3	7	22
1981-82—Toronto Marlboros		OHL	62	14	16	30	79
1982-83—Toronto Marlboros		OHL	59	13	37	50	60
1982-83—Indianapolis Checkers		CHL	3	0	1	1	0
1983-84—Toledo Goaldiggers		IHL	5	1	3	4	0
1983-84—Indianapolis Checkers		CHL	58	7	10	17	25
1984-85—Springfield Indians		AHL	2	1	0	1	0
1984-85—Indianapolis Checkers		IHL	82	31	26	57	95
1985-86—Springfield Indians		AHL	60	17	9	26	92
1985-86—New York Islanders		NHL	16	3	4	7	4
1986-87—Springfield Indians		AHL	47	12	13	25	63
1986-87—New York Islanders		NHL	9	2	1	3	7
1987-88—Springfield Indians		AHL	27	11	4	15	33
1987-88—New York Islanders		NHL	1	0	0	0	0
NHL TOTALS			26	5	5	10	11

(c)—June, 1981—Drafted as underage junior by New York Islanders in 1981 NHL entry draft. Fourth Islanders pick, 63rd overall, third round.

YVES COURTEAU

Right Wing ... 5'11" ... 183 lbs. ... Born, Montreal, Que., April 25, 1964 ... Shoots right ... (October, 1987)—Missed 54 games due to a pulled stomach muscle.

Year	Team	League	Games	G.	A.	Pts.	Pen.
1980-81—Laval Voisins		QMJHL	70	24	39	63	80
1981-82—Laval Voisins (c)		QMJHL	64	30	38	68	15
1982-83—Laval Voisins (d)		QHL	68	44	78	122	52
1983-84—Laval Voisins		QHL	62	45	75	120	52
1984-85—Moncton Golden Flames		AHL	59	19	21	40	32
1984-85—Calgary Flames		NHL	14	1	4	5	4
1985-86—Moncton Golden Flames		AHL	70	26	22	48	19
1985-86—Calgary Flames		NHL	4	1	1	2	0

Year	Team	League	Games	G.	A.	Pts.	Pen.
1986-87—Hartford Whalers (e)		NHL	4	0	0	0	0
1986-87—Binghamton Whalers		AHL	57	15	28	43	8
1987-88—Binghamton Whalers		AHL	25	15	22	37	22
NHL TOTALS			22	2	5	7	4

(c)—June, 1982—Drafted as underage junior by Detroit Red Wings in 1982 NHL entry draft. Second Red Wings pick, 23rd overall, second round.

(d)—December, 1982—NHL rights traded by Detroit Red Wings to Calgary Flames for Bobby Francis.

(e)—October, 1987—Traded by Calgary Flames to Hartford Whalers for Mark Paterson.

GEOFF COURTNALL

Left Wing . . . 6' . . . 165 lbs. . . . Born, Victoria, B.C., August 18, 1962 . . . Shoots left.

Year	Team	League	Games	G.	A.	Pts.	Pen.
1980-81—Victoria Cougars		WHL	11	3	5	8	6
1981-82—Victoria Cougars		WHL	72	35	57	92	100
1983-84—Victoria Cougars		WHL	71	41	73	114	186
1983-84—Hershey Bears (c)		AHL	74	14	12	26	51
1983-84—Boston Bruins		NHL	5	0	0	0	0
1984-85—Hershey Bears		AHL	9	8	4	12	4
1984-85—Boston Bruins		NHL	64	12	16	28	82
1985-86—Moncton Golden Flames		AHL	12	8	8	16	6
1985-86—Boston Bruins		NHL	64	21	17	38	61
1986-87—Boston Bruins		NHL	65	13	23	36	117
1987-88—Boston Bruins (d)		NHL	62	32	26	58	108
1987-88—Edmonton Oilers (e)		NHL	12	4	4	8	15
NHL TOTALS			272	82	86	168	383

(c)—September, 1983—Signed by Boston Bruins as a free agent.

(d)—March, 1988—Traded with Bill Ranford by Boston Bruins to Edmonton Oilers for Andy Moog.

(e)—July, 1988—Traded by Edmonton Oilers to Washington Capitals for Greg Adams.

RUSS COURTNALL

Center . . . 5'10" . . . 175 lbs. . . . Born, Victoria, B.C., June 3, 1965 . . . Shoots right . . . Member of 1984 Canadian Olympic Team . . . (November, 1987)—Bruised knee . . . (February, 1988)—Virus . . . (March, 1988)—Back spasms at Vancouver.

Year	Team	League	Games	G.	A.	Pts.	Pen.
1982-83—Victoria Cougars (c)		WHL	60	36	61	97	33
1983-84—Victoria Cougars		WHL	32	29	37	66	63
1983-84—Canadian Olympic Team		Int'l	16	4	7	11	10
1983-84—Toronto Maple Leafs		NHL	14	3	9	12	6
1984-85—Toronto Maple Leafs		NHL	69	12	10	22	44
1985-86—Toronto Maple Leafs		NHL	73	22	38	60	52
1986-87—Toronto Maple Leafs		NHL	79	29	44	73	90
1987-88—Toronto Maple Leafs		NHL	65	23	26	49	47
NHL TOTALS			300	89	127	216	239

(c)—June, 1983—Drafted by Toronto Maple Leafs as underage junior in NHL entry draft. First Maple Leafs pick, seventh overall, first round.

SYLVAIN COUTURIER

Center . . . 6'1" . . . 200 lbs. . . . Born, Greenfield Park, Que., April 23, 1968 . . . Shoots left . . . Also plays Left Wing.

Year	Team	League	Games	G.	A.	Pts.	Pen.
1984-85—Richelieu Riverain Midget		Que.	42	41	70	111	62
1985-86—Laval Titans (c)		QHL	68	21	37	58	649
1986-87—Laval Titans		QHL	67	39	51	90	77
1987-88—Laval Titans		QHL	67	70	67	137	115

(c)—June, 1986—Drafted as underage junior by Los Angeles Kings in 1986 NHL entry draft. Third Kings pick, 65th overall, fourth round.

ERIC COUVRETTE

Left Wing . . . 5'11" . . . 185 lbs. . . . Born, Pointe Claire, Que., March 11, 1969 . . . Shoots left.

Year	Team	League	Games	G.	A.	Pts.	Pen.
1986-87—Longueuil Chevaliers		QHL	55	24	49	73	29
1987-88—Victoriaville-St. Jean Castors (c)		QHL	55	34	60	94	37

(c)—June, 1988—Drafted by New York Rangers in 1988 NHL entry draft. Seventh Rangers pick, 152nd overall, eighth round.

CRAIG COXE

Center . . . 6'4" . . . 185 lbs. . . . Born, Chula Vista, Calif., January 21, 1964 . . . Shoots left . . . (October, 1985)—Broke hand in pre-season game with Calgary and missed 13 games . . . (September, 1987)—Suspended for first three regular season games by NHL after leaving the penalty box in a pre-season game vs. Los Angeles.

Year	Team	League	Games	G.	A.	Pts.	Pen.
1980-81—Los Angeles Midgets		Calif.	..	..	..	..	..
1981-82—St. Albert Saints (c)		AJHL	51	17	48	65	212
1982-83—Belleville Bulls		OHL	64	14	27	41	102
1983-84—Belleville Bulls		OHL	45	17	28	45	90
1984-85—Vancouver Canucks (d)		NHL	9	0	0	0	49
1984-85—Fredericton Express		AHL	62	8	7	15	242
1985-86—Vancouver Canucks		NHL	57	3	5	8	176
1986-87—Fredericton Express		AHL	46	1	12	13	168
1986-87—Vancouver Canucks		NHL	15	1	0	1	31
1987-88—Vancouver Canucks (e)		NHL	64	5	12	17	186
1987-88—Calgary Flames		NHL	7	2	3	5	32
NHL TOTALS			152	11	20	31	474

(c)—June, 1982—Drafted as underage junior by Detroit Red Wings in 1982 NHL entry draft. Fourth Red Wings pick, 66th overall, fourth round.

(d)—October, 1984—WHL rights traded by Portland Winter Hawks to Saskatoon Blades for future considerations.

(e)—March, 1988—Traded by Vancouver Canucks to Calgary Flames for Brian Bradley, Peter Bakovic and future considerations (Kevan Guy).

MURRAY CRAVEN

Center . . . 6'2" . . . 175 lbs. . . . Born, Medicine Hat, Alta., July 20, 1964 . . . Shoots left . . . Also plays Left Wing . . . (January 15, 1983)—Injured left knee cartilage vs. Toronto . . . (April 16, 1987)—Broke foot in playoff game vs. N.Y. Rangers.

Year	Team	League	Games	G.	A.	Pts.	Pen.
1980-81—Medicine Hat Tigers		WHL	69	5	10	15	18
1981-82—Medicine Hat Tigers (c)		WHL	72	35	46	81	49
1982-83—Medicine Hat Tigers		WHL	28	17	29	46	35
1982-83—Detroit Red Wings		NHL	31	4	7	11	6
1983-84—Medicine Hat Tigers		WHL	48	38	56	94	53
1983-84—Detroit Red Wings		NHL	15	0	4	4	6
1984-85—Philadelphia Flyers (d)		NHL	80	26	35	61	30
1985-86—Philadelphia Flyers		NHL	78	21	33	54	34
1986-87—Philadelphia Flyers		NHL	77	19	30	49	38
1987-88—Philadelphia Flyers		NHL	72	30	46	76	58
NHL TOTALS			353	100	155	255	172

(c)—June, 1982—Drafted as underage junior by Detroit Red Wings in 1982 NHL entry draft. First Red Wings pick, 17th overall, first round.

(d)—October, 1984—Traded with Joe Paterson by Detroit Red Wings to Philadelphia Flyers for Darryl Sittler.

LOUIS CRAWFORD

Left Wing . . . 5'11" . . . 175 lbs. . . . Born, Belleville, Ont., November 5, 1962 . . . Shoots left.

Year	Team	League	Games	G.	A.	Pts.	Pen.
1979-80—Belleville Jr. B		OHA	10	7	11	18	60
1980-81—Kitchener Rangers		OHL	53	2	7	9	134
1981-82—Kitchener Rangers		OHL	64	11	17	28	243
1982-83—Rochester Americans (c)		AHL	64	5	11	16	142
1983-84—Rochester Americans		AHL	76	7	6	13	234
1984-85—Rochester Americans		AHL	65	12	29	41	173
1985-86—Nova Scotia Oilers (d)		AHL	78	8	11	19	214
1986-87—Nova Scotia Oilers		AHL	35	3	4	7	48
1987-88—Nova Scotia Oilers		AHL	65	15	15	30	170

(c)—August, 1984—Signed by Buffalo Sabres as a free agent.

(d)—October, 1985—Signed by Nova Scotia Oilers as a free agent.

MARC JOSEPH JOHN CRAWFORD

Left Wing . . . 5'11" . . . 181 lbs. . . . Born, Belleville, Ont., February 13, 1961 . . . Shoots left . . . Son of Floyd Crawford (Member of Belleville MacFarlands, 1959 Canadian World Cup Winners) . . . Brother of Peter and Bob Crawford . . . (February 3, 1987)—Given three-game suspension by NHL for being the first player off the bench . . . (October, 1987)—Named player-assistant coach of Fredericton Express.

Year	Team	League	Games	G.	A.	Pts.	Pen.
1978-79—Cornwall Royals		QMJHL	70	28	41	69	206
1979-80—Cornwall Royals (c)		QMJHL	54	27	36	63	127
1980-81—Cornwall Royals		QMJHL	63	42	57	99	242
1981-82—Dallas Black Hawks		CHL	34	13	21	34	71
1981-82—Vancouver Canucks		NHL	40	4	8	12	29
1982-83—Fredericton Express		AHL	30	15	9	24	59
1982-83—Vancouver Canucks		NHL	41	4	5	9	28
1983-84—Vancouver Canucks		NHL	19	0	1	1	9
1983-84—Fredericton Express		AHL	56	9	22	31	96
1984-85—Fredericton Express		AHL	65	12	29	41	173
1984-85—Vancouver Canucks		NHL	1	0	0	0	4
1985-86—Fredericton Express		AHL	26	10	14	24	55
1985-86—Vancouver Canucks		NHL	54	11	14	25	92
1986-87—Vancouver Canucks		NHL	21	0	3	3	67
1986-87—Fredericton Express		AHL	25	8	11	19	21
1987-88—Fredericton Express		AHL	43	5	13	18	90
NHL TOTALS			176	19	31	50	229

(c)—June, 1980—Drafted as underage junior by Vancouver Canucks in 1980 NHL entry draft. Third Canucks pick, 70th overall, fourth round.

ADAM CREIGHTON

Center . . . 6'5" . . . 210 lbs. . . . Born, Burlington, Ont., June 2, 1965 . . . Shoots left . . . Son of Dave Creighton (NHL, '50s-'60s) . . . (May, 1984)—Named MVP of 1984 Memorial Cup . . . (January, 1988)—Knee surgery.

Year	Team	League	Games	G.	A.	Pts.	Pen.
1981-82—Ottawa 67's		OHL	60	14	27	42	73
1982-83—Ottawa 67's (c)		OHL	68	44	46	90	88
1983-84—Ottawa 67's		OHL	56	42	49	91	79
1983-84—Buffalo Sabres		NHL	7	2	2	4	4
1984-85—Ottawa 67's		OHL	10	4	14	18	23
1984-85—Rochester Americans		AHL	6	5	3	8	2
1984-85—Buffalo Sabres		NHL	30	2	8	10	33
1985-86—Rochester Americans		AHL	32	17	21	38	27
1985-86—Buffalo Sabres		NHL	20	1	1	2	2
1986-87—Buffalo Sabres		NHL	56	18	22	40	26
1987-88—Buffalo Sabres		NHL	36	10	17	27	87
NHL TOTALS			149	33	50	83	152

(c)—June, 1983—Drafted as underage junior by Buffalo Sabres in 1983 NHL entry draft. Third Sabres pick, 11th overall, first round.

SHAWN CRONIN

Defense . . . 6'2" . . . 210 lbs. . . . Born, Flushing, Mich., August 20, 1963 . . . Shoots left.

Year	Team	League	Games	G.	A.	Pts.	Pen.
1982-83—U. of Illinois-Chicago		CCHA	36	1	5	6	52
1983-84—U. of Illinois-Chicago		CCHA	32	0	4	4	41
1984-85—U. of Illinois-Chicago		CCHA	31	2	6	8	52
1985-86—U. of Illinois-Chicago (c)		CCHA	38	3	8	11	70
1986-87—Binghamton Whalers		AHL	12	0	1	1	60
1986-87—Salt Lake Golden Eagles		IHL	53	8	16	24	118
1987-88—Binghamton Whalers (d)		AHL	66	3	8	11	212

(c)—March, 1986—Signed by Hartford Whalers as a free agent.
(d)—June, 1988—Signed by Washington Capitals as a free agent.

DOUG CROSSMAN

Defense . . . 6'2" . . . 190 lbs. . . . Born, Peterborough, Ont., June 30, 1960 . . . Shoots left . . . (February, 1983)—Injured thumb.

Year	Team	League	Games	G.	A.	Pts.	Pen.
1976-77—London Knights		OMJHL	1	0	0	0	0
1977-78—Ottawa 67's		OMJHL	65	4	17	21	17
1978-79—Ottawa 67's (c)		OMJHL	67	12	51	63	63
1979-80—Ottawa 67's (a)		OMJHL	66	20	96	116	48
1980-81—Chicago Black Hawks		NHL	9	0	2	2	2
1980-81—New Brunswick Hawks		AHL	70	13	43	56	90
1981-82—Chicago Black Hawks		NHL	70	12	28	40	24
1982-83—Chicago Black Hawks (d)		NHL	80	13	40	53	46
1983-84—Philadelphia Flyers		NHL	78	7	28	35	63
1984-85—Philadelphia Flyers		NHL	80	4	33	37	65

Year	Team	League	Games	G.	A.	Pts.	Pen.
1985-86—Philadelphia Flyers		NHL	80	6	37	43	55
1986-87—Philadelphia Flyers		NHL	78	9	31	40	29
1987-88—Philadelphia Flyers		NHL	76	9	29	38	43
NHL TOTALS			551	60	228	288	327

(c)—August, 1979—Drafted by Chicago Black Hawks as underage junior in 1979 NHL entry draft. Sixth Black Hawks pick, 112th overall, sixth round.

(d)—June, 1983—Traded by Chicago Black Hawks with second-round draft pick (Scott Mellanby) in 1984 to Philadelphia Flyers for Behn Wilson.

JEFF CROSSMAN

Center . . . 6' . . . 200 lbs. . . . Born, Detroit, Mich., December 3, 1964 . . . Shoots left.

Year	Team	League	Games	G.	A.	Pts.	Pen.
1982-83—Western Michigan Univ.		CCHA	30	3	2	5	43
1983-84—Western Michigan Univ. (c)		CCHA	39	9	12	21	91
1984-85—Western Michigan Univ.		CCHA	35	5	12	17	87
1985-86—Western Michigan Univ.		CCHA	39	13	19	32	*154
1986-87—New Haven Nighthawks (d)		AHL	61	2	3	5	133
1987-88—Colorado Rangers		IHL	60	13	12	25	103

(c)—June, 1984—Drafted by Los Angeles Kings in 1984 NHL entry draft. Tenth Kings pick, 191st overall, 10th round.

(d)—March, 1987—Traded with Marcel Dionne and a third-round 1989 draft pick by Los Angeles Kings to New York Rangers for Bobby Carpenter and Tom Laidlaw.

KEITH SCOTT CROWDER

Right Wing . . . 6' . . . 190 lbs. . . . Born, Windsor, Ont., January 6, 1959 . . . Shoots right . . . Also plays Center . . . Brother of former NHLer Bruce Crowder . . . (February, 1978)—Broken ankle . . . Set Bruins team record for most penalty minutes by a rookie (172) in 1980-81 . . . (December, 1983)—Sprained right knee and missed 16 games . . . (October 26, 1986)—Separated right shoulder at Calgary . . . (May, 1987)—Surgery to right shoulder . . . (February, 1988)—Strained abdominal muscle . . . (March, 1988)—Strained right shoulder.

Year	Team	League	Games	G.	A.	Pts.	Pen.
1976-77—Peterborough Petes		Jr."A"OHA	58	13	19	32	99
1977-78—Peterborough Petes (c)		Jr."A"OHA	58	30	30	60	139
1978-79—Birmingham Bulls (d)		WHA	5	1	0	1	17
1978-79—Peterborough Petes (e)		OMJHL	43	25	41	66	76
1979-80—Binghamton Dusters		AHL	13	4	0	4	15
1979-80—Grand Rapids Owls		IHL	20	10	13	23	22
1980-81—Springfield Indians		AHL	26	12	18	30	34
1980-81—Boston Bruins		NHL	47	13	12	25	172
1981-82—Boston Bruins		NHL	71	23	21	44	101
1982-83—Boston Bruins		NHL	74	35	39	74	105
1983-84—Boston Bruins		NHL	63	24	28	52	128
1984-85—Boston Bruins		NHL	79	32	38	70	142
1985-86—Boston Bruins		NHL	78	38	46	84	177
1986-87—Boston Bruins		NHL	58	22	30	52	106
1987-88—Boston Bruins		NHL	68	17	26	43	173
WHA TOTALS			5	1	0	1	17
NHL TOTALS			538	204	240	444	1104

(c)—July, 1978—Signed by Birmingham Bulls (WHA) as underage player.

(d)—November, 1978—Returned to Peterborough to play final year of junior eligibility.

(e)—August, 1979—Drafted by Boston Bruins in entry draft. Fourth Boston pick, 57th overall, third round.

TROY CROWDER

Right Wing . . . 6'3" . . . 200 lbs. . . . Born, Sudbury, Ont., May 3, 1968 . . . Shoots right.

Year	Team	League	Games	G.	A.	Pts.	Pen.
1984-85—Walden Midgets		NOHA	28	20	21	41	63
1985-86—Hamilton Steelhawks (c)		OHL	55	4	4	8	178
1986-87—North Bay Centennials		OHL	35	6	11	17	90
1986-87—Belleville Bulls		OHL	21	5	5	10	52
1987-88—North Bay Centennials		OHL	9	1	2	3	44
1987-88—Belleville Bulls		OHL	46	12	27	39	103
1987-88—Utica Devils		AHL	3	0	0	0	36

(c)—June, 1986—Drafted as underage junior by New Jersey Devils in 1986 NHL entry draft. Sixth Devils pick, 108th overall, sixth round.

TED CROWLEY

Defense . . . 6'1" . . . 190 lbs. . . . Born, Concord, Mass., May 3, 1970 . . . Shoots right.

Year	Team	League	Games	G.	A.	Pts.	Pen.
1986-87	Lawrence Academy	Mass. H.S.	..	6	17	23	..
1987-88	Lawrence Academy (c)	Mass. H.S.	..	11	23	34	..

(c)—June, 1988—Drafted by Toronto Maple Leafs in 1988 NHL entry draft. Fourth Maple Leafs pick, 69th overall, fourth round.

JIM CULHANE

Defense . . . 6' . . . 190 lbs. . . . Born, Haileybury, Ont., August 8, 1960 . . . Shoots left.

Year	Team	League	Games	G.	A.	Pts.	Pen.
1983-84	Western Michigan Univ. (c)	CCHA	42	1	14	15	88
1984-85	Western Michigan Univ.	CCHA	37	2	8	10	84
1985-86	Western Michigan Univ.	CCHA	40	1	21	22	61
1986-87	Western Michigan Univ.	CCHA	41	9	13	22	*163
1987-88	Binghamton Whalers	AHL	76	5	17	22	169

(c)—June, 1984—Drafted by Hartford Whalers in 1984 NHL entry draft. Sixth Whalers pick, 214th overall, 11th round.

RANDY WILLIAM CUNNEYWORTH

Center and Left Wing . . . 6' . . . 180 lbs. . . . Born, Etobicoke, Ont., May 10, 1961 . . . Shoots left . . . (January, 1988)—Suspended by NHL for three games and five games.

Year	Team	League	Games	G.	A.	Pts.	Pen.
1979-80	Ottawa 67's (c)	OMJHL	63	16	25	41	145
1980-81	Ottawa 67's	OHL	67	54	74	128	240
1980-81	Rochester Americans	AHL	1	0	1	1	2
1980-81	Buffalo Sabres	NHL	1	0	0	0	2
1981-82	Rochester Americans	AHL	57	12	15	27	86
1981-82	Buffalo Sabres	NHL	20	2	4	6	47
1982-83	Rochester Americans	AHL	78	23	33	56	111
1983-84	Rochester Americans	AHL	54	18	17	35	85
1984-85	Rochester Americans	AHL	72	30	38	68	148
1985-86	Pittsburgh Penguins (d)	NHL	75	15	30	45	74
1986-87	Pittsburgh Penguins	NHL	79	26	27	53	142
1987-88	Pittsburgh Penguins	NHL	71	35	39	74	141
	NHL TOTALS		246	78	100	178	406

(c)—June, 1980—Drafted as underage junior by Buffalo Sabres in 1980 NHL entry draft. Ninth Sabres pick, 167th overall, eighth round.

(d)—October, 1985—After attending Pittsburgh's training camp as an unsigned free agent, his equalization rights were traded with Mike Moller by Buffalo Sabres to Pittsburgh Penguins for future considerations.

BRIAN CURRAN

Defense . . . 6'4" . . . 200 lbs. . . . Born, Toronto, Ont., November 5, 1963 . . . Shoots left . . . (November, 1981)—Appendectomy . . . (September, 1982)—Broken ankle . . . (November, 1984)—Charley Horse . . . (October 6, 1985)—Missed five games with fractured thumb . . . (February 1, 1986)—Broken leg at Montreal . . . Set a N.Y. Islanders record for penalty minutes in a season (356) in 1986-87 . . . (January 12, 1988)—Fractured jaw in game vs. Pittsburgh.

Year	Team	League	Games	G.	A.	Pts.	Pen.
1980-81	Portland Winter Hawks	WHL	51	2	16	18	132
1981-82	Portland Winter Hawks (c)	WHL	59	2	28	30	275
1982-83	Portland Winter Hawks	WHL	56	1	30	31	187
1983-84	Hershey Bears	AHL	23	0	2	2	94
1983-84	Boston Bruins	NHL	16	1	1	2	57
1984-85	Hershey Bears	AHL	4	0	0	0	19
1984-85	Boston Bruins	NHL	56	0	1	1	158
1985-86	Boston Bruins	NHL	43	2	5	7	192
1986-87	New York Islanders (d)	NHL	68	0	10	10	356
1987-88	Springfield Indians	AHL	8	1	0	1	43
1987-88	New York Islanders (e)	NHL	22	0	1	1	68
1987-88	Toronto Maple Leafs	NHL	7	0	1	1	19
	NHL TOTALS		212	3	19	22	850

(c)—June, 1982—Drafted as underage junior by Boston Bruins in 1982 NHL entry draft. Second Bruins pick, 22nd overall, second round.

(d)—August, 1986—Signed by New York Islanders as a free agent with compensation due Boston. When the two clubs could not agree, an arbitration judge awarded the Bruins Paul Boutilier.

DAN CURRIE

Left Wing . . . 6'1" . . . 180 lbs. . . . Born, Burlington, Ont., March 15, 1968 . . . Shoots left.

Year	Team	League	Games	G.	A.	Pts.	Pen.
1984-85—Burlington Midgets		OHA	29	28	27	55	35
1985-86—Sault Ste. Marie Greyhounds (c)		OHL	66	21	22	43	37
1986-87—Sault Ste. Marie Greyhounds		OHL	66	31	52	83	53
1987-88—Sault Ste. Marie Greyhounds (a)		OHL	57	50	59	109	53
1987-88—Nova Scotia Oilers		AHL	3	4	2	6	0

(c)—June, 1986—Drafted as underage junior by Edmonton Oilers in 1986 NHL entry draft. Fourth Oilers pick, 84th overall, fourth round.

GLEN CURRIE

Center . . . 6'1" . . . 175 lbs. . . . Born, Lachine, Que., July 18, 1958 . . . Shoots left . . . Nephew of Jim Peters (NHL player in late '40s and early '50s) . . . (September, 1985)—Injured back during training camp.

Year	Team	League	Games	G.	A.	Pts.	Pen.
1975-76—Laval National		QJHL	72	15	54	69	20
1976-77—Laval National		QJHL	72	28	51	79	42
1977-78—Laval National (b-c)		QJHL	72	63	82	145	29
1978-79—Port Huron Flags		IHL	69	27	36	63	43
1979-80—Hershey Bears		AHL	45	17	26	43	16
1979-80—Washington Capitals		NHL	32	2	0	2	2
1980-81—Washington Capitals		NHL	40	5	13	18	16
1980-81—Hershey Bears		AHL	35	18	21	39	10
1981-82—Hershey Bears		AHL	31	12	12	24	6
1981-82—Washington Capitals		NHL	43	7	7	14	14
1982-83—Hershey Bears		AHL	12	5	11	16	6
1982-83—Washington Capitals		NHL	68	11	28	39	20
1983-84—Washington Capitals		NHL	80	12	24	36	20
1984-85—Binghamton Whalers		AHL	17	1	5	6	6
1984-85—Washington Capitals		NHL	44	1	5	6	19
1985-86—Los Angeles Kings (d)		NHL	12	1	2	3	9
1985-86—New Haven Nighthawks		AHL	8	0	4	4	2
1986-87—New Haven Nighthawks		AHL	54	12	16	28	16
1987-88—Los Angeles Kings		NHL	7	0	0	0	0
1987-88—New Haven Nighthawks		AHL	55	15	19	34	14
NHL TOTALS			326	39	79	118	100

(c)—Drafted from Laval National by Washington Capitals in third round of 1978 amateur draft.
(d)—September, 1985—Traded by Washington Capitals to Los Angeles Kings for Daryl Evans.

PAUL CYR

Left Wing . . . 5'10" . . . 180 lbs. . . . Born, Port Alberni, B.C., October 31, 1963 . . . Shoots left . . . (December 16, 1982)—Injured thumb while playing for Team Canada at World Junior Championships . . . (March 6, 1984)—Broke knuckle in finger at Montreal . . . (December 13, 1985)—Pulled groin vs. Hartford . . . (August, 1986)—Broke ankle in charity softball game and missed training camp . . . (March 20, 1987)—Missed four games with pulled groin vs. Montreal . . . (October 16, 1987)—Sprained knee.

Year	Team	League	Games	G.	A.	Pts.	Pen.
1979-80—Nanaimo		BCJHL	60	28	52	80	202
1980-81—Victoria Cougars		WHL	64	36	22	58	85
1981-82—Victoria Cougars (b-c)		WHL	58	52	56	108	167
1982-83—Victoria Cougars		WHL	20	21	22	43	61
1982-83—Buffalo Sabres		NHL	36	15	12	27	59
1983-84—Buffalo Sabres		NHL	71	16	27	43	52
1984-85—Buffalo Sabres		NHL	71	22	24	46	63
1985-86—Buffalo Sabres		NHL	71	20	31	51	120
1986-87—Buffalo Sabres		NHL	73	11	16	27	122
1987-88—Buffalo Sabres (d)		NHL	20	1	1	2	38
1987-88—New York Rangers		NHL	40	4	13	17	41
NHL TOTALS			382	89	124	213	495

(c)—June, 1982—Drafted as underage junior by Buffalo Sabres in 1982 NHL entry draft. Second Sabres pick, ninth overall, first round.
(d)—December, 1987—Traded with 10th-round 1988 draft pick (Eric Fenton) by Buffalo Sabres to New York Rangers for Mike Donnelly and a fifth-round 1988 draft pick (Alexander Mogilny).

MIKE DAGENAIS

Defense . . . 6'3" . . . 200 lbs. . . . Born, Ottawa, Ont., July 22, 1969 . . . Shoots left . . . Son of Dennis Degenais, 1967 scoring leader of the Quebec Professional Lacrosse League.

Year	Team	League	Games	G.	A.	Pts.	Pen.
1984-85—Gloucester Major Midget		ODHA	40	12	22	34	78
1985-86—Peterborough Petes		OHL	45	1	3	4	40
1986-87—Peterborough Petes (c)		OHL	56	1	17	18	66
1987-88—Peterborough Petes		OHL	66	11	23	34	125

(c)—June, 1987—Drafted by Chicago Black Hawks in 1979 NHL entry draft. Fourth Black Hawks pick, 60th overall, third round.

KEVIN DAHL

Defense . . . 5'11" . . . 190 lbs. . . . Born, Regina, Sask., December 30, 1968 . . . Shoots right.

Year	Team	League	Games	G.	A.	Pts.	Pen.
1986-87—Bowling Green Univ.		CCHA	32	2	6	8	54
1987-88—Bowling Green Univ. (c)		CCHA	44	2	23	25	78

(c)—June, 1988—Drafted by Montreal Canadiens in 1988 NHL entry draft. Twelfth Canadiens pick, 230th overall, 11th round.

ULF DAHLEN

Center . . . 6'2" . . . 194 lbs. . . . Born, Ostersund, Sweden, January 12, 1967 . . . Shoots right . . . (November, 1987)—Bruised shin.

Year	Team	League	Games	G.	A.	Pts.	Pen.
1983-84—Ostersund		Sweden	36	15	11	26	10
1984-85—Ostersund (c)		Sweden	36	33	26	59	20
1985-86—Bjorkloven		Sweden	22	4	3	7	8
1986-87—Bjorkloven		Sweden	37	15	14	29	25
1987-88—New York Rangers		NHL	70	29	23	52	26
1987-88—Colorado Rangers		IHL	2	2	2	4	0
NHL TOTALS			70	29	23	52	26

(c)—June, 1985—Drafted by New York Rangers in 1985 NHL entry draft. First Rangers pick, seventh overall, first round.

KJELL DAHLIN

Right Wing . . . 6' . . . 176 lbs. . . . Born, Timra, Sweden, February 2, 1963 . . . Shoots left . . . (January 7, 1987)—Damaged knee ligaments vs. Vancouver . . . (November, 1987)— Missed eight games due to back and rib injuries.

Year	Team	League	Games	G.	A.	Pts.	Pen.
1984-85—Farjestad (c)		Sweden	35	21	26	47	..
1985-86—Montreal Canadiens		NHL	77	32	39	71	4
1986-87—Montreal Canadiens		NHL	41	12	8	20	0
1987-88—Montreal Canadiens (d)		NHL	48	13	12	25	6
NHL TOTALS			166	57	59	116	10

(c)—June, 1981—Drafted by Montreal Canadiens in NHL entry draft. Seventh Canadiens pick, 82nd overall, fourth round.

(d)—May, 1988—Announced he was leaving Montreal Canadiens to play for Farjestads in Sweden.

CHRIS DAHLQUIST

Defense . . . 6'1" . . . 190 lbs. . . . Born, Fridley, Minn., December 14, 1962. . . . Shoots left.

Year	Team	League	Games	G.	A.	Pts.	Pen.
1981-82—Lake Superaor State		CCHA	39	4	10	14	18
1982-83—Lake Superior State		CCHA	35	0	12	12	63
1983-84—Lake Superior State		CCHA	40	4	19	23	76
1984-85—Lake Superior State (c)		CCHA	44	4	15	19	112
1985-86—Baltimore Skipjacks		AHL	65	4	21	25	64
1985-86—Pittsburgh Penguins		NHL	5	1	2	3	2
1986-87—Baltimore Skipjacks		AHL	51	1	16	17	50
1986-87—Pittsburgh Penguins		NHL	19	0	1	1	20
1987-88—Pittsburgh Penguins		NHL	44	3	6	9	69
NHL TOTALS			68	4	9	13	91

(c)—May, 1985—Signed by Pittsburgh Penguins as a free agent.

JEAN-JACQUES DAIGNEAULT

Defense . . . 5'11" . . . 180 lbs. . . . Born, Montreal, Que., October 12, 1965 . . . Shoots left . . . (March, 1984)—Knee surgery . . . (March 19, 1986)—Broke finger vs. Toronto . . . (April 12, 1987)—Sprained ankle in playoff game vs. N.Y. Rangers.

Year	Team	League	Games	G.	A.	Pts.	Pen.
1981-82—Laval Voisins	QMJHL	64	4	25	29	41
1982-83—Longueuil Chevaliers (a)	QHL	70	26	58	84	58
1983-84—Canadian Olympic Team	Int'l	62	6	15	21	40
1983-84—Longueuil Chevaliers (c)	QHL	10	2	11	13	6
1984-85—Vancouver Canucks	NHL	67	4	23	27	69
1985-86—Vancouver Canucks (d)	NHL	64	5	23	28	45
1986-87—Philadelphia Flyers	NHL	77	6	16	22	56
1987-88—Philadelphia Flyers	NHL	28	2	2	4	12
1987-88—Hershey Bears	AHL	10	1	5	6	8
NHL TOTALS		236	17	64	81	182

(c)—June, 1984—Drafted as underage junior by Vancouver Canucks in 1984 NHL entry draft. First Canucks pick, 10th overall, first round.

(d)—June, 1986—Traded by Vancouver Canucks with second-round draft choice (Kent Hawley) in 1986 and a fifth round choice in 1987 to Philadelphia Flyers for Rich Sutter, Dave Richter and third-round choice in 1986.

BRAD DALGARNO

Right Wing . . . 6'3" . . . 205 lbs. . . . Born, Vancouver, B.C., August 8, 1967 . . . Shoots right.

Year	Team	League	Games	G.	A.	Pts.	Pen.
1983-84—Markham Travelways	MTJHL	40	17	11	28	59
1984-85—Hamilton Steelhawks (c)	OHL	66	23	30	53	86
1985-86—Hamilton Steelhawks	OHL	54	22	43	65	79
1985-86—New York Islanders	NHL	2	1	0	1	0
1986-87—Hamilton Steelhawks	OHL	60	27	32	59	100
1986-87—New York Islanders (d)	NHL	....	...	....	....	....
1987-88—New York Islanders	NHL	38	2	8	10	58
1987-88—Springfield Indians	AHL	39	13	11	24	76
NHL TOTALS		40	3	8	11	58

(c)—June, 1985—Drafted as underage junior by New York Islanders in 1985 NHL entry draft. First Islanders pick, sixth overall, first round.

(d)—No regular season record. Played one playoff game (one assist).

MARTY DALLMAN

Center . . . 5'10" . . . 183 lbs. . . . Born, Niagara Falls, Ont., February 15, 1963 . . . Shoots right . . . (December, 1986)—Injured knee.

Year	Team	League	Games	G.	A.	Pts.	Pen.
1979-80—Niagara Falls Canucks	OPJHL	40	39	43	82	....
1980-81—R.P.I. (c)	ECAC	22	8	10	18	6
1981-82—R.P.I.	ECAC	28	22	18	40	27
1982-83—R.P.I.	ECAC	29	21	29	50	42
1983-84—R.P.I.	ECAC	38	30	24	54	32
1984-85—New Haven Nighthawks	AHL	78	18	39	57	26
1985-86—New Haven Nighthawks	AHL	69	23	33	56	92
1986-87—Baltimore Skipjacks (d)	AHL	6	0	1	1	0
1986-87—Newmarket Saints (e)	AHL	42	24	24	48	44
1987-88—Newmarket Saints	AHL	76	50	39	89	52
1987-88—Toronto Maple Leafs	NHL	2	0	1	1	0
NHL TOTALS		2	0	1	1	0

(c)—June, 1981—Drafted as underage junior by Los Angeles Kings in 1981 NHL entry draft. Third Kings pick, 81st overall, fourth round.

(d)—October, 1986—Signed by Baltimore Skipjacks as a free agent.

(e)—November, 1986—Signed by Newmarket Saints as a free agent after being released by Baltimore Skipjacks.

ROD DALLMAN

Left Wing . . . 5'11" . . . 185 lbs. . . . Born, Quesnel, B.C., January 26, 1967 . . . Shoots left . . . (October, 1984)—Broken left ankle . . . (October, 1986)—Injured shoulder.

Year	Team	League	Games	G.	A.	Pts.	Pen.
1983-84—P. Albert Midget Raiders	BC-Midget	21	14	6	20	69
1984-85—Prince Albert Raiders (c)	WHL	40	8	11	19	133
1985-86—Prince Albert Raiders	WHL	59	20	21	41	198
1986-87—Prince Albert Raiders	WHL	47	13	21	34	240
1987-88—New York Islanders	NHL	3	1	0	1	6
1987-88—Springfield Indians	AHL	59	9	17	26	355
NHL TOTALS		3	1	0	1	6

(c)—June, 1985—Drafted as underage junior by New York Islanders in 1985 NHL entry draft. Eighth Islanders pick, 118th overall, eighth round.

TREVOR DAM

Right Wing . . . 5'10" . . . 205 lbs. . . . Born, Scarborough, Ont., April 20, 1970 . . . Shoots right.

Year	Team	League	Games	G.	A.	Pts.	Pen.
1986-87	London Knights	OHL	64	6	17	23	88
1987-88	London Knights (c)	OHL	66	25	38	63	169

(c)—June, 1988—Drafted by Chicago Black Hawks in 1988 NHL entry draft. Second Black Hawks pick, 50th overall, third round.

VINCENT DAMPHOUSSE

Left Wing . . . 6'1" . . . 190 lbs. . . . Born, Montreal, Que., December 17, 1967 . . . Shoots left . . . Also plays Center.

Year	Team	League	Games	G.	A.	Pts.	Pen.
1983-84	Laval Voisins	QHL	66	29	36	65	25
1984-85	Laval Voisins	QHL	68	35	68	103	62
1985-86	Laval Titans (b-c)	QHL	69	45	110	155	70
1986-87	Toronto Maple Leafs	NHL	80	21	25	46	26
1987-88	Toronto Maple Leafs	NHL	75	12	36	48	40
	NHL TOTALS		155	33	61	94	66

(c)—June, 1986—Drafted as underage junior by Toronto Maple Leafs in 1986 NHL entry draft. First Maple Leafs pick, sixth overall, first round.

KENNETH DANEYKO

Defense . . . 6'1" . . . 195 lbs. . . . Born, Windsor, Ont., April 17, 1964 . . . Shoots left. . . . (November 2, 1983)—Broke right fibula at Hartford . . . (October, 1985)—Given one game suspension and fined $500 by the NHL for playing hockey in West Germany (Manheim) without NHL permission . . . (February 25, 1987)—Injured wrist during an altercation with Mitch Wilson at Pittsburgh.

Year	Team	League	Games	G.	A.	Pts.	Pen.
1980-81	Spokane Flyers	WHL	62	6	13	19	140
1981-82	Spokane Flyers	WHL	26	1	11	12	147
1981-82	Seattle Breakers (c-d)	WHL	38	1	22	23	151
1982-83	Seattle Breakers	WHL	69	17	43	60	150
1983-84	Kamloops Junior Oilers	WHL	19	6	28	34	52
1983-84	New Jersey Devils	NHL	11	1	4	5	17
1984-85	New Jersey Devils	NHL	1	0	0	0	10
1984-85	Maine Mariners	AHL	80	4	9	13	206
1985-86	Maine Mariners	AHL	21	3	2	5	75
1985-86	New Jersey Devils	NHL	44	0	10	10	100
1986-87	New Jersey Devils	NHL	79	2	12	14	183
1987-88	New Jersey Devils	NHL	80	5	7	12	239
	NHL TOTALS		215	8	33	41	549

(c)—December, 1981—Drafted by Seattle Breakers in WHL Dispersal draft of players from Spokane Flyers.

(d)—June, 1982—Drafted as underage junior by New Jersey Devils in 1982 entry draft. Second Devils pick, 18th overall, first round.

JEFF DANIELS

Left Wing . . . 6' . . . 190 lbs. . . . Born, Oshawa, Ont., June 24, 1968 . . . Shoots left.

Year	Team	League	Games	G.	A.	Pts.	Pen.
1984-85	Oshawa Generals	OHL	59	7	11	18	16
1985-86	Oshawa Generals (c)	OHL	62	13	19	32	23
1986-87	Oshawa Generals	OHL	54	14	9	23	22
1987-88	Oshawa Generals	OHL	64	29	39	68	59

(c)—June, 1986—Drafted as underage junior by Pittsburgh Penguins in 1986 NHL entry draft. Sixth Penguins pick, 109th overall, sixth round.

DAN ARMAND DAOUST

Center . . . 5'11" . . . 160 lbs. . . . Born, Kirkland Lake, Ont., February 29, 1960 . . . Shoots left . . . (November 2, 1986)—Missed 45 games when he broke left ankle during an altercation with Gerard Gallant vs. Detroit . . . (March, 1988)—Strained right ankle ligaments.

Year	Team	League	Games	G.	A.	Pts.	Pen.
1977-78	Cornwall Royals	QMJHL	68	24	44	68	74
1978-79	Cornwall Royals	QMJHL	72	42	55	97	85
1979-80	Cornwall Royals (c)	QMJHL	70	40	62	102	82
1980-81	Nova Scotia Voyageurs (a)	AHL	80	38	60	98	106
1981-82	Nova Scotia Voyageurs	AHL	61	25	40	65	75
1982-83	Montreal Canadiens (d)	NHL	4	0	1	1	4

Year	Team	League	Games	G.	A.	Pts.	Pen.
1982-83—Toronto Maple Leafs		NHL	48	18	33	51	31
1983-84—Toronto Maple Leafs		NHL	78	18	56	74	88
1984-85—Toronto Maple Leafs		NHL	79	17	37	54	98
1985-86—Toronto Maple Leafs		NHL	80	7	13	20	88
1986-87—Newmarket Saints		AHL	1	0	0	0	4
1986-87—Toronto Maple Leafs		NHL	33	4	3	7	35
1987-88—Toronto Maple Leafs		NHL	67	9	8	17	57
NHL TOTALS			389	73	151	224	401

(c)—September, 1980—Signed by Montreal Canadiens as a free agent.
(d)—December, 1982—Traded by Montreal Canadiens with Gaston Gingras to Toronto Maple Leafs for future draft considerations.

MICHAEL DARK

Defense and Right Wing . . . 6'3" . . . 225 lbs. . . . Born, Sarnia, Ont., September 17, 1963 . . . Shoots right.

Year	Team	League	Games	G.	A.	Pts.	Pen.
1982-83—Rensselaer Poly. Inst. (c)		ECAC	29	3	16	19	54
1983-84—Rensselaer Poly. Inst.		ECAC	38	2	12	14	60
1984-85—Rensselaer Poly. Inst. (d)		ECAC	36	7	26	33	76
1985-86—Rensselaer Poly. Inst. (a-e)		ECAC	32	7	29	36	58
1986-87—Peoria Rivermen		IHL	42	4	11	15	93
1986-87—St. Louis Blues		NHL	13	2	0	2	2
1987-88—St. Louis Blues		NHL	30	3	6	9	12
1987-88—Peoria Riverman		IHL	37	21	12	33	97
NHL TOTALS			43	5	6	11	14

(c)—June, 1982—Drafted by Montreal Canadiens in NHL entry draft. Tenth Canadiens pick, 124th overall, sixth round.
(d)—June, 1985—NHL rights traded by Montreal Canadiens to St. Louis Blues along with Mark Hunter and future considerations for St. Louis' first-round draft choice (Jose Charbonneau) and a switch of other choices.
(e)—Named to East All-America.

GUY DARVEAU

Defense . . . 6' . . . 200 lbs. . . . Born, Montreal, Que., April 7, 1968 . . . Shoots left.

Year	Team	League	Games	G.	A.	Pts.	Pen.
1985-86—Longueuil Chevaliers		QHL	55	0	8	8	139
1986-87—Longueuil Chevaliers		QHL	67	9	24	33	175
1987-88—Victoriaville Tigers (c)		QHL	57	19	16	35	274

(c)—June, 1988—Drafted by Calgary Flames in 1988 NHL entry draft. Tenth Flames pick, 210th overall, 10th round.

LEE DAVIDSON

Center . . . 5'10" . . . 160 lbs. . . . Born, Winnipeg, Manitoba, June 30, 1968 . . . Shoots left . . . Son of Roy Davidson (Former Univ. of North Dakota player).

Year	Team	League	Games	G.	A.	Pts.	Pen.
1985-86—Penticton Knights (c)		BCJHL	46	34	72	106	37
1986-87—Univ. of North Dakota		WCHA	41	16	12	28	65
1987-88—Univ. of North Dakota		WCHA	40	22	24	46	74

(c)—June, 1986—Drafted by Washington Capitals in 1986 NHL entry draft. Ninth Capitals pick, 166th overall, eighth round.

ROBERT SEAN DAVIDSON
(Known by middle name)

Right Wing . . . 5'11" . . . 180 lbs. . . . Born, Toronto, Ont., April 13, 1968 . . . Shoots right . . . (January, 1985)—Broken wrist.

Year	Team	League	Games	G.	A.	Pts.	Pen.
1984-85—Toronto Nationals		MTHL	60	58	55	113	80
1985-86—Toronto Marlboros (c)		OHL	65	18	34	52	23
1986-87—Toronto Marlboros		OHL	66	30	32	62	24
1987-88—Toronto Marlboros		OHL	66	34	47	81	61

(c)—June, 1986—Drafted by Toronto Maple Leafs as an underage junior in 1986 NHL entry draft. Tenth Maple Leafs pick, 195th overall, 10th round.

JOSEPH DAY

Left Wing . . . 5'11" . . . 175 lbs. . . . Born, Chicago, Ill., May 11, 1968 . . . Shoots left.

Year	Team	League	Games	G.	A.	Pts.	Pen.
1985-86—Chicago Minor Hawks		Ill.	30	23	18	41	69
1986-87—St. Lawrence Univ. (c)		ECAC	33	9	11	20	25
1987-88—St. Lawrence Univ.		ECAC	33	23	17	40	40

(c)—June, 1987—Drafted by Hartford Whalers in 1987 NHL entry draft. Eighth Whalers pick, 186th overall, ninth round.

BRYAN THOMAS DEASLEY

Left Wing . . . 6'3" . . . 200 lbs. . . . Born, Toronto, Ont., November 26, 1968 . . . Shoots left . . . (February, 1986)—Broken ribs . . . (January, 1987)—Fractured wrist . . . (July, 1987)—Off-season ankle injury.

Year	Team	League	Games	G.	A.	Pts.	Pen.
1985-86—St. Michael's Jr. B		OHA	30	17	20	37	88
1986-87—Univ. of Michigan (c)		CCHA	38	13	10	23	74
1987-88—Univ. of Michigan		CCHA	27	18	4	22	38

(c)—June, 1987—Drafted by Calgary Flames in 1987 NHL entry draft. First Flames pick, 19th overall, first round.

LUCIEN DeBLOIS

Right Wing . . . 5'11" . . . 200 lbs. . . . Born, Joliette, Que., June 21, 1957 . . . Shoots right . . . (November, 1980)—Groin pull . . . (November 6, 1984)—Pulled groin at Detroit . . . (January 2, 1985)—Pulled stomach muscles at Detroit . . . (October 16, 1985)—Sprained right knee vs. Buffalo and missed 16 games . . . (January, 1988)—Hyper-extended right knee . . . (March, 1988)—Bursitis in right knee.

Year	Team	League	Games	G.	A.	Pts.	Pen.
1973-74—Sorel Black Hawks		QJHL	56	30	35	65	53
1974-75—Sorel Black Hawks		QJHL	72	46	53	99	62
1975-76—Sorel Black Hawks (a)		QJHL	70	56	55	111	112
1976-77—Sorel Black Hawks (a-c-d)		QJHL	72	56	78	134	131
1977-78—New York Rangers		NHL	71	22	8	30	27
1978-79—New York Rangers		NHL	62	11	17	28	26
1978-79—New Haven Nighthawks		AHL	7	4	6	10	6
1979-80—New York Rangers (e)		NHL	6	3	1	4	7
1979-80—Colorado Rockies		NHL	70	24	19	43	36
1980-81—Colorado Rockies (f)		NHL	74	26	16	42	78
1981-82—Winnipeg Jets		NHL	65	25	27	52	87
1982-83—Winnipeg Jets		NHL	79	27	27	54	69
1983-84—Winnipeg Jets (g)		NHL	80	34	45	79	50
1984-85—Montreal Canadiens		NHL	51	12	11	23	20
1985-86—Montreal Canadiens		NHL	61	14	17	31	48
1986-87—New York Rangers (h)		NHL	40	3	8	11	27
1987-88—New York Rangers		NHL	74	9	21	30	103
NHL TOTALS			733	210	217	427	578

(c)—Won Most Valuable Player Award.
(d)—Drafted from Sorel Black Hawks by New York Rangers in first round of 1977 amateur draft.
(e)—November, 1979—Traded with Mike McEwen, Pat Hickey, Dean Turner and future considerations (Bobby Sheehan and Bobby Crawford) by New York Rangers to Colorado Rockies for Barry Beck.
(f)—July, 1981—Traded by Colorado Rockies to Winnipeg Jets for Brent Ashton and a third-round 1982 draft pick (Dave Kasper).
(g)—June, 1984—Traded by Winnipeg Jets to Montreal Canadiens for Perry Turnbull.
(h)—September, 1986—Signed by New York Rangers as a free agent.

DEAN DeFAZIO

Left Wing . . . 5'11" . . . 183 lbs. . . . Born, Ottawa, Ont., April 16, 1963 . . . Shoots left.

Year	Team	League	Games	G.	A.	Pts.	Pen.
1979-80—Ottawa Senators		OPJHL	47	27	25	52	80
1980-81—Brantford Alexanders (c)		OHL	60	6	13	19	104
1981-82—Brantford Alexanders (d)		OHL	10	2	6	8	30
1981-82—Sudbury Wolves		OHL	50	21	32	53	81
1982-83—Oshawa Generals (e)		OHL	52	22	23	45	108
1983-84—Pittsburgh Penguins		NHL	22	0	2	2	28
1983-84—Baltimore Skipjacks		AHL	46	18	13	31	114
1984-85—Baltimore Skipjacks		AHL	78	10	17	27	88
1985-86—Baltimore Skipjacks		AHL	75	14	24	38	171
1986-87—Newmarket Saints		AHL	76	7	13	20	116
1987-88—Flint Spirits		IHL	30	8	6	14	39
1987-88—Baltimore Skipjacks		AHL	21	1	2	3	75
1987-88—New Haven Nighthawks		AHL	26	5	12	17	21
NHL TOTALS			22	0	2	2	28

(c)—June, 1981—Drafted as underage junior by Pittsburgh Penguins in 1981 NHL entry draft. Eighth Penguins pick, 175th overall, ninth round.

(d)—October, 1981—Traded with Tom DellaMaestra by Brantford Alexanders to Sudbury Wolves for Dan Zavarise and Gary Corbiere.

(e)—October, 1982—Traded by Sudbury Wolves to Oshawa Generals for Ali Butorac, Jim Uens and future considerations.

PHIL DeGAETANO

Defense . . . 6'1" . . . 200 lbs. . . . Born, Roslyn, N.Y., August 9, 1963 . . . Shoots right.

Year	Team	League	Games	G.	A.	Pts.	Pen.
1981-82—Northern Michigan Univ.		CCHA	36	4	10	14	34
1982-83—Northern Michigan Univ.		CCHA	37	5	9	14	56
1983-84—Northern Michigan Univ.		CCHA	35	2	9	11	45
1984-85—Northern Michigan Univ.		WCHA	40	5	20	25	98
1985-86—Indianapolis Checkers (c)		IHL	80	9	39	48	109
1986-87—Adirondack Red Wings		AHL	78	7	23	30	75
1987-88—Adirondack Red Wings		AHL	65	4	27	31	105

(c)—June, 1986—Signed by Detroit Red Wings as a free agent.

DALE DeGRAY

Defense . . . 5'10" . . . 190 lbs. . . . Born, Oshawa, Ont., September 3, 1963 . . . Shoots right . . . (January, 1988)—Missed 15 games with separated left shoulder.

Year	Team	League	Games	G.	A.	Pts.	Pen.
1979-80—Oshawa Legionaires		Metro Jr.B	42	14	14	28	34
1979-80—Oshawa Generals		OMJHL	1	0	0	0	2
1980-81—Oshawa Generals (c)		OHL	61	11	10	21	93
1981-82—Oshawa Generals		OHL	66	11	22	33	162
1982-83—Oshawa Generals		OHL	69	20	30	50	149
1983-84—Colorado Flames		CHL	67	16	14	30	67
1984-85—Moncton Golden Flames (b)		AHL	77	24	37	61	63
1985-86—Moncton Golden Flames		AHL	76	10	31	41	128
1985-86—Calgary Flames		NHL	1	0	0	0	0
1986-87—Moncton Golden Flames		AHL	45	10	22	32	57
1986-87—Calgary Flames		NHL	27	6	7	13	29
1987-88—Toronto Maple Leafs (d)		NHL	56	6	18	24	63
1987-88—Newmarket Saints		AHL	8	2	10	12	8
NHL TOTALS			84	12	25	37	92

(c)—June, 1981—Drafted as underage junior by Calgary Flames in 1981 NHL entry draft. Seventh Flames pick, 162nd overall, eighth round.

(d)—September, 1987—Traded by Calgary Flames to Toronto Maple Leafs for future considerations.

GILBERT DELORME

Defense . . . 5'11" . . . 205 lbs. . . . Born, Boucherville, Que., November 25, 1962 . . . Shoots right . . . (January 3, 1982)—Dislocated left shoulder at Buffalo . . . (November 19, 1985)— Injured throat vs. Edmonton and missed two games . . . (January 25, 1986)—Bruised knee vs. Buffalo and missed seven games . . . (February, 1988)—Injured ankle.

Year	Team	League	Games	G.	A.	Pts.	Pen.
1978-79—Chicoutimi Sagueneens		QMJHL	72	13	47	60	53
1979-80—Chicoutimi Sagueneens		QMJHL	71	25	86	111	68
1980-81—Chicoutimi Sagueneens (b-c)		QMJHL	70	27	79	106	77
1981-82—Montreal Canadiens		NHL	60	3	8	11	55
1982-83—Montreal Canadiens		NHL	78	12	21	33	89
1983-84—Montreal Canadiens (d)		NHL	27	2	7	9	8
1983-84—St. Louis Blues		NHL	44	0	5	5	41
1984-85—St. Louis Blues		NHL	74	2	12	14	53
1985-86—Quebec Nordiques (e)		NHL	65	2	18	20	55
1986-87—Quebec Nordiques (f)		NHL	19	2	0	2	14
1986-87—Detroit Red Wings		NHL	24	2	3	5	33
1987-88—Detroit Red Wings		NHL	55	2	8	10	81
NHL TOTALS			446	27	82	109	429

(c)—June, 1981—Drafted as underage junior by Montreal Canadiens in 1981 NHL entry draft. Second Canadiens pick, 18th overall, first round.

(d)—December, 1983—Traded with Doug Wickenheiser and Greg Paslawski by Montreal Canadiens to St. Louis Blues for Perry Turnbull.

(e)—October, 1985—Traded by St. Louis Blues to Quebec Nordiques for Bruce Bell.

(f)—January, 1987—Traded with Brent Ashton and Mark Kumpel by Quebec Nordiques to Detroit Red Wings for John Ogrodnick, Doug Shedden and Basil McRae.

LARRY DePALMA

Left Wing . . . 6' . . . 180 lbs. . . . Born, Trenton, Mich., October 27, 1965 . . . Shoots left . . . (October, 1987)—Injured wrist.

Year	Team	League	Games	G.	A.	Pts.	Pen.
1984-85—New Westminister Bruins		WHL	65	14	16	30	87
1985-86—Saskatoon Blades (b)		WHL	65	61	51	112	232
1985-86—Minnesota North Stars (c)		NHL	1	0	0	0	0
1986-87—Springfield Indians		AHL	9	2	2	4	82
1986-87—Minnesota North Stars		NHL	56	9	6	15	219
1987-88—Baltimore Skipjacks		AHL	16	8	10	18	121
1987-88—Kalamazoo Wings		IHL	22	6	11	17	215
1987-88—Minnesota North Stars		NHL	7	1	1	2	15
NHL TOTALS			64	10	7	17	234

(c)—March, 1986—Signed by Minnesota North Stars as a free agent.

ERIC DESJARDINS

Defense . . . 6'1" . . . 185 lbs. . . . Born, Rouyn, Que., June 14, 1969 . . . Shoots right.

Year	Team	League	Games	G.	A.	Pts.	Pen.
1985-86—Laval Laurentides Midget		Que. Midget	42	6	30	36	54
1986-87—Granby Bisons (b-c)		QHL	66	14	24	38	75
1987-88—Granby Bisons		QHL	62	18	49	67	138
1987-88—Sherbrooke Canadiens		AHL	3	0	0	0	6

(c)—June, 1987—Drafted as an underage junior by Montreal Canadiens in 1987 NHL entry draft. Third Canadiens pick, 38th overall, second round.

MARTIN DESJARDINS

Center . . . 5'11" . . . 165 lbs. . . . Born, Ste. Rose, Que., January 28, 1967 . . . Shoots left.

Year	Team	League	Games	G.	A.	Pts.	Pen.
1984-85—Trois-Rivieres Draveurs (c)		QHL	66	29	34	63	76
1985-86—Trois-Rivieres Draveurs		QHL	71	49	69	118	103
1986-87—Longueuil Chevaliers		QHL	68	39	61	100	89
1987-88—Sherbrooke Canadiens		AHL	75	34	36	70	117

(c)—June, 1985—Drafted by Montreal Canadiens in 1985 NHL entry draft. Fifth Canadiens pick, 75th overall, fourth round.

JOHN DEVEREAUX

Center . . . 6' . . . 174 lbs. . . . Born, Scituate, Mass., June 8, 1965 . . . Shoots right.

Year	Team	League	Games	G.	A.	Pts.	Pen.
1983-84—Scituate H.S. (c)		Mass. H.S.	20	41	34	75	..
1984-85—Boston College		H. East	19	3	3	6	6
1985-86—Boston College		H. East	41	8	6	14	24
1986-87—Boston College		H. East	39	14	20	34	6
1987-88—Boston College		H. East	34	14	24	38	48

(c)—June, 1984—Drafted by Hartford Whalers in 1984 NHL entry draft. Fourth Whalers pick, 173rd overall, ninth round.

GERALD DIDUCK

Defense . . . 6'2" . . . 195 lbs. . . . Born, Edmonton, Alta., April 6, 1965 . . . Shoots right . . . (November, 1987)—Fractured left foot.

Year	Team	League	Games	G.	A.	Pts.	Pen.
1981-82—Lethbridge Broncos		WHL	71	1	15	16	81
1982-83—Lethbridge Broncos (c)		WHL	67	8	16	24	151
1983-84—Lethbridge Broncos		WHL	65	10	24	34	133
1984-85—New York Islanders		NHL	65	2	8	10	80
1985-86—New York Islanders		NHL	10	1	2	3	2
1985-86—Springfield Indians		AHL	61	6	14	20	175
1986-87—Springfield Indians		AHL	45	6	8	14	120
1986-87—New York Islanders		NHL	30	2	3	5	67
1987-88—New York Islanders		NHL	68	7	12	19	113
NHL TOTALS			173	12	25	37	262

(c)—June, 1983—Drafted as underage junior by New York Islanders in 1983 NHL entry draft. Second Islanders pick, 16th overall, first round.

BOB DIMAIO

Center . . . 5'8" . . . 175 lbs. . . . Born, Calgary, Alta., February 19, 1968 . . . Shoots right . . . (January 28, 1988)—Suspended two games for leaving the bench to enter on-ice altercation.

Year	Team	League	Games	G.	A.	Pts.	Pen.
1984-85—Kamloops Blazers		WHL	55	9	18	27	29
1985-86—Kamloops Blazers (c)		WHL	6	1	0	1	0
1985-86—Medicine Hat Tigers		WHL	55	20	30	50	82
1986-87—Medicine Hat Tigers (d)		WHL	70	27	43	70	130
1987-88—Medicine Hat Tigers		WHL	54	47	43	90	120

(c)—December, 1985—Traded with Dave MacKay and Calvin Knibbs by Kamloops Blazers to Medicine Hat Tigers for Doug Pickel and Sean Pass.

(d)—June, 1987—Drafted by New York Islanders in 1987 NHL entry draft. Sixth Islanders pick, 118th overall, sixth round.

GORDON DINEEN

Defense . . . 5'11" . . . 180 lbs. . . . Born, Toronto, Ont., September 21, 1962 . . . Shoots right . . . Brother of Shawn, Peter, Jerry and Kevin Dineen and son of Bill Dineen (Detroit and Chicago, mid-1950s) . . . (January 15, 1985)—Bruised ribs vs. Vancouver . . . (February, 1988)—Sprained left ankle.

Year	Team	League	Games	G.	A.	Pts.	Pen.
1979-80—St. Michaels Junior 'B'		....	42	15	35	50	103
1980-81—Sault Ste. Marie Greyhounds (c)		OHL	68	4	26	30	158
1981-82—Sault Ste. Marie Greyhounds		OHL	68	9	45	54	185
1982-83—Indianapolis Racers (a-d-e)		CHL	73	10	47	57	78
1982-83—New York Islanders		NHL	2	0	0	0	4
1983-84—Indianapolis Checkers		IHL	26	4	13	17	63
1983-84—New York Islanders		NHL	43	1	11	12	32
1984-85—Springfield Indians		AHL	25	1	8	9	46
1984-85—New York Islanders		NHL	48	1	12	13	89
1985-86—New York Islanders		NHL	57	1	8	9	81
1985-86—Springfield Indians		AHL	11	2	3	5	20
1986-87—New York Islanders		NHL	71	4	10	14	110
1987-88—New York Islanders (f)		NHL	57	4	12	16	62
1987-88—Minnesota North Stars		NHL	13	1	1	2	21
NHL TOTALS			291	12	54	66	399

(c)—June, 1981—Drafted as underage junior by New York Islanders in 1981 NHL entry draft. Second Islanders pick, 42nd overall, second round.

(d)—Won Bobby Orr Trophy (Most Valuable CHL Defenseman).

(e)—Won Bob Gassoff Award (Most Improved CHL Defenseman).

(f)—March, 1988—Traded with future considerations by New York Islanders to Minnesota North Stars for Chris Pryor.

KEVIN DINEEN

Right Wing . . . 5'10" . . . 180 lbs. . . . Born, Toronto, Ont., October 28, 1963 . . . Shoots right . . . Brother of Shawn, Peter, Jerry and Gordon Dineen and son of Bill Dineen (Detroit and Chicago, mid-1950s.) . . . Set University of Denver penalty-minute record (105) as a freshman . . . Member of 1984 Canadian Olympic Team . . . (October 24, 1985)—Sprained left shoulder at Philadelphia and missed nine games . . . (January 12, 1986)—Broke knuckle at Chicago and missed seven games . . . (February 14, 1986)—Sprained knee at Winnipeg . . . (January, 1988)—Missed five games with a sprained right shoulder.

Year	Team	League	Games	G.	A.	Pts.	Pen.
1980-81—St. Michaels Jr. B		MTJHL	40	15	28	43	167
1981-82—University of Denver (c)		WCHA	38	12	22	34	105
1982-83—University of Denver		WCHA	36	16	13	29	108
1983-84—Canadian Olympic Team		Int'l.	..	..	..	..	..
1984-85—Binghamton Whalers		AHL	25	15	8	23	41
1984-85—Hartford Whalers		NHL	57	25	16	41	120
1985-86—Hartford Whalers		NHL	57	33	35	68	124
1986-87—Hartford Whalers		NHL	78	40	69	109	110
1987-88—Hartford Whalers		NHL	74	25	25	50	219
1987-88—Hartford Whalers		NHL	74	25	25	50	219
NHL TOTALS			266	123	145	268	573

(c)—June, 1982—Drafted as underage player by Hartford Whalers in 1982 NHL entry draft. Third Whalers pick, 56th overall, third round.

PETER DINEEN

Defense . . . 5'11" . . . 181 lbs. . . . Born, Kingston, Ont., November 19, 1960 . . . Shoots right . . . Brother of Shawn, Gordon, Jerry and Kevin Dineen and son of Bill Dineen (Detroit and Chicago, mid-1950s) . . . (October, 1980)—Broken ankle.

Year	Team	League	Games	G.	A.	Pts.	Pen.
1977-78—Seattle Breakers		WCHL	2	0	0	0	0
1978-79—Kingston Canadians		OMJHL	60	7	14	21	70

Year	Team	League	Games	G.	A.	Pts.	Pen.
1979-80—Kingston Canadians (c)		OMJHL	32	4	10	14	54
1980-81—Maine Mariners		AHL	41	6	7	13	100
1981-82—Maine Mariners		AHL	71	6	14	20	156
1982-83—Maine Mariners (d)		AHL	2	0	0	0	0
1982-83—Moncton Alpines		AHL	59	0	10	10	76
1983-84—Moncton Alpines		AHL	63	0	10	10	120
1983-84—Hershey Bears (e)		AHL	12	0	1	1	32
1984-85—Hershey Bears (f)		AHL	79	4	19	23	144
1985-86—Binghamton Whalers		AHL	11	0	1	1	35
1985-86—Moncton Golden Flames (g)		AHL	55	5	13	18	136
1986-87—Los Angeles Kings		NHL	11	0	2	2	8
1986-87—New Haven Nighthawks		AHL	59	2	17	19	140
1987-88—Adirondack Red Wings		AHL	76	8	26	34	137
NHL TOTALS			11	0	2	2	8

(c)—June, 1980—Drafted by Philadelphia Flyers in 1980 NHL entry draft. Ninth Flyers pick, 189th overall, ninth round.

(d)—October, 1982—Traded by Philadelphia Flyers to Edmonton Oilers for Bob Hoffmeyer.

(e)—September, 1984—Signed by Boston Bruins as a free agent.

(f)—August, 1985—Signed as free agent by Hartford Whalers.

(g)—July, 1986—Signed by Los Angeles Kings as a free agent.

MARCEL ELPHEGE DIONNE

Center . . . 5'8" . . . 185 lbs. . . . Born, Drummondville, Que., August 3, 1951 . . . Shoots right . . . Missed part of 1970-71 season with broken collarbone . . . Set NHL record for points in rookie season in 1971-72 (broken by Bryan Trottier in 1975-76) . . . Established record for shorthanded goals (10) in single season, 1974-75 (broken by Wayne Gretzky in 1983-84) . . . Missed part of 1977-78 season with shoulder separations . . . (January 7, 1981)—Collected 1,000th NHL point in 740th NHL game, the fastest by any player in history (record broken by Guy Lafleur, 720th game) . . . (January 11, 1984)—Sprained left ankle vs. Washington . . . (February 14, 1984)—Aggravated ankle injury at New Jersey . . . (December, 1987)—Arthritic inflammation of left knee.

Year	Team	League	Games	G.	A.	Pts.	Pen.
1967-68—Drummondville Rangers		QJHL	....	...	....	....	....
1968-69—St. Cath. Black Hawks		Jr."A"OHA	48	37	63	100	38
1969-70—St. Cath. B. Hawks (b-c)		Jr."A"OHA	54	*55	*77	*132	46
1970-71—St. Cath. B. Hawks (a-c-d)		Jr."A"OHA	46	62	81	*143	20
1971-72—Detroit Red Wings		NHL	78	28	49	77	14
1972-73—Detroit Red Wings		NHL	77	40	50	90	21
1973-74—Detroit Red Wings		NHL	74	24	54	78	10
1974-75—Detroit Red Wings (e-f)		NHL	80	47	74	121	14
1975-76—Los Angeles Kings		NHL	80	40	54	94	38
1976-77—Los Angeles Kings (a-f)		NHL	80	53	69	122	12
1977-78—Los Angeles Kings		NHL	70	36	43	79	37
1978-79—Los Angeles Kings (b)		NHL	80	59	71	130	30
1979-80—Los Angeles Kings (a-g-h)		NHL	80	53	84	*137	32
1980-81—Los Angeles Kings (b)		NHL	80	58	77	135	70
1981-82—Los Angeles Kings		NHL	78	50	67	117	50
1982-83—Los Angeles Kings		NHL	80	56	51	107	22
1983-84—Los Angeles Kings		NHL	66	39	53	92	28
1984-85—Los Angeles Kings		NHL	80	46	80	126	46
1985-86—Los Angeles Kings		NHL	80	36	58	94	42
1986-87—Los Angeles Kings (i)		NHL	67	24	50	74	54
1986-87—New York Rangers		NHL	14	4	6	10	6
1987-88—New York Rangers		NHL	67	31	34	65	54
NHL TOTALS			1311	724	1024	1748	580

(c)—Won Eddie Powers Memorial Trophy (leading scorer award).

(d)—Drafted from St. Catharines Black Hawks by Detroit Red Wings in first round of 1971 amateur draft.

(e)—June, 1975—Signed by Los Angeles Kings as free agent after playing out option. Kings sent Terry Harper, Dan Maloney and second-round 1976 draft choice to Red Wings as compensation. L.A. received Bart Crashley from Detroit as part of deal.

(f)—Won Lady Byng Memorial Trophy (Combination of Sportsmanship and Quality play.)

(g)—Won Art Ross Trophy (NHL Leading Scorer.)

(h)—Selected NHL Player of the Year by THE SPORTING NEWS in poll of players.

(i)—March, 1987—Traded with Jeff Crossman and a third-round 1989 draft pick by Los Angeles Kings to New York Rangers for Bobby Carpenter and Tom Laidlaw.

ROBERT DIRK

Defense . . . 6'4" . . . 210 lbs. . . . Born, Regina, Sask., August 20, 1966 . . . Shoots left.

Year	Team	League	Games	G.	A.	Pts.	Pen.
1982-83—Regina Pats		WHL	1	0	0	0	0
1983-84—Regana Pats (c)		WHL	62	2	10	12	64
1984-85—Regina Pats		WHL	69	10	34	44	97
1985-86—Regina Pats (b)		WHL	72	19	60	79	140
1986-87—Peoria Rivermen		IHL	76	5	17	22	155
1987-88—St. Louis Blues		NHL	7	0	1	1	16
1987-88—Peoria Rivermen		IHL	54	4	21	25	126
NHL TOTALS			7	0	1	1	16

(c)—June, 1984—Drafted as underage junior by St. Louis Blues in 1984 NHL entry draft. Fourth Blues pick, 53rd overall, third round.

DAVID DiVITA

Defense . . . 6'2" . . . 205 lbs. . . . Born, Detroit, Mich., February 3, 1969 . . . Shoots right . . . (February 5, 1988)—Separated shoulder.

Year	Team	League	Games	G.	A.	Pts.	Pen.
1987-88—Lake Superior State Univ. (c)	CCHA	26	1	0	1	20

(c)—June, 1988—Drafted by Buffalo Sabres in 1988 NHL entry draft. Sixth Sabres pick, 106th overall, sixth round.

BRIAN DOBBIN

Right Wing . . . 5'11" . . . 195 lbs. . . . Born, Petrolia, Ont., August 18, 1966 . . . Shoots right . . . (September, 1986)—Damaged ligament in right knee during Philadelphia training camp and required surgery.

Year	Team	League	Games	G.	A.	Pts.	Pen.
1981-82—Mooretown Flags Jr. C	GLOHA	38	31	24	55	50
1982-83—Kingston Canadians	OHL	69	16	39	55	35
1983-84—London Knights (c)	OHL	70	30	40	70	70
1984-85—London Knights	OHL	53	42	57	99	63
1985-86—London Knights	OHL	59	38	55	93	113
1985-86—Hershey Bears	AHL	2	1	0	1	0
1986-87—Hershey Bears	AHL	52	26	35	61	66
1986-87—Philadelphia Flyers	NHL	12	2	1	3	14
1987-88—Hershey Bears	AHL	54	36	47	83	58
1987-88—Philadelpia Flyers	NHL	21	3	5	8	6
NHL TOTALS		33	5	6	11	20

(c)—June, 1984—Drafted as underage junior by Philadelphia Flyers in 1984 NHL entry draft. Sixth Flyers pick, 100th overall, fifth round.

BOBBY DOLLAS

Defense . . . 6'2" . . . 220 lbs. . . . Born, Montreal, Que., January 31, 1965 . . . Shoots left.

Year	Team	League	Games	G.	A.	Pts.	Pen.
1981-82—Lac St. Louis AAA	Que. Midget	44	9	31	40	138
1982-83—Laval Voisins (b-c-d)	QHL	63	16	45	61	144
1983-84—Laval Voisins	QHL	54	12	33	45	80
1983-84—Winnipeg Jets	NHL	1	0	0	0	0
1984-85—Winnipeg Jets	NHL	9	0	0	0	0
1984-85—Sherbrooke Canadiens	AHL	8	1	3	4	4
1985-86—Sherbrooke Canadiens	AHL	25	4	7	11	29
1985-86—Winnipeg Jets	NHL	46	0	5	5	66
1986-87—Sherbrooke Canadiens	AHL	75	6	18	24	87
1987-88—Quebec Nordiques (e)	NHL	9	0	0	0	2
1987-88—Moncton Golden Flames	AHL	26	4	10	14	20
1987-88—Fredericton Express	AHL	33	4	8	12	27
NHL TOTALS		56	0	5	5	68

(c)—Won Raymond Lagace Trophy (Top rookie defenseman).
(d)—June, 1983—Drafted as underage junior by Winnipeg Jets in 1983 NHL entry draft. Second Jets pick, 14th overall, first round.
(e)—December, 1987—Traded by Winnipeg Jets to Quebec Nordiques for Stu Kulak.

TAHIR (Tie) DOMI

Right Wing . . . 5'10" . . . 200 lbs. . . . Born, Windsor, Ont., November 1, 1969 . . . (November 2, 1986)—Given an indefinite suspension by OHL for leaving the bench during an on-ice altercation.

Year	Team	League	Games	G.	A.	Pts.	Pen.
1985-86—Windsor Junior B	OHL	32	8	17	25	346
1986-87—Peterborough Petes	OHL	18	1	1	2	79
1987-88—Peterborough Petes (c)	OHL	60	22	21	43	292

(c)—June, 1988—Drafted by Toronto Maple Leafs in 1988 NHL entry draft. Second Maple Leafs pick, 27th overall, second round.

CLARK DONATELLI

Left Wing . . . 5'10" . . . 190 lbs. . . . Born, Providence, R.I., November 22, 1965 . . . Shoots left.

Year	Team	League	Games	G.	A.	Pts.	Pen.
1983-84—Stratford Collitons Jr. B (c)		MWOHA	38	41	49	90	46
1984-85—Boston University		H. East	40	17	18	35	46
1985-86—Boston University		H. East	43	28	34	62	30
1986-87—Boston University (d)		H. East	37	15	23	38	46
1987-88—U.S. Olympic Team		Int'l	53	12	28	40	..

(c)—June, 1984—Drafted by New York Rangers in 1984 NHL entry draft. Fourth Rangers pick, 98th overall, fifth round.

(d)—October, 1986—Traded with Reijo Ruotsalainen, Ville Horava and Jim Wiemer by New York Rangers to Edmonton Oilers to complete an earlier deal that saw the Rangers acquire Don Jackson and Mike Golden.

GORDON DONNELLY

Defense . . . 6'2" . . . 202 lbs. . . . Born, Montreal, Que., April 5, 1962 . . . Shoots right . . . (October 29, 1987)—Suspended five games by NHL for kneeing . . . (February 26, 1988)— Suspended five games and fined $100 for engaging in a pre-game fight at Montreal.

Year	Team	League	Games	G.	A.	Pts.	Pen.
1978-79—Laval Nationals		QMJHL	71	1	14	15	79
1979-80—Laval Nationals		QMJHL	44	5	10	15	47
1979-80—Chicoutimi Sagueneens		QMJHL	24	1	5	6	64
1980-81—Sherbrooke Beavers (c)		QMJHL	67	15	23	38	252
1981-82—Sherbrooke Beavers (d)		QMJHL	60	8	41	49	250
1982-83—Salt Lake Golden Eagles (e)		CHL	67	3	12	15	222
1983-84—Fredericton Express		AHL	30	2	3	5	146
1983-84—Quebec Nordiques		NHL	38	0	5	5	60
1984-85—Fredericton Express		AHL	42	1	5	6	134
1984-85—Quebec Nordiques		NHL	22	0	0	0	33
1985-86—Fredericton Express		AHL	37	3	5	8	103
1985-86—Quebec Nordiques		NHL	36	2	2	4	85
1986-87—Quebec Nordiques		NHL	38	0	2	2	143
1987-88—Quebec Nordiques		NHL	63	4	3	7	301
NHL TOTALS			197	6	12	18	622

(c)—June, 1981—Drafted by St. Louis Blues in 1981 NHL entry draft. Third Blues pick, 62nd overall, third round.

(d)—Led QMJHL Playoffs with 106 penalty minutes.

(e)—August, 1983—Sent by St. Louis Blues along with Claude Julien to Quebec Nordiques as compensation for St. Louis signing coach Jacques Demers.

MIKE DONNELLY

Left Wing . . . 5'11" . . . 185 lbs. . . . Born, Livonia, Mich., October 10, 1963 . . . Shoots left . . . Set a CCHA single-season record with 59 goals in 1985-86 . . . (November, 1987)—Dislocated and fractured right index finger.

Year	Team	League	Games	G.	A.	Pts.	Pen.
1982-83—Michigan State University		CCHA	24	7	13	20	8
1983-84—Michigan State University		CCHA	44	18	14	32	40
1984-85—Michigan State University		CCHA	44	26	21	47	48
1985-86—Michigan State Univeristy (c-d)		CCHA	44	*59	38	97	65
1986-87—New York Rangers		NHL	5	1	1	2	0
1986-87—New Haven Nighthawks		AHL	58	27	34	61	52
1987-88—Colorado Rangers		IHL	8	7	11	19	15
1987-88—New York Rangers (e)		NHL	17	2	2	4	8
1987-88—Buffalo Sabres		NHL	40	6	8	14	44
NHL TOTALS			62	9	11	20	52

(c)—Named to first team (West) All-America.

(d)—August, 1986—Signed by New York Rangers as a free agent

(e)—December, 1987—Traded with a fifth-round 1988 draft pick (Alexander Mogilny) by New York Rangers to Buffalo Sabres for Paul Cyr and a 10th-round 1988 draft pick (Eric Fenton).

SEAN DOOLEY

Defense . . . 6'3" . . . 215 lbs. . . . Born, Ipswich, Mass., March 22, 1969 . . . Shoots left.

Year	Team	League	Games	G.	A.	Pts.	Pen.
1985-86—Groton H.S.		Mass. H.S.	....	11	18	29	....
1986-87—Groton H.S. (c)		Mass. H.S.	....	9	17	26	....
1987-88—Merrimack College		ECAC	3	0	0	0	0

DANIEL DORE

Right Wing . . . 6'3" . . . 200 lbs. . . . Born, St. Jerome, Que., April 9, 1970 . . . Shoots right.

Year	Team	League	Games	G.	A.	Pts.	Pen.
1986-87	Drummondville Voltigeurs	QHL	68	23	41	64	229
1987-88	Drummondville Voltigeurs (c)	QHL	64	24	39	63	218

(c)—June, 1988—Drafted by Quebec Nordiques in 1988 NHL entry draft. Second Nordiques pick, fifth overall, first round.

DAN DORION

Right Wing . . . 5'8" . . . 169 lbs. . . . Born, New York, N.Y., March 2, 1963 . . . Shoots right.

Year	Team	League	Games	G.	A.	Pts.	Pen.
1981-82	Austin Mavericks (c)	USHL	50	52	44	96	....
1982-83	U. of Western Michigan	CCHA	34	11	20	31	23
1983-84	U. of Western Michigan	CCHA	42	41	50	91	42
1984-85	U. of Western Michigan	CCHA	39	21	46	67	28
1985-86	U. of Western Michigan (d)	CCHA	42	42	62	104	48
1985-86	New Jersey Devils	NHL	3	1	1	2	0
1986-87	Maine Mariners	AHL	70	16	22	38	47
1987-88	New Jersey Devils	NHL	1	0	0	0	2
1987-88	Utica Devils	AHL	65	30	35	65	98
	NHL TOTALS		4	1	1	2	2

(c)—June, 1982—Drafted by New Jersey Devils in 1982 NHL entry draft. Thirteenth Devils pick, 232nd overall, 12th round.

(d)—Named first team (West) All-America.

WAYNE DOUCET

Left Wing . . . 6'1" . . . 200 lbs. . . . Born, Etobicoke, Ont., June 19, 1970 . . . Shoots left . . . (October, 1986)—Separated shoulder.

Year	Team	League	Games	G.	A.	Pts.	Pen.
1985-86	Toronto Marlboro Midget	OHA	34	17	18	35	101
1986-87	Sudbury Wolves	OHL	64	20	28	48	85
1987-88	Sudbury Wolves	OHL	23	9	4	13	53
1987-88	Hamilton Steelhawks (c)	OHL	37	11	14	25	74

(c)—June, 1988—Drafted by New York Islanders in 1988 NHL entry draft. Second Islanders pick, 29th overadl, second round.

PETER DOURIS

Center . . . 6' . . . 195 lbs. . . . Born, Toronto, Ont., February 19, 1966 . . . Shoots right.

Year	Team	League	Games	G.	A.	Pts.	Pen.
1983-84	Univ. of New Hampshire (c)	ECAC	38	19	15	34	14
1984-85	Univ. of New Hampshire	H. East	42	27	24	51	34
1985-86	Team Canada	Int'l	33	16	7	23	18
1985-86	Winnipeg Jets	NHL	11	0	0	0	0
1986-87	Sherbrooke Canadiens	AHL	62	14	28	42	24
1986-87	Winnipeg Jets	NHL	6	0	0	0	0
1987-88	Moncton Golden Flames	AHL	73	42	37	79	53
1987-88	Winnipeg Jets	NHL	4	0	2	2	0
	NHL TOTALS		21	0	2	2	0

(c)—June, 1984—Drafted by Winnipeg Jets in 1984 NHL entry draft. First Jets pick, 30th overall, second round.

JIM DOWD

Right Wing . . . 6'1" . . . 185 lbs. . . . Born, Brick, N.J., December 25, 1968 . . . Shoots right.

Year	Team	League	Games	G.	A.	Pts.	Pen.
1985-86	Brick H.S.	N.J.H.S.	..	47	51	98	..
1986-87	Brick H.S. (c)	N.J.H.S.	24	22	33	55	..
1987-88	Lake Superior State Univ.	CCHA	45	18	27	45	16

(c)—June, 1987—Drafted by New Jersey Devils in 1987 NHL entry draft. Seventh Devils pick, 149th overall, eighth round.

ROB DOYLE

Defense . . . 5'11" . . . 185 lbs. . . . Born, Lindsay, Ont., February 10, 1964 . . . Shoots left.

Year	Team	League	Games	G.	A.	Pts.	Pen.
1983-84—Colorado College		WCHA	34	5	29	34	112
1984-85—Colorado College		WCHA	37	11	44	55	136
1985-86—Colorado College (b-c)		WCHA	40	18	41	59	73
1986-87—Colorado College (a-d)		WCHA	42	17	37	54	72
1987-88—Adirondack Red Wings		AHL	40	11	28	39	48
1987-88—Flint Spirits		IHL	37	22	22	44	85

(c)—June, 1986—Selected by Detroit Red Wings in NHL supplemental draft.

(d)—Named second team All-America (West).

SHANE DOYLE

Defense . . . 6'2" . . . 195 lbs. . . . Born, Lindsay, Ont., April 26, 1967 . . . Shoots left . . . Brother of Rob Doyle (Colorado College) . . . (November 2, 1986)—Suspended by OHL for being involved in a bench clearing incident vs. Peterborough.

Year	Team	League	Games	G.	A.	Pts.	Pen.
1983-84—Newmarket Flyers		OHA	37	6	15	21	337
1984-85—Belleville Bulls (c)		OHL	59	2	26	28	129
1985-86—Belleville Bulls (d)		OHL	13	1	5	6	41
1985-86—Hamilton Steelhawks (e)		OHL	10	0	7	7	24
1985-86—Cornwall Royals		OHL	32	3	16	19	139
1986-87—Oshawa Generals (f)		OHL	46	9	13	22	168
1987-88—Utica Devils		AHL	14	0	1	1	38
1987-88—Flint Spirits		IHL	13	1	1	2	81

(c)—June, 1985—Drafted as underage junior by Vancouver Canucks in 1985 NHL entry draft. Third Canucks pick, 46th overall, third round.

(d)—November, 1985—Traded with John Purves and Brian Hood by Belleville Bulls to Hamilton Steelhawks for Jason Lafreniere, Lawrence Hinch and Peter Choma.

(e)—January, 1986—Traded by Hamilton Steelhawks to Cornwall Royals for Brad Hyatt and Brent Thompson.

(f)—June, 1987—Traded by Vancouver Canucks to New Jersey Devils for a 12th-round 1987 draft pick (Neil Eisenhut).

BRUCE DRIVER

Defense . . . 6' . . . 174 lbs. . . . Born, Toronto, Ont., April 29, 1962 . . . Shoots left . . . Member of 1984 Canadian Olympic Team . . . (February, 1985)—Surgery to left knee . . . (April 2, 1985)—Reinjured knee when struck by stick at St. Louis . . . (March 9, 1986)—Bruised shoulder at Buffalo . . . (February, 1987)—Stiff neck . . . (February, 1988)—Sprained ankle.

Year	Team	League	Games	G.	A.	Pts.	Pen.
1979-80—Royal York Royals		OPJHL	43	13	57	70	102
1980-81—University of Wisconsin (c)		WCHA	42	5	15	20	42
1981-82—University of Wisconsin (a-d)		WCHA	46	7	37	44	84
1982-83—University of Wisconsin (b)		WCHA	39	16	34	50	50
1983-84—Canadian Olympic Team		Int'l	61	11	17	28	44
1983-84—Maine Mariners		AHL	12	2	6	8	15
1983-84—New Jersey Devils		NHL	4	0	2	2	0
1984-85—New Jersey Devils		NHL	67	9	23	32	36
1985-86—Maine Mariners		AHL	15	4	7	11	16
1985-86—New Jersey Devils		NHL	40	3	15	18	32
1986-87—New Jersey Devils		NHL	74	6	28	34	36
1987-88—New Jersey Devils		NHL	74	15	40	55	68
NHL TOTALS			259	33	108	141	172

(c)—June, 1981—Drafted as underage junior by Colorado Rockies in 1981 NHL entry draft. Sixth Rockies pick, 108th overall, sixth round.

(d)—Named to All-America Team (West).

JOHN DRUCE

Right Wing . . . 6'1" . . . 190 lbs. . . . Born, Peterborough, Ont., February 23, 1966 . . . Shoots right . . . (October, 1983)—Broken collarbone . . . (December, 1984)—Partially torn ligaments in ankle . . . (October, 1985)—Torn thumb ligaments.

Year	Team	League	Games	G.	A.	Pts.	Pen.
1983-84—Peterborough Jr. B		OHA	40	15	18	33	69
1984-85—Peterborough Petes (c)		OHL	54	12	14	26	90
1985-86—Peterborough Petes		OHL	49	22	24	46	84
1986-87—Binghamton Whalers		AHL	77	13	9	22	131
1987-88—Binghamton Whalers		AHL	68	32	29	61	82

(c)—June, 1985—Drafted by Washington Capitals in 1985 NHL entry draft. Second Capitals pick, 40th overall, second round.

STAN DRULIA

Right Wing . . . 5'10" . . . 180 lbs. . . . Born, Elmira, N.Y., January 5, 1968 . . . Shoots right.

Year	Team	League	Games	G.	A.	Pts.	Pen.
1984-85—Belleville Bulls		OHL	63	24	31	55	33
1985-86—Belleville Bulls (c)		OHL	66	43	37	80	73
1986-87—Hamilton Steelhawks		OHL	55	27	51	78	26
1987-88—Hamilton Steelhawks		OHL	65	52	69	121	44

(c)—June, 1986—Drafted as underage junior by Pittsburgh Penguins in 1986 NHL entry draft. Eleventh Penguins pick, 214th overall, 11th round.

GAETAN DUCHESNE

Left Wing . . . 5'11" . . . 195 lbs. . . . Born, Quebec City, Que., July 11, 1962 . . . Shoots left . . . (December 30, 1981)—Bruised right ankle at Pittsburgh . . . (October 11, 1984)—Broke index finger of left hand on a shot at Philadelphia . . . (January 26, 1988)—Sprained left knee on goal post.

Year	Team	League	Games	G.	A.	Pts.	Pen.
1979-80—Quebec Remparts		QJHL	46	9	28	37	22
1980-81—Quebec Remparts (c)		QJHL	72	27	45	72	63
1981-82—Washington Capitals		NHL	74	9	14	23	46
1982-83—Hershey Bears		AHL	1	1	0	1	0
1982-83—Washington Capitals		NHL	77	18	19	37	52
1983-84—Washington Capitals		NHL	79	17	19	36	29
1984-85—Washington Capitals		NHL	67	15	23	38	32
1985-86—Washington Capitals		NHL	80	11	28	39	39
1986-87—Washington Capitals (d)		NHL	74	17	35	52	53
1987-88—Quebec Nordiques		NHL	80	24	23	47	83
NHL TOTALS			531	111	161	272	334

(c)—June, 1981—Drafted by Washington Capitals in 1981 NHL entry draft. Eighth Capitals pick, 152nd overall, eighth round.

(d)—June, 1987—Traded with Alan Haworth and a first-round 1987 draft pick (Joe Sakic) by Washington Capitals to Quebec Nordiques for Dale Hunter and Clint Malarchuk.

STEVE DUCHESNE

Defense . . . 5'11" . . . 195 lbs. . . . Born, Sept-Iles, Que., June 30, 1965 . . . Shoots left.

Year	Team	League	Games	G.	A.	Pts.	Pen.
1983-84—Drummondville Voltigeurs		QHL	67	1	34	35	79
1984-85—Drummondville Voltigeurs (c)		QHL	65	22	54	76	94
1985-86—New Haven Nighthawks		AHL	75	14	35	49	76
1986-87—Los Angeles Kings		NHL	75	13	25	38	74
1987-88—Los Angeles Kings		NHL	71	16	39	55	109
NHL TOTALS			146	29	64	93	183

(c)—October, 1984—Signed by Los Angeles Kings as a free agent.

TOBY DUCOLON

Left Wing . . . 6' . . . 195 lbs. . . . Born, St. Albans, Vt., June 18, 1966 . . . Shoots right.

Year	Team	League	Games	G.	A.	Pts.	Pen.
1983-84—Bellows Free Academy (c)		Ver. H.S.	22	38	26	64	36
1984-85—University of Vermont		ECAC	24	7	4	11	14
1985-86—University of Vermont		ECAC	30	10	6	16	48
1986-87—University of Vermont		ECAC	32	9	11	20	42
1987-88—University of Vermont		ECAC	34	21	18	39	62

(c)—June, 1984—Drafted by St. Louis Blues in 1984 NHL entry draft. Third Blues pick, 50th overall, third round.

DONALD DUFRESNE

Defense . . . 6' . . . 187 lbs. . . . Born, Quebec City, Que., April 10, 1967 . . . Shoots left . . . (November, 1984)—Pneumonia . . . (January 8, 1988)—Dislocated shoulder in AHL game at Rochester.

Year	Team	League	Games	G.	A.	Pts.	Pen.
1983-84—Trois-Rivieres Draveurs		QHL	67	7	12	19	97
1984-85—Trois-Rivieres Draveurs (c)		QHL	65	5	30	35	112
1985-86—Trois-Rivieres Draveurs (b)		QHL	63	8	32	40	160
1986-87—Longueuil Chevaliers (b)		QHL	67	5	29	34	97
1987-88—Sherbrooke Canadiens		AHL	47	1	8	9	107

(c)—June, 1985—Drafted as underage junior by Montreal Canadiens in 1985 entry draft. Eighth Canadiens pick, 117th overall, sixth round.

KEN DUGGAN

Defense . . . 6'3" . . . 210 lbs. . . . Born, Toronto, Ont., February 21, 1963 . . . Shoots left.

Year	Team	League	Games	G.	A.	Pts.	Pen.
1985-86—University of Toronto (c)		CWUAA	44	12	32	44	106
1986-87—Flint Spirit		IHL	67	2	23	25	51
1987-88—Minnesota North Stars (d)		NHL	1	0	0	0	0
1987-88—Flint Spirits		IHL	1	0	0	0	0
NHL TOTALS			1	0	0	0	0

(c)—July, 1986—Signed by New York Rangers as a free agent.
(d)—January, 1988—Signed tryout agreement with Minnesota North Stars.

RON DUGUAY

Right Wing . . . 6'2" . . . 210 lbs. . . . Born, Sudbury, Ont., July 6, 1957 . . . Shoots right . . . Missed part of 1977-78 season with strained groin . . . (October 30, 1980)—Lacerated tendons in right leg . . . (January, 1982)—Separated left shoulder . . . (February, 1983)—Pulled stomach muscle . . . Does not wear a helmet . . . (January, 1988)—Strained lower back.

Year	Team	League	Games	G.	A.	Pts.	Pen.
1973-74—Sudbury Wolves		Jr."A"OHA	59	20	20	40	73
1974-75—Sudbury Wolves		Jr."A"OHA	64	26	52	78	43
1975-76—Sudbury Wolves		Jr."A"OHA	61	42	92	134	101
1976-77—Sudbury Wolves (c)		Jr."A"OHA	61	43	66	109	109
1977-78—New York Rangers		NHL	71	20	20	40	43
1978-79—New York Rangers		NHL	79	27	36	63	35
1979-80—New York Rangers		NHL	73	28	22	50	37
1980-81—New York Rangers		NHL	50	17	21	38	83
1981-82—New York Rangers		NHL	72	40	36	76	82
1982-83—New York Rangers (d)		NHL	72	19	25	44	58
1983-84—Detroit Red Wings		NHL	80	33	47	80	34
1984-85—Detroit Red Wings		NHL	80	38	51	89	51
1985-86—Detroit Red Wings (e)		NHL	67	19	29	48	26
1985-86—Pittsburgh Penguins		NHL	13	6	7	13	6
1986-87—Pittsburgh Penguins (f)		NHL	40	5	13	18	30
1986-87—New York Rangers		NHL	34	9	12	21	9
1987-88—Colorado Rangers		IHL	2	0	0	0	0
1987-88—New York Rangers (g)		NHL	48	4	4	8	23
1987-88—Los Angeles Kings		NHL	15	2	6	8	17
NHL TOTALS			794	267	329	596	534

(c)—Drafted from Sudbury Wolves by New York Rangers in first round of 1977 amateur draft.
(d)—June, 1983—Traded with Eddie Johnstone and Ed Mio by New York Rangers to Detroit Red Wings for Mark Osborne, Mike Blaisdell and Willie Huber.
(e)—March, 1986—Traded by Detroit Red Wings to Pittsburgh Penguins for Doug Shedden.
(f)—March, 1987—Traded by Pittsburgh Penguins to New York Rangers for Chris Kontos.
(g)—February, 1988—Traded by New York Rangers to Los Angeles Kings for Mark Hardy.

CLAUDE DUMAS

Center . . . 6' . . . 161 lbs. . . . Born, Thetford Mines, Que., January 10, 1967 . . . (February, 1985)—Sprained ankle.

Year	Team	League	Games	G.	A.	Pts.	Pen.
1983-84—Magog Cantoniers		Que. Midget	42	22	45	67	44
1984-85—Granby Bisons (c)		QHL	62	19	37	56	34
1985-86—Granby Bisons		QHL	64	31	58	89	78
1985-86—Binghamton Whalers		AHL	7	2	2	4	0
1986-87—Granby Bisons		QHL	67	50	82	132	59
1986-87—Fort Wayne Komets		IHL	3	1	3	4	2
1987-88—Fort Wayne Komets		IHL	80	28	45	73	32

(c)—June, 1985—Drafted as underage junior by Washington Capitals in 1985 NHL entry draft. Sixth Capitals pick, 103rd overall, fifth round.

ROBERT DUMAS

Defense . . . 5'11" . . . 195 lbs. . . . Born, Spirit River, Alta., March 19, 1969 . . . Shoots right.

Year	Team	League	Games	G.	A.	Pts.	Pen.
1983-84—Coquitlam Chiefs		Alta. Midget	50	10	15	25	40
1984-85—Seattle Breakers		WHL	38	0	0	0	26
1985-86—Seattle Thunderbirds		WHL	68	4	11	15	121
1986-87—Seattle Thunderbirds (c)		WHL	72	8	29	37	259
1987-88—Seattle Thunderbirds		WHL	67	12	25	37	218

DALE DUNBAR

Defense . . . 6'1" . . . 200 lbs. . . . Born, Winthrop, Mass., October 14, 1961 . . . Shoots left . . . (September 22, 1985)—Concussion when struck by a deflected puck in pre-season game and missed three weeks.

Year Team	League	Games	G.	A.	Pts.	Pen.
1981-82—Boston University	ECAC	6	0	0	0	0
1982-83—Boston University	ECAC	21	1	7	8	32
1983-84—Boston University	ECAC	34	0	15	15	49
1984-85—Boston University (c)	H. East	39	2	19	21	62
1985-86—Vancouver Canucks	NHL	1	0	0	0	2
1985-86—Fredericton Express	AHL	32	2	10	12	26
1986-87—Peoria Rivermen	IHL	46	2	8	10	32
1987-88—Maine Mariners	AHL	66	1	7	8	120
NHL TOTALS		1	0	0	0	2

(c)—May, 1985—Signed by Vancouver Canucks as a free agent.

IAIN DUNCAN

Left Wing . . . 6'1" . . . 180 lbs. . . . Born, Weston, Ont., October 6, 1964 . . . Shoots left . . . (February, 1988)—Injured groin.

Year Team	League	Games	G.	A.	Pts.	Pen.
1983-84—Bowling Green Univ. (c)	CCHA	44	9	11	20	65
1984-85—Bowling Green Univ.	CCHA	37	9	21	30	105
1985-86—Bowling Green Univ.	CCHA	41	26	26	52	124
1986-87—Bowling Green Univ. (a)	CCHA	39	28	41	69	141
1986-87—Winnipeg Jets	NHL	6	1	2	3	0
1987-88—Winnipeg Jets (d)	NHL	62	19	23	42	73
1987-88—Moncton Golden Flames	AHL	8	1	3	4	26
NHL TOTALS		68	20	25	45	73

(c)—June, 1983—Drafted by Winnipeg Jets in 1983 NHL entry draft. Eighth Jets pick, 129th overall, seventh round.

(d)—Named to NHL All-Rookie team.

CRAIG DUNCANSON

Left Wing . . . 6' . . . 190 lbs. . . . Born, Sudbury, Ont., March 17, 1967 . . . Shoots left . . . (September, 1984)—Torn knee ligaments . . . (November 23, 1986)—Deep leg bruise in OHL game at Hamilton.

Year Team	League	Games	G.	A.	Pts.	Pen.
1982-83—St. Michaels Jr. B	OHA	32	14	19	33	68
1983-84—Sudbury Wolves	OHL	62	38	38	76	178
1984-85—Sudbury Wolves (c)	OHL	53	35	28	63	129
1985-86—Sudbury Wolves	OHL	21	12	17	29	55
1985-86—Cornwall Royals	OHL	40	31	50	81	135
1985-86—Los Angeles Kings	NHL	2	0	1	1	0
1985-86—New Haven Nighthawks (d)	AHL	..	..	..	..	..
1986-87—Cornwall Royals	OHL	52	22	45	67	88
1986-87—Los Angeles Kings	NHL	2	0	0	0	24
1987-88—New Haven Nighthawks	AHL	57	15	25	40	170
1987-88—Los Angeles Kings	NHL	9	0	0	0	12
NHL TOTALS		13	0	1	1	36

(c)—June, 1985—Drafted as underage junior by Los Angeles Kings in 1985 NHL entry draft. First Kings pick, ninth overall, first round.

(d)—No regular season record. Played two playoff games.

ROCKY DUNDAS

Right Wing . . . 6' . . . 195 lbs. . . . Born, Edmonton, Alta., January 30, 1967 . . . Shoots right . . . Brother of R.J. Dundas . . . Son of Ron Dundas (former CFL player).

Year Team	League	Games	G.	A.	Pts.	Pen.
1983-84—Kelowna Wings	WHL	72	15	24	39	57
1984-85—Kelowna Wings (c)	WHL	71	32	44	76	117
1985-86—Spokane Chiefs	WHL	71	31	70	101	160
1986-87—Medicine Hat Tigers	WHL	48	35	41	76	132
1987-88—Baltimore Skipjacks	AHL	9	0	1	1	46
1987-88—Sherbrooke Canadiens	AHL	38	9	6	15	104

(c)—June, 1985—Drafted as underage junior by Montreal Canadiens in 1985 NHL entry draft. Fourth Canadiens pick, 47th overall, third round.

RICHARD DUNN

Defense . . . 6' . . . 192 lbs. . . . Born, Canton, Mass., May 12, 1957 . . . Shoots left . . . (December, 1981)—Shoulder injury.

Year	Team	League	Games	G.	A.	Pts.	Pen.
1975-76—Kingston Canadians		Jr."A"OHA	61	7	18	25	62
1976-77—Windsor Spitfires (c)		Jr."A"OHA	65	5	21	26	98
1977-78—Hershey Bears		AHL	54	7	22	29	17
1977-78—Buffalo Sabres		NHL	25	0	3	3	16
1978-79—Buffalo Sabres		NHL	24	0	3	3	14
1978-79—Hershey Bears		AHL	34	5	18	23	10
1979-80—Buffalo Sabres		NHL	80	7	31	38	61
1980-81—Buffalo Sabres		NHL	79	7	42	49	34
1981-82—Buffalo Sabres (d)		NHL	72	7	19	26	73
1982-83—Calgary Flames (e)		NHL	80	3	11	14	47
1983-84—Hartford Whalers		NHL	63	5	20	25	30
1984-85—Hartford Whalers		NHL	13	1	4	5	2
1984-85—Binghamton Whalers (a-f-g)		AHL	64	9	39	48	43
1985-86—Buffalo Sabres		NHL	29	4	5	9	25
1985-86—Rochester Americans		AHL	34	6	17	23	12
1986-87—Buffalo Sabres		NHL	2	0	1	1	2
1986-87—Rochester Americans (a)		AHL	64	6	26	32	47
1987-88—Rochester Americans		AHL	68	12	35	47	52
1987-88—Buffalo Sabres		NHL	12	2	0	2	8
NHL TOTALS			479	36	139	175	310

(c)—September, 1977—Signed by Buffalo Sabres as free agent.
(d)—June, 1982—Traded by Buffalo Sabres with goaltender Don Edwards and a second-round choice in 1982 NHL entry draft to Calgary Flames for Calgary's first and second round draft choices in 1982 and their second round pick in 1983 plus the option to switch first-round picks in '83.
(e)—July, 1983—Traded by Calgary Flames with Joel Quenneville to Hartford Whalers for Mickey Volcan.
(f)—Won Eddie Shore Plaque (Top AHL defenseman).
(g)—August, 1985—Signed by Buffalo Sabres as a free agent.

GUY DUPUIS

Defense . . . 6'2" . . . 200 lbs. . . . Born, Moncton, N.B., May 10, 1970 . . . Shoots right.

Year	Team	League	Games	G.	A.	Pts.	Pen.
1986-87—Hull Olympiques		QHL	69	5	10	15	35
1987-88—Hull Olympiques (c)		QHL	69	14	34	48	72

(c)—June, 1988—Drafted by Detroit Red Wings in 1988 NHL entry draft. Third Red Wings pick, 47th overall, third round.

MURRAY DUVAL

Defense . . . 6' . . . 195 lbs. . . . Born, Thompson, Manitoba, January 22, 1970 . . . Shoots left . . . (January, 1987)—Stretched left knee ligaments.

Year	Team	League	Games	G.	A.	Pts.	Pen.
1986-87—Spokane Chiefs		WHL	27	2	6	8	21
1987-88—Spokane Chiefs (c)		WHL	70	26	37	63	104

(c)—June, 1988—Drafted by New York Rangers in 1988 NHL entry draft. Second Rangers pick, 26th overall, second round.

DEAN DYER

Center . . . 6'3" . . . 195 lbs. . . . Born, Edmonton, Alta., April 11, 1969 . . . Shoots right.

Year	Team	League	Games	G.	A.	Pts.	Pen.
1987-88—Lake Superior State Univ. (c)		CCHA	45	6	17	23	38

(c)—June, 1988—Drafted by Hartford Whalers in 1988 NHL entry draft. Third Whalers pick, 74th overall, fourth round.

STEVE DYKSTRA

Defense . . . 6'2" . . . 190 lbs. . . . Born, Edmonton, Alta., February 3, 1962 . . . Shoots left . . . (February 19, 1986)—Injured shoulder at Hartford . . . (August 27, 1986)—Hospitalized after an automobile accident . . . (January, 1987)—Back spasms . . . (December, 1987)—Knee injury.

Year	Team	League	Games	G.	A.	Pts.	Pen.
1981-82—Seattle Flyers		WHL	57	8	26	34	139
1982-83—Rochester Americans (c)		AHL	70	2	16	18	100
1983-84—Rochester Americans		AHL	64	3	19	22	141

Year	Team	League	Games	G.	A.	Pts.	Pen.
1984-85—Rochester Americans		AHL	51	9	23	32	113
1984-85—Flint Generals		IHL	15	1	7	8	36
1985-86—Buffalo Sabres		NHL	65	4	21	25	108
1986-87—Rochester Americans		AHL	18	0	0	0	77
1986-87—Buffalo Sabres		NHL	37	0	1	1	179
1987-88—Rochester Americans		AHL	7	0	1	1	33
1987-88—Buffalo Sabres (d)		NHL	27	1	1	2	91
1987-88—Edmonton Oilers		NHL	15	2	3	5	39
NHL TOTALS			144	7	26	33	417

(c)—October, 1982—Signed by Buffalo Sabres as a free agent.
(d)—February, 1988—Traded by Buffalo Sabres to Edmonton Oilers for Scott Metcalfe.

MICHAEL EAGLES

Center . . . 5'10" . . . 180 lbs. . . . Born, Susex, N.B., March 7, 1963 . . . Shoots left . . . (October, 1984)—Broken hand . . . (February 21, 1986)—Injured ribs at Minnesota.

Year	Team	League	Games	G.	A.	Pts.	Pen.
1979-80—Melville		SJHL	55	46	30	76	77
1980-81—Kitchener Rangers (c)		OHL	56	11	27	38	64
1981-82—Kitchener Rangers		OHL	62	26	40	66	148
1982-83—Kitchener Rangers		OHL	58	26	36	62	133
1982-83—Quebec Nordiques		NHL	2	0	0	0	2
1983-84—Fredericton Express		AHL	68	13	29	42	85
1984-85—Fredericton Express		AHL	36	4	20	24	80
1985-86—Quebec Nordiques		NHL	73	11	12	23	49
1986-87—Quebec Nordiques		NHL	73	13	19	32	55
1987-88—Quebec Nordiques (d)		NHL	76	10	10	20	74
NHL TOTALS			224	34	41	75	180

(c)—June, 1981—Drafted as underage junior by Quebec Nordiques in 1981 NHL entry draft. Fifth Nordiques pick, 116th overall, sixth round.
(d)—July, 1988—Traded by Quebec Nordiques to Chicago Black Hawks for Bob Mason.

DALLAS EAKINS

Defense . . . 6'1" . . . 180 lbs. . . . Born, Dade City, Fla., January 20, 1967 . . . Shoots left.

Year	Team	League	Games	G.	A.	Pts.	Pen.
1983-84—Peterborough Midgets		OHA	29	7	20	27	67
1984-85—Peterborough Petes (c)		OHL	48	0	8	8	96
1985-86—Peterborough Petes		OHL	60	6	16	22	134
1986-87—Peterborough Petes		OHL	54	3	11	14	145
1987-88—Peterborough Petes		OHL	64	11	27	38	129

(c)—June, 1985—Drafted as underage junior by Washington Capitals in 1985 NHL entry draft. Eleventh Capitals pick, 208th overall, 10th round.

MICHAEL EASTWOOD

Center . . . 6'2" . . . 190 lbs. . . . Born, Cornwall, Ont., July 1, 1967 . . . Shoots right . . . Also plays Right Wing.

Year	Team	League	Games	G.	A.	Pts.	Pen.
1986-87—Pembrooke Lumberkings (c)		OHA	....	...	....	....	....
1987-88—Western Michigan Univ.		CCHA	42	5	8	13	14

(c)—June, 1987—Drafted by Toronto Maple Leafs in 1987 NHL entry draft. Fifth Maple Leafs pick, 91st overall, fifth round.

MURRAY EAVES

Center . . . 5'10" . . . 185 lbs. . . . Born, Calgary, Alta., May 10, 1960 . . . Shoots right . . . Brother of Mike Eaves . . . (September, 1984)—Sprained ankle in training camp.

Year	Team	League	Games	G.	A.	Pts.	Pen.
1977-78—Windsor Spitfires		OMJHL	3	0	0	0	0
1978-79—University of Michigan		WCHA	23	12	22	34	14
1979-80—University of Michigan (a-c)		WCHA	33	36	49	85	34
1980-81—Winnipeg Jets		NHL	12	1	2	3	5
1980-81—Tulsa Oilers		CHL	59	24	34	58	59
1981-82—Tulsa Oilers		CHL	68	30	49	79	33
1981-82—Winnipeg Jets		NHL	2	0	0	0	0
1982-83—Winnipeg Jets		NHL	26	2	7	9	2
1982-83—Sherbrooke Jets		AHL	40	25	34	59	16
1983-84—Winnipeg Jets		NHL	2	0	0	0	0
1983-84—Sherbrooke Jets (a)		AHL	78	47	68	115	40
1984-85—Winnipeg Jets		NHL	3	0	3	3	0

Year	Team	League	Games	G.	A.	Pts.	Pen.
1984-85—Sherbrooke Jets		AHL	47	26	42	68	28
1985-86—Sherbrooke Canadiens		AHL	68	22	51	73	26
1985-86—Winnipeg Jets (d)		NHL	4	1	0	1	0
1986-87—Nova Scotia Oilers		AHL	76	26	38	64	46
1987-88—Detroit Red Wings (e)		NHL	7	0	1	1	2
1987-88—Adirondack Red Wings		AHL	65	39	54	93	65
NHL TOTALS			149	29	93	122	16

(c)—June, 1980—Drafted by Winnipeg Jets in 1980 NHL entry draft. Third Jets pick, 44th overall, third round.

(d)—July, 1986—Traded by Winnipeg Jets to Edmonton Oilers for future considerations.

(e)—July, 1987—Signed by Detroit Red Wings as a free agent.

PER-ERIK (Pelle) EKLUND

Center . . . 5'10" . . . 170 lbs. . . . Born, Stockholm, Sweden, March 22, 1963 . . . Shoots left . . . (October, 1985)—Named Sweden's Athlete of the Year for 1984. He was the second leading scorer in the elite league . . . (March, 1988)—Bruised hip.

Year	Team	League	Games	G.	A.	Pts.	Pen.
1983-84—Stockholm AIK (c)		Sweden	35	9	18	27	24
1984-85—Stockholm AIK		Sweden	35	16	33	49	10
1985-86—Philadelphia Flyers		NHL	70	15	51	66	12
1986-87—Philadelphia Flyers		NHL	72	14	41	55	2
1987-88—Philadelphia Flyers		NHL	71	10	32	42	12
NHL TOTALS			213	39	124	163	26

(c)—June, 1983—Drafted by Philadelphia Flyers in 1983 NHL entry draft. Seventh Flyers pick, 161st overall, eighth round.

DAVE ELLETT

Defense . . . 6'1" . . . 200 lbs. . . . Born, Cleveland, O., March 30, 1964 . . . Shoots left . . . Son of Dave Ellett Sr., who played for Cleveland Barons in AHL . . . (March 6, 1988)—Missed 10 games with a bruised thigh.

Year	Team	League	Games	G.	A.	Pts.	Pen.
1981-82—Ottawa Senators		CJOHL	50	9	35	44	..
1982-83—Bowling Green Univ. (c)		CCHA	40	4	13	17	34
1983-84—Bowling Green Univ.		CCHA	43	15	39	54	9
1984-85—Winnipeg Jets		NHL	80	11	27	38	85
1985-86—Winnipeg Jets		NHL	80	15	31	46	96
1986-87—Winnipeg Jets		NHL	78	13	31	44	53
1987-88—Winnipeg Jets		NHL	68	13	45	58	106
NHL TOTALS			306	52	134	186	340

(c)—June, 1982—Drafted as underage player by Winnipeg Jets in NHL entry draft. Third Jets pick, 75th overall, fourth round.

PAT ELYNUIK

Right Wing . . . 6' . . . 185 lbs. . . . Born, Foam Lake, Sask., October 30, 1967 . . . Shoots right.

Year	Team	League	Games	G.	A.	Pts.	Pen.
1983-84—Prince Albert Midget Raiders		SAHA	26	33	30	63	54
1984-85—Prince Albert Raiders		WHL	70	23	20	43	54
1985-86—Prince Albert Raiders (a-c)		WHL	68	53	53	106	62
1986-87—Prince Albert Raiders (a)		WHL	64	51	62	113	40
1987-88—Winnipeg Jets		NHL	13	1	3	4	12
1987-88—Moncton Golden Flames		AHL	30	11	18	29	35
NHL TOTALS			13	1	3	4	12

(c)—June 1986—Drafted as underage junior by Winnipeg Jets in 1986 NHL entry draft. First Jets pick, eighth overall, first round.

NELSON EMERSON

Center . . . 5'11" . . . 165 lbs. . . . Born, Hamilton, Ont., August 17, 1967 . . . Shoots right.

Year	Team	League	Games	G.	A.	Pts.	Pen.
1984-85—Stratford Cullitans Jr.B (c)		OHA	40	23	38	61	70
1985-86—Stratford Cullitans Jr.B		OHA	39	54	58	112	91
1986-87—Bowling Green Univ. (d)		CCHA	45	26	35	61	28
1987-88—Bowling Green Univ. (e)		CCHA	45	34	49	83	54

(c)—June, 1985—Drafted by St. Louis Blues in 1985 NHL entry draft. Second Blues pick, 44th overall, third round.

(d)—Named CCHA Rookie-of-the-Year.

(e)—Named second team All-America (West).

CRAIG T. ENDEAN

Right Wing . . . 6' . . . 170 lbs. . . . Born, Kamloops, B.C., April 13, 1968 . . . Shoots left . . . Also plays Center and Left Wing . . . Holds WHL career records for games played (351) and career points (529).

Year	Team	League	Games	G.	A.	Pts.	Pen.
1983-84—Seattle Breakers		WHL	67	16	6	22	14
1984-85—Seattle Breakers		WHL	69	37	60	97	28
1985-86—Seattle Thunderbirds (c)		WHL	70	58	70	128	34
1986-87—Regina Pats (b)		WHL	76	*69	77	*146	34
1986-87—Winnipeg Jets		NHL	2	0	1	1	0
1987-88—Regina Pats (d)		WHL	69	50	86	136	50
NHL TOTALS			2	0	1	1	0

(c)—June, 1986—Drafted as underage junior by Winnipeg Jets in 1986 NHL entry draft. Fifth Jets pick, 92nd overall, fifth round.

(d)—Won Brad Hornung Trophy (Most Sportsmanlike player).

T. JACOB ENEBAK

Left Wing . . . 6'2" . . . 200 lbs. . . . Born, Northfield, Minn., October 12, 1968 . . . Shoots left.

Year	Team	League	Games	G.	A.	Pts.	Pen.
1986-87—Northfield H.S. (c)		Minn. H.S.	22	40	26	66	....
1987-88—Univ. of Minnesota		WCHA	9	1	1	2	15

(c)—June, 1987—Drafted by Quebec Nordiques in 1987 NHL entry draft. Eighth Nordiques pick, 156th overall, eighth round.

JOHN ENGLISH

Defense . . . 6'2" . . . 185 lbs. . . . Born, Toronto, Ont., May 3, 1966 . . . Shoots right.

Year	Team	League	Games	G.	A.	Pts.	Pen.
1982-83—St. Michaels Jr.		..	34	2	10	12	92
1983-84—Sault Ste. Marie Greyhounds (c)		OHL	64	6	11	17	144
1984-85—Sault Ste. Marie Greyhounds		OHL	15	0	3	3	61
1984-85—Hamilton Steelhawks		OHL	41	2	22	24	105
1985-86—Hamilton Steelhawks (d)		OHL	12	2	10	12	57
1985-86—Ottawa 67's		OHL	43	8	28	36	120
1986-87—New Haven Nighthawks		AHL	3	0	0	0	6
1986-87—Flint Spirit		IHL	18	1	2	3	83
1987-88—Los Angeles Kings		NHL	3	1	3	4	4
1987-88—New Haven Nighthawks		AHL	65	4	22	26	236
NHL TOTALS			3	1	3	4	4

(c)—June, 1984—Drafted as underage junior by Los Angeles Kings in 1984 NHL entry draft. Third Kings pick, 48th overall, third round.

(d)—November, 1985—Traded by Hamilton Steelhawks to Ottawa 67's for a sixth round pick in 1986 OHL priority draft.

JIM ENNIS

Defense . . . 6' . . . 200 lbs. . . . Born, Edmonton, Alta., July 10, 1967 . . . Shoots left.

Year	Team	League	Games	G.	A.	Pts.	Pen.
1985-86—Boston University (c)		H. East	40	1	4	5	22
1986-87—Boston University		H. East	26	3	4	7	27
1987-88—Nova Scotia Oilers		AHL	59	8	12	20	102
1987-88—Edmonton Oilers		NHL	5	1	0	1	10
NHL TOTALS			5	1	0	1	10

(c)—June, 1986—Drafted by Edmonton Oilers in 1986 NHL entry draft. Sixth Oilers pick, 126th overall, sixth round.

BRYAN (BUTSY) ERICKSON

Right Wing . . . 5'9" . . . 170 lbs. . . . Born, Roseau, Minn., March 7, 1960 . . . Shoots right . . . (January, 1983)—Fractured wrist . . . (October, 1984)—Broken thumb . . . (October 23, 1986)—Injured cartilage in left knee at New Jersey . . . (March, 1988)—Separated shoulder.

Year	Team	League	Games	G.	A.	Pts.	Pen.
1979-80—University of Minnesota		WCHA	23	10	15	25	14
1980-81—University of Minnesota		WCHA	44	39	47	86	30
1981-82—University of Minnesota (b)		WCHA	35	25	20	45	20
1982-83—University of Minnesota (a-c)		WCHA	42	35	47	82	30
1982-83—Hershey Bears		AHL	1	0	1	1	0
1983-84—Hershey Bears		AHL	31	16	12	28	11

Year	Team	League	Games	G.	A.	Pts.	Pen.
1983-84—Washington Capitals		NHL	45	12	17	29	16
1984-85—Binghamton Whalers		AHL	13	6	11	17	8
1984-85—Washington Capitals		NHL	57	15	13	28	23
1985-86—Binghamton Whalers (d)		AHL	7	5	3	8	2
1985-86—New Haven Nighthawks		AHL	14	8	3	11	11
1985-86—Los Angeles Kings		NHL	55	20	23	43	36
1986-87—Los Angeles Kings		NHL	68	20	30	50	26
1987-88—Los Angeles Kings (e)		NHL	42	6	15	21	20
1987-88—Pittsburgh Penguins		NHL	11	1	4	5	0
1987-88—New Haven Nighthawks		AHL	3	0	0	0	0
NHL TOTALS			278	74	102	176	121

(c)—April, 1983—Signed by Washington Capitals as a free agent.
(d)—October, 1985—Traded by Washington Capitals to Los Angeles Kings for Bruce Shoebottom.
(e)—February, 1988—Traded by Los Angeles Kings to Pittsburgh Penguins for Chris Kontos and a sixth-round 1988 draft pick (Micah Aivazoff).

JAN ERIXON

Right Wing . . . 6' . . . 190 lbs. . . . Born, Skelleftea, Sweden, July 8, 1962 . . . Shoots left . . . (February, 1985)—Bruised foot . . . (December 8, 1985)—Bruised leg vs. Philadelphia . . . (January 12, 1986)—Fractured tibia vs. St. Louis . . . (December, 1986)—Hip injury.

Year	Team	League	Games	G.	A.	Pts.	Pen.
1979-80—Skelleftea AIK		Sweden	32	9	3	12	22
1980-81—Skelleftea AIK (c)		Sweden	32	6	6	12	4
1981-82—Skelleftea AIK		Sweden	30	7	7	14	26
1982-83—Skelleftea AIK		Sweden	36	10	18	28	..
1983-84—New York Rangers		NHL	75	5	25	30	16
1984-85—New York Rangers		NHL	66	7	22	29	33
1985-86—New York Rangers		NHL	31	2	17	19	4
1986-87—New York Rangers		NHL	68	8	18	26	24
1987-88—New York Rangers		NHL	70	7	19	26	33
NHL TOTALS			310	29	101	130	110

(c)—June, 1981—Drafted by New York Rangers in 1981 NHL entry draft. Second Rangers pick, 30th overall, second round.

BOB ERREY

Left Wing . . . 5'10" . . . 185 lbs. . . . Born, Montreal, Que., September 21, 1964 . . . Shoots left . . . (March 18, 1987)—Sprained right knee at St. Louis . . . (October, 1987)—Broken right wrist.

Year	Team	League	Games	G.	A.	Pts.	Pen.
1981-82—Peterborough Petes		OHL	68	29	31	60	39
1982-83—Peterborough Petes (a-c)		OHL	67	53	47	100	74
1983-84—Pittsburgh Penguins		NHL	65	9	13	22	29
1984-85—Baltimore Skipjacks		AHL	59	17	24	41	14
1984-85—Pittsburgh Penguins		NHL	16	0	2	2	7
1985-86—Baltimore Skipjacks		AHL	18	8	7	15	28
1985-86—Pittsburgh Penguins		NHL	37	11	6	17	8
1986-87—Pittsburgh Penguins		NHL	72	16	18	34	46
1987-88—Pittsburgh Penguins		NHL	17	3	6	9	18
NHL TOTALS			207	39	45	84	108

(c)—June, 1983—Drafted as underage junior by Pittsburgh Penguins in 1983 NHL entry draft. First Penguins pick, 15th overall, first round.

LEONARD ESAU

Defense . . . 6'3" . . . 190 lbs. . . . Born, Meadow Lake, Sask., March 16, 1968 . . . Shoots right . . . Enrolled at St. Cloud State.

Year	Team	League	Games	G.	A.	Pts.	Pen.
1986-87—Humboldt Broncos		SJHL	57	4	26	30	278
1987-88—Humboldt Broncos (c)		SJHL	57	16	37	53	229

(c)—June, 1988—Drafted by Toronto Maple Leafs in 1988 NHL entry draft. Fifth Maple Leafs pick, 86th overall, fifth round.

DAVID ESPE

Defense . . . 6' . . . 185 lbs. . . . Born, St. Paul, Minn., November 3, 1966 . . . Shoots left.

Year	Team	League	Games	G.	A.	Pts.	Pen.
1984-85—White Bear Lake H.S. (c)		Minn. H.S.	21	11	16	27	30
1985-86—Univ. of Minnesota		WCHA	27	0	6	6	18

Year	Team	League	Games	G.	A.	Pts.	Pen.
1986-87—Univ. of Minnesota		WCHA	45	4	8	12	28
1987-88—Univ. of Minnesota		WCHA	43	4	10	14	68

(c)—June, 1985—Drafted by Quebec Nordiques in 1985 NHL entry draft. Fifth Nordiques pick, 78th overall, fourth round.

DARYL THOMAS EVANS

Left Wing . . . 5'9" . . . 180 lbs. . . . Born, Toronto, Ont., January 12, 1961 . . . Shoots left . . . (1981-82)—Broken wrist while playing for New Haven Nighthawks . . . Set an AHL record with goals in 14 straight games in 1986-87 . . . (February, 1988)—Injured left knee.

Year	Team	League	Games	G.	A.	Pts.	Pen.
1977-78—Senaca Nats		OHA Jr. B	40	25	35	60	50
1978-79—Niagara Falls Flyers		OMJHL	65	38	26	64	110
1979-80—Niagara Falls Flyers (c)		OMJHL	63	43	52	95	47
1980-81—Niagara Falls Flyers (d)		OHL	5	3	4	7	11
1980-81—Brantford Alexanders (a)		OHL	58	58	54	112	50
1980-81—Saginaw Gears		IHL	3	3	2	5	0
1981-82—New Haven Nighthawks		AHL	41	14	14	28	10
1981-82—Los Angeles Kings		NHL	14	2	6	8	2
1982-83—Los Angeles Kings		NHL	80	18	22	40	21
1983-84—New Haven Nighthawks (b)		AHL	69	51	35	86	14
1983-84—Los Angeles Kings		NHL	4	0	1	1	0
1984-85—Los Angeles Kings		NHL	7	1	0	1	2
1984-85—New Haven Nighthawks		AHL	59	22	24	46	12
1985-86—Washington Capitals (e)		NHL	6	0	1	1	0
1985-86—Binghamton Whalers		AHL	69	40	52	92	50
1986-87—Newmarket Saints		AHL	74	27	46	73	17
1986-87—Toronto Maple Leafs		NHL	2	1	0	1	0
1987-88—Newmarket Saints		AHL	57	29	36	65	10
NHL TOTALS			113	22	30	52	25

(c)—June, 1980—Drafted as underage junior by Los Angeles Kings in 1980 NHL entry draft. Eleventh Kings pick, 178th overall, ninth round.

(d)—October, 1980—Traded by Niagara Falls Flyers to Brantford Alexanders for Venci Sebek.

(e)—September, 1985—Traded by Los Angeles Kings to Washington Capitals for Glen Currie.

DOUG EVANS

Center . . . 5'9" . . . 178 lbs. . . . Born, Peterborough, Ont., June 2, 1963 . . . Shoots left . . . (September, 1987)—Separated left shoulder during St. Louis training camp.

Year	Team	League	Games	G.	A.	Pts.	Pen.
1980-81—Peterborough Petes		OHL	51	9	24	33	139
1981-82—Peterborough Petes		OHL	56	17	49	66	176
1982-83—Peterborough Petes		OHL	65	31	55	86	165
1983-84—Peterborough Petes		OHL	61	45	79	124	98
1984-85—Peoria Prancers (c)		IHL	81	36	61	97	189
1985-86—St. Louis Blues		NHL	13	1	0	1	2
1985-86—Peoria Rivermen (a)		IHL	69	46	51	97	179
1986-87—Peoria Rivermen		IHL	18	10	15	25	39
1986-87—St. Louis Blues		NHL	53	3	13	16	91
1987-88—Peoria Rivermen		IHL	11	4	16	20	64
1987-88—St. Louis Blues		NHL	41	5	7	12	49
NHL TOTALS			107	9	20	29	142

(c)—June, 1985—Signed by St. Louis Blues as a free agent.

SHAWN EVANS

Defense . . . 6'3" . . . 195 lbs. . . . Born, Kingston, Ont., September 7, 1965 . . . Shoots left . . . Cousin of Dennis Kearns (Vancouver, 1970s).

Year	Team	League	Games	G.	A.	Pts.	Pen.
1981-82—Kitchener Rangers MW Jr. B		OHA	21	9	13	22	55
1982-83—Peterborough Petes (c)		OHL	58	7	41	48	116
1983-84—Peterborough Petes (b)		OHL	67	21	88	109	116
1984-85—Peterborough Petes		OHL	66	16	83	99	78
1985-86—Peoria Rivermen		IHL	55	8	26	34	36
1985-86—St. Louis Blues (d)		NHL	7	0	0	0	2
1986-87—Nova Scotia Oilers (e)		AHL	55	7	28	35	29
1987-88—Nova Scotia Oilers (f)		AHL	79	8	62	70	109
NHL TOTALS			7	0	0	0	2

(c)—June, 1983—Drafted by New Jersey Devils as underage junior in 1983 NHL entry draft. Second Devils pick, 24th overall, second round.

(d)—September, 1985—Traded with a fifth round 1986 draft pick (Mike Wolak) by New Jersey Devils to St. Louis Blues for Mark Johnson.

(e)—October, 1986—Traded by St. Louis Blues to Edmonton Oilers for Todd Ewen.

(f)—July, 1988—Traded by Edmonton Oilers to New Jersey Devils for future considerations.

DEAN EVASON

Center . . . 5'10" . . . 175 lbs. . . . Born, Flin Flon, Man., August 22, 1964 . . . Shoots left . . . Brother of Dan Evason (1984-85 assistant coach of Brandon Wheat Kings).

Year	Team	League	Games	G.	A.	Pts.	Pen.
1980-81—Spokane Flyers		WHL	3	1	1	2	0
1981-82—Kamloops Junior Oilers (c-d)		WHL	70	29	69	98	112
1982-83—Kamloops Junior Oilers		WHL	70	71	93	164	102
1983-84—Kamloops Junior Oilers (a-e)		WHL	57	49	88	137	89
1983-84—Washington Capitals		NHL	2	0	0	0	2
1984-85—Binghamton Whalers		AHL	65	27	49	76	38
1984-85—Washington Capitals (f)		NHL	15	3	4	7	2
1984-85—Hartford Whalers		NHL	2	0	0	0	0
1985-86—Binghamton Whalers		AHL	26	9	17	26	29
1985-86—Hartford Whalers		NHL	55	20	28	48	65
1986-87—Hartford Whalers		NHL	80	22	37	59	67
1987-88—Hartford Whalers		NHL	77	10	18	28	117
NHL TOTALS			231	55	87	142	253

(c)—December, 1981—Drafted by Kamloops Junior Oilers in WHL disperal draft of players of Spokane Flyers.

(d)—June, 1982—Drafted as underage junior by Washington Capitals in 1982 NHL entry draft. Third Capitals pick, 89th overall, fifth round.

(e)—Shared WHL playoff scoring with Taylor Hall, each had 21 goals.

(f)—March, 1985—Traded with Peter Sidorkiewicz by Washington Capitals to Hartford Whalers for David A. Jensen.

DEAN EWEN

Left Wing . . . 6'1" . . . 185 lbs. . . . Born, St. Albert, Alta., February 28, 1969 . . . Shoots left . . . Brother of Todd Ewen . . . (November 1, 1987)—Suspended 12 games by WHL for fighting.

Year	Team	League	Games	G.	A.	Pts.	Pen.
1984-85—St. Albert Saints		AJHL	30	2	4	6	25
1985-86—New Westminster Bruins		WHL	61	7	15	22	154
1986-87—Spokane Chiefs (c)		WHL	66	8	14	22	236
1987-88—Spokane Chiefs		WHL	49	12	12	24	302

(c)—June, 1987—Drafted as underage junior by New York Islanders in 1987 NHL entry draft. Third Islanders pick, 55th overall, third round.

TODD EWEN

Right Wing . . . 6'2" . . . 185 lbs. . . . Born, Saskatoon, Sask., March 26, 1966 . . . Shoots right . . . Brother of Dean Ewen . . . (October, 1987)—Sprained ankle . . . (November 5, 1987)—Suspended one game by St. Louis Blues for a curfew violation . . . (January, 1988)—Suspended one game by NHL for his third game misconduct of the season.

Year	Team	League	Games	G.	A.	Pts.	Pen.
1982-83—Vernon Lakers		BCJHL	42	20	23	53	195
1982-83—Kamloops Junior Oilers		WHL	3	0	0	0	2
1983-84—New Westminster Bruins (c)		WHL	68	11	13	24	176
1984-85—New Westminster Bruins		WHL	56	11	20	31	304
1985-86—New Westminster Bruins		WHL	60	28	24	52	289
1985-86—Maine Mariners (d)		AHL	....	...	....	....	....
1986-87—Peoria Rivermen		IHL	16	3	3	6	110
1986-87—St. Louis Blues (e)		NHL	23	2	0	2	84
1987-88—St. Louis Blues		NHL	64	4	2	6	227
NHL TOTALS			87	6	2	8	311

(c)—June, 1984—Drafted as underage junior by Edmonton Oilers in 1984 NHL entry draft. Eighth Oilers pick, 168th overall, eighth round.

(d)—No regular season record. Played three playoff games.

(e)—October, 1986—Traded by Edmonton Oilers to St. Louis Blues for Shawn Evans.

SEAN FABIAN

Defense . . . 6'1" . . . 205 lbs. . . . Born, St. Paul, Minn., May 11, 1969 . . . Shoots right . . . Son of Bill Fabian, former hockey player at University of Minnesota.

Year	Team	League	Games	G.	A.	Pts.	Pen.
1985-86—Hill Murray H.S.		Minn. H.S.	26	6	13	19	....
1986-87—Hill Murray H.S. (c)		Minn. H.S.	26	7	20	27	....
1987-88—Univ. of Minnesota		WCHA	10	0	1	1	11

(c)—June, 1987—Drafted by Vancouver Canucks in 1987 NHL entry draft. Fourth Canucks pick, 87th overall, fifth round.

TED FAUSS

Defense . . . 6'2" . . . 218 lbs. . . . Born, Clinton, N.Y., June 30, 1961 . . . Shoots left.

Year	Team	League	Games	G.	A.	Pts.	Pen.
1979-80—Clarkson College		ECAC	34	2	4	6	36
1980-81—Clarkson College		ECAC	37	0	5	5	56
1981-82—Clarkson College		ECAC	35	3	6	9	79
1982-83—Clarkson College (c)		ECAC	25	4	6	10	60
1982-83—Nova Scotia Voyageurs		AHL	5	0	1	1	11
1983-84—Nova Scotia Voyageurs		AHL	71	4	11	15	123
1984-85—Sherbrooke Canadiens		AHL	77	1	9	10	62
1985-86—Did not play		....	..	..	..	..	..
1986-87—Newmarket Saints (d)		AHL	59	0	5	5	81
1986-87—Toronto Maple Leafs		NHL	15	0	1	1	11
1987-88—Toronto Maple Leafs		NHL	13	0	1	1	4
1987-88—Newmarket Saints		AHL	49	0	11	11	86
NHL TOTALS			28	0	2	2	15

(c)—March, 1983—Signed by Montreal Canadiens as a free agent.
(d)—July, 1986—Signed by Toronto Maple Leafs as a free agent.

GLEN FEATHERSTONE

Defense . . . 6'4" . . . 209 lbs. . . . Born, Toronto, Ont., July 8, 1968 . . . Shoots left . . . Father (Roy Featherstone) played professional soccer in Ireland.

Year	Team	League	Games	G.	A.	Pts.	Pen.
1984-85—Toronto National Midget		MTHL	45	7	24	31	94
1985-86—Windsor Spitfires (c)		OHL	49	0	6	6	135
1986-87—Windsor Spitfires		OHL	47	6	11	17	154
1987-88—Windsor Spitfires		OHL	53	7	27	34	201

(c)—June, 1986—Drafted as underage junior by St. Louis Blues in 1986 NHL entry draft. Fourth Blues pick, 73rd overall, fourth round.

BERNARD ALLAN FEDERKO

Center . . . 6' . . . 185 lbs. . . . Born, Foam Lake, Sask., May 12, 1956 . . . Shoots left . . . Brother of Ken Federko (Salt Lake—CHL 1980-82) . . . Missed final games of 1978-79 season with broken right wrist . . . (December 29, 1981)—Tore rib cartilage vs. Hartford . . . (November 20, 1984)—Bruised left ankle at Vancouver . . . (January, 1985)—Bruised lung and ribs . . . All-Time leading St. Louis Blues career goal scorer . . . (January 9, 1987)—Broken jaw when struck by teammate Mark Hunter's stick at Edmonton.

Year	Team	League	Games	G.	A.	Pts.	Pen.
1973-74—Saskatoon Blades		WCHL	68	22	28	50	19
1974-75—Saskatoon Blades (c)		WCHL	66	39	68	107	30
1975-76—Saskatoon Blades (a-d-e-f)		WCHL	72	72	*115	*187	108
1976-77—Kansas City Blues (b-g)		CHL	42	30	39	69	41
1976-77—St. Louis Blues		NHL	31	14	9	23	15
1977-78—St. Louis Blues		NHL	72	17	24	41	27
1978-79—St. Louis Blues		NHL	74	31	64	95	14
1979-80—St. Louis Blues		NHL	79	38	56	94	24
1980-81—St. Louis Blues		NHL	78	31	73	104	47
1981-82—St. Louis Blues		NHL	74	30	62	92	70
1982-83—St. Louis Blues		NHL	75	24	60	84	24
1983-84—St. Louis Blues		NHL	79	41	66	107	43
1984-85—St. Louis Blues		NHL	76	30	73	103	27
1985-86—St. Louis Blues		NHL	80	34	68	102	34
1986-87—St. Louis Blues		NHL	64	20	52	72	32
1987-88—St. Louis Blues		NHL	79	20	69	89	52
NHL TOTALS			861	330	676	1006	409

(c)—Led in goals (15) during playoffs.
(d)—Named Most Valuable Player in WCHL.
(e)—Drafted from Saskatoon Blades by St. Louis Blues in first round of 1976 amateur draft.
(f)—Led in assists (27) and points (45) during playoffs.
(g)—CHL Rookie-of-the-Year.

BRENT FEDYK

Right Wing . . . 6' . . . 180 lbs. . . . Born, Yorkton, Sask., March 8, 1967 . . . Shoots right . . . (Septmeber, 1985)—Strained hip in Detroit training camp and missed three weeks of WHL season.

Year	Team	League	Games	G.	A.	Pts.	Pen.
1982-83—Regina Pats	WHL	1	0	0	0	0
1983-84—Regina Pats	WHL	63	15	28	43	30
1984-85—Regina Pats (c)	WHL	66	35	35	70	48
1985-86—Regina Pats (b)	WHL	50	43	34	77	47
1986-87—Portland Winter Hawks	WHL	36	19	21	40	24
1987-88—Detroit Red Wings	NHL	2	0	1	1	2
1987-88—Adirondack Red Wings	AHL	34	9	11	20	22
NHL TOTALS		2	0	1	1	2

(c)—June, 1985—Drafted as underage junior by Detroit Red Wings in 1985 NHL entry draft. First Red Wings pick, eighth overall, first round.

CHRIS FELIX

Defense . . . 5'11" . . . 185 lbs. . . . Born, Bramalea, Ont., May 27, 1964 . . . Shoots right.

Year	Team	League	Games	G.	A.	Pts.	Pen.
1982-83—Sault Ste. Marie Greyhounds	OHL	68	16	57	73	39
1983-84—Sault Ste. Marie Greyhounds	OHL	70	32	61	93	75
1984-85—Sault Ste. Marie Greyhounds	OHL	66	29	72	101	89
1985-86—Canadian National Team	Int'l	73	7	33	40	33
1986-87—Canadian National Team (c)	Int'l	78	14	38	52	36
1987-88—Canadian Olympic Team	Int'l	68	7	27	34	68
1987-88—Fort Wayne Komets	IHL	19	5	17	22	24

(c)—March, 1987—Signed by Washington Capitals as a free agent.

PAUL FENTON

Center . . . 5'11" . . . 180 lbs. . . . Born, Springfield, Mass., December 22, 1959 . . . Shoots left.

Year	Team	League	Games	G.	A.	Pts.	Pen.
1979-80—Boston University	ECAC	28	12	21	33	18
1980-81—Boston University	ECAC	7	4	4	8	0
1981-82—Boston University	ECAC	28	20	13	33	28
1982-83—Peoria Prancers (b-c)	IHL	82	60	51	111	53
1982-83—Colorado Flames	CHL	1	0	1	1	0
1983-84—Binghamton Whalers (d)	AHL	78	41	24	65	67
1984-85—Binghamton Whalers	AHL	45	26	21	47	18
1984-85—Hartford Whalers	NHL	33	7	5	12	10
1985-86—Hartford Whalers	NHL	1	0	0	0	0
1985-86—Binghamton Whalers (a-e)	AHL	75	53	35	88	87
1986-87—New York Rangers (f)	NHL	8	0	0	0	2
1986-87—New Haven Nighthawks (b)	AHL	70	37	38	75	45
1987-88—New Haven Nighthawks	AHL	5	11	5	16	9
1987-88—Los Angeles Kings (g)	NHL	71	20	23	43	46
NHL TOTALS		113	27	28	55	58

(c)—Won Ken McKenzie Trophy (Top U.S. born IHL Rookie)
(d)—October, 1983—Signed by Hartford Whalers as a free agent.
(e)—July, 1986—Released by Hartford Whalers.
(f)—September, 1986—Signed by New York Rangers as a free agent.
(g)—October, 1988—Acquired by Los Angeles Kings on waivers from New York Rangers.

WILLIAM (ERIC) FENTON

Center . . . 6'2" . . . 190 lbs. . . . Born, Troy, N.Y., July 17, 1969 . . . Shoots right . . . Also plays Right Wing.

Year	Team	League	Games	G.	A.	Pts.	Pen.
1986-87—North Yarmouth Acad.	Maine H.S.	..	30	23	53	..
1987-88—North Yarmouth Acad. (c)	Maine H.S.	..	37	33	70	..

(c)—June, 1988—Drafted by New York Rangers in 1988 NHL entry draft. Tenth Rangers pick, 202nd overall, 10th round.

DAVE ALAN FENYVES

Defense . . . 5'10" . . . 188 lbs. . . . Born, Dunnville, Ont., April 29, 1960 . . . Shoots left . . . (October, 1977)—Separated shoulder . . . (December 26, 1985)—Missed five games with a concussion vs. N.Y. Rangers.

Year	Team	League	Games	G.	A.	Pts.	Pen.
1977-78—Peterborough Petes	OMJHL	59	3	12	15	36
1978-79—Peterborough Petes	OMJHL	66	2	23	25	122
1979-80—Peterborough Petes (c)	OMJHL	66	9	36	45	92
1980-81—Rochester Americans	AHL	77	6	16	22	146
1981-82—Rochester Americans	AHL	73	3	14	17	68
1982-83—Rochester Americans	AHL	51	2	19	21	45

Year	Team	League	Games	G.	A.	Pts.	Pen.
1982-83—Buffalo Sabres		NHL	24	0	8	8	14
1983-84—Buffalo Sabres		NHL	10	0	4	4	9
1983-84—Rochester Americans		AHL	70	3	16	19	55
1984-85—Rochester Americans		AHL	9	0	3	3	8
1984-85—Buffalo Sabres		NHL	60	1	8	9	27
1985-86—Buffalo Sabres		NHL	47	0	7	7	37
1986-87—Rochester Americans (b-d)		AHL	71	6	16	22	57
1986-87—Buffalo Sabres		NHL	7	1	0	1	0
1987-88—Philadelphia Flyers (e)		NHL	5	0	0	0	0
1987-88—Hershey Bears		AHL	75	11	40	51	47
NHL TOTALS			153	2	27	29	87

(c)—October, 1979—Signed by Buffalo Sabres as a free agent.

(d)—Won Jack Butterfield Trophy (AHL Playoff MVP).

(e)—October, 1987—Selected by Philadelphia Flyers during 1988 NHL waiver draft as compensation for Buffalo Sabres drafting of Ed Hospodar.

TOM JOSEPH FERGUS

Center ... 6' ... 176 lbs. ... Born, Chicago, Ill., June 16, 1962 ... Shoots left ... (January 20, 1982)—Tore ligaments in left knee at Pittsburgh ... (February, 1984)—Damaged knee ligaments ... (March, 1987)—Missed 23 games with a viral infection ... (November, 1987)—Pulled groin ... (March, 1988)—Bruised ribs.

Year	Team	League	Games	G.	A.	Pts.	Pen.
1979-80—Peterborough Petes (c)		OMJHL	63	8	6	14	14
1980-81—Peterborough Petes		OMJHL	63	43	45	88	33
1981-82—Boston Bruins		NHL	61	15	24	39	12
1982-83—Boston Bruins		NHL	80	28	35	63	39
1983-84—Boston Bruins		NHL	69	25	36	61	12
1984-85—Boston Bruins		NHL	79	30	43	73	75
1985-86—Toronto Maple Leafs (d)		NHL	78	31	42	73	64
1986-87—Newmarket Saints		AHL	1	0	1	1	0
1986-87—Toronto Maple Leafs		NHL	57	21	28	49	57
1987-88—Toronto Maple Leafs		NHL	63	19	31	50	81
NHL TOTALS			487	169	239	408	340

(c)—June, 1980—Drafted as underage junior by Boston Bruins in 1980 NHL entry draft. Second Bruins pick, 60th overall, third round.

(d)—September, 1985—Traded by Boston Bruins to Toronto Maple Leafs for Bill Derlago.

MARK FERNER

Defense ... 6' ... 170 lbs. ... Born, Regina, Sask., September 5, 1965 ... Shoots left ... (March, 1986)—Broken foot.

Year	Team	League	Games	G.	A.	Pts.	Pen.
1982-83—Kamloops Junior Oilers (c)		WHL	69	6	15	21	81
1983-84—Kamloops Junior Oilers		WHL	72	9	30	39	162
1984-85—Kamloops Blazers (a)		WHL	69	15	39	54	91
1985-86—Rochester Americans		AHL	63	3	14	17	87
1986-87—Buffalo Sabres		NHL	13	0	3	3	9
1986-87—Rochester Americans		AHL	54	0	12	12	157
1987-88—Rochester Americans		AHL	69	1	25	26	165
NHL TOTALS			13	0	3	3	9

(c)—June, 1983—Drafted as underage junior by Buffalo Sabres in 1983 NHL entry draft. Twelfth Sabres pick, 194th overall, 10th round.

JAMES FERNHOLZ

Right Wing ... 6'1" ... 200 lbs. ... Born, Minneapolis, Minn., March 16, 1969 ... Shoots right ... Also plays Defense.

Year	Team	League	Games	G.	A.	Pts.	Pen.
1985-86—White Bear Lake H.S.		Minn. H.S.	24	12	23	35	....
1986-87—White Bear Lake H.S. (c)		Minn. H.S.	20	13	17	30	....
1987-88—Univ. of Vermont		ECAC	23	3	5	8	12

(c)—June, 1987—Drafted by Winnipeg Jets in 1987 NHL entry draft. Ninth Jets pick, 184th overall, ninth round.

RAY FERRARO

Center ... 5'10" ... 180 lbs. ... Born, Trail, B.C., August 23, 1964 ... Shoots left ... (1983-84) Set WHL record for most goals in a season (108), most power-play goals (43) and most three-goal games (15) ... (December 7, 1985)—Separated shoulder vs. Boston and missed four games.

Year	Team	League	Games	G.	A.	Pts.	Pen.
1981-82—Penticton (c)	BCJHL	48	65	70	135	50
1982-83—Portland Winter Hawks	WHL	50	41	49	90	39
1983-84—Brandon Wheat Kings (a-d-e-f)	WHL	72	*108	84	*192	84
1984-85—Binghamton Whalers	AHL	37	20	13	33	29
1984-85—Hartford Whalers	NHL	44	11	17	28	40
1985-86—Hartford Whalers	NHL	76	30	47	77	57
1986-87—Hartford Whalers	NHL	80	27	32	59	42
1987-88—Hartford Whalers	NHL	68	21	29	50	81
NHL TOTALS			268	89	125	214	220

(c)—June, 1982—Drafted as underage junior by Hartford Whalers in 1982 NHL entry draft. Fifth Whalers pick, 88th overall, fifth round.
(d)—Named WHL's Most Valuable Player.
(e)—Won Bob Brownridge Memorial Trophy (Top WHL Scorer).
(f)—WHL's Molson Player of the Year.

BRIAN P. FERREIRA

Right Wing . . . 6' . . . 180 lbs. . . . Born, Falmouth, Mass., February 1, 1968 . . . Shoots right . . . Also plays Center.

Year	Team	League	Games	G.	A.	Pts.	Pen.
1984-85—Falmouth H.S.	Mass.	24	31	32	63	....
1985-86—Falmouth H.S. (c)	Mass.	22	37	43	80	12
1986-87—R.P.I.	ECAC	30	19	17	36	24
1987-88—R.P.I.	ECAC	32	18	19	37	48

(c)—June, 1986—Drafted by Boston Bruins in 1986 NHL entry draft. Seventh Bruins pick, 160th overall, eighth round.

JEFF FINLEY

Defense . . . 6'2" . . . 185 lbs. . . . Born, Edmonton, Alta., April 14, 1967 . . . Shoots left.

Year	Team	League	Games	G.	A.	Pts.	Pen.
1983-84—Portland Winter Hawks	WHL	5	0	0	0	0
1983-84—Summarland Buckeroos	BCJHL	49	0	21	21	14
1984-85—Portland Winter Hawks (c)	WHL	69	6	44	50	57
1985-86—Portland Winter Hawks	WHL	70	11	59	70	83
1986-87—Portland Winter Hawks	WHL	72	13	53	66	113
1987-88—Springfield Indians	AHL	52	5	18	23	50
1987-88—New York Islanders	NHL	10	0	5	5	15
NHL TOTALS			10	0	5	5	15

(c)—June, 1985—Drafted as underage junior by New York Islanders in 1985 NHL entry draft. Fourth Islanders pick, 55th overall, third round.

STEVEN FINN

Defense . . . 6' . . . 190 lbs. . . . Born, Laval, Que., August 20, 1966 . . . Shoots left.

Year	Team	League	Games	G.	A.	Pts.	Pen.
1982-83—Laval Voisins	QHL	69	7	30	37	108
1983-84—Laval Voisins (c)	QHL	68	7	39	46	159
1984-85—Laval Voisins	QHL	61	20	33	53	169
1984-85—Fredericton Express	AHL	4	0	0	0	14
1985-86—Laval Titans	QHL	29	4	15	19	111
1985-86—Quebec Nordiques	NHL	17	0	1	1	28
1986-87—Fredericton Express	AHL	38	7	19	26	73
1986-87—Quebec Nordiques	NHL	36	2	5	7	40
1987-88—Quebec Nordiques	NHL	75	3	7	10	198
NHL TOTALS			128	5	13	18	266

(c)—June, 1984—Drafted as underage junior by Quebec Nordiques in 1984 NHL entry draft. Third Nordiques pick, 57th overall, third round.

PETER FIORENTINO

Defense . . . 6'1" . . . 200 lbs. . . . Born, Niagara Falls, Ont., December 22, 1968 . . . Shoots right.

Year	Team	League	Games	G.	A.	Pts.	Pen.
1984-85—Niagara Falls Junior 'B'	OHA	38	7	10	17	149
1985-86—Sault Ste. Marie Greyhounds	OHL	58	1	6	7	87
1986-87—Sault Ste. Marie Greyhounds	OHL	64	1	12	13	187
1987-88—Sault Ste. Marie Greyhounds (c)	OHL	65	5	27	32	252

(c)—June, 1988—Drafted by New York Rangers in 1988 NHL entry draft. Eleventh Rangers pick, 215th overall, 11th round.

CRAIG FISHER

Center . . . 6'1" . . . 170 lbs. . . . Born, Oshawa, Ont., June 30, 1970 . . . Shoots left . . . (October, 1987)—Concussion.

Year	Team	League	Games	G.	A.	Pts.	Pen.
1986-87—Oshawa Legionaires Jr. B		OHA	34	22	26	48	18
1987-88—Oshawa Legionaires Jr. B (c)		OHA	36	42	34	76	48

(c)—June, 1988—Drafted by Philadelphia Flyers in 1988 NHL entry draft. Third Flyers pick, 56th overall, third round.

THOMAS FITZGERALD

Center . . . 6'1" . . . 190 lbs. . . . Born, Melrose, Mass., August 28, 1968 . . . Shoots right . . . Also plays Right Wing.

Year	Team	League	Games	G.	A.	Pts.	Pen.
1984-85—Austin Prep.		Mass.	18	20	21	41	....
1985-86—Austin Prep. (c)		Mass.	24	35	38	73	....
1986-87—Providence College		H. East	15	2	0	2	2
1987-88—Providence College		H. East	36	19	15	34	50

(c)—June, 1986—Drafted by New York Islanders in 1986 NHL entry draft. First Islanders pick, 17th overall, first round.

ROSS FITZPATRICK

Left Wing . . . 6'1" . . . 190 lbs. . . . Born, Penticton, B.C., October 7, 1960 . . . Shoots left . . . (December, 1982)—Broke hand vs. Hershey in AHL game . . . (January 19, 1985)—Surgery for shoulder separation suffered in AHL game vs. Sherbrooke . . . (January, 1987)—Knee surgery . . . (September, 1987)—Knee surgery.

Year	Team	League	Games	G.	A.	Pts.	Pen.
1979-80—Univ. of Western Mich. (c)		CCHA	34	26	33	59	22
1980-81—Univ. of Western Mich. (a)		CCHA	36	28	43	71	22
1981-82—Univ. of Western Mich.		CCHA	33	30	28	58	34
1982-83—Maine Mariners		AHL	66	29	28	57	32
1982-83—Philadelphia Flyers		NHL	1	0	0	0	0
1983-84—Springfield Indians		AHL	45	33	30	63	28
1983-84—Philadelphia Flyers		NHL	12	4	2	6	0
1984-85—Hershey Bears		AHL	35	26	15	41	8
1984-85—Philadelphia Flyers		NHL	5	1	0	1	0
1985-86—Philadelphia Flyers		NHL	2	0	0	0	0
1985-86—Hershey Bears (b)		AHL	77	50	47	97	28
1986-87—Hershey Bears		AHL	66	45	40	85	34
1987-88—Hershey Bears		AHL	35	14	17	31	12
NHL TOTALS			20	5	2	7	0

(c)—June, 1980—Drafted by Philadelphia Flyers in 1980 NHL entry draft. Seventh Flyers pick, 147th overall, seventh round.

JEFFREY FLAHERTY

Center . . . 6'3" . . . 210 lbs. . . . Born, Boston, Mass., July 16, 1968 . . . Shoots right . . . Also plays Right Wing . . . (February, 1988)—Suspended three games for fighting.

Year	Team	League	Games	G.	A.	Pts.	Pen.
1984-85—Weymouth North H.S.		Mass.	....	19	18	37	....
1985-86—Weymouth North H.S. (c)		Mass.	19	27	23	50	12
1986-87—University of Lowell		H. East	28	4	5	9	37
1987-88—University of Lowell		H. East	34	27	12	39	126

(c)—June, 1986—Drafted by Boston Bruins in 1986 NHL entry draft. Eighth Bruins pick, 181st overall, ninth round.

PATRICK FLATLEY

Right Wing . . . 6'3" . . . 200 lbs. . . . Born, Toronto, Ont., October 3, 1963 . . . Shoots right . . . Member of 1984 Canadian Olympic hockey team . . . (April, 1985)—Broke bone in left hand during playoff series with Washington . . . (November 16, 1985)—Injured shoulder vs. Edmonton and missed three games . . . (February 4, 1987)—Strained left knee ligaments at Vancouver . . . (November, 1987)—Separated right shoulder . . . (January, 1988)—Injured right knee . . . (February, 1988)—Reconstructive knee surgery.

Year	Team	League	Games	G.	A.	Pts.	Pen.
1980-81—Henry Carr H.S.		Ont. Tier II	42	30	61	91	122
1981-82—University of Wisconsin (c)		WCHA	33	17	20	37	65
1982-83—University of Wisconsin (a-d)		WCHA	43	25	44	69	76
1983-84—Canadian Olympic Team		Int'l	57	33	17	50	136
1983-84—New York Islanders		NHL	16	2	7	9	6

Year	Team	League	Games	G.	A.	Pts.	Pen.
1984-85—New York Islanders		NHL	78	20	31	51	106
1985-86—New York Islanders		NHL	73	18	34	52	66
1986-87—New York Islanders		NHL	63	16	35	51	81
1987-88—New York Islanders		NHL	40	9	15	24	28
NHL TOTALS			270	65	122	187	287

(c)—June, 1982—Drafted as underage player by New York Islanders in 1982 NHL entry draft. First Islanders pick, 21st overall, first round.

(d)—Named to All-America Team (West).

STEVEN FLETCHER

Defense . . . 6'2" . . . 180 lbs. . . . Born, Montreal, Que., March 31, 1962 . . . Shoots left.

Year	Team	League	Games	G.	A.	Pts.	Pen.
1979-80—Hull Olympics (c)		QMJHL	61	2	14	16	183
1980-81—Hull Olympics		QMJHL	66	4	13	17	231
1981-82—Hull Olympics		QMJHL	60	4	20	24	230
1982-83—Fort Wayne Komets		IHL	34	1	9	10	115
1982-83—Sherbrooke Jets		AHL	36	0	1	1	119
1983-84—Sherbrooke Jets		AHL	77	3	7	10	208
1984-85—Sherbrooke Canadiens		AHL	50	2	4	6	192
1985-86—Sherbrooke Canadiens		AHL	64	2	12	14	293
1986-87—Sherbrooke Canadiens		AHL	70	15	11	26	261
1987-88—Sherbrooke Canadiens		AHL	76	8	21	29	138

(c)—June, 1980—Drafted as underage junior by Calgary Flames in 1980 NHL entry draft. Eleventh Flames pick, 202nd overall, 10th round.

THEOREN FLEURY

Center . . . 5'5" . . . 155 lbs. . . . Born, Oxbow, Sask., June 29, 1968 . . . Shoots right.

Year	Team	League	Games	G.	A.	Pts.	Pen.
1983-84—St. James Canadians		Wpg. Midget	22	33	31	64	88
1984-85—Moose Jaw Warriors		WHL	71	29	46	75	82
1985-86—Moose Jaw Warriors		WHL	72	43	65	108	124
1986-87—Moose Jaw Warriors (a-c)		WHL	66	61	68	129	110
1987-88—Moose Jaw Warriors (b)		WHL	65	68	92	*160	235
1987-88—Salt Lake Golden Eagles		IHL	2	3	4	7	7

(c)—June, 1987—Drafted by Calgary Flames in 1987 NHL entry draft. Ninth Flames pick, 166th overall, eighth round.

TODD FLICHEL

Defense . . . 6'3" . . . 195 lbs. . . . Born, Osgoode, Ont., March 31, 1962 . . . Shoots right.

Year	Team	League	Games	G.	A.	Pts.	Pen.
1983-84—Bowling Green Univ. (c)		CCHA	44	1	3	4	12
1984-85—Bowling Green Univ.		CCHA	42	5	7	12	62
1985-86—Bowling Green Univ.		CCHA	42	3	10	13	84
1986-87—Bowling Green Univ.		CCHA	42	4	15	19	75
1987-88—Winnipeg Jets		NHL	2	0	0	0	14
1987-88—Moncton Golden Flames		AHL	65	5	12	17	102
NHL TOTALS			2	0	0	0	14

(c)—June, 1983—Drafted by Winnipeg Jets in 1983 NHL entry draft. Tenth Jets pick, 169th overall, ninth round.

RON FLOCKHART

Center and Left Wing . . . 5'11" . . . 185 lbs. . . . Born, Smithers, B.C., October 10, 1960 . . . Shoots left . . . Brother of Rob Flockhart . . . (January, 1984)—Missed games due to atopic dermitis (body rash) . . . (January 17, 1985)—Separated left shoulder at N.Y. Islanders and missed 17 games . . . (January 17, 1987) Soft tissue injury to right knee at Minnesota . . . (December, 1987)—Rheumatoid arthritis.

Year	Team	League	Games	G.	A.	Pts.	Pen.
1978-79—Revelstoke		BCJHL	61	47	41	88	54
1979-80—Regina Pats		WHL	65	54	76	130	63
1980-81—Philadelphia Flyers (c)		NHL	14	3	7	10	11
1980-81—Maine Mariners		AHL	59	33	33	66	76
1981-82—Philadelphia Flyers		NHL	72	33	39	72	44
1982-83—Philadelphia Flyers		NHL	73	29	31	60	49
1983-84—Philadelphia Flyers (d)		NHL	8	0	3	3	4
1983-84—Pittsburgh Penguins		NHL	68	27	18	45	40
1984-85—Pittsburgh Penguins (e)		NHL	12	0	5	5	4
1984-85—Montreal Canadiens (f)		NHL	42	10	12	22	14

Year	Team	League	Games	G.	A.	Pts.	Pen.
1985-86—St. Louis Blues		NHL	79	22	45	67	26
1986-87—St. Louis Blues		NHL	60	16	19	35	12
1987-88—St. Louis Blues		NHL	21	5	4	9	4
NHL TOTALS			449	145	183	328	208

(c)—September, 1980—Signed by Philadelphia Flyers as a free agent.
(d)—October, 1983—Traded with Mark Taylor, Andy Brickley and first (Roger Belanger) and third (traded to Vancouver) round 1984 draft picks by Philadelphia Flyers to Pittsburgh Penguins for Rich Sutter and second (Greg Smyth) and third (David McLay) round 1984 draft picks.
(e)—November, 1984—Traded by Pittsburgh Penguins to Montreal Canadiens for John Chabot.
(f)—August, 1985—Traded by Montreal Canadiens to St. Louis Blues for Perry Ganchar.

LARRY FLOYD

Center ... 5'8" ... 180 lbs. ... Born, Peterborough, Ont., May 1, 1961 ... Shoots left.

Year	Team	League	Games	G.	A.	Pts.	Pen.
1979-80—Peterborough Petes	OMJHL	66	21	37	58	54
1980-81—Peterborough Petes	OHL	44	26	37	63	43
1981-82—Peterborough Petes	OHL	39	32	37	69	26
1981-82—Rochester Americans	AHL	1	0	2	2	0
1982-83—New Jersey Devils (c)	NHL	5	1	0	1	2
1982-83—Wichita Wind (d)	CHL	75	40	43	83	16
1983-84—New Jersey Devils	NHL	7	1	3	4	7
1983-84—Maine Mariners	AHL	69	37	49	86	40
1984-85—Maine Mariners	AHL	72	30	51	81	24
1985-86—Maine Mariners	AHL	80	29	58	87	25
1986-87—Maine Mariners	AHL	77	30	44	74	50
1987-88—Played in Austria		..	..	..	..	..
1987-88—Utica Devils	AHL	28	21	21	42	14
NHL TOTALS		12	2	3	5	9

(c)—September, 1982—Signed by New Jersey Devils as a free agent.
(d)—Won Ken McKenzie Trophy (Top CHL Rookie).

BRYAN FOGARTY

Defense ... 6'1" ... 190 lbs. ... Born, Montreal, Que., June 11, 1969 ... Shoots left.

Year	Team	League	Games	G.	A.	Pts.	Pen.
1984-85—Aurora Tigers Jr. A	OHA	66	18	39	57	180
1985-86—Kingston Canadians	OHL	47	2	19	21	14
1986-87—Kingston Canadians (a-c)	OHL	56	20	50	70	46
1987-88—Kingston Canadians	OHL	48	11	36	47	50

(c)—June, 1987—Drafted as an underage junior by Quebec Nordiques in 1987 NHL entry draft. First Nordiques pick, ninth overall, first round.

MIKE ANTHONY FOLIGNO

Right Wing ... 6'2" ... 190 lbs. ... Born, Sudbury, Ont., January 29, 1959 ... Shoots right ... (December 27, 1980)—Set Detroit record for most penalty minutes in one game (37 vs. Philadelphia) ... (October 31, 1982)—Injured tailbone vs. Montreal ... (February 12, 1983)—Injured shoulder at Calgary ... (December 7, 1986)—Bruised kidney when he struck a goal post at New Jersey ... (February, 1988)—Back spasms.

Year	Team	League	Games	G.	A.	Pts.	Pen.
1975-76—Sudbury Wolves	OMJHL	57	22	14	36	45
1976-77—Sudbury Wolves	OMJHL	66	31	44	75	62
1977-78—Sudbury Wolves	OMJHL	67	47	39	86	112
1978-79—Sudbury Wolves (a-c-d-e-f)	OMJHL	68	65	85	*150	98
1979-80—Detroit Red Wings	NHL	80	36	35	71	109
1980-81—Detroit Red Wings	NHL	80	28	35	63	210
1981-82—Detroit Red Wings (g)	NHL	26	13	13	26	28
1981-82—Buffalo Sabres	NHL	56	20	31	51	149
1982-83—Buffalo Sabres	NHL	66	22	25	47	135
1983-84—Buffalo Sabres	NHL	70	32	31	63	151
1984-85—Buffalo Sabres	NHL	77	27	29	56	154
1985-86—Buffalo Sabres	NHL	79	41	39	80	168
1986-87—Buffalo Sabres	NHL	75	30	29	59	176
1987-88—Buffalo Sabres	NHL	74	29	28	57	220
NHL TOTALS		683	278	295	573	1500

(c)—Won Red Tilson Memorial Trophy (OMJHL-MVP).
(d)—Won Eddie Powers Memorial Trophy (OMJHL Leading Scorer).
(e)—Won Jim Mahon Memorial Trophy (OMJHL Top Scoring Right Wing).

(f)—August, 1979—Drafted by Detroit Red Wings in 1979 NHL entry draft. First Red Wings pick, third overall, first round.
(g)—December, 1981—Traded with Dale McCourt, Brent Peterson and future considerations by Detroit Red Wings to Buffalo Sabres for Bob Sauve, Jim Schoenfeld and Derek Smith.

MARC FORTIER

Center ... 6' ... 190 lbs. ... Born, Sherbrooke, Que., February 26, 1966 ... Shoots right.

Year	Team	League	Games	G.	A.	Pts.	Pen.
1984-85	Chicoutimi Sagueneens	QHL	68	35	63	98	114
1985-86	Chicoutimi Sagueneens	QHL	71	47	86	133	49
1986-87	Chicoutimi Sagueneens (a-c)	QHL	65	66	*135	*201	39
1987-88	Quebec Nordiques	NHL	27	4	10	14	12
1987-88	Fredericton Express	AHL	50	26	36	62	48
	NHL TOTALS		27	4	10	14	12

(c)—February, 1987—Signed by Quebec Nordiques as a free agent.

COREY FOSTER

Defense ... 6'3" ... 200 lbs. ... Born, Ottawa, Ont., October 27 ,1969 ... Shoots left.

Year	Team	League	Games	G.	A.	Pts.	Pen.
1985-86	Ottawa West Minor Midget	OHA	37	15	35	50	30
1986-87	Peterborough Petes	OHL	30	3	4	7	4
1987-88	Peterborough Petes (c)	OHL	66	13	31	44	58

(c)—June, 1988—Drafted by New Jersey Devils in 1988 NHL entry draft. First Devils pick, 12th overall, first round.

NICHOLAS EVLAMPIOS FOTIU

Left Wing ... 6'2" ... 200 lbs. ... Born, Staten Island, N.Y., May 25, 1952 ... Shoots left ... Missed entire 1972-73 season with knee injury and part of 1975-76 season with severed tendons in right hand ... (March, 1981)—Given eight-game suspension by NHL for going into stands at Detroit on February 19, 1981 ... (January 31, 1982)—Slight shoulder separation vs. Los Angeles ... First New York City-born player to play with N.Y. Rangers ... (November, 1983)—Bruised left instep ... (January, 1984)—Bruised ribs ... (March 20, 1984)—Confrontation with fan at Madison Square Garden cost $500 and three-game suspension ... Does not wear a helmet.

Year	Team	League	Games	G.	A.	Pts.	Pen.
1971-72	New Hyde Park Arrows	N.Y. MJHA	32	6	17	23	135
1972-73	Did not play		....	...	....	....	....
1973-74	Cape Cod Cubs (c)	NAHL	72	12	24	36	*371
1974-75	Cape Codders	NAHL	5	2	1	3	13
1974-75	New England Whalers	WHA	61	2	2	4	144
1975-76	Cape Codders	NAHL	6	2	1	3	15
1975-76	New England Whalers (d)	WHA	49	3	2	5	94
1976-77	New York Rangers	NHL	70	4	8	12	174
1977-78	New Haven Nighthawks	AHL	5	1	1	2	9
1977-78	New York Rangers	NHL	59	2	7	9	105
1978-79	New York Rangers (e)	NHL	71	3	5	8	190
1979-80	Hartford Whalers	NHL	74	10	8	18	107
1980-81	Hartford Whalers (f)	NHL	42	4	3	7	79
1980-81	New York Rangers	NHL	27	5	6	11	91
1981-82	New York Rangers	NHL	70	8	10	18	151
1982-83	New York Rangers	NHL	72	8	13	21	90
1983-84	New York Rangers	NHL	40	7	6	13	115
1984-85	New York Rangers	NHL	46	4	7	11	54
1985-86	New Haven Nighthawks	AHL	9	4	2	6	21
1985-86	Calgary Flames (g)	NHL	9	0	1	1	21
1986-87	Calgary Flames	NHL	42	5	3	8	145
1987-88	Philadelphia Flyers (h)	NHL	23	0	0	0	40
	WHA TOTALS		110	6	15	21	279
	NHL TOTALS		645	60	77	137	1362

(c)—Tied for lead in penalty minutes (80) during playoffs.
(d)—June, 1976—Signed by New York Rangers.
(e)—June, 1979—Selected by Hartford Whalers in NHL expansion draft.
(f)—January, 1981—Traded by Hartford Whalers to New York Rangers for New York's fifth-round draft pick in 1981 (Bill McGuire).
(g)—March, 1986—Traded by New York Rangers to Calgary Flames for future considerations.
(h)—October, 1987—Signed by Philadelphia Flyers as a free agent.

BOB FOWLER

Defense ... 6'1" ... 195 lbs. ... Born, Tewksbury, Mass., July 9, 1965 ... Shoots left.

Year	Team	League	Games	G.	A.	Pts.	Pen.
1983-84—Merrimack College		ECAC	28	4	8	12	18
1984-85—Merrimack College		ECAC	32	8	19	27	42
1985-86—Merrimack College		ECAC	32	3	20	23	50
1986-87—Merrimack College (c)		ECAC	35	2	25	27	49
1987-88—Moncton Golden Flames		AHL	68	2	11	13	51

(c)—June, 1987—Selected by Winnipeg Jets in 1987 NHL supplementary draft.

DAN FOWLER

Defense . . . 6'3" . . . 205 lbs. . . . Born, Fredericton, N.B., March 4, 1969 . . . Shoots left.

Year	Team	League	Games	G.	A.	Pts.	Pen.
1986-87—Stratford Jr. B		OHA	38	2	17	19	121
1187-88—University of Maine (c)		H. East	20	1	4	5	20

(c)—June, 1988—Drafted by St. Louis Blues in 1988 NHL entry draft. Sixth Blues pick, 114th overall, sixth round.

JAMES CHARLES FOX

Right Wing . . . 5'8" . . . 183 lbs. . . . Born, Coniston, Ont., May 18, 1960 . . . Shoots right . . . (November 6, 1985)—Injured disc at Los Angeles and missed 24 games . . . (January 29, 1986)—Bruised hip vs. Minnesota . . . (March 10, 1988)—Injured right knee at Boston.

Year	Team	League	Games	G.	A.	Pts.	Pen.
1975-76—North Bay Trappers		OPJHL	44	30	45	75	16
1976-77—North Bay Trappers (c)		OPJHL	38	44	64	*108	4
1977-78—Ottawa 67's		OMJHL	59	44	83	127	12
1978-79—Ottawa 67's		OMJHL	53	37	66	103	4
1979-80—Ottawa 67's (d-e-f-g)		OMJHL	52	65	*101	*166	30
1980-81—Los Angeles Kings		NHL	71	18	25	43	8
1981-82—Los Angeles Kings		NHL	77	30	38	68	23
1982-83—Los Angeles Kings		NHL	77	28	40	68	8
1983-84—Los Angeles Kings		NHL	80	30	42	72	26
1984-85—Los Angeles Kings		NHL	79	30	53	83	10
1985-86—Los Angeles Kings		NHL	39	14	17	31	2
1986-87—Los Angeles Kings		NHL	76	19	42	61	48
1987-88—Los Angeles Kings		NHL	68	16	35	51	18
NHL TOTALS			567	185	292	477	143

(c)—Led OPJHL Playoffs in points (38) and assists (25) in 19 games, and was co-leader (with teammate Jim Omiciolli) in goals (13).

(d)—Won Eddie Powers Memorial Trophy (OMJHL Leading Scorer).

(e)—Won Albert (Red) Tilson Memorial Trophy (OMJHL—MVP).

(f)—Won Jim Mahon Memorial Trophy (Top Scoring OMJHL Right Wing).

(g)—June, 1980—Drafted by Los Angeles Kings in 1980 NHL entry draft. Second Kings pick, 10th overall, first round.

LOU FRANCESCHETTI

Left Wing . . . 6' . . . 190 lbs. . . . Born, Toronto, Ont., March 28, 1958 . . . Shoots left . . . (March, 1988)—Bruised right leg.

Year	Team	League	Games	G.	A.	Pts.	Pen.
1975-76—St. Catharines Black Hawks		OMJHL	1	0	0	0	0
1976-77—Niagara Falls Flyers		OMJHL	61	23	30	53	80
1977-78—Niagara Falls Flyers (c)		OMJHL	62	40	50	90	46
1978-79—Saginaw Gears		IHL	2	1	1	2	0
1978-79—Port Huron Flags		IHL	76	45	58	103	131
1979-80—Port Huron Flags		IHL	15	3	8	11	31
1979-80—Hershey Bears		AHL	65	27	29	56	58
1980-81—Hershey Bears		AHL	79	32	36	68	173
1981-82—Washington Capitals		NHL	30	2	10	12	23
1981-82—Hershey Bears		AHL	50	22	33	55	89
1982-83—Hershey Bears		AHL	80	31	44	75	176
1983-84—Washington Capitals		NHL	2	0	0	0	0
1983-84—Hershey Bears		AHL	73	26	34	60	130
1984-85—Binghamton Whalers		AHL	52	29	43	72	75
1984-85—Washington Capitals		NHL	22	4	7	11	45
1985-86—Washington Capitals		NHL	76	7	14	21	131
1986-87—Washington Capitals		NHL	75	12	9	21	127
1987-88—Washington Capitals		NHL	59	4	8	12	113
1987-88—Binghamton Whalers		AHL	6	2	4	6	4
NHL TOTALS			264	29	48	77	439

(c)—June, 1978—Drafted by Washington Capitals in the 1978 NHL amateur draft. Seventh Capitals pick, 71st overall, fifth round.

RONALD FRANCIS

Center . . . 6'1" . . . 170 lbs. . . . Born, Sault Ste. Marie, Ont. . . . Shoots left . . . Cousin of Mike Liut . . . (January 27, 1982)—Out of lineup for three weeks with eye injury . . . (November 30, 1983)—Strained ligaments in right knee vs. Vancouver . . . (January 18, 1986)—Broke left ankle at Quebec and missed 27 games.

Year	Team	League	Games	G.	A.	Pts.	Pen.
1979-80—Sault Ste. Marie Legion		OMHL	45	57	92	149	....
1980-81—Sault Ste. Marie Greyhounds (c)		OHL	64	26	43	69	33
1981-82—Sault Ste. Marie Greyhounds		OHL	25	18	30	48	46
1981-82—Hartford Whalers		NHL	59	25	43	68	51
1982-83—Hartford Whalers		NHL	79	31	59	90	60
1983-84—Hartford Whalers		NHL	72	23	60	83	45
1984-85—Hartford Whalers		NHL	80	24	57	81	66
1985-86—Hartford Whalers		NHL	53	24	53	77	24
1986-87—Hartford Whalers		NHL	75	30	63	93	45
1987-88—Hartford Whalers		NHL	80	25	50	75	89
NHL TOTALS			498	182	385	567	380

(c)—June, 1981—Drafted as underage junior by Hartford Whalers in 1981 NHL entry draft. First Whalers pick, fourth overall, first round.

GORDIE FRANTTI

Center . . . 6'4" . . . 225 lbs. . . . Born, Detroit, Mich., July 17, 1970 . . . Shoots left.

Year	Team	League	Games	G.	A.	Pts.	Pen.
1986-87—Calumet H.S.		Mich. H.S.	24	35	32	67	40
1987-88—Calumet H.S. (c)		Mich. H.S.	26	41	39	80	36

(c)—June, 1988—Drafted by Philadelphia Flyers in 1988 NHL entry draft. Seventh Flyers pick, 119th overall, sixth round.

CURT FRASER

Left Wing . . . 6' . . . 190 lbs. . . . Born, Cincinnati, Ohio, January 12, 1958 . . . Shoots left . . . (November, 1983)—Torn knee ligaments . . . (January 13, 1985)—Multiple fractures to face when struck by goalie stick of Billy Smith vs. N.Y. Islanders. Smith was given a six-game suspension by NHL for the incident . . . (December 14, 1985)—Sprained shoulder at Montreal and missed 19 games . . . (October, 1987)—Bruised ribs . . . (November, 1987)—Bacterial infection complicated by diabetes.

Year	Team	League	Games	G.	A.	Pts.	Pen.
1973-74—Kelowna Buckaroos		Jr."A"BCHL	52	32	32	64	85
1974-75—Victoria Cougars		WCHL	68	17	32	49	105
1975-76—Victoria Cougars		WCHL	71	43	64	107	167
1976-77—Victoria Cougars		WCHL	60	34	41	75	82
1977-78—Victoria Cougars (c)		WCHL	66	48	44	92	256
1978-79—Vancouver Canucks		NHL	78	16	19	35	116
1979-80—Vancouver Canucks		NHL	78	17	25	42	143
1980-81—Vancouver Canucks		NHL	77	25	24	49	118
1981-82—Vancouver Canucks		NHL	79	28	39	67	175
1982-83—Vancouver Canucks (d)		NHL	36	6	7	13	99
1982-83—Chicago Black Hawks		NHL	38	6	13	19	77
1983-84—Chicago Black Hawks		NHL	29	5	12	17	26
1984-85—Chicago Black Hawks		NHL	73	25	25	50	109
1985-86—Chicago Black Hawks		NHL	61	29	39	68	84
1986-87—Chicago Black Hawks		NHL	75	25	25	50	182
1987-88—Chicago Black Hawks		NHL	27	4	6	10	57
1987-88—Minnesota North Stars (e)		NHL	10	1	1	2	20
NHL TOTALS			661	187	235	422	1206

(c)—Drafted from Victoria Cougars by Vancouver Canucks in second round of 1978 amateur draft.

(d)—January, 1983—Traded by Vancouver Canucks to Chicago Black Hawks for Tony Tanti.

(e)—January, 1988—Traded by Chicago Black Hawks to Minnesota North Stars for Dirk Graham.

WILLIAM DANNY FRAWLEY
(Known by middle name.)

Right Wing . . . 6' . . . 193 lbs. . . . Born, Sturgeon Falls, Ont., June 2, 1962 . . . Shoots right . . . (December, 1987)—Knee surgery.

Year	Team	League	Games	G.	A.	Pts.	Pen.
1979-80—Sudbury Wolves (c)		OHL	63	21	26	47	67
1980-81—Cornwall Royals		QMJHL	28	10	14	24	76
1981-82—Cornwall Royals		OHL	64	27	50	77	239
1982-83—Springfield Indians		AHL	80	30	27	57	107
1983-84—Chicago Black Hawks		NHL	3	0	0	0	0

Year	Team	League	Games	G.	A.	Pts.	Pen.
1983-84—Springfield Indians		AHL	69	22	34	56	137
1984-85—Milwaukee Admirals		IHL	26	11	12	23	125
1984-85—Chicago Black Hawks		NHL	30	4	3	7	64
1985-86—Pittsburgh Penguins (d)		NHL	69	10	11	21	174
1986-87—Pittsburgh Penguins		NHL	78	14	14	28	218
1987-88—Pittsburgh Penguins		NHL	47	6	8	14	152
NHL TOTALS			227	34	36	70	608

(c)—June, 1980—Drafted as underage junior by Chicago Black Hawks in 1980 NHL entry draft. Fifteenth Black Hawks pick, 204th overall, 10th round.

(d)—October, 1985—Acquired by Pittsburgh Penguins in 1985 NHL waiver draft.

MARK FREER

Center . . . 5'11" . . . 175 lbs. . . . Born, Peterborough, Ont., July 14, 1968 . . . Shoots left.

Year	Team	League	Games	G.	A.	Pts.	Pen.
1984-85—Peterborough Midget		OHA	49	53	68	121	63
1985-86—Peterborough Petes		OHL	65	16	28	44	24
1986-87—Peterborough Petes		OHL	65	39	43	82	44
1986-87—Philadelphia Flyers (c)		NHL	1	0	1	1	0
1987-88—Philadelphia Flyers		NHL	1	0	0	0	0
1987-88—Peterborough Petes		OHL	63	38	71	109	63
NHL TOTALS			2	0	1	1	0

(c)—September, 1986—Signed by Philadelphia Flyers as a free agent.

MIROSLAV OPAVA FRYCER

Right Wing . . . 6' . . . 200 lbs. . . . Born, Ostrava, Czech., September 27, 1959 . . . Shoots left . . . (December 26, 1982)—Strained stomach muscles during team practice . . . Member of Czechoslovakian National team in 1979, 1980 and 1981 . . . (January, 1984)—Knee injury . . . (February 25, 1984)—Injured shoulder at Edmonton . . . (March 8, 1984)—Torn knee ligaments vs. New Jersey . . . (March, 1985)—Broken bone in foot . . . (September, 1985)—Injured shoulder in training camp . . . (January 13, 1986)—Injured groin vs. Detroit . . . (January 22, 1986)—Bruised knee vs. N.Y. Rangers . . . (November, 1986)—Injured hip . . . (December, 1986)—Missed 18 games with sprained knee ligaments . . . (February 18, 1987)—Cracked pelvis bone at Edmonton . . . (November, 1987)—Strep throat . . . (December, 1987)—Torn cartilage in right knee vs. Washington.

Year	Team	League	Games	G.	A.	Pts.	Pen.
1977-78—VZKG Ostrava		Czech. Jr.	....	...	....	....	....
1978-79—Tj Vitkovice (b)		Czech.	44	22	12	34	....
1979-80—Tj Vitkovice		Czech.	44	31	15	46	....
1980-81—Tj Vitkovice		Czech.	34	33	24	57	....
1981-82—Fredericton Express (c)		AHL	11	9	5	14	16
1981-82—Quebec Nordiques		NHL	49	20	17	37	47
1981-82—Toronto Maple Leafs (d)		NHL	10	4	6	10	31
1982-83—Toronto Maple Leafs		NHL	67	25	30	55	90
1983-84—Toronto Maple Leafs		NHL	47	10	16	26	55
1984-85—Toronto Maple Leafs		NHL	65	25	30	55	55
1985-86—Toronto Maple Leafs		NHL	73	32	43	75	74
1986-87—Toronto Maple Leafs		NHL	29	7	8	15	28
1987-88—Toronto Maple Leafs (e)		NHL	38	12	20	32	41
NHL TOTALS			378	135	170	305	421

(c)—April, 1980—Signed by Quebec Nordiques as a free agent.

(d)—March, 1982—Traded with seventh round 1982 draft pick (Toronto drafted Jeff Triano) by Quebec Nordiques to Toronto Maple Leafs for Wilf Paiement.

(e)—June, 1988—Traded by Toronto Maple Leafs to Detroit Red Wings for Darren Veitch.

LINK GAETZ

Defense . . . 6'2" . . . 205 lbs. . . . Born, Vancouver, B.C., October 2, 1968 . . . Shoots left . . . (April 12, 1988)—Suspended indefinitely by Spokane Chiefs.

Year	Team	League	Games	G.	A.	Pts.	Pen.
1986-87—New Westminster Bruins		WHL	44	2	7	9	52
1987-88—Spokane Chiefs (c)		WHL	59	9	20	29	313

(c)—June, 1988—Drafted by Minnesota North Stars in 1988 NHL entry draft. Second North Stars pick, 40th overall, second round.

JOSEPH (JODY) GAGE

Right Wing . . . 5'11" . . . 182 lbs. . . . Born, Toronto, Ont., November 29, 1959 . . . Shoots right.

Year	Team	League	Games	G.	A.	Pts.	Pen.
1976-77—St. Catharines Black Hawks		OMJHL	47	13	20	33	2
1977-78—Hamilton Fincups		OMJHL	32	15	18	33	19
1977-78—Kitchener Rangers		OMJHL	36	17	27	44	21
1978-79—Kitchener Rangers (c)		OMJHL	59	46	43	89	40
1979-80—Adirondack Red Wings		AHL	63	25	21	46	15
1979-80—Kalamazoo Wings		IHL	14	17	12	29	0
1980-81—Detroit Red Wings		NHL	16	2	2	4	22
1980-81—Adirondack Red Wings		AHL	59	17	31	48	44
1981-82—Adirondack Red Wings		AHL	47	21	20	41	21
1981-82—Detroit Red Wings		NHL	31	9	10	19	2
1982-83—Adirondack Red Wings		AHL	65	23	30	53	33
1983-84—Detroit Red Wings		NHL	3	0	0	0	0
1983-84—Adirondack Red Wings		AHL	73	40	32	72	32
1984-85—Adirondack Red Wings		AHL	78	27	33	60	55
1985-86—Buffalo Sabres (d)		NHL	7	3	2	5	0
1985-86—Rochester Americans (a)		AHL	73	42	57	99	56
1986-87—Rochester Americans		AHL	70	26	39	65	60
1987-88—Rochester Americans		AHL	76	60	44	104	46
1987-88—Buffalo Sabres		NHL	2	0	0	0	0
NHL TOTALS			59	14	14	28	24

(c)—August, 1979—Drafted by Detroit Red Wings in 1979 NHL Entry draft. Second Detroit pick, 46th overall, third round.
(d)—August, 1985—Signed by Buffalo Sabres as a free agent.

PAUL GAGNE

Left Wing . . . 5'10" . . . 178 lbs. . . . Born, Iroquois Falls, Ont., February 6, 1962 . . . Shoots left . . . (December 18, 1980)—Tore knee ligaments . . . (October, 1981)—Fractured cheekbone . . . (January 2, 1982)—Shoulder separation vs. Detroit . . . (February 15, 1986)—Injured back at N.Y. Islanders . . . (March 2, 1986)—Injured back vs. Winnipeg . . . (March 25, 1986)—Injured back vs. N.Y. Rangers . . . (September, 1986)—Reinjured back in training camp and returned home for back therapy, missing the entire season.

Year	Team	League	Games	G.	A.	Pts.	Pen.
1978-79—Windsor Spitfires		OMJHL	67	24	18	42	64
1979-80—Windsor Spitfires (b-c)		OMJHL	65	48	53	101	67
1980-81—Colorado Rockies		NHL	61	25	16	41	12
1981-82—Colorado Rockies		NHL	59	10	12	22	17
1982-83—Wichita Wind		CHL	16	1	9	10	9
1982-83—New Jersey Devils		NHL	53	14	15	29	13
1983-84—New Jersey Devils		NHL	66	14	18	32	33
1984-85—New Jersey Devils		NHL	79	24	19	43	28
1985-86—New Jersey Devils		NHL	47	19	19	38	14
1986-87—Did not play			....	...	....	....	....
1987-88—Did not play (d)			....	...	....	....	....
NHL TOTALS			365	106	99	205	117

(c)—June, 1980—Drafted by Colorado Rockies in 1980 NHL entry draft as an underage junior. First Rockies pick, 19th overall, first round.
(d)—July, 1988—Signed by Toronto Maple Leafs as a free agent.

SIMON GAGNE

Right Wing . . . 6'4" . . . 202 lbs. . . . Born, Montreal, Que., September 29, 1968 . . . Shoots right.

Year	Team	League	Games	G.	A.	Pts.	Pen.
1984-85—Shawinigan Cataracts		QHL	34	3	1	4	16
1985-86—Laval Titans		QHL	71	15	16	31	150
1986-87—Laval Titans (c)		QHL	66	19	35	54	90
1987-88—Drummondville Voltigeurs		QHL	68	17	43	60	197

(c)—June, 1987—Drafted by New York Rangers in 1987 NHL entry draft. Third Rangers pick, 46th overall, third round.

DAVE GAGNER

Center . . . 5'10" . . . 185 lbs. . . . Born, Chatham, Ont., December 11, 1964 . . . Shoots left . . . Member of 1984 Canadian Olympic Team . . . (February 5, 1986)—Fractured ankle at St. Louis . . . (December, 1986)—Emergency appendectomy.

Year	Team	League	Games	G.	A.	Pts.	Pen.
1981-82—Brantford Alexanders		OHL	68	30	46	76	31
1982-83—Brantford Alexanders (b-c)		OHL	70	55	66	121	57
1983-84—Canadian Olympic Team		Int'l	50	19	18	37	26
1983-84—Brantford Alexanders		OHL	12	7	13	20	4

Year	Team	League	Games	G.	A.	Pts.	Pen.
1984-85—New Haven Nighthawks		AHL	38	13	20	33	23
1984-85—New York Rangers		NHL	38	6	6	12	16
1985-86—New York Rangers		NHL	32	4	6	10	19
1985-86—New Haven Nighthawks		AHL	16	10	11	21	11
1986-87—New York Rangers		NHL	10	1	4	5	12
1986-87—New Haven Nighthawks		AHL	56	22	41	63	50
1987-88—Kalamazoo Wings		IHL	14	16	10	26	26
1987-88—Minnesota North Stars (d)		NHL	51	8	11	19	55
NHL TOTALS			131	19	27	46	102

(c)—June, 1983—Drafted as underage junior by New York Rangers in 1983 NHL entry draft. First Rangers pick, 12th overall, first round.

(d)—October, 1987—Traded with Jay Caufield by New York Rangers to Minnesota North Stars for Jari Gronstrad and Paul Boutilier.

ROBERT MICHAEL GAINEY

Left Wing . . . 6'2" . . . 195 lbs. . . . Born, Peterborough, Ont., December 13, 1953 . . . Shoots left . . . Missed part of 1977-78 season with shoulder separation . . . (October 5, 1986)— Tore ligaments in left knee when checked by Gord Donnelly in pre-season game vs. Quebec . . . (March 14, 1987)—Pulled groin vs. Pittsburgh . . . (April, 1988)—Bruised ankle.

Year	Team	League	Games	G.	A.	Pts.	Pen.
1970-71—Peterborough TPTs		Jr."A" OHA	4	0	0	0	0
1971-72—Peterborough TPTs		Jr."A" OHA	4	2	1	3	33
1972-73—Peterborough TPTs (c)		Jr."A" OHA	52	22	21	43	99
1973-74—Nova Scotia Voyageurs		AHL	6	2	5	7	4
1973-74—Montreal Canadiens		NHL	66	3	7	10	34
1974-75—Montreal Canadiens		NHL	80	17	20	37	49
1975-76—Montreal Canadiens		NHL	78	15	13	28	57
1976-77—Montreal Canadiens		NHL	80	14	19	33	41
1977-78—Montreal Canadiens (d)		NHL	66	15	16	31	57
1978-79—Montreal Canadiens (d-e)		NHL	79	20	18	38	44
1979-80—Montreal Canadiens (d)		NHL	64	14	19	33	32
1980-81—Montreal Canadiens (d)		NHL	78	23	24	47	36
1981-82—Montreal Canadiens		NHL	79	21	24	45	24
1982-83—Montreal Canadiens		NHL	80	12	18	30	43
1983-84—Montreal Canadiens		NHL	77	17	22	39	41
1984-85—Montreal Canadiens		NHL	79	19	13	32	40
1985-86—Montreal Canadiens		NHL	80	20	23	43	20
1986-87—Montreal Canadiens		NHL	47	8	8	16	19
1987-88—Montreal Canadiens		NHL	78	11	11	22	14
NHL TOTALS			1111	229	255	484	551

(c)—Drafted from Peterborough TPTs by Montreal Canadiens in first round of 1973 amateur draft.

(d)—Won Frank J. Selke Trophy (Best Defensive Forward).

(e)—Won Conn Smythe Trophy (MVP-NHL Playoffs).

GERARD GALLANT

Left Wing . . . 5'11" . . . 164 lbs. . . . Born, Summerside, P.E.I., September 2, 1963 . . . Shoots left . . . Also plays Center . . . (December 11, 1985)—Broke jaw vs. Minnesota and missed 25 games.

Year	Team	League	Games	G.	A.	Pts.	Pen.
1979-80—Summerside		PEIHA	45	60	55	115	90
1980-81—Sherbrooke Beavers (c)		QMJHL	68	41	60	101	220
1981-82—Sherbrooke Beavers		QMJHL	58	34	58	92	260
1982-83—St. Jean Beavers		QHL	33	28	25	53	139
1982-83—Verdun Juniors		QHL	29	26	49	75	105
1983-84—Adirondack Red Wings		AHL	77	31	33	64	195
1984-85—Adirondack Red Wings		AHL	46	18	29	47	131
1984-85—Detroit Red Wings		NHL	32	6	12	18	66
1985-86—Detroit Red Wings		NHL	52	20	19	39	106
1986-87—Detroit Red Wings		NHL	80	38	34	72	216
1987-88—Detroit Red Wings		NHL	73	34	39	73	242
NHL TOTALS			237	98	104	202	630

(c)—June, 1981—Drafted as underage junior by Detroit Red Wings in 1981 NHL entry draft. Fourth Red Wings pick, 107th overall, sixth round.

GARRY GALLEY

Defense . . . 5'11" . . . 190 lbs. . . . Born, Ottawa, Ont., April 16, 1963 . . . Shoots left . . . (December 8, 1985)—Injured knee at Winnipeg.

Year	Team	League	Games	G.	A.	Pts.	Pen.
1981-82—Bowling Green Univ.		CCHA	42	3	36	39	48
1982-83—Bowling Green Univ. (a-c)		CCHA	40	17	29	46	40
1983-84—Bowling Green Univ.		CCHA	44	15	52	67	61
1984-85—Los Angeles Kings		NHL	78	8	30	38	82
1985-86—Los Angeles Kings		NHL	49	9	13	22	46
1985-86—New Haven Nighthawks		AHL	4	2	6	8	6
1986-87—Los Angeles Kings (d)		NHL	30	5	11	16	57
1986-87—Washington Capitals		NHL	18	1	10	11	10
1987-88—Washington Capitals (e)		NHL	58	7	23	30	44
NHL TOTALS			233	30	87	117	239

(c)—June, 1983—Drafted by Los Angeles Kings in 1983 NHL entry draft. Fourth Kings pick, 100th overall, fifth round.

(d)—February, 1987—Traded by Los Angeles Kings to Washington Capitals for Al Jensen.

(e)—July, 1988—Signed by Boston Bruins as a free agent with Washington Capitals getting third round draft choice in 1989 as compensation.

PERRY GANCHAR

Right Wing . . . 5'9" . . . 175 lbs. . . . Born, Saskatoon, Sask., October 28, 1963 . . . Shoots right . . . (January, 1988)—Injured knee.

Year	Team	League	Games	G.	A.	Pts.	Pen.
1977-78—Saskatoon Blades		WHL	4	2	0	2	2
1978-79—Saskatoon		SJHL	50	21	33	54	72
1978-79—Saskatoon Blades		WHL	14	5	3	8	15
1979-80—Saskatoon Blades		WHL	70	41	24	65	116
1980-81—Saskatoon Blades		WHL	68	36	20	56	195
1981-82—Saskatoon Blades (c)		WHL	53	38	52	90	82
1982-83—Saskatoon Blades		WHL	68	68	48	116	105
1982-83—Salt Lake Golden Eagles (d)		CHL	..	..	..	..	..
1983-84—Montana Magic		CHL	59	23	22	45	77
1983-84—St. Louis Blues		NHL	1	0	0	0	0
1984-85—Peoria Rivermen (b)		IHL	63	41	29	70	114
1984-85—St. Louis Blues (e)		NHL	7	0	2	2	0
1985-86—Sherbrooke Canadiens		AHL	75	25	29	54	42
1986-87—Sherbrooke Canadiens		AHL	68	22	29	51	64
1987-88—Sherbrooke Canadiens		AHL	28	12	18	30	61
1987-88—Montreal Canadiens (f)		NHL	1	1	0	1	0
1987-88—Pittsburgh Penguins		NHL	30	2	5	7	36
NHL TOTALS			39	3	7	10	36

(c)—June, 1982—Drafted as underage junior by St. Louis Blues in 1982 NHL entry draft. Third Blues pick, 113th overall, sixth round.

(d)—No regular season record. Played one playoff game (1 assist).

(e)—August, 1985—Traded by St. Louis Blues to Montreal Canadiens for Ron Flockhart.

(f)—December, 1987—Traded by Montreal Canadiens to Pittsburgh Penguins for future considerations.

WILLIAM SCOTT GARDNER

Center . . . 5'10" . . . 170 lbs. . . . Born, Toronto, Ont., March 19, 1960 . . . Shoots left . . . (February, 1985)—Pinched nerve in neck.

Year	Team	League	Games	G.	A.	Pts.	Pen.
1976-77—Peterborough Petes		OMJHL	1	0	0	0	0
1977-78—Peterborough Petes		OMJHL	65	23	32	55	10
1978-79—Peterborough Petes (c)		OMJHL	68	33	71	104	19
1979-80—Peterborough Petes		OMJHL	59	43	63	106	17
1980-81—New Brunswick Hawks		AHL	48	19	29	48	12
1980-81—Chicago Black Hawks		NHL	1	0	0	0	0
1981-82—Chicago Black Hawks		NHL	69	8	15	23	20
1982-83—Chicago Black Hawks		NHL	77	15	25	40	12
1983-84—Chicago Black Hawks		NHL	79	27	21	48	12
1984-85—Chicago Black Hawks		NHL	74	17	34	51	12
1985-86—Chicago Black Hawks (d)		NHL	46	3	10	13	6
1985-86—Hartford Whalers		NHL	18	1	8	9	4
1986-87—Hartford Whalers		NHL	8	0	1	1	0
1986-87—Binghamton Whalers (e)		AHL	50	17	44	61	18
1987-88—Saginaw Hawks		IHL	54	18	49	67	46
1987-88—Chicago Black Hawks		NHL	2	1	0	1	2
NHL TOTALS			374	72	114	186	68

(c)—August, 1979—Drafted by Chicago Black Hawks as underage junior in entry draft. Third Chicago pick, 49th overall, third round.

(e)—August, 1987—Signed by Chicago Black Hawks as a free agent without compensation.

MICHAEL ALFRED GARTNER

Right Wing . . . 6' . . . 180 lbs. . . . Born, Ottawa, Ont., October 29, 1959 . . . Shoots right . . . (February, 1983)—Eye injury . . . (March, 1986)—Arthroscopic surgery to repair torn cartilage in left knee.

Year	Team	League	Games	G.	A.	Pts.	Pen.
1975-76—St. Cath. Black Hawks	Jr."A"OHA		3	1	3	4	0
1976-77—Niagara Falls Flyers	Jr."A"OHA		62	33	42	75	125
1977-78—Niagara Falls Flyers (a-c)	Jr."A"OHA		64	41	49	90	56
1978-79—Cincinnati Stingers (d)	WHA		78	27	25	52	123
1979-80—Washington Capitals	NHL		77	36	32	68	66
1980-81—Washington Capitals	NHL		80	48	46	94	100
1981-82—Washington Capitals	NHL		80	35	45	80	121
1982-83—Washington Capitals	NHL		73	38	38	76	54
1983-84—Washington Capitals	NHL		80	40	45	85	90
1984-85—Washington Capitals	NHL		80	50	52	102	71
1985-86—Washington Capitals	NHL		74	35	40	75	63
1986-87—Washington Capitals	NHL		78	41	32	73	61
1987-88—Washington Capitals	NHL		80	48	33	81	73
WHA TOTALS			78	27	25	52	123
NHL TOTALS			702	371	363	734	699

(c)—August, 1978—Signed by Cincinnati Stingers (WHA) as underage junior.

(d)—August, 1979—Drafted by Washington Capitals in 1979 entry draft. First Capitals pick, fourth overall, first round.

JAMES GASSEAU

Defense . . . 6'2" . . . 200 lbs. . . . Born, Carleton, Que., May 4, 1966 . . . Shoots right . . . (October, 1986)—Separated shoulder when checked by Ed Kastelic vs. Binghamton.

Year	Team	League	Games	G.	A.	Pts.	Pen.
1983-84—Drummondville Voltigeurs (c)	QHL		68	6	25	31	72
1984-85—Drummondville Voltigeurs	QHL		64	8	43	51	158
1985-86—Drummondville Voltigeurs (b)	QHL		46	20	31	51	155
1986-87—Rochester Americans	AHL		7	0	2	2	6
1987-88—Rochester Americans	AHL		75	9	21	30	109

(c)—June, 1984—Drafted as underage junior by Buffalo Sabres in 1984 NHL entry draft. Sixth Sabres pick, 123rd overall, sixth round.

YVES GAUCHER

Center . . . 5'11" . . . 190 lbs. . . . Born, Valleyfield, Que., July 14, 1968 . . . Shoots right.

Year	Team	League	Games	G.	A.	Pts.	Pen.
1986-87—Chicoutimi Sagueneens	QHL		55	22	25	47	304
1987-88—Chicoutimi Sagueneens (b-c)	QHL		68	37	60	97	388

(c)—June, 1988—Drafted by New York Islanders in 1988 NHL entry draft. Ninth Islanders pick, 142nd overall, seventh round.

ROBERT GAUDREAU

Right Wing . . . 6' . . . 180 lbs. . . . Born, Providence, R.I., January 20, 1970 . . . Shoots right . . . (February, 1987)—Separated shoulder.

Year	Team	League	Games	G.	A.	Pts.	Pen.
1986-87—Bishop Hendricken	R.I. Met. 'A'		33	41	39	80	..
1987-88—Bishop Hendricken (c)	R.I. Met. 'A'		..	52	60	112	..

(c)—June, 1988—Drafted by Pittsburgh Penguins in 1988 NHL entry draft. Eighth Penguins pick, 127nd overall, ninth round.

DALLAS GAUME

Center . . . 5'10" . . . 180 lbs. . . . Born, Innisfal, Alta., August 27, 1963 . . . Shoots left . . . Broke Bill Masterton record for career points at University of Denver.

Year	Team	League	Games	G.	A.	Pts.	Pen.
1982-83—University of Denver	WCHA		37	19	47	66	12
1983-84—University of Denver	WCHA		32	12	25	37	22
1984-85—University of Denver	WCHA		39	15	48	63	28
1985-86—University of Denver (a-c-d)	WCHA		47	32	*67	*99	18
1986-87—Binghamton Whalers	AHL		77	18	39	57	31
1987-88—Binghamton Whalers	AHL		63	24	49	73	39

(c)—Named WCHA MVP.

(d)—July, 1986—Signed by Hartford Whalers as a free agent.

DANIEL GAUTHIER

Left Wing . . . 6'1" . . . 180 lbs. . . . Born, Charlemagne, Que., May 17, 1970 . . . Shoots left.

Year	Team	League	Games	G.	A.	Pts.	Pen.
1986-87—Longueuil Chevaliers		QHL	64	23	22	45	23
1987-88—Victoriaville Tigers (c)		QHL	66	43	47	90	53

(c)—June, 1988—Drafted by Pittsburgh Penguins in 1988 NHL entry draft. Third Penguins pick, 62nd overall, third round.

ROBERT STEWART GAVIN
(Known By middle name.)

Left Wing . . . 6' . . . 180 lbs. . . . Born, Ottawa, Ont., March 15, 1960 . . . Shoots left . . . (October, 1981)—Shoulder separation . . . (December, 1981)—Reinjured shoulder . . . (October, 1982)—Sprained ankle . . . (December 8, 1987)—Missed 22 games with strained ligaments in right ankle at Quebec.

Year	Team	League	Games	G.	A.	Pts.	Pen.
1976-77—Ottawa 67's		OMJHL	1	0	0	0	0
1977-78—Toronto Marlboros		OMJHL	67	16	24	40	19
1978-79—Toronto Marlboros		OMJHL	61	24	25	49	83
1979-80—Toronto Marlboros (c)		OMJHL	66	27	30	57	52
1980-81—Toronto Maple Leafs		NHL	14	1	2	3	13
1980-81—New Brunswick Hawks		AHL	46	7	12	19	42
1981-82—Toronto Maple Leafs		NHL	38	5	6	11	29
1982-83—St. Catharines Saints		OHL	6	2	4	6	17
1982-83—Toronto Maple Leafs		NHL	63	6	5	11	44
1983-84—Toronto Maple Leafs		NHL	80	10	22	32	90
1984-85—Toronto Maple Leafs		NHL	73	12	13	25	38
1985-06—Hartford Whalers (d)		NHL	76	26	29	55	51
1986-87—Hartford Whalers		NHL	79	20	22	42	28
1987-88—Hartford Whalers		NHL	56	11	10	21	59
NHL TOTALS			479	91	109	200	352

(c)—June, 1980—Drafted by Toronto Maple Leafs in 1980 NHL entry draft. Fourth Maple Leafs pick, 74th overall, fourth round.

(d)—October, 1985—Traded by Toronto Maple Leafs to Hartford Whalers for Chris Kotsopoulos.

DEREK GEARY

Right Wing . . . 6'3" . . . 180 lbs. . . . Born, Gloucester, Mass., February 18, 1970 . . . Shoots right.

Year	Team	League	Games	G.	A.	Pts.	Pen.
1987-88—Gloucester H.S. (c)		Mass. H.S.	..	26	24	50	..

(c)—June, 1988—Drafted by Boston Bruins in 1988 NHL entry draft. Fifth Bruins pick, 123rd overall, sixth round.

GREG GELDHART

Center . . . 6'1" . . . 200 lbs. . . . Born, Edmonton, Alta., May 12, 1968 . . . Shoots left.

Year	Team	League	Games	G.	A.	Pts.	Pen.
1987-88—St. Albert Saints (c)		AJHL	58	38	67	105	160

(c)—June, 1988—Drafted by Vancouver Canucks in 1988 NHL entry draft. Seventh Canucks pick, 149th overall, eighth round.

MARTIN GELINAS

Left Wing . . . 5'10" . . . 195 lbs. . . . Born, Shawinigan, Que., June 5, 1970 . . . Shoots left . . . (November, 1983)—Broken left clavicle . . . (July, 1986)—Hairline fracture of clavicle.

Year	Team	League	Games	G.	A.	Pts.	Pen.
1986-87—Magog Midgets		Quebec	41	36	42	78	36
1987-88—Hull Olympiques (c-d)		QHL	65	63	68	131	74

(c)—June, 1988—Drafted by Los Angeles Kings in 1988 NHL entry draft. First Kings pick, seventh overall, first round.

(d)—August, 1988—Traded with Jimmy Carson, first-round draft choices in 1989, '91 and '93, plus cash in excess of $10 million by Los Angeles Kings to Edmonton Oilers for Wayne Gretzky, Marty McSorley and Mike Krushelnyski.

ERIC GERMAIN

Defense . . . 6'1" . . . 190 lbs. . . . Born, Quebec City, Que., June 26, 1966 . . . Shoots left.

Year	Team	League	Games	G.	A.	Pts.	Pen.
1983-84—St. Jean Beavers		QHL	57	2	15	17	60
1984-85—St. Jean Beavers		QHL	66	10	31	41	243
1985-86—St. Jean Castors (c)		QHL	66	5	38	43	183

Year	Team	League	Games	G.	A.	Pts.	Pen.
1986-87—Flint Spirit		IHL	21	0	2	2	23
1986-87—Fredericton Express		AHL	44	2	8	10	28
1987-88—Los Angeles Kings		NHL	4	0	1	1	13
1987-88—New Haven Nighthawks		AHL	69	0	10	10	82
NHL TOTALS			4	0	1	1	13

(c)—June, 1986—Signed by Los Angeles Kings as a free agent.

KENNETH GERNANDER

Center . . . 5'10" . . . 155 lbs. . . . Born, Grand Rapids, Minn., June 30, 1969 . . . Shoots left . . . Son of Bob Gernander (Head coach of Greenway-Coleraine High School hockey team).

Year	Team	League	Games	G.	A.	Pts.	Pen.
1985-86—Greenway H.S.		Minn. H.S.	23	14	23	37	....
1986-87—Greenway H.S. (c)		Minn. H.S.	26	35	34	69	....
1987-88—Univ. of Minnesota		WCHA	44	14	14	28	14

(c)—June, 1987—Drafted by Winnipeg Jets in 1987 NHL entry draft. Fourth Jets pick, 96th overall, fifth round.

DONALD SCOTT GIBSON

Defense . . . 6'1" . . . 210 lbs. . . . Born, Deloraine, Man., March 17, 1967 . . . Shoots right . . . (February, 1988)—Suspended three CCHA games for spearing and fighting.

Year	Team	League	Games	G.	A.	Pts.	Pen.
1985-86—Winkler Flyers (c)		MJHL	34	24	29	53	210
1986-87—Michigan State Univ.		CCHA	43	3	3	6	74
1987-88—Michigan State Univ.		CCHA	43	7	12	19	118

(c)—June, 1986—Drafted by Vancouver Canucks in 1986 NHL entry draft. Second Canucks pick, 49th overall, third round.

LEE GIFFIN

Right Wing . . . 5'11" . . . 177 lbs. . . . Born, Chatham, Ont., April 1, 1967 . . . Shoots right . . . (September, 1987)—Scratched left eye cornea and cut eyelid during a training camp scrimmage.

Year	Team	League	Games	G.	A.	Pts.	Pen.
1982-83—Newmarket Flyers		OHA	47	10	21	31	123
1983-84—Oshawa Generals		OHL	70	23	27	50	88
1984-85—Oshawa Generals (c)		OHL	62	36	42	78	78
1985-86—Oshawa Generals		OHL	54	29	37	66	28
1986-87—Oshawa Generals (a)		OHL	48	31	69	100	46
1986-87—Pittsburgh Penguins		NHL	8	1	1	2	0
1987-88—Pittsburgh Penguins		NHL	19	0	2	2	9
1987-88—Muskegon Lumberjacks		IHL	48	26	37	63	61
NHL TOTALS			27	1	3	4	9

(c)—June, 1985—Drafted as underage junior by Pittsburgh Penguins in 1985 NHL entry draft. Second Penguins pick, 23rd overall, second round.

STEPHANE GIGUERE

Left Wing . . . 6' . . . 185 lbs. . . . Born, Montreal, Que., February 21, 1968 . . . Shoots left.

Year	Team	League	Games	G.	A.	Pts.	Pen.
1984-85—Laval Midget AAA		Que.	41	25	37	62	70
1985-86—St. Jean Castors (c)		QHL	71	13	20	33	110
1986-87—St. Jean Castors		QHL	69	45	45	90	129
1987-88—St. Jean Castors		QHL	66	39	48	87	162

(c)—June, 1986—Drafted as underage junior by Toronto Maple Leafs in 1986 NHL entry draft. Sixth Maple Leafs pick, 111th overall, sixth round.

GREG SCOTT GILBERT

Left Wing . . . 6' . . . 190 lbs. . . . Born, Mississauga, Ont., January 22, 1962 . . . Shoots left . . . (December, 1979)—Sprained ankle . . . (September, 1984)—Stretched ligaments in left ankle while jogging prior to training camp . . . (February 27, 1985)—Injured ligaments when checked into open door at players bench by Jamie Macoun in game at Calgary. He required major reconstructive surgery when the knee did not respond to therapy following arthroscopic surgery . . . (October 11, 1986)—Broke jaw in altercation with Tiger Williams at Los Angeles. He lost 13 pounds and missed 10 games . . . (December 7, 1986)—Bruised thigh at Boston . . . (February, 1987)—Bruised hip . . . (March, 1987)—Separated right shoulder . . . (February 20, 1988)—Bruised right knee . . . (April, 1988)—Injured left foot.

Year	Team	League	Games	G.	A.	Pts.	Pen.
1979-80—Toronto Marlboros (c)		OMJHL	68	10	11	21	35
1980-81—Toronto Marlboros		OHL	64	30	37	67	73
1981-82—Toronto Marlboros		OHL	65	41	67	108	119
1981-82—New York Islanders		NHL	1	1	0	1	0
1982-83—Indianapolis Checkers		CHL	24	11	16	27	23
1982-83—New York Islanders		NHL	45	8	11	19	30
1983-84—New York Islanders		NHL	79	31	35	66	59
1984-85—New York Islanders		NHL	58	13	25	38	36
1985-86—Springfield Indians		AHL	2	0	0	0	2
1985-86—New York Islanders		NHL	60	9	19	28	82
1986-87—New York Islanders		NHL	51	6	7	13	26
1987-88—New York Islanders		NHL	76	17	28	45	46
NHL TOTALS			370	85	125	210	279

(c)—June, 1980—Drafted as underage junior by New York Islanders in 1980 NHL entry draft. Fifth Islanders pick, 80th overall, fourth round.

BRENT GILCHRIST

Center . . . 5'10" . . . 175 lbs. . . . Born, Moose Jaw, Sask., April 3, 1967 . . . Shoots left . . . (January, 1985)—Strained medial collateral ligament at Portland . . . (January, 1987)—Injured knee . . . (January, 1987)—Injured knee.

Year	Team	League	Games	G.	A.	Pts.	Pen.
1983-84—Kelowna Wings		WHL	69	16	11	27	16
1984-85—Kelowna Wings (c)		WHL	51	35	38	73	58
1985-86—Spokane Chiefs		WHL	52	45	45	90	57
1986-87—Spokane Chiefs		WHL	46	45	55	100	71
1986-87—Sherbrooke Canadiens (d)		AHL	....	...	....	....	....
1987-88—Sherbrooke Canadiens		AHL	77	26	48	74	83

(c)—June, 1985—Drafted as underage junior by Montreal Canadiens in 1985 NHL entry draft. Sixth Canadiens pick, 79th overall, sixth round.

(d)—No regular season record. Played 10 playoff games (2 goals, 7 assists).

CURT GILES

Defense . . . 5'8" . . . 180 lbs. . . . Born, The Pas, Manitoba, November 30, 1958 . . . Shoots left . . . Named to All-American College teams in 1978 and 1979 . . . (February, 1981)—Right knee strain . . . (January, 1984)—Knee injury . . . (January 25, 1986)—Sprained knee vs. Washington and missed three games . . . (March 24, 1986)—Left ring finger amputated due to a tumor that had grown into the bone. He returned for the playoffs . . . (April 14, 1987)—Fractured elbow in playoff game vs. Philadelphia.

Year	Team	League	Games	G.	A.	Pts.	Pen.
1975-76—Univ. of Minnesota-Duluth		WCHA	34	5	17	22	76
1976-77—Univ. of Minnesota-Duluth		WCHA	37	12	37	49	64
1977-78—Univ. of Minn.-Duluth (a-c)		WCHA	34	11	36	47	62
1978-79—Univ. of Minnesota-Duluth (a)		WCHA	30	3	38	41	38
1979-80—Oklahoma City Stars		CHL	42	4	24	28	35
1979-80—Minnesota North Stars		NHL	37	2	7	9	31
1980-81—Minnesota North Stars		NHL	67	5	22	27	56
1981-82—Minnesota North Stars		NHL	74	3	12	15	87
1982-83—Minnesota North Stars		NHL	76	2	21	23	70
1983-84—Minnesota North Stars		NHL	70	6	22	28	59
1984-85—Minnesota North Stars		NHL	77	5	25	30	49
1985-86—Minnesota North Stars		NHL	69	6	21	27	30
1986-87—Minnesota North Stars (d)		NHL	11	0	3	3	4
1986-87—New York Rangers		NHL	61	2	17	19	50
1987-88—New York Rangers (e)		NHL	13	0	0	0	10
1987-88—Minnesota North Stars		NHL	59	1	12	13	66
NHL TOTALS			614	32	162	194	512

(c)—June, 1978—Drafted by Minnesota North Stars in NHL amateur draft. Fourth North Stars pick, 54th overall, fourth round.

(d)—November, 1986—Traded with Tony McKegney and a second round 1988 draft pick by Minnesota North Stars to New York Rangers for Bob Brooke and a fourth-round draft pick.

(e)—November, 1987—Traded by New York Rangers to Minnesota North Stars for Byron Lomow and future considerations.

RANDY GILHEN

Left Wing . . . 5'11" . . . 195 lbs. . . . Born, Zweibrucken, West Germany, June 13, 1963 . . . Shoots left.

Year	Team	League	Games	G.	A.	Pts.	Pen.
1979-80—Saskatoon	SJHL	55	18	34	52	112
1979-80—Saskatoon Blades	WHL	9	2	2	4	20
1980-81—Saskatoon Blades	WHL	68	10	5	15	154
1981-82—Winnipeg Warriors (c)	WHL	61	41	37	78	87
1982-83—Winnipeg Warriors	WHL	71	57	44	101	84
1982-83—Hartford Whalers	NHL	2	0	1	1	0
1982-83—Binghamton Whalers (d)	AHL	..	..	..	..	..
1983-84—Binghamton Whalers	AHL	73	8	12	20	72
1984-85—Salt Lake Golden Eagles	IHL	57	20	20	40	28
1984-85—Binghamton Whalers (e)	AHL	18	3	3	6	9
1985-86—Fort Wayne Komets	IHL	82	44	40	84	48
1986-87—Winnipeg Jets	NHL	2	0	0	0	0
1986-87—Sherbrooke Canadiens	AHL	75	36	29	65	44
1987-88—Winnipeg Jets	NHL	13	3	2	5	15
1987-88—Moncton Golden Flames	AHL	68	40	47	87	51
NHL TOTALS		17	3	3	6	15

(c)—June, 1982—Drafted as underage junior by Hartford Whalers in 1982 NHL entry draft. Sixth Whalers pick, 109th overall, sixth round.
(d)—No regular season record. Played five playoff games.
(e)—August, 1985—Signed by Winnipeg Jets as a free agent.

TODD GILL

Defense . . . 6'1" . . . 175 lbs. . . . Born, Brockville, Ont., November 9, 1965 . . . Shoots left . . . (October, 1987)—Cracked bone in right foot.

Year	Team	League	Games	G.	A.	Pts.	Pen.
1982-83—Windsor Spitfires	OHL	70	12	24	36	108
1983-84—Windsor Spitfires (c)	OHL	68	9	48	57	184
1984-85—Toronto Maple Leafs	NHL	10	1	0	1	13
1984-85—Windsor Spitfires	OHL	53	17	40	57	148
1985-86—St. Catharines Saints	AHL	58	8	25	33	90
1985-86—Toronto Maple Leafs	NHL	15	1	2	3	28
1986-87—Newmarket Saints	AHL	11	1	8	9	33
1986-87—Toronto Maple Leafs	NHL	61	4	27	31	92
1987-88—Newmarket Saints	AHL	2	0	1	1	2
1987-88—Toronto Maple Leafs	NHL	65	8	17	25	131
NHL TOTALS		151	14	46	60	264

(c)—June, 1984—Drafted as underage junior by Toronto Maple Leafs in 1984 NHL entry draft. Second Maple Leafs pick, 25th overall, second round.

CLARK GILLIES

Left Wing . . . 6'3" . . . 215 lbs. . . . Born, Moose Jaw, Sask., April 7, 1954 . . . Shoots left . . . Played three seasons of baseball with Houston Astros (NL) Covington, Virginia farm team . . . (April, 1983)—Arthroscopic surgery to left knee . . . Holds New York Islanders club record for goals by a left wing in a season (38) . . . (February, 1985)—Sprained ankle . . . (October 29, 1985)—Bruised shoulder vs. Boston and missed four games . . . (January 28, 1986)—Injured back vs. Toronto and missed eight games . . . (October, 1986)—Back spasms . . . (December, 1986)—Missed games due to pulled groin . . . (November 7, 1987)—Torn knee ligament at Edmonton.

Year	Team	League	Games	G.	A.	Pts.	Pen.
1971-72—Regina Pats	WCHL	68	31	48	79	199
1972-73—Regina Pats	WCHL	68	40	52	92	192
1973-74—Regina Pats (a-c)	WCHL	65	46	66	112	179
1974-75—New York Islanders	NHL	80	25	22	47	66
1975-76—New York Islanders	NHL	80	34	27	61	96
1976-77—New York Islanders	NHL	70	33	22	55	93
1977-78—New York Islanders (a)	NHL	80	35	50	85	76
1978-79—New York Islanders (a)	NHL	75	35	56	91	68
1979-80—New York Islanders	NHL	73	19	35	54	49
1980-81—New York Islanders	NHL	80	33	45	78	99
1981-82—New York Islanders	NHL	79	38	39	77	75
1982-83—New York Islanders	NHL	70	21	20	41	76
1983-84—New York Islanders	NHL	76	12	16	28	65
1984-85—New York Islanders	NHL	54	15	17	32	73
1985-86—New York Islanders	NHL	55	4	10	14	55
1986-87—Buffalo Sabres (d)	NHL	61	10	17	27	81
1987-88—Buffalo Sabres	NHL	25	5	2	7	51
NHL TOTALS		958	319	378	697	1023

(c)—Drafted from Regina Pats by New York Islanders in first round of 1974 amateur draft.
(d)—October, 1986—Selected by Buffalo Sabres in 1986 NHL waiver draft.

PAUL C. GILLIS

Center . . . 6' . . . 195 lbs. . . . Born, Toronto, Ont., December 31, 1963 . . . Shoots left . . . Brother of Mike Gillis . . . (November 2, 1986)—Three-game NHL suspension for scratching Dean Evanson's face in a fight vs. Hartford.

Year	Team	League	Games	G.	A.	Pts.	Pen.
1980-81—Niagara Falls Flyers		OHL	59	14	19	33	165
1981-82—Niagara Falls Flyers (c)		OHL	66	27	62	89	247
1982-83—North Bay Centennials		OHL	61	34	52	86	151
1982-83—Quebec Nordiques		NHL	7	0	2	2	2
1983-84—Fredericton Express		AHL	18	7	8	15	47
1983-84—Quebec Nordiques		NHL	57	8	9	17	59
1984-85—Quebec Nordiques		NHL	77	14	28	42	168
1985-86—Quebec Nordiques		NHL	80	19	24	43	203
1986-87—Quebec Nordiques		NHL	76	13	26	39	267
1987-88—Quebec Nordiques		NHL	80	7	10	17	164
NHL TOTALS			377	61	99	160	863

(c)—June, 1982—Drafted as underage junior by Quebec Nordiques in 1982 NHL entry draft. Second Nordiques pick, 34th overall, second round.

DOUGLAS GILMOUR

Center . . . 5'11" . . . 164 lbs. . . . Born, Kingston, Ont., June 25, 1963 . . . Shoots left . . . (October 7, 1985)—Sprained ankle in training camp and missed four regular season games . . . (January, 1988)—Concussion . . . (March, 1988)—Bruised shoulder.

Year	Team	League	Games	G.	A.	Pts.	Pen.
1980-81—Cornwall Royals		QMJHL	51	12	23	35	35
1981-82—Cornwall Royals (c)		OHL	67	46	73	119	42
1982-83—Cornwall Royals (a-d-e)		OHL	68	*70	*107	*177	62
1983-84—St. Louis Blues		NHL	80	25	28	53	57
1984-85—St. Louis Blues		NHL	78	21	36	57	49
1985-86—St. Louis Blues		NHL	74	25	28	53	41
1986-87—St. Louis Blues		NHL	80	42	63	105	58
1987-88—St. Louis Blues		NHL	72	36	50	86	59
NHL TOTALS			384	149	205	354	264

(c)—June, 1982—Drafted as underage junior by St. Louis Blues in 1982 NHL entry draft. Fourth Blues pick, 134th overall, seventh round.
(d)—Won Red Tilson Trophy (Outstanding OHL Player).
(e)—Won Eddie Powers Memorial Trophy (OHL Scoring Champion).

GASTON REGINALD GINGRAS

Defense . . . 6' . . . 191 lbs. . . . Born, Temiscaming, Que., February 13, 1959 . . . Shoots left . . . (October, 1980)—Severe Charley horse . . . (October, 1981)—Injured back . . . (September 18, 1982)—Injured back in preseason game vs. Buffalo . . . (February, 1983)—Back spasms . . . (April, 1988)—Hyperextended left elbow in playoff game vs. Toronto.

Year	Team	League	Games	G.	A.	Pts.	Pen.
1974-75—North Bay Trappers		OPJHL	41	11	27	38	74
1975-76—Kitchener Rangers		Jr. "A" OHA	66	13	31	44	94
1976-77—Kitchener Rangers		Jr. "A" OHA	59	13	62	75	134
1977-78—Kitchener Rangers (c)		Jr. "A" OHA	32	13	24	37	31
1977-78—Hamilton Fincups (d)		Jr. "A" OHA	29	11	19	30	37
1978-79—Birmingham Bulls (e)		WHA	60	13	21	34	35
1979-80—Nova Scotia Voyageurs		AHL	30	11	27	38	17
1979-80—Montreal Canadiens		NHL	34	3	7	10	18
1980-81—Montreal Canadiens		NHL	55	5	16	21	22
1981-82—Montreal Canadiens		NHL	34	6	18	24	28
1982-83—Montreal Canadiens (f)		NHL	22	1	8	9	8
1982-83—Toronto Maple Leafs		NHL	45	10	18	28	10
1983-84—Toronto Maple Leafs		NHL	59	7	20	27	16
1984-85—Toronto Maple Leafs (g)		NHL	5	0	2	2	0
1984-85—St. Catharines Saints		AHL	36	7	12	19	13
1984-85—Sherbrooke Canadiens		AHL	21	3	14	17	6
1985-86—Sherbrooke Canadiens		AHL	42	11	20	31	14
1985-86—Montreal Canadiens		NHL	34	8	18	26	12
1986-87—Montreal Canadiens		NHL	66	11	34	45	21
1987-88—Montreal Canadiens (h)		NHL	2	0	1	1	0
1987-88—St. Louis Blues		NHL	68	7	22	29	18
WHA TOTALS			60	13	21	34	35
NHL TOTALS			424	58	164	222	153

(c)—December, 1977—Traded to Hamilton Fincups by Kitchener Rangers for Jody Gage and future considerations.

(d)—June, 1978—Signed by Birmingham Bulls (WHA) as underage junior.

(e)—June, 1979—Drafted by Montreal Canadiens in entry draft. First Canadiens pick, 27th overall, second round.

(f)—December, 1982—Traded with Dan Daoust by Montreal Canadiens to Toronto Maple Leafs for future draft considerations.

(g)—February, 1985—Traded by Toronto Maple Leafs to Montreal Canadiens to complete earlier trade involving Larry Landon.

(h)—October, 1987—Traded with third or fourth round 1989 draft pick by Montreal Canadiens to St. Louis Blues for Larry Trader and a third or fourth round 1989 draft pick.

MATT GLENNON

Left Wing . . . 6' . . . 185 lbs. . . . Born, Quincy, Mass., September 20, 1968 . . . Shoots left . . . Brother of Mike Glennon (Currently playing at University of New Hampshire).

Year	Team	League	Games	G.	A.	Pts.	Pen.
1985-86—Archbishop Williams H.S.		Mass. H.S.	18	18	22	40	6
1986-87—Archbishop Williams H.S. (c)		Mass. H.S.	18	22	36	58	20
1987-88—Boston College		H. East	16	3	3	6	16

(c)—June, 1987—Drafted by Boston Bruins in 1987 NHL entry draft. Seventh Bruins pick, 119th overall, sixth round.

MIKE GLOVER

Right Wing . . . 5'11" . . . 195 lbs. . . . Born, Ottawa, Ont., July 23, 1968 . . . Shoots right . . . (July, 1987)—Broken nose.

Year	Team	League	Games	G.	A.	Pts.	Pen.
1984-85—Gloucester Major Midget		OHL	40	13	25	38	48
1985-86—Sault Ste. Marie Greyhounds		OHL	61	14	19	33	133
1986-87—Sault Ste. Marie Greyhounds		OHL	57	26	22	48	112
1987-88—Sault Ste. Marie Greyhounds (c)		OHL	63	41	42	83	130

(c)—June, 1988—Drafted by Edmonton Oilers in 1988 NHL entry draft. Eighth Oilers pick, 145th overall, seventh round.

BRIAN GLYNN

Defense . . . 6'4" . . . 224 lbs. . . . Born, Iserlohn, West Germany, November 23, 1967 . . . Shoots left.

Year	Team	League	Games	G.	A.	Pts.	Pen.
1984-85—Melville Millionaires		SAJHL	12	1	0	1	2
1985-86—Saskatoon Blades (c)		WHL	66	7	25	32	131
1986-87—Saskatoon Blades		WHL	44	2	26	28	163
1987-88—Calgary Flames		NHL	67	5	14	19	87
NHL TOTALS			67	5	14	19	87

(c)—June, 1986—Drafted by Calgary Flames in 1986 NHL entry draft. Second Flames pick, 37th overall, second round.

MICHAEL GOBER

Left Wing . . . 6' . . . 190 lbs. . . . Born, St. Louis, Mo., April 10, 1967 . . . Shoots left . . . (January, 1986)—Injured shoulder . . . (May, 1987)—Broke pelvis in automobile accident.

Year	Team	League	Games	G.	A.	Pts.	Pen.
1984-85—Verdun Jr. Canadiens		QHL	46	9	20	29	125
1985-86—Trois-Rivieres Draveurs		QHL	57	27	23	50	151
1986-87—Laval Titans (c)		QHL	63	49	47	96	292
1987-88—Trois-Rivieres Draveurs		QHL	19	5	10	15	96

(c)—June, 1987—Drafted by Detroit Red Wings in 1987 NHL entry draft. Eighth Red Wings pick, 137th overall, seventh round.

DAVE GOERTZ

Defense . . . 5'11" . . . 205 lbs. . . . Born, Edmonton, Alta., March 28, 1965 . . . Shoots right.

Year	Team	League	Games	G.	A.	Pts.	Pen.
1981-82—Regina Pats		WHL	67	5	19	24	181
1982-83—Regina Pats (c)		WHL	69	4	22	26	132
1983-84—Prince Albert Raiders		WHL	60	13	47	60	111
1983-84—Baltimore Skipjacks		AHL	1	0	0	0	0
1984-85—Prince Albert Raiders		WHL	48	3	48	51	62
1984-85—Baltimore Skipjacks (d)		AHL	....	...	....	....	....
1985-86—Baltimore Skipjacks		AHL	74	1	15	16	76

Year	Team	League	Games	G.	A.	Pts.	Pen.
1986-87—Muskegon Lumberjacks		IHL	44	3	17	20	44
1986-87—Baltimore Skipjacks		IHL	16	0	3	3	8
1987-88—Pittsburgh Penguins		NHL	2	0	0	0	2
1987-88—Muskegon Lumberjacks		IHL	73	8	36	44	87
NHL TOTALS			2	0	0	0	2

(c)—June, 1983—Drafted as underage junior by Pittsburgh Penguins in 1983 NHL entry draft. Tenth Penguins pick, 223rd overall, 12th round.

(d)—No regular season record. Played two playoff games.

MICHAEL GOLDEN

Center . . . 6'1" . . . 194 lbs. . . . Born, Boston, Mass., June 17, 1965 . . . Shoots right.

Year	Team	League	Games	G.	A.	Pts.	Pen.
1982-83—Reading H.S. (c)		Mass. H.S.	23	22	41	63	..
1983-84—Univ. of New Hampshire		ECAC	7	1	1	2	2
1984-85—Stratford Jr. B.		OHL	23	..	..	66	..
1985-86—University of Maine (d)		H. East	24	13	16	29	10
1986-87—University of Maine		H. East	44	31	44	75	46

(c)—June, 1983—Drafted as underage junior by Edmonton Oilers in 1983 NHL entry draft. Second Oilers pick, 40th overall, second round.

(d)—October, 1986—Traded with Don Jackson by Edmonton Oilers to New York Rangers for Reijo Ruotsalainen, NHL rights to Ville Horava, Clark Donatelli and Jim Wiemer.

GLEN GOODALL

Center . . . 5'8" . . . 168 lbs. . . . Born, Fort Nelson, B.C., January 22, 1970 . . . Shoots right . . . Set WHL records for points by a 16-year-old (112) and goals (63).

Year	Team	League	Games	G.	A.	Pts.	Pen.
1983-84—Thompson Bantam		Manitoba	74	163	157	320	40
1984-85—Seattle Breakers		WHL	59	5	21	26	6
1985-86—Seattle Thunderbirds		WHL	65	13	28	41	53
1986-87—Seattle Thunderbirds (b)		WHL	68	63	49	112	64
1987-88—Seattle Thunderbirds (c)		WHL	70	53	64	117	88

(c)—June, 1988—Drafted by Detroit Red Wings in 1988 NHL entry draft. Ninth Red Wings pick, 206th overall, 10th round.

SEAN GORMAN

Defense . . . 6'3" . . . 185 lbs. . . . Born, Cambridge, Mass., February 1, 1969 . . . Shoots right.

Year	Team	League	Games	G.	A.	Pts.	Pen.
1985-86—Matignon H.S.		Mass. H.S.	16	5	8	13	6
1986-87—Matignon H.S. (c)		Mass. H.S.	....	1	9	10	....
1987-88—Princeton University		ECAC	28	0	3	3	6

(c)—June, 1987—Drafted by Boston Bruins in 1987 NHL entry draft. Thirteenth Bruins pick, 245th overall, 12th round.

GUY GOSSELIN

Defense . . . 5'10" . . . 185 lbs. . . . Born, Rochester, Minn., January 6, 1964 . . . Shoots left . . . Son of Gordon Gosselin, a member of 1952 Fort Francis, Ontario Allen Cup Champions.

Year	Team	League	Games	G.	A.	Pts.	Pen.
1981-82—Rochester J. Marshall H.L. (c)		Minn.H.S.	22	14	15	29	48
1982-83—Univ. of Minn.-Duluth		WCHA	4	0	0	0	0
1983-84—Univ. of Minn.-Duluth		WCHA	37	3	3	6	26
1984-85—Univ. of Minn.-Duluth		WCHA	47	3	7	10	50
1985-86—Univ. of Minn.-Duluth		WCHA	39	2	16	18	53
1986-87—Univ. of Minn.-Duluth (b)		WCHA	33	7	8	15	66
1987-88—U.S. Olympic Team		Int'l	53	3	22	25	....
1987-88—Winnipeg Jets		NHL	5	0	0	0	6
NHL TOTALS			5	0	0	0	6

(c)—June, 1982—Drafted as underage player by Winnipeg Jets in 1982 NHL entry draft. Sixth Jets pick, 159th overall, eighth round.

STEVE GOTAAS

Center . . . 5'9" . . . 170 lbs. . . . Born, Cumrose, Sask., May 10, 1967 . . . Shoots right . . . (May, 1984)—Shoulder surgery . . . (September, 1987)—Bursitis in hip during Pittsburgh training camp.

Year	Team	League	Games	G.	A.	Pts.	Pen.
1983-84—Prince Albert Raiders		WHL	65	10	22	32	47
1984-85—Prince Albert Raiders (c)		WHL	72	32	41	73	66

Year	Team	League	Games	G.	A.	Pts.	Pen.
1985-86—Prince Albert Raiders		WHL	61	40	61	101	31
1986-87—Prince Albert Raiders		WHL	68	53	55	108	94
1987-88—Pittsburgh Penguins		NHL	36	5	6	11	45
1987-88—Muskegon Lumberjacks		IHL	34	16	22	38	4
NHL TOTALS			36	5	6	11	45

(c)—June, 1985—Drafted as underage junior by Pittsburgh Penguins in 1985 NHL entry draft. Fourth Penguins pick, 86th overall, fifth round.

ROBERT GOULD

Right Wing . . . 5'11" . . . 195 lbs. . . . Born, Petrolia, Ont., September 2, 1957 . . . Shoots right . . . (October, 1987)—Hairline fracture of right foot.

Year	Team	League	Games	G.	A.	Pts.	Pen.
1975-76—University of New Hampshire		ECAC	31	13	14	27	16
1976-77—University of New Hampshire (c)		ECAC	39	24	25	49	36
1977-78—University of New Hampshire		ECAC	30	23	34	57	40
1978-79—University of New Hampshire		ECAC	....	24	17	41	....
1978-79—Tulsa Oilers		CHL	5	2	0	2	4
1979-80—Atlanta Flames		NHL	1	0	0	0	0
1979-80—Birmingham Bulls		CHL	79	27	33	60	73
1980-81—Calgary Flames		NHL	3	0	0	0	0
1980-81—Birmingham Bulls		CHL	58	25	25	50	43
1980-81—Fort Worth Texans		CHL	18	8	6	14	6
1981-82—Oklahoma City Stars		CHL	1	0	1	1	0
1981-82—Calgary Flames (d)		NHL	16	3	0	3	4
1981-82—Washington Capitals		NHL	60	18	13	31	69
1982-83—Washington Capitals		NHL	80	22	18	40	43
1983-84—Washington Capitals		NHL	78	21	19	40	74
1984-85—Washington Capitals		NHL	78	14	19	33	69
1985-86—Washington Capitals		NHL	79	19	19	38	26
1986-87—Washington Capitals		NHL	78	23	27	50	74
1987-88—Washington Capitals		NHL	72	12	14	26	56
NHL TOTALS			546	132	129	261	415

(c)—June, 1977—Drafted by Atlanta Flames in 1977 amateur draft. Sixth Flames pick, 118th overall, seventh round.

(d)—November, 1981—Traded with Randy Holt by Calgary Flames to Washington Capitals for Pat Ribble.

MICHEL GOULET

Left Wing . . . 6'1" . . . 195 lbs. . . . Born, Peribonqua, Que., April 21, 1960 . . . Shoots left . . . Set Nordiques NHL record for most goals in a season in 1982-83 (57) . . . (1983-84) Set NHL record for most points by left wing in a season (121) and tied record for assists by a left wing (65) set by John Bucyk of Boston in 1970-71 . . . (January 2, 1985)—Fractured thumb vs. Hartford Whalers . . . (September, 1985)—Left training camp to renegotiate contract. He was suspended by Quebec and did not return until after the regular season had started . . . (October 13, 1986)—Broke finger on right hand when slashed by Brad Maxwell at Vancouver.

Year	Team	League	Games	G.	A.	Pts.	Pen.
1976-77—Quebec Remparts		QJHL	37	17	18	35	9
1977-78—Quebec Remparts (b-c)		QJHL	72	73	62	135	109
1978-79—Birmingham Bulls (d)		WHA	78	28	30	58	64
1979-80—Quebec Nordiques		NHL	77	22	32	54	48
1980-81—Quebec Nordiques		NHL	76	32	39	71	45
1981-82—Quebec Nordiques		NHL	80	42	42	84	48
1982-83—Quebec Nordiques (b)		NHL	80	57	48	105	51
1983-84—Quebec Nordiques (a)		NHL	75	56	65	121	76
1984-85—Quebec Nordiques		NHL	69	55	40	95	55
1985-86—Quebec Nordiques (a)		NHL	75	53	50	103	64
1986-87—Quebec Nordiques (a)		NHL	75	49	47	96	61
1987-88—Quebec Nordiques		NHL	80	48	58	106	56
WHA TOTALS			78	28	30	58	64
NHL TOTALS			687	414	421	835	504

(c)—July, 1978—Signed by Birmingham Bulls (WHA) as underage player.

(d)—August, 1979—Drafted by Quebec Nordiques in 1979 NHL entry draft. First Nordiques pick, 20th overall, first round.

CHRIS GOVEDARIS

Left Wing . . . 6' . . . 200 lbs. . . . Born, Toronto, Ont., February 2, 1970 . . . Shoots left . . . Also plays Center . . . (October, 1986)— Suspended two games by OHL.

Year	Team	League	Games	G.	A.	Pts.	Pen.
1985-86—Toronto Young Nationals		MTHL	38	35	50	85	....
1986-87—Toronto Marlboros		OHL	64	36	28	64	148
1987-88—Toronto Marlboros (c)		OHL	62	42	38	80	118

(c)—June, 1988—Drafted by Hartford Whalers in 1988 NHL entry draft. First Whalers pick, 11th overall, first round.

DIRK GRAHAM

Right Wing . . . 5'11" . . . 190 lbs. . . . Born, Regina, Sask., July 29, 1959 . . . Shoots right . . . (November, 1987)—Missed seven games with a sprained wrist.

Year	Team	League	Games	G.	A.	Pts.	Pen.
1975-76—Regina Blues		SJHL	54	36	32	68	82
1975-76—Regina Pats		WCHL	2	0	0	0	0
1976-77—Regina Pats		WCHL	65	37	28	65	66
1977-78—Regina Pats		WCHL	72	49	61	110	87
1978-79—Regina Pats (b-c)		WHL	71	48	60	108	252
1979-80—Dallas Black Hawks		CHL	62	17	15	32	96
1980-81—Fort Wayne Komets		IHL	6	1	2	3	12
1980-81—Toledo Goaldiggers		IHL	61	40	45	85	88
1981-82—Toledo Goaldiggers		IHL	72	49	56	105	68
1982-83—Toledo Goaldiggers (a-d)		IHL	78	70	55	125	86
1983-84—Minnesota North Stars		NHL	6	1	1	2	0
1983-84—Salt Lake Golden Eagles (a)		CHL	57	37	57	94	72
1984-85—Springfield Indians		AHL	37	20	28	48	41
1984-85—Minnesota North Stars		NHL	36	12	11	23	23
1985-86—Minnesota North Stars		NHL	80	22	33	55	87
1986-87—Minnesota North Stars		NHL	76	25	29	54	142
1987-88—Minnesota North Stars (e)		NHL	28	7	5	12	39
1987-88—Chicago Black Hawks		NHL	42	17	19	36	32
NHL TOTALS			268	84	98	182	323

(c)—August, 1979—Drafted by Vancouver Canucks in 1979 NHL entry draft. Fifth Canucks pick, 89th overall, fifth round.

(d)—Co-leader, with teammate Rick Hendricks, during IHL playoffs with 20 points.

(e)—January, 1988—Traded by Minnesota North Stars to Chicago Black Hawks for Curt Fraser.

ROBB GRAHAM

Right Wing . . . 6'3" . . . 205 lbs. . . . Born, Bellevue, Wash., April 7, 1968 . . . Shoots right.

Year	Team	League	Games	G.	A.	Pts.	Pen.
1984-85—Guelph Platers		OHL	62	3	4	7	28
1985-86—Guelph Platers (c)		OHL	62	10	18	28	78
1986-87—Guelph Platers		OHL	45	13	14	27	37
1987-88—Sudbury Wolves		OHL	58	17	17	34	59
1987-88—Colorado Rangers		IHL	5	1	1	2	0

(c)—June, 1986—Drafted as underage junior by New York Rangers in 1986 NHL entry draft. Seventh Rangers pick, 135th overall, seventh round.

DAVID GRANNIS

Right Wing . . . 6' . . . 190 lbs. . . . Born, St. Paul, Minn., January 18, 1966 . . . Shoots right.

Year	Team	League	Games	G.	A.	Pts.	Pen.
1983-84—South St. Paul H.S. (c)		Minn. H.S.	20	20	23	43	14
1984-85—University of Minnesota		WCHA	23	2	6	8	17
1985-86—University of Minnesota		WCHA	25	5	7	12	14
1986-87—University of Minnesota		WCHA	46	10	12	22	32
1987-88—University of Minnesota		WCHA	43	9	12	21	45

(c)—June, 1984—Drafted by Los Angeles Kings in 1984 NHL entry draft. Fifth Kings pick, 87th overall, fifth round.

KEVIN GRANT

Defense . . . 6'4" . . . 210 lbs. . . . Born, Toronto, Ont., January 9, 1969 . . . Shoots right . . . (February 1, 1987)—Injured knee ligaments at North Bay.

Year	Team	League	Games	G.	A.	Pts.	Pen.
1984-85—Halifax McDonalds		N.S. Midget	35	15	20	35	50
1985-86—Kitchener Rangers		OHL	63	2	15	17	204
1986-87—Kitchener Rangers (c)		OHL	52	5	18	23	125
1987-88—Kitchener Rangers		OHL	48	3	20	23	138

(c)—June, 1987—Drafted as underage junior by Calgary Flames in 1987 NHL entry draft. Third Flames pick, 40th overall, second round.

DANNY GRATTON

Center and Left Wing . . . 6'1" . . . 185 lbs. . . . Born, Brantford, Ont., December 7, 1966 . . . Shoots left . . . Son of Ken Gratton (minor league player, 1967-1976).

Year	Team	League	Games	G.	A.	Pts.	Pen.
1981-82—Guelph Platers		OJHL	40	14	26	40	70
1982-83—Oshawa Generals		OHL	64	15	28	43	55
1983-84—Oshawa Generals		OHL	65	40	34	74	55
1984-85—Oshawa Generals (c)		OHL	56	24	48	72	67
1985-86—Oshawa Generals		OHL	10	3	5	8	15
1985-86—Belleville Bulls (d)		OHL	20	12	14	26	11
1985-86—Ottawa 67's		OHL	25	18	18	36	19
1986-87—New Haven Nighthawks		AHL	49	6	10	16	45
1987-88—New Haven Nighthawks		AHL	57	18	28	46	77
1987-88—Los Angeles Kings		NHL	7	1	0	1	5
NHL TOTALS			7	1	0	1	5

(c)—June, 1985—Drafted as underage junior by Los Angeles Kings in 1985 NHL entry draft. Second Kings pick, 10th overall, first round.

(d)—February, 1986—Traded by Belleville Bulls to Ottawa 67's for Frank Dimuzio.

ADAM GRAVES

Center . . . 6' . . . 185 lbs. . . . Born, Toronto, Ont., April 12, 1968 . . . Shoots left . . . Also plays Left Wing . . . (February, 1986)—Bruised shoulder.

Year	Team	League	Games	G.	A.	Pts.	Pen.
1984-85—King City Jr. B.		OHL	25	23	33	56	29
1985-86—Windsor Spitfires (c)		OHL	62	27	37	64	35
1986-87—Windsor Spitfires		OHL	66	45	55	100	70
1986-87—Adirondack Red Wings (d)		AHL	....	...	....	....	....
1987-88—Detroit Red Wings		NHL	9	0	1	1	8
1987-88—Windsor Spitfires		OHL	37	28	32	60	107
NHL TOTALS			9	0	1	1	8

(c)—June, 1986—Drafted as underage junior by Detroit Red Wings in 1986 NHL entry draft. Second Red Wings pick, 22nd overall, second round.

(d)—No regular season record. Played five playoff games (1 assist).

STEVE GRAVES

Left Wing and Center . . . 6' . . . 180 lbs. . . . Born, Kingston, Ont., April 7, 1964 . . . Shoots left . . . (February, 1986)—Torn groin muscle.

Year	Team	League	Games	G.	A.	Pts.	Pen.
1980-81—Ottawa Senators		OPJHL	44	21	17	38	47
1981-82—Sault Ste. Marie Greyhounds (c)		OHL	66	12	15	27	49
1982-83—Sault Ste. Marie Greyhounds		OHL	60	21	20	41	48
1983-84—Sault Ste. Marie Greyhounds		OHL	67	41	48	81	47
1983-84—Edmonton Oilers		NHL	2	0	0	0	0
1984-85—Nova Scotia Oilers		AHL	80	17	15	32	20
1985-86—Nova Scotia Oilers		AHL	78	19	18	37	22
1986-87—Edmonton Oilers		NHL	12	2	0	2	0
1986-87—Nova Scotia Oilers		AHL	59	18	10	28	22
1987-88—Edmonton Oilers		NHL	21	3	4	7	10
1987-88—Nova Scotia Oilers		AHL	11	6	2	8	4
NHL TOTALS			35	5	4	9	10

(c)—June, 1982—Drafted as underage junior by Edmonton Oilers in 1982 NHL entry draft. Second Oilers pick, 41st overall, second round.

RICHARD DOUGLAS (RICK) GREEN

Defense . . . 6'3" . . . 200 lbs. . . . Born, Belleville, Ont., February 20, 1956 . . . Shoots left . . . Missed part of 1976-77 season with broken right wrist . . . (November, 1980)—Broken hand . . . (December 14, 1981)—Separated shoulder at Montreal . . . (March, 1983)—Hip injury . . . (October, 1983)—Broken right wrist . . . (February 21, 1984)—Broke rib at Buffalo . . . (September, 1985)—Injured ankle during training camp and missed first eight games of season . . . (December 31, 1985)—Broken thumb . . . (February 24, 1986)—Reinjured thumb at Edmonton . . . (October, 1986)—Cut eyelid . . . (October, 1987)—Bruised right foot . . . (March, 1988)—Injured back.

Year	Team	League	Games	G.	A.	Pts.	Pen.
1972-73—London Knights		Jr."A"OHA	7	0	1	1	2
1973-74—London Knights		Jr."A"OHA	65	6	30	36	45
1974-75—London Knights		Jr."A"OHA	65	8	45	53	68
1975-76—London Knights (a-c-d)		Jr."A"OHA	61	13	47	60	69

Year	Team	League	Games	G.	A.	Pts.	Pen.
1976-77—Washington Capitals		NHL	45	3	12	15	16
1977-78—Washington Capitals		NHL	60	5	14	19	67
1978-79—Washington Capitals		NHL	71	8	33	41	62
1979-80—Washington Capitals		NHL	71	4	20	24	52
1980-81—Washington Capitals		NHL	65	8	23	31	91
1981-82—Washington Capitals (e)		NHL	65	3	25	28	93
1982-83—Montreal Canadiens		NHL	66	2	24	26	58
1983-84—Montreal Canadiens		NHL	7	0	1	1	7
1984-85—Montreal Canadiens		NHL	77	1	18	19	30
1985-86—Montreal Canadiens		NHL	46	3	2	5	20
1986-87—Montreal Canadiens		NHL	72	1	9	10	10
1987-88—Montreal Canadiens		NHL	59	2	11	13	33
NHL TOTALS			704	40	192	232	539

(c)—Won Max Kaminsky Memorial Trophy (Outstanding Defenseman).
(d)—Drafted from London Knights by Washington Capitals in first round of 1976 amateur draft.
(e)—September, 1982—Traded by Washington Capitals with Ryan Walter to Montreal Canadiens for Rod Langway, Brian Engblom, Doug Jarvis and Craig Laughlin.

JEFF GREENLAW

Left Wing . . . 6'2" . . . 200 lbs. . . . Born, Toronto, Ont., February 28, 1968 . . . Shoots left . . . (April, 1987)—Fitted for body cast to allow healing of a stress fracture of a vertebrae.

Year	Team	League	Games	G.	A.	Pts.	Pen.
1984-85—St. Catharines Jr. B		OHA	33	21	29	50	141
1985-86—Team Canada (c)		Int'l.	57	3	16	19	81
1986-87—Washington Capitals		NHL	22	0	3	3	44
1986-87—Binghamton Whalers		AHL	4	0	2	2	0
1987-88—Binghamton Whalers		AHL	56	8	7	15	142
NHL TOTALS			22	0	3	3	44

(c)—June, 1986—Drafted by Washington Capitals in 1986 NHL entry draft. First Capitals pick, 19th overall, first round.

GLENN GREENOUGH

Right Wing . . . 5'11" . . . 195 lbs. . . . Born, Sudbury, Ont., July 20, 1966 . . . Shoots right . . . (December 19, 1986)—Separated shoulder vs. Indianapolis.

Year	Team	League	Games	G.	A.	Pts.	Pen.
1982-83—Sudbury Wolves		OHL	60	10	9	19	9
1983-84—Sudbury Wolves (c)		OHL	67	26	43	69	33
1984-85—Sudbury Wolves		OHL	15	12	11	23	13
1985-86—Sudbury Wolves		OHL	64	30	41	71	34
1986-87—Saginaw Gears		IHL	70	38	43	81	63
1987-88—Saginaw Wings		IHL	74	35	33	68	65

(c)—June, 1984—Drafted as underage junior by Chicago Black Hawks in 1984 NHL entry draft. Eighth Black Hawks pick, 153rd overall, eighth round.

RANDY GREGG

Defense . . . 6'4" . . . 215 lbs. . . . Born, Edmonton, Alta., February 19, 1956 . . . Shoots left . . . Has a degree in medicine . . . Furthered medical studies while he played hockey in Japan . . . (December, 1984)—Bruised left shoulder . . . (January, 1985)—Sprained left knee . . . (October 28, 1985)—Separated ribs at Calgary and missed 16 games . . . Won Senator Joseph Sullivan Award as the top Canadian College player in 1979 . . . (March 17, 1987)—Dislocated left shoulder.

Year	Team	League	Games	G.	A.	Pts.	Pen.
1975-76—University of Alberta		CWUAA	20	3	14	17	27
1976-77—University of Alberta		CWUAA	24	9	17	26	34
1977-78—University of Alberta		CWUAA	24	7	23	30	37
1978-79—University of Alberta		CWUAA	24	5	16	21	47
1979-80—Canadian National Team		Int'l	56	7	17	24	36
1979-80—Canadian Olympic Team		Int'l	6	1	1	2	2
1980-81—Kokudo Bunnies (c)		Japan	35	12	18	30	30
1981-82—Kokudo Bunnies		Japan	36	12	20	32	25
1981-82—Edmonton Oilers (d)		NHL	....	...	....	....	....
1982-83—Edmonton Oilers		NHL	80	6	22	28	54
1983-84—Edmonton Oilers		NHL	80	13	27	40	56
1984-85—Edmonton Oilers		NHL	57	3	20	23	32
1985-86—Edmonton Oilers		NHL	64	2	26	28	47
1986-87—Edmonton Oilers (e)		NHL	52	8	16	24	42

Year	Team	League	Games	G.	A.	Pts.	Pen.
1987-88—Canadian Olympic Team	Int'l	45	3	8	11	45
1987-88—Edmonton Oilers	NHL	15	1	2	3	8
NHL TOTALS		348	33	113	146	239

(c)—March, 1981—Signed by Edmonton Oilers as a free agent.
(d)—No regular season record. Played four playoff games.
(e)—September, 1986—Announced he was retiring. He returned to the Oilers in November.

BILL GREGOIRE

Defense . . . 6' . . . 175 lbs. . . . Born, Victoria, B.C., April 9, 1967 . . . Shoots left . . . (November, 1986)—Strained knee in a WHL game.

Year	Team	League	Games	G.	A.	Pts.	Pen.
1984-85—Victoria Cougars (c)	WHL	67	2	12	14	144
1985-86—Victoria Cougars	WHL	41	13	19	32	122
1986-87—Calgary Wranglers	WHL	49	13	17	30	173
1986-87—Moncton Golden Flames	AHL	7	0	0	0	29
1987-88—Salt Lake Golden Eagles	IHL	17	2	2	4	59
1987-88—Lethbridge Hurricanes	WHL	10	1	3	4	51
1987-88—New Westminster Bruins	WHL	34	11	16	27	159

(c)—June, 1985—Drafted as underage junior by Calgary Flames in 1985 NHL entry draft. Thirteenth Flames pick, 248th overall, 12th round.

RONALD JOHN GRESCHNER

Defense . . . 6'2" . . . 205 lbs. . . . Born, Goodsoil, Sask., December 22, 1954 . . . Shoots left . . . Set WCHL record for points by defenseman in season in 1973-74 (broken by Kevin McCarthy in 1975-76) . . . Missed part of 1978-79 season with shoulder separation . . . (November 18, 1981)—Pinched nerve in back vs. Philadelphia . . . (September, 1982)—Injured back in training camp and out until February, 1983 . . . (March, 1983)—Reinjured back . . . (November, 1984)—Shoulder separation that cost him 31 games at various points of the season . . . (May, 1985)—Surgery to resection the distal clavical of left shoulder . . . (April 15, 1986)—Fractured right hand in playoff game at Philadelphia . . . Also plays Center . . . (October, 1986)—Fractured left foot . . . (March, 1988)—Strained left shoulder.

Year	Team	League	Games	G.	A.	Pts.	Pen.
1971-72—New Westminster Bruins	WCHL	44	1	9	10	126
1972-73—New Westminster Bruins	WCHL	68	22	47	69	169
1973-74—New Westminster Bruins (c)	WCHL	67	33	70	103	170
1974-75—Providence Reds	AHL	7	5	6	11	10
1974-75—New York Rangers	NHL	70	8	37	45	94
1975-76—New York Rangers	NHL	77	6	21	27	93
1976-77—New York Rangers	NHL	80	11	36	47	89
1977-78—New York Rangers	NHL	78	24	48	72	100
1978-79—New York Rangers	NHL	60	17	36	53	66
1979-80—New York Rangers	NHL	76	21	37	58	103
1980-81—New York Rangers	NHL	74	27	41	68	112
1981-82—New York Rangers	NHL	29	5	11	16	16
1982-83—New York Rangers	NHL	10	3	5	8	0
1983-84—New York Rangers	NHL	77	12	44	56	117
1984-85—New York Rangers	NHL	48	16	29	45	42
1985-86—New York Rangers	NHL	78	20	28	48	104
1986-87—New York Rangers	NHL	61	6	34	40	62
1987-88—New York Rangers	NHL	51	1	5	6	82
NHL TOTALS		869	177	412	589	1080

(c)—Drafted from New Westminster Bruins by New York Rangers in second round of 1974 amateur draft.

KEITH GRETZKY

Center . . . 5'9" . . . 155 lbs. . . . Born, Brantford, Ont., February 16, 1967 . . . Shoots left . . . Brother of Wayne Gretzky.

Year	Team	League	Games	G.	A.	Pts.	Pen.
1981-82—Brantford Midgets	OHL	78	70	74	144	10
1982-83—Brantford Alexanders	OHL	37	5	9	14	0
1983-84—Windsor Spitfires	OHL	70	15	38	53	8
1984-85—Windsor Spitfires (c)	OHL	66	31	62	93	12
1985-86—Windsor Spitfires (d)	OHL	43	24	36	60	10
1985-86—Belleville Bulls	OHL	18	3	11	14	2
1986-87—Belleville Bulls (e)	OHL	29	17	36	53	10
1986-87—Hamilton Steelhawks (f)	OHL	35	18	30	48	8
1987-88—Rochester Americans	AHL	43	8	24	32	6
1987-88—Flint Spirits	IHL	25	9	18	27	0

(c)—June, 1985—Drafted as underage junior by Buffalo Sabres in 1985 NHL entry draft. Third Sabres pick, 56th overall, third round.

(d)—February, 1986—Traded by Windsor Compuware Spitfires to Belleville Bulls for Ken Hulst and future considerations.

(e)—December, 1986—Traded by Belleville Bulls to Hamilton Steelhawks for Paul Wilkinson, Darryl Williams and future considerations.

(f)—Co-winner of William Hanley Trophy (Most Gentlemanly Player) with Scott McCrory.

WAYNE GRETZKY

Center . . . 6' . . . 170 lbs. . . . Born, Brantford, Ont., January 26, 1961 . . . Shoots left . . . In 1979-80, his first NHL season, he became the youngest player in history to win an NHL trophy, to score 50 goals, to collect 100 points (Broken by Dale Hawerchuk) and the youngest to ever be named to the NHL All-Star team . . . Set new regular season NHL record for goals (92 in 1981-82), assists (135 in 1984-85) and points (212 in 1981-82) . . . Set new NHL records for goals (97 in 1981-82), assists (165 in 1984-85) and points (255 in 1984-85) regular season plus playoffs . . . Set new NHL playoff records for assists (31) in 1987-88 and points (47) in 1984-85 . . . Tied single game record in playoffs for most assists in a period (3), and a game (5), in first game of 1981 playoffs (April 8, 1981) in a 6-3 win at Montreal despite not taking a single shot on goal . . . In 1981-82, also set NHL records for fastest (50) goals from the start of the year (39 games), fastest 500 career points (234 games), largest margin over second-place finisher in scoring race (65 points) and most 3-or-more goals in a season (10-later tied in 1983-84) . . . (December 27, 1981)—Became first hockey player to be named THE SPORTING NEWS MAN-OF-THE-YEAR . . . (March 19, 1982)—Youngest player to reach 500 NHL career points (21 years, 1 month, 21 days) . . . (February 8, 1983)—Set All-Star game record with four goals . . . Set NHL playoff record for most points in one game with 7 (vs. Calgary, April 17, 1983, vs. Winnipeg, April 25, 1985 and vs. Los Angeles, April 9, 1987—Broken by Patrik Sundstrom with 8 in 1987-88) . . . (October 5, 1983-January 27, 1984)—Set NHL record by collecting points in 51 consecutive games (61g, 92a), the first 51 games of the season . . . (January 28, 1984)—Bruised right shoulder vs. Los Angeles and ended consecutive games played streak at 362, an Oilers club record . . . (June, 1984)—Surgery on left ankle to remove benign growth caused by lacing his skates too tight . . . Set NHL record for most shorthanded goals in a season (12 in 1983-84) . . . (November 26, 1983-January 4, 1984)—Set NHL record for collecting assists in 17 straight games . . . (December 19, 1984)—Collected his 1000th NHL point in fewer games than any player in history, 424 games (Previous fastest was 720 games by Guy Lafleur). He is also the youngest player to ever reach the plateau at 23 yrs., 10 mos., 23 days. The previous youngest was Lafleur at 29 yrs., 3 mos., 18 days . . . Set playoff record for most assists in a single series (14 vs. Chicago, 1985 . . . First player to have 100 point seasons in first nine years of NHL . . . Brother of Keith Gretzky . . . Named 1985 Canadian Athlete of the Year . . . Set new regular season NHL records for assists (163) and points (215) in 1985-86 . . . Set new NHL playoff records for most career assists (171) and points (252) . . . Tied playoff record for most assists in single playoff game (6 on April 9, 1987) . . . (December 30, 1987)—Twisted right knee as he scored a goal at Philadelphia . . . (February 19, 1988)—Missed three games due to corneal abrasion to left eye vs. Pittsburgh . . . All-time NHL career assist leader.

Year	Team	League	Games	G.	A.	Pts.	Pen.
1976-77—Peterborough Petes		OMJHL	3	0	3	3	0
1977-78—S. Ste. M. G'hounds (b-c)		OMJHL	64	70	112	182	14
1978-79—Indianapolis Racers (d)		WHA	8	3	3	6	0
1978-79—Edmonton Oilers (b-e-f-g)		WHA	72	43	61	104	19
1979-80—Edmonton Oilers (b-h-i)		NHL	79	51	*86	*137	21
1980-81—Edmonton Oilers (a-h-j-l)		NHL	80	55	*109	*164	28
1981-82—Edmonton Oilers (a-h-j-l-p)		NHL	80	*92	*120	*212	26
1982-83—Edmonton Oilers (a-h-j-k-l-p)		NHL	80	*71	*125	*196	59
1983-84—Edmonton Oilers (a-h-j-l-m-p)		NHL	74	*87	*118	*205	39
1984-85—Edmonton Oilers (a-h-j-l-n-o-p)		NHL	80	*73	*135	*208	52
1985-86—Edmonton Oilers (a-h-j-l)		NHL	80	52	*163	*215	46
1986-87—Edmonton Oilers (a-h-j-q)		NHL	79	*62	*121	*183	28
1987-88—Edmonton Oilers (b-o-r-s)		NHL	64	40	*109	149	24
NHL TOTALS			696	583	1086	1669	323
WHA TOTALS			80	46	64	110	19

(c)—May, 1978—Signed to multi-year contract by Indianapolis Racers (WHA) as an underage junior.

(d)—November, 1978—Traded by Indianapolis to Edmonton with Peter Driscoll, Ed Mio for cash and future considerations.

(e)—Won WHA Rookie award.

(f)—Named WHA Rookie of the Year in poll of players by THE SPORTING NEWS.

(g)—Led in points (20) and tied for lead in goals (10) during playoffs.

(h)—Won Hart Memorial Trophy (Most Valuable Player).

(i)—Won Lady Byng Memorial Trophy (Most Gentlemanly Player).

(j)—Won Art Ross Memorial Trophy (NHL Leading Scorer).

(k)—Led Stanley Cup Playoffs with 26 assists and 38 points.

(l)—Selected NHL Player of Year by THE SPORTING NEWS in poll of players.

(m)—Led Stanley Cup Playoffs with 22 assists and 35 points.
(n)—Led Stanley Cup Playoffs with 30 assists and 47 points.
(o)—Won Conn Smythe Trophy (Stanley Cup Playoff MVP).
(p)—Won Lester Pearson Award (NHL Players MVP).
(q)—Led Stanley Cup Playoffs with 29 assists and 34 points.
(r)—Led Stanley Cup Playoffs with 31 assists and 43 points.
(s)—August, 1988—Traded with Marty McSorley and Mike Krushelnyski by Edmonton Oilers to Los Angeles Kings for Jimmy Carson, Martin Gelinas, first-round draft choices in 1989, '91 and '93, plus cash in excess of $10 million.

MIKE GRIFFITH

Right Wing . . . 5'11" . . . 205 lbs. . . . Born, Toronto, Ont., January 3, 1969 . . . Shoots right.

Year	Team	League	Games	G.	A.	Pts.	Pen.
1984-85—Nepean Tier II Jr. A		OHA	54	9	33	42	46
1985-86—Ottawa 67's		OHL	59	14	13	27	38
1986-87—Ottawa 67's		OHL	66	26	66	92	28
1987-88—Ottawa 67's (c)		OHL	66	46	37	83	39

(c)—June, 1988—Drafted by Buffalo Sabres in 1988 NHL entry draft. Eighth Sabres pick, 139th overall, seventh round.

JARI GRONSTRAND

Defense . . . 6'3" . . . 197 lbs. . . . Born, Tampere, Finland, November 14, 1962 . . . Shoots left . . . (October, 1986)—Missed three games with bruised ribs . . . (December 16, 1986)—Separated shoulder at N.Y. Islanders . . . (February, 1987)—Strained knee ligaments . . . (March 11, 1987)—Hospitalized after being struck in the eye with a stick vs. Toronto . . . (February, 1988)—Strained ligaments in right knee.

Year	Team	League	Games	G.	A.	Pts.	Pen.
1984-85—Tappara		Finland	33	9	6	15	..
1985-86—Tappara (c)		Finland	44	10	7	17	32
1986-87—Minnesota North Stars		NHL	47	1	6	7	27
1987-88—New York Rangers (d)		NHL	62	3	11	14	63
1987-88—Colorado Rangers (e)		IHL	3	1	3	4	0
NHL TOTALS			109	4	17	21	90

(c)—June, 1986—Drafted by Minnesota North Stars in 1986 NHL entry draft. Eighth North Stars pick, 96th overall, fifth round.
(d)—October, 1987—Traded with Paul Boutilier by Minnesota North Stars to New York Rangers for Dave Gagner and Jay Caufield.
(e)—August, 1988—Traded with Walt Poddubny, Bruce Bell and fourth-round draft choice in 1989 by New York Rangers to Quebec Nordiques for Normand Rochefort and Jason Lafreniere.

SCOTT KENNETH GRUHL

Left Wing . . . 5'11" . . . 185 lbs. . . . Born, Port Colborne, Ont., September 13, 1959 . . . Shoots left . . . Also plays Defense . . . (March, 1988)—Fractured left hand in IHL game.

Year	Team	League	Games	G.	A.	Pts.	Pen.
1976-77—Northeastern University		ECAC	17	6	4	10	....
1977-78—Northeastern University		ECAC	28	21	38	59	46
1978-79—Sudbury Wolves		OMJHL	68	35	49	84	78
1979-80—Binghamton Dusters		AHL	4	1	0	1	6
1979-80—Saginaw Gears (b-c)		IHL	75	53	40	93	100
1980-81—Houston Apollos		CHL	4	0	0	0	0
1980-81—Saginaw Gears (d)		IHL	77	56	34	90	87
1981-82—New Haven Nighthawks		AHL	73	28	41	69	107
1981-82—Los Angeles Kings		NHL	7	2	1	3	2
1982-83—New Haven Nighthawks		AHL	68	25	38	63	114
1982-83—Los Angeles Kings		NHL	7	0	2	2	4
1983-84—Muskegon Mohawks (a)		IHL	56	40	56	96	49
1984-85—Muskegon Lumberjacks (a-e-f)		IHL	82	62	64	126	102
1985-86—Muskegon Lumberjacks		IHL	82	59	50	109	178
1986-87—Muskegon Lumberjacks		IHL	67	34	39	73	157
1987-88—Pittsburgh Penguins		NHL	6	1	0	1	0
1987-88—Muskegon Lumberjacks		IHL	55	28	47	75	115
NHL TOTALS			20	3	3	6	6

(c)—September, 1980—Signed by Los Angeles Kings as free agent.
(d)—Led IHL playoff with 11 goals and 19 assists.
(e)—Won James Gatchene Memorial Trophy (IHL MVP).
(f)—Led IHL playoffs with 16 assists.

FRANCOIS GUAY

Center . . . 6' . . . 185 lbs. . . . Born, Gatineau, Que., June 8, 1968 . . . Shoots left.

Year	Team	League	Games	G.	A.	Pts.	Pen.
1984-85—Laval Voisins		QHL	66	13	18	31	21
1985-86—Laval Titans (c)		QHL	71	19	55	74	46
1986-87—Laval Titans		QHL	63	52	77	129	67
1987-88—Laval Titans		QHL	66	60	84	144	142

(c)—June, 1986—Drafted as underage junior by Buffalo Sabres in 1986 NHL entry draft. Ninth Sabres pick, 152nd overall, eighth round.

PAUL GUAY

Right Wing . . . 6' . . . 185 lbs. . . . Born, Providence, R.I., September 2, 1963 . . . Shoots right . . . Member of 1984 U.S. Olympic Team.

Year	Team	League	Games	G.	A.	Pts.	Pen.
1979-80—Mt. St. Charles H.S.		R.I.H.S.	23	18	19	37	....
1980-81—Mt. St. Charles H.S. (c)		R.I.H.S.	23	28	38	66	....
1981-82—Providence College		ECAC	33	23	17	40	38
1982-83—Providence College (b)		ECAC	42	34	31	65	83
1983-84—U.S. National Team		Int'l	62	20	18	38	44
1983-84—U.S. Olympic Team		Int'l	6	1	0	1	8
1983-84—Philadelphia Flyers (d)		NHL	14	2	6	8	14
1984-85—Hershey Bears		AHL	74	23	30	53	123
1984-85—Philadelphia Flyers		NHL	2	0	1	1	0
1985-86—Los Angeles Kings (e)		NHL	23	3	3	6	18
1985-86—New Haven Nighthawks		AHL	57	15	36	51	101
1986-87—Los Angeles Kings		NHL	35	2	5	7	16
1986-87—New Haven Nighthawks		AHL	6	1	3	4	11
1987-88—New Haven Nighthawks		AHL	42	21	26	47	53
1987-88—Los Angeles Kings		NHL	33	4	4	8	40
NHL TOTALS			107	11	19	30	88

(c)—June, 1981—Drafted as underage player by Minnesota North Stars in 1981 NHL entry draft. Tenth North Stars pick, 118th overall, sixth round.

(d)—February, 1984—Traded with third round 1985 draft pick by Minnesota North Stars to Philadelphia Flyers for Paul Holmgren.

(e)—October, 1985—Traded by Philadelphia Flyers to Los Angeles Kings for Steve Seguin.

DAVID (JAY) GUDEN

Left Wing . . . 6'1" . . . 180 lbs. . . . Born, Brighton, Mass., April 26, 1968 . . . Shoots left . . . Also plays Center.

Year	Team	League	Games	G.	A.	Pts.	Pen.
1984-85—Roxbury Latin H.S.		Mass.	..	25	27	52	..
1985-86—Roxbury Latin H.S. (c)		Mass.	15	22	26	48	25
1986-87—Providence College		H. East	33	4	2	6	22
1987-88—Providence College		H. East	34	1	5	6	8

(c)—June, 1986—Drafted by Los Angeles Kings in 1986 NHL entry draft. Fourth Kings pick, 86th overall, fifth round.

STEPHANE GUERARD

Defense . . . 6'2" . . . 185 lbs. . . . Born, St. Elisabeth, Que., April 12, 1968 . . . Shoots left . . . (November 5, 1987)—Surgery to right knee.

Year	Team	League	Games	G.	A.	Pts.	Pen.
1984-85—Laurentides Midget		Que.	36	6	12	18	140
1985-86—Shawinigan Cataracts (c-d)		QHL	59	4	16	20	167
1986-87—Shawinigan Cataracts		QHL	31	5	16	21	57
1987-88—Quebec Nordiques		NHL	30	0	0	0	34
NHL TOTALS			30	0	0	0	34

(c)—Won Raymond Lagace Trophy (Top Rookie Defenseman or Goaltender).

(d)—June, 1986—Drafted as underage junior by Quebec Nordiques in 1986 NHL entry draft. Third Nordiques pick, 41st overall, second round.

VINCENT GUIDOTTI

Defense . . . 6' . . . 180 lbs. . . . Born, Sacramento, Calif., April 29, 1967 . . . Shoots left.

Year	Team	League	Games	G.	A.	Pts.	Pen.
1984-85—Noble Greenough H.S. (c)		Maine H.S.	25	14	24	38	32
1985-86—University of Maine		H. East	16	0	0	0	8
1986-87—University of Maine		H. East	39	1	3	4	40
1987-88—University of Maine		H. East	44	7	19	26	69

(c)—June, 1985—Drafted by St. Louis Blues in 1985 NHL entry draft. Ninth Blues pick, 201st overall, 10th round.

BENGT-AKE GUSTAFSSON

Left Wing . . . 6' . . . 185 lbs. . . . Born, Karlskoga, Sweden, March 23, 1958 . . . Shoots left . . . (November 12, 1980)—Cervical strain in back at Pittsburgh . . . (December 23, 1981)— Pulled tendons in right ankle vs. Boston . . . (March 17, 1984)—Partial tear of medial collateral ligament of left knee at N.Y. Islanders . . . (February, 1985)—Pulled left hamstring . . . (April, 1986)—Broken leg.

Year	Team	League	Games	G.	A.	Pts.	Pen.
1977-78	Farjestads (c)	Sweden	32	15	10	25	10
1978-79	Farjestads	Sweden	32	13	11	24	10
1978-79	Edmonton Oilers (d-e)	WHA	....	...	....	....	....
1979-80	Washington Capitals	NHL	80	22	38	60	17
1980-81	Washington Capitals	NHL	72	21	34	55	26
1981-82	Washington Capitals	NHL	70	26	34	60	40
1982-83	Washington Capitals	NHL	67	22	42	64	16
1983-84	Washington Capitals	NHL	69	32	43	75	16
1984-85	Washington Capitals	NHL	51	14	29	43	8
1985-86	Washington Capitals (f)	NHL	70	23	52	75	26
1986-87	Bofors	Sweden-II	28	16	26	42	22
1987-88	Washington Capitals	NHL	78	18	36	54	29
	NHL TOTALS		557	178	308	486	178

(c)—June, 1978—Drafted by Washington Capitals in NHL amateur draft. Seventh Washington pick, 55th overall, fourth round.

(d)—April, 1979—Signed by Edmonton Oilers. Played in two playoff games before being ruled ineligible by WHA office.

(e)—September, 1979—After being priority selection by Edmonton Oilers in NHL expansion draft in June, NHL President overturned case and ruled that Gustafsson was legally property of Washington Capitals because of rules governing expansion proceedings.

(f)—June, 1986—Signed to play with Bofors, a division II team in Sweden, for 1986-87.

KEVAN GUY

Defense . . . 6'2" . . . 190 lbs. . . . Born, Edmonton, Alta., July 16, 1965 . . . Shoots right.

Year	Team	League	Games	G.	A.	Pts.	Pen.
1982-83	Medicine Hat Tigers (c)	WHL	69	7	20	27	89
1983-84	Medicine Hat Tigers	WHL	72	15	42	57	117
1984-85	Medicine Hat Tigers	WHL	31	7	17	24	46
1985-86	Moncton Golden Flames	AHL	73	4	20	24	56
1986-87	Moncton Golden Flames	AHL	46	2	10	12	38
1986-87	Calgary Flames	NHL	24	0	4	4	19
1987-88	Calgary Flames	NHL	11	0	3	3	8
1987-88	Salt Lake Golden Eagles (d)	IHL	61	6	30	36	49
	NHL TOTALS		35	0	7	7	27

(c)—June, 1983—Drafted as underage junior by Calgary Flames in 1983 NHL entry draft. Fifth Flames pick, 71st overall, fourth round

(d)—June, 1988—Traded by Calgary Flames to Vancouver Canucks to complete March, 1988 deal in which Calgary sent Brian Bradley and Peter Backovic to Vancouver for Craig Coxe.

ARI EERIK HAANPAA

Right and Left Wing . . . 6'1" . . . 185 lbs. . . . Born, Nokia, Finland, November 28, 1965 . . . Shoots right . . . (1984-85)—Knee injury . . . (December, 1986)—Bruised right thigh . . . (February, 1987)—Sore back.

Year	Team	League	Games	G.	A.	Pts.	Pen.
1984-85	Ilves (c)	Finland	13	5	..	..	..
1985-86	Springfield Indians	AHL	20	3	1	4	13
1985-86	New York Islanders	NHL	18	0	7	7	20
1986-87	New York Islanders	NHL	41	6	4	10	17
1987-88	New York Islanders (d)	NHL	1	0	0	0	0
1987-88	Springfield Indians	AHL	61	14	19	33	34
	NHL TOTALS		60	6	11	17	37

(c)—June, 1984—Drafted by New York Islanders in 1984 NHL entry draft. Fifth Islanders pick, 83rd overall, fourth round.

(d)—June, 1988—Released by New York Islanders.

DAVID HAAS

Left Wing . . . 6'2" . . . 185 lbs. . . . Born, Toronto, Ont., July 23, 1968 . . . Shoots left.

Year	Team	League	Games	G.	A.	Pts.	Pen.
1984-85	Don Mills Flyers Midgets	MTHL	38	38	38	76	80
1985-86	London Knights (c)	OHL	62	4	13	17	91

Year	Team	League	Games	G.	A.	Pts.	Pen.
1986-87—London Knights (d)		OHL	5	1	0	1	5
1986-87—Kitchener Rangers		OHL	4	0	1	1	4
1986-87—Belleville Bulls		OHL	55	10	13	23	86
1987-88—Belleville Bulls		OHL	5	1	1	2	9
1987-88—Windsor Spitfires (b)		OHL	58	59	46	105	237

(c)—June, 1986—Drafted as underage junior by Edmonton Oilers in 1986 NHL entry draft. Fifth Oilers pick, 105th overall, fifth round.

(d)—October, 1986—Traded with Kelly Cain and Ed Kister by London Knights to Kitchener Rangers for Peter Lisy, Ian Pound, Stebe Marcolini and Greg Hankkio.

MARC JOSEPH HABSCHEID

Center . . . 6'2" . . . 180 lbs. . . . Born, Swift Current, Sask., March 1, 1963 . . . Shoots right . . . (November, 1982)—Head injury . . . (October, 1985)—Suspended by Edmonton Oilers for refusing to report to Nova Scotia Oilers (AHL).

Year	Team	League	Games	G.	A.	Pts.	Pen.
1980-81—Saskatoon Blades (c)		WHL	72	34	63	97	50
1981-82—Saskatoon Blades (b)		WHL	55	64	87	151	74
1981-82—Edmonton Oilers		NHL	7	1	3	4	2
1981-82—Wichita Wind (d)		CHL	..	..	..	..	..
1982-83—Kamloops Junior Oilers		WHL	6	7	16	23	8
1982-83—Edmonton Oilers		NHL	32	3	10	13	14
1983-84—Edmonton Oilers		NHL	9	1	0	1	6
1983-84—Moncton Alpines		AHL	71	19	37	56	32
1984-85—Edmonton Oilers		NHL	26	5	3	8	4
1984-85—Nova Scotia Oilers		AHL	48	29	29	58	65
1985-86—Minnesota North Stars (e)		NHL	6	2	3	5	0
1985-86—Springfield Indians		AHL	41	18	32	50	21
1986-87—Minnesota North Stars (f)		NHL	15	2	0	2	2
1987-88—Canadian Olympic Team		Int'l	69	24	37	61	48
1987-88—Minnesota North Stars		NHL	16	4	11	15	6
NHL TOTALS			111	18	30	48	34

(c)—June, 1981—Drafted as underage junior by Edmonton Oilers in 1981 NHL entry draft. Sixth Oilers pick, 113th overall, sixth round.

(d)—No regular season record. Played three playoff games.

(e)—December, 1985—Traded with Don Barber and Emanuel Viveiros by Edmonton Oilers to Minnesota North Stars for Gord Sherven and Don Biggs.

(f)—November, 1986—Assigned to Springfield Indians (AHL) but refused to report. He was then allowed to join the Canadian National team in Calgary.

LEONARD HACHBORN

Center . . . 5'10" . . . 171 lbs. . . . Born, Brantford, Ont., September 9, 1961 . . . Shoots left . . . (December, 1982)—Knee injury . . . (December, 1984)—Separated left shoulder . . . (January 10, 1986)—Injured groin at Minnesota.

Year	Team	League	Games	G.	A.	Pts.	Pen.
1979-80—Hamilton Tier II		OPJHL	43	25	20	45	42
1980-81—Brantford Alexanders (c)		OHL	66	34	52	86	94
1981-82—Brantford Alexanders		OHL	55	43	50	93	141
1982-83—Maine Mariners		AHL	75	28	55	83	32
1983-84—Springfield Indians		AHL	28	18	42	60	15
1983-84—Philadelphia Flyers		NHL	38	11	21	32	4
1984-85—Hershey Bears		AHL	14	6	7	13	14
1984-85—Philadelphia Flyers		NHL	40	5	17	22	23
1985-86—Hershey Bears (d)		AHL	23	12	22	34	34
1985-86—New Haven Nighthawks		AHL	12	5	8	13	21
1985-86—Los Angeles Kings		NHL	24	4	1	5	2
1986-87—Hershey Bears (e)		AHL	17	4	10	14	2
1987-88—Maine Mariners (f)		AHL	29	16	17	33	16
NHL TOTALS			102	20	39	59	29

(c)—June, 1981—Drafted by Philadelphia Flyers in 1981 NHL entry draft. Twelfth Flyers pick, 184th overall, ninth round.

(d)—December, 1986—Sold by Philadelphia Flyers to Los Angeles Kings.

(e)—February, 1987—Signed by Philadelphia Flyers as a free agent after completing a season in Italy.

(f)—January, 1988—Signed by Maine Mariners after playing in Austria.

RICHARD HAJDU

Left Wing . . . 6' . . . 175 lbs. . . . Born, Victoria, B.C., April 10, 1965 . . . Shoots left.

Year	Team	League	Games	G.	A.	Pts.	Pen.
1981-82—Kamloops Junior Oilers	WHL	64	19	21	40	50
1982-83—Kamloops Junior Oilers (c-d)	WHL	70	22	36	58	101
1983-84—Victoria Cougars	WHL	42	17	10	27	106
1984-85—Victoria Cougars	WHL	24	12	16	28	33
1984-85—Rochester Americans	AHL	2	0	2	2	0
1985-86—Buffalo Sabres	NHL	3	0	0	0	4
1985-86—Rochester Americans	AHL	54	10	27	37	95
1986-87—Buffalo Sabres	NHL	2	0	0	0	0
1986-87—Rochester Americans	AHL	58	7	15	22	90
1987-88—Rochester Americans	AHL	37	7	11	18	24
NHL TOTALS			5	0	0	0	4

(c)—June, 1983—Drafted as underage junior by Buffalo Sabres in 1983 NHL entry draft. Fifth Sabres pick, 34th overall, second round.

(d)—July, 1983—Traded with Doug Kostynski by Kamdoops Junior Oilers to Victoria Cougars for Ron Viglasi and Brian Bertuzzi.

BOB HALKIDIS

Defense . . .5'11" . . . 195 lbs. . . . Born, Toronto, Ont., March 5, 1966 . . . Shoots left . . . (September, 1982)—Broke ankle during training camp. In first game back, in November, he reinjured ankle and missed another two weeks . . . (December 4, 1985)—Dislocated right shoulder at St. Louis and missed 15 games . . . (October 23, 1987)—Given six-game AHL suspension for fighting . . . (December, 1987)—Injured ankle.

Year	Team	League	Games	G.	A.	Pts.	Pen.
1981-82—Toronto Young Nationals	MTMHL	40	9	27	36	54
1982-83—London Knights	OHL	37	3	12	15	52
1983-84—London Knights (c)	OHL	51	9	22	31	123
1984-85—London Knights (a-d)	OHL	62	14	50	64	154
1984-85—Buffalo Sabres (e)	NHL	..	..	..	..	..
1985-86—Buffalo Sabres	NHL	37	1	9	10	115
1986-87—Buffalo Sabres	NHL	6	1	1	2	19
1986-87—Rochester Americans	AHL	59	1	8	9	144
1987-88—Rochester Americans	AHL	15	2	5	7	50
1987-88—Buffalo Sabres	NHL	30	0	3	3	115
NHL TOTALS			73	2	13	15	249

(c)—June, 1984—Drafted as underage junior by Buffalo Sabres in 1984 NHL entry draft. Fourth Sabres pick, 81st overall, fourth round.

(d)—Won Max Kaminsky Trophy (Top OHL Defenseman).

(e)—No regular season record. Played four playoff games.

DEAN HALL

Center . . . 6'2" . . . 190 lbs. . . . Born, Winnipeg, Manitoba, January 14, 1968 . . . Shoots left.

Year	Team	League	Games	G.	A.	Pts.	Pen.
1985-86—St. James Jr. Canadians (c)	MJHL	47	31	49	80	94
1986-87—Northern Michigan Univ.	WCHA	20	4	5	9	16
1987-88—Northern Michigan Univ.	WCHA	31	5	6	11	22

(c)—June, 1986—Drafted by Boston Bruins in 1986 NHL entry draft. Third Bruins pick, 76th overall, fourth round.

TAYLOR HALL

Left Wing . . . 5'11' . . . 177 lbs. . . . Born, Regina, Sask., February 20, 1964 . . . Shoots left . . . (October, 1984)—Damaged knee ligaments.

Year	Team	League	Games	G.	A.	Pts.	Pen.
1980-81—Regina Canadians	Midget	26	51	28	79	35
1981-82—Regina Pats (c)	WHL	48	14	15	29	43
1982-83—Regina Pats	WHL	72	37	57	94	78
1983-84—Regina Pats (a-d)	WHL	69	63	79	142	42
1983-84—Vancouver Canucks	NHL	4	1	0	1	0
1984-85—Vancouver Canucks	NHL	7	1	4	5	19
1985-86—Fredericton Express	AHL	45	21	14	35	28
1985-86—Vancouver Canucks	NHL	19	5	5	10	6
1986-87—Fredericton Express	AHL	36	21	20	41	23
1986-87—Vancouver Canucks (e)	NHL	4	0	0	0	0
1987-88—Maine Mariners	AHL	71	33	41	74	58
1987-88—Boston Bruins	NHL	7	0	0	0	4
NHL TOTALS			41	7	9	16	29

(c)—June, 1982—Drafted as underage junior by Vancouver Canucks in 1982 NHL entry draft. Fourth Canucks pick, 116th overall, sixth round.

(e)—July, 1987—Signed by Boston Bruins as a free agent.

DOUGLAS ROBERT HALWARD

Defense . . . 6'1" . . . 198 lbs. . . . Born, Toronto, Ont., November 1, 1955 . . . Shoots left . . . Missed part of 1979-80 season with a bruised shoulder . . . (December, 1983)—Fractured ankle . . . (October 20, 1985)—Bruised hand at N.Y. Rangers . . . (February, 1987)—Sidelined with phlebitis . . . (May, 1988)—Groin injury.

Year	Team	League	Games	G.	A.	Pts.	Pen.
1973-74—Peterborough TPTs		Jr."A"OHA	69	1	15	16	103
1974-75—Peterborough TPTs (c)		Jr."A"OHA	68	11	52	63	97
1975-76—Rochester Americans		AHL	54	6	11	17	51
1975-76—Boston Bruins		NHL	22	1	5	6	6
1976-77—Rochester Americans		AHL	54	4	28	32	26
1976-77—Boston Bruins		NHL	18	2	2	4	6
1977-78—Rochester Americans		AHL	42	8	14	22	17
1977-78—Boston Bruins (d)		NHL	25	0	2	2	2
1978-79—Los Angeles Kings		NHL	27	1	5	6	13
1978-79—Springfield Indians		AHL	14	5	1	6	10
1979-80—Los Angeles Kings		NHL	63	11	45	56	52
1980-81—Los Angeles Kings (e)		NHL	51	4	15	19	96
1980-81—Vancouver Canucks		NHL	7	0	1	1	4
1981-82—Dallas Black Hawks		CHL	22	8	18	26	49
1981-82—Vancouver Canucks		NHL	37	4	13	17	40
1982-83—Vancouver Canucks		NHL	75	19	33	52	83
1983-84—Vancouver Canucks		NHL	54	7	16	23	35
1984-85—Vancouver Canucks		NHL	71	7	27	34	82
1985-86—Vancouver Canucks		NHL	70	8	25	33	111
1986-87—Vancouver Canucks (f)		NHL	10	0	3	3	34
1986-87—Detroit Red Wings		NHL	11	0	3	3	19
1987-88—Detroit Red Wings		NHL	70	5	21	26	130
NHL TOTALS			611	69	216	285	713

(c)—Drafted from Peterborough TPTs by Boston Bruins in first round of 1975 amateur draft.
(d)—September, 1978—Traded to Los Angeles Kings by Boston Bruins for future considerations.
(e)—March, 1981—Traded by Los Angeles Kings to Vancouver Canucks for future considerations. (Canucks sent goaltender Gary Bromley to Kings to complete deal, June, 1981.)
(f)—November, 1986—Traded by Vancouver Canucks to Detroit Red Wings for future considerations.

GILLES HAMEL

Left Wing . . . 6' . . . 183 lbs. . . . Born, Asbestos, Que., March 18, 1960 . . . Shoots left . . . (January, 1981)—Knee injury . . . Brother of Jean Hamel . . . (April, 1988)—Bruised shoulder.

Year	Team	League	Games	G.	A.	Pts.	Pen.
1977-78—Laval National		QMJHL	72	44	37	81	68
1978-79—Laval National (b-c)		QMJHL	72	56	55	111	130
1979-80—Trois-Rivieres Draveurs		QMJHL	12	13	8	21	8
1979-80—Chicoutimi Sagueneens (a)		QMJHL	58	78	62	135	87
1979-80—Rochester Americans (d)		AHL	...	...	...	...	...
1980-81—Rochester Americans		AHL	14	8	7	15	7
1980-81—Buffalo Sabres		NHL	51	10	9	19	53
1981-82—Rochester Americans		AHL	57	31	44	75	55
1981-82—Buffalo Sabres		NHL	16	2	7	9	2
1982-83—Buffalo Sabres		NHL	66	22	20	42	26
1983-84—Buffalo Sabres		NHL	75	21	23	44	37
1984-85—Buffalo Sabres		NHL	80	18	30	48	36
1985-86—Buffalo Sabres (e)		NHL	77	19	25	44	61
1986-87—Winnipeg Jets		NHL	79	27	21	48	24
1987-88—Winnipeg Jets		NHL	63	8	11	19	35
NHL TOTALS			507	127	146	273	274

(c)—August, 1979—Drafted by Buffalo Sabres as underage junior in entry draft. Fifth Sabres pick, 74th overall, fourth round.
(d)—No regular season record. Played one playoff game.
(e)—June, 1986—Traded by Buffalo Sabres to Winnipeg Jets for Scott Arniel.

BRADLEY HAMILTON

Defense . . . 6' . . . 175 lbs. . . . Born, Calgary, Alta., March 30, 1967 . . . Shoots left.

Year	Team	League	Games	G.	A.	Pts.	Pen.
1983-84—North York Rangers		OHA	42	4	25	29	126
1984-85—Aurora Tigers (c)		OHA	43	9	29	38	149

Year	Team	League	Games	G.	A.	Pts.	Pen.
1985-86—Michigan State Univ.		CCHA	43	3	10	13	52
1986-87—Michigan State Univ.		CCHA	45	3	29	32	54
1987-88—Michigan State Univ.		CCHA	40	7	22	29	56

(c)—June, 1985—Drafted by Chicago Black Hawks in 1985 NHL entry draft. Tenth Black Hawks pick, 200th overall, 10th round.

KEN HAMMOND

Defense . . . 6'1" . . . 190 lbs. . . . Born, London, Ont., August 23, 1963 . . . Shoots left . . . (March 13, 1988)—Sprained knee vs. St. Louis.

Year	Team	League	Games	G.	A.	Pts.	Pen.
1981-82—R.P.I.		ECAC	29	2	3	5	54
1982-83—R.P.I. (c)		ECAC	28	4	13	17	54
1983-84—R.P.I.		ECAC	34	5	11	16	72
1984-85—R.P.I (a-d)		ECAC	38	11	28	39	90
1984-85—Los Angeles Kings		NHL	3	1	0	1	0
1985-86—New Haven Nighthawks		AHL	67	4	12	16	96
1985-86—Los Angeles Kings		NHL	3	0	1	1	2
1986-87—New Haven Nighthawks		AHL	66	1	15	16	76
1986-87—Los Angeles Kings		NHL	10	0	2	2	11
1987-88—New Haven Nighthawks		AHL	26	3	8	11	27
1987-88—Los Angeles Kings		NHL	46	7	9	16	69
NHL TOTALS			62	8	12	20	82

(c)—June, 1983—Drafted by Los Angeles Kings in 1983 NHL entry draft. Eighth Kings pick, 147th overall, eighth round.

(d)—Named first team All-America (East).

RON HANDY

Left Wing . . . 5'11" . . . 165 lbs. . . . Born, Toronto, Ont., January 15, 1963 . . . Shoots left . . . (January, 1984)—Broken nose in CHL game.

Year	Team	League	Games	G.	A.	Pts.	Pen.
1979-80—Toronto Marlboro Midgets		Midget	39	48	60	108	....
1980-81—Sault Ste. Marie Greyhounds (c)		OHL	66	43	43	86	45
1981-82—Sault Ste. Marie		OHL	20	15	10	25	20
1981-82—Kingston Canadians		OHL	44	35	38	73	23
1982-83—Kingston Canadians		OHL	67	52	96	148	64
1982-83—Indianapolis Checkers		CHL	9	2	7	9	0
1983-84—Indianapolis Checkers (b)		CHL	66	29	46	75	40
1984-85—New York Islanders		NHL	10	0	2	2	0
1984-85—Springfield Indians		AHL	69	29	35	64	38
1985-86—Springfield Indians		AHL	79	31	30	61	66
1986-87—Indianapolis Checkers (b-d)		IHL	82	*55	80	135	57
1987-88—Peoria Rivermen (a)		IHL	78	53	63	116	61
1987-88—St. Louis Blues		NHL	4	0	1	1	0
NHL TOTALS			14	0	3	3	0

(c)—June, 1981—Drafted as underage junior by New York Islanders in 1981 NHL entry draft. Third Islanders pick, 57th overall, third round.

(d)—September, 1987—Signed by St. Louis Blues as a free agent.

BENJAMIN HANKINSON

Center . . . 6'2" . . . 180 lbs. . . . Born, Edina, Minn., January 5, 1969 . . . Shoots right . . . Also plays Right Wing . . . Son of John Hankinson, former NFL player with Philadelphia Eagles and Minnesota Vikings.

Year	Team	League	Games	G.	A.	Pts.	Pen.
1985-86—Edina H.S.		Minn. H.S.	....	9	21	30	....
1986-87—Edina H.S. (c)		Minn. H.S.	26	14	20	34	....
1987-88—University of Minnesota		WCHA	24	4	7	11	36

(c)—June, 1987—Drafted by New Jersey Devils in 1987 NHL entry draft. Fifth Devils pick, 107th overall, sixth round.

TIMOTHY HANLEY

Center . . . 6' . . . 200 lbs. . . . Born, Greenfield, Mass., October 10, 1964 . . . Shoots right.

Year	Team	League	Games	G.	A.	Pts.	Pen.
1983-84—Deerfield Academy (c)		Mass. H.S.	22	18	25	43	..
1984-85—Univ. of New Hampshire		H. East	42	22	18	40	21
1985-86—Univ. of New Hampshire		H. East	29	9	13	22	22

Year	Team	League	Games	G.	A.	Pts.	Pen.
1986-87—Univ. of New Hampshire		H. East	37	11	23	34	34
1987-88—Univ. of New Hampshire		H. East	30	13	17	30	38

(c)—June, 1984—Drafted by Los Angeles Kings in 1984 NHL entry draft. Seventh Kings pick, 129th overall, seventh round.

DAVE HANNAN

Center . . . 5'11" . . . 174 lbs. . . . Born, Sudbury, Ont., November 26, 1961 . . . Shoots left . . . Missed part of '80-81 season with a bruised shoulder . . . (January 9, 1987)—Injured knee at Washington and required surgery.

Year	Team	League	Games	G.	A.	Pts.	Pen.
1977-78—Windsor Spitfires		OMJHL	68	14	16	30	43
1978-79—Sault Ste. Marie Greyhounds		OMJHL	26	7	8	15	13
1979-80—Sault Ste. Marie Greyhounds		OMJHL	28	11	10	21	31
1979-80—Brantford Alexanders		OMJHL	25	5	10	15	26
1980-81—Brantford Alexanders (c)		OHL	56	46	35	81	155
1981-82—Erie Blades		AHL	76	33	37	70	129
1981-82—Pittsburgh Penguins		NHL	1	0	0	0	0
1982-83—Baltimore Skipjacks		AHL	5	2	2	4	13
1982-83—Pittsburgh Penguins		NHL	74	11	22	33	127
1983-84—Baltimore Skipjacks		AHL	47	18	24	42	98
1983-84—Pittsburgh Penguins		NHL	24	2	3	5	33
1984-85—Baltimore Skipjacks		AHL	49	20	25	45	91
1984-85—Pittsburgh Penguins		NHL	30	6	7	13	43
1985-86—Pittsburgh Penguins		NHL	75	17	18	35	91
1986-87—Pittsburgh Penguins		NHL	58	10	15	25	56
1987-88—Pittsburgh Penguins (d)		NHL	21	4	3	7	23
1987-88—Edmonton Oilers		NHL	51	9	11	20	43
NHL TOTALS			334	59	79	138	416

(c)—June, 1981—Drafted by Pittsburgh Penguins in 1981 NHL entry draft. Ninth Penguins pick, 196th overall, 10th round.

(d)—November, 1987—Traded with Craig Simpson, Chris Joseph and Moe Mantha by Pittsburgh Penguins to Edmonton Oilers for Paul Coffey, Dave Hunter and Wayne Van Dorp.

JEFFREY HARDING

Right Wing . . . 6'4" . . . 207 lbs. . . . Born, Toronto, Ont., April 6, 1969 . . . Shoots right . . . Also plays Center . . . (October, 1985)—Injured knee.

Year	Team	League	Games	G.	A.	Pts.	Pen.
1985-86—Henry Carr Crusaders		OHA	23	14	10	24	30
1986-87—St. Michael's Buzzers (c)		OHA	22	22	8	30	97
1987-88—Michigan State Univ.		CCHA	43	17	10	27	129

(c)—June, 1987—Drafted as underage junior by Philadelphia Flyers in 1987 NHL entry draft. Second Flyers pick, 30th overall, second round.

MARK LEA HARDY

Defense . . . 5'11" . . . 190 lbs. . . . Born, Semaden, Switzerland, February 1, 1959 . . . Shoots left . . . Mother was a member of 1952 Olympic Figure Skating team from England . . . (October, 1985)—Missed 25 games due to surgery to sublexation tendon in left wrist injured in final pre-season game vs. Calgary . . . (January, 1988)—Viral infection.

Year	Team	League	Games	G.	A.	Pts.	Pen.
1975-76—Montreal Juniors		QMJHL	64	6	17	23	44
1976-77—Montreal Juniors		QMJHL	72	20	40	60	137
1977-78—Montreal Juniors (a-c)		QMJHL	72	25	57	82	150
1978-79—Montreal Juniors (d)		QMJHL	67	18	52	70	117
1979-80—Binghamton Dusters		AHL	56	3	13	16	32
1979-80—Los Angeles Kings		NHL	15	0	1	1	10
1980-81—Los Angeles Kings		NHL	77	5	20	25	77
1981-82—Los Angeles Kings		NHL	77	6	39	45	130
1982-83—Los Angeles Kings		NHL	74	5	34	39	101
1983-84—Los Angeles Kings		NHL	79	8	41	49	122
1984-85—Los Angeles Kings		NHL	78	14	39	53	97
1985-86—Los Angeles Kings		NHL	55	6	21	27	71
1986-87—Los Angeles Kings		NHL	73	3	27	30	120
1987-88—Los Angeles Kings (e)		NHL	61	6	22	28	99
1987-88—New York Rangers (f)		NHL	19	2	2	4	31
NHL TOTALS			608	55	246	301	858

(c)—Named top defenseman in QMJHL.

(d)—August, 1979—Drafted by Los Angeles Kings in 1979 entry draft. Third Kings pick, 30th overall, second round.

(e)—February, 1988—Traded by Los Angeles Kings to New York Rangers for Ron Duguay.
(f)—June, 1988—Traded by New York Rangers to Minnesota North Stars for future draft considerations.

TODD HARKINS

Right Wing . . . 6'3" . . . 210 lbs. . . . Born, Cleveland, Ohio, October 8, 1968 . . . Shoots right.

Year	Team	League	Games	G.	A.	Pts.	Pen.
1986-87—Aurora Eagles		OHA	40	19	29	48	102
1987-88—Miami Univ. of Ohio (c)		CCHA	34	9	7	16	133

(c)—June, 1988—Drafted by Calgary Flames in 1988 NHL entry draft. Second Flames pick, 42nd overall, second round.

SCOTT HARLOW

Left Wing . . . 6' . . . 190 lbs. . . . Born, East Bridgewater, Mass., October 11, 1963 . . . Shoots left.

Year	Team	League	Games	G.	A.	Pts.	Pen.
1982-83—Boston College (c)		ECAC	24	6	19	25	19
1984-85—Boston College		ECAC	39	27	20	47	17
1984-85—Boston College		H. East	44	34	38	72	45
1985-86—Bostgn College (d)		H. East	42	38	41	79	48
1986-87—Sherbrooke Canadiens		AHL	66	22	26	48	6
1987-88—St. Louis Blues (e)		NHL	1	0	1	1	0
1987-88—Sherbrooke Canadiens		AHL	18	6	12	18	8
1987-88—Baltimore Skipjacks		AHL	29	24	27	51	21
1987-88—Peoria Rivermen		IHL	39	30	25	55	46
NHL TOTALS			1	0	1	1	0

(c)—June, 1982—Drafted by Montreal Canadiens in 1982 entry draft. Sixth Canadiens pick, 61st overall, third round.
(d)—Selected first team All-America (East).
(e)—January, 1988—Traded by Montreal Canadiens to St. Louis Blues for future considerations.

WARREN HARPER

Right Wing . . . 5'11" . . . 176 lbs. . . . Born, Prince Albert, Sask., May 10, 1963 . . . Shoots left.

Year	Team	League	Games	G.	A.	Pts.	Pen.
1979-80—Prince Albert AA		Midget	34	20	17	37	58
1980-81—Prince Albert Raiders (c)		SJHL	60	35	35	70	158
1981-82—Prince Albert Raiders		SJHL	39	23	29	52	108
1982-83—Prince Albert Raiders		WHL	41	17	15	32	38
1983-84—Rochester Americans		AHL	78	25	28	53	56
1984-85—Rochester Americans		AHL	78	29	34	63	43
1985-86—Rochester Americans		AHL	80	18	30	48	83
1986-87—Flint Spirit		IHL	15	4	7	11	14
1986-87—Rochester Americans		AHL	61	13	27	40	50
1987-88—Adirondack Red Wings		AHL	80	24	33	57	76

(c)—June, 1981—Drafted as underage junior by Buffalo Sabres in 1981 NHL entry draft. Twelfth Sabres pick, 206th overall, 10th round.

TIM HARRIS

Right Wing . . . 6'1" . . . 180 lbs. . . . Born, Toronto, Ont., October 16, 1967 . . . Shoots right.

Year	Team	League	Games	G.	A.	Pts.	Pen.
1985-86—Pickering Jr. B		OHA	34	13	25	38	91
1986-87—Pickering Jr. B (c)		OHA	36	20	36	56	142
1987-88—Lake Superior State Univ.		CCHA	43	8	10	18	79

(c)—June, 1987—Drafted by Calgary Flames in 1987 NHL entry draft. Fifth Flames pick, 70th overall, fourth round.

TODD HARTJE

Center . . . 6' . . . 175 lbs. . . . Born, Anoka, Minn., February 27, 1968 . . . Shoots left.

Year	Team	League	Games	G.	A.	Pts.	Pen.
1985-86—Anoka H.S.		Minn. H.S.	22	25	34	59	....
1986-87—Harvard Univ. (c)		ECAC	34	3	9	12	36
1987-88—Harvard Univ.		ECAC	32	5	17	22	40

(c)—June, 1987—Drafted by Winnipeg Jets in 1987 NHL entry draft. Seventh Jets pick, 142nd overall, seventh round.

MIKE HARTMAN

Left Wing ... 5'11" ... 190 lbs. ... Born, West Bloomfield, Mich., February 7, 1967 ... Shoots left ... Also plays Right Wing.

Year	Team	League	Games	G.	A.	Pts.	Pen.
1984-85—Belleville Bulls		OHL	49	13	12	25	119
1985-86—Belleville Bulls		OHL	4	2	1	3	5
1985-86—North Bay Centennials (c)		OHL	53	19	16	35	205
1986-87—North Bay Centennials		OHL	32	15	24	39	144
1986-87—Buffalo Sabres		NHL	17	3	3	6	69
1987-88—Rochester Americans		AHL	57	13	14	27	283
1987-88—Buffalo Sabres		NHL	18	3	1	4	90
NHL TOTALS			35	6	4	10	159

(c)—June, 1986—Drafted by Buffalo Sabres in 1986 NHL entry draft. Eighth Sabres pick, 131th overall, seventh round.

CRAIG HARTSBURG

Defense ... 6'1" ... 190 lbs. ... Born, Stratford, Ont., June 29, 1959 ... Shoots left ... (September, 1977)—Torn ligaments in left knee ... (September, 1980)—Separated shoulder ... Member of Team Canada in 1981 Canada Cup ... Son of Bill Hartsburg (WHL, 1960s) ... (October 10, 1983)—Surgery to remove bone spur on knee, returned November 15 ... (January 10, 1984)—Injured ligaments in left knee vs. Hartford and required arthoscopic surgery ... Holds Minnesota club records for most assists (60) and points (77) in a season by a defenseman ... (October, 1984)—Hip pointer in training camp ... (December, 1984)—Fractured femur ... (January 16, 1986)—Injured groin vs. St. Louis and missed four games ... (February, 1987)—Herniated disc ... (March, 1987)—Strained knee ligaments ... (November 7, 1987)—Suffered concussion when he collided with referee Mike Noeth in game vs. Vancouver ... (December, 1987)—Injured left hip and separated left shoulder ... (March, 1988)—Shoulder surgery.

Year	Team	League	Games	G.	A.	Pts.	Pen.
1975-76—S. Ste. Marie Greyhounds		Jr."A"OHA	64	9	19	28	65
1976-77—S. Ste. M. Greyhounds (b-c)		Jr."A"OHA	61	29	64	93	142
1977-78—S. Ste. M. Greyhounds (d)		Jr."A"OHA	36	15	42	57	101
1978-79—Birmingham Bulls (e)		WHA	77	9	40	49	73
1979-80—Minnesota North Stars		NHL	79	14	30	44	81
1980-81—Minnesota North Stars		NHL	74	13	30	43	124
1981-82—Minnesota North Stars		NHL	76	17	60	77	117
1982-83—Minnesota North Stars		NHL	78	12	50	62	109
1983-84—Minnesota North Stars		NHL	26	7	7	14	37
1984-85—Minnesota North Stars		NHL	32	7	11	18	54
1985-86—Minnesota North Stars		NHL	75	10	47	57	127
1986-87—Minnesota North Stars		NHL	73	11	50	61	93
1987-88—Minnesota North Stars		NHL	27	3	16	19	29
WHA TOTALS			77	9	40	49	73
NHL TOTALS			540	94	301	395	769

(c)—Won Max Kaminsky Memorial Trophy (Outstanding Defenseman).
(d)—July, 1978—Signed by Birmingham Bulls (WHA) as underage junior.
(e)—June, 1979—Drafted by Minnesota North Stars in 1979 NHL entry draft. First North Stars pick, sixth overall, first round.

KEVIN HATCHER

Defense ... 6'3" ... 185 lbs. ... Born, Detroit, Mich., September 9, 1966 ... Shoots right ... (October, 1987)—Torn cartilage in left knee.

Year	Team	League	Games	G.	A.	Pts.	Pen.
1982-83—Detroit Compuware		Mich. Midget	75	30	45	75	120
1983-84—North Bay Centennials (c)		OHL	67	10	39	49	61
1984-85—North Bay Centennials (b)		OHL	58	26	37	63	75
1984-85—Washington Capitals		NHL	2	1	0	1	0
1985-86—Washington Capitals		NHL	79	9	10	19	119
1986-87—Washington Capitals		NHL	78	8	16	24	144
1987-88—Washington Capitals		NHL	71	14	27	41	137
NHL TOTALS			230	32	53	85	400

(c)—June, 1984—Drafted as underage junior by Washington Capitals in 1984 NHL entry draft. First Capitals pick, 17th overall, first round.

DALE HAWERCHUK

Center ... 5'11" ... 170 lbs. ... Born, Toronto, Ont., April 4, 1963 ... Shoots left ... Youngest player to have 100-point season (18 years, 351 days) ... (March 7, 1984)—Set NHL record with five assists in a period at Los Angeles ... (April 13, 1985)—Broken rib in

playoff game when checked by Jamie Macoun at Calgary . . . President and part owner of Cornwall Royals of Quebec Junior League.

Year	Team	League	Games	G.	A.	Pts.	Pen.
1979-80—Cornwall Royals (c-d)		OMJHL	72	37	66	103	21
1980-81—Cornwall Royals (a-e-f-g-h-i)		OHL	72	*81	*102	*183	69
1981-82—Winnipeg Jets (j-k)		NHL	80	45	58	103	47
1982-83—Winnipeg Jets		NHL	79	40	51	91	31
1983-84—Winnipeg Jets		NHL	80	37	65	102	73
1984-85—Winnipeg Jets (b)		NHL	80	53	77	130	74
1985-86—Winnipeg Jets		NHL	80	46	59	105	44
1986-87—Winnipeg Jets		NHL	80	47	53	100	54
1987-88—Winnipeg Jets		NHL	80	44	77	121	59
NHL TOTALS			559	312	440	752	382

(c)—Winner of The Instructeurs Trophy (QMJHL Top Rookie).
(d)—Winner of Guy Lafleur Trophy (QMJHL Playoff MVP).
(e)—Winner of Jean Beliveau Trophy (QMJHL Leading Scorer).
(f)—Winner of Michel Briere Trophy (QMJHL MVP).
(g)—Winner of The Association of Journalists for Major Junior League Hockey Trophy (Best Pro Prospect). First year awarded.
(h)—Winner of CCM Trophy (Top Canadian Major Junior League Player).
(i)—Drafted as underage junior by Winnipeg Jets in 1981 NHL entry draft. First Jets pick, first overall, first round.
(j)—Named NHL Rookie of the Year by The Sporting News in poll of players.
(k)—Winner of Calder Memorial Trophy (NHL Rookie of the Year).

GREG HAWGOOD

Defense . . . 5'8" . . . 175 lbs. . . . Born, St. Albert, Alta., August 10, 1968 . . . Shoots left . . . Holds record for career points by a WHL defenseman.

Year	Team	League	Games	G.	A.	Pts.	Pen.
1983-84—Kamloops Junior Oilers		WHL	49	10	23	33	39
1984-85—Kamloops Blazers		WHL	66	25	40	65	72
1985-86—Kamloops Blazers (a-c)		WHL	71	34	85	119	86
1986-87—Kamloops Blazers (a)		WHL	61	30	93	123	139
1987-88—Boston Bruins		NHL	1	0	0	0	0
1987-88—Kamloops Blazers		WHL	63	48	85	133	142
NHL TOTALS			1	0	0	0	0

(c)—June, 1986—Drafted as underage junior by Boston Bruins in 1986 NHL entry draft. Ninth Bruins pick, 202nd overall, 10th round.

TODD HAWKINS

Right Wing . . . 5'11" . . . 190 lbs. . . . Born, Kingston, Ont., August 2, 1966 . . . Shoots right . . . (October 1, 1986)—Suspended two games by OHL.

Year	Team	League	Games	G.	A.	Pts.	Pen.
1984-85—Belleville Bulls		OHL	58	7	16	23	117
1985-86—Belleville Bulls (c)		OHL	60	14	13	27	172
1986-87—Belleville Bulls (b)		OHL	60	47	40	87	187
1987-88—Flint Spirits		IHL	50	13	13	26	337
1987-88—Fredericton Express		AHL	2	0	0	0	11

(c)—June, 1986—Drafted by Vancouver Canucks in 1986 NHL entry draft. Tenth Canucks pick, 217th overall, 11th round.

KENT HAWLEY

Center . . . 6'3" . . . 215 lbs. . . . Born, Kingston, Ont., February 20, 1968 . . . Shoots left.

Year	Team	League	Games	G.	A.	Pts.	Pen.
1984-85—Ottawa Senators		CJHL	54	19	37	56	119
1985-86—Ottawa 67's (c)		OHL	64	21	30	51	96
1986-87—Ottawa 67's		OHL	64	29	53	82	86
1987-88—Ottawa 67's		OHL	55	29	49	78	84

(c)—June, 1986—Drafted as underage junior by Philadelphia Flyers in 1986 NHL entry draft. Third Flyers pick, 28th overall, second round.

ALAN JOSEPH GORDON HAWORTH

Center . . . 5'10" . . . 188 lbs. . . . Born, Drummondville, Que., September 1, 1960 . . . Shoots right . . . (February 4, 1981)—Bruised shoulder . . . (March 11, 1986)—Fractured wrist vs. Pittsburgh . . . (February, 1987)—Missing games with recurring knee pain . . . (November, 1987)—Injured right knee playing badminton . . . (March, 1988)—Concussion.

Year	Team	League	Games	G.	A.	Pts.	Pen.
1977-78—Chicoutimi Sagueneens	QMJHL	59	17	33	50	40
1978-79—Sherbrooke Beavers (c)	QMJHL	70	50	70	120	63
1979-80—Sherbrooke Beavers	QMJHL	45	28	36	64	50
1980-81—Rochester Americans	AHL	21	14	18	32	19
1980-81—Buffalo Sabres	NHL	49	16	20	36	34
1981-82—Rochester Americans	AHL	14	5	12	17	10
1981-82—Buffalo Sabres (d)	NHL	57	21	18	39	30
1982-83—Washington Capitals	NHL	74	23	27	50	34
1983-84—Washington Capitals	NHL	75	24	31	55	52
1984-85—Washington Capitals	NHL	76	23	26	49	48
1985-86—Washington Capitals	NHL	71	34	39	73	72
1986-87—Washington Capitals (e)	NHL	50	25	16	41	43
1987-88—Quebec Nordiques (f)	NHL	72	23	34	57	112
NHL TOTALS			524	189	211	400	425

(c)—August, 1979—Drafted by Buffalo Sabres as underage junior in 1979 entry draft. Sixth Sabres pick, 95th overall, fifth round.

(d)—June, 1982—Traded by Buffalo Sabres with third-round pick in 1982 entry draft to Washington Capitals for second and fourth-round choices in 1982.

(e)—June, 1987—Traded with Gaetan Duchesne and a first-round 1987 draft pick (Joe Sakic) by Washington Capitals to Quebec Nordiques for Dale Hunter and Clint Malarchuk.

(f)—April, 1988—Signed two-year contract with Bern (Switzerland).

BRIAN HAYTON

Defense . . . 6' . . . 197 lbs. . . . Born, Peterborough, Ont., January 22, 1968 . . . Shoots left . . . Also plays Left Wing.

Year	Team	League	Games	G.	A.	Pts.	Pen.
1984-85—Peterborough Jr. B	OHA	30	7	5	12	118
1985-86—Guelph Platers (c)	OHL	56	6	11	17	99
1986-87—Guelph Platers	OHL	63	6	19	25	113
1987-88—Guelph Platers	OHL	63	11	37	48	138
1987-88—New Haven Nighthawks	AHL	6	1	1	2	2

(c)—June, 1986—Drafted as underage junior by Los Angeles Kings in 1986 NHL entry draft. Eleventh Kings pick, 223rd overall, 12th round.

RICK HAYWARD

Defense . . . 6' . . . 173 lbs. . . . Born, Toledo, O., February 25, 1966 . . . Shoots left.

Year	Team	League	Games	G.	A.	Pts.	Pen.
1984-85—Hull Olympiques	QMJHL	56	7	27	34	367
1985-86—Hull Olympiques (c)	QMJHL	59	3	40	43	354
1986-87—Sherbrooke Canadiens	AHL	43	2	3	5	153
1987-88—Sherbrooke Canadiens (d)	AHL	22	1	5	6	91
1987-88—Saginaw Hawks	IHL	24	3	4	7	129
1987-88—Salt Lake Golden Eagles	IHL	17	1	3	4	124

(c)—June, 1986—Drafted by Montreal Canadiens in 1986 NHL entry draft. Ninth Canadiens pick, 162nd overall, eighth round.

(d)—February, 1988—Traded by Montreal Canadiens to Calgary Flames for Martin Nicoletti.

KEVIN HEFFERNAN

Center . . . 6'1" . . . 185 lbs. . . . Born, Weymouth, Mass., January 18, 1966 . . . Shoots left.

Year	Team	League	Games	G.	A.	Pts.	Pen.
1983-84—Weymouth H.S. (c)	Mass. H.S.	24	22	35	57	..
1984-85—Northeastern Univ.	H. East	38	18	25	43	20
1985-86—Northeastern Univ.	H. East	35	8	21	29	12
1986-87—Northeastern Univ.	H. East	36	14	22	36	30
1987-88—Northeastern Univ.	H. East	36	19	28	47	27

(c)—June, 1984—Drafted by Boston Bruins in 1984 NHL entry draft. Ninth Bruins pick, 186th overall, ninth round.

STEPHEN HEINZE

Center . . . 5'11" . . . 180 lbs. . . . Born, Lawrence, Mass., January 30, 1970 . . . Shoots right.

Year	Team	League	Games	G.	A.	Pts.	Pen.
1986-87—Lawrence Academy	Mass. H.S.	....	26	24	50	....
1987-88—Lawrence Academy (c)	Mass. H.S.	....	30	25	55	....

(c)—June, 1988—Drafted by Boston Bruins in 1988 NHL entry draft. Second Bruins pick, 60th overall, second round.

KEVIN HEISE

Left Wing . . . 6'1" . . . 170 lbs. . . . Born, Regina, Sask., September 9, 1968 . . . Shoots left.

Year	Team	League	Games	G.	A.	Pts.	Pen.
1986-87	Calgary Wranglers	WHL	68	20	16	36	125
1987-88	Lethbridge Hurricanes (c)	WHL	70	26	20	46	223

(c)—June, 1988—Drafted by Winnipeg Jets in 1988 NHL entry draft. Thirteenth Jets pick, 220th overall, 11th round.

ANTHONY J. HEJNA

Left Wing . . . 6' . . . 190 lbs. . . . Born, Buffalo, N.Y., January 8, 1968 . . . Shoots left.

Year	Team	League	Games	G.	A.	Pts.	Pen.
1984-85	Nichols H.S.	N.Y.	34	46	40	86	20
1985-86	Nichols H.S. (c)	N.Y.	33	51	27	78	26
1986-87	R.P.I.	ECAC	33	12	18	30	18
1987-88	R.P.I.	ECAC	32	17	19	36	48

(c)—June, 1986—Drafted by St. Louis Blues in 1986 NHL entry draft. Third Blues pick, 52nd overall, third round.

RAIMO HELMINEN

Center . . . 6' . . . 183 lbs. . . . Born, Tampere, Finland, March 11, 1964 . . . Shoots left . . . (October, 1985)—Hip injury . . . (October, 1986)—Fractured left thumb . . . (September, 1987)—Injured wrist.

Year	Team	League	Games	G.	A.	Pts.	Pen.
1983-84	Ilves (c)	Finland	37	17	13	30	14
1984-85	Ilves	Finland	36	21	36	57	20
1985-86	New York Rangers	NHL	66	10	30	40	10
1986-87	New York Rangers (d)	NHL	21	2	4	6	2
1986-87	New Haven Nighthawks	AHL	6	0	2	2	0
1986-87	Minnesota North Stars	NHL	6	0	1	1	0
1987-88	Ilves Tampere (e)	Finland	31	20	23	43	42
	NHL TOTALS		93	12	35	47	12

(c)—June, 1983—Drafted by New York Rangers in NHL entry draft. Second Rangers pick, 35th overall, second round.
(d)—March, 1987—Traded by New York Rangers to Minnesota North Stars for future considerations.
(e)—June, 1988—Signed by New York Islanders as a free agent.

ARCHIE HENDERSON

Right Wing . . . 6'6" . . . 216 lbs. . . . Born, Calgary, Alta., February 17, 1957 . . . Shoots right . . . Missed part of 1976-77 season with knee injury . . . (November, 1980)—Hand injury . . . (October 25, 1985)—Given six-game suspension by AHL for stick-swinging incident with Jim Archibald at Springfield. Henderson had received a match penalty . . . (December 7, 1985)—Given 12-game AHL suspension for crosschecking incident with Robin Bartel in Moncton.

Year	Team	League	Games	G.	A.	Pts.	Pen.
1974-75	Lethbridge Broncos	WCHL	65	3	10	13	177
1975-76	Lethbridge Broncos (c)	WCHL	21	1	2	3	110
1975-76	Victoria Cougars	WCHL	31	8	7	15	205
1976-77	Victoria Cougars (d)	WCHL	47	14	10	24	208
1977-78	Port Huron Flags	IHL	71	16	16	32	419
1978-79	Hershey Bears	AHL	78	17	11	28	337
1979-80	Hershey Bears	AHL	8	0	2	2	37
1979-80	Fort Worth Texans (e)	CHL	49	8	9	17	199
1980-81	Washington Capitals	NHL	7	1	0	1	28
1980-81	Hershey Bears	AHL	60	3	5	8	251
1981-82	Minnesota North Stars (f)	NHL	1	0	0	0	0
1981-82	Nashville South Stars	CHL	77	12	23	35	*320
1982-83	Hartford Whalers (g)	NHL	15	2	1	3	64
1982-83	Binghamton Whalers (h)	AHL	50	8	9	17	172
1983-84	New Haven Nighthawks (i-j)	AHL	48	1	8	9	164
1984-85	Nova Scotia Oilers	AHL	72	5	7	12	271
1985-86	Maine Mariners (k)	AHL	57	4	6	10	72
1986-87	Maine Mariners	AHL	67	4	6	10	246
1987-88	Saginaw Hawks (l)	IHL	55	4	9	13	231
	NHL TOTALS		23	3	1	4	92

(c)—December, 1975—Traded to Victoria Cougars by Lethbridge Broncos for Rick Peter.
(d)—Drafted from Victoria Cougars by Washington Capitals in 10th round of 1977 amateur draft.
(e)—Led in penalty minutes (58) during playoffs.

(f)—September, 1981—Signed with Minnesota North Stars as a free agent after being released by Washington Capitals.
(g)—September, 1982—Signed by Hartford Whalers as a free agent.
(h)—March, 1983—Released by Hartford Whalers.
(i)—September, 1983—Signed by New Haven Nighthawks as a free agent.
(j)—February, 1984—Released by New Haven Nighthawks.
(k)—September, 1985—Signed by New Jersey Devils as a free agent.
(l)—July, 1988—Named head coach of Indianapolis Ice.

DALE HENRY

Left Wing . . . 6' . . . 205 lbs. . . . Born, Prince Albert, Sask., September 24, 1964 . . . Shoots left . . . (December, 1986)—Missed 12 games with a bruised left thigh . . . (March 3, 1987)—Sprained left knee ligaments vs. Boston . . . (November 20, 1987)—Given a four-game suspension by AHL for fighting.

Year	Team	League	Games	G.	A.	Pts.	Pen.
1981-82—Saskatoon Blades		WHL	32	5	4	9	50
1982-83—Saskatoon Blades (c)		WHL	63	21	19	40	213
1983-84—Saskatoon Blades		WHL	71	41	36	77	162
1984-85—Springfield Indians		AHL	67	11	20	31	133
1984-85—New York Islanders		NHL	16	2	1	3	19
1985-86—Springfield Indians		AHL	64	14	26	40	162
1985-86—New York Islanders		NHL	7	1	3	4	15
1986-87—Springfield Indians		AHL	23	9	14	23	49
1986-87—New York Islanders		NHL	19	3	3	6	46
1987-88—Springfield Indians		AHL	24	9	12	21	103
1987-88—New York Islanders		NHL	48	5	15	20	115
NHL TOTALS			90	11	22	33	195

(c)—June, 1983—Drafted as underage junior by New York Islanders in 1983 NHL entry draft. Tenth Islanders pick, 157th overall, eighth round.

MATHEW HENTGES

Defense . . . 6'4" . . . 200 lbs. . . . Born, St. Paul, Minn., December 19, 1969 . . . Shoots left.

Year	Team	League	Games	G.	A.	Pts.	Pen.
1986-87—Edina H.S.		Minn. H.S.	24	3	10	13	34
1987-88—Edina H.S. (c)		Minn. H.S.	27	3	18	21	..

(c)—June, 1988—Drafted by Chicago Black Hawks in 1988 NHL entry draft. Eighth Black Hawks pick, 176th overall, ninth round.

ALAN HEPPLE

Defense . . . 5'10" . . . 200 lbs. . . . Born, Blaudon-on-Tyne, England, August 16, 1963 . . . Shoots right . . . Also plays Center . . . (October, 1980)—Eye injury.

Year	Team	League	Games	G.	A.	Pts.	Pen.
1980-81—Ottawa 67's		OHL	64	3	13	16	110
1981-82—Ottawa 67's (c)		OHL	66	6	22	28	160
1982-83—Ottawa 67's		OHL	64	10	26	36	168
1983-84—Maine Mariners		AHL	64	4	23	27	117
1983-84—New Jersey Devils		NHL	1	0	0	0	7
1984-85—Maine Marifers		AHL	80	7	17	24	125
1984-85—New Jersey Devils		NHL	1	0	0	0	0
1985-86—Maine Mariners		AHL	69	4	21	25	104
1985-86—New Jersey Devils		NHL	1	0	0	0	0
1986-87—Maine Mariners		AHL	74	6	19	25	137
1987-88—Utica Devils		AHL	78	3	16	19	213
NHL TOTALS			3	0	0	0	7

(c)—June, 1982—Drafted as underage junior by New Jersey Devils in 1982 NHL entry draft. Ninth Devils pick, 169th overall, ninth round.

IAN HERBERS

Defense . . . 6'4" . . . 210 lbs. . . . Born, Sherwood Park, Alta., July 18, 1967 . . . Shoots left.

Year	Team	League	Games	G.	A.	Pts.	Pen.
1984-85—Kelowna Wings		WHL	68	3	14	17	120
1985-86—Spokane Chiefs (c)		WHL	29	1	6	7	85
1985-86—Lethbridge Broncos		WHL	32	1	4	5	109
1986-87—Swift Current Broncos (d)		WHL	72	5	8	13	230
1987-88—Swift Current Broncos		WHL	56	5	14	19	238

(c)—January, 1986—Traded with Landis Chaulk and Mike Weigleitner by Spokane Chiefs to Lethbridge Broncos for Mike Berger.
(d)—June, 1987—Drafted by Buffalo Sabres in 1987 NHL entry draft. Eleventh Sabres pick, 190th overall, 10th round.

STEVE HERNIMAN

Defense ... 6'4" ... 200 lbs. ... Born, Windsor, Ont., June 9, 1968 ... Shoots left.

Year	Team	League	Games	G.	A.	Pts.	Pen.
1984-85—Kitchener Midgets		OHA	29	3	20	23	50
1984-85—Cornwall Royals (c)		OHL	55	3	12	15	128
1986-87—Cornwall Royals		OHL	64	2	8	10	121
1987-88—Cornwall Royals		OHL	5	1	0	1	8
1987-88—Sault Ste. Marie Greyhounds		OHL	52	3	14	17	111

(c)—June, 1986—Drafted as underage junior by Vancouver Canucks in 1986 NHL entry draft. Fifth Canucks pick, 112th overall, sixth round.

KEVIN HEROM

Left Wing ... 6' ... 195 lbs. ... Born, Regina, Sask., July 6, 1967 ... Shoots left.

Year	Team	League	Games	G.	A.	Pts.	Pen.
1983-84—Regina Pat Canadians		Sask. Midget	26	22	24	46	39
1984-85—Moose Jaw Warriors (c)		WHL	61	20	18	38	44
1985-86—Moose Jaw Warriors		WHL	66	22	18	40	103
1986-87—Moose Jaw Warriors		WHL	72	34	33	67	111
1987-88—Springfield Indians		AHL	66	9	8	17	74
1987-88—Peoria Rivermen		IHL	3	0	0	0	19

(c)—June, 1985—Drafted as underage junior by New York Islanders in 1985 NHL entry draft. Fifth Islanders pick, 76th overall, fourth round.

BRYAN HERRING

Center ... 6'1" ... 170 lbs. ... Born, Seattle, Wash., February 12, 1969 ... Shoots left ... Also plays Left Wing ... (March, 1986)—Broken hand.

Year	Team	League	Games	G.	A.	Pts.	Pen.
1986-87—Dubuque Fighting Saints (c)		USHL	48	26	27	53	2
1987-88—Univ. of Illinois/Chicago		CCHA	26	1	1	2	10

(c)—June, 1987—Drafted by Montreal Canadiens in 1987 NHL entry draft. Fourteenth Canadiens pick, 248th overall, 12th round.

DANNY HIE

Center ... 6' ... 178 lbs. ... Born, Mississauga, Ont., June 21, 1968 ... Shoots left ... Also plays Left Wing ... (February, 1986)—Shoulder separation.

Year	Team	League	Games	G.	A.	Pts.	Pen.
1984-85—North York Jr. A		Tier II	37	12	12	24	100
1985-86—Ottawa 67's (c)		OHL	55	7	18	25	75
1986-87—Ottawa 67's (d)		OHL	4	3	6	9	16
1986-87—Hamilton Steelhawks (e)		OHL	15	2	14	16	25
1986-87—Sudbury Wolves		OHL	19	1	5	6	47
1987-88—Sudbury Wolves		OHL	1	0	0	0	2
1987-88—London Knights		OHL	39	8	14	22	54

(c)—June, 1986—Drafted as underage junior by Toronto Maple Leafs in 1986 NHL entry draft. Seventh Maple Leafs pick, 132nd overall, seventh round.

(d)—October, 1986—Traded by Ottawa 67's to Hamilton Steelhawks for Řod Thacker and Willie Popp.

(e)—December, 1986—Traded with Steve Locke, Shawn Heaphy, Jordon Fois and Joe Simon by Hamilton Steelhawks to Sudbury Wolves for Ken McRae, Andy Paquette and Ken Alexander.

TIM RAY HIGGINS

Right Wing ... 6'1" ... 185 lbs. ... Born, Ottawa, Ont., February 7, 1958 ... Shoots right ... (January 16, 1983)—Broke index finger of right hand during a fight with Colin Campbell vs. Detroit ... (February, 1983)—Strained knee ligaments ... (October, 1985)—Missed two games with a stomach virus ... (February 13, 1986)—Missed four games with infected foot blisters ... (December 16, 1986)—Bruised thigh at Calgary ... (December, 1987)—Dislocated left shoulder ... (March, 1988)—Scored two goals after suffering a broken nose during game at Vancouver.

Year	Team	League	Games	G.	A.	Pts.	Pen.
1974-75—Ottawa 67's		Jr."A"OHA	22	1	3	4	6
1975-76—Ottawa 67's		Jr."A"OHA	59	15	10	25	59
1976-77—Ottawa 67's		Jr."A"OHA	66	36	52	88	82
1977-78—Ottawa 67's (c)		Jr."A"OHA	50	41	60	101	99
1978-79—Chicago Black Hawks		NHL	36	7	16	23	30
1978-79—New Brunswick Hawks		AHL	17	3	5	8	14
1979-80—Chicago Black Hawks		NHL	74	13	12	25	50
1980-81—Chicago Black Hawks		NHL	78	24	35	59	86
1981-82—Chicago Black Hawks		NHL	74	20	30	50	85

Year	Team	League	Games	G.	A.	Pts.	Pen.
1982-83—Chicago Black Hawks		NHL	64	14	9	23	63
1983-84—Chicago Black Hawks (d)		NHL	32	1	4	5	21
1983-84—New Jersey Devils		NHL	37	18	10	28	27
1984-85—New Jersey Devils		NHL	71	19	29	48	30
1985-86—New Jersey Devils (e)		NHL	59	9	17	26	47
1986-87—Detroit Red Wings		NHL	77	12	14	26	124
1987-88—Detroit Red Wings		NHL	62	12	13	25	94
NHL TOTALS			664	149	189	338	657

(c)—Drafted from Ottawa 67's by Chicago Black Hawks in first round of 1978 amateur draft.
(d)—January, 1984—Traded by Chicago Black Hawks to New Jersey Devils for Jeff Larmer.
(e)—June, 1986—Traded by New Jersey Devils to Detroit Red Wings for Claude Loiselle.

ALAN DOUGLAS HILL

Left Wing and Center . . . 6' . . . 175 lbs. . . . Born, Nanaimo, B. C., April 22, 1955 . . . Shoots left . . . Set NHL record for most points in first NHL game with 2 goals, 3 assists, February 14, 1977 . . . (November 20, 1980)—Fractured hand.

Year	Team	League	Games	G.	A.	Pts.	Pen.
1973-74—Nanaimo		Jr.''A''BCHL	64	29	41	70	60
1974-75—Victoria Cougars		WCHL	70	21	36	57	75
1975-76—Victoria Cougars (c)		WCHL	68	26	40	66	172
1976-77—Springfield Kings		AHL	63	13	28	41	125
1976-77—Philadelphia Flyers		NHL	9	2	4	6	27
1977-78—Maine Mariners (a)		AHL	80	32	59	91	118
1977-78—Philadelphia Flyers		NHL	3	0	0	0	2
1978-79—Philadelphia Flyers		NHL	31	5	11	16	28
1978-79—Maine Mariners		AHL	35	11	14	25	59
1979-80—Philadelphia Flyers		NHL	61	16	10	26	53
1980-81—Philadelphia Flyers		NHL	57	10	15	25	45
1981-82—Philadelphia Flyers		NHL	41	6	13	19	58
1982-83—Moncton Alpines		AHL	78	22	22	44	78
1983-84—Maine Mariners (d)		AHL	51	8	16	24	51
1984-85—Hershey Bears		AHL	73	11	30	41	77
1985-86—Hershey Bears		AHL	80	17	40	57	129
1986-87—Hershey Bears		AHL	76	13	35	48	124
1986-87—Philadelphia Flyers		NHL	7	0	2	2	4
1987-88—Philadelphia Flyers		NHL	12	1	0	1	10
1987-88—Hershey Bears		AHL	57	10	21	31	62
NHL TOTALS			221	40	55	95	227

(c)—September, 1976—Signed by Philadelphia Flyers as a free agent.
(d)—January, 1984—Signed by Maine Mariners as a free agent.

RANDY GEORGE HILLIER

Defense . . . 6'1" . . . 170 lbs. . . . Born, Toronto, Ont., March 30, 1960 . . . Shoots right . . . (April 19, 1982)—Injured knee in playoff series vs. Quebec . . . (December, 1982)—Injured left knee . . . (April 2, 1983)—Strained ligaments in right knee at Montreal . . . (December, 1984)—Surgery to remove bone chips from left shoulder and missed 20 games . . . (March, 1985)—Broken finger . . . (November 30, 1985)—Tore knee ligaments vs. N.Y. Rangers . . . (November, 1986)—Injured shoulder . . . (March 12, 1987)—Bruised left hand vs. Quebec . . . (October, 1987)—Torn hip muscles . . . (November, 1987)—Bruised heel.

Year	Team	League	Games	G.	A.	Pts.	Pen.
1977-78—Sudbury Wolves		OMJHL	60	1	14	15	67
1978-79—Sudbury Wolves		OMJHL	61	9	25	34	173
1979-80—Sudbury Wolves (c)		OMJHL	60	16	49	65	143
1980-81—Springfield Indians		AHL	64	3	17	20	105
1981-82—Erie Blades		AHL	35	6	13	19	52
1981-82—Boston Bruins		NHL	25	0	8	8	29
1982-83—Boston Bruins		NHL	70	0	10	10	99
1983-84—Boston Bruins		NHL	69	3	12	15	125
1984-85—Pittsburgh Penguins (d)		NHL	45	2	19	21	56
1985-86—Baltimore Skipjacks		AHL	8	0	5	5	14
1985-86—Pittsburgh Penguins		NHL	28	0	3	3	53
1986-87—Pittsburgh Penguins		NHL	55	4	8	12	97
1987-88—Pittsburgh Penguins		NHL	55	1	12	13	144
NHL TOTALS			347	10	72	82	603

(c)—June, 1980—Drafted by Boston Bruins in 1980 NHL entry draft. Fourth Bruins pick, 102nd overall, fifth round.
(d)—October, 1984—Traded by Boston Bruins to Pittsburgh Penguins for 1985 fourth round draft pick.

MIKE HILTNER

Right Wing . . . 6'1" . . . 195 lbs. . . . Born, St. Cloud, Minn., March 22, 1966 . . . Shoots right.

Year	Team	League	Games	G.	A.	Pts.	Pen.
1984-85	Univ. of Alaska/Anchorage	GWHC	30	8	9	17	58
1985-86	Univ. of Alaska/Anchorage	GWHC	26	8	12	20	50
1986-87	Univ. of Alaska/Anchorage (c)	GWHC	30	19	20	39	76
1987-88	Univ. of Alaska/Anchorage	GWHC	35	28	21	49	123

(c)—June, 1987—Selected by Quebec Nordiques in 1987 NHL supplemental draft.

MARK HIRTH

Center . . . 6'2" . . . 180 lbs. . . . Born, Ann Arbor, Mich., January 7, 1969 . . . Shoots left.

Year	Team	League	Games	G.	A.	Pts.	Pen.
1987-88	Michigan State Univ. (c)	CCHA	9	0	2	2	0

(c)—June, 1988—Drafted by Hartford Whalers in 1988 NHL entry draft. Eighth Whalers pick, 179th overall, ninth round.

DOUG HOBSON

Defense . . . 6' . . . 185 lbs. . . . Born, Prince Albert, Sask., April 9, 1968 . . . Shoots left.

Year	Team	League	Games	G.	A.	Pts.	Pen.
1984-85	Prince Albert Raiders	WHL	59	7	12	19	73
1985-86	Prince Albert Raiders (c)	WHL	66	2	17	19	70
1986-87	Prince Albert Raiders	WHL	69	3	20	23	83
1987-88	Prince Albert Raiders	WHL	69	9	26	35	96

(c)—June, 1986—Drafted as underage junior by Pittsburgh Penguins in 1986 NHL entry draft. Seventh Penguins pick, 130th overall, seventh round.

KENNETH HODGE JR.

Center . . . 6'2" . . . 190 lbs. . . . Born, Windsor, Ontario, April 13, 1966 . . . Shoots left . . . Son of former NHL star Ken Hodge, who played for Chicago, Boston and New York Rangers in 1965 through 1978 . . . (November, 1987)—Injured his shoulders twice in IHL pre-season games.

Year	Team	League	Games	G.	A.	Pts.	Pen.
1983-84	St. John's Prep. (c)	Mass. H.S.	22	25	38	63	..
1984-85	Boston College (d)	H. East	41	20	44	64	28
1985-86	Boston College	H. East	21	11	17	28	16
1986-87	Boston College	H. East	37	29	33	62	30
1987-88	Kalamazoo Wings	IHL	70	15	35	50	24

(c)—June, 1984—Drafted by Minnesota North Stars in 1984 NHL entry draft. Second North Stars pick, 46th overall, third round.

(d)—Named top Hockey East Freshman.

DAN HODGSON

Center . . . 5'11" . . . 173 lbs. . . . Born, Fort McMurray, Alta., August 29, 1965 . . . Shoots right . . . (October, 1985)—Broken nose and cheekbone . . . (November 25, 1987)—Fractured left leg after a collision with Brad McCrimmon vs. Calgary.

Year	Team	League	Games	G.	A.	Pts.	Pen.
1982-83	Prince Albert Raiders (c-d)	WHL	72	56	74	130	66
1983-84	Prince Albert Raiders (b)	WHL	66	62	*119	181	65
1984-85	Prince Albert Raiders (a-e-f)	WHL	64	70	*112	182	86
1985-86	Toronto Maple Leafs	NHL	40	13	12	25	12
1985-86	St. Catharines Saints	AHL	22	13	16	29	15
1986-87	Newmarket Saints (g)	AHL	20	7	12	19	16
1986-87	Vancouver Canucks	NHL	43	9	13	22	25
1987-88	Fredericton Express	AHL	13	8	18	26	16
1987-88	Vancouver Canucks	NHL	8	3	7	10	2
	NHL TOTALS		91	25	32	57	39

(c)—Won Stuart "Butch" Paul Memorial Trophy (Top WHL Rookie).

(d)—June, 1983—Drafted as underage junior by Toronto Maple Leafs in 1983 NHL entry draft. Fourth Maple Leafs pick, 83rd overall, fifth round.

(e)—Named WHL Molson Player of the Year.

(f)—Led WHL Playoffs with 26 assists and 36 points.

(g)—December, 1986—Traded with Jim Benning by Toronto Maple Leafs to Vancouver Canucks for Rick Lanz.

MICHAEL HOFFMAN

Left Wing . . . 5'11" . . . 179 lbs. . . . Born, Cambridge, Ont., February 26, 1963 . . . Shoots left . . . (March, 1980)—Shoulder dislocation.

Year Team	League	Games	G.	A.	Pts.	Pen.
1979-80—Barrie	Midget	60	40	35	75	....
1980-81—Brantford Alexanders (c)	OHL	68	15	19	34	71
1981-82—Brantford Alexanders	OHL	66	34	47	81	169
1982-83—Brantford Alexanders	OHL	63	26	49	75	128
1982-83—Binghamton Whalers	AHL	1	0	0	0	0
1982-83—Hartford Whalers	NHL	2	0	1	1	0
1983-84—Binghamton Whalers	AHL	64	11	13	24	92
1984-85—Binghamton Whalers	AHL	76	19	26	45	95
1984-85—Hartford Whalers	NHL	1	0	0	0	0
1985-86—Binghamton Whalers	AHL	40	14	14	28	79
1985-86—Hartford Whalers	NHL	6	1	2	3	2
1986-87—Binghamton Whalers	AHL	74	9	32	41	120
1987-88—Flint Spirits	IHL	64	35	28	63	49
NHL TOTALS		9	1	3	4	2

(c)—June, 1981—Drafted as underage junior by Hartford Whalers in 1981 NHL entry draft. Third Whalers pick, 67th overall, fourth round.

JIM HOFFORD

Defense . . . 6' . . . 190 lbs. . . . Born, Sudbury, Ont., October 4, 1964 . . . Shoots right . . . (September, 1981)—Broken nose . . . (November, 1987)—Concussion . . . (January, 1988) —Broke jaw.

Year Team	League	Games	G.	A.	Pts.	Pen.
1981-82—Windsor Spitfires	OHL	67	5	9	14	214
1982-83—Windsor Spitfires (c)	OHL	63	8	20	28	171
1983-84—Windsor Spitfires	OHL	1	0	0	0	2
1984-85—Rochester Americans	AHL	70	2	13	15	166
1985-86—Rochester Americans	AHL	40	2	7	9	148
1985-86—Buffalo Sabres	NHL	5	0	0	0	5
1986-87—Rochester Americans	AHL	54	1	8	9	204
1986-87—Buffalo Sabres	NHL	12	0	0	0	40
1987-88—Rochester Americans	AHL	69	3	15	18	322
NHL TOTALS		17	0	0	0	45

(c)—June, 1983—Drafted as underage junior by Buffalo Sabres in 1983 NHL entry draft. Eighth Sabres pick, 114th overall, sixth round.

BENOIT HOGUE

Center . . . 5'11" . . . 170 lbs. . . . Born, Repentigny, Que., October 28, 1966 . . . Shoots left . . . (October, 1987)—Suspended six games for fighting by AHL.

Year Team	League	Games	G.	A.	Pts.	Pen.
1984-85—St. Jean Beavers	QHL	59	14	11	25	42
1984-85—St. Jean Beavers (c)	QHL	63	46	44	90	92
1985-86—St. Jean Beavers	QHL	65	54	54	108	115
1986-87—Rochester Americans	AHL	52	14	20	34	52
1987-88—Buffalo Sabres	NHL	3	1	1	2	0
1987-88—Rochester Americans	AHL	62	24	31	55	141
NHL TOTALS		3	1	1	2	0

(c)—June, 1985—Drafted as underage junior by Buffalo Sabres in 1985 NHL entry draft. Second Sabres pick, 35th overall, second round.

PAUL HOLDEN

Defense . . . 6'3" . . . 210 lbs. . . . Born, Kitchener, Ont., March 15, 1970 . . , Shoots left.

Year Team	League	Games	G.	A.	Pts.	Pen.
1986-87—St. Thomas Jr. B	OHL	23	5	11	16	112
1987-88—London Knights (c)	OHL	65	8	12	20	87

(c)—June, 1988—Drafted by Los Angeles Kings in 1988 NHL entry draft. Second Kings pick, 28th overall, second round.

DENNIS HOLLAND

Center . . . 5'10" . . . 167 lbs. . . . Born, Vernon, B.C., January 30, 1969 . . . Shoots left . . . Brother of Ken Holland, former AHL goaltender and currently Detroit Red Wings western scout.

Year Team	League	Games	G.	A.	Pts.	Pen.
1985-86—Vernon Lakers	BCJHL	51	43	62	105	40
1985-86—Portland Winter Hawks	WHL	1	3	2	5	0
1986-87—Portland Winter Hawks (c)	WHL	72	36	77	113	96
1987-88—Portland Winter Hawks	WHL	67	58	86	144	115

(c)—June, 1987—Drafted by Detroit Red Wings in 1987 NHL entry draft as an underage junior. Fourth Red Wings pick, 52nd overall, third round.

STEVE HOLLETT

Center ... 6'1" ... 168 lbs. ... Born, St. John's, N.B., June 12, 1967 ... Shoots left.

Year	Team	League	Games	G.	A.	Pts.	Pen.
1983-84—Niagara Falls Midget		OHA	30	46	54	100	95
1984-85—Sault Ste. Marie Greyhounds (c)		OHL	60	12	17	29	25
1985-86—Sault Ste. Marie Greyhounds		OHL	63	31	34	65	81
1985-86—Binghamton Whalers		AHL	8	0	0	0	2
1986-87—Sault Ste. Marie Greyhounds		OHL	65	35	41	76	63
1987-88—Fort Wayne Komets		IHL	76	42	32	74	56

(c)—June, 1985—Drafted as underage junior by Washington Capitals in 1985 NHL entry draft. Tenth Capitals pick, 187th overall, ninth round.

TODD HOOEY

Right Wing ... 6'1" ... 180 lbs. ... Born, Oshawa, Ont., June 23, 1963 ... Shoots right ... Nephew of Tom and Tim O'Connor (1958 World Champion Whitby Dunlops) ... (October, 1984)—Knee injury.

Year	Team	League	Games	G.	A.	Pts.	Pen.
1979-80—Oshawa Reps		Midget	53	31	20	51	....
1980-81—Windsor Spitfires (c)		OHL	68	18	25	43	132
1981-82—Windsor Spitfires		OHL	68	39	62	101	158
1981-82—Oklahoma City Stars		CHL	4	1	1	2	0
1982-83—Windsor Spitfires (d)		OHL	4	0	1	1	6
1982-83—Oshawa Generals		OHL	62	31	34	65	64
1983-84—Colorado Flames		CHL	67	19	21	40	40
1984-85—Moncton Golden Flames		AHL	61	4	14	18	52
1985-86—Salt Lake Golden Eagles		IHL	80	15	23	38	95
1986-87—Salt Lake Golden Eagles (b-e-f)		IHL	82	47	48	95	60
1987-88—New Haven Nighthawks		AHL	45	6	12	18	45

(c)—June, 1981—Drafted as underage junior by Calgary Flames in 1981 NHL entry draft. Fifth Flames pick, 120th overall, sixth round.

(d)—October, 1982—Traded by Windsor Spitfires to Oshawa Generals for Ray Flaherty.

(e)—Led IHL playoffs with 14 goals and 22 assists.

(f)—August, 1987—Signed by Los Angeles Kings as a free agent.

RON HOOVER

Defense ... 5'10" ... 165 lbs. ... Born, North Bay, Ont., January 9, 1965 ... Shoots left.

Year	Team	League	Games	G.	A.	Pts.	Pen.
1985-86—Western Michigan Univ. (c)		CCHA	43	10	23	33	36
1986-87—Western Michigan Univ.		CCHA	34	7	10	17	22
1987-88—Western Michigan Univ.		CCHA	42	39	23	62	40

(c)—June, 1986—Drafted by Hartford Whalers in 1986 NHL entry draft. Seventh Whalers' pick, 158th overall, eighth round.

TIM HOOVER

Defense ... 5'10" ... 165 lbs. ... Born, North Bay, Ont., January 9, 1965 ... Shoots left ... (March, 1986)—Broken foot.

Year	Team	League	Games	G.	A.	Pts.	Pen.
1982-83—Sault Ste. Marie Greyhounds (c)		OHL	60	6	21	27	53
1983-84—Sault Ste. Marie Greyhounds		OHL	70	8	34	42	50
1984-85—Sault Ste. Marie Greyhounds		OHL	49	6	28	34	29
1985-86—Rochester Americans		AHL	49	2	5	7	34
1986-87—Flint Spirits		IHL	75	3	23	26	26
1987-88—Baltimore Skipjacks		AHL	73	2	6	8	39

(c)—June, 1983—Drafted as underage junior by Buffalo Sabres in 1983 NHL entry draft. Eleventh Sabres pick, 174th overall, ninth round.

DEAN ROBERT HOPKINS

Right Wing ... 6'1" ... 205 lbs. ... Born, Cobourg, Ont., June 6, 1959 ... Shoots right ... Played Center prior to 1978-79 ... Missed 14 games during 1979-80 season with broken ankle ... (December, 1981)—Dislocated elbow ... Brother of Brent Hopkins ... (March, 1986)—Broken jaw.

Year	Team	League	Games	G.	A.	Pts.	Pen.
1975-76—London Knights		OMJHL	53	4	14	18	50
1976-77—London Knights		OMJHL	63	19	26	45	67

Year	Team	League	Games	G.	A.	Pts.	Pen.
1977-78—London Knights		OMJHL	67	19	34	53	70
1978-79—London Knights (c)		OMJHL	65	37	55	92	149
1979-80—Los Angeles Kings		NHL	60	8	6	14	39
1980-81—Los Angeles Kings		NHL	67	8	18	26	118
1981-82—Los Angeles Kings		NHL	41	2	13	15	102
1982-83—New Haven Nighthawks		AHL	20	9	8	17	58
1982-83—Los Angeles Kings		NHL	49	5	12	17	43
1983-84—New Haven Nighthawks		AHL	79	35	47	82	162
1984-85—New Haven Nighthawks (d)		AHL	20	7	10	17	38
1984-85—Nova Scotia Voyageurs		AHL	49	13	17	30	93
1985-86—Edmonton Oilers (e)		NHL	1	0	0	0	0
1985-86—Nova Scotia Voyageurs		AHL	60	23	32	55	131
1986-87—Nova Scotia Oilers		AHL	59	20	25	45	84
1987-88—Nova Scotia Oilers		AHL	44	20	22	42	122
NHL TOTALS			218	23	49	72	302

(c)—August, 1979—Drafted by Los Angeles Kings in 1979 entry draft. Second Kings pick, 29th overall, second round.

(d)—November, 1984—Traded with Mark Morrison by New Haven Nighthawks to Nova Scotia Oilers for Rob Tudor and Gerry Minor.

(e)—September, 1985—Signed by Edmonton Oilers as a free agent.

TONY HORACEK

Left Wing ... 6'3" ... 200 lbs. ... Born, Vancouver, B.C., February 3, 1967 ... Shoots left ... (November 1, 1987)—Suspended one WHL game for swinging his stick at fans ... (November 27, 1987)—Suspended eight WHL games for fighting.

Year	Team	League	Games	G.	A.	Pts.	Pen.
1984-85—Kelowna Wings (c)		WHL	67	9	18	27	114
1985-86—Spokane Chiefs		WHL	64	19	28	47	129
1986-87—Spokane Chiefs		WHL	64	23	37	60	177
1986-87—Hershey Bears		AHL	1	0	0	0	0
1987-88—Hershey Bears		AHL	1	0	0	0	0
1987-88—Spokane Chiefs		WHL	24	17	23	40	63
1987-88—Kamloops Blazers		WHL	26	14	17	31	51

(c)—June, 1985—Drafted as underage junior by Philadelphia Flyers in 1985 NHL entry draft. Eighth Flyers pick, 147th overall, seventh round.

STEVE HORNER

Right Wing ... 6'1" ... 195 lbs. ... Born, Cowansville, Que., June 4, 1966 ... Shoots right.

Year	Team	League	Games	G.	A.	Pts.	Pen.
1984-85—Henry Carr H.S. (c)		OHA	35	21	20	41	38
1985-86—Univ. of New Hampshire		H. East	30	3	5	8	14
1986-87—Univ. of New Hampshire		H. East	33	19	17	36	14
1987-88—Univ. of New Hampshire		H. East	27	10	8	18	10

(c)—June, 1985—Drafted by Los Angeles Kings in 1985 NHL entry draft. Eighth Kings pick, 177th overall, ninth round.

ED HOSPODAR

Defense and Right Wing ... 6'2" ... 210 lbs. ... Born, Bowling Green, Ohio, February 9, 1959 ... Shoots right ... (September, 1977)—Surgery to remove cartilage from left knee ... (September, 1978)—Injured ligaments in right knee ... (October, 1980)—Bruised left ankle ... (December 28, 1980)—Strained back ... (December 30, 1981)—Suffered broken jaw and loss of several teeth in altercation with Clark Gillies ... (December, 1983)—Hamstring injury ... (December 16, 1984)—Broke hand vs. Montreal ... (October 13, 1985)—Missed four games with elbow infection ... (January 21, 1986)—Strained back at Washington and missed five games ... (February 10, 1986)—Strained knee at Montreal and missed seven games.

Year	Team	League	Games	G.	A.	Pts.	Pen.
1976-77—Ottawa 67's		OMJHL	51	3	19	22	140
1977-78—Ottawa 67's		OMJHL	62	7	26	33	172
1978-79—Ottawa 67's (b-c)		OMJHL	46	7	16	23	208
1979-80—New Haven Nighthawks		AHL	25	3	9	12	131
1979-80—New York Rangers		NHL	20	0	1	1	76
1980-81—New York Rangers (d)		NHL	61	5	14	19	214
1981-82—New York Rangers (e)		NHL	41	3	8	11	152
1982-83—Hartford Whalers		NHL	72	1	9	10	199
1983-84—Hartford Whalers (f)		NHL	59	0	9	9	163
1984-85—Philadelphia Flyers		NHL	50	3	4	7	130
1985-86—Philadelphia Flyers (g)		NHL	17	3	1	4	55

Year	Team	League	Games	G.	A.	Pts.	Pen.
1985-86—Minnesota North Stars (h)		NHL	43	0	2	2	91
1986-87—Philadelphia Flyers (i)		NHL	45	2	2	4	136
1987-88—Buffalo Sabres		NHL	42	0	1	1	98
NHL TOTALS			450	17	51	68	1314

(c)—August, 1979—Drafted by New York Rangers in 1979 entry draft. Second Rangers pick, 34th overall, second round.

(d)—Led NHL playoffs with 93 penalty minutes.

(e)—October, 1982—Traded by New York Rangers to Hartford Whalers for Kent-Erik Andersson.

(f)—July, 1983—Released by Hartford Whalers and signed by Philadelphia Flyers as a free agent.

(g)—November, 1985—Traded with Todd Bergen by Philadelphia Flyers to Minnesota North Stars for Dave Richter and Bo Berglund.

(h)—June, 1986—Released by Minnesota North Stars and signed by Philadelphia Flyers as a free agent.

(i)—October, 1987—Selected by Buffalo Sabres in NHL waiver draft.

GREG HOTHAM

Defense . . . 5'11" . . . 183 lbs. . . . Born, London, Ont., March 7, 1956 . . . Shoots right . . . (November, 1982)—Injured knee . . . Missed parts of 1982-83 season with sprained knee, separated shoulder and injured back . . . (September, 1984)—Missed first 20 games of the season with mononucleosis.

Year	Team	League	Games	G.	A.	Pts.	Pen.
1973-74—Aurora Tigers		OPJHL	44	10	22	32	120
1974-75—Aurora Tigers		OPJHL	27	14	10	24	46
1974-75—Kingston Canadians		Jr."A"OHA	31	1	14	15	49
1975-76—Kingston Canadians (c)		Jr."A"OHA	49	10	32	42	76
1976-77—Saginaw Gears		IHL	69	4	33	37	100
1977-78—Saginaw Gears (b)		IHL	80	13	59	72	56
1977-78—Dallas Black Hawks (d)		CHL	....	...	...	...	....
1978-79—New Brunswick Hawks		AHL	76	9	27	36	88
1979-80—Toronto Maple Leafs		NHL	46	3	10	13	10
1979-80—New Brunswick Hawks		AHL	21	1	6	7	10
1980-81—Toronto Maple Leafs		NHL	11	1	1	2	11
1980-81—New Brunswick Hawks		AHL	68	8	48	56	80
1981-82—Cincinnati Tigers		CHL	46	10	33	43	94
1981-82—Toronto Maple Leafs (e)		NHL	3	0	0	0	0
1981-82—Pittsburgh Penguins		NHL	25	4	6	10	16
1982-83—Pittsburgh Penguins		NHL	58	2	30	32	39
1983-84—Pittsburgh Penguins		NHL	76	5	25	30	59
1984-85—Baltimore Skipjacks		AHL	44	4	27	31	43
1984-85—Pittsburgh Penguins		NHL	11	0	2	2	4
1985-86—Baltimore Skipjacks		AHL	78	2	26	28	94
1986-87—Newmarket Saints		AHL	51	4	9	13	60
1987-88—Newmarket Saints		AHL	78	12	27	39	102
NHL TOTALS			230	15	74	89	139

(c)—Drafted from Kingston Canadians by Toronto Maple Leafs in fifth round of 1976 amateur draft.

(d)—No regular season record. Played five playoff games.

(e)—January, 1982—Traded by Toronto Maple Leafs to Pittsburgh Penguins for future draft considerations.

PAUL HOUCK

Right Wing . . . 5'11" . . . 185 lbs. . . . . Born, North Vancouver, B.C., August 12, 1963 . . . Shoots right.

Year	Team	League	Games	G.	A.	Pts.	Pen.
1980-81—Kelowna Buckaroos (c)		BCJHL	....	...	....	....	....
1981-82—Univ. of Wisconsin		WCHA	43	9	16	25	38
1982-83—Univ. of Wisconsin		WCHA	47	38	33	71	56
1983-84—Univ. of Wisconsin		WCHA	37	20	20	40	29
1984-85—Univ. of Wisconsin (d)		WCHA	38	15	26	41	34
1984-85—Nova Scotia Oilers		AHL	10	1	0	1	0
1985-86—Minnesota North Stars		NHL	3	1	0	1	0
1985-86—Springfield Indians		AHL	61	15	17	32	27
1986-87—Springfield Indians		AHL	64	29	18	47	58
1986-87—Minnesota North Stars		NHL	12	0	2	2	2
1987-88—Kalamazoo Wings		IHL	74	27	29	56	73
1987-88—Minnesota North Stars		NHL	1	0	0	0	0
NHL TOTALS			16	1	2	3	2

(c)—June, 1981—Drafted by Edmonton Oilers in 1981 NHL entry draft. Third Oilers pick, 71st overall, fourth round.

(d)—June, 1985—Traded by Edmonton Oilers to Minnesota North Stars for Gilles Meloche.

DOUG HOUDA

Defense . . . 6'2" . . . 195 lbs. . . . Born, Blairmore, Alta., June 3, 1966 . . . Shoots right.

Year	Team	League	Games	G.	A.	Pts.	Pen.
1981-82—Calgary Wranglers		WHL	3	0	0	0	0
1982-83—Calgary Wranglers		WHL	71	5	23	28	99
1983-84—Calgary Wranglers (c)		WHL	69	6	30	36	195
1984-85—Calgary Wranglers (b)		WHL	65	20	54	74	182
1984-85—Kalamazoo Wings (d)		IHL	....	...	....	....	....
1985-86—Calgary Wranglers		WHL	16	4	10	14	60
1985-86—Medicine Hat Tigers		WHL	35	9	23	32	80
1985-86—Detroit Red Wings		NHL	6	0	0	0	4
1986-87—Adirondack Red Wings		AHL	77	6	23	29	142
1987-88—Detroit Red Wings		NHL	11	1	1	2	10
1987-88—Adirondack Red Wings		AHL	71	10	32	42	169
NHL TOTALS			17	1	1	2	14

(c)—June, 1984—Drafted as underage junior by Detroit Red Wings in 1984 NHL entry draft. Second Red Wings pick, 28th overall, second round.

(d)—No regular season record. Played seven playoff games.

MIKE L. HOUGH

Left Wing . . . 6'1" . . . 195 lbs. . . . Born, Montreal, Que., February 6, 1963 . . . Shoots left.

Year	Team	League	Games	G.	A.	Pts.	Pen.
1980-81—Dixie Beehives		OPJHL	24	15	20	35	84
1981-82—Kitchener Rangers (c)		OHL	58	14	34	48	172
1982-83—Kitchener Rangers		OHL	61	17	27	44	156
1983-84—Fredericton Express		AHL	69	11	16	27	142
1984-85—Fredericton Express		AHL	76	21	27	48	49
1985-86—Fredericton Express		AHL	74	21	33	54	68
1986-87—Quebec Nordiques		NHL	56	6	8	14	79
1986-87—Fredericton Express		AHL	10	1	3	4	20
1987-88—Fredericton Express		AHL	46	16	25	41	133
1987-88—Quebec Nordiques		NHL	17	3	2	5	2
NHL TOTALS			73	9	10	19	81

(c)—June, 1982—Drafted as underage junior by Quebec Nordiques in 1982 NHL entry draft. Seventh Nordiques pick, 181st overall, ninth round.

WILLIAM HOULDER

Defense . . . 6'2" . . . 192 lbs. . . . Born, Thunder Bay, Ont., March 11, 1967 . . . Shoots left.

Year	Team	League	Games	G.	A.	Pts.	Pen.
1983-84—Thunder Bay Beavers		TBAHA	23	4	18	22	37
1984-85—North Bay Centennials (c)		OHL	66	4	20	24	37
1985-86—North Bay Centennials		OHL	59	5	30	35	97
1986-87—North Bay Centennials		OHL	62	17	51	68	68
1987-88—Washington Capitals		NHL	30	1	2	3	10
1987-88—Fort Wayne Komets		IHL	43	10	14	24	32
NHL TOTALS			30	1	2	3	10

(c)—June, 1985—Drafted as underage junior by Washington Capitals in 1985 NHL entry draft. Fourth Capitals pick, 82nd overall, fourth round.

PHIL HOUSLEY

Defense . . . 5'11" . . . 170 lbs. . . . Born, St. Paul, Minn., March 9, 1964 . . . Shoots left . . . Member of Team U.S.A. at World Junior Championships, 1982 . . . Also plays Center . . . Member of Team U.S.A. at World Cup Tournament, 1982 . . . Set Buffalo record for most assists by a rookie (47) in 1982-83 . . . (January, 1984)—Bruised shoulder . . . (March 18, 1984)—Became youngest defenseman in NHL history to have 30-goal season (20 years, 9 days—Bobby Orr was 22 years, 2 days) . . . Set Buffalo record for points by a defenseman with 77 in 1983-84 . . . (October, 1984)—Given three-game NHL suspension . . . Also plays Center . . . (November, 1987)—Injured back.

Year	Team	League	Games	G.	A.	Pts.	Pen.
1980-81—St. Paul Volcans		USHL	6	7	7	14	6
1981-82—South St. Paul H.S. (c)		Minn. H.S.	22	31	34	65	18
1982-83—Buffalo Sabres		NHL	77	19	47	66	39
1983-84—Buffalo Sabres		NHL	75	31	46	77	33
1984-85—Buffalo Sabres		NHL	73	16	53	69	28
1985-86—Buffalo Sabres		NHL	79	15	47	62	54
1986-87—Buffalo Sabres		NHL	78	21	46	67	57
1987-88—Buffalo Sabres		NHL	74	29	37	66	96
NHL TOTALS			456	131	276	407	307

MARK STEVEN HOWE

Defense . . . 5'11" . . . 180 lbs. . . . Born, Detroit, Mich., May 28, 1955 . . . Shoots left . . . Brother of Marty Howe and son of Hall-of-Famer Gordie Howe . . . Was member of 1972 USA Olympic team . . . Missed most of 1971-72 season following corrective knee surgery and part of 1976-77 season with shoulder separation . . . Missed part of 1977-78 season with rib injury . . . (October 9, 1980)—First defenseman in NHL to score two shorthanded goals in one period at St. Louis . . . (December 27, 1980)—Five-inch puncture wound to upper thigh . . . Set NHL record for most assists (56) and points (80) by an American born player in 1979-80 (Broken by Neal Broten in '81-82) . . . (February, 1984)—Injured shoulder . . . (January, 1985)—Bruised collarbone . . . Also plays Left Wing . . . (January, 1987)— Back spasms . . . (September, 1987)—Broken rib and cracked vertebra when struck by a Ray Bourque shot during a pre-season game vs. Boston . . . (March, 1988)—Strained back.

Year	Team	League	Games	G.	A.	Pts.	Pen.
1970-71—Detroit Jr. Wings (a-c)		SOJHL	44	37	*70	*107	....
1971-72—Detroit Jr. Wings		SOJHL	9	5	9	14	....
1971-72—USA Olympic Team		....	...	....	....	....
1972-73—Toronto Marlboros (d-e-f)		Jr."A"OHA	60	38	66	104	27
1973-74—Houston Aeros (b-g-h)		WHA	76	38	41	79	20
1974-75—Houston Aeros (i)		WHA	74	36	40	76	30
1975-76—Houston Aeros		WHA	72	39	37	76	38
1976-77—Houston Aeros (b-j)		WHA	57	23	52	75	46
1977-78—New England Whalers		WHA	70	30	61	91	32
1978-79—New England Whalers (a-k)		WHA	77	42	65	107	32
1979-80—Hartford Whalers		NHL	74	24	56	80	20
1980-81—Hartford Whalers		NHL	63	19	46	65	54
1981-82—Hartford Whalers (l)		NHL	76	8	45	53	18
1982-83—Philadelphia Flyers (a)		NHL	76	20	47	67	18
1983-84—Philadelphia Flyers		NHL	71	19	34	53	44
1984-85—Philadelphia Flyers		NHL	73	18	39	57	31
1985-86—Philadelphia Flyers (a)		NHL	77	24	58	82	36
1986-87—Philadelphia Flyers (a)		NHL	69	15	43	58	37
1987-88—Philadelphia Flyers		NHL	75	19	43	62	62
WHA TOTALS			426	208	296	504	198
NHL TOTALS			654	166	411	577	320

(c)—Won Most Valuable Player and Outstanding Forward Awards.
(d)—August, 1972—Traded to Toronto Marlboros by London Knights for Larry Goodenough and Dennis Maruk.
(e)—Led in points (26) during playoffs.
(f)—June, 1972—Signed by Houston Aeros (WHA).
(g)—Won WHA Rookie Award.
(h)—Drafted from Toronto Marlboros by Boston Bruins in second round of 1974 amateur draft.
(i)—Tied for lead in goals (10) and led in points (22) during playoffs.
(j)—June, 1977—Signed by New England Whalers as free agent.
(k)—June, 1979—Selected by Boston Bruins in NHL reclaim draft, but remained Hartford Whalers property as a priority selection for the expansion draft.
(l)—August, 1982—Traded by Hartford Whalers to Philadelphia Flyers for Ken Linseman, Greg Adams and Philadelphia's first-round choice (David A. Jensen) in 1983 entry draft. Philadelphia and Hartford also agreed to exchange third-round choices in 1983.

JIRI HRDINA

Center . . . 6' . . . 195 lbs. . . . Born, Prague, Czechoslovakia, January 5, 1958 . . . Shoots right.

Year	Team	League	Games	G.	A.	Pts.	Pen.
1985-86—Sparta Prava (c)		Czech.	44	18	19	37	30
1986-87—Sparta Prava		Czech.	31	18	18	36	24
1987-88—Sparta Prava		Czech.	....	...	....	....	....
1987-88—Calgary Flames		NHL	9	2	5	7	2
NHL TOTALS			9	2	5	7	2

(c)—June, 1984—Drafted by Calgary Flames in 1984 NHL entry draft. Eighth Flames pick, 159th overall, eighth round.

ANTHONY HRKAC

Center . . . 5'11" . . . 165 lbs. . . . Born, Thunder Bay, Ont., July 7, 1966 . . . Shoots left . . . (January, 1985)—Suspended six games by coach for disciplinary reasons . . . (January, 1987)—Bruised left leg . . . (January 12, 1988)—Sprained shoulder when checked by Dave Andreychuk vs. Buffalo . . . (March, 1988)—Lacerated ankle.

Year	Team	League	Games	G.	A.	Pts.	Pen.
1983-84—Orillia Travelways (c)		OJHL	42	*52	54	*106	20
1984-85—Univ. of North Dakota		WCHA	36	18	36	54	16
1985-86—Team Canada		Int'l.	62	19	30	49	36
1986-87—Univ. of North Dakota (a-d-e-f-g)		WCHA	48	46	*70	*116	48
1986-87—St. Louis Blues (h)		NHL	..	..	..	..	..
1987-88—St. Louis Blues		NHL	67	11	37	48	22
NHL TOTALS			67	11	37	48	22

(c)—June, 1984—Drafted as underage junior by St. Louis Blues in 1984 NHL entry draft. Second Blues pick, 32nd overall, second round.
(d)—Named to NCAA All-Tournament Team.
(e)—Named NCAA Tournament MVP.
(f)—Named WCHA Player of the Year.
(g)—Won 1987 Hobey Baker Award (Top U.S. College Player).
(h)—No regular season record. Played three playoff games.

TIM HRYNEWICH

Left Wing . . . 6' . . . 191 lbs. . . . Born, Leamington, Ont., October 2, 1963 . . . Shoots left.

Year	Team	League	Games	G.	A.	Pts.	Pen.
1980-81—Sudbury Wolves		OHL	65	25	17	42	104
1981-82—Sudbury Wolves (c)		OHL	64	29	41	70	144
1982-83—Sudbury Wolves		OHL	23	21	16	37	65
1982-83—Baltimore Skipjacks		AHL	9	2	1	3	6
1982-83—Pittsburgh Penguins		NHL	30	2	3	5	48
1983-84—Baltimore Skipjacks		AHL	52	13	17	30	65
1983-84—Pittsburgh Penguins		NHL	25	4	5	9	34
1984-85—Baltimore Skipjacks		AHL	21	4	3	7	31
1984-85—Muskegon Lumberjacks		IHL	30	10	13	23	42
1985-86—Muskegon Lumberjacks (d)		IHL	67	25	26	51	110
1985-86—Toledo Goaldiggers		IHL	13	8	13	21	25
1986-87—Milwaukee Admirals		IHL	82	39	37	76	78
1987-88—Milwaukee Admirals		IHL	28	6	8	14	39
NHL TOTALS			55	6	8	14	82

(c)—June, 1982—Drafted as underage junior by Pittsburgh Penguins in 1982 NHL entry draft. Second Penguins pick, 38th overall, second round.
(d)—September, 1985—NHL rights traded with Marty McSorley by Pittsburgh Penguins to Edmonton Oilers for Gilles Meloche.

WILHEILM HEINRICH (WILLIE) HUBER

Defense . . . 6'5" . . . 228 lbs. . . . Born, Strasskirchen, West Germany, January 15, 1958 . . . Shoots right . . . (March, 1982)—Fractured left cheekbone . . . (February 12, 1983)—Cracked rib vs. Winnipeg . . . (November, 1983)—Strained left thigh muscle . . . (January 2, 1984)—Tore ligaments in right knee at Washington and required arthoscopic surgery . . . (January, 1985)—Surgery for torn knee ligaments . . . (December 21, 1986)—Strained left knee vs. Hartford . . . (December, 1987)—Strained left knee . . . (March, 1988)—Restrained left knee.

Year	Team	League	Games	G.	A.	Pts.	Pen.
1975-76—Hamilton Fincups		Jr. "A" OHA	58	2	8	10	64
1976-77—St. Catharines Fincups		Jr."A" OHA	36	10	24	34	111
1977-78—Hamilton Fincups (b-c)		Jr."A" OHA	61	12	45	57	168
1978-79—Detroit Red Wings		NHL	68	7	24	31	114
1978-79—Kansas City Red Wings		CHL	10	2	7	9	12
1979-80—Adirondack Red Wings		AHL	4	1	3	4	2
1979-80—Detroit Red Wings		NHL	76	17	23	40	164
1980-81—Detroit Red Wings		NHL	80	15	34	49	130
1981-82—Detroit Red Wings		NHL	74	15	30	45	98
1982-83—Detroit Red Wings (d)		NHL	74	14	29	43	106
1983-84—New York Rangers		NHL	42	9	14	23	60
1984-85—New York Rangers		NHL	49	3	11	14	55
1985-86—New York Rangers		NHL	70	7	8	15	85
1986-87—New York Rangers		NHL	66	8	22	30	70
1987-88—New York Rangers (e)		NHL	11	1	3	4	14
1987-88—Vancouver Canucks (f)		NHL	35	4	10	14	40
1987-88—Philadelphia Flyers		NHL	10	4	9	13	16
NHL TOTALS			655	104	217	321	952

(c)—Drafted from Hamilton Fincups by Detroit Red Wings in first round of 1978 amateur draft.
(d)—July, 1983—Traded by Detroit Red Wings with Mark Osborne and Mike Blaisdell to New York Rangers for Ron Duguay, Eddie Mio and Ed Johnstone.
(e)—November, 1987—Traded with Larry Melnyk by New York Rangers to Vancouver Canucks for Michel Petit.

(f)—March, 1988—Traded by Vancouver Canucks to Philadelphia Flyers for Paul Lawless and the return of Canucks fifth-round 1989 draft pick.

CHARLES WILLIAM HUDDY

Defense . . . 6' . . . 200 lbs. . . . Born, Oshawa, Ont., June 2, 1959 . . . Shoots left . . . (November 10, 1980)—Injured shoulder vs. N.Y. Islanders . . . (February, 1986)—Missed three games with back spasms . . . (April, 1986)—Broken finger . . . (May 7, 1988)—Charley Horse in thigh after colliding with Tim Higgins in playoff game vs. Detroit and required surgery.

Year	Team	League	Games	G.	A.	Pts.	Pen.
1977-78—Oshawa Generals		OMJHL	59	17	18	35	81
1978-79—Oshawa Generals		OMJHL	64	20	38	58	108
1979-80—Houston Apollos (c)		CHL	79	14	34	48	46
1980-81—Edmonton Oilers		NHL	12	2	5	7	6
1980-81—Wichita Wind		CHL	47	8	36	44	71
1981-82—Wichita Wind		CHL	32	7	19	26	51
1981-82—Edmonton Oilers		NHL	41	4	11	15	46
1982-83—Edmonton Oilers		NHL	76	20	37	57	58
1983-84—Edmonton Oilers		NHL	75	8	34	42	43
1984-85—Edmonton Oilers		NHL	80	7	44	51	46
1985-86—Edmonton Oilers		NHL	76	6	35	41	55
1986-87—Edmonton Oilers		NHL	58	4	15	19	35
1987-88—Edmonton Oilers		NHL	77	13	28	41	71
NHL TOTALS			495	64	209	273	360

(c)—September, 1979—Signed by Edmonton Oilers as a free agent.

MICHAEL HUDSON

Left Wing . . . 6'1" . . . 185 lbs. . . . Born, Guelph, Ont., February 6, 1967 . . . Shoots left . . . Also plays Center.

Year	Team	League	Games	G.	A.	Pts.	Pen.
1984-85—Hamilton Steelhawks		OHL	50	10	12	22	13
1985-86—Hamilton Steelhawks (c)		OHL	7	3	2	5	4
1985-86—Sudbury Wolves (d)		OHL	59	35	42	77	20
1986-87—Sudbury Wolves		OHL	63	40	57	97	18
1987-88—Saginaw Hawks		IHL	75	18	30	48	44

(c)—October, 1985—Traded with Keith Vanrooyen by Hamilton Steelhawks to Sudbury Wolves for Brad Belland.

(d)—June, 1986—Drafted as underage junior by Chicago Black Hawks in 1986 NHL entry draft. Sixth Black Hawks pick, 140th overall, seventh round.

KERRY HUFFMAN

Defense . . . 6'3" . . . 185 lbs. . . . Born, Peterborough, Ont., January 3, 1968 . . . Shoots left . . . Brother-in-law of Mike Posavad (St. Louis Blues) . . . (November, 1987)—Sprained ankle . . . (January, 1988)—Missed 22 games with calcium deposits in thigh.

Year	Team	League	Games	G.	A.	Pts.	Pen.
1984-85—Peterborough Jr. B		Metro Jr.B	24	2	5	7	53
1985-86—Guelph Platers (c)		OHL	56	3	24	27	35
1986-87—Guelph Platers (a-d)		OHL	44	4	31	35	20
1986-87—Hershey Bears		AHL	3	0	1	1	0
1986-87—Philadelphia Flyers		NHL	9	0	0	0	2
1987-88—Philadelphia Flyers		NHL	52	6	17	23	34
NHL TOTALS			61	6	17	23	36

(c)—June, 1986—Drafted as underage junior by Philadelphia Flyers in 1986 NHL entry draft. First Flyers pick, 20th overall, first round.

(d)—Won Max Kaminsky Trophy (Top OHL Defenseman).

BRENT HUGHES

Left Wing . . . 5'11" . . . 180 lbs. . . . Born, New Westminster, B.C., April 5, 1966 . . . Shoots left.

Year	Team	League	Games	G.	A.	Pts.	Pen.
1983-84—New Westminster Bruins		WHL	67	21	18	39	133
1984-85—New Westminster Bruins		WHL	64	25	32	57	135
1985-86—New Westminster Bruins		WHL	71	28	52	80	180
1986-87—Victoria Cougars (a-c)		WHL	69	43	65	108	168
1987-88—Moncton Golden Flames (d)		AHL	77	13	19	32	206

(c)—October, 1986—Traded by New Westminster Bruins to Victoria Cougars for future considerations.

(d)—July, 1987—Signed by Winnipeg Jets as a free agent.

BRETT HULL

Right Wing . . . 5'11" . . . 190 lbs. . . . Born, Belleville, Ont., August 9, 1964 . . . Shoots right . . . Brother of Blake Hull, son of Hall-of-Fame left wing Bobby Hull and nephew of Dennis Hull . . . (February-March, 1987)—Set AHL record by scoring goals in 14 straight games.

Year	Team	League	Games	G.	A.	Pts.	Pen.
1983-84—Penticton (c)		BCJHL	56	105	83	188	20
1984-85—Univ. of Minn.-Duluth (d)		WCHA	48	32	28	60	24
1985-86—Univ. of Minn.-Duluth (a)		WCHA	42	*52	32	84	46
1985-86—Calgary Flames (e)		NHL	....	...	....	....	....
1986-87—Moncton Golden Flames (a-f)		AHL	67	50	42	92	16
1986-87—Calgary Flames		NHL	5	1	0	1	0
1987-88—Calgary Flames (g)		NHL	52	26	24	50	12
1987-88—St. Louis Blues		NHL	13	6	8	14	4
NHL TOTALS			70	33	32	65	16

(c)—June, 1984—Drafted by Calgary Flames in 1984 NHL entry draft. Sixth Flames pick, 117th overall, sixth round.

(d)—WCHA Freshman of the Year.

(e)—No regular season record. Played two playoff games.

(f)—Won Red Garrett Trophy (AHL Top Rookie).

(g)—March, 1988—Traded with Steve Bozek by Calgary Flames to St. Louis Blues for Rob Ramage and Rick Wamsley.

JODY HULL

Center and Right Wing . . . 6'1" . . . 200 lbs. . . . Born, Petrolia, Ont., February 2, 1969 . . . Shoots right . . . (September, 1986)—Strained ankle ligaments . . . (February, 1987)—Pulled groin.

Year	Team	League	Games	G.	A.	Pts.	Pen.
1984-85—Cambridge Winterhawks		OHA	38	13	17	30	39
1985-86—Peterborough Petes		OHL	61	20	22	42	29
1986-87—Peterborough Petes (c)		OHL	49	18	34	52	22
1987-88—Peterborough Petes (b)		OHL	60	50	44	94	33

(c)—June, 1987—Drafted as underage junior by Hartford Whalers in 1987 NHL entry draft. First Whalers pick, 18th overall, first round.

KENT HULST

Center . . . 6'1" . . . 180 lbs. . . . Born, St. Thomas, Ont., April 8, 1968 . . . Shoots left.

Year	Team	League	Games	G.	A.	Pts.	Pen.
1984-85—St. Thomas Jr. B		OHA	47	21	25	46	29
1985-86—Belleville Bulls (c)		OHL	43	6	17	23	20
1985-86—Windsor Spitfires (d)		OHL	17	6	10	16	9
1986-87—Windsor Spitfires		OHL	37	18	20	38	49
1986-87—Belleville Bulls		OHL	27	13	10	23	17
1987-88—Belleville Bulls		OHL	66	42	43	85	48

(c)—February, 1986—Traded with future considerations by Belleville Bulls to Windsor Compuware Spitfires for Keith Gretzky.

(d)—June, 1986—Drafted as underage junior by Toronto Maple Leafs in 1986 NHL entry draft. Fourth Maple Leafs pick, 69th overall, fourth round.

BRIAN HUNT

Center . . . 6' . . . 185 lbs. . . . Born, Toronto, Ont., February 12, 1969 . . . Shoots left.

Year	Team	League	Games	G.	A.	Pts.	Pen.
1985-86—Oshawa Jr. B		OHA	17	14	8	22	13
1986-87—Oshawa Generals		OHL	61	13	22	35	22
1987-88—Oshawa Generals (c)		OHL	65	39	56	95	21

(c)—June, 1988—Drafted by Winnipeg Jets in 1988 NHL entry draft. Fourth Jets pick, 73rd overall, fourth round.

JEFF CURTIS HUNT

(Known by middle name.)

Defense . . . 6'1" . . . 175 lbs. . . . Born, North Battleford, Sask., January 28, 1967 . . . Shoots left.

Year	Team	League	Games	G.	A.	Pts.	Pen.
1984-85—Prince Albert Raiders (c)		WHL	64	2	13	15	61
1985-86—Prince Albert Raiders		WHL	72	5	29	34	108
1986-87—Prince Albert Raiders (b)		WHL	47	6	31	37	101
1987-88—Flint Spirits		WHL	76	4	17	21	181
1987-88—Fredericton Express		AHL	1	0	0	0	2

(c)—June, 1985—Drafted as underage junior by Vancouver Canucks in 1985 NHL entry draft. Ninth Canucks pick, 172nd overall, ninth round.

DALE ROBERT HUNTER

Center . . . 5'9" . . . 189 lbs. . . . Born, Petrolia, Ont., July 31, 1960 . . . Shoots left . . . Brother of Dave and Mark Hunter . . . (March, 1984)—Given three-game suspension by NHL . . . (April 21, 1985)—Hand infection occurred during playoff game with Montreal . . . (November 25, 1986)—Broke lower fibula of left leg when skate got caught in a rut at Montreal after checking Petr Svoboda.

Year	Team	League	Games	G.	A.	Pts.	Pen.
1977-78—Kitchener Rangers		Jr."A"OHA	68	22	42	64	115
1978-79—Sudbury Wolves (c)		Jr."A"OHA	59	42	68	110	188
1979-80—Sudbury Wolves		OMJHL	61	34	51	85	189
1980-81—Quebec Nordiques		NHL	80	19	44	63	226
1981-82—Quebec Nordiques		NHL	80	22	50	72	272
1982-83—Quebec Nordiques		NHL	80	17	46	63	206
1983-84—Quebec Nordiques		NHL	77	24	55	79	232
1984-85—Quebec Nordiques (d)		NHL	80	20	52	72	209
1985-86—Quebec Nordiques		NHL	80	28	43	71	265
1986-87—Quebec Nordiques (e)		NHL	46	10	29	39	135
1987-88—Washington Capitals		NHL	79	22	37	59	238
NHL TOTALS			602	162	356	518	1783

(c)—August, 1979—Drafted as underage junior by Quebec Nordiques in entry draft. Second Nordiques pick, 41st overall, second round.

(d)—Led Stanley Cup playoffs with 97 penalty minutes

(e)—June, 1987—Traded with Clint Malarchuk by Quebec Nordiques to Washington Capitals for Alan Haworth, Gaeten Duchesne and a first-round 1987 draft pick (Joe Sakic).

DAVE HUNTER

Left Wing . . . 5'11" . . . 204 lbs. . . . Born, Petrolia, Ont., January 1, 1958 . . . Shoots left . . . Brother of Dale and Mark Hunter . . . (December, 1981)—Knee injury . . . (May, 1984)— Bruised spleen in playoff series with N.Y. Islanders . . . (September 26, 1985)—Sprained left knee ligaments and injured hamstring and missed first seven games of season . . . (December, 1985)—Sentenced to four months in jail for his third conviction of driving while impaired by alcohol and released on bail. He served the sentence at the conclusion of the season.

Year	Team	League	Games	G.	A.	Pts.	Pen.
1975-76—Sudbury Wolves		Jr."A"OHA	53	7	21	28	117
1976-77—Sudbury Wolves		Jr."A"OHA	62	30	56	86	140
1977-78—Sudbury Wolves (c-d)		Jr."A"OHA	68	44	44	88	156
1978-79—Dallas Black Hawks		CHL	6	3	4	7	6
1978-79—Edmonton Oilers (e)		WHA	72	7	25	32	134
1979-80—Edmonton Oilers		NHL	80	12	31	43	103
1980-81—Edmonton Oilers		NHL	78	12	16	28	98
1981-82—Edmonton Oilers		NHL	63	16	22	38	63
1982-83—Edmonton Oilers		NHL	80	13	18	31	120
1983-84—Edmonton Oilers		NHL	80	22	26	48	90
1984-85—Edmonton Oilers		NHL	80	17	19	36	122
1985-86—Edmonton Oilers		NHL	62	15	22	37	77
1986-87—Edmonton Oilers		NHL	77	6	9	15	75
1987-88—Edmonton Oilers (f)		NHL	21	3	3	6	6
1987-88—Pittsburgh Penguins		NHL	59	11	18	29	77
WHA TOTALS			72	7	25	32	134
NHL TOTALS			680	127	184	311	831

(c)—Drafted from Sudbury Wolves by Montreal Canadiens in first round of 1978 amateur draft.

(d)—June, 1978—Selected by Edmonton Oilers in World Hockey Association amateur players draft and signed.

(e)—Led in penalty minutes (42) during playoffs.

(f)—November, 1987—Traded with Paul Coffey and Wayne Van Dorp by Edmonton Oilers to Pittsburgh Penguins for Craig Simpson, Dave Hannan, Moe Mantha and Chris Joseph.

MARK HUNTER

Right Wing . . . 6'1" . . . 200 lbs. . . . Born, Petrolia, Ont., November 12, 1962 . . . Shoots right . . . Brother of Dale and Dave Hunter . . . (November 13, 1982)—Pulled tendon in right knee at Los Angeles . . . (November 29, 1982)—17-stitch cut under right arm vs. Winnipeg . . . (December 26, 1982)—Tore medial ligaments in right knee in collision with brother Dale vs. Quebec. Surgery was required and missed 42 games . . . (October, 1983)—Injured right knee that required surgery . . . (February 21, 1984)—Injured knee at Quebec . . . (February, 1985)—Recurring knee injury . . . (March, 1987)—Strained shoulder . . . (November 3,

1987)—Bruised thigh when checked by Stu Kulak vs. Quebec . . . (March 22, 1988)—Strained left knee at Washington.

Year	Team	League	Games	G.	A.	Pts.	Pen.
1979-80	Brantford Alexanders	OMJHL	66	34	55	89	171
1980-81	Brantford Alexanders (c)	OHL	53	39	40	79	157
1981-82	Montreal Canadiens	NHL	71	18	11	29	143
1982-83	Montreal Canadiens	NHL	31	8	8	16	73
1983-84	Montreal Canadiens	NHL	22	6	4	10	42
1984-85	Montreal Canadiens (d)	NHL	72	21	12	33	123
1985-86	St. Louis Blues	NHL	78	44	30	74	171
1986-87	St. Louis Blues	NHL	74	36	33	69	169
1987-88	St. Louis Blues	NHL	66	32	31	63	136
	NHL TOTALS		414	165	129	294	857

(c)—June, 1981—Drafted as underage junior by Montreal Canadiens in 1981 NHL entry draft. First Canadiens pick, seventh overall, first round.

(d)—June, 1985—Traded with NHL rights to Michael Dark and second-round (Herb Raglan), third (Nelson Emerson), fifth (Dan Brooks) and sixth (Rich Burchill) round 1985 draft picks by Montreal Canadiens to St. Louis Blues for first (Jose Charbonneau), second (Todd Richards), fourth (Martin Desjardins), fifth (Tom Sagissor) and sixth (Donald Dufresne) round 1985 draft picks.

TIM ROBERT HUNTER

Defense . . . 6'2" . . . 186 lbs. . . . Born, Calgary, Alta., September 10, 1960 . . . Shoots right . . . Also plays Right Wing . . . (October, 1987)—Bruised hand.

Year	Team	League	Games	G.	A.	Pts.	Pen.
1977-78	Kamloops	BCJHL	51	9	28	37	266
1977-78	Seattle Breakers	WCHL	3	1	2	3	4
1978-79	Seattle Breakers (c)	WHL	70	8	41	49	300
1979-80	Seattle Breakers	WHL	72	14	53	67	311
1980-81	Birmingham Bulls	CHL	58	3	5	8	*236
1980-81	Nova Scotia Voyageurs	AHL	17	0	0	0	62
1981-82	Oklahoma City Stars	CHL	55	4	12	16	222
1981-82	Calgary Flames	NHL	2	0	0	0	9
1982-83	Calgary Flames	NHL	16	1	0	1	54
1982-83	Colorado Flames	CHL	46	5	12	17	225
1983-84	Calgary Flames	NHL	43	4	4	8	130
1984-85	Calgary Flames	NHL	71	11	11	22	259
1985-86	Calgary Flames	NHL	66	8	7	15	291
1986-87	Calgary Flames	NHL	73	6	15	21	357
1987-88	Calgary Flames	NHL	68	8	5	13	337
	NHL TOTALS		339	38	42	80	1437

(c)—August, 1979—Drafted by Atlanta Flames in 1979 NHL entry draft. Fourth Flames pick, 54th overall, third round.

KELLY HURD

Right Wing . . . 5'11" . . . 185 lbs. . . . Born, Castlegar, B.C., May 13, 1968 . . . Shoots right.

Year	Team	League	Games	G.	A.	Pts.	Pen.
1986-87	Kelowna Packers	BCJHL	50	40	53	93	121
1987-88	Michigan Tech. Univ. (c)	WCHA	41	18	22	40	34

(c)—June, 1988—Drafted by Detroit Red Wings in 1988 NHL entry draft. Sixth Red Wings pick, 143rd overall, seventh round.

JAMES HUSCROFT

Defense . . . 6'2" . . . 200 lbs. . . . Born, Creston, B.C., January 9, 1967 . . . Shoots right . . . (October, 1986)—Missed eight weeks with a broken arm.

Year	Team	League	Games	G.	A.	Pts.	Pen.
1983-84	Portland Winter Hawks	WHL	63	0	12	12	77
1984-85	Seattle Breakers (c)	WHL	69	3	13	16	273
1985-86	Seattle Thunderbirds	WHL	66	6	20	26	394
1986-87	Seattle Thunderbirds (d)	WHL	21	1	18	19	99
1986-87	Medicine Hat Tigers	WHL	35	4	21	25	170
1987-88	Flint Spirits	IHL	3	1	0	1	2
1987-88	Utica Devils	AHL	71	5	7	12	316

(c)—June, 1985—Drafted as underage junior by New Jersey Devils in 1985 NHL entry draft. Ninth Devils pick, 171st overall, ninth round.

(d)—February, 1987—Traded by Seattle Thunderbirds to Medicine Hat Tigers for Mike Schwengler.

JAMIE HUSGEN

Defense . . . 6'3" . . . 205 lbs. . . . Born, St. Louis, Mo., October 13, 1964 . . . Shoots right.

Year	Team	League	Games	G.	A.	Pts.	Pen.
1982-83—Des Moines Buccaneers (c)	MWJHL	45	8	25	33	157
1983-84—Univ. of Illinois/Chicago	CCHA	35	6	17	23	76
1984-85—Univ. of Illinois/Chicago	CCHA	37	3	7	10	44
1985-86—Univ. of Illinois/Chicago	CCHA	29	2	5	7	51
1986-87—Univ. of Illinois/Chicago	CCHA	31	2	8	10	61
1986-87—Sherbrooke Canadiens	AHL	2	0	0	0	0
1987-88—Moncton Golden Flames	AHL	53	7	12	19	54

(c)—June, 1983—Drafted by Winnipeg Jets in 1983 NHL entry draft. Thirteenth Jets pick, 229th overall, 12th round.

DWAINE HUTTON

Center . . . 5'11" . . . 175 lbs. . . . Born, Edmonton, Alta., April 18, 1965 . . . Shoots left . . . (January, 1985)—Broken kneecap.

Year	Team	League	Games	G.	A.	Pts.	Pen.
1982-83—Kelowna Wings (c)	WHL	65	21	47	68	17
1983-84—Regina Pats	WHL	14	2	2	4	2
1983-84—Saskatoon Blades	WHL	35	13	30	43	16
1984-85—Saskatoon Blades	WHL	8	3	5	8	6
1984-85—Kelowna Wings	WHL	37	32	35	67	28
1985-86—Spokane Chiefs	WHL	20	10	21	31	35
1985-86—Team Canada	Int'l	19	3	4	7	24
1986-87—Flint Spirit	IHL	48	13	24	37	71
1986-87—Milwaukee Admirals	IHL	5	2	3	5	0
1987-88—Milwaukee Admirals	IHL	31	6	19	25	6
1987-88—Flint Spirits	IHL	40	12	27	39	59

(c)—June, 1983—Drafted as underage junior by Washington Capitals in 1983 NHL entry draft. Third Capitals pick, 135th overall, seventh round.

BRAD HYATT

Defense . . . 5'11" . . . 205 lbs. . . . Born, Leamington, Ont., July 24, 1968 . . . Shoots right.

Year	Team	League	Games	G.	A.	Pts.	Pen.
1986-87—Belleville Bulls	OHL	16	3	8	11	26
1986-87—Hamilton Steelhawks	OHL	1	0	0	0	0
1986-87—Windsor Spitfires	OHL	39	5	16	21	48
1987-88—Windsor Spitfires (c)	OHL	56	24	64	88	71

(c)—June, 1988—Drafted by Los Angeles Kings in 1988 NHL entry draft. Eleventh Kings pick, 196th overall, 10th round.

GORD HYNES

Defense . . . 6'1" . . . 165 lbs. . . . Born, Montreal, Que., July 22, 1966 . . . Shoots left . . . (July, 1984)—Mononucleosis . . . (October, 1985)—Broken hand.

Year	Team	League	Games	G.	A.	Pts.	Pen.
1983-84—Medicine Hat Tigers	WHL	72	5	14	19	39
1984-85—Medicine Hat Tigers (c)	WHL	70	18	45	63	61
1985-86—Medicine Hat Tigers	WHL	58	22	39	61	45
1986-87—Moncton Golden Flames	AHL	69	2	19	21	21
1987-88—Maine Mariners	AHL	69	5	30	35	65

(c)—June, 1985—Drafted as underage junior by Boston Bruins in 1985 NHL entry draft. Fifth Bruins pick, 115th overall, sixth round.

AL IAFRATE

Defense . . . 6'3" . . . 190 lbs. . . . Born, Dearborn, Mich., March 21, 1966 . . . Shoots left . . . Member of 1984 U.S. Olympic Team . . . (February, 1985)—Bruised knee . . . (October 2, 1985)—Broken nose in fight and missed five games . . . (January 29, 1986)—Strained neck vs. Washington and missed six games . . . (January, 1988)—Stiff back.

Year	Team	League	Games	G.	A.	Pts.	Pen.
1983-84—U.S. National Team	Int'l	55	4	17	21	26
1983-84—U.S. Olympic Team	Int'l	6	0	0	0	2
1983-84—Belleville Bulls (c)	OHL	10	2	4	6	2
1984-85—Toronto Maple Leafs	NHL	68	5	16	21	51
1985-86—Toronto Maple Leafs	NHL	65	8	25	33	40
1986-87—Toronto Maple Leafs	NHL	80	9	21	30	55
1987-88—Toronto Maple Leafs	NHL	77	22	30	52	80
NHL TOTALS		290	44	92	136	226

(c)—June, 1984—Drafted as underage junior by Toronto Maple Leafs in 1984 NHL entry draft. First Maple Leafs pick, fourth overall, first round.

MIROSLAV IHNACAK

Left Wing . . . 6' . . . 185 lbs. . . . Born, Poprad, Czechoslovakia, February 19, 1962 . . . Shoots left . . . Brother of Peter Ihnacak.

Year	Team	League	Games	G.	A.	Pts.	Pen.
1985-86—St. Catharines Saints (c)		AHL	13	4	4	8	2
1985-86—Toronto Maple Leafs		NHL	21	2	4	6	27
1986-87—Newmarket Saints		AHL	32	11	17	28	6
1986-87—Toronto Maple Leafs		NHL	34	6	5	11	12
1987-88—Newmarket Saints		AHL	51	11	17	28	24
NHL TOTALS			55	8	9	17	39

(c)—June, 1982—Drafted by Toronto Maple Leafs in 1982 NHL entry draft. Twelfth Maple Leafs pick, 171st overall, ninth round.

PETER IHNACAK

Center . . . 6' . . . 180 lbs. . . . Born, Prague, Czechoslovakia, May 5, 1957 . . . Shoots right . . . Set Toronto club rookie record with 66 points in 1982-83, and tied rookie record with 28 goals . . . Brother of Miroslav Ihnacak . . . (October 16, 1983)—Injured knee ligaments at New Jersey . . . (February 29, 1984)—Injured shoulder vs. N.Y. Rangers and missed remainder of season . . . (October, 1984)—Knee injury . . . (November 30, 1985)—Suffered concussion vs. Buffalo and missed nine games . . . (January, 1986)—Missed five games with a shoulder injury.

Year	Team	League	Games	G.	A.	Pts.	Pen.
1978-79—Dukla Jihlava		Czech.	44	22	12	34	....
1979-80—Sparta CKD Praha		Czech.	44	19	28	47	....
1980-81—Sparta CKD Praha		Czech.	44	23	22	45	....
1981-82—Sparta CKD Praha		Czech.	39	16	22	38	30
1982-83—Toronto Maple Leafs (c)		NHL	80	28	38	66	44
1983-84—Toronto Maple Leafs		NHL	47	10	13	23	24
1984-85—Toronto Maple Leafs		NHL	70	22	22	44	24
1985-86—Toronto Maple Leafs		NHL	63	18	27	45	16
1986-87—Toronto Maple Leafs		NHL	58	12	27	39	16
1986-87—Newmarket Saints		AHL	8	2	6	8	0
1987-88—Toronto Maple Leafs		NHL	68	10	20	30	41
NHL TOTALS			386	100	147	247	165

(c)—July, 1983—Signed by Toronto Maple Leafs as a free agent.

KIM ISSEL

Right Wing . . . 6'3" . . . 185 lbs. . . . Born, Regina, Sask., September 25, 1967 . . . Shoots left . . . Also plays Left Wing.

Year	Team	League	Games	G.	A.	Pts.	Pen.
1983-84—Prince Albert Raiders		WHL	31	9	9	18	24
1984-85—Prince Albert Raiders		WHL	44	8	15	23	43
1985-86—Prince Albert Raiders (b-c)		WHL	68	29	39	68	41
1986-87—Prince Albert Raiders		WHL	70	31	44	75	55
1987-88—Nova Scotia Oilers		AHL	68	20	25	45	31

(c)—June, 1986—Drafted as underage junior by Edmonton Oilers in 1986 NHL entry draft. First Oilers pick, 21st overall, first round.

JEFF JABLONSKI

Left Wing . . . 6' . . . 175 lbs. . . . Born, Toledo, Ohio, June 20, 1967 . . . Shoots left . . . Brother of Pat Jablonski.

Year	Team	League	Games	G.	A.	Pts.	Pen.
1985-86—London Diamonds Jr. B (c)		OHA	42	28	32	60	47
1986-87—Lake Superior State Univ.		CCHA	40	17	10	27	42
1987-88—Lake Superior State Univ.		CCHA	45	13	12	25	54

(c)—June, 1986—Drafted by New York Islanders in 1986 NHL entry draft. Eleventh Islanders pick, 185th overall, ninth round.

DANE JACKSON

Right Wing . . . 6'1" . . . 190 lbs. . . . Born, Winnipeg, Manitoba, May 17, 1970 . . . Shoots right.

Year	Team	League	Games	G.	A.	Pts.	Pen.
1987-88—Vernon Lakers (c)		BCJHL	50	28	32	60	99

(c)—June, 1988—Drafted by Vancouver Canucks in 1988 NHL entry draft. Third Canucks pick, 44th overall, third round.

JAMES KENNETH JACKSON

Center . . . 5'8" . . . 190 lbs. . . . Born, Oshawa, Ont., February 1, 1960 . . . Shoots right . . . Also plays Right Wing and Defense . . . (January, 1981)—Groin injury.

Year	Team	League	Games	G.	A.	Pts.	Pen.
1976-77	Oshawa Generals	OMJHL	65	13	40	53	26
1977-78	Oshawa Generals	OMJHL	68	33	47	80	60
1978-79	Niagara Falls Flyers	OMJHL	64	26	39	65	73
1979-80	Niagara Falls Flyers	OMJHL	66	29	57	86	55
1980-81	Richmond Rifles (b)	EHL	58	17	43	60	42
1981-82	Muskegon Mohawks (b)	IHL	82	24	51	75	72
1982-83	Colorado Flames	CHL	30	10	16	26	4
1982-83	Calgary Flames	NHL	48	8	12	20	7
1983-84	Calgary Flames	NHL	49	6	14	20	13
1983-84	Colorado Flames	CHL	25	5	27	32	4
1984-85	Moncton Golden Flames	AHL	24	2	5	7	6
1984-85	Calgary Flames	NHL	10	1	4	5	0
1985-86	Rochester Americans (c)	AHL	65	16	32	48	10
1986-87	Rochester Americans	AHL	71	19	38	57	48
1987-88	Buffalo Sabres	NHL	5	2	0	2	0
1987-88	Rochester Americans	AHL	74	23	48	71	23
	NHL TOTALS		112	17	30	47	20

(c)—November, 1985—Signed by Rochester Americans as a free agent.

JEFF JACKSON

Left Wing . . . 6'1" . . . 193 lbs. . . . Born, Chatham, Ont., April 24, 1965 . . . Shoots left . . . Also plays Center . . . (January, 1982)—Stretched knee ligaments . . . (March, 1987)—Has a deteriorating hip condition . . . (January, 1988)—Sprained left knee . . . (March, 1988)—Sprained both knees.

Year	Team	League	Games	G.	A.	Pts.	Pen.
1981-82	Newmarket Flyers	OJHL	45	30	39	69	105
1982-83	Brantford Alexanders (c)	OHL	64	18	25	43	63
1983-84	Brantford Alexanders	OHL	58	27	42	69	78
1984-85	Hamilton Steelhawks	OHL	20	13	14	27	51
1984-85	Toronto Maple Leafs	NHL	17	0	1	1	24
1985-86	St. Catharines Saints	AHL	74	17	28	45	122
1985-86	Toronto Maple Leafs	NHL	5	1	2	3	2
1986-87	Newmarket Saints	AHL	7	3	6	9	13
1986-87	Toronto Maple Leafs (d)	NHL	55	8	7	15	64
1986-87	New York Rangers	NHL	9	5	1	6	15
1987-88	Quebec Nordiques (e)	NHL	68	9	18	27	103
	NHL TOTALS		154	23	29	52	208

(c)—June, 1983—Drafted as underage junior by Toronto Maple Leafs in 1983 NHL entry draft. Second Maple Leafs pick, 28th overall, second round.

(d)—March, 1987—Traded with a third-round 1989 draft pick by Toronto Maple Leafs to New York Rangers for Mark Osborne.

(e)—September, 1987—Traded with Terry Carkner by New York Rangers to Quebec Nordiques for David Shaw and John Ogrodnick.

CRAIG JANNEY

Center . . . 6'1" . . . 180 lbs. . . . Born, Hartford, Conn., September 26, 1967 . . . Shoots left . . . (December, 1985)—Broken collarbone . . . (December, 1986)—Mononucleosis.

Year	Team	League	Games	G.	A.	Pts.	Pen.
1984-85	Deerfield Academy	Conn.	17	33	35	68	6
1985-86	Boston College (c)	H. East	34	13	14	27	8
1986-87	Boston College (a-d)	H. East	37	28	*55	*83	6
1987-88	U.S. Olympic Team	Int'l	54	28	44	72	....
1987-88	Boston Bruins	NHL	15	7	9	16	0
	NHL TOTALS		15	7	9	16	0

(c)—June, 1986—Drafted by Boston Bruins in 1986 NHL entry draft. First Bruins pick, 13th overall, first round.

(d)—Named All-America College first-team All-Star (East).

PAT JANOSTIN

Defense . . . 6' . . . 170 lbs. . . . Born, North Battleford, Sask., November 17, 1966 . . . Shoots right.

Year	Team	League	Games	G.	A.	Pts.	Pen.
1984-85	Notre Dame Hounds (c)	MWIHL	40	5	30	35	30

Year	Team	League	Games	G.	A.	Pts.	Pen.
1985-86—Univ. Minnesota/Duluth		WCHA	26	1	2	3	4
1986-87—Univ. Minnesota/Duluth		WCHA	22	0	1	1	8
1987-88—Univ. Minnesota/Duluth		WCHA	41	1	6	7	12

(c)—June, 1985—Drafted by New York Rangers in 1985 NHL entry draft. Fourth Rangers pick, 70th overall, fourth round.

MARK JANSSENS

Center ... 6'3" ... 195 lbs. ... Born, Surrey, B.C., May 19, 1968 ... Shoots left ... Also plays Left Wing.

Year	Team	League	Games	G.	A.	Pts.	Pen.
1983-84—Surrey Midgets		B.C.	48	40	58	98	64
1984-85—Regina Pats		WHL	70	8	22	30	51
1985-86—Regina Pats (c)		WHL	71	25	38	63	146
1986-87—Regina Pats		WHL	68	24	38	62	209
1987-88—Colorado Rangers		IHL	6	2	2	4	24
1987-88—Regina Pats		WHL	71	39	51	90	202
1987-88—New York Rangers		NHL	1	0	0	0	0
NHL TOTALS			1	0	0	0	0

(c)—June, 1986—Drafted as underage junior by New York Rangers in 1986 NHL entry draft. Fourth Rangers pick, 72nd overall, fourth round.

HANNU JARVENPAA

Right Wing ... 6' ... 195 lbs. ... Born, Ilves, Finland, May 19, 1963 ... Shoots left ... (October 26, 1986)—Charley horse vs. Chicago ... (November, 1986)—Tore knee ligaments in collision with Esa Tikkanen vs. Edmonton.

Year	Team	League	Games	G.	A.	Pts.	Pen.
1981-82—Karpat (c)		Finland	14	11	2	13	18
1982-83—Karpat		Finland	34	15	8	23	56
1983-84—Karpat		Finland	37	15	13	28	46
1984-85—Karpat		Finland	34	12	12	24	45
1985-86—Karpat (d)		Finland	36	26	9	35	48
1986-87—Winnipeg Jets		NHL	20	1	8	9	8
1987-88—Moncton Golden Flames		AHL	5	3	1	4	2
1987-88—Winnipeg Jets		NHL	41	6	11	17	34
NHL TOTALS			61	7	19	26	42

(c)—June, 1982—Drafted by Montreal Canadiens in 1982 NHL entry draft. Eleventh Canadiens pick, 145th overall, seventh round.

(d)—June, 1986—Drafted by Winnipeg Jets in 1986 NHL entry draft. Fourth Jets pick, 71st overall, fourth round.

DOUGLAS JARVIS

Center ... 5'9" ... 172 lbs. ... Born, Brantford, Ont., March 24, 1955 ... Shoots left ... Cousin of Wes Jarvis ... (December 26, 1986)—Set NHL record by playing in his 915th consecutive regular season game ... NHL streak reached 964 games and ended on October 11, 1988 when he was not dressed for a Hartford at Boston game.

Year	Team	League	Games	G.	A.	Pts.	Pen.
1971-72—Brantford Majors		SOJHL	11	2	10	12	0
1972-73—Peterborough TPTs		Jr."A" OHA	63	20	49	69	14
1973-74—Peterborough TPTs		Jr."A" OHA	70	31	53	84	27
1974-75—P'borough TPTs (b-c-d-e)		Jr."A" OHA	64	45	88	133	38
1975-76—Montreal Canadiens		NHL	80	5	30	35	16
1976-77—Montreal Canadiens		NHL	80	16	22	38	14
1977-78—Montreal Canadiens		NHL	80	11	28	39	23
1978-79—Montreal Canadiens		NHL	80	10	13	23	16
1979-80—Montreal Canadiens		NHL	80	13	11	24	28
1980-81—Montreal Canadiens		NHL	80	16	22	38	34
1981-82—Montreal Canadiens (f)		NHL	80	20	28	48	20
1982-83—Washington Capitals		NHL	80	8	22	30	10
1983-84—Washington Capitals (g)		NHL	80	13	29	42	12
1984-85—Washington Capitals		NHL	80	9	28	37	32
1985-86—Washington Capitals (h)		NHL	25	1	2	3	16
1985-86—Hartford Whalers		NHL	57	8	16	24	20
1986-87—Hartford Whalers (i)		NHL	80	9	13	22	20
1987-88—Hartford Whalers (j)		NHL	2	0	0	0	2
1987-88—Binghamton Whalers (k)		AHL	24	5	4	9	4
NHL TOTALS			964	139	264	403	263

(c)—Won William Hanley Trophy (Most Gentlemanly Player).

(d)—Drafted from Peterborough TPTs by Toronto Maple Leafs in second round of 1975 amateur draft.
(e)—June, 1975—Traded to Montreal Canadiens by Toronto Maple Leafs for Greg Hubick.
(f)—September, 1982—Traded by Montreal Canadiens with Rod Langway, Brian Engblom and Craig Laughlin to Washington Capitals for Ryan Walter and Rick Green.
(g)—Won Frank Selke Trophy (Best Defensive Forward).
(h)—December, 1985—Traded by Washington Capitals to Hartford Whalers for Jorgen Pettersson.
(i)—Won Bill Masterton Memorial Trophy (Perserverance, sportsmanship and dedication).
(j)—May, 1988—Released by Hartford Whalers.
(k)—August, 1988—Signed as assistant coach of Minnesota North Stars.

WES JARVIS

Center . . . 5'11" . . . 190 lbs. . . . Born, Toronto, Ont., May 30, 1958 . . . Shoots left . . . Cousin of Doug Jarvis . . . (January, 1984)—Injured ligaments in left knee.

Year	Team	League	Games	G.	A.	Pts.	Pen.
1975-76—Sudbury Wolves		OMJHL	64	26	48	74	22
1976-77—Sudbury Wolves		OMJHL	65	36	60	96	24
1977-78—Sudbury Wolves		OMJHL	21	7	16	23	16
1977-78—Windsor Spitfires (c)		OMJHL	44	27	51	78	37
1978-79—Port Huron Flags (b-d)		IHL	73	44	65	109	39
1979-80—Hershey Bears		AHL	16	6	14	20	4
1979-80—Washington Capitals		NHL	63	11	15	26	8
1980-81—Washington Capitals		NHL	55	9	14	23	30
1980-81—Hershey Bears		AHL	24	15	25	40	39
1981-82—Hershey Bears		AHL	56	31	61	92	44
1981-82—Washington Capitals (e)		NHL	26	1	12	13	18
1982-83—Birmingham South Stars (a-f)		CHL	75	40	*68	*108	36
1982-83—Minnesota North Stars (g)		NHL	3	0	0	0	2
1983-84—Los Angeles Kings		NHL	61	9	13	22	36
1984-85—Toronto Maple Leafs (h)		NHL	26	0	1	1	2
1984-85—St. Catharines Saints		AHL	52	29	44	73	22
1985-86—Toronto Maple Leafs		NHL	2	1	0	1	2
1985-86—St. Catharines Saints		AHL	74	36	60	96	38
1986-87—Newmarket Saints		AHL	70	28	50	78	32
1986-87—Toronto Maple Leafs (i)		NHL	....	...	....	....	....
1987-88—Newmarket Saints		AHL	79	25	59	84	48
1987-88—Toronto Maple Leafs		NHL	1	0	0	0	0
NHL TOTALS			237	31	55	86	98

(c)—June, 1978—Drafted by Washington Capitals in 1978 amateur draft. Fifteenth Capitals pick, 213th overall, 14th round.
(d)—Won Garry F. Longman Memorial Trophy (IHL Top Rookie).
(e)—August, 1982—Traded with Rollie Boutin by Washington Capitals to Minnesota North Stars for Robbie Moore and future considerations.
(f)—Won Phil Esposito Trophy (CHL Scoring Leader).
(g)—August, 1983—Signed by Los Angeles Kings as a free agent.
(h)—September, 1984—Signed by Toronto Maple Leafs as a free agent.
(i)—No regular season record. Played two playoff games.

GRANT JENNINGS

Defense . . . 6'3" . . . 190 lbs. . . . Born, Hudson Bay, Sask., May 5, 1965 . . . Shoots left . . . (1984-85)—Shoulder injury . . . (October, 1986)—Knee injury.

Year	Team	League	Games	G.	A.	Pts.	Pen.
1983-84—Saskatoon Blades		WHL	64	5	13	18	102
1984-85—Saskatoon Blades (c)		WHL	47	10	14	24	134
1985-86—Binghamton Whalers		AHL	51	0	4	4	109
1986-87—Fort Wayne Komets		IHL	3	0	0	0	0
1986-87—Binghamton Whalers		AHL	47	1	5	6	125
1987-88—Binghamton Whalers (d)		AHL	56	2	12	14	195

(c)—June, 1985—Signed by Washington Capitals as a free agent.
(d)—July, 1988—Traded with Ed Kastelic by Washington Capitals to Hartford Whalers for Neil Sheehy and Mike Millar.

CHRIS JENSEN

Center . . . 5'11" . . . 165 lbs. . . . Born, Fort St. John, B.C., October 28, 1963 . . . Shoots right . . . (October, 1985)—Injured knee . . . (October, 1986)—Strained shoulder . . . (April, 1987)—Shoulder surgery.

Year	Team	League	Games	G.	A.	Pts.	Pen.
1980-81—Kelowna		BCJHL	53	51	45	96	120
1981-82—Kelowna (c)		BCJHL	48	46	46	92	212
1982-83—University of North Dakota		WCHA	13	3	3	6	28

Year	Team	League	Games	G.	A.	Pts.	Pen.
1983-84—University of North Dakota	WCHA	44	24	25	49	100
1984-85—University of North Dakota	WCHA	40	25	27	52	80
1985-86—University of North Dakota	WCHA	34	25	40	65	53
1985-86—New York Rangers	NHL	9	1	3	4	0
1986-87—New York Rangers	NHL	37	6	7	13	21
1986-87—New Haven Nighthawks	AHL	14	4	9	13	41
1987-88—New York Rangers	NHL	7	0	1	1	2
1987-88—Colorado Rangers	IHL	43	10	23	33	68
NHL TOTALS		53	7	11	18	23

(c)—June, 1982—Drafted as underage player by New York Rangers in 1982 NHL entry draft. Fourth Rangers pick, 78th overall, fourth round.

DAVID A. JENSEN

Left Wing . . . 6' . . . 175 lbs. . . . Born, Newton, Mass., August 19, 1965 . . . Shoots left . . . Member of 1984 U.S. Olympic Team . . . (November, 1984)—Back injury . . . (September, 1985)—Missed 18 games while recovering from off-season knee surgery . . . (February, 1987)—Separated shoulder.

Year	Team	League	Games	G.	A.	Pts.	Pen.
1982-83—Lawrence Academy (c)	Mass. H.S.	25	41	48	89	....
1983-84—U.S. National Team	Int'l	61	22	56	78	6
1983-84—U.S. Olympic Team	Int'l	6	5	3	8	0
1984-85—Hartford Whalers (d)	NHL	13	0	4	4	6
1984-85—Binghamton Whalers	AHL	40	8	9	17	2
1985-86—Binghamton Whalers	AHL	41	17	14	31	4
1985-86—Washington Capitals	NHL	5	1	0	1	0
1986-87—Washington Capitals	NHL	46	8	8	16	12
1986-87—Binghamton Whalers	AHL	6	2	5	7	0
1987-88—Fort Wayne Komets	IHL	32	10	13	23	8
1987-88—Binghamton Whalers	AHL	9	5	2	7	2
1987-88—Washington Capitals (e)	NHL	5	0	1	1	4
NHL TOTALS		69	9	13	22	22

(c)—June, 1983—Drafted by Hartford Whalers in 1983 NHL entry draft. Second Whalers pick, 20th overall, first round.

(d)—March, 1985—Traded by Hartford Whalers to Washington Capitals for Peter Sidorkiewicz and Dean Evason.

(e)—July, 1988—Signed by Boston Bruins as a free agent.

PAUL JERRARD

Defense . . . 6'1" . . . 185 lbs. . . . Born, Winnipeg, Man., April 20, 1965 . . . Shoots right . . . (October, 1987)—Fractured cheekbone when struck by a shot during an IHL game.

Year	Team	League	Games	G.	A.	Pts.	Pen.
1982-83—Notre Dame H.S. (c)	Man. Juv.	60	34	37	71	150
1983-84—Lake Superior State College	CCHA	40	8	18	26	48
1984-85—Lake Superior State College	CCHA	43	9	25	34	61
1985-86—Lake Superior State College	CCHA	40	13	11	24	34
1986-87—Lake Superior State College	CCHA	34	10	17	27	54
1987-88—Colorado Rangers	IHL	77	20	28	48	182

(c)—June, 1983—Drafted by New York Rangers in 1983 NHL entry draft. Tenth Rangers pick, 173rd overall, ninth round.

TREVOR JOBE

Left Wing . . . 6'1" . . . 192 lbs. . . . Born, Lethbridge, Alta., May 14, 1967 . . . Shoots left.

Year	Team	League	Games	G.	A.	Pts.	Pen.
1983-84—Lethbridge Midget Elks	SAMM	32	22	21	43	44
1984-85—Calgary Wranglers	WHL	66	5	19	24	23
1985-86—Olds Grizzlys	AJHL	11	7	11	18	14
1985-86—Calgary Wranglers	WHL	7	0	2	2	2
1985-86—Spokane Chiefs	WHL	11	1	4	5	0
1985-86—Lethbridge Broncos	WHL	5	1	0	1	0
1986-87—Moose Jaw Warriors (b-c)	WHL	58	54	33	87	53
1987-88—Moose Jaw Warriors	WHL	36	36	35	71	63
1987-88—Prince Albert Raiders	WHL	36	33	28	61	48

(c)—June, 1987—Drafted by Toronto Maple Leafs in 1987 NHL entry draft. Seventh Maple Leafs pick, 133rd overall, seventh round.

JIM JOHANNSON

Center . . . 6'1" . . . 195 lbs. . . . Born, Rochester, Minn., March 10, 1964 . . . Shoots right.

Year	Team	League	Games	G.	A.	Pts.	Pen.
1982-83—Univ. of Wisconsin		WCHA	43	12	9	21	16
1983-84—Univ. of Wisconsin		WCHA	35	17	21	38	52
1984-85—Univ. of Wisconsin		WCHA	40	16	24	40	54
1985-86—Univ. of Wisconsin		WCHA	30	18	13	31	44
1986-87—Landsberg		W. Germ.	57	46	56	102	90
1987-88—U.S. National Team		Int'l	47	16	14	30	64
1987-88—U.S. Olympic Team (c)		Olym.	4	0	1	1	4
1987-88—Salt Lake Golden Eagles		IHL	18	14	7	21	50

(c)—February, 1988—Signed by Calgary Flames as a free agent.

CARL (Calle) JOHANSSON

Defense . . . 5'11" . . . 198 lbs. . . . Goteborg, Sweden, February 14, 1967 . . . Shoots left.

Year	Team	League	Games	G.	A.	Pts.	Pen.
1983-84—Vastra Frolunda		Sweden	34	5	10	15	20
1984-85—Vastra Frolunda (c)		Sweden	36	14	15	29	20
1985-86—Bjorkloven		Sweden	17	1	1	2	14
1986-87—Bjorkloven		Sweden	30	2	13	15	18
1987-88—Buffalo Sabres		NHL	71	4	38	42	37
NHL TOTALS			71	4	38	42	37

(c)—June, 1985—Drafted by Buffalo Sabres in 1985 NHL entry draft. First Sabres pick, 14th overall, first round.

CHAD JOHNSON

Center . . . 5'11" . . . 170 lbs. . . . Born, Grand Forks, N.D., January 10, 1970 . . . Shoots left . . . Brother of Steve Johnson.

Year	Team	League	Games	G.	A.	Pts.	Pen.
1987-88—Rochester Mustangs (c)		USHL	36	15	26	41	43

(c)—June, 1988—Drafted by New Jersey Devils in 1988 NHL entry draft. Seventh Devils pick, 117th overall, sixth round.

JIM JOHNSON

Defense . . . 6' . . . 190 lbs. . . . Born, New Hope, Minn., August 9, 1962 . . . Shoots left . . . (January, 1988)—Torn cartilage in right knee.

Year	Team	League	Games	G.	A.	Pts.	Pen.
1981-82—Univ. of Minnesota-Duluth		WCHA	40	0	10	10	62
1982-83—Univ. of Minnesota-Duluth		WCHA	44	3	18	21	118
1983-84—Univ. of Minnesota-Duluth		WCHA	43	3	13	16	116
1984-85—Univ. of Minnesota-Duluth (c)		WCHA	47	7	29	36	49
1985-86—Pittsburgh Penguins		NHL	80	3	26	29	115
1986-87—Pittsburgh Penguins		NHL	80	5	25	30	116
1987-88—Pittsburgh Penguins		NHL	55	1	12	13	87
NHL TOTALS			215	9	63	72	318

(c)—June, 1985—Signed by Pittsburgh Penguins as a free agent.

MARK JOHNSON

Center . . . 5'9" . . . 160 lbs. . . . Born, Minneapolis, Minn., September 22, 1957 . . . Shoots left . . . Member of 1978 and 1979 U.S. National teams and 1980 U.S. Gold Medal Winning Hockey Team . . . Son of Bob Johnson (Former coach of Calgary Flames and currently Executive Director of U.S. Amateur Hockey Assoc.) . . . (September, 1980)—Took 20 stitches near right eye in preseason game . . . (November, 1980)—Wrist injury . . . (February, 1985)—Rib injury . . . (October, 1987)—Strained left knee . . . (November, 1987)— Knee surgery . . . (January, 1988)—Bruised right instep.

Year	Team	League	Games	G.	A.	Pts.	Pen.
1976-77—University of Wisconsin (c-d)		WCHA	43	36	44	80	16
1977-78—University of Wisconsin (a-e)		WCHA	42	*48	38	86	24
1978-79—Univ. of Wisconsin (a-e-f)		WCHA	40	*41	49	*90	34
1979-80—U.S. Olympic Team		Int'l	60	*38	*54	*92	31
1979-80—Pittsburgh Penguins		NHL	17	3	5	8	4
1980-81—Pittsburgh Penguins		NHL	73	10	23	33	50
1981-82—Pittsburgh Penguins (g)		NHL	46	10	11	21	30
1981-82—Minnesota North Stars (h)		NHL	10	2	2	4	10
1982-83—Hartford Whalers		NHL	73	31	38	69	28
1983-84—Hartford Whalers		NHL	79	35	52	87	27
1984-85—Hartford Whalers (i)		NHL	49	19	28	47	21

Year	Team	League	Games	G.	A.	Pts.	Pen.
1984-85—St. Louis Blues		NHL	17	4	6	10	2
1985-86—New Jersey Devils (j)		NHL	80	21	41	62	16
1986-87—New Jersey Devils		NHL	68	25	26	51	22
1987-88—New Jersey Devils		NHL	54	14	19	33	14
NHL TOTALS			566	174	251	425	224

(c)—June, 1977—Drafted by Pittsburgh Penguins in 1977 NHL amateur draft. Third Penguins pick, 66th overall, fourth round.
(d)—Named WCHA Outstanding Freshman.
(e)—Named to All-America Team (West).
(f)—Named WCHA MVP and NCAA Player of the Year.
(g)—March, 1982—Traded by Pittsburgh Penguins to Minnesota North Stars for second-round 1982 entry draft pick (Tim Hrynewich).
(h)—October, 1982—Traded by Minnesota North Stars with Kent-Erik Andersson to Hartford Whalers for 1984 fifth-round pick (Jiri Poner) in NHL entry draft and future considerations (Jordy Douglas).
(i)—February, 1985—Traded with Greg Millen by Hartford Whalers to St. Louis Blues for Mike Liut and future considerations (Jorgen Pettersson).
(j)—September, 1985—Traded by St. Louis Blues to New Jersey Devils for Shawn Evans and a fifth round 1986 draft pick (Mike Wolak).

SCOTT JOHNSON

Left Wing . . . 5'11" . . . 185 lbs. . . . Born, New Hope, Minn., October 12, 1963 . . . Shoots left.

Year	Team	League	Games	G.	A.	Pts.	Pen.
1982-83—Lake Superior State Univ.		CCHA	32	2	7	9	9
1983-84—Lake Superior State Unvi.		CCHA	39	9	13	22	32
1984-85—Lake Superior State Univ.		CCHA	44	21	23	44	70
1985-86—Lake Superior State Univ. (c)		CCHA	38	21	24	45	55
1986-87—Baltimore Skipjacks		AHL	63	8	7	15	27
1987-88—Saginaw Hawks		IHL	1	0	0	0	2
1987-88—Muskegon Lumberjacks		IHL	51	19	11	30	31

(c)—July, 1986—Signed by Pittsburgh Penguins as a free agent.

STEVE JOHNSON

Right Wing . . . 6'1" . . . 190 lbs. . . . Born, Grand Forks, N.D., March 3, 1966 . . . Shoots right . . . Brother of Chad Johnson.

Year	Team	League	Games	G.	A.	Pts.	Pen.
1984-85—Univ. of North Dakota		WCHA	41	18	16	34	10
1985-86—Univ. of North Dakota		WCHA	38	31	28	59	40
1986-87—Univ. of North Dakota (c)		WCHA	48	26	44	70	38
1987-88—Univ. of North Dakota (d)		WCHA	42	34	51	85	28

(c)—June, 1987—Selected by Vancouver Canucks in 1987 NHL supplemental draft.
(d)—Named to All-America team (West).

TERRANCE JOHNSON

Defense . . . 6'3" . . . 210 lbs. . . . Born, Calgary, Alta., November 28, 1958 . . . Shoots left.

Year	Team	League	Games	G.	A.	Pts.	Pen.
1975-76—Calgary		AJHL	55	3	13	16	100
1976-77—Calgary Canucks		AJHL	60	5	26	31	158
1977-78—Saskatoon Blades		WCHL	70	2	20	22	195
1978-79—University of Alberta		CWAA	24	1	5	6	100
1979-80—Quebec Nordiques (c)		NHL	3	0	0	0	2
1979-80—Syracuse Firebirds		AHL	74	0	13	13	163
1980-81—Quebec Nordiques		NHL	13	0	1	1	46
1980-81—Hershey Bears		AHL	63	1	7	8	207
1981-82—Fredericton Express		AHL	43	0	7	7	132
1981-82—Quebec Nordiques		NHL	6	0	1	1	5
1982-83—Fredericton Express		AHL	78	2	15	17	181
1982-83—Quebec Nordiques		NHL	3	0	0	0	2
1983-84—St. Louis Blues (d)		NHL	65	2	6	8	141
1984-85—St. Louis Blues		NHL	74	0	7	7	120
1985-86—St. Louis Blues (e)		NHL	49	0	4	4	87
1985-86—Calgary Flames		NHL	24	1	4	5	71
1986-87—Newmarket Saints		AHL	24	0	1	1	37
1986-87—Toronto Maple Leafs (f)		NHL	48	0	1	1	104
1987-88—Newmarket Saints		AHL	72	3	3	6	174
NHL TOTALS			285	3	24	27	578

(c)—September, 1979—Signed by Quebec Nordiques as a free agent.

(d)—October, 1983—Selected by St. Louis Blues in NHL waiver draft.
(e)—February, 1986—Traded with Joe Mullen and Rik Wilson by St. Louis Blues to Calgary Flames for Eddy Beers, Gino Cavallini and Charles Bourgeois.
(f)—October, 1986—Traded by Calgary Flames to Toronto Maple Leafs as part of a three-club trade that saw Brian Engblom go from Buffalo to Calgary and Jim Korn go from Toronto to Buffalo.

GREG JOHNSTON

Right Wing . . . 6'1" . . . 195 lbs. . . . Born, Barrie, Ont., January 14, 1965 . . . Shoots right . . . Also plays Center . . . (September, 1982)—Broken ankle.

Year	Team	League	Games	G.	A.	Pts.	Pen.
1981-82—Barrie	OHA Midget	42	31	46	77	74
1982-83—Toronto Marlboros (c)	OHL	58	18	19	37	58
1983-84—Toronto Marlboros	OHL	57	38	35	73	67
1983-84—Boston Bruins	NHL	15	2	1	3	2
1984-85—Boston Bruins	NHL	6	0	0	0	0
1984-85—Hershey Bears	AHL	3	1	0	1	0
1984-85—Toronto Marlboros	OHL	42	22	28	50	55
1985-86—Moncton Golden Flames	AHL	60	19	26	45	56
1985-86—Boston Bruins	NHL	20	0	2	2	0
1986-87—Boston Bruins	NHL	76	12	15	27	79
1987-88—Maine Mariners	AHL	75	21	32	53	105
NHL TOTALS		117	14	18	32	81

(c)—June, 1983—Drafted as underage junior by Boston Bruins in 1983 NHL entry draft. Second Bruins pick, 42nd overall, second round.

BRAD JONES

Center . . . 6' . . . 175 lbs. . . . Born, Sterling Heights, Mich., June 26, 1965 . . . Shoots left . . . (November, 1984)—Injured knee vs. Lake Superior State . . . (February, 1987)—Set record for career assists at Michigan.

Year	Team	League	Games	G.	A.	Pts.	Pen.
1983-84—University of Michigan (c)	CCHA	37	8	26	34	32
1984-85—University of Michigan	CCHA	34	21	27	48	69
1985-86—University of Michigan (b)	CCHA	36	28	39	67	40
1986-87—University of Michigan (a-d)	CCHA	40	32	46	78	64
1986-87—Winnipeg Jets	NHL	4	1	0	1	0
1987-88—Winnipeg Jets	NHL	19	2	5	7	15
1987-88—U.S. Olympic Team	Int'l	47	27	23	50	....
NHL TOTALS		23	3	5	8	15

(c)—June, 1984—Drafted by Winnipeg Jets in 1984 NHL entry draft. Eighth Jets pick, 156th overall, eighth round.
(d)—Named U.S. College All-America Second-Team All-Star (West).

CASEY JONES

Center . . . 5'11" . . . 170 lbs. . . . Born, North Bay, Ont., May 30, 1968 . . . Shoots left.

Year	Team	League	Games	G.	A.	Pts.	Pen.
1986-87—Cornell University (c)	ECAC	27	6	12	18	38
1987-88—Cornell University	ECAC	27	10	22	32	26

(c)—June, 1987—Drafted by Boston Bruins in 1987 NHL entry draft. Eleventh Bruins pick, 203rd overall, 10th round.

DOUG JONES

Defense . . . 5'11" . . . 180 lbs. . . . Born, Powell River, B.C., May 21, 1969 . . . Shoots right.

Year	Team	League	Games	G.	A.	Pts.	Pen.
1984-85—Miramichi Beavers	OHA Midget	56	30	26	56	80
1985-86—Kitchener Rangers	OHL	46	5	4	9	4
1986-87—Kitchener Rangers	OHL	43	4	5	9	19
1987-88—Kitchener Rangers (c)	OHL	54	7	42	49	65

(c)—June, 1988—Drafted by Boston Bruins in 1988 NHL entry draft. Ninth Bruins pick, 249th overall, 12th round.

RONALD JONES

Right Wing . . . 6'2" . . . 198 lbs. . . . Born, Detroit, Mich., January 7, 1969 . . . Shoots right . . . (October, 1986)—Injured knee ligaments.

Year	Team	League	Games	G.	A.	Pts.	Pen.
1984-85—Detroit Compuware Midget	Michigan	75	65	87	152	88
1985-86—Portland Winter Hawks	WHL	71	22	26	48	113

Year	Team	League	Games	G.	A.	Pts.	Pen.
1986-87—Windsor Spitfires		OHL	49	7	20	27	76
1987-88—Windsor Spitfires (c)		OHL	64	22	33	55	173

(c)—June, 1988—Drafted by Winnipeg Jets in 1988 NHL entry draft. Seventh Jets pick, 115th overall, sixth round.

TOMAS JONSSON

Defense . . . 5'10" . . . 176 lbs. . . . Born, Falun, Sweden, April 12, 1960 . . . Shoots left . . . (January 13, 1985)—Separated left shoulder at Chicago . . . (January 22, 1987)—Broken jaw at New Jersey . . . (January, 1987)—Fractured jaw in automobile accident in Detroit . . . (February, 1988)—Bruised left thigh . . . (March, 1988)—Concussion.

Year	Team	League	Games	G.	A.	Pts.	Pen.
1980-81—Ornskoldsvik Modo AIK (c)		Sweden	35	8	12	20	58
1981-82—New York Islanders		NHL	70	9	25	34	51
1982-83—New York Islanders		NHL	72	13	35	48	50
1983-84—New York Islanders		NHL	72	11	36	47	54
1984-85—New York Islanders		NHL	69	16	34	50	58
1985-86—New York Islanders		NHL	77	14	30	44	62
1986-87—New York Islanders		NHL	47	6	25	31	36
1987-88—New York Islanders		NHL	72	6	41	47	115
NHL TOTALS			479	75	226	301	426

(c)—August, 1979—Drafted by New York Islanders in 1979 NHL entry draft. Second Islanders pick, 25th overall, second round.

ANTHONY JOSEPH

Right Wing . . . 6'4" . . . 203 lbs. . . . Born, Cornwall, Ont., March 1, 1969 . . . Shoots right.

Year	Team	League	Games	G.	A.	Pts.	Pen.
1984-85—Cornwall Midget		OHA	37	33	30	63	48
1985-86—Oshawa Generals		OHL	41	3	1	4	28
1986-87—Oshawa Generals		OHL	44	2	5	7	93
1987-88—Oshawa Generals (c)		OHL	49	9	18	27	126

(c)—June, 1988—Drafted by Winnipeg Jets in 1988 NHL entry draft. Fifth Jets pick, 94th overall, fifth round.

CHRIS JOSEPH

Defense . . . 6'1" . . . 195 lbs. . . . Born, Burnaby, B.C., September 10, 1969 . . . Shoots right.

Year	Team	League	Games	G.	A.	Pts.	Pen.
1984-85—Burnaby Midget		B.C. Midget	52	18	48	66	52
1985-86—Seattle Breakers		WHL	72	4	8	12	50
1986-87—Seattle Thunderbirds (c)		WHL	67	13	45	58	155
1987-88—Pittsburgh Penguins (d)		NHL	17	0	4	4	12
1987-88—Edmonton Oilers		NHL	7	0	4	4	6
1987-88—Nova Scotia Oilers		AHL	8	0	2	2	8
1987-88—Seattle Thunderbirds		WHL	23	5	14	19	49
NHL TOTALS			24	0	8	8	18

(c)—June, 1987—Drafted by Pittsburgh Penguins in 1988 NHL entry draft. First Penguins pick, fifth overall, first round.

(d)—November, 1987—Traded with Craig Simpson, Dave Hannan and Moe Mantha by Pittsburgh Penguins to Edmonton Oilers for Paul Coffey, Dave Hunter and Wayne Van Dorp.

FABIAN JOSEPH

Center . . . 5'8" . . . 165 lbs. . . . Born, Sydney, N.S., December 5, 1965 . . . Shoots left.

Year	Team	League	Games	G.	A.	Pts.	Pen.
1982-83—Victoria Cougars		WHL	69	42	48	90	50
1983-84—Victoria Cougars (c)		WHL	72	52	75	127	27
1984-85—Toronto Marlboros		OHL	60	32	43	75	16
1985-86—Canadian Olympic Team		Int'l	71	26	18	44	51
1986-87—Canadian Olympic Team		Int'l	74	15	30	45	26
1987-88—Nova Scotia Oilers		AHL	77	31	39	70	20

(c)—June, 1984—Drafted as underage junior by Toronto Maple Leafs in 1984 NHL entry draft. Fifth Maple Leafs pick, 109th overall, sixth round.

GARTH JOY

Defense . . . 5'11" . . . 180 lbs. . . . Born, Kirkland Lake, Ont., March 8, 1968 . . . Shoots left . . . (October, 1985)—Broken ankle . . . (November, 1985)—Broken foot.

Year	Team	League	Games	G.	A.	Pts.	Pen.
1984-85—Hamilton Steelhawks		OHL	58	4	23	27	36

Year	Team	League	Games	G.	A.	Pts.	Pen.
1985-86—Hamilton Steelhawks (c)		OHL	50	6	31	37	64
1986-87—Hamilton Steelhawks		OHL	66	6	43	49	56
1987-88—Hamilton Steelhawks		OHL	62	10	36	46	105

(c)—June, 1986—Drafted as underage junior by Minnesota North Stars in 1986 NHL entry draft. Twelfth North Stars pick, 222nd overall, 11th round.

ROBERT JOYCE

Left Wing . . . 6'1" . . . 180 lbs. . . . Born, St. Johns, N.B., July 11, 1966 . . . Shoots left . . . (October, 1985)—Tied a WCHA record with five goals vs. Michigan Tech . . . (January 24, 1987)—Set WCHA record with six goals vs. Michigan Tech. He also had three assists to tie a WCHA record with a nine-point game.

Year	Team	League	Games	G.	A.	Pts.	Pen.
1983-84—Wilcox Notre Dame H.S. (c)		Sask. HS	30	33	37	70	..
1984-85—Univ. of North Dakota		WCHA	41	18	16	34	10
1985-86—Univ. of North Dakota		WCHA	38	31	28	59	40
1986-87—Univ. of North Dakota (a-d)		WCHA	48	*52	37	89	42
1987-88—Canadian Olympic Team		Int'l	50	13	10	23	28
1987-88—Boston Bruins		NHL	15	7	5	12	10
NHL TOTALS			15	7	5	12	10

(c)—June, 1984—Drafted by Boston Bruins in 1984 NHL entry draft. Fourth Bruins pick, 82nd overall, fourth round.
(d)—Named U.S. College All-America First Team All-Star (West).

CLAUDE JULIEN

Defense . . . 6' . . . 195 lbs. . . . Born, Orleans, Ont., November 11, 1958 . . . Shoots right . . . (February 1, 1986)—Broken nose at Quebec.

Year	Team	League	Games	G.	A.	Pts.	Pen.
1977-78—Newmarket Flyers		OPJHL	45	18	26	44	137
1977-78—Oshawa Generals		OMJHL	11	0	5	5	14
1978-79—		....	....	...	....	....	....
1979-80—Windsor Spitfires		OMJHL	68	14	37	51	148
1980-81—Windsor Spitfires		OHL	3	1	2	3	21
1980-81—Port Huron Flags		IHL	77	15	40	55	153
1981-82—Salt Lake Golden Eagles (c)		CHL	70	4	18	22	134
1982-83—Salt Lake Golden Eagles (b-d)		CHL	76	14	47	61	176
1983-84—Milwaukee Admirals		IHL	5	0	3	3	2
1983-84—Fredericton Express		AHL	57	7	22	29	58
1984-85—Fredericton Express		AHL	77	6	28	34	97
1984-85—Quebec Nordiques		NHL	1	0	0	0	0
1985-86—Quebec Nordiques		NHL	13	0	1	1	25
1985-86—Fredericton Express		AHL	49	3	18	21	74
1986-87—Fredericton Express (e)		AHL	17	1	6	7	22
1987-88—Fredericton Express		AHL	35	1	14	15	52
1987-88—Baltimore Skipjacks		AHL	30	6	14	20	22
NHL TOTALS			14	0	1	1	25

(c)—September, 1981—Signed by St. Louis Blues as a free agent.
(d)—August, 1983—Sent by St. Louis Blues along with Gordon Donnelly to Quebec Nordiques as compensation for St. Louis signing coach Jacques Demers.
(e)—March, 1987—Signed by Fredericton Express after completing a season in Europe.

JOE JUNEAU

Center . . . 6' . . . 175 lbs. . . . Born, Pont-Rouge, Que., January 5, 1968 . . . Shoots right.

Year	Team	League	Games	G.	A.	Pts.	Pen.
1986-87—Levis-Lauzon Cegep AAA		Que. Midget	38	27	57	84	....
1987-88—R.P.I. (c)		ECAC	31	16	29	45	18

(c)—June, 1988—Drafted by Boston Bruins in 1988 NHL entry draft. Third Bruins pick, 81st overall, fourth round.

MARK KACHOWSKI

Left Wing . . . 5'10" . . . 195 lbs. . . . Born, Edmonton, Alta., February 20, 1965 . . . Shoots left.

Year	Team	League	Games	G.	A.	Pts.	Pen.
1983-84—Kamloops Blazers		WHL	57	6	9	15	156
1984-85—Kamloops Blazers		WHL	68	22	15	37	185
1985-86—Kamloops Blazers		WHL	61	21	31	52	182
1986-87—Flint Spirits (c)		IHL	75	18	13	31	273
1987-88—Pittsburgh Penguins		NHL	38	5	3	8	126

Year	Team	League	Games	G.	A.	Pts.	Pen.
1987-88—Muskegon Lumberjacks		IHL	25	3	6	9	72
NHL TOTALS			38	5	3	8	126

(c)—August, 1987—Signed by Pittsburgh Penguins as a free agent.

TRENT KAESE

Right Wing . . . 6' . . . 205 lbs. . . . Born, Nanaimo, B.C., September 4, 1967 . . . Shoots right.

Year	Team	League	Games	G.	A.	Pts.	Pen.
1983-84—Lethbridge Broncos		WHL	64	6	6	12	33
1984-85—Lethbridge Broncos (c)		WHL	67	20	18	38	107
1985-86—Lethbridge Broncos		WHL	67	24	41	65	67
1986-87—Flint Spirits		IHL	1	0	0	0	0
1986-87—Calgary Wranglers		WHL	70	31	24	55	121
1987-88—Rochester Americans		AHL	37	6	11	17	32
1987-88—Flint Spirits		IHL	43	11	26	37	58

(c)—June, 1985—Drafted as underage junior by Buffalo Sabres in 1985 NHL entry draft. Eighth Sabres pick, 161st overall, eighth round.

KEVIN KAMINSKI

Center . . . 5'9" . . . 168 lbs. . . . Born, Churchbridge, Sask., March 13, 1969 . . . Shoots left . . . (November 4, 1987)—Suspended 12 WHL games for cross checking.

Year	Team	League	Games	G.	A.	Pts.	Pen.
1984-85—Saskatoon Blades		WHL	5	0	1	1	17
1985-86—Saskatoon Blades		WHL	4	1	1	2	35
1986-87—Saskatoon Blades (c)		WHL	67	26	44	70	235
1987-88—Saskatoon Blades		WHL	55	38	61	99	247

(c)—June, 1987—Drafted by Minnesota North Stars in 1987 NHL entry draft as an underage junior. Third North Stars pick, 48th overall, third round.

SHAUN KANE

Defense . . . 6'2" . . . 180 lbs. . . . Born, Holyoke, Mass., February 24, 1970 . . . Shoots left.

Year	Team	League	Games	G.	A.	Pts.	Pen.
1986-87—Springfield Olympics		NEJHL	....	20	36	56	....
1987-88—Springfield Olympics (c)		NEJHL	....	23	40	63	....

(c)—June, 1988—Drafted by Minnesota North Stars in 1988 NHL entry draft. Third North Stars pick, 43rd overall, third round.

STEPHEN NEIL KASPER

Center . . . 5'8" . . . 159 lbs. . . . Born, Montreal, Que., September 28, 1961 . . . Shoots left . . . Brother of David Kasper (New Jersey, '82 draft pick) . . . (October 17, 1981)—Hip pointer at Los Angeles . . . (November 9, 1982)—Surgery to remove torn shoulder cartilage . . . (December 7, 1982)—Surgery to left shoulder for a torn capsule . . . (April, 1983)—Concussion during playoff series vs. Buffalo . . . (November, 1983)—Separated left shoulder . . . (January 7, 1984)—Surgery to shoulder . . . (February, 1984)—Reinjured shoulder.

Year	Team	League	Games	G.	A.	Pts.	Pen.
1977-78—Verdun Black Hawks		QMJHL	63	26	45	71	16
1978-79—Verdun Black Hawks		QMJHL	67	37	67	104	53
1979-80—Sorel Black Hawks (c)		QMJHL	70	57	65	122	117
1980-81—Sorel Black Hawks		QMJHL	2	5	2	7	0
1980-81—Boston Bruins		NHL	76	21	35	56	94
1981-82—Boston Bruins (d)		NHL	73	20	31	51	72
1982-83—Boston Bruins		NHL	24	2	6	8	24
1983-84—Boston Bruins		NHL	27	3	11	14	19
1984-85—Boston Bruins		NHL	77	16	24	40	33
1985-86—Boston Bruins		NHL	80	17	23	40	73
1986-87—Boston Bruins		NHL	79	20	30	50	51
1987-88—Boston Bruins		NHL	79	26	44	70	35
NHL TOTALS			513	125	204	329	401

(c)—June, 1980—Drafted by Boston Bruins in 1980 NHL entry draft. Third Bruins pick, 81st overall, fourth round.

(d)—Winner of Frank Selke Trophy (Best Defensive Forward).

EDWARD KASTELIC

Right Wing . . . 6'3" . . . 203 lbs. . . . Born, Toronto, Ont., January 29, 1964 . . . Shoots right . . . Played Defense prior to 1981-82 season . . . (September 30, 1985)—Fractured left cheekbone in pre-season game at Hartford . . . (January 20, 1986)—Suspended by Washington Capitals.

Year	Team	League	Games	G.	A.	Pts.	Pen.
1980-81—Mississauga Reps		Midget	51	4	10	14	....
1981-82—London Knights (c)		OHL	68	5	18	23	63
1982-83—London Knights		OHL	68	12	11	23	96
1983-84—London Knights		OHL	68	17	16	33	218
1984-85—Fort Wayne Komets		IHL	5	1	0	1	37
1984-85—Binghamton Whalers		AHL	4	0	0	0	7
1984-85—Moncton Golden Flames		AHL	62	5	11	16	187
1985-86—Washington Capitals		NHL	15	0	0	0	73
1985-86—Binghamton Whalers		AHL	23	7	9	16	76
1986-87—Binghamton Whalers		AHL	48	17	11	28	124
1986-87—Washington Capitals		NHL	23	1	1	2	83
1987-88—Binghamton Whalers		AHL	6	4	1	5	6
1987-88—Washington Capitals (d)		NHL	35	1	0	1	78
NHL TOTALS			73	2	1	3	234

(c)—June, 1982—Selected by Washington Capitals in 1982 NHL entry draft as an underage junior. Fourth Capitals pick, 110th overall, sixth round.

(d)—July, 1988—Traded with Grant Jennings by Washington Capitals to Hartford Whalers for Neil Sheehy and Mike Millar.

MIKE KEANE

Right Wing . . . 5'11" . . . 170 lbs. . . . Born, Winnipeg, Man., May 29, 1967 . . . Shoots right.

Year	Team	League	Games	G.	A.	Pts.	Pen.
1983-84—Winnipeg Warriors		WHL	1	0	0	0	0
1984-85—Moose Jaw Warriors		WHL	65	17	26	43	141
1985-86—Moose Jaw Warriors		WHL	67	34	49	83	162
1986-87—Moose Jaw Warriors (c)		WHL	53	25	45	70	107
1986-87—Sherbrooke Canadiens (d)		AHL	....	...	....	....	....
1987-88—Sherbrooke Canadiens		AHL	78	25	43	68	70

(c)—March, 1987—Signed by Montreal Canadiens as a free agent.

(d)—No regular season record. Played nine playoff games (2 goals, 2 assists).

DANIEL KECZMER

Defense . . . 6'1" . . . 180 lbs. . . . Born, Mt. Clemens, Mich., May 25, 1968 . . . Shoots left.

Year	Team	League	Games	G.	A.	Pts.	Pen.
1985-86—Little Caesars Midget (c)		Mich.	65	6	48	54	116
1986-87—Lake Superior State Univ.		CCHA	38	3	5	8	28
1987-88—Lake Superior State Univ.		CCHA	41	2	15	17	34

(c)—June, 1986—Drafted by Minnesota North Stars in 1986 NHL entry draft. Eleventh North Stars pick, 201st overall, 10th round.

MICHAEL KELFER

Center . . . 5'10" . . . 180 lbs. . . . Born, Peabody, Mass., January 2, 1967 . . . Shoots right.

Year	Team	League	Games	G.	A.	Pts.	Pen.
1984-85—St. John's Prep. (c)		Mass. H.S.	25	33	48	81	....
1985-86—Boston University		H. East	39	13	14	27	40
1986-87—Boston University		H. East	33	21	19	40	20
1987-88—Boston University		H. East	54	26	27	53	33

(c)—June, 1985—Drafted by Minnesota North Stars in 1985 NHL entry draft. Fifth North Stars pick, 132nd overall, seventh round.

TONY KELLIN

Defense . . . 6'2" . . . 195 lbs. . . . Born, Grand Rapids, Minn., March 19, 1963 . . . Shoots right . . . Played quarterback for high school football team and named to All-State team.

Year	Team	League	Games	G.	A.	Pts.	Pen.
1980-81—Gr. Rapids High School (c)		Minn. HS	27	19	24	43	38
1981-82—Gr. Rapids High School		Minn. HS	20	22	18	40	30
1982-83—University of Minnesota		WCHA	38	8	6	14	38
1983-84—University of Minnesota		WCHA	38	12	21	33	66
1984-85—University of Minnesota		WCHA	45	7	24	31	82
1985-86—University of Minnesota		WCHA	44	10	24	34	61
1986-87—Binghamton Whalers		AHL	66	8	27	35	65
1987-88—Binghamton Whalers (d)		AHL	48	6	12	18	77

(c)—June, 1981—Drafted by Washington Capitals as underage player in 1981 NHL entry draft. Third Capitals pick, 68th overall, third round.

(d)—May, 1988—Released by Washington Capitals.

PAUL KELLY

Defense . . . 6' . . . 190 lbs. . . . Born, Hamilton, Ont., April 17, 1967 . . . Shoots left.

Year	Team	League	Games	G.	A.	Pts.	Pen.
1983-84	Hamilton Midget	OHA	36	37	32	69	52
1984-85	Guelph Platers	OHL	64	15	27	42	50
1985-86	Guelph Platers (c)	OHL	59	26	32	58	95
1986-87	Guelph Platers	OHL	61	27	48	75	67
1987-88	New Haven Nighthawks	AHL	60	14	25	39	23

(c)—June, 1986—Drafted by Los Angeles Kings in 1986 NHL entry draft. Ninth Kings pick, 191st overall, 10th round.

EDWARD DEAN KENNEDY
(Known by middle name.)

Defense . . . 6'2" . . . 200 lbs. . . . Born, Redvers, Sask., January 18, 1963 . . . Shoots right . . . (February 18, 1983)—Given four-game suspension by NHL after off-ice altercation with Ken Linseman at Edmonton (February 3) . . . Missed part of 1981-82 season with a knee injury . . . (March, 1987)—Hip pointer . . . (November, 1987)—Broken finger . . . (March, 1988)—Injured groin.

Year	Team	League	Games	G.	A.	Pts.	Pen.
1979-80	Weyburn Red Wings	SJHL	57	12	20	32	64
1979-80	Brandon Wheat Kings	WHL	1	0	0	0	0
1980-81	Brandon Wheat Kings (c)	WHL	71	3	29	32	157
1981-82	Brandon Wheat Kings	WHL	49	5	38	43	103
1982-83	Brandon Wheat Kings	WHL	14	2	15	17	22
1982-83	Los Angeles Kings	NHL	55	0	12	12	97
1982-83	Saskatoon Blades (d)	WHL	....	...	....	....	....
1983-84	New Haven Nighthawks	AHL	26	1	7	8	23
1983-84	Los Angeles Kings	NHL	37	1	5	6	50
1984-85	New Haven Nighthawks	AHL	76	3	14	17	104
1985-86	Los Angeles Kings	NHL	78	2	10	12	132
1986-87	Los Angeles Kings	NHL	66	6	14	20	91
1987-88	Los Angeles Kings	NHL	58	1	11	12	158
NHL TOTALS			294	10	52	62	528

(c)—June, 1981—Drafted as underage junior by Los Angeles Kings in 1981 NHL entry draft. Second Kings pick, 39th overall, second round.

(d)—No regular season record. Played four playoff games.

SHELDON KENNEDY

Right Wing . . . 5'10" . . . 170 lbs. . . . Born, Brandon, Manitoba, June 15, 1969 . . . Shoots right . . . Brother of Troy Kennedy . . . (January 18, 1987)—Missed six weeks with a broken ankle.

Year	Team	League	Games	G.	A.	Pts.	Pen.
1986-87	Swift Current Broncos	WHL	49	23	41	64	64
1987-88	Swift Current Broncos (c)	WHL	59	53	64	117	45

(c)—June, 1988—Drafted by Detroit Red Wings in 1988 NHL entry draft. Fifth Red Wings pick, 80th overall, fourth round.

TROY KENNEDY

Right Wing . . . 5'11" . . . 170 lbs. . . . Born, Brandon, Manitoba, March 12, 1968 . . . Shoots right . . . Brother of Sheldon Kennedy.

Year	Team	League	Games	G.	A.	Pts.	Pen.
1983-84	Winnipeg Warriors	WHL	1	0	0	0	0
1984-85	Moose Jaw Warriors	WHL	23	7	5	12	4
1985-86	Moose Jaw Warriors	WHL	24	5	10	15	6
1985-86	Kamloops Blazers	WHL	45	4	19	23	21
1986-87	New Westminster Bruins (c)	WHL	26	13	17	30	11
1986-87	Brandon Wheat Kings	WHL	41	10	26	36	40
1987-88	Brandon Wheat Kings (d)	WHL	70	55	72	127	42

(c)—December, 1986—Traded with Kory Sundstrom by New Westminster Bruins to Brandon Wheat Kings for Jayson More.

(d)—June, 1988—Drafted by Calgary Flames in 1988 NHL entry draft. Eighth Flames pick, 168th overall, eighth round.

ALAN KERR

Right Wing . . . 5'11" . . . 190 lbs. . . . Born, Hazelton, B.C., March 28, 1964 . . . Shoots right . . . (April, 1988)—Took 40 stitches above right eye when grazed by a Ken Daneyko skate in playoff game vs. New Jersey . . . Cousin of former NHLer Reg Kerr.

Year	Team	League	Games	G.	A.	Pts.	Pen.
1981-82—Seattle Breakers (c)		WHL	68	15	18	33	1079
1982-83—Seattle Breakers		WHL	71	38	53	91	183
1983-84—Seattle Breakers (a)		WHL	66	46	66	112	141
1984-85—Springfield Indians		AHL	62	32	27	59	140
1984-85—New York Islanders		NHL	19	3	1	4	24
1985-86—Springfield Indians		AHL	71	35	36	71	127
1985-86—New York Islanders		NHL	7	0	1	1	16
1986-87—New York Islanders		NHL	72	7	10	17	175
1987-88—New York Islanders		NHL	80	24	34	58	198
NHL TOTALS			178	34	46	80	413

(c)—June, 1982—Drafted by New York Islanders as underage junior in 1982 NHL entry draft. Fourth Islanders pick, 84th overall, fourth round.

KEVIN KERR

Right Wing . . . 5'10" . . . 175 lbs. . . . Born, North Bay, Ont., September 18, 1967 . . . Shoots right.

Year	Team	League	Games	G.	A.	Pts.	Pen.
1984-85—Windsor Spitfires		OHL	57	5	16	21	189
1985-86—Windsor Spitfires (c)		OHL	59	21	51	72	*266
1986-87—Windsor Spitfires		OHL	63	27	41	68	*264
1987-88—Rochester Americans		AHL	72	18	11	29	352

(c)—June, 1986—Drafted as underage junior by Buffalo Sabres in 1986 NHL entry draft. Fourth Sabres pick, 56th overall, third round.

TIM KERR

Right Wing and Center . . . 6'3" . . . 215 lbs. . . . Born, Windsor, Ont., January 5, 1960 . . . Shoots right . . . (November 1, 1980)—Injured shoulder . . . (October, 1981)—Injured knee cartilage . . . (September, 1982)—Hernia surgery . . . (November 10, 1982)—Stretched knee ligaments at Buffalo that required surgery . . . (March, 1983)—Cracked fibula of left leg . . . (March, 1985)—Strained knee ligaments . . . (April 13, 1985)—Set NHL playoff records for most goals (4) and power-play goals (3) in a single period in the 2nd period at N.Y. Rangers . . . (May 5, 1985)—Strained right knee in collision with teammate Todd Bergen in opening playoff game with Quebec . . . (September, 1985)—Hospitalized with aseptic meningitis, a viral infection of the brain lining . . . (1985-86)—Set NHL record for most power-play goals in one season with 34, breaking mark of 28 held jointly by Phil Esposito (1971-72) and Mike Bossy (1980-81) . . . (November 29, 1986)—Missed three games with pulled hamstring at N.Y. Islanders . . . (June, 1987)—Had two off-season operations to repair injury to his left shoulder that caused him to miss last two rounds of playoffs . . . (October, 1987)—Two more shoulder surgeries . . . (November, 1987)—A fifth shoulder operation since June, 1987, to remove a screw that was causing an infection . . . (December, 1987)—Served as assistant coach behind the Flyer's bench . . . (March, 1988) —Returned to the Flyers' lineup after missing 315 days.

Year	Team	League	Games	G.	A.	Pts.	Pen.
1976-77—Windsor Spitfires		OMJHL	9	2	4	6	7
1977-78—Kingston Canadians		OMJHL	67	14	25	39	33
1978-79—Kingston Canadians		OMJHL	57	17	25	42	27
1979-80—Kingston Canadians (c)		OMJHL	63	40	33	73	39
1979-80—Maine Mariners		AHL	7	2	4	6	2
1980-81—Philadelphia Flyers		NHL	68	22	23	45	84
1981-82—Philadelphia Flyers		NHL	61	21	30	51	138
1982-83—Philadelphia Flyers		NHL	24	11	8	19	6
1983-84—Philadelphia Flyers		NHL	79	54	39	93	29
1984-85—Philadelphia Flyers		NHL	74	54	44	98	57
1985-86—Philadelphia Flyers		NHL	76	58	26	84	79
1986-87—Philadelphia Flyers (b)		NHL	75	58	37	95	57
1987-88—Philadelphia Flyers		NHL	8	3	2	5	12
NHL TOTALS			465	281	209	490	462

(c)—January, 1980—Signed by Philadelphia Flyers as a free agent.

IAN KIDD

Defense . . . 6' . . . 197 lbs. . . . Born, Gresham, Ore., May 11, 1964 . . . Shoots right.

Year	Team	League	Games	G.	A.	Pts.	Pen.
1985-86—Univ. of North Dakota (c)		WCHA	37	6	16	22	65
1986-87—Univ. of North Dakota (d-e)		WCHA	47	13	47	60	58
1987-88—Fredericton Express		AHL	53	1	21	22	70
1987-88—Vancouver Canucks		NHL	19	4	7	11	25
NHL TOTALS			19	4	7	11	25

(c)—October, 1986—First overall selection in NHL supplemental draft by Detroit Red Wings. However, choice was later voided by NHL.
(d)—Selected first team All-America (West).
(e)—August, 1987—Signed by Vancouver Canucks as a free agent.

DARIN KIMBLE

Right Wing . . . 6'2" . . . 210 lbs. . . . Born, Lucky Lake, Sask., November 22, 1968 . . . Shoots right.

Year	Team	League	Games	G.	A.	Pts.	Pen.
1984-85—Swift Current Jr. A		SAJHL	59	28	32	60	264
1984-85—Calgary Wranglers (c)		WHL	..	..	..	..	..
1985-86—Calgary Wranglers		WHL	37	14	8	22	93
1985-86—New Westminster Bruins		WHL	11	1	1	2	22
1985-86—Brandon Wheat Kings		WHL	15	1	6	7	39
1986-87—Prince Albert Raiders (d)		WHL	68	17	13	30	190
1987-88—Prince Albert Raiders (e)		WHL	67	35	36	71	307

(c)—No regular season record. Played one playoff game.
(d)—September, 1986—Traded with Kerry Angus by Brandon Wheat Kings to Prince Albert Raiders for Graham Garden, Ryan Stewart and Kim Rasmussen.
(e)—June, 1988—Drafted by Quebec Nordiques in 1988 NHL entry draft. Fifth Nordiques pick, 66th overall, fourth round.

DEREK KING

Left Wing . . . 6'1" . . . 210 lbs. . . . Born, Hamilton, Ont., February 11, 1967 . . . Shoots left . . . (September, 1985)—Sprained right knee in N.Y. Islanders training camp . . . (December 12, 1987)—Fractured left wrist at Pittsburgh.

Year	Team	League	Games	G.	A.	Pts.	Pen.
1983-84—Hamilton Jr.A.		OHA	37	10	14	24	142
1984-85—Sault Ste. Marie Greyhounds (c-d)		OHL	63	35	38	73	106
1985-86—Sault Ste. Marie Greyhounds		OHL	25	12	17	29	33
1985-86—Oshawa Generals		OHL	19	8	13	21	15
1986-87—Oshawa Generals (a)		OHL	57	53	53	106	74
1986-87—New York Islanders		NHL	2	0	0	0	0
1987-88—New York Islanders		NHL	55	12	24	36	30
1987-88—Springfield Indians		AHL	10	7	6	13	6
NHL TOTALS			57	12	24	36	30

(c)—Won Emms Family Award (OHL Top Rookie).
(d)—June, 1985—Drafted as underage junior by New York Islanders in 1985 NHL entry draft. Second Islanders pick, 13th overall, first round.

KRIS KING

Center . . . 5'10" . . . 185 lbs. . . . Born, Bracebridge, Ont., February 18, 1966 . . . Shoots left.

Year	Team	League	Games	G.	A.	Pts.	Pen.
1982-83—Gravenhurst		SOJHL	32	72	53	125	115
1983-84—Peterborough Petes (c)		OHL	62	13	18	31	168
1984-85—Peterborough Petes		OHL	61	18	35	53	222
1985-86—Peterborough Petes		OHL	58	19	40	59	254
1986-87—Peterborough Petes		OHL	46	23	33	56	160
1986-87—Binghamton Whalers (d)		AHL	7	0	0	0	18
1987-88—Adirondack Red Wings		AHL	78	21	32	53	337
1987-88—Detroit Red Wings		NHL	3	1	0	1	2
NHL TOTALS			3	1	0	1	2

(c)—June, 1984—Drafted as underage junior by Washington Capitals in 1984 NHL entry draft. Fourth Capitals pick, 80th overall, fourth round.
(d)—June, 1987—Signed by Detroit Red Wings as a free agent.

DOUG KIRTON

Right Wing . . . 6'2" . . . 190 lbs. . . . Born, Pentanguishene, Ont., March 21, 1966 . . . Shoots right . . . (November, 1987)—Broken kneecap.

Year	Team	League	Games	G.	A.	Pts.	Pen.
1985-86—Orilla (c)		OHL	46	34	45	79	158
1986-87—Colorado College		WCHA	38	10	10	20	42
1987-88—Colorado College		WCHA	31	11	17	28	42

(c)—June, 1986—Drafted by New Jersey Devils in 1986 NHL entry draft. Twelfth Devils pick, 236th overall, 12th round.

MARK ROBERT KIRTON

Center . . . 5'10" . . . 170 lbs. . . . Born, Regina, Sask., February 3, 1958 . . . Shoots left . . . (March 7, 1981)—Separated left shoulder.

Year	Team	League	Games	G.	A.	Pts.	Pen.
1975-76—Peterborough Petes		Jr."A"OHA	65	22	38	60	10
1976-77—Peterborough Petes		Jr."A"OHA	48	18	24	42	41
1977-78—Peterborough Petes (c)		Jr."A"OHA	68	27	44	71	29
1978-79—New Brunswick Hawks		AHL	79	20	30	50	14
1979-80—Toronto Maple Leafs		NHL	2	1	0	1	2
1979-80—New Brunswick Hawks		AHL	61	19	42	61	33
1980-81—Toronto Maple Leafs (d)		NHL	11	0	0	0	0
1980-81—Detroit Red Wings		NHL	50	18	13	31	24
1981-82—Detroit Red Wings		NHL	74	14	28	42	62
1982-83—Adirondack Red Wings		AHL	20	6	10	16	12
1982-83—Detroit Red Wings (e)		NHL	10	1	1	2	6
1982-83—Vancouver Canucks		NHL	31	4	6	10	4
1982-83—Fredericton Express		AHL	3	2	0	2	2
1983-84—Vancouver Canucks		NHL	26	2	3	5	2
1983-84—Fredericton Express		AHL	35	8	10	18	8
1984-85—Fredericton Express		AHL	15	5	9	14	18
1984-85—Vancouver Canucks		NHL	62	17	5	22	21
1985-86—Fredericton Express		AHL	77	23	36	59	33
1986-87—Fredericton Express		AHL	80	27	37	64	20
1987-88—Newmarket Saints		AHL	73	17	30	47	42
NHL TOTALS			266	57	56	113	121

(c)—Drafted from Peterborough Petes by Toronto Maple Leafs in third round 1978 amateur draft.
(d)—December, 1980—Traded by Toronto Maple Leafs to Detroit Red Wings for Jim Rutherford.
(e)—January, 1983—Traded by Detroit Red Wings to Vancouver Canucks for Ivan Boldirev.

KELLY KISIO

Center . . . 5'9" . . . 170 lbs. . . . Born, Wetaskwin, Alta., September 18, 1959 . . . Shoots right . . . Also plays Right Wing . . . (February, 1985)—Given five-game suspension by NHL for stick-swinging incident . . . (October, 1986)—Dislocated left shoulder . . . (April, 1987)—Surgery on shoulder . . . (February, 1988)—Bruised and twisted left knee.

Year	Team	League	Games	G.	A.	Pts.	Pen.
1976-77—Red Deer Rustlers		AJHL	60	53	48	101	101
1977-78—Red Deer Rustlers (a)		AJHL	58	74	68	142	66
1978-79—Calgary Wranglers		WHL	70	60	61	121	73
1979-80—Calgary Wranglers		WHL	71	65	73	138	64
1980-81—Adirondack Red Wings		AHL	41	10	14	24	43
1980-81—Kalamazoo Wings (c)		IHL	31	27	16	43	48
1981-82—Dallas Black Hawks (d)		CHL	78	*62	39	101	59
1982-83—Davos HC		Switz.	....	49	38	87	....
1982-83—Detroit Red Wings (e)		NHL	15	4	3	7	0
1983-84—Detroit Red Wings		NHL	70	23	37	60	34
1984-85—Detroit Red Wings		NHL	75	20	41	61	56
1985-86—Detroit Red Wings (f)		NHL	76	21	48	69	85
1986-87—New York Rangers		NHL	70	24	40	64	73
1987-88—New York Rangers		NHL	77	23	55	78	88
NHL TOTALS			383	115	224	339	336

(c)—February, 1981—Traded by Toledo Goaldiggers to Kalamazoo Wings for Jean Chouinard.
(d)—Led CHL Adams Cup Playoffs with 12 goals and 29 points and was co-leader (with Bruce Affleck) with 17 assists.
(e)—February, 1983—Signed by Detroit as a free agent at the conclusion of season in Switzerland.
(f)—July, 1986—Traded with Lane Lambert, Jim Leavins and a fifth-round 1988 draft pick by Detroit Red Wings to New York Rangers for Glen Hanlon, third round 1987 (Dennis Holland) and 1988 draft picks and future considerations.

SCOT KLEINENDORST

Defense . . . 6'3" . . . 205 lbs. . . . Born, Grand Rapids, Minn., January 16, 1960 . . . Shoots left . . . (September, 1982)—Preseason surgery for off-season knee injury . . . Brother of Kurt Kleinendorst . . . (February, 1984)—Suffered groin injury and out for the season . . . (February, 1985)—Knee sprain . . . (October 30, 1985)—Broken right foot vs. Quebec and missed 18 games . . . (February 11, 1986)—Bruised ribs at St. Louis . . . (August, 1987)—Broken foot while training for Team USA in Canada Cup Tournament . . . (November, 1987)—Injured back . . . (February, 1988)—Separated shoulder.

Year	Team	League	Games	G.	A.	Pts.	Pen.
1979-80—Providence College (b-c-d)		ECAC	30	1	12	13	38
1980-81—Providence College		ECAC	32	3	31	34	75

Year	Team	League	Games	G.	A.	Pts.	Pen.
1981-82—Providence College (a)	ECAC	33	30	27	57	14
1981-82—Springfield Indians	AHL	5	0	4	4	11
1982-83—Tulsa Oilers	CHL	10	0	7	7	14
1982-83—New York Rangers	NHL	30	2	9	11	8
1983-84—Tulsa Oilers	CHL	24	4	9	13	10
1983-84—New York Rangers (e)	NHL	23	0	2	2	35
1984-85—Binghamton Whalers	AHL	30	3	7	10	42
1984-85—Hartford Whalers	NHL	35	1	8	9	69
1985-86—Hartford Whalers	NHL	41	2	7	9	62
1986-87—Hartford Whalers	NHL	66	3	9	12	130
1987-88—Hartford Whalers	NHL	44	3	6	9	86
NHL TOTALS		239	11	41	52	390

(c)—Named to All-New England Collegiate All-Star Team (Second team).

(d)—June, 1980—Drafted by New York Rangers in 1980 NHL entry draft. Fourth Rangers pick, 98th overall, fifth round.

(e)—February, 1984—Traded by New York Rangers to Hartford Whalers for Blaine Stoughton.

PETR KLIMA

Left Wing . . . 6' . . . 190 lbs. . . . Born, Chaomutov, Czechoslovakia, December 23, 1964 . . . Shoots right . . . (January 18, 1986)—Injured hip vs. Calgary and missed five games . . . (May, 1988)—Broke right thumb in playoff game at Edmonton when slashed by Charlie Huddy.

Year	Team	League	Games	G.	A.	Pts.	Pen.
1982-83—Czechoslovakian Nationals (c)	Czech.	44	19	17	36	74
1983-84—Dukla Jihlava	Czech.	41	20	16	36	46
1983-84—Czechoslovakian Nationals	Czech.	7	6	5	11	....
1984-85—Dukla Jihlava	Czech.	35	23	22	45	....
1985-86—Detroit Red Wings	NHL	74	32	24	56	16
1986-87—Detroit Red Wings	NHL	77	30	23	53	42
1987-88—Detroit Red Wings	NHL	78	37	25	62	46
NHL TOTALS		229	99	72	171	104

(c)—June, 1983—Drafted by Detroit Red Wings in NHL entry draft. Fifth Red Wings pick, 88th overall, fifth round.

GORD KLUZAK

Defense . . . 6'3" . . . 214 lbs. . . . Born, Climax, Sask., March 4, 1964 . . . Shoots left . . . (February 9, 1982)—Injured knee vs. Medicine Hat that required surgery . . . (March 12, 1983)—Eye injured vs. Philadelphia . . . (October 7, 1984)—Tore ligaments in left knee when he collided with Dave Lewis in final pre-season game with New Jersey at Portland, Maine. Underwent major reconstructive surgery the following day and was lost for the season . . . (January 29, 1986)—Injured shoulder at Washington and missed nine games . . . (September, 1986)—Surgery to left knee and missed season . . . (May 29, 1987)—Had his fourth knee operation . . . (October, 1987)—Sprained left knee . . . (February, 1988)— Sprained right knee.

Year	Team	League	Games	G.	A.	Pts.	Pen.
1980-81—Billings Bighorns	WHL	68	4	34	38	160
1981-82—Billings Bighorns (b-c)	WHL	38	9	24	33	110
1982-83—Boston Bruins	NHL	70	1	6	7	105
1983-84—Boston Bruins	NHL	80	10	27	37	135
1984-85—Boston Bruins	NHL	....	...	....	....	....
1985-86—Boston Bruins	NHL	70	8	31	39	155
1986-87—Boston Bruins	NHL	....	...	....	....	....
1987-88—Boston Bruins	NHL	66	6	31	37	135
NHL TOTALS		286	25	95	120	530

(c)—June, 1982—Drafted as underage junior by Boston Bruins in 1982 NHL entry draft. First Bruins pick, first overall, first round.

JOE KOCUR

Right Wing . . . 6' . . . 204 lbs. . . . Born, Calgary, Alta., December 21, 1964 . . . Shoots right . . . (December, 1981)—Stretched knee ligaments . . . (January, 1985)—Took 20 stitches to back of right hand in fight with Jim Playfair in game with Nova Scotia Oilers . . . (December 11, 1985)—Sprained thumb at Minnesota . . . (March 26, 1986)—Strained ligaments at Chicago . . . (October, 1987)—Sore right elbow . . . (November, 1987)—Strained sternum and collarbone . . . (December, 1987)—Injured shoulder . . . (May, 1988)—Separated shoulder . . . Cousin of Kory Kocur.

Year	Team	League	Games	G.	A.	Pts.	Pen.
1980-81—Yorkton Terriers	SJHL	48	6	9	15	307
1981-82—Yorkton Terriers	SJHL	47	20	21	41	199

Year	Team	League	Games	G.	A.	Pts.	Pen.
1982-83—Saskatoon Blades (c)		WHL	62	23	17	40	289
1983-84—Saskatoon Blades		WHL	69	40	41	81	258
1984-85—Detroit Red Wings		NHL	17	1	0	1	64
1984-85—Adirondack Red Wings		AHL	47	12	7	19	171
1985-86—Adirondack Red Wings		AHL	9	6	2	8	34
1985-86—Detroit Red Wings		NHL	59	9	6	15	*377
1986-87—Detroit Red Wings		NHL	77	9	9	18	276
1987-88—Detroit Red Wings		NHL	64	7	7	14	263
NHL TOTALS			217	26	22	48	980

(c)—June, 1983—Drafted as underage junior by Detroit Red Wings in 1983 NHL entry draft. Sixth Red Wings pick, 88th overall, fifth round.

KORY KOCUR

Right Wing . . . 5'11" . . . 188 lbs. . . . Born, Kelvington, Sask., March 6, 1969 . . . Shoots right . . . Cousin of Joe Kocur.

Year	Team	League	Games	G.	A.	Pts.	Pen.
1986-87—Saskatoon Blades		WHL	62	13	17	30	98
1987-88—Saskatoon Blades (c)		WHL	69	34	37	71	95

(c)—June, 1988—Drafted by Detroit Red Wings in 1988 NHL entry draft. First Red Wings pick, 17th overall, first round.

DEAN KOLSTAD

Defense . . . 6'6" . . . 200 lbs. . . . Born, Edmonton, Alta., June 16, 1968 . . . Shoots left.

Year	Team	League	Games	G.	A.	Pts.	Pen.
1984-85—New Westminster Bruins		WHL	13	0	0	0	16
1985-86—New Westminster Bruins		WHL	16	0	5	5	19
1985-86—Prince Albert Raiders (c)		WHL	54	2	15	17	80
1986-87—Prince Albert Raiders (a)		WHL	72	17	37	54	112
1987-88—Prince Albert Raiders		WHL	72	14	37	51	121

(c)—June, 1986—Drafted as underage junior by Minnesota North Stars in 1986 NHL entry draft. Third North Stars pick, 33rd overall, second round.

STEPHEN MARK KONROYD

Defense . . . 6'1" . . . 195 lbs. . . . Born, Scarborough, Ont., February 10, 1961 . . . Shoots left . . . (December, 1984)—Dislocated elbow . . . (February, 1986)—Pulled chest muscle vs. Toronto . . . (December, 1986)—Bruised collarbone . . . (January, 1988)—Suspended four NHL games for stick-swinging incident with Randy Cunneyworth vs. Pittsburgh.

Year	Team	League	Games	G.	A.	Pts.	Pen.
1978-79—Oshawa Generals		OMJHL	65	4	19	23	63
1979-80—Oshawa Generals (c-d)		OMJHL	62	11	23	34	133
1980-81—Calgary Flames		NHL	4	0	0	0	4
1980-81—Oshawa Generals (b)		OHL	59	19	49	68	232
1981-82—Oklahoma City Stars		CHL	14	2	3	5	15
1981-82—Calgary Flames		NHL	63	3	14	17	78
1982-83—Calgary Flames		NHL	79	4	13	17	73
1983-84—Calgary Flames		NHL	80	1	13	14	94
1984-85—Calgary Flames		NHL	64	3	23	26	73
1985-86—Calgary Flames (e)		NHL	59	7	20	27	64
1985-86—New York Islanders		NHL	14	0	5	5	16
1986-87—New York Islanders		NHL	72	5	16	21	70
1987-88—New York Islanders		NHL	62	2	15	17	99
NHL TOTALS			497	25	119	144	571

(c)—June, 1980—Drafted as underage junior by Calgary Flames in 1980 NHL entry draft. Fourth Flames pick, 39th overall, second round.

(d)—Named winner of Bobby Smith Award (OHL player who best combines high standards of play with academic excellence).

(e)—March, 1986—Traded by Calgary Flames with Richard Kromm to New York Islanders for John Tonelli.

CHRIS KONTOS

Center . . . 6'1" . . . 200 lbs. . . . Born, Toronto, Ont., December 10, 1963 . . . Shoots left . . . Also plays Left Wing . . . (November, 1983)—Suspended by N.Y. Rangers when he refused to report to Tulsa Oilers. He was reinstated in January, 1984.

Year	Team	League	Games	G.	A.	Pts.	Pen.
1979-80—North York Flames		OPJHL	42	39	55	94	37
1980-81—Sudbury Wolves		OHL	56	17	27	44	36
1981-82—Sudbury Wolves (c)		OHL	12	6	6	12	18

Year	Team	League	Games	G.	A.	Pts.	Pen.
1981-82—Toronto Marlboros (d)		OHL	59	36	56	92	68
1982-83—Toronto Marlboros		OHL	28	21	33	54	23
1982-83—New York Rangers		NHL	44	8	7	15	33
1983-84—New York Rangers		NHL	6	0	1	1	8
1983-84—Tulsa Oilers		CHL	21	5	13	18	8
1984-85—New Haven Nighthawks		AHL	48	19	24	43	30
1984-85—New York Rangers		NHL	28	4	8	12	24
1985-86—New Haven Nighthawks		AHL	21	8	15	23	12
1986-87—New Haven Nighthawks (e)		AHL	36	14	17	31	29
1986-87—Pittsburgh Penguins		NHL	31	8	9	17	6
1987-88—Pittsburgh Penguins (f)		NHL	36	1	7	8	12
1987-88—Los Angeles Kings		NHL	6	2	10	12	2
1987-88—New Haven Nighthawks		AHL	16	8	16	24	4
1987-88—Muskegon Lumberjacks		IHL	10	3	6	9	8
NHL TOTALS			151	23	42	65	85

(c)—October, 1981—Traded by Sudbury Wolves to Toronto Marlboros for Keith Knight.

(d)—June, 1982—Drafted as underage junior by New York Rangers in 1982 NHL entry draft. First Rangers pick, 15th overall, first round.

(e)—January, 1987—Traded by New York Rangers to Pittsburgh Penguins for Ron Duguay.

(f)—February, 1988—Traded with a sixth-round 1988 draft pick (Micah Aivazoff) by Pittsburgh Penguins to Los Angeles Kings for Bryan Erickson.

BILL KOPECKY

Center . . . 5'11" . . . 170 lbs. . . . Born, Ipswich, Mass., January 11, 1966 . . . Shoots left.

Year	Team	League	Games	G.	A.	Pts.	Pen.
1983-84—Austin H.S. (c)		Minn. H.S.	21	31	36	67	..
1984-85—Boston College		H. East	29	6	10	16	18
1985-86—Rensselaer Poly. Inst.		ECAC	29	9	15	24	26
1986-87—Rensselaer Poly. Inst.		ECAC	32	13	9	22	29
1987-88—Rensselaer Poly. Inst.		ECAC	29	13	21	34	38

(c)—June, 1984—Drafted by Boston Bruins in 1984 NHL entry draft. Eleventh Bruins pick, 227th overall, 11th round.

JOHN KORDIC

Right Wing . . . 6'1" . . . 190 lbs. . . . Born, Edmonton, Alta., March 22, 1965 . . . Shoots right . . . Uncle played pro soccer in Yugoslavia . . . (February 26, 1988)—Suspended five NHL games and fined $100 for fighting prior to a game vs. Quebec.

Year	Team	League	Games	G.	A.	Pts.	Pen.
1981-82—Edmonton K. of C. AA		Edm. Midget	48	23	41	64	178
1982-83—Portland Winter Hawks (c)		WHL	72	3	22	25	235
1983-84—Portland Winter Hawks		WHL	67	9	50	59	232
1984-85—Portland Winter Hawks		WHL	25	6	22	28	73
1984-85—Seattle Breakers (b)		WHL	46	17	36	53	154
1984-85—Sherbrooke Canadiens		AHL	4	0	0	0	4
1985-86—Sherbrooke Canadiens		AHL	68	3	14	17	238
1985-86—Montreal Canadiens		NHL	5	0	1	1	12
1986-87—Sherbrooke Canadiens		AHL	10	4	4	8	49
1986-87—Montreal Canadiens		NHL	44	5	3	8	151
1987-88—Montreal Canadiens		NHL	60	2	6	8	159
NHL TOTALS			109	7	10	17	322

(c)—June, 1983—Drafted as underage junior by Montreal Canadiens in 1983 NHL entry draft. Sixth Canadiens pick, 78th overall, fourth round.

JAMES A. KORN

Defense . . . 6'5" . . . 220 lbs. . . . Born, Hopkins, Minn., July 28, 1957 . . . Shoots left . . . (January 13, 1981)—Injured ligaments in right knee . . . (February 8, 1984)—Injured ribs vs. Boston . . . (November 5, 1984)—Dislocated shoulder when he collided with goal post at Minnesota . . . (January, 1985)—Given three-game NHL suspension . . . (February 9, 1985)—Separated shoulder during fight with Chris Nilan at Montreal . . . Missed entire 1985-86 season with knee injury . . . (February 12, 1988)—Surgery to remove cartilage, calcium and tissue from rotator cuff in left shoulder.

Year	Team	League	Games	G.	A.	Pts.	Pen.
1976-77—Providence College (c)		ECAC	29	6	9	15	73
1977-78—Providence College		ECAC	33	7	14	21	47
1978-79—Providence College		ECAC	27	5	19	24	72
1979-80—Adirondack Red Wings		AHL	14	2	7	9	40
1979-80—Detroit Red Wings		NHL	63	5	13	18	108
1980-81—Adirondack Red Wings		AHL	9	3	7	10	53

Year	Team	League	Games	G.	A.	Pts.	Pen.
1980-81—Detroit Red Wings		NHL	63	5	15	20	246
1981-82—Detroit Red Wings (d)		NHL	59	1	7	8	104
1981-82—Toronto Maple Leafs		NHL	11	1	3	4	44
1982-83—Toronto Maple Leafs		NHL	80	8	21	29	238
1983-84—Toronto Maple Leafs		NHL	65	12	14	26	257
1984-85—Toronto Maple Leafs		NHL	41	5	5	10	171
1985-86—Toronto Maple Leafs		NHL	..	..	..	..	..
1986-87—Buffalo Sabres (e-f)		NHL	51	4	10	14	158
1987-88—New Jersey Devils		NHL	52	8	13	21	140
NHL TOTALS			485	49	101	150	1466

(c)—June, 1977—Drafted by Detroit Red Wings in 1977 amateur draft. Fourth Detroit pick, 73rd overall, fifth round.

(d)—March, 1982—Traded by Detroit Red Wings to Toronto Maple Leafs for 1982 fourth-round pick (Craig Coxe) and a 1983 fifth-round pick (Joey Kocur) in the NHL entry draft.

(e)—October, 1986—Traded by Toronto Maple Leafs to Buffalo Sabres as part of a three-club trade that saw the Sabres send Brian Engblom to Calgary and the Flames send Terry Johnson to Toronto.

(f)—May, 1987—Traded by Buffalo Sabres to New Jersey Devils for Jan Ludvig.

DAVID KOROL

Defense . . . 6' . . . 180 lbs. . . . Born, Winnipeg, Man., March 1, 1965 . . . Shoots left . . . (January, 1982)—Thumb surgery.

Year	Team	League	Games	G.	A.	Pts.	Pen.
1981-82—Winnipeg Warriors		WHL	64	4	22	26	55
1982-83—Winnipeg Warriors (c)		WHL	72	14	43	57	90
1983-84—Winnipeg Warriors		WHL	57	15	48	63	49
1983-84—Adirondack Red Wings		AHL	2	0	4	4	0
1984-85—Regina Pats		WHL	48	4	30	34	61
1985-86—Adirondack Red Wings		AHL	74	3	9	12	56
1986-87—Adirondack Red Wings		AHL	48	1	4	5	67
1987-88—Adirondack Red Wings		AHL	53	2	17	19	61

(c)—June, 1983—Drafted by Detroit Red Wings in 1983 NHL entry draft. Fourth Red Wings pick, 68th overall, fourth round.

ROGER KORTKO

Center . . . 5'11" . . . 175 lbs. . . . Born, Hafford, Sask., February 1, 1963 . . . Shoots left . . . (October, 1984 and January, 1985)—Sprained ankle . . . (November 1, 1985)—Missed five games with a virus infection . . . (March, 1986)—Damaged ligaments in left knee vs. St. Louis.

Year	Team	League	Games	G.	A.	Pts.	Pen.
1980-81—Humbolt Broncos		SJHL	60	43	82	125	52
1981-82—Saskatoon Blades (c)		WHL	65	33	51	84	82
1982-83—Saskatoon Blades		WHL	72	62	99	161	79
1983-84—Indianapolis Checkers		CHL	64	16	27	43	48
1984-85—Springfield Indians		AHL	30	8	30	38	6
1984-85—New York Islanders		NHL	27	2	9	11	9
1985-86—Springfield Indians		AHL	12	2	10	12	10
1985-86—New York Islanders		NHL	52	5	8	13	19
1986-87—Springfield Indians (d)		AHL	75	16	30	46	54
1987-88—Binghamton Whalers		AHL	72	26	45	71	46
NHL TOTALS			79	7	17	24	28

(c)—June, 1982—Drafted as underage junior by New York Islanders in 1982 NHL entry draft. Sixth Islanders pick, 126th overall, sixth round.

(d)—August, 1987—Signed as free agent by Hartford Whalers.

CHRIS KOTSOPOULOS

Defense . . . 6'3" . . . 215 lbs. . . . Born, Toronto, Ont., November 27, 1958 . . . Shoots right . . . Brother of George Kotsopoulos . . . (October, 1980)—Broke right thumb during exhibition game . . . (January, 1981)—Infection in right arm . . . (January 24, 1981)—Hand infection developed after treatment for cut hand . . . (February, 1983)—Pulled stomach muscles . . . (January 24, 1984)—Strained ligaments in right knee at Montreal . . . (December 28, 1984)—Broke bone in left foot when hit by a Moe Mantha shot at Pittsburgh . . . (March 3, 1985)—Sprained left knee and ankle vs. Vancouver . . . (November 16, 1985)—Sprained ankle vs. Chicago and missed two games . . . (January 13, 1985)—Bruised shoulder vs. Detroit . . . (March 8, 1986)—Strained Achilles tendon vs. Chicago . . . (January, 1987)—Missed 38 games with a groin pull . . . (October, 1987)—Concussion . . . (November, 1987)—Badly stretched groin muscle.

Year	Team	League	Games	G.	A.	Pts.	Pen.
1975-76—Windsor Spitfires		OMJHL	59	3	13	16	169
1978-79—Toledo Goaldiggers		IHL	64	6	22	28	153
1979-80—New Haven Nighthawks		AHL	75	7	27	34	149
1980-81—New York Rangers (c)		NHL	54	4	12	16	153
1981-82—Hartford Whalers		NHL	68	13	20	33	147
1982-83—Hartford Whalers		NHL	68	6	24	30	125
1983-84—Hartford Whalers		NHL	72	5	13	18	118
1984-85—Hartford Whalers		NHL	33	5	3	8	53
1985-86—Toronto Maple Leafs (d)		NHL	61	6	11	17	83
1986-87—Toronto Maple Leafs		NHL	43	2	10	12	75
1987-88—Toronto Maple Leafs		NHL	21	2	2	4	19
NHL TOTALS			420	43	95	138	773

(c)—October, 1981—Traded with Doug Sulliman and Gerry McDonald by New York Rangers to Hartford Whalers for Mike Rogers and a 10th-round 1982 draft pick (Simo Saarinen).
(d)—October, 1985—Traded by Hartford Whalers to Toronto Maple Leafs for Stewart Gavin.

SEAN KRAKIWSKY

Right Wing ... 6' ... 175 lbs. ... Born, Calgary, Alta., December 29, 1967 ... Shoots left.

Year	Team	League	Games	G.	A.	Pts.	Pen.
1985-86—Univ. of Minnesota/Duluth		WCHA	10	0	4	4	2
1985-86—Calgary Wranglers (c)		WHL	39	9	32	41	27
1986-87—Spokane Chiefs		WHL	57	19	42	61	57
1987-88—New Haven Nighthawks		AHL	51	17	26	43	18

(c)—June, 1986—Drafted as underage junior by Los Angeles Kings in 1986 NHL entry draft. Sixth Kings pick, 128th overall, seventh round.

ROB KRAUSS

Defense ... 6'1" ... 210 lbs. ... Born, Grand Prairie, Alta., October 28, 1969 ... Shoots left.

Year	Team	League	Games	G.	A.	Pts.	Pen.
1983-84—Red Deer Moose Bantams		WHL	27	12	33	45	77
1984-85—Lethbridge Broncos		WHL	20	0	0	0	9
1985-86—Olds Grizzlys		AJHL	19	1	10	11	100
1985-86—Lethbridge Broncos		WHL	12	0	2	2	15
1986-87—Calgary Wranglers		WHL	70	3	17	20	130
1987-88—Lethbridge Hurricanes (c)		WHL	69	6	21	27	245

(c)—June, 1988—Drafted by Washington Capitals in 1988 NHL entry draft. Fifth Capitals pick, 78th overall, fourth round.

DALE KRENTZ

Left Wing ... 5'11" ... 185 lbs. ... Born, Steinbach, Man., December 19, 1961 ... Shoots left.

Year	Team	League	Games	G.	A.	Pts.	Pen.
1982-83—Michigan State Univ.		CCHA	42	11	24	35	50
1983-84—Michigan State Univ.		CCHA	44	12	20	32	34
1984-85—Michigan State Univ. (c)		CCHA	44	24	30	54	26
1985-86—Adirondack Red Wings		AHL	79	19	27	46	27
1986-87—Adirondack Red Wings		AHL	71	32	39	71	68
1986-87—Detroit Red Wings		NHL	8	0	0	0	0
1987-88—Adirondack Red Wings		AHL	67	39	43	82	65
1987-88—Detroit Red Wings		NHL	6	2	0	2	5
NHL TOTALS			14	2	0	2	5

(c)—June, 1985—Signed by Detroit Red Wings as a free agent.

RICHARD KROMM

Left Wing ... 5'11" ... 180 lbs. ... Born, Trail, B.C., March 29, 1964 ... Shoots left ... Son of Bobby Kromm (Member of World Champion 1961 Trail Smoke Eaters, and former WHA/NHL coach) ... (October, 1981)—Broken ankle ... Brother of David Kromm ... Also plays Center ... (February, 1985)—Pinched nerve ... (December 2, 1986)—Missed seven games with a sprained left knee at Edmonton ... (March, 1987)—Reinjured knee ... (February, 1988)—Fractured rib.

Year	Team	League	Games	G.	A.	Pts.	Pen.
1980-81—Windsor Royals		Jr. 'B'	39	22	31	53	40
1981-82—Portland Winter Hawks (c)		WHL	60	16	38	54	30
1982-83—Portland Winter Hawks		WHL	72	35	68	103	64
1983-84—Portland Winter Hawks		WHL	10	10	4	14	13
1983-84—Calgary Flames		NHL	53	11	12	23	27
1984-85—Calgary Flames		NHL	73	20	32	52	32

Year	Team	League	Games	G.	A.	Pts.	Pen.
1985-86—Calgary Flames (d)		NHL	63	12	17	29	31
1985-86—New York Islanders		NHL	14	7	7	14	4
1986-87—New York Islanders		NHL	70	12	17	29	20
1987-88—New York Islanders		NHL	71	5	10	15	20
NHL TOTALS			344	67	95	162	134

(c)—June, 1982—Drafted as underage junior by Calgary Flames in 1982 NHL entry draft. Second Flames pick, 37th overall, second round.

(d)—March, 1986—Traded by Calgary Flames with Steve Konroyd to New York Islanders for John Tonelli.

UWE KRUPP

Defense . . . 6'6" . . . 230 lbs. . . . Born, Cologne, West Germany, June 24, 1965 . . . Shoots right . . . (November, 1987)—Bruised hip . . . (April, 1988)—Injured head in playoff game vs. Boston.

Year	Team	League	Games	G.	A.	Pts.	Pen.
1986-87—Rochester Americans (c)		AHL	42	3	19	22	50
1986-87—Buffalo Sabres		NHL	26	1	4	5	23
1987-88—Buffalo Sabres		NHL	75	2	9	11	151
NHL TOTALS			101	3	13	16	174

(c)—June, 1983—Drafted by Buffalo Sabres in 1983 NHL entry draft. Thirteenth Sabres pick, 214th overall, 11th round.

GORDON KRUPPKE

Defense . . . 6'1" . . . 200 lbs. . . . Born, Edmonton, Alta., April 2, 1969 . . . Shoots right . . . (December, 1986)—Had his spleen removed . . . (October, 1987)—Injured left knee ligaments in WHL game.

Year	Team	League	Games	G.	A.	Pts.	Pen.
1984-85—Calgary Buffaloes		Alta. Midget	36	3	22	25	77
1985-86—Prince Albert Raiders		WHL	62	1	8	9	81
1985-86—Prince Albert Raiders (c)		WHL	49	2	10	12	129
1987-88—Prince Albert Raiders		WHL	54	8	8	16	113

(c)—June, 1987—Drafted as underage junior by Detroit Red Wings in 1987 NHL entry draft. Second Red Wings pick, 32nd overall, second round.

MIKE KRUSHELNYSKI

Left Wing and Center . . . 6'2" . . . 200 lbs. . . . Born, Montreal, Que., April 27, 1960 . . . Shoots left . . . Started the 1978-79 season at St. Louis University but left to return to junior hockey . . . (January, 1984)—Separated right shoulder . . . (December 10, 1985)—Sprained right knee at St. Louis and missed 17 games . . . (February 14, 1986)—Twisted knee vs. Quebec and missed nine games . . . (September, 1987)—Suspended by Edmonton Oilers for not reporting to training camp.

Year	Team	League	Games	G.	A.	Pts.	Pen.
1978-79—Montreal Juniors		QMJHL	46	15	29	44	42
1979-80—Montreal Juniors (c)		QMJHL	72	39	61	100	78
1980-81—Springfield Indians		AHL	80	25	38	53	47
1981-82—Erie Blades		AHL	62	31	52	83	44
1981-82—Boston Bruins		NHL	17	3	3	6	2
1982-83—Boston Bruins		NHL	79	23	42	65	43
1983-84—Boston Bruins (d)		NHL	66	25	20	45	55
1984-85—Edmonton Oilers		NHL	80	43	45	88	60
1985-86—Edmonton Oilers		NHL	54	16	24	40	22
1986-87—Edmonton Oilers		NHL	80	16	35	51	67
1987-88—Edmonton Oilers (e)		NHL	76	20	27	47	64
NHL TOTALS			452	146	196	342	313

(c)—August, 1979—Drafted by Boston Bruins as an underage junior in 1979 NHL entry draft. Seventh Bruins pick, 120th overall, sixth round.

(d)—June, 1984—Traded by Boston Bruins to Edmonton Oilers for Ken Linseman.

(e)—August, 1988—Traded with Wayne Gretzky and Marty McSorley by Edmonton Oilers to Los Angeles Kings for Jimmy Carson, Martin Gelinas, first-round draft choices in 1989, '91 and '93, plus cash in excess of $10 million.

MARK KRYS

Defense . . . 6' . . . 185 lbs. . . . Born, Timmons, Ont., May 29, 1969 . . . Shoots left.

Year	Team	League	Games	G.	A.	Pts.	Pen.
1986-87—St. Mike's Jr. A.		OHA	34	4	22	26	61
1987-88—Boston University (c)		H. East	34	0	6	6	40

(c)—June, 1988—Drafted by Boston Bruins in 1988 NHL entry draft. Sixth Bruins pick, 165th overall, eighth round.

BOB KUDELSKI

Center . . . 6'1" . . . 200 lbs. . . . Born, Springfield, Mass., March 3, 1964 . . . Shoots right.

Year	Team	League	Games	G.	A.	Pts.	Pen.
1983-84—Yale University		ECAC	21	14	12	26	12
1984-85—Yale University		ECAC	32	21	23	44	38
1985-86—Yale University (c)		ECAC	31	18	23	41	48
1986-87—Yale University		ECAC	30	25	22	47	34
1987-88—New Haven Nighthawks		AHL	50	15	19	34	41
1987-88—Los Angeles Kings		NHL	26	0	1	1	8
NHL TOTALS			26	0	1	1	8

(c)—October, 1986—Drafted by Los Angeles Kings in 1986 NHL supplemental draft.

STUART KULAK

Right Wing . . . 5'10" . . . 175 lbs. . . . Born, Edmonton, Alta., March 10, 1963 . . . Shoots right . . . Missed entire 1984-85 season with a torn abdominal muscle that required surgery . . . (January 27, 1987)—Separated shoulder at Vancouver . . . (March 14, 1987)—Struck in left eye by a deflected shot at Pittsburgh and required 12 stitches . . . (October, 1987)—Broken left thumb.

Year	Team	League	Games	G.	A.	Pts.	Pen.
1979-80—Sherwood Park Crusaders		AJHL	53	30	23	53	111
1979-80—Victoria Cougars		WHL	3	0	0	0	0
1980-81—Victoria Cougars (c)		WHL	72	23	24	47	43
1981-82—Victoria Cougars		WHL	71	38	50	88	92
1982-83—Victoria Cougars		WHL	50	29	33	62	130
1982-83—Vancouver Canucks		NHL	4	1	1	2	0
1983-84—Fredericton Express		AHL	52	12	16	28	55
1984-85—Vancouver Canucks		NHL	....	...	....	....	....
1985-86—Kalamazoo Wings		IHL	30	14	8	22	38
1985-86—Fredericton Express		AHL	3	1	0	1	0
1986-87—Vancouver Canucks (d)		NHL	28	1	1	2	37
1986-87—Edmonton Oilers (e)		NHL	23	3	1	4	41
1986-87—New York Rangers		NHL	3	0	0	0	0
1987-88—Moncton Golden Flames		AHL	37	9	12	21	58
1987-88—Quebec Nordiques (f)		NHL	14	1	1	2	28
NHL TOTALS			72	6	4	10	106

(c)—June, 1981—Drafted as underage junior by Vancouver Canucks in 1981 NHL entry draft. Fifth Canucks pick, 115th overall, sixth round.

(d)—December, 1986—Acquired by Edmonton Oilers on waivers from Vancouver Canucks.

(e)—March, 1987—Sent to New York Rangers by Edmonton Oilers as compensaton for Reijo Ruotsalainen signing with Edmonton. The Rangers also sent a 12th-round 1987 draft pick (Jesper Duus) to the Oilers as part of the deal.

(f)—December, 1987—Traded by Quebec Nordiques to Winnipeg Jets for Bobby Dollas.

RYAN KUMMU

Defense . . . 6'3" . . . 205 lbs. . . . Born, Kitchener, Ont., June 5, 1967 . . . Shoots left.

Year	Team	League	Games	G.	A.	Pts.	Pen.
1985-86—Rensselaer Poly. Inst.		ECAC	30	2	2	4	40
1985-86—Rensselaer Poly. Inst. (c)		ECAC	20	0	2	2	34
1987-88—Rensselaer Poly. Inst.		ECAC	29	5	10	15	16

(c)—June, 1987—Drafted by Washington Capitals in 1987 NHL entry draft. Eleventh Capitals pick, 246th overall, 12th round.

MARK KUMPEL

Right Wing . . . 6' . . . 190 lbs. . . . Born, Wakefield, Mass., March 7, 1961 . . . Shoots right . . . Member of 1984 U.S. Olympic team . . . (October, 1980)—Suffered knee ligament damage in first game and missed remainder of season . . . (October 21, 1985)—Missed three games after breaking hand at Montreal . . . (February 16, 1986)—Separated shoulder at Calgary . . . (March, 1987)—Broken wrist . . . (December, 1987)—Dislocated left thumb.

Year	Team	League	Games	G.	A.	Pts.	Pen.
1979-80—Lowell University (c)		ECAC	30	18	18	36	12
1980-81—Lowell University		ECAC	1	2	0	2	0
1981-82—Lowell University		ECAC	35	17	13	30	23
1982-83—Lowell University		ECAC	7	8	5	13	0
1982-83—U.S. National Team		Int'l	30	14	18	32	6
1983-84—U.S. National Team		Int'l	61	14	19	33	19
1983-84—U.S. Olympic Team		Int'l	6	1	0	1	2
1983-84—Fredericton Express		AHL	16	1	1	2	5
1984-85—Fredericton Express		AHL	18	9	6	15	17
1984-85—Quebec Nordiques		NHL	42	8	7	15	26
1985-86—Fredericton Express		AHL	7	4	2	6	4
1985-86—Quebec Nordiques		NHL	47	10	12	22	17
1986-87—Quebec Nordiques (d)		NHL	40	1	8	9	16
1986-87—Detroit Red Wings		NHL	5	0	1	1	0
1986-87—Adirondack Red Wings		AHL	7	2	3	5	0
1987-88—Adirondack Red Wings		AHL	4	5	0	5	2
1987-88—Detroit Red Wings (e)		NHL	13	0	2	2	4
1987-88—Winnipeg Jets		NHL	32	4	4	8	19
NHL TOTALS			179	23	34	57	82

(c)—June, 1980—Drafted by Quebec Nordiques in NHL entry draft. Fourth Nordiques pick, 108th overall, sixth round.

(d)—January, 1987—Traded with Brent Ashton and Gilbert Delorme by Quebec Nordiques to Detroit Red Wings for John Ogrodnick, Doug Shedden and Basil McRae.

(e)—January, 1988—Traded by Detroit Red Wings to Winnipeg Jets for Jim Nill.

RISTO KURKINEN

Right Wing . . . 5'9" . . . 185 lbs. . . . Born, Jyvaskyla, Finland, January 21, 1963 . . . Shoots right . . . (October, 1987)—Knee surgery.

Year	Team	League	Games	G.	A.	Pts.	Pen.
1986-87—Jypht (c)		Finland	44	41	19	60	25
1987-88—Muskegon Lumberjacks		IHL	40	17	22	39	10

(c)—June, 1987—Drafted by Pittsburgh Penguins in 1987 NHL entry draft. Fourth Penguins pick, 68th overall, fourth round.

JARI KURRI

Right Wing . . . 6' . . . 183 lbs. . . . Born, Helsinki, Finland, May 18, 1960 . . . Shoots right . . . Played on Finnish Olympic Team in 1980 . . . (November 24, 1981)—Pulled groin during Oilers practice . . . First Finland-born player to have 100-point season in NHL . . . (January, 1984)—Missed 16 games with a pulled groin muscle . . . (May, 1985)—Set NHL playoff record for hat tricks (4) and goals (12) in a single series (vs. Chicago) . . . (May, 1985)—Tied NHL playoff record with 19 goals for a single playoff season . . . (November 17, 1986)—Injured eye at N.Y. Rangers and missed two games . . . (1985-86)—First European to lead NHL in goals in one season.

Year	Team	League	Games	G.	A.	Pts.	Pen.
1977-78—Jokerit		Fin. Elite	29	2	9	11	12
1978-79—Jokerit		Fin. Elite	33	16	14	30	12
1979-80—Jokerit (c)		Fin. Elite	33	23	16	39	22
1980-81—Edmonton Oilers		NHL	75	32	43	75	40
1981-82—Edmonton Oilers		NHL	71	32	54	86	32
1982-83—Edmonton Oilers		NHL	80	45	59	104	22
1983-84—Edmonton Oilers (b-d)		NHL	64	52	61	113	14
1984-85—Edmonton Oilers (a-e-f)		NHL	73	71	64	135	30
1985-86—Edmonton Oilers (b)		NHL	78	*68	63	131	22
1986-87—Edmonton Oilers (a-g)		NHL	79	54	54	108	41
1987-88—Edmonton Oilers (d)		NHL	80	43	53	96	30
NHL TOTALS			600	397	451	848	231

(c)—June, 1980—Drafted by Edmonton Oilers in NHL entry draft. Third Oilers pick, 69th overall, fourth round.

(d)—Led Stanley Cup Playoffs with 14 goals.

(e)—Led Stanley Cup Playoffs with 19 goals.

(f)—Won Lady Byng Memorial Trophy (Combination of Sportsmanship and Quality play).

(g)—Led Stanley Cup Playoffs with 15 goals.

TOM KURVERS

Defense . . . 6' . . . 190 lbs. . . . Born, Minneapolis, Minn., October 14, 1962 . . . Shoots left . . . Set UMD record with 149 career assists . . . (October 23, 1984)—Missed five games when Mario Marois' shot deflected off Chris Chelios' stick and struck Kurvers in the nose and above the right eye . . . (November, 1987)—Fractured left index finger . . . (February, 1988)—Pulled groin . . . (May, 1988)—Injured right thumb in fight with Moe Lemay during playoff series vs. Boston.

Year	Team	League	Games	G.	A.	Pts.	Pen.
1980-81	University of Minnesota/Duluth (c)	WCHA	39	6	24	30	48
1981-82	University of Minnesota/Duluth	WCHA	37	11	31	42	18
1982-83	University of Minnesota/Duluth	WCHA	45	8	36	44	42
1983-84	University of Minn/Duluth (a-d-e)	WCHA	43	18	58	76	46
1984-85	Montreal Canadiens	NHL	75	10	35	45	30
1985-86	Montreal Canadiens	NHL	62	7	23	30	36
1986-87	Montreal Canadiens (f)	NHL	1	0	0	0	0
1986-87	Buffalo Sabres (g)	NHL	55	6	17	23	24
1987-88	New Jersey Devils	NHL	56	5	29	34	46
	NHL TOTALS		249	28	104	132	136

(c)—June, 1981—Drafted as underage player by Montreal Canadiens in 1981 NHL entry draft. Tenth Canadiens pick, 145th overall, seventh round.
(d)—Named to All-American Team (West).
(e)—Won Hobey Baker Award (Top NCAA Hockey Player).
(f)—November, 1986—Traded by Montreal Canadiens to Buffalo Sabres for a second-round 1988 draft pick (Martin St. Amour).
(g)—June, 1987—Traded by Buffalo Sabres to New Jersey Devils for a third-round 1988 draft pick.

MARK KURZAWSKI

Defense . . . 6'3" . . . 200 lbs. . . . Born, Chicago, Ill., February 25, 1968 . . . Shoots right.

Year	Team	League	Games	G.	A.	Pts.	Pen.
1984-85	Chicago Americans	Ill. Midget	63	23	37	60	88
1985-86	Windsor Spitfires (c)	OHL	66	11	26	37	66
1986-87	Windsor Spitfires	OHL	65	5	23	28	96
1987-88	Windsor Spitfires	OHL	62	8	13	21	150

(c)—June, 1986—Drafted by Chicago Black Hawks as an underage junior in 1986 NHL entry draft. Second Black Hawks pick, 35th overall, second round.

DALE KUSHNER

Left Wing . . . 6'1" . . . 205 lbs. . . . Born, Terrace, B.C., June 13, 1966 . . . Shoots left.

Year	Team	League	Games	G.	A.	Pts.	Pen.
1983-84	Fort McMurray	AJHL	44	15	6	21	139
1983-84	Prince Albert Raiders	WHL	1	0	0	0	5
1984-85	Prince Albert Raiders	WHL	2	0	0	0	2
1984-85	Moose Jaw Warriors	WHL	17	5	2	7	23
1984-85	Medicine Hat Tigers	WHL	48	23	17	40	173
1985-86	Medicine Hat Tigers	WHL	66	25	19	44	218
1986-87	Medicine Hat Tigers (c)	WHL	65	34	34	68	250
1987-88	Springfield Indians	AHL	68	13	23	36	201

(c)—March, 1987—Signed by New York Islanders as a free agent.

MARKKU KYLLONEN

Right Wing . . . 6'2" . . . 200 lbs. . . . Born, Joensgo, Finland, February 15, 1962 . . . Shoots right.

Year	Team	League	Games	G.	A.	Pts.	Pen.
1987-88	Karpat (c)	Finland	43	8	24	32	32

(c)—June, 1987—Drafted by Winnipeg Jets in 1987 NHL entry draft. Eighth Jets pick, 163rd overall, eighth round.

NICK KYPREOS

Left Wing . . . 6' . . . 190 lbs. . . . Born, Toronto, Ont., June 4, 1966 . . . Shoots left.

Year	Team	League	Games	G.	A.	Pts.	Pen.
1983-84	North Bay Centennials (c)	OHL	51	12	11	23	36
1984-85	North Bay Centennials	OHL	64	41	36	77	71
1985-86	North Bay Centennials (a)	OHL	64	62	35	97	112
1986-87	North Bay Centennials (b)	OHL	46	49	41	90	54
1986-87	Hershey Bears	AHL	10	0	1	1	4
1987-88	Hershey Bears	AHL	71	24	20	44	101

(c)—September, 1984—Signed by Philadelphia Flyers as a free agent.

JIM KYTE

Defense . . . 6'5" . . . 200 lbs. . . . Born, Ottawa, Ont., March 21, 1964 . . . Shoots left . . . Wears hearing aids when he plays . . . (March, 1980)—Broken left wrist . . . (February, 1988)—Stress fracture in lower back.

Year	Team	League	Games	G.	A.	Pts.	Pen.
1980-81—Hawksbury Hawks		Tier II	42	2	24	26	133
1981-82—Cornwall Royals (c)		OHL	52	4	13	17	148
1982-83—Cornwall Royals		OHL	65	6	30	36	195
1982-83—Winnipeg Jets		NHL	2	0	0	0	0
1983-84—Winnipeg Jets		NHL	58	1	2	3	55
1984-85—Winnipeg Jets		NHL	71	0	3	3	111
1985-86—Winnipeg Jets		NHL	71	1	3	4	126
1986-87—Winnipeg Jets		NHL	72	5	5	10	162
1987-88—Winnipeg Jets		NHL	51	1	3	4	128
NHL TOTALS			325	8	16	24	582

(c)—June, 1982—Drafted as underage junior by Winnipeg Jets in 1982 NHL entry draft. First Jets pick, 12th overall, first round.

NORMAND LACOMBE

Right Wing . . . 5'11" . . . 205 lbs. . . .Born, Pierrefond, Que., October 18, 1964 . . . Shoots right . . . (February 21, 1986)—Fractured jaw vs. N.Y. Islanders . . . (April, 1987)—Surgery for chronic compartment syndrome (a form of shin splints).

Year	Team	League	Games	G.	A.	Pts.	Pen.
1981-82—Univ. New Hampshire		ECAC	35	18	16	34	38
1982-83—Univ. New Hampshire (b-c)		ECAC	35	18	25	43	48
1983-84—Rochester Americans		AHL	44	10	16	26	45
1984-85—Rochester Americans		AHL	33	13	16	29	33
1984-85—Buffalo Sabres		NHL	30	2	4	6	25
1985-86—Rochester Americans		AHL	32	10	13	23	56
1985-86—Buffalo Sabres		NHL	25	6	7	13	13
1986-87—Rochester Americans		AHL	13	6	5	11	4
1986-87—Buffalo Sabres (d)		NHL	39	4	7	11	8
1986-87—Edmonton Oilers		NHL	1	0	0	0	2
1986-87—Nova Scotia Oilers		AHL	10	3	5	8	4
1987-88—Edmonton Oilers		NHL	53	8	9	17	36
NHL TOTALS			148	20	27	47	84

(c)—June, 1983—Drafted by Buffalo Sabres in 1983 NHL entry draft. Second Sabres pick, 10th overall, first round.

(d)—March, 1987—Traded with Wayne Van Dorp and future considerations by Buffalo Sabres to Edmonton Oilers for Lee Fogolin and Mark Napier.

DAVID LACOUTURE

Right Wing . . . 6'2" . . . 205 lbs. . . . Born, Framingham, Mass., December 30, 1969 . . . Shoots right . . . Brother of Billy Lacouture.

Year	Team	League	Games	G.	A.	Pts.	Pen.
1986-87—Natick H.S.		Mass. H.S.	..	15	33	48	..
1987-88—Natick H.S. (c)		Mass. H.S.	19	31	53	84	..

(c)—June, 1988—Drafted by St. Louis Blues in 1988 NHL entry draft. Fifth Blues pick, 105th overall, fifth round.

WILLIAM LACOUTURE

Right Wing . . . 6'2" . . . 192 lbs. . . . Born, Framingham, Mass., May 28, 1968 . . . Shoots right . . . Brother of David Lacouture.

Year	Team	League	Games	G.	A.	Pts.	Pen.
1985-86—Natick H.S.		Mass. H.S.	....	20	18	38	....
1986-87—Natick H.S. (c)		Mass. H.S.	19	15	39	54	....
1987-88—Univ. of New Hampshire		H. East	13	1	3	4	2

(c)—June, 1987—Drafted by Chicago Black Hawks in 1987 NHL entry draft. Eleventh Black Hawks pick, 218th overall, 11th round.

DANIEL LACROIX

Left Wing . . . 6'2" . . . 185 lbs. . . . Born, Montreal, Que., March 11, 1969 . . . Shoots left.

Year	Team	League	Games	G.	A.	Pts.	Pen.
1985-86—Hull Frontaliers		Que. Midget	37	10	13	23	46
1986-87—Granby Bisons (c)		QHL	54	9	16	25	311
1987-88—Granby Bisons		QHL	58	24	50	74	468

(c)—June, 1987—Drafted as underage junior by New York Rangers in 1987 NHL entry draft. Second Rangers pick, 31st overall, second round.

RANDY LADOUCEUR

Defense . . . 6'2" . . . 220 lbs. . . . Born, Brockville, Ont., June 30, 1960 . . . Shoots left . . . (March, 1986)—Back spasms.

Year	Team	League	Games	G.	A.	Pts.	Pen.
1978-79—Brantford Alexanders		OMJHL	64	3	17	20	141
1979-80—Brantford Alexanders (c)		OMJHL	37	6	15	21	125
1980-81—Kalamazoo Wings		IHL	80	7	30	37	52
1981-82—Adirondack Red Wings		AHL	78	4	28	32	78
1982-83—Adirondack Red Wings		AHL	48	11	21	32	54
1982-83—Detroit Red Wings		NHL	27	0	4	4	16
1983-84—Adirondack Red Wings		AHL	11	3	5	8	12
1983-84—Detroit Red Wings		NHL	71	3	17	20	58
1984-85—Detroit Red Wings		NHL	80	3	27	30	108
1985-86—Detroit Red Wings		NHL	78	5	13	18	196
1986-87—Detroit Red Wings (d)		NHL	34	3	6	9	70
1986-87—Hartford Whalers		NHL	36	2	3	5	51
1987-88—Hartford Whalers		NHL	68	1	7	8	91
NHL TOTALS			394	17	77	94	590

(c)—November, 1979—Signed by Detroit Red Wings as a free agent
(d)—January, 1987—Traded by Detroit Red Wings to Hartford Whalers for Dave Barr.

JUSTIN LAFAYETTE

Left Wing . . . 6'6" . . . 200 lbs. . . . Born, Vancouver, B.C., January 23, 1970 . . . Shoots left . . . Son of David Lafayette (Played professional football with the B.C. Lions).

Year	Team	League	Games	G.	A.	Pts.	Pen.
1986-87—Mississauga Reps. Midget		OHA	42	24	28	52	....
1987-88—Ferris State College (c)		CCHA	36	1	2	3	20

(c)—June, 1988—Drafted by Chicago Black Hawks in 1988 NHL entry draft. Fifth Black Hawks pick, 113th overall, sixth round.

GUY DAMIEN LAFLEUR

Right Wing and Center . . . 6' . . . 175 lbs. . . . Born, Thurso, Que., September 20, 1951 . . . Shoots right . . . Missed part of 1974-75 season with fractured index finger . . . Youngest player to score 400 NHL-career goals (Broken by Wayne Gretzky) . . . Missed conclusion of 1979-80 season and playoffs with knee injury . . . (October 8, 1980)—Pulled right hamstring . . . (November, 1980)—Tonsilitis . . . (December 30, 1980)—Injured his right eye when struck by errant stick . . . (February, 1981)—Nine stitch cut under eye . . . (March 4, 1981)—Collected 1,000th NHL point in his 720th game, faster than any player in NHL history (Broken by Wayne Gretzky) . . . (March, 1981)—Charley horse . . . (March 24, 1981)—Fell asleep at the wheel of his car, hit a fence and a metal sign post sliced off the top part of his right ear after the post went through his windshield . . . (November 10, 1981)—Errant stick entered eye at Los Angeles . . . (March 11, 1982)—Bruised bone of left foot when hit by puck vs. Chicago . . . (October 11, 1982)—Eye injured at Quebec . . . (November 4, 1982)—Broke little toe on right foot at Minnesota . . . Holds Montreal Canadien club career records for most assists and points . . . 1988 Hall-of-Fame Inductee.

Year	Team	League	Games	G.	A.	Pts.	Pen.
1966-67—Quebec Jr. Aces		QJHL	8	1	1	2	0
1967-68—Quebec Jr. Aces		QJHL	43	30	19	49	....
1968-69—Quebec Jr. Aces		QJHL	49	50	60	110	83
1969-70—Quebec Remparts		QJHL	56	*103	67	170	89
1970-71—Quebec Remparts (c)		QJHL	62	*130	79	*209	135
1971-72—Montreal Canadiens		NHL	73	29	35	64	48
1972-73—Montreal Canadiens		NHL	69	28	27	55	51
1973-74—Montreal Canadiens		NHL	73	21	35	56	29
1974-75—Montreal Canadiens (a-d-e)		NHL	70	53	66	119	37
1975-76—Montreal Canadiens (a-f)		NHL	80	56	69	*125	36
1976-77—Montreal Canadiens (a-f-g-h-i-j)		NHL	80	56	*80	*136	20
1977-78—Montreal Canadiens (a-f-g-h-k)		NHL	78	*60	72	*132	26
1978-79—Montreal Canadiens (a-l)		NHL	80	52	77	129	28
1979-80—Montreal Canadiens (a)		NHL	74	50	75	125	12
1980-81—Montreal Canadiens		NHL	51	27	43	70	29
1981-82—Montreal Canadiens		NHL	66	27	99	84	24
1982-83—Montreal Canadiens		NHL	68	27	49	76	12
1983-84—Montreal Canadiens		NHL	80	30	40	70	19
1984-85—Montreal Canadiens (m)		NHL	19	2	3	5	10
1985-86—Did not play			....	...	...	...	...
1986-87—Did not play			....	...	...	...	...
1987-88—Did not play (n)			....	...	...	...	...
NHL TOTALS			961	518	728	1246	381

(c)—Drafted from Quebec Remparts by Montreal Canadiens in first round of 1971 amateur draft.
(d)—Led Stanley Cup Playoffs with 12 goals.
(e)—Selected Most Valuable Player in Prince of Wales Conference in poll of players by THE SPORTING NEWS.

(f)—Won Art Ross Memorial Trophy (NHL Leading Scorer).
(g)—Won Hart Memorial Trophy (Most Valuable Player).
(h)—Selected THE SPORTING NEWS' NHL Player-of-the-Year in poll of NHL players.
(i)—Led Stanley Cup Playoffs with 17 assists and 26 points.
(j)—Won Conn Smythe Trophy (MVP in Stanley Cup playoffs).
(k)—Led Stanley Cup Playoffs with 10 goals and tied for lead with 21 points.
(l)—Tied for lead in Stanley Cup Playoffs with 13 assists and 23 points.
(m)—November, 1984—Announced retirement.
(n)—August, 1988—Signed by New York Rangers as a free agent.

PAT La FONTAINE

Center . . . 5'9" . . . 170 lbs. . . . Born, St. Louis, Mo., February 22, 1965 . . . Shoots right . . . Set Quebec Junior League records (1982-83) with points in 43 consecutive games (since broken by Mario Lemieux), and most goals (104), assists (130) and points (234) by a Quebec Junior League Rookie . . . Member of 1984 U.S. Olympic team . . . (August 16, 1984)—Damaged ligaments in left knee when checked by Team Canada's Scott Stevens in pre-Canada Cup game at Bloomington, Minn. . . . (January, 1985)—Mononucleosis . . . (January 25, 1986)—Separated right shoulder vs. Chicago . . . (March, 1988)—Bruised knee.

Year	Team	League	Games	G.	A.	Pts.	Pen.
1981-82—Detroit Compuware		Mich. Midget	79	175	149	324	...
1982-83—Verdun Juniors (a-c-d-e-f-g)		QHL	70	*104	*130	*234	10
1983-84—U.S. National Team		Int'l	58	56	55	111	22
1983-84—U.S. Olympic Team		Int'l	6	5	5	10	0
1983-84—New York Islanders		NHL	15	13	6	19	6
1984-85—New York Islanders		NHL	67	19	35	54	32
1985-86—New York Islanders		NHL	65	30	23	53	43
1986-87—New York Islanders		NHL	80	38	32	70	70
1987-88—New York Islanders		NHL	75	47	45	92	52
NHL TOTALS			302	147	141	288	203

(c)—Won Frank Selke Trophy (Most Gentlemanly Player).
(d)—Won Des Instructeurs Trophy (Top Rookie Forward).
(e)—Won Jean Beliveau Trophy (Leading Scorer).
(f)—Won Guy Lafleur Trophy (Playoff MVP).
(g)—June, 1983—Drafted as underage junior by New York Islanders in 1983 NHL entry draft. First Islanders pick, third overall, first round.

MARC LAFORGE

Defense . . . 6'2" . . . 200 lbs. . . . Born, Sudbury, Ont., January 3, 1968 . . . Shoots left . . . (October, 1986)—Suspended for nine games by OHL . . . (November 6, 1987)—Given a two-year suspension by OHL for attacking several members of the Guelph Platers after a game.

Year	Team	League	Games	G.	A.	Pts.	Pen.
1984-85—Kingston Canadians		OHL	57	1	5	6	214
1985-86—Kingston Canadians (c)		OHL	60	1	13	14	248
1986-87—Kingston Canadians		OHL	53	2	10	12	224
1986-87—Binghamton Whalers (d)		AHL	..	..	..	..	..
1987-88—Sudbury Wolves		OHL	14	0	2	2	68

(c)—June, 1986—Drafted as underage junior by Hartford Whalers in 1986 NHL entry draft. Second Whalers pick, 32nd overall, second round.
(d)—No regular season record. Played four playoff games.

JASON LAFRENIERE

Center . . . 6' . . . 185 lbs. . . . Born, St. Catharines, Ont., December 6, 1966 . . . Shoots right . . . Son of Roger Lafreniere (Detroit 1962-63, and St. Louis 1972-73. He played several seasons in the old WHL, AHL and CPHL).

Year	Team	League	Games	G.	A.	Pts.	Pen.
1982-83—Orillia Travelways		OHA	48	17	40	57	9
1983-84—Brantford Alexanders		OHL	70	24	57	81	4
1984-85—Hamilton Steelhawks (c)		OHL	59	26	69	95	10
1985-86—Hamilton Steelhawks (d)		OHL	14	12	10	22	2
1985-86—Belleville Bulls (a-e)		OHL	48	37	73	110	2
1986-87—Fredericton Express		AHL	11	3	11	14	0
1986-87—Quebec Nordiques		NHL	56	13	15	28	8
1987-88—Fredericton Express		AHL	32	12	19	31	38
1987-88—Quebec Nordiques (f)		NHL	40	10	19	29	4
NHL TOTALS			96	23	34	57	12

(c)—June, 1985—Drafted as underage junior by Quebec Nordiques in 1985 NHL entry draft. Second Nordiques pick, 36th overall, second round.

(d)—November, 1985—Traded with Lawrence Hinch and Peter Choma by Hamilton Steelhawks to Belleville Bulls for Sean Doyl, John Purves and Brian Hoard.
(e)—Won William Hanley Trophy (Most Gentlemanly Player).
(f)—August, 1988—Traded with Normand Rochefort by Quebec Nordiques to New York Rangers for Walt Poddubny, Bruce Bell, Jari Gronstrand and fourth-round draft choice in 1989.

TOM LAIDLAW

Defense . . . 6'2" . . . 215 lbs. . . . Born, Brampton, Ont., April 15, 1958 . . . Shoots left . . . (December, 1984)—Spleen surgery . . . (March 12, 1986)—Back spasms . . . (October 8, 1987)—Sprained medial collateral ligament in right knee in opening game of season at Edmonton.

Year	Team	League	Games	G.	A.	Pts.	Pen.
1978-79	Northern Michigan Univ. (c)	CCHA	29	10	20	30	137
1979-80	Northern Michigan Univ. (a-d)	CCHA	39	8	30	38	83
1979-80	New Haven Nighthawks	AHL	1	0	0	0	0
1980-81	New York Rangers	NHL	80	6	23	29	100
1981-82	New York Rangers	NHL	79	3	18	21	104
1982-83	New York Rangers	NHL	80	0	10	10	75
1983-84	New York Rangers	NHL	79	3	15	18	62
1984-85	New York Rangers	NHL	61	1	11	12	52
1985-86	New York Rangers	NHL	68	6	12	18	103
1986-87	New York Rangers (e)	NHL	63	1	10	11	65
1986-87	Los Angeles Kings	NHL	11	0	3	3	4
1987-88	Los Angeles Kings	NHL	57	1	12	13	47
	NHL TOTALS		578	21	114	135	612

(c)—June, 1978—Drafted by New York Rangers in 1978 NHL amateur draft. Seventh Rangers pick, 93rd overall, sixth round.
(d)—Named to All-NCAA-Tournament team.
(e)—March, 1987—Traded with Bobby Carpenter by New York Rangers to Los Angeles Kings for Marcel Dionne, Jeff Crossman and a third round 1989 draft pick.

BOB LAKSO

Left Wing . . . 6' . . . 180 lbs. . . . Born, Baltimore, Md., April 3, 1962 . . . Shoots left.

Year	Team	League	Games	G.	A.	Pts.	Pen.
1980-81	Univ. of Minnesota/Duluth (c)	WCHA	36	7	6	13	2
1981-82	Univ. of Minnesota/Duluth	WCHA	28	12	11	23	8
1982-83	Univ. of Minnesota/Duluth	WCHA	45	18	25	43	8
1983-84	Univ. of Minnesota/Duluth	WCHA	43	32	34	66	12
1984-85	Indianapolis Checkers	IHL	76	26	32	58	4
1984-85	Springfield Indians	AHL	8	2	1	3	0
1985-86	Indianapolis Checkers	IHL	58	41	35	76	4
1985-86	Springfield Indians	AHL	17	3	6	9	2
1986-87	Indianapolis Checkers	IHL	79	39	55	94	6
1987-88	Milwaukee Admirals	IHL	80	43	28	71	10

(c)—June, 1980—Drafted by Minnesota North Stars in NHL entry draft. Ninth North Stars pick, 184th overall, ninth round.

TODD LALONDE

Left Wing . . . 6' . . . 190 lbs. . . . Born, Sudbury, Ont., August 4, 1969 . . . Shoots left . . . (December, 1986)—Sprained knee.

Year	Team	League	Games	G.	A.	Pts.	Pen.
1984-85	Garson Midget	OHA	29	38	38	76	42
1985-86	Sudbury Wolves	OHL	57	17	30	47	43
1986-87	Sudbury Wolves (c)	OHL	29	5	11	16	71
1987-88	Sudbury Wolves	OHL	59	27	43	70	79

(c)—June, 1987—Drafted as underage junior by Boston Bruins in 1987 NHL entry draft. Third Bruins pick, 56th overall, third round.

JOHN MICHAEL (MIKE) LALOR

Defense . . . 6' . . . 190 lbs. . . . Born, Fort Erie, Ont., March 8, 1963 . . . Shoots left . . . (September, 1987)—Bursitis in right ankle during Montreal training camp.

Year	Team	League	Games	G.	A.	Pts.	Pen.
1981-82	Brantford Alexanders	OHL	64	3	13	16	114
1982-83	Brantford Alexanders	OHL	65	10	30	40	113
1983-84	Nova Scotia Voyageurs (c)	AHL	67	5	11	16	80
1984-85	Sherbrooke Canadiens	AHL	79	9	23	32	114
1985-86	Montreal Canadiens	NHL	62	3	5	8	56

Year	Team	League	Games	G.	A.	Pts.	Pen.
1986-87—Montreal Canadiens		NHL	57	0	10	10	47
1987-88—Montreal Canadiens		NHL	66	1	10	11	113
NHL TOTALS			185	4	25	29	216

(c)—September, 1983—Signed by Nova Scotia Voyageurs as a free agent.

ERIC LaMARQUE

Right Wing . . . 5'10" . . . 183 lbs. . . . Born, Canoga Park, Calif., July 1, 1969 . . . Shoots right.

Year	Team	League	Games	G.	A.	Pts.	Pen.
1986-87—Northern Michigan Univ. (c)		WCHA	38	5	12	17	49
1987-88—Northern Michigan Univ.		WCHA	39	8	22	30	54

(c)—June, 1987—Drafted by Boston Bruins in 1987 NHL entry draft. Twelfth Bruins pick, 224th overall, 11th round.

JEFF LAMB

Center . . . 5'11" . . . 170 lbs. . . . Born, Waterloo, Iowa, July 14, 1964 . . . Shoots left.

Year	Team	League	Games	G.	A.	Pts.	Pen.
1983-84—Austin Mavericks		USHL	24	25	21	46	18
1983-84—Univ. of Denver		WCHA	15	0	2	2	8
1984-85—Univ. of Denver		WCHA	39	14	25	39	62
1985-86—Univ. of Denver (c)		WCHA	45	23	31	54	75
1986-87—Univ. of Denver		WCHA	40	10	24	34	58
1987-88—Maine Mariners		AHL	57	7	12	19	96

(c)—June, 1986—Selected by Pittsburgh Penguins in 1986 NHL supplemental draft.

MARK LAMB

Left Wing . . . 5'9" . . . 170 lbs. . . . Born, Swift Current, Sask., August 3, 1964 . . . Shoots left . . . (December, 1982)—Refused, with team captain Bob Rouse, to dress for a game after Nanaimo (WHL) released coach Les Calder. Both players asked to be traded . . . Also plays Center . . . Brother of Garth Lamb (Currently in WHL).

Year	Team	League	Games	G.	A.	Pts.	Pen.
1980-81—Billings Bighorns		WHL	24	1	8	9	12
1981-82—Billings Bighorns (c)		WHL	72	45	56	101	46
1982-83—Nanaimo Islanders (d)		WHL	30	14	37	51	16
1982-83—Medicine Hat Tigers		WHL	46	22	43	65	33
1983-84—Medicine Hat Tigers (a-e)		WHL	72	59	77	136	30
1984-85—Medicine Hat Tigers (f)		WHL	..	..	..	..	..
1984-85—Moncton Golden Flames		AHL	80	23	49	72	53
1985-86—Calgary Flames		NHL	1	0	0	0	0
1985-86—Moncton Golden Flames		AHL	79	26	50	76	51
1986-87—Detroit Red Wings		NHL	22	2	1	3	8
1986-87—Adirondack Red Wings		AHL	49	14	36	50	45
1987-88—Nova Scotia Oilers (g)		AHL	69	27	61	88	45
1987-88—Edmonton Oilers		NHL	2	0	0	0	0
NHL TOTALS			25	2	1	3	8

(c)—June, 1982—Drafted as underage junior by Calgary Flames in 1982 NHL entry draft. Fifth Flames pick, 72nd overall, fourth round.

(d)—December, 1982—Traded by Nanaimo Islanders to Medicine Hat Tigers for Glen Kulka and Daryl Reaugh.

(e)—Won Frank Boucher Memorial Trophy (Most Gentlemanly Player).

(f)—Played six playoff games (3 goals, 2 assists).

(g)—October, 1987—Acquired by Edmonton Oilers on waivers from Detroit Red Wings.

LANE LAMBERT

Right Wing . . . 6' . . . 175 lbs. . . . Born, Melfort, Sask., November 18, 1964 . . . Shoots right . . . (September, 1982)—Eye injured vs. Brandon . . . (March, 1985)—Surgery to left knee . . . (October, 1986)—Missed 26 games with an injured hip flexor . . . (December, 1987)—Complex fracture of second finger on left hand.

Year	Team	League	Games	G.	A.	Pts.	Pen.
1980-81—Swift Current Broncos		SJHL	55	43	54	97	63
1981-82—Saskatoon Blades		WHL	72	45	69	114	111
1982-83—Saskatoon Blades (b-c)		WHL	64	59	60	119	126
1983-84—Detroit Red Wings		NHL	73	20	15	35	115
1984-85—Detroit Red Wings		NHL	69	14	11	25	104
1985-86—Adirondack Red Wings		AHL	45	16	25	41	69
1985-86—Detroit Red Wings (d)		NHL	34	2	3	5	130
1986-87—New Haven Nighthawks		AHL	11	3	3	6	19
1986-87—New York Rangers (e)		NHL	18	2	2	4	33

Year	Team	League	Games	G.	A.	Pts.	Pen.
1986-87—Quebec Nordiques		NHL	15	5	6	11	18
1987-88—Quebec Nordiques		NHL	61	13	27	40	98
NHL TOTALS			270	56	64	120	498

(c)—June, 1983—Drafted as underage junior by Detroit Red Wings in 1983 NHL entry draft. Second Red Wings pick, 25th overall, second round.

(d)—July, 1986—Traded with Kelly Kisio, Jim Leavins and a fifth-round 1988 draft pick by Detroit Red Wings to New York Rangers for Glen Hanlon, third round 1987 (Dennis Holland) and 1988 draft picks and future considerations.

(e)—March, 1987—Traded by New York Rangers to Quebec Nordiques for Pat Price.

RICHARD LAMBERT

Left Wing . . . 6' . . . 196 lbs. . . . Born, Toronto, Ont., September 9, 1966 . . . Shoots left.

Year	Team	League	Games	G.	A.	Pts.	Pen.
1983-84—Henry Carr H.S. (c)		MTJHL	81	41	62	103	108
1984-85—......			..	..	..	..	..
1985-86—Univ. of New Hampshire		H. East	37	9	7	16	39
1986-87—Univ. of New Hampshire		H. East	34	1	5	6	63
1987-88—Univ. of New Hampshire		H. East	25	4	4	8	48

(c)—June, 1984—Drafted by Edmonton Oilers in 1984 NHL entry draft. Fifth Oilers pick, 105th overall, fifth round.

HANK LAMMENS

Defense . . . 6'2" . . . 196 lbs. . . . Born, Brockville, Ont., February 21, 1966 . . . Shoots left . . . (November, 1984)—Broken wrist and separated shoulder.

Year	Team	League	Games	G.	A.	Pts.	Pen.
1983-84—Brockville Braves		OHA	46	7	11	18	106
1984-85—St. Lawrence Univ. (c)		ECAC	21	1	7	8	16
1985-86—St. Lawrence Univ.		ECAC	30	3	14	17	60
1986-87—St. Lawrence Univ. (b-d)		ECAC	35	6	13	19	92
1987-88—St. Lawrence Univ.		ECAC	36	3	7	10	70

(c)—June, 1985—Drafted by New York Islanders in 1985 NHL entry draft. Tenth Islanders pick, 160th overall, 10th round.

(d)—Named to U.S. College second-team All-America (East).

MITCH LAMOUREUX

Center . . . 5'6" . . . 185 lbs. . . . Born, Ottawa, Ont., August 22, 1962 . . . Shoots left . . . Set AHL record for most goals by a rookie (57) in 1982-83, and most goals by an AHL player.

Year	Team	League	Games	G.	A.	Pts.	Pen.
1979-80—Oshawa Generals		OMJHL	67	28	48	76	63
1980-81—Oshawa Generals (c)		OMJHL	63	50	69	119	256
1981-82—Oshawa Generals		OHL	66	43	78	121	275
1982-83—Baltimore Skipjacks (b-d)		AHL	80	*57	50	107	107
1983-84—Baltimore Skipjacks		AHL	68	30	38	68	136
1983-84—Pittsburgh Penguins		NHL	8	1	1	2	6
1984-85—Pittsburgh Penguins		NHL	62	11	8	19	53
1984-85—Baltimore Skipjacks		AHL	18	10	14	24	34
1985-86—Baltimore Skipjacks		AHL	75	22	31	53	129
1986-87—Hershey Bears		AHL	78	43	46	89	122
1987-88—Philadelphia Flyers		NHL	3	0	0	0	0
1987-88—Hershey Bears		AHL	78	35	52	87	171
NHL TOTALS			73	12	9	21	59

(c)—June, 1981—Drafted as underage junior by Pittsburgh Penguins in 1981 NHL entry draft. Sixth Penguins pick, 154th overall, eighth round.

(d)—Won Dudley (Red) Garrett Memorial Trophy (Top AHL Rookie).

ROD CORRY LANGWAY

Defense . . . 6'3" . . . 215 lbs. . . . Born, Maag, Taiwan, May 3, 1957 . . . Shoots left . . . Attended University of New Hampshire and was member of football and hockey teams . . . Brother of Kim Langway . . . (January 5, 1982)—Bruised left foot vs. Boston . . . (February 9, 1982)—Injured left knee in NHL All-Star game. Examination in March discovered dried blood in the knee which had weakened the muscle in his left leg . . . (October 23, 1985)—Bruised right knee vs. Calgary and missed eight games . . . (November, 1987)—Ruptured disc in back . . . (February, 1988)—Pulled thigh muscle . . . (April, 1988)—Charley Horse . . . Does not wear a helmet.

Year	Team	League	Games	G.	A.	Pts.	Pen.
1975-76—University of New Hampshire	ECAC	..	..	..	..	....
1976-77—Univ. of New Hampshire (c-d)	ECAC	34	10	43	53	52
1977-78—Hampton Gulls	AHL	30	6	16	22	50
1977-78—Birmingham Bulls	WHA	52	3	18	21	52
1978-79—Montreal Canadiens (e)	NHL	45	3	4	7	30
1978-79—Nova Scotia Voyageurs	AHL	18	6	13	19	29
1979-80—Montreal Canadiens	NHL	77	7	29	36	81
1980-81—Montreal Canadiens	NHL	80	11	34	45	120
1981-82—Montreal Canadiens (f)	NHL	66	5	34	39	116
1982-83—Washington Capitals (a-g)	NHL	80	3	29	32	75
1983-84—Washington Capitals (a-g)	NHL	80	9	24	33	61
1984-85—Washington Capitals (b)	NHL	79	4	22	26	54
1985-86—Washington Capitals	NHL	71	1	17	18	61
1986-87—Washington Capitals	NHL	78	2	25	27	53
1987-88—Washington Capitals	NHL	63	3	13	16	28
WHA TOTALS			52	3	18	21	53
NHL TOTALS			719	48	231	279	679

(c)—Drafted from University of New Hampshire by Montreal Canadiens in second round of 1977 amateur draft.
(d)—May, 1977—Selected by Birmingham Bulls in World Hockey Association amateur players' draft.
(e)—October, 1978—Signed by Montreal Canadiens as free agent.
(f)—September, 1982—Traded by Montreal Canadiens with Brian Engblom, Doug Jarvis and Craig Laughlin to Washington Capitals for Ryan Walter and Rick Green.
(g)—Won James Norris Memorial Trophy (Top NHL Defenseman).

MARC LANIEL

Defense . . . 6'1" . . . 185 lbs. . . . Born, Oshawa, Ont., January 16, 1968 . . . Shoots left.

Year	Team	League	Games	G.	A.	Pts.	Pen.
1984-85—Toronto Red Wings	MTHL	37	15	28	43	68
1985-86—Oshawa Generals (c)	OHL	66	9	25	34	27
1986-87—Oshawa Generals	OHL	63	14	31	45	42
1987-88—Oshawa Generals	OHL	41	8	32	40	56
1987-88—Utica Devils	AHL	2	0	0	0	0

(c)—June, 1986—Drafted as underage junior by New Jersey Devils in 1986 NHL entry draft. Fourth Devils pick, 62nd overall, third round.

JEAN-MARC LANTHIER

Right Wing . . . 6'2" . . . 198 lbs. . . . Born, Montreal, Que., March 27, 1963 . . . Shoots right.

Year	Team	League	Games	G.	A.	Pts.	Pen.
1979-80—Quebec Remparts	QMJHL	63	14	32	46	4
1980-81—Quebec Remparts (c)	QMJHL	37	13	32	45	18
1980-81—Sorel Black Hawks (d)	QMJHL	35	6	33	39	29
1981-82—Laval Voisins (e)	QMJHL	60	44	34	78	48
1982-83—Laval Voisins	QHL	69	39	71	110	54
1983-84—Fredericton Express	AHL	60	25	17	42	29
1983-84—Vancouver Canucks	NHL	11	2	1	3	2
1984-85—Fredericton Express	AHL	50	21	21	42	13
1984-85—Vancouver Canucks	NHL	27	6	4	10	13
1985-86—Fredericton Express	AHL	7	5	5	10	2
1985-86—Vancouver Canucks	NHL	62	7	10	17	12
1986-87—Fredericton Express	AHL	78	15	38	53	24
1987-88—Vancouver Canucks	NHL	5	1	1	2	2
1987-88—Fredericton Express (f)	AHL	74	35	71	106	37
NHL TOTALS			105	16	16	32	29

(c)—December, 1980—Traded by Quebec Remparts to Sorel Black Hawks for Andre Cote.
(d)—June, 1981—Drafted as underage junior by Vancouver Canucks in 1981 NHL entry draft. Second Canucks pick, 52nd overall, third round.
(e)—August, 1981—Acquired by Laval Voisins in QMJHL dispersal draft of players from defunct Sorel Black Hawks.
(f)—July, 1988—Signed by Boston Bruins as a free agent.

RICK ROMAN LANZ

Defense . . . 6'1" . . . 195 lbs. . . . Born, Karlouyvary, Czechoslovakia, September 16, 1961 . . . Shoots right . . . (January, 1982)—Surgery to repair torn knee ligaments . . . (December, 1984)—Dislocated disk in neck and missed 23 games . . . (October 16, 1986)—Broke jaw when struck by Derrick Smith at Philadelphia . . . (January, 1988)—Asthma . . . (April, 1988)—Sprained neck.

Year	Team	League	Games	G.	A.	Pts.	Pen.
1977-78—Oshawa Generals		OMJHL	65	1	41	42	51
1978-79—Oshawa Generals		OMJHL	65	12	47	59	88
1979-80—Oshawa Generals (b-c)		OMJHL	52	18	38	56	51
1980-81—Vancouver Canucks		NHL	76	7	22	29	40
1981-82—Vancouver Canucks		NHL	39	3	11	14	48
1982-83—Vancouver Canucks		NHL	74	10	38	48	46
1983-84—Vancouver Canucks		NHL	79	18	39	57	45
1984-85—Vancouver Canucks		NHL	57	2	17	19	69
1985-86—Vancouver Canucks		NHL	75	15	38	53	73
1986-87—Vancouver Canucks (d)		NHL	17	1	6	7	10
1986-87—Toronto Maple Leafs		NHL	44	2	19	21	32
1987-88—Toronto Maple Leafs		NHL	75	6	22	28	65
NHL TOTALS			536	64	212	276	428

(c)—June, 1980—Drafted as underage junior in 1980 NHL entry draft by Vancouver Canucks. First Canucks pick, seventh overall, first round

(d)—December, 1986—Traded by Vancouver Canucks to Toronto Maple Leafs for Jim Benning and Dan Hodgson.

CLAUDE LAPOINTE

Left Wing . . . 5'9" . . . 173 lbs. . . . Born, Ville Emard, Que., October 11, 1968 . . . Shoots left.

Year	Team	League	Games	G.	A.	Pts.	Pen.
1985-86—Trois-Rivieres Draveurs		QHL	72	19	38	57	74
1986-87—Trois-Rivieres Draveurs (c)		QHL	70	47	57	104	123
1987-88—Laval Titans (d)		QHL	69	37	83	120	143

(c)—May, 1987—Traded with Alain Dubeau and a third-round draft pick (Patrice Brisbois) by Trois-Rivieres Draveurs to Laval Titans for Raymond Saumier, Mike Gober, Eric Gobeil and a second round draft pick (Eric Charron).

(d)—June, 1988—Drafted by Quebec Nordiques in 1988 NHL entry draft. Twelfth Nordiques pick, 234th overall, 12th round.

PETER LAPPIN

Center . . . 5'11' . . . 180 lbs. . . . Born, St. Charles, Ill., December 31, 1965 . . . Shoots right . . . (January, 1988)—Injured knee.

Year	Team	League	Games	G.	A.	Pts.	Pen.
1984-85—St. Lawrence Univ.		ECAC	32	10	12	22	22
1985-86—St. Lawrence Univ.		ECAC	30	20	26	46	64
1986-87—St. Lawrence Univ. (b-c)		ECAC	35	34	24	58	32
1987-88—St. Lawrence Univ. (d)		ECAC	34	21	39	60	30
1987-88—Salt Lake Golden Eagles		IHL	3	1	1	2	0

(c)—June, 1987—Selected by Calgary Flames in 1987 NHL supplemental draft.

(d)—Named to second All-America team (East).

JAMES LARKIN

Left Wing . . . 6' . . . 170 lbs. . . . Born, South Weymouth, Mass., April 15, 1970 . . . Shoots left.

Year	Team	League	Games	G.	A.	Pts.	Pen.
1986-87—Mt. St. Joseph H.S.		Vt. H.S.	..	30	26	56	..
1987-88—Mt. St. Joseph H.S. (c)		Vt. H.S.	..	44	41	85	..

(c)—June, 1988—Drafted by Los Angeles Kings in 1988 NHL entry draft. Tenth Kings pick, 175th overall, ninth round.

STEVE DONALD LARMER

Right Wing . . . 5'10" . . . 185 lbs. . . . Born, Peterborough, Ont., June 16, 1961 . . . Shoots left . . . Brother of Jeff Larmer . . . (1982-83)—Set Chicago club records for most goals by a right wing (43), most goals by a Chicago rookie (43) and most points by a Chicago rookie (90). He also tied club record for most assists by a Chicago rookie (47) set by Denis Savard in 1980-81 . . . Has current longest game-played streak in the NHL (480 through 1987-88).

Year	Team	League	Games	G.	A.	Pts.	Pen.
1977-78—Peterborough Petes		OMJHL	62	24	17	41	51
1978-79—Niagara Falls Flyers		OMJHL	66	37	47	84	108
1979-80—Niagara Falls Flyers (c)		OMJHL	67	45	69	114	71
1980-81—Niagara Falls Flyers (b)		OHL	61	55	78	133	73
1980-81—Chicago Black Hawks		NHL	4	0	1	1	0
1981-82—New Brunswick Hawks (b)		AHL	74	38	44	82	46
1981-82—Chicago Black Hawks		NHL	3	0	0	0	0
1982-83—Chicago Black Hawks (d-e)		NHL	80	43	47	90	28
1983-84—Chicago Black Hawks		NHL	80	35	40	75	34

Year	Team	League	Games	G.	A.	Pts.	Pen.
1984-85—Chicago Black Hawks		NHL	80	46	40	86	16
1985-86—Chicago Black Hawks		NHL	80	31	45	76	47
1986-87—Chicago Black Hawks		NHL	80	28	56	84	22
1987-88—Chicago Black Hawks		NHL	80	41	48	89	42
NHL TOTALS			487	224	277	501	189

(c)—June, 1980—Drafted as underage junior in 1980 NHL entry draft by Chicago Black Hawks. Eleventh Black Hawks pick, 120th overall, sixth round.

(d)—Selected as NHL Rookie of the Year in vote of players conducted by THE SPORTING NEWS.

(e)—Won Calder Memorial Trophy (Top NHL Rookie).

DENIS LAROCQUE

Defense . . . 6'1" . . . 200 lbs. . . . Born, Hawkesbury, Ont., October 5, 1967 . . . Shoots left . . . (October, 1986)—Suspended eight games by OHL for a stick fight with Gary Callaghan vs. Belleville.

Year	Team	League	Games	G.	A.	Pts.	Pen.
1982-83—Hawkesbury Hawks		CJHL	31	0	13	13	83
1983-84—Guelph Platers		OHL	65	1	5	6	74
1984-85—Guelph Platers		OHL	62	1	15	16	67
1985-86—Guelph Platers (c)		OHL	66	2	16	18	144
1986-87—Guelph Platers		OHL	45	4	10	14	82
1987-88—New Haven Nighthawks		AHL	58	4	10	14	154
1987-88—Los Angeles Kings		NHL	8	0	1	1	18
NHL TOTALS			8	0	1	1	18

(c)—June, 1986—Drafted by Los Angeles Kings in 1986 NHL entry draft. Second Kings pick, 44th overall, third round.

GUY LAROSE

Center . . . 5'10" . . . 175 lbs. . . . Born, Hull, Que., July 31, 1967 . . . Shoots left . . . Son of Claude Larose (NHL 1960s and 70s, and currently assistant coach of Hartford Whalers) . . . (February 22, 1985)—Fractured third left metacarpal.

Year	Team	League	Games	G.	A.	Pts.	Pen.
1983-84—Ottawa Senators		COJL	54	37	66	103	66
1984-85—Guelph Platers (c)		OHL	58	30	30	60	639
1985-86—Guelph Platers		OHL	37	12	36	48	55
1985-86—Ottawa 67's		OHL	28	19	25	44	63
1986-87—Ottawa 67's		OHL	66	28	49	77	77
1987-88—Moncton Golden Flames		AHL	77	22	31	53	127

(c)—June, 1985—Drafted as underage junior by Buffalo Sabres in 1985 NHL entry draft. Eleventh Sabres pick, 224th overall, 11th round.

PIERRE LAROUCHE

Center . . . 5'11" . . . 175 lbs. . . . Born, Taschereau, Que., November 16, 1955 . . . Shoots right . . . Missed part of 1976-77 season with broken left thumb . . . Missed part of 1978-79 season with injury to left knee . . . (March, 1980)—Injured shoulder . . . (November 1, 1980)—Broken left hand . . . (November 2, 1981)—Severe cut over eye at Quebec . . . (January 20, 1983)—Injured back at Los Angeles and missed remainder of season with recurring back spasms . . . Only player to have 50-goal seasons with two different NHL clubs . . . (March, 1985)—Injured wrist and bruised tailbone . . . (November, 1985)—Cut knee in AHL game . . . (March 11, 1986)—Broke right thumb at New Jersey . . . (November, 1987)—Pinched nerve in lower back. Underwent traction treatments.

Year	Team	League	Games	G.	A.	Pts.	Pen.
1972-73—Sorel Black Hawks		QJHL	63	52	62	114	44
1973-74—Sorel Black Hawks (b-c)		QJHL	67	94	*157	*251	53
1974-75—Pittsburgh Penguins (d)		NHL	79	31	37	68	52
1975-76—Pittsburgh Penguins		NHL	76	53	58	111	33
1976-77—Pittsburgh Penguins		NHL	65	29	34	63	14
1977-78—Pittsburgh Penguins (e)		NHL	20	6	5	11	0
1977-78—Montreal Canadiens		NHL	44	17	32	49	11
1978-79—Montreal Canadiens		NHL	36	9	13	22	4
1979-80—Montreal Canadiens		NHL	73	50	41	91	16
1980-81—Montreal Canadiens		NHL	61	25	28	53	28
1981-82—Montreal Canadiens (f)		NHL	22	9	12	21	0
1981-82—Hartford Whalers		NHL	45	25	25	50	12
1982-83—Hartford Whalers		NHL	38	18	22	40	8
1983-84—New York Rangers (g)		NHL	77	48	33	81	22
1984-85—New York Rangers		NHL	65	24	36	60	8
1985-86—Hershey Bears (h)		AHL	32	22	17	39	16

Year	Team	League	Games	G.	A.	Pts.	Pen.
1985-86—New York Rangers		NHL	28	20	7	27	4
1986-87—New York Rangers		NHL	73	28	35	63	12
1987-88—New York Rangers		NHL	10	3	9	12	13
NHL TOTALS			812	395	427	822	237

(c)—Drafted from Sorel Black Hawks by Pittsburgh Penguins in first round of 1974 amateur draft.

(d)—Named Prince of Wales Conference Rookie of the Year in poll of players by THE SPORTING NEWS.

(e)—November, 1977—Traded to Montreal Canadiens by Pittsburgh Penguins for Peter Lee and Peter Mahovlich.

(f)—December, 1981—Traded with first-round 1984 and third-round 1985 entry draft picks by Montreal Canadiens to Hartford Whalers for first-round 1984 and third-round 1985 entry draft picks.

(g)—September, 1983—Signed by New York Rangers as a free agent.

(h)—October, 1985—Assigned with Andre Dore to Hershey Bears by New York Rangers as compensation to Philadelphia Flyers for the Rangers' signing of coach Ted Sator.

REED DAVID LARSON

Defense . . . 6' . . . 195 lbs. . . . Born, Minneapolis, Minn., July 30, 1956 . . . Shoots right . . . (July, 1981)—Surgery to remove bone chips from right elbow . . . Holds NHL record for defensemen, scoring 20 goals in five straight seasons . . . Holds Detroit club record for most goals (27 in 1980-81), most assists (52 in 1982-83) and points (74 in 1982-83) by a defenseman in one season . . . (1983-84)—Passed Tommy Williams to become all-time U.S.-born NHL career leader in points (Williams had 430) and assists (Williams had 269) . . . (1984-85)—Passed Tommy Williams to become highest goal scoring U.S. born player ever (Williams had 161 goals) . . . Holds Detroit Red Wings career record for goals, assists and points by a defenseman . . . (October, 1986)—Separated shoulder in Boston training camp . . . (June, 1987)—Crushed artery in his left arm in automobile accident . . . (October 14, 1987)—Injured left arm . . . (April, 1988)—Separated right shoulder.

Year	Team	League	Games	G.	A.	Pts.	Pen.
1974-75—University of Minnesota		WCHA	41	11	17	28	37
1975-76—University of Minnesota (a-c)		WCHA	42	13	29	42	94
1976-77—University of Minnesota		WCHA	21	10	15	25	30
1976-77—Detroit Red Wings		NHL	14	0	1	1	23
1977-78—Detroit Red Wings		NHL	75	19	41	60	95
1978-79—Detroit Red Wings		NHL	79	18	49	67	169
1979-80—Detroit Red Wings		NHL	80	22	44	66	101
1980-81—Detroit Red Wings		NHL	78	27	31	58	153
1981-82—Detroit Red Wings		NHL	80	21	39	60	112
1982-83—Detroit Red Wings		NHL	80	22	52	74	104
1983-84—Detroit Red Wings		NHL	78	23	39	62	122
1984-85—Detroit Red Wings		NHL	77	17	45	62	139
1985-86—Detroit Red Wings (d)		NHL	67	19	41	60	109
1985-86—Boston Bruins		NHL	13	3	4	7	8
1986-87—Boston Bruins		NHL	66	12	24	36	95
1987-88—Boston Bruins		NHL	62	10	24	34	93
1987-88—Maine Mariners		AHL	2	2	0	2	4
NHL TOTALS			849	213	434	647	1323

(c)—Drafted from University of Minnesota by Detroit Red Wings in second round of 1976 amateur draft.

(d)—March, 1986—Traded by Detroit Red Wings to Boston Bruins for Mike O'Connell.

TYLER LARTER

Center . . . 5'10" . . . 180 lbs. . . . Born, Charlottetown, P.E.I., March 12, 1968 . . . Shoots left.

Year	Team	League	Games	G.	A.	Pts.	Pen.
1983-84—Charlottetown Tigers		PEIJHL	26	24	32	56	....
1984-85—Sault Ste. Marie Greyhounds		OHL	64	14	26	40	48
1985-86—Sault Ste. Marie Greyhounds		OHL	60	15	40	55	137
1986-87—Sault Ste. Marie Greyhounds (c)		OHL	59	34	59	93	122
1987-88—Sault Ste. Marie Greyhounds		OHL	65	44	65	109	155

(c)—June, 1987—Drafted by Washington Capitals in 1987 NHL entry draft. Third Capitals pick, 78th overall, fourth round.

MARTIN LATREILLE

Defense . . . 6'1" . . . 200 lbs. . . . Born, Montreal, Que., September 14, 1968 . . . Shoots left . . . (November, 1985)—Injured knee ligaments.

Year	Team	League	Games	G.	A.	Pts.	Pen.
1984-85—Montreal Concordia Midget		Que.	38	2	11	13	81
1985-86—Laval Titans (c)		QHL	65	1	11	12	48
1986-87—Laval Titans		QHL	59	1	16	17	118
1987-88—Drummondville Voltigeurs		QHL	60	2	22	24	134

(c)—June, 1986—Drafted as underage junior by Quebec Nordiques in 1986 NHL entry draft. Thirteenth Nordiques pick, 228th overall, 11th round.

DAVE LATTA

Left Wing . . . 6' . . . 185 lbs. . . . Born, Thunder Bay, Ont., January 3, 1967 . . . Shoots left . . . Brother of Ken Latta . . . (December, 1984)—Shoulder injury . . . (October, 1987)—Separated shoulder.

Year	Team	League	Games	G.	A.	Pts.	Pen.
1982-83	Orillia Travelways	OJHL	43	16	25	41	26
1983-84	Kitchener Rangers	OHL	66	17	26	43	54
1984-85	Kitchener Rangers (c)	OHL	52	38	27	65	26
1985-86	Kitchener Rangers	OHL	55	36	34	70	60
1985-86	Fredericton Express	AHL	3	1	0	1	0
1985-86	Quebec Nordiques	NHL	1	0	0	0	0
1986-87	Kitchener Rangers	OHL	50	32	46	78	46
1987-88	Fredericton Express	AHL	34	11	21	32	28
1987-88	Quebec Nordiques	NHL	10	0	0	0	0
	NHL TOTALS		11	0	0	0	0

(c)—June, 1985—Drafted as underage junior by Quebec Nordiques in 1985 NHL entry draft. First Nordiques pick, 15th overall, first round.

BRAD LAUER

Right Wing . . . 6' . . . 195 lbs. . . . Born, Humbolt, Sask., October 27, 1966 . . . Shoots left.

Year	Team	League	Games	G.	A.	Pts.	Pen.
1983-84	Regina Pats	WHL	60	5	7	12	51
1984-85	Regina Pats (c)	WHL	72	33	46	79	57
1985-86	Regina Pats	WHL	57	36	38	74	69
1986-87	New York Islanders	NHL	61	7	14	21	65
1987-88	New York Islanders	NHL	69	17	18	35	67
	NHL TOTALS		130	24	32	56	132

(c)—June, 1985—Drafted as underage junior by New York Islanders in 1985 NHL entry draft. Third Islanders pick, 34th overall, second round.

CRAIG LAUGHLIN

Right Wing . . . 5'11" . . . 198 lbs. . . . Born, Toronto, Ont., September 19, 1957 . . . Shoots right . . . (February 22, 1986)—Sprained ankle at Philadelphia . . . (April 8, 1987)—Strained knee ligaments in playoffs vs. N.Y. Islanders.

Year	Team	League	Games	G.	A.	Pts.	Pen.
1976-77	Clarkson College (c)	ECAC	33	12	13	25	44
1977-78	Clarkson College	ECAC	30	17	31	48	56
1978-79	Clarkson College	ECAC	30	18	29	47	22
1979-80	Clarkson College	ECAC	34	18	30	48	38
1979-80	Nova Scotia Voyageurs	AHL	2	0	0	0	2
1980-81	Nova Scotia Voyageurs	AHL	46	32	29	61	15
1981-82	Nova Scotia Voyageurs	AHL	26	14	15	29	16
1981-82	Montreal Canadiens (d)	NHL	36	12	11	23	33
1982-83	Washington Capitals	NHL	75	17	27	44	41
1983-84	Washington Capitals	NHL	80	20	32	52	69
1984-85	Washington Capitals	NHL	78	16	34	50	38
1985-86	Washington Capitals	NHL	75	30	45	75	43
1986-87	Washington Capitals	NHL	80	22	30	52	67
1987-88	Washington Capitals (e)	NHL	40	5	5	10	26
1987-88	Los Angeles Kings (f)	NHL	19	4	8	12	6
	NHL TOTALS		483	126	192	318	323

(c)—June, 1977—Drafted by Montreal Canadiens in 1977 NHL amateur draft. Seventeenth Canadiens pick, 162nd overall, 10th round.

(d)—September, 1982—Traded by Montreal Canadiens with Rod Langway, Brian Engblom and Doug Jarvis to Washington Capitals for Ryan Walter and Rick Green.

(e)—February, 1988—Traded by Washington Capitals to Los Angeles Kings for Grant Ledyard.

(f)—June, 1988—Signed by Toronto Maple Leafs as a free agent.

MARK J. LaVARRE

Right Wing . . . 5'11" . . . 170 lbs. . . . Born, Evanston, Ill., February 21, 1965 . . . Shoots right . . . Also plays Defense . . . (February, 1981)—Fractured two vertebras in back.

Year	Team	League	Games	G.	A.	Pts.	Pen.
1982-83	Stratford Cullitons (c)	MWJBHL	40	33	62	95	88
1983-84	North Bay Centennials	OHL	41	19	22	41	15

Year	Team	League	Games	G.	A.	Pts.	Pen.
1984-85—Windsor Compuware Spitfires (d)		OHL	46	15	30	45	30
1985-86—Chicago Black Hawks		NHL	2	0	0	0	0
1985-86—Nova Scotia Oilers		AHL	62	15	19	34	32
1986-87—Nova Scotia Oilers		AHL	17	12	8	20	8
1986-87—Chicago Black Hawks		NHL	58	8	15	23	33
1987-88—Saginaw Hawks		IHL	39	27	18	45	121
1987-88—Chicago Black Hawks		NHL	18	1	1	2	25
NHL TOTALS			78	9	16	25	58

(c)—June, 1983—Drafted as underage junior by Chicago Black Hawks in 1983 NHL entry draft. Seventh Black Hawks pick, 119th overall, sixth round.

(d)—October, 1984—Traded with Peter McGrath by North Bay Centennials to Windsor Compuware Spitfires for Jamie Jefferson, J.D. Urbanic and OHL rights to Rick Flamminio.

PETER LAVIOLETTE

Defense . . . 6'2" . . . 200 lbs. . . . Born, Franklin, Mass., December 7, 1964 . . . Shoots left.

Year	Team	League	Games	G.	A.	Pts.	Pen.
1986-87—Indianapolis Checkers		IHL	72	10	20	30	146
1987-88—U. S. Olympic Team (c)		Int'l.	56	3	22	25	....
1987-88—Colorado Rangers		IHL	19	2	5	7	27

(c)—June, 1987—Signed by New York Rangers as a free agent.

DOMINIC LAVOIE

Defense . . . 6'2" . . . 187 lbs. . . . Born, Montreal, Que., November 21, 1967 . . . Shoots right.

Year	Team	League	Games	G.	A.	Pts.	Pen.
1984-85—St. Jean Castors		QMJHL	30	1	1	2	10
1985-86—St. Jean Castors (c)		QMJHL	70	12	37	49	99
1986-87—St. Jean Castors		QMJHL	64	12	42	54	97
1987-88—Peoria Rivermen		IHL	65	7	26	33	54

(c)—September, 1986—Signed by St. Louis Blues as a free agent.

PAUL LAWLESS

Left Wing . . . 6' . . . 190 lbs. . . . Born, Scarborough, Ont., July 2, 1964 . . . Shoots left . . . (January 7, 1987)—Strained ligaments in left knee and missed 18 games . . . (April 1, 1987)—Broke finger in right hand when slashed by Claude Lemieux at Montreal . . . (November, 1987)—Bruised ribs.

Year	Team	League	Games	G.	A.	Pts.	Pen.
1980-81—Wexford Midgets		MTHL	40	38	40	78	....
1981-82—Windsor Spitfires (c)		OHL	68	24	25	49	47
1982-83—Windsor Spitfires		OHL	33	15	20	35	25
1982-83—Hartford Whalers		NHL	47	6	9	15	4
1983-84—Hartford Whalers		NHL	6	0	3	3	0
1983-84—Windsor Spitfires (b)		OHL	55	31	49	80	26
1984-85—Binghamton Whalers		AHL	8	1	1	2	0
1984-85—Salt Lake Golden Eagles		IHL	72	49	48	97	14
1985-86—Hartford Whalers		NHL	64	17	21	38	20
1986-87—Hartford Whalers		NHL	60	22	32	54	14
1987-88—Hartford Whalers (d)		NHL	27	4	5	9	16
1987-88—Philadelphia Flyers (e)		NHL	8	0	5	5	0
1987-88—Vancouver Canucks		NHL	13	0	1	1	0
NHL TOTALS			225	49	76	125	54

(c)—June, 1982—Selected by Hartford Whalers in 1982 NHL entry draft. First Whalers pick, 14th overall, first round.

(d)—January, 1988—Traded by Hartford Whalers to Philadelphia Flyers for Lindsay Carson.

(e)—March, 1988—Traded with Vancouver's fifth-round 1989 draft pick by Philadelphia Flyers to Vancouver Canucks for Willie Huber.

BRETT LAWRENCE

Right Wing . . . 6'2" . . . 180 lbs. . . . Born, Rochester, N.Y., November 4, 1968 . . . Shoots right . . . Brother-in-law of Clint Fehr (former AHL player with Rochester).

Year	Team	League	Games	G.	A.	Pts.	Pen.
1984-85—Rochester Jr. Americans		NEJBHL	57	49	43	92	62
1985-86—Rochester Jr. Americans (c)		NEJBHL	38	45	40	85	60
1986-87—Colgate Univ.		ECAC	33	8	7	15	22
1987-88—Colgate Univ.		ECAC	29	6	5	11	12

(c)—June, 1986—Drafted by Philadelphia Flyers in 1986 NHL entry draft. Tenth Flyers pick, 230th overall, 11th round.

BRIAN LAWTON

Center . . . 6' . . . 180 lbs. . . . Born, New Brunswick, N.J., June 29, 1965 . . . Shoots left . . . First American-born player to be a first overall draft choice in the NHL . . . (November, 1983)—Separated shoulder . . . (October, 1984)—Injured shoulder during training camp . . . (October, 1987)—Broken thumb . . . (February, 1988)—Bruised ribs when struck by teammate Frantisek Musil at Toronto.

Year	Team	League	Games	G.	A.	Pts.	Pen.
1981-82—Mount St. Charles H.S.		R.I. H.S.	26	45	43	88	..
1982-83—Mount St. Charles H.S. (c)		R.I. H.S.	23	40	43	83	..
1982-83—U.S. National Team		Int'l	7	3	2	5	6
1983-84—Minnesota North Stars		NHL	58	10	21	31	33
1984-85—Springfield Indians		AHL	42	14	28	42	37
1984-85—Minnesota North Stars		NHL	40	5	6	11	24
1985-86—Minnesota North Stars		NHL	65	18	17	35	36
1986-87—Minnesota North Stars		NHL	66	21	23	44	86
1987-88—Minnesota North Stars		NHL	74	17	24	41	71
NHL TOTALS			303	71	91	162	250

(c)—June, 1983—Drafted by Minnesota North Stars in 1983 NHL entry draft. First North Stars pick, first overall, first round.

DEREK LAXDAL

Right Wing . . . 6'1" . . . 180 lbs. . . . Born, St. Boniface, Man., February 21, 1966 . . . Shoots right . . . (January, 1985)—Broken hand.

Year	Team	League	Games	G.	A.	Pts.	Pen.
1982-83—Portland Winter Hawks		WHL	39	4	9	13	27
1983-84—Brandon Wheat Kings (c)		WHL	70	23	20	43	86
1984-85—Brandon Wheat Kings		WHL	69	61	41	102	72
1984-85—St. Catharines Saints		AHL	5	3	2	5	2
1984-85—Toronto Maple Leafs		NHL	3	0	0	0	6
1985-86—Brandon Wheat Kings		WHL	42	34	35	69	62
1985-86—New Westminister Bruins		WHL	18	9	6	15	14
1985-86—St. Catharines Saints		AHL	7	0	1	1	15
1986-87—Newmarket Saints		AHL	78	24	20	44	89
1986-87—Toronto Maple Leafs		NHL	2	0	0	0	7
1987-88—Toronto Maple Leafs		NHL	5	0	0	0	6
1987-88—Newmarket Saints		AHL	67	18	25	43	81
NHL TOTALS			10	0	0	0	19

(c)—June, 1984—Drafted as an underage junior by Toronto Maple Leafs in 1984 NHL entry draft. Seventh Maple Leafs pick, 151st overall, eighth round.

STEPHEN LEACH

Right Wing . . . 5'11" . . . 180 lbs. . . . Born, Cambridge, Mass., January 16, 1966 . . . Shoots right.

Year	Team	League	Games	G.	A.	Pts.	Pen.
1983-84—Matignon H.S. (c)		Mass. H.S.	21	27	22	49	49
1984-85—Univ. of New Hampshire		H. East	41	12	25	37	53
1985-86—Univ. of New Hampshire		H. East	25	22	6	28	30
1985-86—Washington Capitals		NHL	11	1	1	2	2
1986-87—Binghamton Whalers		AHL	54	18	21	39	39
1986-87—Washington Capitals		NHL	15	1	0	1	6
1987-88—U.S. Olympic Team		Int'l	53	26	20	46	..
1987-88—Washington Capitals		NHL	8	1	1	2	17
NHL TOTALS			34	3	2	5	25

(c)—June, 1984—Drafted by Washington Capitals in 1984 NHL entry draft. Second Capitals pick, 34th overall, second round.

WILLIAM (JAMIE) LEACH

Right Wing . . . 6'1" . . . 190 lbs. . . . Born, Winnipeg, Man., August 25, 1969 . . . Shoots right . . . Son of Reggie Leach (Philadelphia Flyer in 1970s) . . . (February, 1986)—Hip injury.

Year	Team	League	Games	G.	A.	Pts.	Pen.
1984-85—Cherry Hill East H.S.		NJHS	60	48	51	99	68
1985-86—New Westminster Bruins		WHL	58	8	7	15	20
1986-87—Hamilton Steelhawks (c)		OHL	64	12	19	31	67
1987-88—Hamilton Steelhawks		OHL	64	24	19	43	79

(c)—June, 1987—Drafted as underage junior by Pittsburgh Penguins in 1987 NHL entry draft. Third Penguins pick, 47th overall, third round.

JAMES T. LEAVINS

Defense . . . 5'11" . . . 185 lbs. . . . Born, Dinsmore, Sask., July 28, 1960 . . . Shoots left . . . (October, 1986)—Lower back spasms.

Year	Team	League	Games	G.	A.	Pts.	Pen.
1980-81—Univ. of Denver		WCHA	40	8	18	26	18
1981-82—Univ. of Denver		WCHA	41	8	34	42	56
1982-83—Univ. of Denver		WCHA	33	16	24	40	20
1983-84—Univ. of Denver		WCHA	39	13	24	37	38
1983-84—Tulsa Oilers		CHL	1	0	0	0	0
1984-85—Fort Wayne Komets		IHL	76	5	50	55	57
1985-86—Adirondack Red Wings		AHL	36	4	21	25	19
1985-86—Detroit Red Wings (c-d)		NHL	37	2	11	13	26
1986-87—New Haven Nighthawks		AHL	54	7	21	28	16
1986-87—New York Rangers		NHL	4	0	1	1	4
1987-88—New Haven Nighthawks		AHL	11	2	5	7	6
1987-88—Salt Lake Golden Eagles (b-e)		IHL	68	12	45	57	45
NHL TOTALS			41	2	12	14	30

(c)—November, 1985—Signed by Detroit Red Wings as a free agent.

(d)—July, 1986—Traded with Kelly Kisio, Lane Lambert and a fifth-round 1988 draft pick by Detroit Red Wings to New York Rangers for Glen Hanlon, third-round 1987 (Dennis Holland) and 1988 draft pick and future considerations.

(e)—November, 1987—Traded by New York Rangers to Calgary Flames for Don Mercier.

BENOIT LEBEAU

Left Wing . . . 6'1" . . . 185 lbs. . . . Born, Montreal, Que., June 4, 1968 . . . Shoots left.

Year	Team	League	Games	G.	A.	Pts.	Pen.
1987-88—Merrimack College (c)		ECAC	40	35	38	73	52

(c)—June, 1988—Drafted by Winnipeg Jets in 1988 NHL entry draft. Sixth Jets pick, 101st overall, fifth round.

STEPHANE LeBEAU

Center . . . 5'10" . . . 180 lbs. . . . Born, Sherbrooke, Que., February 28, 1968 . . . Shoots right.

Year	Team	League	Games	G.	A.	Pts.	Pen.
1984-85—Shawinigan Cataracts		QHL	66	41	38	79	18
1985-86—Shawinigan Cataracts		QHL	72	69	77	146	22
1986-87—Shawinigan Cataracts (a-c)		QHL	65	77	90	167	60
1987-88—Shawinigan Cataracts (b-d)		QHL	67	*94	94	188	66

(c)—September, 1986—Signed as a free agent by Montreal Canadiens.

(d)—Won Frank Selke Trophy (Most Gentlemanly Player).

JOHN LeBLANC

Left Wing . . . 6'1" . . . 190 lbs. . . . Born, Campellton, N.B., January 21, 1964 . . . Shoots left.

Year	Team	League	Games	G.	A.	Pts.	Pen.
1985-86—U. of New Brunswick (c-d)		CIAU	24	38	26	64	32
1986-87—Fredericton Express		AHL	75	40	30	70	27
1986-87—Vancouver Canucks		NHL	2	1	0	1	0
1987-88—Fredericton Express		AHL	35	26	25	51	54
1987-88—Vancouver Canucks		NHL	41	12	10	22	18
NHL TOTALS			43	13	10	23	18

(c)—Named winner of the Senator Joseph A. Sullivan Trophy to the top Canadian college player.

(d)—April, 1986—Signed by Vancouver Canucks as a free agent.

SEAN LeBRUN

Left Wing . . . 6'2" . . . 200 lbs. . . . Born, Prince George, B.C., May 2, 1969 . . . Shoots left.

Year	Team	League	Games	G.	A.	Pts.	Pen.
1984-85—Prince George Midget		B.C. Midget	53	61	51	112	46
1985-86—Spokane Chiefs		WHL	70	6	11	17	41
1986-87—Spokane Chiefs		WHL	6	2	5	7	9
1986-87—New Westminster Bruins		WHL	55	21	32	53	47
1987-88—New Westminster Bruins (b-c)		WHL	72	36	53	89	59

(c)—June, 1988—Drafted by New York Islanders in 1988 NHL entry draft. Third Islanders pick, 37th overall, third round.

JOHN LeCLAIR

Center . . . 6'1" . . . 185 lbs. . . . Born, St. Albans, Vt., July 5, 1969 . . . Shoots left.

Year	Team	League	Games	G.	A.	Pts.	Pen.
1985-86—Bellows Free Acad.		Ver. H.S.	22	41	28	69	14
1986-87—Bellows Free Acad. (c)		Ver. H.S.	23	44	40	84	25
1987-88—University of Vermont		ECAC	31	12	22	34	62

(c)—June, 1987—Drafted by Montreal Canadiens in 1987 NHL entry draft. Second Canadiens pick, 33rd overall, second round.

GRANT LEDYARD

Defense . . . 6'2" . . . 190 lbs. . . . Born, Winnipeg, Man., November 19, 1961 . . . Shoots left . . . (October, 1984)—Hip injury . . . (October, 1987)—Sprained ankle.

Year	Team	League	Games	G.	A.	Pts.	Pen.
1979-80—Fort Garry Blues		MJHL	49	13	24	37	90
1980-81—Saskatoon Blades		WHL	71	9	28	37	148
1981-82—Fort Garry Blues (a-c)		MJHL	63	25	45	70	150
1982-83—Tulsa Oilers (d)		CHL	80	13	29	42	115
1983-84—Tulsa Oilers (e)		CHL	58	9	17	26	71
1984-85—New Haven Nighthawks		AHL	36	6	20	26	18
1984-85—New York Rangers		NHL	42	8	12	20	53
1985-86—New York Rangers (f)		NHL	27	2	9	11	20
1985-86—Los Angeles Kings		NHL	52	7	18	25	78
1986-87—Los Angeles Kings		NHL	67	14	23	37	93
1987-88—New Haven Nighthawks		AHL	3	2	1	3	4
1987-88—Los Angeles Kings (g)		NHL	23	1	7	8	52
1987-88—Washington Capitals		NHL	21	4	3	7	14
NHL TOTALS			232	36	72	108	310

(c)—Named Manitoba Junior Hockey League Most Valuable Player.
(d)—July, 1982—Signed by New York Rangers as a free agent.
(e)—Won Max McNab Trophy (Playoff MVP).
(f)—December, 1986—Traded by New York Rangers to Los Angeles Kings for Brian MacLellan and a fourth round 1987 draft pick (Michael Sullivan). The Rangers also sent a second round 1986 (Neil Wilkinson) and a fourth round 1987 draft pick (John Weisbrod) to Minnesota and the North Stars sent Roland Melanson to the Kings as part of the same deal.
(g)—February, 1988—Traded by Los Angeles Kings to Washington Capitals for Craig Laughlin.

GARY LEEMAN

Defense and Right Wing . . . 6' . . . 175 lbs. . . . Born, Toronto, Ont., February 19, 1964 . . . Shoots right . . . (January, 1984)—Broken finger . . . (March, 1984)—Broken wrist . . . (March, 1985)—Shoulder separation . . . (April 14, 1987)—Cracked kneecap in playoff game at St. Louis . . . (April, 1988)—Cracked bone in right hand.

Year	Team	League	Games	G.	A.	Pts.	Pen.
1980-81—Notre Dame Midgets		SCMHL	24	15	23	38	28
1981-82—Regina Pats (c)		WHL	72	19	41	60	112
1982-83—Regina Pats (a-d)		WHL	63	24	62	86	88
1983-84—Toronto Maple Leafs		NHL	52	4	8	12	31
1984-85—St. Catharines Saints		AHL	7	2	2	4	11
1984-85—Toronto Maple Leafs		NHL	53	5	26	31	72
1985-86—St. Catharines Saints		AHL	25	15	13	28	6
1985-86—Toronto Maple Leafs		NHL	53	9	23	32	20
1986-87—Toronto Maple Leafs		NHL	80	21	31	52	66
1987-88—Toronto Maple Leafs		NHL	80	30	31	61	62
NHL TOTALS			318	69	119	188	251

(c)—June, 1982—Drafted by Toronto Maple Leafs as underage junior in 1982 NHL entry draft. Second Maple Leafs pick, 24th overall, second round.
(d)—Won WHL Top Defenseman Trophy.

BRIAN LEETCH

Defense . . . 5'11" . . . 170 lbs. . . . Born, Corpus Christi, Tex., March 3, 1968 . . . Shoots left . . . (July, 1987)—Suffered sprained ligaments in his left knee at U.S. Olympic Sports Festival.

Year	Team	League	Games	G.	A.	Pts.	Pen.
1984-85—Avon Old Farms H.S.		Conn.	26	30	46	76	15
1985-86—Avon Old Farms H.S. (c)		Conn.	28	40	44	84	18
1986-87—Boston College (a-d-e-f)		H. East	37	9	38	47	10
1987-88—U.S. Olympic Team		Int'l	53	13	64	77	..
1987-88—New York Rangers		NHL	17	2	12	14	0
NHL TOTALS			17	2	12	14	0

(c)—June, 1986—Drafted by New York Rangers in 1986 NHL entry draft. First Rangers pick, ninth overall, first round.
(d)—Named Hockey East Rookie-of-the-Year.
(e)—Named Hockey East Player-of-the-Year.
(f)—Named to U.S. College First-Team All-America Team.

SYLVAIN LEFEBVRE

Left Wing . . . 6'2" . . . 185 lbs. . . . Born, Richmond, Que., October 14, 1967 . . . Shoots left.

Year	Team	League	Games	G.	A.	Pts.	Pen.
1984-85	Laval Voisins	QHL	66	7	5	12	31
1985-86	Laval Voisins (c)	QHL	71	8	17	25	48
1986-87	Laval Voisins	QHL	70	10	36	46	44
1987-88	Sherbrooke Canadiens	AHL	79	3	24	27	73

(c)—September, 1986—Signed by Montreal Canadiens as a free agent.

TOMMY LEHMAN

Center . . . 6'1" . . . 185 lbs. . . . Born, Solna, Sweden, February 3, 1964 . . . Shoots left . . . (October, 1987)—Sprained left knee . . . (February, 1988)—Pneumonia . . . (March, 1988) —Inflamed left kneecap.

Year	Team	League	Games	G.	A.	Pts.	Pen.
1985-86	AIK Sweden (c)	Sweden	23	6	9	15	10
1986-87	AIK Sweden	Sweden	....	25	26	51	....
1987-88	Maine Mariners	AHL	11	3	5	8	2
1987-88	Boston Bruins	NHL	9	1	3	4	6
	NHL TOTALS		9	1	3	4	6

(c)—June, 1982—Drafted by Boston Bruins in 1982 NHL entry draft. Eleventh Bruins pick, 228th overall, 11th round.

KEN LEITER

Defense . . . 6'1" . . . 195 lbs. . . . Born, Detroit, Mich., April 19, 1961 . . . Shoots left . . . (November, 1987)—Pneumonia in left lung . . . (December, 1987)—Strained abdominal muscle . . . (February, 1988)—Back spasms.

Year	Team	League	Games	G.	A.	Pts.	Pen.
1979-80	Michigan State Univ.	CCHA	38	0	10	10	96
1980-81	Michigan State Univ. (c)	CCHA	31	2	13	15	48
1981-82	Michigan State Univ.	CCHA	31	7	13	20	50
1982-83	Michigan State Univ.	CCHA	32	3	24	27	50
1983-84	Indianapolis Checkers	CHL	68	10	26	36	46
1984-85	Springfield Indians	AHL	39	3	12	15	12
1984-85	New York Islanders	NHL	5	0	2	2	2
1985-86	New York Islanders	NHL	9	1	1	2	6
1985-86	Springfield Indians	AHL	68	7	27	34	51
1986-87	New York Islanders	NHL	74	9	20	29	30
1987-88	Springfield Indians	AHL	2	0	4	4	0
1987-88	New York Islanders	NHL	54	4	13	17	24
	NHL TOTALS		142	14	36	50	62

(c)—June, 1980—Drafted by New York Islanders in NHL entry draft. Sixth Islanders pick, 101st overall, fifth round.

MAURICE (MOE) LEMAY

Left Wing . . . 5'11" . . . 180 lbs. . . . Born, Saskatoon, Sask., February 18, 1962 . . . Shoots left . . . (March, 1983)—Hip injury . . . (April, 1983)—Injured knee during AHL playoffs . . . (January 10, 1986)—Injured hip at Hartford . . . (February 16, 1986)—Injured knee at Toronto.

Year	Team	League	Games	G.	A.	Pts.	Pen.
1979-80	Ottawa 67's	OMJHL	62	16	23	39	20
1980-81	Ottawa 67's (c)	OHL	63	32	45	77	102
1981-82	Ottawa 67's (a-d)	OHL	62	*68	70	138	48
1981-82	Vancouver Canucks	NHL	5	1	2	3	0
1982-83	Fredericton Express	AHL	26	7	8	15	6
1982-83	Vancouver Canucks	NHL	44	11	9	20	41
1983-84	Fredericton Express	AHL	23	9	7	16	32
1983-84	Vancouver Canucks	NHL	56	12	18	30	38
1984-85	Vancouver Canucks	NHL	56	0	0	0	4
1985-86	Vancouver Canucks	NHL	48	16	15	31	92
1986-87	Vancouver Canucks (e)	NHL	52	9	17	26	128
1986-87	Edmonton Oilers	NHL	10	1	2	3	36
1987-88	Edmonton Oilers (f)	NHL	4	0	0	0	2
1987-88	Boston Bruins	NHL	2	0	0	0	0
1987-88	Nova Scotia Oilers	AHL	39	14	25	39	89
1987-88	Maine Mariners	AHL	11	5	6	11	14
	NHL TOTALS		277	50	63	113	341

(c)—June, 1981—Drafted as an underage junior by Vancouver Canucks in 1981 NHL entry draft. Fourth Canucks pick, 105th overall, fifth round.

(d)—Led J. Ross Robertson Cup playoffs (OHL) with 19 assists.
(e)—March, 1987—Traded by Vancouver Canucks to Edmonton Oilers for Raimo Summanen.
(f)—March, 1988—Traded by Edmonton Oilers to Boston Bruins for Allan May.

ALAIN LEMIEUX

Center . . . 6' . . . 185 lbs. . . . Born, Montreal, Que., May 24, 1961 . . . Shoots left . . . Brother of Mario Lemieux . . . (September, 1985)—Separated shoulder at Quebec Nordiques training camp.

Year	Team	League	Games	G.	A.	Pts.	Pen.
1978-79—Chicoutimi Sagueneens		QMJHL	31	15	27	42	5
1978-79—Montreal Juniors		QMJHL	39	7	5	12	2
1979-80—Chicoutimi Sagueneens (c)		QMJHL	72	47	95	142	36
1980-81—Chicoutimi Sagueneens (d)		QMJHL	1	0	0	0	2
1980-81—Trois-Rivieres Draveurs (b-e)		QMJHL	69	68	98	166	62
1981-82—Salt Lake Golden Eagles		CHL	74	41	42	83	61
1981-82—St. Louis Blues		NHL	3	0	1	1	0
1982-83—Salt Lake Golden Eagles		CHL	29	20	24	44	35
1982-83—St. Louis Blues		NHL	42	9	25	34	18
1983-84—St. Louis Blues		NHL	17	4	5	9	6
1983-84—Montana Magic		CHL	38	28	41	69	36
1983-84—Springfield Indians		AHL	14	11	14	25	18
1984-85—Peoria Rivermen		IHL	2	1	0	1	0
1984-85—St. Louis Blues (f)		NHL	19	4	2	6	0
1984-85—Quebec Nordiques		NHL	30	11	11	22	12
1985-86—Quebec Nordiques		NHL	7	0	0	0	0
1985-86—Fredericton Express		AHL	64	29	46	75	54
1986-87—Pittsburgh Penguins (g)		NHL	1	0	0	0	0
1986-87—Baltimore Skipjacks (b)		AHL	72	41	56	97	62
1987-88—Springfield Indians		AHL	15	7	10	17	4
1987-88—Hershey Bears		AHL	20	8	10	18	10
1987-88—Baltimore Skipjacks		AHL	16	2	14	16	4
NHL TOTALS			119	28	44	72	36

(c)—June, 1980—Drafted as underage junior by St. Louis Blues in 1980 NHL entry draft. Fourth Blues pick, 96th overall, fifth round.
(d)—October, 1980—Traded by Chicoutimi Sagueneens to Trois-Rivieres Draveurs for Rene Labbe and Daniel Courcy.
(e)—Winner of Guy Lafleur Trophy (Playoff MVP).
(f)—January, 1985—Traded by St. Louis Blues to Quebec Nordiques for Luc Dufour.
(g)—November, 1986—Signed as a free agent by Pittsburgh Penguins.

CLAUDE LEMIEUX

Right Wing . . . 6'1" . . . 215 lbs. . . . Born, Buckingham, Que., July 16, 1965 . . . Shoots right . . . Brother of Jocelyn Lemieux . . . (October, 1987)—Torn ankle ligaments during Canada Cup . . . (January 14, 1988)—Fractured orbital bone above right eye when elbowed by Gord Kluzak vs. Boston.

Year	Team	League	Games	G.	A.	Pts.	Pen.
1981-82—Richelieu Eclairevrs		Que. Midget	48	24	48	72	96
1982-83—Trois-Rivieres Draveurs (c)		QHL	62	28	38	66	187
1983-84—Verdun Juniors (b)		QHL	51	41	45	86	225
1983-84—Montreal Canadiens		NHL	8	1	1	2	12
1984-85—Verdun Juniors (a-d)		QHL	52	58	66	124	152
1984-85—Montreal Canadiens		NHL	1	0	1	1	7
1985-86—Sherbrooke Canadiens		AHL	58	21	32	53	145
1985-86—Montreal Canadiens		NHL	10	1	2	3	22
1986-87—Montreal Canadiens		NHL	76	27	26	53	156
1987-88—Montreal Canadiens		NHL	80	31	30	61	137
NHL TOTALS			175	60	60	120	334

(c)—June, 1983—Drafted as underage junior by Montreal Canadiens in 1983 NHL entry draft. Second Canadiens pick, 26th overall, second round.
(d)—Won Guy Lafleur Trophy (Playoff MVP).

JOCELYN LEMIEUX

Left Wing . . . 5'11" . . . 205 lbs. . . . Born, Mont Laurier, Que., November 18, 1967 . . . Shoots left . . . Brother of Claude Lemieux . . . Also plays Right Wing . . . (December, 1986)—Severed tendon in little finger of left hand . . . (January, 1988)—Broke left leg and tore ligaments.

Year	Team	League	Games	G.	A.	Pts.	Pen.
1984-85—Laval Voisins		QHL	68	13	19	32	92
1985-86—Laval Titans (a-c)		QHL	71	57	68	125	131

Year	Team	League	Games	G.	A.	Pts.	Pen.
1986-87—St. Louis Blues		NHL	53	10	8	18	94
1987-88—Peoria Rivermen		IHL	8	0	5	5	35
1987-88—St. Louis Blues (d)		NHL	23	1	0	1	42
NHL TOTALS			76	11	8	19	136

(c)—June, 1986—Drafted as underage junior by St. Louis Blues in 1986 NHL entry draft. First Blues pick, 10th overall, first round.

(d)—August, 1988—Traded with Darrell May and second-round draft choice in 1989 by St. Louis Blues to Montreal Canadiens for Sergio Momesso and Vincent Riendeau.

MARIO LEMIEUX

Center ... 6'4" ... 200 lbs.... Born, Montreal, Que., October 5, 1965 ... Shoots right ... Set single-season record in Quebec Junior League in 1983-84 for goals (133) and points (282) as well as a Quebec League record for most career assists (315) ... Brother of Alain Lemieux ... (September, 1984)—Sprained left knee in training camp and fitted with a playing brace.... (December 2, 1984)—Resprained knee in collision with Darren Veitch at Washington ... (November 24, 1985)—Missed one game with back injury at Philadelphia ... (December 20, 1986)—Sprained right knee when checked by Ron Sutter vs. Philadelphia ... (March, 1987)—Fitted for two knee braces ... (November, 1987)—Bruised right shoulder when checked by Alan Kerr vs. N.Y. Islanders.

Year	Team	League	Games	G.	A.	Pts.	Pen.
1981-82—Laval Voisins		QMJHL	64	30	66	96	22
1982-83—Laval Voisins (b)		QHL	66	84	100	184	76
1983-84—Laval Voisins (a-c)		QHL	70	*133	*149	*282	92
1984-85—Pittsburgh Penguins (d-e)		NHL	73	43	57	100	54
1985-86—Pittsburgh Penguins (b-f)		NHL	79	48	93	141	43
1986-87—Pittsburgh Penguins (b)		NHL	63	54	53	107	57
1987-88—Pittsburgh Penguins (a-g-h-i)		NHL	77	*70	98	*168	92
NHL TOTALS			292	215	301	516	246

(c)—June, 1984—Drafted as underage junior by Pittsburgh Penguins in 1984 NHL entry draft. First Penguins pick, first overall, first round.

(d)—Won Calder Memorial Trophy (NHL Top Rookie).

(e)—Named NHL Rookie of the Year in poll of players by THE SPORTING NEWS.

(f)—Won 1986 Lester B. Pearson Award as the NHL's outstanding player. Voting is done by the NHLPA.

(g)—Won Art Ross Memorial Trophy (NHL Leading Scorer).

(h)—Won Hart Memorial Trophy (Most Valuable Player).

(i)—Named NHL Player of the Year in poll of players by THE SPORTING NEWS.

TIM LENARDON

Center ... 6'2" ... 185 lbs.... Born, Trail, B.C., May 11, 1962 ... Shoots left ... (December, 1986)—Separated shoulder in AHL game.

Year	Team	League	Games	G.	A.	Pts.	Pen.
1981-82—Trail		KIHL	40	48	61	138	....
1982-83—Trail		KIHL	38	86	86	172	....
1983-84—Univ. of Brandon		CWUAA	24	22	21	43	....
1984-85—Univ. of Brandon		CWUAA	24	21	39	60	....
1985-86—Univ. of Brandon (c-d)		CWUAA	26	26	40	66	33
1986-87—New Jersey Devils		NHL	7	1	1	2	0
1986-87—Maine Mariners		AHL	61	28	35	63	30
1987-88—Utica Devils		AHL	79	38	53	91	72
NHL TOTALS			7	1	1	2	0

(c)—Named Canadian College Player of the Year.

(d)—August, 1986—Signed by New Jersey Devils as a free agent.

FRANCOIS LEROUX

Defense ... 6'5" ... 217 lbs.... Born, St. Adele, Que., April 18, 1970 ... Shoots left.

Year	Team	League	Games	G.	A.	Pts.	Pen.
1986-87—Laval Laurentides Midget		Quebec	42	5	11	16	76
1987-88—St. Jean Casters (c)		QHL	58	3	8	11	143

(c)—June, 1988—Drafted by Edmonton Oilers in 1988 NHL entry draft. First Oilers pick, 19th overall, first round.

CURTIS LESCHYSHYN

Defense ... 6' ... 205 lbs.... Born, Thompson, Manitoba, September 21, 1969 ... Shoots left.

Year	Team	League	Games	G.	A.	Pts.	Pen.
1985-86—Saskatoon Blades		WHL	1	0	0	0	0

Year	Team	League	Games	G.	A.	Pts.	Pen.
1986-87—Saskatoon Blades		WHL	70	14	26	40	107
1987-88—Saskatoon Blades (a-c)		WHL	56	14	41	55	86

(c)—June, 1988—Drafted by Quebec Nordiques in 1988 NHL entry draft. First Nordiques pick, third overall, first round.

RICHARD LESSARD

Defense . . . 6'2" . . . 200 lbs. . . . Born, Timmons, Ont., January 9, 1968 . . . Shoots left.

Year	Team	League	Games	G.	A.	Pts.	Pen.
1984-85—Ottawa 67's		OHL	60	2	13	15	128
1985-86—Ottawa 67's (c)		OHL	64	1	20	21	231
1986-87—Ottawa 67's		OHL	66	5	36	41	188
1987-88—Ottawa 67's		OHL	58	5	34	39	210

(c)—June, 1986—Drafted as an underage junior by Calgary Flames in 1986 NHL entry draft. Sixth Flames pick, 142nd overall, seventh round.

CHRIS LEVASSEUR

Center . . . 6'2" . . . 200 lbs. . . . Born, Grand Rapids, Minn., March 6, 1964 . . . Shoots left.

Year	Team	League	Games	G.	A.	Pts.	Pen.
1984-85—Univ. of Alaska/Anchorage		GWHC	31	17	30	47	22
1985-86—Univ. of Alaska/Anchorage (c)		GWHC	19	9	12	21	50
1986-87—Univ. of Alaska/Anchorage		GWHC	28	15	17	32	34
1987-88—Moncton Golden Flames		AHL	49	15	12	27	30

(c)—June, 1986—Selected by Winnipeg Jets in 1986 NHL supplemental draft.

IGOR LIBA

Left Wing . . . 6' . . . 197 lbs. . . . Czechoslovakia, November 4, 1960 . . . Shoots left.

Year	Team	League	Games	G.	A.	Pts.	Pen.
1987-88—VSZ. Kosice (c-d)		Czech.	39	14	26	40	....

(c)—June, 1983—Drafted by Calgary Flames in NHL entry draft. Seventh Flames pick, 91st overall, fifth round.

(d)—May, 1988—Traded by Calgary Flames to Minnesota North Stars for a fifth-round draft choice (Thomas Forslund) in 1988.

DOUG LIDSTER

Defense . . . 6'1" . . . 195 lbs. . . . Born, Kamloops, B.C., October 18, 1960 . . . Shoots right . . . (1982-83)—Tied Colorado College record for most points by a defenseman in a season (56) . . . Member of 1984 Canadian Olympic Team . . . (January 3, 1986)—Injured knee vs. Winnipeg and missed two games . . . (January, 1988)—Strained left knee vs. Chicago.

Year	Team	League	Games	G.	A.	Pts.	Pen.
1979-80—Colorado College (c)		WCHA	39	18	25	43	52
1980-81—Colorado College		WCHA	36	10	30	40	54
1981-82—Colorado College (a)		WCHA	36	13	22	35	32
1982-83—Colorado College		WCHA	34	15	41	56	30
1983-84—Canadian Olympic Team		Int'l	59	6	20	26	28
1983-84—Vancouver Canucks		NHL	8	0	0	0	4
1984-85—Vancouver Canucks		NHL	78	6	24	30	55
1985-86—Vancouver Canucks		NHL	78	12	16	28	56
1986-87—Vancouver Canucks		NHL	80	12	51	63	40
1987-88—Vancouver Canucks		NHL	64	4	32	36	105
NHL TOTALS			308	34	123	157	260

(c)—June, 1980—Drafted by Vancouver Canucks in 1980 NHL entry draft. Sixth Canucks pick, 133rd overall, seventh round.

TREVOR LINDEN

Center . . . 6'3" . . . 185 lbs. . . . Born, Medicine Hat, Alta., April 11, 1970 . . . Shoots right.

Year	Team	League	Games	G.	A.	Pts.	Pen.
1985-86—Medicine Hat Tigers		WHL	5	2	0	2	0
1986-87—Medicine Hat Tigers		WHL	72	14	22	36	59
1987-88—Medicine Hat Tigers (b-c)		WHL	67	46	64	110	76

(c)—June, 1988—Drafted by Vancouver Canucks in 1988 NHL entry draft. First Canucks pick, second overall, first round.

KEN LINSEMAN

Center . . . 5'11" . . . 175 lbs. . . . Born, Kingston, Ont., August 11, 1958 . . . Shoots left . . . (September, 1980)—Broke tibia bone in leg in preseason game vs. N.Y. Rangers . . .

Brother of John, Ted and Steve Linseman . . . (February, 1983)—Suspended for four games for fight in stands at Vancouver . . . (November, 1984)—Shoulder injury . . . (November 21, 1985)—Broke right hand vs. N.Y. Islanders and missed 10 games . . . (December 28, 1985)—Injured hand at St. Louis and missed six games . . . (March, 1988)—Sprained right ankle.

Year	Team	League	Games	G.	A.	Pts.	Pen.
1974-75—Kingston Canadians		Jr."A" OHA	59	19	28	47	70
1975-76—Kingston Canadians		Jr."A" OHA	65	61	51	112	92
1976-77—Kingston Canadians (b-c)		Jr"A" OHA	63	53	74	127	210
1977-78—Birmingham Bulls (d)		WHA	71	38	38	76	126
1978-79—Maine Mariners		AHL	38	17	23	40	106
1978-79—Philadelphia Flyers		NHL	30	5	20	25	23
1979-80—Philadelphia Flyers (e)		NHL	80	22	57	79	107
1980-81—Philadelphia Flyers		NHL	51	17	30	47	150
1981-82—Philadelphia Flyers (f)		NHL	79	24	68	92	275
1982-83—Edmonton Oilers		NHL	72	33	42	75	181
1983-84—Edmonton Oilers (g)		NHL	72	18	49	67	119
1984-85—Boston Bruins		NHL	74	25	49	74	126
1985-86—Boston Bruins		NHL	64	23	58	81	97
1986-87—Boston Bruins		NHL	64	15	34	49	126
1987-88—Boston Bruins		NHL	77	29	45	74	167
WHA TOTALS			71	38	38	76	126
NHL TOTALS			663	211	452	663	1371

(c)—June, 1977—Selected by Birmingham Bulls in World Hockey Association amateur player draft as underage junior.

(d)—Drafted from Birmingham Bulls by Philadelphia Flyers (with choice obtained from N. Y. Rangers) in first round of 1978 amateur draft.

(e)—Led Stanley Cup Playoffs with 18 assists.

(f)—August, 1982—Traded with Greg Adams and first and third-round 1983 draft picks by Philadelphia Flyers to Hartford Whalers for Mark Howe and Whalers third-round '83 pick. Linseman was then traded with Don Nachbaur by Hartford Whalers to Edmonton Oilers for Risto Siltanen and Brent Loney.

(g)—June, 1984—Traded by Edmonton Oilers to Boston Bruins for Mike Krushelnyski.

LONNIE LOACH

Left Wing . . . 5'10" . . . 180 lbs. . . . Born, New Liskeard, Ont., April 14, 1968 . . . Shoots left.

Year	Team	League	Games	G.	A.	Pts.	Pen.
1984-85—St. Mary's Jr. B		OHA	44	26	36	62	113
1985-86—Guelph Platers (c-d)		OHL	65	41	42	83	63
1986-87—Guelph Platers		OHL	56	31	24	55	42
1987-88—Guelph Platers		OHL	66	43	49	92	75

(c)—Won Emms Family Award (OHL Rookie of the Year).

(d)—June, 1986—Drafted as underage junior by Chicago Black Hawks in 1986 NHL entry draft. Fourth Black Hawks pick, 98th overall, fifth round.

JOE LOCKWOOD

Right Wing . . . 6' . . . 180 lbs. . . . Born, Milford, Mich., March 21, 1965 . . . Shoots right.

Year	Team	League	Games	G.	A.	Pts.	Pen.
1984-85—Univ. of Michigan		CCHA	38	5	9	14	42
1985-86—Univ. of Michigan		CCHA	38	7	6	13	45
1986-87—Univ. of Michigan (c)		CCHA	39	13	5	18	62
1987-88—Univ. of Michigan		CCHA	32	11	13	24	42

(c)—June, 1987—Selected by New York Rangers in 1987 NHL supplemental draft.

DARCY LOEWEN

Left Wing . . . 5'10" . . . 180 lbs. . . . Born, Calgary, Alta., February 26, 1969 . . . Shoots left.

Year	Team	League	Games	G.	A.	Pts.	Pen.
1985-86—Spokane Chiefs		WHL	8	2	1	3	19
1986-87—Spokane Chiefs		WHL	68	15	25	40	129
1987-88—Spokane Chiefs (c)		WHL	72	30	44	74	231

(c)—June, 1988—Drafted by Buffalo Sabres in 1988 NHL entry draft. Second Sabres pick, 55th overall, third round.

MARK LOFTHOUSE

Right Wing . . . 6'1" . . . 185 lbs. . . . Born, New Westminster, B.C., April 21, 1957 . . . Shoots right . . . (February, 1983)—Injured back.

Year	Team	League	Games	G.	A.	Pts.	Pen.
1973-74—Kelowna Buckaroos		Jr."A"BCHL	62	44	42	86	59
1974-75—New Westminster Bruins		WCHL	61	36	28	64	53
1975-76—New Westminster Bruins		WCHL	72	68	48	116	55
1976-77—New Westminster Bruins (b-c)		WCHL	70	54	58	112	59
1977-78—Hershey Bears		AHL	35	8	6	14	39
1977-78—Salt Lake City Golden Eagles		CHL	13	0	1	1	4
1977-78—Washington Capitals		NHL	18	2	1	3	8
1978-79—Washington Capitals		NHL	52	13	10	23	10
1978-79—Hershey Bears		AHL	16	7	7	14	6
1979-80—Hershey Bears		AHL	9	7	3	10	6
1979-80—Washington Capitals		NHL	68	15	18	33	20
1980-81—Washington Capitals		NHL	3	1	1	2	4
1980-81—Hershey Bears (a-d-e)		AHL	74	*48	55	*103	131
1981-82—Adirondack Red Wings		AHL	69	33	38	71	75
1981-82—Detroit Red Wings		NHL	12	3	4	7	13
1982-83—Adirondack Red Wings		AHL	39	27	18	45	20
1982-83—Detroit Red Wings (f)		NHL	28	8	4	12	18
1983-84—New Haven Nighthawks (b)		AHL	79	37	64	101	45
1984-85—New Haven Nighthawks		AHL	12	11	4	15	4
1985-86—New Haven Nighthawks		AHL	70	32	35	67	56
1986-87—New Haven Nighthawks (g)		AHL	47	18	27	45	34
1987-88—Hershey Bears		AHL	51	21	21	42	64
NHL TOTALS			181	42	38	80	73

(c)—Drafted from New Westminster Bruins by Washington Capitals in second round of 1977 amateur draft.
(d)—Winner of John B. Sollenberger Trophy (Leading Scorer).
(e)—August, 1981—Traded by Washington Capitals to Detroit Red Wings for Al Jensen.
(f)—August, 1983—Signed by Los Angeles Kings as a free agent.
(g)—August, 1987—Signed by Philadelphia Flyers as a free agent.

BOB LOGAN

Right Wing . . . 6' . . . 190 lbs. . . . Born, Montreal, Que., February 22, 1964 . . . Shoots right.

Year	Team	League	Games	G.	A.	Pts.	Pen.
1982-83—Yale University (c)		ECAC	28	13	12	25	8
1983-84—Yale University		ECAC	22	9	13	22	25
1984-85—Yale University		ECAC	32	19	12	31	18
1985-86—Yale University (b)		ECAC	31	21	23	44	24
1986-87—Buffalo Sabres		NHL	22	7	3	10	0
1986-87—Rochester Americans		AHL	56	30	14	44	27
1987-88—Rochester Americans		AHL	45	23	15	38	35
1987-88—Buffalo Sabres		NHL	16	3	2	5	0
NHL TOTALS			38	10	5	15	0

(c)—June, 1982—Drafted by Buffalo Sabres in 1982 NHL entry draft. Eighth Sabres pick, 100th overall, fifth round.

CLAUDE LOISELLE

Center . . . 5'11" . . . 195 lbs. . . . Born, Ottawa, Ont., May 29, 1963 . . . Shoots left . . . (January 7, 1984)—Given six-game suspension by NHL for a stick-swinging incident with Paul Holmgren of Philadelphia . . . (December 17, 1985)—Injured knee at Minnesota and missed 11 games . . . (February, 1988)—Separated right shoulder.

Year	Team	League	Games	G.	A.	Pts.	Pen.
1979-80—Gloucester Rangers		OPJHL	50	21	38	59	26
1980-81—Windsor Spitfires (c)		OHL	68	38	56	94	103
1981-82—Windsor Spitfires		OHL	68	36	73	109	192
1981-82—Detroit Red Wings		NHL	4	1	0	1	2
1982-83—Detroit Red Wings		NHL	18	2	0	2	15
1982-83—Windsor Spitfires		OHL	46	39	49	88	75
1982-83—Adirondack Red Wings		AHL	6	1	7	8	0
1983-84—Adirondack Red Wings		AHL	29	13	16	29	59
1983-84—Detroit Red Wings		NHL	28	4	6	10	32
1984-85—Adirondack Red Wings		AHL	47	22	29	51	24
1984-85—Detroit Red Wings		NHL	30	8	1	9	45
1985-86—Adirondack Red Wings		AHL	21	15	11	26	32
1985-86—Detroit Red Wings (d)		NHL	48	7	15	22	142
1986-87—New Jersey Devils		NHL	75	16	24	40	137
1987-88—New Jersey Devils		NHL	68	17	18	35	118
NHL TOTALS			271	55	64	119	491

(c)—June, 1981—Drafted as underage junior by Detroit Red Wings in 1981 NHL entry draft. First Red Wings pick, 23rd overall, second round.
(d)—June, 1986—Traded by Detroit Red Wings to New Jersey Devils for Tim Higgins.

BYRON LOMOW

Center ... 5'11" ... 180 lbs. ... Born, Sherwood Park, Alta., April 27, 1965 ... Shoots right.

Year	Team	League	Games	G.	A.	Pts.	Pen.
1982-83	Kamloops Junior Oilers	WHL	40	13	17	30	21
1982-83	Brandon Wheat Kings	WHL	22	6	9	15	9
1983-84	Brandon Wheat Kings	WHL	71	44	57	101	44
1984-85	Brandon Wheat Kings	WHL	71	42	70	112	90
1985-86	Brandon Wheat Kings (c)	WHL	72	52	67	119	77
1985-86	Indianapolis Checkers	IHL	9	8	3	11	10
1986-87	Indianapolis Checkers	IHL	81	28	43	71	225
1987-88	Baltimore Skipjacks (d)	AHL	71	14	26	40	77
1987-88	Colorado Rangers	IHL	10	2	10	12	7

(c)—April, 1986—Signed by Minnesota North Stars as a free agent.
(d)—November, 1987—Traded by Minnesota North Stars to New York Rangers for Curt Giles.

TROY LONEY

Left Wing ... 6'3" ... 215 lbs. ... Born, Bow Island, Alta., September 21, 1963 ... Shoots left ... (December, 1986)—Suspended by AHL ... (January 17, 1987)—Sprained right shoulder at Boston ... (October, 1987)—Knee surgery.

Year	Team	League	Games	G.	A.	Pts.	Pen.
1980-81	Lethbridge Broncos	WHL	71	18	13	31	100
1981-82	Lethbridge Broncos (c)	WHL	71	26	31	57	152
1982-83	Lethbridge Broncos	WHL	72	33	34	67	156
1983-84	Baltimore Skipjacks	AHL	63	18	13	31	147
1983-84	Pittsburgh Penguins	NHL	13	0	0	0	9
1984-85	Baltimore Skipjacks	AHL	15	4	2	6	25
1984-85	Pittsburgh Penguins	NHL	46	10	8	18	59
1985-86	Baltimore Skipjacks	AHL	33	12	11	23	84
1985-86	Pittsburgh Penguins	NHL	47	3	9	12	95
1986-87	Baltimore Skipjacks	AHL	40	13	14	27	134
1986-87	Pittsburgh Penguins	NHL	23	8	7	15	22
1987-88	Pittsburgh Penguins	NHL	65	5	13	18	151
	NHL TOTALS		194	26	37	63	336

(c)—June, 1982—Drafted as underage junior by Pittsburgh Penguins in 1982 NHL entry draft. Third Penguins pick, 52nd overall, third round.

HAKAN LOOB

Right Wing ... 5'9" ... 180 lbs. ... Born, Karlstad, Sweden, July 3, 1960 ... Shoots right ... Set Swedish records in 1982-83 for goals (42), assists (34) and points (76) in a season ... Brother of Peter Loob ... (March 8, 1987)—Broke baby finger on left hand when slashed by Pat Price at N.Y. Rangers ... (August, 1987)—Surgery to right shoulder.

Year	Team	League	Games	G.	A.	Pts.	Pen.
1978-79	Karlskrona IK	Sweden Jr.	....	...	....	....	....
1979-80	Karlstad Farjestads BK (c)	Sweden	36	15	4	19	20
1980-81	Karlstad Farjestads BK (d-e)	Sweden	36	23	6	29	14
1981-82	Karlstad Farjestads BK	Sweden	36	26	15	41	28
1982-83	Karlstad Farjestads BK	Sweden	36	*42	*34	*76	18
1983-84	Calgary Flames	NHL	77	30	25	55	22
1984-85	Calgary Flames	NHL	78	37	35	72	14
1985-86	Calgary Flames	NHL	68	31	36	67	36
1986-87	Calgary Flames	NHL	68	18	26	44	26
1987-88	Calgary Flames (a)	NHL	80	50	56	106	47
	NHL TOTALS		371	166	178	344	145

(c)—June, 1980—Drafted by Calgary Flames in 1980 NHL entry draft. Tenth Flames pick, 181st overall, ninth round.
(d)—Shared Swedish National League playoffs goal scoring lead with teammate Jan Ingman (5 goals).
(e)—Shared Swedish National League playoff point lead with teammate Robin Eriksson (8 points).

GARY LORDEN

Center ... 6'2" ... 190 lbs. ... Born, St. Paul, Minn., January 17, 1966 ... Shoots right.

Year	Team	League	Games	G.	A.	Pts.	Pen.
1984-85	Univ. of Michigan (c)	CCHA	38	1	2	3	22
1985-86	Univ. of Michigan	CCHA	18	0	2	2	6
1986-87	Univ. of Michigan	CCHA	1	0	1	1	2
1987-88	Univ. of Michigan	CCHA	38	1	5	6	33

(c)—June, 1984—Drafted by Winnipeg Jets in 1984 NHL entry draft. Fifth Jets pick, 114th overall, sixth round.

KEVIN HUGH LOWE

Defense . . . 6' . . . 185 lbs. . . . Born, Lachute, Que., April 15, 1959 . . . Shoots left . . . Cousin of Mike Lowe (St. Louis 1969 draft pick) . . . (March 7, 1986)—Broke index finger vs. Pittsburgh and missed six games . . . (March 9, 1988)—Broke left wrist vs. Montreal.

Year	Team	League	Games	G.	A.	Pts.	Pen.
1976-77—Quebec Remparts		QMJHL	69	3	19	22	39
1977-78—Quebec Remparts		QMJHL	64	13	52	65	86
1978-79—Quebec Remparts (b-c)		QMJHL	68	26	60	86	120
1979-80—Edmonton Oilers		NHL	64	2	19	21	70
1980-81—Edmonton Oilers		NHL	79	10	24	34	94
1981-82—Edmonton Oilers		NHL	80	9	31	40	63
1982-83—Edmonton Oilers		NHL	80	6	34	40	43
1983-84—Edmonton Oilers		NHL	80	4	42	46	59
1984-85—Edmonton Oilers		NHL	80	4	22	26	104
1985-86—Edmonton Oilers		NHL	74	2	16.	18	90
1986-87—Edmonton Oilers		NHL	77	8	29	37	94
1987-88—Edmonton Oilers		NHL	70	9	15	24	89
NHL TOTALS			684	54	232	286	706

(c)—August, 1979—Drafted by Edmonton Oilers in 1979 entry draft. First Oilers pick, 21st overall, first round.

GLEN LOWES

Left Wing . . . 6' . . . 190 lbs. . . . Born, Burlington, Ont., January 17, 1968 . . . Shoots left.

Year	Team	League	Games	G.	A.	Pts.	Pen.
1984-85—Burlington Midgets		OMHA	41	22	39	61	168
1985-86—Toronto Marlboros (c)		OHL	64	8	14	22	134
1986-87—Toronto Marlboros		OHL	49	10	14	24	118
1987-88—Toronto Marlboros		OHL	44	12	12	24	125

(c)—June, 1986—Drafted as underage junior by Chicago Black Hawks in 1986 NHL entry draft. Ninth Black Hawks pick, 203rd overall, 10th round.

DAVE LOWRY

Left Wing . . . 6'2" . . . 175 lbs. . . . Born, Sudbury, Ont., January 14, 1965 . . . Shoots left . . . (December, 1982)—Arthroscopic surgery on knee.

Year	Team	League	Games	G.	A.	Pts.	Pen.
1981-82—Nepean Midgets		Ont. Midget	60	50	64	114	46
1982-83—London Knights (c)		OHL	42	11	16	27	48
1983-84—London Knights		OHL	66	29	47	76	125
1984-85—London Knights (a)		OHL	61	60	60	120	94
1985-86—Vancouver Canucks		NHL	73	10	8	18	143
1986-87—Vancouver Canucks		NHL	70	8	10	18	176
1987-88—Fredericton Express		AHL	46	18	27	45	59
1987-88—Vancouver Canucks		NHL	22	1	3	4	38
NHL TOTALS			165	19	21	40	357

(c)—June, 1983—Drafted as underage junior by Vancouver Canucks in 1983 NHL entry draft. Fourth Canucks pick, 110th overall, sixth round.

JAN LUDVIG

Right Wing . . . 5'10" . . . 187 lbs. . . . Born, Liberec, Czechoslovakia, September 17, 1961 . . . Shoots right . . . (December, 1982)—Bruised ribs . . . (January, 1984)—Hip Injury . . . (December, 1985)—Injured left tibula . . . (January 21, 1986)—Missed two games with a bruised knee . . . (November, 1986)—Dislocated left shoulder . . . (October, 1987)—Torn cartilage in right knee.

Year	Team	League	Games	G.	A.	Pts.	Pen.
1981-82—St. Albert Saints (c)		AJHL	4	2	4	6	20
1981-82—Kamloops Oilers		WHL	37	31	34	65	36
1982-83—Wichita Wind (d)		CHL	9	3	0	3	19
1982-83—New Jersey Devils		NHL	51	7	10	17	30
1983-84—New Jersey Devils		NHL	74	22	32	54	70
1984-85—New Jersey Devils		NHL	74	12	19	31	53
1985-86—New Jersey Devils		NHL	42	5	9	14	63
1986-87—Maine Mariners		AHL	14	6	4	10	46
1986-87—New Jersey Devils (e)		NHL	47	7	9	16	98
1987-88—Buffalo Sabres		NHL	13	1	6	7	65
NHL TOTALS			301	54	85	139	379

(c)—October, 1981—Signed by Edmonton Oilers as a free agent.
(d)—November, 1982—Signed by New Jersey Devils as a free agent.
(e)—May, 1987—Traded by New Jersey Devils to Buffalo Sabres for Jim Korn.

CRAIG LEE LUDWIG

Defense . . . 6'3" . . . 212 lbs. . . . Born, Rhinelander, Wis., March 15, 1961 . . . Shoots left . . . (October, 1984)—Fractured knuckle in left hand in pre-season game . . . (December 2, 1985)—Broke hand vs. Vancouver and missed nine games . . . (January, 1988)—Missed five games with a broken right facial bone in a collision with Mikael Andersson vs. Buffalo.

Year	Team	League	Games	G.	A.	Pts.	Pen.
1979-80—University of North Dakota (c)		WCHA	33	1	8	9	32
1980-81—University of North Dakota		WCHA	34	4	8	12	48
1981-82—University of North Dakota (b)		WCHA	47	5	26	31	70
1982-83—Montreal Canadiens		NHL	80	0	25	25	59
1983-84—Montreal Canadiens		NHL	72	4	13	17	45
1984-85—Montreal Canadiens		NHL	72	5	14	19	90
1985-86—Montreal Canadiens		NHL	69	2	4	6	63
1986-87—Montreal Canadiens		NHL	75	4	12	16	105
1987-88—Montreal Canadiens		NHL	74	4	10	14	69
NHL TOTALS			442	19	78	97	431

(c)—June, 1980—Drafted by Montreal Canadiens in 1980 NHL entry draft. Fifth Canadiens pick, 61st overall, third round.

STEVE LUDZIK

Center . . . 5'11" . . . 185 lbs. . . . Born, Toronto, Ont., April 3, 1961 . . . Shoots left . . . (October 19, 1985)—Broke left foot at Detroit . . . (December 29, 1985)—Injured foot vs. Boston and missed four games . . . (January 26, 1987)—Broke collarbone at Montreal.

Year	Team	League	Games	G.	A.	Pts.	Pen.
1977-78—Markham Waxers		OPJHL	34	15	24	39	20
1978-79—Niagara Falls Flyers		OMJHL	68	32	65	97	138
1979-80—Niagara Falls Flyers (c)		OMJHL	67	43	76	119	102
1980-81—Niagara Falls Flyers		OHL	58	50	92	142	108
1981-82—Chicago Black Hawks		NHL	8	2	1	3	2
1981-82—New Brunswick Hawks		AHL	75	21	41	62	142
1982-83—Chicago Black Hawks		NHL	66	6	19	25	63
1983-84—Chicago Black Hawks		FHL	80	9	20	29	73
1984-85—Chicago Black Hawks		NHL	79	11	20	31	86
1985-86—Chicago Black Hawks		NHL	49	6	5	11	21
1986-87—Chicago Black Hawks		NHL	52	5	12	17	34
1987-88—Chicago Black Hawks		NHL	73	6	15	21	40
NHL TOTALS			407	45	92	137	319

(c)—June, 1980—Drafted as underage junior by Chicago Black Hawks in 1980 NHL entry draft. Third Black Hawks pick, 28th overall, second round.

JAAN LUIK

Defense . . . 6'1" . . . 210 lbs. . . . Born, Scarborough, Ont., January 15, 1970 . . . Shoots left . . . Twin brother of Scott Luik.

Year	Team	League	Games	G.	A.	Pts.	Pen.
1986-87—Toronto Marlboro Midget		MTHL	66	7	27	34	125
1987-88—Miami Univ. of Ohio (c)		CCHA	35	2	5	7	93

(c)—June, 1988—Drafted by St. Louis Blues in 1988 NHL entry draft. Fourth Blues pick, 72nd overall, fourth round.

SCOTT LUIK

Right Wing . . . 6'1" . . . 210 lbs. . . . Born, Scarborough, Ont., January 15, 1970 . . . Shoots right . . . Twin brother of Jaan Luik.

Year	Team	League	Games	G.	A.	Pts.	Pen.
1986-87—Toronto Marlboro Midget		MTHL	65	34	37	71	102
1987-88—Miami Univ. of Ohio (c)		CCHA	34	4	10	14	47

(c)—June, 1988—Drafted by New Jersey Devils in 1988 NHL entry draft. Fifth Devils pick, 75th overall, fourth round.

CHRISTOPHER LUONGO

Defense . . . 6' . . . 180 lbs. . . . Born, Detroit, Mich., March 17, 1967 . . . Shoots right.

Year	Team	League	Games	G.	A.	Pts.	Pen.
1984-85—St. Clair Shores Falcons (c)		NAJHL	41	2	25	27	....
1985-86—Michigan State Univ.		CCHA	38	1	5	6	29
1986-87—Michigan State Univ.		CCHA	27	4	16	20	38
1987-88—Michigan State Univ.		CCHA	45	3	15	18	49

(c)—June, 1985—Drafted by Detroit Red Wings in 1985 NHL entry draft. Fifth Red Wings pick, 92nd overall, fifth round.

KEN MacARTHUR

Defense . . . 6'1" . . . 185 lbs. . . . Born, Rossland, B.C., March 15, 1968 . . . Shoots left . . . (November, 1986)—Strained knee.

Year	Team	League	Games	G.	A.	Pts.	Pen.
1986-87—Penticton Knights		BCJHL	30	20	23	43	25
1987-88—University of Denver (c)		WCHA	38	6	16	22	69

(c)—June, 1988—Drafted by Minnesota North Stars in 1988 NHL entry draft. Fifth North Stars pick, 148th overall, eighth round.

PAUL MacDERMID

Center . . . 6' . . . 188 lbs. . . . Born, Chesley, Ont., April 14, 1963 . . . Shoots right . . . (December, 1982)—Injured knee.

Year	Team	League	Games	G.	A.	Pts.	Pen.
1979-80—Port Elgin Bears		OHA Jr.'C'	30	23	20	43	87
1980-81—Windsor Spitfires (c)		OHL	68	15	17	32	106
1981-82—Windsor Spitfires		OHL	65	26	45	71	179
1981-82—Hartford Whalers		NHL	3	1	0	1	2
1982-83—Windsor Spitfires		OHL	42	35	45	80	90
1982-83—Hartford Whalers		NHL	7	0	0	0	2
1983-84—Hartford Whalers		NHL	3	0	1	1	0
1983-84—Binghamton Whalers		AHL	70	31	30	61	130
1984-85—Binghamton Whalers		AHL	48	9	31	40	87
1984-85—Hartford Whalers		NHL	31	4	7	11	299
1985-86—Hartford Whalers		NHL	74	13	10	23	160
1986-87—Hartford Whalers		NHL	72	7	11	18	202
1987-88—Hartford Whalers		NHL	80	20	14	34	139
NHL TOTALS			270	45	43	88	534

(c)—June, 1981—Drafted as underage junior in 1981 NHL entry draft by Hartford Whalers. Second Whalers pick, 61st overall, third round.

BRETT MacDONALD

Defense . . . 6' . . . 195 lbs. . . . Born, Bothwell, Ont., January 5, 1966 . . . Shoots left.

Year	Team	League	Games	G.	A.	Pts.	Pen.
1982-83—Dixie Beehives		MTJHL	44	5	18	23	28
1983-84—North Bay Centennials (c)		OHL	70	8	18	26	83
1984-85—North Bay Centennials		OHL	58	6	27	33	72
1985-86—North Bay Centennials		OHL	15	0	6	6	42
1985-86—Kitchener Rangers		OHL	53	10	27	37	52
1986-87—Fredericton Express		AHL	49	0	9	9	29
1987-88—Vancouver Canucks		NHL	1	0	0	0	0
1987-88—Fredericton Express		AHL	15	1	5	6	23
1987-88—Flint Spirits		IHL	49	2	21	23	43
NHL TOTALS			1	0	0	0	0

(c)—June, 1984—Drafted as underage junior by Vancouver Canucks in NHL entry draft. Sixth Canucks pick, 94th overall, fifth round.

BRUCE MacDONALD

Right Wing . . . 6'1" . . . 190 lbs. . . . . Born, Utica, N.Y., December 16, 1967 . . . Shoots right.

Year	Team	League	Games	G.	A.	Pts.	Pen.
1984-85—Loomis Chaffee H.S.		Pa. H.S.	24	17	25	42	....
1985-86—Loomis Chaffee H.S.		Pa. H.S.	28	27	42	69	20
1986-87—Loomis Chaffee H.S. (c)		Pa. H.S.	25	30	33	63	54
1987-88—Univ. of New Hampshire		H. East	12	0	1	1	8

(c)—June, 1987—Drafted by Philadelphia Flyers in 1987 NHL entry draft. Ninth Flyers pick, 188th overall, ninth round.

SHANE MacEACHERN

Center . . . 5'11" . . . 179 lbs. . . . Born, Charlottetown, PEI, December 14, 1967 . . . Shoots left.

Year	Team	League	Games	G.	A.	Pts.	Pen.
1983-84—Verdun Juniors		QMJHL	65	13	27	40	62
1984-85—Verdun Juniors		QMJHL	57	14	21	35	109
1985-86—Hull Olympiques (c)		QMJHL	70	20	45	65	128
1986-87—Hull Olympiques		QMJHL	69	44	58	102	126
1987-88—Peoria Rivermen		IHL	68	18	30	48	67
1987-88—St. Louis Blues		NHL	1	0	0	0	0
NHL TOTALS			1	0	0	0	0

(c)—September, 1986—Signed by St. Louis Blues as a free agent.

ALLAN MacINNIS

Defense . . . 6'1" . . . 183 lbs. . . . Born, Inverness, N.S., July 11, 1963 . . . Shoots right . . . (February, 1985)—Twisted knee . . . (March 23, 1986)—Lacerated hand at Winnipeg.

Year	Team	League	Games	G.	A.	Pts.	Pen.
1979-80	Regina Blues	SJHL	59	20	28	48	110
1980-81	Kitchener Rangers (c)	OHL	47	11	28	39	59
1981-82	Kitchener Rangers (a)	OHL	59	25	50	75	145
1981-82	Calgary Flames	NHL	2	0	0	0	0
1982-83	Kitchener Rangers (a-d)	OHL	51	38	46	84	67
1982-83	Calgary Flames	NHL	14	1	3	4	9
1983-84	Colorado Flames	CHL	19	5	14	19	22
1983-84	Calgary Flames	NHL	51	11	34	45	42
1984-85	Calgary Flames	NHL	67	14	52	66	75
1985-86	Calgary Flames (e)	NHL	77	11	57	68	76
1986-87	Calgary Flames (b)	NHL	79	20	56	76	97
1987-88	Calgary Flames	NHL	80	25	58	83	114
	NHL TOTALS		370	82	260	342	413

(c)—June, 1981—Drafted as underage junior by Calgary Flames in 1981 NHL entry draft. First Flames pick, 15th overall, first round.
(d)—Won Max Kaminsky Trophy (Outstanding Defenseman).
(e)—Led Stanley Cup Playoffs with 15 assists.

JOSEPH MacINNIS

Center . . . 6' . . . 165 lbs. . . . Born, Cambridge, Mass., May 25, 1966 . . . Shoots left.

Year	Team	League	Games	G.	A.	Pts.	Pen.
1983-84	Watertown H.S. (c)	Mass. H.S.	18	28	18	46	....
1984-85	Northeastern University	H. East	33	4	3	7	20
1985-86	Northeastern University	H. East	20	4	3	7	10
1986-87	Northeastern University	H. East	29	7	8	15	33
1987-88	Northeastern University	H. East	30	10	4	14	36

(c)—June, 1984—Drafted by Toronto Maple Leafs in NHL entry draft. Sixth Maple Leafs pick, 130th overall, seventh round.

NORM MACIVER

Defense . . . 5'11" . . . 180 lbs. . . . Born, Thunder Bay, Ont., September 8, 1964 . . . Shoots left . . . (March, 1988)—Dislocated right shoulder.

Year	Team	League	Games	G.	A.	Pts.	Pen.
1982-83	Univ. of Minn./Duluth	WCHA	45	1	26	27	40
1983-84	Univ. of Minn./Duluth	WCHA	31	13	28	41	28
1984-85	Univ. of Minn./Duluth	WCHA	47	14	47	61	63
1985-86	Univ. of Minn./Duluth	WCHA	42	11	51	62	36
1985-86	New Haven Nighthawks	AHL	71	6	30	36	73
1985-86	New York Rangers (c)	NHL	3	0	1	1	0
1987-88	Colorado Rangers	IHL	27	6	20	26	22
1987-88	New York Rangers	NHL	37	9	15	24	14
	NHL TOTALS		40	9	16	25	14

(c)—September, 1986—Signed by New York Rangers as a free agent.

JEAN-MARC MacKENZIE

Center . . . 5'10" . . . 180 lbs. . . . Born, Sydney, N.S., October 29, 1966 . . . Shoots left.

Year	Team	League	Games	G.	A.	Pts.	Pen.
1982-83	Cape Breton	N.S. Midget	32	33	34	67	20
1983-84	Sault Ste. Marie Greyhounds	OHL	29	5	10	15	12
1984-85	Sault Ste. Marie Greyhounds	OHL	60	16	29	45	13
1985-86	Sault Ste. Marie Greyhounds	OHL	64	28	26	54	10
1986-87	London Knights (c)	OHL	63	49	56	105	20
1986-87	Binghamton Whalers	AHL	3	0	0	0	0
1987-88	Milwaukee Admirals	IHL	56	16	18	34	21

(c)—March, 1987—Signed by Hartford Whalers as a free agent.

DAVID MACKEY

Left Wing . . . 6'3" . . . 190 lbs. . . . Born, New Westminster, B.C., July 24, 1966 . . . Shoots left.

Year	Team	League	Games	G.	A.	Pts.	Pen.
1981-82	Seafair	B.C. Midgets	60	48	62	110	99
1982-83	Victoria Cougars	WHL	69	16	16	32	53
1983-84	Victoria Cougars (c)	WHL	69	15	15	30	97

Year	Team	League	Games	G.	A.	Pts.	Pen.
1984-85—Victoria Cougars		WHL	16	5	6	11	45
1984-85—Portland Winter Hawks		WHL	56	28	32	60	122
1985-86—Kamloops Blazers (d)		WHL	9	3	4	7	13
1985-86—Medicine Hat Tigers		WHL	60	25	32	57	167
1986-87—Saginaw Gears		IHL	81	26	49	75	173
1987-88—Saginaw Hawks		IHL	62	29	22	51	211
1987-88—Chicago Black Hawks		NHL	23	1	3	4	71
NHL TOTALS			23	1	3	4	71

(c)—June, 1984—Drafted as underage junior by Chicago Black Hawks in NHL entry draft. Twelfth Black Hawks pick, 224th overall, 11th round.

(d)—December, 1986—Traded with Rob Dimaio and Calvin Knibbs by Kamloops Blazers to Medicine Hat Tigers for Doug Pickel and Sean Pass.

JOHN MacLEAN

Right Wing . . . 6' . . . 195 lbs. . . . Born, Oshawa, Ont., November 20, 1964 . . . Shoots right . . . (November, 1984)—Bruised shoulder vs. N.Y. Rangers . . . (January 25, 1985)—Injured right knee at Edmonton . . . (January 31, 1985)—Reinjured knee and underwent arthroscopic surgery . . . (November 2, 1986)—Bruised ankle vs. N.Y. Rangers.

Year	Team	League	Games	G.	A.	Pts.	Pen.
1981-82—Oshawa Generals		OHL	67	17	22	39	197
1982-83—Oshawa Generals (c-d)		OHL	66	47	51	98	138
1983-84—New Jersey Devils		NHL	23	1	0	1	10
1983-84—Oshawa Generals		OHL	30	23	36	59	58
1984-85—New Jersey Devils		NHL	61	13	20	33	44
1985-86—New Jersey Devils		NHL	74	21	37	58	112
1986-87—New Jersey Devils		NHL	80	31	36	67	120
1987-88—New Jersey Devils		NHL	76	23	16	39	145
NHL TOTALS			314	89	109	198	431

(c)—Led OHL playoffs with 18 goals and shared OHL playoff point lead with teammate Dave Gans with 38 points.

(d)—June, 1983—Drafted as underage junior by New Jersey Devils in 1983 NHL entry draft. First Devils pick, sixth overall, first round.

PAUL MacLEAN

Right Wing . . . 6' . . . 205 lbs. . . . Born, Grostenquin, France, March 9, 1958 . . . Shoots right . . . Member of 1980 Canadian Olympic team . . . (October, 1985)—Jammed thumb . . . (March 8, 1987)—Stretched knee ligaments in a collision with Mario Lemieux vs. Pittsburgh.

Year	Team	League	Games	G.	A.	Pts.	Pen.
1977-78—Hull Festivals (c)		QMJHL	66	38	33	71	125
1978-79—Canadian National Team		Int'l	....	...	....	....	....
1979-80—Canadian National Team		Int'l	50	21	11	32	90
1979-80—Canadian Olympic Team		Oly.	6	2	3	5	6
1980-81—Salt Lake City		CHL	80	36	42	78	160
1980-81—St. Louis Blues (d)		NHL	1	0	0	0	0
1981-82—Winnipeg Jets		NHL	74	36	25	61	106
1982-83—Winnipeg Jets		NHL	80	32	44	76	121
1983-84—Winnipeg Jets		NHL	76	40	31	71	155
1984-85—Winnipeg Jets		NHL	79	41	60	101	119
1985-86—Winnipeg Jets		NHL	69	27	29	56	74
1986-87—Winnipeg Jets		NHL	72	32	42	74	75
1987-88—Winnipeg Jets (e)		NHL	77	40	39	79	76
NHL TOTALS			528	248	270	518	726

(c)—June, 1978—Drafted by St. Louis Blues in 1978 NHL amateur draft. Sixth Blues pick, 109th overall, seventh round.

(d)—July, 1981—Traded by St. Louis Blues with Ed Staniowski and Bryan Maxwell to Winnipeg Jets for John Markell and Scott Campbell.

(e)—June, 1988—Traded by Winnipeg Jets to Detroit Red Wings for Brent Ashton.

TERRY MacLEAN

Center . . . 6'1" . . . 178 lbs. . . . Born, Montreal, Que., January 14, 1968 . . . Shoots left.

Year	Team	League	Games	G.	A.	Pts.	Pen.
1984-85—Quebec Remparts		QMJHL	69	21	45	66	10
1985-86—Longueuil Chevaliers (c)		QMJHL	70	36	45	81	18
1986-87—Longueuil-Trois-Rivieres		QMJHL	69	41	76	117	20
1987-88—Trois-Rivieres Draveurs		QMJHL	69	52	91	143	44

(c)—June, 1986—Drafted by St. Louis in 1986 NHL entry draft. Eleventh Blues pick, 220th overall, 11th round.

BRIAN MacLELLAN

Left Wing ... 6'3" ... 212 lbs. ... Born, Guelph, Ont., October 27, 1958 ... Shoots left.

Year	Team	League	Games	G.	A.	Pts.	Pen.
1978-79	Bowling Green University	CCHA	44	34	29	63	94
1979-80	Bowling Green University	CCHA	38	8	15	23	46
1980-81	Bowling Green University	CCHA	37	11	14	25	96
1981-82	Bowling Green University (c)	CCHA	41	11	21	32	109
1982-83	Los Angeles Kings	NHL	8	0	3	3	7
1982-83	New Haven Nighthawks	AHL	71	11	15	26	40
1983-84	New Haven Nighthawks	AHL	2	0	2	2	0
1983-84	Los Angeles Kings	NHL	72	25	29	54	45
1984-85	Los Angeles Kings	NHL	80	31	54	85	53
1985-86	Los Angeles Kings (d)	NHL	27	5	8	13	19
1985-86	New York Rangers	NHL	51	11	21	32	47
1986-87	Minnesota North Stars (e)	NHL	76	32	31	63	69
1987-88	Minnesota North Stars	NHL	75	16	32	48	74
	NHL TOTALS		389	120	178	298	314

(c)—April, 1982—Signed by Los Angeles Kings as a free agent.
(d)—December, 1985—Traded with a fourth round 1987 draft pick by Los Angeles Kings to New York Rangers for Roland Melanson and Grant Ledyard. The Rangers had earlier traded a second round 1986 pick (Neil Wilkinson) and a fourth round 1987 draft pick to Minnesota for Melanson. Melanson was then traded with Ledyard to Los Angeles.
(e)—September, 1986—Traded by New York Rangers to Minnesota North Stars for a third-round 1987 draft pick (Simon Gagne).

JAMIE MACOUN

Defense ... 6'2" ... 200 lbs. ... Born, Newmarket, Ont., August 17, 1961 ... Shoots left ... (December 26, 1984)—Cheekbone fractured in altercation with Mark Messier vs. Edmonton. Messier was given a 10-game NHL suspension because of the incident ... (May, 1987)—Nerve damage to left arm in automobile accident.

Year	Team	League	Games	G.	A.	Pts.	Pen.
1980-81	Ohio State University	CCHA	38	9	20	29	83
1981-82	Ohio State University	CCHA	25	2	18	20	89
1982-83	Ohio State University (c)	CCHA	.....	...	.....	....	....
1982-83	Calgary Flames	NHL	22	1	4	5	25
1983-84	Calgary Flames	NHL	72	9	23	32	97
1984-85	Calgary Flames	NHL	70	9	30	39	67
1985-86	Calgary Flames	NHL	77	11	21	32	81
1986-87	Calgary Flames	NHL	79	7	33	40	111
1987-88	Did not play		...	...	.....	....	....
	NHL TOTALS		320	37	111	148	381

(c)—January, 1983—Left Ohio State University to sign with Calgary Flames as a free agent.

DUNCAN MacPHERSON

Defense ... 6'1" ... 190 lbs. ... Born, Saskatoon, Sask., February 3, 1966 ... Shoots left ... Missed almost half of the 1983-84 season with an ankle injury ... (September, 1984)—Bruised left knee in N.Y. Islanders training camp ... (October, 1986)—Knee injury.

Year	Team	League	Games	G.	A.	Pts.	Pen.
1982-83	Battleford Barons	SAJHL	59	6	11	17	215
1983-84	Saskatoon Blades (c)	WHL	45	0	14	14	74
1984-85	Saskatoon Blades	WHL	69	9	26	35	116
1985-86	Saskatoon Blades	WHL	70	10	54	64	147
1986-87	Springfield Indians	AHL	26	1	0	1	86
1987-88	Springfield Indians	AHL	74	5	14	19	213

(c)—June, 1984—Drafted as underage junior by New York Islanders in NHL entry draft. First Islanders pick, 20th overall, first round.

STEVE MacSWAIN

Center ... 5'8" ... 190 lbs. ... Born, Anchorage, Alaska, August 8, 1965 ... Shoots right.

Year	Team	League	Games	G.	A.	Pts.	Pen.
1983-84	Univ. of Minnesota	WCHA	28	8	10	18	12
1984-85	Univ. of Minnesota	WCHA	10	2	0	2	18
1985-86	Univ. of Minnesota (c)	WCHA	48	26	35	61	61
1986-87	Univ. of Minnesota	WCHA	48	31	29	60	24
1987-88	Salt Lake Golden Eagles	IHL	61	16	20	36	52

(c)—June, 1986—Selected by Calgary Flames in 1986 NHL supplemental draft.

CRAIG MacTAVISH

Center . . . 6' . . . 185 lbs. . . . Born, London, Ont., August 15, 1958 . . . Shoots left . . . Also plays Left Wing . . . (January, 1984)—Involved in automobile accident in which Kim Lea Radley was killed. He was charged with vehicular homicide, driving while under the influence of alcohol and reckless driving. In May he pleaded guilty and was convicted by Essex, Mass., Superior court and sentenced to a year in prison.

Year	Team	League	Games	G.	A.	Pts.	Pen.
1977-78—University of Lowell (b-c-d)	ECAC	....	...	....	....	....
1978-79—University of Lowell (a-e)	ECAC-II	....	36	52	*88	....
1979-80—Binghamton Dusters	AHL	34	17	15	32	20
1979-80—Boston Bruins	NHL	46	11	17	28	8
1980-81—Boston Bruins	NHL	24	3	5	8	13
1980-81—Springfield Indians	AHL	53	19	24	43	89
1981-82—Erie Blades	AHL	72	23	32	55	37
1981-82—Boston Bruins	NHL	2	0	1	1	0
1982-83—Boston Bruins	NHL	75	10	20	30	18
1983-84—Boston Bruins	NHL	70	20	23	43	35
1984-85—Boston Bruins (f)	NHL	....	...	....	....	....
1985-86—Edmonton Oilers	NHL	74	23	24	47	70
1986-87—Edmonton Oilers	NHL	79	20	19	39	55
1987-88—Edmonton Oilers	NHL	80	15	17	32	47
NHL TOTALS			450	102	126	228	246

(c)—June, 1978—Drafted by Boston Bruins in amateur draft. Ninth Bruins pick, 153rd overall, ninth round.
(d)—Named ECAC Division II Rookie of the Year.
(e)—Named ECAC Division II Player of the Year.
(f)—February, 1984—Signed by Edmonton Oilers as a free agent.

ANDREW MacVICAR

Left Wing . . . 6'1" . . . 195 lbs. . . . Born, Halifax, N.S., March 12, 1969 . . . Shoots left.

Year	Team	League	Games	G.	A.	Pts.	Pen.
1985-86—Halifax Midget	N.S. Midget	34	29	32	61	77
1986-87—Peterborough Petes (c)	OHL	64	6	13	19	33
1987-88—Peterborough Petes	OHL	62	30	51	81	45

(c)—June, 1987—Drafted as underage junior by Buffalo Sabres in 1987 NHL entry draft. Third Sabres pick, 53rd overall, third round.

JEFF MADILL

Right Wing . . . 5'11" . . . 195 lbs. . . . Born, Oshawa, Ont., June 21, 1965 . . . Shoots right.

Year	Team	League	Games	G.	A.	Pts.	Pen.
1984-85—Ohio State Univ.	CCHA	12	5	6	11	18
1985-86—Ohio State Univ.	CCHA	41	32	25	57	65
1986-87—Ohio State Univ. (c)	CCHA	43	38	32	70	139
1987-88—Utica Devils	AHL	58	18	15	33	127

(c)—June, 1987—Selected by New Jersey Devils in 1987 NHL supplemental draft.

KEVIN MAGUIRE

Right Wing . . . 6'2" . . . 200 lbs. . . . Born, Toronto, Ont., January 5, 1963 . . . Shoots right . . . (February, 1988)—Fractured ankle vs. Winnipeg.

Year	Team	League	Games	G.	A.	Pts.	Pen.
1983-84—Orillia Travelways	OHA	....	35	42	77	....
1984-85—St. Catharines Saints (c)	AHL	76	10	15	25	112
1985-86—St. Catharines Saints	AHL	61	6	9	15	161
1986-87—Newmarket Saints	AHL	51	4	2	6	131
1986-87—Toronto Maple Leafs	NHL	17	0	0	0	74
1987-88—Buffalo Sabres (d)	NHL	46	4	6	10	162
NHL TOTALS			63	4	6	10	236

(c)—September, 1984—Signed by Toronto Maple Leafs as a free agent.
(d)—October, 1988—Acquired by Buffalo Sabres in 1987 NHL waiver draft.

SCOTT MAHONEY

Left Wing . . . 6' . . . 188 lbs. . . . Born, Peterborough, Ont., April 19, 1969 . . . Shoots right.

Year	Team	League	Games	G.	A.	Pts.	Pen.
1986-87—Oshawa Generals (c)	OHL	54	13	9	22	161
1987-88—Oshawa Generals	OHL	60	10	21	31	272

(c)—June, 1987—Drafted by Calgary Flames as an underage junior in 1987 NHL entry draft. Fourth Flames pick, 61st overall, third round.

BRUCE MAJOR

Center . . . 6'3" . . . 180 lbs. . . . Born, Vernon, B.C., January 3, 1967 . . . Shoots left.

Year	Team	League	Games	G.	A.	Pts.	Pen.
1984-85—Richmond Sockeyes (c)		BCJHL	48	43	56	99	56
1985-86—University of Maine		H. East	38	14	14	28	39
1986-87—University of Maine		H. East	37	14	10	24	12
1987-88—University of Maine		H. East	26	0	5	5	14

(c)—June, 1985—Drafted by Quebec Nordiques in 1985 NHL entry draft. Sixth Nordiques pick, 99th overall, fifth round.

MARK MAJOR

Left Wing . . . 6'3" . . . 205 lbs. . . . Born, Toronto, Ont., March 20, 1970 . . . Shoots left.

Year	Team	League	Games	G.	A.	Pts.	Pen.
1986-87—Don Mills Flyers Midget		MTHL	36	12	14	26	81
1987-88—North Bay Centennials (c)		OHL	57	16	17	33	272

(c)—June, 1988—Drafted by Pittsburgh Penguins in 1988 NHL entry draft. Second Penguins pick, 25th overall, second round.

MIKKO MAKELA

Right Wing . . . 6'2" . . . 195 lbs. . . . Born, Tampere, Finland, February 28, 1965 . . . Shoots left . . . Also plays Center . . . (November 1, 1985)—Injured back at Washington and missed 15 games . . . (February, 1988)—Infected elbow.

Year	Team	League	Games	G.	A.	Pts.	Pen.
1984-85—Ilves Tampere		Finland	35	17	11	28	....
1984-85—Ilves Tampere (a-c-d)		Finland	36	*34	25	59	24
1985-86—Springfield Indians		AHL	2	1	1	2	0
1985-86—New York Islanders		NHL	58	16	20	36	28
1986-87—New York Islanders		NHL	80	24	33	57	24
1987-88—New York Islanders		NHL	73	36	40	76	22
NHL TOTALS			211	76	93	169	74

(c)—June, 1983—Drafted by New York Islanders in 1983 NHL entry draft. Fifth Islanders pick, 65th overall, fourth round.

(d)—Won Most Gentlemanly Player Trophy.

DAVID MALEY

Center . . . 6'3" . . . 200 lbs. . . . Born, Beaver Dam, Wis., April 24, 1963 . . . Shoots left . . . (May, 1987)—Suspended prior to a playoff game with Rochester.

Year	Team	League	Games	G.	A.	Pts.	Pen.
1981-82—Edina H.S. (c)		Minn. H.S.	26	22	28	50	26
1982-83—University of Wisconsin		WCHA	47	17	23	40	24
1983-84—University of Wisconsin		WCHA	38	10	28	38	56
1984-85—University of Wisconsin		WCHA	35	19	9	28	86
1985-86—University of Wisconsin		WCHA	42	20	40	60	*135
1985-86—Montreal Canadiens		NHL	3	0	0	0	0
1986-87—Sherbrooke Canadiens		AHL	11	1	5	6	25
1986-87—Montreal Canadiens (d)		NHL	48	6	12	18	55
1987-88—Utica Devils		AHL	9	5	3	8	40
1987-88—New Jersey Devils		NHL	44	4	2	6	65
NHL TOTALS			95	10	14	24	120

(c)—June, 1982—Drafted by Montreal Canadiens as underage player in 1982 NHL entry draft. Fourth Canadiens pick, 33rd overall, second round.

(d)—June, 1987—Traded by Montreal Canadiens to New Jersey Devils for a third-round 1987 draft pick (Mathieu Schneider).

TROY MALLETTE

Center . . . 6'2" . . . 190 lbs. . . . Born, Sudbury, Ont., February 25, 1970 . . . Shoots left . . . Also plays Left Wing.

Year	Team	League	Games	G.	A.	Pts.	Pen.
1985-86—Rayside-Belfour Midget		OHA	27	24	26	50	75
1986-87—Sault Ste. Marie Greyhounds		OHL	65	20	25	45	157
1987-88—Sault Ste. Marie Greyhounds (c)		OHL	62	18	30	48	186

(c)—June, 1988—Drafted by New York Rangers in 1988 NHL entry draft. First Rangers pick, 22nd overall, second round.

DONALD MICHAEL MALONEY

Left Wing . . . 6'1" . . . 190 lbs. . . . Born, Lindsay, Ont., September 5, 1958 . . . Shoots left . . . Brother of Dave Maloney . . . (October, 1980)—Mononucleosis . . . Set record for most

points by a rookie in playoffs (20) in 1979 (broken in 1981 by Dino Ciccarelli with 21) . . . (October 24, 1981)—Partial ligament tear in right knee at Toronto. He missed 25 games and returned to lineup December 23, 1981 . . . (November 28, 1983)—Broke ring finger of right hand with Vancouver . . . (October, 1984)—Pulled abdominal muscle injury . . . (November 18, 1984)—Broke leg and ankle in collision with Bruce Driver vs. New Jersey. He required surgery and a pin was inserted in his leg . . . (October 1, 1985)—Suspended by NHL for first three games of season for fighting in a pre-season game with Philadelphia . . . (November 20, 1985)—Injured knee vs. Toronto and missed nine games . . . (November, 1987)—Injured left shoulder rotator cuff . . . (December, 1987)—Groin injury.

Year	Team	League	Games	G.	A.	Pts.	Pen.
1974-75—Kitchener Rangers		Jr."A"OHA	5	1	3	4	0
1975-76—Kitchener Rangers		Jr."A"OHA	61	27	41	68	132
1976-77—Kitchener Rangers		Jr."A"OHA	38	22	34	56	126
1977-78—Kitchener Rangers (c)		Jr."A"OHA	62	30	74	104	143
1978-79—New Haven Nighthawks		AHL	38	18	26	44	62
1978-79—New York Rangers (d)		NHL	28	9	17	26	39
1979-80—New York Rangers		NHL	79	25	48	73	97
1980-81—New York Rangers		NHL	61	29	23	52	99
1981-82—New York Rangers		NHL	54	22	36	58	73
1982-83—New York Rangers		NHL	78	29	40	69	88
1983-84—New York Rangers		NHL	79	24	42	66	62
1984-85—New York Rangers		NHL	37	11	16	27	32
1985-86—New York Rangers		NHL	68	11	17	28	56
1986-87—New York Rangers		NHL	72	19	38	57	117
1987-88—New York Rangers		NHL	66	12	21	33	60
NHL TOTALS			622	191	298	489	723

(c)—Drafted from Kitchener Rangers by New York Rangers in second round of 1978 amateur draft.
(d)—Tied for lead in assists (13) during playoffs.

STEVE MALTAIS

Left Wing . . . 6'1" . . . 190 lbs. . . . Born, Ottawa, Ont., January 25, 1969 . . . Shoot left.

Year	Team	League	Games	G.	A.	Pts.	Pen.
1985-86—Wexford Raiders		MTHL	33	35	19	54	38
1986-87—Cornwall Royals (c)		OHL	65	32	12	44	29
1987-88—Cornwall Royals		OHL	59	39	46	85	30

(c)—June, 1987—Drafted as underage junior by Washington Capitals in 1987 NHL entry draft. Second Capitals pick, 57th overall, third round.

JAMES EDWARD MANN

Right Wing . . . 6' . . . 202 lbs. . . . Born, Montreal, Que., April 17, 1959 . . . Shoots right . . . (March, 1980)—Served two-game suspension for his fourth game misconduct of 1979-80 season . . . (December 9, 1981)—Pushed NHL linesman Gord Broseker in game vs. Toronto. Mann was fined $500 and given a three-game suspension . . . (January 13, 1982)—Left Winnipeg bench and entered altercation on ice, breaking the jaw of Pittsburgh Penguin Paul Gardner in two places. Mann was given a 10-game suspension by NHL . . . He also was charged with assault by Province of Manitoba, found guilty and given a suspended sentence . . . (December, 1982)—Stretched knee ligaments . . . Set Winnipeg NHL club penalty-minute record in 1979-80 . . . (December, 1984)—Pulled abdominal muscles in AHL game . . . (November, 1985)—Missed seven games with the flu . . . (October, 1987)—Elbow surgery . . . (March, 1988)—Pulled groin.

Year	Team	League	Games	G.	A.	Pts.	Pen.
1975-76—Laval National		QMJHL	65	8	9	17	107
1976-77—Sherbrooke Beavers		QMJHL	69	12	14	26	200
1977-78—Sherbrooke Beavers		QMJHL	67	27	54	81	277
1978-79—Sherbrooke Beavers (a-c)		QMJHL	65	35	47	82	260
1979-80—Winnipeg Jets		NHL	72	3	5	8	*287
1980-81—Tulsa Oilers		CHL	26	4	7	11	175
1980-81—Winnipeg Jets		NHL	37	3	3	6	105
1981-82—Winnipeg Jets		NHL	37	3	2	5	79
1982-83—Winnipeg Jets		NHL	40	0	1	1	73
1983-84—Sherbrooke Jets		AHL	20	6	3	9	94
1983-84—Winnipeg Jets (d)		NHL	16	0	1	1	54
1983-84—Quebec Nordiques		NHL	22	1	1	2	42
1984-85—Fredericton Express		AHL	13	4	4	8	97
1984-85—Quebec Nordiques		NHL	25	0	4	4	54
1985-86—Quebec Nordiques		NHL	35	0	3	3	148
1986-87—Did not play (e)			....	...	....	....	....
1987-88—Muskegon Lumberjacks		IHL	10	0	2	2	61
1987-88—Pittsburgh Penguins		NHL	9	0	0	0	53
NHL TOTALS			293	10	20	30	895

(c)—August, 1979—Drafted by Winnipeg Jets in NHL entry draft. First Winnipeg pick, 19th overall, first round.

(d)—January, 1984—Traded by Winnipeg Jets to Quebec Nordiques for future considerations.

(e)—July, 1987—Signed by Pittsburgh Penguins as a free agent.

RUSSELL MANN

Defense . . . 6'2" . . . 205 lbs. . . . Born, Metuen, Mass., July 8, 1967 . . . Shoots right . . . Also plays Right Wing.

Year	Team	League	Games	G.	A.	Pts.	Pen.
1984-85—Tewksbury H.S.		Mass	19	19	19	38	....
1985-86—St. Lawrence University (c)		ECAC	31	3	4	7	44
1986-87—St. Lawrence University		ECAC	34	2	14	16	30
1987-88—St. Lawrence University		ECAC	38	6	9	15	50

(c)—June, 1986—Drafted by Los Angeles Kings in 1986 NHL entry draft. Tenth Kings pick, 212th overall, 11th round.

MAURICE MANSI

Center . . . 5'11" . . . 172 lbs. . . . Born, Montreal, Que., September 3, 1965 . . . Shoots left . . . Also plays Left Wing.

Year	Team	League	Games	G.	A.	Pts.	Pen.
1984-85—R.P.I (c)		ECAC	21	4	6	10	12
1985-86—R.P.I.		ECAC	31	16	21	37	35
1986-87—R.P.I.		ECAC	22	3	7	10	19
1987-88—R.P.I.		ECAC	30	15	20	35	24

(c)—June, 1985—Drafted by Montreal Canadiens in 1985 NHL entry draft. Twelfth Canadiens pick, 198th overall, tenth round.

DAVID MANSON

Defense . . . 6'2" . . . 192 lbs. . . . Born, Prince Albert, Sask., January 27, 1967 . . . Shoots left.

Year	Team	League	Games	G.	A.	Pts.	Pen.
1983-84—Prince Albert Raiders		WHL	70	2	7	9	233
1984-85—Prince Albert Raiders (c)		WHL	72	8	30	38	247
1985-86—Prince Albert Raiders (b)		WHL	70	14	34	48	177
1986-87—Chicago Black Hawks		NHL	63	1	8	9	146
1987-88—Sagniaw Hawks		IHL	6	0	3	3	37
1987-88—Chicago Black Hawks		NHL	54	1	6	7	185
NHL TOTALS			117	2	14	16	331

(c)—June, 1985—Drafted as underage junior by Chicago Black Hawks in 1985 NHL entry draft. First Black Hawks pick, 11th overall, first round.

MAURICE (MOE) WILLIAM MANTHA

Defense . . . 6'2" . . . 197 lbs. . . . Born, Lakewood, O., January 21, 1961 . . . Shoots right . . . Son of Maurice Mantha (AHL early 1960s) . . . Missed 20 games during 1980-81 season with recurring back problems . . . (October, 1981)—Eye injury . . . (October, 1982)—Surgery for injured shoulder . . . (December 7, 1984)—Broke nose when hit by a puck at N.Y. Rangers . . . (February, 1985)—Bruised spine . . . (February 16, 1986)—Sprained knee at New Jersey . . . (November 26, 1986)—Fractured right wrist at N.Y. Islanders . . . (February 26, 1987)—Missed four games with eye injury at N.Y. Islanders . . . (March 24, 1987)—Sprained left knee vs. Philadelphia . . . (February 29, 1988)—Bruised kneecap vs. New Jersey.

Year	Team	League	Games	G.	A.	Pts.	Pen.
1978-79—Toronto Marlboros		OMJHL	68	10	38	48	57
1979-80—Toronto Marlboros (c)		OMJHL	58	8	38	46	86
1980-81—Winnipeg Jets		NHL	58	2	23	25	35
1981-82—Tulsa Oilers		CHL	33	8	15	23	56
1981-82—Winnipeg Jets		NHL	25	0	12	12	28
1982-83—Sherbrooke Jets		AHL	13	1	4	5	13
1982-83—Winnipeg Jets		NHL	21	2	7	9	6
1983-84—Sherbrooke Jets		AHL	7	1	1	2	10
1983-84—Winnipeg Jets (d)		NHL	72	16	38	54	67
1984-85—Pittsburgh Penguins		NHL	71	11	40	51	54
1985-86—Pittsburgh Penguins		NHL	78	15	52	67	102
1986-87—Pittsburgh Penguins		NHL	62	9	31	40	44
1987-88—Pittsburgh Penguins (e)		NHL	21	2	8	10	23
1987-88—Edmonton Oilers (f)		NHL	25	0	6	6	26
1987-88—Minnesota North Stars		NHL	30	9	13	22	4
NHL TOTALS			463	66	230	296	389

(c)—June, 1980—Drafted as underage junior by Winnipeg Jets in 1980 NHL entry draft. Second Jets pick, 23rd overall, second round.
(d)—May, 1984—Traded by Winnipeg Jets to Pittsburgh Penguins to complete March trade for Randy Carlyle.
(e)—November, 1987—Traded with Craig Simpson, Dave Hannan and Chris Joseph by Pittsburgh Penguins to Edmonton Oilers for Paul Coffey, Dave Hunter and Wayne Van Dorp.
(f)—January, 1988—Traded by Edmonton Oilers to Minnesota North Stars for Keith Acton.

BRYAN MARCHMENT

Defense . . . 6'1" . . . 195 lbs. . . . Born, Scarborough, Ont., May 1, 1969 . . . Shoots left . . . (October 1, 1986)—Suspended for three games by OHL.

Year	Team	League	Games	G.	A.	Pts.	Pen.
1984-85—Toronto Nats.		MTHL	....	14	35	49	229
1985-86—Belleville Bulls		OHL	57	5	15	20	225
1986-87—Belleville Bulls (c)		OHL	52	6	38	44	238
1987-88—Belleville Bulls		OHL	56	7	51	58	200

(c)—June, 1987—Drafted as underage junior by Winnipeg Jets in 1987 NHL entry draft. First Jets pick, 16th overall, first round.

DAVID MARCINYSHYN

Defense . . . 6'3" . . . 195 lbs. . . . Born, Edmonton, Alta., February 4, 1967 . . . Shoots left.

Year	Team	League	Games	G.	A.	Pts.	Pen.
1984-85—Fort Saskatchewan		AJHL	55	11	41	52	311
1985-86—Kamloops Blazers		WHL	57	2	7	9	211
1986-87—Kamloops Blazers (c)		WHL	68	5	27	32	106
1987-88—Utica Devils		AHL	73	2	7	9	179
1987-88—Flint Spirits		IHL	3	0	0	0	4

(c)—September, 1986—Signed by New Jersey Devils as a free agent.

GORDON MARK

Defense . . . 6'3" . . . 210 lbs. . . . Born, Edmonton, Alta., September 10, 1964 . . . Shoots right . . . (December, 1984)—Knee injury . . . (January 6, 1987)—Separated shoulder in NHL debut . . . (October, 1987)—Fractured fifth knuckle on right hand . . . (November, 1987)— Fractured left eye orbit.

Year	Team	League	Games	G.	A.	Pts.	Pen.
1982-83—Kamloops Junior Oilers (c)		WHL	71	12	20	32	135
1983-84—Kamloops Junior Oilers (b)		WHL	67	12	30	42	202
1984-85—Kamloops Blazers		WHL	32	11	23	34	68
1985-86—Maine Mariners		AHL	77	9	13	22	134
1986-87—Maine Mariners		AHL	29	4	10	14	69
1986-87—New Jersey Devils		NHL	36	3	5	8	82
1987-88—Utica Devils		AHL	50	5	21	26	96
1987-88—New Jersey Devils		NHL	19	0	2	2	27
NHL TOTALS			55	3	7	10	109

(c)—June, 1983—Drafted as underage junior by New Jersey Devils in 1983 NHL entry draft. Fourth Devils pick, 105th overall, sixth round.

NEVIN MARKWART

Left Wing . . . 5'11" . . . 175 lbs. . . . Born, Toronto, Ont., December 9, 1964 . . . Shoots left . . . (January, 1983)—Shoulder separation . . . (October, 1984)—Bruised hip . . . (December 28, 1985)—Hip-pointer at St. Louis and missed four games . . . (March 22, 1986)—Sprained right knee vs. N.Y. Islanders . . . (October, 1987)—Dislocated left shoulder . . . (April, 1988)—Strained groin.

Year	Team	League	Games	G.	A.	Pts.	Pen.
1981-82—Regina Blues		SJHL	....	...	....	....	....
1981-82—Regina Pats		WHL	25	2	12	14	56
1982-83—Regina Pats (c)		WHL	43	27	39	66	91
1983-84—Boston Bruins		NHL	70	14	16	30	121
1984-85—Hershey Bears		AHL	38	13	18	31	79
1984-85—Boston Bruins		NHL	26	0	4	4	36
1985-86—Boston Bruins		NHL	65	7	15	22	207
1986-87—Boston Bruins		NHL	64	10	9	19	225
1986-87—Moncton Golden Flames		AHL	3	3	3	6	11
1987-88—Boston Bruins		NHL	25	1	12	13	85
NHL TOTALS			250	32	56	88	674

(c)—June, 1983—Drafted as underage junior by Boston Bruins in 1983 NHL entry draft. First Bruins pick, 21st overall, first round.

DANIEL MAROIS

Right Wing . . . 6' . . . 180 lbs. . . . Born, Montreal, Que., October 3, 1968 . . . Shoots right.

Year	Team	League	Games	G.	A.	Pts.	Pen.
1985-86—Verdun Junior Canadiens		QHL	58	42	35	77	110
1986-87—Chicoutimi Sagueneens (c)		QHL	40	22	26	48	143
1987-88—Verdun Junior Canadiens		QHL	67	52	36	88	153
1987-88—Newmarket Saints		AHL	8	4	4	8	4

(c)—June, 1987—Drafted as underage junior by Toronto Maple Leafs in 1987 NHL entry draft. Second Maple Leafs pick, 28th overall, second round.

MARIO JOSEPH MAROIS

Defense . . . 5'11" . . . 170 lbs. . . . Born, Ancienne Lorette, Que., December 15, 1957 . . . Shoots right . . . Missed part of 1977-78 season with broken ankle . . . (March 27, 1982)—Broke right wrist at Montreal . . . (December 30, 1982)—Broke right leg in exhibition game vs. USSR National Team.

Year	Team	League	Games	G.	A.	Pts.	Pen.
1975-76—Quebec Remparts		QJHL	67	11	42	53	270
1976-77—Quebec Remparts (b-c)		QJHL	72	17	67	84	249
1977-78—New Haven Nighthawks		AHL	52	8	23	31	147
1977-78—New York Rangers		NHL	8	1	1	2	15
1978-79—New York Rangers		NHL	71	5	26	31	153
1979-80—New York Rangers		NHL	79	8	23	31	142
1980-81—New York Rangers (d)		NHL	8	1	2	3	46
1980-81—Vancouver Canucks (e)		NHL	50	4	12	16	115
1980-81—Quebec Nordiques		NHL	11	0	7	7	20
1981-82—Quebec Nordiques		NHL	71	11	32	43	161
1982-83—Quebec Nordiques		NHL	36	2	12	14	108
1983-84—Quebec Nordiques		NHL	80	13	36	49	151
1984-85—Quebec Nordiques		NHL	76	6	37	43	91
1985-86—Quebec Nordiques (f)		NHL	20	1	12	13	42
1985-86—Winnipeg Jets		NHL	56	4	28	32	110
1986-87—Winnipeg Jets		NHL	79	4	40	44	106
1987-88—Winnipeg Jets		NHL	79	7	44	51	111
NHL TOTALS			724	67	312	379	1371

(c)—Drafted from Quebec Remparts by New York Rangers in fourth round of 1977 amateur draft.

(d)—November, 1980—Traded by New York Rangers with Jim Mayer to Vancouver Canucks for Jere Gillis and Jeff Bandura.

(e)—March, 1981—Traded by Vancouver Canucks to Quebec Nordiques for Garry Lariviere in a three-way deal that saw Lariviere then go to Edmonton Oilers for Blair MacDonald.

(f)—November, 1985—Traded by Quebec Nordiques to Winnipeg Jets for Robert Picard.

DALE MARQUETTE

Left Wing . . . 5'11" . . . 190 lbs. . . . Born, Prince George, B.C., March 8, 1968 . . . Shoots left.

Year	Team	League	Games	G.	A.	Pts.	Pen.
1984-85—Lethbridge Broncos		WHL	50	4	4	8	46
1985-86—Lethbridge Broncos		WHL	64	12	14	26	83
1986-87—Brandon Wheat Kings (c)		WHL	68	41	29	70	59
1987-88—Saginaw Hawks (d)		IHL	....	...	....	....	....
1987-88—Brandon Wheat Kings		WHL	62	51	52	103	48

(c)—June, 1987—Drafted by Chicago Black Hawks in 1987 NHL entry draft. Tenth Black Hawks pick, 197th overall, 10th round.

(d)—No regular season record. Played three playoff games (one goals, two penalty minutes).

CHARLES BRADLEY (BRAD) MARSH

Defense . . . 6'2" . . . 215 lbs. . . . Born, London, Ont., March 31, 1958 . . . Shoots left . . . Brother of Paul Marsh . . . Set NHL record by playing a total of 83 games in 1981-82 . . . (January 2, 1983)—Bruised knee tendon at Chicago . . . (March 24, 1983)—Broken fibula vs. Toronto . . . (December, 1987)—Concussion . . . (February, 1988)—Bruised knee.

Year	Team	League	Games	G.	A.	Pts.	Pen.
1974-75—London Knights		Jr."A"OHA	70	4	17	21	160
1975-76—London Knights		Jr."A"OHA	61	3	26	29	184
1976-77—London Knights		Jr."A"OHA	63	7	33	40	121
1977-78—London Knights (a-c-d)		Jr."A"OHA	62	8	55	63	192
1978-79—Atlanta Flames		NHL	80	0	19	19	101
1979-80—Atlanta Flames		NHL	80	2	9	11	119
1980-81—Calgary Flames		NHL	80	1	12	13	87
1981-82—Calgary Flames (e)		NHL	17	0	1	1	10

Year	Team	League	Games	G.	A.	Pts.	Pen.
1981-82—Philadelphia Flyers		NHL	66	2	22	24	106
1982-83—Philadelphia Flyers		NHL	68	2	11	13	52
1983-84—Philadelphia Flyers		NHL	77	3	14	17	83
1984-85—Philadelphia Flyers		NHL	77	2	18	20	91
1985-86—Philadelphia Flyers		NHL	79	0	13	13	123
1986-87—Philadelphia Flyers		NHL	77	2	9	11	124
1987-88—Philadelphia Flyers		NHL	70	3	9	12	57
NHL TOTALS			771	17	137	154	953

(c)—Drafted from London Knights by Atlanta Flames in first round of 1978 amateur draft.
(d)—Shared Max Kaminsky Memorial Trophy (Outstanding Defenseman) with Rob Ramage.
(e)—November, 1981—Traded by Calgary Flames to Philadelphia Flyers for Mel Bridgman.

PAUL MARSHALL

Defense . . . 6'2" . . . 180 lbs. . . . Born, Quincy, Mass., October 22, 1966 . . . Shoots right . . . Brother of Chris Marshall . . . (February, 1988)—Set Hockey East record for most goals by a defenseman in a season.

Year	Team	League	Games	G.	A.	Pts.	Pen.
1984-85—Northwood Prep. (c)		Mass. H.S.	32	14	30	44	34
1985-86—Boston College		H. East	40	0	12	12	28
1986-87—Boston College		H. East	36	4	10	14	30
1987-88—Boston College		H. East	34	12	23	35	50

(c)—June, 1985—Drafted by Philadelphia Flyers in 1985 NHL entry draft. Fifth Flyers pick, 84th overall, fourth round.

DON MARTIN

Left Wing . . . 6' . . . 200 lbs. . . . Born, London, Ont., March 29, 1968 . . . Shoots left.

Year	Team	League	Games	G.	A.	Pts.	Pen.
1985-86—Hamilton Steelhawks (c)		OHL	7	0	0	0	21
1985-86—London Knights		OHL	55	7	6	13	112
1986-87—London Knights		OHL	63	19	38	57	127
1987-88—London Knights (d)		OHL	57	30	32	62	190

(c)—November, 1985—Traded with Ray Gallagher by North Bay Centennials to London Knights for a six-round 1987 draft pick (Brock Shyiak) and future considerations.
(d)—June, 1988—Drafted by Edmonton Oilers in 1988 NHL entry draft. Sixth Oilers pick, 103rd overall, fifth round.

GRANT MICHAEL MARTIN

Left Wing . . . 5'10" . . . 190 lbs. . . . Born, Smooth Rock Falls, Ont., March 13, 1962 . . . Shoots left . . . (January 27, 1988)—Suspended for 10 AHL games for stick-swinging incident vs. Newmarket . . . (February, 1988)—Knee injury.

Year	Team	League	Games	G.	A.	Pts.	Pen.
1979-80—Kitchener Rangers (c)		OMJHL	65	31	21	52	62
1980-81—Kitchener Rangers		OHL	66	41	57	98	77
1981-82—Kitchener Rangers		OHL	54	33	63	96	97
1982-83—Fredericton Express		AHL	80	19	27	46	73
1983-84—Fredericton Express		AHL	57	36	24	60	46
1983-84—Vancouver Canucks		NHL	12	0	2	2	6
1984-85—Vancouver Canucks		NHL	12	0	1	1	39
1984-85—Fredericton Express (d)		AHL	65	31	47	78	78
1985-86—Binghamton Whalers		AHL	54	27	49	76	97
1985-86—Washington Capitals		NHL	11	0	1	1	6
1986-87—Washington Capitals		NHL	9	0	0	0	4
1986-87—Binghamton Whalers		AHL	63	30	23	53	86
1987-88—Rochester Americans (e)		AHL	22	11	15	26	18
NHL TOTALS			44	0	4	4	55

(c)—June, 1980—Drafted as underage junior by Vancouver Canucks in 1980 NHL entry draft. Ninth Canucks pick, 196th overall, 10th round.
(d)—August, 1985—Signed by Washington Capitals as a free agent.
(e)—January, 1988—Signed as a free agent by Rochester Americans after playing in Austria.

TOM MARTIN

Left Wing . . . 6'2" . . . 190 lbs. . . . Born, Kelowna, B.C., May 11, 1964 . . . Shoots left . . . Set University of Denver record for penalty minutes during his freshman year (1982-83).

Year	Team	League	Games	G.	A.	Pts.	Pen.
1981-82—Kelowna (c)		BCJHL	51	35	45	80	293
1982-83—University of Denver (d)		WCHA	37	8	18	26	128
1983-84—Victoria Cougars		WHL	60	30	45	75	261

Year	Team	League	Games	G.	A.	Pts.	Pen.
1983-84—Sherbrooke Jets		AHL	5	0	0	0	16
1984-85—Sherbrooke Canadiens		AHL	58	4	15	19	212
1984-85—Winnipeg Jets		NHL	8	1	0	1	42
1985-86—Winnipeg Jets		NHL	5	0	0	0	0
1985-86—Sherbrooke Canadiens		AHL	69	11	18	29	227
1986-87—Adirondack Red Wings		AHL	18	5	6	11	57
1986-87—Winnipeg Jets (e)		NHL	11	1	0	1	49
1987-88—Binghamton Whalers		AHL	71	28	61	89	344
1987-88—Hartford Whalers		NHL	5	1	2	3	14
NHL TOTALS			29	3	2	5	105

(c)—June, 1982—Drafted as underage player by Winnipeg Jets in 1982 NHL entry draft. Second Jets pick, 74th overall, fourth round.

(d)—January, 1983—WHL rights traded by Seattle Breakers with cash to Victoria Cougars for used team bus and player to be named later.

(e)—August, 1987—Signed as free agent by Hartford Whalers.

STEVE MARTINSON

Left Wing . . . 6'1" . . . 205 lbs. . . . Born, Minnetonka, Minn., June 21, 1957 . . . Shoots left . . . Set AHL single-season penalty minute record in 1985-86 . . . (May, 1986)—Disc operation . . . (March 12, 1988)—Suspended six AHL games for fighting with Mark Ferner vs. Rochester.

Year	Team	League	Games	G.	A.	Pts.	Pen.
1981-82—Toledo Goaldiggers		IHL	35	12	18	30	128
1982-83—Birmingham Bulls (c)		CHL	43	4	5	9	184
1982-83—Toledo Goaldiggers		IHL	32	9	10	19	111
1983-84—Tulsa Oilers (d)		CHL	42	3	6	9	*240
1984-85—Salt Lake Golden Eagles		IHL	32	4	7	11	140
1984-85—Toledo Goaldiggers (e)		IHL	22	0	3	3	160
1984-85—New Haven Nighthawks		AHL	4	0	0	0	17
1985-86—Hershey Bears (f)		AHL	69	3	6	9	*432
1986-87—Hershey Bears		AHL	17	0	3	3	85
1986-87—Adirondack Red Wings (g)		AHL	14	1	1	2	78
1987-88—Adirondack Red Wings		AHL	32	6	8	14	146
1987-88—Detroit Red Wings		NHL	10	1	1	2	84
NHL TOTALS			10	1	1	2	84

(c)—Led CHL playoffs with 80 penalty minutes.

(d)—Led CHL playoffs with 43 penalty minutes.

(e)—February, 1985—Traded with Kurt Kleinendorst by Salt Lake Golden Eagles to Toledo Goaldiggers for Kevin Conway, Blake Stephan, Grant Rezansoff and Steve Harrison.

(f)—September, 1985—Signed by Philadelphia Flyers as a free agent.

(g)—March, 1987—Signed by Adirondack Red Wings as a free agent.

DENNIS JOHN MARUK

Center . . . 5'8" . . . 170 lbs. . . . Born, Toronto, Ont., November 17, 1955 . . . Shoots left . . . (October, 1979)—Torn ligaments in right knee and out for four months . . . Set NHL record for most shorthanded goals by a rookie (5) in 1975-76 . . . (December, 1984)—Sprained knee ligaments . . . (October, 1987)—Torn foot tendons . . . (January 13, 1988)—Suspended three NHL games for crosschecking Wendel Clark vs. Toronto . . . (February 20, 1988)—Kneecap broken vs. Washington.

Year	Team	League	Games	G.	A.	Pts.	Pen.
1971-72—Toronto Marlboros		Jr. "A" OHA	8	2	1	3	4
1972-73—London Knights		Jr. "A" OHA	59	46	67	113	54
1973-74—London Knights		Jr. "A" OHA	69	47	65	112	61
1974-75—London Knights (c-d)		Jr. "A" OHA	65	66	79	145	53
1975-76—California Seals		NHL	80	30	32	62	44
1976-77—Cleveland Barons		NHL	80	28	50	78	68
1977-78—Cleveland Barons		NHL	76	36	35	71	50
1978-79—Minnesota North Stars (e)		NHL	2	0	0	0	0
1978-79—Washington Capitals		NHL	76	31	59	90	71
1979-80—Washington Capitals		NHL	27	10	17	27	8
1980-81—Washington Capitals		NHL	80	50	47	97	87
1981-82—Washington Capitals		NHL	80	60	76	136	128
1982-83—Washington Capitals (f)		NHL	80	31	50	81	71
1983-84—Minnesota North Stars		NHL	71	17	43	60	42
1984-85—Minnesota North Stars		NHL	71	19	41	60	56
1985-86—Minnesota North Stars		NHL	70	21	37	58	67
1986-87—Minnesota North Stars		NHL	67	16	30	46	50
1987-88—Minnesota North Stars		NHL	22	7	4	11	15
NHL TOTALS			882	356	521	877	757

(c)—Won Red Tilson Memorial Trophy (MVP).
(d)—Drafted from London Knights by California Seals in second round of 1975 amateur draft.
(e)—October, 1978—Traded by Minnesota North Stars to Washington Capitals for second of Washington's two picks in the first round, 10th overall, of the 1979 entry draft (Tom McCarthy).
(f)—July, 1983—Traded by Washington Capitals to Minnesota for second round draft pick in 1984 (Stephen Leach) and cash.

DWIGHT MATHIASEN

Right Wing ... 6'2" ... 190 lbs. ... Born, New Westminster, B.C., December 5, 1963 ... Shoots right ... (February 1, 1987)—Sprained left ankle vs. Hartford.

Year	Team	League	Games	G.	A.	Pts.	Pen.
1983-84	University of Denver	WCHA	36	24	27	51	48
1984-85	University of Denver	WCHA	39	26	32	58	64
1985-86	University of Denver (b-c)	WCHA	48	40	49	89	48
1985-86	Pittsburgh Penguins	NHL	4	1	0	1	2
1986-87	Baltimore Skipjacks	AHL	61	23	22	45	49
1987-88	Muskegon Lumberjacks	IHL	46	19	42	61	35
1987-88	Pittsburgh Penguins	NHL	23	0	6	6	14
	NHL TOTALS		27	1	6	7	16

(c)—March, 1986—Signed by Pittsburgh Penguins as a free agent.

STEPHANE MATTEAU

Left Wing ... 6'3" ... 185 lbs. ... Born, Rouyn, Que., September 2, 1969 ... Shoots left.

Year	Team	League	Games	G.	A.	Pts.	Pen.
1985-86	Hull Olympiques	QHL	60	6	8	14	19
1986-87	Hull Olympiques (c)	QHL	69	27	48	75	113
1987-88	Hull Olympiques	QHL	57	17	40	57	179

(c)—June, 1987—Drafted as underage junior by Calgary Flames in 1987 NHL entry draft. Second Flames pick, 25th overall, second round.

IVAN MATULIK

Left Wing ... 6' ... 194 lbs. ... Born, Nitra, Czechoslovakia, June 17, 1968 ... Shoots left.

Year	Team	League	Games	G.	A.	Pts.	Pen.
1986-87	Slovan Bratislava (c)	Czech.	25	1	3	4	..
1987-88	Nova Scotia Oilers	AHL	46	13	10	23	29

(c)—June, 1986—Drafted by Edmonton Oilers in 1986 NHL entry draft. Seventh Oilers pick, 147th overall, seventh round.

SCOTT MATUSOVICH

Defense ... 6'2" ... 205 lbs. ... Born, Derby, Conn., January 31, 1969 ... Shoots left.

Year	Team	League	Games	G.	A.	Pts.	Pen.
1986-87	Canterbury H.S.	Ct. H.S.	..	10	22	32	..
1987-88	Canterbury H.S. (c)	Ct. H.S.	..	20	31	51	..

(c)—June, 1988—Drafted by Calgary Flames in 1988 NHL entry draft. Fifth Flames pick, 90th overall, fifth round.

DANIEL MAURICE

Center ... 6' ... 175 lbs. ... Repentigny, Que., April 19, 1969 ... Shoots left.

Year	Team	League	Games	G.	A.	Pts.	Pen.
1985-86	Chicoutimi Sagueneens	QHL	67	6	22	28	41
1986-87	Chicoutimi Sagueneens	QHL	68	31	61	92	151
1987-88	Chicoutimi Sagueneens (c)	QHL	69	56	90	146	150

(c)—June, 1988—Drafted by Chicago Black Hawks in 1988 NHL entry draft. Ninth Black Hawks pick, 197th overall, 10th round.

PAUL MAURICE

Defense ... 6'2" ... 190 lbs. ... Born, Sault Ste. Marie, Ont., January 30, 1967 ... Shoots right.

Year	Team	League	Games	G.	A.	Pts.	Pen.
1983-84	Soo Legion Midget	OHA	38	6	17	23	44
1984-85	Windsor Spitfires (c)	OHL	38	0	3	3	47
1985-86	Windsor Spitfires	OHL	56	3	10	13	89
1986-87	Windsor Spitfires	OHL	63	4	15	19	87
1987-88	Windsor Spitfires	OHL	32	1	4	5	33

(c)—June, 1985—Drafted by Philadelphia Flyers in 1985 NHL entry draft. Twelfth Flyers pick, 252nd overall, 12th round.

KEVIN MAXWELL

Center . . . 5'8" . . . 170 lbs. . . . Born, Edmonton, Alta., March 30, 1960 . . . Shoots right . . . (February, 1981)—Broke thumb . . . (October, 1981)—Back surgery . . . (December, 1981)—Groin injury . . . (January, 1987)—Knee surgery.

Year	Team	League	Games	G.	A.	Pts.	Pen.
1978-79—Univ. of North Dakota (a-c-d)	WCHA	42	31	51	82	79
1979-80—Canadian National Team	Int'l	....	25	41	66	....
1979-80—Canadian Olympic Team	Olympic	6	0	5	5	4
1980-81—Oklahoma City Stars	CHL	31	8	13	21	38
1980-81—Minnesota North Stars	NHL	6	0	3	3	7
1981-82—Minnesota North Stars (e)	NHL	12	1	4	5	8
1981-82—Colorado Rockies	NHL	34	5	5	10	44
1982-83—Wichita Wind	CHL	68	24	41	65	47
1983-84—New Jersey Devils	NHL	14	0	3	3	2
1983-84—Maine Mariners	AHL	56	21	27	48	59
1984-85—Maine Mariners	AHL	52	25	21	46	70
1985-86—Maine Mariners	AHL	49	14	17	31	77
1986-87—Hershey Bears	AHL	56	12	20	32	139
1987-88—Hershey Bears	AHL	77	36	49	85	55
NHL TOTALS			66	6	15	21	61

(c)—Named to All-American Team (West).
(d)—August, 1979—Drafted as underage player in 1979 NHL entry draft by Minnesota North Stars. Fourth North Stars pick, 63rd overall, third round.
(e)—December, 1981—Traded with Jim Dobson by Minnesota North Stars to Colorado Rockies for cash.

ALAN MAY

Right Wing . . . 6'1" . . . 215 lbs. . . . Born, Barrhead, Alta., January 14, 1965 . . . Shoots right.

Year	Team	League	Games	G.	A.	Pts.	Pen.
1987-88—Maine Mariners (c)	AHL	61	14	11	25	357
1987-88—Boston Bruins (d)	NHL	3	0	0	0	15
1987-88—Nova Scotia Oilers	AHL	12	4	1	5	54
NHL TOTALS			3	0	0	0	15

(c)—September, 1987—Signed by Boston Bruins as a free agent.
(d)—March, 1988—Traded by Boston Bruins to Edmonton Oilers for Moe Lemay.

ANDY MAY

Center . . . 6'2" . . . 180 lbs. . . . Born, Mississauga, Ont., May 2, 1968 . . . Shoots left.

Year	Team	League	Games	G.	A.	Pts.	Pen.
1985-86—Bramalea Jr. B (c)	OHA	35	21	26	47	41
1986-87—Northeastern Univ.	H. East	36	4	8	12	25
1987-88—Northeastern Univ.	H. East	17	2	5	7	10

(c)—June, 1986—Drafted by St. Louis Blues in 1986 NHL entry draft. Seventh Blues pick, 136th overall, seventh round.

DEREK MAYER

Defense . . . 6' . . . 190 lbs. . . . Born, Rossland, B.C., May 21, 1967 . . . Shoots right . . . (January, 1986)—Dislocated shoulder . . . (December, 1987)—Separated shoulder.

Year	Team	League	Games	G.	A.	Pts.	Pen.
1985-86—University of Denver (c)	WCHA	44	2	7	9	42
1986-87—University of Denver	WCHA	38	5	17	22	87
1987-88—University of Denver	WCHA	34	5	16	21	82

(c)—June, 1986—Drafted by Detroit Red Wings in 1986 NHL entry draft. Third Red Wings pick, 43rd overall, third round.

PAT MAYER

Defense . . . 6'3" . . . 227 lbs. . . . Born, Royal Oak, Mich., July 24, 1961 . . . Shoots right.

Year	Team	League	Games	G.	A.	Pts.	Pen.
1982-83—U.S. International Univ.	GWHC	30	3	6	9	68
1983-84—U.S. International Univ.	GWHC	35	1	15	16	89
1984-85—U.S. International Univ.	GWHC	28	3	14	17	94
1985-86—Toledo Goaldiggers	IHL	61	1	13	14	216
1985-86—Muskegon Lumberjacks	IHL	13	1	2	3	17
1986-87—Muskegon Lumberjacks (c)	IHL	71	4	14	18	387
1987-88—Muskegon Lumberjacks	IHL	73	3	10	13	*450
1987-88—Pittsburgh Penguins	NHL	1	0	0	0	4
NHL TOTALS			1	0	0	0	4

(c)—July, 1987—Signed by Pittsburgh Penguins as a free agent.

ANDREW McBAIN

Right Wing . . . 6'1" . . . 190 lbs. . . . Born, Toronto, Ont., February 18, 1965 . . . Shoots right . . . (November, 1982)—Fractured cheekbone . . . (March, 1983)—Separated sterno clavicular joint . . . Also plays Center . . . (April 25, 1985)—Lost for the playoffs with mononucleosis . . . (September, 1985)—Switched to center . . . (December 8, 1985)—Injured knee vs. Los Angeles . . . (March, 1987)—Suspended four games by NHL for stick-swinging incident.

Year	Team	League	Games	G.	A.	Pts.	Pen.
1981-82—Niagara Falls Flyers		OHL	68	19	25	44	35
1982-83—North Bay Centennials (b-c)		OHL	67	33	87	120	61
1983-84—Winnipeg Jets		NHL	78	11	19	30	37
1984-85—Winnipeg Jets		NHL	77	7	15	22	45
1985-86—Winnipeg Jets		NHL	28	3	3	6	17
1986-87—Winnipeg Jets		NHL	71	11	21	32	106
1987-88—Winnipeg Jets		NHL	74	32	31	63	145
NHL TOTALS			328	64	89	153	350

(c)—June, 1983—Drafted as underage junior by Winnipeg Jets in 1983 NHL entry draft. First Jets pick, eighth overall, first round.

WAYNE McBEAN

Defense . . . 6'2" . . . 190 lbs. . . . Born, Calgary, Alta., February 21, 1969 . . . Shoots left.

Year	Team	League	Games	G.	A.	Pts.	Pen.
1984-85—Calgary North Stars		Alta. Midget	38	8	34	42	46
1985-86—Medicine Hat Tigers		WHL	67	1	14	15	73
1986-87—Medicine Hat Tigers (a-c-d)		WHL	71	12	41	53	163
1987-88—Los Angeles Kings		NHL	27	0	1	1	26
1987-88—Medicine Hat Tigers		WHL	30	15	30	45	48
NHL TOTALS			27	0	1	1	26

(c)—Named WHL Top Defenseman (East Division).

(d)—June, 1987—Drafted as underage junior by Los Angeles Kings in 1987 NHL entry draft. First Kings pick, fourth overall, first round.

DARYN McBRIDE

Center . . . 5'9" . . . 180 lbs. . . . Born, Ft. Saskatchewan, Alta., March 29, 1968 . . . Shoots right.

Year	Team	League	Games	G.	A.	Pts.	Pen.
1985-86—Sherwood Park Crusaders		AJHL	47	16	23	39	150
1986-87—Univ. of Denver (c)		WCHA	39	19	13	32	54
1987-88—Univ. of Denver		WCHA	39	30	28	58	122

(c)—June, 1987—Drafted by Pittsburgh Penguins in 1987 NHL entry draft. Tenth Penguins pick, 194th overall, 10th round.

KEVIN McCARTHY

Defense . . . 5'11" . . . 197 lbs. . . . Born, Winnipeg, Man., July 14, 1957 . . . Shoots right . . . Set WCHL record for points by a defenseman in 1975-76 (121) and broke own record in 1976-77 (127) and assists by a defenseman (105) in 1976-77 . . . Holds all-time WCHL record for career assists (276) . . . (December, 1979)—Bone chip lodged in hip muscles caused disabling pain . . . (January, 1982)—Slight shoulder separation . . . (February, 1983)—Sprained wrist.

Year	Team	League	Games	G.	A.	Pts.	Pen.
1973-74—Winnipeg Clubs		WCHL	66	5	22	27	65
1974-75—Winnipeg Clubs		WCHL	66	20	61	81	102
1975-76—Winnipeg Clubs (a-c)		WCHL	72	33	88	121	160
1976-77—Winnipeg Monarchs (a-d)		WCHL	72	22	*105	127	110
1977-78—Philadelphia Flyers		NHL	62	2	15	17	32
1978-79—Philadelphia Flyers (e)		NHL	22	1	2	3	21
1978-79—Vancouver Canucks		NHL	1	0	0	0	0
1979-80—Vancouver Canucks		NHL	79	15	30	45	70
1980-81—Vancouver Canucks		NHL	80	16	37	53	85
1981-82—Vancouver Canucks		NHL	71	6	39	45	84
1982-83—Vancouver Canucks		NHL	74	12	28	40	88
1983-84—Vancouver Canucks (f)		NHL	47	2	14	16	61
1983-84—Pittsburgh Penguins		NHL	31	4	16	20	52
1984-85—Pittsburgh Penguins (g)		NHL	64	9	10	19	30
1985-86—Philadelphia Flyers		NHL	4	0	0	0	4
1985-86—Hershey Bears (a)		AHL	64	15	40	55	157
1986-87—Philadelphia Flyers		NHL	2	0	0	0	0
1986-87—Hershey Bears		AHL	74	6	44	50	86
1987-88—Hershey Bears		AHL	61	9	30	39	83
NHL TOTALS			537	67	191	258	527

(c)—Named Outstanding Defenseman.
(d)—Drafted from Winnipeg Monarchs by Philadelphia Flyers in first round of 1977 amateur draft.
(e)—December, 1978—Traded with Drew Callander by Philadelphia Flyers to Vancouver Canucks for Dennis Ververgaert.
(f)—January, 1984—Traded by Vancouver Canucks to Pittsburgh Penguins for third round 1985 draft pick.
(g)—July, 1985—Signed by Philadelphia Flyers as a free agent.

TOM JOSEPH McCARTHY

Left Wing ... 6'2" ... 202 lbs. ... Born, Toronto, Ont., July 31, 1960 ... Shoots left ... Rib injury (February, 1980) ... (February, 1981)—Wrist surgery ... (September 25, 1981)—Strained tendon in ankle during training camp ... (November, 1981)—Tore calf muscle while conditioning from ankle injury ... (April, 1984)—Injured back when a jeep over-turned (he was a passenger). Ten days later he broke a bone in his back during playoff game with St. Louis when he collided with a goalpost ... (October 18, 1984)—Torn tricep muscle vs. Edmonton ... (December 21, 1984)—Sprained ankle ... (February, 1985)—Vision problem ... (September, 1985)—Moved to center, injured knee during training camp and missed the first five games of season ... (November 23, 1985)—Bell's palsey ... (December 14, 1985)—Injured shoulder vs. Toronto and missed 16 games ... (March 5, 1986)—Broken thumb vs. Toronto ... (October, 1987)—Strained hamstring ... (November, 1987)—Sprained right knee ... (January, 1988)—Deteriorating cartilage in jaw.

Year	Team	League	Games	G.	A.	Pts.	Pen.
1976-77—Kingston Canadians		OMJHL	2	1	0	1	0
1976-77—North York Rangers		OPJHL	43	49	47	96	12
1977-78—Oshawa Generals		OMJHL	62	47	46	93	72
1978-79—Oshawa Generals (a-c)		OMJHL	63	69	75	144	98
1979-80—Minnesota North Stars		NHL	68	16	20	36	39
1980-81—Minnesota North Stars		NHL	62	23	25	48	62
1981-82—Minnesota North Stars		NHL	40	12	30	42	36
1982-83—Minnesota North Stars		NHL	80	28	48	76	59
1983-84—Minnesota North Stars		NHL	66	39	31	70	49
1984-85—Minnesota North Stars		NHL	44	16	21	37	36
1985-86—Minnesota North Stars (d)		NHL	25	12	12	24	12
1986-87—Boston Bruins		NHL	68	30	29	59	31
1986-87—Moncton Golden Flames		AHL	2	0	1	1	0
1987-88—Boston Bruins		NHL	7	2	5	7	6
1987-88—Maine Mariners		AHL	17	7	6	13	14
NHL TOTALS			460	178	221	399	330

(c)—August, 1979—Drafted as underage player by Minnesota North Stars in 1979 entry draft. Second North Stars pick, 10th overall, first round.
(d)—May, 1986—Traded by Minnesota North Stars to Boston Bruins for third round 1986 draft pick (Rob Zettler) and second round pick in 1987 (Scott McCrady).

BRAD McCAUGHEY

Right Wing ... 6' ... 180 lbs. ... Born, Ann Arbor, Mich., June 10, 1966 ... Shoots right.

Year	Team	League	Games	G.	A.	Pts.	Pen.
1984-85—Univ. of Michigan (c)		CCHA	35	16	11	27	49
1985-86—Univ. of Michigan		CCHA	32	24	26	50	51
1986-87—Univ. of Michigan		CCHA	30	26	23	49	53
1987-88—Univ. of Michigan		CCHA	33	20	14	34	36

(c)—June, 1984—Drafted by Montreal Canadiens in 1984 NHL entry draft. Tenth Canadiens pick, 158th overall, eighth round.

KEVIN WILLIAM McCLELLAND

Center ... 6' ... 180 lbs. ... Born, Oshawa, Ont., July 4, 1962 ... Shoots right ... (September 21, 1981)—Dislocated shoulder in preseason game ... (January 24, 1983)—Dislocated shoulder in fight with Paul Higgins at Toronto. He required surgery on the shoulder and was lost for the season ... (January, 1985)—Sprained left knee ... (December 10, 1986)—Suspended for three games by NHL for being the first off the bench during a fight at Winnipeg ... (November, 1987)—Sprained knee ... (February, 1988)—Bruised right knee vs. Vancouver.

Year	Team	League	Games	G.	A.	Pts.	Pen.
1979-80—Niagara Falls Flyers (c)		OMJHL	67	14	14	28	71
1980-81—Niagara Falls Flyers (d)		OHL	68	36	72	108	184
1981-82—Niagara Falls Flyers		OHL	46	36	47	83	184
1981-82—Pittsburgh Penguins		NHL	10	1	4	5	4
1982-83—Pittsburgh Penguins		NHL	38	5	4	9	73
1983-84—Baltimore Skipjacks		AHL	3	1	1	2	0
1983-84—Pittsburgh Penguins (e)		NHL	24	2	4	6	62
1983-84—Edmonton Oilers		NHL	52	8	20	28	127

Year	Team	League	Games	G.	A.	Pts.	Pen.
1984-85—Edmonton Oilers		NHL	62	8	15	23	205
1985-86—Edmonton Oilers		NHL	79	11	25	36	266
1986-87—Edmonton Oilers		NHL	72	12	13	25	238
1987-88—Edmonton Oilers		NHL	74	10	6	16	281
NHL TOTALS			411	57	91	148	1256

(c)—June, 1980—Drafted as underage junior by Hartford Whalers in 1980 NHL entry draft. Fourth Whalers pick, 71st overall, fourth round.

(d)—July, 1981—Acquired by Pittsburgh Penguins with Pat Boutette as compensation from Hartford Whalers for Hartford signing free agent Greg Millen. Decision required by NHL Arbitrator Judge Joseph Kane when Hartford and Pittsburgh were unable to agree on compensation.

(e)—December, 1983—Traded with sixth round 1984 draft pick (Emanuel Viveiros) by Pittsburgh Penguins to Edmonton Oilers for Tom Roulston.

GARY McCOLGAN

Left Wing . . . 6' . . . 192 lbs. . . . Born, Scarborough, Ont., March 27, 1966 . . . Shoots left . . . (October, 1986)—Separated shoulder.

Year	Team	League	Games	G.	A.	Pts.	Pen.
1982-83—Don Mills Midgets		MTMHL	40	32	27	59	28
1983-84—Oshawa Generals (c)		OHL	66	11	28	39	14
1984-85—Hamilton Steelhawks (d)		OHL	12	4	3	7	0
1984-85—Oshawa Generals		OHL	51	25	23	48	17
1985-86—Oshawa Generals		OHL	57	49	55	104	22
1986-87—Indianapolis Checkers		IHL	75	30	25	55	15
1987-88—Kalamazoo Wings		IHL	66	17	35	52	13

(c)—June, 1984—Drafted as underage junior by Minnesota North Stars in NHL entry draft. Sixth North Stars pick, 118th overall, sixth round.

(d)—December, 1984—Traded with Brent Loney by Hamilton Steelhawks to Oshawa Generals for Steve Hedington, John Hutchings and a sixth round pick in OHL 1985 priority draft (Andy May).

STEVEN McCOOL

Defense . . . 6'2" . . . 195 lbs. . . . Born, Boston, Mass., April 26, 1968 . . . Shoots left.

Year	Team	League	Games	G.	A.	Pts.	Pen.
1985-86—Hill School		N.J.H.S.	26	15	29	44	....
1986-87—Hill School (c)		N.J.H.S.	23	14	29	43	24
1987-88—Boston College		H. East	19	0	1	1	6

(c)—June, 1987—Drafted by Montreal Canadiens in 1987 NHL entry draft. Seventh Canadiens pick, 101st overall, fifth round.

SCOTT McCRADY

Defense . . . 6'1" . . . 190 lbs. . . . Born, Bassang, Alta., October 10, 1968 . . . Shoots right . . . (October 5, 1987)—Injured left knee ligament during Minnesota North Stars training camp.

Year	Team	League	Games	G.	A.	Pts.	Pen.
1985-86—Medicine Hat Tigers		WHL	65	8	25	33	114
1985-86—Calgary Spurs		AJHL	6	0	4	4	37
1986-87—Medicine Hat Tigers (c)		WHL	70	10	66	76	157
1987-88—Medicine Hat Tigers (a)		WHL	65	7	70	77	132

(c)—June, 1987—Drafted by Minnesota North Stars as underage junior in 1987 NHL entry draft. Second North Stars pick, 35th overall, second round.

BILL McCREARY, JR.

Left Wing . . . 6' . . . 200 lbs. . . . Born, Springfield, Mass., April 15, 1960 . . . Shoots left . . . Son of Bill McCreary, Sr., nephew of Keith McCreary and Ron Attwell and a cousin of Bob Attwell.

Year	Team	League	Games	G.	A.	Pts.	Pen.
1978-79—Colgate University (c)		ECAC	24	19	25	44	70
1979-80—Colgate University		ECAC	12	7	13	20	44
1980-81—Toronto Maple Leafs		NHL	12	1	0	1	4
1980-81—New Brunswick Hawks		AHL	61	19	24	43	120
1981-82—Cincinnati Tigers		CHL	69	8	27	35	61
1982-83—Saginaw Gears		IHL	60	19	28	47	17
1982-83—Peoria Prancers		IHL	16	4	6	10	11
1982-83—St. Catharines Saints (d)		AHL	4	0	1	1	2
1983-84—Milwaukee Admirals		IHL	81	28	35	63	44
1984-85—Milwaukee Admirals		IHL	10	1	10	11	4
1985-86—Milwaukee Admirals		IHL	80	30	31	61	83

Year	Team	League	Games	G.	A.	Pts.	Pen.
1986-87—Milwaukee Admirals		IHL	74	30	35	65	64
1987-88—Milwaukee Admirals		IHL	67	23	30	53	51
NHL TOTALS			12	1	0	1	4

(c)—August, 1979—Drafted by Toronto Maple Leafs in 1979 NHL entry draft. Fifth Maple Leafs pick, 114th overall, sixth round.

(d)—June, 1983—Released by Toronto Maple Leafs.

BYRON BRAD McCRIMMON
(Known by middle name.)

Defense . . . 5'11" . . . 193 lbs. . . . Born, Dodsland, Sask., March 29, 1959 . . . Shoots left . . . (February 2, 1985)—Broke bone in right hand during pre-game warmups and missed 13 games . . . (May 9, 1985)—Separated left shoulder, requiring surgery, during playoff game vs. Quebec when he was checked by Wilf Paiement . . . Missed start of 1986-87 season in contract dispute.

Year	Team	League	Games	G.	A.	Pts.	Pen.
1976-77—Brandon Wheat Kings (b)		WCHL	72	18	66	84	96
1977-78—Brandon Wheat Kings (a-c)		WCHL	65	19	78	97	245
1978-79—Brandon Wheat Kings (a-d)		WHL	66	24	74	98	139
1979-80—Boston Bruins		NHL	72	5	11	16	94
1980-81—Boston Bruins		NHL	78	11	18	29	148
1981-82—Boston Bruins (e)		NHL	78	1	8	9	83
1982-83—Philadelphia Flyers		NHL	79	4	21	25	61
1983-84—Philadelphia Flyers		NHL	71	0	24	24	76
1984-85—Philadelphia Flyers		NHL	66	8	25	33	81
1985-86—Philadelphia Flyers		NHL	80	13	42	55	85
1986-87—Philadelphia Flyers (f)		NHL	71	10	29	39	52
1987-88—Calgary Flames (b)		NHL	80	7	35	42	98
NHL TOTALS			675	59	213	272	778

(c)—Named outstanding defenseman.

(d)—August, 1979—Drafted by Boston Bruins in 1979 entry draft. Second Boston pick, 15th overall, first round.

(e)—June, 1982—Traded by Boston Bruins to Philadelphia Flyers for Pete Peeters.

(f)—August, 1987—Traded by Philadelphia Flyers to Calgary Flames for a first-round draft choice in 1989 and a third-round draft choice in 1988 (Dominic Roussel).

SCOTT McCRORY

Center . . . 5'10" . . . 175 lbs. . . . Born, Sudbury, Ont., February 27, 1967 . . . Shoots right.

Year	Team	League	Games	G.	A.	Pts.	Pen.
1983-84—Sudbury Midget		OHA	65	92	76	168	32
1984-85—Oshawa Generals		OHL	64	9	24	33	28
1985-86—Oshawa Generals (c)		OHL	66	52	80	132	40
1986-87—Oshawa Generals (a-d-e-f-g-h)		OHL	66	51	*99	*150	35
1987-88—Binghamton Whalers		AHL	72	18	33	51	29

(c)—June, 1986—Drafted as underage junior by Washington Capitals in 1986 NHL entry draft. Thirteenth Capitals pick, 250th overall, 12th round.

(d)—Won Eddie Powers Memorial Trophy (Scoring Champion).

(e)—Won Red Tilson Trophy (Outstanding Player).

(f)—Co-Winner of William Hanley Trophy (Most Gentlemanly) with Keith Gretzky.

(g)—Named OHL Player of the Year.

(h)—Led OHL Playoffs with 22 assists and 37 points.

DARWIN McCUTCHEON

Defense . . . 6'5" . . . 210 lbs. . . . Born, Listowel, Ont., April 19, 1962 . . . Shoots right . . . (April, 1987)—Suspended during AHL playoffs.

Year	Team	League	Games	G.	A.	Pts.	Pen.
1979-80—Kitchener Rangers		OMJHL	28	0	3	3	30
1979-80—Toronto Maple Leafs (c)		OMJHL	18	0	1	1	2
1980-81—Toronto Marlboros		OMJHL	38	1	3	4	50
1981-82—Windsor Spitfires		OMJHL	26	1	7	8	36
1981-82—Toronto Maple Leafs		NHL	1	0	0	0	2
1981-82—Windsor Spitfires		OHL	67	5	24	29	141
1982-83—Kitchener Rangers		OHL	11	4	7	11	25
1983-84—............			....	...	....	....	....
1984-85—Univ. of P.E.I.		AUAA	24	5	30	35	73
1985-86—Moncton Golden Flames (d)		AHL	12	0	2	2	31
1986-87—Moncton Golden Flames		AHL	69	1	10	11	187
1987-88—Salt Lake Golden Eagles		IHL	64	2	8	10	150
NHL TOTALS			1	0	0	0	2

(c)—June, 1980—Drafted as underage junior by Toronto Maple Leafs in 1980 NHL entry draft. Ninth Maple Leafs pick, 179th overall, ninth round.

(d)—March, 1986—Signed by Calgary Flames as a free agent.

LANNY KING McDONALD

Right Wing . . . 6' . . . 185 lbs. . . . Born, Hanna, Alta., February 16, 1953 . . . Shoots right . . . Voted Colorado Athlete of the Year (1980) by state media . . . (February 18, 1984)—Fractured bone in right foot vs. Boston . . . (October, 1984)—Strained abdominal muscles in collision with Scott Stevens during pre-season game vs. Washington . . . (March, 1985)—Torn knee ligaments.

Year	Team	League	Games	G.	A.	Pts.	Pen.
1969-70—Lethbridge Sugar Kings		AJHL	34	2	9	11	19
1970-71—Lethbridge Sugar Kings (b)		AJHL	45	37	45	82	56
1970-71—Calgary Centennials		WCHL	6	0	2	2	6
1971-72—Medicine Hat Tigers		WCHL	68	50	64	114	54
1972-73—Medicine Hat Tigers (a-c)		WCHL	68	62	77	139	84
1973-74—Toronto Maple Leafs		NHL	70	14	16	30	43
1974-75—Toronto Maple Leafs		NHL	64	17	27	44	86
1975-76—Toronto Maple Leafs		NHL	75	37	56	93	70
1976-77—Toronto Maple Leafs (b)		NHL	80	46	44	90	77
1977-78—Toronto Maple Leafs		NHL	74	47	40	87	54
1978-79—Toronto Maple Leafs		NHL	79	43	42	85	32
1979-80—Toronto Maple Leafs (d)		NHL	35	15	15	30	10
1979-80—Colorado Rockies		NHL	46	25	20	45	43
1980-81—Colorado Rockies		NHL	80	35	46	81	56
1981-82—Colorado Rockies (e)		NHL	16	6	9	15	20
1981-82—Calgary Flames		NHL	55	34	33	67	37
1982-83—Calgary Flames (b-f)		NHL	80	66	32	98	90
1983-84—Calgary Flames		NHL	65	33	33	66	64
1984-85—Calgary Flames		NHL	43	19	18	37	36
1985-86—Calgary Flames		NHL	80	28	43	71	44
1986-87—Calgary Flames		NHL	58	14	12	26	54
1987-88—Calgary Flames (g)		NHL	60	10	13	23	57
NHL TOTALS			1060	489	499	988	973

(c)—Drafted from Medicine Hat Tigers by Toronto Maple Leafs in first round of 1973 amateur draft.

(d)—December, 1979—Traded with Joel Quenneville by Toronto Maple Leafs to Colorado Rockies for Wilf Paiement and Pat Hickey.

(e)—December, 1981—Traded with fourth-round 1983 entry draft pick by Colorado Rockies to Calgary Flames for Bob MacMillan and Don Lever.

(f)—Won Bill Masterton Memorial Trophy (Perseverance, sportsmanship and dedication).

(g)—Winner of King Clancy Trophy (Humanitarian Award).

PETER McGEOUGH

Defense . . . 6'1" . . . 190 lbs. . . . Born, Watertown, N.Y., April 15, 1965 . . . Shoots left.

Year	Team	League	Games	G.	A.	Pts.	Pen.
1984-85—St. Lawrence Univ. (c)		ECAC	32	1	8	9	70
1985-86—St. Lawrence Univ.		ECAC	27	9	8	17	83
1986-87—St. Lawrence Univ.		ECAC	30	7	14	21	90
1987-88—St. Lawrence Univ.		ECAC	38	2	25	27	70

(c)—June, 1983—Drafted by New York Islanders in 1983 NHL entry draft. Fourteenth Islanders pick, 247th overall, 12th round.

ROBERT PAUL McGILL

Defense . . . 6' . . . 202 lbs. . . . Born, Edmonton, Alta., April 27, 1962 . . . Shoots right . . . (January, 1985)—Given three-game NHL suspension . . . (January 4, 1986)—Separated shoulder vs. Los Angeles and missed three games . . . (March 1, 1986)—Suspended by NHL for seven games . . . (October, 1986)—Ankle injury.

Year	Team	League	Games	G.	A.	Pts.	Pen.
1978-79—Abbotsford		BCJHL	46	3	20	23	242
1979-80—Victoria Cougars (c)		WHL	70	3	18	21	230
1980-81—Victoria Cougars		WHL	66	5	36	41	295
1981-82—Toronto Maple Leafs		NHL	68	1	10	11	263
1982-83—Toronto Maple Leafs		NHL	30	0	0	0	146
1982-83—St. Catharines Saints		AHL	32	2	5	7	95
1983-84—Toronto Maple Leafs		NHL	11	0	2	2	51
1983-84—St. Catharines Saints		AHL	55	1	15	16	217
1984-85—Toronto Maple Leafs		NHL	72	0	5	5	250
1985-86—Toronto Maple Leafs		NHL	61	1	4	5	141

Year	Team	League	Games	G.	A.	Pts.	Pen.
1986-87—Toronto Maple Leafs (d)		NHL	56	1	4	5	103
1987-88—Chicago Blacks Hawks		NHL	67	4	7	11	131
NHL TOTALS			365	7	32	39	1085

(c)—June, 1980—Drafted as underage junior by Toronto Maple Leafs in 1980 NHL entry draft. Second Maple Leafs pick, 26th overall, second round.

(d)—September, 1987—Traded with Rick Vaive and Steve Thomas by Toronto Maple Leafs to Chicago Black Hawks for Al Secord and Ed Olczyk.

RYAN McGILL

Defense . . . 6'2" . . . 198 lbs. . . . Born, Prince Albert, Sask., February 28, 1969 . . . Shoots right . . . (January, 1986)—Sprained ankle . . . (July, 1986)—Knee operation.

Year	Team	League	Games	G.	A.	Pts.	Pen.
1985-86—Lethbridge Broncos		WHL	64	5	10	15	171
1986-87—Swift Current Broncos (c)		WHL	71	12	36	48	226
1987-88—Medicine Hat Tigers (d)		WHL	67	5	30	35	224

(c)—June, 1987—Drafted as underage junior by Chicago Black Hawks in 1987 NHL entry draft. Second Black Hawks pick, 29th overall, second round.

(d)—September, 1987—Traded by Swift Current Broncos to Medicine Hat Tigers for Kelly Hitching.

MARTY McINNIS

Center . . . 5'11" . . . 175 lbs. . . . Born, Weymouth, Mass., June 2, 1970 . . . Shoots right.

Year	Team	League	Games	G.	A.	Pts.	Pen.
1986-87—Milton Academy		Mass. H.S.	..	21	19	40	..
1987-88—Milton Academy (c)		Mass. H.S.	..	26	25	51	..

(c)—June, 1988—Drafted by New York Islanders in 1988 NHL entry draft. Tenth Islanders pick, 163rd overall, eighth round.

JOHN McINTYRE

Center . . . 6'1" . . . 175 lbs. . . . Born, Ravenswood, Ont., April 29, 1969 . . . Shoots left . . . Also plays Left Wing . . . (November, 1985)—Broken ankle . . . (February, 1987)—Severed nerve in right leg at Sault Ste. Marie.

Year	Team	League	Games	G.	A.	Pts.	Pen.
1984-85—Strathroy Jr. B		OHA	48	21	23	44	49
1985-86—Guelph Platers		OHL	30	4	6	10	25
1986-87—Guelph Platers (c)		OHL	47	8	22	30	95
1987-88—Guelph Platers		OHL	39	24	18	42	109

(c)—June, 1987—Drafted as underage junior by Toronto Maple Leafs in 1987 NHL entry draft. Third Maple Leafs pick, 49th overall, third round.

DARREN McKAY

Defense . . . 5'9" . . . 190 lbs. . . . Born, Lloydminster, Sask., February 10, 1962 . . . Shoots left.

Year	Team	League	Games	G.	A.	Pts.	Pen.
1977-78—Red Deer Rustlers		AJHL	59	2	11	13	50
1978-79—Red Deer Rustlers		AJHL	....	...	....	....	....
1978-79—Billings Bighorns		WHL	2	0	0	0	0
1979-80—Red Deer Rustlers		AJHL	....	...	....	....	....
1979-80—Billings Bighorns		WHL	14	6	2	8	23
1980-81—Billings Bighorns		WHL	68	10	29	39	183
1981-82—Billings Bighorns		WHL	70	12	64	76	176
1982-83—Binghamton Whalers (c)		AHL	65	4	32	36	113
1983-84—Binghamton Whalers		AHL	71	11	40	51	206
1984-85—Muskegon Mohawks		IHL	64	8	28	36	90
1985-86—Indianapolis Checkers		IHL	30	4	14	18	42
1985-86—Muskegon Lumberjacks		IHL	36	4	22	26	62
1986-87—Milwaukee Admirals		IHL	58	9	29	38	64
1987-88—Milwaukee Admirals		IHL	28	2	8	10	66

(c)—August, 1982—Signed by Hartford Whalers as a free agent.

RANDY McKAY

Right Wing . . . 6'1" . . . 170 lbs. . . . Born, Montreal, Que., January 25, 1967 . . . Shoots right.

Year	Team	League	Games	G.	A.	Pts.	Pen.
1983-84—Lac. St. Louis Midget		Que. Midget	38	18	28	46	62
1984-85—Michigan Tech. (c)		WCHA	25	4	5	9	32
1985-86—Michigan Tech.		WCHA	40	12	22	34	46
1986-87—Michigan Tech.		WCHA	39	5	11	16	46
1987-88—Michigan Tech		WCHA	41	17	24	41	70
1987-88—Adirondack Red Wings		AHL	10	0	3	3	12

(c)—June, 1985—Drafted by Detroit Red Wings in 1985 NHL entry draft. Sixth Red Wings pick, 113th overall, sixth round.

ANTHONY SYIIYD (TONY) McKEGNEY

Left Wing . . . 6'1" . . . 195 lbs. . . . Born, Montreal, Que., February 15, 1958 . . . Shoots left . . . Brother of Mike (1974 Montreal draft pick) and Ian (Dallas-CHL) McKegney and adopted son of Lawrey McKegney . . . (February, 1985)—Separated shoulder that required surgery . . . (January 16, 1986)—Injured shoulder vs. St. Louis and missed seven games.

Year	Team	League	Games	G.	A.	Pts.	Pen.
1974-75—Kingston Canadians		Jr. "A" OHA	52	27	48	75	36
1975-76—Kingston Canadians		Jr. "A" OHA	65	24	56	80	20
1976-77—Kingston Canadians (a)		Jr. "A" OHA	66	58	77	135	30
1977-78—Kingston Canadians (b-c)		Jr. "A" OHA	55	43	49	92	19
1978-79—Buffalo Sabres		NHL	52	8	14	22	10
1978-79—Hershey Bears		AHL	24	21	18	39	4
1979-80—Buffalo Sabres		NHL	80	23	29	52	24
1980-81—Buffalo Sabres		NHL	80	37	32	69	24
1981-82—Buffalo Sabres		NHL	73	23	29	52	41
1982-83—Buffalo Sabres (d)		NHL	78	36	37	73	18
1983-84—Quebec Nordiques		NHL	75	24	27	51	23
1984-85—Quebec Nordiques (e)		NHL	30	12	9	21	12
1984-85—Minnesota North Stars		NHL	27	11	13	24	4
1985-86—Minnesota North Stars		NHL	70	15	25	40	48
1986-87—Minnesota North Stars (f)		NHL	11	2	3	5	15
1986-87—New York Rangers (g)		NHL	64	29	17	46	56
1987-88—St. Louis Blues		NHL	80	40	38	78	82
NHL TOTALS			720	260	273	533	357

(c)—Drafted from Kingston Canadians by Buffalo Sabres in second round of 1978 amateur draft.

(d)—June, 1983—Traded by Buffalo Sabres with Andre Savard, Jean-Francois Sauve and Buffalo's third-round pick in 1983 (Iiro Jarvi) to Quebec Nordiques for Real Cloutier and Quebec's first-round draft choice in 1983 (Adam Creighton).

(e)—December, 1984—Traded with Bo Berglund by Quebec Nordiques to Minnesota North Stars for Brad Maxwell and Brent Ashton.

(f)—November, 1986—Traded with Curt Giles and a second-round 1988 draft pick by Minnesota North Stars to New York Rangers for Bob Brooke and a fourth-round 1988 draft pick.

(g)—June, 1987—Traded with Rob Whistle by New York Rangers to St. Louis Blues for Bruce Bell, a fourth-round 1988 draft pick and future considerations.

SEAN MICHAEL McKENNA

Right Wing . . . 6' . . . 186 lbs. . . . Born, Asbestos, Que., March 7, 1962 . . . Shoots right . . . (March, 1987)—Hip pointer.

Year	Team	League	Games	G.	A.	Pts.	Pen.
1978-79—Montreal Juniors		QMJHL	66	9	14	23	14
1979-80—Sherbrooke Beavers (c)		QMJHL	59	20	19	39	24
1980-81—Sherbrooke Beavers (a)		QMJHL	71	57	47	104	122
1981-82—Sherbrooke Beavers (b-d-e)		QMJHL	59	57	33	90	29
1981-82—Buffalo Sabres		NHL	3	0	1	1	2
1982-83—Buffalo Sabres		NHL	46	10	14	24	4
1982-83—Rochester Americans (f)		AHL	26	16	10	26	14
1983-84—Buffalo Sabres		NHL	78	20	10	30	45
1984-85—Buffalo Sabres		NHL	65	20	16	36	41
1985-86—Buffalo Sabres (g)		NHL	45	6	12	18	28
1985-86—Los Angeles Kings		NHL	30	4	0	4	7
1986-87—Los Angeles Kings (h)		NHL	69	14	19	33	10
1987-88—Los Angeles Kings		NHL	30	3	2	5	12
1987-88—Toronto Maple Leafs		NHL	40	5	5	10	12
NHL TOTALS			406	82	79	161	161

(c)—June, 1980—Drafted as underage junior by Buffalo Sabres in 1980 NHL entry draft. Third Sabres pick, 56th overall, third round.

(d)—Led QMJHL President Cup Playoffs with 26 goals.

(e)—Named MVP of 1982 Memorial Cup Tournament.

(f)—Led AHL playoffs with a record 14 goals.

(g)—January, 1986—Traded with Larry Playfair and Ken Baumgartner by Buffalo Sabres to Los Angeles Kings for Brian Engblom and Doug Smith.

(h)—December, 1987—Traded by Los Angeles Kings to Toronto Maple Leafs for Mike Allison.

BARRY McKINLAY

Defense . . . 6' . . . 195 lbs. . . . Born, Edmonton, Alta., August 8, 1967 . . . Shoots right.

Year	Team	League	Games	G.	A.	Pts.	Pen.
1985-86—St. Albert Saints		AJHL	52	21	51	72	202
1986-87—Univ. of Illinois-Chicago (c)		CCHA	33	9	16	25	37
1987-88—Univ. of Illinois-Chicago		CCHA	38	15	31	46	81

(c)—June, 1987—Drafted by Montreal Canadiens in 1987 NHL entry draft. Twelfth Canadiens pick, 206th overall, 10th round.

JAMIE McKINLEY

Center ... 6'1" ... 165 lbs. ... Born, Moncton, N.B., May 1, 1967 ... Shoots right.

Year	Team	League	Games	G.	A.	Pts.	Pen.
1983-84—Fredericton Midgets		OHA	49	51	52	103	26
1984-85—Guelph Platers (c)		OHL	64	25	22	47	7
1985-86—Guelph Platers		OHL	66	23	30	53	48
1986-87—Guelph Platers		OHL	57	23	50	73	109
1987-88—Guelph Platers		OHL	47	29	28	57	39

(c)—June, 1985—Drafted as underage junior by New Jersey Devils in 1985 NHL entry draft. Eleventh Devils pick, 213th overall, 11th round.

MICHAEL McLAUGHLIN

Left Wing ... 6'1" ... 185 lbs. ... Born, Springfield, Mass., March 29, 1970 ... Shoots left.

Year	Team	League	Games	G.	A.	Pts.	Pen.
1986-87—Choate H.S.		Mass. H.S.	..	19	18	37	..
1987-88—Choate H.S. (c)		Mass. H.S.	..	17	18	35	..

(c)—June, 1988—Drafted by Buffalo Sabres in 1988 NHL entry draft. Seventh Sabres pick, 118th overall, sixth round.

DAVID McLAY

Left Wing ... 5'11" ... 175 lbs. ... Born, Chilliwak, B.C., May 13, 1966 ... Shoots left.

Year	Team	League	Games	G.	A.	Pts.	Pen.
1983-84—Kelowna Wings (c)		WHL	71	34	34	68	112
1984-85—Kelowna Wings		WHL	17	9	10	19	44
1984-85—Portland Winter Hawks		WHL	53	23	26	49	176
1985-86—Portland Winter Hawks		WHL	80	37	49	86	219
1986-87—Portland Winter Hawks		WHL	57	35	42	77	151
1986-87—Hershey Bears		AHL	7	1	2	3	15
1987-88—Hershey Bears		AHL	37	1	7	8	60
1987-88—Flint Spirits		IHL	26	2	10	12	45

(c)—June, 1984—Drafted as underage junior by Philadelphia Flyers in NHL entry draft. Third Flyers pick, 43rd overall, third round.

TODD McLELLAN

Center ... 5'10" ... 185 lbs. ... Born, Melville, Sask., October 3, 1967 ... Shoots left ... (October, 1985)—Dislocated left shoulder ... (May, 1988)—Surgery to right thumb tendons.

Year	Team	League	Games	G.	A.	Pts.	Pen.
1982-83—Saskatoon Blazers Midgets		Sask.	25	6	9	15	6
1983-84—Saskatoon Blades		WHL	50	8	14	22	15
1984-85—Saskatoon Blades		WHL	41	15	35	50	33
1985-86—Saskatoon Blades (c)		WHL	27	9	10	19	13
1986-87—Saskatoon Blades		WHL	60	34	39	73	66
1987-88—Springfield Indians		AHL	70	18	26	44	32
1987-88—New York Islanders		NHL	5	1	1	2	0
NHL TOTALS			5	1	1	2	0

(c)—June, 1986—Drafted by New York Islanders in 1986 NHL entry draft. Sixth Islanders pick, 104th overall, fifth round.

DONALD McLENNAN

Defense ... 6'4" ... 200 lbs. ... Born, Winnipeg, Man., October 4, 1968 ... Shoots left.

Year	Team	League	Games	G.	A.	Pts.	Pen.
1985-86—Winnipeg South Blues		MJHL	45	2	10	12	65
1986-87—University of Denver (c)		WCHA	35	2	2	4	38
1987-88—University of Denver		WCHA	29	0	3	3	24

(c)—June, 1987—Drafted by Winnipeg Jets in 1987 NHL entry draft. Third Jets pick, 79th overall, fourth round.

DAVID McLLWAIN

Right Wing . . . 6' . . . 190 lbs. . . . Born, Seaforth, Ont., January 9, 1967 . . . Shoots right.

Year	Team	League	Games	G.	A.	Pts.	Pen.
1984-85—Kitchener Rangers		OHL	61	13	21	34	29
1985-86—Kitchener Rangers (c)		OHL	13	7	7	14	12
1985-86—North Bay Centennials (d)		OHL	51	30	28	58	25
1986-87—North Bay Centennials (b)		OHL	60	46	73	119	35
1987-88—Muskegon Lumberjacks		IHL	9	4	6	10	23
1987-88—Pittsburgh Penguins		NHL	66	11	8	19	40
NHL TOTALS			66	11	8	19	40

(c)—November, 1985—Traded with John Keller and Todd Stromback by Kitchener Rangers to North Bay Centennials for Ron Sanko, Peter Lisy, Richard Hawkins and Brett McDonald.

(d)—June, 1986—Drafted as underage junior by Pittsburgh Penguins in 1986 NHL entry draft. Ninth Penguins pick, 172nd overall, ninth round.

BILL McMILLAN

Right Wing . . . 6'2" . . . 185 lbs. . . . Born, North Bay, Ont., April 3, 1967 . . . Shoots right.

Year	Team	League	Games	G.	A.	Pts.	Pen.
1983-84—North Bay Midget		OHA	74	63	71	134	36
1984-85—Peterborough Petes (c)		OHL	61	12	22	34	10
1985-86—Peterborough Petes		OHL	56	16	33	49	67
1986-87—Peterborough Petes		OHL	38	14	14	28	32
1987-88—London Knights		OHL	2	1	2	3	0
1987-88—North Bay Centennials		OHL	52	30	46	76	12

(c)—June, 1985—Drafted by New Jersey Devils in 1985 NHL entry draft. Sixth Devils pick, 108th overall, sixth round.

TOM McMURCHY

Right Wing . . . 5'10" . . . 170 lbs. . . . Born, New Westminster, B.C., December 2, 1963 . . . Shoots left . . . Also plays Center and Left Wing . . . Brother of Anthony McMurchy . . . (October, 1986)—Broken toe.

Year	Team	League	Games	G.	A.	Pts.	Pen.
1980-81—Medicine Hat Tigers (c)		WHL	14	5	0	5	46
1980-81—Brandon Wheat Kings		WHL	46	20	33	53	101
1981-82—Brandon Wheat Kings (d)		WHL	68	59	63	122	179
1982-83—Brandon Wheat Kings		WHL	42	43	38	81	48
1982-83—Springfield Indians		AHL	8	2	2	4	0
1983-84—Springfield Indians		AHL	43	16	14	30	54
1983-84—Chicago Black Hawks		NHL	27	3	1	4	42
1984-85—Milwaukee Admirals		IHL	69	30	26	56	61
1984-85—Chicago Blacks Hawks		NHL	15	1	2	3	13
1985-86—Chicago Black Hawks		NHL	4	0	0	0	2
1985-86—Nova Scotia Oilers (e)		AHL	49	26	21	47	73
1985-86—Moncton Golden Flames		AHL	16	7	3	10	27
1986-87—Nova Scotia Oilers		AHL	67	21	35	56	99
1987-88—Nova Scotia Oilers		AHL	61	40	21	61	132
1987-88—Edmonton Oilers		NHL	9	4	1	5	8
NHL TOTALS			55	8	4	12	65

(c)—November, 1980—Traded with Syd Cranston and future considerations by Medicine Hat Tigers to Brandon Wheat Kings for Mike Winther.

(d)—June, 1982—Drafted as underage junior by Chicago Black Hawks in 1982 NHL entry draft. Third Black Hawks pick, 49th overall, third round.

(e)—March, 1986—Traded by Chicago Black Hawks to Calgary Flames for Rik Wilson.

GEORGE McPHEE

Left Wing . . . 5'9" . . . 170 lbs. . . . Born, Guelph, Ont., July 2, 1958 . . . Shoots left . . . (January, 1983)—Back injury . . . (October, 1984)—Hip injury . . . (November 4, 1985)—Injured thumb in Pittsburgh and missed seven games . . . (October, 1986)—Injured shoulder in final pre-season game and needed surgery . . . (October, 1987)—Sprained left wrist . . . (November, 1987)—Pulled groin . . . (December, 1987)—Reinjured groin . . . (March, 1988)—Reinjured groin.

Year	Team	League	Games	G.	A.	Pts.	Pen.
1977-78—Guelph Platers		OPJHL	48	53	57	110	150
1978-79—Bowling Green St. Univ.		CCHA	43	*40	48	*88	58
1979-80—Bowling Green St. Univ.		CCHA	34	21	24	45	51
1980-81—Bowling Green St. Univ. (b)		CCHA	36	25	29	54	68
1981-82—Bowling Green U. (a-c-d-e)		CCHA	40	28	52	80	57

Year	Team	League	Games	G.	A.	Pts.	Pen.
1982-83—Tulsa Oilers (f)		CHL	61	17	43	60	145
1982-83—New York Rangers (g)		NHL	....	...	....	....	....
1983-84—New York Rangers		NHL	9	1	1	2	11
1983-84—Tulsa Oilers		CHL	49	20	28	48	133
1984-85—New Haven Nighthawks		AHL	3	2	2	4	13
1984-85—New York Rangers		NHL	49	12	15	27	139
1985-86—New York Rangers		NHL	30	4	4	8	63
1986-87—New York Rangers		NHL	21	4	4	8	34
1987-88—New Jersey Devils (h-i)		NHL	5	3	0	3	8
NHL TOTALS			114	24	24	48	255

(c)—CCHA Player of the Year.
(d)—Named to All-America Team (West).
(e)—Winner of Hobey Baker Award (Top NCAA hockey player).
(f)—May, 1983—Signed by New York Rangers as a free agent.
(g)—No regular-season record. Played nine playoff games (3 goals, 3 assists).
(h)—September, 1987—Traded by New York Rangers to Winnipeg Jets for a fourth-round 1989 draft pick.
(i)—October, 1987—Traded by Winnipeg Jets to New Jersey Devils for a fourth-round 1989 draft pick.

MICHAEL JOSEPH McPHEE

Left Wing . . . 6'2" . . . 200 lbs. . . . Born, Sydney, N.S., February 14, 1960 . . . Shoots left . . . (September, 1982)—Broke hand in training camp . . . (January 10, 1986)—Injured ankle at N.Y. Rangers and missed 10 games.

Year	Team	League	Games	G.	A.	Pts.	Pen.
1978-79—R.P.I.		ECAC	26	14	19	33	16
1979-80—R.P.I. (c)		ECAC	27	15	21	36	22
1980-81—R.P.I.		ECAC	29	28	18	46	22
1981-82—R.P.I.		ECAC	6	0	3	3	4
1982-83—Nova Scotia Voyageurs		AHL	42	10	15	25	29
1983-84—Nova Scotia Voyageurs		AHL	67	22	33	55	101
1983-84—Montreal Canadiens		NHL	14	5	2	7	41
1984-85—Montreal Canadiens		NHL	70	17	22	39	120
1985-86—Montreal Canadiens		NHL	70	19	21	40	69
1986-87—Montreal Canadiens		NHL	79	18	21	39	58
1987-88—Montreal Canadiens		NHL	77	23	20	43	53
NHL TOTALS			310	82	86	168	341

(c)—June, 1980—Drafted by Montreal Canadiens in 1980 NHL entry draft. Eighth Canadiens pick, 124th overall, sixth round.

DARWIN McPHERSON

Defense . . . 6'1" . . . 195 lbs. . . . Born, Flin Flon, Man., May 16, 1968 . . . Shoots left.

Year	Team	League	Games	G.	A.	Pts.	Pen.
1984-85—Brandon Wheat Kings		WHL	39	2	0	2	36
1985-86—New Westminster Bruins		WHL	63	2	8	10	149
1986-87—New Westminster Bruins (c)		WHL	65	10	22	32	242
1987-88—New Westminster Bruins		WHL	47	1	17	18	192

(c)—June, 1987—Drafted by Boston Bruins in 1987 NHL entry draft. Fourth Bruins pick, 67th overall, fourth round.

BASIL PAUL McRAE

Left Wing . . . 6'2" . . . 200 lbs. . . . Born, Orillia, Ont., January 1, 1961 . . . Shoots left . . . Brother of Chris McRae.

Year	Team	League	Games	G.	A.	Pts.	Pen.
1977-78—Seneca Nats		OHA Jr. "B"	36	21	38	59	80
1978-79—London Knights		OMJHL	66	13	28	41	79
1979-80—London Knights (c)		OMJHL	67	23	35	58	116
1980-81—London Knights		OHL	65	29	23	52	266
1981-82—Fredericton Express		AHL	47	11	15	26	175
1981-82—Quebec Nordiques		NHL	20	4	3	7	69
1982-83—Fredericton Express		AHL	53	22	19	41	146
1982-83—Quebec Nordiques		NHL	22	1	1	2	59
1983-84—Toronto Maple Leafs (d)		NHL	3	0	0	0	19
1983-84—St. Catharines Saints		AHL	78	14	25	39	187
1984-85—St. Catharines Saints		AHL	72	30	25	55	186
1984-85—Toronto Maple Leafs		NHL	1	0	0	0	0
1985-86—Detroit Red Wings		NHL	4	0	0	0	5
1985-86—Adirondack Red Wings		AHL	69	22	30	52	259
1986-87—Detroit Red Wings (f)		NHL	36	2	2	4	193

Year	Team	League	Games	G.	A.	Pts.	Pen.
1986-87—Quebec Nordiques (g)		NHL	33	9	5	14	149
1987-88—Minnesota North Stars		NHL	80	5	11	16	378
NHL TOTALS			199	21	22	43	872

(c)—June, 1980—Drafted as underage junior by Quebec Nordiques in 1980 NHL entry draft. Third Nordiques pick, 87th overall, fifth round.

(d)—August, 1983—Traded by Quebec Nordiques to Toronto Maple Leafs for Richard Trumel.

(e)—August, 1985—Signed by Detroit Red Wings as a free agent.

(f)—January, 1987—Traded with John Ogrodnick and Doug Shedden by Detroit Red Wings to Quebec Nordiques for Brent Ashton, Mark Kumpel and Gilbert Delorme.

(g)—July, 1987—Signed by Minnesota North Stars as a free agent.

CHRIS McRAE

Left Wing . . . 6' . . . 180 lbs. . . . Born, Newmarket, Ont., August 26, 1965 . . . Shoots left . . . Brother of Basil McRae.

Year	Team	League	Games	G.	A.	Pts.	Pen.
1982-83—Newmarket Tier II		OHA	42	11	22	33	207
1983-84—Sudbury Wolves		OHL	53	14	31	45	120
1983-84—Belleville Bulls		OHL	9	0	0	0	19
1984-85—Sudbury Wolves		OHL	6	0	2	2	10
1984-85—Oshawa Generals		OHL	43	8	7	15	118
1984-85—St. Catharines Saints		AHL	6	4	3	7	24
1985-86—St. Catharines Saints (c)		AHL	59	1	1	2	233
1986-87—Newmarket Saints		AHL	51	3	6	9	193
1987-88—Newmarket Saints		AHL	34	7	6	13	165
1987-88—Toronto Maple Leafs		NHL	11	0	0	0	65
NHL TOTALS			11	0	0	0	65

(c)—October, 1985—Signed by Toronto Maple Leafs as a free agent.

KEN McRAE

Center . . . 6'1" . . . 195 lbs. . . . Born, Finch, Ont., April 23, 1968 . . . Shoots right.

Year	Team	League	Games	G.	A.	Pts.	Pen.
1984-85—Hawkesbury Tier II		OHA	51	38	50	88	77
1985-86—Sudbury Wolves (c)		OHL	66	25	40	65	127
1986-87—Sudbury Wolves (d)		OHL	21	12	15	27	40
1986-87—Hamilton Steelhawks		OHL	20	7	12	19	25
1987-88—Quebec Nordiques		NHL	1	0	0	0	0
1987-88—Hamilton Steelhawks		OHL	62	30	55	85	158
NHL TOTALS			1	0	0	0	0

(c)—June, 1986—Drafted as underage junior by Quebec Nordiques in 1986 NHL entry draft. First Nordiques pick, 18th overall, first round.

(d)—December, 1986—Traded with Andy Paquette and Ken Alexander by Sudbury Wolves to Hamilton Steelhawks for Dan Hie, Joe Simon, Steve Locke, Shawn Heaphy and Jordan Fois.

BRIAN McREYNOLDS

Center . . . 6'1" . . . 180 lbs. . . . Born, Penetanguishene, Ont., January 5, 1965 . . . Shoots left.

Year	Team	League	Games	G.	A.	Pts.	Pen.
1984-85—Orillia Travelways (c)		OHA	48	40	54	94	....
1985-86—Michigan State Univ.		CCHA	45	14	24	38	78
1986-87—Michigan State Univ.		CCHA	45	16	24	40	68
1987-88—Michigan State Univ.		CCHA	43	10	24	34	50

(c)—June, 1985—Drafted by New York Rangers in 1985 NHL entry draft. Sixth Rangers pick, 112th overall, sixth round.

CHRISTOPHER McSORLEY

Center . . . 5'11" . . . 185 lbs. . . . Born, Hamilton, Ont., March 22, 1962 . . . Shoots right . . . Also plays Right Wing.

Year	Team	League	Games	G.	A.	Pts.	Pen.
1984-85—Kalamazoo Wings		IHL	9	2	2	4	32
1984-85—Toledo Goaldiggers		IHL	42	13	12	25	253
1985-86—Toledo Goaldiggers (c)		OHL	75	27	28	55	*546
1986-87—New Haven Nighthawks		AHL	22	2	2	4	116
1986-87—Muskegon Lumberjacks		IHL	47	18	17	35	293
1987-88—Flint Spirits		IHL	30	5	10	15	222
1987-88—New Haven Nighthawks		AHL	44	10	9	19	186

(c)—May, 1986—Signed by Los Angeles Kings as a free agent.

MARTY McSORLEY

Right Wing and Defense . . . 6'1" . . . 190 lbs. . . . Born, Hamilton, Ont., May 18, 1963 . . . Shoots right . . . (March, 1987)—Suspended by the NHL for an AHL incident . . . (November, 1987)—Sprained knee vs. New Jersey . . . (April 23, 1988)—Suspended three NHL playoff games for spearing Mike Bullard vs. Calgary.

Year	Team	League	Games	G.	A.	Pts.	Pen.
1981-82—Belleville Bulls		OHL	58	6	13	19	234
1982-83—Belleville Bulls		OHL	70	10	41	51	183
1982-83—Baltimore Skipjacks (c)		AHL	2	0	0	0	22
1983-84—Pittsburgh Penguins		NHL	72	2	7	9	224
1984-85—Baltimore Skipjacks		AHL	58	6	24	30	154
1984-85—Pittsburgh Penguins		NHL	15	0	0	0	15
1985-86—Edmonton Oilers (d)		NHL	59	11	12	23	265
1985-86—Nova Scotia Oilers		AHL	9	2	4	6	34
1986-87—Edmonton Oilers		NHL	41	2	4	6	159
1986-87—Nova Scotia Oilers		AHL	7	2	2	4	48
1987-88—Edmonton Oilers (e)		NHL	60	9	17	26	223
NHL TOTALS			247	24	40	64	886

(c)—April, 1983—Signed by Pittsburgh Penguins as a free agent.
(d)—August, 1985—Traded with Tim Hrynewich by Pittsburgh Penguins to Edmonton Oilers for Gilles Meloche.
(e)—August 1988—Traded with Wayne Gretzky and Mike Krushelnyski by Edmonton Oilers to Los Angeles Kings for Jimmy Carson, Martin Gelinas, first-round draft choices in 1989, '91 and '93, plus cash in excess of $10 million.

DON McSWEEN

Defense . . . 5'10" . . . 190 lbs. . . . Born, Detroit, Mich., June 9, 1964 . . . Shoots left.

Year	Team	League	Games	G.	A.	Pts.	Pen.
1983-84—Michigan State Univ. (c)		CCHA	46	10	26	36	30
1984-85—Michigan State Univ.		CCHA	44	2	23	25	52
1985-86—Michigan State Univ.		CCHA	45	9	29	38	18
1986-87—Michigan State Univ. (a-d)		CCHA	45	7	23	30	34
1987-88—Rochester Americans		AHL	63	9	29	38	108
1987-88—Buffalo Sabres		NHL	5	0	1	1	4
NHL TOTALS			5	0	1	1	4

(c)—June, 1983—Drafted by Buffalo Sabres in 1983 NHL entry draft. Tenth Sabres pick, 154th overall, eighth round.
(d)—Named second-team All-American (West).

NEIL ROBERT MEADMORE

Right Wing . . . 6'4" . . . 180 lbs. . . . Born, Winnipeg, Man., October 23, 1959 . . . Shoots right . . . Son of Ronald Meadmore, who played several seasons in CFL . . . Brother of Jim Meadmore . . . (November, 1983)—Knee surgery.

Year	Team	League	Games	G.	A.	Pts.	Pen.
1977-78—Flin Flon Bombers		WCHL	25	7	8	15	30
1977-78—New Westminster Bruins		WCHL	29	5	7	12	19
1978-79—New Westminster Bruins		WHL	71	30	36	66	128
1979-80—Kalamazoo Wings		IHL	79	23	37	60	160
1980-81—Kalamazoo Wings		IHL	82	31	41	78	179
1981-82—Adirondack Red Wings		AHL	52	13	11	24	106
1981-82—Kalamazoo Wings		IHL	24	18	11	29	51
1982-83—Kalamazoo Wings		IHL	26	10	7	17	97
1983-84—Kalamazoo Wings		IHL	82	39	48	87	267
1984-85—Kalamazoo Wings		IHL	45	10	23	33	167
1985-86—Kalamazoo Wings		IHL	37	12	17	29	118
1986-87—Kalamazoo Wings (c)		IHL	14	5	4	9	37
1986-87—Milwaukee Admirals		IHL	64	30	31	61	122
1987-88—Milwaukee Admirals		IHL	76	16	31	47	380

(c)—November, 1986—Ended holdout and signed with Kalamazoo Wings.

RICK MEAGHER

Center . . . 5'8" . . . 175 lbs. . . . Born, Belleville, Ont., November 4, 1953 . . . Shoots left . . . Member of Boston University Hall of Fame . . . Named Boston University Athlete of the Decade (1970-79) . . . Elected to ECAC All-Decade Team (1970-79) . . . Brother of Terry Meagher . . . (December, 1981)—Back and knee problems . . . (November, 1982)—Missed eight games with shoulder separation suffered at Montreal . . . (January, 1984)—Fractured rib . . . (October, 1984)—Cut right forearm when run over by a skate in pre-season game with Hartford . . . (January, 1985)—Bruised ribs.

Year	Team	League	Games	G.	A.	Pts.	Pen.
1973-74—Boston University		ECAC	30	19	21	40	26

Year	Team	League	Games	G.	A.	Pts.	Pen.
1974-75—Boston University		ECAC	32	25	28	53	80
1975-76—Boston University		ECAC	28	12	25	37	22
197_-77—Boston University (a-c)		ECAC	34	34	46	80	42
1977-78—Nova Scotia Voyageurs		AHL	57	20	27	47	33
1978-79—Nova Scotia Voyageurs		AHL	79	35	46	81	57
1979-80—Nova Scotia Voyageurs		AHL	64	32	44	76	53
1979-80—Montreal Canadiens (d)		NHL	2	0	0	0	0
1980-81—Binghamton Whalers		AHL	50	23	35	58	54
1980-81—Hartford Whalers		NHL	27	7	10·	17	19
1981-82—Hartford Whalers		NHL	65	24	19	43	51
1982-83—Hartford Whalers		NHL	4	0	0	0	0
1982-83—New Jersey Devils		NHL	57	15	14	29	11
1983-84—Maine Mariners		AHL	10	6	4	10	2
1983-84—New Jersey Devils		NHL	52	14	14	28	16
1984-85—New Jersey Devils (e)		NHL	71	11	20	31	22
1985-86—St. Louis Blues		NHL	79	11	19	30	28
1986-87—St. Louis Blues		NHL	80	18	21	39	54
1987-88—St. Louis Blues		NHL	76	18	16	34	76
NHL TOTALS			513	118	133	251	277

(c)—Named to first team (East) All-America.
(d)—June, 1980—Traded with third (Paul MacDermid) and fifth (Dan Bourbonnais) round picks in 1981 draft by Montreal Canadiens to Hartford Whalers for third (Dieter Hegen) and fifth (Steve Rooney) round Whalers picks in 1981 draft.
(e)—August, 1985—Traded with 1986 12th round draft choice (Bill Butler) by New Jersey Devils to St. Louis Blues for Perry Anderson.

CHARLES MEITNER

Left Wing . . . 6'2" . . . 205 lbs. . . . Born, Whitby, Ont., July 8, 1962 . . . Shoots left.

Year	Team	League	Games	G.	A.	Pts.	Pen.
1982-83—Clarkson College		ECAC	24	6	6	12	2
1983-84—Clarkson College		ECAC	34	9	15	24	10
1984-85—Clarkson College		ECAC	34	18	23	41	38
1985-86—Clarkson College		ECAC	28	18	23	41	42
1986-87—Peoria Rivermen (c)		IHL	38	12	10	22	12
1987-88—Baltimore Skipjacks		AHL	28	12	15	27	18

(c)—September, 1986—Signed by New York Islanders as a free agent.

SCOTT MELLANBY

Right Wing . . . 6'1" . . . 195 lbs. . . . Born, Montreal, Que., June 11, 1966 . . . Shoots right . . . (October, 1987)—Cut index finger on right hand.

Year	Team	League	Games	G.	A.	Pts.	Pen.
1983-84—Henry Carr H.S. (c)		MTJHL	39	37	37	74	97
1984-85—University of Wisconsin		WCHA	40	14	24	38	60
1985-86—University of Wisconsin		WCHA	32	21	23	44	89
1985-86—Philadelphia Flyers		NHL	2	0	0	0	0
1986-87—Philadelphia Flyers		NHL	71	11	21	32	94
1987-88—Philadelphia Flyers		NHL	75	25	26	51	185
NHL TOTALS			148	36	47	83	279

(c)—June, 1984—Drafted as underage junior by Philadelphia Flyers in NHL entry draft. First Flyers pick, 27th overall, second round.

LARRY JOSEPH MELNYK

Defense . . . 6' . . . 180 lbs. . . . Born, New Westminster, B.C., February 21, 1960 . . . Shoots left . . . (January 16, 1985)—Twisted knee vs. N.Y. Islanders . . . (December, 1985)—Separated shoulder . . . (November, 1987)—Cut eye and concussion . . . (April 1, 1988)—Severed tendon in right arm in final regular season game vs. Minnesota.

Year	Team	League	Games	G.	A.	Pts.	Pen.
1977-78—Abbotsford		BCJHL	39	10	9	19	100
1977-78—New Westminster Bruins		WCHL	44	3	22	25	71
1978-79—New Westminster Bruins (c)		WHL	71	7	33	40	142
1979-80—New Westminster Bruins		WHL	67	13	38	51	236
1980-81—Boston Bruins		NHL	26	0	4	4	39
1980-81—Springfield Indians		AHL	47	1	10	11	109
1981-82—Erie Blades		AHL	10	0	3	3	36
1981-82—Boston Bruins		NHL	48	0	8	8	84
1982-83—Baltimore Skipjacks		AHL	72	2	24	26	215
1982-83—Boston Bruins		NHL	1	0	0	0	0
1983-84—Hershey Bears (d)		AHL	51	0	18	18	156
1983-84—Moncton Alpines		AHL	14	0	3	3	17

Year	Team	League	Games	G.	A.	Pts.	Pen.
1983-84—Edmonton Oilers (e)		NHL	....	...	....	....	....
1984-85—Nova Scotia Voyageurs		AHL	37	2	10	12	97
1984-85—Edmonton Oilers		NHL	28	0	11	11	25
1985-86—Nova Scotia Oilers		AHL	19	2	8	10	72
1985-86—Edmonton Oilers (f)		NHL	6	2	3	5	11
1985-86—New York Rangers		NHL	46	1	8	9	65
1986-87—New York Rangers		NHL	73	3	12	15	182
1987-88—New York Rangers (g)		NHL	14	0	1	1	34
1987-88—Vancouver Canucks		NHL	49	2	3	5	73
NHL TOTALS			291	8	50	58	513

(c)—August, 1979—Drafted as underage junior by Boston Bruins in 1979 NHL entry draft. Fifth Bruins pick, 78th overall, fourth round.

(d)—March, 1983—Traded by Boston Bruins to Edmonton Oilers for John Blum.

(e)—No regular season record. Played six playoff games (1 assist).

(f)—December, 1985—Traded with Todd Strueby by Edmonton Oilers to New York Rangers for Mike Rogers.

(g)—November, 1987—Traded with Willie Huber by New York Rangers to Vancouver Canucks for Michel Petit.

KEVAN MELROSE

Defense . . . 5'10" . . . 180 lbs. . . . Born, Calgary, Alta., March 28, 1966 . . . Shoots left . . . (Summer, 1984)—Knee surgery.

Year	Team	League	Games	G.	A.	Pts.	Pen.
1983-84—Red Deer Rustlers (c)		AJHL	42	9	26	35	89
1984-85—Penticton		BCJHL	24	15	10	25	42
1985-86—Penticton		BCJHL	22	18	15	33	56
1986-87—Canadian Olympic Team		Int'l	8	1	0	1	4
1987-88—Harvard Univ.		ECAC	31	4	6	10	50

(c)—June, 1984—Drafted by Calgary Flames in 1984 NHL entry draft. Seventh Flames pick, 138th overall, seventh round.

ROBERT MENDEL

Defense . . . 6'1" . . . 185 lbs. . . . Born, Los Angeles, Calif., September 19, 1968 . . . Shoots left.

Year	Team	League	Games	G.	A.	Pts.	Pen.
1985-86—Edina High School		Minn. H.S.	21	2	27	29	....
1986-87—Univ. of Wisconsin (c)		WCHA	42	1	7	8	26
1987-88—Univ. of Wisconsin		WCHA	40	0	7	7	22

(c)—June, 1987—Drafted by Quebec Nordiques in 1987 NHL entry draft. Fifth Nordiques pick, 93rd overall, fifth round.

DON MERCIER

Defense . . . 6'4" . . . 210 lbs. . . . Born, Grimshaw, Alaska, January 21, 1963 . . . Shoots left.

Year	Team	League	Games	G.	A.	Pts.	Pen.
1983-84—Univ. of Denver		WCHA	35	2	10	12	44
1984-85—Univ. of Denver		WCHA	33	4	12	16	62
1985-86—Univ. of Denver (c)		WCHA	48	3	10	13	60
1986-87—Moncton Golden Flames		AHL	74	5	11	16	107
1987-88—Salt Lake Golden Eagles (d)		IHL	11	0	1	1	16
1987-88—Colorado Rangers		IHL	51	3	13	16	137

(c)—July, 1986—Signed by Calgary Flames as a free agent.

(d)—November, 1987—Traded by Calgary Flames to New York Rangers for Jim Leavins.

GLENN MERKOSKY

Center . . . 5'10" . . . 175 lbs. . . . Born, Edmonton, Alta., April 8, 1960 . . . Shoots left.

Year	Team	League	Games	G.	A.	Pts.	Pen.
1977-78—Seattle Breakers		WCHL	6	4	3	7	2
1978-79—Michigan Tech		WCHA	38	14	29	43	22
1979-80—Calgary Wranglers		WHL	72	49	40	89	95
1980-81—Binghamton Whalers (c)		AHL	80	26	35	61	61
1981-82—Hartford Whalers		NHL	7	0	0	0	2
1981-82—Binghamton Whalers		AHL	72	29	40	69	83
1982-83—New Jersey Devils (d)		NHL	34	4	10	14	20
1982-83—Wichita Wind		CHL	45	26	23	49	15
1983-84—Maine Mariners		AHL	75	28	28	56	56
1983-84—New Jersey Devils		NHL	5	1	0	1	0
1984-85—Maine Mariners (b)		AHL	80	38	38	76	19

Year	Team	League	Games	G.	A.	Pts.	Pen.
1985-86—Adirondack Red Wings		AHL	59	24	33	57	22
1985-86—Detroit Red Wings (e)		NHL	17	0	2	2	0
1986-87—Adirondack Red Wings (a-f)		AHL	77	*54	31	85	66
1987-88—Rosenheim SB		W. Germany	16	2	3	5	17
1987-88—Adirondack Red Wings		AHL	66	34	42	76	34
NHL TOTALS			63	5	12	17	22

(c)—August, 1980—Signed by Hartford Whalers as a free agent.
(d)—September, 1982—Signed by New Jersey Devils as a free agent.
(e)—August, 1985—Signed by Detroit Red Wings as a free agent.
(f)—Won Fred Hunt Trophy (Sportsmanship Trophy).

MIKE MERSH

Defense . . . 6'2" . . . 210 lbs. . . . Born, Skokie, Ill., September 29, 1964 . . . Shoots left . . . (January, 1987)—Missed 32 games with a separated shoulder.

Year	Team	League	Games	G.	A.	Pts.	Pen.
1983-84—Univ. of Illinois/Chicago		CCHA	29	0	5	5	18
1984-85—Univ. of Illinois/Chicago		CCHA	35	1	14	15	36
1985-86—Univ. of Illinois/Chicago (c)		CCHA	36	4	19	23	30
1986-87—Salt Lake Golden Eagles		IHL	43	3	12	15	101
1987-88—Salt Lake Golden Eagles		IHL	1	0	0	0	2
1987-88—Flint Spirits		IHL	58	1	14	15	118

(c)—April, 1986—Signed by Calgary Flames as a free agent.

MARK MESSIER

Center and Left Wing . . . 6' . . . 205 lbs. . . . Born, Edmonton, Alta., January 18, 1961 . . . Shoots left . . . Son of Doug Messier (WHL), brother of Paul Messier and cousin of Mitch Messier . . . (November 7, 1981)—Injured ankle at Chicago . . . (March, 1983)—Chipped bone in wrist . . . (January 18, 1984)—Given six-game suspension by NHL for hitting Vancouver's Thomas Gradin over the head with his stick . . . Brother-in-law of John Blum . . . (November, 1984)—Sprained knee ligaments . . . (December 26, 1984)—Given 10-game NHL suspension for cracking cheekbone of Jamie Macoun at Calgary . . . (December 3, 1985)—Bruised left foot at Los Angeles and missed 17 games . . . (October, 1987)—Suspended and fined by Edmonton Oilers after refusing to report to training camp. He missed three weeks of camp.

Year	Team	League	Games	G.	A.	Pts.	Pen.
1976-77—Spruce Grove Mets		AJHL	57	27	39	66	91
1977-78—St. Albert Saints		AJHL	....	...	....	....	....
1978-79—Indianapolis Racers (c)		WHA	5	0	0	0	0
1978-79—Cincinnati Stingers (d-e)		WHA	47	1	10	11	58
1979-80—Houston Apollos		CHL	4	0	3	3	4
1979-80—Edmonton Oilers		NHL	75	12	21	33	120
1980-81—Edmonton Oilers		NHL	72	23	40	63	102
1981-82—Edmonton Oilers (a)		NHL	78	50	38	88	119
1982-83—Edmonton Oilers (a)		NHL	77	48	58	106	72
1983-84—Edmonton Oilers (b-f)		NHL	73	37	64	101	165
1984-85—Edmonton Oilers		NHL	55	23	31	54	57
1985-86—Edmonton Oilers		NHL	63	35	49	84	68
1986-87—Edmonton Oilers		NHL	77	37	70	107	73
1987-88—Edmonton Oilers		NHL	77	37	74	111	103
WHA TOTALS			52	1	10	11	58
NHL TOTALS			647	302	445	747	879

(c)—November, 1978—Given five-game trial by Indianapolis Racers.
(d)—January, 1979—Signed by Cincinnati Stingers as free agent.
(e)—August, 1979—Drafted by Edmonton Oilers in NHL entry draft. Second Edmonton pick, 48th overall, third round.
(f)—Won Conn Smythe Trophy (Stanley Cup Playoff MVP).

MITCH MESSIER

Center . . . 6'2" . . . 185 lbs. . . . Born, Regina, Sask., August 21, 1965 . . . Shoots right . . . Cousin of Mark Messier . . . Brother of Jody Messier . . . (November, 1987)—Bruised knee.

Year	Team	League	Games	G.	A.	Pts.	Pen.
1981-82—Notre Dame H.S.		Sask. Midget	26	8	20	28	..
1982-83—Notre Dame H.S. (c)		Sask. Juvenile	60	108	73	181	160
1983-84—Michigan State University		CCHA	37	6	15	21	22
1984-85—Michigan State University		CCHA	42	12	21	33	46
1985-86—Michigan State University		CCHA	38	24	40	64	36
1986-87—Michigan St. Univ.(a-d)		CCHA	45	44	48	92	89

Year	Team	League	Games	G.	A.	Pts.	Pen.
1987-88—Kalamazoo Wings		IHL	69	29	37	66	42
1987-88—Minnesota North Stars		NHL	13	0	1	1	11
NHL TOTALS			13	0	1	1	11

(c)—June, 1983—Drafted by Minnesota North Stars in 1983 NHL entry draft. Fourth North Stars pick, 56th overall, third round.

(d)—Named U.S. College All-America First-Team All-Star.

SCOTT METCALFE

Left Wing . . . 6' . . . 195 lbs. . . . Born, Toronto, Ont., January 6, 1967 . . . Shoots left.

Year	Team	League	Games	G.	A.	Pts.	Pen.
1982-83—Toronto Young Nats		OHA	39	22	43	65	74
1983-84—Kingston Canadians		OHL	68	25	49	74	154
1984-85—Kingston Canadians (c)		OHL	58	27	33	60	100
1985-86—Kingston Canadians		OHL	66	36	43	79	213
1986-87—Kingston Canadians (d)		OHL	39	15	45	60	14
1986-87—Windsor Spitfires		OHL	18	10	12	22	52
1987-88—Nova Scotia Oilers		AHL	43	9	19	28	87
1987-88—Rochester Americans		AHL	22	2	13	15	56
1987-88—Edmonton Oilers (e)		NHL	2	0	0	0	0
1987-88—Buffalo Sabres		NHL	1	0	1	1	0
NHL TOTALS			3	0	1	1	0

(c)—June, 1985—Drafted as underage junior by Edmonton Oilers in 1985 NHL entry draft. First Oilers pick, 20th overall, first round

(d)—February, 1987—Traded by Kingston Canadians to Windsor Spitfires for future draft considerations.

(e)—February, 1988—Traded by Edmonton Oilers to Buffalo Sabres for Steve Dykstra.

DAVID MICHAYLUK

Right Wing . . . 5'10" . . . 175 lbs. . . . Born, Wakaw, Sask., May 18, 1962 . . . Shoots left . . . Also plays Left Wing.

Year	Team	League	Games	G.	A.	Pts.	Pen.
1979-80—Prince Albert Saints		AJHL	60	46	67	113	49
1980-81—Regina Pats (b-c-d)		WHL	72	62	71	133	39
1981-82—Regina Pats (b-e)		WHL	72	62	111	173	128
1981-82—Philadelphia Flyers		NHL	1	0	0	0	0
1982-83—Philadelphia Flyers		NHL	13	2	6	8	8
1982-83—Maine Mariners		AHL	69	32	40	72	16
1983-84—Springfield Indians		AHL	79	18	44	62	37
1984-85—Hershey Bears		AHL	3	0	2	2	2
1984-85—Kalamazoo Wings (b)		IHL	82	*66	33	99	49
1985-86—Nova Scotia Oilers		AHL	3	0	1	1	0
1985-86—Muskegon Lumberjacks		IHL	77	52	52	104	73
1986-87—Muskegon Lumberjacks (b)		IHL	82	47	53	100	69
1987-88—Muskegon Lumberjacks (a)		IHL	81	56	81	137	46
NHL TOTALS			14	2	6	8	8

(c)—Winner of Stewart "Butch" Paul Memorial Trophy (Top Rookie).

(d)—June, 1981—Drafted as underage junior by Philadelphia Flyers in 1981 NHL entry draft. Fifth Flyers pick, 65th overall, fourth round.

(e)—Led WHL playoffs with 40 points.

PAT MICHELETTI

Right Wing . . . 5'9" . . . 170 lbs. . . . Born, Hibbing, Minn., December 11, 1963 . . . Shoots right . . . Brother of former NHL defenseman Joe Micheletti . . . (October, 1987)—Injured knee in pre-season IHL game.

Year	Team	League	Games	G.	A.	Pts.	Pen.
1982-83—University of Minnesota (c)		WCHA	31	14	19	33	74
1983-84—University of Minnesota		WCHA	39	26	34	60	62
1984-85—University of Minnesota		WCHA	44	48	48	96	154
1985-86—University of Minnesota		WCHA	48	32	48	80	113
1985-86—Springfield Indians		AHL	2	1	0	1	0
1986-87—Springfield Indians		AHL	67	17	26	43	39
1987-88—Minnesota North Stars		NHL	12	2	0	2	8
1987-88—Kalamazoo Wings		IHL	19	12	6	18	12
NHL TOTALS			12	2	0	2	8

(c)—June, 1982—Drafted by Minnesota North Stars in 1982 NHL entry draft. Ninth North Stars pick, 185th overall, ninth round.

TROY MICK

Left Wing . . . 6' . . . 180 lbs. . . . Born, Burnaby, B.C., March 30, 1969 . . . Shoots left . . . (March, 1987)—Left knee surgery.

Year	Team	League	Games	G.	A.	Pts.	Pen.
1985-86—Portland Winter Hawks		WHL	6	2	5	7	2
1986-87—Portland Winter Hawks		WHL	57	30	33	63	60
1987-88—Portland Winter Hawks (a-c)		WHL	72	63	84	147	78

(c)—June, 1988—Drafted by Pittsburgh Penguins in 1988 NHL entry draft. Sixth Penguins pick, 130th overall, seventh round.

MAX MIDDENDORF

Right Wing . . . 6'4" . . . 195 lbs. . . . Born, Syracuse, N.Y., August 18, 1967 . . . Shoots right . . . (February 1, 1987)—Dislocated thumb.

Year	Team	League	Games	G.	A.	Pts.	Pen.
1983-84—New Jersey Rockets		N.J. Midget	58	94	74	168	....
1984-85—Sudbury Wolves (c)		OHL	63	16	28	44	106
1985-86—Sudbury Wolves		OHL	61	40	42	82	71
1986-87—Quebec Nordiques		NHL	6	1	4	5	4
1986-87—Sudbury Wolves		OHL	31	31	29	60	7
1986-87—Kitchener Rangers		OHL	17	7	15	22	6
1987-88—Fredericton Express		AHL	38	11	13	24	57
1987-88—Quebec Nordiques		NHL	1	0	0	0	0
NHL TOTALS			7	1	4	5	4

(c)—June, 1985—Drafted as underage junior by Quebec Nordiques in 1985 NHL entry draft. Third Nordiques pick, 57th overall, third round.

RICHARD DAVID (RICK) MIDDLETON

Right Wing . . . 5'11" . . . 170 lbs. . . . Born, Toronto, Ont., December 4, 1953 . . . Shoots right . . . Missed parts of 1974-75 season with broken left leg and fractured cheek . . . (March 11, 1982)—Scored hat trick vs. Winnipeg despite suffering sprained right shoulder . . . (July, 1982)—Surgery to replace torn tendon in right shoulder . . . (November 10, 1985)—Neck and shoulder spasms . . . (February, 1986)—Hit in head by shot in practice. Suffered dizzy spells and missed remainder of season . . . (January, 1988)—Pulled hamstring . . . (February 6, 1988)—Fractured rib vs. Quebec.

Year	Team	League	Games	G.	A.	Pts.	Pen.
1971-72—Oshawa Generals		Jr."A"OHA	53	36	34	70	24
1972-73—Oshawa Generals (b-c-d)		Jr."A"OHA	62	*67	70	137	14
1973-74—Providence Reds (a-e)		AHL	63	36	48	84	14
1974-75—New York Rangers		NHL	47	22	18	40	19
1975-76—New York Rangers (f)		NHL	77	24	26	50	14
1976-77—Boston Bruins		NHL	72	20	22	42	2
1977-78—Boston Bruins		NHL	79	25	35	60	8
1978-79—Boston Bruins		NHL	71	38	48	86	7
1979-80—Boston Bruins		NHL	80	40	52	92	24
1980-81—Boston Bruins		NHL	80	44	59	103	16
1981-82—Boston Bruins (b-g)		NHL	75	51	43	94	12
1982-83—Boston Bruins		NHL	80	49	47	96	8
1983-84—Boston Bruins		NHL	80	47	58	105	14
1984-85—Boston Bruins		NHL	80	30	46	76	6
1985-86—Boston Bruins		NHL	49	14	30	44	10
1986-87—Boston Bruins		NHL	76	31	37	68	6
1987-88—Boston Bruins		NHL	59	13	19	32	11
NHL TOTALS			1005	448	540	988	157

(c)—Won Red Tilson Memorial Trophy (MVP).
(d)—Drafted from Oshawa Generals by New York Rangers in first round of 1973 amateur draft.
(e)—Won Dudley (Red) Garrett Memorial Trophy (leading rookie).
(f)—May, 1976—Traded to Boston Bruins by New York Rangers for Ken Hodge.
(g)—Winner of Lady Byng Memorial Trophy (Combination of Sportsmanship and Quality play).

KEVIN MIEHM

Center . . . 6'2" . . . 190 lbs. . . . Born, Kitchener, Ont., September 10, 1969 . . . Shoots left.

Year	Team	League	Games	G.	A.	Pts.	Pen.
1985-86—Kitchener Greenshirts		OHA	20	20	37	57	65
1986-87—Oshawa Generals (c)		OHL	61	12	27	39	19
1987-88—Oshawa Generals		OHL	52	16	36	52	30

(c)—June, 1987—Drafted as underage junior by St. Louis Blues in 1987 NHL entry draft. Second Blues pick, 54th overall, third round.

MARIO MILANI

Right Wing . . . 6' . . . 176 lbs. . . . Born, Jonquiere, Que., January 9, 1968 . . . Shoots left.

Year	Team	League	Games	G.	A.	Pts.	Pen.
1984-85—Montreal Concordia Midget		Que.	41	21	32	53	63
1985-86—Verdun Junior Canadiens (c)		QHL	71	16	31	47	74
1986-87—Verdun Junior Canadiens		QHL	60	15	27	42	83
1987-88—Verdun Junior Canadiens		QHL	68	15	26	41	75

(c)—June, 1986—Drafted as underage junior by Montreal Canadiens in 1986 NHL entry draft. Sixth Canadiens pick, 99th overall, fifth round.

MIKE MILLAR

Right Wing . . . 5'10" . . . 170 lbs. . . . Born, St. Catharines, Ont., April 28, 1965 . . . Shoots left.

Year	Team	League	Games	G.	A.	Pts.	Pen.
1981-82—St. Catharines Midgets		Ont. Midget	30	32	32	64	24
1982-83—Brantford Alexanders		OHL	53	20	29	49	10
1983-84—Brantford Alexanders (c)		OHL	69	50	45	95	48
1984-85—Hamilton Steelhawks		OHL	63	*66	60	126	54
1985-86—Team Canada		Int'l.	69	50	38	88	74
1986-87—Hartford Whalers		NHL	10	2	2	4	0
1986-87—Binghamton Whalers		AHL	61	45	32	77	38
1987-88—Binghamton Whalers		AHL	31	32	17	49	42
1987-88—Hartford Whalers (d)		NHL	28	7	7	14	6
NHL TOTALS			38	9	9	18	6

(c)—June, 1984—Drafted as underage junior by Hartford Whalers in 1984 NHL entry draft. Second Whalers pick, 110th overall, sixth round.

(d)—July, 1988—Traded with Neil Sheehy by Hartford Whalers to Washington Capitals for Ed Kastelic and Grant Jennings.

COREY MILLEN

Center . . . 5'7" . . . 165 lbs. . . . Born, Cloquet, Minn., April 29, 1964 . . . Shoots right . . . (November, 1982)—Injured knee in WCHA game vs. Colorado College, requiring surgery . . . Member of 1984 U.S. Olympic team . . . (October, 1984)—Shoulder injury.

Year	Team	League	Games	G.	A.	Pts.	Pen.
1981-82—Cloquet H.S. (c)		Minn. H.S.	18	46	35	81	....
1982-83—University of Minnesota		WCHA	21	14	15	29	18
1983-84—U.S. National Team		Int'l	45	15	11	26	10
1983-84—U.S. Olympic Team		Int'l	6	0	0	0	2
1984-85—University of Minnesota (b)		WCHA	38	28	36	64	60
1985-86—University of Minnesota (b)		WCHA	48	41	42	83	64
1986-87—University of Minnesota (b)		WCHA	42	36	29	65	62
1987-88—U.S. Olympic Team		Int'l	51	46	45	91	..

(c)—June, 1982—Drafted by New York Rangers in 1982 NHL entry draft as underage player. Third Rangers pick, 57th overall, third round.

BRAD MILLER

Defense . . . 6'4" . . . 205 lbs. . . . Born, Edmonton, Alta., July 23, 1969 . . . Shoots left.

Year	Team	League	Games	G.	A.	Pts.	Pen.
1984-85—Edmonton K. of C.		Alta. Midget	42	7	26	33	154
1985-86—Regina Pats		WHL	71	2	14	16	99
1986-87—Regina Pats (c)		WHL	67	10	38	48	154
1987-88—Regina Pats		WHL	61	9	34	43	148
1987-88—Rochester Americans		AHL	3	0	0	0	4

(c)—June, 1987—Drafted as underage junior by Buffalo Sabres in 1987 NHL entry draft. Second Sabres pick, 22nd overall, second round.

JAY MILLER

Left Wing . . . 6'2" . . . 215 lbs. . . . Born, Wellesley, Mass., July 16, 1960 . . . Shoots left . . . (November, 1984)—Broken bone in right hand . . . Also plays Defense . . . (April, 1988)—Strained right knee ligaments.

Year	Team	League	Games	G.	A.	Pts.	Pen.
1979-80—Univ. New Hampshire		ECAC	28	7	12	19	53
1981-82—Univ. New Hampshire		ECAC	10	4	8	12	14
1982-83—Univ. New Hampshire		ECAC	24	6	4	10	34
1983-84—Toledo Goaldiggers		IHL	2	0	0	0	4
1983-84—Mohawk Valley Comets		ACHL	48	15	36	51	167
1983-84—Maine Mariners		AHL	15	1	1	2	27
1984-85—Muskegon Mohawks		IHL	56	5	29	34	177

Year	Team	League	Games	G.	A.	Pts.	Pen.
1985-86—Moncton Golden Flames		AHL	18	4	6	10	113
1985-86—Boston Bruins (c)		NHL	46	3	0	3	178
1986-87—Boston Bruins		NHL	55	1	4	5	208
1987-88—Boston Bruins		NHL	78	7	12	19	304
NHL TOTALS			179	11	16	27	690

(c)—September, 1985—Signed by Boston Bruins as a free agent.

KEITH MILLER

Left Wing . . . 6'2" . . . 212 lbs. . . . Born, Toronto, Ont., March 18, 1967 . . . Shoots left.

Year	Team	League	Games	G.	A.	Pts.	Pen.
1984-85—Guelph Platers		OHL	18	1	3	4	7
1984-85—Aurora Tigers Tier II		OJHL	24	7	11	18	31
1985-86—Guelph Platers (c)		OHL	61	32	17	49	30
1986-87—Guelph Platers		OHL	66	50	31	81	44
1987-88—Baltimore Skipjacks		AHL	21	6	5	11	12

(c)—June, 1986—Drafted by Quebec Nordiques in 1986 NHL entry draft. Tenth Nordiques pick, 165th overall, eighth round.

KELLY MILLER

Left Wing . . . 5'11" . . . 185 lbs. . . . Born, Lansing, Mich., March 3, 1963 . . . Shoots left . . . (September, 1985)—Injured ankle in training camp . . . (January 27, 1986)—Sprained knee at Quebec and missed five games . . . Brother of Kip and Kevin Miller.

Year	Team	League	Games	G.	A.	Pts.	Pen.
1981-82—Michigan State University (c)		CCHA	40	11	19	30	21
1982-83—Michigan State University		CCHA	36	16	19	35	12
1983-84—Michigan State University		CCHA	46	28	21	49	12
1984-85—Michigan State University (d)		CCHA	43	27	23	50	21
1984-85—New York Rangers		NHL	5	0	2	2	2
1985-86—New York Rangers		NHL	74	13	20	33	52
1986-87—New York Rangers (e)		NHL	38	6	14	20	22
1986-87—Washington Capitals		NHL	39	10	12	22	26
1987-88—Washington Capitals		NHL	80	9	23	32	35
NHL TOTALS			236	38	71	109	137

(c)—June, 1982—Drafted by New York Rangers in NHL entry draft. Ninth Rangers pick, 183rd overall, ninth round.

(d)—First-Team (West) All-America.

(e)—January, 1987—Traded with Mike Ridley and Bobby Crawford by New York Rangers to Washington Capitals for Bobby Carpenter and a second-round 1989 draft pick.

KEVIN MILLER

Center . . . 5'9" . . . 170 lbs. . . . Born, Lansing, Mich., August 9, 1965 . . . Shoots right . . . Brother of Kip and Kelly Miller . . . Also plays Right Wing.

Year	Team	League	Games	G.	A.	Pts.	Pen.
1984-85—Michigan State Univ. (c)		CCHA	44	11	29	40	84
1985-86—Michigan State Univ.		CCHA	45	19	52	71	112
1986-87—Michigan State Univ.		CCHA	42	25	56	81	63
1987-88—Michigan State Univ.		CCHA	9	6	3	9	18
1987-88—U.S. Olympic Team		Int'l	50	32	34	66	..

(c)—June, 1984—Drafted by New York Rangers in 1984 NHL entry draft. Tenth Rangers pick, 202nd overall, 10th round.

KIP MILLER

Center . . . 5'10" . . . 160 lbs. . . . Born, Lansing, Mich., June 11, 1969 . . . Shoots left . . . Brother of Kevin Miller and Kelly Miller . . . (November, 1987)—Accidentally put hand and forearm through a storm-door window.

Year	Team	League	Games	G.	A.	Pts.	Pen.
1986-87—Michigan State Univ. (c)		CCHA	45	22	19	41	96
1987-88—Michigan State Univ.		CCHA	39	16	25	41	51

(c)—June, 1987—Drafted by Quebec Nordiques in 1987 NHL entry draft. Fourth Nordiques pick, 72nd overall, fourth round.

KRIS MILLER

Defense . . . 6' . . . 185 lbs. . . . Born, Bemidji, Minn., March 30, 1969 . . . Shoots left.

Year	Team	League	Games	G.	A.	Pts.	Pen.
1985-86—Greenway H.S.		Minn. H.S.	20	9	16	25	....
1986-87—Greenway H.S. (c)		Minn. H.S.	26	10	33	43	....
1987-88—Univ. Minnesota/Duluth		WCHA	30	1	6	7	30

(c)—June, 1987—Drafted by Montreal Canadiens in 1987 NHL entry draft. Sixth Canadiens pick, 80th overall, fourth round.

CHRIS MILLS

Defense . . . 6'1" . . . 185 lbs. . . . Born, Scarborough, Ont., May 30, 1966 . . . Shoots left.

Year	Team	League	Games	G.	A.	Pts.	Pen.
1983-84—Bramalea Blues (c)		MTJHL	42	9	27	36	50
1984-85—Clarkson College		ECAC	29	0	1	1	22
1985-86—Clarkson College		ECAC	32	2	3	5	36
1986-87—Clarkson College		ECAC	30	3	14	17	32
1987-88—Clarkson College		ECAC	35	5	15	20	38

(c)—June, 1984—Drafted as underage junior by Winnipeg Jets in NHL entry draft. Second Jets pick, 68th overall, fourth round.

JOHN MINER

Defense . . . 5'10" . . . 170 lbs. . . . Born, Moose Jaw, Sask., August 28, 1965 . . . Shoots right . . . (September, 1982)—Eye injury . . . (November, 1986)—Injured foot.

Year	Team	League	Games	G.	A.	Pts.	Pen.
1981-82—Regina Pats		SJHL	..	..	..	..	..
1981-82—Regina Pats		WHL	10	0	1	1	11
1982-83—Regina Pats (c)		WHL	71	11	23	34	126
1983-84—Regina Pats (b)		WHL	70	27	42	69	132
1984-85—Regina Pats (a)		WHL	66	30	54	84	128
1984-85—Nova Scotia Oilers (d)		AHL	....	...	....	.....	....
1985-86—Nova Scotia Oilers		AHL	79	10	33	43	90
1986-87—Nova Scotia Oilers		AHL	45	5	28	33	38
1987-88—Nova Scotia Oilers		AHL	61	8	26	34	61
1987-88—Edmonton Oilers (e)		NHL	14	2	3	5	16
NHL TOTALS			14	2	3	5	16

(c)—June, 1983—Drafted as underage junior by Edmonton Oilers in 1983 NHL entry draft. Tenth Oilers pick, 220th overall, 11th round.

(d)—No regular season record. Played three playoff games (2 goals, 2 assists).

(e)—August, 1988—Traded by Edmonton Oilers to Los Angeles Kings for Craig Redmond.

MIKE MODANO

Center . . . 6'1" . . . 175 lbs. . . . Born, Detroit, Mich., June 7, 1970 . . . Shoots left.

Year	Team	League	Games	G.	A.	Pts.	Pen.
1986-87—Prince Albert Raiders		WHL	70	32	30	62	96
1987-88—Prince Albert Raiders (c)		WHL	65	47	80	127	80

(c)—June, 1988—Drafted by Minnesota North Stars in 1988 NHL entry draft. First North Stars pick, first overall, first round.

CARL MOKOSAK

Left Wing . . . 6'1" . . . 181 lbs. . . . Born, Fort Saskatchewan, Alta., September 22, 1962 . . . Shoots left . . . Brother of John Mokosak.

Year	Team	League	Games	G.	A.	Pts.	Pen.
1978-79—Brandon		MJHL	44	12	11	23	146
1979-80—Brandon Wheat Kings		WHL	61	12	21	33	226
1980-81—Brandon Wheat Kings		WHL	70	20	40	60	118
1981-82—Brandon Wheat Kings (c)		WHL	69	46	61	107	363
1981-82—Oklahoma City Stars		CHL	2	1	1	2	2
1981-82—Calgary Flames		NHL	1	0	1	1	0
1982-83—Colorado Flames		CHL	28	10	12	22	106
1982-83—Calgary Flames (d)		NHL	41	7	6	13	87
1983-84—New Haven Nighthawks		AHL	80	18	21	39	206
1984-85—New Haven Nighthawks		AHL	11	6	6	12	26
1984-85—Los Angeles Kings (e)		NHL	30	4	8	12	43
1985-86—Philadelphia Flyers		NHL	1	0	0	0	5
1985-86—Hershey Bears (f)		AHL	79	30	42	72	312
1986-87—Pittsburgh Penguins		NHL	3	0	0	0	4
1986-87—Baltimore Skipjacks		AHL	67	23	27	50	228
1987-88—Muskegon Lumberjacks		IHL	81	29	37	66	308
NHL TOTALS			76	11	15	26	139

(c)—August, 1981—Signed by Calgary Flames as a free agent.

(d)—June, 1983—Traded by Calgary Flames with Kevin LaVallee to Los Angeles Kings for Steve Bozek.

(e)—June, 1985—Released by Los Angeles Kings and subsequently signed by Philadelphia Flyers as a free agent.

(f)—July, 1986—Signed by Pittsburgh Penguins as a free agent.

JOHN MOKOSAK

Defense . . . 5'11" . . . 185 lbs. . . . Born, Edmonton, Alta., September 7, 1963 . . . Shoots left . . . Brother of Carl Mokosak.

Year	Team	League	Games	G.	A.	Pts.	Pen.
1979-80—Fort Saskatchewan Traders		SJHL	58	5	13	18	57
1980-81—Victoria Cougars (c)		WHL	71	2	18	20	59
1981-82—Victoria Cougars		WHL	69	6	45	51	102
1982-83—Victoria Cougars		WHL	70	10	33	43	102
1983-84—Binghamton Whalers		AHL	79	3	21	24	80
1984-85—Salt Lake Golden Eagles		CHL	22	1	10	11	41
1984-85—Binghamton Whalers		AHL	54	1	13	14	109
1985-86—Binghamton Whalers		AHL	64	0	9	9	196
1986-87—Binghamton Whalers		AHL	72	2	15	17	187
1987-88—Springfield Indians		AHL	77	1	16	17	178

(c)—June, 1981—Drafted as underage junior by Hartford Whalers in 1981 NHL entry draft. Sixth Whalers pick, 130th overall, seventh round.

JIM MOLLARD

Left Wing . . . 6' . . . 190 lbs. . . . Born, Stonewall, Man., November 11, 1963 . . . Shoots left.

Year	Team	League	Games	G.	A.	Pts.	Pen.
1985-86—Brandon Univ. (c)		CWUAA	22	21	27	48	117
1986-87—Nova Scotia Oilers		AHL	2	0	1	1	0
1986-87—Muskegon Lumberjacks		IHL	67	25	38	63	78
1987-88—Nova Scotia Oilers		AHL	32	4	10	14	33

(c)—August, 1986—Signed by Edmonton Oilers as a free agent.

MICHAEL JOHN MOLLER

Right Wing . . . 6' . . . 189 lbs. . . . Born, Calgary, Alta., June 16, 1962 . . . Shoots right . . . Brother of Randy Moller.

Year	Team	League	Games	G.	A.	Pts.	Pen.
1978-79—Red Deer Midgets		RDMHL	....	...	....	....	....
1979-80—Lethbridge Broncos (c)		WHL	72	30	41	71	55
1980-81—Lethbridge Broncos (a)		WHL	70	39	69	108	71
1980-81—Buffalo Sabres		NHL	5	2	2	4	0
1981-82—Lethbridge Broncos (a-d)		WHL	49	41	81	122	38
1981-82—Buffalo Sabres		NHL	9	0	0	0	0
1982-83—Rochester Americans		AHL	10	1	6	7	2
1982-83—Buffalo Sabres		NHL	49	6	12	18	14
1983-84—Buffalo Sabres		NHL	59	5	11	16	27
1984-85—Rochester Americans		AHL	73	19	46	65	27
1984-85—Buffalo Sabres		NHL	5	0	2	2	0
1985-86—Edmonton Oilers (e-f)		NHL	1	0	0	0	0
1985-86—Nova Scotia Oilers		AHL	62	16	15	31	24
1986-87—Nova Scotia Oilers		AHL	70	14	33	47	28
1986-87—Edmonton Oilers		NHL	6	2	1	3	0
1987-88—Nova Scotia Oilers		AHL	60	12	31	43	14
NHL TOTALS			134	15	28	43	41

(c)—June, 1980—Drafted by Buffalo Sabres as underage junior in 1980 NHL entry draft. Second Sabres pick, 41st overall, second round.

(d)—Winner of Frank Bouchar Memorial Trophy (Most Gentlemanly Player).

(e)—October, 1985—Traded with equalization rights of Randy Cunneyworth by Buffalo Sabres to Pittsburgh Penguins for future considerations.

(f)—October, 1985—Traded by Pittsburgh Penguins to Edmonton Oilers to complete earlier Gilles Meloche deal.

RANDY MOLLER

Defense . . . 6'2" . . . 205 lbs. . . . Born, Red Deer, Alta., August 23, 1963. . . Shoots right . . . (December, 1980)—Torn knee ligaments required surgery . . . Brother of Mike Moller . . . (October 28, 1986)—Broken hand when slashed by Morris Lukowich vs. Los Angeles . . . (November, 1987)—Lingering neck problem . . . (January, 1988)—Knee injury . . . (March, 1988)—Back spasms.

Year	Team	League	Games	G.	A.	Pts.	Pen.
1979-80—Red Deer Rustlers		AJHL	56	3	34	37	253
1980-81—Lethbridge Broncos (c)		WHL	46	4	21	25	176
1981-82—Lethbridge Broncos (b)		WHL	60	20	55	75	249
1982-83—Quebec Nordiques		NHL	75	2	12	14	145
1983-84—Quebec Nordiques		NHL	74	4	14	18	147
1984-85—Quebec Nordiques		NHL	79	7	22	29	120

Year	Team	League	Games	G.	A.	Pts.	Pen.
1985-86—Quebec Nordiques		NHL	69	5	18	23	141
1986-87—Quebec Nordiques		NHL	71	5	9	14	144
1987-88—Quebec Nordiques		NHL	66	3	22	25	169
NHL TOTALS			434	26	97	123	866

(c)—June, 1981—Drafted by Quebec Nordiques in 1981 NHL entry draft. First Nordiques pick, 11th overall, first round.

SERGIO MOMESSO

Left Wing . . . 6'3" . . . 205 lbs. . . . Born, Montreal, Que, September 4, 1965 . . . Shoots left . . . Also plays Center . . . (December 5, 1985)—Torn cruciate ligament in left knee. He required surgery and missed remainder of season . . . (December 5, 1986)—Tore ligaments, injured cartilage and fractured left knee in a collision with Michael Thelvin vs. Boston . . . (February, 1988)—Cut leg.

Year	Team	League	Games	G.	A.	Pts.	Pen.
1982-83—Shawinigan Cataracts (c)		QHL	70	27	42	69	93
1983-84—Shawinigan Cataracts		QHL	68	42	88	130	235
1983-84—Montreal Canadiens		NHL	1	0	0	0	0
1984-85—Shawinigan Sagueneens (a)		QHL	64	56	90	146	216
1985-86—Montreal Canadiens		NHL	24	8	7	15	46
1986-87—Montreal Canadiens		NHL	59	14	17	31	96
1986-87—Sherbrooke Canadiens		AHL	6	1	6	7	10
1987-88—Montreal Canadiens (d)		NHL	53	7	14	21	91
NHL TOTALS			137	29	38	67	233

(c)—June, 1983—Drafted as underage junior by Montreal Canadiens in 1983 NHL entry draft. Third Canadiens pick, 27th overall, second round.

(d)—August, 1988—Traded with Vincent Riendeau by Montreal Canadiens to St. Louis Blues for Jocelyn Lemieux, Darrell May and second-round draft choice in 1989.

JOHN MOORE

Center . . . 6'3" . . . 200 lbs. . . . Born, Montreal, Que., January 9, 1967 . . . Shoots right . . . Grandson of Jack McGill (Montreal Canadiens, 1934-37).

Year	Team	League	Games	G.	A.	Pts.	Pen.
1985-86—Yale University J.V.		ECAC	....	...	....	....	....
1986-87—Yale University (c)		ECAC	30	4	2	6	38
1987-88—Yale University		ECAC	26	3	18	21	22

(c)—June, 1987—Drafted by Hartford Whalers in 1987 NHL entry draft. Seventh Whalers pick, 165th overall, eighth round.

STEVE MOORE

Defense . . . 6'2" . . . 185 lbs. . . . Born, Toronto, Ont., January 21, 1967 . . . Shoots right . . . (November, 1988)—Surgery to right thumb tendon.

Year	Team	League	Games	G.	A.	Pts.	Pen.
1983-84—London Diamonds Jr. B		OHA	46	6	21	27	43
1984-85—London Diamonds Jr. B (c)		OHA	46	12	26	38	112
1985-86—Rensselaer Poly. Inst.		ECAC	24	4	3	7	32
1986-87—Rensselaer Poly. Inst.		ECAC	32	3	16	19	47
1987-88—Rensselaer Poly. Inst.		ECAC	27	3	9	12	26

(c)—June, 1985—Drafted by Boston Bruins in 1985 NHL entry draft. Fourth Bruins pick, 94th overall, fifth round.

JAYSON MORE

Defense . . . 6'1" . . . 191 lbs. . . . Born, Souris, Man., January 1, 1969 . . . Shoots right.

Year	Team	League	Games	G.	A.	Pts.	Pen.
1984-85—Lethbridge Broncos		WHL	71	3	9	12	101
1985-86—Lethbridge Broncos		WHL	61	7	18	25	155
1986-87—New Westminster Bruins (c)		WHL	64	8	29	37	217
1987-88—New Westminster Bruins (a)		WHL	70	13	47	60	270

(c)—June, 1987—Drafted as underage junior by New York Rangers in 1987 NHL entry draft. First Rangers pick, 10th overall, first round.

JON MORRIS

Center . . . 6' . . . 165 lbs. . . . Born, Lowell, Mass., May 6, 1966 . . . Shoots right.

Year	Team	League	Games	G.	A.	Pts.	Pen.
1983-84—Chelmsford H.S. (c)		Mass. H.S.	24	31	50	81	....
1984-85—University of Lowell		H. East	42	29	31	60	16
1985-86—University of Lowell		H. East	39	25	31	56	52

Year	Team	League	Games	G.	A.	Pts.	Pen.
1986-87—University of Lowell (a-d)		H. East	36	28	33	61	48
1987-88—University of Lowell		H. East	37	15	39	54	39

(c)—June, 1984—Drafted by New Jersey Devils in NHL entry draft. Fifth Devils pick, 86th overall, fifth round.

(d)—Named second team All-America (East).

KEN MORROW

Defense . . . 6'4" . . . 210 lbs. . . . Born, Flint, Mich., October 17, 1956 . . . Shoots right . . . Member of 1980 U.S. Olympic Gold Medal Team . . . Member of 1979 Team U.S.A. . . . First ever All-American at Bowling Green University . . . First person in history to play for Gold Medal Olympic team and Stanley Cup Team in same season. . . . (October, 1983)—Water on the knee . . . (December, 1983)—Arthroscopic surgery on right knee . . . (May, 1983)— Missed one game in playoff series with Boston due to further arthroscopic surgery on right knee . . . (September, 1984)—Right knee swollen after first week of training camp . . . (October, 1984)—Knee surgery . . . (October, 1985)—Injured shoulder . . . (December 1, 1985)—Injured back . . . (February 18, 1987)—Bruised ribs vs. Montreal . . . (February, 1988)—Separated right shoulder at Philadelphia.

Year	Team	League	Games	G.	A.	Pts.	Pen.
1975-76—Bowling Green Univ. (a-c)		CCHA	31	4	15	19	34
1976-77—Bowling Green Univ. (b)		CCHA	39	7	22	29	22
1977-78—Bowling Green Univ. (a-d)		CCHA	39	8	18	26	26
1978-79—Bowling Green Univ. (a-e)		CCHA	45	15	37	52	22
1979-80—U.S. Olympic Team		Int'l	63	5	20	25	12
1979-80—New York Islanders		NHL	18	0	3	3	4
1980-81—New York Islanders		NHL	80	2	11	13	20
1981-82—New York Islanders		NHL	75	1	18	19	56
1982-83—New York Islanders		NHL	79	5	11	16	44
1983-84—New York Islanders		NHL	63	3	11	14	45
1984-85—New York Islanders		NHL	15	1	7	8	14
1985-86—New York Islanders		NHL	69	0	12	12	22
1986-87—New York Islanders		NHL	64	3	8	11	32
1987-88—New York Islanders		NHL	53	1	4	5	40
NHL TOTALS			516	16	85	101	277

(c)—May, 1976—Drafted by New York Islanders in 1976 NHL amateur draft. Fourth Islanders pick, 68th overall, fourth round.

(d)—All-American Team (West).

(e)—Named CCHA Player of the Year.

DEAN MORTON

Defense . . . 6'1" . . . 195 lbs. . . . Born, Peterborough, Ont., February 27, 1968 . . . Shoots right . . . (October, 1986)—Suspended by OHL for being involved in a bench clearing incident vs. Peterborough.

Year	Team	League	Games	G.	A.	Pts.	Pen.
1984-85—Peterborough Midgets		OHA	47	9	38	47	158
1985-86—Ottawa 67's (c)		OHL	16	3	1	4	32
1986-87—Oshawa Generals		OHL	62	1	11	12	165
1987-88—Oshawa Generals		OHL	57	6	19	25	187

(c)—June, 1986—Drafted as underage junior by Detroit Red Wings in 1986 NHL entry draft. Eighth Red Wings pick, 148th overall, eighth round.

DAVID MOYLAN

Defense . . . 6'1" . . . 195 lbs. . . . Born, Tillsonburg, Ont., August 13, 1967 . . . Shoots left . . . (November, 1983)—Separated shoulder.

Year	Team	League	Games	G.	A.	Pts.	Pen.
1983-84—St. Mary's Lincolns		OHA	46	7	13	20	143
1984-85—Sudbury Wolves (c)		OHL	66	1	15	16	108
1985-86—Sudbury Wolves		OHL	52	10	25	35	87
1986-87—Sudbury Wolves		OHL	13	5	6	11	41
1986-87—Kitchener Rangers		OHL	38	1	7	8	57
1987-88—Flint Spirits		IHL	9	0	2	2	10
1987-88—Rochester Americans		AHL	16	0	0	0	2
1987-88—Baltimore Skipjacks		AHL	20	4	5	9	35

(c)—June, 1985—Drafted as underage junior by Buffalo Sabres in 1985 entry draft. Fourth Sabres pick, 77th overall, fourth round.

BRIAN MULLEN

Left Wing . . . 5'10" . . . 170 lbs. . . . Born, New York, N.Y., March 16, 1962 . . . Shoots left . . . Brother of Joe Mullen . . . (January, 1988)—Bruised left knee.

Year	Team	League	Games	G.	A.	Pts.	Pen.
1977-78—New York Westsiders		NYMJHL	33	21	36	57	38
1978-79—New York Westsiders		NYMJHL	....	...	....	....	....
1979-80—New York Westsiders		NYMJHL	....	...	....	....	....
1980-81—University of Wisconsin (c)		WCHA	38	11	13	24	28
1981-82—University of Wisconsin		WCHA	33	20	17	37	10
1982-83—Winnipeg Jets		NHL	80	24	26	50	14
1983-84—Winnipeg Jets		NHL	75	21	41	62	28
1984-85—Winnipeg Jets		NHL	69	32	39	71	32
1985-86—Winnipeg Jets		NHL	79	28	34	62	38
1986-87—Winnipeg Jets (d)		NHL	69	19	32	51	20
1987-88—New York Rangers		NHL	74	25	29	54	42
NHL TOTALS			446	149	201	350	174

(c)—June, 1980—Drafted by Winnipeg Jets in 1981 NHL entry draft. Seventh Jets pick, 128th overall, seventh round.

(d)—June, 1987—Traded with 10th round draft choice in 1987 by Winnipeg Jets to New York Rangers for fifth round draft choice in 1988 and third round draft choice in 1989.

JOE MULLEN

Right Wing ... 5'9" ... 180 lbs. ... Born, New York, N.Y., February 26, 1957 ... Shoots right ... Brother of Brian Mullen ... (1981-82)—First player to have 20-goal year in minors and majors in the same season ... (October 18, 1982)—Leg injury at Minnesota ... (January 29, 1983)—Tore ligaments in left knee vs. Los Angeles, requiring surgery. He was lost for remainder of season ... Established record for goals in single season by U.S.-born player in 1983-84 (Broken by Bobby Carpenter) ... (April, 1988)—Bruised knee in playoff game vs. Los Angeles.

Year	Team	League	Games	G.	A.	Pts.	Pen.
1971-72—New York 14th Precinct		NYMJHL	30	13	11	24	2
1972-73—New York Westsiders		NYMJHL	40	14	28	42	8
1973-74—New York Westsiders		NYMJHL	42	71	49	120	41
1974-75—New York Westsiders (c)		NYMJHL	40	110	72	*182	20
1975-76—Boston College		ECAC	24	16	18	34	4
1976-77—Boston College		ECAC	28	28	26	54	8
1977-78—Boston College (a)		ECAC	34	34	34	68	12
1978-79—Boston College (a-d)		ECAC	25	32	24	56	8
1979-80—Salt Lake Golden Eagles (b-e-g)		CHL	75	40	32	72	21
1979-80—St. Louis Blues (f)		NHL	....	...	....	....	....
1980-81—Salt Lake Golden Eagles (a-h-i)		CHL	80	59	58	*117	8
1981-82—Salt Lake Golden Eagles		CHL	27	21	27	48	12
1981-82—St. Louis Blues		NHL	45	25	34	59	4
1982-83—St. Louis Blues		NHL	49	17	30	47	6
1983-84—St. Louis Blues		NHL	80	41	44	85	19
1984-85—St. Louis Blues		NHL	79	40	52	92	6
1985-86—St. Louis Blues (j)		NHL	48	28	24	52	10
1985-86—Calgary Flames (k)		NHL	29	16	22	38	11
1986-87—Calgary Flames (l)		NHL	79	47	40	87	14
1987-88—Calgary Flames		NHL	80	40	44	84	30
NHL TOTALS			489	254	290	544	100

(c)—Named Most Valuable Player.

(d)—August, 1979—Signed as free agent by St. Louis Blues.

(e)—Co-leader with Red Laurence in goals (9) during CHL playoffs.

(f)—No regular season record. Played one playoff game.

(g)—Won Ken McKenzie Trophy (Top Rookie).

(h)—Winner of Phil Esposito Trophy (Leading Scorer).

(i)—Winner of Tommy Ivan Trophy (MVP).

(j)—February, 1986—Traded with Terry Johnson and Rik Wilson by St. Louis Blues to Calgary Flames for Eddy Beers, Gino Cavallini and Charles Bourgeois.

(k)—Led Stanley Cup Playoffs with 12 goals.

(l)—Won Lady Byng Trophy (Combination of Sportsmanship and Quality play.)

KIRK MULLER

Center ... 5'11" ... 185 lbs. ... Born, Kingston, Ont., February 8, 1966 ... Shoots left ... Member of 1984 Canadian Olympic team ... (January 13, 1986)—Strained knee ... (April, 1986)—Fractured ribs at world championships in Soviet Union.

Year	Team	League	Games	G.	A.	Pts.	Pen.
1980-81—Kingston Canadians		OHL	2	0	0	0	0
1981-82—Kingston Canadians		OHL	67	12	39	51	27
1982-83—Guelph Platers (c)		OHL	66	52	60	112	41
1983-84—Canadian Olympic Team		Int'l	15	2	2	4	6
1983-84—Guelph Platers (d)		OHL	49	31	63	94	27

Year	Team	League	Games	G.	A.	Pts.	Pen.
1984-85—New Jersey Devils		NHL	80	17	37	54	69
1985-86—New Jersey Devils		NHL	77	25	42	67	45
1986-87—New Jersey Devils		NHL	79	26	50	76	75
1987-88—New Jersey Devils		NHL	80	37	57	94	114
NHL TOTALS			316	105	186	291	303

(c)—Won William Hanley Trophy (Most Gentlemanly).

(d)—June, 1984—Drafted as underage junior by New Jersey Devils in NHL entry draft. First Devils pick, second overall, first round.

DWIGHT MULLINS

Center ... 5'11" ... 190 lbs. ... Born, Calgary, Alta., February 28, 1967 ... Shoots right ... Also plays Right Wing.

Year	Team	League	Games	G.	A.	Pts.	Pen.
1982-83—Lethbridge Broncos		WHL	66	5	2	7	71
1983-84—Lethbridge Broncos		WHL	70	20	23	43	101
1984-85—Lethbridge Broncos (c)		WHL	62	21	18	39	94
1985-86—Lethbridge Broncos		WHL	72	52	37	89	99
1986-87—Calgary Wranglers		WHL	31	12	8	20	71
1987-88—Saskatoon Blades (d)		WHL	52	12	17	29	71

(c)—June, 1985—Drafted as underage junior by Minnesota North Stars in 1985 NHL entry draft. Third North Stars pick, 90th overall, fifth round.

(d)—October, 1987—Traded by Lethbridge Broncos to Saskatoon Blades for Calvin Wiltshire and Marty Frazma.

MICHAEL MULLOWNEY

Defense ... 6'1" ... 190 lbs. ... Born, Brighton, Mass., January 17, 1966 ... Shoots left.

Year	Team	League	Games	G.	A.	Pts.	Pen.
1984-85—Deerfield Academy (c)		Mass. H.S.	17	17	30	47	18
1985-86—Boston College		H. East	26	0	2	2	20
1986-87—Boston College		H. East	30	0	2	2	22
1987-88—Boston College		H. East	25	1	7	8	48

(c)—June, 1985—Drafted by Minnesota North Stars in 1985 NHL entry draft. Fourth North Stars pick, 111th overall, sixth round.

CRAIG DOUGLAS MUNI

Defense ... 6'2" ... 201 lbs. ... Born, Toronto, Ont., July 19, 1962 ... Shoots left ... (September, 1981)—Tore left knee ligaments while skating in Windsor, Ont., prior to the opening of Toronto training camp ... (January, 1983)—Broken ankle in AHL game at Fredericton ... (May, 1987)—Bruised kidney in playoffs ... (January, 1988)—Bruised ankle vs. Calgary.

Year	Team	League	Games	G.	A.	Pts.	Pen.
1979-80—Kingston Canadians (c)		OMJHL	66	6	28	34	114
1980-81—Kingston Canadians		OHL	38	2	14	16	65
1980-81—Windsor Spitfires		OHL	25	5	11	16	41
1980-81—New Brunswick Hawks (d)		AHL	....	...	....	....	....
1981-82—Windsor Spitfires		OHL	49	5	32	37	92
1981-82—Cincinnati Tigers (e)		CHL	....	...	....	....	....
1982-83—Toronto Maple Leafs		NHL	2	0	1	1	0
1982-83—St. Catharines Saints		AHL	64	6	32	38	52
1983-84—St. Catharines Saints		AHL	64	4	16	20	79
1984-85—St. Catharines Saints		AHL	68	7	17	24	54
1984-85—Toronto Maple Leafs		NHL	8	0	0	0	0
1985-86—Toronto Maple Leafs		NHL	6	0	1	1	4
1985-86—St. Catharines Saints		AHL	73	3	34	37	91
1986-87—Edmonton Oilers (f)		NHL	79	7	22	29	85
1987-88—Edmonton Oilers		NHL	72	4	15	19	77
NHL TOTALS			167	11	39	50	166

(c)—June, 1980—Drafted as underage junior by Toronto Maple Leafs in 1980 NHL entry draft. First Maple Leafs pick, 25th overall, second round.

(d)—No regular season appearance. Played two playoff games.

(e)—No regular season appearance. Played three playoff games.

(f)—August, 1986—Signed by Edmonton Oilers as a free agent.

ERIC A. MURANO

Center ... 6' ... 190 lbs. ... Born, LaSalle, Que., May 4, 1967 ... Shoots right.

Year	Team	League	Games	G.	A.	Pts.	Pen.
1985-86—Calgary Canucks (c)		AJHL	52	34	47	81	32

Year	Team	League	Games	G.	A.	Pts.	Pen.
1986-87—University of Denver		WCHA	31	5	7	12	12
1987-88—University of Denver		WCHA	37	8	13	21	26

(c)—June, 1986—Drafted by Vancouver Canucks in 1986 NHL entry draft. Fourth Canucks pick, 91st overall, fifth round.

DANIEL MURPHY

Defense . . . 6' . . . 195 lbs. . . . Born, New Haven, Conn., June 13, 1970 . . . Shoots left.

Year	Team	League	Games	G.	A.	Pts.	Pen.
1986-87—The Gunnery Prep.		Ct. H.S.	26	12	18	30	..
1987-88—The Gunnery Prep. (c)		Ct. H.S.	..	12	24	36	..

(c)—June, 1988—Drafted by Boston Bruins in 1988 NHL entry draft. Fourth Bruins pick, 102nd overall, fifth round.

GARY MURPHY

Defense . . . 6'1" . . . 175 lbs. . . . Born, Winchester, Mass., March 23, 1967 . . . Shoots left.

Year	Team	League	Games	G.	A.	Pts.	Pen.
1983-84—Arlington Catholic H.S.		Mass. H.S.	....	9	18	27	....
1984-85—Arlington Catholic H.S. (c)		Mass. H.S.	20	7	26	33	40
1985-86—University of Lowell		H. East	27	0	9	9	32
1986-87—University of Lowell		H. East	21	3	4	7	13
1987-88—University of Lowell		H. East	36	5	10	15	20

(c)—June, 1985—Drafted by Quebec Nordiques in 1985 NHL entry draft. Twelfth Nordiques pick, 225th overall, 11th round.

GORDON MURPHY

Defense . . . 6'1" . . . 180 lbs. . . . Born, Willowdale, Ont., February 23, 1967 . . . Shoots right . . . (January, 1985)—Injured clavicle.

Year	Team	League	Games	G.	A.	Pts.	Pen.
1983-84—Don Mills Flyers		MTHL	65	24	42	66	130
1984-85—Oshawa Generals (c)		OHL	59	3	12	15	25
1985-86—Oshawa Generals		OHL	64	7	15	22	56
1986-87—Oshawa Generals		OHL	56	7	30	37	95
1987-88—Hershey Bears		AHL	62	8	20	28	44

(c)—June, 1985—Drafted as underage junior by Philadelphia Flyers in 1985 NHL entry draft. Tenth Flyers pick, 189th overall, ninth round.

JOSEPH PATRICK MURPHY

Center . . . 6'1" . . . 185 lbs. . . . Born, London, Ont., October 16, 1967 . . . Shoots left . . . Also plays Left Wing . . . First college player to be taken first-overall in an NHL draft . . . (January, 1988)—Sprained right ankle.

Year	Team	League	Games	G.	A.	Pts.	Pen.
1984-85—Penticton Knights (c)		BCJHL	51	68	84	*152	92
1985-86—Michigan State Univ. (d-e)		CCHA	35	24	37	61	50
1985-86—Team Canada		Int'l	8	3	3	6	2
1986-87—Adirondack Red Wings		AHL	71	21	38	59	61
1986-87—Detroit Red Wings		NHL	5	0	1	1	2
1987-88—Adirondack Red Wings		AHL	6	5	6	11	4
1987-88—Detroit Red Wings		NHL	50	10	9	19	37
NHL TOTALS			55	10	10	20	39

(c)—Named AJHL Rookie of the Year.
(d)—Named CCHA Rookie of the Year.
(e)—June, 1986—Drafted by Detroit Red Wings in 1986 NHL entry draft. First Red Wings pick, first overall, first round.

KELLY MURPHY

Defense . . . 6'1" . . . 175 lbs. . . . Born, Regina, Sask., April 24, 1966 . . . Shoots right.

Year	Team	League	Games	G.	A.	Pts.	Pen.
1983-84—Wilcox Notre Dame H.S.(c)		Sask.H.S.	40	15	45	60	..
1984-85—Michigan Tech.		WCHA	40	2	8	10	16
1985-86—Michigan Tech.		WCHA	40	0	11	11	20
1986-87—Michigan Tech.		WCHA	14	0	1	1	14
1987-88—Michigan Tech.		WCHA	35	0	4	4	38

(c)—June, 1984—Drafted by New York Islanders in NHL entry draft. Eighth Islanders pick, 146th overall, seventh round.

LAWRENCE THOMAS MURPHY

Defense . . . 6'1" . . . 210 lbs. . . . Born, Scarborough, Ont., March 8, 1961 . . . Shoots right . . . Set record for most points by NHL rookie defenseman in 1980-81 (76 points) . . . Holds Los Angeles Kings club record for most goals, assists and points by a defenseman in a career as well as L.A. records for assists and points by a rookie . . . (1981-82)—Set club record for most goals by a defenseman in a season (22) . . . (1980-81)—Set NHL record for most assists (60) and points (76) by a rookie defenseman . . . (October 29, 1985)—Injured foot . . . (May, 1988)—Broken ankle in swimming pool accident.

Year	Team	League	Games	G.	A.	Pts.	Pen.
1978-79	Peterborough Petes	OMJHL	66	6	21	27	82
1979-80	Peterborough Petes (a-c-d)	OMJHL	68	21	68	89	88
1980-81	Los Angeles Kings	NHL	80	16	60	76	79
1981-82	Los Angeles Kings	NHL	79	22	44	66	95
1982-83	Los Angeles Kings	NHL	77	14	48	62	81
1983-84	Los Angeles Kings	NHL	6	0	3	3	0
1983-84	Washington Capitals (e)	NHL	72	13	33	46	50
1984-85	Washington Capitals	NHL	79	13	42	55	51
1985-86	Washington Capitals	NHL	78	21	44	65	50
1986-87	Washington Capitals (b)	NHL	80	23	58	81	39
1987-88	Washington Capitals	NHL	79	8	53	61	72
	NHL TOTALS		630	130	385	515	517

(c)—Won Max Kaminsky Memorial Trophy (Outstanding Defenseman).
(d)—June, 1980—Drafted as underage junior by Los Angeles Kings in 1980 NHL entry draft. First Kings pick, fourth overall, first round. (L.A. obtained draft pick from Detroit Red Wings as part of the Dale McCourt/Andre St. Laurent trade of August, 1979).
(e)—October, 1983—Traded by Los Angeles Kings to Washington Capitals for Brian Engblom and Ken Houston.

ROBERT MURPHY

Center . . . 6'2" . . . 195 lbs. . . . Born, Hull, Que., April 7, 1969 . . . Shoots left.

Year	Team	League	Games	G.	A.	Pts.	Pen.
1985-86	Outaouais Midget	Que. Mdgt.	41	17	33	50	47
1986-87	Laval Titans (c)	QHL	70	35	54	89	86
1987-88	Vancouver Canucks	NHL	5	0	0	0	2
1987-88	Drummondville Voltigeurs	QHL	59	27	53	80	123
	NHL TOTALS		5	0	0	0	2

(c)—June, 1987—Drafted as underage junior by Vancouver Canucks in 1987 NHL entry draft. First Canucks pick, 24th overall, second round.

MIKE MURRAY

Center . . . 6' . . . 183 lbs. . . . Born, Kingston, Ont., April 29, 1966 . . . Shoots left.

Year	Team	League	Games	G.	A.	Pts.	Pen.
1982-83	Sarnia	Ont. Midget	57	61	39	100	48
1983-84	London Knights (c)	OHL	70	8	24	32	14
1984-85	London Knights (d)	OHL	43	21	35	56	19
1984-85	Guelph Platers	OHL	23	10	9	19	8
1985-86	Guelph Platers (e)	OHL	56	27	38	65	19
1986-87	Hershey Bears	AHL	70	8	16	24	10
1987-88	Hershey Bears	AHL	57	14	14	28	34
1987-88	Philadelphia Flyers	NHL	1	0	0	0	0
	NHL TOTALS		1	0	0	0	0

(c)—June, 1984—Drafted as underage junior by New York Islanders in 1984 NHL entry draft. Sixth Islanders pick, 104th overall, fifth round.
(d)—January, 1985—Traded with Ron Coutts by Kitchener Rangers to Guelph Platers for Trevor Stienburg.
(e)—June, 1986—Traded by New York Islanders to Philadelphia Flyers for a fifth round 1986 draft pick (Todd McLellan).

PAT MURRAY

Left Wing . . . 6'2" . . . 180 lbs. . . . Born, Stratford, Ont., August 20, 1969 . . . Shoots left.

Year	Team	League	Games	G.	A.	Pts.	Pen.
1986-87	Stratford Jr. B	OHA	42	34	75	109	38
1987-88	Michigan State Univ. (c)	CCHA	44	14	23	37	26

(c)—June, 1988—Drafted by Philadelphia Flyers in 1988 NHL entry draft. Second Flyers pick, 35th overall, second round.

ROBERT MURRAY

Center ... 6'1" ... 175 lbs. .... Born, Toronto, Ont., April 4, 1967 ... Shoots right ...
(November 2, 1986)—Suspended for two games by OHL.

Year Team	League	Games	G.	A.	Pts.	Pen.
1983-85—Mississauga Reps	OHA	35	18	36	54	32
1984-85—Peterborough Petes (c)	OHL	63	12	9	21	155
1985-86—Peterborough Petes	OHL	52	14	18	32	125
1986-87—Peterborough Petes	OHL	62	17	37	54	204
1987-88—Fort Wayne Komets	IHL	80	12	21	33	139

(c)—June, 1985—Drafted as underage junior by Washington Capitals in 1985 NHL entry draft. Third Capitals pick, 61st overall, third round.

ROBERT FREDERICK MURRAY

Defense ... 5'9" ... 175 lbs. .... Born, Kingston, Ont., November 26, 1954 ... Shoots right ...
(December 20, 1981)—Tore ligaments in left knee vs. Toronto and required surgery ...
(November, 1987)—Twisted left knee.

Year Team	League	Games	G.	A.	Pts.	Pen.
1971-72—Cornwall Royals	QJHL	62	14	49	63	88
1972-73—Cornwall Royals	QJHL	32	9	26	35	34
1973-74—Cornwall Royals (c)	QJHL	63	23	76	99	88
1974-75—Dallas Black Hawks	CHL	75	14	43	57	130
1975-76—Chicago Black Hawks	NHL	64	1	2	3	44
1976-77—Chicago Black Hawks	NHL	77	10	11	21	71
1977-78—Chicago Black Hawks	NHL	70	14	17	31	41
1978-79—Chicago Black Hawks	NHL	79	19	32	51	38
1979-80—Chicago Black Hawks	NHL	74	16	34	50	60
1980-81—Chicago Black Hawks	NHL	77	13	47	60	93
1981-82—Chicago Black Hawks	NHL	45	8	22	30	48
1982-83—Chicago Black Hawks	NHL	79	7	32	39	73
1983-84—Chicago Black Hawks	NHL	78	11	37	48	78
1984-85—Chicago Black Hawks	NHL	80	5	38	43	56
1985-86—Chicago Black Hawks	NHL	80	9	29	38	75
1986-87—Chicago Black Hawks	NHL	79	6	38	44	80
1987-88—Chicago Black Hawks	NHL	63	6	20	26	44
NHL TOTALS		945	125	359	484	801

(c)—Drafted from Cornwall Royals by Chicago Black Hawks in third round of 1974 amateur draft.

TROY NORMAN MURRAY

Center ... 6'1" ... 195 lbs. .... Born, Winnipeg, Man., July 31, 1962 ... Shoots right ...
(November, 1983)—Knee ligament injury.

Year Team	League	Games	G.	A.	Pts.	Pen.
1979-80—St. Albert Saints (c)	AJHL	60	53	47	100	101
1980-81—Univ. of North Dakota (b-d)	WCHA	38	33	45	78	28
1981-82—Univ. of North Dakota (b)	WCHA	42	22	29	51	62
1981-82—Chicago Black Hawks	NHL	1	0	0	0	0
1982-83—Chicago Black Hawks	NHL	54	8	8	16	27
1983-84—Chicago Black Hawks	NHL	61	15	15	30	45
1984-85—Chicago Black Hawks	NHL	80	26	40	66	82
1985-86—Chicago Black Hawks (e)	NHL	80	45	54	99	94
1986-87—Chicago Black Hawks	NHL	77	28	43	71	59
1987-88—Chicago Black Hawks	NHL	79	22	36	58	96
NHL TOTALS		432	144	196	340	403

(c)—June, 1980—Drafted by Chicago Black Hawks in 1980 NHL entry draft. Sixth Black Hawks pick, 57th overall, third round.
(d)—Named Outstanding Freshman in WCHA.
(e)—Won Frank Selke Trophy (Best Defensive Forward).

DANA MURZYN

Defense ... 6'3" ... 205 lbs. ... Born, Regina, Sask., December 9, 1966 ... Shoots left.

Year Team	League	Games	G.	A.	Pts.	Pen.
1983-84—Calgary Wranglers	WHL	65	11	20	31	135
1984-85—Calgary Wranglers (a-c)	WHL	72	32	60	92	233
1985-86—Hartford Whalers	NHL	78	3	23	26	125
1986-87—Hartford Whalers	NHL	74	9	19	28	95
1987-88—Hartford Whalers (d)	NHL	33	1	6	7	45
1987-88—Calgary Flames	NHL	41	6	5	11	94
NHL TOTALS		226	19	53	72	359

(c)—June, 1985—Drafted as underage junior by Hartford Whalers in 1985 NHL entry draft. First Whalers pick, fifth overall, first round.

(d)—January, 1988—Traded with Shane Churla by Hartford Whalers to Calgary Flames for Carey Wilson, Neil Sheehy and Lane MacDonald.

FRANTISEK MUSIL

Defense . . . 6'3" . . . 205 lbs. . . . Born, Pardubice, Czechoslovakia, December 17, 1964 . . . Shoots left . . . (December 9, 1986)—Shoulder separation vs. Edmonton.

Year	Team	League	Games	G.	A.	Pts.	Pen.
1985-86	Dukla Jihlava (c)	Czech.	35	3	7	10	85
1986-87	Minnesota North Stars	NHL	72	2	9	11	148
1987-88	Minnesota North Stars	NHL	80	9	8	17	213
	NHL TOTALS		152	11	17	28	361

(c)—June, 1983—Drafted by Minnesota North Stars in 1983 NHL entry draft. Third North Stars pick, 38th overall, second round.

DONALD KENNETH NACHBAUR

Center . . . 6'2" . . . 200 lbs. . . . Born, Kitimat, B.C., January 30, 1959 . . . Shoots left . . . Also plays Left Wing . . . (October 20, 1984)—Injured forearm at Baltimore and spent remainder of season as assistant coach of Hershey Bears . . . (March, 1988)—Sprained back.

Year	Team	League	Games	G.	A.	Pts.	Pen.
1976-77	Merritt Luckies	......	54	22	27	49	31
1977-78	Billings Bighorns	WCHL	68	23	27	50	128
1978-79	Billings Bighorns (c)	WHL	69	44	52	96	175
1979-80	Springfield Indians	AHL	70	12	17	29	119
1980-81	Hartford Whalers	NHL	77	16	17	33	139
1981-82	Hartford Whalers (d)	NHL	77	5	21	26	117
1982-83	Edmonton Oilers	NHL	4	0	0	0	17
1982-83	Moncton Alpines	AHL	70	33	33	66	125
1983-84	New Haven Nighthawks (e)	AHL	70	33	32	65	194
1984-85	Hershey Bears	AHL	7	2	3	5	21
1985-86	Philadelphia Flyers (f)	NHL	5	1	1	2	7
1985-86	Hershey Bears	AHL	74	23	24	47	301
1986-87	Philadelphia Flyers	NHL	23	0	2	2	89
1986-87	Hershey Bears	AHL	57	18	17	35	274
1987-88	Philadelphia Flyers	NHL	20	0	4	4	61
1987-88	Hershey Bears	AHL	42	19	21	40	174
	NHL TOTALS		206	22	45	67	430

(c)—August, 1979—Drafted by Hartford Whalers in entry draft. Third Hartford pick, 60th overall, third round.

(d)—August, 1982—Traded with Ken Linseman by Hartford Whalers to Edmonton Oilers for Risto Siltanen and Brent Loney.

(e)—October, 1983—Selected by Los Angeles Kings in NHL waiver draft.

(f)—July, 1985—Signed by Philadelphia Flyers as a free agent.

MARK NAPIER

Right Wing . . . 5'10" . . . 182 lbs. . . . Born, Toronto, Ont., January 28, 1957 . . . Shoots left . . . Brother of Steve Napier, Cornell goalie in mid 1970's . . . (October 20, 1983)—Ankle tendon partially severed by skate of Dan Mandich at Minnesota . . . (March, 1988)—Bruised ribs.

Year	Team	League	Games	G.	A.	Pts.	Pen.
1972-73	Wexford Raiders	OPHL	44	41	27	68	201
1973-74	Toronto Marlboros	Jr."A"OHA	70	47	46	93	63
1974-75	Toronto Marlboros (a-c)	Jr."A"OHA	61	66	64	130	106
1975-76	Toronto Toros (d-e)	WHA	78	43	50	93	20
1976-77	Birmingham Bulls (f)	WHA	80	60	36	96	24
1977-78	Birmingham Bulls (g)	WHA	79	33	32	65	90
1978-79	Montreal Canadiens	NHL	54	11	20	31	11
1979-80	Montreal Canadiens	NHL	76	16	33	49	7
1980-81	Montreal Canadiens	NHL	79	35	36	71	24
1981-82	Montreal Canadiens	NHL	80	40	41	81	14
1982-83	Montreal Canadiens	NHL	73	40	27	67	6
1983-84	Montreal Canadiens (h)	NHL	5	3	2	5	0
1983-84	Minnesota North Stars	NHL	58	13	28	41	17
1984-85	Minnesota North Stars (i)	NHL	39	10	18	28	2
1984-85	Edmonton Oilers	NHL	33	9	26	35	19
1985-86	Edmonton Oilers	NHL	80	24	32	56	14
1986-87	Edmonton Oilers (j)	NHL	62	8	13	21	2

Year	Team	League	Games	G.	A.	Pts.	Pen.
1986-87—Buffalo Sabres		NHL	15	5	5	10	0
1987-88—Buffalo Sabres		NHL	47	10	8	18	8
WHA TOTALS			237	136	118	254	134
NHL TOTALS			701	224	289	513	124

(c)—May, 1975—Signed by Toronto Toros (WHA).
(d)—Won WHA Rookie Award.
(e)—Named WHA Rookie of the Year in poll of players by THE SPORTING NEWS.
(f)—Drafted from Birmingham Bulls (WHA) by Montreal Canadiens in first round of 1977 amateur draft.
(g)—September, 1978—Signed by Montreal Canadiens.
(h)—October, 1983—Traded with Keith Acton and third-round 1984 draft pick (Kenneth Hodge) by Montreal Canadiens to Minnesota North Stars for Bobby Smith.
(i)—January, 1985—Traded by Minnesota North Stars to Edmonton Oilers for Terry Martin and Gord Sherven.
(j)—March, 1987—Traded with Lee Fogolin and a fourth-round 1987 draft pick (Peter Eriksson) by Edmonton Oilers to Buffalo Sabres for Wayne Van Dorp, Norm Lacombe and a fourth-round 1987 draft pick (John Bradley).

MATS NASLUND

Left Wing ... 5'7" ... 158 lbs. ... Born, Timra, Sweden, October 31, 1959 ... Shoots left.

Year	Team	League	Games	G.	A.	Pts.	Pen.
1980-81—Brynas IF (c)		Sweden	....	17	25	42	....
1981-82—Brynas IF		Sweden	....	25	20	45	....
1982-83—Montreal Canadiens		NHL	74	26	45	71	10
1983-84—Montreal Canadiens		NHL	77	29	35	64	4
1984-85—Montreal Canadiens		NHL	80	42	37	79	14
1985-86—Montreal Canadiens		NHL	80	43	67	110	16
1986-87—Montreal Canadiens		NHL	79	25	55	80	16
1987-88—Montreal Canadiens (d)		NHL	78	24	59	83	14
NHL TOTALS			468	189	298	487	74

(c)—August, 1979—Drafted by Montreal Canadiens in 1979 NHL entry draft. Second Canadiens pick, 37th overall, second round.
(d)—Won Lady Byng Memorial Trophy (Most Gentlemanly Player).

ERIC RIC NATTRESS
(Known by middle name.)

Defense ... 6'2" ... 208 lbs. ... Born, Hamilton, Ont., May 25, 1962 ... Shoots right ... (August, 1983)—Fined $150 in Brantford, Ontario for possession of three grams of marijuana and one gram of hashish ... (September, 1983)—Given 40-game suspension by NHL following his conviction in Ontario court ... (March, 1984)—Fractured finger ... (March 17, 1986)—Injured shoulder at Minnesota ... (February, 1987)—Strained knee ... (March, 1988)—Bruised right shoulder ... (March, 1988)—Knee surgery.

Year	Team	League	Games	G.	A.	Pts.	Pen.
1979-80—Brantford Alexanders (c)		OMJHL	65	3	21	24	94
1980-81—Brantford Alexanders		OHL	51	8	34	42	106
1981-82—Brantford Alexanders		OHL	59	11	50	61	126
1982-83—Nova Scotia Voyageurs		AHL	9	0	4	4	16
1982-83—Montreal Canadiens		NHL	40	1	3	4	19
1983-84—Montreal Canadiens		NHL	34	0	12	12	15
1984-85—Sherbrooke Canadiens		AHL	72	8	40	48	37
1984-85—Montreal Canadiens		NHL	5	0	1	1	2
1985-86—St. Louis Blues (d)		NHL	78	4	20	24	52
1986-87—St. Louis Blues (e)		NHL	73	6	22	28	24
1987-88—Calgary Flames		NHL	63	2	13	15	37
NHL TOTALS			293	13	71	84	149

(c)—June, 1980—Drafted as underage junior by Montreal Canadiens in 1980 NHL entry draft. Second Canadiens pick, 27th overall, second round.
(d)—September, 1985—Traded by Montreal Canadiens to St. Louis Blues to complete June deal for Mark Hunter
(e)—June, 1987—Traded by St. Louis Blues to Calgary Flames for a fourth-round 1987 draft pick (Andy Rymsha) and a fifth-round 1988 draft pick.

MIKE NATYSHAK

Right Wing ... 6'2" ... 210 lbs. ... Born, Belle River, Ont., November 29, 1963 ... Shoots right.

Year	Team	League	Games	G.	A.	Pts.	Pen.
1983-84—Bowling Green Univ.		CCHA	19	0	0	0	0
1984-85—Bowling Green Univ.		CCHA	38	4	9	13	79

Year	Team	League	Games	G.	A.	Pts.	Pen.
1985-86—Bowling Green Univ. (c)		CCHA	40	3	5	8	62
1986-87—Bowling Green Univ.		CCHA	45	5	10	15	101
1987-88—Quebec Nordiques		NHL	4	0	0	0	0
1987-88—Fredericton Express		AHL	46	5	9	14	84
NHL TOTALS			4	0	0	0	0

(c)—June, 1986—Selected in 1986 NHL supplemental draft by Quebec Nordiques.

JEAN-FRANCOIS NAULT

Center . . . 6'2" . . . 180 lbs. . . . Born, Montreal, Que., May 12, 1967 . . . Shoots left.

Year	Team	League	Games	G.	A.	Pts.	Pen.
1984-85—Levis Lauzon College		Que.	41	13	16	29	28
1985-86—Granby Bisons (c)		QHL	39	13	20	33	20
1986-87—Granby Bisons		QHL	53	36	49	85	68
1987-88—Baltimore Skipjacks		AHL	67	18	18	36	46

(c)—June, 1986—Drafted as underage junior by Quebec Nordiques in 1986 NHL entry draft. Ninth Nordiques pick, 144th overall, seventh round.

CAM NEELY

Right Wing . . . 6'1" . . . 185 lbs. . . . Born, Comox, B.C., June 6, 1965 . . . Shoots right . . . (October, 1984)—Dislocated kneecap . . . (March, 1988)—Slipped right kneecap.

Year	Team	League	Games	G.	A.	Pts.	Pen.
1981-82—Ridge Meadow		B.C. Midget	64	73	68	141	134
1982-83—Portland Winter Hawks (c)		WHL	72	56	64	120	130
1983-84—Portland Winter Hawks		WHL	19	8	18	26	29
1983-84—Vancouver Canucks		NHL	56	16	15	31	57
1984-85—Vancouver Canucks		NHL	72	21	18	39	137
1985-86—Vancouver Canucks (d)		NHL	73	14	20	34	126
1986-87—Boston Bruins		NHL	75	36	36	72	143
1987-88—Boston Bruins (b)		NHL	69	42	27	69	175
NHL TOTALS			345	129	116	245	638

(c)—June, 1983—Drafted as underage junior by Vancouver Canucks in 1983 NHL entry draft. First Canucks pick, ninth overall, first round.

(d)—June, 1986—Traded with first-round draft choice in 1987 (Glen Wesley) by Vancouver Canucks to Boston Bruins for Barry Pederson.

MIKE NEILL

Defense . . . 6' . . . 195 lbs. . . . Born, Kenora, Ont., August 6, 1965 . . . Shoots left.

Year	Team	League	Games	G.	A.	Pts.	Pen.
1981-82—Kenora Thistles		MJHL	60	12	32	44	65
1982-83—Sault Ste. Marie Greyhounds (c)		OHL	65	4	13	17	115
1983-84—Sault Ste. Marie Greyhounds		OHL	20	2	6	8	42
1983-84—Windsor Spitfires		OHL	49	9	17	26	101
1984-85—Windsor Compuware Spitfires		OHL	62	3	17	20	143
1984-85—Springfield Indians		AHL	7	0	0	0	16
1984-85—Indianapolis Checkers (d)		IHL	....	...	....	....	....
1985-86—Indianapolis Checkers		IHL	71	2	11	13	117
1985-86—Springfield Indians		AHL	8	0	2	2	11
1986-87—Springfield Indians		AHL	32	3	4	7	67
1986-87—Peoria Rivermen		IHL	43	2	10	12	83
1987-88—Peoria Rivermen		IHL	56	4	19	23	148
1987-88—Springfield Indians		AHL	11	0	1	1	39

(c)—June, 1983—Drafted as underage junior by New York Islanders in 1983 NHL entry draft. Fourth Islanders pick, 57th overall, third round.

(d)—No regular season record. Played one playoff game.

CHRISTOPHER NELSON

Defense . . . 6'2" . . . 190 lbs. . . . Born, Philadelphia, Pa., February 12, 1969 . . . Shoots right.

Year	Team	League	Games	G.	A.	Pts.	Pen.
1987-88—Rochester Mustangs (c)		USHL	48	6	29	35	82

(c)—June, 1988—Drafted by New Jersey Devils in 1988 NHL entry draft. Sixth Devils pick, 96th overall, fifth round.

STEVE NEMETH

Center . . . 5'8" . . . 167 lbs. . . . Born, Calgary, Alta., February 11, 1967 . . . Shoots left . . . (November, 1984)—Dislocated left shoulder . . . (March, 1987)—Given a one-year suspen-

sion from international competition by the IIHF for being involved in an on-ice fight between National Junior Canadian and Soviet Teams in Prague, Czechoslovakia.

Year	Team	League	Games	G.	A.	Pts.	Pen.
1983-84—Lethbridge Broncos		WHL	68	22	20	42	33
1984-85—Lethbridge Broncos (c)		WHL	67	39	55	94	39
1985-86—Lethbridge Broncos		WHL	70	42	69	111	47
1986-87—Kamloops Blazers		WHL	10	10	4	14	0
1986-87—Canadian Olympic Team		Int'l	43	14	7	21	12
1987-88—Colorado Rangers		IHL	57	13	24	37	28
1987-88—New York Rangers		NHL	12	2	0	2	2
NHL TOTALS			12	2	0	2	2

(c)—June, 1985—Drafted as underage junior by New York Rangers in 1985 NHL entry draft. Tenth Rangers pick, 196th overall, 10th round.

JIM NESICH

Right Wing and Center . . . 5'11" . . . 160 lbs. . . . Born, Dearborn, Mich., February 22, 1966 . . . Shoots right.

Year	Team	League	Games	G.	A.	Pts.	Pen.
1983-84—Verdun Juniors (c)		WHL	70	22	24	46	35
1984-85—Verdun Juniors		QHL	65	19	33	52	72
1985-86—Verdun Juniors		OHL	71	26	55	81	114
1985-86—Sherbrooke Canadiens		AHL	4	0	1	1	0
1986-87—Verdun Junior Canadiens		QHL	62	20	50	70	133
1987-88—Sherbrooke Canadiens		AHL	53	4	10	14	51

(c)—June, 1984—Drafted by Montreal Canadiens in NHL entry draft. Eighth Canadiens pick, 116th overall, sixth round.

RAY NEUFELD

Right Wing . . . 6'2" . . . 215 lbs. . . . Born, St. Boniface, Man., April 15, 1959 . . . Shoots right . . . (September, 1978)—Broken ribs . . . (January 7, 1985)—Injured shoulder when checked by Gary Leeman at Toronto . . . (April 11, 1987)—Stretched knee ligaments when checked by Craig Muni in a playoff game vs. Edmonton.

Year	Team	League	Games	G.	A.	Pts.	Pen.
1976-77—Flin Flon Bombers		WCHL	68	13	19	32	63
1977-78—Flin Flon Bombers		WCHL	72	23	46	69	224
1978-79—Edmonton Oil Kings (c)		WCHL	57	54	48	102	138
1979-80—Springfield Indians		AHL	73	23	29	52	51
1979-80—Hartford Whalers		NHL	8	1	0	1	0
1980-81—Binghamton Whalers		AHL	25	7	7	14	43
1980-81—Hartford Whalers		NHL	52	5	10	15	44
1981-82—Binghamton Whalers (d)		AHL	61	28	31	59	81
1981-82—Hartford Whalers		NHL	19	4	3	7	4
1982-83—Hartford Whalers		NHL	80	26	31	57	86
1983-84—Hartford Whalers		NHL	80	27	42	69	97
1984-85—Hartford Whalers		NHL	76	27	35	62	129
1985-86—Hartford Whalers (e)		NHL	16	5	10	15	40
1985-86—Winnipeg Jets		NHL	60	20	28	48	62
1986-87—Winnipeg Jets		NHL	80	18	18	36	105
1987-88—Winnipeg Jets		NHL	78	18	18	36	167
NHL TOTALS			549	151	195	346	734

(c)—August, 1979—Drafted by Hartford Whalers in 1979 entry draft. Fourth Whalers pick, 81st overall, fourth round.

(d)—Co-leader (with Florent Robidoux of New Brunswick) during AHL Calder Cup Playoffs with nine goals.

(e)—November, 1985—Traded by Hartford Whalers to Winnipeg Jets for Dave Babych.

JIM NEWHOUSE

Left Wing . . . 5'10" . . . 180 lbs. . . . Born, Winchester, Mass., April 1, 1966 . . . Shoots left . . . (January, 1988)—Declared academically ineligible at Lowell University.

Year	Team	League	Games	G.	A.	Pts.	Pen.
1983-84—Matignon H.S. (c)		Mass. H.S.	22	18	30	48	..
1984-85—University of Lowell		H. East	37	6	7	13	16
1985-86—University of Lowell		H. East	39	20	13	33	32
1986-87—University of Lowell		H. East	31	12	24	36	17
1987-88—University of Lowell		H. East	14	10	2	12	4

(c)—June, 1984—Drafted by Boston Bruins in NHL entry draft. Twelfth Bruins pick, 248th overall, 12th round.

TOM NEZOIL

Left Wing . . . 6'1" . . . 190 lbs. . . . Born, Burlington, Ont., August 7, 1967 . . . Shoots left.

Year	Team	League	Games	G.	A.	Pts.	Pen.
1986-87—Miami of Ohio Univ. (c)		CCHA	39	11	18	29	80
1987-88—Miami of Ohio Univ.		CCHA	34	13	13	26	52

(c)—June, 1987—Drafted by New Jersey Devils in 1987 NHL entry draft. Sixth Devils pick, 128th overall, seventh round.

MARTIN NICHOLETTI

Right Wing . . . 6' . . . 200 lbs. . . . Born, LaSalle, Que., January 15, 1963 . . . Shoots right.

Year	Team	League	Games	G.	A.	Pts.	Pen.
1983-84—Univ. of Que./Trois-Riv.		QUAA	24	8	12	20	30
1984-85—Univ. of Que./Trois-Riv.		QUAA	18	7	8	15	30
1985-86—Univ. of Que./Trois-Riv.		QUAA	12	5	6	11	25
1986-87—Univ. of Que./Trois-Riv. (c)		QUAA	18	7	20	27	45
1987-88—Salt Lake Golden Eagles (d)		IHL	49	10	13	23	37
1987-88—Sherbrooke Canadiens		AHL	18	6	8	14	22

(c)—May, 1987—Signed by Calgary Flames as a free agent.
(d)—February, 1988—Traded by Calgary Flames to Montreal Canadiens for Rick Hayward.

BERNIE IRVINE NICHOLLS

Center . . . 6' . . . 185 lbs. . . . Born, Haliburton, Ont., June 24, 1961 . . . Shoots right . . . (November 18, 1982)—Partial tear of medial colateral ligament in right knee vs. Detroit when hit by Willie Huber . . . (February, 1984)—Broken jaw, missed only two games but lost 13 pounds before the end of season with jaw wired shut . . . (October 8, 1987)—Fractured left index finger in three places in opening game of season vs. St. Louis.

Year	Team	League	Games	G.	A.	Pts.	Pen.
1978-79—Kingston Canadians		OMJHL	2	0	1	1	0
1979-80—Kingston Canadians (c)		OMJHL	68	36	43	79	85
1980-81—Kingston Canadians		OHL	65	63	89	152	109
1981-82—New Haven Nighthawks		AHL	55	41	30	71	31
1981-82—Los Angeles Kings		NHL	22	14	18	32	27
1982-83—Los Angeles Kings		NHL	71	28	22	50	124
1983-84—Los Angeles Kings		NHL	78	41	54	95	83
1984-85—Los Angeles Kings		NHL	80	46	54	100	76
1985-86—Los Angeles Kings		NHL	80	36	61	97	78
1986-87—Los Angeles Kings		NHL	80	33	48	81	101
1987-88—Los Angeles Kings		NHL	65	32	46	78	114
NHL TOTALS			**476**	**230**	**303**	**533**	**603**

(c)—June, 1980—Drafted by Los Angeles Kings as underage junior in 1980 NHL entry draft. Fourth Kings pick, 73rd overall, fourth round.

ROB NICHOLS

Left Wing . . . 5'11" . . . 172 lbs. . . . Born, Hamilton, Ontario, August 4, 1964 . . . Shoots left.

Year	Team	League	Games	G.	A.	Pts.	Pen.
1982-83—Kitchener Rangers (c)		OHL	54	17	26	43	208
1983-84—Kitchener Rangers		OHL	12	5	8	13	46
1983-84—North Bay Centennials		OHL	46	36	32	68	98
1984-85—North Bay Centennials		OHL	41	27	39	66	72
1984-85—Fredericton Express		AHL	1	0	0	0	2
1984-85—Kalamazoo Wings		IHL	8	2	1	3	0
1985-86—Kalamazoo Wings		IHL	73	38	41	79	406
1986-87—Kalamazoo Wings		IHL	71	29	27	56	357
1987-88—Adirondack Red Wings		AHL	65	21	16	37	256

(c)—June, 1983—Drafted as underage junior by Philadelphia Flyers in 1983 NHL entry draft. Eighth Flyers pick, 181st overall, ninth round.

JAMIE NICOLLS

Left Wing . . . 6'1" . . . 193 lbs. . . . Born, Vancouver, B.C., March 27, 1968 . . . Shoots left . . . Also plays Right Wing.

Year	Team	League	Games	G.	A.	Pts.	Pen.
1983-84—Portland Winter Hawks		WHL	44	7	12	19	14
1984-85—Portland Winter Hawks		WHL	70	12	24	36	56
1985-86—Portland Winter Hawks (c)		WHL	65	15	37	52	60
1986-87—Portland Winter Hawks		WHL	59	28	37	65	42
1987-88—Portland Winter Hawks		WHL	14	3	6	9	13
1987-88—Seattle Thunderbirds		WHL	56	31	20	51	30
1987-88—Nova Scotia Oilers		AHL	5	2	2	4	0

(c)—June, 1986—Drafted as underage junior by Edmonton Oilers in 1986 NHL entry draft. Second Oilers pick, 42nd overall, second round.

LEN NIELSEN

Center . . . 5'9" . . . 172 lbs. . . . Born, Moose Jaw, Sask., March 28, 1967 . . . Shoots left.

Year	Team	League	Games	G.	A.	Pts.	Pen.
1983-84—Regina Pats		WHL	57	9	15	24	20
1984-85—Regina Pats (c)		WHL	72	35	74	109	43
1985-86—Regina Pats		WHL	66	30	77	107	49
1985-86—Team Canada		Int'l	1	0	0	0	0
1986-87—Regina Pats (d)		WHL	72	36	*100	136	32
1986-87—Sherbrooke Canadiens		AHL	3	1	0	1	0
1987-88—Moncton Golden Flames		AHL	66	9	29	38	28

(c)—September, 1985—Invited to Winnipeg Jets training camp and signed as a free agent.
(d)—Won Frank Boucher Memorial Trophy (East Division Most Gentlemanly Player).

KRAIG NIENHUIS

Left Wing . . . 6'3" . . . 205 lbs. . . . Born, Sarnia, Ont., May 9, 1962 . . . Shoots left . . . (October, 1987)—Missed two months with mononucleosis.

Year	Team	League	Games	G.	A.	Pts.	Pen.
1982-83—Rensselaer Poly. Inst.		ECAC	24	9	11	20	34
1983-84—Rensselaer Poly. Inst.		ECAC	35	10	12	22	26
1984-85—Rensselaer Poly. Inst. (c)		ECAC	36	11	10	21	55
1985-86—Boston Bruins		NHL	70	16	14	30	37
1986-87—Moncton Golden Flames		AHL	54	10	17	27	44
1986-87—Boston Bruins		NHL	16	4	2	6	2
1987-88—Maine Mariners (d)		AHL	36	16	17	33	57
1987-88—Boston Bruins		NHL	1	0	0	0	0
NHL TOTALS			87	20	16	36	39

(c)—June, 1985—Signed by Boston Bruins as a free agent.
(d)—March, 1988—Released by Boston Bruins.

JOE NIEUWENDYK

Center . . . 6'2" . . . 185 lbs. . . . Born, Oshawa, Ont., September 10, 1966 . . . Shoots left . . . Cousin of Jeff, John and Brian Beukeboom . . . (November, 1987)—Concussion vs. N.Y. Rangers.

Year	Team	League	Games	G.	A.	Pts.	Pen.
1983-84—Pickering Panthers Jr. B.		MTJHL	38	30	28	58	35
1984-85—Cornell University (c-d)		ECAC	29	21	24	45	30
1985-86—Cornell University (a)		ECAC	29	26	28	54	67
1986-87—Cornell University (a-e-f)		ECAC	23	26	26	52	26
1986-87—Calgary Flames		NHL	9	5	1	6	0
1987-88—Calgary Flames (g-h)		NHL	75	51	41	92	23
NHL TOTALS			84	56	42	98	23

(c)—Won Ivy-League Rookie of the Year Trophy.
(d)—June, 1985—Drafted by Calgary Flames in 1985 NHL entry draft. Second Flames pick, 27th overall, second round.
(e)—Named ECAC Player-of-the-Year.
(f)—Named to U.S. College First-Team All-America Team.
(g)—Won Calder Memorial Trophy (Top NHL Rookie).
(h)—Named NHL Rookie of the Year in poll of players by THE SPORTING NEWS.

CHRIS NILAN

Right Wing . . . 6' . . . 200 lbs. . . . Born, Boston, Mass., February 9, 1958 . . . Shoots right . . . (November 21, 1981)—Threw puck at Paul Baxter of Pittsburgh while sitting in penalty box. Was given a three-game suspension by NHL . . . (January 22, 1985)—Became all-time Montreal Canadien career penalty minute leader (previous record held by Maurice Richard with 1285 minutes) . . . (October 13, 1985)—Given eight-game suspension by NHL for intentional injury of Rick Middleton at Boston . . . (November 20, 1986)—Given three-game suspension by NHL after an altercation with Ken Linseman at Boston . . . (February, 1987)—Left knee braced . . . (March, 1987)—Hip injury . . . (February 2, 1988)—Sprained medial colateral ligament in right knee when he collided with Mikko Makela vs. N.Y. Islanders in his first game with Rangers.

Year	Team	League	Games	G.	A.	Pts.	Pen.
1977-78—Northeastern University (c)		ECAC	....	...	....	....	....
1978-79—Northeastern University		ECAC	32	9	13	22	....
1979-80—Nova Scotia Voyageurs		AHL	49	15	10	25	*304

Year	Team	League	Games	G.	A.	Pts.	Pen.
1979-80—Montreal Canadiens		NHL	15	0	2	2	50
1980-81—Montreal Canadiens		NHL	57	7	8	15	262
1981-82—Montreal Canadiens		NHL	49	7	4	11	204
1982-83—Montreal Canadiens		NHL	66	6	8	14	213
1983-84—Montreal Canadiens (d)		NHL	76	16	10	26	*338
1984-85—Montreal Canadiens		NHL	77	21	16	37	*358
1985-86—Montreal Canadiens (e)		NHL	72	19	15	34	274
1986-87—Montreal Canadiens		NHL	44	4	16	20	266
1987-88—Montreal Canadiens (f)		NHL	50	7	5	12	209
1987-88—New York Rangers		NHL	22	3	5	8	96
NHL TOTALS			528	90	89	179	2270

(c)—June, 1978—Drafted by Montreal Canadiens in 1978 amateur draft. Twenty-first Canadiens pick, 231st overall, 19th round.

(d)—Led Stanley Cup Playoffs with 81 penalty minutes.

(e)—Led Stanley Cup Playoffs with 141 penalty minutes.

(f)—January 27, 1988—Traded by Montreal Canadiens to New York Rangers for the option to flip first round 1989 draft picks.

JIM EDWARD NILL

Right Wing . . . 6' . . . 185 lbs. . . . Born, Hanna, Alta., April 11, 1958 . . . Shoots right . . . (March, 1983)—Concussion . . . (October 10, 1985)—Dislocated shoulder at Edmonton and missed 15 games . . . (October 14, 1986)—Injured knee vs. Boston.

Year	Team	League	Games	G.	A.	Pts.	Pen.
1974-75—Drumheller Falcons		AJHL	59	30	30	60	103
1975-76—Medicine Hat Tigers		WCHL	62	5	11	16	69
1976-77—Medicine Hat Tigers		WCHL	71	23	24	47	140
1977-78—Medicine Hat Tigers (c)		WCHL	72	47	46	93	252
1978-79—Canadian National Team		Int'l	....	...	....	....	....
1979-80—Canadian National Team		Int'l	51	14	21	35	58
1979-80—Canadian Olympic Team		Olympics	6	1	2	3	4
1980-81—Salt Lake Golden Eagles (b)		CHL	79	28	34	62	222
1981-82—St. Louis Blues (d)		NHL	61	9	12	21	127
1981-82—Vancouver Canucks		NHL	8	1	2	3	5
1982-83—Vancouver Canucks		NHL	65	7	15	22	136
1983-84—Vancouver Canucks (e)		NHL	51	9	6	15	78
1983-84—Boston Bruins		NHL	27	3	2	5	81
1984-85—Boston Bruins (f)		NHL	49	1	9	10	62
1984-85—Winnipeg Jets		NHL	20	8	8	16	38
1985-86—Winnipeg Jets		NHL	61	6	8	14	75
1986-87—Winnipeg Jets		NHL	36	3	4	7	52
1987-88—Moncton Golden Flames		AHL	3	0	0	0	6
1987-88—Winnipeg Jets (g)		NHL	24	0	1	1	44
1987-88—Detroit Red Wings		NHL	36	3	11	14	55
NHL TOTALS			438	50	78	128	753

(c)—June, 1978—Drafted by St. Louis Blues in 1978 NHL amateur draft. Fourth Blues pick, 89th overall, sixth round.

(d)—March, 1982—Traded with Tony Currie and Rick Heinz by St. Louis Blues to Vancouver Canucks for Glen Hanlon and a fourth-round 1982 draft pick (Shawn Kilroy).

(e)—February, 1984—Traded by Vancouver Canucks to Boston Bruins for Peter McNab.

(f)—January, 1985—Traded by Boston Bruins to Winnipeg Jets for Morris Lukowich.

(g)—January, 1988—Traded by Winnipeg Jets to Detroit Red Wings for Mark Kumpel.

JEFFREY NOBLE

Center . . . 5'10" . . . 170 lbs. . . . Born, Mount Forest, Ont., May 20, 1968 . . . Shoots left.

Year	Team	League	Games	G.	A.	Pts.	Pen.
1984-85—Kitchener Greenshirts Midgets		OHA	63	63	39	102	150
1985-86—Kitchener Rangers (c)		OHL	58	22	33	55	65
1986-87—Kitchener Rangers		OHL	66	29	57	86	55
1987-88—Kitchener Rangers		OHL	55	37	64	101	97

(c)—June, 1986—Drafted as underage junior by Vancouver Canucks in 1986 NHL entry draft. Seventh Canucks pick, 154th overall, eighth round.

BRIAN NOONAN

Center . . . 6'1" . . . 180 lbs. . . . Born, Boston, Mass., May 29, 1965 . . . Shoots right . . . (April 3, 1988)—Separated shoulder in final regular season game vs. New Jersey.

Year	Team	League	Games	G.	A.	Pts.	Pen.
1982-83—Archbishop Williams H.S. (c)		Mass. H.S.	21	26	17	43	....
1983-84—Archbishop Williams H.S.		Mass. H.S.	17	14	23	37	....

Year	Team	League	Games	G.	A.	Pts.	Pen.
1984-85—New Westminister Bruins		WHL	72	50	66	116	76
1985-86—Saginaw Generals (d)		IHL	76	39	39	78	69
1985-86—Nova Scotia Oilers		AHL	2	0	0	0	0
1986-87—Nova Scotia Oilers		AHL	70	25	26	51	30
1987-88—Chicago Black Hawks		NHL	77	10	20	30	44
NHL TOTALS			77	10	20	30	44

(c)—June, 1983—Drafted by Chicago Black Hawks in 1983 NHL entry draft. Tenth Black Hawks pick, 179th overall, ninth round.

(d)—Won Ken McKenzie Trophy (Top IHL U.S.-Born player).

ROBERT NORDMARK

Defense . . . 6'1" . . . 190 lbs. . . . Born, Lulea, Sweden, August 20, 1962 . . . Shoots right . . . (September, 1987)—Separated shoulder during St. Louis training camp.

Year	Team	League	Games	G.	A.	Pts.	Pen.
1986-87—Lulea (c-d)		Sweden	32	7	8	15	42
1987-88—St. Louis Blues		NHL	67	3	18	21	60
NHL TOTALS			67	3	18	21	60

(c)—June, 1981—Drafted by Detroit Red Wings in 1981 NHL entry draft. Eighth Red Wings pick, 191st overall, 10th round.

(d)—June, 1987—Drafted by St. Louis Blues in 1987 NHL entry draft. Third Blues pick, 59th overall, third round.

CHRIS NORTON

Defense . . . 6'2" . . . 200 lbs. . . . Born, Oakville, Ont., March 11, 1965 . . . Shoots right . . . Holds career point record for Cornell defensemen.

Year	Team	League	Games	G.	A.	Pts.	Pen.
1984-85—Cornell Univ. (c)		ECAC	29	4	19	23	34
1985-86—Cornell Univ.		ECAC	21	8	15	23	56
1986-87—Cornell Univ.		ECAC	24	10	21	31	79
1987-88—Cornell Univ.		ECAC	27	9	25	34	53

(c)—June, 1985—Drafted by Winnipeg Jets in 1985 NHL entry draft. Eleventh Jets pick, 228th overall, 11th round.

D'ARCY NORTON

Left Wing . . . 6' . . . 175 lbs. . . . Born, Camrose, Alta., May 2, 1967 . . . Shoots left.

Year	Team	League	Games	G.	A.	Pts.	Pen.
1984-85—Lethbridge Broncos		WHL	50	4	11	15	49
1985-86—Lethbridge Broncos		WHL	69	19	25	44	69
1986-87—Kamloops Blazers (c)		WHL	71	45	57	102	66
1987-88—Kamloops Blazers (a)		WHL	68	64	43	107	82

(c)—June, 1987—Drafted by Minnesota North Stars in 1987 NHL entry draft. Sixth North Stars pick, 109th overall, sixth round.

JEFF NORTON

Defense . . . 6'2" . . . 190 lbs. . . . Born, Cambridge, Mass., November 25, 1965 . . . Shoots left.

Year	Team	League	Games	G.	A.	Pts.	Pen.
1983-84—Cushing Academy (c)		Mass. H.S.	21	22	33	55	..
1984-85—University of Michigan		CCHA	37	8	16	24	103
1985-86—University of Michigan		CCHA	37	15	30	45	99
1986-87—University of Michigan (b)		CCHA	39	12	37	49	92
1987-88—U.S. Olympic Team		Int'l	57	7	25	32	..
1987-88—New York Islanders		NHL	15	1	6	7	14
NHL TOTALS			15	1	6	7	14

(c)—June, 1984—Drafted by New York Islanders in NHL entry draft. Third Islanders pick, 62nd overall, third round.

LEE CHARLES NORWOOD

Defense . . . 6' . . . 190 lbs. . . . Born, Oakland, Calif., February 2, 1960 . . . Shoots left . . . (February, 1987)—Pulled stomach muscle . . . (October, 1987)—Groin injury . . . (December, 1987)—Knee injury.

Year	Team	League	Games	G.	A.	Pts.	Pen.
1977-78—Hull Olympiques		QMJHL	51	3	17	20	83
1978-79—Oshawa Generals (c)		OMJHL	61	23	38	61	171
1979-80—Oshawa Generals		OMJHL	60	13	39	52	143
1980-81—Hershey Bears		AHL	52	11	32	43	78
1980-81—Quebec Nordiques		NHL	11	1	1	2	9

Year	Team	League	Games	G.	A.	Pts.	Pen.
1981-82—Fredericton Express		AHL	29	6	13	19	74
1981-82—Quebec Nordiques (d)		NHL	2	0	0	0	2
1981-82—Washington Capitals		NHL	26	7	10	17	115
1982-83—Washington Capitals		NHL	8	0	1	1	14
1982-83—Hershey Bears		AHL	67	12	36	48	90
1983-84—St. Catharines Saints		AHL	75	13	46	59	91
1984-85—Peoria Rivermen (a-e)		IHL	80	17	60	77	229
1985-86—St. Louis Blues (f)		NHL	71	5	24	29	134
1986-87—Adirondack Red Wings		AHL	3	0	3	3	0
1986-87—Detroit Red Wings		NHL	57	6	21	27	163
1987-88—Detroit Red Wings		NHL	51	9	22	31	131
NHL TOTALS			226	28	79	107	568

(c)—August, 1979—Drafted by Quebec Nordiques as underage junior in 1979 NHL entry draft. Third Nordiques pick, 62nd overall, third round.
(d)—January, 1982—Traded by Quebec Nordiques to Washington Capitals for Tim Tookey.
(e)—Won Governor's Trophy (Top Defenseman).
(f)—August, 1986—Traded by St. Louis Blues to Detroit Red Wings for Larry Trader.

TEPPO KALEVI NUMMINEN

Defense . . . 6'1" . . . 190 lbs. . . . Born, Tampere, Finland, July 3, 1968 . . . Shoots right.

Year	Team	League	Games	G.	A.	Pts.	Pen.
1984-85—Tappara (c)		Finland	30	14	17	31	10
1985-86—Tappara		Finland	39	2	4	6	6
1986-87—Tappara		Finland	..	..	..	..	..
1987-88—Tappara		Finland	44	10	10	20	29

(c)—June, 1986—Drafted by Winnipeg Jets in 1986 NHL entry draft. Second Jets pick, 29th overall, second round.

GARY NYLUND

Defense . . . 6'4" . . . 210 lbs. . . . Born, Surrey, B.C., October 28, 1963 . . . Shoots left . . . (September, 1982)—Injury to left knee in exhibition game, requiring surgery . . . (October, 1983)—Knee surgery . . . (November 5, 1984)—Concussion at Minnesota . . . (October, 1987)—Bruised elbow.

Year	Team	League	Games	G.	A.	Pts.	Pen.
1978-79—Delta		BCJHL	57	6	29	35	107
1978-79—Portland Winter Hawks		WHL	2	0	0	0	0
1979-80—Portland Winter Hawks		WHL	72	5	21	26	59
1980-81—Portland Winter Hawks (b)		WHL	70	6	40	46	186
1981-82—Portland Winter Hawks (a-c-d)		WHL	65	7	59	66	267
1982-83—Toronto Maple Leafs		NHL	16	0	3	3	16
1983-84—Toronto Maple Leafs		NHL	47	2	14	16	103
1984-85—Toronto Maple Leafs		NHL	76	3	17	20	99
1985-86—Toronto Maple Leafs (e)		NHL	79	2	16	18	180
1986-87—Chicago Black Hawks		NHL	80	7	20	27	190
1987-88—Chicago Black Hawks		NHL	76	4	15	19	208
NHL TOTALS			374	18	85	103	796

(c)—Winner of WHL Top Defenseman Trophy.
(d)—June, 1982—Drafted as underage junior by Toronto Maple Leafs in 1982 NHL entry draft. First Maple Leafs pick, third overall, first round.
(e)—August, 1986—Signed by Chicago Black Hawks as a free agent. An NHL arbitrator subsequently ruled that the Black Hawks had to send Ken Yaremchuk, Jerome Dupont and a fourth-round 1987 draft pick (Joe Sacco) to compensate the Maple Leafs.

ADAM OATES

Center . . . 5'11" . . . 190 lbs. . . . Born, Weston, Ont., August 27, 1962 . . . Shoots right . . . Holds All-time career record for assists at R.P.I. (150) . . . (1984-85)—Set R.P.I. record for assists and points in a single season . . . (March 3, 1986)—Strained knee vs. Minnesota and missed three games . . . (October, 1987)—Pulled abdominal muscle.

Year	Team	League	Games	G.	A.	Pts.	Pen.
1982-83—R.P.I.		ECAC	22	9	33	42	8
1983-84—R.P.I. (b)		ECAC	38	26	57	83	15
1984-85—R.P.I. (a-c-d)		ECAC	38	31	60	91	29
1985-86—Adirondack Red Wings		AHL	34	18	28	46	4
1985-86—Detroit Red Wings		NHL	38	9	11	20	10
1986-87—Detroit Red Wings		NHL	76	15	32	47	21
1987-88—Detroit Red Wings		NHL	63	14	40	54	20
NHL TOTALS			177	38	83	121	51

(c)—Named to All America Team (East).
(d)—June, 1985—Signed by Detroit Red Wings as a free agent.

ERIK O'BORSKY

Center . . . 6'3" . . . 210 lbs. . . . Born, Los Angeles, Calif., June 2, 1968 . . . Shoots left.

Year	Team	League	Games	G.	A.	Pts.	Pen.
1986-87	Yale University (c)	ECAC	27	1	5	6	24
1987-88	Yale University	ECAC	14	4	3	7	24

(c)—June, 1987—Drafted by New York Rangers in 1987 NHL entry draft. Fifth Rangers pick, 94th overall, fifth round.

DAVID O'BRIEN

Right Wing . . . 6'1" . . . 180 lbs. . . . Born, Brighton, Mass., September 13, 1966 . . . Shoots right.

Year	Team	League	Games	G.	A.	Pts.	Pen.
1984-85	Northeastern Univ.	H. East	30	8	7	15	6
1985-86	Northeastern Univ. (c)	H. East	39	23	16	39	18
1986-87	Northeastern University	H. East	35	16	24	40	12
1987-88	Northeastern University	H. East	37	18	29	47	18

(c)—June, 1986—Drafted by St. Louis Blues in 1986 NHL entry draft. Thirteenth Blues pick, 241st overall, 12th round.

JACK O'CALLAHAN

Defense . . . 6'1" . . . 185 lbs. . . . Born, Charlestown, Mass., July 24, 1957 . . . Shoots right . . . Member of Gold Medal Winning U.S. Olympic Hockey team . . . (December 28, 1983)— Given eight-game suspension by NHL for slashing Dave Maloney vs. N.Y. Rangers . . . (November, 1984)—Bruised shoulder . . . (October 21, 1987)—Fractured left eye orbital bone when elbowed by Mark Kachowski vs. Pittsburgh. O'Callahan was given a three-game NHL suspension for kicking Kachowski following the incident.

Year	Team	League	Games	G.	A.	Pts.	Pen.
1975-76	Boston University	ECAC	....	...	....	....	....
1976-77	Boston University (c)	ECAC	31	1	23	24	90
1977-78	Boston University (a)	ECAC	31	8	47	55	61
1978-79	Boston University (a)	ECAC	29	6	16	22	72
1979-80	U.S. Olympic Team	Int'l.	55	7	30	37	*85
1980-81	New Brunswick Hawks	AHL	78	9	25	34	167
1981-82	New Brunswick Hawks	AHL	79	15	33	48	130
1982-83	Springfield Indians	AHL	35	2	24	26	25
1982-83	Chicago Black Hawks	NHL	39	0	11	11	46
1983-84	Chicago Black Hawks	NHL	70	4	13	17	67
1984-85	Chicago Black Hawks	NHL	66	6	8	14	105
1985-86	Chicago Black Hawks	NHL	80	4	19	23	116
1986-87	Chicago Black Hawks	NHL	48	1	13	14	59
1987-88	New Jersey Devils (d)	NHL	50	7	19	26	97
	NHL TOTALS		353	22	83	105	490

(c)—June, 1977—Drafted by Chicago Black Hawks in 1977 NHL amateur draft. Fifth Black Hawks pick, 96th overall, sixth round.

(d)—October, 1987—Selected by New Jersey Devils in 1987 NHL waiver draft.

MICHAEL THOMAS O'CONNELL

Defense . . . 5'11" . . . 176 lbs. . . . Born, Chicago, Ill., November 25, 1955 . . . Shoots right . . . Son of former Cleveland Browns quarterback Tommy O'Connell . . . Brother of Tim O'Connell . . . Missed part of 1976-77 season with torn muscle in right shoulder . . . First member of the Black Hawks to be born in Chicago . . . (February 11, 1986)—Pulled rib muscles at Quebec and missed three games . . . (November 27, 1987)—Suspended eight NHL games for high sticking Doug Evans vs. St. Louis . . . (February, 1988)—Broken left index finger.

Year	Team	League	Games	G.	A.	Pts.	Pen.
1973-74	Kingston Canadiens	Jr."A"OHA	70	16	43	59	81
1974-75	King. Canadiens (a-c-d)	Jr."A"OHA	50	18	55	73	47
1975-76	Dallas Black Hawks (e)	CHL	70	6	37	43	50
1976-77	Dallas Black Hawks (a-f)	CHL	63	15	53	68	30
1977-78	Dallas Black Hawks (g)	CHL	62	6	45	51	75
1977-78	Chicago Black Hawks	NHL	6	1	1	2	2
1978-79	Chicago Black Hawks	NHL	48	4	22	26	20
1978-79	New Brunswick Hawks	AHL	35	5	20	25	21
1979-80	Chicago Black Hawks	NHL	78	8	22	30	52
1980-81	Chicago Black Hawks (h)	NHL	34	5	16	21	32

Year	Team	League	Games	G.	A.	Pts.	Pen.
1980-81—Boston Bruins		NHL	48	10	22	32	42
1981-82—Boston Bruins		NHL	80	5	34	39	75
1982-83—Boston Bruins		NHL	80	14	39	53	42
1983-84—Boston Bruins		NHL	75	18	42	60	42
1984-85—Boston Bruins		NHL	78	15	40	55	64
1985-86—Boston Bruins (i)		NHL	63	8	21	29	47
1985-86—Detroit Red Wings		NHL	13	1	7	8	16
1986-87—Detroit Red Wings		NHL	77	5	26	31	70
1987-88—Detroit Red Wings		NHL	48	6	13	19	38
NHL TOTALS			728	100	305	405	542

(c)—Drafted from Kingston Canadians by Chicago Black Hawks in third round of 1975 amateur draft.
(d)—Won Max Kaminsky Memorial Trophy (outstanding Defenseman).
(e)—Tied for lead in assists (5) during playoffs.
(f)—Won CHL Most Valuable Defenseman Award.
(g)—Tied for lead in assists (11) during playoffs.
(h)—December, 1980—Traded by Chicago Black Hawks to Boston Bruins for Al Secord.
(i)—March, 1986—Traded by Detroit Red Wings to Boston Bruins for Reed Larson.

MYLES O'CONNOR

Defense . . . 5'11" . . . 165 lbs. . . . Born, Calgary, Alta., April 2, 1967 . . . Shoots left.

Year	Team	League	Games	G.	A.	Pts.	Pen.
1984-85—Notre Dame Hounds (c)		MICHL	40	20	35	55	40
1985-86—University of Michigan		CCHA	37	6	19	25	73
1985-86—Team Canada		Int'l	8	0	0	0	0
1986-87—University of Michigan		CCHA	39	15	30	45	111
1987-88—University of Michigan		CCHA	40	9	25	34	78

(c)—June, 1985—Drafted by New Jersey Devils in 1985 NHL entry draft. Fourth Devils pick, 45th overall, third round.

JAY OCTEAU

Defense . . . 5'10" . . . 180 lbs. . . . Born, Providence, R.I., March 24, 1965 . . . Shoots right.

Year	Team	League	Games	G.	A.	Pts.	Pen.
1983-84—Boston Univ. (c)		H. East	27	1	6	7	20
1984-85—Boston Univ.		H. East	38	2	14	16	42
1985-86—Boston Univ. (d)		H. East	41	8	27	35	47
1986-87—Boston Univ.		H. East	37	5	23	28	40
1987-88—Flint Spirits		IHL	38	1	8	9	12
1987-88—New Haven Nighthawks		AHL	1	0	0	0	0

(c)—June, 1983—Drafted by New Jersey Devils in 1983 NHL entry draft. Seventh Devils pick, 171st overall, ninth round.
(d)—Named second-team All-America (East).

LYLE ODELEIN

Defense . . . 6' . . . 180 lbs. . . . Born, Quill Lake, Sask., July 21, 1968 . . . Shoots right . . . Brother of Selmar Odelein.

Year	Team	League	Games	G.	A.	Pts.	Pen.
1984-85—Regina Pat Canadians		Sask. Midget	26	12	13	25	30
1985-86—Moose Jaw Warriors (c)		WHL	67	9	37	46	117
1986-87—Moose Jaw Warriors		WHL	59	9	50	59	70
1987-88—Moose Jaw Warriors		WHL	63	15	43	58	166

(c)—June, 1986—Drafted as underage junior by Montreal Canadiens in 1986 NHL entry draft. Eighth Canadiens pick, 141st overall, seventh round.

SELMAR ODELEIN

Defense . . . 6' . . . 195 lbs. . . . Born, Quill Lake, Sask., April 11, 1966 . . . Shoots right . . . Brother of Lyle Odelein . . . (October, 1986)—Knee injury.

Year	Team	League	Games	G.	A.	Pts.	Pen.
1982-83—Regina Canadians		Sask. Midget	70	30	84	114	38
1983-84—Regina Pats (c)		WHL	71	9	42	51	45
1984-85—Regina Pats		WHL	64	24	35	59	121
1985-86—Regina Pats		WHL	36	13	28	41	57
1985-86—Edmonton Oilers		NHL	4	0	0	0	0
1986-87—Nova Scotia Oilers		AHL	2	0	1	1	2
1987-88—Nova Scotia Oilers		AHL	43	9	14	23	75
1987-88—Edmonton Oilers		NHL	12	0	2	2	33
NHL TOTALS			16	0	2	2	33

(c)—June, 1984—Drafted as underage junior by Edmonton Oilers in NHL entry draft. First Oilers pick, 21st overall, first round.

BILL O'DWYER

Center . . . 5'11" . . . 187 lbs. . . . Born, South Boston, Mass., January 25, 1960 . . . Shoots left . . . (October, 1985)—Injured jaw . . . (October, 1986)—Broken jaw . . . (March, 1988)—Strained right hip . . . (April, 1988)—Injured left knee.

Year	Team	League	Games	G.	A.	Pts.	Pen.
1978-79	Boston College	ECAC	30	9	30	39	14
1979-80	Boston College (b-c-d)	ECAC	33	20	22	42	22
1980-81	Boston College (b)	ECAC	31	20	20	40	6
1981-82	Boston College (b)	ECAC	30	15	26	41	10
1982-83	New Haven Nighthawks	AHL	77	24	23	47	29
1983-84	Los Angeles Kings	NHL	5	0	0	0	0
1983-84	New Haven Nighthawks	AHL	58	15	42	57	39
1984-85	New Haven Nighthawks	AHL	46	19	24	43	27
1984-85	Los Angeles Kings (e)	NHL	13	1	0	1	15
1985-86	New Haven Nighthawks	AHL	41	10	15	25	41
1986-87	New Haven Nighthawks	AHL	65	22	42	64	74
1987-88	Boston Bruins (f)	NHL	77	7	10	17	83
	NHL TOTALS		95	8	10	18	98

(c)—Named to second team All-New England Team (Division I).
(d)—June, 1980—Drafted by Los Angeles Kings in 1980 NHL entry draft. Ninth Kings pick, 157th overall, eighth round.
(e)—August, 1985—Signed by New York Rangers as a free agent.
(f)—July, 1987—Signed by Boston Bruins as a free agent.

JOHN ALEXANDER OGRODNICK

Left Wing . . . 6' . . . 190 lbs. . . . Born, Ottawa, Ont., June 20, 1959 . . . Shoots left . . . (February 26, 1984)—Fractured left wrist at Chicago . . . (January 21, 1986)—Missed three games with a sprained ankle . . . (October, 1986)—Sprained ankle . . . (December, 1987)—Ligaments damage and cracked bone in left instep . . . (February, 1988)—Bruised ribs.

Year	Team	League	Games	G.	A.	Pts.	Pen.
1976-77	Maple Ridge Bruins	BCJHL	67	54	56	110	63
1976-77	New Westminster Bruins	WCHL	14	2	4	6	0
1977-78	New Westminster Bruins (c)	WCHL	72	59	29	88	47
1978-79	New Westminster Bruins (d)	WHL	72	48	36	84	38
1979-80	Adirondack Red Wings	AHL	39	13	20	33	21
1979-80	Detroit Red Wings	NHL	41	8	24	32	8
1980-81	Detroit Red Wings	NHL	80	35	35	70	14
1981-82	Detroit Red Wings	NHL	80	28	26	54	28
1982-83	Detroit Red Wings	NHL	80	41	44	85	30
1983-84	Detroit Red Wings	NHL	64	42	36	78	14
1984-85	Detroit Red Wings (a)	NHL	79	55	50	105	30
1985-86	Detroit Red Wings	NHL	76	38	32	70	18
1986-87	Detroit Red Wings (e)	NHL	39	12	28	40	6
1986-87	Quebec Nordiques	NHL	32	11	16	27	4
1987-88	New York Rangers (f)	NHL	64	22	32	54	16
	NHL TOTALS		635	292	323	615	168

(c)—Shared Rookie of Year award in WCHL with Keith Brown.
(d)—August, 1979—Drafted by Detroit Red Wings in 1979 entry draft. Fourth Red Wings pick, 66th overall, fourth round.
(e)—January, 1987—Traded with Doug Shedden and Basil McRae by Detroit Red Wings to Quebec Nordiques for Brent Ashton, Mark Kumpel and Gilbert Delorme.
(f)—September, 1987—Traded with David Shaw by Quebec Nordiques to New York Rangers for Jeff Jackson and Terry Carkner.

ROGER OHMAN

Defense . . . 6'3" . . . 215 lbs. . . . Born, Stockholm, Sweden, June 5, 1967 . . . Shoots left . . . Also plays Left Wing.

Year	Team	League	Games	G.	A.	Pts.	Pen.
1983-84	Leksands	Sweden	36	31	21	52	80
1984-85	Leksands (c)	Sweden	40	32	44	76	60
1985-86	Leksands	Sweden	...	...	...	...	...
1986-87	Frolunda	Sweden	34	3	8	11	26
1987-88	Moncton Golden Flames	AHL	67	11	17	28	38

(c)—June, 1985—Drafted by Winnipeg Jets in 1985 NHL entry draft. Second Jets pick, 39th overall, second round.

JANNE OJANEN

Center . . . 6'2" . . . 190 lbs. . . . Born, Tampere, Finland, April 9, 1968 . . . Shoots left.

Year	Team	League	Games	G.	A.	Pts.	Pen.
1985-86	Tappara (c)	Finland	14	5	17	22	...
1986-87	Tappara	Finland	...	...	...	...	...
1987-88	Tappara	Finland	44	21	31	52	30

(c)—June, 1986—Drafted by New Jersey Devils in 1984 NHL entry draft. Third Devils pick, 45th overall, third round.

TODD OKERLUND

Right Wing . . . 6' . . . 195 lbs. . . . Born, St. Paul, Minn., September 6, 1964 . . . Shoots right . . . (October 18, 1986)—Tore medial and anterior ligaments in right knee vs. Univ. Minn./Duluth. He finished the game but required surgery the next day.

Year	Team	League	Games	G.	A.	Pts.	Pen.
1981-82	Burnsville H.S. (c)	Minn. H.S.	25	12	20	32	8
1982-83	Burnsville H.S.	Minn. H.S.	...	...	...	...	...
1983-84	Univ. of Minnesota	WCHA	34	11	20	31	18
1984-85	Univ. of Minnesota	WCHA	47	16	27	43	80
1985-86	Univ. of Minnesota	WCHA	48	17	32	49	58
1986-87	Univ. of Minnesota	WCHA	4	0	7	7	0
1987-88	New York Islanders	NHL	4	0	0	0	2
1987-88	Springfield Indians	AHL	13	2	1	3	9
1987-88	U.S. Olympic Team	Int'l	42	10	16	26	...
	NHL TOTALS		4	0	0	0	2

(c)—June, 1982—Drafted by New York Islanders in 1982 NHL entry draft. Eighth Islanders pick, 168th overall, eighth round.

FREDRIK OLAUSSON

Defense . . . 6'2" . . . 200 lbs. . . . Born, Vaxsjo, Sweden, October 5, 1966 . . . Shoots right . . . (August, 1987)—Dislocated shoulder in training for Canada Cup tournament . . . (November, 1987)—Shoulder surgery.

Year	Team	League	Games	G.	A.	Pts.	Pen.
1983-84	Nybro	Sweden	28	8	14	22	32
1984-85	Farjestad (c)	Sweden	34	6	12	18	24
1985-86	Farjestad	Sweden	33	5	12	17	14
1986-87	Winnipeg Jets	NHL	72	7	29	36	24
1987-88	Winnipeg Jets	NHL	38	5	10	15	18
	NHL TOTALS		110	12	39	51	42

(c)—June, 1985—Drafted by Winnipeg Jets in NHL entry draft. Fourth Jets pick, 81st overall, fourth round.

ED OLCZYK

Right Wing . . . 6'1" . . . 195 lbs. . . . Born, Chicago, Ill., August 16, 1966 . . . Shoots left . . . (September, 1984)—Hyperextended knee during training camp . . . (December 16, 1984)—Broken bone in left foot when hit by shot of Doug Wilson vs. Minnesota . . . Also plays Center.

Year	Team	League	Games	G.	A.	Pts.	Pen.
1983-84	U.S. National Team	Int'l	56	19	40	59	36
1983-84	U.S. Olympic Team (c)	Int'l	6	2	7	9	0
1984-85	Chicago Black Hawks	NHL	70	20	30	50	67
1985-86	Chicago Black Hawks	NHL	79	29	50	79	47
1986-87	Chicago Black Hawks (d)	NHL	79	16	35	51	119
1987-88	Toronto Maple Leafs	NHL	80	42	33	75	55
	NHL TOTALS		308	107	148	255	288

(c)—June, 1984—Drafted by Chicago Black Hawks in NHL entry draft. First Black Hawks pick, 3rd overall, first round. (Black Hawks traded Rich Preston and Don Dietrich to New Jersey, who had the second overall pick, not to draft Olczyk. Devils also sent Bob MacMillan to Chicago in the deal).

(d)—September, 1987—Traded with Al Secord by Chicago Black Hawks to Toronto Maple Leafs for Rick Vaive, Steve Thomas and Bob McGill.

DEVON OLENIUK

Defense . . . 6'1" . . . 186 lbs. . . . Born, Kinstin, Sask., March 28, 1968 . . . Shoots left.

Year	Team	League	Games	G.	A.	Pts.	Pen.
1984-85	Saskatoon Blades	WHL	71	1	4	5	37
1985-86	Saskatoon Blades	WHL	70	4	12	16	104
1986-87	Kamloops Blazers (c)	WHL	55	2	10	12	54
1987-88	Kamloops Blazers	WHL	69	3	11	14	103

(c)—June, 1987—Drafted by Washington Capitals in 1987 NHL entry draft. Sixth Capitals pick, 141st overall, seventh round.

DARRYL OLSEN

Defense . . . 6' . . . 180 lbs. . . . Born, Calgary, Alta., October 7, 1966 . . . Shoots left.

Year	Team	League	Games	G.	A.	Pts.	Pen.
1984-85	St. Albert Saints (c)	AJHL	57	19	48	67	77
1985-86	Univ. of Northern Michigan	WCHA	37	5	20	25	46
1986-87	Northern Michigan University	WCHA	37	5	20	25	96
1987-88	Northern Michigan University	WCHA	35	11	20	31	59

(c)—June, 1985—Drafted by Calgary Flames in 1985 NHL entry draft. Tenth Flames pick, 185th overall, ninth round.

MARK OLSEN

Defense . . . 6'3" . . . 215 lbs. . . . Born, Irvine, Tex., September 6, 1966 . . . Shoots left.

Year	Team	League	Games	G.	A.	Pts.	Pen.
1985-86	Colorado College (c)	WCHA	39	2	4	6	48
1986-87	Colorado College	WCHA	42	2	4	6	38
1987-88	Colorado College	WCHA	36	2	11	13	81

(c)—June, 1986—Drafted by Calgary Flames in 1986 NHL entry draft. Seventh Flames pick, 163rd overall, eighth round.

GATES ORLANDO

Center . . . 5'8" . . . 175 lbs. . . . Born, LaSalle, Que., November 13, 1962 . . . Shoots right . . . (February, 1985)—Sprained right knee.

Year	Team	League	Games	G.	A.	Pts.	Pen.
1980-81	Providence College (c)	ECAC	31	24	32	56	45
1981-82	Providence College	ECAC	28	18	18	36	31
1982-83	Providence College	ECAC	40	30	39	69	32
1983-84	Providence College	ECAC	34	23	30	53	52
1983-84	Rochester Americans	AHL	11	8	7	15	2
1984-85	Rochester Americans	AHL	49	26	30	56	62
1984-85	Buffalo Sabres	NHL	11	3	6	9	6
1985-86	Rochester Americans	AHL	3	4	0	4	10
1985-86	Buffalo Sabres	NHL	61	13	12	25	29
1986-87	Rochester Americans	AHL	44	22	42	64	42
1986-87	Buffalo Sabres	NHL	27	2	8	10	16
1987-88	Rochester Americans	AHL	13	4	13	17	18
	NHL TOTALS		99	18	26	44	51

(c)—Drafted by Buffalo Sabres as underage player in 1981 NHL entry draft. Tenth Sabres pick, 164th overall, eighth round.

MIKE ORN

Center . . . 5'11" . . . 170 lbs. . . . Born, Moorehead, Minn., April 26, 1966 . . . Shoots left.

Year	Team	League	Games	G.	A.	Pts.	Pen.
1984-85	Miami Univ. of Ohio (c)	CCHA	40	13	15	28	52
1985-86	Miami Univ. of Ohio	CCHA	31	13	19	32	58
1986-87	Miami Univ. of Ohio	CCHA	36	22	23	45	70
1987-88	Miami Univ. of Ohio	CCHA	31	28	15	43	34

(c)—June, 1984—Drafted by Minnesota North Stars in 1984 NHL entry draft. Tenth North Stars pick, 201st overall, 10th round.

KEITH OSBORNE

Right Wing . . . 6'1" . . . 181 lbs. . . . Born, Toronto, Ont., April 2, 1969 . . . Shoots right . . . (September, 1987)—Broken wrist . . . (October, 1987)—Broken ankle.

Year	Team	League	Games	G.	A.	Pts.	Pen.
1985-86	Toronto Red Wings Midget	MTHL	42	48	63	111	36
1986-87	North Bay Centennials (c)	OHL	61	34	55	89	31
1987-88	North Bay Centennials	OHL	30	14	22	36	20

(c)—June, 1987—Drafted as underage junior by St. Louis Blues in 1987 NHL entry draft. First Blues pick, 12th overall, first round.

MARK ANATOLE OSBORNE

Left Wing . . . 6'2" . . . 200 lbs. . . . Born, Toronto, Ont., August 13, 1961 . . . Shoots left . . . (October, 1984)—Hip Injury . . . (February 12, 1986)—Sprained ankle vs. Vancouver and missed 12 games . . . (February, 1987)—Skate cut behind left knee . . . (April, 1988)—Separated left shoulder.

Year	Team	League	Games	G.	A.	Pts.	Pen.
1978-79—Niagara Falls Flyers		OMJHL	62	17	25	42	53
1979-80—Niagara Falls Flyers (c)		OMJHL	52	10	33	43	104
1980-81—Niagara Falls Flyers		OHL	54	39	41	80	140
1980-81—Adirondack Red Wings (d)		AHL	....	...	....	....	....
1981-82—Detroit Red Wings		NHL	80	26	41	67	61
1982-83—Detroit Red Wings (e)		NHL	80	19	24	43	83
1983-84—New York Rangers		NHL	73	23	28	51	88
1984-85—New York Rangers		NHL	23	4	4	8	33
1985-86—New York Rangers		NHL	62	16	24	40	80
1986-87—New York Rangers (f)		NHL	58	17	15	32	101
1986-87—Toronto Maple Leafs		NHL	16	5	10	15	12
1987-88—Toronto Maple Leafs		NHL	79	23	37	60	102
NHL TOTALS			471	133	183	316	560

(c)—June, 1980—Drafted as underage junior by Detroit Red Wings in 1980 NHL entry draft. Second Red Wings pick, 46th overall, third round.

(d)—No regular season record. Played 13 playoff games.

(e)—June, 1983—Traded by Detroit Red Wings with Willie Huber and Mike Blaisdell to New York Rangers for Ron Duguay, Eddie Mio and Ed Johnstone.

(f)—March, 1987—Traded by New York Rangers to Toronto Maple Leafs for a third-round 1989 draft pick.

MIKE O'TOOLE

Right Wing . . . 6'1" . . . 180 lbs. . . . Born, Toronto, Ont., July 2, 1966 . . . Shoots right.

Year	Team	League	Games	G.	A.	Pts.	Pen.
1986-87—Michigan State Univ. (c)		CCHA	43	2	13	15	74
1987-88—Michigan State Univ.		CCHA	44	12	10	22	76

(c)—June, 1988—Drafted by St. Louis Blues in 1988 NHL entry draft. Sixth Blues pick, 115th overall, sixth overall.

JOEL OTTO

Center . . . 6'4" . . . 220 lbs. . . . Born, St. Cloud, Minn., October 29, 1961 . . . Shoots right . . . (March 10, 1987)—Torn cartilage in right knee at Washington . . . (October 8, 1987)— Strained right knee ligaments in season opening game vs. Detroit.

Year	Team	League	Games	G.	A.	Pts.	Pen.
1980-81—Bemidji State Univ.		NCAA-II	23	5	11	16	10
1981-82—Bemidji State Univ.		NCAA-II	31	19	33	52	24
1982-83—Bemidji State Univ.		NCAA-II	37	33	28	61	68
1983-84—Bemidji State Univ. (c)		NCAA-II	31	32	43	75	32
1984-85—Moncton Golden Flames		AHL	56	27	36	63	89
1984-85—Calgary Flames		NHL	17	4	8	12	20
1985-86—Calgary Flames		NHL	79	25	34	59	188
1986-87—Calgary Flames		NHL	68	19	31	50	185
1987-88—Calgary Flames		NHL	62	13	39	52	194
NHL TOTALS			226	61	112	173	587

(c)—September, 1984—Signed by Calgary Flames as a free agent.

GORDON PADDOCK

Defense . . . 6' . . . 180 lbs. . . . Born, Hamiota, Man., February 15, 1964 . . . Shoots right . . . Brother of John Paddock.

Year	Team	League	Games	G.	A.	Pts.	Pen.
1981-82—Saskatoon Jays		SJHL	59	8	21	29	232
1982-83—Saskatoon Blades		WHL	67	4	25	29	158
1983-84—Brandon Wheat Kings		WHL	72	14	37	51	151
1984-85—Indianapolis Checkers		IHL	65	10	21	31	92
1984-85—Springfield Indians		AHL	12	0	2	2	24
1985-86—Indianapolis Checkers (c)		IHL	11	1	1	2	11
1985-86—Muskegon Lumberjacks		IHL	47	1	20	21	87
1985-86—Springfield Indians		AHL	20	1	1	2	52
1986-87—Springfield Indians		AHL	78	6	11	17	127
1987-88—Springfield Indians		AHL	74	8	26	34	127

(c)—November, 1985—Traded by Indianapolis Checkers to Muskegon Lumberjacks for Don Murdoch.

JIM PAEK

Defense . . . 6' . . . 188 lbs. . . . Born, Weston, Ont., April 7, 1967 . . . Shoots left . . . (November 2, 1986)—Suspended for two games by OHL for being involved in a bench clearing incident vs. Peterborough.

Year	Team	League	Games	G.	A.	Pts.	Pen.
1983-84—St. Michael's Midget		OHA	39	8	26	34	21
1984-85—Oshawa Generals (c)		OHL	54	2	13	15	57
1985-86—Oshawa Generals		OHL	64	5	21	26	122
1986-87—Oshawa Generals		OHL	57	5	17	22	75
1987-88—Muskegon Lumberjacks		IHL	82	7	52	59	141

(c)—June, 1985—Drafted as underage junior by Pittsburgh Penguins in 1985 NHL entry draft. Ninth Penguins pick, 170th overall, ninth round.

WILFRED (WILF) PAIEMENT JR.

Right Wing . . . 6'1" . . . 205 lbs. . . . Born, Earlton, Ont., October 16, 1955 . . . Shoots right . . . Brother of Rosaire Paiement . . . Missed final part of 1975-76 season with thigh injury . . . Suspended for 15 games by NHL for stick swinging incident in 1978-79 season . . . (October 12, 1980)—Credited with scoring NHL's 100,000th regular season goal in 4-2 win at Philadelphia into an empty net . . . (March 27, 1982)—Sprained right knee at Montreal . . . (September 26, 1985)—Tore knee ligaments in training camp and missed first six games of season . . . (February 8, 1986)—Fractured left foot in first game with N.Y. Rangers at Boston and missed 19 games . . . (February 28, 1987)—Sprained right knee at Boston that required surgery . . . (January 18, 1988)—Strained left knee ligaments in IHL game.

Year	Team	League	Games	G.	A.	Pts.	Pen.
1971-72—Niagara Falls Flyers		Jr."A" OHA	34	6	13	19	74
1972-73—St. Cath. Black Hawks (c)		Jr."A" OHA	61	18	27	45	173
1973-74—St. Cath. Black Hawks (a-d)		Jr."A" OHA	70	50	73	123	134
1974-75—Kansas City Scouts		NHL	78	26	13	39	101
1975-76—Kansas City Scouts		NHL	57	21	22	43	121
1976-77—Colorado Rockies		NHL	78	41	40	81	101
1977-78—Colorado Rockies		NHL	80	31	56	87	114
1978-79—Colorado Rockies		NHL	65	24	36	60	80
1979-80—Colorado Rockies (e)		NHL	34	10	16	26	41
1979-80—Toronto Maple Leafs		NHL	41	20	28	48	72
1980-81—Toronto Maple Leafs		NHL	77	40	57	97	145
1981-82—Toronto Maple Leafs (f)		NHL	69	18	40	58	203
1981-82—Quebec Nordiques		NHL	8	7	6	13	18
1982-83—Quebec Nordiques		NHL	80	26	38	64	170
1983-84—Quebec Nordiques		NHL	80	39	37	76	121
1984-85—Quebec Nordiques		NHL	68	23	28	51	165
1985-86—Quebec Nordiques (g)		NHL	44	7	12	19	145
1985-86—New York Rangers		NHL	8	1	6	7	13
1986-87—Buffalo Sabres (h-i)		NHL	56	20	17	37	108
1987-88—Muskegon Lumberjacks		IHL	28	17	18	35	52
1987-88—Pittsburgh Penguins		NHL	23	2	6	8	39
NHL TOTALS			946	356	458	814	1757

(c)—Traded to St. Catharines Black Hawks by Sudbury Wolves for midget draft choice.

(d)—Drafted from St. Catharines Black Hawks by Kansas City Scouts in first round of 1974 amateur draft.

(e)—December, 1979—Traded with Pat Hickey by Colorado Rockies to Toronto Maple Leafs for Lanny McDonald and Joel Quenneville.

(f)—March, 1982—Traded by Toronto Maple Leafs to Quebec Nordiques for Miroslav Frycer and seventh-round 1982 entry draft pick (Jeff Triano).

(g)—February, 1986—Traded by Quebec Nordiques to New York Rangers for Stephen Patrick.

(h)—October, 1986—Claimed by Buffalo Sabres in 1986 NHL waiver draft.

(i)—July, 1987—Signed by Pittsburgh Penguins as a free agent.

SCOTT PALUCH

Defense . . . 6'3" . . . 185 lbs. . . . Born, Chicago, III., March 9, 1966 . . . Shoots left . . . Named to second all-star team at 1986 IIHF World Junior Championships as a member of Team USA.

Year	Team	League	Games	G.	A.	Pts.	Pen.
1983-84—Chicago Jets (c)		CJHL	50	44	46	90	42
1984-85—Bowling Green University		CCHA	42	11	25	36	64
1985-86—Bowling Green University		CCHA	34	10	11	21	44
1986-87—Bowling Green University		CCHA	45	13	38	51	88
1987-88—Bowling Green University (d)		CCHA	44	14	47	61	88

(c)—June, 1984—Drafted by St. Louis Blues in NHL entry draft. Seventh Blues pick, 92nd overall, fifth round.

(d)—Named first team All-America (West).

DONALD PANCOE

Defense . . . 6'1" . . . 190 lbs. . . . Born, Brantford, Ont., February 23, 1969 . . . Shoots left . . . Also plays Left Wing.

Year	Team	League	Games	G.	A.	Pts.	Pen.
1984-85—Cambridge Winter Hawks		OHA	32	2	14	16	62
1985-86—Hamilton Steelhawks		OHL	57	1	11	12	108
1986-87—Hamilton Steelhawks		OHL	44	4	8	12	120
1987-88—Hamilton Steelhawks (c)		OHL	60	2	12	14	144

(c)—June, 1988—Drafted by Pittsburgh Penguins in 1988 NHL entry draft. Ninth Penguins pick, 193rd overall, 10th round.

RYAN PARDOSKI

Left Wing . . . 6' . . . 165 lbs. . . . Born, Calgary, Alta., August 19, 1968 . . . Shoots left.

Year	Team	League	Games	G.	A.	Pts.	Pen.
1985-86—Calgary Canucks (c)		AJHL	50	16	27	43	61
1986-87—University of Michigan		CCHA	39	4	9	13	26
1987-88—University of Michigan		CCHA	31	4	9	13	36

(c)—June, 1986—Drafted by New Jersey Devils in 1986 NHL entry draft. Eighth Devils pick, 150th overall, eighth round.

RUSSELL L. PARENT

Defense . . . 5'9" . . . 180 lbs. . . . Born, Winnipeg, Manitoba, May 6, 1968 . . . Shoots left . . . (November, 1987)—Broken kneecap.

Year	Team	League	Games	G.	A.	Pts.	Pen.
1985-86—South Winnipeg Blues (c)		MJHL	47	16	65	81	106
1986-87—Univ. of North Dakota		WCHA	47	2	17	19	50
1987-88—Univ. of North Dakota		WCHA	30	4	20	24	38

(c)—June, 1986—Drafted by New York Rangers in 1986 NHL entry draft. Eleventh Rangers pick, 219th overall, 11th round.

JEFF PARKER

Right Wing . . . 6'3" . . . 198 lbs. . . . Born, St. Paul, Minn., September 7, 1964 . . . Shoots right . . . Brother of John Parker . . . (December, 1988)—Missed 28 games with a back injury.

Year	Team	League	Games	G.	A.	Pts.	Pen.
1983-84—Michigan State University (c)		CCHA	44	8	13	21	82
1984-85—Michigan State University		CCHA	42	10	12	22	85
1985-86—Michigan State University		CCHA	41	15	20	35	88
1986-87—Rochester Americans		AHL	54	14	8	22	75
1986-87—Buffalo Sabres		NHL	15	3	3	6	7
1987-88—Buffalo Sabres		NHL	4	0	2	2	2
1987-88—Rochester Americans		AHL	34	13	31	44	60
NHL TOTALS			19	3	5	8	9

(c)—June, 1982—Drafted by Buffalo Sabres in 1982 NHL entry draft. Ninth Sabres pick, 111th overall, sixth round.

DUSAN PASEK

Center . . . 6' . . . 187 lbs. . . . Born, Czechoslovakia, September 7, 1960 . . . Shoots right.

Year	Team	League	Games	G.	A.	Pts.	Pen.
1987-88—Bratislava (c)		Czech.	28	13	10	23	..

(c)—June, 1982—Drafted by Minnesota North Stars in NHL entry draft. Fourth North Stars pick, 81st overall, fourth round.

DAVE PASIN

Right Wing . . . 6'1" . . . 195 lbs. . . . Born, Edmonton, Alta., July 8, 1966 . . . Shoots right . . . (November 25, 1985)—Missed five games with sprained left knee . . . (November, 1987)—Injured eye during Maine Mariners practice when struck by a puck.

Year	Team	League	Games	G.	A.	Pts.	Pen.
1982-83—Prince Albert Raiders		WHL	62	40	42	82	48
1983-84—Prince Albert Raiders (b-c)		WHL	71	68	54	122	68
1984-85—Prince Albert Raiders (b)		WHL	65	64	52	116	88
1985-86—Boston Bruins		NHL	71	18	19	37	50
1986-87—Moncton Golden Flames		AHL	66	27	25	52	47
1987-88—Maine Mariners		AHL	30	8	14	22	39
NHL TOTALS			71	18	19	37	50

(c)—June, 1984—Drafted as underage junior by Boston Bruins in 1984 NHL entry draft. First Bruins pick, 19th overall, first round.

GREGORY STEPHEN PASLAWSKI

Right Wing . . . 5'11" . . . 195 lbs. . . . Born, Kindersley, Sask., August 25, 1961 . . . Shoots right

... (February 20, 1986)—Injured knee at N.Y. Rangers ... (December, 1986)—Injured knee ... (October, 1987)—Pinched nerve in left leg ... (November, 1987)—Disc surgery.

Year	Team	League	Games	G.	A.	Pts.	Pen.
1980-81—Prince Albert Raiders		SJHL	59	55	60	115	106
1981-82—Nova Scotia Voyageurs (c)		AHL	43	15	11	26	31
1982-83—Nova Scotia Voyageurs		AHL	75	46	42	88	32
1983-84—Montreal Canadiens (d)		NHL	26	1	4	5	4
1983-84—St. Louis Blues		NHL	34	8	6	14	7
1984-85—St. Louis Blues		NHL	72	22	20	42	21
1985-86—St. Louis Blues		NHL	56	22	11	33	18
1986-87—St. Louis Blues		NHL	76	29	35	64	27
1987-88—St. Louis Blues		NHL	17	2	1	3	4
NHL TOTALS			281	84	77	161	91

(c)—January, 1982—Signed by Montreal Canadiens as a free agent.
(d)—December, 1983—Traded with Doug Wickenheiser and Gilbert Delorme by Montreal Canadiens to St. Louis Blues for Perry Turnbull.

JOE ANDREW PATERSON

Left Wing and Center ... 6'1" ... 208 lbs. ... Born, Toronto, Ont., June 25, 1960 ... Shoots left ... (October, 1982)—Pulled groin muscle ... (October, 1987)—Pulled groin.

Year	Team	League	Games	G.	A.	Pts.	Pen.
1977-78—London Knights		OMJHL	68	17	16	33	100
1978-79—London Knights (c)		OMJHL	60	22	19	41	158
1979-80—London Knights		OMJHL	65	21	50	71	156
1979-80—Kalamazoo Wings		IHL	4	1	2	3	2
1980-81—Detroit Red Wings		NHL	38	2	5	7	53
1980-81—Adirondack Red Wings		AHL	39	9	16	25	68
1981-82—Adirondack Red Wings		AHL	74	22	28	50	132
1981-82—Detroit Red Wings		NHL	3	0	0	0	0
1982-83—Adirondack Red Wings		AHL	36	11	10	21	85
1982-83—Detroit Red Wings		NHL	33	2	1	3	14
1983-84—Detroit Red Wings		NHL	41	2	5	7	148
1983-84—Adirondack Red Wings (d)		AHL	20	10	15	25	43
1984-85—Hershey Bears		AHL	67	26	27	53	173
1984-85—Philadelphia Flyers		NHL	6	0	0	0	31
1985-86—Hershey Bears		AHL	20	5	10	15	68
1985-86—Philadelphia Flyers (e)		NHL	5	0	0	0	12
1985-86—Los Angeles Kings		NHL	47	9	18	27	153
1986-87—Los Angeles Kings		NHL	45	2	1	3	158
1987-88—Los Angeles Kings (f)		NHL	32	1	3	4	113
1987-88—New York Rangers		NHL	21	1	3	4	65
NHL TOTALS			271	19	36	55	747

(c)—August, 1979—Drafted by Detroit Red Wings as underage junior in 1979 NHL entry draft. Fifth Red Wings pick, 87th overall, fifth round.
(d)—October, 1984—Traded with Murray Craven by Detroit Red Wings to Philadelphia Flyers for Darryl Sittler.
(e)—December, 1985—Traded by Philadelphia Flyers to Los Angeles Kings for future considerations.
(f)—January, 1988—Traded by Los Angeles Kings to New York Rangers for Mike Siltala and Gord Walker.

MARK PATERSON

Defense ... 6' ... 185 lbs. ... Born, Ottawa, Ont., February 22, 1964 ... Shoots left ... (September, 1984)—Missed training camp and early part of season with mononucleosis ... (September 29, 1986)—Suspended by Hartford Whalers for failure to report to Binghamton Whalers.

Year	Team	League	Games	G.	A.	Pts.	Pen.
1980-81—Nepean Raiders		OPJHL	50	6	13	19	98
1981-82—Ottawa 67's (c)		OHL	64	4	14	18	66
1982-83—Ottawa 67's		OHL	57	7	14	21	140
1982-83—Hartford Whalers		NHL	2	0	0	0	0
1983-84—Ottawa 67's		OHL	45	8	16	24	114
1983-84—Hartford Whalers		NHL	9	2	0	2	4
1984-85—Binghamton Whalers		AHL	44	2	18	20	74
1984-85—Hartford Whalers		NHL	13	1	3	4	24
1985-86—Hartford Whalers		NHL	5	0	0	0	5
1985-86—Binghamton Whalers		AHL	67	2	16	18	121
1986-87—Moncton Golden Flames (d)		AHL	70	6	21	27	112
1987-88—Saginaw Hawks		IHL	23	1	5	6	55
NHL TOTALS			29	3	3	6	33

(c)—June, 1982—Drafted as underage junior by Hartford Whalers in 1982 NHL entry draft. Second Whalers pick, 35th overall, second round.

(d)—October, 1986—Traded by Hartford Whalers to Calgary Flames for Yves Courteau.

RICHARD DAVID (RICK) PATERSON

Center . . . 5'10" . . . 185 lbs. . . . Born, Kingston, Ont., February 10, 1958 . . . Shoots right . . . (January, 1981)—Chipped ankle bone . . . Also plays Right Wing.

Year	Team	League	Games	G.	A.	Pts.	Pen.
1974-75—Cornwall Royals		QJHL	68	18	20	38	50
1975-76—Cornwall Royals		QJHL	71	20	60	80	59
1976-77—Cornwall Royals		QJHL	72	31	63	94	90
1977-78—Cornwall Royals (c)		QJHL	71	58	80	138	105
1978-79—New Brunswick Hawks		AHL	74	21	19	40	30
1979-80—Chicago Black Hawks		NHL	11	0	2	2	0
1979-80—New Brunswick Hawks		AHL	55	22	30	52	18
1980-81—Chicago Black Hawks		NHL	49	8	2	10	18
1980-81—New Brunswick Hawks		CHL	21	7	8	15	6
1981-82—New Brunswick Hawks		AHL	30	8	16	24	45
1981-82—Chicago Black Hawks		NHL	48	4	7	11	8
1982-83—Chicago Black Hawks		NHL	79	14	9	23	14
1983-84—Chicago Black Hawks		NHL	72	7	6	13	41
1984-85—Chicago Black Hawks		NHL	79	7	12	19	25
1985-86—Chicago Black Hawks		NHL	70	9	3	12	24
1986-87—Nova Scotia Oilers		AHL	31	5	7	12	2
1986-87—Chicago Black Hawks		NHL	22	1	2	3	6
1987-88—Saginaw Hawks		IHL	82	19	26	45	83
NHL TOTALS			430	50	43	93	136

(c)—Drafted from Cornwall Royals by Chicago Black Hawks in third round of 1978 amateur draft.

JAMES PATRICK

Defense . . . 6'2" . . . 185 lbs. . . . Born, Winnipeg, Man., June 14, 1963 . . . Shoots right . . . Brother of Steve Patrick . . . Member of 1984 Canadian Olympic Team . . . (October, 1984)—Groin injury . . . (October 24, 1985)—Pinched nerve in neck and missed two games . . . (December 15, 1985)—Pinched nerve vs. Pittsburgh . . . (March, 1988)—Strained left knee ligaments.

Year	Team	League	Games	G.	A.	Pts.	Pen.
1980-81—Prince Albert Raiders (a-c-d)		SJHL	59	21	61	82	162
1981-82—Univ. of North Dakota (b-e)		WCHA	42	5	24	29	26
1982-83—Univ. of North Dakota		WCHA	36	12	36	48	29
1983-84—Canadian Olympic Team		Int'l	63	7	24	31	52
1983-84—New York Rangers		NHL	12	1	7	8	2
1984-85—New York Rangers		NHL	75	8	28	36	71
1985-86—New York Rangers		NHL	75	14	29	43	88
1986-87—New York Rangers		NHL	78	10	45	55	62
1987-88—New York Rangers		NHL	70	17	45	62	52
NHL TOTALS			310	50	154	204	275

(c)—June, 1981—Drafted by New York Rangers as underage player in 1981 NHL entry draft. First Rangers pick, ninth overall, first round.

(d)—Named Chapstick Player-of-the-Year as top Tier II Canadian Junior Player.

(e)—Named WCHA Rookie-of-the-Year.

COLIN PATTERSON

Right Wing . . . 6'2" . . . 195 lbs. . . . Born, Rexdale, Ont., May 11, 1960 . . . Shoots right . . . (March 14, 1984)—Shoulder injury . . . (January, 1985)—Torn knee ligaments . . . (October, 1987)—Pulled hamstring . . . (December, 1987)—Sprained ankle.

Year	Team	League	Games	G.	A.	Pts.	Pen.
1980-81—Clarkson College		ECAC	34	20	31	51	8
1981-82—Clarkson College		ECAC	35	21	31	52	32
1982-83—Clarkson College (b)		ECAC	31	23	29	52	30
1982-83—Colorado Flames (c)		CHL	7	1	1	2	0
1983-84—Colorado Flames		CHL	6	2	3	5	9
1983-84—Calgary Flames		NHL	56	13	14	27	15
1984-85—Calgary Flames		NHL	57	22	21	43	5
1985-86—Calgary Flames		NHL	61	14	13	27	22
1986-87—Calgary Flames		NHL	68	13	14	27	41
1987-88—Calgary Flames		NHL	39	7	11	18	28
NHL TOTALS			281	69	73	142	111

(c)—March, 1983—Signed by Calgary Flames as a free agent.

JAMES PETER PAVESE

Defense . . . 6'2" . . . 204 lbs. . . . Born, New York, N.Y., June 8, 1962 . . . Shoots left . . . (October, 1981)—Infected hand requiring hospitalization . . . (December 10, 1985)— Sprained ankle vs. Edmonton . . . (April, 1987)—Sore knee . . . .(November, 1987)—Low grade viral infection . . . (May, 1988)—Hospitalized with infected elbow.

Year	Team	League	Games	G.	A.	Pts.	Pen.
1976-77—Suffolk Royals (c)		NYMJHL	32	6	31	37	32
1977-78—Suffolk Royals		NYMJHL	34	18	40	58	102
1978-79—Peterborough Petes		OMJHL	16	1	1	2	22
1979-80—Kitchener Rangers (d)		OMJHL	68	10	26	36	206
1980-81—Kitchener Rangers (e)		OHL	19	3	12	15	93
1980-81—Sault Ste. Marie Greyhounds		OHL	43	3	25	28	127
1981-82—Sault Ste. Marie Greyhounds		OHL	26	4	21	25	110
1981-82—Salt Lake Golden Eagles (f)		CHL	....	...	....	....	....
1981-82—St. Louis Blues		NHL	42	2	9	11	101
1982-83—Salt Lake Golden Eagles		CHL	36	5	6	11	165
1982-83—St. Louis Blues		NHL	24	0	2	2	45
1983-84—Montana Magic		CHL	47	1	19	20	147
1983-84—St. Louis Blues		NHL	4	0	1	1	19
1984-85—St. Louis Blues		NHL	51	2	5	7	69
1985-86—St. Louis Blues		NHL	69	4	7	11	116
1986-87—St. Louis Blues		NHL	69	2	9	11	127
1987-88—St. Louis Blues (g)		NHL	4	0	1	1	8
1987-88—New York Rangers (h)		NHL	14	0	1	1	48
1987-88—Detroit Red Wings		NHL	7	0	3	3	21
1987-88—Colorado Rangers		IHL	1	0	0	0	2
NHL TOTALS			**284**	**10**	**38**	**48**	**548**

(c)—Named co-winner of Most Valuable Defenseman award (Shared award with Tom Matthews)

(d)—June, 1980—Drafted as underage junior by St. Louis Blues in 1980 NHL entry draft. Second Blues pick, 54th overall, third round.

(e)—December, 1980—Traded by Kitchener Rangers with Rick Morrocco to Sault Ste. Marie Greyhounds for Scott Clements, Bob Hicks and Mario Michieli.

(f)—No regular-season record. Played one playoff game.

(g)—October, 1987—Traded by St. Louis Blues to New York Rangers for the St. Louis Blues 1989 draft pick that had been sent to the Rangers as part of the Bruce Bell trade.

(h)—March, 1988—Traded by New York Rangers to Detroit Red Wings for future considerations.

KENT PAYNTER

Defense . . . 6' . . . 186 lbs. . . . Born, Summerside, P.E.I., April 27, 1965 . . . Shoots left.

Year	Team	League	Games	G.	A.	Pts.	Pen.
1981-82—Western Capitals		P.E.I.JHL	35	7	23	30	66
1982-83—Kitchener Rangers (c)		OHL	65	4	11	15	97
1983-84—Kitchener Rangers		OHL	65	9	27	36	94
1984-85—Kitchener Rangers		OHL	58	7	28	35	93
1985-86—Nova Scotia Oilers		AHL	23	1	2	3	36
1985-86—Saginaw Generals		IHL	4	0	1	1	2
1986-87—Nova Scotia Oilers		AHL	66	2	6	8	57
1987-88—Saginaw Hawks		IHL	74	8	20	28	141

(c)—June, 1983—Drafted by Chicago Black Hawks as underage junior in 1983 NHL entry draft. Ninth Black Hawks pick, 159th overall, eighth round.

SCOTT PEARSON

Left Wing . . . 6'1" . . . 205 lbs. . . . Born, Cornwall, Ont., December 19, 1969 . . . Shoots left . . . (May, 1988)—Surgery to left wrist.

Year	Team	League	Games	G.	A.	Pts.	Pen.
1984-85—Cornwall Midgets		OHA	60	40	40	80	60
1985-86—Kingston Canadians		OHL	63	16	23	39	56
1986-87—Kingston Canadians		OHL	62	30	24	54	101
1987-88—Kingston Canadians (c)		OHL	46	26	32	58	118

(c)—June, 1988—Drafted by Toronto Maple Leafs in 1988 NHL entry draft. First Maple Leafs pick, sixth overall, first round.

TED PEARSON

Left Wing . . . 5'10" . . . 175 lbs. . . . Born, Kitchener, Ont., January 9, 1962 . . . Shoots left . . . Son of Mel Pearson (Played pro hockey between 1957 and 1973 with QHL, AHL, WHL, EPHL, NHL, CPHL and WHA) . . . (October, 1984)—Shoulder injury . . . (March, 1987)— Ankle injury.

Year	Team	League	Games	G.	A.	Pts.	Pen.
1980-81—University of Wisconsin		WCHA	36	6	9	15	59
1981-82—University of Wisconsin (c)		WCHA	41	15	23	38	85
1982-83—University of Wisconsin		WCHA	42	6	9	15	90
1983-84—University of Wisconsin		WCHA	35	13	20	33	60
1984-85—Moncton Golden Flames		AHL	65	9	17	26	70
1985-86—Salt Lake Golden Eagles		IHL	77	28	27	55	68
1986-87—Salt Lake Golden Eagles		IHL	17	6	8	14	10
1987-88—Milwaukee Admirals		IHL	68	18	23	41	60

(c)—June, 1982—Drafted by Calgary Flames in 1982 NHL entry draft. Eleventh Flames pick, 177th overall, ninth round.

ALLEN PEDERSEN

Defense . . . 6'3" . . . 180 lbs. . . . Born, Edmonton, Alta., January 13, 1965 . . . Shoots left.

Year	Team	League	Games	G.	A.	Pts.	Pen.
1982-83—Medicine Hat Tigers (c)		WHL	63	3	10	13	49
1983-84—Medicine Hat Tigers		WHL	44	0	11	11	47
1984-85—Medicine Hat Tigers		WHL	72	6	16	22	66
1985-86—Moncton Golden Flames		AHL	59	1	8	9	39
1986-87—Boston Bruins		NHL	79	1	11	12	71
1987-88—Boston Bruins		NHL	78	0	6	6	90
NHL TOTALS			157	1	17	18	161

(c)—June, 1983—Drafted as underage junior by Boston Bruins in 1983 NHL entry draft. Fifth Bruins pick, 102nd overall, fifth round.

BARRY ALAN PEDERSON

Center . . . 5'11" . . . 171 lbs. . . . Born, Big River, Sask., March 13, 1961 . . . Shoots right . . . (1981-82)—Set Boston Bruin rookie records with 44 goals and 92 points . . . (1982-83)—Became youngest player to ever lead Boston in scoring . . . (October 2, 1984)—Broke knuckle on right hand during fight with Mario Marois in pre-season game at Quebec . . . (January, 1985)—Surgery to remove a benign fibrous tumor from rear shoulder muscle of right arm. Doctors had to cut away parts of the muscle when they removed the growth and he missed remainder of season . . . Cousin of Brian Skrudland . . . (December 12, 1987)—Whiplash injury when he struck the back of a truck on the way to a game in Vancouver.

Year	Team	League	Games	G.	A.	Pts.	Pen.
1977-78—Nanaimo		BCJHL	....	...	....	....	....
1977-78—Victoria Cougars		WCHL	3	1	4	5	2
1978-79—Victoria Cougars		WHL	72	31	53	84	41
1979-80—Victoria Cougars (b-c)		WHL	72	52	88	140	50
1980-81—Victoria Cougars (a)		WHL	55	65	82	147	65
1980-81—Boston Bruins		NHL	9	1	4	5	6
1981-82—Boston Bruins		NHL	80	44	48	92	53
1982-83—Boston Bruins		NHL	77	46	61	107	47
1983-84—Boston Bruins		NHL	80	39	77	116	64
1984-85—Boston Bruins		NHL	22	4	8	12	10
1985-86—Boston Bruins (d)		NHL	79	29	47	76	60
1986-87—Vancouver Canucks		NHL	79	24	52	76	50
1987-88—Vancouver Canucks		NHL	76	19	52	71	92
NHL TOTALS			502	206	349	555	382

(c)—June, 1980—Drafted as underage junior by Boston Bruins in 1980 NHL entry draft. First Bruins pick, 18th overall, first round.

(d)—June, 1986—Traded by Boston Bruins to Vancouver Canucks for Cam Neely and first round 1987 draft pick (Glen Wesley).

MARK PEDERSON

Left Wing . . . 6'1" . . . 195 lbs. . . . Born, Prelate, Sask., January 14, 1968 . . . Shoots left . . . (March, 1985)—Shoulder injury.

Year	Team	League	Games	G.	A.	Pts.	Pen.
1983-84—Cablevision Tigers		Alta. Midget	42	43	47	90	64
1984-85—Medicine Hat Tigers		WHL	71	42	40	82	63
1985-86—Medicine Hat Tigers (c)		WHL	72	46	60	106	46
1986-87—Medicine Hat Tigers (a)		WHL	69	56	46	102	58
1987-88—Medicine Hat Tigers (b)		WHL	62	53	58	111	55

(c)—June, 1986—Drafted as underage junior by Montreal Canadiens in 1986 NHL entry draft. First Canadiens pick, 15th overall, first round.

MIKE PELUSO

Defense . . . 6'4" . . . 200 lbs. . . . Born, Hibbing, Minn., November 8, 1965 . . . Shoots left.

Year	Team	League	Games	G.	A.	Pts.	Pen.
1984-85—Stratford (c)		OPJHL	52	11	45	56	114
1985-86—Univ. of Alaska/Anchorage		GWHC	32	2	11	13	59
1986-87—Univ. of Alaska/Anchorage		GWHC	30	5	21	26	68
1987-88—Univ. of Alaska/Anchorage		GWHC	35	4	33	37	76

(c)—June, 1985—Drafted by New Jersey Devils in 1985 NHL entry draft. Tenth Devils pick, 190th overall, 10th round.

JIM DESMOND PEPLINSKI

Center ... 6'2" ... 201 lbs. ... Born, Renfrew, Ont., October 24, 1960 ... Shoots right ... (September, 1987)—Fractured sinus in pre-season game vs. Winnipeg.

Year	Team	League	Games	G.	A.	Pts.	Pen.
1977-78—Toronto Marlboros		OMJHL	66	13	28	41	44
1978-79—Toronto Marlboros (c)		OMJHL	66	23	32	55	60
1979-80—Toronto Marlboros		OMJHL	67	35	66	101	89
1980-81—Calgary Flames		NHL	80	13	25	38	108
1981-82—Calgary Flames		NHL	74	30	37	67	115
1982-83—Calgary Flames		NHL	80	15	26	41	134
1983-84—Calgary Flames		NHL	74	11	22	33	114
1984-85—Calgary Flames		NHL	80	16	29	45	111
1985-86—Calgary Flames		NHL	77	24	35	59	214
1986-87—Calgary Flames		NHL	80	18	32	50	185
1987-88—Calgary Flames		NHL	75	20	31	51	234
1987-88—Canadian Olympic Team		Olympics	7	0	1	1	6
NHL TOTALS			620	147	237	384	1215

(c)—August, 1979—Drafted by Atlanta Flames as underage junior in 1979 NHL entry draft. Fifth Flames pick, 75th overall, fourth round.

DAVE PERGOLA

Right Wing ... 6' ... 185 lbs. ... Born, Waltham, Mass., March 4, 1969 ... Shoots right.

Year	Team	League	Games	G.	A.	Pts.	Pen.
1985-86—Belmont Hill		Mass. H.S.	....	13	22	35	....
1986-87—Belmont Hill (c)		Mass. H.S.	....	24	17	41	....
1987-88—Boston College		H. East	33	5	7	12	22

(c)—June, 1987—Drafted by Buffalo Sabres in 1987 NHL entry draft. Fifth Sabres pick, 85th overall, fifth round.

TERRY PERKINS

Right Wing ... 6'1" ... 190 lbs. ... Born, Campbell River, B.C., June 21, 1966 ... Shoots right.

Year	Team	League	Games	G.	A.	Pts.	Pen.
1983-84—Portland Winter Hawks (c)		WHL	68	35	30	65	75
1984-85—Portland Winter Hawks		WHL	63	33	38	71	81
1985-86—Portland Winter Hawks		WHL	6	5	4	9	9
1985-86—Spokane Chiefs (b)		WHL	60	66	42	108	65
1986-87—Fredericton Express		AHL	44	10	11	21	35
1986-87—Muskegon Lumberjacks		IHL	12	4	8	12	31
1987-88—Baltimore Skipjacks		AHL	65	28	41	69	65

(c)—June, 1984—Drafted as underage junior by Quebec Nordiques in NHL entry draft. Fourth Nordiques pick, 78th overall, fourth round.

RON PESETTI

Defense ... 5'11" ... 190 lbs. ... Born, Laval, Que., May 3, 1963 ... Shoots right.

Year	Team	League	Games	G.	A.	Pts.	Pen.
1982-83—Western Michigan Univ. (c)		CCHA	31	2	8	10	34
1983-84—Western Michigan Univ.		CCHA	33	3	11	14	44
1984-85—Western Michigan Univ.		CCHA	29	1	6	7	32
1985-86—Western Michigan Univ.		CCHA	42	8	20	28	62
1986-87—Fort Wayne Komets		IHL	79	12	39	51	62
1987-88—Moncton Golden Flames		AHL	60	8	21	29	41
1987-88—Fort Wayne Komets		IHL	3	0	2	2	4

(c)—June, 1983—Drafted by Winnipeg Jets in 1983 NHL entry draft. Ninth Jets pick, 149th overall, eighth round.

MATTHEW PESKLEWIS

Left Wing ... 6'2" ... 185 lbs. ... Born, Edmonton, Alta., May 21, 1968 ... Shoots left.

Year	Team	League	Games	G.	A.	Pts.	Pen.
1984-85—St. Albert Midget Raiders	Alta.Midg	28	23	8	31	96
1985-86—St. Albert Saints (c)	WHL	51	13	26	39	259
1986-87—Boston University	H. East	24	0	2	2	28
1987-88—Boston University	H. East	28	6	11	17	54

(c)—June, 1986—Drafted as underage junior by Boston Bruins in 1986 NHL entry draft. Fourth Bruins pick, 97th overall, fifth round.

BRENT RONALD PETERSON

Center . . . 6'1" . . . 195 lbs. . . . Born, Calgary, Alta., February 15, 1958 . . . Shoots right . . . Missed most of 1978-79 season with broken leg . . . (October 15, 1980)—Fractured right cheekbone . . . (November 12, 1980)—Fractured left ankle . . . (February 10, 1983)—Dislocated shoulder at Los Angeles . . . (November, 1987)—Cracked rib . . . (January, 1988)—Pulled groin.

Year	Team	League	Games	G.	A.	Pts.	Pen.
1974-75—Edmonton Oil Kings	WCHL	66	17	26	43	44
1975-76—Edmonton Oil Kings	WCHL	70	22	39	61	57
1976-77—Portland Winter Hawks	WCHL	69	34	78	112	98
1977-78—Portland Winter Hawks (c)	WCHL	51	33	50	83	95
1978-79—Detroit Red Wings	NHL	5	0	0	0	0
1979-80—Adirondack Red Wings	AHL	52	9	22	31	61
1979-80—Detroit Red Wings	NHL	18	1	2	3	2
1980-81—Detroit Red Wings	NHL	53	6	18	24	24
1980-81—Adirondack Red Wings	AHL	3	1	0	1	10
1981-82—Detroit Red Wings (d)	NHL	15	1	0	1	6
1981-82—Buffalo Sabres	NHL	46	9	5	14	43
1982-83—Buffalo Sabres	NHL	75	13	24	37	38
1983-84—Buffalo Sabres	NHL	70	9	12	21	52
1984-85—Buffalo Sabres	NHL	74	12	22	34	47
1985-86—Vancouver Canucks (e)	NHL	77	8	23	31	94
1986-87—Vancouver Canucks	NHL	69	7	15	22	77
1987-88—Hartford Whalers (f)	NHL	52	2	7	9	40
NHL TOTALS		554	68	128	196	423

(c)—Drafted from Portland Winter Hawks by Detroit Red Wings (with choice obtained from Toronto Maple Leafs) in first round of 1978 amateur draft.

(d)—December, 1981—Traded with Mike Foligno, Dale McCourt and future considerations by Detroit Red Wings to Buffalo Sabres for Danny Gare, Jim Schoenfeld, Derek Smith and Bob Sauve.

(e)—October, 1985—Acquired by Vancouver Canucks in 1985 NHL waiver draft.

(f)—October, 1987—Acquired by Hartford Whalers in 1987 NHL waiver draft as compensation from Vancouver Canucks for their drafting of Doug Wickenheiser.

BRETT PETERSON

Defense . . . 6'2" . . . 195 lbs. . . . Born, St. Paul, Minn., February 1, 1969 . . . Shoots right.

Year	Team	League	Games	G.	A.	Pts.	Pen.
1986-87—Roseville H.S.	Minn. H.S.	26	7	15	22	....
1987-88—St. Paul Vulcans (c)	USHL	37	2	9	11	68

(c)—June, 1988—Drafted by Calgary Flames in 1988 NHL entry draft. Ninth Flames pick, 189th overall, ninth round.

MICHEL PETIT

Defense . . . 6'1" . . . 185 lbs. . . . Born, St. Malo, Que., February 12, 1964 . . . Shoots right . . . (March, 1984)—Separated shoulder . . . (February, 1987)—Knee injury . . . (December, 1987)—Pulled groin.

Year	Team	League	Games	G.	A.	Pts.	Pen.
1980-81—St. Foy Midget AAA	QAAAMHL	48	10	45	55	84
1981-82—Sherbrooke Beavers (a-c-d-e)	QMJHL	63	10	39	49	106
1982-83—St. Jean Beavers (a)	QHL	62	19	67	86	196
1982-83—Vancouver Canucks	NHL	2	0	0	0	0
1983-84—Vancouver Canucks	NHL	44	6	9	15	53
1984-85—Vancouver Canucks	NHL	69	5	26	31	127
1985-86—Fredericton Express	AHL	25	0	13	13	79
1985-86—Vancouver Canucks	NHL	32	1	6	7	27
1986-87—Vancouver Canucks	NHL	69	12	13	25	131
1987-88—Vancouver Canucks (f)	NHL	10	0	3	3	35
1987-88—New York Rangers	NHL	64	9	24	33	223
NHL TOTALS		290	33	81	114	596

(c)—Winner of Raymond Lagace Trophy (Top Rookie Defenseman).

(d)—Winner of the Association of Journalist of Hockey Trophy (Top Pro Prospect).

(e)—June, 1982—Drafted as underage junior by Vancouver Canucks in 1982 NHL entry draft. First Canucks pick, 11th overall, first round.

(f)—November, 1987—Traded by Vancouver Canucks to New York Rangers for Willie Huber and Larry Melnyk.

LYLE PHAIR

Left Wing . . . 6'1" . . . 188 lbs. . . . Born, Pilot Mound, Man., March 8, 1961 . . . Shoots left.

Year	Team	League	Games	G.	A.	Pts.	Pen.
1981-82—Michigan State University		CCHA	42	24	19	43	49
1982-83—Michigan State University		CCHA	41	20	15	35	64
1983-84—Michigan State University		CCHA	45	15	16	31	58
1984-85—Michigan State University (c)		CCHA	43	23	27	50	84
1985-86—Los Angeles Kings		NHL	15	0	1	1	2
1985-86—New Haven Nighthawks		AHL	35	9	9	18	15
1986-87—New Haven Nighthawks		AHL	65	19	27	46	77
1986-87—Los Angeles Kings		NHL	5	2	0	2	2
1987-88—Los Angeles Kings		NHL	28	4	6	10	8
1987-88—New Haven Nighthawks		AHL	45	15	12	27	26
NHL TOTALS			48	6	7	13	12

(c)—June, 1985—Signed by Los Angeles Kings as a free agent.

ROBERT RENE JOSEPH PICARD

Defense . . . 6'2" . . . 203 lbs. . . . Born, Montreal, Que., May 25, 1957 . . . Shoots left . . . Nephew of former NHL defenseman Noel Picard . . . (November 12, 1980)—Strained knee ligaments . . . (January, 1983)—Broken bone in foot . . . (September, 1985)—Concussion in training camp . . . (January 4, 1986)—Cut hand at Detroit . . . (February 25, 1986)—Broke ribs vs. Boston and missed five games . . . (October, 1987)—Injured ligaments in left knee . . . (February 6, 1988)—Crushed lumbar vertebrae at Boston.

Year	Team	League	Games	G.	A.	Pts.	Pen.
1973-74—Montreal Red, White and Blue		QJHL	70	7	46	53	296
1974-75—Montreal Red, White and Blue		QJHL	70	13	74	87	339
1975-76—Montreal Juniors (b)		QJHL	72	14	67	81	282
1976-77—Montreal Juniors (a-c-d)		QJHL	70	32	60	92	267
1977-78—Washington Capitals		NHL	75	10	27	37	101
1978-79—Washington Capitals		NHL	77	21	44	65	85
1979-80—Washington Capitals (e)		NHL	78	11	43	54	122
1980-81—Toronto Maple Leafs (f)		NHL	59	6	19	25	68
1980-81—Montreal Canadiens		NHL	8	2	2	4	6
1981-82—Montreal Canadiens		NHL	62	2	26	28	106
1982-83—Montreal Canadiens		NHL	64	7	31	38	60
1983-84—Montreal Canadiens (g)		NHL	7	0	2	2	0
1983-84—Winnipeg Jets		NHL	62	6	16	22	34
1984-85—Winnipeg Jets		NHL	78	12	22	34	107
1985-86—Winnipeg Jets (h)		NHL	20	2	5	7	17
1985-86—Quebec Nordiques		NHL	48	7	27	34	36
1986-87—Quebec Nordiques		NHL	78	8	20	28	71
1987-88—Quebec Nordiques		NHL	65	3	13	16	103
NHL TOTALS			781	97	297	394	916

(c)—Outstanding Defenseman in QJHL.

(d)—Drafted from Montreal Juniors by Washington Capitals in first round of 1977 amateur draft.

(e)—June, 1980—Traded with Tim Coulis and second round draft choice in 1980 (Bob McGill) by Washington Capitals to Toronto Maple Leafs for Mike Palmateer and third round draft choice (Torrie Robertson).

(f)—March, 1981—Traded by Toronto Maple Leafs with a future eighth round draft pick to Montreal Canadiens for Michel Larocque.

(g)—November, 1983—Traded by Montreal Canadiens to Winnipeg Jets for third-round 1984 draft pick (Patrick Roy).

(h)—November, 1985—Traded by Winnipeg Jets to Quebec Nordiques for Mario Marois.

DAVE PICHETTE

Defense . . . 6'3" . . . 195 lbs. . . . Born, Grand Falls, N. B., February 4, 1960 . . . Shoots left . . . (January, 1983)—Back injury . . . (January 8, 1986)—Concussion at Chicago and missed eight games.

Year	Team	League	Games	G.	A.	Pts.	Pen.
1978-79—Quebec Remparts		QMJHL	57	10	16	26	134
1979-80—Quebec Remparts		QMJHL	56	8	19	27	129
1980-81—Quebec Nordiques (c)		NHL	46	4	16	20	62
1980-81—Hershey Bears		AHL	20	2	3	5	37
1981-82—Quebec Nordiques		NHL	67	7	30	37	152

Year	Team	League	Games	G.	A.	Pts.	Pen.
1982-83—Fredericton Express	AHL	16	3	11	14	14
1982-83—Quebec Nordiques	NHL	53	3	21	24	49
1983-84—Fredericton Express	AHL	10	2	1	3	13
1983-84—Quebec Nordiques (d)	NHL	23	2	7	9	12
1983-84—St. Louis Blues	NHL	23	0	11	11	6
1984-85—New Jersey Devils (e)	NHL	71	17	40	57	41
1985-86—Maine Mariners	AHL	25	4	15	19	28
1985-86—New Jersey Devils	NHL	33	7	12	19	22
1987-88—New York Rangers	NHL	6	1	3	4	4
1987-88—New Haven Nighthawks	AHL	46	10	21	31	37
NHL TOTALS		322	41	140	181	348

(c)—September, 1980—Signed by Quebec Nordiques as a free agent.

(d)—February, 1984—Traded by Quebec Nordiques to St. Louis Blues for Andre Dore.

(e)—October, 1984—Drafted by New Jersey Devils in NHL waiver draft.

DOUG PICKELL

Left Wing . . . 6' . . . 185 lbs. . . . Born, London, Ont., May 7, 1968 . . . Shoots left.

Year	Team	League	Games	G.	A.	Pts.	Pen.
1983-84—Sherwood Park Midgets	WHL	40	31	33	64	84
1984-85—Medicine Hat Tigers	WHL	69	4	13	17	124
1985-86—Medicine Hat Tigers (c)	WHL	8	2	4	6	11
1985-86—Kamloops Blazers (d)	WHL	62	25	16	41	101
1986-87—Kamloops Blazers	WHL	70	34	24	58	182
1987-88—Kamloops Blazers	WHL	39	10	11	21	144
1987-88—Spokane Chiefs	WHL	28	4	8	12	60

(c)—December, 1985—Traded with Sean Pass by Medicine Hat Tigers to Kamloops Blazers for Rob Dimaio, Dave MacKey and Calvin Knibbs.

(d)—June, 1986—Drafted as underage junior by Calgary Flames in 1986 NHL entry draft. Ninth Flames pick, 205th overall, 10th round.

NEIL PILON

Defense . . . 6'4" . . . 185 lbs. . . . Born, Merritt, B.C., April 26, 1967 . . . Shoots right . . . (October, 1984)—Sprained wrist . . . (December, 1984)—Shoulder separation.

Year	Team	League	Games	G.	A.	Pts.	Pen.
1983-84—Williams Lake Mustangs	PCJHL	60	10	39	49	200
1983-84—Kamloops Blazers	WHL	9	0	2	2	0
1984-85—Kamloops Blazers (c)	WHL	52	1	6	7	40
1985-86—Moose Jaw Warriors	WHL	59	2	18	20	112
1986-87—Moose Jaw Warriors	WHL	72	2	23	25	119
1987-88—Seattle Thunderbirds	WHL	71	5	18	23	137

(c)—June, 1985—Drafted as underage junior by New York Rangers in 1985 NHL entry draft. Seventh Rangers pick, 133rd overall, seventh round.

RICHARD PILON

Defense . . . 5'11" . . . 197 lbs. . . . Born, Saskatoon, Sask., April 30, 1968 . . . Shoots left.

Year	Team	League	Games	G.	A.	Pts.	Pen.
1984-85—Prince Albert Midget Raiders	Sask. Midg.	26	3	11	14	41
1985-86—Prince Albert Midget Raiders	Sask. Midg.	35	3	28	31	142
1985-86—Prince Albert Raiders (c)	WHL	6	0	0	0	0
1986-87—Prince Albert Raiders	WHL	68	4	21	25	192
1987-88—Prince Albert Raiders (b)	WHL	65	13	34	47	177

(c)—June, 1986—Drafted as underage junior by New York Islanders in 1986 NHL entry draft. Ninth Islanders pick, 143rd overall, seventh round.

LANCE PITLICK

Defense . . . 6' . . . 185 lbs. . . . Born, Fridley, Minn., November 5, 1967 . . . Shoots right.

Year	Team	League	Games	G.	A.	Pts.	Pen.
1984-85—Cooper H.S.	Minn.	23	8	4	12	....
1985-86—Cooper H.S. (c)	Minn.	21	17	8	25	....
1986-87—Univ. of Minnesota	WCHA	45	0	9	9	88
1987-88—Univ. of Minnesota	WCHA	38	3	9	12	76

(c)—June, 1986—Drafted by Minnesota North Stars in 1986 NHL entry draft. Tenth North Stars pick, 180th overall, ninth round.

MICHAL PIVONKA

Center . . . 6'2" . . . 192 lbs. . . . Born, Kladno, Czechoslovakia, January 28, 1966 . . . Shoots

left . . . (March, 1987)—Strained ankle ligaments . . . (October, 1987)—Sprained right wrist . . . (March, 1988)—Sprained left ankle.

Year	Team	League	Games	G.	A.	Pts.	Pen.
1985-86—Dukla Jihlava (c)		Czech.	....	...	....	....	....
1986-87—Washington Capitals		NHL	73	18	25	43	41
1987-88—Washington Capitals		NHL	71	11	23	34	28
NHL TOTALS			144	29	48	77	69

(c)—June, 1984—Drafted by Washington Capitals in 1984 NHL entry draft. Third Capitals pick, 59th overall, third round.

ADRIEN PLAVSIC

Defense . . . 6' . . . 190 lbs. . . . Born, Montreal, Que., January 13, 1970 . . . Shoots left.

Year	Team	League	Games	G.	A.	Pts.	Pen.
1986-87—Lac St. Louis Midget		Que. Midget	42	8	27	35	22
1987-88—Univ. of New Hampshire (c)		H. East	30	5	6	11	45

(c)—June, 1988—Drafted by St. Louis Blues in 1988 NHL entry draft. Second Blues pick, 30th overall, second round.

JIM PLAYFAIR

Defense . . . 6'3" . . . 200 lbs. . . . Born, Vanderhoof, B.C., May 22, 1964 . . . Shoots left . . . Brother of Larry Playfair . . . (November, 1984)—Severe groin pull . . . (February, 1987)—Bruised liver at Sherbrooke.

Year	Team	League	Games	G.	A.	Pts.	Pen.
1980-81—Fort Saskatchewan		AJHL	31	2	17	19	105
1981-82—Portland Winter Hawks (c)		WHL	70	4	13	17	121
1982-83—Portland Winter Hawks		WHL	63	8	27	35	218
1983-84—Portland Winter Hawks		WHL	16	5	6	11	38
1983-84—Calgary Wranglers		WHL	44	6	9	15	96
1983-84—Edmonton Oilers		NHL	2	1	1	2	2
1984-85—Nova Scotia Oilers		AHL	41	0	4	4	107
1985-86—Nova Scotia Oilers		AHL	73	2	12	14	160
1986-87—Nova Scotia Oilers (d)		AHL	60	1	21	22	82
1987-88—Saginaw Hawks		IHL	50	5	21	26	133
1987-88—Chicago Black Hawks		NHL	12	1	3	4	21
NHL TOTALS			14	2	4	6	23

(c)—June, 1982—Drafted by Edmonton Oilers in 1982 NHL entry draft. First Oilers pick, 20th overall, first round.

(d)—August, 1987—Signed by Chicago Black Hawks as a free agent.

LARRY WILLIAM PLAYFAIR

Defense . . . 6'4" . . . 215 lbs. . . . Born, Fort St. James, B. C., June 23, 1958 . . . Shoots left . . . (October 9, 1980)—Severely cut right hand kept him out of Sabres lineup for 10 days . . . Brother of Jim Playfair . . . (April, 1983)—Chipped bone in right elbow in playoff series vs. Boston . . . (January, 1986)—Injured shoulder . . . (March 1, 1986)—Injured left knee . . . (May, 1986)—Shoulder surgery . . . (December 17, 1986)—Injured left knee when he collided with Terry Ruskowski vs. Pittsburgh . . . (January, 1987)—Surgery to left knee . . . (January 31, 1987)—Reinjured knee at Montreal . . . (February 19, 1987)—Reconstructive surgery to left knee . . . (November, 1987)—Reconstructive knee surgery . . . (March, 1988)—Bruised chest.

Year	Team	League	Games	G.	A.	Pts.	Pen.
1975-76—Langley		Jr. "A"BCHL	72	10	20	30	162
1976-77—Portland Winter Hawks		WCHL	65	2	17	19	199
1977-78—Portland Winter Hawks (a-c)		WCHL	71	13	19	32	402
1978-79—Buffalo Sabres		NHL	26	0	3	3	60
1978-79—Hershey Bears		AHL	45	0	12	12	148
1979-80—Buffalo Sabres		NHL	79	2	10	12	145
1980-81—Buffalo Sabres		NHL	75	3	9	12	169
1981-82—Buffalo Sabres		NHL	77	6	10	16	258
1982-83—Buffalo Sabres		NHL	79	4	13	17	180
1983-84—Buffalo Sabres		NHL	76	5	11	16	209
1984-85—Buffalo Sabres		NHL	72	3	14	17	157
1985-86—Buffalo Sabres (d)		NHL	47	1	2	3	100
1985-86—Los Angeles Kings		NHL	14	0	1	1	26
1986-87—Los Angeles Kings		NHL	37	2	7	9	181
1987-88—Los Angeles Kings		NHL	54	0	7	7	197
NHL TOTALS			636	26	87	113	1682

(c)—Drafted from Portland Winter Hawks by Buffalo Sabres in first round of 1978 amateur draft.

(d)—January, 1986—Traded with Sean McKenna and Ken Baumgartner by Buffalo Sabres to Los Angeles Kings for Brian Engblom and Doug Smith.

WILLIAM (WILLI) PLETT

Right Wing . . . 6'3" . . . 205 lbs. . . . Born, Paraguay, South America, June 7, 1955 . . . Shoots right . . . (October, 1982)—Suspended for seven games for swinging his stick at Detroit goalie Greg Stefan . . . (October 18, 1984)—Dislocated shoulder in fight with Don Jackson vs. Edmonton . . . (October 19, 1985)—Separated shoulder at Philadelphia and missed four weeks . . . (January 21, 1986)—Dislocated shoulder at Philadelphia and missed four games . . . (March 11, 1986)—Bruised shoulder vs. Edmonton and missed six games . . . (September, 1986)—Pulled back muscle in training camp.

Year	Team	League	Games	G.	A.	Pts.	Pen.
1974-75—Niagara Falls Flyers		SOJHL	....	...	....	....	....
1974-75—St. Cath. Black Hawks (c)		Jr."A"OHA	22	6	8	14	63
1975-76—Tulsa Oilers (d)		CHL	73	30	20	50	163
1975-76—Atlanta Flames		NHL	4	0	0	0	2
1976-77—Tulsa Oilers		CHL	14	8	4	12	68
1976-77—Atlanta Flames (e)		NHL	64	33	23	56	123
1977-78—Atlanta Flames		NHL	78	22	21	43	171
1978-79—Atlanta Flames		NHL	74	23	20	43	213
1979-80—Atlanta Flames		NHL	76	13	19	32	231
1980-81—Calgary Flames		NHL	78	38	30	68	239
1981-82—Calgary Flames (f)		NHL	78	21	36	57	288
1982-83—Minnesota North Stars		NHL	71	25	14	39	170
1983-84—Minnesota North Stars		NHL	73	15	23	38	316
1984-85—Minnesota North Stars		NHL	47	14	14	28	157
1985-86—Minnesota North Stars		NHL	59	10	7	17	231
1986-87—Minnesota North Stars (g)		NHL	67	6	5	11	263
1987-88—Boston Bruins (h)		NHL	65	2	3	5	170
NHL TOTALS			834	222	215	437	2574

(c)—Drafted from St. Catharines Black Hawks by Atlanta Flames in fifth round of 1975 amateur draft.
(d)—Tied for lead in goals (5) during playoffs.
(e)—Won Calder Memorial Trophy and named THE SPORTING NEWS NHL Rookie-of-the-Year.
(f)—June, 1982—Traded by Calgary Flames with a fourth-round draft choice in 1982 to Minnesota North Stars for Bill Nyrop, Steve Christoff and a second-round draft choice in 1982.
(g)—September, 1987—Traded by Minnesota North Stars to New York Rangers for Pat Price.
(h)—October, 1987—Selected by Boston Bruins in 1987 NHL waiver draft.

WALT MICHAEL PODDUBNY

Center . . . 6'1" . . . 203 lbs. . . . Born, Thunder Bay, Ont. February 14, 1960 . . . Shoots left . . . (October, 1982)—Injured leg . . . Shares Toronto goal scoring record for rookies (28) with Peter Ihnacak . . . (October, 1983)—Broken ankle . . . (February, 1985)—Broke thumb in AHL game . . . (September, 1985)—Infected foot during training camp . . . (December, 1986)—Injured hip . . . (December 21, 1986)—Concussion vs. Hartford.

Year	Team	League	Games	G.	A.	Pts.	Pen.
1978-79—Brandon Wheat Kings		WHL	20	11	11	22	12
1979-80—Kitchener Rangers		OMJHL	19	3	9	12	35
1979-80—Kingston Canadians (c)		OMJHL	43	30	17	47	36
1980-81—Milwaukee Admirals		IHL	5	4	2	6	4
1980-81—Wichita Wind		CHL	70	21	29	50	207
1981-82—Edmonton Oilers (d)		NHL	4	0	0	0	0
1981-82—Wichita Wind		CHL	60	35	46	81	79
1981-82—Toronto Maple Leafs		NHL	11	3	4	7	8
1982-83—Toronto Maple Leafs		NHL	72	28	31	59	71
1983-84—Toronto Maple Leafs		NHL	38	11	14	25	48
1984-85—St. Catharines Saints		AHL	8	5	7	12	10
1984-85—Toronto Maple Leafs		NHL	32	5	15	20	26
1985-86—St. Catharines Saints		AHL	37	28	27	55	52
1985-86—Toronto Maple Leafs (e)		NHL	33	12	22	34	25
1986-87—New York Rangers		NHL	75	40	47	87	49
1987-88—New York Rangers (f)		NHL	77	38	50	88	76
NHL TOTALS			342	137	183	320	303

(c)—June, 1980—Drafted by Edmonton Oilers in 1980 NHL entry draft. Fourth Oilers pick, 90th overall, fifth round.
(d)—March, 1982—Traded with NHL rights to Phil Drouillard by Edmonton Oilers to Toronto Maple Leafs for Laurie Boschman.
(e)—August, 1986—Traded by Toronto Maple Leafs to New York Rangers for Mike Allison.
(f)—August, 1988—Traded with Bruce Bell and Jari Gronstrand and a fourth-round draft choice in 1989 by New York Rangers to Quebec Nordiques for Normand Rochefort and Jason Lafreniere.

RAY PODLOSKI

Center . . . 6'2" . . . 210 lbs. . . . Born, Edmonton, Alta., January 5, 1966 . . . Shoots left . . . (November 1, 1987)—Missed 13 games with ankle and knee injury at Sherbrooke.

Year	Team	League	Games	G.	A.	Pts.	Pen.
1982-83—Red Deer Rustlers		AJHL	59	49	49	98	47
1982-83—Portland Winter Hawks		WHL	2	0	1	1	0
1983-84—Portland Winter Hawks (c)		WHL	66	46	50	96	44
1984-85—Portland Winter Hawks		WHL	67	63	75	138	41
1985-86—Portland Winter Hawks		WHL	66	59	75	134	68
1986-87—Moncton Golden Flames		AHL	70	23	27	50	12
1987-88—Maine Mariners		AHL	36	12	20	32	12

(c)—June, 1984—Drafted by Boston Bruins as underage junior in NHL entry draft. Second Bruins pick, 40th overall, second round.

RUDY POESCHUK

Defense ... 6'2" ... 205 lbs. ... Born, Terrace, B.C., September 19, 1966 ... Shoots right ... (December, 1984)—Knee injury ... (November, 1986)—Injured shoulder.

Year	Team	League	Games	G.	A.	Pts.	Pen.
1983-84—Kamloops Jr. Oilers		WHL	47	3	9	12	93
1984-85—Kamloops Blazers (c)		WHL	34	6	7	13	100
1985-86—Kamloops Blazers		WHL	32	3	13	16	92
1986-87—Kamloops Blazers		WHL	54	13	18	31	153
1987-88—New York Rangers		NHL	1	0	0	0	2
1987-88—Colorado Rangers		IHL	82	7	31	38	210
NHL TOTALS			1	0	0	0	2

(c)—June, 1985—Drafted as underage junior by New York Rangers in 1985 NHL entry draft. Twelfth Rangers pick, 238th overall, 12th round.

JON POJAR

Left Wing ... 5'11" ... 180 lbs. ... Born, St. Paul, Minn., May 5, 1970 ... Shoots left.

Year	Team	League	Games	G.	A.	Pts.	Pen.
1986-87—Roseville H.S.		Minn. H.S.	23	10	23	33	..
1987-88—Roseville H.S. (c)		Minn. H.S.	19	9	11	20	..

(c)—June, 1988—Drafted by Chicago Black Hawks in 1988 NHL entry draft. Seventh Black Hawks pick, 155th overall, eighth round.

DAVID PORTER

Right and Left Wing ... 6'1" ... 170 lbs. ... Born, Milford, Mich., June 2, 1967 ... Shoots left.

Year	Team	League	Games	G.	A.	Pts.	Pen.
1986-87—Northern Michigan Univ. (c)		WCHA	39	10	12	22	20
1987-88—Northern Michigan Univ.		WCHA	38	9	19	28	16

(c)—June, 1987—Drafted by New York Rangers in 1987 NHL entry draft. Tenth Rangers pick, 199th overall, 10th round.

VICTOR POSA

Defense ... 6'1" ... 195 lbs. ... Born, Bari, Italy, May 11, 1966 ... Shoots left ... Also plays Left Wing.

Year	Team	League	Games	G.	A.	Pts.	Pen.
1983-84—Henry Carr H.S.		OHA	25	16	21	37	139
1984-85—University of Wisconsin (c)		WCHA	33	1	5	6	47
1985-86—Toronto Marlboros		OHL	48	28	34	62	116
1985-86—Chicago Black Hawks		NHL	2	0	0	0	2
1986-87—Saginaw Generals		IHL	61	13	27	40	203
1986-87—Nova Scotia Oilers		AHL	2	1	0	1	2
1987-88—Saginaw Hawks		IHL	2	0	0	0	0
1987-88—Flint Spirits		IHL	9	1	0	1	36
1987-88—Peoria Rivermen		IHL	10	0	2	2	106
NHL TOTALS			2	0	0	0	2

(c)—June, 1985—Drafted by Chicago Black Hawks in 1985 NHL entry draft. Seventh Black Hawks pick, 137th overall, seventh round.

MICHAEL POSMA

Defense ... 6'1" ... 195 lbs. ... Born, Utica, N.Y., December 16, 1967 ... Shoots right.

Year	Team	League	Games	G.	A.	Pts.	Pen.
1984-85—Buffalo Junior Sabres		NAJHL	43	4	28	32	....
1985-86—Buffalo Junior Sabres (c)		NAJHL	40	16	47	63	62
1986-87—Western Michigan Univ.		CCHA	35	12	20	32	46
1987-88—Western Michigan Univ.		CCHA	42	16	38	54	30

(c)—June, 1986—Drafted by St. Louis Blues in 1986 NHL entry draft. Second Blues pick, 31st overall, second round.

DENIS CHARLES POTVIN

Defense . . . 6' . . . 204 lbs. . . . Born, Hull, Que., October 29, 1953 . . . Shoots left . . . Brother of Jean Potvin . . . Missed part of 1971-72 season with broken wrist . . . Set Jr. "A" OHA record for points by a defenseman in season (1972-73) . . . Set NHL record for goals in rookie season by defenseman with 17 in 1973-74 (broken by Barry Beck in 1977-78) . . . (October 14, 1978)—Set NHL defenseman record with three goals in one period in 10-7 loss at Toronto . . . Missed much of 1979-80 season after surgery to correct stretched ligaments in thumb . . . Set NHL record for most points by a defenseman (25) in the playoffs in 1981 (Broken by Paul Coffey in 1985 playoffs) . . . (May 21, 1981)—Pulled groin in final game of Stanley Cup Playoffs, aggravated injury during Canada Cup Tournament in August, 1981 and did not play until November 14, 1981 . . . Set NHL record for most career playoff assists with 101 (broke Jean Beliveau's record of 97 career playoff assists) . . . (November 21, 1985)—Missed four games with an ear infection . . . (February 5, 1986)—Injured ankle at Chicago and missed one game . . . (1985-86)—Became all-time NHL leader in goals and points by a defenseman, breaking records of Bobby Orr . . . (February 21, 1987)—Sprained left knee when checked by Bob Gainey vs. Montreal . . . (February, 1988)—Sprained left knee in game at Washington.

Year	Team	League	Games	G.	A.	Pts.	Pen.
1968-69—Ottawa 67's		Jr. "A" OHA	46	12	25	37	83
1969-70—Ottawa 67's		Jr. "A" OHA	42	13	18	31	97
1970-71—Ottawa 67's (a)		Jr. "A" OHA	57	20	58	78	200
1971-72—Ottawa 67's (a-c)		Jr. "A" OHA	48	15	45	60	188
1972-73—Ottawa 67's (a-c-d)		Jr. "A" OHA	61	35	88	123	232
1973-74—New York Islanders (e-f)		NHL	77	17	37	54	175
1974-75—New York Islanders (a)		NHL	79	21	55	76	105
1975-76—New York Islanders (a-g-h)		NHL	78	31	67	98	100
1976-77—New York Islanders (b)		NHL	80	25	55	80	103
1977-78—New York Islanders (a-g)		NHL	80	30	64	94	81
1978-79—New York Islanders (a-g)		NHL	73	31	70	101	58
1979-80—New York Islanders		NHL	31	8	33	41	44
1980-81—New York Islanders (a)		NHL	74	20	56	76	104
1981-82—New York Islanders		NHL	60	24	37	61	83
1982-83—New York Islanders		NHL	69	12	54	66	60
1983-84—New York Islanders		NHL	78	22	63	85	87
1984-85—New York Islanders		NHL	77	17	51	68	96
1985-86—New York Islanders		NHL	74	21	38	59	78
1986-87—New York Islanders		NHL	58	12	30	42	70
1987-88—New York Islanders (i)		NHL	72	19	32	51	112
NHL TOTALS			1060	310	742	1052	1356

(c)—Won Max Kaminsky Memorial Trophy (Outstanding Defenseman).
(d)—Drafted from Ottawa 67's by New York Islanders in first round of 1973 amateur draft.
(e)—Won Calder Memorial Trophy (NHL Rookie of the Year).
(f)—Named NHL's East Division rookie of the year in poll of players by THE SPORTING NEWS.
(g)—Won James Norris Memorial Trophy (Outstanding Defenseman).
(h)—Tied for lead in assists (14) during playoffs.
(i)—September, 1987—Announced his retirement after the 1987-88 season.

MARC POTVIN

Right Wing . . . 6'1" . . . 185 lbs. . . . Born, Ottawa, Ont., January 29, 1967 . . . Shoots right.

Year	Team	League	Games	G.	A.	Pts.	Pen.
1985-86—Stratford (c)		OPJHL	63	5	6	11	117
1986-87—Bowling Green Univ.		CCHA	43	5	15	20	74
1987-88—Bowling Green Univ.		CCHA	45	15	21	36	80

(c)—June, 1986—Drafted by Detroit Red Wings in 1986 NHL entry draft. Ninth Red Wings pick, 169th overall, ninth round.

DANIEL POUDRIER

Defense . . . 6'2" . . . 175 lbs. . . . Born, Thetford Mines, Que., February 15, 1964 . . . Shoots left.

Year	Team	League	Games	G.	A.	Pts.	Pen.
1980-81—Magog AAA Midget		QAAAMHL	26	8	8	16	18
1981-82—Shawinigan Cataracts (c)		QMJHL	64	6	18	24	26
1982-83—Shawinigan Cataracts		QHL	67	6	28	34	31
1983-84—Drummondville Voltigeurs		QHL	64	7	28	35	15
1984-85—Fredericton Express		AHL	1	0	0	0	0
1984-85—Muskegon Lumberjacks		IHL	82	9	30	39	10
1985-86—Fredericton Express		AHL	65	5	26	31	9
1985-86—Quebec Nordiques		NHL	13	1	5	6	10
1986-87—Fredericton Express		AHL	69	8	18	26	11

Year	Team	League	Games	G.	A.	Pts.	Pen.
1986-87—Quebec Nordiques		NHL	6	0	0	0	0
1987-88—Quebec Nordiques		NHL	6	0	0	0	0
1987-88—Fredericton Express		AHL	66	13	30	43	18
NHL TOTALS			25	1	5	6	10

(c)—June, 1982—Drafted as underage junior by Quebec Nordiques in 1982 NHL entry draft. Sixth Nordiques pick, 131st overall, seventh round.

DAVE POULIN

Center ... 5'11" ... 175 lbs. ... Born, Mississauga, Ont., December 17, 1958 ... Shoots left ... (1983-84)—Set Philadelphia record for most points by a rookie ... (February 13, 1986)—Missed one game with back spasms ... (November, 1986)—Pulled hamstring and groin muscle ... (April 16, 1987)—Cracked rib in playoff game at N.Y. Rangers ... (February, 1988)—Pulled groin.

Year	Team	League	Games	G.	A.	Pts.	Pen.
1978-79—University of Notre Dame		WCHA	37	28	31	59	32
1979-80—University of Notre Dame		WCHA	24	19	24	43	46
1980-81—University of Notre Dame		WCHA	35	13	22	35	53
1981-82—University of Notre Dame		CCHA	39	29	30	59	44
1982-83—Rogle (c)		Sweden	33	35	18	53	..
1982-83—Maine Mariners		AHL	16	7	9	16	2
1982-83—Philadelphia Flyers		NHL	2	2	0	2	2
1983-84—Philadelphia Flyers		NHL	73	31	45	76	47
1984-85—Philadelphia Flyers		NHL	73	30	44	74	59
1985-86—Philadelphia Flyers		NHL	79	27	42	69	49
1986-87—Philadelphia Flyers (d)		NHL	75	25	45	70	53
1987-88—Philadelphia Flyers		NHL	68	19	32	51	32
NHL TOTALS			370	134	208	342	242

(c)—February, 1983—Signed by Philadelphia Flyers as a free agent.
(d)—Won Frank J. Selke Trophy (Best Defensive Forward).

WILLIAM POWERS

Center ... 6' ... 175 lbs. ... Born, Cambridge, Mass., April 10, 1966 ... Shoots right.

Year	Team	League	Games	G.	A.	Pts.	Pen.
1985-86—Univ. of Michigan (c)		CCHA	38	15	28	43	10
1986-87—Univ. of Michigan		CCHA	36	13	16	29	18
1987-88—Univ. of Michigan		CCHA	39	22	19	41	8

(c)—June, 1984—Drafted by Philadelphia Flyers in 1984 NHL entry draft. Eleventh Flyers pick, 184th overall, ninth round.

PETR PRAJSLER

Defense ... 6'3" ... 200 lbs. ... Born, Hradec Kralove, Czechoslovakia, September 21, 1965 ... Shoots left ... (October, 1987)—Pulled groin.

Year	Team	League	Games	G.	A.	Pts.	Pen.
1985-86—Pardubice (c)		Czech.	27	5	5	10	34
1986-87—Pardubice		Czech.	41	3	4	7	..
1987-88—Los Angeles Kings		NHL	7	0	0	0	2
1987-88—New Haven Nighthawks		AHL	41	3	8	11	58
NHL TOTALS			7	0	0	0	2

(c)—June, 1985—Drafted by Los Angeles Kings in 1985 NHL entry draft. Fifth Kings pick, 93rd overall, fifth round.

TOM PRATT

Defense ... 6'3" ... 190 lbs. ... Born, Lake Placid, N.Y., August 28, 1965 ... Shoots left.

Year	Team	League	Games	G.	A.	Pts.	Pen.
1983-84—St. Lawrence Univ. (c)		ECAC	32	4	8	12	70
1984-85—St. Lawrence Univ.		ECAC	31	2	4	6	32
1985-86—Bowling Green Univ.		CCHA	38	1	4	5	74
1986-87—Bowling Green Univ.		CCHA	41	1	7	8	46
1987-88—Salt Lake Golden Eagles		IHL	41	2	6	8	146

(c)—June, 1983—Drafted by Calgary Flames in 1983 NHL entry draft. Twelfth Flames pick, 191st overall, 10th round.

JODY PRAZNIK

Defense ... 6'1" ... 180 lbs. ... Born, Winnipeg, Man., June 28, 1969 ... Shoots right.

Year	Team	League	Games	G.	A.	Pts.	Pen.
1986-87—Selkirk Steelers		MJHL	46	11	25	36	63
1987-88—Colorado College (c)		WCHA	37	5	10	15	46

(c)—June, 1988—Drafted by Detroit Red Wings in 1988 NHL entry draft. Eighth Red Wings pick, 185th overall, ninth round.

GARTH PREMAK

Defense . . . 6'1" . . . 185 lbs. . . . Born, Ituna, Sask., March 15, 1968 . . . Shoots left . . . (November, 1984)—Broken hand.

Year	Team	League	Games	G.	A.	Pts.	Pen.
1984-85—Red Deer Rustlers		AJHL	46	8	30	38	56
1985-86—New Westminister Bruins (c)		WHL	72	10	18	28	55
1986-87—Kamloops Blazers		WHL	70	8	28	36	18
1987-88—Kamloops Blazers		WHL	68	10	43	53	72

(c)—June, 1986—Drafted as underage junior by Boston Bruins in 1986 NHL entry draft. Fifth Bruins pick, 118th overall, sixth round.

WAYNE PRESLEY

Right Wing . . . 5'11" . . . 175 lbs. . . . Born, Dearborn, Mich., March 23, 1965 . . . Shoots right . . . (November, 1987)—Missed 36 games following surgery to repair ligaments and cartilage in right knee.

Year	Team	League	Games	G.	A.	Pts.	Pen.
1981-82—Detroit Little Ceasars		Mich. Midget	61	38	56	94	146
1982-83—Kitchener Rangers (c)		OHL	70	39	48	87	99
1983-84—Kitchener Rangers (a-d)		OHL	70	63	76	139	156
1984-85—Kitchener Rangers (e)		OHL	31	25	21	46	77
1984-85—Sault Ste. Marie Greyhounds		OHL	11	5	9	14	14
1984-85—Chicago Black Hawks		NHL	3	0	1	1	0
1985-86—Nova Scotia Oilers		AHL	29	6	9	15	22
1985-86—Chicago Black Hawks		NHL	38	7	8	15	38
1986-87—Chicago Black Hawks		NHL	80	32	29	61	114
1987-88—Chicago Black Hawks		NHL	42	12	10	22	52
NHL TOTALS			163	51	48	99	204

(c)—June, 1983—Drafted as underage junior by Chicago Black Hawks in 1983 NHL entry draft. Second Black Hawks pick, 39th overall, second round.

(d)—Won Jim Mahon Memorial Trophy (Highest scoring right wing).

(e)—January, 1985—Traded by Kitchener Rangers to Sault Ste. Marie Greyhounds for Shawn Tyers.

SHAUN PATRICK (PAT) PRICE

Defense . . . 6'2" . . . 200 lbs. . . . Born, Nelson, B.C., March 24, 1955 . . . Shoots left . . . (January, 1983)—Headaches and nervous disorder . . . (November, 1984)—Separated shoulder . . . (January 2, 1986)—Sprained knee at Quebec and missed 11 games . . . (February 12, 1986)—Apendectomy and missed 13 games.

Year	Team	League	Games	G.	A.	Pts.	Pen.
1970-71—Saskatoon Blades		WCHL	66	2	16	18	56
1971-72—Saskatoon Blades		WCHL	66	10	48	58	85
1972-73—Saskatoon Blades		WCHL	67	12	56	68	134
1973-74—Saskatoon Blades (a-c-d)		WCHL	67	27	68	81	147
1974-75—Vancouver Blazers (e)		WHA	69	5	29	34	54
1975-76—Fort Worth Texans		CHL	72	6	44	50	119
1975-76—New York Islanders		NHL	4	0	2	2	2
1976-77—New York Islanders		NHL	71	3	22	25	25
1977-78—Rochester Americans		AHL	5	2	1	3	9
1977-78—New York Islanders		NHL	52	2	10	12	27
1978-79—New York Islanders (f)		NHL	55	3	11	14	50
1979-80—Edmonton Oilers		NHL	75	11	21	32	134
1980-81—Edmonton Oilers (g)		NHL	59	8	24	32	193
1980-81—Pittsburgh Penguins		NHL	13	0	10	10	33
1981-82—Pittsburgh Penguins		NHL	77	7	31	38	322
1982-83—Pittsburgh Penguins (h)		NHL	38	1	11	12	104
1982-83—Quebec Nordiques		NHL	14	1	2	3	28
1983-84—Quebec Nordiques		NHL	72	3	25	28	188
1984-85—Quebec Nordiques		NHL	68	1	26	27	118
1985-86—Quebec Nordiques		NHL	53	3	13	16	78
1986-87—Fredericton Express		AHL	7	0	0	0	14
1986-87—Quebec Nordiques (i)		NHL	47	0	6	6	81
1986-87—New York Rangers		NHL	13	0	2	2	49
1987-88—Minnesota North Stars (j)		NHL	14	0	2	2	20
1987-88—Kalamazoo Wings		IHL	2	1	1	2	15
WHA TOTALS			69	5	29	34	54
NHL TOTALS			725	43	218	261	1452

(c)—May, 1974—Selected by Vancouver Blazers in WHA amateur player draft.
(d)—Named Outstanding Defenseman in WCHL.
(e)—Drafted from Saskatoon Blades by New York Islanders in first round of 1975 amateur draft.
(f)—June, 1979—Selected by Edmonton Oilers in NHL expansion draft.
(g)—March, 1981—Traded by Edmonton Oilers to Pittsburgh Penguins for Pat Hughes.
(h)—December, 1982—Released by Pittsburgh Penguins and subsequently claimed on waivers by Quebec Nordiques for $2,500.
(i)—March, 1987—Traded by Quebec Nordiques to New York Rangers for Lane Lambert.
(j)—October, 1987—Named playing-assistant coach of Minnesota North Stars.

KEN PRIESTLAY

Center . . . 5'11" . . . 175 lbs. . . . Born, Vancouver, B.C., August 24, 1967 . . . Shoots left . . . (November, 1984)—Shoulder separation.

Year	Team	League	Games	G.	A.	Pts.	Pen.
1983-84—Victoria Cougars		WHL	55	10	18	28	31
1984-85—Victoria Cougars (c)		WHL	50	25	37	62	48
1985-86—Victoria Cougars (b)		WHL	72	73	72	145	45
1985-86—Rochester Americans		AHL	4	0	2	2	0
1986-87—Victoria Cougars (b)		WHL	33	43	39	82	37
1986-87—Buffalo Sabres		NHL	34	11	6	17	8
1986-87—Rochester Americans (d)		AHL	..	..	..	..	..
1987-88—Buffalo Sabres		NHL	33	5	12	17	35
1987-88—Rochester Americans		AHL	43	27	24	51	47
NHL TOTALS			67	16	18	34	43

(c)—June, 1985—Drafted as underage junior by Buffalo Sabres in 1985 NHL entry draft. Fifth Sabres pick, 98th overall, fifth round.
(d)—No regular season record. Played eight playoff games (3 goals, 2 assists).

ROBERT PROBERT

Left Wing . . . 6'3" . . . 205 lbs. . . . Born, Windsor, Ont., June 5, 1965 . . . Shoots left . . . (July 22, 1986)—Entered Hazelden Foundation . . . (July, 1986)—Entered Lindstrom, Minn. Hospital to deal with alcohol abuse problem . . . (November 2, 1986)—Not allowed to re-enter U.S. by customs agents. He was on probation for assaulting a police officer and driving while impaired in July . . . (December 19, 1986)—Suspended by the Detroit Red Wings . . . (1987-88)—Suspended six games during the season for game misconduct penalties.

Year	Team	League	Games	G.	A.	Pts.	Pen.
1981-82—Windsor Club 240		Ont. Midget	55	60	40	100	40
1982-83—Brantford Alexanders (c)		OHL	51	12	16	28	133
1983-84—Brantford Alexanders		OHL	65	35	38	73	189
1984-85—Hamilton Steelhawks		OHL	4	0	1	1	21
1984-85—Sault Ste. Marie Greyhounds		OHL	44	20	52	72	172
1985-86—Adirondack Red Wings		AHL	32	12	15	27	152
1985-86—Detroit Red Wings		NHL	44	8	13	21	186
1986-87—Detroit Red Wings		NHL	63	13	11	24	221
1986-87—Adirondack Red Wings		AHL	7	1	4	5	15
1987-88—Detroit Red Wings		NHL	74	29	33	62	*398
NHL TOTALS			181	50	57	107	805

(c)—June, 1983—Drafted as underage junior by Detroit Red Wings in 1983 NHL entry draft. Third Red Wings pick, 46th overall, third round.

BRIAN PROPP

Left Wing . . . 5'9" . . . 185 lbs. . . . Born, Lanigan, Sask., February 15, 1959 . . . Shoots left . . . Was all-time Western Hockey League scoring leader with 511 points (Broken by Rob Brown in 1986-87) . . . Brother of Ron Propp . . . (January, 1985)—Given four-game suspension . . . (March 4, 1986)—Injured eye vs. Buffalo and missed eight games . . . (December 7, 1986)—Fractured left knee vs. Edmonton . . . (December, 1987)—Sprained left knee.

Year	Team	League	Games	G.	A.	Pts.	Pen.
1975-76—Melville Millionaires		SJHL	57	76	92	168	36
1976-77—Brandon Wheat Kings (b-c-d)		WCHL	72	55	80	135	47
1977-78—Brandon Wheat Kings (a-e)		WCHL	70	70	*112	*182	200
1978-79—Brandon Wheat Kings (a-e-f)		WHL	71	*94	*100	*194	127
1979-80—Philadelphia Flyers		NHL	80	34	41	75	54
1980-81—Philadelphia Flyers		NHL	79	26	40	66	110
1981-82—Philadelphia Flyers		NHL	80	44	47	91	117
1982-83—Philadelphia Flyers		NHL	80	40	42	82	72
1983-84—Philadelphia Flyers		NHL	79	39	53	92	37
1984-85—Philadelphia Flyers		NHL	76	43	53	96	43
1985-86—Philadelphia Flyers		NHL	72	40	57	97	47

Year	Team	League	Games	G.	A.	Pts.	Pen.
1986-87—Philadelphia Flyers		NHL	53	31	36	67	45
1987-88—Philadelphia Flyers		NHL	74	27	49	76	76
NHL TOTALS			673	324	418	742	601

(c)—Named WCHL Rookie of the Year.
(d)—Shared lead in goals (14) during playoffs.
(e)—WCHL leading scorer.
(f)—August, 1979—Drafted by Philadelphia Flyers in entry draft. First Flyers pick, 14th overall, first round.

CHRIS PRYOR

Defense . . . 5'11" . . . 210 lbs. . . . Born, St. Paul, Minn., January 31, 1961 . . . Shoots right.

Year	Team	League	Games	G.	A.	Pts.	Pen.
1979-80—Univ. of New Hampshire		ECAC	27	9	13	22	27
1980-81—Univ. of New Hampshire		ECAC	33	10	27	37	36
1981-82—Univ. of New Hampshire		ECAC	35	3	16	19	36
1982-83—Univ. of New Hampshire		ECAC	34	4	9	13	23
1983-84—Salt Lake Golden Eagles		CHL	72	7	21	28	215
1984-85—Springfield Indians		AHL	77	3	21	24	158
1984-85—Minnesota North Stars (c)		NHL	4	0	0	0	16
1985-86—Springfield Indians		AHL	55	4	16	20	104
1985-86—Minnesota North Stars		NHL	7	0	1	1	0
1986-87—Minnesota North Stars		NHL	50	1	3	4	49
1986-87—Springfield Indians		AHL	5	0	2	2	17
1987-88—Minnesota North Stars (d)		NHL	3	0	0	0	6
1987-88—New York Islanders		NHL	1	0	0	0	2
1987-88—Kalamazoo Wings		IHL	56	4	16	20	171
NHL TOTALS			65	1	4	5	73

(c)—January, 1985—Signed by Minnesota North Stars as a free agent.
(d)—March, 1988—Traded with future considerations by Minnesota North Stars to New York Islanders for Gord Dineen.

JOHN PURVES

Right Wing . . . 6'2" . . . 185 lbs. . . . Born, Toronto, Ont., February 12, 1968 . . . Shoots right . . . (October, 1986)—Broken wrist.

Year	Team	League	Games	G.	A.	Pts.	Pen.
1984-85—Belleville Bulls		OHL	55	15	14	29	39
1984-85—Belleville Bulls		OHL	16	3	9	12	6
1984-85—Hamilton Steelhawks (c)		OHL	36	13	28	41	36
1986-87—Hamilton Steelhawks		OHL	28	12	11	23	37
1987-88—Hamilton Steelhawks		OHL	64	39	44	83	65

(c)—June, 1986—Drafted as underage junior by Washington Capitals in 1986 NHL entry draft. Sixth Capitals pick, 103rd overall, fifth round.

JEFF PYLE

Center . . . 6' . . . 175 lbs. . . . Born, Ft. Leonard Wood, Mo., October 7, 1958 . . . Shoots left.

Year	Team	League	Games	G.	A.	Pts.	Pen.
1978-79—Univ. of Northern Michigan		CCHA	34	15	27	42	4
1979-80—Univ. of Northern Michigan		CCHA	41	26	37	63	12
1980-81—Univ. of Northern Mich.(a-c-d)		CCHA	40	*35	53	88	20
1981-82—Saginaw Gears		IHL	4	2	3	5	0
1981-82—Mohawk Valley Stars		ACHL	29	16	34	50	16
1981-82—Binghamton Whalers		AHL	16	1	1	2	15
1982-83—Mohawk Valley Stars (a)		ACHL	59	53	48	101	44
1983-84—Flint Generals (e)		IHL	80	44	59	103	20
1984-85—Flint Generals		IHL	82	35	59	94	51
1985-86—Saginaw Generals		IHL	80	39	70	109	49
1986-87—Saginaw Generals (b-f-g)		IHL	82	49	*87	*136	34
1987-88—Saginaw Hawks (b)		IHL	66	30	47	77	19

(c)—Named CCHA Most Valuable Player.
(d)—September, 1981—Signed by Hartford Whalers as a free agent.
(e)—Led IHL playoffs with seven goals and shared point lead (15) with Toledo's Kevin Conway and Jim Bissett and Flint's Lawrie Nisker.
(f)—Co-winner of James Gatschene Memorial Trophy (MVP) with Jock Callander.
(g)—Co-winner of Leo P. Lamoureux Memorial Trophy (Top Scorer) with Jock Callander.

JOEL NORMAN QUENNEVILLE

Defense . . . 6' . . . 187 lbs. . . . Born, Windsor, Ont., September 15, 1958 . . . Shoots left . . . (March, 1980)—Rib-cage injury . . . (March, 1980)—Surgery to repair torn ligaments in

ring finger of left hand . . . (January 4, 1982)—Sprained ankle, twisted knee and suffered facial cuts when he crashed into boards during a Rockies practice . . . (December 16, 1985)—Pulled stomach muscle at Montreal and missed four games . . . (December 18, 1986)—Broke right shoulder at Boston and missed 42 games.

Year	Team	League	Games	G.	A.	Pts.	Pen.
1975-76—Windsor Spitfires		Jr."A"OHA	66	15	33	48	61
1976-77—Windsor Spitfires		Jr."A"OHA	65	19	59	78	169
1977-78—Windsor Spitfires (b-c)		Jr."A"OHA	66	27	76	103	114
1978-79—Toronto Maple Leafs		NHL	61	2	9	11	60
1978-79—New Brunswick Hawks		AHL	16	1	10	11	10
1979-80—Toronto Maple Leafs (d)		NHL	32	1	4	5	24
1979-80—Colorado Rockies		NHL	35	5	7	12	26
1980-81—Colorado Rockies		NHL	71	10	24	34	86
1981-82—Colorado Rockies		NHL	64	5	10	15	55
1982-83—New Jersey Devils (e-f)		NHL	74	5	12	17	46
1983-84—Hartford Whalers		NHL	80	5	8	13	95
1984-85—Hartford Whalers		NHL	79	6	16	22	96
1985-86—Hartford Whalers		NHL	71	5	20	25	83
1986-87—Hartford Whalers		NHL	37	3	7	10	24
1987-88—Hartford Whalers		NHL	77	1	8	9	44
NHL TOTALS			681	48	125	173	639

(c)—Drafted from Windsor Spitfires by Toronto Maple Leafs in second round of 1978 amateur draft.
(d)—December, 1979—Traded with Lanny McDonald by Toronto Maple Leafs to Colorado Rockies for Wilf Paiement and Pat Hickey.
(e)—July, 1983—Traded by New Jersey Devils with Steve Tambellini to Calgary Flames for Mel Bridgman and Phil Russell.
(f)—August, 1983—Traded by Calgary Flames with Richie Dunn to Hartford Whalers for Mickey Volcan and third-round draft choice in 1984.

DAN QUINN

Center . . . 5'11" . . . 175 lbs. . . . Born, Ottawa, Ont., June 1, 1965 . . . Shoots left . . . Son of Peter Quinn (former CFL player with Ottawa) . . . (October, 1987)—Broken left wrist.

Year	Team	League	Games	G.	A.	Pts.	Pen.
1981-82—Belleville Bulls		OHL	67	19	32	51	41
1982-83—Belleville Bulls (c)		OHL	70	59	88	147	27
1983-84—Belleville Bulls		OHL	24	23	36	59	12
1983-84—Calgary Flames		NHL	54	19	33	52	20
1984-85—Calgary Flames		NHL	74	20	38	58	22
1985-86—Calgary Flames		NHL	78	30	42	72	44
1986-87—Calgary Flames (d)		NHL	16	3	6	9	14
1986-87—Pittsburgh Penguins		NHL	64	28	43	71	40
1987-88—Pittsburgh Penguins		NHL	70	40	39	79	50
NHL TOTALS			356	140	201	341	190

(c)—June, 1983—Drafted as underage junior by Calgary Flames in 1983 NHL entry draft. First Flames pick, 13th overall, first round.
(d)—November, 1986—Traded by Calgary Flames to Pittsburgh Penguins for Mike Bullard.

JOSEPH D. QUINN

Right Wing . . . 6'1" . . . 185 lbs. . . . Born, Calgary, Alta., February 19, 1967 . . . Shoots right.

Year	Team	League	Games	G.	A.	Pts.	Pen.
1984-85—Abbotsford Flyers		BCJHL	31	7	29	36	52
1985-86—Calgary Canucks (c)		AJHL	29	17	24	41	20
1986-87—Bowling Green Univ.		CCHA	40	4	13	17	22
1987-88—Bowling Green Univ.		CCHA	39	14	13	27	24

(c)—June, 1986—Drafted by Hartford Whalers in 1986 NHL entry draft. Fifth Whalers pick, 116th overall, sixth round.

KEN QUINNEY

Right Wing . . . 5'10" . . . 195 lbs. . . . Born, New Westminster, B.C., May 23, 1965 . . . Shoots right . . . (February, 1986)—Broken wrist.

Year	Team	League	Games	G.	A.	Pts.	Pen.
1981-82—Calgary Wranglers		WHL	63	11	17	28	55
1982-83—Calgary Wranglers		WHL	71	26	25	51	71
1983-84—Calgary Wranglers (c)		WHL	71	64	54	118	38
1984-85—Calgary Wranglers (a)		WHL	56	47	67	114	65
1985-86—Fredericton Express		AHL	61	11	26	37	34
1986-87—Quebec Nordiques		NHL	25	2	7	9	16
1986-87—Fredericton Express		AHL	48	14	27	41	20

Year	Team	League	Games	G.	A.	Pts.	Pen.
1987-88—Fredericton Express	AHL	58	37	39	76	39
1987-88—Quebec Nordiques	NHL	15	2	2	4	5
NHL TOTALS			40	4	9	13	21

(c)—June, 1984—Drafted as underage junior by Quebec Nordiques in NHL entry draft. Ninth Nordiques pick, 203rd overall, 10th round.

STEPHANE QUINTAL

Defense . . . 6'3" . . . 215 lbs. . . . Born, Boucherville, Que., October 22, 1968 . . . Shoots right . . . (December, 1985)—Broken wrist.

Year	Team	League	Games	G.	A.	Pts.	Pen.
1985-86—Granby Bisons	QHL	67	2	17	19	144
1986-87—Granby Bisons (a-c)	QHL	67	13	41	54	178
1987-88—Hull Olympiques	QHL	38	13	23	36	138

(c)—June, 1987—Drafted as underage junior by Boston Bruins in 1987 NHL entry draft. Second Bruins pick, 14th overall, first round.

YVES RACINE

Defense . . . 6' . . . 183 lbs. . . . Born, Matane, Que., February 7, 1969 . . . Shoots left.

Year	Team	League	Games	G.	A.	Pts.	Pen.
1985-86—Ste. Foy Gouverneurs	Que. Midget	42	4	38	42	66
1986-87—Longueuil Chevaliers (c)	QHL	70	7	43	50	50
1987-88—Victoriaville Tigers (a)	QHL	69	10	84	94	150

(c)—June, 1987—Drafted by Detroit Red Wings as underage junior in 1987 NHL entry draft. First Red Wings pick, 11th overall, first round.

HERB RAGLAN

Right Wing . . . 6' . . . 200 lbs. . . . Born, Peterborough, Ont., August 5, 1967 . . . Shoots right . . . Son of Clare Raglan (Detroit and Chicago in early '50s) . . . (December, 1985)—Severely sprained ankle . . . (November, 1987)—Strained right knee ligaments.

Year	Team	League	Games	G.	A.	Pts.	Pen.
1983-84—Peterborough Midget	OHA	26	39	21	60	60
1984-85—Kingston Canadians (c)	OHL	58	20	22	42	166
1985-86—Kingston Canadians	OHL	28	10	9	19	88
1985-86—St. Louis Blues	NHL	7	0	0	0	5
1986-87—St. Louis Blues	NHL	62	6	10	16	159
1987-88—St. Louis Blues	NHL	73	10	15	25	190
NHL TOTALS			142	16	25	41	354

(c)—June, 1985—Drafted as underage junior by St. Louis Blues in 1985 NHL entry draft. First Blues pick, 37th overall, second round.

GEORGE ROBERT (ROB) RAMAGE

Defense . . . 6'2" . . . 210 lbs. . . . Born, Byron, Ont., January 11, 1959 . . . Shoots right . . . (March 22, 1986)—Sprained knee vs. Montreal . . . (November 24, 1986)—Missed 21 games with tendinitis around left kneecap.

Year	Team	League	Games	G.	A.	Pts.	Pen.
1975-76—London Knights	Jr."A"OHA	65	12	31	43	113
1976-77—London Knights	Jr."A"OHA	65	15	58	73	177
1977-78—London Knights (a-c-d)	Jr."A"OHA	59	17	47	64	162
1978-79—Birmingham Bulls (a-e)	WHA	80	12	36	48	165
1979-80—Colorado Rockies	NHL	75	8	20	28	135
1980-81—Colorado Rockies	NHL	79	20	42	62	193
1981-82—Colorado Rockies (f)	NHL	80	13	29	42	201
1982-83—St. Louis Blues	NHL	78	16	35	51	193
1983-84—St. Louis Blues	NHL	80	15	45	60	121
1984-85—St. Louis Blues	NHL	80	7	31	38	178
1985-86—St. Louis Blues	NHL	77	10	56	66	171
1986-87—St. Louis Blues	NHL	59	11	28	39	106
1987-88—St. Louis Blues (g)	NHL	67	8	34	42	127
1987-88—Calgary Flames	NHL	12	1	6	7	37
WHA TOTALS			80	12	36	48	165
NHL TOTALS			687	109	326	435	1462

(c)—July, 1978—Signed by Birmingham Bulls (WHA) as underage junior.

(d)—Shared Max Kaminsky Memorial Trophy (Outstanding Defenseman) with Brad Marsh.

(e)—Drafted by Colorado Rockies in 1979 entry draft. First Rockies pick, first overall, first round.

(f)—June, 1982—Traded by Colorado Rockies to St. Louis Blues for St. Louis' first-round draft choices in 1982 (Rocky Trottier) and 1983 (John MacLean).

(g)—March, 1988—Traded with Rick Wamsley by St. Louis Blues to Calgary Flames for Brett Hull and Steve Bozek.

MICHAEL ALLEN RAMSEY

Defense ... 6'2" ... 185 lbs. ... Born, Minneapolis, Minn., December 3, 1960 ... Shoots left ... Member of 1980 gold-medal U.S. Olympic hockey team ... (December 4, 1983)—Dislocated thumb vs. Montreal ... (October, 1987)—Injured groin ... (January, 1988)—Charlie Horse.

Year	Team	League	Games	G.	A.	Pts.	Pen.
1978-79—University of Minnesota (c)		WCHA	26	6	11	17	30
1979-80—U.S. Olympic Team		Int'l	63	11	24	35	63
1979-80—Buffalo Sabres		NHL	13	1	6	7	6
1980-81—Buffalo Sabres		NHL	72	3	14	17	56
1981-82—Buffalo Sabres		NHL	80	7	23	30	56
1982-83—Buffalo Sabres		NHL	77	8	30	38	55
1983-84—Buffalo Sabres		NHL	72	9	22	31	82
1984-85—Buffalo Sabres		NHL	79	8	22	30	102
1985-86—Buffalo Sabres		NHL	76	7	21	28	117
1986-87—Buffalo Sabres		NHL	80	8	31	39	109
1987-88—Buffalo Sabres		NHL	63	5	16	21	77
NHL TOTALS			612	56	185	241	660

(c)—August, 1979—Drafted by Buffalo Sabres in entry draft. First Sabres pick, 11th overall, first round.

PAUL RANHEIM

Left Wing ... 6' ... 195 lbs. ... Born, St. Louis, Mo., January 25, 1966 ... Shoots right.

Year	Team	League	Games	G.	A.	Pts.	Pen.
1982-83—Edina H.S.		Minn. H.S.	26	12	25	37	4
1983-84—Edina H.S. (c)		Minn. H.S.	26	16	24	40	6
1984-85—Univ. of Wisconsin		WCHA	42	11	11	22	40
1985-86—Univ. of Wisconsin		WCHA	33	17	17	34	34
1986-87—Univ. of Wisconsin		WCHA	42	24	35	59	54
1987-88—Univ. of Wisconsin		WCHA	44	36	26	62	63

(c)—June, 1983—Drafted by Calgary Flames in 1983 NHL entry draft. Flames third pick, 38th overall, second round.

JASON RATHBONE

Right Wing ... 6' ... 175 lbs. ... Born, Syracuse, N.Y., April 13, 1970 ... Shoots right.

Year	Team	League	Games	G.	A.	Pts.	Pen.
1986-87—Brookline H.S.		Mass. H.S.	..	9	11	20	..
1987-88—Brookline H.S. (c)		Mass. H.S.	..	23	23	46	..

(c)—June, 1988—Drafted by New York Islanders in 1988 NHL entry draft. Eighth Islanders pick, 121st overall, sixth round.

MARTY RAUS

Defense ... 6'3" ... 205 lbs. ... Born, Mississauga, Ont., August 4, 1965 ... Shoots right.

Year	Team	League	Games	G.	A.	Pts.	Pen.
1985-86—Northeastern Univ. (c)		H. East	38	4	21	25	30
1986-87—Northeastern Univ.		H. East	26	0	7	7	24
1987-88—Northeastern Univ.		H. East	9	2	3	5	2

(c)—June, 1986—Selected by St. Louis Blues in 1986 NHL supplemental draft.

DEREK RAY

Right Wing ... 5'11" ... 200 lbs. ... Born, Auburn, Mass., October 30, 1963 ... Shoots right.

Year	Team	League	Games	G.	A.	Pts.	Pen.
1982-83—Clarkson University (c)		ECAC	30	1	5	6	50
1983-84—Clarkson University		ECAC	33	12	16	28	102
1984-85—Clarkson University		ECAC	31	6	6	12	94
1985-86—Clarkson University		ECAC	28	8	4	12	142
1986-87—Fort Wayne Komets		IHL	75	16	23	39	156
1987-88—Fort Wayne Komets		IHL	56	13	10	23	99

(c)—June, 1982—Drafted by Winnipeg Jets in 1982 NHL entry draft. Fifth Jets pick, 138th overall, seventh round.

ROB RAY

Left Wing ... 6' ... 200 lbs. ... Born, Belleville, Ont., June 8, 1968 ... Shoots left ... (January, 1987)—Broken jaw.

Year	Team	League	Games	G.	A.	Pts.	Pen.
1984-85—Whitby Lawmen		OPJHL	35	5	10	15	318
1985-86—Cornwall Royals		OHL	53	6	13	19	253
1986-87—Cornwall Royals		OHL	46	17	20	37	158
1987-88—Cornwall Royals (c)		OHL	61	11	41	52	179

(c)—June, 1988—Drafted by Buffalo Sabres in 1988 NHL entry draft. Fifth Sabres pick, 97th overall, fifth round.

MARK RECCHI

Center . . . 5'9" . . . 185 lbs. . . . . Born, Kamloops, B.C., February 1, 1968 . . . Shoots left . . . (January, 1987)—Broken ankle.

Year	Team	League	Games	G.	A.	Pts.	Pen.
1984-85—Langley Eagles		BCJHL	51	26	39	65	39
1985-86—New Westminster Bruins		WHL	72	21	40	61	55
1986-87—Kamloops Blazers		WHL	40	26	50	76	63
1987-88—Kamloops Blazers (c)		WHL	62	61	93	154	75

(c)—June, 1988—Drafted by Pittsburgh Penguins in 1988 NHL entry draft. Fourth Penguins pick, 67th overall, fourth round.

CRAIG REDMOND

Defense . . . 5'10" . . . 190 lbs. . . . Born, Dawson Creek, B.C., September 22, 1965 . . . Shoots left . . . Cousin of Mickey and Dick Redmond (former NHL players through the 1970s) . . . (November 6, 1986)—Right knee cartilage surgery . . . (February, 1987)—Tendinitis and inflammation of right knee . . . (October 15, 1987)—Suspended by Los Angeles Kings for failing to report to New Haven.

Year	Team	League	Games	G.	A.	Pts.	Pen.
1980-81—Abbotsford Flyers		BCJHL	40	15	22	37	..
1981-82—Abbotsford Flyers		BCJHL	45	30	76	106	..
1982-83—University of Denver (c)		WCHA	34	18	36	54	44
1983-84—Canadian Olympic Team (d)		Int'l	55	10	11	21	38
1984-85—Los Angeles Kings		NHL	79	6	33	39	57
1985-86—Los Angeles Kings		NHL	73	6	18	24	57
1986-87—New Haven Nighthawks		AHL	5	2	2	4	6
1986-87—Los Angeles Kings		NHL	16	1	7	8	8
1987-88—Los Angeles Kings (e)		NHL	2	0	0	0	0
NHL TOTALS			170	13	58	71	122

(c)—Won WCHA Rookie of the Year Award.

(d)—June, 1984—Drafted by Los Angeles Kings in NHL entry draft. First Kings pick, sixth overall, first round.

(e)—August, 1988—Traded by Los Angeles Kings to Edmonton Oilers for John Miner.

MARK REEDS

Right Wing . . . 5'10" . . . 188 lbs. . . . Born, Burlington, Ont., January 24, 1960 . . . Shoots right . . . (November 19, 1983)—Cryotherapy to repair the margins of his retina.

Year	Team	League	Games	G.	A.	Pts.	Pen.
1976-77—Markham Waxers		OPJHL	24	17	23	40	62
1976-77—Toronto Marlboros		OMJHL	18	6	7	13	6
1977-78—Peterborough Petes		OMJHL	68	11	27	36	67
1978-79—Peterborough Petes (c)		OMJHL	66	25	25	50	91
1979-80—Peterborough Petes		OMJHL	54	34	45	79	51
1980-81—Salt Lake Golden Eagles		CHL	74	15	45	60	81
1981-82—Salt Lake Golden Eagles		CHL	59	22	24	46	55
1981-82—St. Louis Blues		NHL	9	1	3	4	0
1982-83—Salt Lake Golden Eagles		CHL	55	16	26	42	32
1982-83—St. Louis Blues		NHL	20	5	14	19	6
1983-84—St. Louis Blues		NHL	65	11	14	25	23
1984-85—St. Louis Blues		NHL	80	9	30	39	25
1985-86—St. Louis Blues		NHL	78	10	28	38	28
1986-87—St. Louis Blues		NHL	68	9	16	25	16
1987-88—Hartford Whalers (d)		NHL	38	0	7	7	31
NHL TOTALS			358	45	112	157	129

(c)—August, 1979—Drafted by St. Louis Blues as an underage junior in NHL entry draft. Third St. Louis pick, 86th overall, fifth round.

(d)—October 5, 1987—Traded by St. Louis Blues to Hartford Whalers for a third-round 1989 draft pick.

JOE JAMES REEKIE

Defense . . . 6'2" . . . 176 lbs. . . . Born, Victoria, B.C., February 22, 1965 . . . Shoots left . . .

(March 14, 1987)—Injured ankle at Edmonton . . . (October, 1987)—Injured shoulder . . . (November 15, 1987)—Broken kneecap at Toronto.

Year	Team	League	Games	G.	A.	Pts.	Pen.
1981-82—Nepean Raiders		CJHL	16	2	5	7	4
1982-83—North Bay Centennials (c)		OHL	59	2	9	11	49
1983-84—North Bay Centennials		OHL	9	1	0	1	18
1983-84—Cornwall Royals (d)		OHL	53	6	27	33	166
1984-85—Cornwall Royals (e)		OHL	65	19	63	82	134
1985-86—Rochester Americans		AHL	77	3	25	28	178
1985-86—Buffalo Sabres		NHL	3	0	0	0	14
1986-87—Buffalo Sabres		NHL	56	1	8	9	82
1986-87—Rochester Americans		AHL	22	0	6	6	52
1987-88—Buffalo Sabres		NHL	30	1	4	5	68
NHL TOTALS			89	2	12	14	164

(c)—June, 1983—Drafted as underage junior by Hartford Whalers in 1983 NHL entry draft. Eighth Whalers pick, 124th overall, seventh round.
(d)—June, 1984—Released by Hartford Whalers.
(e)—June, 1985—Drafted by Buffalo Sabres in 1985 NHL entry draft. Sixth Sabres pick, 119th overall, sixth round.

BRENT REGAN

Left Wing . . . 6' . . . 175 lbs. . . . Born, Edmonton, Alta., March 4, 1966 . . . Shoots left.

Year	Team	League	Games	G.	A.	Pts.	Pen.
1984-85—Bowling Green Univ. (c)		CCHA	42	6	18	24	12
1985-86—Bowling Green Univ.		CCHA	32	4	2	6	28
1986-87—Bowling Green Univ.		CCHA	43	12	17	29	22
1987-88—Bowling Green Univ.		CCHA	42	28	22	50	34

(c)—June, 1984—Drafted by Hartford Whalers in 1984 NHL entry draft. Fifth Whalers pick, 194th overall, 10th round.

DAVID REID

Left Wing . . . 6'1" . . . 205 lbs. . . . Born, Toronto, Ont., May 15, 1964 . . . Shoots left . . . (November 14, 1985)—Sprained ankle at Toronto and missed four games . . . (December, 1986)—Knee surgery . . . (November, 1987)—Missed 10 games with separated shoulder in AHL game.

Year	Team	League	Games	G.	A.	Pts.	Pen.
1980-81—Mississauga Midgets		Ont. Midget	39	21	32	53	....
1981-82—Peterborough Petes (c)		OHL	68	10	32	42	41
1982-83—Peterborough Petes		OHL	70	23	34	57	33
1983-84—Peterborough Petes		OHL	60	33	64	97	12
1983-84—Boston Bruins		NHL	8	1	0	1	2
1984-85—Hershey Bears		AHL	43	10	14	24	6
1984-85—Boston Bruins		NHL	35	14	13	27	27
1985-86—Moncton Golden Flames		AHL	26	14	18	32	4
1985-86—Boston Bruins		NHL	37	10	10	20	10
1986-87—Boston Bruins		NHL	12	3	3	6	0
1986-87—Moncton Golden Flames		AHL	40	12	22	34	23
1987-88—Maine Mariners		AHL	63	21	37	58	40
1987-88—Boston Bruins		NHL	3	0	0	0	0
NHL TOTALS			95	28	26	54	39

(c)—June, 1982—Drafted by Boston Bruins as underage junior in 1982 NHL entry draft. Fourth Bruins pick, 60th overall, third round.

DAVE REIERSON

Defense . . . 5'11" . . . 172 lbs. . . . Born, Bashaw, Alta., August 30, 1964 . . . Shoots right.

Year	Team	League	Games	G.	A.	Pts.	Pen.
1980-81—Prince Albert Raiders		SAJHL	73	14	39	53	..
1981-82—Prince Albert Raiders (c)		SAJHL	87	23	76	99	..
1982-83—Michigan Tech.		CCHA	38	2	14	16	58
1983-84—Michigan Tech.		CCHA	38	4	15	19	63
1984-85—Michigan Tech.		WCHA	36	5	27	32	76
1985-86—Michigan Tech.		WCHA	39	7	16	23	51
1986-87—Moncton Golden Flames (d)		AHL	..	..	..	..	..
1987-88—Canadian Olympic Team		Int'l	61	1	17	18	36
1987-88—Salt Lake Golden Eagles		IHL	48	10	19	29	42

(c)—June, 1982—Drafted as underage junior by Calgary Flames in 1982 NHL entry draft. First Flames pick, 29th overall, second round.
(d)—No regular season record. Played six playoff games.

PAUL REINHART

Defense . . . 5'11" . . . 216 lbs. . . . Born, Kitchener, Ont., January 8, 1960 . . . Shoots left . . . (January 13, 1981)—Strained ligaments . . . (September, 1981)—Injured ligaments in right ankle during Canada Cup . . . Brother of Kevin Reinhart (Toronto '78 draft pick, 132nd overall) . . . Set Flames club records for goals (18 in '80-81), assists (58 in '82-83) and points (75 in '82-83) by a defenseman in one season . . . (November 24, 1983)—Injured back in game vs. Winnipeg . . . (April, 1984)—Reinjured back in playoff series with Edmonton . . . (December, 1984)—Recurring back problems . . . (November, 1987)—Deteriorating back disc.

Year	Team	League	Games	G.	A.	Pts.	Pen.
1975-76—Kitchener Rangers		OMJHL	53	6	33	39	42
1976-77—Kitchener Rangers		OMJHL	51	4	14	18	16
1977-78—Kitchener Rangers		OMJHL	47	17	28	45	15
1978-79—Kitchener Rangers (c)		OMJHL	66	51	78	129	57
1979-80—Atlanta Flames		NHL	79	9	38	47	31
1980-81—Calgary Flames		NHL	74	18	49	67	52
1981-82—Calgary Flames		NHL	62	13	48	61	17
1982-83—Calgary Flames		NHL	78	17	58	75	28
1983-84—Calgary Flames		NHL	27	6	15	21	10
1984-85—Calgary Flames		NHL	75	23	46	69	18
1985-86—Calgary Flames		NHL	32	8	25	33	15
1986-87—Calgary Flames		NHL	76	15	54	69	22
1987-88—Calgary Flames		NHL	14	0	4	4	10
NHL TOTALS			517	109	337	446	203

(c)—August, 1979—Drafted by Atlanta Flames as underage junior in NHL entry draft. First Flames pick, 12th overall, first round.

ERIC REISMAN

Defense . . . 6'2" . . . 220 lbs. . . . Born, Manhatten, N.Y., May 19, 1968 . . . Shoots left.

Year	Team	League	Games	G.	A.	Pts.	Pen.
1987-88—Ohio State Univ. (c)		CCHA	29	0	3	3	45

(c)—June, 1988—Drafted by Boston Bruins in 1988 NHL entry draft. Eighth Bruins pick, 228th overall, 11th round.

BRUCE RENDALL

Left Wing . . . 6'1" . . . 180 lbs. . . . Born, Thunder Bay, Ont., April 8, 1967 . . . Shoots left . . . (December, 1987)—Broken left wrist.

Year	Team	League	Games	G.	A.	Pts.	Pen.
1984-85—Chatham Maroons (c)		OHA	46	32	33	65	62
1985-86—Michigan State Univ.		CCHA	45	14	18	32	68
1986-87—Michigan State Univ.		CCHA	44	11	15	25	113
1987-88—Michigan State Univ.		CCHA	39	10	2	12	70

(c)—June, 1985—Drafted by Philadelphia Flyers in 1985 NHL entry draft. Second Flyers pick, 42nd overall, second round.

ROBERT REYNOLDS

Center . . . 5'11" . . . 175 lbs. . . . Born, Flint, Mich., July 14, 1967 . . . Shoots left . . . Also plays Left Wing.

Year	Team	League	Games	G.	A.	Pts.	Pen.
1983-84—St. Clair Shores Falcons		GLJHL	60	25	34	59	....
1984-85—St. Clair Shores Falcons (c)		GLJHL	43	20	30	50	....
1985-86—Michigan State Univ.		CCHA	45	9	10	19	26
1986-87—Michigan State Univ.		CCHA	40	20	13	33	40
1987-88—Michigan State Univ.		CCHA	46	42	25	67	52

(c)—June, 1985—Drafted by Toronto Maple Leafs in 1985 NHL entry draft. Tenth Maple Leafs pick, 190th overall, 10th round.

GRANT REZANSOFF

Center . . . 5'11" . . . 181 lbs. . . . Born, Surrey, B.C., March 3, 1961 . . . Shoots right.

Year	Team	League	Games	G.	A.	Pts.	Pen.
1978-79—Delta		BCJHL	61	42	45	87	22
1979-80—Victoria Cougars		WHL	67	17	19	36	7
1980-81—Victoria Cougars (c)		WHL	72	40	57	97	27
1981-82—Muskegon Mohawks		IHL	37	15	11	26	4
1981-82—Oklahoma City Stars		CHL	45	15	20	35	10
1982-83—Colorado Flames		CHL	22	4	3	7	16
1982-83—Peoria Prancers		IHL	49	23	42	65	23
1983-84—Peoria Prancers		IHL	82	36	46	82	11

Year	Team	League	Games	G.	A.	Pts.	Pen.
1984-85—Toledo Goaldiggers		IHL	25	9	10	19	0
1984-85—Salt Lake Golden Eagles (d)		IHL	37	12	17	29	29
1985-86—Peoria Rivermen (e)		IHL	80	30	47	77	23
1986-87—Peoria Rivermen		IHL	82	25	44	69	33
1987-88—Peoria Rivermen		IHL	78	21	38	59	42

(c)—August, 1981—Signed by Calgary Flames as a free agent.
(d)—February, 1985—Traded with Kevin Conway, Blake Stephan and Steve Harrison by Toledo Goaldiggers to Salt Lake Golden Eagles for Steve Martinson and Kurt Kleinendorst.
(e)—September, 1985—Signed by Peoria Rivermen as a free agent.

JEAN-MARC RICHARD

Defense ... 5'11" ... 170 lbs. ... Born, St. Raymond, Que., October 8, 1966 ... Shoots left.

Year	Team	League	Games	G.	A.	Pts.	Pen.
1983-84—Chicoutimi Sagueneens		QHL	61	1	20	21	41
1984-85—Chicoutimi Sagueneens		QHL	68	10	61	71	57
1985-86—Chicoutimi Sagueneens (a)		QHL	72	19	88	107	111
1986-87—Chicoutimi Sagueneens (a-c)		QHL	67	21	81	102	105
1987-88—Fredericton Express		AHL	68	14	42	56	52
1987-88—Quebec Nordiques		NHL	4	2	1	3	2
NHL TOTALS			4	2	1	3	2

(c)—April, 1987—Signed by Quebec Nordiques as a free agent.

MIKE RICHARD

Center ... 5'9" ... 175 lbs. ... Born, Toronto, Ont., July 9, 1966 ... Shoots left ... (December, 1987)—Set AHL record with points in 31 straight games between October 18 and December 26, 1987 (25g, 30a).

Year	Team	League	Games	G.	A.	Pts.	Pen.
1982-83—Don Mills Midgets		OHA	40	25	30	55	10
1983-84—Toronto Marlboros		OHL	66	19	17	36	12
1984-85—Toronto Marlboros		OHL	66	31	41	72	15
1985-86—Toronto Marlboros		OHL	63	32	48	80	28
1986-87—Toronto Marlboros (c)		OHL	66	*57	50	107	38
1986-87—Baltimore Skipjacks (d)		AHL	9	5	2	7	2
1987-88—Washington Capitals (e)		NHL	4	0	0	0	0
1987-88—Binghamton Whalers		AHL	72	46	48	94	23
NHL TOTALS			4	0	0	0	0

(c)—Won Leo Lalonde Memorial Trophy (Top Overage Player).
(d)—April, 1987—Signed by Baltimore Skipjacks as a free agent.
(e)—October, 1988—Signed by Washington Capitals as a free agent.

TODD RICHARDS

Defense ... 6' ... 180 lbs. ... Born, Robbinsdale, Minn., October 20, 1966 ... Shoots right ... (January 8, 1988)—Separated shoulder vs. North Dakota.

Year	Team	League	Games	G.	A.	Pts.	Pen.
1984-85—Armstrong H.S. (c)		Minn. H.S.	24	10	23	33	24
1985-86—Univ. of Minnesota		WCHA	38	6	23	29	38
1986-87—Univ. of Minnesota (b)		WCHA	49	8	43	51	70
1987-88—Univ. of Minnesota		WCHA	34	10	30	40	26

(c)—June, 1985—Drafted by Montreal Canadiens in 1985 NHL entry draft. Third Canadiens pick, 33rd overall, second round.

TRAVIS RICHARDS

Defense ... 6' ... 180 lbs. ... Born, Robbinsdale, Minn., March 3, 1970 ... Shoots right ... (January, 1988)—Separated shoulder.

Year	Team	League	Games	G.	A.	Pts.	Pen.
1986-87—Armstrong H.S.		Minn. H.S.	22	6	16	22	20
1987-88—Armstrong H.S. (c)		Minn. H.S.	24	14	14	28	....

(c)—June, 1988—Drafted by Minnesota North Stars in 1988 NHL entry draft. Sixth North Stars pick, 169th overall, ninth round.

LUKE RICHARDSON

Defense ... 6'4" ... 210 lbs. ... Born, Ottawa, Ont., March 26, 1969 ... Shoots left.

Year	Team	League	Games	G.	A.	Pts.	Pen.
1984-85—Ottawa Golden Knights		OHA	35	5	26	31	72
1985-86—Peterborough Petes		OHL	63	6	18	24	57

Year	Team	League	Games	G.	A.	Pts.	Pen.
1986-87—Peterborough Petes (c)		OHL	59	13	32	45	70
1987-88—Toronto Maple Leafs		NHL	78	4	6	10	90
NHL TOTALS			78	4	6	10	90

(c)—June, 1987—Drafted as underage junior by Toronto Maple Leafs in 1987 NHL entry draft. First Maple Leafs pick, seventh overall, first round.

STEPHANE RICHER

Center . . . 6' . . . 190 lbs. . . . Born, Buckingham, Que., June 7, 1966 . . . Shoots right . . . (November 18, 1985)—Sprained ankle vs. Boston and missed 13 games . . . (November, 1987)—Missed three games with knee injury . . . (March 12, 1988)—Bruised right hand in fight with Kevin Dineen vs. Hartford . . . (April, 1988)—Broke right thumb when slashed by Michael Thelven in playoff game vs. Boston.

Year	Team	League	Games	G.	A.	Pts.	Pen.
1983-84—Granby Bisons (c)		QHL	67	39	37	76	58
1984-85—Granby Bisons/Chic. Sags. (b-d)		QHL	57	61	59	120	71
1984-85—Montreal Canadiens		NHL	1	0	0	0	0
1984-85—Sherbrooke Canadiens (e)		AHL	....	...	....	....	....
1985-86—Montreal Canadiens		NHL	65	21	16	37	50
1986-87—Sherbrooke Canadiens		AHL	12	10	4	14	11
1986-87—Montreal Canadiens		NHL	57	20	19	39	80
1987-88—Montreal Canadiens		NHL	72	50	28	78	72
NHL TOTALS			194	91	63	154	202

(c)—June, 1984—Drafted as underage junior by Montreal Canadiens in NHL entry draft. Third Canadiens pick, 29th overall, second round.

(d)—January, 1985—Traded with Greg Choules by Granby Bisons to Chicoutimi Sagueneens for Stephane Roy, Marc Bureau, Lee Duhemee, Sylvain Demers and Rene Lecuyer.

(e)—No regular season record. Played nine playoff games (6 goals, 3 assists).

STEVE RICHMOND

Defense . . . 6'1" . . . 205 lbs. . . . Born, Chicago, Ill., December 11, 1959 . . . Shoots left . . . (December, 1986)—Three-game NHL suspension . . . (February, 1987)—Strained left knee.

Year	Team	League	Games	G.	A.	Pts.	Pen.
1978-79—University of Michigan		WCHA	34	2	5	7	38
1979-80—University of Michigan		WCHA	38	10	19	29	26
1980-81—University of Michigan		WCHA	39	22	32	54	46
1981-82—University of Michigan (b-c)		CCHA	38	6	30	36	68
1982-83—Tulsa Oilers		CHL	78	5	13	18	187
1983-84—Tulsa Oilers		CHL	38	1	17	18	114
1983-84—New York Rangers		NHL	26	2	5	7	110
1984-85—New Haven Nighthawks		AHL	37	3	10	13	122
1984-85—New York Rangers		NHL	34	0	5	5	90
1985-86—New Haven Nighthawks		AHL	11	2	6	8	32
1985-86—New York Rangers (d)		NHL	17	0	2	2	63
1985-86—Adirondack Red Wings		AHL	20	1	7	8	23
1985-86—Detroit Red Wings (e)		NHL	29	1	2	3	82
1986-87—New Jersey Devils		NHL	44	1	7	8	143
1987-88—Utica Devils		AHL	79	6	27	33	141
1987-88—Flint Spirits		IHL	2	0	2	2	2
NHL TOTALS			150	4	21	25	488

(c)—July, 1982—Signed by New York Rangers as a free agent.

(d)—December, 1985—Traded by New York Rangers to Detroit Red Wings for Mike McEwen.

(e)—August, 1986—Traded by Detroit Red Wings to New Jersey Devils for Sam St. Laurent.

BARRY RICHTER

Defense . . . 6'2" . . . 190 lbs. . . . Born, Madison, Wis., September 11, 1970 . . . Shoots left . . . Son of Pat Richter (Former Washington Redskins football player).

Year	Team	League	Games	G.	A.	Pts.	Pen.
1986-87—Culver Academy		Indiana H.S.	35	19	26	45	..
1987-88—Culver Academy (c)		Indiana H.S.	35	24	29	53	18

(c)—June, 1988—Drafted by Hartford Whalers in 1988 NHL entry draft. Second Whalers pick, 32nd overall, second round.

DAVE RICHTER

Defense . . . 6'5" . . . 217 lbs. . . . Born, Winnipeg, Man., April 8, 1960 . . . Shoots right . . . (November, 1982)—Strained knee ligaments . . . (Summer, 1983)—Elbow surgery . . .

(October, 1984)—Strained abdominal muscle during training camp . . . (February, 1985)—Shoulder injury . . . (September, 1985)—Missed first seven games of season due to a pulled groin from training camp . . . (January 17, 1986)—Sprained knee vs. N.Y. Islanders and missed six games . . . (November, 1987)—Strained left knee . . . (February, 1988)—Bruised eye . . . (March 9, 1988)—Suspended 10 NHL games.

Year	Team	League	Games	G.	A.	Pts.	Pen.
1979-80—University of Michigan		WCHA	34	0	4	4	54
1980-81—University of Michigan		WCHA	36	2	13	15	56
1981-82—University of Michigan		CCHA	36	9	12	21	78
1981-82—Nashville South Stars		CHL	2	0	1	1	0
1981-82—Minnesota North Stars (c)		NHL	3	0	0	0	11
1982-83—Minnesota North Stars		NHL	6	0	0	0	4
1982-83—Birmingham South Stars		CHL	69	6	17	23	211
1983-84—Salt Lake Golden Eagles		CHL	10	1	4	5	39
1983-84—Minnesota North Stars		NHL	42	2	3	5	132
1984-85—Springfield Indians		AHL	3	0	0	0	2
1984-85—Minnesota North Stars		NHL	55	2	8	10	221
1985-86—Minnesota North Stars (d)		NHL	14	0	3	3	29
1985-86—Philadelphia Flyers (e)		NHL	50	0	2	2	138
1986-87—Vancouver Canucks		NHL	78	2	15	17	172
1987-88—Vancouver Canucks		NHL	49	2	4	6	224
NHL TOTALS			297	8	35	43	931

(c)—June, 1982—Signed by Minnesota North Stars as a free agent.
(d)—November, 1985—Traded with Bo Berglund by Minnesota North Stars to Philadelphia Flyers for Todd Bergen and Ed Hospodar.
(e)—June, 1986—Traded by Philadelphia Flyers with Rich Sutter and a third-round draft choice in 1986 to Vancouver Canucks for J.J. Daigneault, a second-round draft choice (Kent Hawley) in 1986 and a fifth-round pick in 1987.

MIKE RIDLEY

Center . . . 6'1" . . . 200 lbs. . . . Born, Winnipeg, Man., July 8, 1963 . . . Shoots left.

Year	Team	League	Games	G.	A.	Pts.	Pen.
1983-84—University of Manitoba (c)		GPAC	46	39	41	80	..
1984-85—University of Manitoba		GPAC	30	29	38	67	..
1985-86—New York Rangers (d)		NHL	80	22	43	65	69
1986-87—New York Rangers (e)		NHL	38	16	20	36	20
1986-87—Washington Capitals		NHL	40	15	19	34	20
1987-88—Washington Capitals		NHL	70	28	31	59	22
NHL TOTALS			228	81	113	194	131

(c)—Won Sen. Joseph Sullivan Award as the top Canadian College hockey player.
(d)—September, 1985—Signed by New York Rangers as a free agent.
(e)—January, 1987—Traded with Kelly Miller and Bobby Crawford by New York Rangers to Washington Capitals for Bobby Carpenter and a second-round 1989 draft pick.

GARY ROBERTS

Left Wing . . . 6'1" . . . 190 lbs. . . . Born, North York, Ont., May 23, 1966 . . . Shoots left.

Year	Team	League	Games	G.	A.	Pts.	Pen.
1981-82—Whitby Midgets		Ont. Midgets	44	55	31	86	133
1982-83—Ottawa 67's		OHL	53	12	8	20	83
1983-84—Ottawa 67's (c-d)		OHL	48	27	30	57	144
1984-85—Ottawa 67's (b)		OHL	59	44	62	106	186
1984-85—Moncton Golden Flames		AHL	7	4	2	6	7
1985-86—Ottawa 67's		OHL	24	26	25	51	83
1985-86—Guelph Platers (b)		OHL	23	18	15	33	65
1986-87—Moncton Golden Flames		AHL	38	20	18	38	72
1986-87—Calgary Flames		NHL	32	5	9	14	6
1987-88—Calgary Flames		NHL	74	13	15	28	282
NHL TOTALS			106	18	24	42	288

(c)—Led OHL playoffs with 62 penalty minutes.
(d)—June, 1984—Drafted as underage junior by Calgary Flames in 1984 NHL entry draft. First Flames pick, 12th overall, first round.

GORDON ROBERTS

Defense . . . 6' . . . 195 lbs. . . . Born, Detroit, Mich., October 2, 1957 . . . Shoots left . . . Brother of former NHLers Dave and Doug Roberts . . . (April, 1984)—Bruised hip during playoff series with Edmonton . . . (November 13, 1985)—Injured foot at Hartford and missed four games . . . (October, 1986)—Dislocated shoulder . . . (January, 1988)—Bruised shoulder.

Year	Team	League	Games	G.	A.	Pts.	Pen.
1973-74—Detroit Jr. Red Wings	SOJHL	70	25	55	80	340
1974-75—Victoria Cougars (c)	WCHL	53	19	45	64	145
1975-76—New England Whalers	WHA	77	3	19	22	102
1976-77—New England Whalers (d)	WHA	77	13	33	46	169
1977-78—New England Whalers	WHA	78	15	46	61	118
1978-79—New England Whalers	WHA	79	11	46	57	113
1979-80—Hartford Whalers	NHL	80	8	28	36	89
1980-81—Hartford Whalers (e)	NHL	27	2	11	13	81
1980-81—Minnesota North Stars	NHL	50	6	31	37	94
1981-82—Minnesota North Stars	NHL	79	4	30	34	119
1982-83—Minnesota North Stars	NHL	80	3	41	44	103
1983-84—Minnesota North Stars	NHL	77	8	45	53	132
1984-85—Minnesota North Stars	NHL	78	6	36	42	112
1985-86—Minnesota North Stars	NHL	76	2	21	23	101
1986-87—Minnesota North Stars	NHL	67	3	10	13	68
1987-88—Minnesota North Stars (f)	NHL	48	1	10	11	103
1987-88—Philadelphia Flyers (g)	NHL	11	1	2	3	15
1987-88—St. Louis Blues	NHL	11	1	3	4	25
WHA TOTALS		311	42	144	186	502
NHL TOTALS		684	45	268	313	1042

(c)—September, 1975—Signed by New England Whalers (WHA).

(d)—Drafted from New England Whalers (WHA) by Montreal Canadiens in third round of 1977 amateur draft.

(e)—December, 1980—Traded by Hartford Whalers to Minnesota North Stars for Mike Fidler.

(f)—February, 1988—Traded by Minnesota North Stars to Philadelphia Flyers for a fourth round 1989 draft pick.

(g)—March, 1988—Traded by Philadelphia Flyers to St. Louis Blues for a fifth-round 1989 draft pick.

TIM ROBERTS

Center . . . 6'2" . . . 180 lbs. . . . Born, Boston, Mass., March 6, 1969 . . . Shoots left.

Year	Team	League	Games	G.	A.	Pts.	Pen.
1985-86—Deerfield Academy	Mass. H.S.	..	20	22	42	..
1986-87—Deerfield Academy (c)	Mass. H.S.	..	18	15	33	..
1987-88—R.P.I.	ECAC	28	5	9	14	40

(c)—June, 1987—Drafted by Buffalo Sabres in 1987 NHL entry draft. Ninth Sabres pick, 153rd overall, eighth round.

TORRIE ANDREW ROBERTSON

Left Wing . . . 5'11" . . . 185 lbs. . . . Born, Victoria, B.C., August 2, 1961 . . . Shoots left . . . Brother of Geordie Robertson . . . (November 29, 1986)—Multiple fracture of left leg at Montreal and missed remainder of season . . . (November 16, 1987)—Returned to Hartford lineup.

Year	Team	League	Games	G.	A.	Pts.	Pen.
1978-79—Victoria Cougars	WHL	69	18	23	41	141
1979-80—Victoria Cougars (c)	WHL	72	23	24	47	298
1980-81—Victoria Cougars (b)	WHL	59	45	66	111	274
1980-81—Washington Capitals	NHL	3	0	0	0	0
1981-82—Hershey Bears	AHL	21	5	3	8	60
1981-82—Washington Capitals	NHL	54	8	13	21	204
1982-83—Washington Capitals	NHL	5	2	0	2	4
1982-83—Hershey Bears	AHL	69	21	33	54	187
1983-84—Hartford Whalers (d)	NHL	66	7	14	21	198
1984-85—Hartford Whalers	NHL	74	11	30	41	337
1985-86—Hartford Whalers	NHL	76	13	24	37	358
1986-87—Hartford Whalers	NHL	20	1	0	1	98
1987-88—Hartford Whalers	NHL	63	2	8	10	293
NHL TOTALS		361	44	89	133	1492

(c)—June, 1980—Drafted by Washington Capitals as underage junior in 1980 NHL entry draft. Third Capitals pick, 55th overall, third round.

(d)—October, 1983—Traded by Washington Capitals to Hartford Whalers for Greg Adams.

JEFFREY ROBINSON

Defense . . . 6'1" . . . 180 lbs. . . . Born, Norwood, Mass., June 3, 1970 . . . Shoots left . . . (January, 1988)—Broken wrist.

Year	Team	League	Games	G.	A.	Pts.	Pen.
1986-87—Mt. St. Charles	R.I. H.S.	24	11	14	25	..
1987-88—Mt. St. Charles (c)	R.I. H.S.	..	5	30	35	..

(c)—June, 1988—Drafted by Los Angeles Kings in 1988 NHL entry draft. Fifth Kings pick, 91st overall, fifth round.

LARRY CLARK ROBINSON

Defense ... 6'3" ... 210 lbs. ... Born, Winchester, Ont., June 2, 1951 ... Shoots left ... Also plays Left Wing ... Brother of Moe Robinson ... Missed part of 1978-79 season with water on the knee ... (March 6, 1980)—Right shoulder separation vs. Edmonton ... (October, 1980)—Groin injury ... (November 14, 1980)—Separated left shoulder ... (January 8, 1981)—Broken nose ... (October, 1982)—Sore left shoulder ... (October, 1983)—Skin infection behind right knee ... (March, 1985)—Hyperextended left elbow ... (March 9, 1987)—Strained ligaments in right ankle when checked by Dennis Maruk at Minnesota ... (August, 1987)—Broke right leg in a polo accident ... (December, 1987)—Sprained right wrist.

Year	Team	League	Games	G.	A.	Pts.	Pen.
1968-69—Brockville Braves	Cent. Jr. OHA	....	...	....	....	....	....
1969-70—Brockville Braves (a)	Cent. Jr. OHA	40	22	29	51	74
1970-71—Kitchener Rangers (c)	Jr."A" OHA	61	12	39	51	65
1971-72—Nova Scotia Voyageurs	AHL	74	10	14	24	54
1972-73—Nova Scotia Voyageurs	AHL	38	6	33	39	33
1972-73—Montreal Canadiens	NHL	36	2	4	6	20
1973-74—Montreal Canadiens	NHL	78	6	20	26	66
1974-75—Montreal Canadiens	NHL	80	14	47	61	76
1975-76—Montreal Canadiens	NHL	80	10	30	40	59
1976-77—Montreal Canadiens (a-d)	NHL	77	19	66	85	45
1977-78—Montreal Canadiens (b-e-f)	NHL	80	13	52	65	39
1978-79—Montreal Canadiens (a)	NHL	67	16	45	61	33
1979-80—Montreal Canadiens (a-d)	NHL	72	14	61	75	39
1980-81—Montreal Canadiens (b)	NHL	65	12	38	50	37
1981-82—Montreal Canadiens	NHL	71	12	47	59	41
1982-83—Montreal Canadiens	NHL	71	14	49	63	33
1983-84—Montreal Canadiens	NHL	74	9	34	43	39
1984-85—Montreal Canadiens	NHL	76	14	33	47	44
1985-86—Montreal Canadiens (b)	NHL	78	19	63	82	39
1986-87—Montreal Canadiens	NHL	70	13	37	50	44
1987-88—Montreal Canadiens	NHL	53	6	34	40	30
NHL TOTALS			1128	193	660	853	684

(c)—Drafted from Kitchener Rangers by Montreal Canadiens in second round of 1971 amateur draft.
(d)—Won James Norris Memorial Trophy (Outstanding Defenseman).
(e)—Led in assists (17) and tied for lead in points (21) during playoffs.
(f)—Won Conn Smythe Trophy (MVP in Stanley Cup playoffs).

ROB ROBINSON

Defense ... 6'3" ... 210 lbs. ... Born, St. Catharines, Ont., April 19, 1967 ... Shoots left ... Son of former NHL defenseman Doug Robinson.

Year	Team	League	Games	G.	A.	Pts.	Pen.
1985-86—Miami of Ohio Univ.	CCHA	38	1	9	10	24
1986-87—Miami of Ohio Univ. (c)	CCHA	33	3	5	8	32
1987-88—Miami of Ohio Univ.	CCHA	35	1	3	4	56

(c)—June, 1987—Drafted by St. Louis Blues in 1987 NHL entry draft. Sixth Blues pick, 117th overall, sixth round.

LUC ROBITAILLE

Left Wing ... 6' ... 180 lbs. ... Born, Montreal, Que., February 17, 1966 ... Shoots left.

Year	Team	League	Games	G.	A.	Pts.	Pen.
1983-84—Hull Olympiques (c)	QHL	70	32	53	85	48
1984-85—Hull Olympiques	QHL	64	55	94	148	115
1985-86—Hull Olympiques (a-d-e)	QHL	63	68	*123	*191	93
1986-87—Los Angeles Kings (b-f)	NHL	79	45	39	84	28
1987-88—Los Angeles Kings (a)	NHL	80	53	58	111	82
NHL TOTALS			159	98	97	195	110

(c)—June, 1984—Drafted as underage junior by Los Angeles Kings in NHL entry draft. Ninth Kings pick, 171st overall, ninth round.
(d)—Named Canadian Major Junior Hockey League Player of the Year.
(e)—Shared Guy Lafleur Trophy (Playoff MVP) with Sylvain Cote.
(f)—Won Calder Memorial Trophy (NHL Rookie of the Year).

NORMAND ROCHEFORT

Defense ... 6'1" ... 200 lbs. ... Born, Trois-Rivieres, Que., January 28, 1961 ... Shoots left ... (November, 1980)—Neck injury ... Missed parts of 1982-83 season with injured knee

... Nephew of Leon Rochefort (NHL, 1961-1976) ... (October 19, 1985)—Sprained ankle vs. Pittsburgh ... (February 8, 1986)—Separated shoulder vs. Chicago ... (October, 1987)—Injured neck and upper back ... (January, 1988)—Bruised left foot ... (February, 1988)—Sprained right knee.

Year	Team	League	Games	G.	A.	Pts.	Pen.
1977-78—Trois-Rivieres Draveurs	QMJHL	72	9	37	46	36
1978-79—Trois-Rivieres Draveurs	QMJHL	72	17	57	74	80
1979-80—Trois-Rivieres Draveurs	QMJHL	20	5	25	30	22
1979-80—Quebec Remparts (b-c)	QMJHL	52	8	39	47	68
1980-81—Quebec Remparts	QMJHL	9	2	6	8	14
1980-81—Quebec Nordiques	NHL	56	3	7	10	51
1981-82—Quebec Nordiques	NHL	72	4	14	18	115
1982-83—Quebec Nordiques	NHL	62	6	17	23	40
1983-84—Quebec Nordiques	NHL	75	2	22	24	47
1984-85—Quebec Nordiques	NHL	73	3	21	24	74
1985-86—Quebec Nordiques	NHL	26	5	4	9	30
1986-87—Quebec Nordiques	NHL	70	6	9	15	46
1987-88—Quebec Nordiques (d)	NHL	46	3	10	13	49
NHL TOTALS		480	32	104	136	452

(c)—June, 1980—Drafted by Quebec Nordiques as underage junior in 1980 NHL entry draft. First Nordiques pick, 24th overall, second round.

(d)—August, 1988—Traded with Jason Lafreniere by Quebec Nordiques to New York Rangers for Walt Poddubny, Bruce Bell, Jari Gronstrand and a fourth-round draft choice in 1989.

JEREMY ROENICK

Center ... 5'11" ... 170 lbs. ... Born, Boston, Mass., January 17, 1970 ... Shoots right.

Year	Team	League	Games	G.	A.	Pts.	Pen.
1986-87—Thayer Academy	Mass. H.S.	24	31	34	65	..
1987-88—Thayer Academy (c)	Mass. H.S.	..	34	50	84	..

(c)—June, 1988—Drafted by Chicago Black Hawks in 1988 NHL entry draft. First Black Hawks pick, eighth overall, first round.

JEFF ROHLICEK

Left Wing ... 5'11" ... 165 lbs. ... Born, Park Ridge, Ill., January 27, 1966 ... Shoots left.

Year	Team	League	Games	G.	A.	Pts.	Pen.
1983-84—Portland Winter Hawks (b-c)	WHL	71	44	53	97	22
1984-85—Portland Winter Hawks	WHL	16	5	13	18	2
1984-85—Kelowna Wings (b)	WHL	49	34	39	73	24
1985-86—Spokane Chiefs	WHL	57	50	52	102	39
1986-87—Fredericton Express	AHL	70	19	37	56	22
1987-88—Vancouver Canucks	NHL	7	0	0	0	4
1987-88—Fredericton Express	AHL	65	26	31	57	50
NHL TOTALS		7	0	0	0	4

(c)—June, 1984—Drafted as underage junior by Vancouver Canucks in NHL entry draft. Second Canucks pick, 31st overall, second round.

STEVE ROHLIK

Left Wing ... 6' ... 180 lbs. ... Born, St. Paul, Minn., May 15, 1968 ... Shoots left.

Year	Team	League	Games	G.	A.	Pts.	Pen.
1984-85—Hill Murray H.S.	Minn.	25	16	24	40	....
1985-86—Hill Murray H.S. (c)	Minn.	27	26	33	59	....
1986-87—Univ. of Wisconsin	WCHA	31	3	0	3	34
1987-88—Univ. of Wisconsin	WCHA	44	3	10	13	59

(c)—June, 1986—Drafted by Pittsburgh Penguins in 1986 NHL entry draft. Eighth Penguins pick, 151st overall, eighth round.

JON ROHLOFF

Defense ... 6' ... 200 lbs. ... Born, Mankato, Minn., October 3, 1969 ... Shoots right.

Year	Team	League	Games	G.	A.	Pts.	Pen.
1986-87—Grand Rapids H.S.	Minn. H.S.	21	12	23	35	16
1987-88—Grand Rapids H.S. (c)	Minn. H.S.	23	10	13	23	...

(c)—June, 1988—Drafted by Boston Bruins in 1988 NHL entry draft. Seventh Bruins pick, 186th overall, ninth round.

RUSSELL ROMANIUK

Left Wing ... 6'1" ... 186 lbs. ... Born, Winnipeg, Man., June 9, 1970 ... Shoots left ...

(December, 1987)—Chip fracture of left knee . . . (February, 1988)—Sprained right shoulder.

Year	Team	League	Games	G.	A.	Pts.	Pen.
1987-88—St. Boniface Saints (c)		MJHL	...	...	...	...	...

  (c)—June, 1988—Drafted by Winnipeg Jets in 1988 NHL entry draft. Second Jets pick, 31st overall, second round.

CLIFF RONNING

Center . . . 5'8" . . . 160 lbs. . . . Born, Vancouver, B.C., October 1, 1965 . . . Shoots left . . . (1984-85)—Set WHL record with goals in 18 straight games . . . (1984-85)—Set WHL single season record with 197 points (Broken by Rob Brown in 1986-87).

Year	Team	League	Games	G.	A.	Pts.	Pen.
1982-83—New Westminster Royals	BCJHL	52	82	68	150	42
1983-84—New Westminster Bruins (b-c-d)	WHL	71	69	67	136	10
1984-85—New Westminster Bruins (a-e-f-g)	WHL	70	*89	108	*197	20
1985-86—Team Canada	Int'l	71	55	63	118	53
1985-86—St. Louis Blues (h)	NHL	...	...	...	...	...
1986-87—Canadian National Team	Int'l	...	...	...	...	...
1986-87—Canadian Olympic Team	Int'l	71	55	63	118	53
1986-87—St. Louis Blues	NHL	42	11	14	25	6
1987-88—Canadian Olympic Team	Int'l	...	...	...	...	...
1987-88—St. Louis Blues	NHL	26	5	8	13	12
NHL TOTALS		68	16	22	38	18

  (c)—Won Stewart Paul Memorial Trophy (Top Rookie).
  (d)—June, 1984—Drafted by St. Louis Blues as underage junior in NHL entry draft. Ninth Blues pick, 134th overall, seventh round.
  (e)—Won Bob Brownridge Memorial Trophy (Scoring Leader).
  (f)—Won Frank Boucher Memorial Trophy (Most Gentlemanly).
  (g)—Won MVP Trophy.
  (h)—No regular season record. Played five playoff games (1 goal).

LARRY ROONEY

Left Wing . . . 5'11" . . . 165 lbs. . . . Born, Boston, Mass., January 30, 1968 . . . Shoots left.

Year	Team	League	Games	G.	A.	Pts.	Pen.
1985-86—Thayer H.S. (c)	Mass. H.S.	24	20	35	55	...
1986-87—Thayer H.S.	Mass. H.S.	26	15	26	41	...
1987-88—Providence College	H. East	33	1	9	10	34

  (c)—June, 1986—Drafted by Buffalo Sabres in 1986 NHL entry draft. Sixth Sabres pick, 89th overall, fifth round.

STEVEN PAUL ROONEY

Left Wing . . . 6'2" . . . 195 lbs. . . . Born, Canton, Mass., June 28, 1962 . . . Shoots left . . . (November 26, 1985)—Shoulder surgery . . . (November 1, 1987)—Broken ankle . . . (February, 1988)—Fractured rib.

Year	Team	League	Games	G.	A.	Pts.	Pen.
1981-82—Providence College (c)	ECAC	31	7	10	17	41
1982-83—Providence College	ECAC	42	10	20	30	31
1983-84—Providence College	ECAC	33	11	16	27	46
1984-85—Providence College	H. East	42	28	22	50	63
1984-85—Montreal Canadiens	NHL	3	1	0	1	7
1985-86—Montreal Canadiens	NHL	38	2	3	5	114
1986-87—Sherbrooke Canadiens	AHL	22	4	11	15	66
1986-87—Montreal Canadiens (d)	NHL	2	0	0	0	22
1986-87—Winnipeg Jets	NHL	30	2	3	5	57
1987-88—Winnipeg Jets (e)	NHL	56	7	6	13	217
NHL TOTALS		129	12	12	24	417

  (c)—June, 1981—Drafted by Montreal Canadiens in NHL entry draft. Eighth Canadiens pick, 88th overall, fifth round.
  (d)—January, 1987—Traded by Montreal Canadiens to Winnipeg Jets for a third-round 1987 draft pick (Francois Gravel).
  (e)—July, 1988—Traded with fourth-round draft choice in 1989 by Winnipeg Jets to New Jersey Devils for Alain Chevrier and seventh-round draft choice in 1989.

WILLIAM JOHN ROOT

Defense . . . 6' . . . 197 lbs. . . . Born, Toronto, Ont., September 6, 1959 . . . Shoots right . . . (March, 1985)—Broken finger . . . (October, 1985)—Broke foot when struck by a puck vs. Winnipeg . . . (February, 1988)—Pulled groin.

Year	Team	League	Games	G.	A.	Pts.	Pen.
1976-77—Niagara Falls Flyers		OMJHL	66	3	19	22	114
1977-78—Niagara Falls Flyers		OMJHL	67	6	11	17	61
1978-79—Niagara Falls Flyers (c)		OMJHL	67	4	31	35	119
1979-80—Nova Scotia Voyageurs		AHL	55	4	15	19	57
1980-81—Nova Scotia Voyageurs		AHL	63	3	12	15	76
1981-82—Nova Scotia Voyageurs		AHL	77	6	25	31	105
1982-83—Montreal Canadiens		NHL	46	2	3	5	24
1982-83—Nova Scotia Voyageurs		AHL	24	0	7	7	29
1983-84—Montreal Canadiens (d)		NHL	72	4	13	17	45
1984-85—St. Catharines Saints		AHL	28	5	9	14	10
1984-85—Toronto Maple Leafs		NHL	35	1	1	2	23
1985-86—Toronto Maple Leafs		NHL	27	0	1	1	29
1985-86—St. Catharines Saints		AHL	14	7	4	11	11
1986-87—Toronto Maple Leafs		NHL	34	3	3	6	37
1986-87—Newmarket Saints		AHL	32	4	11	15	23
1987-88—St. Louis Blues (e-f)		NHL	9	0	0	0	6
1987-88—Philadelphia Flyers (g)		NHL	24	1	2	3	16
NHL TOTALS			247	11	23	34	180

(c)—October, 1979—Signed by Montreal Canadiens as a free agent.
(d)—August, 1984—Traded by Montreal Canadiens to Toronto Maple Leafs for future considerations.
(e)—October, 1987—Selected by St. Louis Blues in 1987 NHL waiver draft.
(f)—November, 1987—Claimed on Waivers by Philadelphia Flyers from St. Louis Blues for $7,500.
(g)—June, 1988—Traded by Philadelphia Flyers to Toronto Maple Leafs for Mike Stothers.

JAY ROSE

Defense . . . 6' . . . 180 lbs. . . . Born, Newton, Mass., July 6, 1966 . . . Shoots right.

Year	Team	League	Games	G.	A.	Pts.	Pen.
1983-84—Boston New Prep. (c)		Mass. H.S.	30	3	26	29	..
1984-85—Clarkson College		ECAC	15	1	4	5	18
1985-86—Clarkson College		ECAC	32	1	7	8	40
1986-87—Clarkson College		ECAC	29	2	10	12	74
1987-88—Clarkson College		ECAC	33	1	9	10	50
1987-88—Adirondack Red Wings		AHL	2	0	0	0	0

(c)—June, 1984—Drafted by Detroit Red Wings in NHL entry draft. Tenth Red Wings pick, 195th overall, 10th round.

MARC ROSSEAU

Defense . . . 6' . . . 185 lbs. . . . Born, North Vancouver, B.C., May 17, 1968 . . . Shoots left . . . (August, 1984)—Torn knee ligaments.

Year	Team	League	Games	G.	A.	Pts.	Pen.
1985-86—Penticton Knights		BCJHL	42	7	23	30	176
1986-87—Univ. of Denver (c)		WCHA	39	3	18	21	70
1987-88—Univ. of Denver		WCHA	38	6	22	28	92

(c)—June, 1987—Drafted by Hartford Whalers in 1987 NHL entry draft. Fourth Whalers pick, 102nd overall, fifth round.

GUY ROULEAU

Center . . . 5'8" . . . 165 lbs. . . . Born, Beloeil, Que., February 16, 1965 . . . Shoots left.

Year	Team	League	Games	G.	A.	Pts.	Pen.
1982-83—Longueuil Chevaliers		QHL	68	25	31	56	23
1983-84—Longueuil Chevaliers		QHL	70	60	73	133	28
1984-85—Longueuil Chevaliers		QHL	60	*76	87	*163	68
1985-86—Hull Olympiques (a-c-d-e-f)		QHL	62	*92	99	*191	72
1986-87—Sherbrooke Canadiens		AHL	10	4	3	7	2
1987-88—Sherbrooke Canadiens		AHL	76	26	47	73	42

(c)—October, 1985—Traded with Stephane Provost by Longueuil Chevaliers to Hull Olympiques for Michel Thibodeau, Mark Saumier and second and fifth round draft picks.
(d)—Won Michel Briere Trophy (Regular Season MVP).
(e)—Won Jean Beliveau Trophy (Leading Scorer).
(f)—May, 1986—Signed by Montreal Canadiens as a free agent.

MAGNUS ROUPE

Left Wing . . . 6'1" . . . 190 lbs. . . . Born, Stockholm, Sweden, March 23, 1963 . . . Shoots left.

Year	Team	League	Games	G.	A.	Pts.	Pen.
1986-87—Farjestad (c)		Sweden	31	11	6	17	58
1987-88—Hershey Bears		AHL	23	6	16	22	10
1987-88—Philadelphia Flyers		NHL	33	2	4	6	32
NHL TOTALS			33	2	4	6	32

(c)—June, 1982—Drafted by Philadelphia Flyers in 1982 NHL entry draft. Ninth Flyers pick, 182nd overall, ninth round.

BOB ROUSE

Defense . . . 6'1" . . . 210 lbs. . . . Born, Surrey, B.C., June 18, 1964 . . . Shoots right . . . (January 2, 1986)—Injured thumb vs. Vancouver and missed two games . . . (January, 1988)—Hip contusions vs. Toronto.

Year	Team	League	Games	G.	A.	Pts.	Pen.
1980-81—Billings Bighorns		WHL	70	0	13	13	116
1981-82—Billings Bighorns (c)		WHL	71	7	22	29	209
1982-83—Nanaimo Islanders		WHL	29	7	20	27	86
1982-83—Lethbridge Broncos		WHL	71	15	50	65	168
1983-84—Lethbridge Broncos (a-d)		WHL	71	18	42	60	101
1983-84—Minnesota North Stars		NHL	1	0	0	0	0
1984-85—Springfield Indians		AHL	8	0	3	3	6
1984-85—Minnesota North Stars		NHL	63	2	9	11	113
1985-86—Minnesota North Stars		NHL	75	1	14	15	151
1986-87—Minnesota North Stars		NHL	72	2	10	12	179
1987-88—Minnesota North Stars		NHL	74	0	12	12	168
NHL TOTALS			285	5	45	50	611

(c)—June, 1982—Drafted as underage junior by Minnesota North Stars in 1982 NHL entry draft. Third North Stars pick, 80th overall, fourth round.
(d)—Won WHL Top Defenseman Trophy.

JEAN-MARC ROUTHIER

Right Wing . . . 6'2" . . . 180 lbs. . . . Born, Quebec City, Que., February 2, 1968 . . . Shoots right.

Year	Team	League	Games	G.	A.	Pts.	Pen.
1984-85—Ste. Foy Midgets		Quebec	41	13	22	35	68
1985-86—Hull Olympiques (c)		QHL	71	18	16	34	111
1986-87—Hull Olympiques		QHL	59	17	18	35	98
1987-88—Victoriaville Tigers (d)		QHL	57	16	28	44	267

(c)—June, 1986—Drafted as underage junior by Quebec Nordiques in 1986 NHL entry draft. Second Nordiques pick, 39th overall, second round.
(d)—July, 1987—Traded by Hull Olympiques to Victoriaville Tigers for Marc Saumier.

MICHAEL ROWE

Defense . . . 6'1" . . . 208 lbs. . . . Born, Kingston, Ont., March 8, 1965 . . . Shoots left.

Year	Team	League	Games	G.	A.	Pts.	Pen.
1981-82—Toronto Marlboros		OHL	58	4	4	8	214
1982-83—Toronto Marlboros (c)		OHL	64	4	29	33	*262
1983-84—Toronto Marlboros		OHL	59	9	36	45	208
1984-85—Toronto Marlboros		OHL	66	17	34	51	202
1984-85—Pittsburgh Penguins		NHL	6	0	0	0	7
1984-85—Baltimore Skipjacks (d)		AHL	..	..	..	..	..
1985-86—Pittsburgh Penguins		NHL	3	0	0	0	4
1985-86—Baltimore Skipjacks		AHL	67	0	5	5	107
1986-87—Baltimore Skipjacks		AHL	79	1	18	19	64
1986-87—Pittsburgh Penguins		NHL	2	0	0	0	0
1987-88—Muskegon Lumberjacks		IHL	80	8	21	29	137
NHL TOTALS			11	0	0	0	11

(c)—June, 1983—Drafted as underage junior by Pittsburgh Penguins in 1983 NHL entry draft. Third Penguins pick, 58th overall, third round.
(d)—No regular season record. Played three playoff games.

STEPHANE ROY

Left Wing . . . 5'11" . . . 185 lbs. . . . Born, Ste. Foy, Que., June 29, 1967 . . . Shoots left . . . Also plays Center . . . Brother of Patrick Roy.

Year	Team	League	Games	G.	A.	Pts.	Pen.
1983-84—Chicoutimi Sagueneens		QHL	67	12	26	38	25
1984-85—Chicoutimi/Granby (c-d)		QHL	68	28	53	81	34
1985-86—Granby Bisons		QHL	61	33	52	85	68
1985-86—Team Canada		Int'l	10	0	1	1	4
1986-87—Canadian Olympic Team		Int'l	9	1	2	3	4
1986-87—Granby Bisons		QHL	45	23	44	67	54
1987-88—Kalamazoo Wings		IHL	58	21	12	33	52
1987-88—Minnesota North Stars		NHL	12	1	0	1	0
NHL TOTALS			12	1	0	1	0

(c)—January, 1985—Traded with Marc Bureau, Lee Duhemee, Sylvain Demers and Rene Lecuyer by Chicoutimi Sagueneens to Granby Bisons for Stephane Richer and Greg Choules.
(d)—June, 1985—Drafted as underage junior by Minnesota North Stars in 1985 NHL entry draft. First North Stars pick, 51st overall, third round.

MATTHEW RUCHTY

Left Wing . . . 6'1" . . . 205 lbs. . . . Born, Kitchener, Ont., November 27, 1969 . . . Shoots left.

Year	Team	League	Games	G.	A.	Pts.	Pen.
1986-87—Kitchener Greenshirts Midget		OHA	75	58	44	102	...
1987-88—Bowling Green Univ. (c)		CCHA	41	6	15	21	78

(c)—June, 1988—Drafted by New Jersey Devils in 1988 NHL entry draft. Fourth Devils pick, 65th overall, fourth round.

MIKE RUCINSKI

Center . . . 6' . . . 193 lbs. . . . Born, Chicago, Ill., December 12, 1963 . . . Shoots right . . . Also plays Right Wing . . . (February, 1985)—Broke arm vs. Bowling Green University.

Year	Team	League	Games	G.	A.	Pts.	Pen.
1983-84—Univ. Illinois/Chicago		CCHA	33	17	26	43	12
1984-85—Univ. Illinois/Chicago		CCHA	40	29	32	61	28
1985-86—Univ. Illinois/Chicago		CCHA	37	16	31	47	18
1986-87—Salt Lake Golden Eagles (c)		IHL	28	16	25	41	19
1986-87—Moncton Golden Flames (d)		AHL	42	5	9	14	14
1987-88—Saginaw Hawks		IHL	44	19	31	50	32

(c)—August, 1986—Signed by Calgary Flames as a free agent.
(d)—August, 1987—Signed by Chicago Black Hawks as a free agent.

LINDY CAMERON RUFF

Defense . . . 6'2" . . . 190 lbs. . . . Born, Warburg, Alta., February 17, 1960 . . . Shoots left . . . (December, 1980)—Fractured ankle . . . Also plays Left Wing . . . Brother of Marty Ruff and brother of Brent Ruff, one of four junior hockey players who died in December, 1986 when the team bus of the Swift Current Broncos overturned . . . (March, 1983)—Broke hand . . . (January 14, 1984)—Injured shoulder at Detroit . . . (October 26, 1984)—Separated shoulder at Detroit . . . (November 30, 1985)—Broke foot at Toronto and missed four games . . . (December 29, 1985)—Bruised knee vs. N.Y. Islanders and missed four games . . . (March 5, 1986)—Broke left clavicle at Hartford.

Year	Team	League	Games	G.	A.	Pts.	Pen.
1976-77—Taber Golden Suns		AJHL	60	13	33	46	112
1976-77—Lethbridge Broncos		WCHL	2	0	2	2	0
1977-78—Lethbridge Broncos		WCHL	66	9	24	33	219
1978-79—Lethbridge Broncos (c)		WHL	24	9	18	27	108
1979-80—Buffalo Sabres		NHL	63	5	14	19	38
1980-81—Buffalo Sabres		NHL	65	8	18	26	121
1981-82—Buffalo Sabres		NHL	79	16	32	48	194
1982-83—Buffalo Sabres		NHL	60	12	17	29	130
1983-84—Buffalo Sabres		NHL	58	14	31	45	101
1984-85—Buffalo Sabres		NHL	39	13	11	24	45
1985-86—Buffalo Sabres		NHL	54	20	12	32	158
1986-87—Buffalo Sabres		NHL	50	6	14	20	74
1987-88—Buffalo Sabres		NHL	77	2	23	25	179
NHL TOTALS			545	96	172	268	1040

(c)—August, 1979—Drafted by Buffalo Sabres as underage junior in entry draft. Second Buffalo pick, 32nd overall, second round.

DARREN RUMBLE

Defense . . . 6'1" . . . 185 lbs. . . . Born, Barrie, Ont., January 23, 1969 . . . Shoots left.

Year	Team	League	Games	G.	A.	Pts.	Pen.
1985-86—Barrie Jr. B		OHA	46	14	32	46	91
1986-87—Kitchener Rangers (c)		OHL	64	11	32	43	44
1987-88—Kitchener Rangers		OHL	55	15	50	65	64

(c)—June, 1987—Drafted as underage junior by Philadelphia Flyers in 1987 NHL entry draft. First Flyers pick, 20th overall, first round.

TERRY WALLACE RUSKOWSKI

Center . . . 5'10" . . . 178 lbs. . . . Born, Prince Albert, Sask., December 31, 1954 . . . Shoots left . . . Missed part of 1974-75 season with injured right hand and part of 1975-76 season with broken middle finger on right hand . . . (Summer, 1980)—Surgery to right knee . . . (March, 1981)—Viral infection . . . (December 9, 1981)—Ruptured ligaments in right

thumb during fight with Timo Blomqvist of Washington . . . (December 31, 1985)—Sprained thumb at St. Louis . . . (March 26, 1986)—Sprained left knee vs. Edmonton . . . (January 3, 1987)—Sprained left knee vs. Montreal . . . (January 18, 1987)—Reinjured left knee vs. Detroit . . . (September, 1987)—Missed first two weeks of Minnesota North Stars training camp with a hip flexor injury . . . (January, 1988)—Back spasms . . . (January 21, 1988)—Tore knee ligaments vs. Boston.

Year	Team	League	Games	G.	A.	Pts.	Pen.
1971-72—Swift Current Broncos		WCHL	67	13	38	51	177
1972-73—Swift Current Broncos		WCHL	53	25	64	89	136
1973-74—Swift Current Broncos (c-d)		WCHL	68	40	93	133	243
1974-75—Houston Aeros		WHA	71	10	36	46	134
1975-76—Houston Aeros (e)		WHA	65	14	35	49	100
1976-77—Houston Aeros		WHA	80	24	60	84	146
1977-78—Houston Aeros (f)		WHA	78	15	57	72	170
1978-79—Winnipeg Jets (g-h)		WHA	75	20	66	86	211
1979-80—Chicago Black Hawks		NHL	74	15	55	70	252
1980-81—Chicago Black Hawks		NHL	72	8	51	59	225
1981-82—Chicago Black Hawks		NHL	60	7	30	37	120
1982-83—Chicago Black Hawks (i)		NHL	5	0	2	2	12
1982-83—Los Angeles Kings		NHL	71	14	30	44	127
1983-84—Los Angeles Kings		NHL	77	7	25	32	92
1984-85—Los Angeles Kings (j)		NHL	78	16	33	49	144
1985-86—Pittsburgh Penguins		NHL	73	26	37	63	162
1986-87—Pittsburgh Penguins (k)		NHL	70	14	37	51	147
1987-88—Minnesota North Stars		NHL	47	5	12	17	76
WHA TOTALS			369	83	254	337	761
NHL TOTALS			627	112	312	424	1357

(c)—Drafted from Swift Current Broncos by Chicago Black Hawks in third round of 1974 amateur draft.
(d)—May, 1974—Selected by Houston Aeros in WHA amateur draft.
(e)—Led in assists (23) and penalty minutes (64) during playoffs.
(f)—July, 1978—Sold to Winnipeg Jets with Houston Aeros' franchise.
(g)—Led in assists (12) during playoffs.
(h)—June, 1979—Selected by Chicago Black Hawks in NHL reclaim draft.
(i)—October, 1982—Traded by Chicago Black Hawks to Los Angeles Kings for Larry Goodenough and future considerations.
(j)—July, 1985—Signed by Pittsburgh Penguins as a free agent.
(k)—July, 1987—Signed by Minnesota North Stars as a free agent.

CAM RUSSELL

Defense . . . 6'3" . . . 180 lbs. . . . Born, Halifax, N.S., January 12, 1969 . . . Shoots left.

Year	Team	League	Games	G.	A.	Pts.	Pen.
1985-86—Hull Olympiques		QHL	56	3	4	7	24
1986-87—Hull Olympiques (c)		QHL	66	3	16	19	119
1987-88—Hull Olympiques		QHL	53	9	18	27	141

(c)—June, 1987—Drafted as underage junior by Chicago Black Hawks in 1987 NHL entry draft. Third Black Hawks pick, 50th overall, third round.

KERRY RUSSELL

Right Wing . . . 5'11" . . . 165 lbs. . . . Born, Kamloops, B.C., June 23, 1969 . . . Shoots right.

Year	Team	League	Games	G.	A.	Pts.	Pen.
1987-88—Michigan State Univ. (c)		CCHA	46	16	23	39	50

(c)—June, 1988—Drafted by Hartford Whalers in 1988 NHL entry draft. Sixth Whalers pick, 137th overall, seventh round.

PAUL RUTHERFORD

Center . . . 6' . . . 190 lbs. . . . Born, Sudbury, Ont., January 1, 1969 . . . Shoots left.

Year	Team	League	Games	G.	A.	Pts.	Pen.
1986-87—Richmond Sockeyes		BCJHL	40	22	17	39	33
1987-88—Ohio State Univ. (c)		CCHA	40	18	23	41	40

(c)—June, 1988—Drafted by New York Islanders in 1988 NHL entry draft. Fifth Islanders pick, 100th overall, fifth round.

CHRISTIAN RUUTTU

Center . . . 5'11" . . . 180 lbs. . . . Born, Lappeenranta, Finland, February 20, 1964 . . . Shoots left . . . (February, 1988)—Knee injury.

Year	Team	League	Games	G.	A.	Pts.	Pen.
1985-86—Helsinki IFK (c)		Sweden	36	14	42	56	41

Year	Team	League	Games	G.	A.	Pts.	Pen.
1986-87—Buffalo Sabres		NHL	76	22	43	65	62
1987-88—Buffalo Sabres		NHL	73	26	45	71	85
NHL TOTALS			149	48	88	136	147

(c)—June, 1983—Drafted by Buffalo Sabres in 1983 entry draft. Ninth Sabres pick, 134th overall, seventh round.

TOM RYAN

Defense . . . 5'11" . . . 180 lbs. . . . Born, Boston, Mass., January 12, 1966 . . . Shoots right.

Year	Team	League	Games	G.	A.	Pts.	Pen.
1983-84—Newton North H.S. (c)		Mass.H.S.	..	..	..	..	..
1984-85—Boston University		H. East	34	6	8	14	14
1985-86—Boston University		H. East	42	2	8	10	22
1986-87—Boston University		H. East	37	1	7	8	20
1987-88—Boston University		H. East	33	9	14	23	12

(c)—June, 1984—Drafted by Pittsburgh Penguins in NHL entry draft. Sixth Penguins pick, 127th overall, seventh round.

WARREN RYCHEL

Left Wing . . . 6' . . . 190 lbs. . . . Born, Tecumseh, Ont., May 12, 1967 . . . Shoots left.

Year	Team	League	Games	G.	A.	Pts.	Pen.
1983-84—Essex Jr. "C"		OHA	24	11	16	27	86
1984-85—Sudbury Wolves		OHL	35	5	8	13	74
1984-85—Guelph Platers		OHL	29	1	3	4	48
1985-86—Guelph Platers		OHL	38	14	5	19	119
1985-86—Ottawa 67's		OHL	29	11	18	29	54
1986-87—Ottawa 67's (c)		OHL	28	11	7	18	57
1986-87—Kitchener Rangers		OHL	21	5	5	10	39
1987-88—Saginaw Hawks		IHL	51	2	7	9	113
1987-88—Peoria Rivermen		IHL	7	2	1	3	7

(c)—September, 1986—Signed by Chicago Black Hawks as a free agent.

ANDY RYMSHA

Left Wing . . . 6'1" . . . 203 lbs. . . . Born, St. Catharines, Ont., December 10, 1968 . . . Shoots left.

Year	Team	League	Games	G.	A.	Pts.	Pen.
1985-86—St. Catharines Falcons		OHA	39	6	13	19	170
1986-87—Western Michigan Univ. (c)		CCHA	42	7	10	17	122
1987-88—Western Michigan Univ.		CCHA	42	5	6	11	114

(c)—June, 1987—Drafted by St. Louis Blues in 1987 NHL entry draft. Fifth Blues pick, 82nd overall, fourth round.

SHAWN SABOL

Defense . . . 6'3" . . . 215 lbs. . . . Born, Fargo, N.D., July 13, 1966 . . . Shoots left.

Year	Team	League	Games	G.	A.	Pts.	Pen.
1983-84—St. Paul Volcans		USHL	47	6	10	16	32
1984-85—St. Paul Volcans		USHL	47	4	13	17	137
1985-86—St. Paul Volcans (c)		USHL	46	10	19	29	129
1986-87—Univ. of Wisconsin		WCHA	40	7	16	23	98
1987-88—Univ. of Wisconsin		WCHA	8	4	3	7	10
1987-88—Hershey Bears		AHL	51	1	9	10	66

(c)—June, 1986—Drafted by Philadelphia Flyers in 1986 NHL entry draft. Ninth Flyers pick, 209th overall, 10th round.

KEN SABOURIN

Defense . . . 6'4" . . . 200 lbs. . . . Born, Scarborough, Ont., April 28, 1966 . . . Shoots left.

Year	Team	League	Games	G.	A.	Pts.	Pen.
1981-82—Don Mills Midgets		MTHL	40	10	20	30	..
1982-83—Sault Ste. Marie Greyhounds		OHL	58	0	8	8	90
1983-84—Sault Ste. Marie Greyhounds (c)		OHL	63	7	13	20	157
1984-85—Sault Ste. Marie Greyhounds		OHL	63	5	19	24	139
1985-86—Sault Ste. Marie Greyhounds (d)		OHL	25	1	5	6	77
1985-86—Cornwall Royals		OHL	37	3	12	15	94
1985-86—Moncton Golden Flames		AHL	3	0	0	0	0
1986-87—Moncton Golden Flames		AHL	75	1	10	11	166
1987-88—Salt Lake Golden Eagles		IHL	71	2	8	10	186

(c)—June, 1984—Drafted as underage junior by Washington Capitals in NHL entry draft. Second Capitals pick, 34th overall, second round.

(d)—March, 1986—Traded by Sault Ste. Marie Greyhounds to Cornwall Royals for Kent Trolley and a fifth round 1986 OHL priority draft pick.

JOSEPH SACCO

Left Wing . . . 6'1" . . . 180 lbs. . . . Born, Medford, Mass., February 4, 1969 . . . Shoots left.

Year	Team	League	Games	G.	A.	Pts.	Pen.
1985-86—Medford H.S.		Mass. H.S.	20	30	30	60	..
1986-87—Medford H.S. (c)		Mass. H.S.	21	22	32	54	..
1987-88—Boston University		H. East	34	14	22	36	38

(c)—June, 1987—Drafted by Toronto Maple Leafs in 1987 NHL entry draft. Fourth Maple Leafs pick, 71st overall, fourth round.

THOMAS SAGISSOR

Center . . . 5'11" . . . 180 lbs. . . . Born, Hastings, Minn., September 12, 1967 . . . Shoots left.

Year	Team	League	Games	G.	A.	Pts.	Pen.
1985-86—Hastings H.S. (c)		Minn. H.S.	25	26	38	64	28
1986-87—Univ. of Wisconsin		WCHA	41	1	4	5	32
1987-88—Univ. of Wisconsin		WCHA	38	4	5	9	65

(c)—June, 1985—Drafted by Montreal Canadiens in 1985 NHL entry draft. Seventh Canadiens pick, 96th overall, fifth round.

MARTIN ST. AMOUR

Left Wing . . . 6'2" . . . 195 lbs. . . . Born, Montreal, Que., January 30, 1970 . . . Shoots left.

Year	Team	League	Games	G.	A.	Pts.	Pen.
1986-87—Laval Laurentides Midget		Quebec	52	55	95	150	58
1987-88—Verdun Junior Canadiens (c)		QHL	61	20	50	70	111

(c)—June, 1988—Drafted by Montreal Canadiens in 1988 NHL entry draft. Second Canadiens pick, 34th overall, second round.

TOM ST. JAMES

Left Wing . . . 5'11" . . . 175 lbs. . . . Born, Iroquois Falls, Ont., February 18, 1963 . . . Shoots left.

Year	Team	League	Games	G.	A.	Pts.	Pen.
1981-82—Sudbury Wolves		OHL	67	18	25	43	64
1982-83—Kitchener Rangers		OHL	64	32	48	80	35
1983-84—Rochester Americans (c)		AHL	31	6	7	13	8
1984-85—Flint Generals		IHL	80	40	38	78	54
1985-86—Saginaw Gears		IHL	53	16	34	50	36
1986-87—Saginaw Generals		IHL	53	30	25	55	33
1987-88—Milwaukee Admirals		IHL	18	7	11	18	8

(c)—March, 1984—Signed by Rochester Americans as a free agent.

JOE SAKIC

Center . . . 5'11" . . . 185 lbs. . . . Born, Vancouver, B.C. July 7, 1969 . . . Shoots left . . . Brother of Brian Sakic.

Year	Team	League	Games	G.	A.	Pts.	Pen.
1985-86—Burnaby Hawks		BC Midgets	60	83	73	156	96
1986-87—Swift Current Broncos (b-c-d-e)		WHL	72	60	73	133	31
1987-88—Swift Current Broncos (a-e-f-g)		WHL	64	*78	82	*160	64

(c)—June, 1987—Drafted as underage junior by Quebec Nordiques in 1987 NHL entry draft. Second Nordiques pick, 15th overall, first round.
(d)—Named WHL East Division Rookie-of-the-Year.
(e)—Named WHL East Division MVP.
(f)—Named WHL Player of the Year.
(g)—Shared WHL scoring title with Theoren Fleury.

ANDERS BORJE SALMING
(Known by middle name.)

Defense . . . 6'1" . . . 185 lbs. . . . Born, Kiruna, Sweden, April 17, 1951 . . . Shoots left . . . Missed part of 1974-75 season with cracked bone in heel and part of the 1978 playoffs with facial injuries . . . (January, 1980)—Surgery to clear sinus problem . . . (March, 1981)—Separated shoulder . . . (December 2, 1981)—Separated shoulder vs. Hartford . . . (December, 1982)—Suffered Charley horse and missed eight games . . . (January 17, 1983)—Cut by skate on knee at St. Louis . . . (March 12, 1984)—Broke kneecap vs. Winnipeg and out for the season . . . (October, 1984)—Eye infection . . . (January 19, 1985)—Injured sinus vs. Boston . . . (October 12, 1985)—Injured ribs vs. Quebec and missed one

game . . . (November 8, 1985)—Injured back at Detroit and missed 38 games . . . (September 4, 1986)—Suspended for first eight games of season for cocaine use . . . (November 5, 1986)—Cracked orbital bone above left eye when struck by Bernie Federko vs. St. Louis . . . (November 26, 1986)—Cut by Gerard Gallant's skate during a goal-mouth pile-up at Detroit, requiring 250 facial stitches . . . (December, 1987)—Sprained back.

Year	Team	League	Games	G.	A.	Pts.	Pen.
1971-72—Swedish National Team			12	0	....	....	....
1972-73—Swedish National Team (c)			23	4	....	....	....
1973-74—Toronto Maple Leafs		NHL	76	5	34	39	48
1974-75—Toronto Maple Leafs (b)		NHL	60	12	25	37	34
1975-76—Toronto Maple Leafs (b-d)		NHL	78	16	41	57	70
1976-77—Toronto Maple Leafs (a-d)		NHL	76	12	66	78	46
1977-78—Toronto Maple Leafs (b)		NHL	80	16	60	76	70
1978-79—Toronto Maple Leafs (b-d)		NHL	78	17	56	73	76
1979-80—Toronto Maple Leafs (b)		NHL	74	19	52	71	96
1980-81—Toronto Maple Leafs		NHL	72	5	61	66	154
1981-82—Toronto Maple Leafs		NHL	69	12	44	56	170
1982-83—Toronto Maple Leafs		NHL	69	7	38	45	104
1983-84—Toronto Maple Leafs		NHL	68	5	38	43	92
1984-85—Toronto Maple Leafs		NHL	73	6	33	39	76
1985-86—Toronto Maple Leafs		NHL	41	7	15	22	48
1986-87—Toronto Maple Leafs		NHL	56	4	16	20	42
1987-88—Toronto Maple Leafs		NHL	66	2	24	26	82
NHL TOTALS			1036	145	603	748	1209

(c)—Selected most valuable player in Sweden.
(d)—Named winner of Viking Award (Top Swedish player in NHL/WHA as selected by poll of Swedish players).

GARY SAMPSON

Center . . . 6' . . . 190 lbs. . . . Born, Atikokan, Ont., August 24, 1959 . . . Shoots left . . . Member of 1984 U.S. Olympic Team . . . (December 27, 1984)—Ligament damage to left knee when checked by Pat Flatley at N.Y. Islanders . . . (February 13, 1985)—Reinjured knee at Winnipeg.

Year	Team	League	Games	G.	A.	Pts.	Pen.
1978-79—Boston College		ECAC	30	10	18	28	4
1979-80—Boston College		ECAC	24	6	8	14	8
1980-81—Boston College		ECAC	31	8	16	24	8
1981-82—Boston College		ECAC	21	7	11	18	22
1982-83—U.S. National Team		Int'l	40	11	20	31	8
1983-84—U.S. National Team		Int'l	56	21	18	39	10
1983-84—U.S. Olympic Team		Int'l	6	1	3	4	2
1983-84—Washington Capitals (c)		NHL	15	1	1	2	6
1984-85—Binghamton Whalers		AHL	5	2	2	4	2
1984-85—Washington Capitals		NHL	46	10	15	25	13
1985-86—Washington Capitals		NHL	19	1	4	5	2
1985-86—Binghamton Whalers		AHL	49	9	21	30	16
1986-87—Washington Capitals		NHL	25	1	2	3	4
1986-87—Binghamton Whalers		AHL	37	12	16	28	10
1987-88—Baltimore Skipjacks		AHL	16	2	4	6	4
NHL TOTALS			105	13	22	35	25

(c)—February, 1984—Signed by Washington Capitals as a free agent.

KJELL SAMUELSSON

Defense . . . 6'6" . . . 227 lbs. . . . Born, Tingsryd, Sweden, October 18, 1956 . . . Shoots right . . . (February, 1988)—Pulled groin.

Year	Team	League	Games	G.	A.	Pts.	Pen.
1983-84—Leksand (c)		Sweden	36	6	7	13	59
1984-85—Leksand		Sweden	35	9	5	14	34
1985-86—New York Rangers		NHL	9	0	0	0	10
1985-86—New Haven Nighthawks		AHL	56	6	21	27	87
1986-87—New York Rangers (d)		NHL	30	2	6	8	50
1986-87—Philadelphia Flyers		NHL	46	1	6	7	86
1987-88—Philadelphia Flyers		NHL	74	6	24	30	184
NHL TOTALS			159	9	36	45	330

(c)—June, 1984—Drafted by New York Rangers in NHL entry draft. Fifth Rangers pick, 119th overall, sixth round
(d)—December, 1986—Traded with second-round 1989 draft pick by New York Rangers to Philadelphia Flyers for Bob Froese.

ULF SAMUELSSON

Defense ... 6'1" ... 195 lbs. ... Born, Leksand, Sweden, March 26, 1964 ... Shoots left.

Year	Team	League	Games	G.	A.	Pts.	Pen.
1983-84—Leksands (c)		Sweden	36	5	10	15	53
1984-85—Binghamton Whalers		AHL	36	5	11	16	92
1984-85—Hartford Whalers		NHL	41	2	6	8	83
1985-86—Hartford Whalers		NHL	80	5	19	24	172
1986-87—Hartford Whalers		NHL	78	2	31	33	162
1987-88—Hartford Whalers		NHL	76	8	34	42	159
NHL TOTALS			275	17	90	107	576

(c)—June, 1982—Drafted by Hartford Whalers in NHL entry draft. Fourth Whalers pick, 67th overall, fourth round.

SCOTT SANDELIN

Defense ... 6' ... 190 lbs. ... Born, Hibbing, Minn., August 8, 1964 ... Shoots right ... (October, 1984)—Stretched knee ligaments.

Year	Team	League	Games	G.	A.	Pts.	Pen.
1981-82—Hibbing High School (c)		Minn. H.S.	20	5	15	20	30
1982-83—Univ. of North Dakota		WCHA	30	1	6	7	10
1983-84—Univ. of North Dakota		WCHA	41	4	23	27	24
1984-85—Univ. of North Dakota		WCHA	38	4	17	21	30
1985-86—Univ. of North Dakota (a)		WCHA	40	7	31	38	38
1985-86—Sherbrooke Canadiens		AHL	6	0	2	2	2
1986-87—Montreal Canadiens		NHL	1	0	0	0	0
1986-87—Sherbrooke Canadiens		AHL	74	7	22	29	35
1987-88—Montreal Canadiens		NHL	8	0	1	1	2
1987-88—Sherbrooke Canadiens		AHL	58	8	14	22	35
NHL TOTALS			9	0	1	1	2

(c)—June, 1982—Drafted as underage player by Montreal Canadiens in 1982 NHL entry draft. Fifth Canadiens pick, 40th overall, second round.

JAMES SANDLAK JR.

Right Wing ... 6'3" ... 205 lbs. ... Born, Kitchener, Ont., December 12, 1966 ... Shoots right ... Named to All-Tournament team at 1986 World Junior Championships as well as being named top forward ... (January, 1986)—Ruptured ligaments in right thumb.

Year	Team	League	Games	G.	A.	Pts.	Pen.
1982-83—Kitchener Rangers		OHA	38	26	25	51	100
1983-84—London Knights		OHL	68	23	18	41	143
1984-85—London Knights (c)		OHL	58	40	24	64	128
1985-86—London Knights		OHL	16	7	13	20	36
1985-86—Vancouver Canucks		NHL	23	1	3	4	10
1986-87—Vancouver Canucks		NHL	78	15	21	36	66
1987-88—Vancouver Canucks		NHL	49	16	15	31	81
1987-88—Fredericton Express		AHL	24	10	15	25	47
NHL TOTALS			150	32	39	71	157

(c)—June, 1985—Drafted as underage junior by Vancouver Canucks in 1985 NHL entry draft. First Canucks pick, fourth overall, first round.

TOMAS SANDSTROM

Right Wing ... 6'2" ... 200 lbs. ... Born, Fagersta, Sweden, September 4, 1964 ... Shoots left ... (October 23, 1985)—Bruised right shoulder vs. New Jersey and missed two games ... (December 7, 1985)—Bruised tailbone at Philadelphia and missed three games ... (February 24, 1986)—Concussion at Minnesota ... (February 11, 1987)—Fractured right ankle vs. Soviet National Team when checked by Andrei Khomutov at Rendez-Vous '87 ... (November, 1987)—Fractured right index finger.

Year	Team	League	Games	G.	A.	Pts.	Pen.
1983-84—Brynas (c)		Sweden	....	20	10	30	....
1984-85—New York Rangers		NHL	74	29	30	59	51
1985-86—New York Rangers		NHL	73	25	29	54	109
1986-87—New York Rangers		NHL	64	40	34	74	60
1987-88—New York Rangers		NHL	69	28	40	68	95
NHL TOTALS			280	122	133	255	315

(c)—June, 1982—Drafted by New York Rangers in NHL entry draft. Second Rangers pick, 36th overall, second round.

EVERETT SANIPASS

Left Wing ... 6'2" ... 190 lbs. ... Born, Big Cove, New Brunswick, February 13, 1968 ...

Shoots left . . . Micmac Indian descendant . . . (December, 1987)—Back spasms . . . (January 17, 1988)—Back spasms and concussion vs. Washington . . . (March, 1988)—Broken hand.

Year	Team	League	Games	G.	A.	Pts.	Pen.
1984-85—Verdun Junior Canadiens		QHL	38	8	11	19	84
1985-86—Verdun Junior Canadiens (c)		QHL	67	28	66	94	320
1986-87—Granby Bisons (a)		QHL	35	34	48	82	220
1986-87—Chicago Black Hawks		NHL	7	1	3	4	2
1987-88—Chicago Black Hawks		NHL	57	8	12	20	126
NHL TOTALS			64	9	15	24	128

(c)—June, 1986—Drafted as underage junior by Chicago Black Hawks in 1986 NHL entry draft. First Black Hawks pick, 14th overall, first round.

DAVID SAUNDERS

Left Wing . . . 6'1" . . . 195 lbs. . . . Born, Ottawa, Ont., May 20, 1966 . . . Shoots left.

Year	Team	League	Games	G.	A.	Pts.	Pen.
1983-84—St. Lawrence Univ. (c)		CCHA	32	10	21	31	26
1984-85—St. Lawrence Univ.		ECAC	27	7	9	16	16
1985-86—St. Lawrence Univ.		ECAC	29	15	19	34	26
1986-87—St. Lawrence Univ.		ECAC	34	18	34	52	44
1987-88—Vancouver Canucks		NHL	56	7	13	20	10
1987-88—Fredericton Express		AHL	14	9	7	16	6
1987-88—Flint Spirits		IHL	8	5	5	10	2
NHL TOTALS			56	7	13	20	10

(c)—June, 1984—Drafted by Vancouver Canucks in NHL entry draft. Third Canucks pick, 52nd overall, third round.

JOEL SAVAGE

Right Wing . . . 5'11' . . . 195 lbs. . . . Born, Surrey, B.C., December 25, 1969 . . . Shoots right . . . (October, 1985)—Concussion.

Year	Team	League	Games	G.	A.	Pts.	Pen.
1986-87—Victoria Cougars		WHL	68	14	13	27	48
1987-88—Victoria Cougars (b-c)		WHL	69	37	32	69	73

(c)—June, 1988—Drafted by Buffalo Sabres in 1988 NHL entry draft. First Sabres pick, 13th overall, first round.

REGINALD SAVAGE

Center . . . 5'10" . . . 177 lbs. . . . Born, Montreal, Que., May 1, 1970 . . . Shoots left.

Year	Team	League	Games	G.	A.	Pts.	Pen.
1986-87—Richelieu Midget AAA		Quebec	42	82	57	139	44
1987-88—Victoriaville Tigers (c)		QHL	68	68	54	122	77

(c)—June, 1988—Drafted by Washington Capitals in 1988 NHL entry draft. First Capitals pick, 15th overall, first round.

DENIS SAVARD

Center . . . 5'9" . . . 157 lbs. . . . Born, Pointe Gatineau, Que., February 4, 1961 . . . Shoots right . . . Cousin of Jean Savard . . . Set Chicago rookie record with 75 points in 1980-81 (broken by Steve Larmer) . . . (October 15, 1980)—Strained knee vs. Vancouver . . . Set Chicago records for assists (87) and points (119) in one season in 1981-82 . . . Broke his own points record in 1982-83 . . . (January 7, 1984)—Broke nose at N.Y. Islanders . . . (October 13, 1984)—Injured ankle when he blocked a shot at N.Y. Islanders . . . (March 22, 1987)—Bruised ribs when checked by Jeff Jackson at N.Y. Rangers.

Year	Team	League	Games	G.	A.	Pts.	Pen.
1977-78—Montreal Juniors		QMJHL	72	37	79	116	22
1978-79—Montreal Juniors		QMJHL	70	46	*112	158	88
1979-80—Montreal Juniors (a-c-d)		QMJHL	72	63	118	181	93
1980-81—Chicago Black Hawks		NHL	76	28	47	75	47
1981-82—Chicago Black Hawks		NHL	80	32	87	119	82
1982-83—Chicago Black Hawks (b)		NHL	78	35	86	121	99
1983-84—Chicago Black Hawks		NHL	75	37	57	94	71
1984-85—Chicago Black Hawks		NHL	79	38	67	105	56
1985-86—Chicago Black Hawks		NHL	80	47	69	116	111
1986-87—Chicago Black Hawks		NHL	70	40	50	90	108
1987-88—Chicago Black Hawks		NHL	80	44	87	131	95
NHL TOTALS			618	301	550	851	669

(d)—June, 1980—Drafted as underage junior by Chicago Black Hawks in 1980 NHL entry draft. First Black Hawks pick, third overall, first round.

KEVIN DEAN SCHAMEHORN

Right Wing . . . 5'10" . . . 185 lbs. . . . Born, Calgary, Alta., July 28, 1956 . . . Shoots right.

Year	Team	League	Games	G.	A.	Pts.	Pen.
1973-74—Bellingham Blazers		Jr. "A" BCHL	58	17	8	25	293
1973-74—New Westminster Bruins		WCHL	2	1	1	2	7
1974-75—New Westminster Bruins		WCHL	37	14	6	20	175
1975-76—New Westminster Bruins (c)		WCHL	62	32	42	74	276
1976-77—Kalamazoo Wings		IHL	77	27	31	58	314
1976-77—Detroit Red Wings		NHL	3	0	0	0	9
1977-78—Kansas City Red Wings		CHL	36	5	3	8	113
1977-78—Kalamazoo Wings		IHL	39	18	14	32	144
1978-79—Kalamazoo Wings		IHL	80	45	57	102	245
1979-80—Detroit Red Wings		NHL	2	0	0	0	4
1979-80—Adirondack Red Wings (d)		AHL	60	10	13	23	145
1980-81—Los Angeles Kings		NHL	5	0	0	0	4
1980-81—Houston Apollos		CHL	26	7	9	16	43
1980-81—Rochester Americans		AHL	27	6	10	16	44
1981-82—Kalamazoo Wings		IHL	75	38	27	65	113
1982-83—Kalamazoo Wings		IHL	58	38	29	67	78
1983-84—Kalamazoo Wings		IHL	76	37	31	68	154
1984-85—Kalamazoo Wings		IHL	80	35	43	78	154
1985-86—Milwaukee Admirals (e)		IHL	82	47	34	81	101
1986-87—Milwaukee Admirals		IHL	82	35	35	70	102
1987-88—Milwaukee Admirals		IHL	57	17	19	36	122
1987-88—Flint Spirits		IHL	19	3	11	14	32
NHL TOTALS			10	0	0	0	17

(c)—Drafted from New Westminster Bruins by Detroit Red Wings in fourth round of 1976 amateur draft.
(d)—September, 1980—Signed by Los Angeles Kings as a free agent.
(e)—October, 1985—Traded by Kalamazoo Wings to Milwaukee Admirals for John Flesch.

STEVE SCHEIFELE

Right Wing . . . 6' . . . 175 lbs. . . . Born, Alexandria, Va., April 18, 1968 . . . Shoots right.

Year	Team	League	Games	G.	A.	Pts.	Pen.
1985-86—Stratford (c)		OPJHL	40	41	39	80	84
1986-87—Boston College		H. East	38	13	13	26	28
1987-88—Boston College		H. East	30	11	16	27	22

(c)—June, 1986—Drafted by Philadelphia Flyers in 1986 NHL entry draft. Fifth Flyers pick, 125th overall, sixth round.

ROB SCHENNA

Defense . . . 6'1" . . . 190 lbs. . . . Born, Saugus, Mass., February 6, 1967 . . . Shoots left.

Year	Team	League	Games	G.	A.	Pts.	Pen.
1985-86—R.P.I. (c)		ECAC	32	0	6	6	63
1986-87—R.P.I.		ECAC	32	1	9	10	34
1987-88—R.P.I.		ECAC	30	5	9	14	56

(c)—June, 1985—Drafted by Detroit Red Wings in 1985 NHL entry draft. Ninth Red Wings pick, 197th overall, 10th round.

BRAD SCHLEGAL

Defense . . . 5'10" . . . 180 lbs. . . . Born, Kitchener, Ont., July 22, 1968 . . . Shoots right.

Year	Team	League	Games	G.	A.	Pts.	Pen.
1984-85—Kitchener Midget		OHA	40	30	50	80	70
1985-86—London Knights		OHA	62	2	13	15	35
1986-87—London Knights		OHA	65	4	23	27	24
1987-88—London Knights (b-c)		OHA	66	13	63	76	49

(c)—June, 1988—Drafted by Washington Capitals in 1988 NHL entry draft. Eighth Capitals pick, 144th overall, seventh round.

DON SCHMIDT

Defense . . . 5'10" . . . 190 lbs. . . . Born, Calgary, Alta., July 13, 1968 . . . Shoots left.

Year	Team	League	Games	G.	A.	Pts.	Pen.
1983-84—Prince Albert Raiders		WHL	..	..	..	..	..
1983-84—Ft. Saskatchewan Traders		AJHL	52	3	3	6	244
1984-85—Prince Albert Raiders		WHL	52	3	14	17	159
1985-86—Kamloops Blazers		WHL	29	2	5	7	168
1985-86—Prince Albert Raiders		WHL	14	0	2	2	48
1985-86—Kamloops Blazers (c)		WHL	49	5	21	26	248
1987-88—Kamloops Blazers		WHL	54	5	28	33	208

(c)—June, 1987—Drafted by Minnesota North Stars in 1987 NHL entry draft. Eighth North Stars pick, 151st overall, eighth round.

NORM SCHMIDT

Defense . . . 5'11" . . . 190 lbs. . . . Born, Sault Ste. Marie, Ont., January 24, 1963 . . . Shoots right . . . (December, 1984)—Knee injury and missed remainder of season . . . (September, 1985)—Arthroscopic surgery to left knee and missed 13 games . . . (March 1, 1986)—Injured mouth vs. Hartford and missed one game . . . (October, 1987)—Back surgery.

Year	Team	League	Games	G.	A.	Pts.	Pen.
1979-80—Sault Ste. Marie Thunderbirds		OPJHL	18	8	16	24	....
1980-81—Oshawa Generals (c)		OMJHL	65	12	25	37	73
1981-82—Oshawa Generals		OHL	67	13	48	61	172
1982-83—Oshawa Generals (b)		OHL	61	21	49	70	114
1983-84—Pittsburgh Penguins		NHL	34	6	12	18	12
1983-84—Baltimore Skipjacks		AHL	43	4	12	16	31
1984-85—Baltimore Skipjacks		AHL	33	0	22	22	31
1985-86—Pittsburgh Penguins		NHL	66	15	14	29	57
1986-87—Pittsburgh Penguins		NHL	10	1	5	6	4
1986-87—Baltimore Skipjacks		AHL	36	4	7	11	25
1987-88—Pittsburgh Penguins		NHL	5	1	2	3	0
NHL TOTALS			115	23	33	56	73

(c)—June, 1981—Drafted as underage junior by Pittsburgh Penguins in 1981 NHL entry draft. Third Penguins pick, 70th overall, fourth round.

MATHIEU SCHNEIDER

Defense . . . 5'11" . . . 180 lbs. . . . Born, New York, N.Y., June 12, 1969 . . . Shoots left.

Year	Team	League	Games	G.	A.	Pts.	Pen.
1985-86—Mt. St. Charles H.S.		RIHS	19	3	27	30	....
1986-87—Cornwall Royals (c)		QHL	63	7	29	36	75
1987-88—Montreal Canadiens		NHL	4	0	0	0	2
1987-88—Cornwall Royals (a)		OHL	48	21	40	61	85
NHL TOTALS			4	0	0	0	2

(c)—June, 1987—Drafted by Montreal Canadiens in 1987 NHL entry draft. Fourth Canadiens pick, 44th overall, third round.

SCOTT SCHNEIDER

Center . . . 6'1" . . . 174 lbs. . . . Born, Rochester, Minn., May 18, 1965 . . . Shoots right.

Year	Team	League	Games	G.	A.	Pts.	Pen.
1983-84—Colorado College (c)		WCHA	35	19	14	33	24
1984-85—Colorado College		WCHA	33	16	13	29	60
1985-86—Colorado College		WCHA	40	16	22	38	32
1986-87—Colorado College		WCHA	42	21	22	43	36
1987-88—Moncton Golden Flames		AHL	68	12	23	35	28

(c)—June, 1984—Drafted by Winnipeg Jets in NHL entry draft. Fourth Jets pick, 93rd overall, fifth round.

DWIGHT SCHOFIELD

Defense . . . 6' . . . 187 lbs. . . . Born, Lynn, Mass., March 25, 1956 . . . Shoots left . . . Missed part of 1977-78 season following knee surgery . . . (October, 1986)—Surgery to left knee.

Year Team	League	Games	G.	A.	Pts.	Pen.
1974-75—London Knights	Jr."A" OHA	70	6	16	22	124
1975-76—London Knights (c)	Jr."A" OHA	59	14	29	43	121
1976-77—Kalamazoo Wings	IHL	73	20	41	61	180
1976-77—Detroit Red Wings	NHL	3	1	0	1	2
1977-78—Kansas City Red Wings	CHL	22	3	7	10	58
1977-78—Kalamazoo Wings	IHL	3	3	6	9	21
1978-79—Kansas City Red Wings	CHL	13	1	4	5	20
1978-79—Kalamazoo Wings	IHL	47	8	29	37	199
1978-79—Fort Wayne Komets	IHL	14	2	3	5	54
1979-80—Tulsa Oilers	CHL	1	0	0	0	0
1979-80—Dayton Gems	IHL	71	15	47	62	257
1980-81—Milwaukee Admirals	IHL	82	18	41	59	327
1981-82—Nova Scotia Voyageurs (d)	AHL	75	7	24	31	*335
1982-83—Montreal Canadiens	NHL	2	0	0	0	7
1982-83—Nova Scotia Voyageurs	AHL	73	10	21	31	248
1983-84—St. Louis Blues (e)	NHL	70	4	10	14	219
1984-85—St. Louis Blues	NHL	43	1	4	5	184
1985-86—Washington Capitals (f)	NHL	50	1	2	3	127
1986-87—Pittsburgh Penguins (g)	NHL	25	1	6	7	59
1986-87—Baltimore Skipjacks	AHL	20	1	5	6	58
1987-88—Kalamazoo Wings (h)	IHL	34	2	7	9	150
1987-88—Winnipeg Jets (i)	NHL	18	0	0	0	33
NHL TOTALS		211	8	22	30	631

(c)—Drafted from London Knights by Detroit Red Wings in fifth round of 1976 amateur draft.
(d)—September, 1981—Signed by Montreal Canadiens as a free agent.
(e)—October, 1983—Selected by St. Louis Blues in NHL waiver draft.
(f)—October, 1985—Acquired by Washington Capitals in 1985 NHL waiver draft.
(g)—October, 1986—Sold by Washington Capitals to Pittsburgh Penguins.
(h)—October, 1987—Released by Detroit Red Wings and signed by Kalamazoo Wings as a free agent.
(i)—January, 1988—Signed by Winnipeg Jets as a free agent.

WALLY SCHREIBER

Left Wing . . . 5'11" . . . 175 lbs. . . . Born, Edmonton, Alta., April 15, 1962 . . . Shoots right.

Year Team	League	Games	G.	A.	Pts.	Pen.
1980-81—Ft. Saskatchewan Traders	SJHL	55	39	41	80	105
1981-82—Regina Pats (c-d)	WHL	68	56	68	124	68
1982-83—Fort Wayne Komets	IHL	67	24	34	58	23
1983-84—Fort Wayne Komets (a-e)	IHL	82	47	66	*113	44
1984-85—Fort Wayne Komets (a)	IHL	81	51	58	109	45
1985-86—Fort Wayne Komets (b)	IHL	72	37	52	89	38
1985-86—Team Canada	Int'l	..	..	..	..	..
1986-87—Canadian Olympic Team	Int'l	..	..	..	..	..
1987-88—Canadian Olympic Team	Int'l	69	25	17	42	36
1987-88—Minnesota North Stars (f)	NHL	16	6	5	11	2
NHL TOTALS		16	6	5	11	2

(c)—September, 1981—Traded by Portland Winter Hawks to Regina Pats for future considerations.
(d)—June, 1982—Drafted by Washington Capitals in 1982 NHL entry draft. Fifth Capitals pick, 152nd overall, eighth round.
(e)—Winner of Leo P. Lamoureux Trophy (Leading Scorer).
(f)—February, 1988—Signed by Minnesota North Stars as a free agent.

KEVIN SCOTT

Center . . . 5'10" . . . 180 lbs. . . . Born, Kimberley, B.C., March 11, 1967 . . . Shoots left.

Year Team	League	Games	G.	A.	Pts.	Pen.
1986-87—Vernon Lakers (c)	BCJHL	52	56	72	128	50
1987-88—Northern Michigan Univ.	WCHA	36	9	12	21	42

(c)—June, 1987—Drafted by Detroit Red Wings in 1987 NHL entry draft. Ninth Red Wings pick, 158th overall, eighth round.

GLEN SEABROOKE

Left Wing . . . 6'1" . . . 175 lbs. . . . Born, Peterborough, Ont., September 11, 1967 . . . Shoots left . . . Also plays Center . . . (July, 1983)—Broken collarbone . . . (February, 1985)—Groin injury . . . (September, 1985)—Summer long injury, thought to be a pulled groin muscle, turned out to be a dislocated pelvis and he missed most of the 1985-86 season following surgery.

Year	Team	League	Games	G.	A.	Pts.	Pen.
1983-84—Peterborough Midget		OHA	29	36	31	67	31
1984-85—Peterborough Petes (c)		OHL	45	21	13	34	59
1985-86—Peterborough Petes		OHL	19	8	12	20	33
1986-87—Peterborough Petes		OHL	48	30	39	69	29
1986-87—Philadelphia Flyers		NHL	10	1	4	5	2
1987-88—Hershey Bears		AHL	73	32	46	78	39
1987-88—Philadelphia Flyers		NHL	6	0	1	1	2
NHL TOTALS			16	1	5	6	4

(c)—June, 1985—Drafted as underage junior by Philadelphia Flyers in 1985 NHL entry draft. First Flyers pick, 21st overall, first round.

ALAN WILLIAM SECORD

Left Wing . . . 6'1" . . . 210 lbs. . . . Born, Sudbury, Ont., March 3, 1958 . . . Shoots left . . . (October, 1980)—Bruised right knee . . . (March, 1981)—Ankle injury . . . (April, 1983)—Suspended for one game in playoffs for abusive language to an official . . . (October, 1983)—Tore abdominal muscles . . . (December 12, 1984)—Pulled abductor muscles in thigh during a team practice . . . (October, 1987)—Separated ribs and torn rib cartilage.

Year	Team	League	Games	G.	A.	Pts.	Pen.
1974-75—Wexford Raiders		OPJHL	41	5	13	18	104
1975-76—Hamilton Fincups		Jr."A" OHA	63	9	13	22	117
1976-77—St. Catharines Fincups		Jr."A" OHA	57	32	34	66	343
1977-78—Hamilton Fincups (c)		Jr."A" OHA	59	28	22	50	185
1978-79—Rochester Americans		AHL	4	4	2	6	40
1978-79—Boston Bruins		NHL	71	16	7	23	125
1979-80—Boston Bruins		NHL	77	23	16	39	170
1980-81—Springfield Indians		AHL	8	3	5	8	21
1980-81—Boston Bruins (d)		NHL	18	0	3	3	42
1980-81—Chicago Black Hawks		NHL	41	13	9	22	145
1981-82—Chicago Black Hawks		NHL	80	44	31	75	303
1982-83—Chicago Black Hawks		NHL	80	54	32	86	180
1983-84—Chicago Black Hawks		NHL	14	4	4	8	77
1984-85—Chicago Black Hawks		NHL	51	15	11	26	193
1985-86—Chicago Black Hawks		NHL	80	40	36	76	201
1986-87—Chicago Black Hawks (e)		NHL	77	29	29	58	196
1987-88—Toronto Maple Leafs		NHL	74	15	27	42	221
NHL TOTALS			663	253	205	458	1853

(c)—Drafted from Hamilton Fincups by Boston Bruins in first round of 1978 amateur draft.
(d)—December, 1980—Traded by Boston Bruins to Chicago Black Hawks for Mike O'Connell.
(e)—September, 1987—Traded with Ed Olczyk by Chicago Black Hawks to Toronto Maple Leafs for Rick Vaive, Steve Thomas and Bob McGill.

STEVEN SEFTEL

Left Wing . . . 6'1" . . . 185 lbs. . . . Born, Kitchener, Ont., May 14, 1968 . . . Shoots left . . . (September, 1985)—Broken ankle.

Year	Team	League	Games	G.	A.	Pts.	Pen.
1984-85—Kitchener Greenshirts		OHA Midget	69	58	52	110	176
1985-86—Kingston Canadians (c)		OHL	42	11	16	27	53
1986-87—Kingston Canadians		OHL	54	21	43	64	55
1987-88—Kingston Canadians		OHL	66	32	43	75	51
1987-88—Binghamton Whalers		AHL	3	0	0	0	2

(c)—June, 1986—Drafted as underage junior by Washington Capitals in 1986 NHL entry draft. Second Capitals pick, 40th overall, second round.

RICHARD JAMES (RIC) SEILING

Right Wing . . . 6'1" . . . 180 lbs. . . . Born, Elmira, Ont., December 15, 1957 . . . Shoots right . . . Brother of Rod and Don Seiling . . . (January 30, 1982)—Injured eye when hit by stick in game vs. Calgary . . . (December 15, 1985)—Pulled groin vs. Quebec and missed eight games . . . (February 16, 1986)—Bruised knee at Edmonton and missed one game.

Year	Team	League	Games	G.	A.	Pts.	Pen.
1974-75—Hamilton Red Wings		Jr."A"OHA	68	33	30	63	74
1975-76—Hamilton Fincups		Jr."A"OHA	59	35	51	86	49
1976-77—St. Catharines Fincups (c)		Jr."A"OHA	62	49	61	110	103
1977-78—Buffalo Sabres		NHL	80	19	19	38	33
1978-79—Buffalo Sabres		NHL	78	20	22	42	56
1979-80—Buffalo Sabres		NHL	80	25	35	60	54
1980-81—Buffalo Sabres		NHL	74	30	27	57	80
1981-82—Buffalo Sabres		NHL	57	22	25	47	58

Year	Team	League	Games	G.	A.	Pts.	Pen.
1982-83—Buffalo Sabres		NHL	75	19	22	41	41
1983-84—Buffalo Sabres		NHL	78	13	22	35	42
1984-85—Buffalo Sabres		NHL	73	16	15	31	86
1985-86—Buffalo Sabres		NHL	69	12	13	25	74
1986-87—Detroit Red Wings (d)		NHL	74	3	8	11	49
1987-88—Adirondack Red Wings		AHL	70	16	13	29	34
NHL TOTALS			738	179	208	387	573

(c)—Drafted from St. Catharines Fincups by Buffalo Sabres in first round of 1977 amateur draft.
(d)—October, 1986—Sold by Buffalo Sabres to Detroit Red Wings.

TEEMU SELANNE

Right Wing . . . 6' . . . 176 lbs. . . . Born, Helsinki, Finland, March 7, 1970 . . . Shoots right.

Year	Team	League	Games	G.	A.	Pts.	Pen.
1987-88—Jokerit (c)		Fin.	33	42	23	65	18

(c)—June, 1988—Drafted by Winnipeg Jets in 1988 NHL entry draft. First Jets pick, 10th overall, first round.

DAVID SEMENKO

Left Wing . . . 6'3" . . . 215 lbs. . . . Born, Winnipeg, Man., July 12, 1957 . . . Shoots left . . . (May 20, 1979)—Scored final WHA goal, sixth game of playoff series vs. Winnipeg Jets (Gary Smith in goal) . . . (January 4, 1984)—Sprained left knee vs. Minnesota.

Year	Team	League	Games	G.	A.	Pts.	Pen.
1974-75—Brandon Travellers		MJHL	42	11	17	28	55
1974-75—Brandon Wheat Kings		WCHL	12	2	1	3	12
1975-76—Brandon Wheat Kings		WCHL	72	8	5	13	194
1976-77—Brandon Wheat Kings (c-d)		WCHL	61	27	33	60	265
1977-78—Brandon Wheat Kings		WCHL	7	10	5	15	40
1977-78—Edmonton Oilers (e)		WHA	65	6	6	12	140
1978-79—Edmonton Oilers (f-g)		WHA	77	10	14	24	158
1979-80—Edmonton Oilers		NHL	67	6	7	13	135
1980-81—Edmonton Oilers		NHL	58	11	8	19	80
1980-81—Wichita Wind		CHL	14	1	2	3	40
1981-82—Edmonton Oilers		NHL	59	12	12	24	194
1982-83—Edmonton Oilers		NHL	75	12	15	27	141
1983-84—Edmonton Oilers		NHL	52	6	11	17	118
1984-85—Edmonton Oilers		NHL	69	6	12	18	172
1985-86—Edmonton Oilers		NHL	69	6	12	18	141
1986-87—Edmonton Oilers		NHL	5	0	0	0	0
1986-87—Hartford Whalers (h)		NHL	51	4	8	12	87
1987-88—Toronto Maple Leafs (i)		NHL	70	2	3	5	107
WHA TOTALS			142	16	20	36	298
NHL TOTALS			575	65	88	153	1175

(c)—Drafted from Brandon Wheat Kings by Minnesota North Stars in second round of 1977 amateur draft.
(d)—June, 1977—Selected by Houston Aeros in World Hockey Association amateur players draft.
(e)—November, 1978—Signed by Edmonton Oilers (WHA).
(f)—June, 1979—Selected by Minnesota North Stars in NHL reclaim draft.
(g)—August, 1979—Traded by Minnesota North Stars to Edmonton Oilers for a draft choice.
(h)—December, 1986—Traded by Edmonton Oilers to Hartford Whalers for third-round 1988 draft pick (Trevor Sim).
(i)—March, 1988—Announced his retirement.

GEORGE SERVINIS

Left Wing . . . 5'11" . . . 180 lbs. . . . Born, Toronto, Ont., April 29, 1962 . . . Shoots left . . . Missed the final 50 games of 1985-86 season due to a separated shoulder.

Year	Team	League	Games	G.	A.	Pts.	Pen.
1980-81—Wexford Raiders		MTJBHL	40	35	45	80	....
1981-82—Aurora Tigers		OJHL	55	62	55	117	....
1982-83—R.P.I. (c)		ECAC	28	35	29	64	22
1983-84—Canadian National Team		Int'l	43	13	11	24	33
1983-84—R.P.I.		ECAC	12	5	13	18	14
1984-85—R.P.I. (d)		ECAC	35	34	25	59	44
1985-86—Springfield Indians		AHL	30	2	14	16	19
1986-87—Indianapolis Checkers		IHL	70	41	54	95	54
1987-88—Minnesota North Stars		NHL	5	0	0	0	0
1987-88—Kalamazoo Wings		IHL	49	34	21	55	54
NHL TOTALS			5	0	0	0	0

(c)—Named ECAC Top Rookie.
(d)—August, 1985—Signed by Minnesota North Stars as a free agent.

JAROSLAV SEVCIK

Left Wing . . . 5'8" . . . 170 lbs. . . . Born, Brno, Czech., May 15, 1965 . . . Shoots left.

Year	Team	League	Games	G.	A.	Pts.	Pen.
1986-87	Zetor Brno (c)	Czech.	34	12	5	17	....
1987-88	Fredericton Express	AHL	32	9	7	16	8

(c)—June, 1987—Drafted by Quebec Nordiques in 1987 NHL entry draft. Ninth Nordiques pick, 177th overall, ninth round.

DEAN SEXSMITH

Center . . . 6'1" . . . 180 lbs. . . . Born, Virden, Manitoba, May 13, 1968 . . . Shoots left.

Year	Team	League	Games	G.	A.	Pts.	Pen.
1983-84	Notre Dame Hounds	Sask. Midget	26	16	7	23	16
1984-85	Brandon Wheat Kings	WHL	47	8	8	16	31
1985-86	Brandon Wheat Kings (c)	WHL	65	13	23	36	34
1986-87	Seattle Thunderbirds	WHL	65	14	24	38	46
1987-88	Seattle Thunderbirds	WHL	16	10	9	19	10
1987-88	Saskatoon Blades	WHL	58	15	26	41	37

(c)—June, 1986—Drafted as underage junior by New York Islanders in 1986 NHL entry draft. Fifth Islanders pick, 101st overall, fifth round.

BRENDON SHANAHAN

Center . . . 6'3" . . . 200 lbs. . . . Born, Mimico, Ont., January 23, 1969 . . . Shoots right . . . (January, 1987)—Bruised tendons in shoulder . . . (December, 1987)—Broken nose.

Year	Team	League	Games	G.	A.	Pts.	Pen.
1984-85	Mississauga Reps	MTHL	36	20	21	41	26
1985-86	London Knights	OHL	59	28	34	62	70
1986-87	London Knights (c)	OHL	56	39	53	92	128
1987-88	New Jersey Devils	NHL	65	7	19	26	131
	NHL TOTALS		65	7	19	26	131

(c)—June, 1987—Drafted as underage junior by New Jersey Devils in 1987 NHL entry draft. First Devils pick, second overall, first round.

DARRIN SHANNON

Left Wing . . . 6'2" . . . 190 lbs. . . . Born, Barrie, Ont., December 8, 1969 . . . Shoots left . . . (November, 1986)—Separated right shoulder . . . (November, 1987)—Dislocated left elbow vs. Toronto Marlboros . . . (January, 1988)—Separated left shoulder . . . Brother of Darryl Shannon.

Year	Team	League	Games	G.	A.	Pts.	Pen.
1985-86	Barrie Colts Jr. B	OHA	40	13	22	35	21
1986-87	Windsor Spitfires (c)	OHL	60	16	67	83	116
1987-88	Windsor Spitfires (a-d-e)	OHL	43	33	41	74	49

(c)—Named to OHL All-Scholastic team.
(d)—Named top scholastic OHL player.
(e)—June, 1988—Drafted by Pittsburgh Penguins in 1988 NHL entry draft. First Penguins pick, fourth overall, first round.

DARRYL SHANNON

Defense . . . 6'2" . . . 190 lbs. . . . Born, Barrie, Ont., June 21, 1968 . . . Shoots left . . . Brother of Darrin Shannon.

Year	Team	League	Games	G.	A.	Pts.	Pen.
1984-85	Barrie Jr. 'B'	OHA	39	5	23	28	50
1985-86	Windsor Spitfires (c)	OHL	57	6	21	27	52
1986-87	Windsor Spitfires (b)	OHL	64	23	27	50	83
1987-88	Windsor Spitfires	OHL	60	16	70	86	116

(c)—June, 1986—Drafted by Toronto Maple Leafs in 1986 NHL entry draft. Second Maple Leafs pick, 36th overall, second round.

JEFF SHARPLES

Defense . . . 6' . . . 190 lbs. . . . Born, Terrace, B.C., July 28, 1967 . . . Shoots left.

Year	Team	League	Games	G.	A.	Pts.	Pen.
1983-84	Kelowna Wings	WHL	72	9	24	33	51
1984-85	Kelowna Wings (b-c)	WHL	72	12	41	53	90
1985-86	Portland Winter Hawks	WHL	19	2	6	8	44

Year	Team	League	Games	G.	A.	Pts.	Pen.
1985-86—Spokane Chiefs		WHL	3	0	0	0	4
1986-87—Portland Winter Hawks		WHL	44	25	35	60	92
1986-87—Detroit Red Wings		NHL	3	0	1	1	2
1987-88—Detroit Red Wings		NHL	56	10	25	35	42
1987-88—Adirondack Red Wings		AHL	4	2	1	3	4
NHL TOTALS			59	10	26	36	44

(c)—June, 1985—Drafted as underage junior by Detroit Red Wings in 1985 NHL entry draft. Second Red Wings pick, 29th overall, second round.

SCOTT SHAUNESSY

Defense . . . 6'4" . . . 220 lbs. . . . Born, Newport, R.I., January 22, 1964 . . . Shoots left . . . (November 20, 1987)—Given a six-game AHL suspension for returning to fight after going to the dressing room vs. Fredericton.

Year	Team	League	Games	G.	A.	Pts.	Pen.
1982-83—St. John's Prep. (c)		R.I. H.S.	23	7	32	39	....
1983-84—Boston University		ECAC	40	6	22	28	48
1984-85—Boston University (b)		H. East	42	7	15	22	87
1985-86—Boston University (a)		H. East	38	4	22	26	60
1986-87—Boston University		H. East	32	2	13	15	71
1986-87—Quebec Nordiques		NHL	3	0	0	0	7
1987-88—Fredericton Express		AHL	60	0	9	9	257
NHL TOTALS			3	0	0	0	7

(c)—June, 1983—Drafted by Quebec Nordiques in 1983 NHL entry draft. Ninth Nordiques pick, 192nd overall, 10th round.

BRAD SHAW

Defense . . . 5'11" . . . 163 lbs. . . . Born, Cambridge, Ont., April 28, 1964 . . . Shoots right . . . (February, 1988)—Fractured finger on left hand.

Year	Team	League	Games	G.	A.	Pts.	Pen.
1980-81—Kitchener Greenshirts		Ont. Midgets	62	14	58	72	14
1981-82—Ottawa 67's (c)		OHL	68	13	59	72	24
1982-83—Ottawa 67's		OHL	63	12	66	78	24
1983-84—Ottawa 67's (a-d-e-f)		OHL	68	11	71	82	75
1984-85—Salt Lake Golden Eagles		IHL	44	3	29	32	25
1984-85—Binghamton Whalers		AHL	24	1	10	11	4
1985-86—Hartford Whalers		NHL	8	0	2	2	4
1985-86—Binghamton Whalers		AHL	64	10	44	54	33
1986-87—Hartford Whalers		NHL	2	0	0	0	0
1986-87—Binghamton Whalers (a-g)		AHL	77	9	30	39	43
1987-88—Binghamton Whalers		AHL	73	12	50	62	50
1987-88—Hartford Whalers		NHL	1	0	0	0	0
NHL TOTALS			11	0	2	2	4

(c)—June, 1982—Drafted as underage junior by Detroit Red Wings in 1982 NHL entry draft. Fifth Red Wings pick, 86th overall, fifth round.
(d)—Won Max Kaminsky Trophy (Top Defenseman).
(e)—Led OHL playoffs with 27 assists.
(f)—May, 1984—Traded by Detroit Red Wings to Hartford Whalers for eighth-round 1984 draft pick (Lars Karlsson).
(g)—Won Eddie Shore Award (Top Defenseman).

DAVE SHAW

Defense . . . 6'2" . . . 190 lbs. . . . Born, St. Thomas, Ont., May 25, 1964 . . . Shoots right . . . (December 18, 1985)—Sprained wrist at Montreal . . . (January 27, 1986)—Charley Horse vs. N.Y. Rangers and missed two games . . . (October, 1987)—Separated shoulder.

Year	Team	League	Games	G.	A.	Pts.	Pen.
1980-81—Stratford Jr. B		OPJHL	41	12	19	31	30
1981-82—Kitchener Rangers (c)		OHL	68	6	25	31	99
1982-83—Kitchener Rangers		OHL	57	18	56	74	78
1982-83—Quebec Nordiques		NHL	2	0	0	0	0
1983-84—Kitchener Rangers (a)		OHL	58	14	34	48	73
1983-84—Quebec Nordiques		NHL	3	0	0	0	0
1984-85—Guelph Platers		OHL	2	0	0	0	0
1984-85—Fredericton Express		AHL	48	7	6	13	73
1984-85—Quebec Nordiques		NHL	14	0	0	0	11
1985-86—Quebec Nordiques		NHL	73	7	19	26	78
1986-87—Quebec Nordiques		NHL	75	0	19	19	69
1987-88—New York Rangers (d)		NHL	68	7	25	32	100
NHL TOTALS			235	14	63	77	258

(c)—June, 1982—Drafted as underage junior by Quebec Nordiques in 1982 NHL entry draft. First Nordiques pick, 13th overall, first round.
(d)—September, 1987—Traded with John Ogrodnick by Quebec Nordiques to New York Rangers for Jeff Jackson and Terry Carkner.

LARRY SHAW

Defense . . . 6' . . . 190 lbs. . . . Born, Guelph, Ont., February 10, 1967 . . . Shoots right . . . (November 2, 1986)—Suspended for two OHL games for being involved in a bench-clearing fight vs. Oshawa.

Year	Team	League	Games	G.	A.	Pts.	Pen.
1981-82—Guelph Midgets		OHA	45	8	20	28	70
1982-83—Guelph Platers		OHL	67	0	13	13	107
1983-84—Peterborough Petes		OHL	64	1	11	12	64
1984-85—Peterborough Petes (c)		OHL	55	1	11	12	93
1985-86—Peterborough Petes		OHL	66	2	17	19	106
1986-87—Peterborough Petes		OHL	61	4	13	17	78
1986-87—Binghamton Whalers (d)		AHL	..	..	..	..	..
1987-88—Binghamton Whalers		AHL	1	0	0	0	2
1987-88—Fort Wayne Komets		IHL	7	0	0	0	36

(c)—June, 1985—Drafted by Washington Capitals in 1985 NHL entry draft as an underage junior. Fifth Capitals pick, 83rd overall, fourth round.
(d)—No regular season record. Played three playoff games.

DAN SHEA

Left Wing . . . 5'9" . . . 165 lbs. . . . Born, Quincy, Mass., March 10, 1965 . . . Shoots left.

Year	Team	League	Games	G.	A.	Pts.	Pen.
1984-85—Boston College		H. East	43	16	20	36	36
1985-86—Boston College		H. East	40	11	25	36	44
1986-87—Boston College (c)		H. East	38	21	45	66	56
1987-88—Boston College		H. East	34	21	31	52	48

(c)—June, 1987—Selected by Pittsburgh Penguins in 1987 NHL supplemental draft.

DOUGLAS ARTHUR SHEDDEN

Right Wing . . . 6' . . . 184 lbs. . . . Born, Wallaceburg, Ont., April 29, 1961 . . . Shoots right . . . (October 25, 1981)—Suffered a broken finger and leg and ankle injuries during a team practice . . . Also plays Center . . . (March 24, 1986)—Kidney infection.

Year	Team	League	Games	G.	A.	Pts.	Pen.
1977-78—Hamilton Fincups		OMJHL	32	1	9	10	32
1977-78—Kitchener Rangers		OMJHL	18	5	7	12	14
1978-79—Kitchener Rangers		OMJHL	66	16	42	58	29
1979-80—Kitchener Rangers		OMJHL	16	10	16	26	26
1979-80—Sault Ste. Marie Greyhounds (c)		OMJHL	45	30	44	74	59
1980-81—Sault Ste. Marie Greyhounds		OHL	66	51	72	123	78
1981-82—Erie Blades		AHL	17	4	6	10	14
1981-82—Pittsburgh Penguins		NHL	38	10	15	25	12
1982-83—Pittsburgh Penguins		NHL	80	24	43	67	54
1983-84—Pittsburgh Penguins		NHL	67	22	35	57	20
1984-85—Pittsburgh Penguins		NHL	80	35	32	67	30
1985-86—Pittsburgh Penguins (d)		NHL	67	32	34	66	32
1985-86—Detroit Red Wings		NHL	11	2	3	5	4
1986-87—Adirondack Red Wings		AHL	5	2	2	4	4
1986-87—Detroit Red Wings (e)		NHL	33	6	12	18	6
1986-87—Fredericton Express		AHL	15	12	6	18	0
1986-87—Quebec Nordiques		NHL	16	0	2	2	8
1987-88—Baltimore Skipjacks (f)		AHL	80	37	51	88	32
NHL TOTALS			392	131	176	307	166

(c)—June, 1980—Drafted as underage junior by Pittsburgh Penguins in 1980 NHL entry draft. Fourth Penguins pick, 93rd overall, sixth round.
(d)—March, 1986—Traded by Pittsburgh Penguins to Detroit Red Wings for Ron Duguay.
(e)—January, 1987—Traded with John Ogrodnick and Basil McRae by Detroit Red Wings to Quebec Nordiques for Brent Ashton, Mark Kumpel and Gilbert Delorme.
(f)—August, 1988—Signed by Toronto Maple Leafs as a free agent.

NEIL SHEEHY

Defense . . . 6'2" . . . 210 lbs. . . . Born, Fort Francis, Ont., February 9, 1960 . . . Shoots right . . . Brother of Shawn and Tim Sheehy (hockey players) and nephew of Bronko Nagurski (football star for University of Minnesota and Hall-of-Famer with Chicago Bears) . . . (October, 1986)—Dislocated shoulder . . . (December, 1986)—Missed games due to re-

curring shoulder problems . . . (March 10, 1987)—Deep thigh bruise when kneed by Lou Franceschetti at Washington . . . (January, 1988)—Injured hip.

Year Team	League	Games	G.	A.	Pts.	Pen.
1979-80—Harvard University	ECAC	13	0	0	0	10
1980-81—Harvard University	ECAC	26	4	8	12	22
1981-82—Harvard University	ECAC	30	7	11	18	46
1982-83—Harvard University	ECAC	34	5	13	18	48
1983-84—Colorado Flames (c)	CHL	74	5	18	23	151
1983-84—Calgary Flames	NHL	1	1	0	1	2
1984-85—Moncton Golden Flames	AHL	34	6	9	15	101
1984-85—Calgary Flames	NHL	31	3	4	7	109
1985-86—Moncton Golden Flames	AHL	4	1	1	2	21
1985-86—Calgary Flames	NHL	65	2	16	18	271
1986-87—Calgary Flames	NHL	54	4	6	10	151
1987-88—Calgary Flames (d)	NHL	36	2	6	8	73
1987-88—Hartford Whalers (e)	NHL	26	1	4	5	116
NHL TOTALS		213	13	36	49	722

(c)—August, 1983—Signed by Calgary Flames as a free agent.
(d)—January, 1988—Traded with Carey Wilson and Lane MacDonald by Calgary Flames to Hartford Whalers for Dana Murzyn and Shane Churla.
(e)—July, 1988—Traded with Mike Millar by Hartford Whalers to Washington Capitals for Ed Kastelic and Grant Jennings.

RAY SHEPPARD

Right Wing . . . 5'11" . . . 175 lbs. . . . Born, Pembroke, Ont., May 27, 1966 . . . Shoots right . . . (September, 1986)—Missed Buffalo training camp with a left knee injury.

Year Team	League	Games	G.	A.	Pts.	Pen.
1982-83—Brockville	OPHL	48	27	36	63	81
1983-84—Cornwall Royals (c)	OHL	68	44	36	80	69
1984-85—Cornwall Royals	OHL	49	25	33	58	51
1985-86—Cornwall Royals (a-d-e-f)	OHL	63	*81	61	*142	25
1986-87—Rochester Americans	AHL	55	18	13	31	11
1987-88—Buffalo Sabres	NHL	74	38	27	65	14
NHL TOTALS		74	38	27	65	14

(c)—June, 1984—Drafted as underage junior by Buffalo Sabres in NHL entry draft. Third Sabres pick, 60th overall, third round.
(d)—Won Eddie Powers Memorial Trophy (Scoring Champion).
(e)—Won Jim Mahon Memorial Trophy (Top Scoring Right Winger).
(f)—Won Red Tilson Trophy (Outstanding Player).

GORD SHERVEN

Right Wing . . . 6' . . . 185 lbs. . . . Born, Gravelbourg, Sask., August 21, 1963 . . . Shoots right.

Year Team	League	Games	G.	A.	Pts.	Pen.
1980-81—Weyburn Red Wings (c)	SJHL	44	35	34	69	....
1981-82—University of North Dakota	WCHA	46	18	25	43	16
1982-83—University of North Dakota	WCHA	36	12	21	33	16
1983-84—Canadian National Team	Int'l	46	9	13	22	13
1983-84—University of North Dakota	WCHA	10	5	5	10	4
1983-84—Edmonton Oilers	NHL	2	1	0	1	0
1984-85—Nova Scotia Oilers	AHL	5	4	5	9	5
1984-85—Edmonton Oilers (d)	NHL	37	9	7	16	10
1984-85—Minnesota North Stars	NHL	32	2	12	14	8
1985-86—Springfield Indians	AHL	11	3	7	10	8
1985-86—Minnesota North Stars (e)	NHL	13	0	2	2	11
1985-86—Edmonton Oilers	NHL	5	1	1	2	4
1985-86—Nova Scotia Oilers	AHL	38	14	17	31	4
1986-87—Canadian National Team	Int'l	..	..	..	..	..
1986-87—Hartford Whalers (f)	NHL	7	0	0	0	0
1987-88—Hartford Whalers	NHL	1	0	0	0	0
1987-88—Canadian Olympic Team	Int'l	61	16	20	36	30
NHL TOTALS		97	13	22	35	33

(c)—June, 1981—Drafted by Edmonton Oilers in 1981 NHL entry draft. Ninth Oilers pick, 197th overall, 10th round.
(d)—January, 1985—Traded with Terry Martin by Edmonton Oilers to Minnesota North Stars for Mark Napier.
(e)—December, 1985—Traded with Don Biggs by Minnesota North Stars to Edmonton Oilers for Marc Habscheid, Emanuel Viveiros and Don Barber.
(f)—October, 1987—Selected by Hartford Whalers in NHL waiver draft.

DAVE SHIELDS

Center . . . 5'9" . . . 170 lbs. . . . Born, Calgary, Alta., April 24, 1967 . . . Shoots left . . . (January, 1988)—Major reconstructive surgery to his right shoulder. He had arthroscopic surgery to same shoulder after 1986-87 season.

Year	Team	League	Games	G.	A.	Pts.	Pen.
1986-87—Univ. of Denver (c-d)		WCHA	40	18	30	48	8
1987-88—Univ. of Denver		WCHA	21	10	7	17	2

(c)—June, 1987—Drafted by Minnesota North Stars in 1987 NHL entry draft. Twelfth North Stars pick, 235th overall, 12th round.

(d)—Named WCHA Rookie-of-the-Year.

BRUCE SHOEBOTTOM

Defense . . . 6'2" . . . 200 lbs. . . . Born, Windsor, Ont., August 20, 1965 . . . Shoots left . . . (December, 1982)—Broken leg . . . (January 24, 1987)—IHL suspension for going into the stands at Salt Lake City . . . (April, 1988)—Broken collarbone.

Year	Team	League	Games	G.	A.	Pts.	Pen.
1981-82—Peterborough Petes		OHL	51	0	4	4	67
1982-83—Peterborough Petes (c)		OHL	34	2	10	12	106
1983-84—Peterborough Petes		OHL	16	0	5	5	73
1984-85—Peterborough Petes		OHL	60	2	15	17	143
1985-86—New Haven Nighthawks (d)		AHL	6	2	0	2	12
1985-86—Binghamton Whalers		AHL	62	7	5	12	249
1986-87—Fort Wayne Komets		IHL	75	2	10	12	309
1987-88—Maine Mariners		AHL	70	2	12	14	138
1987-88—Boston Bruins		NHL	3	0	1	1	0
NHL TOTALS			3	0	1	1	0

(c)—June, 1983—Drafted as underage junior by Los Angeles Kings in 1983 NHL entry draft. First Kings pick, 47th overall, third round.

(d)—October, 1985—Traded by Los Angeles Kings to Washington Capitals for Bryan Erickson.

RONALD SHUDRA

Defense . . . 6'1" . . . 180 lbs. . . . Born, Winnipeg, Manitoba, November 28, 1967 . . . Shoots left . . . Also plays Left Wing.

Year	Team	League	Games	G.	A.	Pts.	Pen.
1984-85—Red Deer Rustlers		AJHL	57	14	57	71	70
1985-86—Kamloops Blazers (b-c-d)		WHL	72	10	40	50	81
1986-87—Kamloops Blazers (b)		WHL	71	49	70	119	68
1987-88—Nova Scotia Oilers		AHL	49	7	15	22	21
1987-88—Edmonton Oilers		NHL	10	0	5	5	6
NHL TOTALS			10	0	5	5	6

(c)—Co-winner of WHL Rookie-of-the-Year Trophy with Dave Waldie.

(d)—June, 1986—Drafted as underage junior by Edmonton Oilers in 1986 NHL entry draft. Third Oilers pick, 63rd overall, third round.

MICHAEL SILTALA

Right Wing . . . 5'10" . . . 173 lbs. . . . Born, Toronto, Ont., August 5, 1963 . . . Shoots right.

Year	Team	League	Games	G.	A.	Pts.	Pen.
1979-80—Sault Ste. Marie		Ont. Midget	57	78	83	161	....
1980-81—Kingston Canadians (c)		OMJHL	63	18	22	40	23
1981-82—Kingston Canadians		OHL	59	38	49	87	70
1981-82—Washington Capitals		NHL	3	1	0	1	2
1982-83—Kingston Canadians (a)		OHL	50	53	61	114	45
1982-83—Hershey Bears		AHL	9	0	3	3	2
1983-84—Hershey Bears		AHL	50	15	17	32	29
1984-85—Binghamton Whalers (b)		AHL	75	42	36	78	53
1985-86—Binghamton Whalers (d)		AHL	50	25	22	47	36
1986-87—New York Rangers		NHL	1	0	0	0	0
1986-87—New Haven Nighthawks		AHL	17	13	6	19	20
1987-88—New York Rangers		NHL	3	0	0	0	0
1987-88—Colorado Rangers (e)		IHL	38	22	28	50	28
1987-88—New Haven Nighthawks		AHL	32	17	20	37	8
NHL TOTALS			7	1	0	1	2

(c)—June, 1980—Drafted as underage junior by Washington Capitals in 1980 NHL entry draft. Fourth Capitals pick, 89th overall, fifth round.

(d)—August, 1986—Signed by New York Rangers as a free agent.

(e)—January, 1988—Traded with Gord Walker by New York Rangers to Los Angeles Kings for Joe Paterson.

TREVOR SIM

Center ... 6'2" ... 180 lbs. ... Born, Calgary, Alta., June 9, 1970 ... Shoots right.

Year	Team	League	Games	G.	A.	Pts.	Pen.
1986-87—Calgary Spurs		AJHL	57	38	50	88	48
1987-88—Seattle Thunderbirds (c)		WHL	67	17	18	35	87

(c)—June, 1988—Drafted by Edmonton Oilers in 1988 NHL entry draft. Third Oilers pick, 53rd overall, third round.

MARTIN SIMARD

Right Wing ... 6'3" ... 215 lbs. ... Born, June 25, 1966, Montreal, Que., ... Shoots right.

Year	Team	League	Games	G.	A.	Pts.	Pen.
1983-84—Quebec Remparts		QHL	59	6	10	16	26
1984-85—Granby Bisons		QHL	58	22	31	53	78
1985-86—Hull Olympiques		QHL	68	40	36	76	184
1986-87—Granby Bisons (c)		QHL	41	30	47	77	105
1987-88—Salt Lake Golden Eagles		IHL	82	8	23	31	281

(c)—May, 1987—Signed by Calgary Flames as a free agent.

CHARLES ROBERT SIMMER

Left Wing ... 6'3" ... 210 lbs. ... Born, Terrace Bay, Ont., March 20, 1954 ... Shoots left ... Also plays Center ... Missed part of 1975-76 season with knee surgery ... Scored goals in 13 straight games in 1979-80 to set modern NHL record ... Missed 15 games in 1979-80 season with strained ligaments in knee ... Only the second player in NHL history to not have a hat trick during a 50-goal season (Vic Hadfield was the first during 1971-72 season with N.Y. Rangers) ... (March 2, 1981)—Broken right leg ... (September, 1984)—Suspended by L.A. Kings for not reporting to training camp. He demanded to be traded ... (October, 1984)—Reported to L.A. camp and suspended ... (January, 1985)—Broken jaw ... (November 10, 1985)—Torn medial collateral ligament of right knee vs. Minnesota and missed 19 games ... (January 4, 1986)—Injured eye when struck by stick vs. Buffalo and missed six games ... (April 8, 1987)—Dislocated thumb and sprained wrist in playoff game vs. Montreal.

Year	Team	League	Games	G.	A.	Pts.	Pen.
1971-72—Kenora Muskies		MJHL	45	14	31	45	77
1972-73—Kenora Muskies (a)		MJHL	48	43	*68	*111	57
1973-74—S Ste. Marie Greyh'ds (c)		Jr."A"OHA	70	45	54	99	137
1974-75—Salt Lake Golden Eagles		CHL	47	12	29	41	86
1974-75—California Seals		NHL	35	8	13	21	26
1975-76—Salt Lake Golden Eagles		CHL	42	23	16	39	96
1975-76—California Seals		NHL	21	1	1	2	22
1976-77—Salt Lake Golden Eagles (b)		CHL	51	32	30	62	37
1976-77—Cleveland Barons (d)		NHL	24	2	0	2	16
1977-78—Springfield Indians (b)		AHL	75	42	41	83	100
1977-78—Los Angeles Kings		NHL	3	0	0	0	2
1978-79—Springfield Indians		AHL	39	13	23	36	33
1978-79—Los Angeles Kings		NHL	38	21	27	48	16
1979-80—Los Angeles Kings (a)		NHL	64	*56	45	101	65
1980-81—Los Angeles Kings (a)		NHL	65	56	49	105	62
1981-82—Los Angeles Kings		NHL	50	15	24	39	42
1982-83—Los Angeles Kings		NHL	80	29	51	80	51
1983-84—Los Angeles Kings		NHL	79	44	48	92	78
1984-85—Los Angeles Kings (e)		NHL	5	1	0	1	4
1984-85—Boston Bruins		NHL	63	33	30	63	35
1985-86—Boston Bruins (f)		NHL	55	36	23	59	42
1986-87—Boston Bruins		NHL	80	29	40	69	59
1987-88—Pittsburgh Penguins (g)		NHL	50	11	17	28	24
NHL TOTALS			712	342	368	710	544

(c)—Drafted from Sault Ste. Marie Greyhounds by California Golden Seals in third round of 1974 amateur draft.

(d)—August, 1977—Signed by Los Angeles Kings as free agent.

(e)—October, 1984—Traded by Los Angeles Kings to Boston Bruins for first round 1985 draft pick (Craig Duncanson).

(f)—Won Bill Masterton Memorial Trophy (Perseverance, Sportsmanship and Dedication).

(g)—October, 1987—Selected by Pittsburgh Penguins in 1987 NHL waiver draft.

FRANK SIMONETTI

Defense ... 6'1" ... 190 lbs. ... Born, Melrose, Mass., Sept. 11, 1962 ... Shoots right ... (Summer, 1985)—Mononucleosis ... (November 12, 1985)—Surgery to left shoulder ... (February, 1988)—Injured knee.

Year	Team	League	Games	G.	A.	Pts.	Pen.
1983-84—Norwick University		ECAC-II	....	...	....	....	....
1984-85—Hershey Bears (c)		AHL	31	0	6	6	14
1984-85—Boston Bruins		NHL	43	1	5	6	26
1985-86—Boston Bruins		NHL	17	1	0	1	14
1985-86—Moncton Golden Flames		AHL	5	0	0	0	2
1986-87—Moncton Golden Flames		AHL	7	0	1	1	6
1986-87—Boston Bruins		NHL	25	1	0	1	17
1987-88—Maine Mariners		AHL	7	0	1	1	4
1987-88—Boston Bruins		NHL	30	2	3	5	19
NHL TOTALS			115	5	8	13	76

(c)—September, 1984—Signed by Boston Bruins as a free agent.

CRAIG SIMPSON

Center . . . 6'2" . . . 185 lbs. . . . Born, London, Ont., February 15, 1967 . . . Shoot right . . . Brother of Dave Simpson . . . Son of Marion Simpson (Member of 1952 Canadian Women's Olympic Track Team) . . . (March, 1987)—Pulled muscle in right hip . . . (March 14, 1987)—Sprained right wrist vs. Philadelphia.

Year	Team	League	Games	G.	A.	Pts.	Pen.
1982-83—London Diamonds Jr. B.		OHA	....	48	63	*111	....
1983-84—Michigan State		CCHA	30	8	28	36	22
1984-85—Michigan State (a-c-d)		CCHA	42	31	53	84	33
1985-86—Pittsburgh Penguins		NHL	76	11	17	28	49
1986-87—Pittsburgh Penguins		NHL	72	26	25	51	57
1987-88—Pittsburgh Penguins (e)		NHL	21	13	13	26	34
1987-88—Edmonton Oilers		NHL	59	43	21	64	43
NHL TOTALS			228	93	76	169	183

(c)—First Team All-America (West).
(d)—June, 1985—Drafted by Pittsburgh Penguins in 1985 NHL entry draft. First Penguins pick, second overall, first round.
(e)—November, 1987—Traded with Dave Hannan, Chris Joseph and Moe Mantha by Pittsburgh Penguins to Edmonton Oilers for Paul Coffey, Dave Hunter and Wayne Van Dorp.

ILKKA SINISALO

Left Wing . . . 6'1" . . . 190 lbs. . . . Born, Valeskoski, Finland, July 10, 1958 . . . Shoots left . . . (September, 1982)—Broke collarbone . . . (December, 1984)—Missed 10 games with back spasms . . . (December 7, 1985)—Infected left ankle and missed three games . . . (December, 1986)—Strained left knee and required surgery . . . (December, 1987)—Back spasms . . . (February, 1988)—Bruised knee . . . (March, 1988)—Twisted left knee.

Year	Team	League	Games	G.	A.	Pts.	Pen.
1979-80—Helsinki IFK		Finland	35	16	9	25	16
1980-81—Helsinki IFK		Finland	36	27	17	44	14
1981-82—Philadelphia Flyers (c)		NHL	66	15	22	37	22
1982-83—Philadelphia Flyers		NHL	61	21	29	50	16
1983-84—Philadelphia Flyers		NHL	73	29	17	46	29
1984-85—Philadelphia Flyers		NHL	70	36	37	73	16
1985-86—Philadelphia Flyers		NHL	74	39	37	76	31
1986-87—Philadelphia Flyers		NHL	42	10	21	31	8
1987-88—Philadelphia Flyers		NHL	68	25	17	42	30
NHL TOTALS			454	175	180	355	152

(c)—February, 1981—Signed by Philadelphia Flyers as a free agent.

VILLE SIREN

Defense . . . 6'2" . . . 185 lbs. . . . Born, Helsinki, Finland, November 2, 1964 . . . Shoots left . . . (October 16, 1985)—Fractured right ankle at Chicago and missed 19 games . . . (March 10, 1987)—Sprained ligaments in left knee vs. N.Y. Islanders . . . (October, 1987)—Sore shoulder . . . (December, 1987)—Missed 17 games with broken foot.

Year	Team	League	Games	G.	A.	Pts.	Pen.
1984-85—Ilves (c-d)		Finland	36	11	3	24	..
1985-86—Pittsburgh Penguins		NHL	60	4	8	12	32
1986-87—Pittsburgh Penguins		NHL	69	5	17	22	50
1987-88—Pittsburgh Penguins		NHL	58	1	20	21	62
NHL TOTALS			187	10	45	55	144

(c)—June, 1983—Drafted by Hartford Whalers in NHL entry draft. Third Whalers pick, 23rd overall, second round.
(d)—November, 1984—Traded by Hartford Whalers to Pittsburgh Penguins for Pat Boutette.

RANDALL SKARDA

Defense . . . 6'1" . . . 195 lbs. . . . Born, St. Paul, Minn., May 5, 1968 . . . Shoots right.

Year	Team	League	Games	G.	A.	Pts.	Pen.
1984-85	St. Thomas Academy	Minn.	23	14	42	56	....
1985-86	St. Thomas Academy (c)	Minn.	23	15	27	42	....
1986-87	Univ. of Minnesota	WCHA	43	3	10	13	77
1987-88	Univ. of Minnesota (d)	WCHA	42	19	26	45	102

(c)—June, 1986—Drafted by St. Louis Blues in 1986 NHL entry draft. Eighth Blues pick, 157th overall, eighth round.

(d)—Named second-team All-American (West).

PETRI SKRIKO

Right Wing . . . 5'10" . . . 172 lbs. . . . Born, Laapeenranta, Finland, March 12, 1962 . . . Shoots left . . . (October, 1984)—Broken thumb . . . (October, 1987)—Bruised knee . . . (January, 1988)—Sprained ankle.

Year	Team	League	Games	G.	A.	Pts.	Pen.
1980-81	Saipa	Finland	36	20	13	33	14
1981-82	Saipa	Finland	33	19	27	46	24
1982-83	Saipa	Finland	36	23	12	35	12
1983-84	Saipa (c)	Finland	32	25	26	51	13
1984-85	Vancouver Canucks	NHL	72	21	14	35	10
1985-86	Vancouver Canucks	NHL	80	38	40	78	34
1986-87	Vancouver Canucks	NHL	76	33	41	74	44
1987-88	Vancouver Canucks	NHL	73	30	34	64	32
	NHL TOTALS		301	122	129	251	120

(c)—June, 1981—Drafted by Vancouver Canucks in NHL entry draft. Seventh Canucks pick, 157th overall, seventh round.

BRIAN SKRUDLAND

Center . . . 6' . . . 180 lbs. . . . Born, Peace River, Alta, July 31, 1963 . . . Shoots left . . . Cousin of Barry Pederson . . . (February, 1988)—Groin injury.

Year	Team	League	Games	G.	A.	Pts.	Pen.
1980-81	Saskatoon Blades	WHL	66	15	27	42	97
1981-82	Saskatoon Blades	WHL	71	27	29	56	135
1982-83	Saskatoon Blades (c)	WHL	71	35	59	94	42
1983-84	Nova Scotia Voyageurs	AHL	56	13	12	25	55
1984-85	Sherbrooke Canadiens	AHL	70	22	28	50	109
1985-86	Montreal Canadiens	NHL	65	9	13	22	57
1986-87	Montreal Canadiens	NHL	79	11	17	28	107
1987-88	Montreal Canadiens	NHL	79	12	24	36	112
	NHL TOTALS		223	32	54	86	286

(c)—August, 1983—Signed as free agent by Montreal Canadiens.

DOUG SMAIL

Left Wing . . . 5'10" . . . 175 lbs. . . . Born, Moose Jaw, Sask., September 2, 1957 . . . Shoots left . . . (January 10, 1981)—Suffered fractured jaw and also broke jaw in a November 1980 practice . . . (December 20, 1981)—Set NHL record for fastest goal at start of game (5 seconds) vs. St. Louis . . . (December, 1983)—Stretched knee ligaments . . . (October 25, 1985)—Pulled leg muscle vs. Washington and missed seven games . . . (September, 1987)—Arthroscopic knee surgery.

Year	Team	League	Games	G.	A.	Pts.	Pen.
1977-78	Univ. of North Dakota	WCHA	38	22	28	50	52
1978-79	Univ. of North Dakota	WCHA	35	24	34	58	46
1979-80	Univ. of North Dakota (b-c-d)	WCHA	40	43	44	87	70
1980-81	Winnipeg Jets	NHL	30	10	8	18	45
1981-82	Winnipeg Jets	NHL	72	17	18	35	55
1982-83	Winnipeg Jets	NHL	80	15	29	44	32
1983-84	Winnipeg Jets	NHL	66	20	17	37	62
1984-85	Winnipeg Jets	NHL	80	31	35	66	45
1985-86	Winnipeg Jets	NHL	73	16	26	42	32
1986-87	Winnipeg Jets	NHL	78	25	18	43	36
1987-88	Winnipeg Jets	NHL	71	15	16	31	34
	NHL TOTALS		550	149	167	316	341

(c)—Named to NCAA Tournament All-Star team and Tournament's Most Valuable Player.

(d)—May, 1980—Signed by Winnipeg Jets as a free agent.

BRAD ALLAN SMITH

Right Wing . . . 6'1" . . . 195 lbs. . . . Born, Windsor, Ont., April 13, 1958 . . . Shoots right . . . (January 19, 1986)—Injured leg vs. Calgary . . . (January, 1987)—Back spasms.

Year	Team	League	Games	G.	A.	Pts.	Pen.
1975-76—Windsor Spitfires		OMJHL	4	4	2	6	4
1976-77—Windsor Spitfires		OMJHL	66	37	53	90	154
1977-78—Windsor Spitfires		OMJHL	20	18	16	34	39
1977-78—Sudbury Wolves (c)		OMJHL	46	21	21	42	183
1978-79—Vancouver Canucks		NHL	2	0	0	0	2
1978-79—Dallas Black Hawks		CHL	60	17	18	35	143
1979-80—Dallas Black Hawks		CHL	51	26	16	42	138
1979-80—Vancouver Canucks (d)		NHL	19	1	3	4	50
1979-80—Atlanta Flames		NHL	4	0	0	0	4
1980-81—Birmingham Bulls		CHL	10	5	6	11	13
1980-81—Calgary Flames (e)		NHL	45	7	4	11	65
1980-81—Detroit Red Wings		NHL	20	5	2	7	93
1981-82—Detroit Red Wings		NHL	33	2	0	2	80
1981-82—Adirondack Red Wings		AHL	34	10	5	15	126
1982-83—Detroit Red Wings		NHL	1	0	0	0	0
1982-83—Adirondack Red Wings		AHL	74	20	30	50	132
1983-84—Adirondack Red Wings		AHL	46	15	29	44	128
1983-84—Detroit Red Wings		NHL	8	2	1	3	36
1984-85—Detroit Red Wings		NHL	1	1	0	1	5
1984-85—Adirondack Red Wings (f)		AHL	75	33	39	72	89
1985-86—St. Catharines Saints		AHL	31	13	29	42	79
1985-86—Toronto Maple Leafs		NHL	42	5	17	22	84
1986-87—Toronto Maple Leafs		NHL	47	5	7	12	174
1987-88—Did not play			..	..	..	..	..
NHL TOTALS			**222**	**28**	**34**	**62**	**593**

(c)—June, 1978—Drafted by Vancouver Canucks in 1978 NHL amateur draft. Fifth Canucks pick, 57th overall, fourth round.

(d)—February, 1980—Traded with Don Lever by Vancouver Canucks to Atlanta Flames for Ivan Boldirev and Darcy Rota.

(e)—February, 1981—Traded by Calgary Flames to Detroit Red Wings for future considerations. (Detroit sent Rick Vasko to Calgary in June to complete deal.)

(f)—August, 1985—Signed by Toronto Maple Leafs as a free agent.

DARIN SMITH

Left Wing . . . 6'2" . . . 200 lbs. . . . Born, St. Catharines, Ont., February 20, 1967 . . . Shoots left . . . (November, 1986)—Broken wrist.

Year	Team	League	Games	G.	A.	Pts.	Pen.
1984-85—London Knights		OHL	52	1	9	10	98
1985-86—London Knights (c)		OHL	9	2	5	7	23
1985-86—North Bay Centennials		OHL	45	7	24	31	131
1986-87—North Bay Centennials (d)		OHL	59	22	25	47	142
1987-88—Peoria Rivermen		IHL	81	21	23	44	144

(c)—November, 1985—Claimed by North Bay Centennials from London Knights to complete an earlier trade.

(d)—June, 1987—Drafted by St. Louis Blues in 1987 NHL entry draft. Fourth Blues pick, 75th overall, fourth round.

DENNIS SMITH

Defense . . . 5'11" . . . 192 lbs. . . . Born, Livonia, Mich., July 27, 1964 . . . Shoots left.

Year	Team	League	Games	G.	A.	Pts.	Pen.
1981-82—Kingston Canadians		OHL	48	2	23	25	83
1982-83—Kingston Canadians		OHL	65	6	24	30	90
1983-84—Kingston Canadians		OHL	62	10	40	50	136
1984-85—Erie Blades		ACHL	19	5	20	25	67
1985-86—Peoria Rivermen		IHL	70	5	15	20	102
1986-87—Adirondack Red Wings (c)		AHL	64	4	24	28	120
1987-88—Adirondack Red Wings		AHL	75	6	24	30	213

(c)—September, 1986—Signed by Detroit Red Wings as a free agent.

DERRICK SMITH

Left Wing . . . 6'1" . . . 185 lbs. . . . Born, Scarborough, Ont., January 22, 1965 . . . Shoots left . . . (November, 1987)—Bruised back.

Year	Team	League	Games	G.	A.	Pts.	Pen.
1981-82—Wexford Midgets		Ont. Midgets	45	35	47	82	40
1982-83—Peterborough Petes (c)		OHL	70	16	19	35	47
1983-84—Peterborough Petes		OHL	70	30	36	66	31
1984-85—Philadelphia Flyers		NHL	77	17	22	39	31
1985-86—Philadelphia Flyers		NHL	69	6	6	12	57
1986-87—Philadelphia Flyers		NHL	71	11	21	32	34
1987-88—Philadelphia Flyers		NHL	76	16	8	24	104
NHL TOTALS			293	50	57	107	226

(c)—June, 1983—Drafted as underage junior by Philadelphia Flyers in 1983 NHL entry draft. Second Flyers pick, 44th overall, third round.

DOUG SMITH

Center . . . 6' . . . 185 lbs. . . . Born, Ottawa, Ont., May 17, 1963 . . . Shoots right . . . (October, 1980)—Knee injury . . . (October 27, 1982)—Broke left wrist and missed 34 games . . . Also plays Right Wing . . . (January 16, 1985)—Partially tore medial collateral ligament in right knee vs. Toronto . . . (January 14, 1987)—Missed two games with injured knee vs. Montreal.

Year	Team	League	Games	G.	A.	Pts.	Pen.
1979-80—Ottawa 67s		OJHL	64	23	34	57	45
1980-81—Ottawa 67s (c)		OHL	54	45	56	101	61
1981-82—Ottawa 67's		OHL	1	1	2	3	17
1981-82—Los Angeles Kings		NHL	80	16	14	30	64
1982-83—Los Angeles Kings		NHL	42	11	11	22	12
1983-84—Los Angeles Kings		NHL	72	16	20	36	28
1984-85—Los Angeles Kings		NHL	62	21	20	41	58
1985-86—Los Angeles Kings (d)		NHL	48	8	9	17	56
1985-86—Buffalo Sabres		NHL	30	10	11	21	73
1986-87—Buffalo Sabres		NHL	62	16	24	40	106
1986-87—Rochester Americans		AHL	15	5	6	11	35
1987-88—Buffalo Sabres		NHL	70	9	19	28	117
NHL TOTALS			466	107	128	235	514

(c)—June, 1981—Drafted by Los Angeles Kings in NHL entry draft. First Kings pick, second overall, first round.

(d)—January, 1986—Traded with Brian Engblom by Los Angeles Kings to Buffalo Sabres for Larry Playfair, Sean McKenna and Ken Baumgartner.

GEOFF SMITH

Defense . . . 6'1" . . . 180 lbs. . . . Born, Edmonton, Alta., March 7, 1969 . . . Shoots left.

Year	Team	League	Games	G.	A.	Pts.	Pen.
1985-86—Carnwood Wireline		Cgy. Midget	41	9	21	30	58
1986-87—St. Albert Saints (c)		AJHL	57	7	28	35	101
1987-88—Univ. of North Dakota		WCHA	42	4	12	16	34

(c)—June, 1987—Drafted by Edmonton Oilers in 1987 NHL entry draft. Third Oilers pick, 63rd overall, third round.

GREGORY JAMES SMITH

Defense . . . 6' . . . 195 lbs. . . . Born, Ponoka, Alta., July 8, 1955 . . . Shoots left . . . Missed early part of 1979-80 season after knee surgery . . . (September, 1982)—Injured right knee during training camp and required arthroscopic surgery . . . (March, 1985)—Knee injury . . . (February 21, 1986)—Bruised ankle vs. Pittsburgh . . . (February, 1987)—Pulled rib muscle . . . (May, 1987)—Broken kneecap.

Year	Team	League	Games	G.	A.	Pts.	Pen.
1973-74—Colorado College		WCHA	31	7	13	20	80
1974-75—Colorado College (c)		WCHA	36	10	24	34	75
1975-76—Colorado College		WCHA	34	18	19	37	123
1975-76—Salt Lake Golden Eagles		CHL	5	0	2	2	2
1975-76—California Seals		NHL	1	0	1	1	2
1976-77—Cleveland Barons		NHL	74	9	17	26	65
1977-78—Cleveland Barons		NHL	80	7	30	37	92
1978-79—Minnesota North Stars		NHL	80	5	27	32	147
1979-80—Minnesota North Stars		NHL	55	5	13	18	103
1980-81—Minnesota North Stars (d)		NHL	74	5	21	26	126
1981-82—Detroit Red Wings		NHL	69	10	22	32	79
1982-83—Detroit Red Wings		NHL	73	4	26	30	79
1983-84—Detroit Red Wings		NHL	75	3	20	23	108
1984-85—Detroit Red Wings		NHL	73	2	18	20	117
1985-86—Detroit Red Wings (e)		NHL	62	5	19	24	84
1985-86—Washington Capitals		NHL	14	0	3	3	10

Year	Team	League	Games	G.	A.	Pts.	Pen.
1986-87—Washington Capitals		NHL	45	0	9	9	31
1987-88—Washington Capitals		NHL	54	1	6	7	67
NHL TOTALS			829	56	232	288	1110

(c)—Drafted from Colorado College by California Seals in fourth round of 1975 amateur draft.

(d)—September, 1981—Traded by Minnesota North Stars with Don Murdoch to Detroit Red Wings giving North Stars option to switch first-round draft choices with Detroit in 1982 entry draft. Minnesota exercised option and drafted Brian Bellows. Detroit drafted Murray Craven.

(e)—March, 1986—Traded with John Barrett by Detroit Red Wings to Washington Capitals for Darren Veitch.

JIM SMITH

Defense . . . 6'1" . . . 215 lbs. . . . Born, Castlegar, B.C., January 18, 1964 . . . Shoots left.

Year	Team	League	Games	G.	A.	Pts.	Pen.
1982-83—Denver University		WCHA	36	10	18	28	10
1983-84—Denver University		WCHA	36	5	15	20	24
1984-85—Denver University		WCHA	37	7	18	25	40
1985-86—Denver University (c)		WCHA	47	10	40	50	37
1986-87—Adirondack Red Wings		AHL	77	8	27	35	43
1987-88—Adirondack Red Wings (d)		AHL	41	3	10	13	36

(c)—July, 1986—Signed by Detroit Red Wings as a free agent.

(d)—February, 1988—Contract bought out by Detroit Red Wings and he was released.

RANDY SMITH

Center . . . 6'2" . . . 180 lbs. . . . Born, Saskatoon, Sask., July 15, 1965 . . . Shoots left.

Year	Team	League	Games	G.	A.	Pts.	Pen.
1982-83—Battleford Barons		SAJHL	64	25	20	45	141
1983-84—Saskatoon Blades		WHL	69	19	21	40	53
1984-85—Saskatoon Blades		WHL	25	6	16	22	9
1984-85—Calgary Wranglers		WHL	46	28	35	63	17
1985-86—Saskatoon Blades (b)		WHL	70	60	86	146	44
1985-86—Minnesota North Stars (c)		NHL	1	0	0	0	0
1986-87—Springfield Indians		AHL	75	20	44	64	24
1986-87—Minnesota North Stars		NHL	2	0	0	0	0
1987-88—Kalamazoo Wings		IHL	77	13	43	56	54
NHL TOTALS			3	0	0	0	0

(c)—March, 1986—Signed by Minnesota North Stars as a free agent.

ROBERT DAVID SMITH

Center . . . 6'4" . . . 210 lbs. . . . Born, N. Sydney, N.S., February 12, 1958 . . . Shoots left . . . Missed part of 1979-80 season with fractured ankle . . . (December, 1984)—Broken Jaw.

Year	Team	League	Games	G.	A.	Pts.	Pen.
1975-76—Ottawa 67's		Jr."A"OHA	62	24	34	58	21
1976-77—Ottawa 67's (b)		Jr."A"OHA	64	*65	70	135	52
1977-78—Ottawa 67's (a-c-d)		Jr."A"OHA	61	69	*123	*192	44
1978-79—Minnesota North Stars (e-f)		NHL	80	30	44	74	39
1979-80—Minnesota North Stars		NHL	61	27	56	83	24
1980-81—Minnesota North Stars		NHL	78	29	64	93	73
1981-82—Minnesota North Stars		NHL	80	43	71	114	84
1982-83—Minnesota North Stars		NHL	77	24	53	77	81
1983-84—Minnesota North Stars (g)		NHL	10	3	6	9	9
1983-84—Montreal Canadiens		NHL	70	26	37	63	62
1984-85—Montreal Canadiens		NHL	65	16	40	56	59
1985-86—Montreal Canadiens		NHL	79	31	55	86	55
1986-87—Montreal Canadiens		NHL	80	28	47	75	72
1987-88—Montreal Canadiens		NHL	78	27	66	93	78
NHL TOTALS			758	284	569	823	636

(c)—Won Eddie Powers Memorial Trophy (Leading Scorer) and Albert "Red" Tilson Memorial Trophy (MVP).

(d)—Drafted from Ottawa 67's by Minnesota North Stars in first round of 1978 amateur draft.

(e)—Won Calder Memorial Trophy (NHL Rookie of the Year).

(f)—Named THE SPORTING NEWS NHL Rookie of the Year in poll of players.

(g)—October, 1983—Traded by Minnesota North Stars to Montreal Canadiens for Mark Napier, Keith Acton and third-round draft pick (Kenneth Hodge).

SANDY SMITH

Center . . . 5'11" . . . 185 lbs. . . . Born, Brainerd, Minn., October 23, 1967 . . . Shoots right . . . (September, 1985)—Torn knee ligaments.

Year	Team	League	Games	G.	A.	Pts.	Pen.
1984-85—Brainerd H.S.		Minn.	21	30	20	50	..
1985-86—Brainerd H.S. (c)		Minn.	17	28	22	50	..
1986-87—Univ. of Minnesota/Duluth		WCHA	35	3	3	6	26
1987-88—Univ. of Minnesota/Duluth		WCHA	41	22	9	31	47

(c)—June, 1986—Drafted by Pittsburgh Penguins in 1986 NHL entry draft. Fifth Penguins pick, 88th overall, fifth round.

JAMES STEPHEN (STEVE) SMITH

Defense . . . 6'2" . . . 190 lbs. . . . Born, Glasgow, Scotland, April 30, 1963 . . . Shoots left . . . Also plays Right Wing . . . (November 1, 1985)—Strained right shoulder in fight vs. Buffalo . . . (February, 1986)—Pulled stomach muscle.

Year	Team	League	Games	G.	A.	Pts.	Pen.
1980-81—London Knights (c)		OMJHL	62	4	12	16	141
1981-82—London Knights		OHL	58	10	36	46	207
1982-83—London Knights		OHL	50	6	35	41	133
1982-83—Moncton Alpines		AHL	2	0	0	0	0
1983-84—Moncton Alpines		AHL	64	1	8	9	176
1984-85—Nova Scotia Oilers		AHL	68	2	28	30	161
1984-85—Edmonton Oilers		NHL	2	0	0	0	2
1985-86—Nova Scotia Oilers		AHL	4	0	2	2	11
1985-86—Edmonton Oilers		NHL	55	4	20	24	166
1986-87—Edmonton Oilers		NHL	62	7	15	22	165
1987-88—Edmonton Oilers		NHL	79	12	43	55	286
NHL TOTALS			198	23	78	101	619

(c)—June, 1981—Drafted as underage junior by Edmonton Oilers in 1981 NHL entry draft. Fifth Oilers pick, 111th overall, sixth round.

STEVE SMITH

Defense . . . 5'9" . . . 202 lbs. . . . Born, Trenton, Ont., April 4, 1963 . . . Shoots left . . . (February, 1987)—Hip flexor injury.

Year	Team	League	Games	G.	A.	Pts.	Pen.
1979-80—Belleville Tier 2		OHL	41	8	25	33	105
1980-81—Sault Ste. Marie Greyhounds (b-c-d)		OHL	61	3	37	40	143
1981-82—Sault Ste. Marie Greyhounds (b)		OHL	50	7	20	27	179
1981-82—Philadelphia Flyers		NHL	8	0	1	1	0
1982-83—Sault Ste. Marie Greyhounds (b)		OHL	55	11	33	44	139
1983-84—Springfield Indians		AHL	70	4	25	29	77
1984-85—Philadelphia Flyers		NHL	2	0	0	0	7
1984-85—Hershey Bears		AHL	65	10	20	30	83
1985-86—Hershey Bears		AHL	49	1	11	12	96
1985-86—Philadelphia Flyers		NHL	2	0	0	0	2
1986-87—Hershey Bears		AHL	66	11	26	37	191
1986-87—Philadelphia Flyers		NHL	2	0	0	0	6
1987-88—Hershey Bears		AHL	66	10	19	29	132
1987-88—Philadelphia Flyers (e)		NHL	1	0	0	0	0
NHL TOTALS			15	0	1	1	15

(c)—Won Max Kaminsky Award (Outstanding Defenseman).
(d)—Drafted by Philadelphia Flyers in NHL entry draft. First Flyers pick, 16th overall, first round.
(e)—July, 1988—Signed by Calgary Flames as a free agent.

VERN SMITH

Defense . . . 6'1" . . . 190 lbs. . . . Born, Winnipeg, Man., May 30, 1964 . . . Shoots left . . . (February 10, 1988)—Torn knee ligaments vs. Utica Devils (AHL).

Year	Team	League	Games	G.	A.	Pts.	Pen.
1981-82—Lethbridge Broncos (c)		WHL	72	5	38	43	73
1982-83—Lethbridge Broncos		WHL	30	2	10	12	54
1982-83—Nanaimo Islanders		WHL	42	6	21	27	62
1983-84—New Westminster Bruins		WHL	69	13	44	57	94
1984-85—Springfield Indians		AHL	76	6	20	26	115
1984-85—New York Islanders		NHL	1	0	0	0	0
1985-86—Springfield Indians		AHL	55	3	11	14	83
1986-87—Springfield Indians		AHL	41	1	10	11	58
1987-88—Springfield Indians		AHL	64	5	22	27	78
NHL TOTALS			1	0	0	0	0

(c)—June, 1982—Drafted as underage junior by New York Islanders in 1982 NHL entry draft. Second Islanders pick, 42nd overall, second round.

STAN SMYL

Right Wing ... 5'8" ... 200 lbs. ... Born, Glendon, Alta., January 28, 1958 ... Shoots right ... Set Vancouver record for points in a season in 1982-83 (Broken by Patrik Sundstrom with 91 in '83-84) ... Only player to ever play in four Memorial Cup Tournaments ... (March 26, 1986)—Twisted knee vs. Quebec that required surgery ... (February 11, 1988)—Pulled groin.

Year	Team	League	Games	G.	A.	Pts.	Pen.
1974-75—Bellingham Blazers		Jr. "A" BCHL	....	...	....	....	....
1974-75—New Westminster Bruins (c)		WCHL	....	...	....	....	....
1975-76—New Westminster Bruins		WCHL	72	32	42	74	169
1976-77—New Westminster Bruins		WCHL	72	35	31	66	200
1977-78—New Westminster Bruins (d)		WCHL	53	29	47	76	211
1978-79—Vancouver Canucks		NHL	62	14	24	38	89
1978-79—Dallas Black Hawks		CHL	3	1	1	2	9
1979-80—Vancouver Canucks		NHL	77	31	47	78	204
1980-81—Vancouver Canucks		NHL	80	25	38	63	171
1981-82—Vancouver Canucks		NHL	80	34	44	78	144
1982-83—Vancouver Canucks		NHL	74	38	50	88	114
1983-84—Vancouver Canucks		NHL	80	24	43	67	136
1984-85—Vancouver Canucks		NHL	80	27	37	64	100
1985-86—Vancouver Canucks		NHL	73	27	35	62	144
1986-87—Vancouver Canucks		NHL	66	20	23	43	84
1987-88—Vancouver Canucks		NHL	57	12	25	37	110
NHL TOTALS			729	252	366	618	1296

(c)—No regular season record. Played three playoff games.

(d)—Drafted from New Westminster Bruins by Vancouver Canucks in third round of 1978 amateur draft.

GREG SMYTH

Defense ... 6'3" ... 195 lbs. ... Born, Oakville, Ont., April 23, 1966 ... Shoots right ... (December, 1984)—Given 10-game OHL suspension for fight with fans in Hamilton ... (October, 1985)—Suspended by London Knights ... (November 7, 1985)—Given eight-game suspension by OHL.

Year	Team	League	Games	G.	A.	Pts.	Pen.
1983-84—London Knights (c)		OHL	64	4	21	25	*252
1984-85—London Knights		OHL	47	7	16	23	188
1985-86—London Knights (b)		OHL	46	12	42	54	197
1985-86—Hershey Bears		AHL	2	0	1	1	5
1986-87—Hershey Bears		AHL	35	0	2	2	158
1986-87—Philadelphia Flyers		NHL	1	0	0	0	0
1987-88—Hershey Bears		AHL	21	0	10	10	102
1988-89—Philadelphia Flyers (d)		NHL	47	1	6	7	192
NHL TOTALS			48	1	6	7	192

(c)—June, 1984—Drafted as underage junior by Philadelphia Flyers in NHL entry draft. First Flyers pick, 22nd overall, second round.

(d)—July, 1988—Traded with third-round draft choice in 1989 by Philadelphia Flyers to Quebec Nordiques for Terry Carkner.

HAROLD JOHN SNEPSTS

Defense ... 6'3" ... 215 lbs. ... Born, Edmonton, Alta., October 24, 1954 ... Shoots left ... (October, 1981)—Knee injury ... (November, 1982)—Fractured orbit bone of right eye ... (January 12, 1983)—Five-game suspension for fight with Doug Risebrough outside Calgary lockerroom ... Holds Vancouver club record for most career games (683) and penalty minutes (1351) ... (October 12, 1985)—Strained left knee ligaments in Boston and missed 13 games ... (November 16, 1985)—Injured knee at Minnesota and missed 19 games ... (February, 1987)—Separated right shoulder against N.Y. Rangers. Injured same shoulder in playoffs and had arthroscopic surgery in July ... (October, 1987)—Shoulder surgery ... Does not wear a helmet.

Year	Team	League	Games	G.	A.	Pts.	Pen.
1972-73—Edmonton Oil Kings		WCHL	68	2	24	26	155
1973-74—Edmonton Oil Kings (c)		WCHL	68	8	41	49	239
1974-75—Seattle Totems		CHL	19	1	6	7	58
1974-75—Vancouver Canucks		NHL	27	1	2	3	30
1975-76—Vancouver Canucks		NHL	78	3	15	18	125
1976-77—Vancouver Canucks		NHL	79	4	18	22	149
1977-78—Vancouver Canucks		NHL	75	4	16	20	118
1978-79—Vancouver Canucks		NHL	76	7	24	31	130
1979-80—Vancouver Canucks		NHL	79	3	20	23	202
1980-81—Vancouver Canucks		NHL	76	3	16	19	212
1981-82—Vancouver Canucks		NHL	68	3	14	17	153

Year	Team	League	Games	G.	A.	Pts.	Pen.
1982-83—Vancouver Canucks		NHL	46	2	8	10	80
1983-84—Vancouver Canucks (d)		NHL	79	4	16	20	152
1984-85—Minnesota North Stars (e)		NHL	71	0	7	7	232
1985-86—Detroit Red Wings		NHL	35	0	6	6	75
1986-87—Detroit Red Wings		NHL	54	1	13	14	129
1987-88—Adirondack Red Wings		AHL	3	0	2	2	14
1987-88—Detroit Red Wings		NHL	31	1	4	5	67
NHL TOTALS			874	36	179	215	1854

(c)—Drafted from Edmonton Oil Kings by Vancouver Canucks in fourth round of 1974 amateur draft.
(d)—June, 1984—Traded by Vancouver Canucks to Minnesota North Stars for Al MacAdam.
(e)—August, 1985—Signed by Detroit Red Wings as a free agent.

DAVE SNUGGERUD

Left Wing . . . 6' . . . 170 lbs. . . . Born, Minnetonka, Minn., June 20, 1966 . . . Shoots left.

Year	Team	League	Games	G.	A.	Pts.	Pen.
1984-85—Minneapolis Junior Stars		USHL	48	38	35	73	26
1985-86—Univ. of Minnesota		WCHA	42	14	18	32	47
1986-87—Univ. of Minnesota (c)		WCHA	39	30	29	59	38
1987-88—U.S. Olympic Team		Int'l	54	16	22	38	....

(c)—June, 1987—Selected by Buffalo Sabres in 1987 NHL supplemental draft.

PETER SOBERLAK

Left Wing . . . 6'2" . . . 185 lbs. . . . Born, Trail, B.C., May 12, 1969 . . . Shoots left . . . (March 18, 1987)—Fractured right ankle.

Year	Team	League	Games	G.	A.	Pts.	Pen.
1985-86—Kamloops Blazers		WHL	55	10	11	21	46
1986-87—Swift Current Broncos (c)		WHL	68	33	42	75	45
1987-88—Swift Current Broncos		WHL	67	43	56	99	47

(c)—June, 1987—Drafted as underage junior by Edmonton Oilers in 1987 NHL entry draft. First Oilers pick, 21st overall, first round.

GARY SOCHA

Center . . . 6'4" . . . 175 lbs. . . . Born, North Attleboro, Mass., December 30, 1969 . . . Shoots left.

Year	Team	League	Games	G.	A.	Pts.	Pen.
1986-87—Tabor Academy		Mass. H.S.	....	8	10	18	....
1987-88—Tabor Academy (c)		Mass. H.S.	....	25	15	40	....

(c)—June, 1988—Drafted by Calgary Flames in 1988 NHL entry draft. Third Flames pick, 84th overall, fourth round.

KENNETH W. SPANGLER

Defense . . . 5'11" . . . 190 lbs. . . . Born, Edmonton, Alta., May 2, 1967 . . . Shoots left.

Year	Team	League	Games	G.	A.	Pts.	Pen.
1983-84—Calgary Wranglers		WHL	71	1	12	13	119
1984-85—Calgary Wranglers (c)		WHL	71	5	30	35	251
1985-86—Calgary Wranglers (a)		WHL	66	19	36	55	237
1985-86—St. Catharines Saints		AHL	7	0	0	0	16
1986-87—Calgary Wranglers		WHL	49	12	24	36	185
1987-88—Newmarket Saints		AHL	64	3	6	9	128

(c)—June, 1985—Drafted as underage junior by Toronto Maple Leafs in 1985 NHL entry draft. Second Maple Leafs pick, 22nd overall, second round.

JIM SPRENGER

Defense . . . 5'11" . . . 175 lbs. . . . Born, Cloquet, Minn., May 28, 1965 . . . Shoots right . . . (February, 1988)—Strained ligaments in left ankle.

Year	Team	League	Games	G.	A.	Pts.	Pen.
1982-83—Cloquet H.S. (c)		Minn. H.S.	23	16	26	42	....
1983-84—Univ. of Minnesota/Duluth		WCHA	42	2	7	9	22
1984-85—Univ. of Minnesota/Duluth		WCHA	48	6	12	18	32
1985-86—Univ. of Minnesota/Duluth		WCHA	42	6	11	17	24
1986-87—Univ. of Minnesota/Duluth		WCHA	39	5	14	19	30
1987-88—Peoria Rivermen		IHL	64	3	17	20	37

(c)—June, 1983—Drafted by New York Islanders in 1983 NHL entry draft. Ninth Islanders pick, 137th overall, seventh round.

JIM SPROTT

Defense ... 6'1" ... 185 lbs. ... Born, Hanover, Ont., April 11, 1969 ... Shoots left.

Year	Team	League	Games	G.	A.	Pts.	Pen.
1985-86—Oakville Blades Jr.B		OHA	26	2	7	9	47
1986-87—London Knights (c)		OHL	66	8	30	38	153
1987-88—London Knights		OHL	65	8	23	31	216

(c)—June, 1987—Drafted as underage junior by Quebec Nordiques in 1987 NHL entry draft. Third Nordiques pick, 51st overall, third round.

DARYL STANLEY

Defense ... 6'2" ... 200 lbs. ... Born, Winnipeg, Man., December 2, 1962 ... Shoots left ... (January 21, 1985)—Dislocated neck vertebrae and bruised kidney in automobile accident and missed several games at start of 1985-86 season ... (February, 1987)—Missed six games with injured left ankle ... (March, 1987)—Reinjured left ankle ligaments ... (October, 1987)—Sprained left ankle ... (December, 1987)—Bruised shoulder ... (January, 1988)—Back spasms ... (March 6, 1988)—Separated shoulder vs. Washington.

Year	Team	League	Games	G.	A.	Pts.	Pen.
1979-80—New Westminster Bruins		WHL	64	2	12	14	110
1980-81—New Westminster Bruins		WHL	66	7	27	34	127
1981-82—Saskatoon Blades (c-d)		WHL	65	7	25	32	175
1981-82—Maine Mariners (e)		AHL	....	...	....	....	....
1982-83—Toledo Goaldiggers		IHL	5	0	2	2	2
1982-83—Maine Mariners		AHL	44	2	5	7	95
1983-84—Springfield Indians		AHL	52	4	10	14	122
1983-84—Philadelphia Flyers		NHL	23	1	4	5	71
1984-85—Hershey Bears		AHL	24	0	7	7	13
1985-86—Philadelphia Flyers		NHL	33	0	2	2	69
1985-86—Hershey Flyers		AHL	27	0	4	4	88
1986-87—Philadelphia Flyers (f)		NHL	33	1	2	3	76
1987-88—Vancouver Canucks		NHL	57	2	7	9	151
NHL TOTALS			146	4	15	19	367

(c)—October, 1981—Signed by Philadelphia Flyers as a free agent.

(d)—September, 1981—Traded by Kamloops Junior Oilers to Saskatoon Blades for Brian Propp and Mike Spencer.

(e)—No regular season record. Played two playoff games.

(f)—August, 1987—Traded by Philadelphia Flyers with Darren Jensen to Vancouver Canucks for Wendell Young and a 1991 third-round draft choice.

PAUL STANTON

Defense ... 6' ... 175 lbs. ... Born, Boston, Mass., June 22, 1967 ... Shoots right.

Year	Team	League	Games	G.	A.	Pts.	Pen.
1983-84—Catholic Memorial H.S.		Mass.H.S.	....	15	20	35	....
1984-85—Catholic Memorial H.S. (c)		Mass.H.S.	20	16	21	37	17
1985-86—Univ. of Wisconsin		WCHA	36	4	6	10	16
1986-87—Univ. of Wisconsin		WCHA	41	5	17	22	70
1987-88—Univ. of Wisconsin (d)		WCHA	45	9	38	47	98

(c)—June, 1985—Drafted by Pittsburgh Penguins in 1985 NHL entry draft. Eighth Penguins pick, 149th overall, eighth round.

(d)—Named first-team All-America (West).

MIKE STAPLETON

Center ... 5'10" ... 165 lbs. ... Born, Sarnia, Ont., May 5, 1966 ... Shoots right ... Son of former Chicago defenseman Pat Stapleton.

Year	Team	League	Games	G.	A.	Pts.	Pen.
1982-83—Strathroy Braves		WOJBHL	40	39	38	77	99
1983-84—Cornwall Royals (c)		OHL	70	24	45	69	94
1984-85—Cornwall Royals		OHL	56	41	44	85	68
1985-86—Cornwall Royals		OHL	56	39	65	104	74
1986-87—Team Canada		Int'l	21	2	4	6	4
1986-87—Chicago Black Hawks		NHL	39	3	6	9	6
1987-88—Saginaw Hawks		IHL	31	11	19	30	52
1987-88—Chicago Black Hawks		NHL	53	2	9	11	59
NHL TOTALS			92	5	15	20	65

(c)—June, 1984—Drafted as underage junior by Chicago Black Hawks in NHL entry draft. Seventh Black Hawks pick, 132nd overall, seventh round.

JAY STARK

Defense ... 6' ... 190 lbs. ... Born, Vernon, B.C., February 29, 1968 ... Shoots right.

Year Team	League	Games	G.	A.	Pts.	Pen.
1984-85—Kelowna Wings	WHL	4	0	0	0	0
1985-86—Portland Winter Hawks (c)	WHL	61	2	11	13	102
1985-86—Spokane Chiefs	WHL	8	0	2	2	13
1986-87—Portland Winter Hawks	WHL	70	2	14	16	321
1987-88—Portland Winter Hawks	WHL	40	1	8	9	195
1987-88—Seattle Thunderbirds	WHL	24	0	1	1	59

(c)—June, 1986—Drafted as underage junior by Detroit Red Wings in 1986 NHL entry draft. Sixth Red Wings pick, 106th overall, sixth round.

ANTON STASTNY

Left Wing . . . 6' . . . 185 lbs. . . . Born, Bratislava, Czechoslovakia, August 5, 1959 . . . Shoots left . . . Brother of Peter, Marian and Bohuslav Stastny . . . (December, 1981)—Pulled knee ligaments . . . (November 9, 1985)—Missed two games with back spasms . . . (December 10, 1985)—Fractured toe at Buffalo and missed one game . . . (February 1, 1986)—Missed two games with broken ribs vs. Philadelphia . . . (November, 1987)—Sprained left ankle when hooked by Ville Siren vs. Pittsburgh.

Year Team	League	Games	G.	A.	Pts.	Pen.
1977-78—Slovan Bratislava	Czech	44	19	17	36	....
1977-78—Czechoslovakian Nat's.	Int'l.	6	1	1	2	....
1978-79—Slovan Bratislava (a-c)	Czech.	44	32	19	51	....
1978-79—Czechoslovakian Nat's.	Int'l.	20	9	6	15	....
1979-80—Slovan Bratislava	Czech.	40	30	30	60	....
1979-80—Czech. Olympic Team (d)	Oly.	6	4	4	8	2
1980-81—Quebec Nordiques	NHL	80	39	46	85	12
1981-82—Quebec Nordiques	NHL	68	26	46	72	16
1982-83—Quebec Nordiques	NHL	79	32	60	92	25
1983-84—Quebec Nordiques	NHL	69	25	37	62	14
1984-85—Quebec Nordiques	NHL	79	38	42	80	30
1985-86—Quebec Nordiques	NHL	74	31	43	74	19
1986-87—Quebec Nordiques	NHL	77	27	35	62	8
1987-88—Quebec Nordiques	NHL	69	27	45	72	14
NHL TOTALS		**595**	**245**	**354**	**599**	**138**

(c)—August, 1979—Drafted by Quebec Nordiques in 1979 NHL entry draft. Fourth Nordiques pick, 83rd overall, fourth round.

(d)—August, 1980—Signed by Quebec Nordiques.

PETER STASTNY

Center . . . 6'1" . . . 200 lbs. . . . Born, Bratislava, Czechoslovakia, September 18, 1956 . . . Shoots left . . . Brother of Anton, Marion and Bohuslav Stastny . . . (December 18, 1982)— Knee injury at Buffalo . . . One of only four players to break in NHL with three straight 100-point seasons (Wayne Gretzky, Mario Lemieux and Mike Rogers being the others) . . . (1980-81)—Set NHL records for most assists and points by a rookie . . . One of only two players (Wayne Gretzky) to have 100-point seasons in their first six NHL seasons . . . (October, 1984)—Served five-game suspension . . . (May 2 and 5, 1985)—Scored overtime goals in consecutive playoff games to tie record by Mel Hill and Maurice Richard . . . (November, 1987)—Injured lower back.

Year Team	League	Games	G.	A.	Pts.	Pen.
1977-78—Slovan Bratislava (b)	Czech.	44	29	24	53	....
1977-78—Czechoslovakia Nat's.	Int'l.	16	5	2	7	....
1978-79—Slovan Bratislava (a)	Czech.	44	32	23	55	....
1978-79—Czechoslovakia Nat's.	Int'l.	18	12	9	21	....
1979-80—Slovan Bratislava	Czech.	40	28	30	58	....
1979-80—Czech. Olympic Team (c)	Oly.	6	7	7	14	6
1980-81—Quebec Nordiques (d-e)	NHL	77	39	70	109	37
1981-82—Quebec Nordiques	NHL	80	46	93	139	91
1982-83—Quebec Nordiques	NHL	75	47	77	124	78
1983-84—Quebec Nordiques	NHL	80	46	73	119	73
1984-85—Quebec Nordiques	NHL	75	32	68	100	95
1985-86—Quebec Nordiques	NHL	76	41	81	122	60
1986-87—Quebec Nordiques	NHL	64	24	52	76	43
1987-88—Quebec Nordiques	NHL	76	46	65	111	69
NHL TOTALS		**603**	**321**	**579**	**900**	**546**

(c)—August, 1980—Signed by Quebec Nordiques as a free agent.

(d)—Winner of Calder Trophy (NHL Rookie of the Year).

(e)—Selected THE SPORTING NEWS NHL Rookie of the Year in a vote of the players.

THOMAS STEEN

Center . . . 5'10" . . . 195 lbs. . . . Born, Tocksmark, Sweden, June 8, 1960 . . . Shoots left . . .

(September, 1981)—Lacerated elbow during Canada Cup as a member of Team Sweden . . . (October, 1981)—Injured knee in training camp.

Year	Team	League	Games	G.	A.	Pts.	Pen.
1978-79—Leksands IF		Sweden	25	13	4	17	35
1979-80—Leksands IF (c)		Sweden	18	7	7	14	14
1980-81—Farjestads BK (d)		Sweden	32	16	23	39	30
1981-82—Winnipeg Jets		NHL	73	15	29	44	42
1982-83—Winnipeg Jets		NHL	75	26	33	59	60
1983-84—Winnipeg Jets		NHL	78	20	45	65	69
1984-85—Winnipeg Jets		NHL	79	30	54	84	80
1985-86—Winnipeg Jets		NHL	78	17	47	64	76
1986-87—Winnipeg Jets		NHL	75	17	33	50	59
1987-88—Winnipeg Jets		NHL	76	16	38	54	53
NHL TOTALS			534	141	279	420	439

(c)—June, 1980—Drafted by Winnipeg Jets in 1980 NHL entry draft. Fifth Jets pick, 103rd overall, fifth round.

(d)—Named Player of the Year in Swedish National League.

RONALD STERN

Right Wing . . . 6'1" . . . 195 lbs. . . . Born, Ste. Agatha Des Mont, Que., January 11, 1967 . . . Shoots right.

Year	Team	League	Games	G.	A.	Pts.	Pen.
1984-85—Longueuil Chevaliers		QHL	67	6	14	20	176
1985-86—Longueuil Chevaliers (c)		QHL	70	39	33	72	317
1986-87—Longueuil Chevaliers		QHL	56	32	39	71	266
1987-88—Fredericton Express		AHL	2	1	0	1	4
1987-88—Flint Spirits		IHL	55	14	19	33	294
1987-88—Vancouver Canucks		NHL	15	0	0	0	52
NHL TOTALS			15	0	0	0	52

(c)—June, 1986—Drafted as underage junior by Vancouver Canucks in 1986 NHL entry draft. Third Canucks pick, 70th overall, fourth round.

JOHN STEVENS

Defense . . . 6'1" . . . 180 lbs. . . . Born, Completon, N.B., May 4, 1966 . . . Shoots left . . . (September, 1984)—Knee surgery.

Year	Team	League	Games	G.	A.	Pts.	Pen.
1982-83—Newmarket Flyers		OJHL	48	2	9	11	111
1983-84—Oshawa Generals (c)		OHL	70	1	10	11	71
1984-85—Oshawa Generals		OHL	45	2	10	12	61
1984-85—Hershey Bears		AHL	3	0	0	0	2
1985-86—Oshawa Generals		OHL	65	1	7	8	146
1985-86—Kalamazoo Wings		IHL	6	0	1	1	8
1986-87—Hershey Bears (d)		AHL	63	1	15	16	131
1986-87—Philadelphia Flyers		NHL	6	0	2	2	14
1987-88—Philadelphia Flyers		NHL	3	0	0	0	0
1987-88—Hershey Bears		AHL	59	1	15	16	108
NHL TOTALS			9	0	2	2	14

(c)—June, 1984—Drafted as underage junior by Chicago Black Hawks in NHL entry draft. Second Black Hawks pick, 45th overall, third round.

(d)—September, 1987—Signed by Philadelphia Flyers as a free agent.

KEVIN STEVENS

Center . . . 6'3" . . . 207 lbs. . . . Born, Brockton, Mass., April 15, 1965 . . . Shoots left . . . Also plays Left Wing.

Year	Team	League	Games	G.	A.	Pts.	Pen.
1982-83—Silver Lake H.S. (c)		Minn. H.S.	18	24	27	51	..
1983-84—Boston College (d)		ECAC	37	6	14	20	36
1984-85—Boston College		H. East	40	13	23	36	36
1985-86—Boston College		H. East	42	17	27	44	56
1986-87—Boston College (a-e)		H. East	39	*35	35	70	54
1987-88—U.S. Olympic Team		Int'l	....	...	....	....	....
1987-88—Pittsburgh Penguins		NHL	16	5	2	7	8
NHL TOTALS			16	5	2	7	8

(c)—June, 1983—Drafted by Los Angeles Kings in 1983 NHL entry draft. Sixth Kings pick, 108th overall, sixth round.

(d)—September, 1983—Traded by Los Angeles Kings to Pittsburgh Penguins for Anders Hakansson.

(e)—Named Second-Team U.S. College All-America (East).

MIKE STEVENS

Center . . . 5'11" . . . 195 lbs. . . . Born, Kitchener, Ont., December 30, 1965 . . . Shoots left . . . (October, 1984)—Arthroscopic knee surgery . . . Brother of Scott Stevens . . . Also plays Left Wing.

Year	Team	League	Games	G.	A.	Pts.	Pen.
1982-83—Kitchener Ranger B's		MWOJBHL	29	5	18	23	86
1983-84—Kitchener Rangers (c)		OHL	66	19	21	40	109
1984-85—Kitchener Rangers		OHL	37	17	18	35	121
1984-85—Vancouver Canucks		NHL	6	0	3	3	6
1985-86—Fredericton Express		AHL	79	12	19	31	208
1986-87—Fredericton Express		AHL	71	7	18	25	258
1987-88—Maine Mariners (d)		AHL	63	30	25	55	265
1987-88—Boston Bruins (e)		NHL	7	0	1	1	9
NHL TOTALS			13	0	4	4	15

(c)—June, 1984—Drafted as underage junior by Vancouver Canucks in NHL entry draft. Fourth Canucks pick, 58th overall, third round.

(d)—October, 1987—Traded by Vancouver Canucks to Boston Bruins for future considerations.

(e)—August, 1988—Signed by New York Islanders as a free agent.

SCOTT STEVENS

Defense . . . 6' . . . 197 lbs. . . . Born, Kitchener, Ont., April 1, 1964 . . . Shoots left . . . Brother of Mike Stevens . . . (November 6, 1985)—Bruised right knee at Pittsburgh and missed seven games . . . (December 14, 1986)—Broke right index finger vs. N.Y. Islanders . . . (April, 1988)—Bruised shoulder vs. Philadelphia in playoffs.

Year	Team	League	Games	G.	A.	Pts.	Pen.
1980-81—Kitchener Jr. B.		OPJHL	39	7	33	40	82
1981-82—Kitchener Rangers (c)		OHL	68	6	36	42	158
1982-83—Washington Capitals		NHL	77	9	16	25	195
1983-84—Washington Capitals		NHL	78	13	32	45	201
1984-85—Washington Capitals		NHL	80	21	44	65	221
1985-86—Washington Capitals		NHL	73	15	38	53	165
1986-87—Washington Capitals		NHL	77	10	51	61	285
1987-88—Washington Capitals (a)		NHL	80	12	60	72	184
NHL TOTALS			465	80	241	321	1251

(c)—June, 1982—Drafted as underage junior by Washington Capitals in 1982 NHL entry draft. First Capitals pick, fifth overall, first round.

ALLAN STEWART

Left Wing . . . 5'11" . . . 173 lbs. . . . Born, Fort St. John, B.C., January 31, 1964 . . . Shoots left . . . (1983-84)—Set WHL record with 14 shorthanded goals . . . (October, 1987)—Missed two months following hernia surgery.

Year	Team	League	Games	G.	A.	Pts.	Pen.
1981-82—Prince Albert Raiders		SJHL	46	9	25	34	53
1982-83—Prince Albert Raiders (c)		WHL	70	25	34	59	272
1983-84—Prince Albert Raiders		WHL	67	44	39	83	216
1984-85—Maine Mariners		AHL	75	8	11	19	241
1985-86—Maine Mariners		AHL	58	7	12	19	181
1985-86—New Jersey Devils		NHL	4	0	0	0	21
1986-87—Maine Mariners		AHL	74	14	24	38	143
1986-87—New Jersey Devils		NHL	7	1	0	1	26
1987-88—New Jersey Devils		NHL	1	0	0	0	0
1987-88—Utica Devils		AHL	49	8	17	25	129
NHL TOTALS			12	1	0	1	47

(c)—June, 1983—Drafted as underage junior by New Jersey Devils in 1983 NHL entry draft. Ninth Devils pick, 205th overall, 11th round.

RYAN STEWART

Center . . . 6'1" . . . 175 lbs. . . . Born, Prince George, B.C., June 1, 1967 . . . Shoots right . . . Also plays Right Wing . . . (January, 1987)—Liver ailment.

Year	Team	League	Games	G.	A.	Pts.	Pen.
1983-84—Kamloops Junior Oilers		WHL	69	31	38	69	88
1984-85—Kamloops Blazers (c)		WHL	54	33	37	70	92
1985-86—Winnipeg Jets		NHL	3	1	0	1	0
1985-86—Kamloops Blazers		WHL	10	7	11	18	27
1985-86—Prince Albert Raiders		WHL	52	45	33	78	55
1986-87—Portland Winter Hawks		WHL	22	12	11	23	27
1987-88—Moncton Golden Flames		AHL	49	15	12	27	30
NHL TOTALS			3	1	0	1	0

TREVOR STIENBURG

Right Wing . . . 6'1" . . . 180 lbs. . . . Born, Kingston, Ont., May 13, 1966 . . . Shoots right . . . (September, 1985)—Torn knee ligaments in Quebec training camp.

Year	Team	League	Games	G.	A.	Pts.	Pen.
1982-83—Brockville Braves		COJHL	47	39	30	69	182
1983-84—Guelph Platers (c)		OHL	65	33	18	51	104
1984-85—Guelph Platers (d)		OHL	18	7	12	19	38
1984-85—London Knights		OHL	22	9	11	20	45
1984-85—Fredericton Express (e)		AHL	....	...	....	....	....
1985-86—Quebec Nordiques		NHL	2	1	0	1	0
1985-86—London Knights		OHL	31	12	18	30	88
1986-87—Fredericton Express		AHL	48	14	12	26	123
1986-87—Quebec Nordiques		NHL	6	1	0	1	12
1987-88—Quebec Nordiques		NHL	8	0	1	1	24
1987-88—Fredericton Express		AHL	55	12	24	36	279
NHL TOTALS			16	2	1	3	36

(c)—June, 1984—Drafted as underage junior by Quebec Nordiques in NHL entry draft. First Nordiques pick, 15th overall, first round.

(d)—January, 1985—Traded by Guelph Platers to London Knights for Mike Murray and Ron Coutts.

(e)—No regular season record. Played two playoff games.

MICHAEL PATRICK STOTHERS

Defense . . . 6'4" . . . 210 lbs. . . . Born, Toronto, Ont., February 22, 1962 . . . Shoots left . . . (December, 1984)—Ankle injury.

Year	Team	League	Games	G.	A.	Pts.	Pen.
1979-80—Kingston Canadians (c)		OMJHL	66	4	23	27	137
1980-81—Kingston Canadians		OHL	65	4	22	26	237
1981-82—Kingston Canadians		OHL	61	1	20	21	203
1981-82—Maine Mariners		AHL	5	0	0	0	4
1982-83—Maine Mariners		AHL	80	2	16	18	139
1983-84—Maine Mariners		AHL	61	2	10	12	109
1984-85—Philadelphia Flyers		NHL	1	0	0	0	0
1984-85—Hershey Bears		AHL	59	8	18	26	142
1985-86—Hershey Bears		AHL	66	4	9	13	221
1985-86—Philadelphia Flyers		NHL	6	0	1	1	6
1986-87—Philadelphia Flyers		NHL	2	0	0	0	4
1986-87—Hershey Bears		AHL	75	5	11	16	283
1987-88—Philadelphia Flyers (d)		NHL	3	0	0	0	13
1987-88—Toronto Maple Leafs		NHL	18	0	1	1	42
1987-88—Hershey Bears		AHL	13	3	2	5	55
1987-88—Newmarket Saints		AHL	38	1	9	10	69
NHL TOTALS			30	0	2	2	65

(c)—June, 1980—Drafted as underage junior by Philadelphia Flyers in NHL entry draft. First Flyers pick, 21st overall, first round.

(d)—November, 1987—Traded by Philadelphia Flyers to Toronto Maple Leafs for future considerations. Returned to Flyers in June of 1988.

DOUGLAS STROMBACK

Right Wing . . . 6' . . . 175 lbs. . . . Born, Farmington, Mich., March 2, 1967 . . . Shoots right . . . Also plays Center.

Year	Team	League	Games	G.	A.	Pts.	Pen.
1983-84—Detroit Compuware		Mich. Midget	65	32	45	77	32
1984-85—Kitchener Rangers (c)		OHL	66	20	24	44	48
1985-86—Kitchener Rangers (d)		OHL	13	7	10	17	13
1985-86—North Bay Centennials		OHL	50	19	22	41	50
1986-87—North Bay Centennials		OHL	24	10	13	23	13
1986-87—Belleville Bulls		OHL	41	22	33	55	10
1987-88—Belleville Bulls		OHL	60	27	35	62	19

(c)—June, 1985—Drafted as underage junior by Washington Capitals in 1985 NHL entry draft. Seventh Capitals pick, 124th overall, sixth round.

(d)—November, 1985—Traded with John Keller and Dave McIlwain by Kitchener Rangers to North Bay Centennials for Ron Sanko, Peter Lisy, Richard Hawkins and Brett McDonald.

TODD STRUEBY

Left Wing . . . 6'1" . . . 186 lbs. . . . Born, Lannigan, Sask., June 15, 1963 . . . Shoots left . . . (October, 1985)—Left Edmonton Oilers' training camp.

Year	Team	League	Games	G.	A.	Pts.	Pen.
1979-80—Notre Dame Midgets		....	58	44	61	105	112
1980-81—Regina Pats (c)		WHL	71	18	27	45	99
1981-82—Saskatoon Blades (a-d)		WHL	61	60	58	118	160
1981-82—Edmonton Oilers		NHL	3	0	0	0	0
1982-83—Saskatoon Blades		WHL	65	40	70	110	119
1982-83—Edmonton Oilers		NHL	1	0	0	0	0
1983-84—Edmonton Oilers		NHL	1	0	1	1	2
1983-84—Moncton Alpines		AHL	72	17	25	42	38
1984-85—Nova Scotia Oilers		AHL	38	2	3	5	29
1984-85—Muskegon Lumberjacks		IHL	27	19	12	31	55
1985-86—Muskegon Lumberjacks (e)		IHL	58	25	40	65	191
1986-87—Muskegon Lumberjacks		IHL	82	28	41	69	208
1987-88—Fort Wayne Komets		IHL	68	29	27	56	211
NHL TOTALS			5	0	1	1	2

(c)—Drafted by Edmonton Oilers in NHL entry draft. Second Oilers pick, 29th overall, second round.
(d)—September, 1981—Traded by Regina Pats to Saskatoon Blades for Lyndon Byers.
(e)—December, 1985—Traded with Larry Melnyk by Edmonton Oilers to New York Rangers for Mike Rogers.

SIMON DOUGLAS SULLIMAN
(Known by middle name.)

Left Wing . . . 5'9" . . . 195 lbs. . . . Born, Glace Bay, Nova Scotia, August 29, 1959 . . . Shoots left . . . Missed part of 1979-80 season with injury to right knee . . . Also plays Right Wing . . . (November, 1983)—Groin pull . . . (December 14, 1985)—Bruised tailbone at Quebec . . . (December, 1987)—Bruised left shoulder . . . (March, 1988)—Strained left knee.

Year	Team	League	Games	G.	A.	Pts.	Pen.
1976-77—Kitchener Rangers		OMJHL	65	30	41	71	123
1977-78—Kitchener Rangers		OMJHL	68	50	39	89	87
1978-79—Kitchener Rangers (c)		OMJHL	68	38	77	115	88
1979-80—New York Rangers		NHL	31	4	7	11	2
1979-80—New Haven Nighthawks		AHL	31	9	7	16	9
1980-81—New Haven Nighthawks		AHL	45	10	16	26	18
1980-81—New York Rangers		NHL	32	4	1	5	32
1981-82—Hartford Whalers (d)		NHL	77	29	40	69	39
1982-83—Hartford Whalers		NHL	77	22	19	41	14
1983-84—Hartford Whalers (e)		NHL	67	6	12	18	20
1984-85—New Jersey Devils		NHL	57	22	16	38	4
1985-86—New Jersey Devils		NHL	73	21	21	42	20
1986-87—New Jersey Devils		NHL	78	27	26	53	14
1987-88—New Jersey Devils		NHL	59	16	14	30	25
NHL TOTALS			551	151	156	307	170

(c)—August, 1979—Drafted by New York Rangers in entry draft. First Rangers pick, 13th overall, first round.
(d)—October, 1981—Traded with Chris Kotsopoulos and Gerry McDonald by New York Rangers to Hartford Whalers for Mike Rogers and a 10th-round 1982 entry draft pick (Simo Saarinen).
(e)—July, 1984—Released by Hartford Whalers and signed by New Jersey Devils as a free agent.

BRIAN SULLIVAN

Right Wing . . . 6'3" . . . 180 lbs. . . . Born, South Windsor, Conn., April 23, 1969 . . . Shoots right . . . Brother of Kevin Sullivan . . . (February, 1988)—Set Northeastern Univ. record for goals by a freshman.

Year	Team	League	Games	G.	A.	Pts.	Pen.
1985-86—South Windsor H.S.		Conn. H.S.	....	39	50	89	....
1986-87—Springfield Olympics (c)		NEJHL	....	30	35	65	....
1987-88—Northeastern Univ.		H. East	37	20	12	32	18

(c)—June, 1987—Drafted by New Jersey Devils in 1987 NHL entry draft. Third Devils pick, 65th overall, fourth round.

MICHAEL SULLIVAN

Center . . . 6'2" . . . 185 lbs. . . . Born, Marshfield, Mass., February 28, 1968 . . . Shoots left.

Year	Team	League	Games	G.	A.	Pts.	Pen.
1985-86—Boston College H.S.		Mass. H.S.	22	26	33	59	....
1986-87—Boston University (c)		H. East	37	13	18	31	18
1987-88—Boston University		H. East	30	18	22	40	30

(c)—June, 1987—Drafted by New York Rangers in 1987 NHL entry draft. Fourth Rangers pick, 69th overall, fourth round.

RAIMO SUMMANEN

Left Wing . . . 5'11" . . . 185 lbs. . . . Born, Jyvaskyla, Finland, March 2, 1962 . . . Shoots left . . . Member of 1984 Finland Olympic team . . . (November, 1987)—Virus.

Year	Team	League	Games	G.	A.	Pts.	Pen.
1981-82—Lahti Kiekkoreipas (c)		Finland	36	15	6	21	17
1981-82—Lahti Kiekkoreipas		Finland	....	...	....	....	....
1983-84—Tampere Ilves		Finland	36	28	19	47	26
1983-84—Finland Olympic Team		Int'l.	4	4	7	11	2
1983-84—Edmonton Oilers		NHL	2	1	4	5	2
1984-85—Nova Scotia Oilers		AHL	66	20	33	53	2
1984-85—Edmonton Oilers		NHL	9	0	4	4	0
1985-86—Edmonton Oilers		NHL	73	19	18	37	16
1986-87—Edmonton Oilers (d)		NHL	48	10	7	17	15
1986-87—Vancouver Canucks		NHL	10	4	4	8	0
1987-88—Flint Spirits		IHL	7	1	1	2	0
1987-88—Fredericton Express		AHL	20	7	15	22	38
1987-88—Vancouver Canucks		NHL	9	2	3	5	2
NHL TOTALS			151	36	40	76	35

(c)—June, 1982—Drafted by Edmonton Oilers in 1982 NHL entry draft. Sixth Oilers pick, 125th overall, sixth round.

(d)—March, 1987—Traded by Edmonton Oilers to Vancouver Canucks for Moe Lemay.

PATRIK SUNDSTROM

Center . . . 6' . . . 195 lbs. . . . Born Skellefteaa, Sweden, December 14, 1961 . . . Shoots left . . . (November, 1982)—Shoulder separation . . . (1983-84)—Set Vancouver club records for most points in a season and most goals by a center . . . Twin brother of Peter Sundstrom . . . (September, 1985)—Broke left wrist in final game of Canada Cup Tournament . . . (January, 1987)—Missed six games with Torn rotator cuff . . . (April 22, 1988)—Set NHL record for most points in playoff game (8) . . . (March, 1988)—Abdominal strain.

Year	Team	League	Games	G.	A.	Pts.	Pen.
1979-80—Umea Bjorkloven IF (c)		Sweden	26	5	7	12	20
1980-81—Umea Bjorkloven IF		Sweden	36	10	18	28	30
1981-82—Umea Bjorkloven IF		Sweden	36	22	13	35	38
1982-83—Vancouver Canucks		NHL	74	23	23	46	30
1983-84—Vancouver Canucks (d)		NHL	78	38	53	91	37
1984-85—Vancouver Canucks		NHL	71	25	43	68	46
1985-86—Vancouver Canucks		NHL	79	18	48	66	28
1986-87—Vancouver Canucks		NHL	72	29	42	71	40
1987-88—New Jersey Devils (e)		NHL	78	15	36	51	42
NHL TOTALS			452	148	245	393	223

(c)—June, 1980—Drafted by Vancouver Canucks in 1980 NHL entry draft. Eighth Canucks pick, 175th overall, ninth round.

(d)—Won Viking Award (Outstanding Swedish-born player in NHL as voted on by fellow Swedish-born NHL players).

(e)—September, 1987—Traded with a fourth-round 1988 NHL entry draft (Matt Ruchty) by Vancouver Canucks to New Jersey Devils for Kirk McLean and Greg Adams.

PETER SUNDSTROM

Left Wing . . . 6' . . . 180 lbs. . . . Born, Skelleftea, Sweden, December 14, 1961 . . . Shoots left . . . Twin brother of Patrik Sundstrom . . . (November, 1987)—Bruised right shoulder when checked by Brian MacLellan vs. Minnesota.

Year	Team	League	Games	G.	A.	Pts.	Pen.
1979-80—Umea Bjorkloven IF		Sweden	8	0	0	0	2
1980-81—Umea Bjorkloven IF (c)		Sweden	29	7	2	9	8
1981-82—Umea Bjorkloven IF		Sweden	35	10	14	24	18
1982-83—Umea Bjorkloven IF		Sweden	36	17	10	27	....
1983-84—New York Rangers		NHL	77	22	22	44	24
1984-85—New York Rangers		NHL	76	18	26	44	34
1985-86—New Haven Nighthawks		AHL	8	3	6	9	4
1985-86—New York Rangers		NHL	53	8	15	23	12
1986-87—Bjorkloven (d)		Sweden	36	22	16	38	44
1987-88—Washington Capitals		NHL	76	8	17	25	34
NHL TOTALS			282	56	80	136	104

(c)—June, 1981—Drafted by New York Rangers in NHL entry draft. Third Rangers pick, 50th overall, third round.

(d)—July, 1987—Signed as free agent by Washington Capitals with Capitals sending a fifth-round draft choice in 1988 (Martin Bergeron) to New York Rangers as compensation.

GARY SUTER

Defense . . . 6' . . . 190 lbs. . . . Born, Madison, Wis., June 24, 1964 . . . Shoots left . . . (December, 1986)—Stretched ligament in knee vs. Chicago . . . (September 4, 1987)—High sticked Andrei Lomakin in a USA/Soviet game at Hartford during Canada Cup. Suter was suspended for the first four NHL games as well as the next six international games in which the NHL is a participant . . . (February, 1988)—Injured left knee vs. Winnipeg.

Year	Team	League	Games	G.	A.	Pts.	Pen.
1983-84—Univ. of Wisconsin (c)		WCHA	35	4	18	22	68
1984-85—Univ. of Wisconsin		WCHA	39	12	39	51	110
1985-86—Calgary Flames (d)		NHL	80	18	50	68	141
1986-87—Calgary Flames		NHL	68	9	40	49	70
1987-88—Calgary Flames (b)		NHL	75	21	70	91	124
NHL TOTALS			223	48	160	208	335

(c)—June, 1984—Drafted by Calgary Flames in NHL entry draft. Ninth Flames pick, 180th overall, ninth round.

(d)—Won Calder Memorial Trophy (NHL Rookie of the Year).

BRENT BOLIN SUTTER

Center . . . 5'11" . . . 175 lbs. . . . Born, Viking, Alta., June 10, 1962 . . . Shoots right . . . Brother of Brian, Darryl, Ron, Gary, Rich and Duane Sutter . . . (January, 1984)—Missed 11 games with damaged tendon and infection in right hand . . . (March, 1985)—Separated shoulder . . . (October 19, 1985)—Bruised left shoulder vs. N.Y. Rangers and missed 12 games . . . (December 21, 1985)—Bruised shoulder vs. N.Y. Rangers and missed seven games . . . (March, 1987)—Strained abductor muscle in right leg . . . (December, 1987)—Non-displaced fracture of right thumb.

Year	Team	League	Games	G.	A.	Pts.	Pen.
1977-78—Red Deer Rustlers		AJHL	60	12	18	30	33
1978-79—Red Deer Rustlers		AJHL	60	42	42	84	79
1979-80—Red Deer Rustlers (c)		AJHL	59	70	101	171	131
1980-81—New York Islanders		NHL	3	2	2	4	0
1980-81—Lethbridge Broncos		WHL	68	54	54	108	116
1981-82—Lethbridge Broncos		WHL	34	46	34	80	162
1981-82—New York Islanders		NHL	43	21	22	43	114
1982-83—New York Islanders		NHL	80	21	19	40	128
1983-84—New York Islanders		NHL	69	34	15	49	69
1984-85—New York Islanders		NHL	72	42	60	102	51
1985-86—New York Islanders		NHL	61	24	31	55	74
1986-87—New York Islanders		NHL	69	27	36	63	73
1987-88—New York Islanders		NHL	70	29	31	60	55
NHL TOTALS			467	200	216	416	564

(c)—June, 1980—Drafted by New York Islanders as underage junior in 1980 NHL entry draft. First Islanders pick, 17th overall, first round.

BRIAN SUTTER

Left Wing . . . 5'11" . . . 172 lbs. . . . Born, Viking, Alta., October 7, 1956 . . . Shoots left . . . Brother of Darryl, Brent, Ron, Rich, Gary and Duane Sutter . . . (November 3, 1983)—Hairline fracture of pelvis at Boston . . . Holds St. Louis record for most career games and power-play goals . . . (January 16, 1986)—Broke left shoulder . . . (March 8, 1986)—Reinjured shoulder vs. Vancouver. It was his first game back from previous injury . . . (November, 1986)—Damaged muscle around left shoulder blade . . . (November, 1987)—Sprained ankle.

Year	Team	League	Games	G.	A.	Pts.	Pen.
1972-73—Red Deer Rustlers		AJHL	51	27	40	67	54
1973-74—Red Deer Rustlers (a)		AJHL	59	42	*54	96	139
1974-75—Lethbridge Broncos		WCHL	53	34	47	81	134
1975-76—Lethbridge Broncos (c)		WCHL	72	36	56	92	233
1976-77—Kansas City Blues		CHL	38	15	23	38	47
1976-77—St. Louis Blues		NHL	35	4	10	14	82
1977-78—St. Louis Blues		NHL	78	9	13	22	123
1978-79—St. Louis Blues		NHL	77	41	39	80	165
1979-80—St. Louis Blues		NHL	71	23	35	58	156
1980-81—St. Louis Blues		NHL	78	35	34	69	232
1981-82—St. Louis Blues		NHL	74	39	36	75	239
1982-83—St. Louis Blues		NHL	79	46	30	76	254
1983-84—St. Louis Blues		NHL	76	32	51	83	162
1984-85—St. Louis Blues		NHL	77	37	37	74	121
1985-86—St. Louis Blues		NHL	44	19	23	42	87
1986-87—St. Louis Blues		NHL	14	3	3	6	18
1987-88—St. Louis Blues (d)		NHL	76	15	22	37	147
NHL TOTALS			779	303	333	636	1786

(c)—Drafted from Lethbridge Broncos by St. Louis Blues in second round of 1976 amateur draft.
(d)—June, 1988—Retired as a player and signed as head coach of St. Louis Blues.

DUANE CALVIN SUTTER

Right Wing ... 6' ... 181 lbs. ... Born, Viking, Alta., March 16, 1960 ... Shoots right ... Brother of Brian, Brent, Ron, Rich, Gary and Darryl Sutter ... (November 11, 1980)—Damaged ligaments in right knee. Injury required surgery ... (April 2, 1981)—Two weeks after coming back from knee surgery he dislocated right shoulder ... (November, 1983)—Strained ligaments in left knee vs. Quebec ... (May, 1986)—Surgery to left shoulder ... (October, 1987)—Damaged right knee cartilage.

Year	Team	League	Games	G.	A.	Pts.	Pen.
1976-77—Red Deer Rustlers		AJHL	60	9	26	35	76
1977-78—Red Deer Rustlers		AJHL	59	47	53	100	218
1977-78—Lethbridge Broncos		WCHL	5	1	5	6	19
1978-79—Lethbridge Broncos (c)		WHL	71	50	75	125	212
1979-80—Lethbridge Broncos		WHL	21	18	16	34	74
1979-80—New York Islanders		NHL	56	15	9	24	55
1980-81—New York Islanders		NHL	23	7	11	18	26
1981-82—New York Islanders		NHL	77	18	35	53	100
1982-83—New York Islanders		NHL	75	13	19	32	118
1983-84—New York Islanders		NHL	78	17	23	40	94
1984-85—New York Islanders		NHL	78	17	24	41	174
1985-86—New York Islanders		NHL	80	20	33	53	157
1986-87—New York Islanders		NHL	80	14	17	31	169
1987-88—Chicago Black Hawks (d)		NHL	37	7	9	16	70
NHL TOTALS			584	128	180	308	963

(c)—August, 1979—Drafted by New York Islanders as underage junior in entry draft. First Islanders pick, 17th overall, first round.
(d)—September, 1987—Traded by New York Islanders to Chicago Black Hawks for a second-round 1988 draft pick (Wayne Doucet).

RICHARD SUTTER

Right Wing ... 5'11" ... 190 lbs. ... Born, Viking, Alta., December 2, 1963 ... Shoots right ... Brother of Brian, Brent, Darryl, Duane, Gary and twin brother of Ron Sutter.

Year	Team	League	Games	G.	A.	Pts.	Pen.
1979-80—Red Deer Rustlers		AJHL	60	13	19	32	157
1980-81—Lethbridge Broncos		WHL	72	23	18	41	255
1981-82—Lethbridge Broncos (c)		WHL	57	38	31	69	263
1982-83—Lethbridge Broncos		WHL	64	37	30	67	200
1982-83—Pittsburgh Penguins		NHL	4	0	0	0	0
1983-84—Baltimore Skipjacks		AHL	2	0	1	1	0
1983-84—Pittsburgh Penguins (d)		NHL	5	0	0	0	0
1983-84—Philadelphia Flyers		NHL	70	16	12	28	93
1984-85—Hershey Bears		AHL	13	3	7	10	14
1984-85—Philadelphia Flyers		NHL	56	6	10	16	89
1985-86—Philadelphia Flyers (e)		NHL	78	14	25	39	199
1986-87—Vancouver Canucks		NHL	74	20	22	42	113
1987-88—Vancouver Canucks		NHL	80	15	15	30	165
NHL TOTALS			367	71	84	155	659

(c)—June, 1982—Drafted as underage junior by Pittsburgh Penguins in 1982 NHL entry draft. First Penguins pick, 10th overall, first round.
(d)—October, 1983—Traded with second (Greg Smyth) and third (David McLay) round 1984 draft picks by Pittsburgh Penguins to Philadelphia Flyers for Ron Flockhart, Mark Taylor, Andy Brickley, first (Roger Belanger) and third-round 1984 draft picks.
(e)—June, 1986—Traded by Philadelphia Flyers with Dave Richter and a third-round draft choice in 1986 to Vancouver Canucks for J.J. Daigneault, a second-round draft choice (Kent Hawley) in 1986 and a fifth-round pick in 1987.

RONALD SUTTER

Center ... 6' ... 180 lbs. ... Born, Viking, Alta., December 2, 1963 ... Shoots right ... Brother of Brian, Brent, Darryl, Duane, Gary and twin brother of Rich Sutter ... (November 27, 1981)—Broke ankle in game against Medicine Hat ... (March, 1985)—Bruised ribs ... (September, 1985)—Pulled hip flexor muscle during training camp and missed the first three games of the season ... (January, 1987)—Lower back stress fracture ... (March, 1988)—Torn rib cartilage.

Year	Team	League	Games	G.	A.	Pts.	Pen.
1979-80—Red Deer Rustlers		AJHL	60	12	33	35	44
1980-81—Lethbridge Broncos		WHL	72	13	32	45	152
1981-82—Lethbridge Broncos (c)		WHL	59	38	54	92	207

Year	Team	League	Games	G.	A.	Pts.	Pen.
1982-83—Lethbridge Broncos		WHL	58	35	48	83	98
1982-83—Philadelphia Flyers		NHL	10	1	1	2	9
1983-84—Philadelphia Flyers		NHL	79	19	32	51	101
1984-85—Philadelphia Flyers		NHL	73	16	29	45	94
1985-86—Philadelphia Flyers		NHL	75	18	41	59	159
1986-87—Philadelphia Flyers		NHL	39	10	17	27	69
1987-88—Philadelphia Flyers		NHL	69	8	25	33	146
NHL TOTALS			345	72	145	217	578

(c)—June, 1982—Drafted as underage junior by Philadelphia Flyers in 1982 NHL entry draft. First Flyers pick, fourth overall, first round.

BOYD SUTTON

Center . . . 5'10" . . . 175 lbs. . . . Born, Anchorage, Alaska, December 6, 1966 . . . Shoots left.

Year	Team	League	Games	G.	A.	Pts.	Pen.
1985-86—Miami Univ. of Ohio (c)		CCHA	33	8	12	20	24
1986-87—Miami Univ. of Ohio		CCHA	39	19	18	37	44
1987-88—Miami Univ. of Ohio		CCHA	37	17	16	33	34

(c)—June, 1985—Drafted by Buffalo Sabres in 1985 NHL entry draft. Tenth Sabres pick, 203rd overall, 10th round.

JEFF SVEEN

Center . . . 5'11" . . . 175 lbs. . . . Born, Barrhead, Alta., February 5, 1967 . . . Shoots right . . . Also plays Right Wing.

Year	Team	League	Games	G.	A.	Pts.	Pen.
1984-85—Boston University (c)		H. East	42	14	10	24	10
1985-86—Boston University		H. East	35	15	8	23	18
1986-87—Boston University		H. East	34	8	6	14	32
1987-88—Boston University		H. East	17	6	5	11	14

(c)—June, 1985—Drafted by New York Islanders in 1985 NHL entry draft. Seventh Islanders pick, 97th overall, fifth round.

PETR SVOBODA

Defense . . . 6'1" . . . 160 lbs. . . . Born, Most, Czechoslovakia, February 14, 1966 . . . Shoots left . . . (January 20, 1986)—Injured shoulder at Quebec and missed three games . . . (January, 1988)—Back spasms . . . (March, 1988)—Hip pointer.

Year	Team	League	Games	G.	A.	Pts.	Pen.
1983-84—Czechoslovakia Jr. (c)		Czech.	40	15	21	36	14
1984-85—Montreal Canadiens		NHL	73	4	27	31	65
1985-86—Montreal Canadiens		NHL	73	1	18	19	93
1986-87—Montreal Canadiens		NHL	70	5	17	22	63
1987-88—Montreal Canadiens		NHL	69	7	22	29	149
NHL TOTALS			285	17	84	101	370

(c)—June, 1984—Drafted by Montreal Canadiens in NHL entry draft. First Canadiens pick, fifth overall, first round.

DON SWEENEY

Defense . . . 5'11" . . . 170 lbs. . . . Born, St. Stephen, N.B., August 17, 1966 . . . Shoots left.

Year	Team	League	Games	G.	A.	Pts.	Pen.
1983-84—St. Paul N.B. H.S. (c)		N.B.H.S.	22	33	26	59	....
1984-85—Harvard University		ECAC	29	3	7	10	30
1985-86—Harvard University		ECAC	31	4	5	9	29
1986-87—Harvard University		ECAC	34	7	14	21	22
1987-88—Harvard University (d)		ECAC	30	6	23	29	37

(c)—June, 1984—Drafted by Boston Bruins in NHL entry draft. Eighth Bruins pick, 166th overall, eighth round.

(d)—Named second-team All-America (East).

ROBERT SWEENEY

Center . . . 6'3" . . . 200 lbs. . . . Born, Boxborough, Mass., January 25, 1964 . . . Shoots right . . . Brother of Timothy Sweeney.

Year	Team	League	Games	G.	A.	Pts.	Pen.
1982-83—Boston College (c)		ECAC	30	17	11	28	10
1983-84—Boston College		ECAC	23	14	7	21	10
1984-85—Boston College		H. East	44	32	32	64	43
1985-86—Boston College		H. East	41	15	24	39	52
1986-87—Boston Bruins		NHL	14	2	4	6	21

Year	Team	League	Games	G.	A.	Pts.	Pen.
1986-87—Moncton Golden Flames		AHL	58	29	26	55	81
1987-88—Boston Bruins		NHL	80	22	23	45	73
NHL TOTALS			94	24	27	51	94

(c)—June, 1982—Drafted by Boston Bruins in 1982 NHL entry draft. Sixth Bruins pick, 123rd overall, sixth round.

TIMOTHY SWEENEY

Center . . . 5'11" . . . 180 lbs. . . . Born, Boston, Mass., April 12, 1967 . . . Shoots left . . . Brother of Bob Sweeney (Boston College All-America hockey player, 1984-85) . . . (January 26, 1988)—Fractured index finger vs. Northeastern Univ.

Year	Team	League	Games	G.	A.	Pts.	Pen.
1983-84—Weymouth North H.S.		Mass. H.S.	23	33	26	59	....
1984-85—Weymouth North H.S. (c)		Mass. H.S.	22	32	56	88	....
1985-86—Boston College		H. East	32	8	4	12	8
1986-87—Boston College		H. East	38	31	16	47	28
1987-88—Boston College		H. East	18	9	11	20	18

(c)—June, 1985—Drafted by Calgary Flames in 1985 NHL entry draft. Seventh Flames pick, 122nd overall, sixth round.

PHIL SYKES

Left Wing . . . 6' . . . 185 lbs. . . . Born, Dawson Creek, B.C., May 18, 1959 . . . Shoots left . . . (January 10, 1986)—Strained groin at Minnesota and missed four games . . . (May, 1986)—Injured left wrist during world championships in Moscow and required surgery in September, 1986 . . . (March, 1987)—Sprained knee . . . (May, 1987)—Injured left wrist during World Championships in Moscow that required surgery . . . (October, 1987)—Partially torn groin muscle . . . (March, 1988)—Strained knee.

Year	Team	League	Games	G.	A.	Pts.	Pen.
1978-79—North Dakota University		WCHA	41	9	5	14	16
1979-80—North Dakota University		WCHA	37	22	27	49	34
1980-81—North Dakota University		WCHA	38	28	34	62	22
1981-82—North Dakota University (c-d)		WCHA	45	39	24	63	20
1982-83—Los Angeles Kings		NHL	7	2	0	2	2
1982-83—New Haven Nighthawks		AHL	71	19	26	45	111
1983-84—New Haven Nighthawks		AHL	77	29	37	66	101
1983-84—Los Angeles Kings		NHL	3	0	0	0	2
1984-85—Los Angeles Kings		NHL	79	17	15	32	38
1985-86—Los Angeles Kings		NHL	76	20	24	44	97
1986-87—Los Angeles Kings		NHL	58	6	15	21	133
1987-88—Los Angeles Kings		NHL	40	9	12	21	82
NHL TOTALS			263	54	66	120	354

(c)—Named to Western All-America Team.
(d)—April, 1982—Signed by Los Angeles Kings as a free agent.

PETER TAGLIANETTI

Defense . . . 6'2" . . . 200 lbs. . . . Born, Framingham, Mass., August 15, 1963 . . . Shoots left . . . (October, 1985)—Dislocated shoulder in fight with Perry Turnbull during Winnipeg Jets' training camp . . . (February 20, 1986)—Dislocated shoulder . . . (March, 1986)—Surgery to correct recurring shoulder dislocations.

Year	Team	League	Games	G.	A.	Pts.	Pen.
1981-82—Providence College		ECAC	2	0	0	0	2
1982-83—Providence College (c)		ECAC	43	4	17	21	68
1983-84—Providence College		ECAC	30	4	25	29	68
1984-85—Providence College (a)		H. East	43	8	21	29	114
1984-85—Winnipeg Jets		NHL	1	0	0	0	0
1985-86—Sherbrooke Canadiens		AHL	24	1	8	9	75
1985-86—Winnipeg Jets		NHL	18	0	0	0	48
1986-87—Winnipeg Jets		NHL	3	0	0	0	12
1986-87—Sherbrooke Canadiens		AHL	54	5	14	19	104
1987-88—Winnipeg Jets		NHL	70	6	17	23	182
NHL TOTALS			92	6	17	23	242

(c)—June, 1983—Drafted by Winnipeg Jets in NHL entry draft. Fourth Jets pick, 43rd overall, third round.

RONALD TALAKOSKI

Right Wing . . . 6'3" . . . 220 lbs. . . . Born, Thunder Bay, Ont., June 1, 1962 . . . Shoots right . . . Also played football at University of Manitoba.

Year	Team	League	Games	G.	A.	Pts.	Pen.
1982-83—Univ. of Manitoba		GPAC	31	12	11	23	51
1983-84—Did not play			..	..	..	..	..
1984-85—Univ. of Manitoba		GPAC	11	4	4	8	77
1985-86—Did not play			..	..	..	..	..
1986-87—New York Rangers (c)		NHL	3	0	0	0	21
1986-87—New Haven Nighthawks		AHL	26	2	2	4	58
1986-87—Flint Spirits		IHL	3	2	1	3	12
1987-88—New York Rangers		NHL	6	0	1	1	12
1987-88—Colorado Rangers		IHL	62	24	19	43	104
NHL TOTALS			9	0	1	1	33

(c)—October, 1986—Signed by New York Rangers as a free agent.

STEVE ANTHONY TAMBELLINI

Center . . . 6' . . . 190 lbs. . . . Born, Trail, B.C., May 14, 1958 . . . Shoots left . . . (December, 1982)—Shoulder separation . . . Son of Adolph Addie Tambellini (member of 1961 World Champion Trail Smoke Eaters) . . . (December, 1984)—Bruised elbow . . . (January 21, 1986)—Injured knee vs. New Jersey and missed 11 games . . . (March 15, 1986)—Broken thumb at Boston . . . (March, 1988)—Bruised hand.

Year	Team	League	Games	G.	A.	Pts.	Pen.
1975-76—Lethbridge Broncos (c)		WCHL	72	38	59	97	42
1976-77—Lethbridge Broncos (d)		WCHL	55	42	42	84	23
1977-78—Lethbridge Broncos (e)		WCHL	66	75	80	155	32
1978-79—New York Islanders		NHL	1	0	0	0	0
1978-79—Fort Worth Texans		CH	73	25	27	52	32
1979-80—New York Islanders		NHL	45	5	8	13	4
1980-81—New York Islanders (f)		NHL	61	19	17	36	17
1980-81—Colorado Rockies		NHL	13	6	12	18	2
1981-82—Colorado Rockies		NHL	79	29	30	59	14
1982-83—New Jersey Devils (g)		NHL	73	25	18	43	14
1983-84—Calgary Flames		NHL	73	15	10	25	16
1984-85—Moncton Golden Flames		AHL	7	2	5	7	0
1984-85—Calgary Flames (h)		NHL	47	19	10	29	4
1985-86—Vancouver Canucks		NHL	48	15	15	30	12
1986-87—Vancouver Canucks		NHL	72	16	20	36	14
1987-88—Canadian Olympic Team		Int'l	10	2	3	5	2
1987-88—Vancouver Canucks (i)		NHL	41	11	10	21	8
NHL TOTALS			553	160	150	310	105

(c)—Won WCHL Rookie of the Year Award.
(d)—Won WCHL Most Gentlemanly Player Award.
(e)—Drafted from Lethbridge Broncos by New York Islanders in first round of 1978 amateur draft.
(f)—March, 1981—Traded by New York Islanders with Glenn Resch to Colorado Rockies for Mike McEwen and Jari Kaarela.
(g)—July, 1983—Traded by New Jersey Devils with Joel Quenneville to Calgary Flames for Mel Bridgman and Phil Russell.
(h)—August, 1985—Signed by Vancouver Canucks as a free agent.
(i)—June, 1988—Signed by Zurich (Switzerland).

DAVID TANNER

Defense . . . 6' . . . 185 lbs. . . . Born, Winnipeg, Manitoba, March 5, 1966 . . . Shoots left.

Year	Team	League	Games	G.	A.	Pts.	Pen.
1984-85—Yale University (c)		ECAC	31	2	10	12	4
1985-86—Yale University		ECAC	22	6	20	26	11
1986-87—Yale University		ECAC	30	10	11	21	20
1987-88—Yale University		ECAC	26	11	11	22	16

(c)—June, 1984—Drafted by Montreal Canadiens in 1984 NHL entry draft. Thirteenth Canadiens pick, 220th overall, 11th round.

TONY TANTI

Right Wing . . . 5'9" . . . 181 lbs. . . . Born, Toronto, Ont., September 7, 1963 . . . Shoots left . . . Broke Wayne Gretzky's record for most goals in rookie OHL season . . . (November, 1981)—Separated shoulder . . . (December, 1981)—Sore hip . . . (1983-84)—Set Vancouver club records for most goals (45) and most power-play goals (19) . . . (November, 1984)—Strained knee . . . Also plays Left Wing . . . (December 8, 1987)—Broken foot when struck by puck vs. Minnesota.

Year	Team	League	Games	G.	A.	Pts.	Pen.
1979-80—St. Michaels Jr. B		OHL	37	31	27	58	67
1980-81—Oshawa Generals (a-c-d)		OHL	67	81	69	150	197
1981-82—Oshawa Generals (b-e)		OHL	57	62	64	126	138

Year	Team	League	Games	G.	A.	Pts.	Pen.
1981-82—Chicago Black Hawks		NHL	2	0	0	0	0
1982-83—Oshawa Generals		OHL	30	34	28	62	35
1982-83—Chicago Black Hawks (f)		NHL	1	1	0	1	0
1982-83—Vancouver Canucks		NHL	39	8	8	16	16
1983-84—Vancouver Canucks		NHL	79	45	41	86	50
1984-85—Vancouver Canucks		NHL	68	39	20	59	45
1985-86—Vancouver Canucks		NHL	77	39	33	72	85
1986-87—Vancouver Canucks		NHL	77	41	38	79	84
1987-88—Vancouver Canucks		NHL	73	40	37	77	90
NHL TOTALS			416	213	177	390	370

(c)—Won Hap Emms OHL Rookie Award.

(d)—June, 1981—Drafted by Chicago Black Hawks in NHL entry draft. First Black Hawks pick, 12th overall, first round.

(e)—Won Jim Mahon Memorial Trophy (Top Scoring Right Wing).

(f)—January, 1983—Traded by Chicago Black Hawks to Vancouver Canucks for Curt Fraser.

DARREN TAYLOR

Center . . . 6'1" . . . 170 lbs. . . . Born, Calgary, Alta., May 28, 1967 . . . Shoots left.

Year	Team	League	Games	G.	A.	Pts.	Pen.
1983-84—Calgary Spurs		AJHL	55	15	21	36	160
1984-85—Calgary Wranglers (c)		WHL	72	11	5	16	54
1985-86—Calgary Wranglers		WHL	41	9	11	20	83
1985-86—Seattle Thunderbirds		WHL	27	2	8	10	54
1986-87—Seattle Thunderbirds		WHL	60	13	13	26	112
1987-88—Medicine Hat Tigers		WHL	60	12	21	33	122

(c)—June, 1985—Drafted as underage junior by Vancouver Canucks in 1985 NHL entry draft. Twelfth Canucks pick, 235th overall, 12th round.

DAVID ANDREW TAYLOR

Right Wing . . . 6' . . . 185 lbs. . . . Born, Levack, Ont., December 4, 1955 . . . Shoots right . . . Set ECAC record and tied NCAA record with 108 points in 1976-77 . . . Missed parts of 1979-80 season with pulled back muscle and sprained left knee . . . (November 5, 1980)— Sprained shoulder . . . (October 29, 1982)—Broke right wrist in collision with Kevin Lowe at Edmonton and missed 33 games . . . (January, 1983)—Right knee injury . . . (May 28, 1983)—Operation on right wrist he broke for second time in World Championships at West Germany . . . Holds single season record for most goals, assists and points by a former college player . . . Holds Los Angeles club records for goals, assists and points by a right wing . . . (November 10, 1983)—Returned from broken wrist vs. St. Louis . . . (November, 1986)—Sprained knee . . . (December, 1987)—Groin injury.

Year	Team	League	Games	G.	A.	Pts.	Pen.
1974-75—Clarkson College (c)		ECAC	....	20	34	54	....
1975-76—Clarkson College		ECAC	....	26	33	59	....
1976-77—Clarkson College (d-e)		ECAC	34	41	67	108	....
1976-77—Fort Worth Texans		CHL	7	2	4	6	6
1977-78—Los Angeles Kings		NHL	64	22	21	43	47
1978-79—Los Angeles Kings		NHL	78	43	48	91	124
1979-80—Los Angeles Kings		NHL	61	37	53	90	72
1980-81—Los Angeles Kings (b)		NHL	72	47	65	112	130
1981-82—Los Angeles Kings		NHL	78	39	67	106	130
1982-83—Los Angeles Kings		NHL	46	21	37	58	76
1983-84—Los Angeles Kings		NHL	63	20	49	69	91
1984-85—Los Angeles Kings		NHL	79	41	51	92	132
1985-86—Los Angeles Kings		NHL	76	33	38	71	110
1986-87—Los Angeles Kings		NHL	67	18	44	62	84
1987-88—Los Angeles Kings		NHL	68	26	41	67	129
NHL TOTALS			752	347	514	861	1125

(c)—Drafted by Los Angeles Kings in 15th round of 1975 amateur draft.

(d)—Named ECAC Player of the Year.

(e)—Named to All-America team (East).

MEL SCOTT TAYLOR
(Known by middle name)

Defense . . . 6' . . . 185 lbs. . . . Born, Toronto, Ont., March 23, 1968 . . . Shoots right.

Year	Team	League	Games	G.	A.	Pts.	Pen.
1984-85—Markham Waxers		OJHL	43	1	13	14	247
1985-86—Kitchener Rangers (c)		OHL	59	4	13	17	211
1986-87—Kitchener Rangers		OHL	53	6	16	22	123
1987-88—Kitchener Rangers		OHL	2	0	0	0	13

Year	Team	League	Games	G.	A.	Pts.	Pen.
1987-88—Windsor Spitfires		OHL	8	0	3	3	37
1987-88—Belleville Bulls		OHL	38	5	9	14	115

(c)—June, 1986—Drafted as underage junior by Toronto Maple Leafs in 1986 NHL entry draft. Fifth Maple Leafs pick, 90th overall, fifth round.

TIM TAYLOR

Center . . . 5'11" . . . 170 lbs. . . . Born, Stratford, Ont., February 6, 1969 . . . Shoots left . . . (October, 1986)—Mononucleosis.

Year	Team	League	Games	G.	A.	Pts.	Pen.
1986-87—London Knights		OHL	34	7	9	16	11
1987-88—London Knights (c)		OHL	64	46	50	96	66

(c)—June, 1988—Drafted by Washington Capitals in 1988 NHL entry draft. Second Capitals pick, 36th overall, second round.

GREG TEBBUTT

Defense . . . 6'2" . . . 215 lbs. . . . Born, North Vancouver, B.C., May 11, 1957 . . . Shoots left . . . (December, 1980)—Surgery to repair severe lacerations of tendons and muscles in left forearm.

Year	Team	League	Games	G.	A.	Pts.	Pen.
1975-76—Victoria Cougars		WCHL	51	3	4	7	217
1976-77—Victoria Cougars (c)		WCHL	29	7	12	19	98
1976-77—Regina Pats (d-e)		WCHL	40	8	17	25	138
1977-78—Flin Flon Bombers		WCHL	55	28	46	74	270
1978-79—Birmingham Bulls (f)		WHA	38	2	5	7	83
1978-79—Binghamton Dusters		AHL	33	8	9	17	50
1979-80—Quebec Nordiques		NHL	2	0	1	1	4
1979-80—Syracuse Firebirds		AHL	14	2	3	5	35
1979-80—Erie Blades (b-g)		EHL	48	20	53	75	138
1980-81—Erie Blades (h)		EHL	35	16	37	53	93
1981-82—Fort Wayne Komets (i)		IHL	49	13	34	47	148
1982-83—Baltimore Skipjacks (a-j)		AHL	80	28	56	84	140
1983-84—Baltimore Skipjacks		AHL	44	12	42	54	125
1983-84—Pittsburgh Penguins (k)		NHL	24	0	2	2	31
1984-85—Muskegon Lumberjacks (b)		IHL	73	23	55	78	220
1984-85—Baltimore Skipjacks		AHL	2	0	0	0	4
1985-86—Milwaukee Admirals		IHL	77	20	49	69	226
1986-87—Saginaw Gears (a)		IHL	81	27	59	86	215
1987-88—Baltimore Skipjacks		AHL	24	1	14	15	72
WHA TOTALS			38	2	5	7	83
NHL TOTALS			26	0	3	3	35

(c)—December, 1976—Traded to Regina Pats by Victoria Cougars with Hugh Ellis and Lorne Schmidt for Ron Trafford, Rick Odegard and Keith Hertz.
(d)—June, 1977—Selected by Birmingham Bulls in World Hockey Association amateur player draft.
(e)—Drafted from Regina Pats by Minnesota North Stars in eighth round of 1977 amateur draft.
(f)—June, 1979—Claimed by Quebec Nordiques in WHA dispersal draft. Selected by Minnesota North Stars in NHL reclaim draft.
(g)—Led EHL playoffs in goals (11) and points (23) and was co-leader with Daniel Poulin in assists (12).
(h)—Led EHL playoffs with 12 assists.
(i)—August, 1981—Released by Quebec Nordiques.
(j)—Won Eddie Shore Plaque (Outstanding AHL Defenseman).
(k)—June, 1983—Signed by Pittsburgh Penguins as a free agent.

MARK TEEVENS

Right Wing . . . 6' . . . 180 lbs. . . . Born, Ottawa, Ont., June 17, 1966 . . . Shoots left . . . (December, 1986)—Charley Horse.

Year	Team	League	Games	G.	A.	Pts.	Pen.
1982-83—Ottawa Senators		COJHL	47	14	26	40	36
1983-84—Peterborough Petes (c)		OHL	70	27	37	64	70
1984-85—Peterborough Petes		OHL	65	43	*90	133	70
1985-86—Peterborough Petes		OHL	50	31	50	81	106
1986-87—Baltimore Skipjacks		AHL	71	15	16	31	34
1987-88—Muskegon Lumberjacks		IHL	53	17	26	43	39

(c)—June, 1984—Drafted as underage junior by Pittsburgh Penguins in NHL entry draft. Fourth Penguins pick, 64th overall, fourth round.

GREG PATRICK TERRION

Center . . . 6' . . . 190 lbs. . . . Born, Peterborough, Ont., May 2, 1960 . . . Shoots left . . .

(December, 1981)—Separated shoulder . . . (January 14, 1984)—Scored second penalty shot goal of the season. Only other NHL player to do that was Pat Egan, New York Americans, in 1941-42 . . . (December 26, 1985)—Bruised knee at Detroit and missed four games . . . (March, 1988)—Injured groin.

Year	Team	League	Games	G.	A.	Pts.	Pen.
1977-78—Hamilton Fincups		OMJHL	64	11	30	41	43
1978-79—Brantford Alexanders		OMJHL	63	27	28	55	48
1979-80—Brantford Alexanders (c)		OMJHL	67	44	78	122	13
1980-81—Los Angeles Kings		NHL	73	12	25	37	99
1981-82—Los Angeles Kings		NHL	61	15	22	37	23
1982-83—New Haven Nighthawks (d)		AHL	4	0	1	1	7
1982-83—Toronto Maple Leafs		NHL	74	16	16	32	59
1983-84—Toronto Maple Leafs		NHL	79	15	24	39	36
1984-85—Toronto Maple Leafs		NHL	72	14	17	31	20
1985-86—Toronto Maple Leafs		NHL	76	10	22	32	31
1986-87—Toronto Maple Leafs		NHL	67	7	8	15	6
1987-88—Newmarket Saints		AHL	4	1	3	4	6
1987-88—Toronto Maple Leafs		NHL	59	4	16	20	65
NHL TOTALS			561	93	150	243	339

(c)—June, 1980—Drafted by Los Angeles Kings in 1980 NHL entry draft. Second Kings pick, 33rd overall, second round.

(d)—October, 1982—Traded by Los Angeles Kings to Toronto Maple Leafs for future considerations.

WILLIAM TERRY

Center . . . 5'8" . . . 165 lbs. . . . Born, Toronto, Ont., July 13, 1961 . . . Shoots right . . . (December, 1986)—Separated shoulder.

Year	Team	League	Games	G.	A.	Pts.	Pen.
1978-79—Sault Ste. Marie Greyhounds		OMJHL	68	28	21	49	85
1979-80—Sault Ste. Marie Greyhounds		OMJHL	68	21	34	55	64
1980-81—Michigan Tech. Univ. (c)		WCHA	40	23	19	42	12
1981-82—Michigan Tech. Univ.		CCHA	35	26	24	50	37
1982-83—Michigan Tech. Univ.		CCHA	37	19	29	48	37
1983-84—Michigan Tech. Univ.		CCHA	40	23	17	40	40
1983-84—Toledo Goaldiggers		IHL	3	2	2	4	4
1984-85—			..	..	..	..	..
1985-86—Kalamazoo Wings (b-d)		IHL	78	43	66	109	28
1986-87—Kalamazoo Wings		IHL	27	11	22	33	36
1987-88—Minnesota North Stars (e)		NHL	5	0	0	0	0
1987-88—Kalamazoo Wings		IHL	77	31	54	85	75
NHL TOTALS			5	0	0	0	0

(c)—Named outstanding freshman athlete at Michigan Tech.

(d)—September, 1986—Signed by Detroit Red Wings as a free agent after a season in Europe.

(e)—September, 1987—Signed by Minnesota North Stars as a free agent.

TOM TERWILLIGER

Defense . . . 6'2" . . . 185 lbs. . . . Born, Denver, Colo., September 1, 1965 . . . Shoots right.

Year	Team	League	Games	G.	A.	Pts.	Pen.
1983-84—Edina H.S. (c)		Minn. H.S.	24	5	11	16	20
1984-85—Miami of Ohio Univ.		CCHA	29	2	3	5	18
1985-86—Miami of Ohio Univ.		CCHA	32	1	3	4	35
1986-87—Miami of Ohio Univ.		CCHA	28	2	1	3	24
1987-88—Miami of Ohio Univ.		CCHA	35	1	4	5	53

(c)—June, 1984—Drafted by Minnesota North Stars in NHL entry draft. Eleventh North Stars pick, 222nd overall, 11th round.

ROD THACKER

Defense . . . 6'2" . . . 200 lbs. . . . Born, Kitchener, Ont., July 16, 1968 . . . Shoots left . . . (December, 1984)—Torn knee ligaments . . . (December, 1985)—Fractured nose.

Year	Team	League	Games	G.	A.	Pts.	Pen.
1984-85—Kitchener Greenshirts Midgets		OHA	19	1	15	16	38
1985-86—Hamilton Steelhawks (c)		OHL	58	2	9	11	60
1986-87—Hamilton Steelhawks		OHL	6	0	0	0	0
1986-87—Ottawa 67's		OHL	31	1	3	4	36
1986-87—Sault Ste. Marie Greyhounds		OHL	26	0	6	6	28
1987-88—Sault Ste. Marie Greyhounds		OHL	41	1	4	5	59

(c)—June, 1986—Drafted as underage junior by St. Louis Blues in 1986 NHL entry draft. Tenth Blues pick, 199th overall, 10th round.

CHRIS THAYER

Center . . . 6'2" . . . 190 lbs. . . . Born, Exeter, N.H., November 9, 1967 . . . Shoots right.

Year	Team	League	Games	G.	A.	Pts.	Pen.
1985-86—Kent Prep. (c)		Conn. H.S.	25	7	16	23	6
1986-87—Kent Prep.		Conn. H.S.	22	15	22	37	..
1987-88—Univ. of New Hampshire		H. East	18	0	0	0	8

(c)—June, 1986—Drafted by Chicago Black Hawks in 1986 NHL entry draft. Tenth Black Hawks pick, 224th overall, 11th round.

MICHAEL THELVEN

Defense . . . 5'11" . . . 180 lbs. . . . Born, Stockholm, Sweden, January 7, 1961 . . . Shoots right . . . (January 13, 1986)—Facial surgery and missed five games . . . (February 6, 1986)—Injured groin vs. Buffalo . . . (February 18, 1986)—Dislocated shoulder at Calgary . . . (September, 1986)—Dislocated left shoulder in Bruins training camp and required surgery . . . (January, 1988)—Sprained neck . . . (March, 1988)—Groin strain . . . (April, 1988)—Strained right shoulder vs. Montreal during playoffs.

Year	Team	League	Games	G.	A.	Pts.	Pen.
1984-85—Djurgardens (c)		Sweden	..	8	13	21	..
1985-86—Boston Bruins		NHL	60	6	20	26	48
1986-87—Boston Bruins		NHL	34	5	15	20	18
1987-88—Boston Bruins		NHL	67	6	25	31	57
NHL TOTALS			161	17	60	77	123

(c)—June, 1980—Drafted by Boston Bruins in NHL entry draft. Eighth Bruins pick, 186th overall, ninth round.

GILLES THIBAUDEAU

Left Wing . . . 5'10" . . . 165 lbs. . . . Born, Montreal, Que., March 4, 1963 . . . Shoots left.

Year	Team	League	Games	G.	A.	Pts.	Pen.
1984-85—Flint Generals (b-c)		IHL	71	52	45	97	91
1984-85—Sherbrooke Canadiens		AHL	7	2	4	6	2
1985-86—Sherbrooke Canadiens (d)		AHL	61	15	21	36	20
1986-87—Sherbrooke Canadiens		AHL	62	27	40	67	26
1986-87—Montreal Canadiens		NHL	9	1	3	4	0
1987-88—Montreal Canadiens		NHL	17	5	6	11	0
1987-88—Sherbrooke Canadiens		AHL	59	39	57	96	45
NHL TOTALS			26	6	9	15	0

(c)—Won Harry F. Longman Memorial Trophy (Rookie-of-the-Year).
(d)—September, 1985—Signed by Montreal Canadiens as a free agent.

STEVE THOMAS

Left Wing . . . 5'10" . . . 180 lbs. . . . Born, Markham, Ont., July 15, 1963 . . . Shoots left . . . (September, 1984)—Broke wrist on second day of training camp . . . Also plays Right Wing . . . (October, 1987)—Pulled stomach muscle . . . (February 20, 1988)—Separated left shoulder at Detroit and required surgery in May.

Year	Team	League	Games	G.	A.	Pts.	Pen.
1981-82—Markham Tier-II		OHA	48	68	57	125	113
1982-83—Toronto Marlboros		OHL	61	18	20	38	42
1983-84—Toronto Marlboros		OHL	70	51	54	105	77
1984-85—Toronto Maple Leafs (c)		NHL	18	1	1	2	2
1984-85—St. Catharines Saints (a-d)		AHL	64	42	48	90	56
1985-86—St. Catharines Saints		AHL	19	18	14	32	35
1985-86—Toronto Maple Leafs		NHL	65	20	37	57	36
1986-87—Toronto Maple Leafs (e)		NHL	78	35	27	62	114
1987-88—Chicago Black Hawks		NHL	30	13	13	26	40
NHL TOTALS			191	69	78	147	192

(c)—June, 1984—Signed by Toronto Maple Leafs as a free agent.
(d)—Won Dudley Red Garrett Memorial Trophy (Top Rookie).
(e)—September, 1987—Traded with Rick Vaive and Bob McGill by Toronto Maple Leafs to Chicago Black Hawks for Al Secord and Ed Olczyk.

DAVE THOMLINSON

Left Wing . . . 6'1" . . . 185 lbs. . . . Born, Edmonton, Alta., October 22, 1966 . . . Shoots left . . . (November, 1983)—Separated shoulder . . . (November, 1984)—Separated shoulder.

Year	Team	League	Games	G.	A.	Pts.	Pen.
1983-84—Brandon Wheat Kings		WHL	41	17	12	29	62
1984-85—Brandon Wheat Kings (c)		WHL	26	13	14	27	70

Year	Team	League	Games	G.	A.	Pts.	Pen.
1985-86—Brandon Wheat Kings		WHL	53	25	20	45	116
1986-87—Moose Jaw Warriors (d)		WHL	71	44	37	81	126
1987-88—Peoria Rivermen		IHL	74	27	30	57	56

(c)—June, 1985—Drafted as underage junior by Toronto Maple Leafs in the 1985 NHL entry draft. Third Maple Leafs pick, 43rd overall, third round.

(d)—July, 1987—Signed by St. Louis Blues as a free agent.

JIM THOMSON

Right Wing . . . 6'2" . . . 180 lbs. . . . Born, Edmonton, Alta., December 30, 1965 . . . Shoots right.

Year	Team	League	Games	G.	A.	Pts.	Pen.
1982-83—Markham Waxers		OJHL	35	6	7	13	81
1983-84—Toronto Marlboros (c)		OHL	60	10	18	28	68
1984-85—Toronto Marlboros		OHL	63	23	28	51	122
1984-85—Binghamton Whalers		AHL	4	0	0	0	2
1985-86—Binghamton Whalers		AHL	59	15	9	24	195
1986-87—Binghamton Whalers		AHL	57	13	10	23	*360
1986-87—Washington Capitals		NHL	10	0	0	0	35
1987-88—Binghamton Whalers		AHL	25	8	9	17	64
NHL TOTALS			10	0	0	0	35

(c)—June, 1984—Drafted as underage junior by Washington Capitals in NHL entry draft. Eighth Capitals pick, 185th overall, ninth round.

ESA TIKKANEN

Left Wing . . . 5'11" . . . 185 lbs. . . . Born, Jyvaskyla, Finland, March 2, 1962 . . . Shoots left . . . (December 10, 1985)—Broke foot at St. Louis . . . (December 9, 1986)—Cut on elbow developed into bursitis that required surgery.

Year	Team	League	Games	G.	A.	Pts.	Pen.
1984-85—IFK Helsinki (c)		Finland	....	21	33	54	....
1984-85—Edmonton Oilers (d)		NHL	....	...	....	....	....
1985-86—Nova Scotia Oilers		AHL	15	4	8	12	17
1985-86—Edmonton Oilers		NHL	35	7	6	13	28
1986-87—Edmonton Oilers		NHL	76	34	44	78	120
1987-88—Edmonton Oilers		NHL	80	23	51	74	153
NHL TOTALS			191	64	101	165	301

(c)—August, 1983—Drafted by Edmonton Oilers in NHL entry draft. Fourth Oilers pick, 82nd overall, fourth round.

(d)—No regular season record. Played three playoff games.

TOM TILLEY

Defense . . . 6' . . . 180 lbs. . . . Born, Trenton, Ont., March 28, 1965 . . . Shoots right.

Year	Team	League	Games	G.	A.	Pts.	Pen.
1983-84—Orillia Travelways (c)		OJHL	38	16	35	51	113
1984-85—Michigan State University		CCHA	37	1	5	6	58
1985-86—Michigan State University		CCHA	42	9	25	34	48
1986-87—Michigan State University		CCHA	42	7	14	21	46
1987-88—Michigan State University		CCHA	46	8	18	26	44

(c)—June, 1984—Drafted as underage junior by St. Louis Blues in NHL entry draft. Thirteenth Blues pick, 196th overall, 10th round.

MARK TINORDI

Defense . . . 6'4" . . . 205 lbs. . . . Born, Reed Deer, Alta., May 9, 1965 . . . Shoots left . . . (January, 1988)—Abdominal pains.

Year	Team	League	Games	G.	A.	Pts.	Pen.
1982-83—Lethbridge Broncos		WHL	64	0	4	4	50
1983-84—Lethbridge Broncos		WHL	72	5	14	19	53
1984-85—Lethbridge Broncos		WHL	58	10	15	25	134
1985-86—Lethbridge Broncos		WHL	58	8	30	37	139
1986-87—Calgary Wranglers (a)		WHL	61	29	37	66	148
1986-87—New Haven Nighthawks (c)		AHL	2	0	0	0	2
1987-88—New York Rangers		NHL	24	1	2	3	50
1987-88—Colorado Rangers		IHL	41	8	19	27	150
NHL TOTALS			24	1	2	3	50

(c)—January, 1987—Signed by New York Rangers as a free agent.

DAVE TIPPETT

Center . . . 5'10" . . . 175 lbs. . . . Born, Moosomin, Sask., August 25, 1961 . . . Shoots left . . . Member of 1984 Canadian Olympic Team.

Year	Team	League	Games	G.	A.	Pts.	Pen.
1979-80—Prince Albert Raiders		SAJHL	85	72	95	177	..
1980-81—Prince Albert Raiders		SAJHL	84	62	93	155	..
1981-82—University of North Dakota		WCHA	43	13	28	41	24
1982-83—University of North Dakota		WCHA	36	15	31	46	44
1983-84—Canadian Olympic Team		Int'l	66	14	19	33	24
1983-84—Hartford Whalers (c)		NHL	17	4	2	6	2
1984-85—Hartford Whalers		NHL	80	7	12	19	12
1985-86—Hartford Whalers		NHL	80	14	20	34	18
1986-87—Hartford Whalers		NHL	80	9	22	31	42
1987-88—Hartford Whalers		NHL	80	16	21	37	30
NHL TOTALS			337	50	77	127	104

(c)—February, 1984—Signed by Hartford Whalers as a free agent.

TIM TISDALE

Center . . . 6'1" . . . 186 lbs. . . . Born, Shaunavon, Sask., May 28, 1968 . . . Shoots right.

Year	Team	League	Games	G.	A.	Pts.	Pen.
1986-87—Swift Current Broncos		WHL	66	20	29	49	25
1987-88—Swift Current Broncos (c)		WHL	32	11	15	26	15

(c)—June, 1988—Drafted by Edmonton Oilers in 1988 NHL entry draft. Thirteenth Oilers pick, 250th overall, 12th round.

GRANT TKACHUK

Left Wing . . . 5'9" . . . 175 lbs. . . . Born, Lac La Bichi, Alta., September 24, 1968 . . . Shoots left.

Year	Team	League	Games	G.	A.	Pts.	Pen.
1983-84—Lac La Bichi		Alta. Midgt.	40	31	35	66	40
1984-85—Saskatoon Blades		WHL	71	8	16	24	55
1985-86—Saskatoon Blades		WHL	52	18	27	45	82
1986-87—Saskatoon Blades (c)		WHL	71	46	36	82	108
1987-88—Saskatoon Blades (a)		WHL	70	51	46	97	126

(c)—June, 1987—Drafted by Buffalo Sabres in 1987 NHL entry draft. Tenth Sabres pick, 169th overall, ninth round.

RICK TOCCHET

Right Wing . . . 6' . . . 195 lbs. . . . Born, Scarborough, Ont., April 9, 1964 . . . Shoots right . . . (October 30, 1985)—Door of team bench slammed on his middle finger at Montreal and he missed four games . . . (November 23, 1985)—Bruised right knee at Philadelphia and missed seven games . . . (February, 1988)—Separated left shoulder.

Year	Team	League	Games	G.	A.	Pts.	Pen.
1981-82—Sault Ste. Marie Greyhounds		OHL	59	7	15	22	184
1982-83—Sault Ste. Marie Greyhounds (c-d-e)		OHL	66	32	34	66	146
1983-84—Sault Ste. Marie Greyhounds (f)		OHL	64	44	64	108	209
1984-85—Philadelphia Flyers		NHL	75	14	25	39	181
1985-86—Philadelphia Flyers		NHL	69	14	21	35	284
1986-87—Philadelphia Flyers		NHL	69	21	26	47	286
1987-88—Philadelphia Flyers		NHL	65	31	33	64	301
NHL TOTALS			278	80	105	185	1052

(c)—Led OHL playoffs with 67 penalty minutes.
(d)—June, 1983—Drafted as underage junior by Philadelphia Flyers in 1983 NHL entry draft. Fifth Flyers pick, 121st overall, sixth round.
(e)—Led OHL playoffs with 62 penalty minutes.
(f)—Led OHL playoffs witth 22 goals and co-leader (with teammate Wayne Groulx) with 36 points.

KEVIN TODD

Center . . . 5'11" . . . 180 lbs. . . . Born, Winnipeg, Manitoba, May 4, 1968 . . . Shoots left . . . (December, 1985)—Stretched knee ligaments.

Year	Team	League	Games	G.	A.	Pts.	Pen.
1984-85—Winnipeg Stars		Man. Midget	60	66	100	166	....
1985-86—Prince Albert Raiders (c)		WHL	55	14	25	39	19
1986-87—Prince Albert Raiders		WHL	71	39	46	85	92
1987-88—Prince Albert Raiders		WHL	72	49	72	121	83

(c)—June, 1986—Drafted as underage junior by New Jersey Devils in 1986 NHL entry draft. Seventh Devils pick, 129th overall, seventh round.

KIRK TOMLINSON

Center . . . 5'10" . . . 175 lbs. . . . Born, Toronto, Ont., March 2, 1968 . . . Shoots left.

Year	Team	League	Games	G.	A.	Pts.	Pen.
1984-85	New Westminster Bruins	WHL	66	9	14	23	48
1985-86	Hamilton Steelhawks (c)	OHL	58	28	23	51	230
1986-87	Hamilton Steelhawks	OHL	65	33	37	70	169
1987-88	Hamilton Steelhawks (d)	OHL	23	10	18	28	72
1987-88	Oshawa Generals	OHL	26	10	13	23	128

(c)—June, 1986—Drafted as underage junior by Minnesota North Stars in 1986 NHL entry draft. Seventh North Stars pick, 75th overall, fourth round.

(d)—January, 1988—Traded by Hamilton Steelhawks to Oshawa Generals for John Andersen.

JOHN TONELLI

Left Wing and Center . . . 6'1" . . . 190 lbs. . . . Born, Hamilton, Ont., March 23, 1957 . . . Shoots left . . . Did not take part in 1975 playoffs after signing pro contract . . . Brother of Ray Tonelli . . . (February, 1981)—Shoulder injury . . . Set N.Y. Islanders club record for left wings with 93 points in 1981-82 . . . (December, 1983)—Knee injury . . . (Fall, 1985)—Sat out 22 days of N.Y. Islanders' training camp in contract dispute.

Year	Team	League	Games	G.	A.	Pts.	Pen.
1973-74	Toronto Marlboros	Jr."A" OHA	69	18	37	55	62
1974-75	Toronto Marlboros (a-c)	Jr."A" OHA	70	49	86	135	85
1975-76	Houston Aeros	WHA	79	17	14	31	66
1976-77	Houston Aeros (d)	WHA	80	24	31	55	109
1977-78	Houston Aeros (e)	WHA	65	23	41	64	103
1978-79	New York Islanders	NHL	73	17	39	56	44
1979-80	New York Islanders	NHL	77	14	30	44	49
1980-81	New York Islanders	NHL	70	20	32	52	57
1981-82	New York Islanders (b)	NHL	80	35	58	93	57
1982-83	New York Islanders	NHL	76	31	40	71	55
1983-84	New York Islanders	NHL	73	27	40	67	66
1984-85	New York Islanders (b)	NHL	80	42	58	100	95
1985-86	New York Islanders (f)	NHL	65	20	41	61	50
1985-86	Calgary Flames	NHL	9	3	4	7	10
1986-87	Calgary Flames	NHL	78	20	31	51	72
1987-88	Calgary Flames (g)	NHL	74	17	41	58	84
	WHA TOTALS		224	64	86	150	278
	NHL TOTALS		755	246	414	660	639

(c)—March, 1975—Signed by Houston Aeros (WHA).

(d)—Drafted from Houston Aeros by New York Islanders in second round of 1977 amateur draft.

(e)—July, 1978—Signed to multi year contract by New York Islanders.

(f)—March, 1986—Traded by New York Islanders to Calgary Flames for Richard Kromm and Steve Konroyd.

(g)—July, 1988—Signed by Los Angeles Kings as a free agent.

TIMOTHY RAYMOND TOOKEY

Center . . . 5'11" . . . 180 lbs. . . . Born, Edmonton, Alta., August 29, 1960 . . . Shoots left . . . (December 30, 1981)—Sprained left ankle at Pittsburgh . . . (February, 1983)—Concussion . . . (April, 1983)—Injured shoulder during AHL playoffs . . . (December, 1987)—Knee surgery.

Year	Team	League	Games	G.	A.	Pts.	Pen.
1977-78	Portland Winter Hawks	WCHL	72	16	15	31	55
1978-79	Portland Winter Hawks (c)	WHL	56	33	47	80	55
1979-80	Portland Winter Hawks	WHL	70	58	83	141	55
1980-81	Hershey Bears	AHL	47	20	38	58	129
1980-81	Washington Capitals	NHL	29	10	13	23	18
1981-82	Washington Capitals (d)	NHL	28	8	8	16	35
1981-82	Hershey Bears	AHL	14	4	9	13	10
1981-82	Fredericton Express	AHL	16	6	10	16	16
1982-83	Quebec Nordiques	NHL	12	1	6	7	4
1982-83	Fredericton Express	AHL	53	24	43	67	24
1983-84	Pittsburgh Penguins (e)	NHL	8	0	2	2	2
1983-84	Baltimore Skipjacks	AHL	58	16	28	44	25
1984-85	Baltimore Skipjacks (f)	AHL	74	25	43	68	74
1985-86	Hershey Bears (a-g-h)	AHL	69	35	*62	97	66
1986-87	Hershey Bears (a-i-j)	AHL	80	51	*73	*124	45
1986-87	Philadelphia Flyers	NHL	2	0	0	0	0
1987-88	Los Angeles Kings (k)	NHL	20	1	6	7	8
1987-88	New Haven Nighthawks	AHL	11	6	7	13	2
	NHL TOTALS		99	20	35	55	67

(c)—August, 1979—Drafted by Washington Capitals as underage junior in 1979 NHL entry draft. Fourth Capitals pick, 88th overall, fifth round.
(d)—January, 1982—Traded by Washington Capitals to Quebec Nordiques for Lee Norwood.
(e)—August, 1983—Signed by Pittsburgh Penguins as a free agent.
(f)—August, 1985—Signed by Philadelphia Flyers as a free agent.
(g)—Led AHL Calder Cup Playoffs with 11 goals.
(h)—Won Jack Butterfield Trophy (Playoff MVP).
(i)—Winner of Les Cunningham Award (MVP).
(j)—Won John Sollenberger Trophy (Leading Scorer).
(k)—October, 1987—Selected by Los Angeles Kings in 1987 NHL waiver draft. The Kings put him on recallable waivers in an attempt to assign him to New Haven. Philadelphia claimed him. The Kings then recalled him from the waiver wire and assigned him to Los Angeles.

SEAN TOOMEY

Center . . . 6'2" . . . 190 lbs. . . . Born, St. Paul, Minn., June 27, 1965 . . . Shoots left.

Year	Team	League	Games	G.	A.	Pts.	Pen.
1982-83	St. Paul Cretin H.S. (c)	Minn. H.S.	23	48	32	80	..
1983-84	Univ. of Minnesota-Duluth	WCHA	29	3	5	8	8
1984-85	Univ. of Minnesota-Duluth	WCHA	43	6	7	13	14
1985-86	Univ. of Minnesota-Duluth	WCHA	33	23	11	34	10
1986-87	Univ. of Minnesota-Duluth	WCHA	39	26	17	43	34
1986-87	Minnesota North Stars	NHL	1	0	0	0	0
1986-87	Indianapolis Checkers	IHL	13	3	3	6	0
1987-88	Baltimore Skipjacks	AHL	49	15	18	33	12
1987-88	Kalamazoo Wings	IHL	23	12	5	17	2
	NHL TOTALS		1	0	0	0	0

(c)—June, 1983—Drafted by Minnesota North Stars in 1983 NHL entry draft. Eighth North Stars pick, 136th overall, seventh round.

LARRY TRADER

Defense . . . 6'2" . . . 186 lbs. . . . Born, Barry's Bay, Ont., July 7, 1963 . . . Shoots left . . . (October, 1984)—Knee surgery . . . (November, 1987)—Strained right knee ligaments.

Year	Team	League	Games	G.	A.	Pts.	Pen.
1979-80	Gloucester Tier II	OPJHL	50	13	20	33	70
1980-81	London Knights (c)	OPJHL	68	5	23	28	132
1981-82	London Knights	OHL	68	19	37	56	171
1982-83	Detroit Red Wings	NHL	15	0	2	2	6
1982-83	London Knights	OHL	39	16	28	44	67
1982-83	Adirondack Red Wings	AHL	6	2	2	4	4
1983-84	Adirondack Red Wings	AHL	80	13	28	41	89
1984-85	Adirondack Red Wings	AHL	6	0	4	4	0
1984-85	Detroit Red Wings	NHL	40	3	7	10	39
1985-86	Adirondack Red Wings (b-d)	AHL	64	10	46	56	77
1986-87	St. Louis Blues	NHL	5	0	0	0	8
1986-87	Team Canada	Int'l.	....	...	....	....	....
1987-88	St. Louis Blues (e)	NHL	1	0	0	0	2
1987-88	Sherbrooke Canadiens	AHL	11	2	2	4	25
1987-88	Montreal Canadiens (f)	NHL	30	2	4	6	19
	NHL TOTALS		91	5	13	18	74

(c)—June, 1981—Drafted as underage junior by Detroit Red Wings in 1981 NHL entry draft. Third Red Wings pick, 86th overall, fifth round.
(d)—August, 1986—Traded by Detroit Red Wings to St. Louis Blues for Lee Norwood.
(e)—October, 1987—Traded with third or fourth round 1989 draft pick by St. Louis Blues to Montreal Canadiens for Gaston Gingras and a third or fourth round 1989 draft pick.
(f)—August, 1989—Signed by Hartford Whalers as a free agent.

LADISLAV TRESL

Center . . . 6'1" . . . 180 lbs. . . . Born, Brno, Czechoslovakia, July 30, 1961 . . . Shoots left.

Year	Team	League	Games	G.	A.	Pts.	Pen.
1986-87	Zetor Brno (c)	Czech.	33	13	11	24	..
1987-88	Fredericton Express	AHL	30	6	16	22	16

(c)—June, 1987—Drafted by Quebec Nordiques in 1987 NHL entry draft. Tenth Nordiques pick, 183rd overall, ninth round.

DAVE TRETOWICZ

Defense . . . 5'11" . . . 186 lbs. . . . Born, Pittsfield, Mass., March 15, 1969 . . . Shoots left . . . Brother of Mark Tretowicz.

Year	Team	League	Games	G.	A.	Pts.	Pen.
1987-88—Clarkson Univ. (c)		ECAC	35	8	14	22	28

(c)—June, 1988—Drafted by Calgary Flames in 1988 NHL entry draft. Eleventh Flames pick, 231st overall, 11th round.

BRYAN JOHN TROTTIER

Center . . . 5'10" . . . 205 lbs. . . . Born, Val Marie, Sask., July 17, 1956 . . . Shoots left . . . (1975-76)—Set NHL records for most assists and points in rookie season (broken by Peter Stastny, 1980-81) . . . Set Stanley Cup Playoff record with 29 points during 1980 playoffs (broken by Mike Bossy's 35 points in 1981) . . . Set NHL record for consecutive playoff games with points (25) covering more than one season . . . Set NHL record for consecutive playoff games with points one season (18) . . . Brother of Monty Trottier and Rocky Trottier . . . (April, 1983)—Sprained left knee during playoff series against N.Y. Rangers . . . (January, 1984)—Injured left knee . . . (July, 1984)—Became U.S. citizen and played with Team USA in 1984 Canada Cup Tournament . . . (October, 1984)—Knee injury . . . (March, 1987)—Fined $1,000 by NHL for being critical of NHL officiating.

Year	Team	League	Games	G.	A.	Pts.	Pen.
1972-73—Swift Current Broncos		WCHL	67	16	29	45	10
1973-74—Swift Current Broncos (c)		WCHL	68	41	71	112	76
1974-75—Lethbridge Broncos (a)		WCHL	67	46	*98	144	103
1975-76—New York Islanders (d-e)		NHL	80	32	63	95	21
1976-77—New York Islanders		NHL	76	30	42	72	34
1977-78—New York Islanders (a)		NHL	77	46	*77	123	46
1978-79—New York Islanders (a-f-g-h)		NHL	76	47	*87	*134	50
1979-80—New York Islanders (i-j)		NHL	78	42	62	104	68
1980-81—New York Islanders (k)		NHL	73	31	72	103	74
1981-82—New York Islanders (b-l)		NHL	80	50	79	129	88
1982-83—New York Islanders		NHL	80	34	55	89	68
1983-84—New York Islanders (b)		NHL	68	40	71	111	59
1984-85—New York Islanders		NHL	68	28	31	59	47
1985-86—New York Islanders		NHL	78	37	59	96	72
1986-87—New York Islanders		NHL	80	23	64	87	50
1987-88—New York Islanders		NHL	77	30	52	82	48
NHL TOTALS			991	470	814	1284	725

(c)—Drafted from Swift Current Broncos by New York Islanders in second round of 1974 amateur draft.
(d)—Won Calder Memorial Trophy (NHL Rookie of the Year).
(e)—Selected NHL Rookie of the Year in poll of players by THE SPORTING NEWS.
(f)—Won Hart Memorial Trophy (NHL MVP).
(g)—Won Art Ross Trophy (NHL Top Scorer).
(h)—Named THE SPORTING NEWS NHL Player of the Year in poll of players.
(i)—Led Stanley Cup Playoffs in points (29) and co-leader, with Bill Barber, in goals (12).
(j)—Won Conn Smythe Trophy (NHL Playoff MVP).
(k)—Tied for Stanley Cup Playoffs assist lead (18 assists) with teammate Mike Bossy.
(l)—Led Stanley Cup Playoffs with 23 assists and 29 points.

STEVE TSUJIURA

Center . . . 5'5" . . . 155 lbs. . . . Born, Coaldale, Alta., February 28, 1962 . . . Shoots left . . . (February, 1985)—Strained knee ligaments.

Year	Team	League	Games	G.	A.	Pts.	Pen.
1977-78—Medicine Hat Tigers		WHL	17	5	8	13	0
1978-79—Medicine Hat Tigers		WHL	62	24	45	69	14
1979-80—Medicine Hat Tigers (c)		WHL	72	25	77	102	36
1980-81—Medicine Hat Tigers (b-c-d-e)		WHL	72	55	84	139	60
1981-82—Calgary Wranglers		WHL	37	26	53	79	33
1981-82—University of Calgary		CWUAA	.....	...	.....	.....	.....
1982-83—Maine Mariners		AHL	78	15	51	66	46
1983-84—Springfield Indians (f)		AHL	78	24	56	80	27
1984-85—Maine Mariners		AHL	69	28	38	66	40
1985-86—Maine Mariners (g)		AHL	80	31	55	86	34
1986-87—Maine Mariners		AHL	80	24	41	65	73
1987-88—Utica Devils (h)		AHL	54	15	32	47	55
1987-88—Maine Mariners		AHL	12	2	8	10	10

(c)—Won Frank Boucher Memorial Trophy (Most Gentlemanly).
(d)—Won WHL Most Valuable Player Trophy.
(e)—June, 1981—Drafted by Philadelphia Flyers in NHL entry draft. Thirteenth Flyers pick, 205th overall, 10th round.
(f)—July, 1984—Signed by New Jersey Devils as a free agent.
(g)—Won Fred Hunt Memorial Award (Sportsmanship, Determination and Dedication).
(h)—March, 1988—Traded by New Jersey Devils to Boston Bruins for a 10th round 1988 draft pick (Alexander Semak).

JOHN TUCKER

Center . . . 6' . . . 185 lbs. . . . Born, Windsor, Ont., September 29, 1964 . . . Shoots right . . . (November 7, 1984)—Broke bone in foot at Minnesota . . . (March 7, 1986)—Bruised shoulder vs. Hartford and missed five games . . . (January 28, 1987)—Injured disc in back vs. Philadelphia and required off-season surgery . . . (November 7, 1987)—Torn knee ligaments at Edmonton . . . (December, 1987)—Shoulder injury . . . (February 25, 1988)—Injured shoulder vs. St. Louis.

Year	Team	League	Games	G.	A.	Pts.	Pen.
1981-82	Kitchener Rangers	OHL	67	16	32	48	32
1982-83	Kitchener Rangers (c)	OHL	70	60	80	140	33
1983-84	Kitchener Rangers (a-d)	OHL	39	40	60	100	25
1983-84	Buffalo Sabres	NHL	21	12	4	16	4
1984-85	Buffalo Sabres	NHL	64	22	27	49	21
1985-86	Buffalo Sabres	NHL	75	31	34	65	39
1986-87	Buffalo Sabres	NHL	54	17	34	51	21
1987-88	Buffalo Sabres	NHL	45	19	19	38	20
	NHL TOTALS		259	101	118	219	105

(c)—June, 1983—Drafted as underage junior by Buffalo Sabres in 1983 NHL entry draft. Fourth Sabres pick, 31st overall, second round.

(d)—Won Red Tilson Trophy (Most Outstanding player).

ALLAN TUER

Defense . . . 6' . . . 175 lbs. . . . Born, North Battleford, Sask., July 19, 1963 . . . Shoots left.

Year	Team	League	Games	G.	A.	Pts.	Pen.
1980-81	Regina Pats (c)	WHL	31	0	7	7	58
1981-82	Regina Pats	WHL	63	2	18	20	*486
1982-83	Regina Pats	WHL	71	3	27	30	229
1983-84	New Haven Nighthawks	AHL	78	0	20	20	195
1984-85	New Haven Nighthawks	AHL	56	0	7	7	241
1985-86	New Haven Nighthawks	AHL	8	1	0	1	53
1985-86	Los Angeles Kings (d)	NHL	45	0	1	1	150
1986-87	Nova Scotia Oilers	AHL	31	0	1	1	4
1987-88	Minnesota North Stars	NHL	6	1	0	1	29
1987-88	Kalamazoo Wings (e-f)	IHL	68	2	15	17	303
	NHL TOTALS		51	1	1	2	179

(c)—June, 1980—Drafted as underage junior by Los Angeles Kings in NHL entry draft. Eighth Kings pick, 186th overall, ninth round.

(d)—August, 1986—Signed by Edmonton Oilers as a free agent.

(e)—October, 1987—Selected by Minnesota North Stars in 1987 NHL waiver draft.

(f)—August, 1988—Signed by Hartford Whalers as a free agent.

ALFIE TURCOTTE

Center . . . 5'10" . . . 175 lbs. . . . Born, Gary, Ind., June 5, 1965 . . . Shoots left . . . Son of Real Turcotte (Former Coach and General Manager of Nanaimo Islanders of WHL).

Year	Team	League	Games	G.	A.	Pts.	Pen.
1981-82	Detroit Compuware	Mich. Midget	93	131	152	283	40
1982-83	Nanaimo Islanders	WHL	36	23	27	50	22
1982-83	Portland Winter Hawks (c)	WHL	39	26	51	77	26
1983-84	Portland Winter Hawks	WHL	32	22	41	63	39
1983-84	Montreal Canadiens	NHL	30	7	7	14	10
1984-85	Montreal Canadiens	NHL	53	8	16	24	35
1985-86	Sherbrooke Canadiens	AHL	75	29	36	65	60
1985-86	Montreal Canadiens (d)	NHL	2	0	0	0	2
1986-87	Nova Scotia Oilers (e)	AHL	70	27	41	68	37
1987-88	Winnipeg Jets (f)	NHL	3	0	0	0	0
1987-88	Baltimore Skipjacks	AHL	33	21	33	54	42
1987-88	Moncton Golden Flames	AHL	25	12	25	37	18
1987-88	Sherbrooke Canadiens	AHL	8	3	8	11	4
	NHL TOTALS		88	15	23	38	47

(c)—June, 1983—Drafted as underage junior by Montreal Canadiens in 1983 NHL entry draft. First Canadiens pick, 17th overall, first round.

(d)—July, 1986—Traded by Montreal Canadiens to Edmonton Oilers for future considerations.

(e)—May, 1987—Sold by Edmonton Oilers to Montreal Canadiens.

(f)—January, 1988—Traded by Montreal Canadiens to Winnipeg Jets for future considerations.

DARREN TURCOTTE

Center . . . 6' . . . 170 lbs. . . . Born, Boston, Mass., March 2, 1968 . . . Shoots left . . . (October, 1987)—Missed 34 games due to shoulder separation.

Year	Team	League	Games	G.	A.	Pts.	Pen.
1984-85—North Bay Centennials		OHL	62	33	32	65	28
1985-86—North Bay Centennials (c)		OHL	62	35	37	72	35
1986-87—North Bay Centennials		OHL	55	30	48	78	20
1987-88—Colorado Rangers		IHL	8	4	3	7	9
1987-88—North Bay Centennials		OHL	32	30	33	63	16

(c)—June, 1986—Drafted as underage junior by New York Rangers in 1986 NHL entry draft. Sixth Rangers pick, 114th overall, sixth round.

PIERRE TURGEON

Center . . . 6'1" . . . 200 lbs. . . . Born, Noranda, Que., August 29, 1969 . . . Shoots left . . . Brother of Sylvain Turgeon . . . (June, 1985)—Knee surgery.

Year	Team	League	Games	G.	A.	Pts.	Pen.
1985-86—Granby Bisons		QHL	69	47	67	114	31
1986-87—Granby Bisons (c)		QHL	58	69	85	154	8
1987-88—Buffalo Sabres		NHL	76	14	28	42	34
NHL TOTALS			76	14	28	42	34

(c)—June, 1987—Drafted as underage junior by Buffalo Sabres in 1987 NHL entry draft. First Sabres pick, first overall, first round.

SYLVAIN TURGEON

Left Wing . . . 6' . . . 190 lbs. . . . Born, Noranda, Que., January 17, 1965 . . . Shoots left . . . Also plays center . . . Set Hartford club record for goals and points by an NHL rookie in 1983-84 . . . (October, 1984)—Pulled abdominal muscles . . . Brother of Pierre Turgeon . . . (November 14, 1986)—Abdominal surgery to repair torn stomach muscle and missed 39 games . . . (August 11, 1987)—Broken left arm when slashed by Ron Hextall during a Team Canada practice.

Year	Team	League	Games	G.	A.	Pts.	Pen.
1981-82—Hull Olympics (c)		QMJHL	57	33	40	73	78
1982-83—Hull Olympics (a-d-e)		QHL	67	54	109	163	103
1983-84—Hartford Whalers		NHL	76	40	32	72	55
1984-85—Hartford Whalers		NHL	64	31	31	62	67
1985-86—Hartford Whalers		NHL	76	45	34	79	88
1986-87—Hartford Whalers		NHL	41	23	13	36	45
1987-88—Hartford Whalers		NHL	71	23	26	49	71
NHL TOTALS			328	162	136	298	326

(c)—Won Des Instructeurs Trophy (Top Rookie Forward).
(d)—Won The Association of Journalist of Hockey Trophy (Top Pro Prospect).
(e)—June, 1983—Drafted as underage junior by Hartford Whalers in 1983 NHL entry draft. First Whalers pick, second overall, first round.

PERRY TURNBULL

Left Wing . . . 6'2" . . . 200 lbs. . . . Born, Bentley, Alta., March 9, 1959 . . . Shoots left . . . Cousin of Randy Turnbull . . . (April, 1982)—Severed tendon just above right knee in playoff mishap when cut by teammate's skate . . . (October 21, 1984)—Strained knee ligaments when checked by Terry O'Reilly vs. Boston . . . (October, 1986)—Dislocated shoulder.

Year	Team	League	Games	G.	A.	Pts.	Pen.
1974-75—The Pass Red Devils		AJHL	69	6	4	10	134
1975-76—The Pass Red Devils		AJHL	45	27	23	50	140
1975-76—Calgary Centennials		WCHL	19	6	7	13	14
1976-77—Calgary Centennials (c)		WCHL	10	8	5	13	33
1976-77—Portland Winter Hawks		WCHL	58	23	30	53	249
1977-78—Portland Winter Hawks		WCHL	57	36	27	63	318
1978-79—Portland Winter Hawks (d-e)		WHL	70	75	43	118	191
1979-80—St. Louis Blues		NHL	80	16	19	35	124
1980-81—St. Louis Blues		NHL	75	34	22	56	209
1981-82—St. Louis Blues		NHL	79	33	26	59	161
1982-83—St. Louis Blues		NHL	79	32	15	47	172
1983-84—St. Louis Blues (f)		NHL	32	14	8	22	81
1983-84—Montreal Canadiens (g)		NHL	40	6	7	13	59
1984-85—Winnipeg Jets		NHL	66	22	21	43	130
1985-86—Winnipeg Jets		NHL	80	20	31	51	183
1986-87—Winnipeg Jets (h)		NHL	26	1	5	6	44
1987-88—St. Louis Blues		NHL	51	10	9	19	82
1987-88—Peoria Rivermen		IHL	3	5	0	5	4
NHL TOTALS			608	188	163	351	1245

(c)—Traded to Portland Winter Hawks by Calgary Centennials for Doug Lecuyer and Dave Morrow, October, 1976.

(d)—Named Most Valuable Player of WHL.
(e)—August, 1979—Drafted by St. Louis Blues in 1979 entry draft. First Blues pick, second overall, first round.
(f)—December, 1983—Traded by St. Louis Blues to Montreal Canadiens for Gilbert Delorme, Greg Paslawski and Doug Wickenheiser.
(g)—June, 1984—Traded by Montreal Canadiens to Winnipeg Jets for Lucien DeBlois.
(h)—June, 1987—Traded by Winnipeg Jets to St. Louis Blues for a fifth-round 1987 draft pick (Ken Gernander).

BRAD TURNER

Defense . . . 6'2" . . . 200 lbs. . . . Born, Winnipeg, Manitoba, May 25, 1968 . . . Shoots right.

Year	Team	League	Games	G.	A.	Pts.	Pen.
1984-85—Darien H.S.		Conn.	24	32	34	66	....
1985-86—Calgary Canucks (c)		AJHL	52	14	21	35	109
1986-87—Univ. of Michigan		CCHA	40	3	10	13	40
1987-88—Univ. of Michigan		CCHA	39	3	11	14	52

(c)—June, 1986—Drafted by Minnesota North Stars in 1986 NHL entry draft. Sixth North Stars pick, 58th overall, third round.

BRIAN TUTT

Defense . . . 6'1" . . . 195 lbs. . . . Born, Swallwell, Alta., June 9, 1962 . . . Shoots left . . . (September, 1981)—Broke leg while attending Philadelphia Flyers training camp.

Year	Team	League	Games	G.	A.	Pts.	Pen.
1979-80—Calgary Canucks		AJHL	59	6	14	20	55
1979-80—Calgary Wranglers (c)		WHL	2	0	0	0	2
1980-81—Calgary Wranglers		WHL	72	10	41	51	111
1981-82—Calgary Wranglers		WHL	40	2	16	18	85
1982-83—Toledo Goaldiggers		IHL	42	7	13	20	56
1982-83—Maine Mariners		AHL	31	0	0	0	28
1983-84—Toledo Goaldiggers (b)		IHL	82	7	44	51	79
1983-84—Springfield Indians		AHL	1	0	0	0	2
1984-85—Hershey Bears		AHL	3	0	0	0	8
1984-85—Kalamazoo Wings (b)		IHL	80	8	45	53	62
1985-86—Kalamazoo Wings		IHL	82	11	39	50	129
1986-87—Maine Mariners		AHL	41	6	15	21	19
1986-87—Kalamazoo Wings		IHL	19	2	7	9	10
1987-88—New Haven Nighthawks		AHL	32	1	12	13	33

(c)—June, 1980—Drafted as underage junior by Philadelphia Flyers in NHL entry draft. Sixth Flyers pick, 126th overall, sixth round.

STEVE TUTTLE

Right Wing . . . 6'1" . . . 180 lbs. . . . Born, Vancouver, B.C., January 5, 1966 . . . Shoots right.

Year	Team	League	Games	G.	A.	Pts.	Pen.
1983-84—Richmond (c)		BCJHL	46	46	34	80	22
1984-85—University of Wisconsin		WCHA	28	3	4	7	0
1985-86—University of Wisconsin		WCHA	32	2	10	12	2
1986-87—University of Wisconsin		WCHA	42	31	21	52	14
1987-88—University of Wisconsin (d)		WCHA	45	27	39	66	18

(c)—June, 1984—Drafted by St. Louis Blues in NHL entry draft. Eighth Blues pick, 113th overall, sixth round.

(d)—Named second-team All-America (West).

TONY TWIST

Defense . . . 6' . . . 210 lbs. . . . Born, Sherwood Park, Alta., May 9, 1968 . . . Shoots left . . . (January 28, 1988)—Suspended three WHL games and fined $250 for leaving the penalty box to fight.

Year	Team	League	Games	G.	A.	Pts.	Pen.
1986-87—Saskatoon Blades		WHL	64	0	8	8	181
1987-88—Saskatoon Blades (c)		WHL	55	1	8	9	226

(c)—June, 1988—Drafted by St. Louis Blues in 1988 NHL entry draft. Ninth Blues pick, 177th overall, ninth round.

RICK VAIVE

Right Wing . . . 6' . . . 180 lbs. . . . Born, Ottawa, Ont., May 14, 1959 . . . Shoots right . . . (February, 1981)—Slight groin pull . . . First Toronto Maple Leafs player to have a 50-goal season when he set a club record with 54 goals in 1981-82 . . . (February 25, 1984)—Injured

ankle at Edmonton . . . (December, 1984)—Knee injury . . . (November 27, 1985)—Injured hand at Pittsburgh and missed five games . . . (December 23, 1985)—Injured hand and missed 12 games . . . (October, 1986)—Pinched nerve in neck.

Year	Team	League	Games	G.	A.	Pts.	Pen.
1976-77—Sherbrooke Beavers (c)		QJHL	68	51	59	110	91
1977-78—Sherbrooke Beavers (d)		QJHL	68	76	79	155	199
1978-79—Birmingham Bulls (e)		WHA	75	26	33	59	*248
1979-80—Vancouver Canucks (f)		NHL	47	13	8	21	111
1979-80—Toronto Maple Leafs		NHL	22	9	7	16	77
1980-81—Toronto Maple Leafs		NHL	75	33	29	62	229
1981-82—Toronto Maple Leafs		NHL	77	54	35	89	157
1982-83—Toronto Maple Leafs		NHL	78	51	28	79	105
1983-84—Toronto Maple Leafs		NHL	76	52	41	93	114
1984-85—Toronto Maple Leafs		NHL	72	35	33	68	112
1985-86—Toronto Maple Leafs		NHL	61	33	31	64	85
1986-87—Toronto Maple Leafs (g)		NHL	73	32	34	66	61
1987-88—Chicago Black Hawks		NHL	76	43	26	69	108
WHA TOTALS			75	26	33	59	248
NHL TOTALS			657	355	272	627	1159

(c)—Won Rookie of the Year Award.
(d)—July, 1978—Signed by Birmingham Bulls (WHA) as underage junior.
(e)—Drafted by Vancouver Canucks in entry draft. First Vancouver pick, fifth overall, first round.
(f)—February, 1980—Traded with Bill Derlago by Vancouver Canucks to Toronto Maple Leafs for Dave Williams and Jerry Butler.
(g)—September, 1987—Traded with Steve Thomas and Bob McGill by Toronto Maple Leafs to Chicago Black Hawks for Al Secord and Ed Olczyk.

CARL VALIMONT

Defense . . . 6'1" . . . 180 lbs. . . . Born, Southington, Conn., March 1, 1966 . . . Shoots left.

Year	Team	League	Games	G.	A.	Pts.	Pen.
1984-85—University of Lowell (c)		H. East	40	4	11	15	24
1985-86—University of Lowell		H. East	26	1	9	10	12
1986-87—University of Lowell		H. East	36	8	9	17	36
1987-88—University of Lowell		H. East	38	6	26	32	59

(c)—June, 1985—Drafted by Vancouver Canucks in 1985 NHL entry draft. Tenth Canucks pick, 193rd overall, 10th round.

GARRY VALK

Left Wing . . . 6'1" . . . 190 lbs. . . . Born, Edmonton, Alta., November 27, 1967 . . . Shoots left . . . Also plays Right Wing.

Year	Team	League	Games	G.	A.	Pts.	Pen.
1985-86—Sherwood Park Crusaders		AJHL	40	20	26	46	116
1986-87—Sherwood Park Crusaders (c)		AJHL	59	42	44	86	204
1987-88—Univ. of North Dakota		WCHA	38	23	12	35	64

(c)—June, 1987—Drafted by Vancouver Canucks in 1987 NHL entry draft. Fifth Canucks pick, 108th overall, sixth round.

SHAWN VAN ALLEN

Center . . . 6'1" . . . 200 lbs. . . . Born, Shaunavon, Sask., August 29, 1967 . . . Shoots left.

Year	Team	League	Games	G.	A.	Pts.	Pen.
1984-85—Swift Current		SAJHL	61	12	20	32	136
1985-86—Saskatoon Blades		WHL	55	12	11	23	43
1986-87—Saskatoon Blades (c)		WHL	72	38	59	97	116
1987-88—Nova Scotia Oilers		AHL	19	4	10	14	17
1987-88—Milwaukee Admirals		IHL	40	14	28	42	34

(c)—June, 1987—Drafted by Edmonton Oilers in 1987 NHL entry draft. Fifth Oilers pick, 105th overall, fifth round.

WAYNE VAN DORP

Right Wing . . . 6'5" . . . 230 lbs. . . . Born, Vancouver, B.C., May 19, 1961 . . . Shoots right . . . (February, 1988)—Injured right knee in collision with Bryan Erickson during a team practice.

Year	Team	League	Games	G.	A.	Pts.	Pen.
1978-79—Billington		BCJHL	61	18	30	48	66
1979-80—Seattle Breakers		WHL	68	8	13	21	195
1980-81—Seattle Breakers		WHL	63	22	30	52	242
1981-82—.......			....	...	....	....	....
1982-83—.......			....	...	....	....	....

Year	Team	League	Games	G.	A.	Pts.	Pen.
1983-84—Erie Blades		ACHL	45	19	18	37	131
1984-85—Erie Blades		ACHL	7	9	8	17	21
1985-86—.......		Holland	29	27	32	59	69
1986-87—Rochester Americans (c)		AHL	47	7	3	10	192
1986-87—Nova Scotia Oilers		AHL	11	2	3	5	37
1986-87—Edmonton Oilers		NHL	3	0	0	0	25
1987-88—Pittsburgh Penguins (d)		NHL	25	1	3	4	75
1987-88—Nova Scotia Oilers		AHL	12	2	2	4	87
NHL TOTALS			28	1	3	4	100

(c)—March, 1987—Traded with Norm Lacombe and future considerations by Buffalo Sabres to Edmonton Oilers for Lee Fogolin and Mark Napier.

(d)—November, 1987—Traded with Paul Coffey and Dave Hunter by Edmonton Oilers to Pittsburgh Penguins for Chris Joseph, Craig Simpson, Dave Hannan and Moe Mantha.

JOHN VanKESSEL

Right Wing . . . 6'4" . . . 180 lbs. . . . Born, Bridgewater, Ont., December 19, 1969 . . . Shoots right.

Year	Team	League	Games	G.	A.	Pts.	Pen.
1985-86—Antigosh Midget		N. Scotia	83	52	65	117	40
1986-87—Belleville Bulls		OHL	61	1	10	11	58
1987-88—North Bay Centennials (c)		OHL	50	13	16	29	214

(c)—June, 1988—Drafted by Los Angeles Kings in 1988 NHL entry draft. Third Kings pick, 49th overall, third round.

ERNESTO VARGAS

Center . . . 6'2" . . . 205 lbs. . . . Born, St. Paul, Minn., January 3, 1964 . . . Shoots left . . . Also plays Left Wing . . . (December 13, 1987)—Injured ankle in AHL game at Baltimore.

Year	Team	League	Games	G.	A.	Pts.	Pen.
1981-82—Coon Rapids H.S. (c)		Minn. H.S.	24	28	28	56	22
1982-83—University of Wisconsin		WCHA	37	2	4	6	32
1983-84—University of Wisconsin		WCHA	36	5	15	20	32
1984-85—University of Wisconsin		WCHA	42	8	16	24	68
1985-86—University of Wisconsin		WCHA	41	20	23	43	67
1986-87—Sherbrooke Canadiens		AHL	69	22	32	54	52
1987-88—Baltimore Skipjacks		AHL	5	1	0	1	2
1987-88—Sherbrooke Canadiens		AHL	31	6	21	27	48
1987-88—Peoria Rivermen (d)		IHL	31	9	13	22	26

(c)—June, 1982—Drafted as underage player by Montreal Canadiens in 1982 NHL entry draft. Ninth Canadiens pick, 117th overall, sixth round.

(d)—February, 1988—Traded by Montreal Canadiens to St. Louis Blues for a conditional 1989 draft pick.

DENNIS VASKE

Defense . . . 6'2" . . . 210 lbs. . . . Born, Rockford, Ill., October 11, 1967 . . . Shoots left.

Year	Team	League	Games	G.	A.	Pts.	Pen.
1984-85—Armstrong H.S.		Minn.	22	5	18	23	..
1985-86—Armstrong H.S. (c)		Minn.	20	9	13	22	..
1986-87—Univ. of Minn./Duluth		WCHA	33	0	2	2	40
1987-88—Univ. of Minn./Duluth		WCH	39	1	6	7	90

(c)—June, 1986—Drafted by New York Islanders in 1986 NHL entry draft. Second Islanders pick, 38th overall, second round.

STEVE VEILLEUX

Defense . . . 6' . . . 190 lbs. . . . Born, Montreal, Que., March 9, 1969 . . . Shoots right . . . Cousin of Corrado Micalef.

Year	Team	League	Games	G.	A.	Pts.	Pen.
1985-86—Trois-Rivieres Draveurs		QHL	67	1	20	21	132
1986-87—Trois-Rivieres Draveurs (c)		QHL	62	6	22	28	227
1987-88—Trois-Rivieres Draveurs (b)		QHL	63	7	25	32	150

(c)—June, 1987—Drafted as underage junior by Vancouver Canucks in 1987 NHL entry draft. Second Canucks pick, 45th overall, third round.

DARREN WILLIAM VEITCH

Defense . . . 5'11" . . . 188 lbs. . . . Born, Saskatoon, Sask., April 24, 1960 . . . Shoots right . . . (October 27, 1982)—Fractured collarbone in three places at Pittsburgh . . . (February 19, 1983)—Broke collarbone again at Los Angeles . . . (February 11, 1984)—Suffered broken ribs vs. Philadelphia . . . (January, 1985)—Bruised ribs . . . (March, 1988)—Injured ankle.

Year	Team	League	Games	G.	A.	Pts.	Pen.
1976-77—Regina Blues		SJHL	60	15	21	36	121
1976-77—Regina Pats		WCHL	1	0	0	0	0
1977-78—Regina Pats		WCHL	71	13	32	45	135
1978-79—Regina Pats		WHL	51	11	36	47	80
1979-80—Regina Pats (a-c)		WHL	71	29	*93	122	118
1980-81—Hershey Bears		AHL	26	6	22	28	12
1980-81—Washington Capitals		NHL	59	4	21	25	46
1981-82—Hershey Bears		AHL	10	5	10	15	16
1981-82—Washington Capitals		NHL	67	9	44	53	54
1982-83—Hershey Bears		AHL	5	0	1	1	2
1982-83—Washington Capitals		NHL	10	0	8	8	0
1983-84—Washington Capitals		NHL	46	6	18	24	17
1983-84—Hershey Bears		AHL	11	1	6	7	4
1984-85—Washington Capitals		NHL	75	3	18	21	37
1985-86—Washington Capitals (d)		NHL	62	3	9	12	27
1985-86—Detroit Red Wings		NHL	13	0	5	5	2
1986-87—Detroit Red Wings		NHL	77	13	45	58	52
1987-88—Detroit Red Wings (e)		NHL	63	7	33	40	45
NHL TOTALS			472	45	201	246	280

(c)—June, 1980—Drafted by Washington Capitals in 1980 NHL entry draft. First Capitals pick, fifth overall, first round.

(d)—March, 1986—Traded by Washington Capitals to Detroit Red Wings for John Barrett and Greg Smith.

(e)—June, 1988—Traded by Detroit Red Wings to Toronto Maple Leafs for Miroslav Frycer.

RANDY VELISCHEK

Defense . . . 6' . . . 200 lbs. . . . Born, Montreal, Que., February 10, 1962 . . . Shoots left.

Year	Team	League	Games	G.	A.	Pts.	Pen.
1979-80—Providence College (c)		ECAC	31	5	5	10	20
1980-81—Providence College		ECAC	33	3	12	15	26
1981-82—Providence College (b)		ECAC	33	1	14	15	34
1982-83—Providence College (a-d-e)		ECAC	41	18	34	52	50
1982-83—Minnesota North Stars		NHL	3	0	0	0	2
1983-84—Salt Lake Golden Eagles		CHL	43	7	21	28	54
1983-84—Minnesota North Stars		NHL	33	2	2	4	10
1984-85—Springfield Indians		AHL	26	2	7	9	22
1984-85—Minnesota North Stars		NHL	52	4	9	13	26
1985-86—New Jersey Devils (f)		NHL	47	2	7	9	39
1985-86—Maine Mariners		AHL	21	0	4	4	4
1986-87—New Jersey Devils		NHL	64	2	16	18	54
1987-88—New Jersey Devils		NHL	51	3	9	12	66
NHL TOTALS			250	13	43	56	197

(c)—June, 1980—Drafted by Minnesota North Stars as underage player in 1980 NHL entry draft. Third North Stars pick, 53rd overall, third round.

(d)—ECAC Player of the Year.

(e)—NCAA All-America Team (East).

(f)—Acquired by New Jersey Devils in 1985 NHL waiver draft.

MIKE VELLUCCI

Defense . . . 6'1" . . . 180 lbs. . . . Born, Farmington, Mich., August 11, 1966 . . . Shoots left . . . (August, 1984)—Missed season with fractured vertebrae in automobile accident . . . (March, 1987)—Injured collarbone.

Year	Team	League	Games	G.	A.	Pts.	Pen.
1982-83—Detroit Compuware		Mich. Midget	70	23	20	43	98
1983-84—Belleville Bulls (c)		OHL	67	2	20	22	83
1984-85—Belleville Bulls		OHL	..	..	..	..	....
1985-86—Belleville Bulls		OHL	64	11	32	43	154
1986-87—Salt Lake Golden Eagles		IHL	60	5	30	35	94
1987-88—Hartford Whalers		NHL	2	0	0	0	11
1987-88—Binghamton Whalers		AHL	3	0	0	0	2
1987-88—Milwaukee Admirals		IHL	66	7	18	25	202
NHL TOTALS			2	0	0	0	11

(c)—June, 1984—Drafted as underage junior by Hartford Whalers in NHL entry draft. Third Whalers pick, 131st overall, seventh round.

CHRIS VENKUS

Right Wing . . . 5'11" . . . 190 lbs. . . . Born, Hinsdale, Ill., April 14, 1969 . . . Shoots right.

Year	Team	League	Games	G.	A.	Pts.	Pen.
1986-87—St. Mike's Jr. B		MTHL	29	12	17	29	104
1987-88—Western Michigan Univ. (c)		CCHA	42	8	9	17	76

(c)—June, 1988—Drafted by Washington Capitals in 1988 NHL entry draft. Thirteenth Capitals pick, 225th overall, 11th round.

STEPHANE VENNE

Defense ... 6'3" ... 210 lbs. ... Born, Montreal, Que., April 29, 1969 ... Shoots right.

Year	Team	League	Games	G.	A.	Pts.	Pen.
1987-88—Univ. of Vermont (c)		ECAC	31	9	12	21	64

(c)—June, 1988—Drafted by Quebec Nordiques in 1988 NHL entry draft. Sixth Nordiques pick, 87th overall, fifth round.

PAT VERBEEK

Center ... 5'9" ... 195 lbs. ... Born, Sarnia, Ont., May 24, 1964 ... Shoots right ... (May 15, 1985)—Left thumb severed between knuckles in a corn planting machine on his farm near Forest, Ontario. Doctors reconnected the thumb surgically ... Brother of Brian Verbeek ... (March, 1987)—Pulled side muscle.

Year	Team	League	Games	G.	A.	Pts.	Pen.
1980-81—Petrolia Jr. B.		OPJHL	42	44	44	88	155
1981-82—Sudbury Wolves (c-d)		OHL	66	37	51	88	180
1982-83—Sudbury Wolves		OHL	61	40	67	107	184
1982-83—New Jersey Devils		NHL	6	3	2	5	8
1983-84—New Jersey Devils		NHL	79	20	27	47	158
1984-85—New Jersey Devils		NHL	78	15	18	33	162
1985-86—New Jersey Devils		NHL	76	25	28	53	79
1986-87—New Jersey Devils		NHL	74	35	24	59	120
1987-88—New Jersey Devils		NHL	73	46	31	77	227
NHL TOTALS			386	144	130	274	754

(c)—Winner of Emms Family Award (Rookie of the Year).
(d)—June, 1982—Drafted as underage junior by New Jersey Devils in 1982 NHL entry draft. Third Devils pick, 43rd overall, third round.

MARK VERMETTE

Right Wing ... 6'1" ... 190 lbs. ... Born, Cochenour, Ont., October 3, 1967 ... Shoots right.

Year	Team	League	Games	G.	A.	Pts.	Pen.
1985-86—Lake Superior State Univ. (c)		CCHA	32	1	4	5	7
1986-87—Lake Superior State Univ.		CCHA	38	19	17	36	59
1987-88—Lake Superior State Univ.		CCHA	46	45	29	74	154

(c)—June, 1988—Drafted by Quebec Nordiques in 1986 NHL entry draft. Eighth Nordiques pick, 134th overall, seventh round.

LEIGH VERSTRAETE

Right Wing ... 5'11" ... 183 lbs. ... Born, Pincher Creek, Alta., January 6, 1962 ... Shoots right.

Year	Team	League	Games	G.	A.	Pts.	Pen.
1981-82—Calgary Wranglers (c)		WHL	49	19	20	39	385
1982-83—Calgary Wranglers		WHL	4	0	1	1	11
1982-83—Toronto Maple Leafs		NHL	3	0	0	0	5
1982-83—St. Catharines Saints		AHL	61	5	3	8	221
1983-84—St. Catharines Saints		AHL	51	0	7	7	183
1983-84—Muskegon Mohawks		IHL	19	5	5	10	123
1984-85—Toronto Maple Leafs		NHL	2	0	0	0	0
1984-85—St. Catharines Saints		AHL	43	5	8	13	164
1985-86—St. Catharines Saints		AHL	75	8	12	20	300
1986-87—Newmarket Saints		AHL	57	9	7	16	179
1987-88—Newmarket Saints		AHL	12	4	3	7	38
1987-88—Toronto Maple Leafs		NHL	3	0	1	1	9
NHL TOTALS			8	0	1	1	14

(c)—June, 1982—Drafted by Toronto Maple Leafs in 1982 NHL entry draft. Thirteenth Maple Leafs pick, 192nd overall, 10th round.

JIM VESEY

Center ... 6'1" ... 200 lbs. ... Born, Columbus, Mass., September 29, 1965 ... Shoots right.

Year	Team	League	Games	G.	A.	Pts.	Pen.
1984-85—Merrimack College (c)		ECAC-II	33	19	11	30	28
1985-86—Merrimack College		ECAC-II	32	29	32	61	67

Year	Team	League	Games	G.	A.	Pts.	Pen.
1986-87—Merrimack College		ECAC	35	22	36	58	57
1987-88—Merrimack College		ECAC	40	40	55	95	95

(c)—June, 1984—Drafted by St. Louis Blues in 1984 NHL entry draft. Eleventh Blues pick, 155th overall, eighth round.

GREG VEY

Center . . . 6'1" . . . 190 lbs. . . . Born, Toronto, Ont., June 20, 1967 . . . Shoots left . . . Also plays either Wing.

Year	Team	League	Games	G.	A.	Pts.	Pen.
1983-84—Pickering Jr. B.		OHA	42	5	19	24	45
1984-85—Peterborough Petes (c)		OHL	61	11	15	26	25
1985-86—Peterborough Petes		OHL	61	14	20	34	49
1986-87—Peterborough Petes		OHL	57	8	22	30	105
1987-88—London Knights (d)		OHL	35	9	11	20	49

(c)—June, 1985—Drafted as underage junior by Toronto Maple Leafs in 1985 NHL entry draft. Fourth Maple Leafs pick, 64th overall, fourth round.

(d)—October, 1987—Traded with Billie MacMillan by Peterborough Petes to London Knights for a 1989 fifth-round draft pick.

DENNIS VIAL

Defense . . . 6'1" . . . 195 lbs. . . . Born, Sault Ste. Marie, Ont., April 10, 1969 . . . Shoots left . . . (October, 1986)—Suspended three OHL games for spearing.

Year	Team	League	Games	G.	A.	Pts.	Pen.
1984-85—Sault Ste. Marie Legion Midgets		OHA	31	4	19	23	40
1985-86—Hamilton Steelhawks		OHL	31	1	1	2	66
1986-87—Hamilton Steelhawks		OHL	53	1	8	9	194
1987-88—Hamilton Steelhawks (c)		OHL	52	3	17	20	229

(c)—June, 1988—Drafted by New York Rangers in 1988 NHL entry draft. Fifth Rangers pick, 110th overall, sixth round.

MARK VICHOREK

Defense . . . 6'3" . . . 207 lbs. . . . Born, Moose Lake, Minn., August 11, 1966 . . . Shoots right.

Year	Team	League	Games	G.	A.	Pts.	Pen.
1981-82—Sioux City Musketeers (c)		USHL	48	11	27	38	111
1982-83—Lake Superior State Univ.		CCHA	36	2	13	15	24
1983-84—Lake Superior State Univ.		CCHA	40	3	8	11	14
1984-85—Lake Superior State Univ.		CCHA	44	4	11	15	36
1985-86—Lake Superior State Univ.		CCHA	41	9	11	20	40
1986-87—Binghamton Whalers (d)		AHL	64	1	12	13	63
1986-87—Salt Lake Golden Eagles		IHL	16	1	0	1	32
1987-88—Binghamton Whalers		AHL	26	0	4	4	48
1987-88—Milwaukee Admirals		IHL	49	4	5	9	67

(c)—June, 1982—Drafted by Philadelphia Flyers in 1982 NHL entry draft. Twelfth Flyers pick, 245th overall, 12th round.

(d)—August, 1986—Signed by Hartford Whalers as a free agent.

CLAUDE VILGRAIN

Right Wing . . . 6'1" . . . 195 lbs. . . . Born, Port-au-Prince, Haiti, March 1, 1963 . . . Shoots right . . . First Haitian-born player in the NHL.

Year	Team	League	Games	G.	A.	Pts.	Pen.
1983-84—Univ. of Moncton (c)		AUAA	20	11	20	31	8
1984-85—Univ. of Moncton		AUAA	24	35	28	63	20
1985-86—Univ. of Moncton		AUAA	19	17	20	37	25
1986-87—Canadian Olympic Team		Int'l	78	28	42	70	38
1987-88—Canadian Olympic Team (d)		Int'l	67	21	20	41	41
1987-88—Vancouver Canucks		NHL	6	1	1	2	0
NHL TOTALS			6	1	1	2	0

(c)—June, 1982—Drafted by Detroit Red Wings in 1982 NHL entry draft. Sixth Red Wings pick, 107th overall, sixth round.

(d)—June, 1987—Signed by Vancouver Canucks as a free agent.

ANDRE VILLENEUVE

Defense . . . 6'3" . . . 190 lbs. . . . Born, Alma, Que., January 19, 1963 . . . Shoots left . . . (September, 1985)—Broken leg.

Year	Team	League	Games	G.	A.	Pts.	Pen.
1979-80—Chicoutimi Sagueneens		QMJHL	4	0	2	2	0
1980-81—Chicoutimi Sagueneens (c)		QMJHL	62	10	23	33	92

Year	Team	League	Games	G.	A.	Pts.	Pen.
1981-82—Chicoutimi Sagueneens		QMJHL	51	11	39	50	97
1982-83—Chicoutimi Sagueneens		QHL	68	24	63	87	76
1983-84—Springfield Indians		AHL	8	1	5	6	6
1984-85—Did not play			..	..	..	..	..
1985-86—Hershey Bears		AHL	33	2	7	9	18
1986-87—Hershey Bears (d)		AHL	5	0	2	2	2
1986-87—Sherbrooke Canadiens		AHL	51	3	16	19	69
1987-88—Sherbrooke Canadiens		AHL	61	4	21	25	122

(c)—June, 1981—Drafted as underage junior by Philadelphia Flyers in 1981 NHL entry draft. Eighth Flyers pick, 121st overall, sixth round.

(d)—November, 1986—Traded by Philadelphia Flyers to Montreal Canadiens for Dominic Campedelli.

DANIEL VINCELETTE

Left Wing . . . 6'1" . . . 202 lbs. . . . Born, Verdun, Que., August 1, 1967 . . . Shoots left . . . (December, 1983)—Knee surgery . . . (February, 1988)—Bruised ribs.

Year	Team	League	Games	G.	A.	Pts.	Pen.
1983-84—Magog Cantonniers		Que. Midget	40	9	13	22	43
1984-85—Drummondville Voltigeurs (c)		QHL	64	11	24	35	124
1985-86—Drummondville Voltigeurs		QHL	70	37	47	84	234
1986-87—Drummondville Voltigeurs		QHL	50	34	35	69	288
1986-87—Chicago Black Hawks (d)		NHL	....	...	....	....	....
1987-88—Chicago Black Hawks		NHL	69	6	11	17	109
NHL TOTALS			69	6	11	17	109

(c)—June, 1985—Drafted as underage junior by Chicago Black Hawks in 1985 NHL entry draft. Third Black Hawks pick, 74th overall, fourth round.

(d)—No regular season record. Played three playoff games.

EMANUEL VIVEIROS

Defense . . . 5'11" . . . 160 lbs. . . . Born, St. Albert, Alta., January 8, 1966 . . . Shoots left.

Year	Team	League	Games	G.	A.	Pts.	Pen.
1982-83—Prince Albert Raiders		WHL	59	6	26	32	55
1983-84—Prince Albert Raiders (b-c)		WHL	67	15	94	109	48
1984-85—Prince Albert Raiders (b)		WHL	68	17	71	88	94
1985-86—Prince Albert Raiders (a-d-e-f)		WHL	57	22	70	92	30
1985-86—Minnesota North Stars		NHL	4	0	1	1	0
1986-87—Minnesota North Stars		NHL	1	0	1	1	0
1986-87—Springfield Indians		AHL	76	7	35	42	38
1987-88—Kalamazoo Wings		IHL	57	15	48	63	41
1987-88—Minnesota North Stars		NHL	24	1	9	10	6
NHL TOTALS			29	1	11	12	6

(c)—June, 1984—Drafted as underage junior by Edmonton Oilers in NHL entry draft. Sixth Oilers pick, 106th overall, sixth round.

(d)—Named best WHL Defenseman (East).

(e)—Named WHL MVP (East).

(f)—December, 1985—Traded by Edmonton Oilers with Marc Habscheid and Don Barber to Minnesota North Stars for Gord Sherven and Don Biggs.

DAVID VOLEK

Right Wing . . . 6' . . . 183 lbs. . . . Born, Czechoslovakia, June 18, 1966 . . . Shoots right.

Year	Team	League	Games	G.	A.	Pts.	Pen.
1986-87—Sparta Praha (c)		Czech.	39	27	25	52	....
1987-88—Sparta Praha		Czech.	30	18	12	30	....

(c)—June, 1984—Drafted by New York Islanders in 1984 NHL entry draft. Eleventh Islanders pick, 208th overall, 10th round.

TROY VOLLHOFFER

Left Wing . . . 5'11" . . . 180 lbs. . . . Born, Regina, Sask., February 9, 1966 . . . Shoots left.

Year	Team	League	Games	G.	A.	Pts.	Pen.
1982-83—Regina Pats		WHL	2	0	1	1	0
1982-83—Regina Canadians		SMJHL	68	65	74	139	96
1983-84—Winnipeg Warriors		WHL	66	22	37	59	92
1984-85—Saskatoon Blades		WHL	50	18	24	42	64
1984-85—New Westminster Bruins		WHL	12	3	7	10	18
1985-86—Saskatoon Blades		WHL	72	55	55	110	118
1986-87—Baltimore Skipjacks (c)		AHL	67	11	25	36	90
1987-88—Muskegon Lumberjacks		IHL	33	4	13	17	54
1987-88—New Haven Nighthawks		AHL	18	2	6	8	30

(c)—October, 1986—Signed by Baltimore Skipjacks as a free agent.

PHIL VonSTEFENELLI

Defense . . . 6'1" . . . 185 lbs. . . . Born, Vancouver, B.C., April 10, 1969 . . . Shoots left.

Year	Team	League	Games	G.	A.	Pts.	Pen.
1986-87	Richmond Jr. A	BCJHL	35	5	19	24	14
1987-88	Boston Univ. (c)	H. East	34	3	13	16	38

(c)—June, 1988—Drafted by Vancouver Canucks in 1988 NHL entry draft. Fifth Canucks pick, 122nd overall, sixth round.

RALPH VOS

Left Wing . . . 6'2" . . . 185 lbs. . . . Born, Guelph, Ont., January 5, 1964 . . . Shoots right.

Year	Team	League	Games	G.	A.	Pts.	Pen.
1983-84	Northern Michigan Univ. (c)	WCHA	39	7	28	35	26
1984-85	Northern Michigan Univ.	WCHA	39	12	37	49	52
1985-86	Northern Michigan Univ.	WCHA	39	12	36	48	42
1986-87	Northern Michigan Univ.	WCHA	18	4	12	16	18
1987-88	Nova Scotia Oilers	AHL	17	0	4	4	10
1987-88	Milwaukee Admirals	IHL	30	10	16	26	17

(c)—June, 1983—Drafted by Edmonton Oilers in 1983 NHL entry draft. Seventh Oilers pick, 166th overall, eighth round.

MICHAEL VUKONICH

Center . . . 6'1" . . . 190 lbs. . . . Born, Duluth, Minn., November 5, 1968 . . . Shoots left . . . Coached by his father at Duluth Denfeld H.S.

Year	Team	League	Games	G.	A.	Pts.	Pen.
1985-86	Duluth Denfeld Hunters	Minn. H.S.	24	14	20	34	....
1986-87	Duluth Denfeld Hunters (c)	Minn. H.S.	22	30	23	53	....
1987-88	Harvard University	ECAC	32	9	14	23	24

(c)—June, 1987—Drafted by Los Angeles Kings in 1987 NHL entry draft. Fourth Kings pick, 90th overall, fifth round.

MICK VUKOTA

Right Wing . . . 6'2" . . . 195 lbs. . . . Born, Saskatoon, Sask., September 14, 1966 . . . Shoots right . . . (November 20, 1987)—Given a six-game AHL suspension for returning to fight after being sent to the dressing room vs. Fredericton.

Year	Team	League	Games	G.	A.	Pts.	Pen.
1983-84	Winnipeg Warriors	WHL	3	1	1	2	10
1984-85	Kelowna Wings	WHL	66	10	6	16	247
1985-86	Spokane Chiefs	WHL	64	19	14	33	369
1986-87	Spokane Chiefs	WHL	61	25	28	53	*337
1987-88	New York Islanders (c)	NHL	17	1	0	1	82
1987-88	Springfield Indians	AHL	52	7	9	16	372
	NHL TOTALS		17	1	0	1	82

(c)—September, 1987—Signed by New York Islanders as a free agent.

DUANE (DEWEY) WAHLIN

Right Wing . . . 5'11" . . . 165 lbs. . . . Born, St. Paul, Minn., June 3, 1965 . . . Shoots right.

Year	Team	League	Games	G.	A.	Pts.	Pen.
1983-84	St. Paul Johnson H.S. (c)	Minn. H.S.	29	55	36	91	30
1984-85	University of Maine	H. East	38	12	6	18	36
1985-86	University of Maine	H. East	12	0	3	3	14
1986-87	U.S. International Univ.	GWHC	34	7	12	19	42
1987-88	U.S. International Univ.	GWHC	26	9	8	17	22

(c)—June, 1984—Drafted by Minnesota North Stars in NHL entry draft. Ninth North Stars pick, 181st overall, ninth round.

GORDON WALKER

Left Wing . . . 6' . . . 178 lbs. . . . Born, Castlegar, B.C., August 12, 1965 . . . Shoots left . . . Also plays Center.

Year	Team	League	Games	G.	A.	Pts.	Pen.
1981-82	Drumheller Miners	AJHL	60	35	44	79	90
1982-83	Portland Winter Hawks (c)	WHL	66	24	30	54	95
1983-84	Portland Winter Hawks	WHL	58	28	41	69	65
1984-85	Kamloops Blazers (a-d-e)	WHL	66	67	67	134	76
1985-86	New Haven Nighthawks	AHL	46	11	28	39	66
1986-87	New York Rangers	NHL	1	1	0	1	2
1986-87	New Haven Nighthawks	AHL	59	24	20	44	58

Year	Team	League	Games	G.	A.	Pts.	Pen.
1987-88—New York Rangers (f)		NHL	18	1	4	5	17
1987-88—Colorado Rangers		IHL	16	4	9	13	4
1987-88—New Haven Nighthawks		AHL	14	10	9	19	17
NHL TOTALS			19	2	4	6	19

(c)—June, 1983—Drafted as underage junior by New York Rangers in 1983 NHL entry draft. Fifth Rangers pick, 53rd overall, third round.

(d)—September, 1984—Traded with Craig Benning by Portland Winter Hawks to Kamloops Blazers for Brad Werenka.

(e)—Led WHL Playoffs with 13 goals.

(f)—January, 1988—Traded with Mike Siltala by New York Rangers to Los Angeles Kings for Joe Paterson.

ROBERT WALLMARK

Center ... 5'11" ... 180 lbs. ... Born, Boston, Mass., March 15, 1968 ... Shoots right.

Year	Team	League	Games	G.	A.	Pts.	Pen.
1987-88—Miami Univ. of Ohio (c)		CCHA	36	6	24	30	59

(c)—June, 1988—Drafted by New Jersey Devils in 1988 NHL entry draft. Fourteenth Devils pick, 243rd overall, 12th round.

MICHAEL WALSH

Left Wing ... 6'2" ... 195 lbs. ... Born, New York, N.Y., April 3, 1962 ... Shoots left.

Year	Team	League	Games	G.	A.	Pts.	Pen.
1985-86—Springfield Indians		AHL	2	1	0	1	0
1986-87—Springfield Indians (c)		AHL	67	20	26	46	32
1987-88—New York Islanders		NHL	1	0	0	0	0
1987-88—Springfield Indians		AHL	77	27	23	50	48
NHL TOTALS			1	0	0	0	0

(c)—August, 1986—Signed by New York Islanders as a free agent.

RYAN WILLIAM WALTER

Left Wing ... 6' ... 195 lbs. ... Born, New Westminster, B. C., April 23, 1958 ... Shoots left ... Brother of George Walter ... (November, 1983)—Injured groin muscle ... (October 27, 1984)—Concussion and twisted knee when checked by Andy Brickley at Pittsburgh ... (December 18, 1985)—Cut on left eyebrow vs. Quebec and missed three games ... (March 8, 1986)—Back spasms ... (March, 1986)—Broke ankle and missed remainder of regular season and all of playoffs except for Stanley Cup finals ... (October, 1987)—Bruised ribs ... (November, 1987)—Back spasms.

Year	Team	League	Games	G.	A.	Pts.	Pen.
1973-74—Langley Lords		Jr."A"BCHL	....	...	....	....	....
1973-74—Kamloops Chiefs		WCHL	2	0	0	0	0
1974-75—Langley Lords		Jr."A"BCHL	....	...	....	....	....
1974-75—Kamloops Chiefs		WCHL	9	8	4	12	2
1975-76—Kamloops Chiefs		WCHL	72	35	49	84	96
1976-77—Kamloops Chiefs		WCHL	71	41	58	99	100
1977-78—Seattle Breakers (a-c)		WCHL	62	54	71	125	148
1978-79—Washington Capitals		NHL	69	28	28	56	70
1979-80—Washington Capitals		NHL	80	24	42	66	106
1980-81—Washington Capitals		NHL	80	24	45	69	150
1981-82—Washington Capitals (d)		NHL	78	38	49	87	142
1982-83—Montreal Canadiens		NHL	80	29	46	75	15
1983-84—Montreal Canadiens		NHL	73	20	29	49	83
1984-85—Montreal Canadiens		NHL	72	19	19	39	59
1985-86—Montreal Canadiens		NHL	69	15	34	49	45
1986-87—Montreal Canadiens		NHL	76	23	23	46	34
1987-88—Montreal Canadiens		NHL	61	13	23	36	39
NHL TOTALS			738	233	338	572	743

(c)—Drafted from Seattle Breakers by Washington Capitals in first round of 1978 amateur draft.

(d)—September, 1982—Traded by Washington Capitals with Rick Green to Montreal Canadiens for Rod Langway, Brian Engblom, Doug Jarvis and Craig Laughlin.

DIXON WARD JR.

Right Wing ... 6'1" ... 195 lbs. ... Born, Edmonton, Alta., September 23, 1968 ... Shoots right.

Year	Team	League	Games	G.	A.	Pts.	Pen.
1986-87—Red Deer Rustlers		AJHL	59	46	40	86	153
1987-88—Red Deer Rustlers (c)		AJHL	51	60	71	131	167

(c)—June, 1988—Drafted by Vancouver Canucks in 1988 NHL entry draft. Sixth Canucks pick, 128th overall, seventh round.

ED WARD

Right Wing . . . 6'3" . . . 190 lbs. . . . Born, Edmonton, Alta., November 10, 1969 . . . Shoots right . . . (August, 1987)—Torn knee cartilage.

Year	Team	League	Games	G.	A.	Pts.	Pen.
1986-87—Sherwood Park Crusaders		AJHL	60	18	28	46	272
1987-88—Northern Michigan Univ. (c)		WCHA	25	0	2	2	40

(c)—June, 1988—Drafted by Quebec Nordiques in 1988 NHL entry draft. Seventh Nordiques pick, 108th overall, sixth round.

MICHAEL WARE

Right Wing . . . 6'5" . . . 200 lbs. . . . Born, York, Ont., March 22, 1967 . . . Shoots right . . . Also plays Defense . . . (October, 1985)—Broken collarbone.

Year	Team	League	Games	G.	A.	Pts.	Pen.
1983-84—Mississauga Reps		OHA	30	14	20	34	50
1984-85—Hamilton Steelhawks (c)		OHL	57	4	14	18	225
1985-86—Hamilton Steelhawks		OHL	44	8	11	19	155
1986-87—Cornwall Royals		OHL	50	5	19	24	173
1987-88—Nova Scotia Oilers		AHL	52	0	8	8	253

(c)—June, 1985—Drafted as underage junior by Edmonton Oilers in 1985 NHL entry draft. Third Oilers pick, 62nd overall, third round.

MIKE WARUS

Right Wing . . . 6'1" . . . 190 lbs. . . . Born, Sudbury, Ont., January 16, 1964 . . . Shoots right . . . (October 10, 1987)—Left Moncton Golden Flames and later returned.

Year	Team	League	Games	G.	A.	Pts.	Pen.
1983-84—Lake Superior State (c)		CCHA	35	6	4	10	33
1984-85—Lake Superior State		CCHA	43	4	11	15	80
1985-86—Lake Superior State		CCHA	40	5	6	11	92
1986-87—Lake Superior State		CCHA	38	7	14	21	111
1987-88—Moncton Golden Flames		AHL	38	11	9	20	63

(c)—June, 1984—Drafted by Winnipeg Jets in 1984 NHL entry draft. Eleventh Jets pick, 218th overall, 11th round.

GERRARD WASLEN

Center . . . 6' . . . 187 lbs. . . . Born, Humbolt, Sask., October 5, 1962 . . . Shoots right.

Year	Team	League	Games	G.	A.	Pts.	Pen.
1982-83—Colgate Univ.		ECAC	28	24	22	46	30
1983-84—Colgate Univ.		ECAC	35	28	33	61	64
1984-85—Colgate Univ.		ECAC	28	20	10	30	55
1985-86—Colgate Univ. (c)		ECAC	32	28	36	64	68
1986-87—Newmarket Saints		AHL	79	22	30	52	64
1987-88—Newmarket Saints		AHL	71	26	36	62	58

(c)—August, 1986—Signed by Toronto Maple Leafs as a free agent.

WILLIAM (BILL) WATSON

Right Wing . . . 6' . . . 180 lbs. . . . Born, Pine Falls, Man., March 30, 1964 . . . Shoots left . . . (October 13, 1985)—Injured left shoulder . . . (January 24, 1987)—Separated right shoulder at Montreal.

Year	Team	League	Games	G.	A.	Pts.	Pen.
1980-81—Prince Albert Raiders		AJHL	54	30	39	69	27
1981-82—Prince Albert Raiders (c)		AJHL	47	43	41	84	37
1982-83—University of Minn./Duluth		WCHA	22	5	10	15	10
1983-84—University of Minn./Duluth		WCHA	40	35	51	86	12
1984-85—U of Minn./Duluth (a-d-e-f)		WCHA	46	49	60	109	48
1985-86—Chicago Black Hawks		NHL	52	8	16	24	2
1986-87—Chicago Black Hawks		NHL	51	13	19	32	6
1987-88—Chicago Black Hawks		NHL	9	2	0	2	0
1987-88—Saginaw Hawks		IHL	35	15	20	35	10
NHL TOTALS			112	23	35	58	8

(c)—June, 1982—Drafted by Chicago Black Hawks in NHL entry draft. Fourth Black Hawks pick, 70th overall, fourth round.
(d)—WCHA MVP.
(e)—First team All-America forward (West).
(f)—Hobey Baker Award Winner (Top American College Hockey Player).

TIM WATTERS

Defense . . . 5'11" . . . 180 lbs. . . . Born, Kamloops, B.C., July 25, 1959 . . . Shoots left . . . Set record for assists and points by a defenseman at Michigan Tech in 1980-81 . . . (October, 1983)—Pulled hamstring . . . (December, 1984)—Broken wrist . . . (February, 1986)—Back spasms . . . (December, 1987)—Strained knee in collision with Kevin Lowe vs. Edmonton.

Year	Team	League	Games	G.	A.	Pts.	Pen.
1977-78—Michigan Tech		WCHA	37	1	15	16	47
1978-79—Michigan Tech (c)		WCHA	31	6	21	27	48
1979-80—Canadian Olympic Team		Int'l	56	8	21	29	43
1979-80—Canadian Olympic Team		Int'l	6	1	1	2	0
1980-81—Michigan Tech (a-d)		WCHA	43	12	38	50	36
1981-82—Tulsa Oilers		CHL	5	1	2	3	0
1981-82—Winnipeg Jets		NHL	69	2	22	24	97
1982-83—Winnipeg Jets		NHL	77	5	18	23	98
1983-84—Winnipeg Jets		NHL	74	3	20	23	169
1984-85—Winnipeg Jets		NHL	63	2	20	22	74
1985-86—Winnipeg Jets		NHL	56	6	8	14	95
1986-87—Winnipeg Jets		NHL	63	3	13	16	119
1987-88—Winnipeg Jets		NHL	36	0	0	0	106
1987-88—Canadian Olympic Team (e)		Int'l	10	0	3	3	2
NHL TOTALS			438	21	101	122	758

(c)—August, 1979—Drafted by Winnipeg Jets in NHL draft. Sixth Jets pick, 124th overall, sixth round.
(d)—Named to All-America Team (West).
(e)—July, 1988—Signed by Los Angeles Kings as a free agent.

JEFF WAVER

Defense . . . 5'11" . . . 195 lbs. . . .Born, St. Boniface, Man., September 28, 1968 . . . Shoots left.

Year	Team	League	Games	G.	A.	Pts.	Pen.
1983-84—Notre Dame Hounds		SAHA	67	43	59	102	83
1984-85—Brandon Wheat Kings		WHL	66	5	14	19	156
1985-86—Brandon Wheat Kings		WHL	68	16	23	39	171
1986-87—Hamilton Steelhawks (c)		OHL	63	12	28	40	132
1987-88—Hamilton Steelhawks		OHL	64	27	34	61	134

(c)—June, 1987—Drafted by Pittsburgh Penguins in 1987 NHL entry draft. Fifth Penguins pick, 89th overall, fifth round.

ERIC WEINRICH

Defense . . . 6'1" . . . 205 lbs. . . . Born, Roanoke, Vir., December 19, 1966 . . . Shoots left . . . (December, 1984)—Dislocated shoulder . . . Brother of Alexander Weinrich.

Year	Team	League	Games	G.	A.	Pts.	Pen.
1983-84—North Yarmouth Acad.		Mass. H.S.	17	23	33	56	..
1984-85—North Yarmouth Acad. (c)		Mass. H.S.	20	6	21	27	..
1985-86—Univ. of Maine		H. East	34	0	15	15	26
1986-87—Univ. of Maine (a-d)		H. East	41	12	32	44	59
1987-88—U.S. Olympic Team		Int'l	39	3	9	12	..
1987-88—Univ. of Maine		H. East	8	4	7	11	22

(c)—June, 1985—Drafted by New Jersey Devils in 1985 NHL entry draft. Third Devils pick, 32nd overall, second round.
(d)—Named to second-team U.S. College All-America team (East).

TOM WEISS

Right Wing . . . 6'4" . . . 220 lbs. . . . Born, Englewood, Colo., January 31, 1962 . . . Shoots right.

Year	Team	League	Games	G.	A.	Pts.	Pen.
1983-84—Denver University		WCHA	38	12	7	19	34
1984-85—Denver University		WCHA	38	14	9	23	26
1985-86—Denver University (c)		WCHA	48	22	26	48	50
1986-87—Peoria Rivermen		IHL	9	3	3	6	6
1986-87—Springfield Indians		AHL	46	6	10	16	47
1987-88—Peoria Rivermen		IHL	29	3	6	9	6
1987-88—Springfield Indians		AHL	3	0	0	0	0

(c)—August, 1986—Signed by New York Islanders as a free agent.

GORDON JAY WELLS
(Known by middle name)

Defense . . . 6'1" . . . 205 lbs. . . . Born, Paris, Ont., May 18, 1959 . . . Shoots left . . . (October

16, 1981)—Broke right hand in team practice when hit by a puck . . . (December 14, 1982)—Tore medial collateral ligament in right knee at Washington . . . (December, 1983)—Sprained ankle . . . (February, 1987)—Struck in eye by a puck during a team practice . . . (November, 1987)—Strained lower back.

Year	Team	League	Games	G.	A.	Pts.	Pen.
1976-77—Kingston Canadians		OMJHL	59	4	7	11	90
1977-78—Kingston Canadians		OMJHL	68	9	13	22	195
1978-79—Kingston Canadians (a-c)		OMJHL	48	6	21	27	100
1979-80—Los Angeles Kings		NHL	43	0	0	0	113
1979-80—Binghamton Dusters		AHL	28	0	6	6	48
1980-81—Los Angeles Kings		NHL	72	5	13	18	155
1981-82—Los Angeles Kings		NHL	60	1	8	9	145
1982-83—Los Angeles Kings		NHL	69	3	12	15	167
1983-84—Los Angeles Kings		NHL	69	3	18	21	141
1984-85—Los Angeles Kings		NHL	77	2	9	11	185
1985-86—Los Angeles Kings		NHL	79	11	31	42	226
1986-87—Los Angeles Kings		NHL	77	7	29	36	155
1987-88—Los Angeles Kings		NHL	58	2	23	25	159
NHL TOTALS			604	34	143	177	1446

(c)—August, 1979—Drafted by Los Angeles Kings in entry draft. First Kings pick, 16th overall, first round.

JEFF WENAAS

Center . . . 5'11" . . . 185 lbs. . . . Born, Eastend, Sask., September 1, 1967 . . . Shoots left . . . Brother of Stu Wenaas (Pittsburgh 10th round 1982 draft pick).

Year	Team	League	Games	G.	A.	Pts.	Pen.
1983-84—Medicine Hat Midget Tigers		AHA	38	16	22	38	77
1984-85—Medicine Hat Tigers (c)		WHL	70	27	27	54	70
1985-86—Medicine Hat Tigers		WHL	65	20	26	46	57
1986-87—Medicine Hat Tigers		WHL	70	42	29	71	68
1987-88—Salt Lake Golden Eagles		IHL	80	23	39	62	109

(c)—June, 1985—Drafted as underage junior by Calgary Flames in 1985 NHL entry draft. Third Flames pick, 38th overall, second round.

BRAD WERENKA

Defense . . . 6'2" . . . 205 lbs. . . . Born, Two Hills, Alta., February 12, 1969 . . . Shoots left.

Year	Team	League	Games	G.	A.	Pts.	Pen.
1985-86—Fort Saskatchewan Traders		SJHL	29	12	23	35	24
1986-87—Northern Michigan Univ. (c)		WCHA	30	4	4	8	35
1987-88—Northern Michigan Univ.		WCHA	34	7	23	30	26

(c)—June, 1987—Drafted as underage junior by Edmonton Oilers in 1987 NHL entry draft. Second Oilers pick, 42nd overall, second round.

LANCE WERNESS

Right Wing . . . 6' . . . 175 lbs. . . . Born, Minneapolis, Minn., March 28, 1969 . . . Shoots right . . . Mother (Diane Werness) is a professional skating instructor . . . Father (Bob) member of University of Minnesota baseball team (1964 NCAA Baseball champions).

Year	Team	League	Games	G.	A.	Pts.	Pen.
1986-87—Burnsville H.S. (c)		Minn. H.S.	26	17	29	46	....
1987-88—Univ. of Minnesota		WCHA	27	8	5	13	20

(c)—June, 1987—Drafted by Chicago Black Hawks in 1987 NHL entry draft. Ninth Black Hawks pick, 176th overall, ninth round.

BLAKE WESLEY

Defense . . . 6'3" . . . 210 lbs. . . . Born, Red Deer, Alta., July 10, 1959 . . . Shoots left . . . Brother of Glen Wesley.

Year	Team	League	Games	G.	A.	Pts.	Pen.
1974-75—Red Deer Rustlers		AJHL	3	1	0	1	4
1975-76—Red Deer Rustlers		AJHL	55	19	41	60	199
1976-77—Portland Winter Hawks		WCHL	63	8	25	33	111
1977-78—Portland Winter Hawks		WCHL	67	7	37	44	190
1978-79—Portland Winter Hawks (b-c)		WHL	69	10	42	52	292
1979-80—Philadelphia Flyers		NHL	2	0	1	1	2
1979-80—Maine Mariners		AHL	65	12	22	34	76
1980-81—Maine Mariners		AHL	24	6	10	16	20
1980-81—Philadelphia Flyers (d)		NHL	50	3	7	10	107
1981-82—Hartford Whalers		NHL	78	9	18	27	123
1982-83—Hartford Whalers (e)		NHL	22	0	1	1	46

Year	Team	League	Games	G.	A.	Pts.	Pen.
1982-83—Quebec Nordiques		NHL	52	4	8	12	84
1983-84—Quebec Nordiques		NHL	46	2	8	10	75
1984-85—Fredericton Express		AHL	25	3	4	7	80
1984-85—Quebec Nordiques (f)		NHL	21	0	2	2	28
1985-86—Toronto Maple Leafs		NHL	27	0	1	1	21
1985-86—St. Catharines Saints		AHL	37	3	4	7	56
1986-87—Newmarket Saints (g)		AHL	79	1	12	13	170
1987-88—Maine Mariners		AHL	34	0	3	3	124
NHL TOTALS			298	18	46	64	486

(c)—August, 1979—Drafted by Philadelphia Flyers in entry draft. Second Flyers pick, 22nd overall, second round.

(d)—July, 1981—Traded with Don Gillen, Rick MacLeish, first (Paul Lawless), second (Mark Paterson) and third (Kevin Dineen) round picks in the 1982 NHL entry draft by Philadelphia Flyers to Hartford Whalers for Ray Allison, Fred Arthur and Whalers first (Ron Sutter) and third (Miroslav Dvorak) round picks in 1982 draft.

(e)—December, 1982—Traded by Hartford Whalers to Quebec Nordiques for Pierre Lacroix.

(f)—August, 1985—Signed by Toronto Maple Leafs as a free agent.

(g)—August, 1987—Signed by Boston Bruins as a free agent.

GLEN WESLEY

Defense . . . 6'1" . . . 195 lbs. . . . Born, Red Deer, Alta., October 2, 1968 . . . Shoots left . . . Brother of Blake Wesley.

Year	Team	League	Games	G.	A.	Pts.	Pen.
1983-84—Red Deer Rustlers		AJHL	57	9	20	29	40
1984-85—Portland Winterhawks		WHL	67	16	52	68	76
1985-86—Portland Winterhawks (a-c)		WHL	69	16	75	91	96
1986-87—Portland Winterhawks (a-d)		WHL	63	16	46	62	72
1987-88—Boston Bruins		NHL	79	7	30	37	69
NHL TOTALS			79	7	30	37	69

(c)—Named Best WHL Defenseman (West).

(d)—June, 1987—Drafted as underage junior by Boston Bruins in 1987 NHL entry draft. First Bruins pick, third overall, first round.

SIMON WHEELDON

Center . . . 5'11" . . . 170 lbs. . . . Born, Vancouver, B.C., August 30, 1966 . . . Shoots left.

Year	Team	League	Games	G.	A.	Pts.	Pen.
1982-83—Kelowna Bucks		BCJHL	60	...	....	86	....
1983-84—Victoria Cougars (c)		WHL	56	14	24	38	43
1984-85—Victoria Cougars (b)		WHL	67	50	76	126	78
1984-85—Nova Scotia Oilers		AHL	4	0	1	1	0
1985-86—Victoria Cougars (b)		WHL	70	61	96	157	85
1986-87—Flint Spirits		IHL	41	17	53	70	67
1986-87—New Haven Nighthawks (d)		AHL	38	11	28	39	39
1987-88—New York Rangers		NHL	5	0	1	1	4
1987-88—Colorado Rangers		AHL	69	45	54	99	80
NHL TOTALS			5	0	1	1	4

(c)—June, 1984—Drafted as underage junior by Edmonton Oilers in NHL entry draft. Eleventh Oilers pick, 229th overall, 11th round.

(d)—August, 1987—Signed by New York Rangers as a free agent.

ROB WHISTLE

Defense . . . 6'2" . . . 195 lbs. . . . Born, Thunder Bay, Ont., April 30, 1961 . . . Shoots right . . . (March 28, 1988)—Broken ankle when struck by a Rob Ramage shot vs. Calgary.

Year	Team	League	Games	G.	A.	Pts.	Pen.
1984-85—Wilfred Laurier (c-d-e)		OUAA	....	...	....	....	....
1985-86—New York Rangers		NHL	32	4	2	6	10
1985-86—New Haven Nighthawks		AHL	20	1	4	5	5
1986-87—New Haven Nighthawks (f)		AHL	55	4	12	16	30
1987-88—Peoria Rivermen		IHL	39	5	21	26	21
1987-88—St. Louis Blues		NHL	19	3	3	6	6
NHL TOTALS			51	7	5	12	16

(c)—Member of All-Canadian Team.

(d)—Won Senator Joseph A. Sullivan Trophy (Top Canadian-College hockey player).

(e)—October, 1985—Signed by New York Rangers as a free agent.

(f)—June, 1987—Traded with Tony McKegney by New York Rangers to St. Louis Blues for Bruce Bell, a fourth-round 1988 draft pick and future considerations.

GORD WHITAKER

Right Wing . . . 6'2" . . . 205 lbs. . . . Born, Edmonton, Alta., January 24, 1966 . . . Shoots right.

Year	Team	League	Games	G.	A.	Pts.	Pen.
1983-84—Colorado College (c)		WCHA	33	10	10	20	44
1984-85—Colorado College		WCHA	31	10	5	15	76
1985-85—Colorado College		WCHA	34	14	16	30	53
1986-87—Colorado College		WCHA	34	21	17	38	69
1987-88—Moncton Golden Flames		AHL	14	2	2	4	12
1987-88—Baltimore Skipjacks		AHL	20	3	4	7	10

(c)—June, 1984—Drafted by Winnipeg Jets in NHL entry draft. Ninth Jets pick, 177th overall, ninth round.

BOB WHITE

Defense . . . 6' . . . 185 lbs. . . . Born, Brockville, Ont., March 9, 1968 . . . Shoots right.

Year	Team	League	Games	G.	A.	Pts.	Pen.
1986-87—St. Lawrence Univ.		ECAC	30	2	9	11	52
1987-88—St. Lawrence Univ. (c)		ECAC	37	4	16	20	29

(c)—June, 1988—Drafted by Hartford Whalers in 1988 NHL entry draft. Tenth Whalers pick, 221st overall, 11th round.

SCOTT WHITE

Defense . . . 6' . . . 190 lbs. . . . Born, Ormstown, Que., April 21, 1968 . . . Shoots right.

Year	Team	League	Games	G.	A.	Pts.	Pen.
1985-86—Michigan Tech. Univ. (c)		WCHA	40	3	15	18	58
1986-87—Michigan Tech. Univ.		WCHA	36	4	15	19	58
1987-88—Michigan Tech. Univ.		WCHA	40	7	25	32	32

(c)—June, 1986—Drafted by Quebec Nordiques in 1986 NHL entry draft. Sixth Nordiques pick, 117th overall, sixth round.

SHAWN WHITHAM

Defense . . . 5'11" . . . 175 lbs. . . . Born, Verdun, Que., March 13, 1967 . . . Shoots left . . . (December, 1987)—Sprained ankle.

Year	Team	League	Games	G.	A.	Pts.	Pen.
1985-86—Providence College (c)		H. East	38	10	14	24	91
1986-87—Providence College		H. East	31	9	11	20	57
1987-88—Providence College		H. East	29	8	17	25	71

(c)—June, 1986—Drafted by Buffalo Sabres in 1986 NHL entry draft. Tenth Sabres pick, 173rd overall, ninth round.

DOUGLAS PETER WICKENHEISER

Center . . . 6' . . . 199 lbs. . . . Born, Regina, Sask., March 30, 1961 . . . Shoots left . . . Brother of Kurt Wickenheiser . . . (March 30, 1983)—Broke rib at Pittsburgh . . . (March 13, 1985)—Suffered complete tears of the entire medial complex and both cruciate ligaments in his left knee . . . (January 21, 1986)—Returned to St. Louis lineup after missing 56 games (12 in '84-85 and 44 in '85-86).

Year	Team	League	Games	G.	A.	Pts.	Pen.
1976-77—Regina Blues		SJHL	59	42	46	88	63
1977-78—Regina Pats		WCHL	68	37	51	88	49
1978-79—Regina Pats		WHL	68	32	62	94	141
1979-80—Regina Pats (a-c-d-e)		WHL	71	*89	81	*170	99
1980-81—Montreal Canadiens		NHL	41	7	8	15	20
1981-82—Montreal Canadiens		NHL	56	12	23	35	43
1982-83—Montreal Canadiens		NHL	78	25	30	55	49
1983-84—Montreal Canadiens (f)		NHL	27	5	5	10	6
1983-84—St. Louis Blues		NHL	46	7	21	28	19
1984-85—St. Louis Blues		NHL	68	23	20	43	36
1985-86—St. Louis Blues		NHL	36	8	11	19	16
1986-87—St. Louis Blues		NHL	80	13	15	28	37
1987-88—Vancouver Canucks (g-h)		NHL	80	7	19	26	36
NHL TOTALS			512	107	152	259	262

(c)—Won Bob Brownridge Memorial Trophy (Leading Scorer).

(d)—Named WHL's Most Valuable Player.

(e)—June, 1980—Drafted as underage junior by Montreal Canadiens in 1980 NHL entry draft. First Canadiens pick, first overall, first round.

(f)—December, 1983—Traded by Montreal Canadiens with Gilbert Delorme and Greg Paslawski to St. Louis Blues for Perry Turnbull.

(g)—October, 1987—Acquired by Hartford Whalers in 1987 NHL waiver draft as compensation for St. Louis Blues drafting Bill Root from Whalers. He was then selected by Vancouver Canucks from the Whalers unprotected list with the Whalers taking Brent Peterson from Vancouver as compensation.

(h)—July, 1988—Signed by New York Rangers as a free agent.

JAMES DUNCAN WIEMER

Defense . . . 6'4" . . . 197 lbs. . . . Born, Sudbury, Ont., January 9, 1961 . . . Shoots left.

Year	Team	League	Games	G.	A.	Pts.	Pen.
1978-79	Peterborough Petes	OMJHL	63	15	12	27	50
1979-80	Peterborough Petes (c)	OMJHL	53	17	32	49	63
1980-81	Peterborough Petes	OHL	65	41	54	95	102
1981-82	Rochester Americans	AHL	74	19	26	45	57
1982-83	Rochester Americans	AHL	74	15	44	59	43
1982-83	Buffalo Sabres (d)	NHL	..	..	..	..	..
1983-84	Buffalo Sabres	NHL	64	5	15	20	48
1983-84	Rochester Americans	AHL	12	4	11	15	11
1984-85	Rochester Americans	AHL	13	1	9	10	24
1984-85	New Haven Nighthawks	AHL	33	9	27	36	39
1984-85	Buffalo Sabres (e)	NHL	10	3	2	5	4
1984-85	New York Rangers	NHL	22	4	3	7	30
1985-86	New Haven Nighthawks (a-f)	AHL	73	24	49	73	108
1985-86	New York Rangers	NHL	7	3	0	3	2
1986-87	New Haven Nighthawks (g)	AHL	6	0	7	7	6
1986-87	Nova Scotia Oilers	AHL	59	9	25	34	72
1987-88	Nova Scotia Oilers	AHL	57	11	32	43	99
1987-88	Edmonton Oilers	NHL	12	1	2	3	15
	NHL TOTALS		115	16	22	38	99

(c)—June, 1980—Drafted by Buffalo Sabres as underage junior in 1980 NHL entry draft. Fifth Sabres pick, 83rd overall, fourth round.

(d)—No regular season record. Played one playoff game.

(e)—December, 1984—Traded with Steve Patrick by Buffalo Sabres to New York Rangers for Chris Renaud and Dave Maloney.

(f)—Won Eddie Shore Plaque (Top Defenseman).

(g)—October, 1986—Traded with NHL rights to Reijo Ruotsalainen, Ville Horava and Clark Donatelli by New York Rangers to Edmonton Oilers to complete an earlier deal that saw the Rangers acquire Don Jackson and Mike Golden.

RICHARD WIEST

Center . . . 5'11" . . . 170 lbs. . . . Born, Lethbridge, Alta., June 22, 1967 . . . Shoots right.

Year	Team	League	Games	G.	A.	Pts.	Pen.
1983-84	Lethbridge Broncos	WHL	71	17	16	33	138
1984-85	Lethbridge Broncos (c)	WHL	65	18	19	37	305
1985-86	Lethbridge Broncos (d)	WHL	31	5	13	18	111
1985-86	Seattle Thunderbirds	WHL	2	0	0	0	2
1985-86	Calgary Wranglers	WHL	23	8	3	11	74
1986-87	Kamloops Blazers	WHL	68	19	27	46	129
1987-88	Lethbridge Hurricanes	WHL	20	3	5	8	41

(c)—June, 1985—Drafted as underage junior by New York Islanders in 1985 NHL entry draft. Eleventh Islanders pick, 181st overall, ninth round.

(d)—January, 1986—Traded by Lethbridge Broncos to Seattle Thunderbirds for Mario Desjardins.

BOB WILKIE

Defense . . . 6'2" . . . 200 lbs. . . . Born, Calgary, Alta., February 11, 1969 . . . Shoots right.

Year	Team	League	Games	G.	A.	Pts.	Pen.
1984-85	Calgary Buffaloes	Atla. Midget	37	20	33	53	116
1985-86	Calgary Wranglers	WHL	63	8	19	27	56
1986-87	Swift Current Broncos (c)	WHL	65	12	38	50	50
1987-88	Swift Current Broncos	WHL	67	12	68	80	124

(c)—June, 1987—Drafted as underage junior by Detroit Red Wings in 1987 NHL entry draft. Third Red Wings pick, 41st overall, second round.

NEIL WILKINSON

Defense . . . 6'3" . . . 190 lbs. . . . Born, Selkirk, Manitoba, August 15, 1967 . . . Shoots right . . . (January, 1986)—Broken nose and concussion.

Year	Team	League	Games	G.	A.	Pts.	Pen.
1985-86	Selkirk Steelers (c)	MJHL	42	14	35	49	91
1986-87	Michigan State Univ.	CCHA	19	3	4	7	18
1987-88	Medicine Hat Tigers	WHL	55	11	21	32	157

(c)—June, 1986—Drafted by Minnesota North Stars in 1986 NHL entry draft. Second North Stars pick, 30th overall, second round.

BRIAN WILKS

Center . . . 5'11" . . . 175 lbs. . . . Born, Toronto, Ont., February 22, 1966 . . . Shoots right.

Year	Team	League	Games	G.	A.	Pts.	Pen.
1981-82—Toronto Marlboro Midgets		MTMHL	36	40	48	88	22
1982-83—Kitchener Rangers		OHL	69	6	17	23	25
1983-84—Kitchener Rangers (c)		OHL	64	21	54	75	36
1984-85—Kitchener Rangers		OHL	58	30	63	93	52
1984-85—Los Angeles Kings		NHL	2	0	0	0	0
1985-86—Los Angeles Kings		NHL	43	4	8	12	25
1986-87—Los Angeles Kings		NHL	1	0	0	0	0
1986-87—New Haven Nighthawks		AHL	43	16	20	36	23
1987-88—New Haven Nighthawks		AHL	18	4	8	12	26
NHL TOTALS			46	4	8	12	25

(c)—June, 1984—Drafted as underage junior by Los Angeles Kings in NHL entry draft. Second Kings pick, 24th overall, second round.

DAVID JAMES (TIGER) WILLIAMS

Left Wing . . . 5'11" . . . 180 lbs. . . . Born, Weyburn, Sask., February 3, 1954 . . . Shoots left . . . (October 10, 1980)—Fracture of lower lombar transverse in a goal-mouth crash in first game of 1980-81 season . . . (1982-83)—Missed 12 games due to various NHL suspensions . . . (October 30, 1983)—Given eight-game suspension by NHL for 'potentially dangerous' attempt to injure Paul Baxter at Calgary . . . All-time NHL penalty minute leader . . . Set career playoff record for most penalty minutes with 455 . . . (January 8, 1986)—Bruised shoulder at Pittsburgh and missed four games . . . (January 27, 1986)—Injured shoulder at Calgary and missed one game . . . (November, 1987)—Bruised sternum.

Year	Team	League	Games	G.	A.	Pts.	Pen.
1971-72—Swift Current Broncos		WCHL	68	12	22	34	278
1972-73—Swift Current Broncos		WCHL	68	44	58	102	266
1973-74—Swift Current Broncos (c)		WCHL	68	52	56	108	310
1974-75—Oklahoma City Blazers		CHL	39	16	11	27	202
1974-75—Toronto Maple Leafs		NHL	42	10	19	29	187
1975-76—Toronto Maple Leafs		NHL	78	21	19	40	299
1976-77—Toronto Maple Leafs		NHL	77	18	25	43	*338
1977-78—Toronto Maple Leafs (d)		NHL	78	19	31	50	351
1978-79—Toronto Maple Leafs (e)		NHL	77	19	20	39	*298
1979-80—Toronto Maple Leafs (f)		NHL	55	22	18	40	197
1979-80—Vancouver Canucks		NHL	23	8	5	13	81
1980-81—Vancouver Canucks		NHL	77	35	27	62	*343
1981-82—Vancouver Canucks (g)		NHL	77	17	21	38	341
1982-83—Vancouver Canucks		NHL	68	8	13	21	265
1983-84—Vancouver Canucks (h)		NHL	67	15	16	31	294
1984-85—Adirondack Red Wings		AHL	8	5	2	7	4
1984-85—Detroit Red Wings (i)		NHL	55	3	8	11	158
1984-85—Los Angeles Kings		NHL	12	4	3	7	43
1985-86—Los Angeles Kings		NHL	72	20	29	49	320
1986-87—Los Angeles Kings		NHL	76	16	18	34	*358
1987-88—Los Angeles Kings (j)		NHL	2	0	0	0	6
1987-88—Hartford Whalers (k)		NHL	26	6	0	6	87
NHL TOTALS			962	241	272	513	3966

(c)—Drafted from Swift Current Broncos by Toronto Maple Leafs in second round of 1974 amateur draft.
(d)—Led Stanley Cup Playoffs in penalty minutes with 63.
(e)—Led Stanley Cup Playoffs in penalty minutes with 48.
(f)—February, 1980—Traded with Jerry Butler by Toronto Maple Leafs to Vancouver Canucks for Rick Vaive and Bill Derlago.
(g)—Led Stanley Cup Playoffs in penalty minutes with 116.
(h)—August, 1984—Traded by Vancouver Canucks to Detroit Red Wings for Rob McClanahan.
(i)—March, 1985—Traded by Detroit Red Wings to Los Angeles Kings for future considerations.
(j)—October, 1987—Sold by Los Angeles Kings to Hartford Whalers.
(k)—February, 1988—Released by Hartford Whalers.

SEAN WILLIAMS

Center . . . 6'2" . . . 180 lbs. . . . Born, Oshawa, Ont., January 28, 1968 . . . Shoots left.

Year	Team	League	Games	G.	A.	Pts.	Pen.
1984-85—Oshawa Generals		OHL	40	6	7	13	28
1985-86—Oshawa Generals (c)		OHL	55	15	23	38	23

Year	Team	League	Games	G.	A.	Pts.	Pen.
1986-87—Oshawa Generals		OHL	62	21	23	44	32
1987-88—Oshawa Generals		OHL	65	58	65	123	38

(c)—June, 1986—Drafted as underage junior by Minnesota North Stars in 1986 NHL entry draft. Eleventh North Stars pick, 245th overall, 12th round.

BEHN BEVAN WILSON

Defense . . . 6'3" . . . 207 lbs. . . . Born, Toronto, Ont., December 19, 1958 . . . Shoots left . . . (October, 1982)—Serious groin pull . . . (February 19, 1983)—Suspended six games for high sticking N. Y. Rangers goalie Glen Hanlon . . . (November, 1985)—Missed two games with a viral infection . . . (February 13, 1986)—Injured knee vs. Toronto . . . (April, 1986)— Injured back in playoff series vs. Toronto . . . (October, 1986)—Missed season due to back spasms . . . (December, 1987)—Pulled groin . . . (January, 1988)—Back spasms.

Year	Team	League	Games	G.	A.	Pts.	Pen.
1975-76—Ottawa 67's		Jr."A"OHA	63	5	16	21	131
1976-77—Ottawa 67's (c)		Jr."A"OHA	31	8	29	37	115
1976-77—Windsor Spitfires		Jr."A"OHA	17	4	16	20	38
1976-77—Kalamazoo Wings		IHL	13	2	7	9	40
1977-78—Kingston Canadians (d)		Jr."A"OHA	52	18	58	76	186
1978-79—Philadelphia Flyers		NHL	80	13	36	49	197
1979-80—Philadelphia Flyers		NHL	61	9	25	34	212
1980-81—Philadelphia Flyers		NHL	77	16	47	63	237
1981-82—Philadelphia Flyers		NHL	59	13	23	36	135
1982-83—Philadelphia Flyers (e)		NHL	62	8	24	32	92
1983-84—Chicago Black Hawks		NHL	59	10	22	32	143
1984-85—Chicago Black Hawks		NHL	76	10	23	33	185
1985-86—Chicago Black Hawks		NHL	69	13	37	50	113
1986-87—Chicago Black Hawks		NHL	..	..	..	..	..
1987-88—Chicago Black Hawks		NHL	58	6	23	29	166
NHL TOTALS			601	98	260	358	1480

(c)—Traded to Windsor Spitfires by Ottawa 67's with John Wilson for Jim Fox, December, 1976.

(d)—Drafted from Kingston Canadians by Philadelphia Flyers (with choice obtained from Pittsburgh Penguins in trade for Tom Bladon, Orest Kindrachuk and Don Saleski) in first round of 1978 amateur draft.

(e)—June, 1983—Traded by Philadelphia Flyers to Chicago Black Hawks for Doug Crossman and a second-round draft choice in 1984 (Scott Mellanby).

CAREY WILSON

Center . . . 6'2" . . . 205 lbs. . . . Born, Winnipeg, Man., May 19, 1962 . . . Shoots right . . . Son of Dr. Gerry Wilson, former vice-president and team doctor of Winnipeg Jets (WHA) . . . (September 28, 1985)—Injured shoulder in pre-season game and missed first three games of regular season . . . (April 28, 1986)—Suffered ruptured spleen and missed re- mainder of playoffs . . . (October, 1987)—Strained shoulder.

Year	Team	League	Games	G.	A.	Pts.	Pen.
1978-79—Calgary Chinooks		AJHL	60	30	34	64	....
1979-80—Dartmouth College (c)		ECAC	31	16	22	38	20
1980-81—Dartmouth College		ECAC	21	9	13	22	52
1981-82—Helsinki IFK		Finland	39	15	17	32	58
1982-83—Helsinki IFK (d)		Finland	36	18	22	40	...
1983-84—Canadian Olympic Team		Int'l	59	21	24	45	34
1983-84—Calgary Flames		NHL	15	2	5	7	2
1984-85—Calgary Flames		NHL	74	24	48	72	27
1985-86—Calgary Flames		NHL	76	29	29	58	24
1986-87—Calgary Flames		NHL	80	20	36	56	42
1987-88—Calgary Flames (e)		NHL	34	9	21	30	18
1987-88—Hartford Whalers		NHL	36	18	20	38	22
NHL TOTALS			315	102	159	261	135

(c)—June, 1980—Drafted by Chicago Black Hawks in NHL entry draft. Eighth Black Hawks pick, 67th overall, fourth round.

(d)—November, 1982—Traded by Chicago Black Hawks to Calgary Flames for Denis Cyr.

(e)—January, 1987—Traded with Neil Sheehy and the NHL rights to Lane MacDonald by Calgary Flames to Hartford Whalers for Shane Churla and Dana Murzyn.

DOUGLAS WILSON

Defense . . . 6'1" . . . 187 lbs. . . . Born, Ottawa, Ont., July 5, 1957 . . . Shoots left . . . Missed part of 1976-77 season with knee surgery . . . Brother of Murray Wilson . . . Missed part of 1978-79 season with shoulder injury that required surgery . . . (November 25, 1981)—Bro- ken jaw at Vancouver. Had his jaw wired shut, lost 25 pounds and has his vision restricted by special protective mask he had to wear . . . Set Chicago Black Hawks record for

defensemen in 1981-82 with 39 goals and 85 points . . . Set Chicago record of 54 assists by a defenseman in 1984-85 (broke own record of 51 set in 1982-83) . . . (November, 1983)—Ankle injury . . . (February 3, 1984)—Broke nose at Winnipeg . . . (March 4, 1984)—Played his first game without a facemask after recovering from broken nose. He was accidently hit by the stick of Walt Poddubny of Toronto, suffered a fractured skull and missed remainder of the season . . . (March 8, 1987)—Sprained right knee vs. N.Y. Islanders . . . Holds Chicago Black Hawks career record for goals, assists and points by a defenseman . . . (December, 1987)—Shoulder surgery.

Year	Team	League	Games	G.	A.	Pts.	Pen.
1974-75—Ottawa 67's		Jr."A"OHA	55	29	58	87	75
1975-76—Ottawa 67's (b)		Jr."A"OHA	58	26	62	88	142
1976-77—Ottawa 67's (a-c)		Jr."A"OHA	43	25	54	79	85
1977-78—Chicago Black Hawks		NHL	77	14	20	34	72
1978-79—Chicago Black Hawks		NHL	56	5	21	26	37
1979-80—Chicago Black Hawks		NHL	73	12	49	61	70
1980-81—Chicago Black Hawks		NHL	76	12	39	51	80
1981-82—Chicago Black Hawks (a-d)		NHL	76	39	46	85	54
1982-83—Chicago Black Hawks		NHL	74	18	51	69	58
1983-84—Chicago Black Hawks		NHL	66	13	45	58	64
1984-85—Chicago Black Hawks (b)		NHL	78	22	54	76	44
1985-86—Chicago Black Hawks		NHL	79	17	47	64	80
1986-87—Chicago Black Hawks		NHL	69	16	32	48	36
1987-88—Chicago Black Hawks		NHL	27	8	24	32	28
NHL TOTALS			751	176	428	604	623

(c)—Drafted from Ottawa 67's by Chicago Black Hawks in first round of 1977 amateur draft.
(d)—Won James Norris Memorial Trophy (Top NHL Defenseman).

MITCH WILSON

Right Wing . . . 5'8" . . . 185 lbs. . . . Born, Kelowna, B.C., February 15, 1962 . . . Shoots right.

Year	Team	League	Games	G.	A.	Pts.	Pen.
1980-81—Seattle Breakers		WHL	64	8	23	31	253
1981-82—Seattle Breakers		WHL	60	18	17	35	436
1982-83—Wichita Wind (c)		CHL	55	4	6	10	186
1983-84—Maine Mariners		AHL	71	6	8	14	*349
1984-85—Maine Mariners		AHL	51	6	3	9	220
1984-85—New Jersey Devils		NHL	9	0	2	2	21
1985-86—Maine Mariners		AHL	64	4	3	7	217
1986-87—Baltimore Skipjacks		AHL	58	8	9	17	353
1986-87—Pittsburgh Penguins		NHL	17	2	1	3	83
1987-88—Muskegon Lumberjacks		IHL	68	27	25	52	400
NHL TOTALS			26	2	3	5	104

(c)—October, 1982—Signed by New Jersey Devils as a free agent.

ROBERT WILSON

Defense . . . 6'3" . . . 195 lbs. . . . Born, Toronto, Ont., July 18, 1968 . . . Shoots left.

Year	Team	League	Games	G.	A.	Pts.	Pen.
1984-85—Mississauga Midget Reps.		OHA	61	11	35	46	106
1985-86—Sudbury Wolves (c)		OHL	61	1	5	6	93
1986-87—Sudbury Wolves		OHL	58	1	27	28	135
1987-88—Sudbury Wolves		OHL	42	3	15	18	93

(c)—June, 1986—Drafted as underage junior by Pittsburgh Penguins in 1986 NHL entry draft. Twelfth Penguins pick, 235th overall, 12th round.

RONALD LAWRENCE WILSON

Defense . . . 5'11" . . . 175 lbs. . . . Born, Windsor, Ont., May 28, 1955 . . . Shoots right . . . Son of former NHL forward Larry Wilson . . . (March 9, 1987)—Separated shoulder when he collided with teammate Paul Houck at Montreal.

Year	Team	League	Games	G.	A.	Pts.	Pen.
1973-74—Providence College		ECAC	26	16	22	38	....
1974-75—Providence College (a-c-d)		ECAC	27	26	61	87	12
1974-75—U.S. National Team		Int'l	27	5	32	47	42
1975-76—Providence College (a-d)		ECAC	28	19	47	66	44
1976-77—Providence College		ECAC	30	17	42	59	62
1976-77—Dallas Black Hawks		CHL	4	1	0	1	2
1977-78—Dallas Black Hawks (a)		CHL	67	31	38	69	18
1977-78—Toronto Maple Leafs		NHL	13	2	1	3	0
1978-79—New Brunswick Hawks		AHL	31	11	20	31	13
1978-79—Toronto Maple Leafs		NHL	5	0	2	2	2
1979-80—New Brunswick Hawks		AHL	43	20	43	63	10

Year	Team	League	Games	G.	A.	Pts.	Pen.
1980-81—Davos	Switz.	....	...	....	....	....	
1981-82—Davos	Switz.	....	...	....	....	....	
1982-83—Davos	Switz.	....	...	....	....	....	
1983-84—Davos	Switz.	....	...	....	....	....	
1984-85—Davos	Switz.	....	...	....	....	....	
1984-85—Minnesota North Stars (e)	NHL	13	4	8	12	2	
1985-86—Davos	Switz.	....	...	....	....	....	
1985-86—Minnesota North Stars	NHL	11	1	3	4	8	
1986-87—Minnesota North Stars	NHL	65	12	29	41	36	
1987-88—Minnesota North Stars (f)	NHL	24	2	12	14	16	
NHL TOTALS			177	26	67	93	68

(c)—June, 1975—Drafted by Toronto Maple Leafs in 1975 amateur draft. Seventh Maple Leafs pick, 132nd overall, seventh round.

(d)—Named to first-team (East) All-America.

(e)—March, 1985—Loaned by Davos club to Minnesota North Stars for remainder of NHL season and playoffs. Teams had same agreement in 1985-86. North Stars sent Craig Levie to Davos club in May, 1986 to secure Wilson for 1986-87 season.

(f)—December, 1987—Released by Minnesota North Stars.

RONALD LEE WILSON

Left Wing . . . 5'9" . . . 170 lbs. . . . Born, Toronto, Ont., May 13, 1956 . . . Shoots left . . . Also plays Center.

Year	Team	League	Games	G.	A.	Pts.	Pen.
1974-75—Markham Waxers	OPJHL	43	26	28	54	24
1974-75—Toronto Marlboros	Jr."A"OHA	16	6	12	18	6
1975-76—St. Cath. Black Hawks (c)	Jr."A"OHA	64	37	62	99	44
1976-77—Nova Scotia Voyageurs	AHL	67	15	21	36	18
1977-78—Nova Scotia Voyageurs	AHL	59	15	25	40	17
1978-79—Nova Scotia Voyageurs (d)	AHL	77	33	42	75	91
1979-80—Winnipeg Jets	NHL	79	21	36	57	28
1980-81—Winnipeg Jets	NHL	77	18	33	51	55
1981-82—Tulsa Oilers	CHL	41	20	38	58	22
1981-82—Winnipeg Jets	NHL	39	3	13	16	49
1982-83—Sherbrooke Jets	AHL	65	30	55	85	71
1982-83—Winnipeg Jets	NHL	12	6	3	9	4
1983-84—Winnipeg Jets	NHL	51	3	12	15	12
1983-84—Sherbrooke Jets	AHL	22	10	30	40	16
1984-85—Winnipeg Jets	NHL	75	10	9	19	31
1985-86—Winnipeg Jets	NHL	54	6	7	13	16
1985-86—Sherbrooke Canadiens	AHL	10	9	8	17	9
1986-87—Winnipeg Jets	NHL	80	3	13	16	13
1987-88—Winnipeg Jets (e)	NHL	69	5	8	13	28
NHL TOTALS		536	75	134	209	236

(c)—Drafted from St. Catharines Black Hawks by Montreal Canadiens in 15th round of 1976 amateur draft.

(d)—June, 1979—Sold by Montreal Canadiens to Winnipeg Jets.

(e)—May, 1988—Named playing/assistant coach of Moncton Golden Flames.

ROSS WILSON

Right Wing . . . 6'3" . . . 200 lbs. . . . Born, The Pas, Man., June 26, 1969 . . . Shoots right.

Year	Team	League	Games	G.	A.	Pts.	Pen.
1985-86—Sudbury Burgess Midget	SMHA	71	53	64	117	52
1986-87—Peterborough Petes (c)	OHL	66	28	11	39	91
1987-88—Peterborough Petes	OHL	66	29	30	59	114

(c)—June, 1987—Drafted as underage junior by Los Angeles Kings in 1987 NHL entry draft. Third Kings pick, 43rd overall, third round.

WILLIAM RICHARD (RIK) WILSON

Defense . . . 6' . . . 195 lbs. . . . Born, Long Beach, Calif., June 17, 1962 . . . Shoots right . . . (October, 1982)—Sprained ankle . . . (December, 1984)—Bruised knee . . . (February, 1985)—Sprained ankle . . . (November, 1986)—Injured knee.

Year	Team	League	Games	G.	A.	Pts.	Pen.
1979-80—Kingston Canadians (c)	OMJHL	67	15	38	53	75
1980-81—Kingston Canadians (a)	OHL	68	30	70	100	108
1981-82—Kingston Canadians	OHL	16	9	10	19	38
1981-82—St. Louis Blues	NHL	48	3	18	21	24
1982-83—St. Louis Blues	NHL	56	3	11	14	50
1982-83—Salt Lake Golden Eagles	CHL	4	0	0	0	0

Year	Team	League	Games	G.	A.	Pts.	Pen.
1983-84—Montana Magic		CHL	6	0	3	3	2
1983-84—St. Louis Blues		NHL	48	7	11	18	53
1984-85—St. Louis Blues		NHL	51	8	16	24	39
1985-86—Nova Scotia Oilers		AHL	13	4	5	9	11
1985-86—Moncton Golden Flames		AHL	8	3	3	6	2
1985-86—St. Louis Blues (d)		NHL	32	0	4	4	48
1985-86—Calgary Flames (e)		NHL	2	0	0	0	0
1986-87—Nova Scotia Oilers		AHL	45	8	13	21	109
1987-88—Chicago Black Hawks		NHL	14	4	5	9	6
1987-88—Saginaw Hawks		AHL	33	4	5	9	105
NHL TOTALS			251	25	65	90	220

(c)—June, 1980—Drafted by St. Louis Blues as underage junior in 1980 NHL entry draft. First Blues pick, 12th overall, first round.

(d)—February, 1986—Traded with Terry Johnson and Joe Mullen by St. Louis Blues to Calgary Flames for Gino Cavallini, Eddy Beers and Charles Bourgeois.

(e)—March, 1986—Traded by Calgary Flames to Chicago Black Hawks for Tom McMurchy.

CHRISTOPHER WINNES

Right Wing . . . 6' . . . 180 lbs. . . . Born, Columbus, Ohio, February 12, 1968 . . . Shoots right.

Year	Team	League	Games	G.	A.	Pts.	Pen.
1985-86—Ridgefield H.S.		Conn. H.S.	24	40	30	70	..
1986-87—Northwood Prep. (c)		Mass. H.S.	27	25	25	50	..
1987-88—Univ. of New Hampshire		H. East	30	17	19	36	28

(c)—June, 1987—Drafted by Boston Bruins in 1987 NHL entry draft. Ninth Bruins pick, 161st overall, eighth round.

MICHAEL LAWRENCE WOLAK

Center . . . 5'11" . . . 170 lbs. . . . Born, Utica, Mich., April 29, 1968 . . . Shoots left.

Year	Team	League	Games	G.	A.	Pts.	Pen.
1984-85—Detroit Compuware Midget		Mich.	75	85	95	180	80
1985-86—Kitchener Rangers (c)		OHL	62	24	44	68	48
1986-87—Kitchener Rangers		OHL	9	3	6	9	6
1986-87—Belleville Bulls		OHL	25	20	16	36	18
1986-87—Windsor Spitfires		OHL	26	7	14	21	26
1987-88—Windsor Spitfires		OHL	63	42	72	114	86

(c)—June, 1986—Drafted as underage junior by St. Louis Blues in 1986 NHL entry draft. Fifth Blues pick, 87th overall, fifth round.

CHRIS WOLANIN

Defense . . . 6'2" . . . 205 lbs. . . . Born, Detroit, Mich., October 21, 1969 . . . Shoots right . . . Brother of Craig Wolanin.

Year	Team	League	Games	G.	A.	Pts.	Pen.
1986-87—St. Mikes Jr. B		MTHL	25	4	9	13	50
1987-88—Univ. of Illinois/Chicago (c)		CCHA	37	1	6	7	38

(c)—June, 1988—Drafted by Vancouver Canucks in 1988 NHL entry draft. Tenth Canucks pick, 212th overall, 11th round.

CRAIG WOLANIN

Defense . . . 6'3" . . . 190 lbs. . . . Born, Grosse Point, Mich., July 27, 1967 . . . Shoots left . . . (October 31, 1985)—Bruised left shoulder vs. Detroit . . . (February 1, 1986)—Broke ring finger on left hand at Washington . . . (February 19, 1986)—Surgery to finger . . . (December, 1987)—Sore left hip . . . Brother of Chris Wolanin.

Year	Team	League	Games	G.	A.	Pts.	Pen.
1983-84—Detroit Compuware		Mich. Midget	69	8	42	50	86
1984-85—Kitchener Rangers (c)		OHL	60	5	16	21	95
1985-86—New Jersey Devils		NHL	44	2	16	18	74
1986-87—New Jersey Devils		NHL	68	4	6	10	109
1987-88—New Jersey Devils		NHL	78	6	25	31	170
NHL TOTALS			190	12	47	59	353

(c)—June, 1985—Drafted as underage junior by New Jersey Devils in 1985 NHL entry draft. First Devils pick, third overall, first round.

RANDY WOOD

Right Wing . . . 6' . . . 190 lbs. . . . Born, Manchester, Mass., October 12, 1963 . . . Shoots left.

Year	Team	League	Games	G.	A.	Pts.	Pen.
1982-83—Yale University		ECAC	26	5	14	19	10
1983-84—Yale University		ECAC	18	7	7	14	10
1984-85—Yale University		ECAC	32	25	28	53	23
1985-86—Yale University		ECAC	31	25	30	55	26
1986-87—Springfield Indians		AHL	75	23	24	47	57
1986-87—New York Islanders (c)		NHL	6	1	0	1	4
1987-88—New York Islanders		NHL	75	22	16	38	80
1987-88—Springfield Indians		AHL	1	0	1	1	0
NHL TOTALS			81	23	16	39	84

(c)—August, 1986—Signed by New York Islanders as a free agent.

CRAIG WOODCROFT

Left Wing . . . 6'1" . . . 185 lbs. . . . Born, Toronto, Ont., December 3, 1969 . . . Shoots left.

Year	Team	League	Games	G.	A.	Pts.	Pen.
1986-87—Pickering Jr. B		OHA	37	21	21	42	42
1987-88—Colgate Univ. (c)		ECAC	29	7	10	17	28

(c)—June, 1988—Drafted by Chicago Black Hawks in 1988 NHL entry draft. Sixth Black Hawks pick, 134th overall, seventh round.

DAN WOODLEY

Center . . . 5'11" . . . 190 lbs. . . . Born, Oklahoma City, Okla., December 29, 1967 . . . Shoots right . . . Also plays either Wing . . . (February 1985)—Torn cartilage in right knee . . . (October, 1986)—Surgery to repair torn abdominal muscle.

Year	Team	League	Games	G.	A.	Pts.	Pen.
1983-84—Summerland Buckeroos		BCJHL	53	17	34	51	100
1984-85—Portland Winter Hawks		WHL	63	21	36	57	108
1985-86—Portland Winter Hawks (c)		WHL	62	45	47	92	100
1986-87—Portland Winter Hawks		WHL	47	30	50	80	81
1987-88—Vancouver Canucks		NHL	5	2	0	2	17
1987-88—Flint Spirits (d)		IHL	69	29	37	66	104
NHL TOTALS			5	2	0	2	17

(c)—June, 1986—Drafted as underage junior by Vancouver Canucks in NHL entry draft. First Canucks pick, seventh overall, first round.

(d)—Winner of Ken McKenzie Trophy (Outstanding American-born Rookie).

BOB WOODS

Defense . . . 6' . . . 175 lbs. . . . Born, Chilliwack, B.C., January 24, 1968 . . . Shoots left.

Year	Team	League	Games	G.	A.	Pts.	Pen.
1987-88—Brandon Wheat Kings (c)		WHL	72	21	56	77	84

(c)—June, 1988—Drafted by New Jersey Devils in 1988 NHL entry draft. Eleventh Devils pick, 201st overall, 10th round.

TERRY YAKE

Center . . . 5'11" . . . 175 lbs. . . . Born, New Westminister, B.C., October 22, 1968 . . . Shoots right.

Year	Team	League	Games	G.	A.	Pts.	Pen.
1984-85—Brandon Wheat Kings		WHL	11	1	1	2	0
1985-86—Brandon Wheat Kings		WHL	72	26	26	52	49
1986-87—Brandon Wheat Kings (c)		WHL	71	44	58	102	64
1987-88—Brandon Wheat Kings		WHL	72	55	85	140	59

(c)—June, 1987—Drafted by Hartford Whalers in 1987 NHL entry draft. Third Whalers pick, 81st overall, fourth round.

KEN YAREMCHUK

Center . . . 5'11" . . . 185 lbs. . . . Born, Edmonton, Alta., January 1, 1964 . . . Shoots right . . . Brother of Gary Yaremchuk . . . (January, 1984)—Serious groin injury and missed two months . . . (November, 1984)—Bruised toe.

Year	Team	League	Games	G.	A.	Pts.	Pen.
1979-80—Fort Saskatchewan		AJHL	59	40	72	112	39
1980-81—Portland Winter Hawks		WHL	72	56	79	135	121
1981-82—Portland Winter Hawks (a-c)		WHL	72	58	99	157	181
1982-83—Portland Winter Hawks (b)		WHL	66	51	*109	160	76
1983-84—Chicago Black Hawks		NHL	47	6	7	13	19
1984-85—Milwaukee Admirals		IHL	7	4	6	10	9
1984-85—Chicago Black Hawks		NHL	63	10	16	26	16
1985-86—Chicago Black Hawks		NHL	78	14	20	34	43

Year	Team	League	Games	G.	A.	Pts.	Pen.
1986-87—Toronto Maple Leafs (d)	NHL	20	3	8	11	16
1986-87—Newmarket Saints	AHL	14	2	4	6	21
1987-88—Canadian Olympic Team	Int'l	46	18	21	39	65
1987-88—Toronto Maple Leafs	NHL	16	2	5	7	10
NHL TOTALS			224	35	56	91	104

(c)—June, 1982—Drafted as underage junior by Chicago Black Hawks in 1982 NHL entry draft. First Black Hawks pick, seventh overall, first round.

(d)—September, 1986—Awarded with Jerome Dupont to Toronto Maple Leafs by arbitration judge for Chicago Black Hawks signing of free agent Gary Nylund. Toronto also received Chicago's fourth-round 1987 draft pick (Joe Sacco).

TRENT YAWNEY

Defense . . . 6'3" . . . 185 lbs. . . . Born, Hudson Bay, Sask., September 29, 1965 . . . Shoots left.

Year	Team	League	Games	G.	A.	Pts.	Pen.
1981-82—Saskatoon Blades	WHL	6	1	0	1	0
1982-83—Saskatoon Blades	WHL	59	6	31	37	44
1983-84—Saskatoon Blades (c)	WHL	72	13	46	59	81
1984-85—Saskatoon Blades	WHL	72	16	51	67	158
1985-86—Team Canada	Int'l.	73	6	15	21	60
1986-87—Team Canada	Int'l.	51	4	15	19	37
1987-88—Canadian Olympic Team	Int'l	68	5	13	18	87
1987-88—Chicago Black Hawks	NHL	15	2	8	10	15
NHL TOTALS			15	2	8	10	15

(c)—June, 1984—Drafted as underage junior by Chicago Black Hawks in NHL entry draft. Second Black Hawks pick, 45th overall, third round.

SCOTT YOUNG

Right Wing . . . 6' . . . 185 lbs. . . . Born, Clinton, Mass., October 1, 1967 . . . Shoots right.

Year	Team	League	Games	G.	A.	Pts.	Pen.
1984-85—St. Marks H.S.	Mass.	23	28	41	69	....
1985-86—Boston University (c)	H. East	38	16	13	29	31
1986-87—Boston University	H. East	33	15	21	36	24
1987-88—U.S. Olympic Team	Int'l	59	13	53	66	..
1987-88—Hartford Whalers	NHL	7	0	0	0	2
NHL TOTALS			7	0	0	0	2

(c)—June, 1986—Drafted by Hartford Whalers in 1986 NHL entry draft. First Whalers pick, 11th overall, first round.

WARREN HOWARD YOUNG

Left Wing . . . 6'3" . . . 195 lbs. . . . Born, Weston, Ont., January 11, 1956 . . . Shoots left.

Year	Team	League	Games	G.	A.	Pts.	Pen.
1974-75—Dixie Beehives	OPJHL	44	32	25	57	50
1975-76—Michigan Tech (c)	WCHA	42	16	15	31	48
1976-77—Michigan Tech	WCHA	37	19	26	45	86
1977-78—Michigan Tech	WCHA	32	14	16	30	54
1978-79—Michigan Tech	WCHA	26	11	7	18	45
1978-79—Oklahoma City Stars	CHL	4	0	1	1	2
1979-80—Oklahoma City Stars	CHL	13	4	8	12	9
1979-80—Baltimore Clippers (b)	EHL	65	*53	53	106	75
1980-81—Oklahoma City Stars	CHL	77	26	33	59	42
1981-82—Minnesota North Stars	NHL	1	0	0	0	0
1981-82—Nashville South Stars	CHL	60	31	28	59	154
1982-83—Minnesota North Stars	NHL	4	1	1	2	0
1982-83—Birmingham South Stars (b)	CHL	75	26	58	84	144
1983-84—Pittsburgh Penguins (d)	NHL	15	1	7	8	19
1983-84—Baltimore Skipjacks	AHL	59	25	38	63	142
1984-85—Pittsburgh Penguins (e)	NHL	80	40	32	72	174
1985-86—Detroit Red Wings (f)	NHL	79	22	24	46	161
1986-87—Baltimore Skipjacks	AHL	22	8	7	15	95
1986-87—Pittsburgh Penguins	NHL	50	8	13	21	103
1987-88—Pittsburgh Penguins	NHL	7	0	0	0	15
1987-88—Muskegon Lumberjacks	IHL	60	25	26	51	325
NHL TOTALS			236	72	77	149	472

(c)—May, 1976—Drafted by California Seals in NHL amateur draft. Fourth Seals pick, 59th overall, fourth round.

(d)—August, 1983—Signed by Pittsburgh Penguins as a free agent.

(e)—July, 1985—Signed by Detroit Red Wings as a free agent.

(f)—October, 1987—Traded to Pittsburgh Penguins for future considerations. Penguins chose not to retain Young for 1987-88 and returned him to Detroit in July.

PAUL YSEBAERT

Center . . . 6'1" . . . 170 lbs. . . . Born, Sarnia, Ont., May 15, 1966 . . . Shoots left.

Year	Team	League	Games	G.	A.	Pts.	Pen.
1983-84—Petrolia Jets (c)		WOJBHL	33	35	42	77	20
1984-85—Bowling Green Univ.		CCHA	42	23	32	55	54
1985-86—Bowling Green Univ. (b)		CCHA	42	23	45	68	50
1986-87—Bowling Green Univ. (b)		CCHA	45	27	58	85	44
1986-87—Canadian Olympic Team		Int'l	5	1	0	1	4
1987-88—Utica Devils		AHL	78	30	49	79	60

(c)—June, 1984—Drafted by New Jersey Devils in NHL entry draft. Fourth Devils pick, 74th overall, fourth round.

STEVE YZERMAN

Center . . . 5'11" . . . 175 lbs. . . . Born, Cranbrook, B.C., May 9, 1965 . . . Shoots right . . . (January 31, 1984)—Became youngest person to ever play in NHL All-Star Game . . . (January 31, 1986)—Broke collarbone vs. St. Louis . . . (March 1, 1988)—Fell into a goal-post vs. Buffalo moments after scoring his 50th goal of the season. He required surgery to his right knee to repair damaged ligaments.

Year	Team	League	Games	G.	A.	Pts.	Pen.
1981-82—Peterborough Petes		OHL	58	21	43	64	65
1982-83—Peterborough Petes (c)		OHL	56	42	49	91	33
1983-84—Detroit Red Wings (d)		NHL	80	39	48	87	33
1984-85—Detroit Red Wings		NHL	80	30	59	89	58
1985-86—Detroit Red Wings		NHL	51	14	28	42	16
1986-87—Detroit Red Wings		NHL	80	31	59	90	43
1987-88—Detroit Red Wings		NHL	64	50	52	102	44
NHL TOTALS			355	164	246	410	194

(c)—June, 1983—Drafted as underage junior by Detroit Red Wings in 1983 NHL entry draft. First Red Wings pick, fourth overall, first round.

(d)—Named NHL Rookie of the Year in poll of players by THE SPORTING NEWS.

ZARLEY ZALAPSKI

Defense . . . 6'1" . . . 195 lbs. . . . Born, Edmonton, Alta., April 22, 1968 . . . Shoots left . . . (October, 1987)—Spondylothesis (Deterioration of the bony structure of the spine).

Year	Team	League	Games	G.	A.	Pts.	Pen.
1984-85—Fort Saskatchewan Traders		AJHL	23	17	30	47	14
1985-86—Fort Saskatchewan Traders		AJHL	27	20	33	53	46
1985-86—Team Canada (c)		Int'l	32	2	4	6	10
1986-87—Team Canada		Int'l	74	11	29	40	28
1987-88—Canadian Olympic Team		Int'l	55	4	16	20	34
1987-88—Pittsburgh Penguins		NHL	15	3	8	11	7
NHL TOTALS			15	3	8	11	7

(c)—June, 1986—Drafted by Pittsburgh Penguins in 1986 NHL entry draft. First Penguins pick, fourth overall, first round.

RICHARD ANDREW ZEMLAK

Center . . . 6'2" . . . 190 lbs. . . . Born, Wynard, Sask., March 3, 1963 . . . Shoots right.

Year	Team	League	Games	G.	A.	Pts.	Pen.
1979-80—Regina Pat Blues		SJHL	30	4	7	11	80
1980-81—Spokane Flyers (c)		WHL	72	19	19	38	132
1981-82—Spokane Flyers (d)		WHL	28	10	22	32	113
1981-82—Medicine Hat Tigers		WHL	41	11	20	31	70
1981-82—Salt Lake Golden Eagles		CHL	6	0	0	0	2
1982-83—Medicine Hat Tigers		WHL	51	20	17	37	119
1982-83—Nanaimo Islanders		WHL	18	2	8	10	50
1983-84—Montana Magic		CHL	14	2	2	4	17
1983-84—Toledo Goaldiggers (e)		IHL	45	8	19	27	101
1984-85—Fredericton Express		AHL	16	3	4	7	59
1984-85—Muskegon Lumberjacks		IHL	64	19	18	37	221
1985-86—Muskegon Lumberjacks		IHL	3	1	2	3	36
1985-86—Fredericton Express		AHL	58	6	5	11	305
1986-87—Fredericton Express		AHL	28	9	6	15	201
1986-87—Quebec Nordiques		NHL	20	0	2	2	47
1987-88—Minnesota North Stars (f)		NHL	54	1	4	5	307
NHL TOTALS			74	1	6	7	354

(c)—June, 1981—Drafted as underage junior by St. Louis Blues in 1981 NHL entry draft. Ninth Blues pick, 209th overall, 10th round.

(d)—December, 1981—Selected by Medicine Hat Tigers in special WHL draft of players from defunct Spokane Flyers.

(e)—August, 1984—Sold by St. Louis Blues to Quebec Nordiques.

(f)—October, 1987—Acquired by the New York Rangers in the 1987 NHL waiver draft as compensation for the Quebec Nordiques drafting of Stu Kulak. The Minnesota North Stars then selected him from the New York Rangers list.

ROB ZETTLER

Defense . . . 6'2" . . . 180 lbs. . . . Born, Sept Illes, Que., March 8, 1968 . . . Shoots left.

Year	Team	League	Games	G.	A.	Pts.	Pen.
1984-85—Sault Ste. Marie Greyhounds		OHL	60	2	14	16	37
1985-86—Sault Ste. Marie Greyhounds (c)		OHL	57	5	23	28	92
1986-87—Sault Ste. Marie Greyhounds		OHL	64	13	22	35	89
1987-88—Sault Ste. Marie Greyhounds		OHL	64	7	41	48	77
1987-88—Kalamazoo Wings		IHL	2	0	1	1	0

(c)—June, 1986—Drafted as underage junior by Minnesota North Stars in 1986 NHL entry draft. Fifth North Stars pick, 55th overall, fifth round.

PETER ZEZEL

Center . . . 5'10" . . . 195 lbs. . . . Born, Toronto, Ont., April 22, 1965 . . . Shoots left . . . (November, 1984)—Broken hand . . . (March, 1987)—Torn medial cartilage in left knee . . . (November, 1987)—Sprained right ankle . . . (March, 1988)—Separated left shoulder.

Year	Team	League	Games	G.	A.	Pts.	Pen.
1981-82—Don Mills Flyers		MTHL	40	43	51	94	36
1982-83—Toronto Marlboros (c)		OHL	66	35	39	74	28
1983-84—Toronto Marlboros		OHL	68	47	86	133	31
1984-85—Philadelphia Flyers		NHL	65	15	46	61	26
1985-86—Philadelphia Flyers		NHL	79	17	37	54	76
1986-87—Philadelphia Flyers		NHL	71	33	39	72	71
1987-88—Philadelphia Flyers		NHL	69	22	35	57	42
NHL TOTALS			284	87	157	244	215

(c)—June, 1983—Drafted as underage junior by Philadelphia Flyers in 1983 NHL entry draft. First Flyers pick, 41st overall, second round.

RICK ZOMBO

Defense . . . 6'1" . . . 190 lbs. . . . Born, Des Plaines, Ill., May 8, 1963 . . . Shoots right . . . (December, 1984)—Injured knee . . . (December, 1987)—Injured shoulder.

Year	Team	League	Games	G.	A.	Pts.	Pen.
1980-81—Austin Mavericks (c)		USHL	43	10	26	36	73
1981-82—Univ. of North Dakota		WCHA	45	1	15	16	31
1982-83—Univ. of North Dakota		WCHA	33	5	11	16	41
1983-84—Univ. of North Dakota		WCHA	34	7	24	31	40
1984-85—Adirondack Red Wings		AHL	56	3	32	35	70
1984-85—Detroit Red Wings		NHL	1	0	0	0	0
1985-86—Adirondack Red Wings		AHL	69	7	34	41	94
1985-86—Detroit Red Wings		NHL	14	0	1	1	16
1986-87—Adirondack Red Wings		AHL	25	0	6	6	22
1986-87—Detroit Red Wings		NHL	44	1	4	5	59
1987-88—Detroit Red Wings		NHL	62	3	14	17	96
NHL TOTALS			121	4	19	23	171

(c)—June, 1981—Drafted by Detroit Red Wings in NHL entry draft. Sixth Red Wings pick, 149th overall, eighth round.

GOALTENDERS

MURRAY BANNERMAN

Goaltender . . . 5'11" . . . 184 lbs. . . . Born, Fort Frances, Ont., April 27, 1957 . . . Shoots left . . . (June, 1985)—Fractured large bone of left index finger when he fell out of tree he was pruning in his backyard.

Year	Team	League	Games	Mins.	Goals	SO.	Avg.	A.	Pen.
1972-73—St. James Canadians (b)		MJHL	31	1788	104	*1	*3.49	1	6
1973-74—St. James Canadians		MJHL	17	930	69	0	4.45	1	16
1973-74—Winnipeg Clubs		WCHL	6	258	29	0	6.74	..	....
1974-75—Winnipeg Clubs		WCHL	28	1351	113	0	5.02	2	6
1975-76—Victoria Cougars		WCHL	44	2450	178	1	4.36	5	25
1976-77—Victoria Cougars (c)		WCHL	67	3893	262	2	4.04	3	24
1977-78—Fort Wayne Komets (a)		IHL	44	2435	133	1	3.28	6	10
1977-78—Vancouver Canucks (d)		NHL	1	20	0	0	0.00	0	0
1978-79—New Brunswick Hawks		AHL	47	2557	152	0	3.57	3	23
1979-80—New Brunswick Hawks (b)		AHL	61	3361	186	*3	3.32	3	25
1980-81—Chicago Black Hawks		NHL	15	865	62	0	4.30	0	0
1981-82—Chicago Black Hawks		NHL	29	1671	116	1	4.17	1	0
1982-83—Chicago Black Hawks		NHL	41	2460	127	4	3.10	1	2
1983-84—Chicago Black Hawks		NHL	56	3335	188	2	3.38	4	17
1984-85—Chicago Black Hawks		NHL	60	3371	215	0	3.83	1	8
1985-86—Chicago Black Hawks		NHL	48	2689	201	1	4.48	2	6
1986-87—Chicago Black Hawks		NHL	39	2059	142	0	4.14	1	4
1987-88—Baltimore Skipjacks		AHL	41	2014	164	0	4.89	3	40
1987-88—Saginaw Wings		IHL	3	140	15	0	6.43	0	0
NHL TOTALS			289	16470	1051	8	3.83	10	37

(c)—Drafted from Victoria Cougars by Vancouver Canucks in fourth round of 1977 amateur draft.
(d)—June, 1978—Sent to Chicago Black Hawks by Vancouver Canucks as the future consideration in a November, 1977 deal that saw Pit Martin go from Chicago to Vancouver. The Canucks had to choose between Bannerman and Glen Hanlon as future considerations.

THOMAS BARRASSO

Goaltender . . . 6'3" . . . 195 lbs. . . . Born, Boston, Mass., March 31, 1965 . . . Shoots right . . . Member of 1983 U.S. National Junior Team . . . Left 1984 U.S. Olympic team to sign with Buffalo Sabres . . . First U.S.-born player to win Calder Trophy (top NHL rookie) since Frank Brimsek (Boston goalie) in 1939 . . . First goaltender to win Calder Trophy since Ken Dryden in 1972 . . . (June, 1985)—Twisted knee during Molson Softball Tournament in Niagara Falls, Ont. . . . (November, 1987)—Chip fracture of ankle . . . (April 9, 1988)—Pulled groin in playoff series vs. Boston.

Year	Team	League	Games	Mins.	Goals	SO.	Avg.	A.	Pen.
1981-82—Acton Boxboro H.S.		Mass. H.S.	23	1035	32	7	1.86	..	....
1982-83—Acton Boxboro H.S. (c)		Mass. H.S.	23	1035	17	10	0.99	..	....
1983-84—Buffalo Sabres (a-d-e)		NHL	42	2475	117	2	2.84	2	20
1984-85—Rochester Americans		AHL	5	267	6	1	1.35	0	2
1984-85—Buffalo Sabres (b)		NHL	54	3248	144	5	2.66	6	41
1985-86—Buffalo Sabres		NHL	60	3561	214	2	3.61	4	28
1986-87—Buffalo Sabres		NHL	46	2501	152	2	3.65	1	22
1987-88—Buffalo Sabres		NHL	54	3133	173	2	3.31	1	50
NHL TOTALS			256	14918	800	13	3.22	14	161

(c)—June, 1983—Drafted by Buffalo Sabres in 1983 NHL entry draft. First Sabres pick, fifth overall, first round.
(d)—Won Calder Memorial Trophy (Top NHL Rookie).
(e)—Won Vezina Trophy (Outstanding NHL Goaltender).

DARREN KELSEY BEALS

Goaltender . . . 6' . . . 185 lbs. . . . Born, Dartmouth, N.S., August 28, 1968 . . . Shoots right . . . (October, 1987)—Suspended eight OHL games for pushing a linesman.

Year	Team	League	Games	Mins.	Goals	SO.	Avg.	A.	Pen.
1984-85—Dartmouth Midget		N. Scotia	11	660	27	0	2.42	..	..
1985-86—Ottawa 67's		OHL	45	2622	*233	1	5.33	2	17
1986-87—Ottawa 67's (c-d)		OHL	4	240	11	1	2.75	0	0
1986-87—Kitchener Rangers		OHL	45	2342	179	0	4.59	3	2
1987-88—Kitchener Rangers		OHL	38	2063	169	0	4.92	2	4

(c)—September, 1986—Signed by Edmonton Oilers as a free agent.
(d)—October, 1986—Traded by Ottawa 67's to Kitchener Rangers for future considerations.

DON BEAUPRE

Goaltender . . . 5'8" . . . 155 lbs. . . . Born, Kitchener, Ont., September 19, 1961 . . . Shoots left . . . (October, 1981)—Bruised ribs . . . (February, 1985)—Sprained knee . . . (December, 1987)—Pulled groin muscle.

Year	Team	League	Games	Mins.	Goals	SO.	Avg.	A.	Pen.
1978-79	Sudbury Wolves	OMJHL	54	3248	259	2	4.78	0	0
1979-80	Sudbury Wolves (a-c)	OMJHL	59	3447	248	0	4.32	4	18
1980-81	Minnesota North Stars	NHL	44	2585	138	0	3.20	1	20
1981-82	Nashville South Stars	CHL	5	299	25	0	5.02	0	4
1981-82	Minnesota North Stars	NHL	29	1634	101	0	3.71	0	19
1982-83	Birmingham South Stars	CHL	10	599	31	0	3.11	0	6
1982-83	Minnesota North Stars	NHL	36	2011	120	0	3.58	2	10
1983-84	Salt Lake Golden Eagles	CHL	7	419	30	0	4.30	0	0
1983-84	Minnesota North Stars	NHL	33	1791	123	0	4.12	0	17
1984-85	Minnesota North Stars	NHL	21	1770	109	1	3.69	0	4
1985-86	Minnesota North Stars	NHL	52	3073	182	1	3.55	0	34
1986-87	Minnesota North Stars	NHL	47	2622	174	1	3.98	0	16
1987-88	Minnesota North Stars	NHL	43	2288	161	0	4.22	0	8
	NHL TOTALS		305	17774	1108	3	3.74	3	128

(c)—June, 1980—Drafted by Minnesota North Stars as underage junior in 1980 NHL entry draft. Second North Stars pick, 37th overall, second round.

STEPHANE BEAUREGARD

Goaltender . . . 5'11" . . . 180 lbs. . . . Born, Cowansville, Que., January 10, 1968 . . . Shoots right.

Year	Team	League	Games	Mins.	Goals	SO.	Avg.	A.	Pen.
1986-87	St. Jean Castors	QHL	13	785	58	0	4.43	0	0
1987-88	St. Jean Castors (a-c-d-e)	QHL	66	3766	229	2	3.65	1	12

(c)—June, 1988—Drafted by Winnipeg Jets in 1988 NHL entry draft. Third Jets pick, 52nd overall, third round.
(d)—Won Raymond Lagace Trophy (Top Rookie Defenseman or Goaltender).
(e)—Won Jacques Plante Trophy (Best Goalie).

ROGER BEEDON

Goaltender . . . 6' . . . 175 lbs. . . . Born, Marysville, Mich., May 30, 1967 . . . Shoots left.

Year	Team	League	Games	Mins.	Goals	SO.	Avg.	A.	Pen.
1985-86	Ohio State Univ. (c)	CCHA	27	1393	115	0	4.95	3	2
1986-87	Ohio State Univ.	CCHA	24	1322	114	1	5.17	1	6
1987-88	Ohio State Univ.	CCHA	24	1119	98	0	5.35	1	2

(c)—June, 1985—Drafted by Montreal Canadiens in 1985 NHL entry draft. Eleventh Canadiens pick, 184th overall, eighth round.

ED BELFOUR

Goaltender . . . 5'11" . . . 170 lbs. . . . Born, Carman, Man., April 21, 1965 . . . Shoots left.

Year	Team	League	Games	Mins.	Goals	SO.	Avg.	A.	Pen.
1985-86	Winkler Flyers (c)	MJHL	....	.....	....	...	.....	..	....
1986-87	Univ. of North Dakota (a-d-e)	WCHA	34	2049	81	3	2.37	2	6
1987-88	Saginaw Gears (a-f)	IHL	61	3446	183	3	3.19	2	23

(c)—Named top goaltender in Manitoba Junior Hockey League.
(d)—Named to second-team All-America college team (West).
(e)—June, 1987—Signed by Chicago Black Hawks as a free agent.
(f)—Shared Garry F. Longham Memorial Trophy (Outstanding Rookie) with John Cullen.

JEAN-CLAUDE BERGERON

Goaltender . . . 6'2" . . . 180 lbs. . . . Born, Havreziue, Que., October 14, 1968 . . . Shoots left.

Year	Team	League	Games	Mins.	Goals	SO.	Avg.	A.	Pen.
1985-86	Shawinigan Cataracts	QHL	33	1796	156	0	5.21	2	17
1986-87	Verdun Junior Canadiens	QHL	52	2991	*306	0	6.14	1	0
1987-88	Verdun Junior Canadiens (c)	QHL	49	2715	265	0	5.86	2	4

(c)—June, 1988—Drafted by Montreal Canadiens in 1988 NHL entry draft. Sixth Canadiens pick, 104th overall, fifth round.

TIMOTHY JOHN BERNHARDT

Goaltender . . . 5'9" . . . 160 lbs. . . . Born, Sarnia, Ont., January 17, 1958 . . . Shoots left . . . (October, 1980)—Surgery to remove abscess at base of spine . . . (November 27, 1985)— Pulled muscle at Pittsburgh and missed four games.

Year	Team	League	Games	Mins.	Goals	SO.	Avg.	A.	Pen.
1975-76—Cornwall Royals		QJHL	51	2985	195	2	3.92	..	....
1976-77—Cornwall Royals (a-c)		QJHL	44	2497	151	0	*3.63	1	2
1977-78—Cornwall Royals (a-d)		QJHL	54	3165	179	2	3.39	..	....
1978-79—Tulsa Oilers		CHL	46	2705	191	0	4.24	1	4
1979-80—Birmingham Bulls		CHL	34	1933	122	1	3.79	0	0
1980-81—Birmingham Bulls		CHL	29	1598	106	1	3.98	1	0
1981-82—Oklahoma City Stars		CHL	10	526	45	0	5.13	0	0
1981-82—Rochester Americans		AHL	29	1586	95	0	3.59	2	0
1982-83—Calgary Flames		NHL	6	280	21	0	4.50	0	0
1982-83—Colorado Flames		CHL	34	1896	122	0	3.86	0	4
1983-84—St. Catharines Saints (b)		AHL	42	2501	154	0	3.69	0	0
1984-85—St. Catharines Saints (e)		AHL	14	801	55	0	4.12	0	2
1984-85—Toronto Maple Leafs		NHL	37	2182	136	0	3.74	2	4
1985-86—St. Catharines Saints		AHL	14	776	38	1	2.94	1	2
1985-86—Toronto Maple Leafs		NHL	23	1266	107	0	5.07	1	0
1986-87—Newmarket Saints		AHL	31	1705	117	1	4.12	2	0
1986-87—Toronto Maple Leafs		NHL	1	20	3	0	9.00	0	0
1987-88—Newmarket Saints		AHL	49	2704	166	0	3.68	1	2
NHL TOTALS			67	3748	267	0	4.27	3	4

(c)—Won leading goalie award.
(d)—Drafted from Cornwall Royals by Atlanta Flames in third round of 1978 amateur draft.
(e)—September, 1984—Signed by Toronto Maple Leafs as a free agent.

DANIEL BERTHIAUME

Goaltender . . . 5'9" . . . 151 lbs. . . . Born, Longueuil, Que., January 26, 1966 . . . Shoots left . . . (March 1, 1988)—Pulled chest muscle.

Year	Team	League	Games	Mins.	Goals	SO.	Avg.	A.	Pen.
1983-84—Drummondville Voltigeurs		QHL	28	1562	131	0	5.03	1	0
1984-85—Drummondville/Chicoutimi (c-d)		QHL	59	3347	215	*2	*3.85	3	16
1985-86—Chicoutimi Sagueneens		QHL	*66	*3718	*286	1	4.62	2	12
1985-86—Winnipeg Jets (e)		NHL	....	......	....	...	.....	..	....
1986-87—Sherbrooke Canadiens		AHL	7	420	23	0	3.29	0	2
1986-87—Winnipeg Jets		NHL	31	1758	93	1	3.17	0	2
1987-88—Winnipeg Jets		NHL	54	3010	176	2	3.51	2	12
NHL TOTALS			85	4768	269	3	3.39	2	14

(c)—October, 1984—Traded by Drummondville Voltigeurs to Chicoutimi Saguenees for Simon Masse.
(d)—June, 1985—Drafted as underage junior by Winnipeg Jets in 1985 NHL entry draft. Third Jets pick, 60th overall, third round.
(e)—No regular season record. Played one playoff game, allowing four goals.

ALLAN J. BESTER

Goaltender . . . 5'7" . . . 152 lbs. . . . Born, Hamilton, Ont., March 26, 1964 . . . Shoots left . . . (February, 1988)—Missed 14 games with sprained left knee ligaments.

Year	Team	League	Games	Mins.	Goals	SO.	Avg.	A.	Pen.
1981-82—Brantford Alexanders		OHL	19	970	68	0	4.21	1	4
1982-83—Brantford Alexanders (a-c-d)		OHL	56	3210	188	0	3.51	0	16
1983-84—Brantford Alexanders		OHL	23	1271	71	1	3.35	1	4
1983-84—Toronto Maple Leafs		NHL	32	1848	134	0	4.35	0	6
1984-85—St. Catharines Saints		AHL	30	1669	133	0	4.78	0	2
1984-85—Toronto Maple Leafs		NHL	15	767	54	1	4.22	1	4
1985-86—St. Catharines Saints		AHL	50	2855	173	1	3.64	1	6
1985-86—Toronto Maple Leafs		NHL	1	20	2	0	6.00	0	0
1986-87—Newmarket Saints		AHL	3	190	6	0	1.89	0	0
1986-87—Toronto Maple Leafs		NHL	36	1808	110	2	3.65	0	8
1987-88—Toronto Maple Leafs		NHL	30	1607	102	2	3.81	3	6
NHL TOTALS			114	6050	402	5	3.99	4	24

(c)—Led OHL playoffs with a 2.50 average and one shutout.
(d)—June, 1983—Drafted as underage junior by Toronto Maple Leafs in 1983 NHL entry draft. Third Maple Leafs pick, 48th overall, third round.

CRAIG BILLINGTON

Goaltender . . . 5'10" . . . 150 lbs. . . . Born, London, Ont., September 11, 1966 . . . Shoots left . . . (July, 1984)—Mononucleosis.

Year	Team	League	Games	Mins.	Goals	SO.	Avg.	A.	Pen.
1982-83—London Diamonds		WOJBHL	23	1338	76	0	3.39	..	..
1983-84—Belleville Bulls (c)		OHL	44	2335	162	1	4.16	2	7
1984-85—Belleville Bulls (a)		OHL	47	2544	180	1	4.25	0	2
1985-86—Belleville Bulls		OHL	3	180	11	0	3.67	0	0

Year	Team	League	Games	Mins.	Goals	SO.	Avg.	A.	Pen.
1985-86—New Jersey Devils		NHL	18	902	77	0	5.12	1	0
1986-87—Maine Mariners		AHL	20	1151	70	0	3.65	1	4
1986-87—New Jersey Devils		NHL	22	1114	89	0	4.79	0	12
1987-88—Utica Devils		AHL	59	3404	208	1	3.67	2	19
NHL TOTALS			40	2016	166	0	4.94	1	12

(c)—June, 1984—Drafted as underage junior by New Jersey Devils in NHL entry draft. Second Devils pick, 23rd overall, second round.

GRANT BLAIR

Goaltender ... 6' ... 150 lbs. ... Born, Stoney Creek, Ont., August 15, 1964 ... Shoots left.

Year	Team	League	Games	Mins.	Goals	SO.	Avg.	A.	Pen.
1981-82—Guelph		Ont. Tier II	25	1506	82	1	3.27	..	..
1982-83—Harvard University (c)		ECAC	26	1575	72	..	2.74	0	0
1983-84—Harvard University (d)		ECAC	23	1391	71	..	3.06	1	8
1984-85—Harvard University (b)		ECAC	31	1785	86	1	2.89	0	26
1985-86—Harvard University		ECAC	31	1812	82	2	2.72	2	6
1986-87—Salt Lake Golden Eagles		IHL	25	1431	108	0	4.53	2	21
1987-88—Kalamazoo Wings		IHL	2	120	11	0	5.20	0	0
1987-88—Salt Lake Golden Eagles		IHL	19	813	51	0	3.76	0	2

(c)—June, 1983—Drafted by Calgary Flames in 1983 NHL entry draft. Eighth Flames pick, 111th overall, sixth round.

(d)—Ivy League Player of the Year.

JOHN BLUE

Goaltender ... 5'9" ... 170 lbs. ... Born, Huntington Beach, Calif., February 9, 1966 ... Shoots left.

Year	Team	League	Games	Mins.	Goals	SO.	Avg.	A.	Pen.
1983-84—Des Moines Buccaneers		USHL	15	753	63	..	5.02	0	4
1984-85—Univ. of Minnesota (b)		WCHA	34	1964	111	2	3.39	1	7
1985-86—Univ. of Minnesota (a-c)		WCHA	29	1588	80	3	3.02	1	4
1986-87—Univ. of Minnesota		WCHA	33	1889	99	3	3.14	6	6
1987-88—Kalamazoo Wings (d)		IHL	15	847	65	0	4.60	0	4
1987-88—U.S. Olympic Team		Int'l	8	...	..	..	3.37	..	..

(c)—June, 1986—Drafted by Winnipeg Jets in 1986 NHL entry draft. Ninth Jets pick, 197th overall, 10th round.

(d)—March, 1988—Traded by Winnipeg Jets to Minnesota North Stars for a seventh-round 1988 draft pick (Markus Akerbloom).

JOHN BRADLEY

Goaltender ... 6' ... 165 lbs. ... Born, Pawtucket, R.I., February 6, 1968 ... Shoots left.

Year	Team	League	Games	Mins.	Goals	SO.	Avg.	A.	Pen.
1986-87—New Hampton H.S. (c)		R.I.H.S.	34	2040	96	4	2.82	..	....
1987-88—Boston University		H. East	9	523	40	0	4.59	0	2

(c)—June, 1987—Drafted by Buffalo Sabres in 1987 NHL entry draft. Fourth Sabres pick, 84th overall, fourth round.

RICHARD BRODEUR

Goaltender ... 5'7" ... 185 lbs. ... Born, Longueuil, Que., September 15, 1952 ... Shoots left ... Missed part of 1977-78 season with surgery on left knee ... (February 15, 1981)—Injured left knee, resulting in surgery to remove bone spurs ... (November, 1982)—Knee injury ... (February 5, 1983)—Suffered 20-stitch cut and perforated eardrum when struck by shot of Toronto's Dan Daoust ... Last player from the WHA's first season (1972-73) to still be playing in the NHL ... (October, 1987)—Bronchitis ... (December, 1987)—Pulled groin.

Year	Team	League	Games	Mins.	Goals	SO.	Avg.	A.	Pen.
1970-71—Cornwall Royals		QJHL	41	.....	191	0	4.66	..	....
1971-72—C'wall Royals (a-c-d-e)		QJHL	58	.....	170	*5	*2.93	..	....
1972-73—Quebec Nordiques		WHA	24	1288	102	0	4.75	0	4
1973-74—Maine Nordiques		NAHL	15	936	47	0	3.01	0	0
1973-74—Quebec Nordiques		WHA	30	1607	89	1	3.32	1	0
1974-75—Quebec Nordiques		WHA	51	2938	188	0	3.84	2	13
1975-76—Quebec Nordiques		WHA	69	3967	244	2	3.69	3	2
1976-77—Quebec Nordiques		WHA	53	2906	167	2	3.45	1	0
1977-78—Quebec Nordiques		WHA	36	1962	121	0	3.70	2	0
1978-79—Quebec Nordiques (b-f-g)		WHA	42	2433	126	*3	3.11	3	2
1979-80—Indianapolis Checkers (a-h-i)		CHL	46	2722	131	*4	2.89	0	12
1979-80—New York Islanders (j)		NHL	2	80	6	0	4.50	0	0
1980-81—Vancouver Canucks		NHL	52	3024	177	0	3.51	0	0

Year	Team	League	Games	Mins.	Goals	SO.	Avg.	A.	Pen.
1981-82—Vancouver Canucks		NHL	52	3010	168	2	3.35	2	0
1982-83—Vancouver Canucks		NHL	58	3291	208	0	3.79	1	2
1983-84—Vancouver Canucks		NHL	36	2107	141	1	4.02	2	0
1984-85—Fredericton Express		AHL	4	249	13	0	3.13	0	0
1984-85—Vancouver Canucks		NHL	51	2930	228	0	4.67	1	4
1985-86—Vancouver Canucks		NHL	64	3541	240	2	4.07	2	16
1986-87—Vancouver Canucks		NHL	53	2972	178	1	3.59	0	2
1987-88—Fredericton Express		AHL	2	99	8	0	4.85	0	0
1987-88—Vancouver Canucks (k)		NHL	11	670	49	0	4.39	0	0
1987-88—Hartford Whalers		NHL	6	340	15	0	2.65	0	2
WHA TOTALS			305	17101	1037	8	3.64	12	21
NHL TOTALS			385	21965	1410	6	3.85	8	26

(c)—Won leading goalie award.

(d)—February, 1972—Selected by Quebec Nordiques in World Hockey Association player selection draft.

(e)—Drafted from Cornwall Royals by New York Islanders in seventh round of 1972 amateur draft.

(f)—June, 1979—Selected by New York Islanders in NHL reclaim draft, but remained with Nordiques and was made a priority selection by Quebec for expansion draft.

(g)—August, 1979—Traded by Quebec Nordiques to New York Islanders for Goran Hogosta.

(h)—Led CHL Adams Playoff goaltenders with a 2.02 average and shared shutout lead (1) with Michel Plasse.

(i)—Shared Terry Sawchuk Trophy (Top Goaltender) with teammate Jim Park.

(j)—October, 1980—Traded with fifth round 1981 draft pick (Moe Lemay) by New York Islanders to Vancouver Canucks for fifth round 1981 draft pick (Jacques Sylvestri).

(k)—March, 1988—Traded by Vancouver Canucks to Hartford Whalers for Steve Weeks.

SCOTT BROWER

Goaltender . . . 6' . . . 185 lbs. . . . Born, Viking, Alta., September 26, 1964 . . . Shoots left.

Year	Team	League	Games	Mins.	Goals	SO.	Avg.	A.	Pen.
1983-84—Lloydminster (c)		SJHL	43	2566	173	2	4.04	..	....
1984-85—University of North Dakota		WCHA	31	1808	99	2	3.29	1	0
1985-86—University of North Dakota		WCHA	20	1096	67	1	3.67	0	0
1986-87—University of North Dakota		WCHA	15	803	44	0	3.29	1	4
1987-88—University of North Dakota		WCHA	24	1450	88	1	3.64	0	2

(c)—June, 1984—Drafted by New York Rangers in NHL entry draft. Twelfth Rangers pick, 243rd overall, 12th round.

MARIO BRUNETTA

Goaltender . . . 6'3" . . . 180 lbs. . . . Born, St. Fidele, Que., January 25, 1967 . . . Shoots left.

Year	Team	League	Games	Mins.	Goals	SO.	Avg.	A.	Pen.
1983-84—Ste. Foy Midget		Que. Midget	39	2169	162	0	4.48	..	..
1984-85—Quebec Remparts (c)		QHL	45	2255	192	0	5.11	1	16
1985-86—Laval Titans		QHL	63	3383	279	0	4.95	3	34
1986-87—Laval Titans		QHL	59	3469	261	1	4.51	0	23
1987-88—Fredericton Express		AHL	5	300	24	0	4.80	0	4
1987-88—Quebec Nordiques		NHL	29	1550	96	0	3.72	0	16
NHL TOTALS			29	1550	96	0	3.72	0	16

(c)—June, 1985—Drafted as underage junior by Quebec Nordiques in 1985 NHL entry draft. Ninth Nordiques pick, 162nd overall, eighth round.

SEAN BURKE

Goaltender . . . 6'2" . . . 183 lbs. . . . Born, Windsor, Ont., January 29, 1967 . . . Shoots left.

Year	Team	League	Games	Mins.	Goals	SO.	Avg.	A.	Pen.
1983-84—St. Michael's H.S.		MTHL	25	1482	120	0	4.85	..	..
1984-85—Toronto Marlboros (c)		OHL	49	2987	211	0	4.24	2	6
1985-86—Toronto Marlboros		OHL	47	2840	*233	0	4.92	5	32
1985-86—Team Canada		Int'l	5	284	22	0	4.65	..	..
1986-87—Team Canada		Int'l	46	2670	138	0	3.10	..	..
1987-88—Canadian Olympic Team		Int'l	41	2200	104	1	2.84	..	..
1987-88—New Jersey Devils		NHL	13	689	35	1	3.05	1	6
NHL TOTALS			13	689	35	1	3.05	1	6

(c)—June, 1985—Drafted as underage junior by New Jersey Devils in 1985 NHL entry draft. Second Devils pick, 24th overall, second round.

FRANK CAPRICE

Goaltender . . . 5'9" . . . 160 lbs. . . . Born, Hamilton, Ont., May 2, 1962 . . . Shoots left . . . (December, 1985)—Injured knee.

Year	Team	League	Games	Mins.	Goals	SO.	Avg.	A.	Pen.
1979-80—London Knights		OHL	18	919	74	1	4.84	0	2
1980-81—London Knights (c)		OHL	42	2171	190	0	5.25	1	9
1981-82—London Knights		OHL	45	2614	196	0	4.50	3	6
1981-82—Dallas Black Hawks		CHL	3	178	19	0	6.40	0	0
1982-83—Vancouver Canucks		NHL	10	20	3	0	9.00	0	0
1982-83—Fredericton Express		AHL	14	819	50	0	3.67	3	0
1983-84—Vancouver Canucks		NHL	19	1099	62	1	3.38	0	2
1983-84—Fredericton Express		AHL	18	1089	49	2	2.70	0	2
1984-85—Vancouver Canucks		NHL	28	1523	122	0	4.81	2	0
1985-86—Fredericton Express		AHL	26	1526	109	0	4.29	0	4
1985-86—Vancouver Canucks		NHL	7	308	28	0	5.45	1	0
1986-87—Fredericton Express		AHL	12	686	47	0	4.11	0	2
1986-87—Vancouver Canucks		NHL	25	1390	89	0	3.84	0	9
1987-88—Vancouver Canucks		NHL	22	1250	87	0	4.18	0	6
NHL TOTALS			111	5590	391	1	4.20	3	17

(c)—June, 1981—Drafted as underage junior by Vancouver Canucks in NHL entry draft. Eighth Canucks pick, 178th overall, ninth round.

JON CASEY

Goaltender . . . 5'10" . . . 155 lbs. . . . Born, Grand Rapids, Minn., March 29, 1962 . . . Shoots left.

Year	Team	League	Games	Mins.	Goals	SO.	Avg.	A.	Pen.
1980-81—Univ. of North Dakota		WCHA	6	300	19	0	3.80	0	....
1981-82—Univ. of North Dakota		WCHA	18	1038	48	1	2.77	0	0
1982-83—Univ. of North Dakota		WCHA	17	1021	42	0	2.47	1	4
1983-84—Univ. of North Dakota (c)		WCHA	37	2180	115	...	3.17	1	20
1983-84—Minnesota North Stars		NHL	2	84	6	0	4.29	0	0
1984-85—Baltimore Skipjacks (a-d)		AHL	46	2646	116	*4	*2.63	2	2
1985-86—Springfield Indians		AHL	9	464	30	0	3.88	0	6
1985-86—Minnesota North Stars		NHL	26	1402	91	0	3.89	0	6
1986-87—Indianapolis Checkers		IHL	31	1794	133	0	4.45	2	28
1986-87—Springfield Indians		AHL	13	770	56	0	4.36	1	8
1987-88—Kalamazoo Wings		IHL	42	2541	154	2	3.64	1	23
1987-88—Minnesota North Stars		NHL	14	663	41	0	3.71	0	2
NHL TOTALS			42	2149	138	0	3.85	0	8

(c)—March, 1984—Signed by Minnesota North Stars as a free agent.
(d)—Won Baz Bastien Award (Coaches pick as Top Goaltender).

FREDERIC CHABOT

Goaltender . . . 5'10" . . . 160 lbs. . . . Born, Hebertville, Que., February 12, 1968 . . . Shoots right.

Year	Team	League	Games	Mins.	Goals	SO.	Avg.	A.	Pen.
1986-87—Drummondville Voltigeurs (c)		QHL	*62	*3508	293	1	5.01	2	14
1987-88—Drummondville Voltigeurs		QHL	58	3276	237	1	4.34	3	20

(c)—June, 1986—Drafted by New Jersey Devils in 1986 NHL entry draft. Tenth Devils pick, 192nd overall, 10th round.

TIM CHEVELDAE

Goaltender . . . 5'11" . . . 175 lbs. . . . Born, Melville, Sask., February 15, 1968 . . . Shoots left.

Year	Team	League	Games	Mins.	Goals	SO.	Avg.	A.	Pen.
1984-85—Melville Millionaires		SAJHL	23	1167	98	0	5.04	..	..
1985-86—Saskatoon Blades (c)		WHL	37	1862	143	0	4.61	3	0
1986-87—Saskatoon Blades		WHL	33	1909	133	2	4.18	4	2
1987-88—Saskatoon Blades (a)		WHL	66	3798	235	1	3.71	7	10

(c)—June, 1986—Drafted as underage junior by Detroit Red Wings in 1986 NHL entry draft. Fourth Red Wings pick, 64th overall, fourth round.

ALAIN CHEVRIER

Goaltender . . . 5'8" . . . 170 lbs. . . . Born, Cornwall, Ont., April 23, 1961 . . . Shoots left.

Year	Team	League	Games	Mins.	Goals	SO.	Avg.	A.	Pen.
1980-81—Miami of Ohio Univ.		Ind.	16	778	44	0	4.01	..	..
1981-82—Miami of Ohio Univ.		CCHA	19	1053	73	..	4.16	..	..
1982-83—Miami of Ohio Univ.		CCHA	33	1894	125	..	3.96	1	..
1983-84—Miami of Ohio Univ.		CCHA	32	1509	123	..	4.89	1	0
1984-85—Fort Wayne Komets (c)		IHL	56	3219	194	0	3.62	1	8
1985-86—New Jersey Devils		NHL	37	1862	143	0	4.61	3	0

Year	Team	League	Games	Mins.	Goals	SO.	Avg.	A.	Pen.
1986-87—New Jersey Devils		NHL	58	3153	227	0	4.32	0	17
1987-88—New Jersey Devils (d)		NHL	45	2354	148	1	3.77	1	8
NHL TOTALS			140	7369	518	1	4.22	4	25

(c)—May, 1985—Signed by New Jersey Devils as a free agent.

(d)—July, 1988—Traded with seventh-round draft choice in 1989 by New Jersey Devils to Winnipeg Jets for Steve Rooney and fourth-round draft choice in 1989.

CHRIS CLIFFORD

Goaltender ... 5'9" ... 140 lbs. ... Born, Kingston, Ont., May 26, 1966 ... Shoots left ... First OHL goalie to score a goal (1985-86).

Year	Team	League	Games	Mins.	Goals	SO.	Avg.	A.	Pen.
1982-83—Brockville Braves		COJHL	32	1746	126	1	4.33	..	....
1983-84—Kingston Canadians (c)		OHL	50	2808	229	2	4.89	3	6
1984-85—Kingston Canadians		OHL	52	2768	241	0	5.22	2	6
1984-85—Chicago Black Hawks		NHL	1	20	0	0	0.00	0	0
1985-86—Kingston Canadians		OHL	50	2988	178	1	3.57	7	16
1986-87—Kingston Canadians		OHL	44	2576	188	1	4.38	2	24
1987-88—Saginaw Hawks		IHL	22	1146	80	0	4.19	0	4
NHL TOTALS			1	20	0	0	0.00	0	0

(c)—June, 1984—Drafted as underage junior by Chicago Black Hawks in NHL entry draft. Sixth Black Hawks pick, 111th overall, sixth round.

JACQUES CLOUTIER

Goaltender ... 5'7" ... 154 lbs. ... Born, Noranda, Que., January 3, 1960 ... Shoots left ... (January, 1982)—Broken collarbone when hit by a slap shot in practice ... (December, 1984)—Tore ligaments in knee and was lost for the season. He spent the year as an assistant coach with Rochester.

Year	Team	League	Games	Mins.	Goals	SO.	Avg.	A.	Pen.
1976-77—Trois-Rivieres Draveurs		QMJHL	24	1109	93	0	5.03	0	0
1977-78—Trois-Rivieres Draveurs		QMJHL	71	4134	240	*4	3.48	..	....
1978-79—Trois-Rivieres Draveurs (a-c)		QMJHL	72	4168	218	*3	*3.14	..	....
1979-80—Trois-Rivieres Draveurs		QMJHL	55	3222	231	*2	4.30	0	0
1980-81—Rochester Americans		AHL	61	3478	209	1	3.61	3	9
1981-82—Rochester Americans		AHL	23	1366	64	0	2.81	2	0
1981-82—Buffalo Sabres		NHL	7	311	13	0	2.51	0	0
1982-83—Buffalo Sabres		NHL	25	1390	81	0	3.50	0	0
1982-83—Rochester Americans		AHL	13	634	42	0	3.97	0	4
1983-84—Rochester Americans		AHL	*51	*2841	172	1	3.63	2	10
1984-85—Rochester Americans		AHL	14	803	36	0	2.69	0	6
1984-85—Buffalo Sabres		NHL	1	65	4	0	3.69	1	0
1985-86—Rochester Americans		AHL	14	835	38	1	2.73	0	4
1985-86—Buffalo Sabres		NHL	15	875	49	1	3.36	2	2
1986-87—Buffalo Sabres		NHL	40	2167	137	0	3.79	2	10
1987-88—Buffalo Sabres		NHL	20	851	67	0	4.72	0	0
NHL TOTALS			108	5659	351	1	3.72	5	12

(c)—August, 1979—Drafted by Buffalo Sabres as underage junior in 1979 entry draft. Fourth Sabres pick, 55th overall, third round.

JEFF COOPER

Goaltender ... 5'10" ... 170 lbs. ... Born, Nepean, Ont., June 12, 1962 ... Shoots left.

Year	Team	League	Games	Mins.	Goals	SO.	Avg.	A.	Pen.
1981-82—Colgate University		ECAC	10	....	36	..	3.71	1	2
1982-83—Colgate University		ECAC	26	1486	100	..	4.03	..	..
1983-84—Colgate University		ECAC	32	1874	121	..	3.88	..	..
1984-85—Colgate University (c)		ECAC	31	1778	110	..	3.71	1	2
1985-86—Baltimore Skipjacks		AHL	23	1099	77	2	4.20	0	4
1986-87—Muskegon Lumberjacks (a)		IHL	45	2673	147	2	*3.30	3	4
1987-88—Muskegon Lumberjacks		IHL	21	1195	80	0	4.02	0	0
1987-88—New Haven Nighthawks		AHL	9	485	37	0	4.58	0	0

(c)—May, 1985—Signed by Pittsburgh Penguins as a free agent.

DOUGLAS DADSWELL

Goaltender ... 5'10" ... 175 lbs. ... Born, Scarborough, Ont., February 7, 1964 ... Shoots left ... (February, 1987)—Injured ankle.

Year	Team	League	Games	Mins.	Goals	SO.	Avg.	A.	Pen.
1984-85—Cornell University		Ivy	28	1654	97	0	3.45	..	....
1985-86—Cornell University (c-d)		Ivy	30	1815	92	1	3.01	..	....

Year	Team	League	Games	Mins.	Goals	SO.	Avg.	A.	Pen.
1986-87—Moncton Golden Flames		AHL	42	2275	138	1	3.64	0	14
1986-87—Calgary Flames		NHL	2	125	10	0	4.80	0	0
1987-88—Calgary Flames		NHL	25	1221	89	0	4.37	2	2
NHL TOTALS			27	1346	99	0	4.41	2	2

(c)—Named first-team (East) All-America.
(d)—August, 1986—Signed by Calgary Flames as a free agent.

CORRIE D'ALESSIO

Goaltender ... 5'11" ... 155 lbs. ... Born, September 9, 1969, Cornwall, Ont., ... Shoots left.

Year	Team	League	Games	Mins.	Goals	SO.	Avg.	A.	Pen.
1986-87—Pembroke Jr. A		BCJHL	25	1327	95	0	4.29	..	....
1987-88—Cornell University (c)		ECAC	25	1457	67	0	2.76	1	0

(c)—June, 1988—Drafted by Vancouver Canucks in 1988 NHL entry draft. Fourth Canucks pick, 107th overall, sixth round.

MARC D'AMOUR

Goaltender ... 5'10" ... 167 lbs. ... Born, Sudbury, Ont., April 29, 1961 ... Shoots left ... (December 17, 1985)—Pulled groin at Pittsburgh and missed five games ... (January 28, 1986)—Pulled groin.

Year	Team	League	Games	Mins.	Goals	SO.	Avg.	A.	Pen.
1978-79—Sault Ste. Marie Greyhounds		OHL	30	1501	149	0	5.96	0	15
1979-80—Sault Ste. Marie Greyhounds		OHL	33	1429	117	0	4.91	2	31
1980-81—Sault Ste. Marie Greyhounds		OHL	16	653	38	0	3.49	0	0
1981-82—Sault Ste. Marie Greyhounds (a-c-d)		OHL	46	2384	130	1	*3.27	1	29
1982-83—Colorado Flames		CHL	42	2373	153	1	3.87	1	23
1983-84—Colorado Flames		CHL	36	1917	131	0	4.10	2	6
1984-85—Salt Lake Golden Eagles		IHL	12	694	33	0	2.85	0	4
1984-85—Moncton Golden Flames		AHL	37	2051	115	0	3.36	0	59
1985-86—Moncton Golden Flames		AHL	21	1129	72	0	3.83	0	10
1985-86—Calgary Flames		NHL	15	560	32	0	3.43	0	22
1986-87—Binghamton Whalers		AHL	8	461	30	0	3.90	0	2
1986-87—Salt Lake Golden Eagles		IHL	10	523	37	0	4.24	0	0
1987-88—Salt Lake Golden Eagles		IHL	62	3245	177	0	3.27	2	99
NHL TOTALS			15	560	32	0	3.43	0	22

(c)—Co-winner with teammate John Vanbiesbrouck, of Dave Pinkey Trophy (Top Team Goaltending).
(d)—April, 1982—Signed by Calgary Flames as a free agent.

CLEON DASKALAKIS

Goaltender ... 5'9" ... 175 lbs. ... Born, Boston, Mass., September 29, 1962 ... Shoots left ... (June, 1985)—Separated shoulder during Molson Softball Tournament in Niagara Falls, Ontario.

Year	Team	League	Games	Mins.	Goals	SO.	Avg.	A.	Pen.
1980-81—Boston University		ECAC	8	399	24	0	3.61	..	..
1981-82—Boston University		ECAC	20	1101	59	..	3.22	0	6
1982-83—Boston University (b)		ECAC	22	1278	69	1	3.24	1	4
1983-84—Boston University (c-d)		ECAC	35	1972	96	..	2.92	0	4
1984-85—Hershey Bears		AHL	30	1614	119	0	4.42	3	8
1984-85—Boston Bruins		NHL	8	289	24	0	4.98	0	0
1985-86—Moncton Golden Flames		AHL	41	2343	141	0	3.61	1	23
1985-86—Boston Bruins		NHL	2	120	10	0	5.00	0	0
1986-87—Moncton Golden Flames		AHL	27	1452	118	0	4.88	0	14
1986-87—Boston Bruins		NHL	2	97	7	0	4.33	0	0
1987-88—Hershey Bears		AHL	3	122	9	0	4.43	0	4
1987-88—Binghamton Whalers		AHL	6	344	27	0	4.71	0	2
1987-88—Rochester Americans		AHL	8	382	22	0	3.46	0	6
1987-88—Milwaukee Admirals		IHL	9	483	47	0	5.84	0	4
NHL TOTALS			12	506	41	0	4.86	0	0

(c)—Won Walter Brown Award (Top U.S.-born player in New England colleges).
(d)—June, 1984—Signed by Boston Bruins as a free agent.

MICHEL DUFOUR

Goaltender ... 5'6" ... 160 lbs. ... Born, Val d'Or, Que., August 31, 1962 ... Shoots left.

Year	Team	League	Games	Mins.	Goals	SO.	Avg.	A.	Pen.
1979-80—Sorel Black Hawks		QMJHL	59	3178	306	0	5.78	2	6
1980-81—Sorel Black Hawks (b-c-d)		QMJHL	54	2703	164	0	*3.64	2	21
1981-82—Trois-Rivieres Draveurs (e)		QMJHL	58	3316	238	*1	4.31	0	33
1982-83—Fredericton Express		AHL	1	60	5	0	5.00	0	0

Year	Team	League	Games	Mins.	Goals	SO.	Avg.	A.	Pen.
1982-83—Milwaukee Admirals		IHL	4	244	16	0	3.93	0	0
1982-83—Kalamazoo Wings		IHL	23	1180	73	0	3.71	1	0
1983-84—Fredericton Express		AHL	6	365	19	0	3.12	0	2
1983-84—Milwaukee Admirals		IHL	21	1255	79	0	3.78	0	4
1984-85—Muskegon Lumberjacks		IHL	50	2937	174	1	3.55	3	16
1985-86—Muskegon Lumberjacks (b)		IHL	52	2935	151	0	3.09	1	12
1986-87—Muskegon Lumberjacks		IHL	3	179	11	0	3.69	0	0
1986-87—Fort Wayne Komets (f)		IHL	41	2247	126	1	3.36	3	27
1987-88—Fort Wayne Komets		IHL	48	2702	163	1	3.62	2	8

(c)—Won Jacques Plante Trophy (Best Goalie).
(d)—August, 1980—Signed by Quebec Nordiques as underage junior.
(e)—Led QMJHL playoffs with two shutouts.
(f)—Co-winner of James Norris Memorial Trophy with teammate Alain Raymond. (Outstanding Goaltender).

DARREN ELIOT

Goaltender . . . 6'1" . . . 175 lbs. . . . Born, Milton, Ont., November 26, 1961 . . . Shoots left . . . Member of 1984 Canadian Olympic team . . . Played every minute of every game on Cornell schedule in 1982-83 . . . (November 27, 1984)—Pulled hamstring vs. Winnipeg . . . (September, 1987)—Pulled groin in Detroit training camp.

Year	Team	League	Games	Mins.	Goals	SO.	Avg.	A.	Pen.
1979-80—Cornell University (c)		ECAC	26	1362	94	0	4.14	..	..
1980-81—Cornell University		ECAC	18	912	52	1	3.42	..	..
1981-82—Cornell University		ECAC	7	338	25	0	4.44	0	2
1982-83—Cornell University (a-d)		ECAC	26	1606	100	1	3.66	0	4
1983-84—Canadian Olympic Team		Int'l	31	1676	111	0	3.97	..	..
1983-84—New Haven Nighthawks		AHL	7	365	30	0	4.93	0	0
1984-85—Los Angeles Kings		NHL	33	1882	137	0	4.37	0	0
1985-86—New Haven Nighthawks		AHL	3	180	19	0	6.33	0	2
1985-86—Los Angeles Kings		NHL	27	1481	121	0	4.90	1	4
1986-87—New Haven Nighthawks		AHL	4	239	15	0	3.77	1	2
1986-87—Los Angeles Kings (e)		NHL	24	1404	103	1	4.40	1	18
1987-88—Detroit Red Wings		NHL	3	97	9	0	5.57	0	2
1987-88—Adirondack Red Wings		AHL	43	2445	136	0	3.34	3	8
NHL TOTALS			87	4864	370	1	4.56	2	24

(c)—June, 1980—Drafted by Los Angeles Kings in NHL entry draft. Eighth Kings pick, 115th overall, sixth round.
(d)—Named to All-America Team (East).
(e)—June, 1987—Signed by Detroit Red Wings as a free agent.

CHAD ERICKSON

Goaltender . . . 5'9" . . . 175 lbs. . . . Born, Minneapolis, Minn., August 21, 1970 . . . Shoots right.

Year	Team	League	Games	Mins.	Goals	SO.	Avg.	A.	Pen.
1986-87—Warroad H.S.		Minn. H.S.	21	945	36	1	2.29	..	..
1987-88—Warroad H.S. (c)		Minn. H.S.	24	1080	33	7	1.83	..	..

(c)—June, 1988—Drafted by New Jersey Devils in 1988 NHL entry draft. Eighth Devils pick, 138th overall, seventh round.

BOB ESSENSA

Goaltender . . . 6' . . . 160 lbs. . . . Born, Toronto, Ont., January 14, 1965 . . . Shoots left . . . (February, 1985)—Severe lacerations to both hands and wrist from broken window.

Year	Team	League	Games	Mins.	Goals	SO.	Avg.	A.	Pen.
1981-82—Henry Carr H.S.		MJBHL	17	948	79	..	5.00	..	..
1982-83—Henry Carr H.S. (c)		MJBHL	31	1840	98	2	3.20	..	..
1983-84—Michigan State University		CCHA	17	947	44	...	2.79	2	0
1984-85—Michigan State University (a)		CCHA	18	1059	29	2	1.64	1	0
1985-86—Michigan State University (b-d)		CCHA	23	1333	74	0	3.33	1	2
1986-87—Michigan State University		CCHA	25	1383	64	*2	*2.78	1	0
1987-88—Moncton Golden Flames		AHL	27	1287	100	1	4.66	1	4

(c)—June, 1983—Drafted by Winnipeg Jets in 1983 NHL entry draft. Fifth Jets pick, 69th overall, fourth round.
(d)—Member of CCHA All-Academic Team.

SEAN EVOY

Goaltender . . . 6'1" . . . 190 lbs. . . . Born, Sudbury, Ont., February 11, 1966 . . . Shoots left.

Year	Team	League	Games	Mins.	Goals	SO.	Avg.	A.	Pen.
1982-83—Don Mills Flyers		MTHL	25	1125	56	4	2.24	..	....
1983-84—Sudbury Wolves		OHL	34	1536	159	1	6.21	1	10
1984-85—Sudbury Wolves		OHL	49	2451	196	1	4.80	2	24
1985-86—Sudbury Wolves		OHL	21	1212	69	0	3.42	2	8
1985-86—Cornwall Royals (c)		OHL	27	1391	122	1	5.26	3	4
1986-87—Oshawa Generals (d)		OHL	31	1702	89	2	3.14	6	4
1987-88—Milwaukee Admirals		IHL	17	933	71	0	4.57	1	8

(c)—June, 1986—Drafted by Hartford Whalers in 1986 NHL entry draft. Ninth Whalers pick, 200th overall, 10th round.

(d)—Co-Winner of Dave Pinkney Trophy with teammate Jeff Hackett (Lowest team goals-against average).

RANDY EXELBY

Goaltender ... 5'9" ... 170 lbs. ... Born, Toronto, Ont., August 13, 1965 ... Shoots left.

Year	Team	League	Games	Mins.	Goals	SO.	Avg.	A.	Pen.
1983-84—Lake Superior State		CCHA	21	905	75	0	4.97	..	..
1984-85—Lake Superior State		CCHA	36	1999	112	..	3.36	..	..
1985-86—Lake Superior State (c)		CCHA	28	1626	98	0	3.62	3	2
1986-87—Lake Superior State		CCHA	27	1358	91	..	4.02	0	4
1987-88—Sherbrooke Canadiens		AHL	19	1050	49	0	2.80	1	27

(c)—June, 1986—Selected by Montreal Canadiens in 1986 NHL supplemental draft.

STEPHANE FISET

Goaltender ... 6' ... 175 lbs. ... Born, Montreal, Que., June 17, 1970 ... Shoots left.

Year	Team	League	Games	Mins.	Goals	SO.	Avg.	A.	Pen.
1986-87—Montreal Midget		Quebec	29	1445	142	0	5.90	..	..
1987-88—Victoriaville Tigers (c)		QHL	40	2221	146	1	3.94	3	6

(c)—June, 1987—Drafted by Quebec Nordiques in 1988 NHL entry draft. Third Nordiques pick, 24th overall, second round.

MARK FITZPATRICK

Goaltender ... 6'1" ... 190 lbs. ... Born, Toronto, Ont., November 13, 1968 ... Shoots left ... (February, 1987)—Injured knee.

Year	Team	League	Games	Mins.	Goals	SO.	Avg.	A.	Pen.
1983-84—Medicine Hat Tigers		AJHL	....	......	....	...	......	..	....
1983-84—Revelstoke Rockets		BCJHL	21	1019	90	0	5.30	..	....
1984-85—Medicine Hat Tigers		WHL	3	180	9	0	3.00	0	0
1985-86—Medicine Hat Tigers (b)		WHL	41	2074	99	1	*2.86	1	6
1986-87—Medicine Hat Tigers (c)		WHL	50	2844	159	*4	*3.35	8	16
1987-88—Medicine Hat Tigers (b)		WHL	63	3600	194	*2	*3.23	9	29

(c)—June, 1987—Drafted as underage junior by Los Angeles Kings in 1987 NHL entry draft. Second Kings pick, 27th overall, second round.

WADE FLAHERTY

Goaltender ... 5'11" ... 160 lbs. ... Born, Terreace, B.C., January 11, 1968 ... Shoots right.

Year	Team	League	Games	Mins.	Goals	SO.	Avg.	A.	Pen.
1986-87—Nanaimo Clippers		BCJHL	15	830	53	0	3.83	..	..
1986-87—Victoria Cougars		WHL	3	127	16	0	7.56	1	0
1987-88—Victoria Cougars (c)		WHL	36	2052	135	0	3.95	3	10

(c)—June, 1988—Drafted by Buffalo Sabres in 1988 NHL Entry draft. Tenth Sabres pick, 181st overall, ninth round.

JOHN FLETCHER

Goaltender ... 5'7" ... 163 lbs. ... Born, Newton, Mass., October 14, 1967 ... Shoots left.

Year	Team	League	Games	Mins.	Goals	SO.	Avg.	A.	Pen.
1986-87—Clarkson Univ. (c)		ECAC	23	1240	62	4	3.00	0	....
1987-88—Clarkson Univ. (d)		ECAC	33	1820	97	1	3.20	0	0

(c)—June, 1987—Drafted by Vancouver Canucks in 1987 NHL entry draft. Ninth Canucks pick, 166th overall, eighth round.

(d)—Named second team All-America (East).

BRIAN FORD

Goaltender ... 5'10" ... 170 lbs. ... Born, Edmonton, Alta., September 22, 1961 ... Shoots left.

Year	Team	League	Games	Mins.	Goals	SO.	Avg.	A.	Pen.
1980-81—Billings Bighorns		WHL	44	2435	204	0	5.03	2	52
1981-82—Billings Bighorns		WHL	53	2791	256	0	5.50	0	0
1982-83—Fredericton Express (c-d)		AHL	27	1444	84	0	3.49	2	0
1982-83—Carolina Thunderbirds		ACHL	4	204	7	0	2.07	0	0
1983-84—Fredericton Express (a-e-f)		AHL	36	2142	105	2	*2.94	4	8
1983-84—Quebec Nordiques		NHL	3	123	13	0	6.34	0	0
1984-85—Pittsburgh Penguins (g)		NHL	8	457	48	0	6.30	0	0
1984-85—Baltimore Skipjacks		AHL	6	363	21	0	3.47	0	0
1984-85—Muskegon Lumberjacks		IHL	22	1321	59	1	2.68	3	4
1985-86—Baltimore Skipjacks		AHL	39	2230	136	1	3.66	1	8
1985-86—Muskegon Lumberjacks (h)		IHL	9	513	33	0	3.86	2	2
1986-87—Baltimore Skipjacks		AHL	32	1541	99	0	3.85	1	2
1987-88—Springfield Indians		AHL	35	1898	118	0	3.73	2	10
NHL TOTALS			11	580	61	0	6.31	0	0

(c)—August, 1982—Signed by Quebec Nordiques as a free agent.
(d)—Co-winner of Harry (Hap) Holmes Memorial Trophy (Top Goaltenders) with teammate Ken Ellacott.
(e)—Won Harry (Hap) Holmes Memorial Trophy (Top Goaltender).
(f)—Won Baz Bastien Trophy (Coaches pick as top goalie; first time awarded).
(g)—December, 1984—Traded by Quebec Nordiques to Pittsburgh Penguins for Tom Thornbury.
(h)—Led IHL playoff goaltenders with 13 games, 793 minutes, 41 goals against and a 3.10 average.

NORM FOSTER

Goaltender . . . 5'9" . . . 175 lbs. . . . Born, Vancouver, B.C., February 10, 1965 . . . Shoots left.

Year	Team	League	Games	Mins.	Goals	SO.	Avg.	A.	Pen.
1981-82—Penticton Knights		BCJHL	21	1187	58	..	2.93	..	..
1982-83—Penticton Knights (c)		BCJHL	33	1999	156	0	4.68	..	..
1983-84—Michigan State University		CCHA	32	1814	83	...	2.75	0	2
1984-85—Michigan State University		CCHA	26	1531	67	1	2.63	1	0
1985-86—Michigan State University (d)		CCHA	24	1414	87	1	3.69	1	0
1986-87—Michigan State University		CCHA	24	1384	90	1	3.90	2	4
1987-88—Milwaukee Admirals		IHL	38	2001	170	0	5.10	2	0

(c)—June, 1983—Drafted by Boston Bruins in 1983 NHL entry draft. Eleventh Bruins pick, 222nd overall, 11th round.
(d)—Named to NCAA All-Tournament team.

ROB FOURNIER

Goaltender . . . 6' . . . 185 lbs. . . . Born, Sudbury, Ont., April 8, 1969 . . . Shoots left . . . (May, 1987)—Broken ankle.

Year	Team	League	Games	Mins.	Goals	SO.	Avg.	A.	Pen.
1985-86—Valley East Midget		OHA	35	1575	84	6	3.20	..	..
1986-87—North Bay Centennials		OHL	25	1281	72	2	3.37	0	12
1987-88—North Bay Centennials (b-c)		OHL	61	3601	210	1	3.50	1	48

(c)—June, 1988—Drafted by St. Louis Blues in 1988 NHL entry draft. Third Blues pick, 51st overall, third round.

BOB FROESE

Goaltender . . . 5'11" . . . 178 lbs. . . . Born, St. Catharines, Ont., June 30, 1958 . . . Shoots left . . . (October, 1980)—Pulled hamstring . . . Set NHL record for most consecutive games without a loss from the start of an NHL career (13 games, 12-0-1) in 1982-83 . . . (December 8, 1984)—Strained left knee ligaments vs. N.Y. Rangers . . . (March 10, 1985)—Pulled groin vs. Pittsburgh . . . (November 13, 1985)—Pulled groin . . . (November, 1987)—Dislocated right shoulder.

Year	Team	League	Games	Mins.	Goals	SO.	Avg.	A.	Pen.
1974-75—St. Cath. Black Hawks		OMJHL	15	871	71	0	4.89	0	2
1975-76—St. Cath. Black Hawks		OMJHL	39	1976	193	0	5.86	0	10
1976-77—Oshawa Generals		OMJHL	39	2063	161	*2	4.68	2	40
1977-78—Niagara Falls Flyers (c)		OMJHL	53	3128	246	0	4.72	1	39
1978-79—Saginaw Gears		IHL	21	1050	58	0	3.31	0	56
1978-79—Milwaukee Admirals		IHL	14	715	42	1	3.52	..	....
1979-80—Maine Mariners (d)		AHL	1	60	5	...	5.00	0	0
1979-80—Saginaw Gears		IHL	52	2827	178	0	3.78	7	45
1980-81—Saginaw Gears (e)		IHL	43	2298	114	3	2.98	2	22
1981-82—Maine Mariners		AHL	33	1900	104	2	3.28	0	2
1982-83—Maine Mariners		AHL	33	1966	110	2	3.36	1	11
1982-83—Philadelphia Flyers		NHL	24	1406	59	4	2.52	2	2
1983-84—Philadelphia Flyers		NHL	48	2863	150	2	3.14	2	10
1984-85—Hershey Bears		AHL	4	245	15	0	3.67	0	0
1984-85—Philadelphia Flyers		NHL	17	923	37	1	2.41	1	2

Year	Team	League	Games	Mins.	Goals	SO.	Avg.	A.	Pen.
1985-86—Philadelphia Flyers (b-f)		NHL	51	2728	116	5	2.55	1	8
1986-87—Philadelphia Flyers (g)		NHL	3	180	8	0	2.67	0	0
1986-87—New York Rangers		NHL	28	1474	92	0	3.74	2	56
1987-88—New York Rangers		NHL	25	1443	85	0	3.53	1	6
NHL TOTALS			196	11017	547	12	2.98	9	84

(c)—June, 1978—Drafted by St. Louis Blues in amateur draft. Eleventh St. Louis pick, 160th overall, 10th round.

(d)—September, 1979—Signed by Philadelphia Flyers as a free agent.

(e)—Led IHL playoffs in goals-against average (2.15) and shutouts (2).

(f)—Shared Bill Jennings Trophy with teammate Darren Jensen (team that allows the fewest goals).

(g)—December, 1986—Traded by Philadelphia Flyers to New York Rangers for Kjell Samuelsson and a second-round 1989 draft pick.

PETER FRY

Goaltender . . . 6' . . . 170 lbs. . . . Born, Toronto, Ont., April 1, 1967 . . . Shoots left.

Year	Team	League	Games	Mins.	Goals	SO.	Avg.	A.	Pen.
1983-84—Portland Winter Hawks		WHL	39	1930	186	0	5.78	..	....
1984-85—Portland Winter Hawks		WHL	35	1581	166	0	6.30	2	50
1985-86—Spokane Chiefs		WHL	1	60	6	0	6.00	0	0
1985-86—Victoria Cougars		WHL	14	610	63	0	6.20	2	2
1986-87—Victoria Cougars (b-c)		WHL	54	2937	255	0	5.21	5	22
1987-88—Victoria Cougars		WHL	39	2227	189	0	5.09	8	28

(c)—June, 1987—Drafted by New Jersey Devils in 1987 NHL entry draft. Ninth Devils pick, 191st overall, 10th round.

GRANT FUHR

Goaltender . . . 5'10" . . . 181 lbs. . . . Born, Spruce Grove, Alta., September 28, 1962 . . . Shoots right . . . (December, 1981)—Partial separation of right shoulder . . . (December 13, 1983)—Strained left knee ligaments vs. Hartford and required surgery . . . (January 27, 1984)—Collected ninth assist of season to set NHL record for goaltenders. He ended the season with 14 . . . First black player to be on Stanley Cup-winning team . . . (February, 1985)—Separated shoulder . . . (November 3, 1985)—Bruised left shoulder vs. Toronto and missed 10 games . . . (November, 1987)—Bruised left shoulder at N.Y. Rangers . . . (March 1988)—Set NHL record for appearances in a single season.

Year	Team	League	Games	Mins.	Goals	SO.	Avg.	A.	Pen.
1979-80—Victoria Cougars (a-c)		WHL	43	2488	130	2	3.14	1	2
1980-81—Victoria Cougars (a-d-e)		WHL	59	*3448	160	*4	*2.78	2	6
1981-82—Edmonton Oilers (b)		NHL	48	2847	157	0	3.31	6	6
1982-83—Moncton Alpines		AHL	10	604	40	0	3.98	0	0
1982-83—Edmonton Oilers		NHL	32	1803	129	0	4.29	0	6
1983-84—Edmonton Oilers		NHL	45	2625	171	1	3.91	14	6
1984-85—Edmonton Oilers		NHL	46	2559	165	1	3.87	3	6
1985-86—Edmonton Oilers		NHL	40	2184	143	0	3.93	2	0
1986-87—Edmonton Oilers		NHL	44	2388	137	0	3.44	2	6
1987-88—Edmonton Oilers (a-f)		NHL	*75	*4304	246	*4	3.43	8	16
NHL TOTALS			330	18710	1148	6	3.68	35	46

(c)—Won Stewart Paul Memorial Trophy (WHL Rookie of the Year).

(d)—Named outstanding goalie in WHL.

(e)—June, 1981—Drafted by Edmonton Oilers in NHL entry draft. First Oilers pick, eighth overall, first round.

(f)—Won Vezina Trophy (Top NHL Goalie).

FRANK FURLAN

Goaltender . . . 5'9" . . . 175 lbs. . . . Born, Nanaimo, B.C., March 8, 1968 . . . Shoots left.

Year	Team	League	Games	Mins.	Goals	SO.	Avg.	A.	Pen.
1985-86—Sherwood Park Crusaders (c)		AJHL	23	1290	91	0	4.23	0	12
1986-87—Michigan Tech. Univ.		WCHA	11	623	66	0	6.36	1	2
1987-88—Michigan Tech. Univ.		WCHA	16	854	77	0	5.41	1	7

(c)—June, 1986—Drafted by Winnipeg Jets in 1986 NHL entry draft. Seventh Jets pick, 155th overall, eighth round.

TROY GAMBLE

Goaltender . . . 5'11" . . . 180 lbs. . . . Born, Toronto, Ont., April 7, 1967 . . . Shoots left.

Year	Team	League	Games	Mins.	Goals	SO.	Avg.	A.	Pen.
1983-84—Hobbema Hawks		AJHL	22	1102	90	0	4.90	..	....
1984-85—Medicine Hat Tigers (a-c-d)		WHL	37	2095	100	*3	*2.86	2	4
1985-86—Medicine Hat Tigers		WHL	45	2264	142	0	3.76	3	29

Year	Team	League	Games	Mins.	Goals	SO.	Avg.	A.	Pen.
1986-87—Medicine Hat Tigers (e)		WHL	11	646	46	0	4.27	1	0
1986-87—Spokane Chiefs		WHL	38	2157	163	0	4.53	2	23
1986-87—Vancouver Canucks		NHL	1	60	4	0	4.00	0	0
1987-88—Spokane Chiefs (a-c)		WHL	67	3824	235	0	3.69	3	47
NHL TOTALS			1	60	4	0	4.00	0	0

  (c)—Won WHL Top Goaltender Trophy.

  (d)—June, 1985—Drafted as underage junior by Vancouver Canucks in 1985 NHL entry draft. Second Canucks pick, 25th overall, second round.

  (e)—December, 1986—Traded with Kevin Ekdahl by Medicine Hat Tigers to Spokane Flyers for Keith Van Rooyen, Kirby Lindal and Rocky Dundas.

DARRYL GILMOUR

Goaltender . . . 5'11" . . . 155 lbs. . . . Born, Winnipeg, Manitoba, February 13, 1967 . . . Shoots left.

Year	Team	League	Games	Mins.	Goals	SO.	Avg.	A.	Pen.
1983-84—St. James Canadiens		MJHL	15	900	45	...	3.00	..	....
1984-85—Moose Jaw Warriors (c)		WHL	58	3004	297	0	5.93	6	4
1985-86—Moose Jaw Warriors (a)		WHL	*62	*3482	*276	1	4.76	2	4
1986-87—Moose Jaw Warriors		WHL	31	1776	123	2	4.16	1	4
1986-87—Portland Winter Hawks		WHL	24	1460	111	0	4.56	2	0
1987-88—Hershey Bears		AHL	25	1273	78	1	3.68	1	2

  (c)—June, 1985—Drafted as underage junior by Philadelphia Flyers in 1985 NHL entry draft. Third Flyers pick, 48th overall, third round.

SCOTT GORDON

Goaltender . . . 5'10" . . . 175 lbs. . . . Born, South Easton, Mass., February 6, 1963 . . . Shoots left.

Year	Team	League	Games	Mins.	Goals	SO.	Avg.	A.	Pen.
1982-83—Boston College		ECAC	9	371	15	...	2.43	0	0
1983-84—Boston College		ECAC	35	2034	127	...	3.75	0	6
1984-85—Boston College		H. East	36	2179	131	1	3.61	1	4
1985-86—Boston College (a)		H. East	32	1851	112	2	3.63	1	14
1986-87—Fredericton Express (c)		AHL	31	1599	119	0	4.47	2	12
1987-88—Baltimore Skipjacks		AHL	34	1638	145	0	5.31	0	10

  (c)—October, 1986—Signed by Quebec Nordiques as a free agent.

MARIO GOSSELIN

Goaltender . . . 5'8" . . . 160 lbs. . . . Born, Thetford Mines, Que., June 15, 1963 . . . Shoots left . . . Member of 1984 Canadian Olympic team . . . (February 25, 1984)—First NHL game was 5-0 shutout of St. Louis Blues . . . (March 8, 1984)—Injured knee vs. Pittsburgh and out for the season . . . (January 16, 1986)—Missed one game with the flu.

Year	Team	League	Games	Mins.	Goals	SO.	Avg.	A.	Pen.
1980-81—Shawinigan Cataracts		QMJHL	21	907	75	0	4.96	1	0
1981-82—Shawinigan Cataracts (b-c)		QMJHL	*60	*3404	230	0	4.50	3	10
1982-83—Shawinigan Cataracts (a-d)		QHL	46	2556	133	*3	*3.12	4	18
1983-84—Canadian Olympic Team		Int'l	36	2007	126	0	3.77	..	....
1983-84—Quebec Nordiques		NHL	3	148	3	1	1.22	0	2
1984-85—Quebec Nordiques		NHL	35	1960	109	1	3.34	0	2
1985-86—Fredericton Express		AHL	5	304	15	0	2.96	0	0
1985-86—Quebec Nordiques		NHL	31	1726	111	2	3.86	3	2
1986-87—Quebec Nordiques		NHL	30	1625	86	0	3.18	3	20
1987-88—Quebec Nordiques		NHL	54	3002	189	2	3.78	0	8
NHL TOTALS			153	8461	498	6	3.53	6	34

  (c)—June, 1982—Drafted as underage junior by Quebec Nordiques in 1982 NHL entry draft. Third Nordiques pick, 55th overall, third round.

  (d)—Won Jacques Plante Trophy (Top Goalie).

MARK GOWANS

Goaltender . . . 6' . . . 160 lbs. . . . Born, Bay City, Mich., March 26, 1967 . . . Shoots left.

Year	Team	League	Games	Mins.	Goals	SO.	Avg.	A.	Pen.
1983-84—Detroit Compuware		Mich. Midget	30	1800	72	5	2.40	..	....
1984-85—Windsor Spitfires (c)		OHL	36	2112	162	0	4.60	2	0
1985-86—Oshawa Generals		OHL	25	1187	84	0	4.25	0	0
1986-87—Oshawa Generals (d)		OHL	10	571	21	0	2.21	1	0
1986-87—Hamilton Steelhawks		OHL	20	1106	82	0	4.45	2	2
1987-88—Toronto Marlboros		OHL	24	1263	108	1	5.13	1	2

(c)—June, 1985—Drafted as underage junior by Detroit Red Wings in 1985 NHL entry draft. Fourth Red Wings pick, 71st overall, fourth round.

(d)—December, 1986—Traded by Oshawa Generals to Hamilton Steelhawks for a fifth-round draft pick and future considerations.

FRANCOIS GRAVEL

Goaltender . . . 6'2" . . . 185 lbs. . . . Born, Ste. Foy, Que., October 21, 1968 . . . Shoots left.

Year	Team	League	Games	Mins.	Goals	SO.	Avg.	A.	Pen.
1985-86—St. Jean Castors		QHL	42	2450	212	0	5.19	2	8
1986-87—Shawinigan Cataracts (c)		QHL	40	2415	194	0	4.82	0	0
1987-88—Shawinigan Cataracts		QHL	44	2499	200	1	4.80	2	30

(c)—June, 1987—Drafted by Montreal Canadiens in 1987 NHL entry draft. Fifth Canadiens pick, 58th overall, third round.

MIKE GREENLAY

Goaltender . . . 6'3" . . . 200 lbs. . . . Born, Calgary, Alta., September 15, 1968 . . . Shoots left.

Year	Team	League	Games	Mins.	Goals	SO.	Avg.	A.	Pen.
1986-87—Lake Superior State (c)		CCHA	17	744	44	..	3.55	0	0
1987-88—Lake Superior State		CCHA	19	1023	57	..	3.34	0	2

(c)—June, 1986—Drafted by Edmonton Oilers in 1986 NHL entry draft. Ninth Oilers pick, 189th overall, ninth round.

STEVE GUENETTE

Goaltender . . . 5'9" . . . 165 lbs. . . . Born, Montreal, Que., November 13, 1965 . . . Shoots left.

Year	Team	League	Games	Mins.	Goals	SO.	Avg.	A.	Pen.
1984-85—Guelph Platers		OHL	47	2593	200	1	4.63	1	2
1985-86—Guelph Platers (b-c)		OHL	50	2910	165	3	3.40	2	16
1986-87—Baltimore Skipjacks		AHL	54	3035	157	*5	3.10	2	13
1986-87—Pittsburgh Penguins		NHL	2	113	8	0	4.25	0	0
1987-88—Pittsburgh Penguins		NHL	19	1092	61	1	3.35	0	2
1987-88—Muskegon Lumberjacks (b-d)		IHL	33	1943	91	*4	2.81	0	22
NHL TOTALS			21	1205	69	1	3.44	0	2

(c)—June, 1985—Signed by Pittsburgh Penguins as a free agent.

(d)—Won James Norris Memorial Trophy (Top Goaltender).

ROYDEN GUNN

Goaltender . . . 5'9" . . . 170 lbs. . . . Born, Saskatoon, Sask., August 5, 1966 . . . Shoots right.

Year	Team	League	Games	Mins.	Goals	SO.	Avg.	A.	Pen.
1982-83—Saskatoon Blazers Midget		Sask.	18	1073	102	0	5.70	..	..
1983-84—Prince Albert Raiders		WHL	6	254	23	0	5.43	..	..
1984-85—Prince Albert Raiders		WHL	36	2085	119	2	3.42	2	12
1985-86—Prince Albert Raiders		WHL	51	3051	183	*2	3.60	5	6
1986-87—Springfield Indians (c)		AHL	29	1599	107	0	4.02	1	17
1987-88—Springfield Indians		AHL	44	2278	154	0	4.06	0	2
1987-88—Baltimore Skipjacks		AHL	18	797	77	0	5.80	0	2

(c)—October, 1986—Signed by New York Islanders as a free agent.

JEFF HACKETT

Goaltender . . . 6' . . . 175 lbs. . . . Born, London, Ont., June 1, 1968 . . . Shoots left.

Year	Team	League	Games	Mins.	Goals	SO.	Avg.	A.	Pen.
1985-86—London Diamonds Jr. B		OHA	19	1150	66	0	3.44	..	..
1986-87—Oshawa Generals (c-d-e)		OHA	31	1672	85	2	3.05	2	0
1987-88—Oshawa Generals		OHL	53	3165	205	0	3.89	4	39

(c)—Won F. W. Dinty Moore Trophy (Lowest average among rookie goaltenders).

(d)—Co-Winner of Dave Pinkney Trophy with teammate Sean Evoy (Lowest team goals-against average).

(e)—June, 1987—Drafted as underage junior by New York Islanders in 1987 NHL entry draft. Second Islanders pick, 34th overall, second round.

GLEN HANLON

Goaltender . . . 6' . . . 175 lbs. . . . Born, Brandon, Man., February 20, 1957 . . . Shoots right . . . Missed part of 1977-78 season with torn ankle ligaments . . . Missed part of 1979-80 season with shoulder injury . . . (October 18, 1980)—Stretched knee ligaments . . . (March, 1981) —Shoulder separation . . . (October 16, 1987)—Cut finger . . . (January, 1988)—Broken left index finger.

Year	Team	League	Games	Mins.	Goals	SO.	Avg.	A.	Pen.
1973-74—Brandon Travellers		MJHL	20	1059	64	*1	3.63	0	5
1974-75—Brandon Wheat Kings		WCHL	43	2498	176	0	4.22	1	6
1975-76—Brandon Wheat Kings (a)		WCHL	64	3523	234	4	3.99	2	35
1976-77—Brandon Wheat K. (a-c-d)		WCHL	65	3784	195	*4	*3.09	5	8
1977-78—Tulsa Oilers (a-e)		CHL	53	3123	160	*3	3.07	4	30
1977-78—Vancouver Canucks		NHL	4	200	9	0	2.70	0	2
1978-79—Vancouver Canucks		NHL	31	1821	94	3	3.10	1	30
1979-80—Vancouver Canucks		NHL	57	3341	193	0	3.47	1	43
1980-81—Dallas Black Hawks		CHL	4	239	8	1	2.01	1	0
1980-81—Vancouver Canucks		NHL	17	798	59	1	4.44	1	10
1981-82—Vancouver Canucks (f)		NHL	28	1610	106	1	3.95	0	22
1981-82—St. Louis Blues		NHL	2	76	8	0	6.32	0	0
1982-83—St. Louis Blues (g)		NHL	14	671	50	0	4.47	0	0
1982-83—New York Rangers		NHL	21	1173	67	0	3.43	0	2
1983-84—New York Rangers		NHL	50	2837	166	1	3.51	2	30
1984-85—New York Rangers		NHL	44	2510	175	0	4.18	0	4
1985-86—Adirondack Red Wings		AHL	10	605	33	0	3.27	0	2
1985-86—New Haven Nighthawks		AHL	5	279	22	0	4.73	1	4
1985-86—New York Rangers (h)		NHL	23	1170	65	0	3.33	1	4
1986-87—Detroit Red Wings		NHL	36	1963	104	1	3.18	0	20
1987-88—Detroit Red Wings		NHL	47	2623	141	*4	3.23	1	30
NHL TOTALS			374	20793	1237	11	3.57	7	197

(c)—Won WCHL Leading Goalie Award.
(d)—Drafted from Brandon Wheat Kings by Vancouver Canucks in third round of 1977 amateur draft.
(e)—Won CHL Rookie-of-the-Year Award.
(f)—March, 1982—Traded by Vancouver Canucks to St. Louis Blues for Tony Currie, Jim Nill, Rick Heinz and fourth-round 1982 entry draft pick (Shawn Kilroy).
(g)—January, 1983—Traded by St. Louis Blues with Vaclav Nedomansky to New York Rangers for Andre Dore and future considerations.
(h)—August, 1986—Traded by New York Rangers with third-round draft choices in 1987 (Dennis Holland) and 1988 (Guy Dupuis) and future considerations to Detroit Red Wings for Kelly Kisio, Lane Lambert and Jim Leavins and a fifth round 1988 draft pick.

BRIAN HAYWARD

Goaltender . . . 5'10" . . . 175 lbs. . . . Born, Georgetown, Ont., June 25, 1960 . . . Shoots left . . . (November, 1987)—Back spasms . . . (December 26, 1987)—Pulled thigh muscle at Toronto . . . (February 23, 1988)—Injured back when checked into boards by Gord Donnelly.

Year	Team	League	Games	Mins.	Goals	SO.	Avg.	A.	Pen.
1978-79—Cornell University		ECAC	25	1469	95	0	3.88	..	....
1979-80—Cornell University		ECAC	12	508	52	0	6.02	..	....
1980-81—Cornell University		ECAC	19	967	58	1	3.54	..	....
1981-82—Cornell University		ECAC	....	1320	68	0	3.09	..	....
1982-83—Sherbrooke Jets (c)		AHL	22	1208	89	1	4.42	0	0
1982-83—Winnipeg Jets		NHL	24	1440	89	1	3.71	1	0
1983-84—Sherbrooke Jets		AHL	15	781	69	0	5.30	1	2
1983-84—Winnipeg Jets		NHL	28	1530	124	0	4.86	1	2
1984-85—Winnipeg Jets		NHL	61	3436	220	0	3.84	4	10
1985-86—Sherbrooke Canadiens		AHL	3	185	5	0	1.62	1	0
1985-86—Winnipeg Jets (d)		NHL	52	2721	217	0	4.79	2	25
1986-87—Montreal Canadiens		NHL	37	2178	102	1	2.81	2	2
1987-88—Montreal Canadiens (e)		NHL	39	2247	107	2	2.86	2	24
NHL TOTALS			241	13552	859	4	3.80	12	63

(c)—September, 1982—Signed by Winnipeg Jets as a free agent.
(d)—August, 1986—Traded by Winnipeg Jets to Montreal Canadiens for Steve Penney and Jan Ingman.
(e)—Co-winner (with teammate Patrick Roy) of Bill Jennings Trophy (Top NHL Goaltending tandem).

GLEN HEALY

Goaltender . . . 5'10" . . . 185 lbs. . . . Born, Pickering, Ont., August 23, 1962 . . . Shoots left.

Year	Team	League	Games	Mins.	Goals	SO.	Avg.	A.	Pen.
1981-82—Western Michigan Univ.		CCHA	27	1569	116	0	4.44	2	2
1982-83—Western Michigan Univ.		CCHA	30	1733	116	0	4.02	3	4
1983-84—Western Michigan Univ.		CCHA	38	2242	146	..	3.91	1	13
1984-85—Western Michigan Univ. (b-c-d)		CCHA	37	2172	118	..	3.26	2	8
1985-86—Toledo Goaldiggers		IHL	7	402	28	0	4.18	0	0
1985-86—New Haven Nighthawks		AHL	43	2410	160	0	3.98	2	18
1985-86—Los Angeles Kings		NHL	1	51	6	0	7.06	0	0
1986-87—New Haven Nighthawks		AHL	47	2828	173	1	3.67	2	24
1987-88—Los Angeles Kings		NHL	34	1869	135	1	4.33	2	6
NHL TOTALS			35	1920	141	1	4.41	2	6

(c)—Second team All-America Goaltender.
(d)—June, 1985—Signed by Los Angeles Kings as a free agent.

ANDY HELMUTH

Goaltender . . . 5'10" . . . 170 lbs. . . . Born, Detroit, Mich., March 18, 1967 . . . Shoots left.

Year	Team	League	Games	Mins.	Goals	SO.	Avg.	A.	Pen.
1983-84	Detroit Little Caesar's	Mich. Midget	38	2466	119	4	3.14	..	....
1984-85	Ottawa 67's (c)	OHL	40	2102	189	0	5.39	3	8
1985-86	Ottawa 67's	OHL	20	1175	97	0	4.95	0	12
1985-86	Guelph Platers	OHL	12	620	39	0	3.77	0	8
1986-87	Guelph Platers	OHL	48	2637	188	*3	4.28	2	21
1987-88	Guelph Platers	OHL	34	1956	137	0	4.20	4	29

(c)—June, 1985—Drafted as underage junior by Chicago Black Hawks in 1985 NHL entry draft. Second Black Hawks pick, 53rd overall, third round.

RON HEXTALL

Goaltender . . . 6'3" . . . 170 lbs. . . . Born, Winnipeg, Manitoba, May 3, 1964 . . . Shoots left . . . (May, 1987)—Given eight-game suspension by the NHL for slashing Kent Nilsson during playoff series vs. Edmonton. The suspension to take affect for the first eight games of the 1987-88 season . . . (1986-87)—Set NHL record for penalty minutes by a goaltender . . . (December 2, 1987)—Scored a goal into an empty Boston Bruins net . . . (1987-88)—Tied his own NHL penalty minute record.

Year	Team	League	Games	Mins.	Goals	SO.	Avg.	A.	Pen.
1980-81	Melville	SJHL	42	2127	254	0	7.17	..	....
1981-82	Brandon Wheat Kings (c)	WHL	30	1398	133	0	5.71	0	0
1982-83	Brandon Wheat Kings	WHL	44	2589	249	0	5.77	4	66
1983-84	Brandon Wheat Kings	WHL	46	2670	190	0	4.27	8	117
1984-85	Kalamazoo Wings	IHL	19	1103	80	0	4.35	2	18
1984-85	Hershey Bears	AHL	11	555	34	0	3.68	2	4
1985-86	Hershey Bears (a-d)	AHL	*53	*3061	*174	*5	3.41	2	54
1986-87	Philadelphia Flyers (a-e-f)	NHL	66	3799	190	1	3.00	6	104
1987-88	Philadelphia Flyers	NHL	62	3560	208	0	3.51	6	104
	NHL TOTALS		128	7359	398	1	3.25	12	208

(c)—June, 1982—Drafted as underage junior by Philadelphia Flyers in 1982 NHL entry draft. Sixth Flyers pick, 119th overall, sixth round.
(d)—Won Dudley (Red) Garrett Memorial Trophy (Top Rookie).
(e)—Won Vezina Trophy (Top NHL Goaltender).
(f)—Won Conn Smythe Trophy (Stanley Cup Playoff MVP).

BILL HORN

Goaltender . . . 5'8" . . . 150 lbs. . . . Born, Regina, Sask., April 16, 1967 . . . Shoots right.

Year	Team	League	Games	Mins.	Goals	SO.	Avg.	A.	Pen.
1985-86	Western Michigan Univ. (c)	CCHA	30	1797	114	0	3.81	1	14
1986-87	Western Michigan Univ. (b)	CCHA	36	2067	136	*2	3.95	0	14
1987-88	Western Michigan Univ.	CCHA	33	1890	139	1	4.41	4	6

(c)—June, 1986—Drafted by Hartford Whalers in 1986 NHL entry draft. Fourth Whalers pick, 95th overall, fifth round.

KELLY HRUDEY

Goaltender . . . 5'10" . . . 183 lbs. . . . Born, Edmonton, Alta., January 13, 1961 . . . Shoots left.

Year	Team	League	Games	Mins.	Goals	SO.	Avg.	A.	Pen.
1978-79	Medicine Hat Tigers	WHL	57	3093	*318	0	6.17	2	43
1979-80	Medicine Hat Tigers (c)	WHL	57	3049	212	1	4.17	6	12
1980-81	Medicine Hat Tigers (b)	WHL	55	3023	200	*4	3.97	0	21
1980-81	Indianapolis Checkers (d)	CHL	....	.....	....	..	.....	..	....
1981-82	Indianapolis Checkers (a-e-f-g)	CHL	51	3033	149	1	*2.95	0	6
1982-83	Indianapolis Checkers (a-e-h-i)	CHL	47	2744	139	2	3.04	0	28
1983-84	Indianapolis Checkers	CHL	6	370	21	0	3.41	1	0
1983-84	New York Islanders	NHL	12	535	28	0	3.14	0	0
1984-85	New York Islanders	NHL	41	2334	141	2	3.62	1	17
1985-86	New York Islanders	NHL	45	2563	137	1	3.21	3	14
1986-87	New York Islanders	NHL	46	2634	145	0	3.30	1	37
1987-88	New York Islanders	NHL	47	2751	153	3	3.34	2	20
	NHL TOTALS		193	10817	604	6	3.35	7	88

(c)—June, 1980—Drafted by New York Islanders as underage junior in 1980 NHL entry draft. Second Islanders pick, 38th overall, second round.
(d)—No regular season games. Played two playoff games.
(e)—Co-winner of Terry Sawchuk Trophy (Top Goaltenders) with teammate Robert Holland.

(f)—Winner of Max McNab Trophy (Playoff MVP).
(g)—Led CHL Playoffs with 2.42 goals-against-average and one shutout.
(h)—Won Tommy Ivan Trophy (MVP).
(i)—Led CHL playoffs with 2.64 average.

JOHN HYDUKE

Goaltender . . . 5'10" . . . 155 lbs. . . . Born, Hibbing, Minn., June 23, 1967 . . . Shoots left . . . (November, 1984)—Arthroscopic knee surgery for torn cartilage.

Year	Team	League	Games	Mins.	Goals	SO.	Avg.	A.	Pen.
1984-85—Hibbing High School (c)		Minn. H.S.	15	645	29	3	1.93	..	..
1985-86—Univ. of Minnesota/Duluth		WCHA	24	1401	84	0	3.60	1	0
1986-87—Univ. of Minnesota/Duluth		WCHA	23	1359	99	0	4.37	1	2
1987-88—Univ. of Minnesota/Duluth		WCHA	31	1883	127	..	4.05	1	2

(c)—June, 1985—Drafted by Los Angeles Kings in 1985 NHL entry draft. Seventh Kings pick, 156th overall, eighth round.

PETER ING

Goaltender . . . 6'2" . . . 165 lbs. . . . Born, Toronto, Ont., April 28, 1969 . . . Shoots left.

Year	Team	League	Games	Mins.	Goals	SO.	Avg.	A.	Pen.
1985-86—Toronto Marlboros Midget		OHA	35	1800	91	4	3.03	..	..
1986-87—Windsor Spitfires		OHL	28	1615	105	0	3.90	1	9
1987-88—Windsor Spitfires (c)		OHL	43	2422	125	2	3.10	3	6

(c)—June, 1988—Drafted by Toronto Maple Leafs in 1988 NHL entry draft. Third Maple Leafs pick, 48th overall, third round.

PAT JABLONSKI

Goaltender . . . 6' . . . 170 lbs. . . . Born, Toledo, O., June 20, 1967 . . . Shoots right.

Year	Team	League	Games	Mins.	Goals	SO.	Avg.	A.	Pen.
1984-85—Detroit Compuware Jr. A. (c)		NASHL	29	1483	95	0	3.84	..	....
1985-86—Windsor Spitfires		OHL	29	1600	119	1	4.46	3	4
1986-87—Windsor Spitfires		OHL	41	2328	128	*3	3.30	1	16
1987-88—Windsor Spitfires		OHL	18	994	48	2	2.90	0	2
1987-88—Peoria Rivermen		IHL	5	285	17	0	3.58	0	2

(c)—June, 1985—Drafted by St. Louis Blues in 1985 NHL entry draft. Sixth Blues pick, 138th overall, seventh round.

ROBERT JANECYK

Goaltender . . . 6'1" . . . 180 lbs. . . . Born, Chicago, Ill., May 18, 1957 . . . Shoots left . . . Led IHL with a combined goals-against average of 3.43 in 1979-80 . . . (February, 1983)—Strained knee ligaments . . . (March, 1987)—Stretched ligaments in right knee.

Year	Team	League	Games	Mins.	Goals	SO.	Avg.	A.	Pen.
1979-80—Flint Generals (b-c)		IHL	2	119	5	0	2.53	0	2
1979-80—Fort Wayne Komets		IHL	40	2208	128	1	3.48	2	14
1980-81—New Brunswick Hawks (d)		AHL	34	1915	131	0	4.10	2	10
1981-82—New Brunswick Hawks (a-e-f)		AHL	53	3224	153	2	2.85	1	20
1982-83—Springfield Indians (a)		AHL	47	2754	167	*3	3.64	4	34
1983-84—Springfield Indians		AHL	30	1664	94	0	3.39	1	2
1983-84—Chicago Black Hawks (g)		NHL	8	412	28	0	4.08	0	2
1984-85—Los Angeles Kings		NHL	51	3002	183	2	3.66	2	27
1985-86—Los Angeles Kings		NHL	38	2083	162	0	4.67	2	11
1986-87—Los Angeles Kings		NHL	7	420	34	0	4.86	0	2
1987-88—Los Angeles Kings		NHL	5	303	23	0	4.55	0	2
1987-88—New Haven Nighthawks		AHL	37	2162	125	1	3.47	1	27
NHL TOTALS			109	6220	430	2	4.15	4	44

(c)—December, 1979—Loaned to Flint Generals by Fort Wayne Komets.
(d)—June, 1980—Signed by Chicago Black Hawks as a free agent.
(e)—Co-winner of Harry (Hap) Holmes Memorial Trophy (Top Goaltenders) with teammate Warren Skorodenski.
(f)—Led AHL Calder Cup Playoffs with 2.35 goals-against average and one shutout.
(g)—June, 1984—Traded with first (Craig Redmond), third (John English) and fourth (Thomas Glavine) round 1984 draft picks by Chicago Black Hawks to Los Angeles Kings for first (Ed Olczyk), third (Trent Yawney) and fourth round (Tommy Eriksson) 1984 draft picks.

MIKE JEFFERY

Goaltender . . . 6'3" . . . 195 lbs. . . . Born, Kamloops, B.C., April 6, 1965 . . . Shoots right.

Year	Team	League	Games	Mins.	Goals	SO.	Avg.	A.	Pen.
1984-85—Northern Michigan Univ.		WCHA	12	573	44	0	4.61	2	0
1985-86—Northern Michigan Univ.		WCHA	15	743	58	0	4.68	0	2

Year	Team	League	Games	Mins.	Goals	SO.	Avg.	A.	Pen.
1986-87—Northern Michigan Univ. (c)		WCHA	28	1601	102	0	3.82	0	....
1987-88—Northern Michigan Univ.		WCHA	30	1801	107	0	3.56	4	0

(c)—June, 1987—Selected by Boston Bruins in 1987 NHL supplemental draft.

ALLAN RAYMOND (AL) JENSEN

Goaltender . . . 5'10" . . . 180 lbs. . . . Born, Hamilton, Ont., November 27, 1958 . . . Shoots left . . . Missed start of 1978-79 season with broken thumb . . . (January, 1984)—Injured back while weightlifting . . . (November, 1984)—Pulled thigh muscle . . . (December, 1984)— Muscle spasms in back.

Year	Team	League	Games	Mins.	Goals	SO.	Avg.	A.	Pen.
1975-76—Hamilton Fincups		Jr."A"OHA	28	1451	97	0	3.97	1	7
1976-77—St. Cath. Fincups (b)		Jr."A"OHA	48	2727	168	*2	3.70	4	6
1977-78—Hamil. Fincups (a-c-d)		Jr."A"OHA	43	2582	146	*3	*3.35	1	6
1978-79—Kalamazoo Wings		IHL	47	2596	156	2	3.61	3	6
1979-80—Adirondack Red Wings		AHL	57	3406	199	2	3.51	0	10
1980-81—Adirondack Red Wings		AHL	60	3169	203	*3	3.84	2	10
1980-81—Detroit Red Wings (e)		NHL	1	60	7	0	7.00	0	0
1981-82—Washington Capitals		NHL	26	1274	81	0	3.81	2	6
1981-82—Hershey Bears		AHL	8	407	24	0	3.54	0	21
1982-83—Hershey Bears		AHL	6	316	14	1	2.66	0	0
1982-83—Washington Capitals		NHL	40	2358	135	1	3.44	0	6
1983-84—Hershey Bears		AHL	3	180	16	0	5.33	0	0
1983-84—Washington Capitals (f)		NHL	43	2414	117	*4	2.91	0	22
1984-85—Binghamton Whalers		AHL	3	180	9	0	3.00	0	2
1984-85—Washington Capitals		NHL	14	803	34	1	2.54	0	6
1985-86—Washington Capitals		NHL	44	2437	129	2	3.18	1	4
1986-87—Binghamton Whalers		AHL	13	684	42	0	3.68	0	6
1986-87—Washington Capitals (g)		NHL	6	328	27	0	4.94	0	0
1986-87—Los Angeles Kings		NHL	5	300	27	0	5.40	1	0
1987-88—New Haven Nighthawks (h)		AHL	20	1129	84	0	4.46	1	6
NHL TOTALS			179	9974	557	8	3.35	2	44

(c)—Shared Dave Pinkney Trophy (leading goalies) with Rick Wamsley.
(d)—Drafted from Hamilton Fincups by Detroit Red Wings in second round of 1978 amateur draft.
(e)—August, 1981—Traded by Detroit Red Wings to Washington Capitals for Mark Lofthouse.
(f)—Co-winner of Bill Jennings Trophy (Top NHL goaltenders) with teammate Pat Riggin.
(g)—February, 1987—Traded by Washington Capitals to Los Angeles Kings for Garry Galley.
(h)—February, 1988—Named assistant coach of Flint Spirits.

DARREN JENSEN

Goaltender . . . 5'9" . . . 165 lbs. . . . Born, Creston, B.C., May 27, 1960 . . . Shoots left.

Year	Team	League	Games	Mins.	Goals	SO.	Avg.	A.	Pen.
1979-80—Univ. of North Dakota (c)		WCHA	15	890	33	1	2.22	..	....
1980-81—Univ. of North Dakota		WCHA	25	1510	110	0	4.37	..	4
1981-82—Univ. of North Dakota (d)		WCHA	16	910	45	1	2.97	0	2
1982-83—Univ. of North Dakota		WCHA	16	905	45	0	2.98	1	0
1983-84—Fort Wayne Komets (a-e-f-g-h-i)		IHL	56	3325	162	*4	*2.92	2	6
1984-85—Hershey Bears		AHL	39	2263	150	1	3.98	1	4
1984-85—Philadelphia Flyers		NHL	1	60	7	0	7.00	0	0
1985-86—Hershey Bears		AHL	14	795	38	1	2.87	0	0
1985-86—Philadelphia Flyers (j)		NHL	29	1436	88	2	3.68	1	2
1986-87—Hershey Bears (k)		AHL	60	3429	215	0	3.76	1	22
1987-88—Fredericton Express		AHL	42	2459	158	0	3.86	1	4
NHL TOTALS			30	1496	95	2	3.81	1	2

(c)—June, 1980—Drafted by Hartford Whalers in NHL entry draft. Fifth Whalers pick, 92nd overall, fifth round.
(d)—Named to NCAA All-Tournament team.
(e)—October, 1983—Released by Hartford Whalers and signed by Fort Wayne Komets as a free agent.
(f)—Won James Gatschene Memorial Trophy (MVP).
(g)—Won Garry F. Longman Memorial Trophy (Outstanding Rookie).
(h)—Won James Norris Memorial Trophy (Top Goaltender).
(i)—May, 1984—Signed by Philadelphia Flyers as a free agent.
(j)—Shared Bill Jennings Trophy with teammate Bob Froese (team that allows the fewest goals).
(k)—August, 1987—Traded with Daryl Stanley by Philadelphia Flyers to Vancouver Canucks for Wendell Young and a 1990 third-round draft choice.

DOUG KEANS

Goaltender . . . 5'7" . . . 174 lbs. . . . Born, Pembroke, Ont., January 7, 1958 . . . Shoots left . . . (March, 1981)—Injury to right ankle that required surgery to repair ligament damage . . .

(February, 1983)—Torn hamstring muscle . . . (December 15, 1983)—Strained ligaments in left knee vs. Hartford and required surgery . . . (February 6, 1986)—Injured left hand vs. Buffalo and missed two games.

Year	Team	League	Games	Mins.	Goals	SO.	Avg.	A.	Pen.
1975-76—Oshawa Generals		OMJHL	1	29	4	0	8.28	0	0
1976-77—Oshawa Generals		OMJHL	48	2632	291	0	6.63	0	4
1977-78—Oshawa Generals (c)		OMJHL	42	2500	172	1	4.13	2	4
1978-79—Saginaw Gears		IHL	59	3207	217	0	4.06	1	11
1979-80—Saginaw Gears		IHL	22	1070	67	1	3.76	3	4
1979-80—Binghamton Dusters		AHL	8	488	31	0	3.81	3	4
1979-80—Los Angeles Kings		NHL	10	559	23	0	2.47	0	0
1980-81—Los Angeles Kings		NHL	9	454	37	0	4.89	0	7
1980-81—Houston Apollos		CHL	11	699	27	0	2.32	0	2
1980-81—Oklahoma City Stars		CHL	9	492	32	1	3.90	0	0
1981-82—New Haven Nighthawks		AHL	13	686	33	2	2.89	1	0
1981-82—Los Angeles Kings		NHL	31	1436	103	0	4.30	0	0
1982-83—Los Angeles Kings		NHL	6	304	24	0	4.73	1	0
1982-83—New Haven Nighthawks		AHL	30	1724	125	0	4.35	2	6
1983-84—Boston Bruins (d)		NHL	33	1779	92	2	3.10	0	2
1984-85—Boston Bruins		NHL	25	1497	82	1	3.29	0	6
1985-86—Boston Bruins		NHL	30	1757	107	1	3.65	1	12
1986-87—Boston Bruins		NHL	36	1942	108	0	3.34	2	34
1987-88—Boston Bruins		NHL	30	1660	90	1	3.25	2	2
1987-88—Maine Mariners		AHL	10	600	34	0	3.40	0	6
NHL TOTALS			210	11388	666	5	3.51	6	63

(c)—June, 1978—Drafted by Los Angeles Kings in amateur draft. Second Los Angeles pick, sixth round.

(d)—June, 1983—Acquired on waivers from Los Angeles Kings by Boston Bruins.

JOHN KEMP

Goaltender . . . 6' . . . 185 lbs. . . . Born, Burlington, Ont., July 31, 1963 . . . Shoots left . . . (December, 1986)—Infected hand.

Year	Team	League	Games	Mins.	Goals	SO.	Avg.	A.	Pen.
1983-84—University of Toronto		CWUAA	29	...	..	0	2.95	...	....
1984-85—University of Toronto		CWUAA	22	....	...	3	2.69	...	..
1985-86—Team Canada		Int'l	....	1368	96	0	4.21	..	....
1985-86—Hershey Bears (c)		AHL	8	440	40	0	5.45	0	0
1986-87—Hershey Bears		AHL	30	1349	80	1	3.56	0	46
1987-88—Hershey Bears		AHL	4	177	16	0	5.42	0	0

(c)—February, 1986—Signed by Philadelphia Flyers as a free agent.

SCOTT KING

Goaltender . . . 6'1" . . . 170 lbs. . . . Born, Thunder Bay, Ont., June 25, 1967 . . . Shoots left.

Year	Team	League	Games	Mins.	Goals	SO.	Avg.	A.	Pen.
1985-86—Vernon (c)		BCJHL	29	1718	134	0	4.68	..	....
1986-87—University of Maine		H. East	21	1111	58	0	3.13	1	0
1987-88—University of Maine		H. East	33	1762	91	0	3.10	1	4

(c)—June, 1986—Drafted by Detroit Red Wings in 1986 NHL entry draft. Tenth Red Wings pick, 190th overall, tenth round.

RICK KNICKLE

Goaltender . . . 5'10" . . . 155 lbs. . . . Born, Chatham, N.B., February 26, 1960 . . . Shoots left . . . (February, 1981)—Sprained thumb.

Year	Team	League	Games	Mins.	Goals	SO.	Avg.	A.	Pen.
1977-78—Brandon Wheat Kings		WCHL	49	2806	182	0	3.89	5	27
1978-79—Brandon Wheat Kings (a-c-d)		WHL	38	2240	118	1	*3.16	3	15
1979-80—Muskegon Mohawks		IHL	16	829	51	0	3.69	0	25
1980-81—Erie Blades (a-e)		EHL	43	2347	125	1	*3.20	0	12
1981-82—Rochester Americans		AHL	31	1753	108	1	3.70	1	0
1982-83—Flint Generals		IHL	27	1638	92	2	3.37	2	6
1982-83—Rochester Americans		AHL	4	143	11	0	4.64	0	0
1983-84—Flint Generals (b-f)		IHL	60	3518	203	3	3.46	6	16
1984-85—Sherbrooke Canadiens		AHL	14	780	53	0	4.08	0	6
1984-85—Flint Generals		IHL	36	2018	115	2	3.42	3	8
1985-86—Saginaw Gears		IHL	39	2235	135	2	3.62	0	6
1986-87—Saginaw Generals		IHL	26	1413	113	0	4.80	0	23
1987-88—Flint Spirits		IHL	1	60	4	0	4.00	0	0
1987-88—Peoria Rivermen		IHL	13	705	58	0	4.94	1	0

(c)—Named top Goaltender in WHL.

(d)—August, 1979—Drafted by Buffalo Sabres as underage junior in entry draft. Seventh Buffalo pick, 116th overall, sixth round.
(e)—Led EHL playoffs with 1.88 goals-against average.
(f)—Led IHL playoffs with 3.00 average.

RICK KOSTI

Goaltender . . . 5'10" . . . 175 lbs. . . . Born, Kincaid, Sask., September 13, 1963 . . . Shoots left.

Year	Team	League	Games	Mins.	Goals	SO.	Avg.	A.	Pen.
1983-84—Univ. of Minnesota-Duluth		WCHA	38	2347	119	...	3.04	0	6
1984-85—Univ. of Minnesota-Duluth (c-d)		WCHA	45	2736	146	...	3.20	0	4
1985-86—Salt Lake Golden Eagles		IHL	25	1330	99	0	4.47	1	2
1985-86—Moncton Golden Flames		AHL	15	705	44	1	3.74	0	6
1986-87—Team Canada		Int'l	30	1736	85	2	2.94	..	...
1987-88—Canadian Olympic Team		Int'l	18	731	54	0	4.43	..	....
1987-88—Salt Lake Golden Eagles		IHL	18	731	54	0	4.43	0	0

(c)—First team (West) All-America.
(d)—May, 1985—Signed by Calgary Flames as a free agent.

JEFFREY KRUESEL

Goaltender . . . 5'11" . . . 180 lbs. . . . Born, Rochester, Minn., June 1, 1970 . . . Shoots left.

Year	Team	League	Games	Mins.	Goals	SO.	Avg.	A.	Pen.
1986-87—Rochester John Marshall H.S.		Minn. H.S.	18	810	32	5	2.37	0	0
1987-88—Rochester John Marshall H.S. (c)		Minn. H.S.	24	2080	41	0	2.28	0	0

(c)—June, 1988—Drafted by Los Angeles Kings in 1988 NHL entry draft. Eighth Kings pick, 133rd overall, seventh round.

GARY KRUZICH

Goaltender . . . 5'5" . . . 173 lbs. . . . Born, Oak Lawn, Ill., April 22, 1965 . . . Shoots left.

Year	Team	League	Games	Mins.	Goals	SO.	Avg.	A.	Pen.
1983-84—Bowling Green State		CCHA	28	1725	83	1	2.89	0	14
1984-85—Bowling Green State		CCHA	31	1739	115	0	3.97	1	10
1985-86—Bowling Green State (c-d)		CCHA	35	2090	124	1	3.56	1	20
1986-87—Bowling Green State (c)		CCHA	38	2229	123	0	3.31	8	19
1987-88—Flint Spirits		IHL	27	1315	91	0	4.15	6	20

(c)—Selected first team All-America (West).
(d)—October, 1986—Drafted by New York Islanders in NHL supplemental draft.

MARK LAFOREST

Goaltender . . . 5'10" . . . 175 lbs. . . . Born, Welland, Ont., July 10, 1962 . . . Shoots left.

Year	Team	League	Games	Mins.	Goals	SO.	Avg.	A.	Pen.
1981-82—Niagara Falls Flyers		OHL	24	1365	105	1	4.62	1	14
1982-83—North Bay Centennials		OHL	54	3140	195	0	3.73	4	20
1983-84—Adirondack Red Wings (c)		AHL	7	351	29	0	4.96	0	2
1983-84—Kalamazoo Wings		IHL	13	718	48	1	4.01	0	11
1984-85—Mohawk Valley Stars		ACHL	8	420	60	0	8.57	1	15
1984-85—Adirondack Red Wings		AHL	11	430	35	0	4.88	0	0
1985-86—Adirondack Red Wings		AHL	19	1142	57	0	2.29	1	14
1985-86—Detroit Red Wings		NHL	28	1383	114	1	4.95	0	23
1986-87—Adirondack Red Wings (d)		AHL	37	2229	105	3	2.83	0	10
1986-87—Detroit Red Wings (e)		NHL	5	219	12	0	3.29	0	10
1987-88—Hershey Bears		AHL	5	309	13	0	2.52	0	2
1987-88—Philadelphia Flyers		NHL	21	972	60	1	3.70	0	8
NHL TOTALS			54	2574	186	2	4.34	0	41

(c)—September, 1983—Signed by Detroit Red Wings as a free agent.
(d)—Won Baz Bastien Trophy (Coaches pick as top Goalie).
(e)—June, 1987—Traded by Detroit Red Wings to Philadelphia Flyers for second-round 1987 draft pick (Bob Wilkie).

REJEAN LEMELIN

Goaltender . . . 5'11" . . . 160 lbs. . . . Born, Sherbrooke, Que., November 19, 1954 . . . Shoots left . . . (February 8, 1981)—Broke thumb on right hand in pre-game warmups at Edmonton . . . (January, 1984)—Back injury.

Year	Team	League	Games	Mins.	Goals	SO.	Avg.	A.	Pen.
1972-73—Sherbrooke Beavers		QJHL	27	1117	146	0	5.21	2	4
1973-74—Sherbrooke Beavers (c)		QJHL	35	.....	158	0	4.60	1	2
1974-75—Philadelphia Firebirds		NAHL	43	2277	131	3	3.45	3	16

Year	Team	League	Games	Mins.	Goals	SO.	Avg.	A.	Pen.
1975-76—Richmond Robins		AHL	7	402	30	0	4.48	0	0
1975-76—Philadelphia Firebirds		NAHL	29	1601	97	1	3.63	1	6
1976-77—Philadelphia Firebirds		NAHL	51	2763	170	1	3.61	2	0
1976-77—Springfield Indians		AHL	3	180	10	0	3.33	0	0
1977-78—Philadelphia Firebirds (a)		AHL	60	3585	177	4	2.96	1	22
1978-79—Atlanta Flames (d)		NHL	18	994	55	0	3.32	0	4
1978-79—Philadelphia Firebirds		AHL	13	780	36	0	2.77	1	12
1979-80—Birmingham Bulls		CHL	38	2188	137	0	3.76	2	14
1979-80—Atlanta Flames		NHL	3	150	15	0	6.00	0	0
1980-81—Birmingham Bulls		CHL	13	757	56	0	4.44	0	4
1980-81—Calgary Flames		NHL	29	1629	88	2	3.24	1	2
1981-82—Calgary Flames		NHL	34	1866	135	0	4.34	1	0
1982-83—Calgary Flames		NHL	39	2211	133	0	3.61	5	7
1983-84—Calgary Flames		NHL	51	2568	150	0	3.50	3	6
1984-85—Calgary Flames		NHL	56	3176	183	1	3.46	0	4
1985-86—Calgary Flames		NHL	60	3369	229	1	4.08	4	10
1986-87—Calgary Flames (e)		NHL	34	1735	94	2	3.25	0	20
1987-88—Boston Bruins		NHL	49	2828	138	3	2.93	0	2
NHL TOTALS			373	20526	1220	9	3.57	14	55

(c)—Drafted from Sherbrooke Beavers by Philadelphia Flyers in sixth round of 1974 amateur draft.
(d)—August, 1978—Signed by Atlanta Flames as free agent.
(e)—August, 1987—Signed by Boston Bruins as a free agent.

DAVID LITTMAN

Goaltender . . . 6' . . . 175 lbs. . . . Born, Cranston, R.I., June 13, 1967 . . . Shoots left.

Year	Team	League	Games	Mins.	Goals	SO.	Avg.	A.	Pen.
1985-86—Boston College		H. East	9	442	22	1	2.99	1	0
1986-87—Boston College (c)		H. East	21	1182	68	0	3.45	0	....
1987-88—Boston College		H. East	30	1726	116	0	4.03	2	10

(c)—June, 1987—Drafted by Buffalo Sabres in 1987 NHL entry draft. Twelfth Sabres pick, 211th overall, 11th round.

MICHAEL LIUT

Goaltender . . . 6'2" . . . 195 lbs. . . . Born, Weston, Ont., January 7, 1956 . . . Shoots left . . . Missed part of 1977-78 season with torn cartilage in left knee . . . (January 10, 1981)— Groin injury vs. Los Angeles . . . (March, 1984)—Strained knee ligaments . . . (October, 1987)—Missed 13 days with muscle spasms in lower back . . . (March, 1988)—Twisted knee . . . (April, 1988)—Sprained shoulder during playoff series vs. Montreal.

Year	Team	League	Games	Mins.	Goals	SO.	Avg.	A.	Pen.
1973-74—Bowling Green State U.		CCHA	24	1272	88	0	4.00	0	4
1974-75—Bowling Green State U. (a)		CCHA	20	1174	78	0	3.99	0	10
1975-76—Bowling Green St. U.(b-c-d)		CCHA	21	1171	50	2	2.56	0	0
1976-77—Bowling Green St. U. (a-e-f)		CCHA	24	1346	61	2	2.72	2	4
1977-78—Cincinnati Stingers		WHA	27	1215	86	0	4.25	1	0
1978-79—Cincinnati Stingers (g)		WHA	54	3181	184	*3	3.47	2	9
1979-80—St. Louis Blues		NHL	64	3661	194	2	3.18	0	2
1980-81—St. Louis Blues (a)		NHL	61	3570	199	1	3.34	0	0
1981-82—St. Louis Blues		NHL	64	3691	250	2	4.06	2	2
1982-83—St. Louis Blues		NHL	68	3794	235	1	3.72	0	2
1983-84—St. Louis Blues		NHL	58	3425	197	3	3.45	4	0
1984-85—St. Louis Blues (h)		NHL	32	1869	119	1	3.82	1	4
1984-85—Hartford Whalers		NHL	12	731	37	1	3.04	0	2
1985-86—Hartford Whalers (i)		NHL	57	3282	197	2	3.60	2	0
1986-87—Hartford Whalers (b)		NHL	59	3476	187	*4	3.23	2	4
1987-88—Hartford Whalers		NHL	60	3532	187	2	3.18	1	4
WHA TOTALS			81	4396	270	3	3.69	3	9
NHL TOTALS			535	31031	1802	19	3.48	12	20

(c)—Drafted from Bowling Green State University by St. Louis Blues in fourth round of 1976 amateur draft.
(d)—May, 1976—Selected by New England Whalers in World Hockey Association amateur player draft.
(e)—May, 1977—WHA rights traded to Cincinnati Stingers by New England Whalers with second-round 1979 draft choice for Greg Carroll and Bryan Maxwell.
(f)—Named CCHA Player-of-the-Year.
(g)—June, 1979—Selected by St. Louis Blues in reclaim draft.
(h)—February, 1985—Traded with future considerations (Jorgen Pettersson) by St. Louis Blues to Hartford Whalers for Greg Millen and Mark Johnson.
(i)—Led Stanley Cup Playoffs with a 1.90 average. He was also one of four goalies to have a shutout.

DANNY LORENZ

Goaltender . . . 5'10" . . . 170 lbs. . . . Born, Murrayville, B.C., December 12, 1969 . . . Shoots left.

Year	Team	League	Games	Mins.	Goals	SO.	Avg.	A.	Pen.
1986-87—Seattle Thunderbirds		WHL	38	2103	199	0	5.68	2	6
1987-88—Seattle Thunderbirds (c)		WHL	62	3302	314	0	5.71	1	9

(c)—June, 1988—Drafted by New York Islanders in 1988 NHL entry draft. Fourth Islanders pick, 58th overall, third round.

CLINT MALARCHUK

Goaltender . . . 5'10" . . . 172 lbs. . . . Born, Grande, Alta., May 1, 1961 . . . Shoots left.

Year	Team	League	Games	Mins.	Goals	SO.	Avg.	A.	Pen.
1978-79—Portland Winter Hawks		WHL	2	120	4	0	2.00	..	....
1979-80—Portland Winter Hawks (c)		WHL	37	1948	147	0	4.53	2	10
1980-81—Portland Winter Hawks		WHL	38	2235	142	3	3.81	7	22
1981-82—Quebec Nordiques		NHL	2	120	14	0	7.00	0	0
1981-82—Fredericton Express		AHL	51	2962	*253	0	5.12	4	22
1982-83—Quebec Nordiques		NHL	15	900	71	0	4.73	0	0
1982-83—Fredericton Express		AHL	25	1506	78	1	*3.11	1	2
1983-84—Fredericton Express		AHL	11	663	40	0	3.62	1	5
1983-84—Quebec Nordiques		NHL	23	1215	80	0	3.95	1	9
1984-85—Fredericton Express		AHL	*56	*3347	*198	2	3.55	1	14
1985-86—Quebec Nordiques		NHL	46	2657	142	4	3.21	2	21
1986-87—Quebec Nordiques (d)		NHL	54	3092	175	1	3.40	2	37
1987-88—Washington Capitals		NHL	54	2926	154	*4	3.16	2	10
NHL TOTALS			194	10910	636	9	3.50	7	77

(c)—October, 1980—Signed by Quebec Nordiques as a free agent.

(d)—June, 1987—Traded with Dale Hunter by Quebec Nordiques to Washington Capitals for Alan Haworth, Gaeten Duchesne and a first-round 1987 draft pick (Joe Sakic).

GEORGE MANELUK

Goaltender . . . 6' . . . 190 lbs. . . . Born, Winnipeg, Man., July 25, 1967 . . . Shoots left . . . Attended University of Manitoba in 1985-86.

Year	Team	League	Games	Mins.	Goals	SO.	Avg.	A.	Pen.
1986-87—Brandon Wheat Kings (c)		WHL	58	3258	315	0	5.80	4	19
1987-88—Brandon Wheat Kings		WHL	64	3651	297	0	4.88	9	14
1987-88—Springfield Indians		AHL	2	125	9	0	4.32	0	0
1987-88—Peoria Rivermen		IHL	3	148	14	0	5.68	0	0

(c)—June, 1987—Drafted by New York Islanders in 1987 NHL entry draft. Fourth Islanders pick, 57th overall, fourth round.

BOB MASON

Goaltender . . . 6'1" . . . 180 lbs. . . . Born, International Falls, Minn., April 22, 1961 . . . Shoots right . . . Member of 1984 U.S. Olympic Team.

Year	Team	League	Games	Mins.	Goals	SO.	Avg.	A.	Pen.
1981-82—Univ. of Minnesota/Duluth		WCHA	26	1521	115	..	4.54	..	..
1982-83—Univ. of Minnesota/Duluth		WCHA	43	2594	151	..	3.49	1	4
1983-84—U.S. National Team		Int'l	33	1895	89	..	2.82	..	..
1983-84—U.S. Olympic Team		Int'l	3	160	10	0	3.75	0	0
1983-84—Washington Capitals (c)		NHL	2	120	3	0	1.50	0	0
1983-84—Hershey Bears		AHL	5	282	26	0	5.53	0	0
1984-85—Washington Capitals		NHL	12	661	31	1	2.81	1	0
1984-85—Binghamton Whalers		AHL	20	1052	58	1	3.31	1	0
1985-86—Binghamton Whalers		AHL	34	1940	126	0	3.90	3	6
1985-86—Washington Capitals		NHL	1	16	0	0	0.00	0	0
1986-87—Binghamton Whalers		AHL	2	119	4	0	2.02	0	2
1986-87—Washington Capitals (d)		NHL	45	2536	137	0	3.24	0	0
1987-88—Chicago Black Hawks (e)		NHL	41	2312	160	0	4.15	2	0
NHL TOTALS			101	5645	331	1	3.52	3	0

(c)—February, 1984—Signed by Washington Capitals as a free agent.

(d)—June, 1987—Signed by Chicago Black Hawks as a free agent.

(e)—July, 1988—Traded by Chicago Black Hawks to Quebec Nordiques for Mike Eagles.

DARRELL MAY

Goaltender . . . 6' . . . 190 lbs. . . . Born, Montreal, Que., March 6, 1962 . . . Shoots left.

Year	Team	League	Games	Mins.	Goals	SO.	Avg.	A.	Pen.
1979-80—Portland Winter Hawks		WHL	21	1113	64	0	3.45	0	2
1979-80—Portland Winter Hawks (c)		WHL	43	2416	143	1	3.55	2	16
1980-81—Portland Winter Hawks		WHL	36	2128	122	3	3.44	3	6
1981-82—Portland Winter Hawks		WHL	52	3097	226	0	4.38	0	0
1982-83—Fort Wayne Komets		IHL	46	2584	177	0	4.11	2	16
1983-84—Erie Golden Blades (b-d)		ACHL	43	2404	163	1	4.07	6	28
1984-85—Peoria Rivermen		IHL	19	1133	56	1	2.97	1	0
1985-87—Peoria Rivermen (a-e-f)		IHL	56	3321	179	1	3.23	0	20
1985-86—St. Louis Blues		NHL	3	184	13	0	4.24	1	2
1986-87—Peoria Rivermen (a)		IHL	58	3420	214	2	3.75	2	22
1987-88—St. Louis Blues		NHL	3	180	18	0	6.00	0	0
1987-88—Peoria Rivermen (g)		IHL	48	2754	162	1	3.53	2	33
NHL TOTALS			6	364	31	0	5.11	1	2

(c)—June, 1980—Drafted by Vancouver Canucks as underage junior in 1980 NHL entry draft. Fourth Canucks pick, 91st overall, fifth round.

(d)—Led ACHL playoffs with 2.08 average and one shutout.

(e)—September, 1985—Signed by St. Louis Blues as a free agent.

(f)—Won James Gatschene Memorial Trophy (MVP).

(g)—August, 1988—Traded with Jocelyn Lemieux and 1989 second-round draft pick by St. Louis Blues to Montreal Canadiens for Sergio Momesso and Vincent Riendeau.

KIRK McLEAN

Goaltender . . . 6' . . . 177 lbs. . . . Born, Willowdale, Ont., June 26, 1966 . . . Shoots left.

Year	Team	League	Games	Mins.	Goals	SO.	Avg.	A.	Pen.
1983-84—Oshawa Generals (c)		OHL	17	940	67	0	4.28	0	11
1984-85—Oshawa Generals		OHL	47	2581	143	1	*3.32	1	6
1985-86—Oshawa Generals		OHL	51	2830	169	1	3.58	0	8
1985-86—New Jersey Devils		NHL	2	111	11	0	5.95	0	0
1986-87—New Jersey Devils		NHL	4	160	10	0	3.75	0	0
1986-87—Maine Mariners		AHL	45	2606	140	1	3.22	1	6
1987-88—Vancouver Canucks		NHL	41	2380	147	1	3.71	2	8
NHL TOTALS			47	2651	168	1	3.80	2	8

(c)—June, 1984—Drafted as underage junior by New Jersey Devils in NHL entry draft. Sixth Devils pick, 10th overall, sixth round.

ROLAND MELANSON

Goaltender . . . 5'10" . . . 178 lbs. . . . Born, Moncton, N.B., June 28, 1960 . . . Shoots left . . . Led OMJHL in games played by goaltenders in 1978-79 and co-leader in 1979-80 (with Bruce Dowie) . . . (November 19, 1985)—Pulled groin at Calgary. After missing 30 days with the injury he was traded to Los Angeles . . . (January 15, 1986)—Injured groin vs. N.Y. Rangers and missed 13 games.

Year	Team	League	Games	Mins.	Goals	SO.	Avg.	A.	Pen.
1977-78—Windsor Spitfires		OMJHL	44	2592	195	1	4.51	2	12
1978-79—Windsor Spitfires (b-c)		OMJHL	*62	*3461	254	1	4.40	7	16
1979-80—Windsor Spitfires		OMJHL	22	1099	90	0	4.91	0	8
1979-80—Oshawa Generals		OMJHL	38	2240	136	*3	3.64	2	14
1980-81—Indianapolis Checkers (a-d)		CHL	*52	*3056	131	2	*2.57	1	16
1980-81—New York Islanders		NHL	11	620	32	0	3.10	0	4
1981-82—New York Islanders		NHL	36	2115	114	0	3.23	0	14
1982-83—New York Islanders (e)		NHL	44	2460	109	1	2.66	3	22
1983-84—New York Islanders		NHL	37	2019	110	0	3.27	2	10
1984-85—New York Islanders (f)		NHL	8	425	35	0	4.94	0	0
1984-85—Minnesota North Stars		NHL	20	1142	78	0	4.10	0	9
1985-86—New Haven Nighthawks		AHL	3	179	13	0	4.36	0	0
1985-86—Minnesota North Stars (g)		NHL	6	325	24	0	4.43	0	0
1985-86—Los Angeles Kings		NHL	22	1246	87	0	4.19	1	8
1986-87—Los Angeles Kings		NHL	46	2734	168	1	3.69	6	22
1987-88—Los Angeles Kings		NHL	47	2676	195	2	4.37	0	16
NHL TOTALS			277	15762	952	4	3.62	12	105

(c)—August, 1979—Drafted by New York Islanders as underage junior in 1979 NHL entry draft. Fourth Islanders pick, 59th overall, third round.

(d)—Winner of Ken McKenzie Trophy (Top Rookie).

(e)—Shared William Jennings Trophy with Billy Smith for NHL's best team goaltending average.

(f)—November, 1984—Traded by New York Islanders to Minnesota North Stars for first round 1985 draft pick (Brad Dalgarno).

(g)—December, 1985—Traded by Minnesota North Stars to N.Y. Rangers for second round 1986 (Neil Wilkinson) and fourth round 1987 (John Weisbrod) draft picks. He was then traded with Grant Ledyard by the Rangers to Los Angeles Kings for Brian MacLellan and a fourth round 1987 draft pick (Michael Sullivan).

GILLES MELOCHE

Goaltender . . . 5'9" . . . 185 lbs. . . . Born, Montreal, Que., July 12, 1950 . . . Shoots left . . . Brother of Denis Meloche . . . Missed part of 1973-74 season with severed tendons in hand requiring surgery . . . Set NHL record for most assists by goalie in season with six in 1974-75 (Broken in 1980-81 by Mike Palmateer with eight) . . . (November 2, 1985)—Broke finger at Montreal and missed 10 games . . . (September 17, 1987)—Right knee surgery.

Year	Team	League	Games	Mins.	Goals	SO.	Avg.	A.	Pen.
1969-70—Verdun Maple Leafs (c)		QJHL	45	.....	221	1	4.95	..	....
1970-71—Flint Generals		IHL	33	1866	104	2	3.34	2	0
1970-71—Chicago Black Hawks (d)		NHL	2	120	6	0	3.00	0	0
1971-72—Calif. Golden Seals (e)		NHL	56	3121	173	4	3.32	2	6
1972-73—California Golden Seals		NHL	59	3473	235	1	4.06	2	4
1973-74—California Golden Seals		NHL	47	2800	198	1	4.24	1	2
1974-75—California Golden Seals		NHL	47	2771	186	1	4.03	*6	14
1975-76—California Golden Seals		NHL	41	2440	140	1	3.44	1	0
1976-77—Cleveland Barons		NHL	51	2961	171	2	3.47	3	18
1977-78—Cleveland Barons		NHL	54	3100	195	1	3.77	0	4
1978-79—Minnesota North Stars		NHL	53	3118	173	2	3.33	1	25
1979-80—Minnesota North Stars		NHL	54	3141	160	1	3.06	1	4
1980-81—Minnesota North Stars		NHL	38	2215	120	2	3.25	0	2
1981-82—Minnesota North Stars		NHL	51	3026	175	1	3.47	1	6
1982-83—Minnesota North Stars		NHL	47	2689	160	1	3.57	1	0
1983-84—Minnesota North Stars		NHL	52	2883	201	2	4.18	1	2
1984-85—Minnesota North Stars (f)		NHL	32	1817	115	0	3.80	0	2
1985-86—Pittsburgh Penguins (g)		NHL	34	1989	119	0	3.59	1	2
1986-87—Pittsburgh Penguins		NHL	43	2343	134	0	3.43	1	20
1987-88—Pittsburgh Penguins		NHL	27	1394	95	0	4.09	0	0
NHL TOTALS			788	45410	2756	20	3.64	22	111

(c)—Drafted from Verdun Maple Leafs by Chicago Black Hawks in fifth round of 1970 amateur draft.
(d)—October, 1971—Traded with Paul Shmyr by Chicago Black Hawks to California Golden Seals for Gerry Desjardins.
(e)—Named Rookie-of-the-Year in NHL's West Division by THE SPORTING NEWS.
(f)—May, 1985—Traded by Minnesota North Stars to Edmonton Oilers for NHL rights to Paul Houck.
(g)—September, 1985—Traded by Edmonton Oilers to Pittsburgh Penguins for Tim Hrynewich, Marty McSorley and future considerations (Mike Moller).

MATT MERTEN

Goaltender . . . 6'3" . . . 190 lbs. . . . Born, Milford, Mass., June 29, 1967 . . . Shoots left.

Year	Team	League	Games	Mins.	Goals	SO.	Avg.	A.	Pen.
1986-87—Providence Univ. (c)		H. East	24	1455	104	0	4.29	1	4
1987-88—Providence Univ.		H. East	25	1328	100	1	4.52	1	8

(c)—June, 1986—Drafted by Vancouver Canucks in 1986 NHL entry draft. Sixth Canucks pick, 175th overall, ninth round.

GREG MILLEN

Goaltender . . . 5'9" . . . 160 lbs. . . . Born, Toronto, Ont., June 25, 1957 . . . Shoots right . . . (October, 1979)—Pulled hamstring muscle and missed 18 games.

Year	Team	League	Games	Mins.	Goals	SO.	Avg.	A.	Pen.
1974-75—Peterborough TPT's		OMJHL	27	1584	90	2	*3.41	..	....
1975-76—Peterborough Petes		OMJHL	58	3282	233	0	4.26	0	6
1976-77—Peterborough Petes (c)		OMJHL	59	3457	244	0	4.23	2	14
1977-78—S. Ste. Marie Greyhounds		OMJHL	25	1469	105	1	4.29	2	0
1977-78—Kalamazoo Wings		IHL	3	180	14	0	4.67	0	0
1978-79—Pittsburgh Penguins		NHL	28	1532	86	1	3.37	0	0
1979-80—Pittsburgh Penguins		NHL	44	2586	157	2	3.64	3	14
1980-81—Pittsburgh Penguins (d)		NHL	63	3721	258	0	4.16	2	6
1981-82—Hartford Whalers		NHL	55	3201	229	0	4.29	5	2
1982-83—Hartford Whalers		NHL	60	3520	282	1	4.81	2	8
1983-84—Hartford Whalers		NHL	*60	*3583	*221	2	3.70	3	10
1984-85—Hartford Whalers (e)		NHL	44	2659	187	1	4.22	0	4
1984-85—St. Louis Blues		NHL	10	605	35	0	3.47	0	0
1985-86—St. Louis Blues		NHL	36	2168	129	1	3.57	1	8
1986-87—St. Louis Blues		NHL	42	2482	146	0	3.53	2	12
1987-88—St. Louis Blues		NHL	48	2854	167	1	3.51	0	4
NHL TOTALS			490	28911	1897	10	3.94	18	68

(c)—June, 1977—Drafted by Pittsburgh Penguins in 1977 NHL amateur draft. Fourth Penguins pick, 102nd overall, sixth round.
(d)—June, 1981—Signed by Hartford Whalers as a free agent. Pat Boutette and Kevin McLelland sent to Pittsburgh as compensation by NHL arbitrator in July.

DONALD ANDREW (ANDY) MOOG

Goaltender . . . 5'8" . . . 165 lbs. . . . Born, Penticton, B.C., February 18, 1960 . . . Shoots left . . . (December, 1983)—While visiting a ward of sick children at a local hospital, he entered a quarantined area, caught a viral infection and lost six pounds . . . (March 1, 1985)—Injured ligaments in both knees vs. Los Angeles.

Year	Team	League	Games	Mins.	Goals	SO.	Avg.	A.	Pen.
1976-77—Kamloops Chiefs		WCHL	1	35	6	0	10.29	..	....
1977-78—Penticton		BCJHL	....	......	....	...	......	..	....
1978-79—Billings Bighorns		WHL	26	1306	90	*3	4.13	0	6
1979-80—Billings Bighorns (b-c)		WHL	46	2435	149	1	3.67	1	17
1980-81—Wichita Wind		CHL	29	1602	89	0	3.33	0	4
1980-81—Edmonton Oilers		NHL	7	313	20	0	3.83	1	0
1981-82—Edmonton Oilers		NHL	8	399	32	0	4.81	1	2
1981-82—Wichita Wind (b)		CHL	40	2391	119	1	2.99	5	8
1982-83—Edmonton Oilers		NHL	50	2833	167	1	3.54	4	16
1983-84—Edmonton Oilers		NHL	38	2212	139	1	3.77	1	4
1984-85—Edmonton Oilers		NHL	39	2019	111	1	3.30	0	8
1985-86—Edmonton Oilers		NHL	47	2664	164	1	3.69	2	8
1986-87—Edmonton Oilers		NHL	46	1461	144	0	3.51	2	8
1987-88—Canadian Olympic Team		Int'l	31	1678	95	0	3.40	..	..
1987-88—Boston Bruins (d)		NHL	6	360	17	1	2.83	0	0
NHL TOTALS			241	12261	794	5	3.89	11	46

(c)—June, 1980—Drafted by Edmonton Oilers in 1980 NHL entry draft. Sixth Oilers pick, 132nd overall, seventh round.

(d)—March, 1988—Traded by Edmonton Oilers to Boston Bruins for Geoff Courtnall, Bill Ranford and second-round 1988 draft choice (Petro Koivunen).

JASON MUZZATTI

Goaltender . . . 6'1" . . . 185 lbs. . . . Born, Toronto, Ont., February 3, 1970 . . . Shoots left.

Year	Team	League	Games	Mins.	Goals	SO.	Avg.	A.	Pen.
1986-87—St. Mikes Jr. B		MTHL	20	1054	69	1	3.93	..	..
1987-88—Michigan State Univ. (c)		CCHA	33	1916	109	1	3.41	4	13

(c)—June, 1988—Drafted by Calgary Flames in 1988 NHL entry draft. First Flames pick, 21st overall, first round.

DARREN PANG

Goaltender . . . 5'5" . . . 155 lbs. . . . Born, Medford, Ont., February 17, 1964 . . . Shoots left.

Year	Team	League	Games	Mins.	Goals	SO.	Avg.	A.	Pen.
1982-83—Belleville Bulls		OHL	12	570	44	0	4.63	1	0
1982-83—Ottawa 67's		OHL	47	2729	166	1	3.65	1	0
1983-84—Ottawa 67's		OHL	43	2313	117	2	3.03	2	8
1984-85—Milwaukee Admirals (c)		IHL	53	3129	226	0	4.33	1	16
1984-85—Chicago Black Hawks		NHL	1	60	4	0	4.00	0	0
1985-86—Saginaw Generals		IHL	44	2638	148	2	3.37	2	4
1986-87—Nova Scotia Oilers		AHL	7	389	21	0	3.24	0	0
1986-87—Saginaw Generals		IHL	44	2500	151	2	3.62	2	12
1987-88—Chicago Black Hawks		NHL	45	2548	163	0	3.84	6	2
NHL TOTALS			46	2608	167	0	3.84	6	2

(c)—September, 1984—Signed by Chicago Black Hawks as a free agent.

PETER PEETERS

Goaltender . . . 6' . . . 180 lbs. . . . Born, Edmonton, Alta., August 1, 1957 . . . Shoots left . . . (November 3, 1983)—Suffered concussion when his head struck crossbar during third period goalmouth pileup vs. St. Louis . . . (September 17, 1984)—Sprained left ankle during Team Canada practice in Canada Cup Tournament . . . (January 28, 1986)—Pulled stomach muscle at Detroit . . . (November 28, 1987)—Strained knee ligaments at Pittsburgh . . . (February, 1988)—Bruised left foot when struck by a Kelly Miller shot during a team practice.

Year	Team	League	Games	Mins.	Goals	SO.	Avg.	A.	Pen.
1975-76—Medicine Hat Tigers		WCHL	37	2074	147	0	4.25	2	29
1976-77—Medicine Hat Tigers (c)		WCHL	62	3423	232	1	4.07	2	30
1977-78—Maine Mariners		AHL	17	855	40	1	2.80	2	6
1977-78—Milwaukee Admirals		IHL	32	1698	93	1	3.29	4	14
1978-79—Philadelphia Flyers		NHL	5	280	16	0	3.43	0	6
1978-79—Maine Mariners (b-d)		AHL	35	2067	100	*2	*2.90	1	8

Year	Team	League	Games	Mins.	Goals	SO.	Avg.	A.	Pen.
1979-80—Philadelphia Flyers		NHL	40	2373	108	1	2.73	0	28
1980-81—Philadelphia Flyers		NHL	40	2333	115	2	2.96	1	8
1981-82—Philadelphia Flyers (e)		NHL	44	2591	160	0	3.71	1	19
1982-83—Boston Bruins (a-f)		NHL	62	*3611	142	*8	*2.36	2	33
1983-84—Boston Bruins		NHL	50	2868	151	0	3.16	0	36
1984-85—Boston Bruins		NHL	51	2975	172	1	3.47	0	20
1985-86—Boston Bruins (g)		NHL	8	485	31	0	3.84	2	4
1985-86—Washington Capitals		NHL	34	2021	113	1	3.35	0	8
1986-87—Binghamton Whalers		AHL	4	245	4	1	0.98	0	2
1986-87—Washington Capitals		NHL	37	2002	107	0	3.21	4	16
1987-88—Washington Capitals		NHL	35	1896	88	2	2.78	1	10
NHL TOTALS			406	23435	1203	15	3.08	11	188

(c)—Drafted from Medicine Hat Tigers by Philadelphia Flyers in eighth round of 1977 amateur draft.
(d)—Shared Harry (Hap) Holmes Memorial Trophy (Top AHL goaltending) with Robbie Moore.
(e)—June, 1982—Traded by Philadelphia Flyers to Boston Bruins for Brad McCrimmon.
(f)—Won Vezina Trophy (Top Goaltender in NHL).
(g)—November, 1985—Traded by Boston Bruins to Washington Capitals for Pat Riggin.

STEVE PENNEY

Goaltender ... 6'1" ... 190 lbs. ... Born, Ste. Foy, Que., February 2, 1961 ... Shoots left ... (February, 1985)—Out for two weeks due to being injured during a team practice ... (December 28, 1985)—Bruised shoulder vs. New Jersey and missed three games ... (March, 1986)—Sprained left knee which required surgery and was out remainder of regular season and playoffs.

Year	Team	League	Games	Mins.	Goals	SO.	Avg.	A.	Pen.
1978-79—Shawinigan Cataracts		QMJHL	36	1631	180	0	6.62	0	8
1979-80—Shawinigan Cataracts (c)		QMJHL	31	1682	143	0	5.10	0	31
1980-81—Shawinigan Cataracts		QMJHL	62	3456	244	0	4.24	6	45
1981-82—Flint Generals		IHL	36	2038	147	1	4.33	0	6
1981-82—Nova Scotia Voyageurs		AHL	6	308	22	0	4.29	1	0
1982-83—Flint Generals		IHL	48	2552	179	0	4.21	1	0
1983-84—Nova Scotia Voyageurs		AHL	27	1571	92	0	3.51	0	15
1983-84—Montreal Canadiens (d)		NHL	4	240	19	0	4.75	0	0
1984-85—Montreal Canadiens		NHL	54	3252	167	1	3.08	1	10
1985-86—Montreal Canadiens (e)		NHL	18	990	72	0	4.36	0	0
1986-87—Sherbrooke Canadiens		AHL	4	199	12	0	3.62	1	2
1986-87—Winnipeg Jets		NHL	7	327	25	0	4.59	0	7
1987-88—Moncton Golden Flames		AHL	28	1541	107	0	4.17	2	4
1987-88—Winnipeg Jets		NHL	8	385	30	0	4.68	0	0
NHL TOTALS			91	5194	313	1	3.62	1	17

(c)—June, 1980—Drafted as underage junior by Montreal Canadiens in NHL entry draft. Tenth Canadiens pick, 166th overall, eighth round.
(d)—Led Stanley Cup Playoffs with 2.20 average and three shutouts.
(e)—August, 1986—Traded by Montreal Canadiens with Jan Ingman to Winnipeg Jets for Brian Hayward.

JOCELYN PERREAULT

Goaltender ... 6'4" ... 210 lbs. ... Born, Montreal, Que., January 8, 1966 ... Shoots right.

Year	Team	League	Games	Mins.	Goals	SO.	Avg.	A.	Pen.
1985-86—St. Laurent College (c)		CEGEP	11	582	30	0	3.09	..	..
1986-87—Sherbrooke Canadiens		AHL	13	722	40	0	3.32	0	0
1986-87—Saginaw Generals		IHL	7	286	21	0	4.41	0	0
1987-88—Sherbrooke Canadiens		AHL	25	1244	77	0	3.71	0	4

(c)—September, 1986—Signed by Montreal Canadiens as a free agent.

ALAN PERRY

Goaltender ... 5'8" ... 155 lbs. ... Born, Providence, R.I., August 30, 1966 ... Shoots right.

Year	Team	League	Games	Mins.	Goals	SO.	Avg.	A.	Pen.
1983-84—Mt. St. Charles H.S. (c)		R.I.H.S.	20	900	28	1	1.87	..	..
1984-85—Windsor Spitfires		OHL	34	1905	135	1	4.25	3	4
1985-86—Windsor Spitfires		OHL	42	2424	131	*3	3.24	2	18
1986-87—Belleville Bulls		OHL	15	843	64	0	4.56	3	10
1986-87—Peoria Rivermen		IHL	6	312	36	0	6.92	0	4
1987-88—Peoria Rivermen		IHL	20	1069	77	0	4.32	1	16

(c)—June, 1984—Drafted by St. Louis Blues in 1984 NHL entry draft. Fifth Blues pick, 56th overall, third round.

FRANK PIETRANGELO

Goaltender . . . 5'10" . . . 178 lbs. . . . Born, Niagara Falls, Ont., December 17, 1964 . . . Shoots left.

Year	Team	League	Games	Mins.	Goals	SO.	Avg.	A.	Pen.
1982-83—University of Minnesota (c)		WCHA	25	1348	80	1	3.56	0	4
1983-84—University of Minnesota		WCHA	20	1141	66	..	3.47	2	0
1984-85—University of Minnesota		WCHA	17	912	52	0	3.42	0	0
1985-86—University of Minnesota		WCHA	23	1284	76	0	3.55	1	0
1986-87—Muskegon Lumberjacks		IHL	35	2090	119	2	3.42	4	2
1987-88—Pittsburgh Penguins		NHL	21	1207	80	1	3.98	2	2
1987-88—Muskegon Lumberjacks		IHL	15	868	43	2	2.97	0	2
NHL TOTALS			21	1207	80	1	3.98	2	2

(c)—June, 1983—Drafted by Pittsburgh Penguins in 1983 NHL entry draft. Fourth Penguins pick, 63rd overall, fourth round.

DAREN PUPPA

Goaltender . . . 6'3" . . . 195 lbs. . . . Born, Kirkland Lake, Ont., March 23, 1965 . . . Shoots right . . . (November 1, 1985)—First NHL game was a 2-0 shutout at Edmonton . . . (February, 1986)—Injured knee in AHL game . . . (October, 1987)—Fractured left index finger.

Year	Team	League	Games	Mins.	Goals	SO.	Avg.	A.	Pen.
1983-84—Rensselaer Poly. Inst. (c)		ECAC	32	1816	89	...	2.94	..	....
1984-85—Rensselaer Poly. Inst.		ECAC	32	1830	78	...	2.56	0	2
1985-86—Buffalo Sabres		NHL	7	401	21	1	3.14	0	0
1985-86—Rochester Americans		AHL	20	1092	79	0	4.34	1	0
1986-87—Buffalo Sabres		NHL	3	185	13	0	4.22	0	2
1986-87—Rochester Americans (a)		AHL	57	3129	146	1	*2.80	1	12
1987-88—Rochester Americans		AHL	26	1415	65	2	2.76	2	8
1987-88—Buffalo Sabres		NHL	17	874	61	0	4.19	1	4
NHL TOTALS			27	1460	95	1	3.90	1	6

(c)—June, 1983—Drafted by Buffalo Sabres in 1983 NHL entry draft. Sixth Sabres pick, 74th overall, fourth round.

BRUCE M. RACINE

Goaltender . . . 6'1" . . . 180 lbs. . . . Born, Cornwall, Ont., August 9, 1966 . . . Shoots left . . . Son of Maurice Racine (17 years in CFL).

Year	Team	League	Games	Mins.	Goals	SO.	Avg.	A.	Pen.
1984-85—Northeastern University (b-c)		H. East	26	1615	103	0	3.83	1	12
1985-86—Northeastern University		H. East	37	2212	171	0	4.64	3	0
1986-87—Northeastern Univ. (a-d)		H. East	33	1966	133	0	4.06	2	0
1987-88—Northeastern Univ. (d)		H. East	30	1809	108	1	3.58	2	0

(c)—June, 1985—Drafted by Pittsburgh Penguins in 1985 NHL entry draft. Third Penguins pick, 58th overall, third round.

(d)—Named to first team All-America Team (East).

JIM RALPH

Goaltender . . . 5'11" . . . 162 lbs. . . . Born, Sault Ste. Marie, Ont., May 13, 1962 . . . Shoots left.

Year	Team	League	Games	Mins.	Goals	SO.	Avg.	A.	Pen.
1979-80—Ottawa 67's (c)		OHL	45	2451	171	0	4.19	1	6
1980-81—Ottawa 67's (a)		OHL	57	3266	202	*2	3.71	3	8
1981-82—Ottawa 67's (b)		OHL	53	3211	185	1	3.45	2	2
1982-83—Colorado Flames		CHL	5	300	18	0	3.60	0	0
1982-83—Springfield Indians		AHL	26	1498	105	0	4.21	0	0
1983-84—Springfield Indians		AHL	9	479	42	0	5.26	1	0
1983-84—Baltimore Skipjacks		AHL	25	1455	87	0	3.59	0	2
1984-85—Milwaukee Admirals		IHL	19	1072	78	0	4.37	0	2
1985-86—Milwaukee Admirals		IHL	14	819	58	1	4.25	0	4
1985-86—Nova Scotia Oilers		AHL	9	549	46	0	5.03	0	0
1986-87—Milwaukee Admirals		IHL	2	120	9	0	4.50	0	2
1987-88—Newmarket Saints (d)		AHL	14	550	45	0	4.91	0	0

(c)—June, 1980—Drafted by Chicago Black Hawks in 1980 NHL entry draft. Twelfth Black Hawks pick, 162nd overall, eighth round.

(d)—October, 1987—Signed by Toronto Maple Leafs as a free agent.

BILL RANFORD

Goaltender . . . 5'11" . . . 165 lbs. . . . Born, Brandon, Manitoba, December 14, 1966 . . . Shoots left.

Year	Team	League	Games	Mins.	Goals	SO.	Avg.	A.	Pen.
1983-84—New Westminster Bruins		WHL	27	1450	130	0	5.38	2	0
1984-85—New Westminster Bruins (c)		WHL	38	2034	142	0	4.19	0	4
1985-86—New Westminster Bruins (b)		WHL	53	2791	225	1	4.84	1	23
1985-86—Boston Bruins		NHL	4	240	10	0	2.50	0	0
1986-87—Moncton Golden Flames		AHL	3	180	6	0	2.00	0	0
1986-87—Boston Bruins		NHL	41	2234	124	3	3.33	1	8
1987-88—Maine Mariners		AHL	51	1856	165	1	3.47	1	4
1987-88—Edmonton Oilers (d)		NHL	6	325	16	0	2.95	2	0
NHL TOTALS			51	2799	150	3	3.22	3	8

(c)—June, 1985—Drafted as underage junior by Boston Bruins in 1985 NHL entry draft. Second Bruins pick, 52nd overall, third round.

(d)—March, 1988—Traded with Geoff Courtnall and second-round 1988 draft choice (Petro Koivunen) by Boston Bruins to Edmonton Oilers for Andy Moog.

ALAIN RAYMOND

Goaltender . . . 5'10" . . . 177 lbs. . . . Born, Rimouski, Que., June 24, 1965 . . . Shoots left.

Year	Team	League	Games	Mins.	Goals	SO.	Avg.	A.	Pen.
1981-82—Cantons de L'Est		Que. Midget	27	1505	128	...	5.10		....
1982-83—Hull Olympics		QHL	17	809	80	0	5.93	0	4
1982-83—Trois-Rivieres Draveurs (c)		QHL	22	1176	124	0	6.33	0	4
1983-84—Trois-Rivieres Draveurs (a)		QHL	53	2725	223	*2	4.91	0	6
1984-85—Trois-Rivieres Draveurs		QHL	58	3295	220	*2	4.01	3	2
1985-86—Team Canada		Int'l	46	2571	151	4	3.52	..	..
1986-87—Fort Wayne Komets (d)		IHL	45	2433	134	1	*3.30	0	27
1987-88—Fort Wayne Komets		IHL	40	2271	142	2	3.75	0	8
1987-88—Washington Capitals		NHL	1	40	2	0	3.00	0	0
NHL TOTALS			1	40	2	0	3.00	0	0

(c)—June, 1983—Drafted as underage junior by Washington Capitals in 1983 NHL entry draft. Seventh Capitals pick, 215th overall, 11th round.

(d)—Co-winner of James Norris Memorial Trophy with teammate Michel Dufour (Top Goaltender).

DARYL REAUGH

Goaltender . . . 6'4" . . . 200 lbs. . . . Born, Prince George, B.C., February 13, 1965 . . . Shoots left.

Year	Team	League	Games	Mins.	Goals	SO.	Avg.	A.	Pen.
1983-84—Kamloops Junior Oilers (b-c-d)		WHL	55	2748	199	1	4.34	5	18
1984-85—Kamloops Blazers (a)		WHL	49	2749	170	2	3.71	3	19
1984-85—Edmonton Oilers		NHL	1	60	5	0	5.00	0	0
1985-86—Nova Scotia Oilers		AHL	38	2205	156	0	4.24	2	4
1986-87—Nova Scotia Oilers		AHL	46	2637	163	1	3.71	2	8
1987-88—Edmonton Oilers		NHL	6	176	14	0	4.77	0	0
1987-88—Nova Scotia Oilers		AHL	8	443	33	0	4.47	0	0
1987-88—Milwaukee Admirals		IHL	9	493	44	0	5.35	1	0
NHL TOTALS			7	236	19	0	4.83	0	0

(c)—Led WHL playoffs with 3.52 average.

(d)—June, 1984—Drafted as underage junior by Edmonton Oilers in 1984 NHL entry draft. Second Oilers pick, 42nd overall, second round.

ELDON (POKEY) REDDICK

Goaltender . . . 5'8" . . . 175 lbs. . . . Born, Halifax, N.S., October 6, 1964 . . . Shoots left.

Year	Team	League	Games	Mins.	Goals	SO.	Avg.	A.	Pen.
1981-82—Billings Bighorns		WHL	1	60	7	0	7.00	0	0
1982-83—Nanaimo Islanders		WHL	*66	*3549	*383	0	6.48	5	6
1983-84—New Westminster Bruins (b)		WHL	50	2930	215	0	4.40	1	6
1984-85—Brandon Wheat Kings (c)		WHL	47	2585	243	0	5.64	4	2
1984-85—Fort Wayne Komets		IHL	10	491	32	2	3.91	0	0
1985-86—Fort Wayne Komets (d-e)		IHL	32	1811	92	*3	*3.05	0	6
1986-87—Winnipeg Jets		NHL	48	2762	149	0	3.24	0	8
1987-88—Winnipeg Jets		NHL	28	1487	102	0	4.12	0	6
1987-88—Moncton Golden Flames		AHL	9	545	26	0	2.86	0	2
NHL TOTALS			76	4249	251	0	3.54	0	14

(c)—October, 1984—Traded by New Westminster Bruins to Brandon Wheat Kings for Jayson Meyer and Lee Trimm.

(d)—September, 1985—Signed by Winnipeg Jets as a free agent.

(e)—Co-winner of James Norris Memorial Trophy (Top Goaltender) with teammate Rick St. Croix.

JEFF REESE

Goaltender . . . 5'9" . . . 155 lbs. . . . Born, Brantford, Ont., March 24, 1966 . . . Shoots left.

Year	Team	League	Games	Mins.	Goals	SO.	Avg.	A.	Pen.
1982-83—Hamilton A's		OJHL	40	2380	176	0	4.43	..	....
1983-84—London Knights (c)		OHL	43	2308	173	0	4.50	1	4
1984-85—London Knights (d)		OHL	50	2878	186	1	3.88	1	4
1985-86—London Knights		OHL	*57	*3281	215	0	3.93	1	25
1986-87—Newmarket Saints		AHL	50	2822	193	1	4.10	2	24
1987-88—Newmarket Saints		AHL	28	1587	103	0	3.89	1	14
1987-88—Toronto Maple Leafs		NHL	5	249	17	0	4.10	0	0
NHL TOTALS			5	249	17	0	4.10	0	0

(c)—June, 1984—Drafted as underage junior by Toronto Maple Leafs in NHL entry draft. Third Maple Leafs pick, 67th overall, fourth round.

(d)—Led OHL playoffs with one shutout and a 2.73 average.

JOHN REID

Goaltender ... 6'1" ... 195 lbs. ... Born, Windsor, Ont., February 18, 1967 ... Shoots right.

Year	Team	League	Games	Mins.	Goals	SO.	Avg.	A.	Pen.
1983-84—Brantford Knights		OHA	30	1350	59	3	1.95	..	..
1984-85—Belleville Bulls (c)		OHL	31	1443	92	0	3.83	1	8
1985-86—Belleville Bulls		OHL	24	1309	100	0	4.58	0	5
1985-86—North Bay Centennials		OHL	23	1318	64	1	2.91	0	6
1986-87—North Bay Centennials		OHL	47	2737	142	1	3.11	1	39
1987-88—Saginaw Wings		IHL	5	260	11	0	2.54	0	2
1987-88—Colorado Rangers		IHL	32	1673	117	0	4.20	0	18

(c)—June, 1985—Drafted as underage junior by Chicago Black Hawks in 1985 NHL entry draft. Eighth Black Hawks pick, 158th overall, eighth round.

MARK REIMER

Goaltender ... 5'11" ... 170 lbs. ... Born, Calgary, Alta., March 23, 1967 ... Shoots left.

Year	Team	League	Games	Mins.	Goals	SO.	Avg.	A.	Pen.
1984-85—Saskatoon Blades		WHL	2	120	7	0	3.50	1	0
1984-85—Calgary Canucks		AJHL	29	1559	132	1	5.08	..	..
1985-86—Saskatoon Blades		WHL	41	2362	192	0	4.88	4	31
1986-87—Saskatoon Blades (b-c)		WHL	42	2442	141	1	3.46	6	4
1987-88—Portland Winter Hawks		WHL	38	2268	208	0	5.50	4	31
1987-88—Flint Spirits		IHL	5	169	22	0	7.86	0	0
1987-88—Adirondack Red Wings		AHL	8	459	24	0	3.14	1	0

(c)—June, 1987—Drafted by Detroit Red Wings in 1987 NHL entry draft. Fifth Red Wings pick, 74th overall, fourth round.

KENTON REIN

Goaltender ... 6' ... 195 lbs. ... Born, Toronto, Ont., September 12, 1967 ... Shoots left ... (September, 1987)—Missed the first four months of the season after being struck in the mask by a shot during training camp.

Year	Team	League	Games	Mins.	Goals	SO.	Avg.	A.	Pen.
1985-86—Prince Albert Raiders (c-d)		WHL	23	1302	71	0	3.27	3	4
1986-87—Prince Albert Raiders (a-e)		WHL	51	2996	159	0	*3.18	3	29
1987-88—Flint Spirits		IHL	1	20	3	0	9.00	0	0

(c)—October, 1984—WHL rights traded with Brent Bobyck by Moose Jaw Warriors to Prince Albert Raiders for Bob Schmidtke, Blaine Gusdal, Dave German and Dale Kushner.

(d)—June, 1986—Drafted as underage junior by Buffalo Sabres in 1986 NHL entry draft. Eleventh Sabres pick, 194th overall, 10th round.

(e)—Named Top Goaltender (East Division).

DAMIAN RHODES

Goaltender ... 6' ... 165 lbs. ... Born, St. Paul, Minn., May 28, 1969 ... Shoots right.

Year	Team	League	Games	Mins.	Goals	SO.	Avg.	A.	Pen.
1985-86—Richfield H.S.		Minn. H.S.	16	720	56	0	4.67	..	..
1986-87—Richfield H.S. (c)		Minn. H.S.	19	673	51	1	4.55	..	..
1987-88—Michigan Tech. Univ.		WCHA	29	1623	114	0	4.21	3	4

(c)—June, 1987—Drafted by Toronto Maple Leafs in 1987 NHL entry draft. Sixth Maple Leafs pick, 112th overall, sixth round.

MIKE RICHTER

Goaltender ... 5'11" ... 170 lbs. ... Born, Philadelphia, Pa., September 22, 1966 ... Shoots left.

Year	Team	League	Games	Mins.	Goals	SO.	Avg.	A.	Pen.
1984-85—Northwood Prep. (c)		Mass. H.S.	24	..	52	2	2.27	..	..
1985-86—Univ. of Wisconsin (b-d)		WCHA	24	1394	92	1	3.96	0	0
1986-87—Univ. of Wisconsin (b)		WCHA	36	2136	126	0	3.54	1	0
1987-88—U.S. Olympic Team		Int'l	30	...	..	..	3.28	..	..
1987-88—Colorado Rangers		IHL	22	1298	68	1	3.14	0	5

(c)—June, 1985—Drafted by New York Rangers in 1985 NHL entry draft. Second Rangers pick, 28th overall, second round.

(d)—Named WCHA Freshman-of-the-Year.

VINCENT RIENDEAU

Goaltender . . . 5'9" . . . 173 lbs. . . . Born, St. Hyacinthe, Que., April 20, 1966 . . . Shoots left . . . (November, 1987)—Skin rash . . . (April 10, 1988)—Broke leg during a team practice.

Year	Team	League	Games	Mins.	Goals	SO.	Avg.	A.	Pen.
1983-84—Verdun Juniors		QMJHL	41	2133	147	2	4.14	1	8
1984-85—Univ. of Sherbrooke (c)		Can. Col.	..	..	..	..	..	..	..
1985-86—Drummondville Voltigeurs (b)		QMJHL	57	3336	215	2	3.87	3	40
1986-87—Sherbrooke Canadiens		AHL	41	2363	114	2	2.89	0	23
1987-88—Sherbrooke Canadiens		AHL	44	2521	112	*4	*2.67	1	22
1987-88—Montreal Canadiens (d)		NHL	1	36	5	0	8.33	0	0
NHL TOTALS			1	36	5	0	8.33	0	0

(c)—October, 1985—Signed by Montreal Canadiens as a free agent.

(d)—August, 1988—Traded with Sergio Momesso by Montreal Canadiens to St. Louis Blues for Jocelyn Lemieux, Darrell May and 1989 second-round draft pick.

PAT RIGGIN

Goaltender . . . 5'9" . . . 163 lbs. . . . Born, Kincardine, Ont., May 26, 1959 . . . Shoots right . . . Son of former Detroit goalie Dennis Riggin.

Year	Team	League	Games	Mins.	Goals	SO.	Avg.	A.	Pen.
1975-76—London Knights		Jr. "A" OHA	29	1385	86	0	3.68	1	0
1976-77—London Knights (a-c)		Jr. "A" OHA	48	2809	138	*2	*2.95	3	4
1977-78—London Knights (b-d)		Jr. "A" OHA	37	2266	140	0	3.65	0	2
1978-79—Birmingham Bulls (e)		WHA	46	2511	158	1	3.78	3	22
1979-80—Birmingham Bulls		CHL	12	746	32	0	2.57	0	2
1979-80—Atlanta Flames		NHL	25	1368	73	2	3.20	0	0
1980-81—Calgary Flames		NHL	42	2411	154	0	3.83	1	7
1981-82—Calgary Flames (f)		NHL	52	2934	207	2	4.23	5	4
1982-83—Washington Capitals		NHL	38	2161	121	0	3.36	0	4
1983-84—Hershey Bears		AHL	3	185	7	0	2.27	1	0
1983-84—Washington Capitals (g)		NHL	41	2299	102	*4	*2.66	0	4
1984-85—Washington Capitals		NHL	57	3388	168	2	2.98	1	2
1985-86—Washington Capitals (h)		NHL	7	369	23	0	3.74	0	2
1985-86—Boston Bruins		NHL	39	2272	127	1	3.35	0	4
1986-87—Boston Bruins (i)		NHL	10	513	29	0	3.39	0	0
1986-87—Moncton Golden Flames		AHL	14	798	34	1	2.56	1	6
1986-87—Pittsburgh Penguins		NHL	17	988	55	0	3.34	1	2
1987-88—Pittsburgh Penguins		NHL	22	1169	76	0	3.90	0	12
1987-88—Muskegon Lumberjacks		IHL	18	956	43	0	2.70	0	22
WHA TOTALS			46	2511	158	1	3.78	3	22
NHL TOTALS			350	19872	1135	11	3.43	8	41

(c)—Won Dave Pinkney Trophy (Leading Goaltender).

(d)—July, 1978—Signed by Birmingham Bulls (WHA) as under-age junior.

(e)—August, 1979—Drafted by Atlanta Flames in entry draft. Third Flames pick, 33rd overall, second round.

(f)—June, 1982—Traded by Calgary Flames with Ken Houston to Washington Capitals for Howard Walker, NHL rights to George White plus sixth round 1982 draft pick (Mats Kihlstrom), third round 1983 draft pick (Perry Berezan) and second round 1984 draft pick (Paul Ranheim).

(g)—Co-winner of Bill Jennings Memorial Trophy (Top NHL Goaltenders) with teammate Al Jensen.

(h)—November, 1985—Traded by Washington Capitals to Boston Bruins for Pete Peeters.

(i)—February, 1987—Traded by Boston Bruins to Pittsburgh Penguins for Roberto Romano.

DAVE ROACH

Goaltender . . . 5'9" . . . 175 lbs. . . . Born, Burnaby, B.C., January 10, 1965 . . . Shoots right.

Year	Team	League	Games	Mins.	Goals	SO.	Avg.	A.	Pen.
1983-84—Michigan Tech (c)		WCHA	24	1407	79	0	3.37	0	0
1984-85—Michigan Tech		WCHA	19	1085	75	0	4.15	0	2
1985-86—Michigan Tech		WCHA	24	1265	104	0	4.93	1	4
1986-87—Michigan Tech		WCHA	30	1811	151	0	5.00	0	0
1987-88—Nova Scotia Oilers		AHL	25	1478	110	1	4.47	0	4

(c)—June, 1983—Drafted by Edmonton Oilers in 1983 NHL entry draft. Eighth Oilers pick, 180th overall, ninth round.

ROBERTO ROMANO

Goaltender . . . 5'5" . . . 172 lbs. . . . Born, Montreal, Que., October 29, 1962 . . . Shoots left . . . (December 5, 1984)—Injured knee at St. Louis.

Year	Team	League	Games	Mins.	Goals	SO.	Avg.	A.	Pen.
1979-80	Quebec Remparts	QMJHL	52	2411	183	0	4.55	0	2
1980-81	Quebec Remparts	QMJHL	59	3174	233	0	4.40	1	0
1981-82	Quebec Remparts (c)	QMJHL	1	60	4	0	4.00	0	0
1981-82	Hull Olympics (a)	QMJHL	56	3090	194	*1	3.77	1	5
1982-83	Baltimore Skipjacks (d)	AHL	38	2164	146	0	4.05	2	6
1982-83	Pittsburgh Penguins	NHL	3	155	18	0	6.97	0	0
1983-84	Pittsburgh Penguins	NHL	18	1020	78	1	4.59	0	0
1983-84	Baltimore Skipjacks	AHL	31	1759	106	0	3.62	0	2
1984-85	Baltimore Skipjacks	AHL	12	719	44	0	3.67	0	0
1984-85	Pittsburgh Penguins	NHL	31	1629	120	1	4.42	0	2
1985-86	Pittsburgh Penguins	NHL	46	2684	159	2	3.55	1	4
1986-87	Pittsburgh Penguins	NHL	25	1438	87	0	3.63	0	0
1986-87	Boston Bruins (e)	NHL	1	60	6	0	6.00	0	0
1986-87	Baltimore Skipjacks	AHL	5	274	18	0	3.94	0	0
1986-87	Moncton Golden Flames	AHL	1	65	3	0	2.77	0	0
1987-88	Maine Mariners (f)	AHL	16	875	52	0	3.57	0	17
	NHL TOTALS		124	6986	468	4	4.02	1	6

(c)—September, 1981—Traded by Quebec Remparts to Hull Olympics for Dan Sanscartier, Alan Bremner and future considerations.
(d)—September, 1983—Signed by Pittsburgh Penguins as a free agent.
(e)—February, 1987—Traded by Pittsburgh Penguins to Boston Bruins for Pat Riggin.
(f)—December, 1987—Left Maine Mariners to play hockey in Italy.

MIKE ROSATI

Goaltender . . . 5'10" . . . 170 lbs. . . . Born, Toronto, Ont., January 7, 1968 . . . Shoots left.

Year	Team	League	Games	Mins.	Goals	SO.	Avg.	A.	Pen.
1985-86	St. Mikes Jr. B.	MTHL	20	1100	95	0	5.18	..	..
1986-87	Hamilton Steelhawks	OHL	26	1334	85	1	3.82	2	12
1987-88	Hamilton Steelhawks (c)	OHL	62	3468	233	1	4.03	2	18

(c)—June, 1988—Drafted by New York Rangers in 1988 NHL entry draft. Sixth Rangers pick, 131st overall, seventh round.

DOMINIC ROUSSEL

Goaltender . . . 6'1" . . . 185 lbs. . . . Born, Hull, Quebec, February 22, 1970 . . . Shoots left.

Year	Team	League	Games	Mins.	Goals	SO.	Avg.	A.	Pen.
1986-87	Lac St. Louis Mid. AAA	Que. Midget	24	1334	85	1	3.82	..	..
1987-88	Trois-Rivieres Draveurs (c)	QHL	51	2905	251	0	5.18	1	14

(c)—June, 1988—Drafted as underage junior by Philadelphia Flyers in 1988 NHL entry draft. Fourth Flyers pick, 63rd overall, third round.

PATRICK ROY

Goaltender . . . 6' . . . 165 lbs. . . . Born, Quebec City, Que., October 5, 1965 . . . Shoots left . . . (October 19, 1987)—Suspended eight NHL games for slashing Warren Babe vs. Minnesota North Stars.

Year	Team	League	Games	Mins.	Goals	SO.	Avg.	A.	Pen.
1982-83	Granby Bisons	QHL	54	2808	293	0	6.26	0	14
1983-84	Granby Bisons (c)	QHL	61	3585	265	0	4.44	6	15
1984-85	Granby Bisons	QHL	44	2463	228	0	5.55	2	74
1984-85	Montreal Canadiens	NHL	1	20	0	0	0.00	0	0
1984-85	Sherbrooke Canadiens (d)	AHL	1	60	4	0	4.00	0	0
1985-86	Montreal Canadiens (e)	NHL	47	2651	150	1	3.39	3	4
1986-87	Montreal Canadiens	NHL	46	2686	131	1	2.93	1	8
1987-88	Montreal Canadiens (b-f)	NHL	45	2586	125	3	2.90	2	14
	NHL TOTALS		139	7943	406	5	3.07	6	26

(c)—June, 1984—Drafted as underage junior by Montreal Canadiens in NHL entry draft. Fourth Canadiens pick, 51st overall, third round.
(d)—Led AHL playoffs with 2.89 average.
(e)—Won Conn Smythe Trophy (Playoff MVP) and was one of four goalies with one shutout.
(f)—Shared Bill Jennings Trophy with teammate Brian Hayward (Top NHL Goaltending tandem).

SAM ST. LAURENT

Goaltender ... 5'10" ... 190 lbs. ... Born, Arvida, Que., February 16, 1959 ... Shoots left.

Year	Team	League	Games	Mins.	Goals	SO.	Avg.	A.	Pen.
1975-76—Chicoutimi Sagueneens		QMJHL	17	889	81	0	5.47	..	....
1976-77—Chicoutimi Sagueneens		QMJHL	21	901	81	0	5.39	0	30
1977-78—Chicoutimi Sagueneens		QMJHL	60	3251	*351	0	6.46	..	....
1978-79—Chicoutimi Sagueneens		QMJHL	70	3806	290	0	4.57	1	0
1979-80—Toledo Goaldiggers (c)		IHL	38	2145	138	2	3.86	1	6
1979-80—Maine Mariners		AHL	4	201	15	0	4.48	0	0
1980-81—Maine Mariners		AHL	7	363	28	0	4.63	0	2
1980-81—Toledo Goaldiggers		IHL	30	1614	113	1	4.20	2	0
1981-82—Maine Mariners		AHL	25	1396	76	0	3.27	0	0
1981-82—Toledo Goaldiggers		IHL	4	248	11	0	2.66	0	0
1982-83—Toledo Goaldiggers		IHL	13	785	52	0	3.97	0	0
1982-83—Maine Mariners		AHL	30	1739	109	0	3.76	0	2
1983-84—Maine Mariners (d)		AHL	38	2158	145	0	4.03	0	0
1984-85—Maine Mariners (b)		AHL	55	3245	168	*4	3.11	1	8
1985-86—New Jersey Devils		NHL	4	188	13	1	4.15	0	0
1985-86—Maine Mariners (b-e-f-g)		AHL	50	2862	161	1	3.38	1	8
1986-87—Adirondack Red Wings		AHL	25	1397	98	1	4.21	1	4
1986-87—Detroit Red Wings		NHL	6	342	16	0	2.81	0	0
1987-88—Adirondack Red Wings		AHL	32	1826	104	2	3.42	1	8
1987-88—Detroit Red Wings		NHL	6	294	16	0	3.27	0	2
NHL TOTALS			16	824	45	1	3.28	0	2

(c)—September, 1979—Signed by Philadelphia Flyers as a free agent.
(d)—August, 1984—Traded by Philadelphia Flyers to New Jersey Devils for future considerations.
(e)—Shared Harry (Hap) Holmes Memorial Trophy with teammate Karl Friesen (Top Goalies).
(f)—Won Baz Bastien Trophy (Coaches pick as top Goalie).
(g)—August, 1986—Traded by New Jersey Devils to Detroit Red Wings for Steve Richmond.

MIKE SANDS

Goaltender ... 5'9" ... 155 lbs. ... Born, Mississauga, Ont., April 6, 1963 ... Shoots left ... (October, 1987)—Suspended by Minnesota North Stars for leaving Baltimore Skipjacks without permission. He was later assigned to Kalamazoo.

Year	Team	League	Games	Mins.	Goals	SO.	Avg.	A.	Pen.
1980-81—Sudbury Wolves (c)		OHL	50	2789	236	0	5.08	5	10
1981-82—Sudbury Wolves		OHL	53	2854	*265	1	5.57	6	25
1981-82—Nashville South Stars		CHL	7	380	26	0	4.11	0	0
1982-83—Sudbury Wolves		OHL	43	2320	204	1	5.28	0	24
1982-83—Birmingham South Stars		CHL	4	169	14	0	4.97	0	0
1983-84—Salt Lake Golden Eagles		CHL	23	1145	93	0	4.87	1	34
1984-85—Springfield Indians		AHL	46	2589	140	2	3.24	2	48
1984-85—Minnesota North Stars		NHL	3	139	14	0	6.04	0	2
1985-86—Springfield Indians		AHL	27	1490	94	0	3.79	0	24
1986-87—Minnesota North Stars		NHL	3	163	12	0	4.42	0	0
1986-87—Springfield Indians		AHL	19	1048	77	0	4.41	0	0
1987-88—Baltimore Skipjacks		AHL	4	185	22	0	7.14	0	4
1987-88—Kalamazoo Wings		IHL	3	184	16	0	5.21	0	2
NHL TOTALS			6	302	26	0	5.17	0	2

(c)—June, 1981—Drafted as underage junior by Minnesota North Stars in 1981 NHL entry draft. Third North Stars pick, 31st overall, second round.

ROBERT SAUVE

Goaltender ... 5'8" ... 165 lbs. ... Born, Ste. Genevieve, Que., June 17, 1955 ... Shoots left ... Brother of Jean-Francois Sauve ... (December, 1984)—Sprained back ... (November 2, 1985)—Pulled hamstring at Boston and missed eight games ... (March 1, 1987)—Pulled back muscle in pre-game warm-up vs. Los Angeles ... (October 10, 1987)—Separated left shoulder at Toronto.

Year	Team	League	Games	Mins.	Goals	SO.	Avg.	A.	Pen.
1971-72—Verdun Maple Leafs		QJHL	33	.....	202	0	6.01	..	....
1972-73—Laval National		QJHL	35	1489	224	0	6.40	2	8
1973-74—Laval National (a)		QJHL	61	.....	341	0	5.65	5	8
1974-75—Laval National (c)		QJHL	57	3403	287	0	5.06	0	6
1975-76—Charlotte Checkers (d)		SHL	17	979	36	2	2.21	1	0
1975-76—Providence Reds (e)		AHL	14	848	44	0	3.11	0	0
1976-77—Rhode Island Reds		AHL	25	1346	94	0	4.14	0	2
1976-77—Hershey Bears		AHL	9	539	38	0	4.23	0	0
1976-77—Buffalo Sabres		NHL	4	184	11	0	3.59	0	0
1977-78—Hershey Bears		AHL	16	872	59	0	4.05	1	0

Year	Team	League	Games	Mins.	Goals	SO.	Avg.	A.	Pen.
1977-78—Buffalo Sabres		NHL	11	480	20	0	2.50	1	0
1978-79—Buffalo Sabres		NHL	29	1610	100	0	3.73	0	2
1978-79—Hershey Bears		AHL	5	278	14	0	3.02	1	0
1979-80—Buffalo Sabres (f-g)		NHL	32	1880	74	4	*2.36	4	2
1980-81—Buffalo Sabres		NHL	35	2100	111	2	3.17	1	0
1981-82—Buffalo Sabres (h)		NHL	14	760	35	0	2.76	0	2
1981-82—Detroit Red Wings (i)		NHL	41	2365	165	0	4.19	0	0
1982-83—Buffalo Sabres		NHL	54	3110	179	1	3.45	1	8
1983-84—Buffalo Sabres		NHL	40	2375	138	0	3.49	0	2
1984-85—Buffalo Sabres (j)		NHL	27	1564	84	0	3.22	1	4
1985-86—Chicago Black Hawks (k)		NHL	38	2099	138	0	3.94	1	27
1986-87—Chicago Black Hawks (l)		NHL	46	2660	159	1	3.59	4	6
1987-88—New Jersey Devils		NHL	34	1803	107	0	3.56	1	4
NHL TOTALS			405	22990	1321	8	3.45	14	57

(c)—Drafted from Laval National by Buffalo Sabres in first round of 1975 amateur draft.
(d)—Leading goalie during playoffs (1.43 average and 2 shutouts).
(e)—January, 1976—Loaned to Providence Reds by Buffalo Sabres.
(f)—Shared Vezina Memorial Trophy (Top NHL Goaltender) with teammate Don Edwards.
(g)—Led Stanley Cup Playoffs with 2.04 goals-against-average and two shutouts.
(h)—December, 1981—Traded by Buffalo Sabres to Detroit Red Wings for future considerations.
(i)—June, 1982—Signed by Buffalo Sabres as a free agent.
(j)—Co-Winner of Bill Jennings Trophy (Top NHL Goaltending) with teammate Tom Barrasso.
(k)—October, 1985—Traded by Buffalo Sabres to Chicago Black Hawks for third round 1986 draft pick (Kevin Kerr).
(l)—July, 1987—Signed by New Jersey Devils as a free agent.

RON SCOTT

Goaltender . . . 5'8" . . . 155 lbs. . . . Born, Guelph, Ont., July 21, 1960 . . . Shoots left . . . (November, 1984)—Severe groin injury and missed three weeks.

Year	Team	League	Games	Mins.	Goals	SO.	Avg.	A.	Pen.
1980-81—Michigan State Univ. (a)		WCHA	33	1899	123	0	3.89	1	4
1981-82—Michigan State Univ. (a-c)		CCHA	39	2298	109	2	2.85	2	2
1982-83—Michigan State Univ. (a-c-d)		CCHA	40	2273	100	...	2.64	5	10
1983-84—Tulsa Oilers		CHL	20	1717	109	0	3.81	0	2
1983-84—New York Rangers		NHL	9	485	29	0	3.59	0	0
1984-85—New Haven Nighthawks		AHL	37	2047	130	0	3.81	1	2
1985-86—New York Rangers		NHL	4	156	11	0	4.23	0	0
1985-86—New Haven Nighthawks		AHL	19	1069	66	1	3.70	2	7
1986-87—New Haven Nighthawks		AHL	29	1744	107	2	3.68	2	4
1986-87—New York Rangers		NHL	1	65	5	0	4.62	0	0
1987-88—New York Rangers		NHL	2	90	6	0	4.00	0	0
1987-88—New Haven Nighthawks		AHL	17	963	49	0	3.05	0	2
1987-88—Colorado Rangers		IHL	8	395	33	0	5.01	0	0
NHL TOTALS			16	796	51	0	3.84	0	0

(c)—Named to All-America Team (West).
(d)—May, 1983—Signed by New York Rangers as a free agent.

WARREN SHARPLES

Goaltender . . . 6' . . . 170 lbs. . . . Born, Calgary, Alta., March 1, 1968 . . . Shoots left.

Year	Team	League	Games	Mins.	Goals	SO.	Avg.	A.	Pen.
1985-86—Penticton Knights (c)		BCJHL	....	......	....	...	......	..	....
1986-87—Univ. of Michigan		CCHA	32	1728	148	1	5.14	3	10
1987-88—Univ. of Michigan		CCHA	33	1930	132	...	4.10	0	12

(c)—June, 1986—Drafted by Calgary Flames in 1986 NHL entry draft. Eighth Flames pick, 184th overall, ninth round.

PETER SIDORKIEWICZ

Goaltender . . . 5'9" . . . 165 lbs. . . . Born, Dabrown Bialostocka, Poland, June 29, 1963 . . . Shoots left.

Year	Team	League	Games	Mins.	Goals	SO.	Avg.	A.	Pen.
1980-81—Oshawa Generals (c)		OHL	7	308	24	0	4.68	0	0
1981-82—Oshawa Generals		OHL	29	1553	123	*2	4.75	1	6
1982-83—Oshawa Generals (d)		OHL	60	3536	213	0	3.61	4	2
1983-84—Oshawa Generals (e)		OHL	52	2966	205	1	4.15	4	16
1984-85—Fort Wayne Komets		IHL	10	590	43	0	4.37	0	0
1984-85—Binghamton Whalers (f)		AHL	45	2691	137	3	3.05	1	14
1985-86—Binghamton Whalers		AHL	49	2819	150	2	*3.19	0	7
1986-87—Binghamton Whalers (b)		AHL	57	3304	161	4	2.92	1	10

Year	Team	League	Games	Mins.	Goals	SO.	Avg.	A.	Pen.
1987-88—Hartford Whalers		NHL	1	60	6	0	6.00	0	0
1987-88—Binghamton Whalers		AHL	42	2346	144	0	3.68	0	17
NHL TOTALS			1	60	6	0	6.00	0	0

(c)—June, 1981—Drafted as underage junior by Washington Capitals in NHL entry draft. Fifth Capitals pick, 91st overall, fifth round.

(d)—Co-winner of Dave Pinkney Trophy (Top Goaltenders) with teammate Jeff Hogg.

(e)—Shared OHL playoff lead with one shutout with Darren Pang of Ottawa.

(f)—March, 1985—Traded with Dean Evason by Washington Capitals to Hartford Whalers for David A. Jensen.

WARREN SKORODENSKI

Goaltender . . . 6'1" . . . 180 lbs. . . . Born, Winnipeg, Man., March 22, 1960 . . . Shoots left . . . (November, 1983)—Suspended by AHL for throwing a stick into the crowd, then charging, pushing and verbally abusing referee Dave Lynch in an AHL game at Sherbrooke.

Year	Team	League	Games	Mins.	Goals	SO.	Avg.	A.	Pen.
1976-77—Kildonan		MJHL	22	1170	78	0	4.00	..	..
1977-78—Calgary Wranglers		WCHL	53	2460	213	1	5.20	1	48
1978-79—Calgary Wranglers (b-c)		WHL	*66	*3595	309	1	5.16	3	58
1979-80—Calgary Wranglers		WHL	66	3724	261	1	4.21	4	60
1980-81—New Brunswick Hawks		AHL	2	124	9	0	4.35	0	0
1980-81—Flint Generals		IHL	47	2602	189	2	4.36	1	64
1981-82—Chicago Black Hawks		NHL	1	60	5	0	5.00	0	0
1981-82—New Brunswick Hawks (d)		AHL	28	1644	70	*3	*2.55	0	2
1982-83—Springfield Indians		AHL	13	592	49	0	4.97	0	0
1982-83—Birmingham South Stars		CHL	25	1450	81	1	3.35	0	2
1983-84—Sherbrooke Jets		AHL	19	1048	88	0	5.04	0	12
1983-84—Springfield Indians		AHL	14	756	67	0	5.32	0	10
1984-85—Chicago Black Hawks		NHL	27	1396	75	2	3.22	0	2
1985-86—Nova Scotia Oilers		AHL	32	1716	109	0	3.81	0	10
1985-86—Chicago Black Hawks		NHL	1	60	6	0	6.00	0	0
1986-87—Chicago Black Hawks		NHL	3	155	7	0	2.71	0	0
1986-87—Nova Scotia Oilers		AHL	32	1813	121	2	4.00	2	13
1986-87—Saginaw Generals		IHL	6	319	21	...	3.95	0	0
1987-88—Edmonton Oilers		NHL	3	61	7	0	6.89	0	0
1987-88—Nova Scotia Oilers		AHL	46	2746	171	0	3.74	3	16
NHL TOTALS			35	1732	100	2	3.46	0	2

(c)—August, 1979—Signed by Chicago Black Hawks as a free agent.

(d)—Co-winner of Harry (Hap) Holmes Memorial Trophy (Top Goalie) with teammate Bob Janecyk.

WILLIAM JOHN SMITH

Goaltender . . . 5'10" . . . 185 lbs. . . . Born, Perth, Ont., December 12, 1950 . . . Shoots left . . . Brother of Gordon and Jack Smith . . . Holds NHL record for most playoff games by a goaltender, career (131) . . . Became first NHL goalie to score a goal November 28, 1979 at Denver vs. Colorado Rockies . . . (September, 1980)—Bell's palsy . . . (September 9, 1981)—Broken finger on left hand during Team Canada practice . . . Member of Long Island Sports Hall of Fame . . . (November, 1987)—Sprained ankle.

Year	Team	League	Games	Mins.	Goals	SO.	Avg.	A.	Pen.
1969-70—Cornwall Royals (c)		QJHL	55	.....	249	*1	4.52	..	....
1970-71—Springfield Kings (d)		AHL	49	2728	160	2	3.51	0	17
1971-72—Springfield Kings		AHL	28	1649	77	*4	2.80	1	38
1971-72—Los Angeles Kings (e)		NHL	5	300	23	0	4.60	0	5
1972-73—New York Islanders		NHL	37	2122	147	0	4.16	0	42
1973-74—New York Islanders		NHL	46	2615	134	0	3.07	0	11
1974-75—New York Islanders		NHL	58	3368	156	3	2.78	0	21
1975-76—New York Islanders		NHL	39	2254	98	3	2.61	1	10
1976-77—New York Islanders		NHL	36	2089	87	2	2.50	1	12
1977-78—New York Islanders		NHL	38	2154	95	2	2.65	0	35
1978-79—New York Islanders		NHL	40	2261	108	1	2.87	2	54
1979-80—New York Islanders		NHL	38	2114	104	2	2.95	0	39
1980-81—New York Islanders (f)		NHL	41	2363	129	2	3.28	0	33
1981-82—New York Islanders (a-g)		NHL	46	2685	133	0	2.97	1	24
1982-83—New York Islanders (h-i)		NHL	41	2340	112	1	2.87	0	41
1983-84—New York Islanders		NHL	42	2279	130	2	3.42	2	23
1984-85—New York Islanders		NHL	37	2090	133	0	3.82	0	25
1985-86—New York Islanders		NHL	41	2308	143	1	3.72	3	49
1986-87—New York Islanders		NHL	40	2252	132	1	3.52	2	37
1987-88—New York Islanders		NHL	38	2107	113	2	3.22	0	20
NHL TOTALS			663	37701	1977	22	3.15	12	481

(c)—Drafted from Cornwall Royals by Los Angeles Kings in fifth round of 1970 amateur draft.
(d)—Leading goalie (2.55 average and 1 shutout) during playoffs.
(e)—June, 1972—Drafted from Los Angeles Kings by New York Islanders in expansion draft.
(f)—Led Stanley Cup Playoffs with a 2.54 goals-against average.
(g)—Winner of Vezina Trophy (Voted as Outstanding NHL Goaltender).
(h)—Winner of Conn Smythe Memorial Trophy (Stanley Cup Playoff MVP).
(i)—Shared William Jennings Trophy with Roland Melanson for NHL's best team goaltending average.

ROBB STAUBER

Goaltender . . . 5'10" . . . 165 lbs. . . . Born, Duluth, Minn., November 25, 1967 . . . Shoots left . . . First Goalie to win the Hobey Baker Award as the top U.S. college player.

Year	Team	League	Games	Mins.	Goals	SO.	Avg.	A.	Pen.
1985-86—Duluth Denfield H.S. (c)		Minn. H.S.	..		..		..	..	..
1986-87—Univ. of Minnesota		WCHA	20	1072	63	0	3.53	1	2
1987-88—Univ. of Minnesota (d-e)		WCHA	44	2621	119	5	2.72	5	18

(c)—June, 1986—Drafted by Los Angeles Kings in 1986 NHL entry draft. Fifth Kings pick, 107th overall, fifth round.

(d)—Named First team All-America (West).

(e)—Won Hobey Baker Award (Top U.S. Collegiate player).

GREG STEFAN

Goaltender . . . 6' . . . 178 lbs. . . . Born, Brantford, Ont., February 11, 1961 . . . Shoots left . . . (March, 1981)—Given six-game suspension by OHL for breaking his goalie stick over shoulder of Bart Wilson of Toronto Marlboros . . . (January, 1985)—Strained left shoulder . . . (April, 1985)—Suspended for first eight games of 1985-86 season for swinging his stick at Al Secord in playoff game vs. Chicago on April 13 . . . (December 14, 1985)—Suspended for six games for high-sticking incident vs. Pittsburgh . . . (January 7, 1986)—Injured back at Washington and missed 17 games . . . (March 20, 1986)—Dislocated thumb vs. St. Louis when he jammed it against the goalpost . . . (January, 1988)—Left knee ligament injury . . . (May, 1988)—Strained neck when struck by Craig Simpson during playoff game vs. Edmonton.

Year	Team	League	Games	Mins.	Goals	SO.	Avg.	A.	Pen.
1978-79—Oshawa Generals		OMJHL	33	1635	133	0	4.88	1	27
1979-80—Oshawa Generals		OMJHL	17	897	58	0	3.88	2	11
1980-81—Oshawa Generals (c)		OHL	46	2407	174	0	4.34	2	92
1981-82—Detroit Red Wings		NHL	2	120	10	0	5.00	0	0
1981-82—Adirondack Red Wings		AHL	29	1571	99	2	3.78	0	36
1982-83—Detroit Red Wings		NHL	35	1847	139	0	4.52	0	35
1983-84—Detroit Red Wings		NHL	50	2600	152	2	3.51	3	14
1984-85—Detroit Red Wings		NHL	46	2633	190	0	4.33	2	23
1985-86—Detroit Red Wings		NHL	37	2068	155	1	4.50	2	23
1986-87—Detroit Red Wings		NHL	43	2351	135	1	3.45	4	24
1987-88—Detroit Red Wings		NHL	33	1854	96	1	3.11	1	36
NHL TOTALS			246	13473	877	5	3.91	12	165

(c)—June, 1981—Drafted by Detroit Red Wings in 1981 NHL entry draft. Fifth Red Wings pick, 128th overall, seventh round.

JEFFERY STOLP

Goaltender . . . 6' . . . 175 lbs. . . . Born, Grand Rapids, Minn., June 20, 1970 . . . Shoots left.

Year	Team	League	Games	Mins.	Goals	SO.	Avg.	A.	Pen.
1986-87—Greenway H.S.		Minn. H.S.	24	1080	39	1	2.17	..	..
1987-88—Greenway H.S. (c)		Minn. H.S.	23	1035	57	1	3.30	..	..

(c)—June, 1988—Drafted by Minnesota North Stars in 1988 NHL entry draft. Fourth North Stars pick, 64th overall, fourth round.

RICHARD TABARACCI

Goaltender . . . 5'10" . . . 185 lbs. . . . Born, Toronto, Ont., January 2, 1969 . . . Shoots left.

Year	Team	League	Games	Mins.	Goals	SO.	Avg.	A.	Pen.
1985-86—Markha Waxers		OHA	40	2176	188	1	5.18	..	....
1986-87—Cornwall Royals (c)		OHL	59	3347	290	1	5.20	1	30
1987-88—Cornwall Royals (a)		OHL	58	3448	200	2	3.48	2	44
1987-88—Muskegon Lumberjacks (d)		IHL	..		..		..	..	..

(c)—June, 1987—Drafted as underage junior by Pittsburgh Penguins in 1987 NHL entry draft. Second Penguins pick, 26th overall, second round.

(d)—No regular season record. Allowed one goal in 13 minutes of one playoff game.

TERRY TAILLEFER

Goaltender . . . 6' . . . 160 lbs. . . . Born, Edmonton, Alta., July 23, 1965 . . . Shoots left.

Year	Team	League	Games	Mins.	Goals	SO.	Avg.	A.	Pen.
1983-84—Boston University (c)		H. East	10	412	20	...	2.91	0	0
1984-85—Boston University		H. East	15	937	47	...	3.01	0	6
1985-86—Boston University		H. East	29	1651	93	...	3.38	0	0
1986-87—Boston University		H. East	22	1260	82	...	3.90	0	0
1987-88—Maine Mariners		AHL	12	506	28	0	3.32	1	4

(c)—June, 1983—Drafted by Boston Bruins in 1983 NHL entry draft. Sixth Bruins pick, 122nd overall, sixth round.

KARI TAKKO

Goaltender . . . 6'2" . . . 182 lbs. . . . Born, Kaupunki, Finland, June 23, 1963 . . . Shoots left.

Year	Team	League	Games	Mins.	Goals	SO.	Avg.	A.	Pen.
1985-86—Springfield Indians (c)		AHL	43	2386	161	1	4.05	0	6
1985-86—Minnesota North Stars (d)		NHL	1	60	3	0	3.00	0	0
1986-87—Springfield Indians		AHL	5	300	16	1	3.20	0	0
1986-87—Minnesota North Stars		NHL	38	2075	119	0	3.44	0	14
1987-88—Minnesota North Stars		NHL	37	1919	143	1	4.47	0	8
NHL TOTALS			76	4054	265	1	3.92	0	22

(c)—June, 1981—Drafted by Quebec Nordiques in 1981 NHL entry draft. Eighth Nordiques pick, 200th overall, 10th round.

(d)—June, 1984—Drafted by Minnesota North Stars in 1984 NHL entry draft. Fifth North Stars pick, 97th overall, fifth round.

CHRISTOPHER ARNOLD TERRERI

Goaltender . . . 5'9" . . . 155 lbs. . . . Born, Warwick, R.I., November 15, 1964 . . . Shoots left . . . (October, 1986)—Strained knee.

Year	Team	League	Games	Mins.	Goals	SO.	Avg.	A.	Pen.
1982-83—Providence College (c)		ECAC	11	529	17	..	1.93	..	..
1983-84—Providence College		ECAC	10	391	20	..	3.07	0	2
1984-85—Providence College (d-e)		H. East	41	2515	131	..	3.12	0	10
1985-86—Providence College		H. East	27	1540	96	0	3.74	0	4
1986-87—Maine Mariners		AHL	14	765	57	0	4.47	0	0
1986-87—New Jersey Devils		NHL	7	286	21	0	4.41	0	0
1987-88—Utica Devils		AHL	7	399	18	0	2.71	0	0
1987-88—U.S. Olympic Team		Int'l	29	1558	95	0	3.66	..	..
NHL TOTALS			7	286	21	0	4.41	0	0

(c)—June, 1983—Drafted by New Jersey Devils in 1983 NHL entry draft. Third Devils pick, 87th overall, fifth round.

(d)—First team (East) All-America.

(e)—Hockey East MVP.

RON TUGNUTT

Goaltender . . . 5'11" . . . 150 lbs. . . . Born, Scarborough, Ont., October 22, 1967 . . . Shoots left.

Year	Team	League	Games	Mins.	Goals	SO.	Avg.	A.	Pen.
1984-85—Peterborough Petes (c)		OHL	18	938	59	0	3.77	1	4
1985-86—Peterborough Petes (d-e)		OHL	26	1543	74	1	2.88	0	4
1986-87—Peterborough Petes		OHL	31	1891	88	2	*2.79	1	4
1987-88—Quebec Nordiques		NHL	6	284	16	0	3.38	1	0
1987-88—Fredericton Express		AHL	34	1962	118	1	3.61	1	13
NHL TOTALS			6	284	16	0	3.38	1	0

(c)—Won F.W. Dinty Moore Trophy (Lowest average by a rookie goalie).

(d)—Shared Dave Pinkney Trophy with teammate Kay Whitmore (Top Goalies).

(e)—June, 1986—Drafted as underage junior by Quebec Nordiques in 1986 NHL entry draft. Fourth Nordiques pick, 81st overall, fourth round.

JOHN VANBIESBROUCK

Goaltender . . . 5'9" . . . 165 lbs. . . . Born, Detroit, Mich., September 4, 1963 . . . Shoots left . . . (October, 1987)—Fractured jaw when struck by shot of teammate Tomas Sundstrom during practice . . . (June, 1988)—Severely cut wrist in accident at home, requiring micro surgery.

Year	Team	League	Games	Mins.	Goals	SO.	Avg.	A.	Pen.
1980-81—Sault Ste. Marie Greyhounds (c-d)		OHL	56	2941	203	0	4.14	2	10
1981-82—Sault Ste. Marie Greyhounds		OHL	31	1686	102	0	3.63	0	23
1981-82—New York Rangers		NHL	1	60	1	0	1.00	0	0
1982-83—Sault Ste. Marie Greyhounds		OHL	*62	3471	209	0	3.61	2	10
1983-84—New York Rangers		NHL	3	180	10	0	3.33	0	2
1983-84—Tulsa Oilers		CHL	37	2153	124	*3	3.46	0	6

Year	Team	League	Games	Mins.	Goals	SO.	Avg.	A.	Pen.
1984-85—New York Rangers		NHL	42	2358	166	1	4.22	5	17
1985-86—New York Rangers (a-e)		NHL	61	3326	184	3	3.32	3	16
1986-87—New York Rangers		NHL	50	2656	161	0	3.64	1	18
1987-88—New York Rangers		NHL	56	3319	187	2	3.38	5	46
NHL TOTALS			213	11899	709	6	3.58	14	99

(c)—Winner of Dinty Moore Trophy (Lowest Individual Goalie average in a rookie season).
(d)—June, 1981—Drafted by New York Rangers in 1981 NHL entry draft. Fifth Rangers pick, 72nd overall, fourth round.
(e)—Won Vezina Trophy (Top NHL Goaltender).

MIKE VERNON

Goaltender . . . 5'7" . . . 150 lbs. . . . Born, Calgary, Alta., February 24, 1963 . . . Shoots left . . . Set NHL record in 1986 playoffs for most minutes played (1229) . . . (March 2, 1988)—Injured hip in team practice.

Year	Team	League	Games	Mins.	Goals	SO.	Avg.	A.	Pen.
1980-81—Calgary Wranglers (c)		WHL	59	3154	198	1	3.77	3	21
1981-82—Calgary Wranglers		WHL	42	2329	143	*3	*3.68	0	0
1982-83—Calgary Wranglers		WHL	50	2856	155	*3	*3.26	2	6
1982-83—Calgary Flames (a-d-e)		NHL	2	100	11	0	6.59	0	0
1983-84—Calgary Flames		NHL	1	11	4	0	21.82	0	0
1983-84—Colorado Flames (b)		CHL	*46	*2648	148	1	*3.35	3	4
1984-85—Moncton Golden Flames		AHL	41	2050	134	0	3.92	1	8
1985-86—Salt Lake Golden Eagles		IHL	10	601	34	1	3.39	2	2
1985-86—Moncton Golden Flames		AHL	6	374	21	0	3.37	0	0
1985-86—Calgary Flames (f)		NHL	18	921	52	1	3.39	1	4
1986-87—Calgary Flames		NHL	54	2957	178	1	3.61	2	14
1987-88—Calgary Flames		NHL	64	3565	210	1	3.53	7	47
NHL TOTALS			139	7554	455	3	3.61	10	65

(c)—June, 1981—Drafted by Calgary Flames in 1981 NHL entry draft. Second Flames pick, 56th overall, third round.
(d)—Named WHL MVP.
(e)—Won WHL goaltending trophy.
(f)—Led NHL playoffs in games played (21), minutes (1229) and goals allowed (60).

JIMMY WAITE

Goaltender . . . 6' . . . 165 lbs. . . . Born, Sherbrooke, Que., April 15, 1969 . . . Shoots right.

Year	Team	League	Games	Mins.	Goals	SO.	Avg.	A.	Pen.
1985-86—Cantonniers de l'est		Que. Midget	29	1643	143	0	5.22	..	....
1986-87—Chicoutimi Sagueneens (c)		QHL	50	2569	209	*2	4.88	2	12
1987-88—Chicoutimi Sagueneens		QHL	36	200	150	0	4.50	0	14

(c)—June, 1987—Drafted as underage junior by Chicago Black Hawks in 1987 NHL entry draft. First Black Hawks pick, eighth overall, first round.

DARCY WAKALUK

Goaltender . . . 5'11" . . . 180 lbs. . . . Born, Pincher Creek, Alta., March 14, 1966 . . . Shoots left . . . (December 5, 1987)—Scored a goal into an empty Maine Mariners net . . . (January 10, 1988)—Played left wing vs. Nova Scotia Oilers.

Year	Team	League	Games	Mins.	Goals	SO.	Avg.	A.	Pen.
1982-83—Pincher Creek Oilers		BC Midget	38	2282	116	0	3.05	..	....
1983-84—Kelowna Wings (c)		WHL	31	1555	163	0	6.29	0	16
1985-86—Kelowna Wings		WHL	54	3094	244	0	4.73	1	46
1985-86—Spokane Chiefs		WHL	47	2562	224	1	5.25	8	18
1986-87—Rochester Americans		AHL	11	545	26	0	2.86	1	12
1987-88—Rochester Americans		AHL	55	2763	159	0	3.45	6	36

(c)—June, 1984—Drafted as underage junior by Buffalo Sabres in 1984 NHL entry draft. Seventh Sabres pick, 144th overall, seventh round.

MARTY WAKELYN

Goaltender . . . 6' . . . 180 lbs. . . . Born, Victoria, B.C., July 18, 1962 . . . Shoots left . . . (February, 1987)—Injured ankle.

Year	Team	League	Games	Mins.	Goals	SO.	Avg.	A.	Pen.
1982-83—Colorado College		WCHA	16	944	89	...	5.66	..	....
1983-84—Colorado College		WCHA	30	1743	140	...	4.82	1	0
1984-85—Colorado College		WCHA	35	2030	154	...	4.55	1	0
1985-86—Colorado College		WCHA	23	1380	100	0	4.35	1	2
1986-87—Springfield Indians (c)		AHL	21	1144	75	0	3.93	1	6
1987-88—Springfield Indians		AHL	44	2278	154	0	4.06	3	9

(c)—September, 1987—Signed by New York Islanders as a free agent.

RICK WAMSLEY

Goaltender . . . 5'11" . . . 185 lbs. . . . Born, Simcoe, Ont., May 25, 1959 . . . Shoots left . . . (October 16, 1985)—Bruised right hand at Calgary and required surgery and missed nine games . . . (March, 1988)—Pulled groin vs. Hartford.

Year	Team	League	Games	Mins.	Goals	SO.	Avg.	A.	Pen.
1976-77	St. Catharines Fincups	OMJHL	12	647	36	0	3.34	0	0
1977-78	Hamilton Fincups (c)	OMJHL	25	1495	74	2	*2.97	1	12
1978-79	Brantford Alexanders (d)	OMJHL	24	1444	128	0	5.32	0	2
1979-80	Nova Scotia Voyageurs	AHL	40	2305	125	2	3.25	3	12
1980-81	Nova Scotia Voyageurs (e)	AHL	43	2372	155	0	3.92	5	10
1980-81	Montreal Canadiens	NHL	5	253	8	1	1.90	0	0
1981-82	Montreal Canadiens (f-g)	NHL	38	2206	101	2	2.75	2	4
1982-83	Montreal Canadiens	NHL	46	2583	151	0	3.51	1	4
1983-84	Montreal Canadiens (h)	NHL	42	2333	144	2	3.70	3	6
1984-85	St. Louis Blues	NHL	40	2319	126	0	3.26	1	0
1985-86	St. Louis Blues	NHL	42	2517	144	1	3.43	0	2
1986-87	St. Louis Blues	NHL	41	2410	142	0	3.54	0	10
1987-88	St. Louis Blues (i)	NHL	31	1818	103	2	3.40	0	14
1987-88	Calgary Flames	NHL	2	73	5	0	4.11	0	0
	NHL TOTALS		287	16512	924	8	3.36	7	40

(c)—Shared Dave Pinkney Trophy (leading goalies) with Al Jensen.
(d)—August, 1979—Drafted by Montreal Canadiens in entry draft. Fifth Canadiens pick, 58th overall, third round.
(e)—Led AHL playoffs with a 1.81 goals-against average.
(f)—Co-winner of Bill Jennings Trophy (Lowest team goaltending average) with teammate Denis Herron.
(g)—Led Stanley Cup Playoffs with 2.20 goals-against average.
(h)—June, 1984—Traded with second round (Brian Benning) and third round (Robert Dirk) 1984 draft picks by Montreal Canadiens to St. Louis Blues for first round (Shayne Corson) and second round (Stephane Richer) 1984 draft picks.
(i)—March, 1988—Traded with Rob Ramage by St. Louis Blues to Calgary Flames for Brett Hull and Steve Bozek.

STEVE WEEKS

Goaltender . . . 5'11" . . . 165 lbs. . . . Born, Scarborough, Ont., June 30, 1958 . . . Shoots left.

Year	Team	League	Games	Mins.	Goals	SO.	Avg.	A.	Pen.
1975-76	Toronto Marlboros	OMJHL	18	873	73	0	4.95	0	0
1976-77	Northern Michigan Univ.	CCHA	16	811	58	0	4.29	..	....
1977-78	Northern Michigan Univ. (c)	CCHA	19	1015	56	1	3.31	..	....
1978-79	Northern Michigan Univ.	CCHA	....	.....	...	...	.....	..	....
1979-80	N. Mich. U. (a-d-e)	CCHA	36	2133	105	0	*2.95	1	2
1980-81	New Haven Nighthawks	AHL	36	2065	142	1	4.13	0	4
1980-81	New York Rangers	NHL	1	60	2	0	2.00	0	0
1981-82	New York Rangers	NHL	49	2852	179	1	3.77	3	0
1982-83	Tulsa Oilers	CHL	19	1116	60	0	3.23	1	0
1982-83	New York Rangers	NHL	18	1040	68	0	3.92	2	0
1983-84	New York Rangers	NHL	26	1361	90	0	3.97	0	4
1983-84	Tulsa Oilers (f)	CHL	3	180	7	0	2.33	0	0
1984-85	Binghamton Whalers	AHL	5	303	13	0	2.57	0	0
1984-85	Hartford Whalers	NHL	24	1457	92	2	3.79	0	0
1985-86	Hartford Whalers	NHL	27	1544	99	1	3.85	1	9
1986-87	Hartford Whalers	NHL	25	1367	78	1	3.42	0	0
1987-88	Hartford Whalers (g)	NHL	18	918	55	0	3.59	0	2
1987-88	Vancouver Canucks	NHL	9	550	31	0	3.38	0	0
	NHL TOTALS		197	11149	694	5	3.73	6	15

(c)—June, 1978—Drafted by New York Rangers in 1978 NHL entry draft. Twelfth Rangers pick, 176th overall, 11th round.
(d)—Named as Most Valuable Player of the CCHA.
(e)—Named to NCAA Tournament All-Star team.
(f)—September, 1984—Traded by New York Rangers to Hartford Whalers for future considerations.
(g)—March, 1988—Traded by Hartford Whalers to Vancouver Canucks for Richard Brodeur.

KAY WHITMORE

Goaltender . . . 6' . . . 170 lbs. . . . Born, Sudbury, Ont., April 10, 1967 . . . Shoots left.

Year	Team	League	Games	Mins.	Goals	SO.	Avg.	A.	Pen.
1982-83	Sudbury Major Midgets	OHA	43	2580	108	4	2.51	..	....
1983-84	Peterborough Petes	OHL	29	1471	110	0	4.49	2	2
1984-85	Peterborough Petes (c)	OHL	53	3077	172	*2	3.35	5	33
1985-86	Peterborough Petes (a-d)	OHL	41	2467	114	*3	*2.77	3	14
1986-87	Peterborough Petes	OHL	36	2159	118	1	3.28	4	13
1987-88	Binghamton Whalers	AHL	38	2137	121	3	3.40	1	20

(c)—June, 1985—Drafted as underage junior by Hartford Whalers in 1985 NHL entry draft. Second Whalers pick, 26th overall, second round.

(d)—Shared Dave Pinkney Trophy with teammate Ron Tugnutt (Top Goalies).

KEN WREGGET

Goaltender . . . 6'1" . . . 180 lbs. . . . Born, Brandon, Man., March 25, 1964 . . . Shoots left . . . (December 26, 1985)—Injured knee at Hartford.

Year	Team	League	Games	Mins.	Goals	SO.	Avg.	A.	Pen.
1981-82	Lethbridge Broncos (c)	WHL	36	1713	118	1	4.13	0	0
1982-83	Lethbridge Broncos (d)	WHL	48	2696	157	1	3.49	1	18
1983-84	Lethbridge Broncos (a)	WHL	53	3052	161	0	*3.16	1	26
1983-84	Toronto Maple Leafs	NHL	3	165	14	0	5.09	0	0
1984-85	Toronto Maple Leafs	NHL	23	1278	103	0	4.84	1	10
1984-85	St. Catharines Saints	AHL	12	688	48	0	4.19	1	0
1985-86	St. Catharines Saints	AHL	18	1058	78	1	4.42	2	8
1985-86	Toronto Maple Leafs	NHL	30	1566	113	0	4.33	0	16
1986-87	Toronto Maple Leafs	NHL	56	3026	200	0	3.97	4	20
1987-88	Toronto Maple Leafs	NHL	56	3000	222	2	4.44	5	40
	NHL TOTALS		168	9035	652	2	4.33	10	86

(c)—June, 1982—Drafted as underage junior by Toronto Maple Leafs in 1982 NHL entry draft. Fourth Maple Leafs pick, 45th overall, third round.

(d)—Led WHL playoffs with 3.02 average and one shutout.

WENDELL YOUNG

Goaltender . . . 5'8" . . . 185 lbs. . . . Born, Halifax, N.S., August 1, 1963 . . . Shoots left.

Year	Team	League	Games	Mins.	Goals	SO.	Avg.	A.	Pen.
1979-80	Cole Harbour	NSJHL	..	1446	94	0	3.90	..	..
1980-81	Kitchener Rangers (c)	OHL	42	2215	164	1	4.44	2	29
1981-82	Kitchener Rangers	OHL	*60	*3470	195	1	3.37	1	4
1982-83	Kitchener Rangers	OHL	61	*3611	231	1	3.84	7	22
1983-84	Salt Lake Golden Eagles	CHL	20	1094	80	0	4.39	1	2
1983-84	Fredericton Express	AHL	11	569	39	1	4.11	2	4
1983-84	Milwaukee Admirals	IHL	6	339	17	0	3.01	0	0
1984-85	Fredericton Express	AHL	22	1242	83	0	4.01	0	0
1985-86	Fredericton Express	AHL	24	1457	78	0	3.21	0	2
1985-86	Vancouver Canucks	NHL	22	1023	61	0	3.58	0	0
1986-87	Fredericton Express	AHL	30	1676	118	0	4.22	4	8
1986-87	Vancouver Canucks (d)	NHL	8	420	35	0	5.00	1	0
1987-88	Philadelphia Flyers	NHL	6	320	20	0	3.75	0	0
1987-88	Hershey Bears	AHL	51	2922	135	1	2.77	2	8
	NHL TOTALS		36	1763	116	0	3.95	1	0

(c)—June, 1981—Drafted as underage junior by Vancouver Canucks in 1981 NHL entry draft. Third Canucks pick, 73rd overall, fourth round.

(d)—August, 1987—Traded with a 1990 third-round draft choice by Vancouver Canucks to Philadelphia Flyers for Daryl Stanley and Darren Jensen.